⚖ NOLO   Products & Services

⇨ Books & Software

Get in-depth information. Nolo publishes hundreds of great books and software programs for consumers and business owners. Order a copy—or download an ebook version instantly—at Nolo.com.

⇨ Legal Encyclopedia

Free at Nolo.com. Here are more than 1,400 free articles and answers to common questions about everyday legal issues including wills, bankruptcy, small business formation, divorce, patents, employment and much more.

⇨ Plain-English Legal Dictionary

Free at Nolo.com. Stumped by jargon? Look it up in America's most up-to-date source for definitions of legal terms.

⇨ Online Legal Documents

Create documents at your computer. Go to Nolo.com to make a will or living trust, form an LLC or corporation or obtain a trademark or provisional patent. For simpler matters, download one of our hundreds of high-quality legal forms, including bills of sale, promissory notes, nondisclosure agreements and many more.

⇨ Lawyer Directory

Find an attorney at Nolo.com. Nolo's consumer-friendly lawyer directory provides in-depth profiles of lawyers all over America. From fees and experience to legal philosophy, education and special expertise, you'll find all the information you need to pick the right lawyer. Every lawyer listed has pledged to work diligently and respectfully with clients.

⇨ Free Legal Updates

Keep up to date. Check for free updates at Nolo.com. Under "Products," find this book and click "Legal Updates." You can also sign up for our free e-newsletters at Nolo.com/newsletters.

13th edition

How to
Buy a House
in California

Ralph Warner, Ira Serkes
& George Devine

edited by Ilona Bray

NOLO
LAW for ALL

Thirteenth Edition	JANUARY 2011
Editor	ILONA BRAY
Cover Design	JALEH DOANE
Production	SUSAN PUTNEY
Proofreading	CATHERINE CAPUTO
Index	VICTORIA BAKER
Printing	DELTA PRINTING SOLUTIONS, INC.

Warner, Ralph E.
  How to buy a house in California / by Ralph Warner, Ira Serkes, & George Devine ; edited by
Ilona Bray. -- 13th ed.
      p. cm.
  Includes index.
  Summary: "Presents expert tips, useful forms, and checklists for people buying a house in
California. The new edition emphasizes that careful research is necessary before deciding
what price and terms to include in an offer and warns of the changing requirements to secure
financing"--Provided by publisher.
  ISBN-13: 978-1-4133-1317-8 (pbk.)
  ISBN-10: 1-4133-1317-5 (pbk.)
  ISBN-13: 978-1-4133-1340-6 (e-book)
  ISBN-10: 1-4133-1340-X (e-book)
  1. House buying--California. 2. Residential real estate--Purchasing--California. 3. Mortgages-
-California. 4. Housing--California--Finance. 5. Real estate business--California. I. Serkes, Ira,
1949- II. Devine, George, 1941- III. Schroeder, Alayna, 1975- IV. Title.
  HD266.C2W37 2011
  643'.1209794--dc22

                                             2010031337

Please note

We believe accurate, plain-English legal information should help you solve many of
your own legal problems. But this text is not a substitute for personalized advice from a
knowledgeable lawyer. If you want the help of a trained professional—and we'll always
point out situations in which we think that's a good idea—consult an attorney licensed
to practice in your state.

Acknowledgments

Collecting and organizing the material for this book turned out to be a daunting task, one that might have defeated us had it not been for the enthusiastic help of Nolo legal editors Ilona Bray, Mary Randolph, Alayna Schroeder, and Marcia Stewart.

Special thanks to Mike Mansel, Certified Insurance Counselor, local insurance specialist, for keeping the book's material on the ever-changing insurance market up-to-date. Also big thanks to Marjo Diehl, loan agent with RPM Mortgage in Alamo, California (www.rpm-mtg.com), who helped update and improve our advice on mortgage funding. And for keeping us up on the latest real-estate activities of the California legislature, thanks go to Senator Alan Lowenthal and legislative assistant Meegan Murray.

Tim Devaney also was a central figure in developing this work. A fine geographer and writer, he contributed much of the original research and writing in Appendix A, Welcome to California.

A number of real estate professionals contributed their good ideas and constructive criticisms. Recognizing that they don't necessarily agree with some of our conclusions or points of emphasis, many thanks to John Murphy, Guy Berry, John Pinto, Terry Moerler, Rob Bader, Judy Cranston, Shel Givens, Elizabeth Hughes, Donald Pearman, author of *The Termite Report;* Martin Reutinger, Temmy Walker, Gene Fama, Robert Jackson, and Judy Rydell.

Our heartfelt thanks to all those house buyers who shared their purchase experiences with us. Many of their stories appear throughout the book, though sometimes slightly edited and with fictitious names. Contributors (and general reviewers) include Mack Babitt, Mike and Carmella Boschetti, Valerie Brown, David Cole, Steve Elias, Jo and Don Gallo, Mary Glaeser, Rose Green, Barry Gustin, Ann Heron, Barbara Hodovan, Wendy Lewis, Jackie and Tony Mancuso, Ken Norwood, Mary Randolph, Barbara Kate Repa, and Ed Shelton.

Thanks, too, to Twila Slesnick, Ph.D., Enrolled Agent, for information on borrowing against retirement plans; Michael Cohen, Berkeley-based loan broker with Schnell Investment Company; Sue Giesberg of the California Attorney General's Office; Xavier Guerrero, Senior Exam Policy Analyst, Internal Revenue Service, for tax information; David Meyers, Real Estate Editor of the *Los Angeles Times;* Susan Tubbesing, Executive Director of the Earthquake Engineering Research Institute in Oakland; and Brian Moggan, Senior Loan Officer at Union Trust Mortgage Services, Inc.

Special thanks to Terri Hearsh, whose creative book design, financial savvy, and cheerful nature made a tremendous difference to this book.

Finally, the work of several prominent real estate writers especially inspired us, including Peter G. Miller, Jack Reed, and Leigh Robinson, and the late Robert Bruss.

Dedications

To Carol Serkes, who showed me how to buy a home when I'd only known how to acquire houses.

To Snidely and Gouger, furry felines and now just beloved memories, who kept me company in the wee hours of the night and helped give birth to the book by sleeping on the manuscript whenever possible; and Lucy The Cat who diligently helped in the revisions on previous editions, plopping herself on my chest whenever I'd lie down on the sofa.

To those of you willing to open your mind to new ideas, especially when your friends tell you that you're dreaming. At 20, I had my entire life planned; at 40, I had no idea what opportunities lay ahead! I'm now past 60 (and 60 is the new 30!). The day after Thanksgiving a few years ago, Puddy Maximus, our cat, strolled away—we did all we could to find her, but she seems to have adopted a new family. It was time to give another fur person a new home, and so Baby T came into our lives.

So our four-legged children continue to rule the roost, the garden is blooming, a 15" Mac Book Pro is our tool of choice, and we continue to live a wonderful life in Berkeley, California, the center of the universe.

Thanks to John & Ellen Pinto, pioneers and experts in the field of Buyer Brokerage. John and Ellen have also set the standard for living La Dolce Vita.

And thanks to Al Gore for inventing The Internet. Without it, I would have never been able to create Berkeleyhomes.com and Berkeleyhomes.com/blog.

—Ira Serkes

To my wife Joanne, son George and daughter-in-law Stephanie, dedicated Realtor®-Associates Joseph G. and Annemarie D. Kurpinsky, and grandchildren, Joseph Gerard Kurpinsky, Jr. and Margaret Devine Kurpinsky, in addition to my students and colleagues in the School of Business and Professional Studies at the University of San Francisco.

—George Devine

Table of Contents

Your Legal Companion to Buying a Home in California

Buying a house should be fun. A good house not only provides shelter, warmth, and a place to lay your head, it has the potential to "come to life" and be a true friend to you and your family.

Unfortunately, locating an affordable house that suits your needs isn't always easy. And even if you find your dream house, that's only the first step to making it yours: You must still bargain with the seller for favorable terms, arrange for a good deal on a mortgage, have the house inspected for physical defects, and make decisions regarding dozens of other potentially daunting issues.

This book gives you the information you need to understand how California houses are financed, inspected, and, finally, purchased. If you've previously bought a house in another part of the United States, the lessons you've learned may be helpful—or may be misleading. While the fundamentals of home sales are similar nationwide, California's fast growth and geographic diversity have resulted in many unique and surprising home-sale customs. Some of these even vary regionally within the state of California.

Some of the concerns that may be on your mind, however, are universal. Maybe you're worried you won't be able to afford a decent house, or you'll pay too much. Or perhaps you wonder whether your bad credit will keep you from getting a loan, whether you'll be taken advantage of by aggressive real estate salespeople, or that you'll hit hard times and be foreclosed on.

Fortunately, this book will help you educate yourself about the process, and overcome those fears. But first, you must commit yourself to doing three things:

1. **Understand all the important aspects of the purchase process.** That's what this book is all about—giving you a thorough, practical discussion of the steps necessary to find and purchase a California house. We recommend reading this whole book, so you can take informed action on dozens of matters, such as finding a suitable agent, deciding how big a down payment you can afford, choosing the best mortgage, and arranging for an inspection that will reveal hidden problems.

2. **Be patient.** By learning all the house-buying basics, you can plan carefully so that you will have time on your side at each stage of the purchase process—and the sale of your old house, if you have one. Being relaxed while others are anxious and hurrying is often the key to saving money.

3. **Trust yourself.** The traditional approach to buying a house is to trust brokers, agents, mortgage lenders, and other "experts" to protect your interests.

While many good, helpful people work in real estate, even the good ones must navigate potential conflicts of interest that are part of the purchase process. No one knows how to meet your needs better than you do.

Whether you're looking for a luxury beachfront home in Southern California, a bungalow in the San Francisco Bay Area, or an affordable new build in Fresno, this book shows you how to buy a house in California.

Describe Your Dream Home

You Know the House You Want to Buy

Given your family's needs, tastes, and finances, you probably already have a good idea of the type of house you want to buy. Because this is true, we skip the typical first chapter in many home buyers' books, in which the author compares such things as the joys of living on a dusty road in outer suburbia to the convenience of living in a townhouse in a major city. If you haven't already thought these things though, you may need to do some critical self-evaluation before beginning your home search.

SKIP AHEAD

Already found the house you want to purchase and are mainly interested in the ins and outs of financing? Skip the rest of this chapter and move on to Chapter 2, How Much House Can You Afford?

Don't Be Talked Into Buying the Wrong House

Like house prices nationwide, those in California fell during the 2008 real estate downturn—but they didn't fall as far. Many California buyers still face an affordability gap between the house they'd like to buy and the one they can afford. Without an organized house-buying approach, you might be talked into compromising on the wrong house by friends, relatives, a real estate agent, or even yourself.

"Not me, I know my own mind," you say. "Don't be too sure," we reply. Every day, confident and knowledgeable home seekers become so anxious and disoriented that they leap into a deal they later come to regret, sometimes bitterly.

Tips on Searching New Places

Perhaps you've heard it said that choosing a house's location wisely is as important as picking a good house. In a state the size of California, it's a vast understatement to say you have a lot of locations to choose from. To help you think about specific California areas, we include Appendix A, Welcome to California.

Despite the title, Welcome to California isn't meant only for newcomers to the state. Whether you're a San Franciscan moving closer to a San Ramon job, a New Yorker relocating to Los Angeles, or simply someone unfamiliar with certain California areas, you'll find a wealth of information. In addition, in Chapter 5 we discuss working with a local real estate agent to get essential information on neighborhoods.

But there's still no substitute for your own legwork. Ask your friends and colleagues, walk and drive around neighborhoods, talk to local residents, read local newspapers, check the library's community resources files, visit the local planning department, and do whatever else will help you get a better sense of a neighborhood or city.

Here is our method to ensure that you buy a house you'll enjoy living in, even if it means you must make some compromises:

- Firmly establish your priorities before you look at a house.
- Insist that any house you offer to buy meets at least your most important priorities.
- Do this even if, in buying a house that meets your top priorities, you must compromise in other areas.

In the following sections, we help you consider a range of house features, establish your priorities, and compare potential houses.

Identify Your Ideal House Profile

When looking for a house, it's easy to become overwhelmed by the array of choices, from size to style to floor plan and fixtures. Then, there's the issue of location—houses come in all sorts of neighborhoods, school districts, and potential hazard zones (fire, earthquake, and flood, to name a few). And, of course, price and purchase terms are crucial consid-erations for most home buyers. To cope with all these and at least a dozen other relevant variables, it's essential to establish your priorities in advance and stick to them.

The first step is to identify house features most important to you by completing our Ideal House Profile, which lists all major categories such as upper price limit, number and type of rooms, and location. A sample is shown below, and a copy is included in Appendix D.

If you're buying with another person, prepare your list of priorities together, so that each person's strong likes and dislikes are respected.

TIP

Getting price and financing inform-ation. Most people will have an upper limit on the house they can afford to buy and the maximum down payment they can make. If you need advice on these issues, be sure to read Chapters 2, 4, and 8 before completing the Ideal House Profile.

Must Haves: Mandatory Priorities

Use the Ideal House Profile to identify the essential features you're looking for (must have) in a house, such as a particular city or neighborhood. Since price is an obvious consideration for most people, fill in the top section first. For example, under *Upper price limit* you might note $400,000, with a *Maximum down payment* of $40,000. Then fill in the rest of the form.

If you have two kids, you might note that three bedrooms, excellent public schools, and a street with lots of children are "must haves." If you plan to live in the house after retirement, a minimal number of stairs and short distances to shops and services may be "must haves."

TIP

Pay close attention to the *School needs* category. If you have children, buying a great house at a great price in a lousy school district may mean years of paying for private schools. By contrast, paying a little more for a good house in an excellent school district may be a bargain in the long run. And if you plan to move in a few years, it will be easier to sell a house in a good school district, because that feature is important to many potential buyers. See Appendix A, Welcome to California, for advice on checking out schools.

Hope to Have: Secondary Priorities

Once you've compiled your list of "must haves," jot down features that you'd like but aren't crucial to your decision of whether to buy. For example, under *Type of yard and grounds,* you might note patio and flat back yard in the "Hope to Have" column. Or under *Number and type of rooms,* you might list finished basement or master bedroom with bath.

Take a second look at your "Must Have" column. If you're typical, you may wonder how you will ever afford a house with the features you've listed. Don't despair—at least, not until you understand the strategies (discussed in Chapter 3) to help you buy an affordable house. For now, you might need to change a couple of "must haves" to "hope to haves."

Absolute No Ways

Be sure to list your "absolute no ways" (you will not buy a house that has any of these features) at the bottom of the Ideal House Profile. Avoiding things you'll always hate— such as a house in a flood zone, poor school district, or high-crime area—can be even more important than finding a house that contains all your mandatory priorities.

If you're moving into a new-house development or condominium, be sure to check into covenants, conditions, and restrictions (CC&Rs), which may be quite detailed and restrictive on everything from the color of your house to your landscaping. (CC&Rs are discussed in more detail in Chapter 7.)

Once you've completed your Ideal House Profile, you're ready to create a House Priorities Worksheet, which will help you see how each house stacks up with your priorities.

Create a House Priorities Worksheet

Now it's time to use the information collected in your Ideal House Profile to create a House Priorities Worksheet for each house you visit.

Start by making several copies of the worksheet (in Appendix D) to allow for mistakes or the eventual scaling back of your priority list if it turns out you can't afford all the features you would like. Then, enter relevant information on a master copy of the House Priorities Worksheet under each major category—"Must have," "Hope to have," and "Absolute no ways." A sample is shown below.

Once you have completed your House Priorities Worksheet to your (and your partner's) satisfaction, make several copies (or install the form on your laptop if you'll be taking it househunting).

For each house you see, fill in the top of the House Priorities Worksheet. Enter the address, asking price, name and phone number of the contact person (listing agent or seller, if it's a For Sale By Owner), and date

Ideal House Profile

Upper price limit: $1,000,000
Maximum down payment: $200,000
Special financing needs: N/A

	Must Have	Hope to Have
Neighborhood or location:		
Northern Berkeley	✓	
Oxford Street		✓
School needs:		
Berkeley High School	✓	
Desired neighborhood features:		
Quiet street with little traffic	✓	
Walking distance to Solano Avenue	✓	
Neighborhood association		✓
Lots of trees		✓
Length of commute:		
Maximum of 15 minutes drive to Berkeley office	✓	
Access to public transportation:		
Walking distance to S.F. express buses	✓	
Size of house:		
Minimum 1,800 square feet	✓	
Number and type of rooms:		
3 bedrooms/2 baths	✓	
Modern kitchen	✓	
Family room for kids		✓
Eat-in kitchen or breakfast nook		✓
Condition, age, and type of house:		
Good shape, less than 100 years old	✓	
Type of yard and grounds:		
Fenced-in yard	✓	
Private yard		✓
Other desired features:		
Easy parking	✓	
Lots of lights		✓
Absolute no ways:		
House in an active or potential slide zone		

you saw the house. As you walk around and talk to the owner or agent, enter a checkmark if the house has a desirable or undesirable feature. Also, make notes next to a particular feature if it can be changed to meet your needs (for example, an okay kitchen that could be modernized for $25,000).

Add comments at the bottom, such as "potential undeveloped lot next door" or "neighbors seem very friendly." If you look at a lot of houses, taking notes such as these will help make sure you don't forget important information.

You should seriously consider only those houses with all or most of your "must haves" and none of your "no ways." If you visit a nice, reasonably priced house that doesn't come close to matching your list and can't be easily changed to do so, say no. Take the time to find a more suitable house; you'll be glad you did.

> **TIP**
>
> **Set up a good filing system.** As the list of houses you look at grows, failing to adopt a good system may lead to revisiting houses you've already seen and rejected or making decisions based on half-remembered facts. For each house that seems like a possible prospect, make a file that includes a completed House Priorities Worksheet, the information materials provided when you toured the home, the Multiple Listing Service information, ads, and your notes. Or, if you are more digitally inclined, set up a simple database with key details on each house you visit. (For advice, see "Organizing Your House Search" in Chapter 6.)

> ### Watch Out for Staged Homes
>
> House "staging" is now a regular practice in home sales. The right paint, furniture, music, and smells can create illusions that would make Martha Stewart and Houdini jealous. The point is to optimize the charms of a house while distracting potential buyers from its flaws.
>
> So if you visit a house that just reeks of charm—look behind, above, and below. Imagine it empty, or with your own furniture.

Prepare a House Comparison Worksheet

If, like many people, you look at a considerable number of houses over an extended period of time—or even in the space of a week—you may soon have trouble distinguishing or comparing their features. That's where our House Comparison Worksheet comes in.

Across the top of the form, list the addresses of the three or four houses you like best. In the left column, fill in your list of priorities and "no ways" from your Ideal House Profile and House Priorities Worksheet. Then put a checkmark on the line under each house that has that feature to allow for a quick comparison.

A sample is shown below, and a copy is included in Appendix D.

House Priorities Worksheet

Date visited: September 15, 2011   Price: $ 950,000

Address: 5 Marin Way, Berkeley

Contact: Jo Tulare, Berkeley Homes   Phone #: 525-5555

Must have:
- ☑ North Berkeley neighborhood
- ☑ Berkeley High School
- ☐ Quiet street with little traffic
- ☑ Walking distance to Solano Avenue
- ☑ Maximum of 15 minutes drive to Berkeley office
- ☑ Walking distance to S.F. express buses
- ☑ Minimum 1,800 square feet
- ☑ 3 bedrooms/2 baths
- ☐ Modern kitchen
- ☑ Good shape, less than 100 years old
- ☐ Fenced-in yard
- ☑ Easy parking

Hope to have:
- ☐ Oxford or Spruce Street
- ☑ Neighborhood association
- ☑ Lots of trees
- ☐ Family room for kids
- ☑ Eat-in kitchen or breakfast nook
- ☐ Private yard
- ☑ Lots of light
- ☐

Absolute no ways:
- ☐ House in an active or potential slide-zone
- ☐
- ☐

Comments about the particular house:

This house is terrific! Our agents found out there are two other interested bidders, so it will probably go for the full list price or more, but well worth trying for. Street is pretty busy, but the house and location meet most of our needs. Neighbors seem very nice.

House Comparison Worksheet

House 1 _____ 257 Loving Avenue, Berkeley
House 2 _____ 1415 Gaylord Street, Berkeley
House 3 _____ 999 Spruce Street, Berkeley
House 4 _____ 5 Marin Way, Berkeley

	1	2	3	4
Must have:				
North Berkeley neighborhood	✓	✓	✓	✓
Berkeley High School	✓	✓	✓	✓
Quiet street with little traffic	✓	✓		
Walking distance to Solano Avenue		✓	✓	✓
Maximum of 15 minutes drive to Berkeley office	✓		✓	✓
Walking distance to S.F. express buses	✓			✓
Minimum 1,800 square feet	✓	✓		✓
3 bedrooms/2 baths	✓	✓		✓
Modern kitchen			✓	
Good shape, less than 100 years old		✓		✓
Fenced-in yard	✓	✓	✓	
Easy parking			✓	✓
Hope to have:				
Oxford or Spruce Street		✓		
Neighborhood association		✓	✓	
Lots of trees	✓		✓	✓
Family room for kids	✓			
Eat-in kitchen or breakfast nook	✓	✓	✓	
Private yard	✓	✓	✓	
Lots of light		✓	✓	✓
Absolute no ways:				
House in an active or potential slide zone	✓	✓	✓	

True Story

Ellen: How Not to Buy a House

I was a first-time buyer on a relatively tight budget when I set out to buy an older, attached row house in San Francisco. I wanted two bedrooms, no (or a very small) yard, proximity to a downtown bus route, and walking access to a neighborhood market and bookstore. I looked for many months at houses that were completely unsuitable, far too expensive, or, with depressing regularity, both. So I broadened my search by reading the classifieds in the Sunday paper. When I saw that prices were more reasonable in the suburbs, I spent a sunny Sunday afternoon browsing in Contra Costa County.

At the first open house I visited, I met an energetic real estate agent who spun a wonderful word picture of the joys of suburban life: lots of sun, room for a tomato garden, and friendly neighbors. She showed me a split-level house with an apple tree in full bloom in my price range. Almost before I realized what I was doing, I signed on the bottom line.

That was the fun part. Soon I was getting up at 6:00 a.m., driving to the train station, and standing for the 40-minute ride to San Francisco. My fantasy about the joy of suburban life was just that. It's hard to believe now, but I seemed to have temporarily overlooked the fact that I'm allergic to direct sun, detest tomatoes, and moved out of the suburbs to get away from overly involved neighbors.

Fortunately, I sold the house six months later, at a small profit. I went in with a friend and together we bought a house in San Francisco that meets my needs perfectly.

How Much House Can You Afford?

t's essential to determine how much you can afford to pay before you look for a house—first off, for your own planning and peace of mind. Crunching a few numbers is also important, however, to help you be either cautious when lenders offer you higher loans than you should realistically take on, or assertive with lenders who don't realize that you're a better credit risk than your records show.

 SKIP AHEAD
If money is no object or you already know how much house you can afford, skip this chapter.

Most readers will find this chapter useful in two ways:

- to help you determine your price range—before you go house hunting, and
- to explain some of the techniques experienced mortgage brokers use to help borrowers qualify for a loan from a bank, savings and loan, or other lender.

The Basics of Determining Housing Affordability

As a broad generalization, most people can afford to purchase a house worth about three times their total (gross) annual income, assuming a 20% down payment and a moderate amount of other long-term debts. With no other debts, they can afford a house worth up to four or five times their annual income.

A much more accurate way to determine how much house you can afford is to compare your monthly carrying costs plus your monthly payments on other long-term debts to your gross (total) monthly income. Carrying costs are the money needed to make a monthly payment (both principal and interest) plus one-twelfth of the yearly bill for property taxes and homeowner's insurance. In real estate industry jargon, monthly carrying costs are often referred to as PITI (pronounced "pity"), which stands for principal, interest, taxes, and insurance.

Assuming you have a decent credit score, lenders traditionally want your regular monthly payments to be less than 36% of your gross monthly income. (Your credit score is a numerical measure that reflects how well you've managed credit in the past.) The lower your other monthly debts, the more of your 36% can be applied to your mortgage costs.

Using these percentages, if your monthly income is $4,000, you should not pay more than $1,440 (0.36 x $4,000) toward your debts. This is called the "debt-to-income ratio."

But if your profile is extremely attractive to a lender, perhaps because you have a particularly high credit score, it may make an exception and approve your loan even if your debt-to-income ratio falls outside its guidelines. Some lenders will accept a higher debt-to-income ratio if you'll take a less-attractive loan, such as one with a higher-than-market interest rate or higher-than-usual points. (Points are an up-front loan fee figured as a percentage of the loan, discussed in Chapter 8.)

How Credit Scores Affect Loan Qualification

When reviewing loan applications and making financing decisions, lenders check a prospective home buyer's credit report. The lenders typically request that the credit agency reporting your file—probably one of three main repositories, Equifax, Experian, or Trans-Union—provide your credit or FICO score.

This score is a statistical summary of the information in your credit report. It's calculated using an elaborate computerized scoring model that takes into account your history of paying bills on time, the level of outstanding debts, how long you've had credit, your credit limit, the number of inquiries for your credit report (too many can lower score), and the number of credit cards and the types of credit you have. These screening models don't consider your race, gender, marital status, age, or neighborhood.

California law (Civil Code § 1785.10) requires credit reporting agencies to provide consumers (upon request) with their scores and related information. Credit scores range from 300 to 850. The higher your credit score, the better. If you routinely pay your bills late or have a poor credit history, expect a lower score. A lender may either reject your loan application or insist on a large down payment or a higher interest rate. Because your credit history is so important, be sure to check your credit report and clean up your file or fix any errors, as discussed below.

For more information on credit scores, check out www.myfico.com.

TIP

Here's what the California Association of Realtors (CAR) says you can afford: According to CAR's statistics for the second quarter of 2010, the minimum household income needed to purchase an entry-level home costing $266,750 in California was $43,960, based on an adjustable effective interest rate of 4.09% and assuming a 10% down payment. (Of course, typical entry-level homes may cost more or less than that amount within the area of California where you're looking.)

Prepare a Family Financial Statement

The first step to determine the purchase price you can afford is to prepare a family financial statement, which includes:

- your monthly income
- your monthly expenses, and
- your net worth (your assets minus your liabilities).

We use the word "family" as shorthand for the economic unit that will buy a house. For our purposes, an unmarried couple or a single person is just as much a family as a married couple with ten kids.

CAUTION

This statement is for you, not your lender. No matter how much debt a lender ultimately says you can handle, the purpose of this statement is to help you develop your own realistic picture of what this debt will mean for your monthly cash flow. The information you collect will help you fill out your loan application, but you won't give this statement directly to the lender. That means that now is not the time to exaggerate your income or underestimate your expenses—you'll only be fooling yourself. (And if you were to compound your error by putting incorrect information on your actual loan application, you'd be committing fraud against the lender.)

Below is a sample family financial statement. A blank copy of the statement itself is in Appendix D, along with instructions for filling it out. Make several photocopies (and fill out the form in pencil) so you'll have a clean copy if you make errors or your financial status changes. If you need more space when filling out any section, include an attachment. Do this work carefully. It will be very useful when you complete a mortgage loan application. (See Chapter 13.)

How Much Down Payment Will You Make?

Generally speaking, the larger the percentage of the total price of a house you can put down, the easier it will be for you to qualify for a mortgage and find a willing seller.

As we discuss below, the monthly mortgage payment (plus taxes and insurance) is the major factor in determining the purchase price of the house you can afford. And with a higher down payment, those payments are lower. A lender's financial interests are better protected: If you default on your mortgage (which is less likely anyway, because the payment is more affordable), a lender has

more room to sell the property and recover its investment.

For now, you need down payment money. How much do you have by way of liquid and nonliquid assets? If you have a house or other property you plan to sell, estimate what you're likely to receive after subtracting costs of sale. If necessary, think about other ways to reasonably raise cash. Can you liquidate other assets or get a gift or loan from a relative or friend? (These and other money-raising techniques are discussed in Chapter 4.)

Once you've calculated the total amount of your liquid assets, do a quick and dirty calculation of how much home you can afford. Start by assuming that you'll pour all these assets into the down payment, and make the standard 20% down payment. For example, if you've got $30,000 in assets, that would work as a 20% down payment on a $150,000 home.

But, as we said, these calculations are quick and dirty—you'll never be able to pour all your liquid assets into the down payment, because this would leave you nothing for closing costs and financial reserves. Closing costs can vary from approximately 2% to 5% of the purchase price. And, lenders will want to see that you have at least two to three months of reserve money left over after you've bought the house, so they may insist that you spend less on a down payment to achieve this. (However, reserve money doesn't have to be liquid; it can also be in the form of retirement money.) The result is that you'll need to fiddle with the figures a bit to figure out a realistic combination of down payment, closing costs, and home

Family Financial Statement

	Borrower	**Coborrower**
Name and address:		
Home phone number:		
Email address:		
Employer's name & address:		
Work phone number:		

WORKSHEET 1: INCOME AND EXPENSES

	Borrower ($)	Coborrower ($)	Total ($)
I. INCOME			
A. Monthly gross income			
1. Employment			
2. Public benefits			
3. Dividends			
4. Royalties			
5. Interest & other investment income			
6. Other (specify):			
B. Total monthly gross income			
II. MONTHLY EXPENSES			
A. Nonhousing			
1. Child care			
2. Clothing & personal expenses			
3. Food			
4. Insurance (auto, life, medical, & dental)			
5. Medical & dental care (not insurance)			
6. Taxes (nonhousing)			
7. Education			
8. Transportation			
9. Other (specify):			
B. Current housing			
1. Mortgage payment or rent			
2. Taxes			
3. Insurance			
4. Utilities			
C. Total monthly expenses			

WORKSHEET 2: ASSETS AND LIABILITIES

I. ASSETS (Cash or Market Value)	Borrower ($)	Coborrower ($)	Total ($)
A. Cash & cash equivalents			
1. Cash			
2. Deposits (list):			
B. Marketable securities			
1. Stocks & bonds (bid price)			
2. Other securities			
3. Mutual funds			
4. Life insurance			
5. Other (specify):			
C. Total cash & marketable securities			
D. Nonliquid assets			
1. Real estate			
2. Retirement funds			
3. Business			
4. Motor vehicles			
5. Other (specify):			
E. Total nonliquid assets			
F. Total all assets			
II. LIABILITIES			
A. Debts			
1. Real estate loans			
2. Student loans			
3. Motor vehicle loans			
4. Child or spousal support			
5. Personal loans			
6. Credit cards (specify):			
7. Other (specify):			
B. Total liabilities			
III. NET WORTH (Total assets minus total liabilities)			

price. If a 20% down payment would deplete your resources, look into government-assisted loans, discussed in Chapter 11.

Remember, in addition to the down payment, you must be able to afford the monthly mortgage, insurance, and property tax payments. If your income is relatively low, you may have to increase your down payment to 25%–30% of the price of a house to bring down the monthly payments. If, however, you have both a good income and enough money set aside for a larger-than-required down payment, you have a choice: You can put more money into the down payment or invest it elsewhere. We discuss your options in Chapter 4.

Once you've completed your family financial statement and done the basic calculations described above, you should have a good sense of how expensive a house you can realistically hope to buy.

Estimate the Mortgage Interest Rate You'll Likely Pay

The next step in arriving at your monthly mortgage is to determine the interest rate you'll pay on a mortgage. This is important because, over the life of your mortgage, you will probably pay much more in interest than you will in principal. A relatively small difference in your interest rate will amount to a big difference in your total debt, and hence the amount of your monthly payments. The table below illustrates the differences by interest rate and mortgage term, using the example of a $100,000 mortgage.

Monthly and Total Payments on a $100,000 Fixed Rate Mortgage				
	15-year period		30-year period	
Interest Rate (%)	Mo. pmt.	Total pmts.	Mo. pmt.	Total pmts.
5.0	790.80	142,344	536.83	193,259
5.5	817.09	147,076	567.79	204,404
6.0	843.86	151,895	599.56	215,842
6.5	871.11	156,799	632.07	227,544
7.0	898.83	161,789	665.30	239,509
7.5	927.01	166,862	699.21	251,717
8.0	955.65	172,017	733.76	264,155
8.5	984.74	177,253	768.91	276,809
9.0	1,014.27	182,569	804.62	298,664
9.5	1,044.22	187,960	840.85	302,708
10.0	1,074.61	193,430	877.57	315,926
10.5	1,105.40	198,972	914.74	329,306
11.0	1,136.60	204,588	952.32	342,836

Because different mortgage types carry different interest rates, start by deciding the mortgage type you want. If you haven't yet decided, read Chapters 8–12 for a thorough review of mortgage options.

Calculate How Much House You Can Afford

When you have a pretty good idea of the size of your down payment and the interest rate you expect to pay, you can calculate how much house you can afford.

The easiest way to do that is to use an online calculator, like those listed below. These calculators use your income and debts, along with the basic terms of the mortgage you expect or hope to get, to determine how much you can afford to borrow.

If you'd rather do the calculation yourself, follow the steps below.

1. **Estimate the amount you need to borrow.** First, you'll have to estimate the purchase price for the home you hope to buy. Reduce that by the amount of the down payment you expect to make (hopefully 20%). That's the amount you'll need to borrow.

2. **Estimate your monthly mortgage payment.** Begin by estimating the mortgage interest rate you expect to pay, based on up-to-date rate information in the Sunday paper or online. (See Chapter 13 for a discussion of gathering information on mortgage rates.) Then, using the Amortization Chart below, find the corresponding mortgage factor. Multiply this number by the number of thousands you'll need to borrow. The result is your estimated monthly principal and interest payment.

3. **Estimate insurance and property taxes.** Add the following factors together: homeowners' insurance (expect to pay $800 to $2,000 per year) and property taxes (approximately 1.2% to 1.8% of the purchase prize). Divide that number by 12 to calculate a monthly cost for insurance and taxes.

4. **Estimate other house-related expenses.** If you're making a down payment of less than 20%, estimate monthly payments for private mortgage insurance or PMI. (See Chapter 4 for more information on PMI.) Also, if you expect to pay fees to a homeowners' association, estimate that monthly fee. Add these numbers together.

5. **Calculate your other fixed monthly debt.** This should include any other monthly debt you have, such as a car loan, student loan, or credit card debt. Add these monthly debt obligations together.

6. **Add items 2–5.** These are your monthly expenses.

7. **Estimate lender qualification.** Generally, lenders will allow your monthly mortgage obligation to be between 0.28 and 0.36 of your gross monthly income (the fewer your debts, and the higher your credit score, the higher the number you use can be).

8. **Divide item 6 by item 7.** That number is the amount of monthly gross income you'll need to get the loan that you want. You can multiply that number by 12 to calculate the yearly gross income you'll need to qualify.

Tips on Improving Your Financial Profile

Bringing your housing costs and monthly debts within the generally acceptable debt-to-income range of 28%–36% should allow you to get a home loan. Many people find, however, that it requires more than 36% of their monthly income to make house payments as well as pay their other debts. If you fit this description, here are some ways to bring yourself within the acceptable range.

Amortization Chart
Mortgage Principal & Interest Payment Factors (Per $1,000)

Interest rates (%)	15-year mortgage	30-year mortgage
4.00	7.39	4.77
4.25	7.52	4.91
4.50	7.64	5.06
4.75	7.77	5.21
5.00	7.90	5.36
5.25	8.03	5.52
5.50	8.18	5.68
5.75	8.31	5.84
6.00	8.44	6.00
6.25	8.58	6.16
6.50	8.72	6.33
6.75	8.85	6.49
7.00	8.99	6.65
7.25	9.13	6.82
7.50	9.27	6.99
7.75	9.41	7.16
8.00	9.56	7.34
8.25	9.70	7.51
8.50	9.85	7.69
8.75	9.99	7.87
9.00	10.14	8.05
9.25	10.29	8.23
9.50	10.44	8.41
9.75	10.59	8.59
10.00	10.75	8.78

Online Mortgage and Financial Calculators

If you hate math, dozens of websites offer calculators to help you determine monthly payments on different-sized mortgages and how much house you can afford. All calculators are not created equal, so sample different ones until you find the calculator that gives you the information you're looking for in the format you prefer.

 WEBSITE RESOURCE

Nolo's website has a variety of real estate calculators to help you, at www.nolo.com/legal-calculators. A few others that appear to have staying power are www.homes.com, www.mortgage-net.com/calculators, www.quickenloans.com, and www.mortgage-calc.com.

Pay Off Debts

The best way to improve your debt-to-income ratio is to pay off some debts. Not only will this reduce your total monthly payments and thus, in the eyes of lenders, leave more of your income to be used for mortgage payments, it will also result in other savings.

First, because the interest rates on consumer debts (such as credit cards) are almost always higher than the rate on mortgage debts, paying off the first type to qualify for more of the second can result in substantial savings. Second, because the interest paid on consumer debts is not tax deductible, while the interest portion of your mortgage is fully tax deductible, you qualify for another substantial saving. For example, if you're in the 28% federal tax bracket and 9.3% state bracket, 34.7% of all interest you pay on your mortgage is subtracted from your taxable income. (This takes into account the fact that state income taxes are a deductible item on your federal tax return. For more on the tax deductibility of mortgage interest, see Chapter 4.)

Check with your lender before deciding which (and how much) of your debts to pay off. You don't want to improve your ratio and then discover you've wiped out a significant part of your down payment. If you do end up short for the down payment, consider selling some of your possessions or tapping friends or relatives for help (discussed below).

Convert Assets to Cash

If you need a few thousand extra dollars to pay off debts or increase your down payment, look for it in your garage, basement, or attic. If you're like most people, you may have many saleable items you don't really need. If you sell them and use the cash to either pay off other debts or increase your down payment, your financial picture can look significantly better.

Also look at your investments as a source of cash. Consider cashing in whole life insurance policies (if the cash value is significantly high) or withdrawing money from a retirement account or plan.

> **TIP**
>
> **Keep records to show "source of funds."** Lenders may suspect that any new savings with a less than two- to three-month history is really a loan.

Emphasize Imminent Income Raises

Lenders commonly require proof that you've been employed, without interruption, for the last two years or so. Exceptions, however, may be made in rare and compelling cases.

For example, if you have just graduated from college, and have started a new, salaried position within your field of expertise, a lender may waive the minimum employment requirement. If you worked part-time within the field you're studying, or worked as an intern, it will help to add that to your employment record on the application.

If future raises are given at the discretion of your employer, consider discussing your house purchase with your boss. If the boss believes that your future with the company is bright, he or she may commit to a pay raise now or, in some cases, even arrange for your employer to make you a loan at a lower-than-market rate of interest.

If You Work for Yourself, Show a Profit or Make a Big Down Payment

Millions of Americans work for themselves, or supplement their income by operating a small business on the side. Few of these businesses show large taxable profits; rather, most owners take advantage of the Internal

Revenue Code rules which make it reasonably easy for small business owners to minimize their taxable earnings. Unfortunately, when a small business owner wishes to borrow money, doing everything legally possible to minimize income for tax purposes is likely to come back to haunt you.

Typically, a small business owner will try to convince a lender that the $28,000 of taxable income reported to the IRS was really closer to $50,000, if deductible business expenses such as transportation, meals, a home work space, depreciation, contributions to an IRA or Keogh plan, self-employment tax, contributions to medical insurance, and entertaining are added back in. But this may be difficult to do. Lenders have heard it all before, and although they may privately acknowledge that an applicant's financial situation is likely to be better than reported to the IRS, they won't normally lend money in this situation unless the buyer can make a down payment of 25% or more. With a high down payment (and excellent credit rating), a borrower may qualify to purchase within accepted debt-to-income ratios even with relatively modest taxable income.

Normally, however, to qualify for a mortgage if your business shows an artificially low profit, you'll need to report a larger taxable profit. If your business really is quite profitable, this should take only a year or two. Instead of writing off every possible personal expense as a business expense while paying yourself a low salary, raise your pay, and treat more expenses as personal. You'll pay more federal income tax, but once

you qualify for a mortgage loan, you can cut it back by deducting your mortgage interest and property tax payments.

TIP

In the past, lenders liberally offered "stated income loans." To get one, you simply told the lender your annual income, without tax returns or pay stubs to back it up. In exchange, you'd pay a higher interest rate. Don't count on getting one of these loans now, some borrowers were taking advantage if these "liar loans" artificially inflating their income, and qualifying for large mortgages they later defaulted on. This made lenders nervous, and means that if you truly need a stated income loan, you'll have a hard time finding one.

Borrow From Friends or Family

We discuss ways to raise money from family and friends in Chapter 12, Private Mortgages. For purposes of showing that you're able to make a solid down payment, you'll need an outright gift, or a loan that doesn't need to be paid back for a considerable period of time, and you may need to get it into your bank account a few months (usually three) prior to loan approval. This is called "seasoning" the funds. A lender wants you to have the money necessary to qualify, not to create another debt that will compete for repayment with your mortgage.

A gift made at the time you're purchasing a house requires documentation that it is a gift, not a loan. (See Chapter 4 for more on gifts.)

Check Your Credit Rating and Clean Up Your File

Your credit report, in particular your credit score, will affect the type and amount of mortgage loan lenders offer you. (See "How Credit Scores Affect Loan Qualification," above.)

Prospective buyers should check their credit files, kept by credit reporting agencies (also called credit bureaus), before applying for a loan. Unfortunately, credit files often contain out-of-date or just plain wrong information. Sometimes they confuse names, addresses, Social Security numbers, or employers. If you have a common name (say John Brown), don't be shocked if you find information in your credit file on other John Browns, or John Brownes, or Jon Browns. Obviously, you don't want this incorrect information given to prospective lenders, especially if the person you're being confused with is in worse financial shape than you are.

A few credit problems doesn't mean you'll never get a loan. It may mean that you'll have to pay a higher interest rate or make a larger down payment. Talk to your mortgage broker—it's the best way to find out how or if you'll qualify for a loan.

How to Get a Copy of Your Credit Report

You can get a free copy of your credit report once a year from each of the three major credit bureaus, which adds up to three free reports per year if you time things right.

You can request your report on the Internet (www.annualcreditreport.com), by phone (877-322-8228), or by mail (Annual Credit Report Request Service, P.O. Box 105281, Atlanta, GA 30348-5281). If you request service by mail, you'll need to include a request form (available on the above website).

You can also contact any of the three major national credit bureaus directly, either to request a copy of your report or ask other report-related questions:

- Equifax, www.equifax.com
- Experian, www.experian.com
- TransUnion, www.transunion.com.

If you need to request more than one credit report per company in the course of a year, you may need to pay, usually no more than $13 apiece.

You are also entitled to a copy of your credit report for free, however, if:

- You have been denied credit because of information in your credit file. You must request your copy within 60 days of being denied credit.
- You are unemployed and planning to apply for a job within 60 days following your request for your credit report.
- You receive public assistance.
- You believe your credit file contains errors due to someone's fraud, such as opening up accounts by using your name or Social Security number.

How to Correct Errors in Your Credit File

If you find any wrong information, take steps to correct the errors. You have the right to insist that the credit bureau verify any wrong, inaccurate, or out-of-date information. Once the credit bureau receives your request, it has 30 days to reinvestigate and tell you its findings. If you need a faster answer, tell them. Items that can't be verified must be removed.

Typical problems include:

- You're a self-employed carpenter, yet your file says you work as a TV repairperson or, worse, are unemployed.
- You're listed as owing a debt that's been repaid.
- A department store bill you owed eight years ago is still listed as outstanding. A credit bureau cannot keep information on file for more than seven years—with one exception: Bankruptcies may be listed for ten years.

If the credit reporting agency insists on retaining inaccurate, wrong, or outdated information, or lists a debt you refused to pay because of a legitimate dispute with the creditor, you have the right to place a brief statement in your file giving your version of the situation.

How to Clean Up Your Credit

If the information in your file is accurate but unfavorable, your best strategy is to clean up your credit before seriously trying to purchase a house. Here are some tips:

- **Remove delinquencies.** Fully pay off small debts ($500 or less). For larger accounts, contact the creditor and attempt to work out a payment plan so that you're no longer listed as delinquent. Then stay current on the account.

Some creditors you've owed for a while may accept less than the total amount owed "as payment in full." A creditor who has given up on collecting may jump at a lump sum payment of two-thirds of what's due. If so, make sure the creditor acknowledges in writing that you've satisfied the debt in full. If the creditor has a court judgment, make sure a "satisfaction of judgment" is filed with the court that issued the judgment. Show the satisfaction of judgment to the credit reporting agency. Be aware that a bank creditor that waives $600 or more must report your "savings" to the IRS. The IRS considers it income to you, and you may have to pay income taxes on it.

- **As a last resort, get professional assistance.** If you owe several creditors varying sums and can't figure out how much to pay whom, you might contact a nonprofit credit advisory group such as Consumer Credit Counseling Services (CCCS). To find the nearest CCCS office, call 800-388-2227 or check the national website at www.nfcc.org, which will link you to local office websites. Be warned, however: There are many different consumer credit counseling organizations, and not all are created equal. Some charge high fees for little service. To find out more about consumer credit counseling, visit the National Consumer Law Center at www.nclc.org.

- **Rebuild your credit.** If you've suffered a major financial setback in the past few years (repossessed automobile, judgment against you for a large debt, foreclosed home, or bankruptcy), you'll need to rebuild your credit, unless a creditworthy person will cosign your mortgage loan, you have cash, or you can borrow from friends or family.

It normally takes two to three years to rebuild your credit. Here are some steps to do so:

1. **Create a budget.** Most of the information you need is in your Family Financial Statement. Compare your monthly income to your total monthly expenses. If your expenses exceed your income, commit to some spending reductions and stick to them.

2. **Get a secured credit card.** Many banks will give you a credit card and a line of credit if you first deposit money into a savings account or certificate of deposit. The line of credit can be up to 150% of the amount you deposit. Use the credit card, and keep absolutely up-to-date on payments. A major drawback with these cards is that the interest rate often nears 20%. To avoid piling up new debts, use the card to charge items that you would have purchased anyway, and pay it off in full each month. After a year or two, banks and other large creditors will likely grant you a higher credit limit and drop the savings account requirement.

3. **Borrow from a bank.** Requesting between $1,500 and $5,000, take out a personal loan. To qualify, you may need a cosigner. Make your monthly payment on time, and your credit will improve rapidly.

If you have enough cash to handle more than one loan payment, deposit the loan you received from the first bank in a second bank, again turning in the passbook in exchange for a loan. Now your credit report shows that two banks have extended you loans.

4. **Obtain a revolving credit card.** Some department stores and gasoline companies will issue credit cards with low lines of credit to almost anyone. Even though you've had a major financial setback, before long you're likely to receive offers for store or gas company credit cards in the mail. Accept one or two and charge small amounts for items you need, paying bills promptly.

    Note: Strategies 2, 3, and 4 are also useful for someone who has never used credit and needs to build a credit history.

5. **Work with a local creditor.** Purchase an item that you really need (such as furniture or possibly a car) on credit. Even if you have a poor credit history, many local businesses will work with you to set up a payment schedule, but be prepared to make a large deposit (up to 30%), pay a high rate of interest, or find someone to cosign your loan.

 RESOURCE

For additional information on credit files and rebuilding credit after a financial setback: See *Credit Repair,* by Robin Leonard and John Lamb (Nolo).

> ⚠ **CAUTION**
>
> **Exaggerating or listing bogus information on your loan application won't help anything.** A lender can and will check the accuracy of your application. Your falsifications will very likely be discovered and held against you—that is, you could be prosecuted for fraud.

Get Loan Preapproval

As an essential step toward purchasing a good house at a reasonable price, it's important to be preapproved for a loan. This means a lender has actually done a credit check on you and evaluated your financial situation, rather than simply relied on your own statement about your income and debts. Preapproval means that the lender would actually fund the loan, pending an appraisal of the property, title report, purchase contract, and any last verifications of your employment and finncial resources.

Get a preapproval letter as soon as you start househunting. Sellers often accept offers from purchasers who can successfully or quickly close the deal (that is, have already arranged financing and have a preapproval letter), even if they don't make the highest offer. A seller who has had earlier deals fall through because of a buyer's financing problems is especially likely to accept an offer, even a low one, backed by a loan preapproval. And even if the seller hasn't seen previous deals fall through, his or her real estate agent no doubt has—it's become an all-too-common occurrence since the real estate meltdown of 2008. Some would-be buyers have even found their lenders unwilling to issue a preapproval letter, and other buyers who got preapproved have found that their lender gets cold feet at the last minute and demands lots of extra documentation or simply refuses to make the loan. The agent will be carefully scrutinizing your financial paperwork to make sure that accepting an offer from you won't be more trouble than it's worth.

> 💡 **TIP**
>
> **Get a preapproval letter for the exact amount of your bid.** When you bid for a home, ask your lender to prepare a new letter stating that you are preapproved for the amount you are offering—no need to tell the seller that you can actually pay more if you wish.

For preapproval, your lender will ask you to pull together various documents, which usually include:

- pay stubs for the last two pay periods
- last two years' tax returns and W-2 forms
- proof of nonsalary income such as rental income or alimony
- three months of bank statements for every account you have (all pages)
- proof of assets such as pension funds, stocks, or life insurance
- source of your down payment, including documentation for any gift funds involved
- names, addresses, and phone numbers of employers for the last two years, and
- names, addresses, and phone numbers of landlords for the last two years.

If you are preparing the application yourself, complete every section. Don't leave any blanks. If an item doesn't apply, write "not applicable" or "N/A."

The lender will review and approve your file, subject to some conditions such as, but not limited to, an acceptable property appraisal, a copy of your purchase contract, and clear title to the property. Your loan officer will review the lender conditions with you to make sure that you will be able to satisfy the lender's requests.

And be ready for follow-up requests right up until the day of your house purchase closes.

Prequalification Versus Preapproval

Once you've completed your financial statement, a lender or loan broker can prepare a prequalification letter saying that loan approval for a specified amount is *likely* based on your income and credit history. Unlike preapproval, prequalification is not even close to a commitment by the lender to lend you that amount, or to lend you money at all. Prequalifying will just help you determine how much you're able to borrow and how much you'll need for a down payment and closing costs.

However, you'll want to do more than prequalify for a loan—you will want to be preapproved for a specific loan amount. Your offer will be more attractive because the seller will know ahead of time that you'll most likely be able to afford the purchase.

Narrowing the Affordability Gap: How to Afford Buying a House

SKIP AHEAD

No money worries. Those few readers with enough money to purchase the house of their dreams and no inclination to bargain hunt can safely skip this chapter. The other 95% should stick around and learn how to overcome the affordability gap.

Why California Houses Are Expensive

The concept of the affordability gap is simple—many house buyers can't afford to buy their ideal house. Some can't afford any house at all. The gap, while particularly acute in urban coastal areas of California, exists in many parts of the state, for several reasons:

- In the past generation, millions of baby boomers have entered their prime house-buying years, creating heavy demand.
- Historically, more people have tended to move to California than leave it (though this has reversed with recent economic downturns).
- Rising construction and lumber costs and, in many areas, restrictive government regulations and taxes, have made it expensive, and sometimes even impossible, to build new housing.
- Recently, interest rates have been at historic lows, allowing more people to enter the real estate market. This has increased demand, keeping prices more stable than they'd otherwise be. Though this trend has leveled

somewhat as many overextended buyers have recently defaulted on their loans, it has still contributed significantly to the growth of demand in recent years.

- Even in a down economy, houses are looked upon as a sound investment.

California House Prices

In mid-2010, the median sales price of an existing California single-family detached house was $311,950, according to the California Association of Realtors®. The median price is the middle point of all sales prices, meaning that one-half of all houses sold for more and one-half sold for less. This is different from the average, which is considerably higher (because high-priced luxury homes pull the average up).

In much of the San Francisco Bay Area and Southern California, the median sales price was considerably higher, reaching $1 million or more in wealthy communities such as Cupertino, Palos Verdes Estates, and Manhattan Beach.

 WEBSITE RESOURCE

For median prices of California houses, see the California Association of Realtors® website at www.car.org. Click the "Newsstand" or the "Market Data" area.

Fortunately, as this chapter shows, there are many creative ways Californians have found to beat affordability problems—such as using equity in a starter house to finance a more expensive one later, having relatives or friends help with the down payment, buying a fixer-upper (substituting sweat equity for capital), and getting the seller to finance part of the purchase by taking back a second mortgage.

Don't Buy a House at All—Rent and Invest Elsewhere

Not everyone should strive to overcome the affordability gap to purchase a house. If you're happy renting and think you'll continue to be for years, there's little point in stretching your finances to the breaking point. In fact, if you live in an area where monthly rents are less than mortgage payments on the same house would be, renting might be a good strategy.

There are many advantages to renting: You don't tie up a lot of money in home equity and improvements, and someone else worries about (and pays for) property maintenance, repairs, insurance, and taxes. In addition, putting all your savings toward a house leaves you with no financial cushion to fall back on in case of an emergency.

A principal advantage of renting is that money not tied up in down payments and improvements can be invested in ways that may produce a better long-term return than a house will. Of course, this depends on interest rates and the housing market at the time you buy and sell. In the early 2000s, people watching their stock portfolios evaporate turned to houses as a more reliable investment. On the other hand, in recent years home buyers in many areas watched home prices stagnate or fall.

The major disadvantage of renting is that your entire monthly payment vanishes. With home ownership, part of each mortgage payment goes toward equity in your home. The remainder (interest), along with local property taxes, is deductible from your income taxes. People in higher tax brackets obviously have the most to gain (in terms of the largest tax break) by buying a house versus renting.

So, what's the bottom line? Is it better to buy or rent? Too many variables make it impossible to produce a definitive answer. Below are a few factors to consider that, depending on your circumstances, may tip the balance one way or the other:

- **The shorter the time you plan to stay put, the more financially advantageous it is to rent.** People who buy and sell often incur transactional costs, such as real estate commissions and closing fees and costs. Commonly, a buyer must own a house for at least three to five years, and sometimes longer, for its increase in value to cover these costs. In other words, a home typically has to appreciate in value by at least 8% to 10% to recover the transaction costs, so if you think you'll sell within two to three years, you're almost always better off renting instead.

- **It's a lot easier to move from a rental unit than from a house.** With a house you own, you can't just give the landlord notice and pick up and leave.
- **Renters have no protection against rent increases beyond the term of their rental agreement or lease.** The exception, of course, is if you live in a rent-controlled area. If you have a fixed rate mortgage, your loan payments remain constant.
- **Rent payments may be less than mortgage payments for the same house.** This depends on the curent economy and local supply and demand, however, so sometimes the reverse is true.
- **A house forces you to be a disciplined investor.** If you're not good at saving and investing money, buying a house is a good way for you to build up a financial nest egg, especially as compared to renting and spending your excess money.

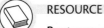

RESOURCE

Rent versus buy: online calculators. To help with your "rent versus buy" decision, see www.realtor.com, www.nolo.com/legal-calculators, or online mortgage broker sites such as E-Loan, www.eloan.com, discussed in Chapter 13.

Fix Up the House You Already Own

If you own a house and plan to sell it to purchase a more expensive one in the same area, consider remodeling rather than selling. You often get more for your money, and possibly a better location. And better yet, you avoid moving to a house that may be many miles from your job, your friends, or your children's school. Indeed, land prices are so high in some cities, such as Santa Monica, that they dwarf the cost of construction to the point that buyers commonly purchase modest houses on desirable lots only to tear them down and build afresh.

There are several other economic advantages to staying put and spending a large sum to redo your house. For one, you save the transactional costs of selling your existing house and closing on a new one.

However, it's easy to underestimate remodeling costs. In figuring out how much it would cost to fix up and perhaps add on to your existing house, don't take shortcuts. Make a detailed plan and cost it out carefully. Here's how to think about the cost of remodeling as compared with the cost of moving.

Moving

- Figure out how much cash you would net for your existing house by subtracting what you owe from its likely sales price.
- From this amount, subtract around 8% of the sales price for real estate commissions and other sales costs.
- Now add any money you've saved for housing. The total is the amount you can put down toward the purchase of a new house.
- Estimate how much you'll need to pay for a suitable new house.
- Add 5% for your share of closing costs and moving expenses.
- Add remodeling costs, if any.

Remodeling

- Estimate the cost of hiring an architect experienced in house remodeling to draw the plans you need.
- Get a hard-eyed contractor's estimate for work you decide on.
- Add 20%–33% to the estimate to cover things you haven't considered and inevitable cost overruns.
- Add these costs to what you already owe on your house plus any costs of temporarily moving out and renting another place while remodeling, if that will be necessary.
- Consider how much you've saved to pay for remodeling or moving. You'll have to borrow any difference between what you have and what you need. If mortgage interest rates have gone down since you bought your house, often the cheapest way to borrow is to get a short-term construction loan and then, when the work is done, refinance the entire loan and your mortgage together. If interest rates have risen, however, keep your original mortgage and take out a second mortgage to refinance the construction.
- Finally, estimate how much the house will be worth in its remodeled condition. Ask local real estate agents and appraisers for their opinions on the house's current value and estimated value after remodeling.

Now ask yourself some big questions. How do the out-of-pocket costs of moving versus remodeling compare? And when the work is done, how much will each house be worth? If the cost of fixing your existing house is only 20%–30% of the purchase price of the new house, you're probably better off staying put.

It's not usually financially wise to remodel an existing house if any of the following are true:

- **You plan to sell the house in a year or two.** Although remodeling will increase the house's value, and you'll get more when you sell it, you're unlikely to get enough more to pay for your investment and trouble. In short, your improvements will benefit the next owner, not you.
- **You live in a marginal area, and your renovated house will be substantially bigger and nicer than its neighbors.** It's always hard to get full value when selling the best house on the block.
- **The work you plan won't substantially increase your house's sales price.** Remodeled kitchens, bathrooms, and extra bedrooms tend to increase the value of a house by 75%–100% of what the remodeling work costs. On the other hand, swimming pools and spas often increase the value by only 50% of what they cost to install—and can sometimes decrease a house's value, because they create maintenance and liability insurance costs. Improvements to the foundation, roof, wiring, or plumbing often result in an even smaller increase in house value, as purchasers assume they should be in good shape to begin with.

RESOURCE

Online resources on remodeling. Everything you need to know about remodeling— from choosing a contractor to setting a budget to design ideas—can be found at ImproveNet at www.improvenet.com. Also see www.nari. org, the website of the National Association of the Remodeling Industry. And the website of *Remodeling* magazine, at www.remodeling.hw.net, offers an annual "Cost vs. Value Report," analyzing which home remodeling projects lead to the greatest rises in property value.

Strategies for Buying an Affordable House

One obvious way to beat the affordability gap is to find a good house at a comparatively reasonable price. Not only are there great differences among houses offered for sale, but the sellers and buyers, who often have little prior experience with real estate, have vastly different family situations, tastes, and even prejudices. For example, the house at 111 Maple St. may be offered for sale by a retired financial planner determined to get top value, while a similar house at 112 Maple may be offered for fast sale by a divorcing couple or an out-of-town seller who has just inherited it. Sometimes, homes sell to the first person who makes an offer, especially if the owner likes the person, without exposing the home to the entire real estate market.

Below we'll discuss 18 strategies to narrow the affordability gap. Most are practical in today's market. A few have less merit but are included because potential home buyers often ask about them. Some of these strategies won't be relevant to you, but skim through them to see if you find one that helps put an affordable home within reach.

What You Can Afford Relates to Your Financing

The focus of this chapter is on how to purchase a good house for 10%–20% below what many others will pay. A major consideration is how you finance the purchase—covered in the following chapters:

- Raising Money for Your Down Payment (Chapter 4)
- Financing Your House: An Overview (Chapter 8)
- Fixed Rate Mortgages (Chapter 9)
- Adjustable Rate Mortgages (Chapter 10)
- Government-Assisted Loans (Chapter 11)
- Private Mortgages (Chapter 12), and
- Obtaining a Mortgage (Chapter 13).

Don't Buy Until You've Saved More Money

First-time purchasers often ask whether it's better to buy a less-than-perfect house now or to save like mad for a few years to afford a better one later. Traditionally, the answer has been "buy now." In California, house prices have tended to increase faster than savings.

However, in recent years, prices in parts of California have dropped significantly and it's unclear how much further they could fall. If you believe that house prices in the area you are interested in are currently too high and are going to level off or drop, you may do better by saving your money and waiting a few years.

Move to a More Affordable Part of the State

There's no better strategy to buying an affordable house than moving from an area with high housing costs to an area where houses cost far less. A house that would cost $750,000 in a posh suburb of Los Angeles or San Francisco would sell for much less in some communities near Bakersfield or Sacramento.

However, unless you work at home or for an employer that pays the same wages no matter where the location (such as the state or federal government), you will probably make less money in low cost areas. But the ratio of your earnings to local house prices is what's important to comparing the affordability of housing in different areas. For example, if you can make 60% of your Orange County salary in Merced, but comparable houses cost 35% as much, your ability to buy a nice house has increased greatly.

Buy a Less Desirable House Than You Really Want

People caught in an affordability squeeze typically must scale down their new-house wish list. A good percentage fall into three broad categories:

- Buy a marginal house in a desirable area.
- Buy a desirable house in a marginal area.
- If you face a severe affordability gap, buy a marginal house in a marginal area.

How Leveraging Can Work When Prices Start to Rise

A main reason why, in an up market, it's possible to trade up to a better house quickly is that investing in a house gives you a unique chance to make a big gain on a small investment. For example, if you buy a house for $400,000, putting $80,000 down and taking a $320,000 mortgage, and a few years later the house goes up in value 20%, you've doubled your $80,000 investment. Pros call this being "highly leveraged." If you put the same $80,000 into a government bond earning 6%, it would take you nearly 12 years to achieve the same result.

Of course, the flip side to being highly leveraged is that if the value of the property drops, your investment can be quickly wiped out. In the example above, if the property's value dropped 20%, the entire $80,000 would be gone.

Buy a Marginal House in a Desirable Area

In older residential areas, where houses were typically built one by one or in small groups, house size, construction techniques, and lot size often vary significantly. On the same block, house prices can differ by a hundred thousand dollars or more. This means that bargains can, and do, pop up where you might not expect to find them, particularly in older neighborhoods.

Here are some houses that seem undesirable but can be greatly improved at modest expense:

- **Houses with ugly exteriors but pleasant interiors.** You'd be amazed at the number of prospective buyers who won't even get out of the car to enter a truly homely house.
- **Houses on busy streets that can be "turned around" to focus on a backyard.** For example, you might spruce up the back by adding a deck or patio.
- **Houses with run-down interiors that need a lot of elbow grease and creative tinkering.** Not only is paint cheap, but replacing wallpaper, linoleum, formica, and light fixtures can normally be done at a reasonable cost.
- **Houses that can be screened from a busy street or other undesirable outdoor feature.** If there's room (and zoning rules allow you) to build a stout redwood fence or plant a thick, tall hedge, you can often block the problem from view. Street noise can often be reduced by walls, fences, and certain types of vegetation. (See, for example, *Sunset* magazine's *Landscaping for Privacy: Hedges, Fences, Arbors.*)

Buy a Desirable House in a Marginal Area

One good way to maximize gain in the short term is to buy a good house in an up-and-coming area that will appreciate quickly after purchase. We don't have a sure-fire technique for spotting a marginal area about to improve. (If we did, this book would cost a lot more than it does!) But we can give you a few useful hints:

- **Avoid the worst neighborhoods.** Prices in desperately poor areas with high crime rates may improve eventually, but not as soon as you'd like; in the meantime, you face the day-to-day reality of living in a dangerous environment.
- **Avoid marginal areas on the immediate periphery of the worst neighborhoods.** As long as the blighted area is there, the marginal area is unlikely to improve much.
- **Look for areas that have been substantially devalued by something no longer, or soon to be no longer, an issue.** For example, house values are likely to be depressed by the proximity of a large, loud, and filthy factory, cannery, or railroad spur-line. If the offending feature is about to close and the surrounding area is otherwise desirable, you may have found a terrific place to buy.
- **Look for blighted areas where a few hardy middle-class pioneers have already settled.** Once these pioneers begin turning things around, small businesses often follow, restaurants and cafes open, and then, seemingly overnight, individuals and developers buy and transform the dilapidated housing stock in the area. If you think you have a good idea about such an area, check with local planning departments. Applications for building permits and plans can tell you a lot about future prospects for a particular area.
- **Look for lower-priced areas touching on more desirable ones.** Many affluent California cities have one or more poorer cousins nearby. Areas particularly likely to improve are pockets of larger old houses.

- **Look for affordable areas where transportation, especially public transportation, is good or will improve soon.** Much of California is already experiencing almost terminal traffic gridlock. The result is that older residential areas convenient to rail or ferry systems are almost sure to increase in value faster than the average residential area.
- **Look for affordable areas within excellent school districts.** It's sometimes possible to find a pocket of affordable housing in an upscale school district.

 TIP

Think twice before buying a nice house in a poor school district. Because house prices (and their chances of appreciating comparatively quickly in the future) are always affected by the quality of local schools, even people without children should think twice about buying

where schools are poor, because values will not appreciate as much.

- **Pay attention to where immigrants are locating.** Property values in many previously depressed areas have jumped substantially as large numbers of new Americans locate there.

Buy a Marginal House in a Marginal Area

There's not much positive to say about buying a relatively undesirable house in a bad neighborhood, even though you can do this comparatively cheaply. We purposely de-emphasize this approach, both because of immediate problems (high crime and run-down public and private services) and because property values in very poor areas usually appreciate far more slowly than in other neighborhoods. But as with any

---

True Story

Problem Houses in Good Areas Can Be a Bargain

Our friend Tim, a savvy real estate professional, recently conducted an experiment. He blindfolded Kim, an experienced agent, and drove her to a house for sale, telling her only that it was located in a particular upscale neighborhood. When Kim entered the house, Tim removed her blindfold and asked her to look around, but not to open the blinds covering the front windows. After ten minutes, Kim was asked how much the house was worth. She replied that if the house didn't have any

major structural problems, she'd guess it would sell for about $525,000.

When Tim told her the actual asking price—$410,000—Kim was flabbergasted. She then opened the blinds and saw that the house was on a busy local street. Even so, she continued to maintain that the house was underpriced.

The point should be readily understood—problem houses in nice neighborhoods are often underpriced, even when a reasonable amount is subtracted to compensate for the problem.

general rule, there are exceptions. Again, the most obvious is an area where large numbers of immigrants move in and quickly change the neighborhood's character. Another involves areas with an extremely desirable location that the city or private developers have already targeted for improvement. For example, plans to build a new ballpark or convention center in an area are often a tip-off that other major changes for the better are likely to follow.

Buy a Fixer-Upper

The era when a dilapidated house in a reasonably decent area could be purchased dirt cheap and fixed up at a moderate cost is past. The demand for this type of house has risen steadily for at least the last two decades, resulting in comparatively high prices for remaining fixer-uppers in all but the most undesirable neighborhoods. Part of the reason is that buying distressed houses, fixing them up quickly, and reselling at a profit is a profitable business for many small contractors, which means house buyers face professional competition.

While most fixer-uppers are no longer great deals, they still cost less than a comparable house in good shape. Ask your real estate agent about special loans available from the Federal Housing Administration for fixer-uppers. (See Chapter 11.) Also, consider purchasing a foreclosed property, which will often be a fixer-upper. (See "Buy a House Subject to Foreclosure," below.)

When you consider the time, effort, and cost of finding and renovating a house, however, a fixer-upper is unlikely to be

a bargain. Indeed, many fixer-uppers sell above their fair market value when you take a hard-eyed approach to the real costs of repair. This is especially true for lower-priced houses, where it will be hard to recover the costs of major repairs in a subsequent sale. Fixer-upper bargains are more likely to be found in higher price ranges, where affluent buyers tend to look for houses already in good condition.

TIP

How to judge whether a fixer-upper is a good deal. If you're seriously interested in a particular fixer-upper, hire a reliable remodeling contractor to check it out carefully and give you an estimate of needed renovation costs. If the total cost of the rehabilitated house is 90% or more of the cost of a comparable house in good shape, keep looking. By the time you factor in the trouble you'll go through and the likelihood of cost overruns, you won't save anything.

How to Find an Ugly Duckling

Bargain hunters who want to find a reasonably priced ugly duckling and turn it into a swan don't always know where to look. Look for ads or write-ups that say "not a drive-by," "a diamond in the rough," "has potential," or "needs TLC."

Buy a Small House and Add On Later

If you find a small house on a relatively large lot priced comparable to, or only slightly above, similar houses on ordinary-sized lots, you pay little or nothing for the extra land. In addition to the added privacy and room to play and garden, you normally have the space to enlarge the house any time you can afford to hire a contractor or have the time to do the work yourself.

Even if the lot isn't that large, consider buying a smaller house with remodeling potential and adding a second-story addition. Of course, check first to be sure that local zoning laws allow the changes you want to make.

Keep in mind, though, that while this strategy will address a short-term lack of cash, it won't necessarily be the most cost-effective in the long term. It's always faster, and almost always less expensive, to buy a larger home in the first place than to build onto an existing home.

Buy a House at a Probate Sale

Probate sales occur when a homeowner dies leaving property to be divided among inheritors, or to be sold to pay debts or taxes. The sale is handled by the executor of the homeowner's will (or a court-appointed administrator if there is no will). It is often supervised by the probate court judge, through a bidding process. The highest bidder gets the property. Some probate sales are handled directly by the executor of an estate without going through the court bidding process.

Occasionally it's possible to buy a house at an estate or probate sale for substantially less than the current market rate. The time and uncertainty involved in bidding discourages many potential buyers from participating. Less buyer competition can mean a lower-than-market price. Also, the cost of bidding

---

True Story

Monica and Dave: Building Additions

Monica and Dave knew they wanted a three-bedroom, two-bath house in the Berkeley-Oakland area for a maximum of $575,000. They also dreamed of a large deck for weekend lounging and parties. But after 18 months of looking at nearly 200 houses, they had not found anything even marginally decent in their price range. So they took a new approach—they looked at smaller houses with expansion potential.

Within weeks, they found a house in North Berkeley with only two bedrooms and one bath (and no deck). At $525,000, the price was right. Best of all, the backyard was deep enough to leave plenty of room to add on to the back. After checking carefully and assuring themselves it was feasible to add on a bedroom later, they said yes. They quickly added a second bathroom (using a space that had been a closet/hallway) and a large deck. After five years, their new equity allowed them to qualify for a home equity loan to add a second-story master bedroom.

How a Court-Supervised Probate Sale Works

Here are the basic steps in a court-supervised probate house sale:

- The house is advertised for sale in a newspaper (often a legal or fairly obscure one) published in the county in which the property is located and, if listed with a broker, in a Multiple Listing Service.
- An appraisal value is established.
- Bids are accepted by a certain date.
- During the court procedure, higher bids are accepted. A cashier's check may be required with each bid. The first higher bid (called an "overbid") must exceed the original highest bid by at least 10% of the first $10,000, plus 5% of the balance. For example, the first overbid on a $200,000 offer must be $210,500:

10% of $10,000	=	$1,000
5% of $190,000	=	9,500
		$ 10,500

- An alternate formula that will get you the same result is 5% of the offer price plus $500.
- Subsequent overbids are allowed in amounts set by the probate judge. For example, the judge might require that each new bid exceed the previous one by $1,000.
- The highest bid, if it is at least 90% of the property's court-appraised value, is accepted.
- Purchase of the property is normally financed in the same way as any other purchase.

(you will likely be required to include a cashier's check for 10% of the price you're offering) discourages people from making casual bids.

The down side is that probate sales aren't subject to disclosure laws (discussed in Chapter 19), so while agents must legally disclose all pertinent facts, many probate-sold houses are sold "as is." Your bid made in court cannot contain financing, inspection, or other contingencies.

If you're considering buying a house at a probate sale, here's some advice for getting the best deal:

- **Hook up with a knowledgeable broker or salesperson who knows the ropes of probate sales.** There are a few in every community.
- **If you plan to bid at a court-supervised probate sale, line up a highly trustworthy and thorough inspector.** Have the inspector check out any house before the court confirmation procedure. (See Chapter 19 for details on inspections.)
- **Find a house that has been appraised too low.** This may be less difficult than you imagine, since a good percentage of houses subject to probate sales are run down. (Chapter 15 discusses how to evaluate sales prices.)
- **For court-supervised sales, consider holding off on your bid until the court procedure begins and the first round of bids are in.** (See "How a Court-Supervised Probate Sale Works," above.) At some probate sales, many bids are placed by investors hoping to pick up a house very cheaply and quickly resell it for a profit. If you can figure out what professional

investors will offer and bid just a little higher, you can sometimes save a bundle. Call the probate court clerk (it's part of your county's superior court) for a list of probate sales on the court calendar. Then check out the property carefully. If it looks like the buyer got a great price, inspect the property, line up your financing, and hope to overbid them at the court confirmation. Contact the attorney handling the estate for the date and time of the confirmation hearing.

Buy a House With a Structural Problem

California law strictly requires that a seller and agent disclose all known problems with a house, using detailed forms entitled "Real Estate Transfer Disclosure Statement" and "Natural Hazard Disclosure Statement." (Copies are in Chapter 19.) In addition (as discussed in Chapter 19), most buyers and lenders insist on careful prepurchase inspections before the sale. As a result, many California houses are inspected two or three times.

Recently, fear of lawsuits for failing to disclose house defects has resulted in some inspectors exaggerating flaws and generally emphasizing the negative. This makes some houses far more difficult to sell than was the case ten years ago. If buyer interest dries up (as it often does when a house has a long list of problems), the asking price of a house will almost surely drop, sometimes precipitously. The house is likely to be perceived by local agents as being stale

(hard to sell at any price), and thus it will be shown to fewer prospective purchasers. Before long, the price may be lowered again, creating a bargain despite the physical problems.

CAUTION

It is often difficult to get loans that include funds for major repairs or renovations. Your best bet is to find a portfolio lender (see Chapter 2) with more flexible policies. To do this, you'll probably need the help of a fairly sophisticated mortgage broker who knows local lending practices well. (See Chapter 13.)

Buy a House Subject to Foreclosure

Foreclosure normally begins when a home-owner misses several mortgage payments and receives a notice of default. During the three months following, the homeowner can make the back payments and cure the default. If he or she does not pay up, the house proceeds to foreclosure. For some people, purchasing a house subject to a foreclosure is a way to buy a house for less than its appraised value.

Home foreclosures aren't usually advertised through the online Multiple Listing Service (MLS) or other normal channels. The best place to check on your own is through websites such as www.realtytrac.com, though you have to pay a weekly membership fee to get anything more than bare-bones details of the listings. Another membership-based service, which contains listings of government foreclosures, is www.hudworks.com.

SEE AN EXPERT

In all stages, it's usually best to hook up with a real estate agent who knows the foreclosure ropes. Many foreclosure markets are dominated by savvy investors, and you'll be at a disadvantage if you aren't represented by someone familiar with the process.

The three broad approaches to buying a house subject to foreclosure are:

1. **Purchase from the owner during the three-month period before the foreclosure sale.** During the three-month period following default the owner may want to sell the property to avoid foreclosure and severe credit damage. At this point, some owners are delighted to sell for little or nothing more than they owe to the lenders, because they've given up hope of keeping the house. In some cases, the owner may even sell the house for less than is owed on the mortgage—this is called a "short sale," and requires the lender's approval, which typically takes months to obtain.

2. **Purchase at the foreclosure sale.** If no one brings the mortgage current or buys the house before the sale, the trustee holds a foreclosure sale and sells the house to the highest bidder. The trustee opens the bidding at the amount of the outstanding mortgage being foreclosed. Potential buyers (often investors) attend the sale or auction with cash or a cashier's check in hand for a little more than the amount they plan to bid (to allow for a small increase). This up-front cash requirement eliminates casual bidders from foreclosure sales.

3. **Purchase after the foreclosure sale if no one bids.** If no one bids at the sale, the foreclosing mortgage holder gets the property back. In recent years, savings and loans and other lenders have ended up with a fair number of houses this way, most of which they want to sell quickly, even if it means taking a loss. (These properties are often called REOs, for "Real Estate-Owned.") Some lenders sell the properties themselves (often with favorable prices and low down payments); the better properties, however, are commonly turned over to real estate brokers, who try to sell them as they would any other house. Even so, the fact that the foreclosed house wasn't prepared for sale by an owner, and thus may be in less than perfect shape, often means there are bargains to be had.

Before purchasing a home through a private or government foreclosure sale, ask these questions:

- **Is the house worth significantly less than you would have to bid to get it on the open market?** If not, don't bother. (See Chapter 15 for how to assess the value of a house.)

- **Are there major problems with the house or property?** Like probate sales, foreclosure sales are an exception to California Civil Code § 1102 requiring sellers to disclose all known problems. Many foreclosed properties are sold "as is," so (if possible) be sure to arrange your own thorough inspection for any structural, mold, or pest control problems before you commit to a purchase. In fact, mold problems have been the cause of some recent foreclosures: Homeowners find themselves in situations where the mold remediation would cost tens or hundreds of thousands of dollars and the insurance company won't pay a cent—so the only choice they can afford is to hand their keys to the bank.

- **Are you taking clear title?** (Title is the history of ownership; see Chapter 18 for more information.) The owner may have had other financial problems, and creditors may have placed liens on the house. Normally, these are paid off or wiped out during the foreclosure process, but before agreeing to buy the house, you'll want to be sure all liens really have been removed.

- **Are there tenants living in the house?** If so, make sure they're gone when you get the house. The last thing you want to do is evict a tenant who doesn't want to leave. If you're buying in a rent controlled area, however, you may have to buy subject to "tenants' rights." Although as an owner you are entitled to live in your house, you may very well have to assert this right by evicting the existing tenants after you purchase. If so, we suggest *The California Landlord's Law Book: Evictions,* by David Brown (Nolo).

Government Foreclosure

If the distressed house had financing guaranteed by the U.S. Department of Veterans Affairs or insured by the Federal Housing Administration (of the U.S. Department of Housing and Urban Development), bidding at a foreclosure sale must follow the agency's rules (typically sealed bids submitted by mail). Buyers frequently must go through a time-consuming and bureaucratic process before the sale is final. But don't let this scare you—government agencies often have good-sized inventories of foreclosed properties and will sometimes offer bargain prices, low down payments, and attractive financing deals to move them.

A real estate agent experienced with government foreclosures can help you locate and buy these types of houses. Government-foreclosed properties are often advertised in local newspapers. For more information, contact the U.S. Department of Veterans Affairs or Department of Housing and Urban Development. (For addresses and websites, see Chapter 11, Government-Assisted Loans.)

 RESOURCE

Foreclosures:

- *The Complete Idiot's Guide to Buying Foreclosures,* by Bobbi Dempsey and Todd Beitler (Alpha).
- *The Smart Money Guide to Bargain Homes: How to Find and Buy Foreclosures,* by James Wiedemer (Dearborn Financial Publishing).

- *Big Money in Real Estate Foreclosures,* by Ted Thomas (Wiley).
- *How to Find Hidden Real Estate Bargains,* by Robert Irwin (McGraw-Hill Trade).

Make Multiple Backup Offers

If you are patient and flexible, you may be able to buy a house at a substantial discount by placing low backup offers on houses for which the seller has already accepted a higher offer. In doing this, you're gambling on three things: that the first offer will fall through (we estimate this happens about 10%–20% of the time, usually because of inspection or financing contingencies), that the seller hasn't already arranged for a backup offer, and that the seller will accept your backup offer rather than put the house back on the market.

Here are some basic rules to follow in making backup offers:

- **Learn the local market.** Remember, it's no bargain to buy a house for 10% less than either the asking price or the amount of the first offer if its price was 15% too high in the first place.
- **Adopt a bidding strategy.** For example, some buyers decide to bid about 5%–10% lower than a house's fair value (not the asking price). If you bid lower than this, you probably won't be taken seriously.
- **Make all backup offers contingent on your subsequent right to approve, should the seller accept.** Reserving a right of approval is essential if you make more than one backup offer; otherwise, if two

or more are accepted simultaneously, you may find yourself in a legal mess and may lose any deposit you've made.

Buy a "Shared Equity" House With Someone You'll Live With

Equity sharing is a fancy term for buying a house with someone other than a spouse. The attraction of equity sharing is that two or more people with pooled resources can buy more house than each can alone. It goes without saying that if you own and live in a house with others, you'd better be personally compatible. Equity sharing tends to be most popular among unmarried couples, although it's also reasonably common with friends and relatives not in romantic relationships. Although many equity-sharing couples live lives similar to married couples, their legal property-ownership arrangements are bound to be different, since California's marital property laws do not apply to them.

Regardless of whether the equity sharers are a couple or not, they should have a written contract. It should spell out the percentage of the house each person owns; who pays how much each month for the mortgage, taxes, insurance, and other costs; what happens if the household breaks up or an owner dies; as well as a number of other practical ownership issues. We discuss a few of these issues in Chapter 20, but to draw up an equity-sharing contract, you'll need additional information. (See "Resource: Writing shared equity contracts," below.)

RESOURCE

Writing shared equity contracts: Nolo publishes the following books to help equity sharers cope with owning property together:

- *The Sharing Solution,* by Emily Doskow and Janelle Orsi, addresses sharing real estate and other property with friends.
- *Living Together: A Legal Guide for Unmarried Couples,* by Ralph Warner, Toni Ihara, and Frederick Hertz, contains several sample house purchasing contracts for unmarried couples.
- *A Legal Guide for Lesbian & Gay Couples,* by Hayden Curry, Frederick Hertz, and Emily Doskow, contains sample contracts similar to those in *Living Together* but adapted to address the special concerns of lesbian and gay couples and groups buying together.
- *Deeds for California Real Estate,* by Mary Randolph, discusses the different ways of taking title to and transferring real property in California.

Buy a "Shared Equity" House With Only One Owner (You) Living on the Property

Equity sharing between a resident owner and an investor is often touted as a good solution for people with affordability problems. The idea is for a nonresident investor to put up a chunk of the down payment in exchange for a share of profits when the house is sold.

Equity sharing is not the best way for one person to help another buy a house. From the house purchaser's point of view, it's usually better to simply borrow the money and own the entire property. Similarly, equity sharing is often a poor idea for the investor. When a house is viewed as an investment

by a lender and as a home by its occupant, the potential conflicts are huge. What if the resident wants to make improvements that will enhance the house's livability but which won't increase its market value? What if the nonresident wants his money back, but the resident doesn't want to sell and can't afford to pay the nonresident his share? Or, even more serious from the investor's point of view, what if the resident owner ceases making payments and refuses to vacate the house? Yes, a written contract can and should deal with these and many other similar questions, but, contract or not, the possibilities for future conflict are considerable.

If, despite these warnings, you want to pursue equity sharing with a nonresident because you've got no other way to raise enough money for a down payment, it may make the most sense to buy with someone who is not a relative or friend, so as to establish that it's clearly a business deal. A good real estate agent should be familiar with programs in your area that bring buyers and investors together.

Typically, the investor supplies all or most of the down payment while the buyer lives in the house, maintains it, and pays all or most of the mortgage, insurance, and tax payments. At an agreed-upon date, the home buyer refinances and pays the investor the down payment plus a specified share of the appreciation. A clear, written agreement is necessary to cover the following:

- the use of the home
- the amount of the initial investment and the percentage of ownership
- buy-out provisions

- the amount and type of insurance to carry, and allocation of the proceeds should the house be damaged or destroyed (for example, by fire)
- the responsibility for daily costs and capital improvements, and
- the details of any sale or refinance (such as time, price, and profit splits).

 CAUTION

Take tax rules seriously. It's crucial that the buyer and investor clearly understand tax laws regarding shared equity arrangements. Consult your tax attorney or accountant for advice on your particular situation.

RESOURCE

Equity sharing:

- *The New Home Buying Strategy: Solve Your Cash Crunch With Team Buying Power,* by Marilyn D. Sullivan (Venture 2000 Publishers), contains sample contracts, useful tax information, and tips on how to make an equity sharing transaction work for both the investor and the resident owner.
- Another good book on equity sharing is *The Home Equity Sharing Manual,* by David A. Sirkin (John Wiley & Sons).

Rent Out Part of the House

One way to overcome affordability problems is to increase monthly income by renting out a room. Renting out a room in an urban area may bring in $800 per month or more, which is $9,600 a year. This increased income may not only help you pay the mortgage, it may also help you qualify for a larger loan amount because your debt-to-income ratio will decrease.

Renting also offers tax advantages. A homeowner can deduct only property taxes and mortgage interest on federal income taxes, while a rental owner can also deduct business expenses, such as repairs and utilities, and take depreciation on the portion of the home that is rented out.

If you're seriously considering renting out a room or two as part of your house-financing strategy, you'll need to do some homework. Start by finding out how much rent you can reasonably charge—that is, what local tenants pay for similar space. Then check with your financial institution or loan broker to be sure they'll let you count the expected rent as part of your monthly income.

Buy a Duplex, Triplex, or House With an In-Law Unit

Another approach to increase income is to buy a duplex or triplex, then live in one unit while renting out the others. A variant of this approach is to buy a large house with a separate, smaller "in-law" unit.

However, there's considerable competition for these types of houses, which means prices are often marked up to the point that rental income is entirely eaten up by the extra monthly costs of the larger mortgage.

Your goal is to find a house selling for little more than if the second (or third) unit wasn't there. The more unconventional the second unit, the more likely you are to be able to accomplish this. For example, if an "in-law" unit is tucked under a hillside house with access down a driveway and around two trees and a rosebush (as opposed to being attached to your unit, with a door facing the street), the real estate market may undervalue it.

 CAUTION

Make sure an extra unit is legal. Especially if an extra living space looks homemade, demand to see necessary permits. If they don't exist, you run the risk that the city or county will close down the unit—or make you fix it—because it doesn't comply with building codes. If there are no permits, don't pay any more for the property than you would if the extra unit didn't exist.

Lease a House You Can't Afford Now With an Option to Buy Later

A lease option is a contract where an owner leases a house (usually from one to three years) to a tenant for a specific monthly rent (which may be scheduled to increase during the contract term) and gives the tenant the right to buy the house for a price established in advance. The tenant pays some money for the option—a lump sum payment at the start of the contract or periodic payments (all nonrefundable). Depending on the contract, the potential buyer normally can exercise the option to purchase at any time during the lease period or at a date specified.

EXAMPLE: Ted and Jane lease Robin's house for $1,700 per month for two

---

True Story

Deborah, Doug, and Rose: The Joy of Living Near Grandma

Deborah and Doug have a two-year-old daughter. Both artists, they wanted at least 1,500 square feet to accommodate their family and need for studio space. Here's how they bridged their affordability gap:

"We wanted to stay in our long-time neighborhood, but, unfortunately, couldn't afford it. Then we heard about a place right around the corner that sounded great—except that it was more expensive and larger than we needed.

"Deborah's mother, Rose, provided an unexpected solution. She offered to help us with the down payment and monthly mortgage payments in exchange for living in one of the units. We quickly struck a two-thirds–one-third financial split. Our family took the three-bedroom unit on the top floor and converted the bottom-floor unit into a home for Rose and the middle unit into a fantastic studio space. We now have our ideal house at a price we can afford, while still retaining our privacy. But the best part is the special relationship between our daughter and her grandma. We wouldn't miss it for the world."

years. In addition, they pay Robin $4,000 for the option to purchase the house for $380,000 at any time during the two years. If Ted and Jane decide to buy, the $4,000 will be credited against the purchase price; if not, Robin keeps it.

This example is deliberately made simple to give you the general idea. Most lease option deals are more complicated. For example, the house purchase price might be a fixed dollar amount, plus an amount tied to any increase in the Consumer Price Index. Or, instead of an up-front option fee, the rent might be set at a higher-than-normal amount, with part, or all, of the extra applied to the purchase price if the option to purchase is ever exercised.

TIP

Buyers want all extra payments credited toward the purchase price. A prospective purchaser who pays a flat fee in exchange for an option to purchase, or agrees to a higher monthly rent to achieve this benefit, makes a good deal only if all money over and above a reasonable rent will be credited toward the purchase price if the option is exercised.

A potential buyer who chooses a lease option will get to move into a home without having to come up with a down payment or financing. It also gives the potential buyer time to clean up any credit problems and to see if he or she can handle the house's maintenance and repair costs and other issues. Even better, it allows the luxury

---

True Story

Author Ira Serkes's Purchase of a Small Berkeley Multiunit Building

"When I first got interested in real estate, I couldn't afford a single-family home. Instead, I looked for a small apartment building where I could live in one unit and have rental income from the others subsidize the mortgage. I originally looked at triplexes but ended up buying a fixer-upper seven-plex. My family invested with the down payment and shared the appreciation. For the next five years, I lived in one of the units. With the help of some tenants, I renovated each apartment as it became vacant. As the value of the building went up, I borrowed against it and used the money for a down payment on another small building.

"My successes inspired a friend of mine to begin investing with me. Now I own a nice house and a number of investment properties, whose monthly rents helped put my nieces through college. And the best fringe benefit of buying this small apartment building is it was where I met my wife, best friend, and business partner Carol! She rented an apartment from me, I broke my rule about going out with a renter, and the rest was history!"

of waiting to see if the value of the house reaches or surpasses the amount of the option price before deciding whether to purchase. If the value does increase, the house will be easier to finance, as the buyer will already have equity (the difference between the sales price and the then-current market value).

Lease options can often fairly easily be arranged in colder markets or when the house is a hard one to sell—don't be afraid to ask, especially if the house has been on the market for awhile.

Here's what to look for:

- An owner having trouble selling the house at the asking price.
- An owner who needs to move now, but who, for tax reasons, doesn't want the profit on the sale to be taxed in the current fiscal year. Often owners about to retire and enter a lower tax bracket fit this description.
- An owner for whom the initial option fee and/or higher-than-normal rent means an excellent short-run return— perhaps filling a house that would have otherwise remained vacant until it sold.
- An owner who hopes you won't exercise the option, giving the owner a premium rent (or up-front option fee payment) while keeping the house.

 RESOURCE

Lease options: *For Sale by Owner in California*, by George Devine (Nolo), includes a sample lease option contract.

Buy a Condominium

Many California condos are priced temptingly low when compared to houses. A condominium (condo) owner owns the unit outright plus an undivided share of common areas (halls, parking areas, roof, plumbing, yard, deck, and the like). To maintain these areas, owners usually must pay fees to a condominium association, in addition to local property taxes assessed on each unit. Condos include a number of restrictions on how the property can be used, such as the type of landscaping you can do or the number or weight of pets you can own. These restrictions are spelled out in a document called the covenants, conditions, and restrictions (CC&Rs).

Condos come in all shapes and sizes, from duplexes to high-rises, and there can be good reasons for buying one. Many people appreciate the decreased maintenance that comes with having some areas held in common. Particularly if you're considering buying in a city or other area where there's limited land on which to build, a condo may be a very good choice.

Historically, however, condos haven't appreciated in value as fast as single-family homes. And you'll need to carefully check out the overall financial situation before buying. A financially unstable developer, or many owners already in foreclosure, could spell trouble for you.

Buy a Town House

Town houses—usually single-family houses with common walls—have surged in

Lease Option Contract (Renter-Buyer's Perspective)

A lease option contract should address the following:

- **When the option can be exercised.** Avoid lease option contracts that allow you to exercise your option only under very restrictive circumstances—for example, for one week at the end of the second and fourth year.
- **The purchase price if you exercise the option.** It's far better to have it fixed at the start of the lease period, even if an increase for inflation is built in, rather than set by an appraisal at the time you exercise the option to purchase.
- **How much of the rent or upfront option payment will be applied toward the down payment or purchase price if the option is exercised.**
- **Exactly how you can exercise the option.** Written notice sent by certified mail is a good approach.
- **Whether the seller will help you finance the house by taking back a second mortgage.** If so, get the details.
- **An inspection of the house.** It is best to have the house thoroughly inspected before the lease option is signed to determine what repairs are needed.
- **Assignability.** If you choose not to exercise your option, it's nice to be able to sell that right to someone else, if possible, for cash or a share of the house's equity.
- **Any other significant terms of the purchase.**

CAUTION

Beware of termination clauses. Avoid any clause in a lease option contract that ends your option if you fail to perform your duties under the rental agreement in a timely manner. Such a clause could let the owner end the option contract if you're late with the rent, even once. Instead, you want a clause that lets you exercise the option to buy if your rent is paid up at the time you choose to exercise the option.

In addition, make sure the lease option contract is notarized and recorded at the County Recorder's Office. This will ensure that your right to purchase will appear on any title search, meaning the owner can't duplicitously sell the house out from under you without your knowledge.

Finally, unless you're experienced in this field, have the contract checked by someone who is. For sample lease option contracts, see "Resource: Lease options," above.

popularity in California because they're relatively inexpensive. And well they should be; they save on land, because common walls and roofs are cheap to build. With most town houses, you hold legal title to your house and the land it's on. You must pay real estate taxes even though you and your neighbors sit on the same piece of land and share common walls.

Town houses may be a better investment than condos. One reason for this is that many town houses, unlike most condos, are two-story, which means they physically look somewhat like single-family houses; condos, which often contain many units, often physically look more like apartment units. Because many people prefer the size and scale of a house (regardless of form of ownership), town houses are a bit more likely than condos to increase in value.

Does this mean that town houses are as good an investment as small detached starter houses? Usually not. Most people prefer living in a house that doesn't share walls with its neighbor. Still, if you can't afford a nice starter house in a decent area, an affordable town house may be a better choice than buying a run-down, detached house in a marginal neighborhood.

Buy Into a Cohousing or Cooperative Arrangement

Another increasingly popular way to find an affordable house is to enter into a cooperative arrangement with others. This usually involves finding or building an apartment building or a series of town houses or small units with shared common areas such as walkways, gardens, or children's play areas. In legal terms, the possible arrangements run the gamut, from condominium-type ownership, in which each buyer purchases his or her own mortgage ("cohousing"), to cooperatives, in which all share a "blanket" mortgage.

A cohousing community is often conceived of, designed, and developed by the people who will live in it. They are not guaranteed to be low cost. However, their emphasis on compact living units with shared resources such as common kitchen and dining areas, walkways, gardens, parking areas, and laundry facilities means that some savings are possible.

For more information on cohousing or similar forms of intentional communities, as well as architects and developers, contact:

- Cohousing Resources, LLC, Langley, Washington-based development consultants, www.cohousingresources. com.
- Fellowship for Intentional Community, in Rutledge, Missouri, 660-883-5545, www.ic.org. You might enjoy their *Communities Directory,* which contains descriptions of over 700 communities in the United States and abroad.
- CoHousing Partners, Nevada City, CA, www.cohousingpartners.com.
- The Cohousing Association of the United States, Bothell, WA, www.cohousing.org.

Unlike cohousing, housing cooperatives are normally set up as nonprofit or public trust corporations. The nonprofit arrangement is referred to as a "limited equity housing cooperative" or "LEHC."

People who want to live in a housing cooperative buy in as shareholders. Shareholders don't own individual units, but their shares entitle them to a proprietary lease on a specific unit. During their ownership, each buyer also pays a monthly carrying charge to cover the mortgage, insurance, and other expenses. If the cooperative will provide housing for low- and moderate-income people, public subsidies can be obtained to help with these carrying charges.

Limited equity housing cooperatives are highly structured, since they're governed by California law. (Civil Code § 817 and Bus. and Prof. Code § 11003.4.) To qualify for entry into an LEHC, you'll need to meet eligibility criteria set by the cooperative (which may or may not include proving that you're low income). You'll also need to get lucky—these cooperatives are being developed only as quickly as nonprofit developers can find land or buildings at low cost, which is no simple matter for anyone in California. Still, the developers sometimes persuade the previous property owners to sell at a below-market price, which translates into savings for the shareholders. And there's nothing to stop you from forming your own nonprofit group to create a cooperative—in fact, some disgruntled tenants have used this method to take control of their living space, by getting together and buying out the landlord of their complex.

While limited equity housing cooperatives are affordable to buy into, the law creates a catch when you sell. You'll receive only a little more than your purchase price back, plus interest (a maximum of 10% per year),

regardless of the property's current market value. That allows your unit to be resold at an affordable price, but it prevents you from following the traditional path of building equity in a starter home and working your way up as property values increase. Still, if your primary goal is to find a decent place to live with comparatively low up-front and monthly payments, an LEHC may be a good choice. And if your monthly payments are low enough, you'll have an opportunity to save—and invest—money that you might not have had if you'd been renting.

To find out more about cooperative housing arrangements, contact your city or county building departments or do a Web search for "limited equity housing," "cooperative housing," or "affordable housing."

 RESOURCE

Our search turned up the following organizations that help create or find this type of housing option:

- National Association of Housing Cooperatives, in Washington, DC, www.coophousing.org.
- Northern California Land Trust, in Berkeley, CA, www.nclt.org.
- Shared Living Resource Center, in Berkeley, CA, at 510-548-6608.

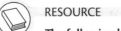 **RESOURCE**

The following books offer information on shared living alternatives, designs, and lifestyles:

- *The Sharing Solution: How to Save Money, Simplify Your Life & Build Community,* by Janelle Orsi and Emily Doskow (Nolo).

- *Cohousing: A Contemporary Approach to Housing Ourselves*, by Kathryn McCamant, Charles Durrett (Contributor), and Ellen Hertzman (Ten Speed Press)
- *The Cohousing Handbook: Building a Place for Community*, by Chris ScottHanson and Kelly ScottHanson (New Society Publishers)
- *Rebuilding Community in America: Housing for Ecological Living, Personal Empowerment, and the New Extended Family*, by Ken Norwood and Kathleen Smith (Shared Living Resource Center).
- *Reinventing Community: Stories from the Walkways of Cohousing*, by David Wann (Fulcrum Publishing).

Buy a House at an Auction

In parts of California where the real estate market has been particularly slow, sellers try to attract buyer interest by auctioning houses. Many auctions are of new houses in situations where developers need to raise quick cash to pay lenders. Foreclosed properties are also sometimes sold at auction.

As a general rule, buying at an auction won't get you a good deal. It should go almost without saying that amateurs (home buyers) rarely beat pros (homesellers familiar with auction procedures and investors who regularly buy at auctions) at their own game. This is especially true when you understand that the seller will take steps to be sure that

True Story

Ken Norwood: Strawberries, Consensus, and Low Monthly Fees.

In the late 1980s, the tenants of our 20-unit property in Berkeley got tired of watching the place go to pot. The tenants decided to organize a cooperative and buy the property. They arranged a private bridge loan for the purchase, which gave them four years to go through the process of organizing as a nonprofit, meet other state requirements, and get long-term financing.

I was interested in cooperative housing and was actually providing architectural services to the group, while renting a room somewhere else. When a unit came open, the group actually loaned me part of the initial purchase price, and I've been happily living here ever since.

Now the property is in great shape—we've just torn up some asphalt to make room for five more fruit trees. We've got four or five green-thumbers, and they voluntarily tend to the strawberries, chard, tomatoes, flowers, and trees around the property. Two common rooms and a roof deck are used for our monthly potluck meetings as well as for parties, exercise (we invested in weight machines), and free laundry. Our monthly meetings are consensus-based. We make decisions on how best to improve the property—such as our planned seismic work and attic insulation—and choose new owners. Sellers get a 4% increase over the amount they paid in. And, best of all, our monthly fees are far less than most people in Berkeley pay for rent.

the house won't sell at a rock-bottom price, including:

- setting a floor price—a price below which the house won't be sold
- advertising extensively—to be sure to collect a crowd
- hiring a professional auctioneer skilled at loosening up the crowd and building auction fever, and
- although it's illegal, sometimes planting shills in the audience to bid up the price.

If auctions are held in your area, a better strategy than actually bidding at the auction is to compare the prices for houses sold at auction with those of houses sold in the normal way. (You may need to attend a few auctions to get this information.) Just learning which sellers are motivated to sell is extremely valuable. And if you like what you see at the auction and the seller has other houses to sell (which is common with developers), stop by on a weekday near the end of the month and offer to buy for slightly less than the auction price. Or make a list of sellers with similar properties not being auctioned, and offer to buy for a little less than the auction price.

If despite this advice you decide to bid at auction, follow these basic rules:

- Research how much comparable houses are selling for in the same area—if you don't know the local market well, you're almost sure to get taken. (See Chapter 15 for how to find out comparable sales prices.)
- Attend several auctions without your checkbook (or paying a bidding fee) to get the hang of how they work. You can also get a sense of how auctions

---

True Story

Anne and Frank: We Bought a Great House at an Auction

We bought a nice house 13 years ago for $200,000 and recently sold it for $450,000. Because we both have fairly good jobs, we had the down payment and the income necessary to move up.

We wanted to live in Marin County and heard that some new luxury houses that had originally been listed at $900,000 had proved unsaleable and were being auctioned with a floor bid requirement of $625,000. We were there for the first sale, but didn't bid. The house went for $710,000, which we figured was too high. On the second and third house to be auctioned, we noticed that one person (let's call him Ollie) who bid at the first sale was bidding again, but each time dropped out at the last minute.

We smelled a rat (a shill) but didn't say anything. We wanted the fourth house and bid several times, until the price was $650,000. Then, when Ollie bid higher, we objected and said we were going to call the District Attorney's Consumer Fraud Unit and the State Real Estate Department and file a complaint. Ollie immediately disappeared, and we got a great house at a good price.

work by doing a Web search for "real estate auctions."

- Research deposit requirements and financing options before you commit yourself to buying property at an auction.
- Ask for brochures that describe the property, and read all the fine print.
- Check out the house's physical condition before buying. Real estate auction companies must disclose known structural problems and defects of property (excluding foreclosures). (See Chapter 19 for details on state disclosure law and inspections.)
- Be sure you're taking clear title to the property. (See Chapter 18 for details.)
- Don't pay more than 10% above the minimum or "floor price," or 70%–75% of the original asking price.
- Get help researching.
- Decide in advance how much you'll pay, and don't bid a penny more.
- If there is lots of bidding on a particular house, drop out fast—if you get into a bidding war, you'll surely pay too much.

Raising Money for Your Down Payment

Let's start with the basics. Down payments are usually discussed as a percentage of a house's purchase price, not a specific dollar figure. A 20% down payment is 20% of the price you pay for the house, such as $60,000 on a $300,000 house. In addition, lenders often use the real estate industry jargon "loan-to-value ratio" (LTV) in referring to the down payment required. A mortgage with an LTV of 90% requires only 10% down, an LTV of 80% requires 20% down, and so on.

The down payment amount depends on the interplay of many factors, including:

- your savings from all sources
- your monthly income
- the house's purchase price
- the type of mortgage you choose
- your credit history, and
- the size of the mortgage.

 SKIP AHEAD

If you're relatively affluent and will put 20% or more down: You can skip most of this chapter, except for "How Much Should Your Down Payment Be?" It discusses the pros and cons of making a big down payment.

Assisted No and Low Down Payment Plans

The Federal Housing Administration, U.S. Department of Veterans Affairs, California Housing Finance Agency, and Cal-Vet program and a few California municipalities offer low down payment mortgage plans. Down payment and eligibility rules for these programs are discussed in Chapter 11, Government-Assisted Loans.

Five and Ten Percent Down Payment Mortgages

Some lenders offer mortgages to people who put 5% or 10% down, but only if the buyer has stellar credit and enough income to make the monthly payments within the lender's debt-to-income guidelines.

If you're really strapped for cash, ask your lender about low down payment plans such as FannieNeighbors and the Community Home Buyer's Program. Some California lenders offer these Fannie Mae mortgage plans, which feature a 5% down payment (even lower in some cases) and flexible qualifying guidelines. FannieNeighbors is a revitalization program, available to buyers who purchase a home within designated central cities or eligible census tracts. The Community Home Buyer's Program is available for loans outside of these designated areas. Both programs, however, are limited to home buyers whose income is equal to or less than the area median income.

 RESOURCE

For more information, contact Fannie Mae at 800-7FANNIE or check out the website, www.fanniemae.com.

If you take out a very low down payment loan, be ready to pay a slightly higher interest rate and loan fee (points) and to purchase private mortgage insurance (PMI), discussed below.

Private Mortgage Insurance

Private mortgage insurance (PMI) policies are designed to reimburse your mortgage lender up to a certain amount if you default on your loan and the foreclosure sale price is less than the amount you owe the lender (the mortgage and the costs of sale).

Today, most California lenders require PMI on loans where the borrower makes a down payment of less than 20%. PMI typically protects lenders for 20%–25% of the purchase price of the house, offsetting at least some of the loss resulting from foreclosure and resale.

The Cost of PMI

Expect to pay between 0.4% and 0.6% of your loan amount for your PMI premiums, depending in part on the size of your down payment. This usually ends up costing buyers somewhere between $80 and $200 a month.

Monthly payments aren't the only possible PMI payment plan. You'll typically be given a choice of whether to pay the full PMI premium amount at closing, split the PMI into a flat fee at closing along with ongoing monthly payments, or simply make monthly payments.

Some lenders offer to pay your PMI, but charge you higher interest in return. This isn't necessarily a worthwhile deal, because you can eventually stop paying PMI when your equity in the house has risen, while you'd be stuck with the higher interest rate for as long as you keep the loan.

TIP

Is PMI tax deductible? For mortgages on your primary residence taken out between 2007 and 2010, PMI was tax deductible. The deduction starts to fade out when your family income reaches $100,000, disappearing completely beyond $109,000. No word at the time this book went to print on whether the deduction would be extended.

Comparing PMI Policies

Some PMI policies are better consumer deals than others. Here's what to look for.

Premium rates. Although you can't choose your own PMI company, you can choose your lender and, if all else is equal, borrow from a lender offering PMI with lower rates.

Impound account. PMI policies also require that you set up an impound account, to pay the lender (or organization that services the loan) the cost of the premium. The lender in turn pays your property taxes and home-owner's insurance. These impound accounts result in your paying for taxes and insurance before you need to, thus losing the interest you'd earn if you kept that money in the bank. Even worse, some lenders require that you pay up to a year's worth of PMI into the impound account when the house purchase closes, thus increasing your up-front costs. And you still pay an amount monthly.

If you're required to set up an impound account, monitor it carefully. In the past, some borrowers have faced significant hassles because the lender forgot to pay the taxes and insurance, with the buyers unfairly receiving a negative credit rating as a result.

How to Drop PMI

Except for some government loans, California law allows you to drop PMI once your loan is no more than 75% of either the original purchase price (so long as its value hasn't dropped) or the current fair market value of the house and you meet the following requirements (Civil Code § 2954.7):

- The house was purchased after January 1, 1991.
- You own and live in a one- to four-unit residential property.
- You've paid at least two years of PMI premiums.
- You are up to date on mortgage payments.
- You have not been more than 30 days overdue on any mortgage payment during the previous two years or otherwise defaulted.
- You make a written request to the lender based on an appraisal you paid for, by an appraiser chosen by the lender.

If you meet the above conditions, the PMI should be automatically canceled—that is, you should not need to take the initiative and request PMI cancellation (Civil Code § 2954.12). There are some exceptions to this law—ask your lender for details.

If your loan is sold to Fannie Mae or Freddie Mac (see Chapter 8), your lender must agree to drop PMI once your equity reaches 20% and you've made timely payments for at least 12 months.

How Much Should Your Down Payment Be?

If you can afford to make a large down payment, should you? Consider the following factors in support of it:

- **The larger your down payment, the lower your monthly payments.** It feels good to have adequate money each month for other expenditures.
- **The larger your down payment, the less it will cost you to borrow.** For example, if you put 20% down on a $300,000 house and borrow $240,000 at 5% for 30 years, you'll pay $223,814 in interest over the life of the loan. If, however, you put 40% down and borrow $180,000 at 4.5%, you'll pay $148,332 in interest.
- **Lenders won't require private mortgage insurance (PMI) if you make a down payment of 20% or more.** That might save you hundreds or thousands of dollars a year.
- **It's easier to get a good loan.** With a large down payment, the lender knows you're unlikely to default, and, even if you do, the house can almost surely be resold for enough to cover the mortgage.
- **It's easier to find a willing seller.** Whether you're in situation where the seller is choosing between offers, or where the seller is worried about finding a buyer who will really be able to get a loan and close the deal, making a large down payment raises you high in the seller's estimation. You may even find the seller willing to make other concessions just to keep you on the hook.

- **A large down payment is like forced savings.** Money tied up in a house can't be spent on frivolous things. But it may be available if you need it in an emergency, by refinancing the house or taking a home equity loan.

- **A large down payment and a short-term mortgage mean you are likely to own your house before you retire** Many people sensibly want to pay off their mortgage before they retire (when their income is likely to decrease) or have to pay other family expenses such as college tuition.

But there are also reasons not to make a big down payment, even if you can afford to:

- **By making a smaller down payment, you can buy a more expensive house than if you make a larger down payment.** (This assumes you qualify for the monthly mortgage payments.)

- **You'll have more cash available.** That will let you spend comfortably on for closing costs, loan fees, and "new house" expenses like moving and redecorating.

- **The interest portion of your mortgage is tax deductible.** Unlike other debts, you can deduct the annual interest paid on mortgage loans up to $1 million from your federal and California income tax returns. This figure is for married couples who file a joint income tax return; you can deduct up to $500,000 if you're single. See IRS Publication 936, *Home Mortgage Interest Deduction*, available at www.irs.gov.

- **You can invest the money.** Whether you'll earn more doing this than it costs you to borrow the money with a large mortgage depends on your rate of investment return.

- **You'll have money available for other needs.** If you tie all your money up with a big down payment, you may find yourself having to borrow it back on a home equity loan (usually at a higher interest rate than the first mortgage) if you want to remodel the house, put your kids through college, or whatever else. And interest paid on a home equity loan is only deductible on your federal income tax for loans up to $100,000. If you need to borrow more, there is no deduction.

- **If your house appreciates, you'll receive a higher return on your investment with a lower down payment.** For example, if you put 20% down and took out a loan for the balance at 10% interest, and the house appreciated 8%, your return on your original investment would be 40%. If you put 10% down, by contrast, your return on that same house would be 80%.

Using Equity in an Existing House as a Down Payment on a New One

Trading up is an integral part of home buying. You buy a starter house, wait for it to appreciate, sell it, and use the profit for the down payment on a nicer house. If the California real estate market regains strength in the next decade, it may take two or three sales to get your dream house.

In a rising real estate market, trading up to raise down payment money works better than saving money or making other investments, because it allows you to maximize your investment leverage. For example, if you put $20,000 down on a $200,000 house (borrowing $180,000) and the house value jumps to $300,000, you've made $100,000 with a $20,000 investment. By contrast, if you deposited the same $20,000 in an unleveraged investment, such as stock or art, and it goes up the same 50%, you'd end up with $30,000.

Using a Gift to Help With the Down Payment

If you're fortunate enough to receive a gift of part or all of the money you need for a down payment, you're in great shape—your monthly payments will be lower, and the amount of house you can afford will be higher than if you borrow for the down payment.

However, you'll need to keep an eye on your lender's rules regarding the source of your down payment. If you get an FHA mortgage, you won't face any restrictions on the amount or percentage of the gift so long as it comes from a blood relative. If you get a conventional mortgage and the gift is for less than 20% of the purchase price, however, you must make at least 5% of the down payment from your own funds, and the gift must be from a blood relative.

Often parents and grandparents will help when it comes to buying a house. Gifts up to $13,000 per year per person (2010 figure—it's indexed to go up with inflation) can be given gift-tax-free. This means, for example, that every year your mother and father can give you and your spouse $48,000 total without having to file a gift tax return.

If a gift will exceed the gift tax exclusion, the gift giver will have to file a gift tax return with the IRS—but, thanks to legislation passed in 2001, there's a good chance he or she won't have to pay gift taxes at all, ever. That's because computing the gift tax debt is now put off until the giver's death—at which time the first $1 million of the person's total gifts given will be exempt from tax. The result is that only the wealthiest of people, who give away more than $1 million over their lifetime, will need to give a second thought to gift tax debt.

However, the estate tax is in flux—it was scheduled to be repealed in 2010, but return in 2011, unless Congress votes to extend the repeal. For more information, see the Wills & Estate Planning section of Nolo's website at www.nolo.com.

RESOURCE

Giving gifts. For detailed information on estate and gift taxes, see *Plan Your Estate*, by Denis Clifford (Nolo).

Borrowing Down Payment Money From a Relative or Friend

Another way to raise money for a down payment is to borrow it from someone you know.

While it's not as advantageous as a gift (since you'll have to pay it back and it will

Get a Gift Letter

If you're lucky enough to receive gift money well in advance of applying for a loan, and three months of your bank statements reflect this extra money, you're in good shape and don't need to ask what a gift letter is. (The lender views money that has been in your account for three months or more as "seasoned," that is, it's been sitting there long enough to be treated as your own.)

If, on the other hand, a large deposit shows up in your bank account closer to the time you apply for a loan, the lender is going to question where that money came from. The lender may suspect that the money was meant to be a loan—for example, from a sympathetic friend—rather than an outright gift. You'll need to allay the lender's concerns by providing a written document stating that the money was indeed a gift, with no expectation of reimbursement.

A sample gift letter is below. The letter should specify the amount of the gift and the type of property for which it will be used. Most important, the letter should say that the money need not be repaid. In addition, if money has not yet been transferred, be prepared to document that it's available, by providing the name of the savings or securities institution where it's kept, the account number, and a signed statement giving the mortgage lender authority to verify the information.

Date _____

To Whom It May Concern:

I/We _____ intend to make a GIFT of _____ to (recipient(s)) _____ , my/our (relationship) _____ , to be applied toward the purchase of property located at: _____

_____ .

There is no repayment expected or implied in this gift, either in the form of cash or by future services, and no lien will be filed by me/us against the property.

The SOURCE of this GIFT is: _____

_____

_____
Signature of Donor(s)

_____
Print or Type Name of Donor(s)

_____
Address of Donor(s): Street, City, and State

_____
Telephone Number of Donor(s)

ATTACHMENTS:

1. **Evidence of Donor(s)' ability to provide funds**

2. **Evidence of receipt of funds by Borrower**

affect your debt-to-income ratio), it can help if:

- **You're short for the down payment, but have a relatively high monthly income.** If lenders conclude that you have enough income to pay a first mortgage and another loan, they may let you borrow some of the down payment. Most lenders will usually require that at least 5% of the purchase price come from your own funds.
- **The person lending you money for the down payment will accept no, or very low, payments for several years.** If you don't need to make payments, your debt burden won't increase. Understanding this, a relative or friend may forgive payments for a few years. If these loan payments are eliminated or substantially reduced for three to eight years, the house may rise in value; you can then refinance the mortgage and pay off the down payment loan. (We discuss this strategy in Chapter 12, Private Mortgages.)

○! **CAUTION**

Before arranging for a loan for the down payment, check with your lender or loan broker. (Loan brokers are discussed in Chapter 13.) There are many ways to structure down payment loans, and you want to be sure that your plan will be approved by the lender. In general, the loan must be at least pegged at "market" interest for a minimum of five years.

Is It a Gift or a Loan? Sometimes It Pays to Be Vague

Some people are tempted to ask for a loan from a friend or relative but tell the lender it's a gift when applying for a mortgage. This scenario may be superficially attractive, but it's technically fraud. While it's unlikely you'd be prosecuted, it's nevertheless a poor idea to obtain a loan under false pretenses.

But, fortunately, you can legally treat money as a gift, as far as a lender is concerned, while reserving the right to repay your benefactor if necessary. For example, if your parents advance you money but worry that circumstances might cause them to need it later, your response might be that you'll do your best to help if they run into problems. As long as there's no written loan agreement and your statement is one of intent (not a promise), the money qualifies as a gift.

Borrowing From Your 401(k) Plan

An excellent source of down payment money is a loan against your 401(k) plan. Check with your employer or the plan administrator to see whether your plan allows for loans. If it does, the maximum loan amount under the law is the lesser of one-half of your vested balance in the plan or $50,000 (unless you have less than $20,000 in the account, in which case you can borrow the amount of your vested balance, but no more than $10,000). Other conditions—including the maximum term, the minimum loan amount, the interest rate, and applicable loan fees—are set by your employer. Any loan must be repaid, with interest, in a "reasonable amount of time," although the Tax Code doesn't define "reasonable."

Be sure to find out what happens if you leave the company before fully repaying a loan from your 401(k) plan. If the loan would become due immediately upon your departure, income tax and penalties may apply to the outstanding balance. But, you may be able to avoid all this hassle by repaying the loan before you leave.

Borrowing against your 401(k) plan has several advantages:

- By borrowing against your own plan, you are receiving the interest payments.
- The loan fees are usually lower than a bank would charge.
- There's less paperwork than is usually required in getting a bank loan.

Tapping Into Your IRA

You can withdraw up to $10,000 penalty-free from an individual retirement account (IRA) for a down payment to purchase your first principal residence. (However, you may have to pay income tax on the withdrawal, and you might have less time than you'd like within which to return it to the IRA if you decide not to use it.) This $10,000 is a lifetime limit—and it must be used within 120 days of the date you receive it.

The law defines a first-time homeowner as someone who hasn't owned a house for the past two years. If a couple is buying a home, both must be first-time homeowners. Ask your tax accountant for more information, or contact the IRS at 800-829-1040 or see their website at www.irs.gov.

Are You Having Too Many Tax Dollars Withheld?

Many people have more of their income tax withheld than is necessary. Some enjoy getting the large refund at the end of the tax year, others want the IRS to protect them from their own spending habits. If you're having too much of your income withheld, ask your employer to adjust the amount to a more realistic level (by filling out a new W-4 form). That way you'll be able to use the money now, instead of letting the feds play with it until next April.

True Story

Juan and Yolanda: Getting Help From Customers of the Family Business

We immigrated to the U.S. from Mexico 15 years ago and started a small landscaping business. Last year, in our mid-30s with two kids, we really wanted to buy our small house. Although we had saved $15,000 for a down payment, we needed another $10,000 to close the deal. With no deep-pocket relatives or friends to call on, we decided to approach our half-dozen best customers to ask if they would be willing to pay in advance for gardening services for the coming year. Most said yes, with the result that we raised the needed money in a few days.

Sharing Equity

One way to enlist the help of family or friends, or even an investor, is to give up a share of the ownership of your house in exchange for a cash contribution. We discuss this approach in Chapter 3.

Getting a Second Mortgage From the Seller

As you should understand by now, a principal function of a down payment is to bridge the gap between what you can borrow and the purchase price of the house. If a lender will lend $350,000 on a $400,000 house, you can make up the balance with a down payment of $50,000. There are other ways as well. One is to get the seller or a private investor to take a second mortgage for some or all of the $50,000.

> **EXAMPLE:** Ralph wants to buy a house but has saved only $12,000 and has no friends or relatives to borrow from. He has an excellent salary with good prospects of earning more, so he looks for a seller who will accept a second mortgage instead of a cash down payment. Ralph finds Mimi, who is anxious to sell him her $290,000 house. She still owes $250,000 on her adjustable rate mortgage, which can be assumed by a qualified purchaser.
>
> Mimi offers Ralph a six-year second mortgage at 6% interest to cover the $40,000 difference between her $250,000

loan, which he'll assume, and the sale price. Because making payments on this second mortgage would increase Ralph's debt-to-income ratio to a level most lenders won't approve, Mimi agrees to a flexible payment schedule with no payments for three years and interest only for the three following. At the end of six years, Ralph will owe Mimi the balance in the form of a large balloon payment. If the property has gone up in value, he can refinance the mortgage and pay Mimi her balance.

The lender, who must approve Ralph assuming the mortgage, likes most of the deal. It demands, however, that Ralph put 10% (or $29,000) down; Mimi's second mortgage is reduced to $11,000. To comply, Ralph uses his savings and sells his new car, which fortunately was paid for.

In addition to reducing the down payment, a second mortgage may eliminate the need for PMI, if it keeps the primary mortgage below 80% of the home's value.

Also consider the down sides of second mortgages:

- **Second mortgage interest rates are often higher than first mortgage interest rates.** That's because the mortgage holder carries greater risk, and if you default, will only get paid after the primary mortgage holder.
- **Most sellers want cash when they sell a house, not a note from the buyer.** Thus, it's not easy to locate a very desirable property that can be financed this way.

- **A short-term second mortgage with low payments may have a lump sum (balloon payment) at the end.** If the house is fairly priced, house prices increase, and interest rates don't go through the roof, you shouldn't have trouble refinancing the first mortgage to pay the balloon payment. But if refinancing proves impossible, you'll need another way to raise the cash (or face foreclosure), unless your second mortgage lets you either gradually increase payments or delay the payment date if you can't refinance when it first comes due.

For more on second mortgages and seller financing, see Chapter 12.

Balloon Payments and Second Mortgages

A balloon payment is the balance owed at the end of a loan term when the loan is not fully paid off. To help buyers qualify for loans, a loan may be amortized (calculated) as though the buyer had 30 years to pay it off when, in fact, the buyer may have a few years—five or seven years is common. The payments are kept artificially low, and, at the end of the five or seven years, the buyer must pay off the balance in a balloon payment.

Working With Real Estate Professionals

This chapter focuses on how California home buyers can work with real estate agents and brokers to find a good house. It also discusses the pros and cons of buying a house without professional help. If you do hire a real estate professional, we recommend you take the following steps, in order:

- Complete your Ideal House Profile in Chapter 1.
- Decide how much you can afford to pay after reading Chapter 2.
- Estimate what it will cost to buy the type of house you want in the area you want by checking prices of recently sold comparable houses. The information in Chapter 15 will help you do this.
- Decide what legal relationship you want to establish with a real estate professional, after reading this chapter.
- Find a good real estate professional. We discuss how to do this in "Finding a Good Agent," below.

Advantages and Disadvantages of Working With a Real Estate Professional

Before describing the different ways you can work with a real estate professional, here are some of the pluses and minuses to consider.

Advantages of Working With a Real Estate Professional

Access detailed market information through the Multiple Listing Service (MLS) and allied computer services. The MLS database lists not only most homes currently on the market, but contains other details not publicly available concerning the homes' sales histories and transaction status. Your real estate agent will usually share this information with you. The agent can also supply a price list of recently sold homes. Together, these lists provide a good overview of the housing market.

Access to a broker's in-house listings. A salesperson employed by a large or well-connected firm will know about houses listed for sale with that firm before they are widely advertised.

Legwork. An energetic salesperson should do lots of house searching for you. This includes going to open houses held for real estate professionals (and often closed to the public), as well as personally checking out all listed houses that seem to meet your criteria.

Business experience. An outstanding real estate salesperson will have successfully completed many transactions. The experience may be valuable in helping your house purchase run smoothly. The salesperson's negotiating skills and relationships with other agents may also help you get the best price and terms.

Knowledge of related professionals. A good salesperson will be one source of referrals to other important professionals like inspectors, title and escrow companies, and loan brokers.

No cost to the buyer. Under the typical contractual arrangement, the seller pays the commission, and the services of the real estate salesperson are free to the buyer.

Real Estate People Defined

Before getting help from someone in the California real estate business, it helps to know who the players are.

Agent or Salesperson. One of the foot soldiers of the real estate business who shows houses, holds open houses, and does most of the other nitty-gritty tasks involved in selling real estate. An agent or salesperson (the terms are used interchangeably) must have a license from the state and must be supervised by a licensed real estate broker.

Broker. A broker may legally represent either the seller or buyer. While brokers (except buyer's brokers) almost always receive compensation from sellers, they owe the highest legal duty (fiduciary duty) to whomever they have agreed in writing to represent (seller and/or buyer). A fiduciary duty is one of utmost care, integrity, honesty, and loyalty, like that of a doctor to a patient. A broker can legally supervise one or more agents and must have two years of full-time experience as a real estate agent or salesperson, pass a state licensing exam, and (like a salesperson) complete a continuing education requirement every four years.

Buyer's Agent (or Broker). An agent (as described above) chosen by the buyer to help find a house. The agent owes a legal duty of trust to the buyer but is typically paid a commission by the seller.

Dual Agent (or Broker). A dual agent is paid by the seller but, at least in legal theory, represents both buyer and seller. This legal arrangement must be confirmed in writing by the buyer, seller, and agent.

Listing Agent. An agent or broker who simply lists the seller's house for sale and markets it for the seller. Unless the listing agent signs a Dual Agency Agreement, he or she represents only the seller.

Real Estate Professional. A term used to include either a real estate broker or a real estate salesperson or agent.

Realtor®. A real estate broker who belongs to the National Association of Realtors®, a business trade group. (An agent or salesperson may also belong.) There are corresponding state associations (California Association of Realtors®) and local Boards of Realtors®; the latter usually operate Multiple Listing Services (MLSs).

Subagent. Another general term for the broker or salesperson who helps a buyer find a house. Unless all parties agree in writing that the subagent exclusively represents the buyer or is a dual agent, he or she is legally a subagent of the seller's broker (the person the seller retains to list the house) and owes a legal duty of trust to the seller, not the buyer. Put slightly differently, although a subagent may work with the buyer and never even meet the seller, his or her legal duty as the seller's subagent is to the seller, who pays the commission, not to the buyer. This arrangement is uncommon.

Disadvantages of Working With a Real Estate Professional

Most real estate professionals are conscientious and honest, but real estate has its share of people who are incompetent or only care about their own self-interest. Because it's a relatively easy field to enter, minimally trained newcomers can have a huge financial impact, and it makes sense to watch out for the bad apples. These bad apples are often late for meetings, are uninterested in showing you houses, take several days to return your phone calls, and make you wonder why they're in the profession at all.

Even though your salesperson has a legal duty to fairly represent your interests (unless representing the seller exclusively as a "seller's agent"), this agent has a more basic conflict of interest. Unless you've agreed to pay by the hour, the agent won't get paid until you buy a home, and the amount of payment depends on the price of the house you buy.

Here are some ways the agent's self-interest (desire to be paid) can manifest itself to your disadvantage, particularly if your agent is a bit of a bad apple:

- The salesperson may try to convince you that a house is worth more than it really is because:
  - If you bid high, you're more likely to get the house and the salesperson will get the commission with the least amount of legwork.
  - The salesperson's commission is a percentage of the sales price; the more you pay, the higher the commission.

  - If the salesperson owes a legal duty of trust (fiduciary duty) to the seller, he or she is legally obligated to protect the seller's interest by maximizing the price. This is true if the salesperson is legally a seller's agent rather than a buyer's agent or a dual agent.
- The salesperson may downplay the shortcomings of a particular home or neighborhood, be it size, commute time, or quality of local schools, in an effort to get you to say yes and hence earn the salesperson a commission.
- The salesperson may show you a long list of unsuitable houses if he or she doesn't know of any houses that meet your specifications at a price you can afford. Rather than admit it, some (especially inexperienced ones) will drag you over half the county muttering something like, "I know this isn't your cup of tea, but I want you to get a feel for the market." The agent is hoping that if he or she wears you out, you'll eventually purchase one of the houses.
- The agent may lack the experience or ethics to best represent the buyer's interest. In unusual situations, the agent may even try to pressure you into buying by misrepresenting the facts (for example, implying that you need to offer the full asking price because of competition that doesn't exist) or withholding material information (not telling you the roof leaks). Sometimes these tactics are subtle, such as, "This place is such a bargain; I'd buy it myself if I could."

Our recommendation: When you evaluate the suitability of a house, don't rely principally on the advice of a person with a major financial stake in your buying it. Take the responsibility to make your own informed choices; among other things, be knowledgeable about the house-buying process, your ideal affordable house and neighborhood, your financing needs and options, your legal rights and the local zoning laws if you're planning to remodel, and how to evaluate comparable prices.

True Story

Barbara Kate and Ray: Touring with Traci

Tired of paying too much rent for too little space in our San Francisco apartment, we began to ponder buying. When we became more serious, we met with Traci, an agent at a large real estate firm. Traci led us to a plush conference room, then through an elaborate list of considerations designed to elicit a Wish List for Our Ideal Home.

"Naive," proclaimed Traci, scanning our list: two bedrooms, good sunlight, lots of closet space, perhaps a little space for a garden, under a half million dollars. "But I'll see what I can find—in this price range." She added a final admonition: "I only work with people I really, really like."

Apparently, Traci really, really liked us—she phoned at seven the next morning with three houses for us to see that very evening. The space in all three was mostly taken up by the kitchen—the one room we confirmed restaurant-goers hadn't even thought of including on the Wish List. None of them had a second bedroom—our number-one priority.

Two nights later, an excited Traci phoned at 11:50 with an exclusive news flash. A nearby two-bedroom owned by her coworker was going on sale the next day. "I've got the keys. I can tour you through right now, before anyone else sees it. I have already prepared the paperwork. I think we can close on this one," whispered Traci. We declined the offer of the midnight ride; the house was still for sale six months later. A week later, Traci had pegged Barbara Kate as the softer sell and suggested that "just the girls" go look at houses. She tracked Barbara Kate down at home, where she was in bed with pneumonia, unwilling and unable to make any girlish outing. But Traci was undaunted. She phoned back that afternoon with a weather report promising a warming of five degrees and "a blanket for you in the trunk."

Two weeks later Traci called, having found our "dream house": two bedrooms, good sunlight, good neighborhood. She never mentioned it had only one small closet—in the pantry. Outside, post-tour, Traci became adamant. "What can I do to get you to buy that place?" she asked, with a Rumpelstiltskin-like stomp for punctuation.

It was our sixth tour with Traci. It was our last. We're still paying too much rent for too little space. But it beats the alternative.

How Brokers and Agents Are Paid

Real estate agents work on commission and get paid only after your home search is over, the contract negotiated and all its terms fulfilled, the loan funded, and the deed recorded.

Most listing brokers get sellers to pay a commission of 5%–7% of the sales price. "Discount" brokers typically charge 4%. However, an increasing number of clients are successfully arguing for lower commissions, pointing out that buyers are doing much of the house-finding legwork—such as scouting out homes using the Internet and visiting them without the agent.

Because most real estate transactions involve two brokers—the one producing the buyer and the one helping the seller—the commission is divided, usually 50-50 between the two brokerage offices. That's $7,500–$10,500 per office on a $300,000 house. Within each office, the salesperson who handled the transaction gets a share, often 50%. In that case, on a $300,000 sale, the salesperson earns a $3,750–$5,250 commission before expenses, which include wear and tear on a car, gas, phone, and the like. The salesperson must sell a considerable number of houses in a year to make a decent living and is under relentless pressure to "close deals."

Still, great agents go out of their way to make sure you get the house for the best price and terms. They know that if they save you $10,000 on the purchase price, after splitting commissions this way it will only affect the size of their check by a few hundred dollars. Knowing you'll refer others to them, and possibly be a repeat customer, is more important than that little bit of extra cash.

Work With a Real Estate Professional Paid by the Seller

Normally, the seller pays the commission of the real estate salesperson who helps the buyer locate the seller's house. Even though the salesperson you work with is typically paid out of the seller's brokerage commission, that doesn't necessarily mean he or she legally represents the seller. Recognizing potential conflicts, California law requires salespeople who help buyers find houses to alert them in writing that they have three different options:

- **Buyer's agent.** The salesperson you work with legally represents you exclusively.
- **Dual agent.** The salesperson you work with legally represents both you and the seller.
- **Seller's agent.** The salesperson you work with legally represents the seller exclusively.

These three choices are outlined in the "Disclosure Regarding Real Estate Agency

Relationships" form you'll be asked to sign as soon as you start working with an agent. You and the seller will confirm your relationships with your agents in the purchase contract as described in Chapter 16 (Clause 16).

Buyer's Agent (Your Best Choice)

A buyer's agent has "a fiduciary duty of the utmost care, integrity, honesty, and loyalty" to you. Your real estate professional rejects any legal duty of care to the seller (called "subagency" in real estate speak) and represents you exclusively. Can you legally insist on this? Unfortunately, no, not if the seller is paying the commission. You can ask, but the seller and the real estate agent helping you must agree—and they may have already committed to another arrangement. However, if you're separately paying your agent, that agent is yours alone. Also, with a little searching, you can find agents (usually independent ones, not working with a firm) who dedicate their services to acting as buyer's agents and can normally count on being paid a commission by the seller. Also, practically speaking, if you cannot get all concerned to agree to the buyer's agent option, they should, at the very least, agree to the dual agent option. After all, you have considerable clout as the one who proposes to buy the house.

Dual Agent (Your Second-Best Choice)

Here the real estate professional is paid by the seller, but represents both the buyer and seller in a house sale and owes the same legal duty of fair conduct to each. Are you in a good legal situation under dual agency? In theory, yes: A dual agent cannot disclose to the seller (without your written permission) that you are willing to pay more than the offering price; conversely, a dual agent cannot tell you if the seller is willing to accept less than the asking price.

A dual agency situation can arise if you've entered into an agency relationship with a real estate agent and subsequently look at a house listed with that agent's company— even if the listing agent is not your agent and works in a different branch office of the company. Your agent should disclose immediately if a property you're interested in is listed by his or her company. Dual agency should only be entered into under a written agreement signed by both buyer and seller.

It's still better, however, to work with a real estate professional as a buyer's agent than a dual agent (often preferred by large brokerage companies that want to sell houses buyers have listed with them and to do so can't solely represent the buyer), because dual agency can mean divided loyalties. For example, a dual agent might not urge you to ask for a lower price, worried that because he knows the seller is desperate, he'd be breaching a duty to the seller.

Seller's Agent (A Poor Choice)

Run, don't walk, from this agency relationship where the seller pays "your" agent's commission, and "your" agent legally represents the seller. This is the way it was in the old days (and still is in most states), and some real estate offices still push it. Why is this such a poor choice? Because "your" real estate agent is legally the subagent of the seller and owes a fiduciary duty of honesty, integrity, and loyalty to the seller, not to you. Specifically, if you make a low offer but the agent knows you will go higher or will pay for repair work, the agent should tell the seller.

The only time you might have to accept the seller's agent option is if you're buying a new home in a development, where all transactions are handled by the developer's sales force directly or by a broker who represents the developer/seller. Chapter 7 discusses using a real estate agent when purchasing a new home.

> **EXAMPLE:** Connie lists her home for sale using Acme Real Estate Associates. Troy, a potential buyer, works with a salesperson from Basic Realty, which represents sellers exclusively. Basic Realty locates Connie's house for Troy. Even though the Basic salesperson has been showing Troy houses for months and has never met Connie, the Basic salesperson is the legal subagent of Connie. This means that while he must act fairly and with good faith toward Troy, he owes the highest duty of trust to Connie. If he knows that Connie needs to sell her house in a hurry and that she'd accept a lower offer than Troy makes, he can't tell Troy this, even though he's been working with Troy for months. Conversely, if he knows Troy will pay more than his first offer,

or accept the house "as is" even though it needs $25,000 worth of pest control work, he can, and should, tell Connie.

Hire and Pay an Exclusive Buyer's Agent

Brokers who market their services directly to buyers are called "buyer's agents" or "exclusive buyer's agents." They owe a fiduciary duty to the buyer, not the seller. They are paid a commission from the buyer, usually a percentage of the purchase price. The buyer's agent agrees to offset his or her fee by the amount the seller offers through the MLS. The arrangement between the buyer and the buyer's agent is often laid out in a written agreement entitled a "Buyer's Listing Agreement" or "Exclusive Authorization to Locate Property (Buyer-Broker Agreement)."

Before California law was changed in the late 1980s to make agency relationships clearer, salespeople who helped buyers find houses were almost always the legal representatives (subagents) of the seller. This led to the types of conflicts of interest discussed above. It also led to some buyers preferring to hire and pay for a buyer's broker. Today, the law has been changed and there is much less reason for a buyer to agree to pay his or her own broker.

One major disadvantage to hiring a buyer's agent is that, in many contracts, the agent gets a commission on any house you purchase during the term of the contract, whether the agent finds it or not. If you consider a buyer's agent, ask that this

Oversight by California Department of Real Estate

Real estate salespeople (agents) and brokers are licensed by the California Department of Real Estate (DRE). Under Business and Professions Code § 10176-7 and DRE regulations, the DRE may suspend or revoke an agent's license for fraudulent or dishonest acts such as:

- making a substantial misrepresentation, such as failing to make a legally required disclosure about a property (see Chapter 19)
- making a false promise that is likely to influence, persuade, or induce
- acting for more than one party to a transaction without the knowledge and consent of all the parties
- commingling money entrusted to the agent with his or her own money
- making a secret profit
- acting fraudulently, negligently, or incompetently, or
- as a broker, failing to reasonably supervise an agent.

To file a complaint or find out whether action has been taken to restrict, suspend, or revoke a license, contact the nearest DRE office. Unfortunately, the DRE won't mediate complaints or order that money be refunded or unfair contracts be canceled. Also, it won't tell you whether any complaints have been filed against a broker or salesperson, or if disciplinary action is pending. Despite these shortcomings, it still pays to complain to the DRE if you believe you've been treated in an illegal or unethical manner.

You can reach the DRE via their website at www.dre.ca.gov. The DRE's website also includes updated information on real estate laws and regulations, frequently asked real estate questions, and links to other useful real estate sites.

condition be limited to the area where the buyer's agent specializes—or be eliminated altogether. You'll have an especially strong argument if you plan to look in two different geographical areas—one with the help of a buyer's agent and the other on your own.

Hire an Agent by the Hour

A few agents market their services directly to potential buyers at an hourly fee. They commonly charge between $50 and $250 per hour, with a typical house purchaser using between 20 and 50 hours of time.

Most of these arrangements are with licensed real estate brokers, particularly those who operate independently of large brokerage companies. A salesperson (agent) can legally provide advice by the hour, but only with the permission of an employing broker.

Advantages of Hiring an Agent by the Hour

The advantages of hiring an agent by the hour are:

Sample Hourly Fee Agreement

This agreement is made between _____ (Buyer)
and _____ (Agent)
on ___*(date)*___ , concerning the contemplated purchase by Buyer of real property generally
described in the Buyer's Ideal House Profile, which is attached. [*You created this Profile in
Chapter 1. A copy should be marked Attachment A and stapled to this agreement.*]

1. Buyer agrees to retain Agent as a consultant on an hourly fee basis to assist Buyer in his or
    her attempt to locate and purchase property described in Buyer's Ideal House Profile. The
    terms of this agreement shall be as follows:

    A. "Agent" shall mean the licensed real estate broker or agent named above, acting directly
       as the employing broker of record or through an agent employed under the Broker's
       license.

    B. Buyer is retaining Agent as an independent contractor and not as an employee.

    C. Agent is a member of a local Multiple Listing Service (MLS); Agent will share with
       Buyer nonconfidential information from any Multiple Listing Service to which Agent
       has access as a participating member concerning properties fitting the description in
       Buyer's Ideal House Profile.

    D. Buyer and Agent agree that Agent shall assist Buyer, to the extent requested by Buyer,
       in completing offer and counteroffer forms, arranging financing, dealing with escrow
       procedures, and completing other paperwork pertaining to the real property purchase.
       This advice shall not include legal or tax advice.

2. Agent shall charge Buyer for consultation services at the rate of $ _____ per hour. Agent's
    services shall not exceed _____ hours for the contemplated purchase unless the parties
    mutually agree in writing. Buyer shall pay no commission to Agent; Agent will accept no
    commission from any Seller from whom Buyer buys.

READ, UNDERSTOOD, AND AGREED TO BY:

Buyer: _____   Date: _____

Buyer: _____   Date: _____

Agent: _____   Date: _____

Supervising Broker: _____   Date: _____

- You get expert help with no built-in conflict of interest, because the agent has no financial stake in whether or not you buy a house.
- You get easy access to market information such as the Multiple Listing Service.

Disadvantages of Hiring an Agent by the Hour

The primary disadvantages of hiring an agent by the hour are:

- You may have trouble locating an outstanding agent by the hour; few experienced agents go this route because more money can be made on commission, and they don't want to take on any potential liability for their involvement with the real estate purchase agreement without proportional compensation.
- You pay for the hours you use, whether or not you buy a house.
- You must do a lot of legwork yourself; it's normally too expensive to pay a person by the hour to look for a house for you.
- An unscrupulous agent may try to "run up the meter" by selling you more time than you need. While this isn't a major concern, it can happen.

Hiring an agent by the hour is cost-effective only if you do most of the grunt work inherent in finding a house, deciding on the offer amount, and negotiating with the seller yourself.

Buy a House Yourself With No Professional Help

Some people enjoy looking for a house alone, feeling that professionals get in the way. If you have the time, you can find and purchase a house without an agent. Be prepared for a lot of details: finding a home that meets your needs and budget, making an offer, negotiating a contract, carrying out inspections and disclosures, and handling the closing.

Routine offer and acceptance forms, along with details on filling them out, are in this book. And there are many useful resources available online to help you buy a house—from checking out comparable sales prices to finding a good inspector. Only in rare situations will serious legal problems develop, and then you'll need a lawyer, not an agent.

Finding a Good Agent

As you read this, a veritable herd of real estate agents are trying to find you—the ready, willing, and able buyer. Almost half a million Californians are licensed real estate salespeople or brokers, and most are underemployed (though the best ones may be quite busy). So the problem isn't finding someone to work with, but finding someone you *want* to work with. The best way to do this is through recommendations from people who've purchased a house in the last few years and whose judgment you trust. (Sellers may give you a good steer, too, but agents who primarily work with sellers have somewhat different skills from those who work with buyers.)

Another possible source for obtaining recommendations is from local title companies. Call two or three title companies to find out who they say the best buyer's agents are.

After collecting the names of several agents, arrange to talk to each before making a decision. While you can always get rid of an agent you don't like, it's better to find someone good in the first place.

RESOURCE

Check out websites of individual real estate agents. These give you a good sense of the real estate agent's listings and the services provided.

If you can't find the website of a particular agent, check the California Association of Realtors website, www.car.org, which includes a directory of California Realtors. Other websites with directories of real estate agents include the National Association of Realtors' site, www.realtor.com; and HomeGain, www.homegain.com.

What to Look for in a Real Estate Agent

The agent or broker you choose should (ideally at least) have the following qualities:

- integrity
- dedication and availability to clients
- good rapport with other agents
- experience in the type of services you need
- knowledge of the area you want to live in, and
- sensitivity to your taste and needs.

While the first trait, integrity, needs little elaboration, here are a few words about the other characteristics you should look for in a real estate agent.

Dedication and availability to clients. Because it's fairly easy to get a real estate license, many dabble in it for a few months or years, often part time, and become discouraged and move on. You don't want to be the guinea pig on which one of these neophytes practices. On the other hand, some agents so overbook themselves with clients that you won't get the time or attention you deserve. Make sure you select

---

True Story

Referrals Mean a Lot

Coauthor Ira Serkes, a Berkeley Realtor whose business is over 50% referral, puts it this way:

"Many real estate agents take a long-term approach. We want our buyers to be satisfied customers, so we try to negotiate the best price possible. If we can save the buyer $5,000 we'll do it, even if that means we earn $150 less in commission. We look upon that $150 as our investment in our future. We know that when clients are happy with our service, they will refer friends, family, and neighbors who want to buy or sell a house. The long-term value of a referral business is much more important than receiving a few hundred dollars more on one sale."

an agent with the skills, knowledge, and time necessary to represent you properly. See "Tough Questions to Ask Real Estate Agents and Brokers," below.

Good rapport with other agents. Although you want an experienced agent, you don't want one who's racked up a history of unpleasant dealings with sellers' agents. That can actually lead to your offer being rejected, even if it's at full price or above. Ask other real estate professionals about a particular agent to see what his or her reputation is.

Experience in the type of services you need. If you're a first-time home buyer you'll probably need more patient guidance, especially with financing issues, than will someone who has owned several houses. If you're looking for a new tract house or a condominium (read Chapter 7 carefully), you may need more specialized help.

Knowledge of the area. Be sure the agent is extremely knowledgeable about the city, county, or, better yet, neighborhood you want to live in.

Sensitivity to your tastes and needs. While it's not essential that you and your real estate agent agree on everything (you're not marrying the person, after all), it certainly helps if you and the agent have compatible tastes or the agent is sensitive to yours.

 RESOURCE

More information on advanced real estate training. These organizations can provide information on and referrals to different real estate specialists:

- **Certified Residential Specialist.** Call the Council of Residential Specialists at 800-462-8841, or check their website at www.crs.com.
- **Accredited Buyer Representatives.** Call the Real Estate Buyer's Agent Council at 800-648-6224, or check their website at www.rebac.net.

One way to get an idea about how well an agent understands the sort of house you want is to provide the agent with a copy of your Ideal House Profile and then ask him or her to show you a few houses. If what you see looks pretty decent (don't expect miracles on the first day), you're probably on the right track. If the agent immediately and repeatedly shows you houses that you simply wouldn't live in, end the relationship politely but firmly.

How to Help a Real Estate Agent Help You

While you're checking out real estate agents, keep in mind that they'll surely be assessing you. The agent will want to know whether you:

- Are highly motivated to buy, or are just a "Looky-Lou" (real estate slang for a person who makes a hobby out of looking at houses and is, essentially, a waste of time).
- Can realistically afford to buy a decent house.
- Are reasonably sensible and considerate. An experienced real estate professional knows how miserable it is to work with people who are demanding and rude.

Tough Questions to Ask Real Estate Agents and Brokers

Here are some questions to ask when interviewing real estate salespeople:

- How long have you been in real estate? How long in this area?
- Are you a licensed real estate broker or an agent?
- Are you full time? If yes, for how long?
- How many buyers have you personally found houses for in the past year? How does this compare with other real estate salespeople in the area?
- Can you give me the names and phone numbers of satisfied customers, or testimonial letters?
- Have you completed any nationally sponsored advanced real estate training programs offering professional designations, such as Graduate Realtor Institute (GRI); Certified Residential Specialist (CRS); Accredited Buyer Representative (ABR); or Certified Relocation Professional (CRP)? (While advanced training doesn't guarantee that an agent will do a good job, typically people who invest time and money in courses take their profession seriously.)

- What systems do you use to make sure all transaction details are completed in a timely manner? (Ask to see sample transaction logs the agent uses to document communications—phone, mail, fax, email, in-person—with house buyers and sellers. Also, ask to see checklists of house-buying details from financing through closing.)
- Do you have the MLS as well as comparable sales information and contracts online? If yes, how will this help you find the right house for me? Do you use other online services that might help me?
- How will we keep in touch? Will you email me home information and updates, preferably daily? Do you have a voicemail system where I can leave detailed messages?
- Do you keep an up-to-date list of lenders, inspectors, roofers, painters, contractors, and other service providers you have personally used and can recommend?
- Can you provide me with a CMA (comparative market analysis) of my home against nearby homes?

If you come across this way, most will back off.

To alleviate an agent's understandable concerns, and show you're really serious about house hunting, here are some tips for your first meeting:

- Give the agent a copy of your Ideal House Profile. (See Chapter 1.)
- Give the agent an idea of your price range and a copy of your financial statement or, even better, a letter from a lender stating that you are preapproved for a mortgage up to a designated amount. (See Chapter 2.)
- Explain why you want to purchase a house in the near future.
- Treat the agent in a businesslike way. This should allay fears that you're demanding, complaining, or neurotic.

How Not to Find an Agent

Here is some advice on how not to find an agent.

Avoid asking an agent where you live now to make a referral in the new area (unless the agent actually knows an experienced colleague there). An agent who receives a referral from someone else in the business is expected to compensate the referrer with a percentage of his or her commission. Some salespeople are overanxious to make referrals and may steer you to someone they met once at a real estate conference or otherwise know only casually. Other salespeople are required to go through their relocation department and can't recommend the best agent for you.

Don't choose an agent just because they're with a nationally advertised chain. Most

---

True Story

Amy and Bruce: Other People's Agents

We found our real estate agent, Kate, through the grapevine of friends and coworkers. We were happy with the choice; she was knowledgeable, efficient, and cooperative, never pushy. We felt comfortable knowing she was looking out for our interests.

We came to feel very differently about the seller's agent, Bob. The annoyances were minor at first. He was always late for meetings. The papers he prepared were sloppy and full of mistakes. He didn't tell our agent that another prospective buyer was making a bid the same day we did, then claimed he'd left a phone message. (Kate rechecked her voicemail; he hadn't.) The last straw was when Bob's failure to relay messages about key points to the sellers nearly made the deal fall through.

By this time, the sellers weren't happy with Bob, either, but they didn't fire him, and we couldn't. Luckily, we could go around him. We went to the broker Bob worked for and told her that from then on, we would either speak to the sellers directly or communicate through her, not Bob. From that point on, we got reliable information—and soon we got the house.

offices of a nationally advertised chain are individually owned and operated, and pay a franchise fee to the national organization. While the national organization may establish some operational standards and provide a degree of training and support, a local branch is no better than its particular owner and staff.

Don't pick someone from the yellow pages, the Internet, a newspaper ad, or a direct mail flyer. As in any business, the best salespeople get plenty of word-of-mouth referrals.

Don't seek referrals from the Better Business Bureau or local Board of Realtors. They either won't make a referral or will simply send you to the next name on their list.

Don't work with someone you meet at an open house, unless and until you thoroughly check the person out. Some real estate salespeople offer to keep houses open for other agents precisely because they're short of business and looking for clients. While you may meet a wonderful agent this way, you can usually do better by getting recommendations from people you trust.

Don't work with someone just because he or she is your first contact when you phone or visit a real estate office. Agents take turns handling cold calls and greeting walk-ins; you'll end up with the person "on the floor" when you call or walk through the door. Many real estate offices have "client protection" policies, meaning that you "belong" to the first agent you happened to talk to or who showed you a house. Obviously, the agent is the only person protected by this sort of arrangement, so if you're treated as if you were the property of someone you don't even know, leave.

CAUTION

Check real estate licenses. Make sure your real estate agent's license has not been suspended or revoked—and that the agent actually has a license in the first place! We've heard stories of people who pose as agents, hoping to make quick money from unwitting buyers. Call the nearest office of the California Department of Real Estate or check the DRE website, www.dre.ca.gov.

Getting Rid of a Broker or Agent You Don't Like

Suppose you realize that your relationship with a real estate professional isn't working. Perhaps the agent repeatedly shows you houses you hate or doesn't show you enough houses. Or maybe you discover that the agent isn't as ethical or careful as you'd like—he or she dismisses your legitimate concerns about the physical condition of the property or pushes you toward a particular lender even though you suspect there are cheaper alternatives. Even if the agent simply doesn't return your phone calls promptly, you may want to work with someone else.

In short, because your home is probably the biggest purchase you'll ever make, you should be very satisfied with your agent. If you're not, don't hesitate to switch. Your agent is a business colleague, not a personal friend. To keep things simple, just make sure you end the relationship before the agent starts negotiating a purchase for you.

Here is how to legally end a relationship with a particular broker or agent:

- If you're working with an agent in a relationship where the seller pays the commission, you need only notify the agent that you no longer want to work together. This is true whether you've signed a Disclosure Regarding Real Estate Agency Relationships form or not. That's it.

- If you've hired an agent by the hour, pay for the services you've used and end the relationship. If you pre-committed to a set number of hours and haven't used them, pay only for what you've used. The agent may demand payment for the rest. If so, point out that the agent has a legal duty to try to earn other income in the remaining hours and to subtract that income from what you owe (this is called "mitigating damages"). You may eventually decide to make a small settlement, but don't be in a hurry or pay for time you haven't used.

- If you've hired a buyer's agent to whom you've agreed to pay a commission, there are three ways to end the relationship:

  - If you're unhappy with the agent before you locate a house, simply write a letter terminating the relation-ship, and don't look at any other houses the agent tries to show you. Even if the contract states that you're bound to work with the agent for a longer period, the letter should legally put you in the clear.

  - If you've found a house you want to buy with the help of the agent, you're legally (and ethically) bound to honor the terms of the contract. In short, pay the agent the commission; he or she has earned it.

  - If you locate a house on your own but it's during the term of an exclusive buyer-broker contract that calls for the agent to get a commission on any house you buy (a rare situation), and you haven't written the agent to terminate the contract, you technically may owe the agent a fee. Should you grit your teeth and pay it? Consider the fairness of the situation. If the agent did a lot of work for you but didn't happen to locate the house you bought, you owe the money and should pay it if that's what the contract says.

But don't pay a large chunk of money to someone who has done nothing to earn it. If you refuse to pay because you received no services, the agent must sue you to collect. This costs time, money, and good will. Few agents want it known publicly that they sued a buyer because the agent didn't do his or her job. Also, before you're actually sued, you'll probably have a chance to settle the dispute for a smaller amount. If you do, get a release of all claims when you make your payment. (See *101 Law Forms for Personal Use,* by Robin Leonard and Ralph Warner (Nolo), for forms.)

When You're Really Thrilled With Your Agent

Buyers often wonder if it's okay to "do something" for their agents. The best thing to do is refer the agent to your friends, coworkers, and relatives. In addition, consider buying the agent a gift. Some people we know bought their agent the finest bottle of Napa wine they could afford. Another couple we know gave their agent some books on topics of interest to him. Another gave a $500 cash bonus. (The deal was a mess—the agent was a savior.)

Use your imagination.

How to Find a House

In Chapter 1, you did an important part of identifying what you want by creating your Ideal House Profile. Now you need to devise a plan to find a house that matches it as closely as possible. Your first task is to pay close attention to your time and financial constraints. For example, the house search of a well-paid executive with money in the bank, who needs to relocate over the summer so her kids' schooling won't be interrupted, differs tremendously from that of a sporadically employed foreign language translator who likes his apartment but eventually wants to buy a modest place with a small down payment.

The Best Time to Look for Houses

When you look at houses may be out of your control. A major event in your life such as a new job or need to move your children before the start of school means you must find a new house quickly. For those people with the luxury of timing their purchase, however, here are a few hints:

- House prices often jump in the spring, absent some major external factor, such as a recession.
- Historically, mid-November through the end of February is a slow time for the housing market.
- Bad news, such as job layoffs, can temporarily depress a local real estate market.
- When interest rates are low, there's often more competition for housing.

Where to Look for Houses

There are lots of places you may find your new home. Below are some of the best places to get started. If you see an interesting listing, especially a For Sale By Owner (FSBO), drive by on Saturday. If you like it, don't be afraid to knock on the door or call to arrange an early showing. It's okay to be a little assertive with FSBOs—after all, the seller is probably at least as anxious to sell as you are to buy.

If the home is listed with a real estate agent, however, and you're already working with an agent, don't disturb the owner or call on signs or ads yourself. Ask your agent to call for you. You may jeopardize your representation by talking directly to the seller's agent or asking him or her to show you the home. The seller's agent may even expect to handle the sale for you or ask for part of your agent's commission.

Find Homes on the Internet

Probably the most powerful tool home buyers have for finding prospective homes with minimal work is the Internet. Many sites will display photos or virtual tours, which may be all you need to determine whether the house is worth a visit.

Here are the best sites for house listings on the Internet.

Real estate sections of local newspapers. If you live in a major metropolitan area such as San Francisco or San Diego, online newspaper classifieds are a good bet. On most websites, you can browse all the listings or customize your search by typing

Organizing Your House Search

Set up a file folder on each house that seems like a prospect. Include a completed House Priorities Worksheet; the information sheet provided at the open house; the Multiple Listing Service information; ads; and your notes. This may seem like overkill, but as the number of houses you look at grows, it will become the best way to keep track of details.

Set up a simple spreadsheet for each house, with columns for the street address and city, price, number of bedrooms and baths, date, comments, or whatever else is important to you. Here's an example:

Address	6938 San Lorenzo	411 Solano Avenue	169 Colusa Avenue
City	Berkeley	Albany	Kensington
Price	$850,000	$650,000	$750,000
Number of bedrooms	3	2	3
Number of bathrooms	1	1	2
Date seen	2/14/09	2/21/09	1/22/09
Comments	Nice home with lots of light	Fixer-upper, but big yard	$14,000 termite report!

You can sort the list by price, date, city, address, or other variable.

House Hunting Tips

Here's advice from seasoned house hunters:
- Bring measurements of your largest pieces of furniture and musical instruments.
- Pace yourself; don't try to see more than six to nine houses in a day. Try to visit a few in the evening after work.
- Visit www.mapquest.com and plot the open house locations to save driving time. Or try the Batch Geocode website at www.batchgeocode.com. Just download their spreadsheet template and enter the address information (and websites!) of the homes you're interested in, and click the "Save/Share/Embed" button to have the map emailed to you.
- Come equipped with a notebook, pen or pencil, calculator, tape measure, graph paper, your House Priorities Worksheet (Chapter 1), and a digital camera or video recorder. (But ask the agent or house owner for permission before using it.)
- If you're interested in the house, fill out the worksheet carefully. Take notes on the layout, condition of major appliances and fixtures, and problems such as stains on the ceiling or cracks in the basement. Use the tape measure to check that the room's dimensions are the same as on the listing sheet and big enough for your needs.
- Don't let the current decor unduly influence you. Remember, the uglier it is, the more likely you are to buy for a lower price. Think creatively about what can be changed.

How to Translate Ads

Anyone who makes a living in the real estate world learns to translate the exaggerated language of classified ads into down-to-earth English. Because most house purchasers aren't around the business long enough to develop this arcane (and only momentarily useful) skill, here is a humorous glossary of some of the most common real estate business euphemisms.

Convenient to shopping. For a month before Christmas, your front lawn will become a parking lot.

Cozy. Rooms are the size of closets; closets don't exist.

Fixer-upper or handyman special. Nothing that an experienced four-person construction crew couldn't fix in nine months.

Fruit trees. Impossible to say anything better.

Half-bath. A small closet contains a 60-year-old toilet located three inches from a basin half the size of a teacup.

Low-maintenance yard. Half-dead Bermuda grass interspersed by an occasional patch of pastel-colored gravel.

Modern kitchen. The rest of the house looks like the birthplace of Abe Lincoln.

Needs tender loving care. Last owner was a recluse with a dozen incontinent dogs.

Not a drive-by. So ugly you have to be dragged by the ear.

Off the beaten path. A bloodhound couldn't find it.

Priced to sell. No one was interested at a higher price.

Quaint. Need you ask?

Starter house. If your alternative is to live in a city shelter, it will look good; otherwise, keep looking.

Water view. Subject to flooding at high tide.

---

in your criteria, such as price range, location, and number of bedrooms and baths. Go to the website of your local paper and see if it has a similar section—most large metropolitan papers do, and even smaller communities may too.

The California Living Network (CLN), at http://ca.realtor.com. The CLN provides real estate listing information from nearly every MLS in California, sponsored by the California Association of Realtors®. The CLN also has a Spanish-language equivalent, at www.sucasa.

net, and a Multilingual Directory of Realtors to assist non-English-speaking home buyers.

Realtor.com, at www.realtor.com (sponsored by the National Association of Realtors®), and MSN's Real Estate, at http://realestate.msn.com. These national sites provide lists of homes for sale throughout the country, including some areas of California. Most of the listings will probably be found in the CLN, but additional features on these sites, such as handy maps to locate the neighborhood of a specific home and useful links to real estate websites, are nice features.

The National Association of Home Builders' site, www.move.com. This provides a listing of new homes and developments in major metropolitan areas of California.

The Owners' Network at www.owners.com. This is the site to see for homes sold without a broker.

Craigslist.org. This is an excellent source for homes listed by real estate professionals or owners. Listings are broken down by major metropolitan area.

Websites sponsored by local real estate brokers. Don't forget this valuable way to check out homes for sale. Some of the best include detailed photographs and downloadable flyers with extensive information on the property for sale and its surrounding neighborhood. Coauthor Ira Serkes's website, for example, at www.berkeleyhomes.com, offers a direct link to the MLS where you can search for San Francisco or East Bay homes.

Once you identify a house that looks interesting, you can give your real estate agent the MLS number or property address. Your agent can send you any additional information that's available and schedule an appointment for homes you want to see in person. If you're not working with an agent, you can call the listing agent directly (or the owner, if it's FSBO).

Check the Classified Ads

All California newspapers publish real estate classifieds, usually on Sundays. Reading them will help you learn the real estate market, and spot new listings and price reductions.

Don't Be a Victim of Illegal Discrimination

Illegal discrimination is the refusal to show property to someone, allow them to make an offer to purchase, or accept an offer from them on the basis of age (except in qualifying for senior citizen housing), ancestry, color, creed, gender, having children, marital status, national origin, physical or mental disability, race, religion, or sexual orientation.

This list is illustrative only. Under California law, any arbitrary or prejudicial action based on a person's personal characteristics such as geographical origin, physical attributes, or personal beliefs could be considered illegal. Thus, if a seller refused to sell to someone with good credit simply because he or she was a member of a particular political party, the seller could be in trouble.

If you believe you've been discriminated against, file a complaint with the California Department of Fair Employment and Housing within 60 days. (Check the Government Pages of your phone book for the nearest office, call 800-233-3212, or check their website at www.dfeh.ca.gov.) You may also want to see a lawyer who handles this type of work.

If you prove the discrimination and the property is still available, you're entitled to buy it for the fair market value and you're eligible to receive substantial damages under California Civil Code § 52. If it's not still for sale, the seller must pay you damages.

Visit Sunday Open Houses

To really get the feel of the market, visit some open houses. Don't be terribly selective at first; your goal is to broadly orient yourself as to general market conditions and current price levels, not to buy the first or second house you see.

CAUTION

While you're looking at open houses, real estate agents are looking at you. Agents view open houses as a way to find more clients, not just to sell property. Be prepared for agents to ask your name and phone number so they can contact you later. Just say no, unless you really do like the person and will take the time to check him or her out. While it's possible to connect with a good agent at an open house, there are better ways, discussed in Chapter 5.

TIP

The sellers may also be looking you over. Open houses are an opportunity for you to make a good impression on the seller—which may tip the balance your way in a bidding situation. Not all sellers attend, but they could be there incognito. Dress respectably, and if you're with someone, keep your comments about the house positive. (You can sneer at their choice of linoleum when you're back in your car.) If there are any tenants who will be staying, try to chat them up—tenants have been known to lobby sellers in favor of a particular future landlord.

Gain Access to the Multiple Listing Service

Local Boards of Realtors for most areas of California maintain a database called the Multiple Listing Service (MLS), which lists most houses for sale. Listings usually include the price, the address, and a photo of the house; the number and type of rooms; the size of the lot; and other features included, such as the kitchen appliances.

Real estate agents also track comparable sales data, including most houses sold through the MLS during the previous three months, arranged by city or neighborhood, each with the original asking price and the selling price.

Until recently, real estate professionals associated with a local Board of Realtors had a monopoly on MLS and comparable sales information. Unless you worked with a sales-person associated with a member broker, you'd have to do without.

The situation has changed dramatically in the past few years, with most MLS infor-mation now available online, as described above. However, the MLS still contains more information than is publicly available, which your agent can look up for you. (See "Use an Agent With Good Skills," below.)

Use an Agent With Good Skills

If you work with an agent, find one with good computer skills who will check new listings several times a day and email you new information as soon as it comes out. Some real estate professionals, such as coauthor Ira Serkes, create customized websites allowing clients to view detailed information on the latest house prospects.

In addition to providing up-to-date sales listings, real estate agents can access a wealth of other data for their clients:

- the date a particular property was bought and for what price, plus property taxes, legal information, and details on the neighborhood
- comparable sales data in bar chart form, with each property's address, asking price, and final selling price
- information on properties that never sold and were taken off the market, in which case you might approach the owners with a new offer, and
- loan origination and mortgage rate comparison programs to speed up loan qualification.

Real estate agents don't have a monopoly on these services, however. Many online services are available to consumers. However, real estate agents and brokers normally have access to houses before they're opened to the public.

Enlist the Help of Personal Contacts

If you know people who live or work near where you want to buy, ask them to become house scouts. When people plan to move, friends, neighbors, and business associates almost always know about it before a house is put on the market.

Approach your friends and acquaintances in a formal, structured way. You want them to understand that you're seriously requesting their assistance, not just fantasizing about owning a new home. Here is how to do it:

- Prepare a cover letter or email containing a brief—perhaps humorous— description of exactly what you want your scouts to do. Generally, this should encourage your scouts to spread the word about your needs and, of course, to call you immediately if they spot a likely house, especially if they hear about it before it goes on the market. Attach your Ideal House Profile.
- Send your letter and worksheet to friends and fairly close acquaintances. Include local businesspeople with whom you have a friendly relationship. Doctors, lawyers, dentists, and insurance brokers may also be good sources of information. They routinely have advance information about impending moves.
- If your house search turns out to be prolonged, contact your scouts with periodic progress reports and reminders that you need help.

Do Your Own House Scouting

In addition to enlisting the help of friends, you can do much looking on your own.

Canvass Neighborhoods

While it may be a little aggressive for some tastes, we know people who have found houses simply by notifying every owner in the area of their interest in their neighborhood. If you have the time, the best

Sample House Scout Letter

Dear Friends:

We have a problem and need your help!

We've been house hunting for months, but without much luck. We're looking for a 3- or 4-bedroom home in Piedmont or the Montclair district of Oakland. Our lender tells us we can pay up to $1,200,000.

It's important that the house be light and airy, with a private backyard that is (or can be) closed in for our old hound, Faithful Fred. We've attached a sheet listing the most important attributes of our ideal house.

Do you know of anyone thinking of selling? Can you help in one or more of the following ways?

- Keep your eyes open for suitable houses already on the market.

- Look for For Sale By Owner houses that we might otherwise miss. (These don't appear in real estate listings and are often hard to find.)

- Tell your friends, neighbors, and business associates—they'll probably hear about a house from someone moving long before it's listed with a broker.

- Ask your doctors, dentists, lawyers, and other service providers, who are often the first to know when people plan to move.

If you hear about or spot a house that seems even remotely likely, give us a call pronto, at 555-4377.

Thanks for your help.

Dennis and Ellen Olson

P.S. As soon as we move in, we plan to throw the best 60s Motown dance party you've ever been to for all our house scouts. And whoever tips us off about the house we buy will be promptly invited to dinner for four at your choice of Chez Panisse in Berkeley or Masa's in San Francisco.

way to do this is to hand carry a flyer door to door and hang signs on notice boards in laundromats and grocery stores.

Another possibility is to mail a friendly letter containing your house specifications to everyone in a particular area after getting the names and addresses from a "reverse directory," available at the public library or at www.reversephonedirectory.com. This type of directory is organized by street address and phone number rather than by last name.

Look for Houses That May Soon Be on the Market

Driving around neighborhoods and looking for run-down houses (peeling paint or weeds in the front yard, no curtains in the window) is one way to find houses that may soon be for sale. For many reasons (foreclosure, ill health, divorce), run-down properties, especially rentals, are often available for purchase, even though they aren't formally listed. If you locate a likely house, ask neighbors if they know whether the house is for sale and the name and phone number of the owner. You can also find the owner's name at the County Assessor's or Recorder's Office, from a local title or escrow company, or using the reverse phone directory described above.

How to Research Property Ownership

Property ownership data collected from tax assessor's records is available from many cities and counties and at most title companies.

The data, often available online, is usually organized by property address, owner's last name, assessor's parcel number, or map corresponding to assessor's parcel number to simplify retrieval.

If you look up properties by address, you'll find the owner's name and where his or her tax bill is sent (probably where he or she lives), the parcel number, and deed of trust recording information. One way to use the information is to pick several streets where you want to live and scan the records for the names of owners who don't live on the premises (out-of-town or out-of-state owners are best). They may be the most motivated to sell, and to sell at a good price. Ask the title company to print the owner's addresses onto 8½" x 11" paper so you can photocopy them directly onto mailing labels.

Advertise for Sellers

Why not let sellers find you by placing a classified ad listing your requirements? Especially if you need help with financing and want the seller to take back a second mortgage, or if you are looking for a house with very particular characteristics (for

Paul and Barbara: Our House Scouts Came Through!

After the birth of our second child, we searched for a bigger house in our general area for almost a year, to no avail.

One technique we used was to tell as many people as possible about our search. One day a friend went for her annual teeth cleaning and her dentist mentioned that he was retiring in about six months and moving out of town. Our scout asked if he and his wife planned to sell their home, which they did. She mentioned us to the dentist and then relayed his invitation for us to call and set up an appointment to look at his house. We did, and loved it.

We suggested to the dentist and his wife that if we could agree on the price, we could jointly handle the entire sale without real estate agents.

They named a moderately high, but fair, price, and we said yes. It turned out, however, that they had promised to list the house with a real estate broker friend. They wanted to honor that promise, and so they paid her a 3% commission in exchange for helping with the contract, inspections, and closing.

We not only got a great house, we got a great deal. If we hadn't heard about the house and it was put on the market months later, the combination of fast-rising local prices and the need to pay an additional $15,000 in real estate commissions would have increased the price by $50,000 or more, effectively putting it out of our price range.

---

example, wheelchair accessibility or within one block of public transit), placing your own ad may be an efficient way to narrow down the possibilities.

How to Approach an Owner You Don't Know

The reason you want to know about houses that may soon be for sale is to contact the owner, preview the house, and, if you like it, make an offer before it's listed. This is often easier said than done. Many people, especially those moving because of health, financial, or marital problems, aren't likely to appreciate an aggressive potential buyer.

It's best to approach a potential seller as politely and nonaggressively as possible. If you have a mutual friend (perhaps a house scout), ask that person to introduce you. If this isn't possible, write the owner a friendly note (use a nice card), saying you've heard he or she might be moving and, if so, would he or she be willing to show you the house. Follow up with a phone call a few days later. If you meet with resistance, back off.

If you get to see a house, and you like it, you'll naturally want to know how much the seller wants. It's fine to ask, but don't be pushy. The seller may not have thought about it, and if he or she thinks you're trying to "steal" the home, you'll probably never hear from him or her again. Do mention that if a sale can be conducted without brokers (or with one broker who gets a 2%–3% commission instead of the customary 5%–7%, or who works by the hour), the seller will save a good bit of money.

Find Foreclosures, Probate Sales, and Lease Option Properties

In Chapter 3, we discuss finding properties subject to foreclosure and probate sale, and houses you may be able to lease option.

Finding a House When You're New to an Area

If you're completely unfamiliar with the area you're moving to, you're at an obvious, and serious, disadvantage—you don't have the basic information normally considered essential to locating a good house, in a congenial location, at a fair price. While a good salesperson can show you the best homes in your price range in different neighborhoods, it will take some time to figure out which communities you'll feel most comfortable in. Getting a real sense of what houses are worth may also be difficult, but a good market analysis can help. Chapter 15 explains how to find the prices of comparable houses.

Some brokers train their agents to be "relocation specialists." While they can't know your personal desires, they have thorough knowledge of schools, community services, and neighborhood features, and if you're clear about what you want, they should be able to answer your questions or send written information such as local maps and home price information.

If you're in a hurry, a sensible alternative to trying to find a house right away is to leave your furniture in storage and rent a furnished place until you have a sense of your new turf. Sure, this means moving twice, but it's better than paying too much for a house in an undesirable area that you may have difficulty reselling when you want to move, which is likely to be soon.

Talk to friends, coworkers, shopkeepers, homeowners, and anyone else familiar with where you're moving to before settling on a geographic area. Emphasize the personal by telling them who you are and what you like. You want to know the specific towns and neighborhoods where you'd fit in. In our view, it's more important to live in such an area than in the perfect house.

Online Help With Community and Neighborhood Information

Many websites will help with your relocation decisions—whether you need to check into home listings, prices, local real estate agents, neighborhoods, schools, or jobs. To check out city, community, and neighborhood information such as schools, housing costs, demographics, crime rates, and jobs visit the California state Web page (www.state.ca.us) and Sperling's Best Places (www.bestplaces. net). (See Appendix A, Welcome to California, and Appendix B, Real Estate Websites, for more resources on specific topics.)

HomeFair, www.homefair.com, has useful links to help you decide where to live based on home prices, schools, crime, salaries, transportation, demographics, and community services. Realtor.com, at www. realtor.com, has neighborhood information that helps you identify communities that meet your preferences as to house type, size, age, and price range, as well as neighborhood demographics, schools, and crime rates.

Finding a Newly Built House

We discuss new houses in Chapter 7. One point worthy of mention here is that to get a good deal on a new house, you need to understand and follow the market for some time. New housing developments, and new sections of old developments, are continually coming on the market. The best tend to sell quickly; the worst hang on for months. It's extremely difficult to accurately judge the new house market in a weekend, or even a week. The best approach is to follow it for some time, making a careful list of all new projects in the geographical area that interests you.

New Houses, Developments, and Condominiums

I f a newly constructed house is definitely not for you, skip this chapter. But if you're open to buying a new house, read on for common problems and pitfalls and for suggestions on ways you can save time, aggravation, and money. Also, while much of this chapter focuses on new houses, there's lots of useful advice for people buying an existing condominium or a property governed by a homeowners' association and CC&Rs.

Pitfalls and Pluses of Buying a New House

Buying a newly built house in California usually means purchasing in a tract development. There are some disadvantages to this, including:

- **Your choice is limited to relatively few models.** Most developers have a few floor plans to choose from, and while you can usually customize features like cabinets or light fixtures, you'll be limited to the available configurations.
- **You may have to deal with a slick sales rep.** Home developers tend to have commissioned sales representatives trained in carefully orchestrated sales techniques designed to make as much money as possible. (We use the terms seller, builder, and developer interchangeably in this chapter to refer to the person, or company representative, who has built the houses and is trying to sell you one.)
- **You'll be lured to the development based on a seemingly impossible low price.** Then you'll be shown model houses that are typically loaded with expensive extras.
- **Many developers make their profit by selling you add-ons and upgrades.** These are commonly overpriced; other developers price their houses high to start with and will resist calling in their workers to install anything extra.
- **You'll get discount financing and extra features only if houses are selling slowly.** But you may get low-quality construction, too. Meanwhile, the seller will charge you top dollar, with no extras, if the market is hot.
- **You'll be asked to sign a contract written primarily to benefit the seller.** The contract will typically be handed to you on a take-it-or-leave-it basis, with little opportunity to negotiate over most terms.

New House Contracts: Special Considerations

As we mention in Chapter 16, you can use the standard California contract when buying a new house. But you will want to complete it very carefully, to allow for homeowners' association membership, optional add-ons, and warranties. You may also want to obtain and review copies of documents relating to the construction of the house. Other clauses unique to new houses relate to developer delays, deposits on optional items, and development and improvement plans in undeveloped areas.

- **Once you place your order, you have little control over when your house is delivered.** The exception, of course, is if you buy a model already in inventory.
- **Lemons happen.** The fact that a home is new doesn't mean it was properly built. In fact, complaints about the quality of new home construction are quite common. For example, Ira Serkes helped a buyer place an offer on a two-year old, $1,500,000 home in the Oakland Hills. When the inspector turned on the bathroom shower, the water flowed down the floor and into the house. The inspector also discovered that half the windows were failing because they'd been improperly installed.
- **If the house turns out to be a lemon, getting problems fixed is extremely difficult.** Getting your money back is next to impossible.
- **The price is seldom negotiable.** When it comes to price, the sellers usually adopt a "take it or leave it" approach. This doesn't mean you shouldn't attempt negotiation, especially if the home seems overpriced—but your most likely bargain is to get the seller to include additional amenities at the same price.

Does this mean you should forget about buying a new house? No. New houses often have many advantages over comparable older houses, such as:

- **Price.** In areas where land is still relatively affordable, many developments are built on large chunks of land, meaning a low per-house land cost. In addition, because many houses are built at once, building supplies are purchased in bulk, bringing construction costs down.

In addition, when new houses don't sell, developers are often under pressure from lenders to raise money quickly, sometimes by slashing prices.

- **Amenities.** Many new house developments include plans for pools, tennis courts, golf courses, and meeting rooms. This is great, as long as the developer has the financial capacity to follow through and actually build them—a problem in recent years. You'll also need to make sure that any user fees are reasonable.
- **Less immediate maintenance and fix-up work.** Since everything is new, you should spend less time and money on repairs or improvements, at least in the early years if the construction was properly done.
- **Lower utility bills.** New homes are usually more energy efficient than older homes, (but, ask the builder to estimate the gas and electric bills).
- **Restrictive rules.** "Covenants, Conditions, and Restrictions" (CC&Rs) regulate many aspects of community life, especially the look of yards, driveways, and exteriors. If you appreciate order, this will be an advantage.

Choose the Developer, Then the House

The most important factor in buying a new house is not what you buy (that is, the particular model), but rather whom you buy from. You want a solid house, delivered on time, from a quality, financially stable builder who stands behind his or her work.

Usually a few developers build in a particular locale, and their reputations are well known. To check out a particular builder, talk to:

- **Existing owners in the development you're considering (or in a recently completed development by the same builder).** If they like or hate the developer, you probably will, too. The homeowners' associations will be an especially good source of information because they often hear about, and sometimes coordinate, complaints from buyers. Also check out postings on homeowner-run websites such as www.hadd.com (Homeowners Against Deficient Dwellings). And see the consumer satisfaction survey on the website of J.D. Power and Associates, at www.jdpower.com.

- **An experienced contractor.** Have your contractor look at other houses the developer is building. It's hard to tell a lot about how good the construction techniques were on a finished model; it's much easier if someone with experience can get access to a house as it's being built.

- **County planning or building office staff who deal with local developers.** For the best results, ask your questions positively. "Do Brady and Jones finish their projects on time, with few complaints?" will probably be answered candidly, while "Is it true Brady and Jones is a real schlock outfit?" might not be.

- **Real estate agents who've worked in the area for some time.** While agents won't usually deal directly with new house sales, they will likely have handled the resale of other houses built by the same developer and will know developers' reputations.

True Story

Marcia and Drew: Boy, Were We Naive

We visited a model home; we liked it and the financing the builder offered. We told the salesperson we had some design changes in mind and were assured that the developer was fair and flexible and would work everything out as we went along. We took him at his word and signed on the dotted line. Within a few days, problems began. For one, we wanted to eliminate some completely nonfunctional pillars in the living room. The builder said "no way." We then asked for different bathroom countertops and offered to pay the extra. Again, we got no cooperation and had to hire an outside contractor to remove the countertop and install the one we wanted. Whatever we requested turned out to be either impossible or prohibitively expensive. When we asked to see the original salesperson who had promised us "total cooperation," we learned that he was now working as a scuba diving instructor in Hawaii.

I guess you can say we learned the hard way. Next time, we'll be better prepared.

- **The Contractors State License Board (CSLB) for any complaints filed against the developer.** You can reach the CSLB at 800-321-CSLB, or see www.cslb.ca.gov. The CSLB will tell you only about complaints that have been fully investigated and referred for legal action. Remember, however, that the lack of complaints doesn't necessarily say anything positive about the builder.

TIP

Green building is a growing trend. If you're looking for a house that was built without excessive waste, is energy efficient (perhaps even solar powered), and uses less water than the typical home, then look for one built by a green builder. You don't need to take the builder's word for his or her environmental concern—there's a certification process, developed by the Building Industry Institute (BII). For more information on the BII standards, see www.thebii.org. To search for builders who've met these standards, see www.greenbuilder.com.

RESOURCE

Look for new houses online. For details on new home developments throughout California, check out specialized new-home websites such as www.newhomeguide.com. or move.com, sponsored by the National Association of Home Builders. The latter allows you to search new houses by city, price range, minimum number of bedrooms and baths and size of the home, move-in date, or other variables such as gated or adult community. You can view floor plans, elevations, color photos, and sometimes virtual tours, and check for details on amenities such as pools or tennis courts.

Of course, don't forget to check other online sources of homes for sale, as discussed in Chapter 6.

Using a Real Estate Agent or Broker

Chapter 5 discusses the legal and practical issues of working with a real estate broker or salesperson. Unfortunately, those rules don't always apply when purchasing a new house:

- Developers don't want to pay a commission to a real estate salesperson, so they hire their own sales staff (who only represent them). Not surprisingly, local real estate people, knowing they won't earn a commission, won't show these houses and may even bad-mouth an entire development in an effort to divert you to houses where commissions are being paid.

- Developers with slow-selling projects may cooperate with local real estate salespeople. This can extend to offering prizes and other come-ons to the salesperson who brings in the most potential buyers. Thus, you may be dragged to completely unsuitable developments for the sole (but unstated) purpose of qualifying the salesperson for a drawing for a trip to Mexico.

- Some developers cooperate with agents under their own (often unusual and not widely published) rules. For example, a developer might not pay a commission if you first visit without your agent, even if your agent is involved in every subsequent step of the purchase; but the developer would pay one if your agent was with you when you first registered. Knowing this, the agent with whom you are working is economically motivated to steer you away from any such tracts you've visited on your own and toward one with rules that will result in a commission if you buy.

If you want professional help negotiating the purchase of a new house, hire an agent familiar with the local new housing scene for a fee before you sign a contract.

If the developer won't pay the commission, you can get a break in the sales price, or provide upgrades such as higher quality carpet, if he or she doesn't have to pay a real estate agent's commission.

Financing a New House

The discussions on how to determine how much house you can afford (Chapter 2) and the various ways to finance your purchase (Chapters 8 through 13) apply to buying new, as well as existing, houses. A few note-worthy differences, however, exist.

Help Arranging a Loan

Often, developers of new housing will help you locate financing by referring you to a local bank or savings and loan that has already appraised the property, or to a loan broker. As discussed in Chapter 13, a lender will check your creditworthiness and appraise the house to see if it's worth what you agree to pay. For new houses, however, a lender often does a blanket appraisal of all development houses and agrees to approve loans for creditworthy borrowers up to a set

---

Find Out How Many Houses or Condos Are Owner-Occupied

When you're considering a house in a new development or a condominium, find out early on what percentage of the units are owner-occupied. The higher the percentage, in general, the better maintained is the development or building. Owners have more at stake (resale value of their property) than do renters, who are more transient.

This information may also affect your ability to get a competitive loan from a conventional lender. If you are buying in a new development, lenders often require at least 50% owner occupancy before granting a loan. In a condominium building, many lenders make loans only where two-thirds or more of the owners occupy their units. If you don't qualify for a loan as a result of low owner occupancy in a new development, you may need to arrange financing with a developer, perhaps on less-favorable terms. In a condo, you may still be able to borrow from a conventional lender, but you may have to put down 20%–30%.

---

amount. If you borrow from one of these lenders, no new appraisal will be necessary.

A developer cannot, however, insist that you accept financing through this network. This is important to remember if the developer pressures you to use its lender or offers incentives to accept a loan with a higher-than-normal interest rate or fees. Such practices have been the subject of consumer complaints, including cases in which the developer secretly offset the supposed discount incentives by raising the house's base price. To get the best deal on a loan, be sure to comparison shop.

Government Housing Programs

Some builders may have their developments qualified for special government loan programs such as the California Housing Financing Agency. For more on this, see Chapter 11, Government-Assisted Loans.

Buydowns and Other Direct Financing Subsidies

In slow markets, developers may increase buyer affordability through a "buydown" of the mortgage. Stripped of jargon, this means the developer pays a part of your monthly mortgage for a set period of time. For example, if you find a house with $1,200 in monthly carrying costs, and you have $300 a month of other debts, you'll need a family income of at least $4,550 per month to qualify. If the builder pays $150 a month toward your mortgage for five years, you'll only need a gross income of $4,100 a month to qualify. (This assumes a debt-to-income ratio of 33%. Most lenders want this ratio to be between 28% and 36%.)

More commonly, the builder will buy down your mortgage by subsidizing the interest rate you pay. One way is through the 3/2/1 subsidy, where the developer subsidizes part of your mortgage for three years, decreasing the subsidy each year. The table below shows how a buydown for a

$100,000, 30-year loan at a fixed rate of 10% might work.

Why would a developer buy down your mortgage? When sales are slow, unsold inventory accumulates. Developers must continue to pay interest on the money borrowed to finance construction. Selling a house, even if it means helping pay your mortgage to do it, reduces this burden. Sure, it reduces the developer's profit as compared to selling all houses with no subsidy, but when this isn't possible, profits (albeit lower ones) depend on selling homes.

How a Builder Buydown Works			
	Your Interest Rate	Your Payment	Mortgage Subsidy From Full 10% Fixed Rate
Year 1	7%	$665.30	24%
Year 2	8%	$733.76	16%
Year 3	9%	$804.62	8%
Years 4–30	10%	$877.57	(none)

If you do not need the lower payment that a buydown would give you, consider bargaining for something else instead, just as you might when buying a new car for cash while dealers are offering low interest rates. For example, you might offer to purchase for a lower price, thereby lowering the down payment, or ask for extra features such as a deck or better-quality light fixtures at no extra cost. In short, the buydown is a tip-off that the market is soft and you have room to bargain for a better deal.

Another reason for substituting a lower price for the buydown is that many buydowns take back many of the benefits they claim to provide—they give you a mortgage that has a higher-than-market interest rate after the buydown period is exhausted.

If you can choose between a buydown of your mortgage and a significantly lower price, a reduced price (resulting in a smaller mortgage) will normally save you more if you plan to own the house for a long time. If you intend to own the house for only a few years, however, a short-term mortgage buydown is probably better, as you'll pay less during this period. (To help with the calculations, use one of the online mortgage calculators listed in Chapter 2.)

Optional Add-Ons and Upgrades

Many developers advertise their houses at comparatively low prices to get you to come out and have a look. The moment you become seriously interested, the price goes up as the developer tries to sell you high-profit extras, such as added features (an extra fireplace, personal spa, or home office), upgrades (replace sliding doors with French doors, or tile countertops with granite), or design changes (greenhouse windows or security and alarm systems).

Buying extras and upgrades may enable you to semi-custom-design your home at a reasonable price. Many buyers appreciate a wide choice of kitchen cabinets, floor coverings, air conditioning systems, windows, skylights, and sprinkler systems. You may even be able to add on a room or two at a reasonable cost. But before you get too carried away, pull out your Ideal House Profile (Chapter 1). What do you really need to add to meet your needs, and how much will it cost? Use this figure to compare one new house to the next.

Be sure you investigate all payment options. Typically, some upgrades must be paid for up front, while others can be added to the price of the house and paid for over time—obviously a much more affordable option if you're on a budget. If you do agree to pay a substantial amount of extra cash, make sure the funds are deposited in an escrow account, to be released when the work is done.

 CAUTION

Negotiate refunds on optional items. If you cancel your contract, some builders will not refund the deposits you paid for optional items. If you plan lots of expensive upgrades, try to negotiate the right to a full (or at least partial) refund if the options (for example, a new security system) haven't been bought or installed. Or negotiate the right to keep any optional items that you've paid for and that haven't been permanently installed.

Upgrades can add 5%–20% or more to the cost of a new home. To get the most for your money, follow these steps:

1. **Make sure prices are fair.** Steer clear of developers who deliberately use poor-quality materials in highly visible spots in their models, almost forcing you to upgrade to overpriced substitutes. Always confirm, in writing, what you

are getting at what price, and whether the developer will allow you to make changes on your own and give you an allowance for materials and labor not used (kitchen cabinets, floor coverings). This can commonly be an issue if you don't like the developer's standard kitchen cabinets, floor coverings, or bathroom fixtures, or the optional upgrades the developer offers, and want to separately purchase and install these items yourself.

To double-check the prices of extras, visit consumer-oriented showrooms, do-it-yourself home stores, and home improvement shops. Also check home improvement magazines.

2. **Negotiate the cost of extras.** Don't be shy about negotiating over the price of extras, even if the developer tells you they're etched in marble. In fact, negotiating over extras is often easier than negotiating over the purchase price. Consider asking for one free extra for every two you buy. For example, if you pay top dollar for a stainless steel refrigerator, tile, and kitchen cabinets, ask the developer to install a better stove at no charge. This is particularly reasonable if the developer does not credit you with the cost of an original item (a plastic countertop) when you upgrade. Also, as mentioned in our discussion of price above, don't be afraid to ask for the right to purchase and install extras or upgrades on your own. If you're considering adding an expensive option such as an oak staircase, built-in window seats, or a deck, you may get a better deal from an outside contractor.

3. **Inspect model houses carefully.** Be sure that the linoleum, tile, rugs, and kitchen cabinets are of good quality, and that

---

True Story

Helen: How I Got the Carpet I Wanted

I bought a new house in El Sobrante that came with low-quality carpeting. The developer offered two better grades, but I didn't like either—they were overpriced and still not really top grade. Thus, my offer to purchase was contingent on the developer installing the carpeting of my choice, at no charge. He balked, but I pointed out that he was planning to install carpet anyway, so what was the difference? He finally agreed and also agreed to give me the carpeting that came with the house. (Why I had to bargain for this is a real mystery, as, of course, I'd paid for it.) At any rate, I purchased my own carpet at a local warehouse for $3,800 and had it delivered. The developer installed it. I then sold the original carpet through a classified ad for $1,500. Not only did I save several hundred dollars over the cost of upgrading to the developer's supposedly top-quality carpet, I also got the carpet I wanted.

Clues to Good Construction and Amenities

The more you pay for a house, the more—and better-quality—amenities you should expect. Here are some things to look for.

Air conditioning. If you live in a hot area, be sure the central air conditioning is adequate. In many tracts in the Central Valley, air conditioning units that supposedly meet minimum standards don't do the job.

Building site. Review a copy of the soils and engineering report, which the builder should have available, and the Transfer Disclosure Statement and the Natural Hazard Disclosure Statement. (See Chapter 19.) You are obviously not interested in buying a house that is likely to flood or slide off a hill, or that is built in immediate proximity to an earthquake fault. If you think the report is incorrect—that is, it says the soil is in better condition than it appears—or fear the consequences of earthquake or flood, check U.S. Geological Survey maps for soil stability and earthquake and flood zones. Federal or state agencies should have these and other impartial information.

Carpets and drapes. Look for good quality. Poor-quality carpets and drapes are often an indication that the house itself is poorly built.

Electrical outlets. You'll want at least four outlets per room, with plenty of phone, cable TV, and computer jacks.

Energy efficiency. Insulation is measured by an "R" factor. In cool areas of California, look for a development that exceeds R19. Good

insulation now will save you enormous heating bills later. Make sure the air conditioning and heating systems are the most efficient.

Entryways. Are the front and back porches covered? Stepping directly into the rain is a nuisance, but eliminating porches saves developers a few dollars.

Floors. The best, but most expensive, floors are hardwood or ceramic tile. Make sure any plywood floor has two layers.

Foundation. Poured concrete is superior to concrete block.

Inside doors. It's usually worth paying extra for solid core doors if they don't come with the house.

Kitchen cabinets. If you're paying top dollar, you want hardwood cabinets, not plywood. Again, this is a good tip-off as to whether you're dealing with a quality developer.

Soundproofing. Make sure you won't hear neighbors or highway noise. In developments where houses are only a few feet apart, or if you're on a busy street, this is particularly important. If some houses in the development are already occupied, check this out with the occupants.

Yard. An underground watering system is a good sign that the builder is committed to quality. Given a choice, it's more efficient and convenient, and it's often less expensive, to install an underground watering system before the yard is graded.

they're the ones you'll get if you buy a house. Many new house contracts contain a clause saying that the model's features are not necessarily the features you'll receive—you are guaranteed only the functional equivalent of what you see, which will almost always be different and will cost the builder far less. If you suspect this problem, shop elsewhere, or make a list of the precise features you're concerned about (include makes and models) and include it in your contract.

 CAUTION

Know what you're buying. Model homes will almost always have the best of everything, including large mirrors to make the rooms seem larger. Don't be fooled into expecting that your home will have the same details. If in doubt, get your understanding in writing or included as a contingency in your purchase contract. And be sure to look at an "unfinished" model, to see exactly what you're buying.

4. **Take care of the essentials before negotiating the flashy add-ons.** Investing in essentials (a fenced yard, wiring for high-speed Internet, or extra office space) tends to add more to the resale value of a home than investing in other add-ons (a hot tub, wine cellar, or home theater). Whatever you do, don't buy the builder's model with all the upgrades unless you get it at a huge discount. Recouping the cost of all the extras at resale is likely to be impossible—resale buyers tend to be far less excited than original owners about add-ons.

5. **Get it in writing.** When dealing with a developer's sales representative, get all promises as to what will be done, and when, in writing. If you haven't yet signed the purchase contract, make sure it includes all agreed-upon changes. If the developer's contract allows installing appliances or using materials different from those in the model, establish exactly what you will get and when. If you've already signed the contract, and you later negotiate for changes, write them down in a separate document.

Developers often resist writing things down, wanting you to rely on oral promises. ("Sure, the deck will be built by March 1.") Oral commitments are notoriously unreliable and, in practice, almost impossible to enforce.

Below is an example of what a supplementary written agreement should cover.

Choosing Your Lot

In some popular new housing developments, you will need to select a lot before your house is built. Sometimes you must choose before any house has been built. This can be tricky, as many builders won't even allow buyers on site for insurance reasons. And even if they will, it can be hard to know what the area will ultimately look like, especially if it's full of earthmovers and construction equipment. Still, if you take your time and really study the developer's

Sample Supplementary Agreement

February 1, 2011

On January 12, 2011, Alex Stevens, Sales Manager for ABC HomeCrafters, presented me with a contract to purchase the house at 8 Warden Crescent. After a discussion, I agreed to sign this contract with the following conditions:

- ABC HomeCrafters agrees to install a drainage system along the rear property line, according to the specifications set out in Attachment A to this agreement, and a redwood deck with railing behind the kitchen, according to the specifications set out in Attachment B. In exchange, I agree to pay $11,000 above the amount agreed to in the purchase contract dated January 17, 2011. Payment will be made by March 10, 2011.

- Work on the drainage system and deck, plus all landscaping called for in the purchase contract, will be completed on or before November 1, 2011. If any work is not completed by this date, we agree that the money to cover the cost will remain in escrow until the work is completed.

_2/1/11_   _Patricia Nelson_
Date   Patricia Nelson

_2/1/11_   _Alex Stevens_
Date   Alex Stevens, for ABC HomeCrafters

maps, paying particular attention to the elevation of various parcels and to traffic-flow patterns, you should get a pretty good picture of what a particular house will be like when the development is complete. Here are some things you will want to consider:

- **Privacy.** Study the elevation of the lot. Will passersby on the street, or neighbors, be able to look into your windows? If so, will they be viewing rooms where you want privacy?

- **Driveway.** Will you have a clear view down the street? It's dangerous to pull out into the middle of a blind curve.

- **Noise.** A lot at the end of a cul-de-sac will be quieter than one on a main access road, especially if you're on a hill or a corner. Also look at how close you'll be to the house next door. Many developments jam numerous houses so close together you can hear the neighbors' TV.

- **Flooding.** Lots on the tops and sides of hills are usually dry. Lots at the bottom are often more prone to flooding, especially if they're near a stream.

- **Geology.** It is impossible to see below the surface of a lot, and most geologic testing is prohibitively expensive. But in a new development, you can ask to see geologic reports that must be done to obtain building permits.

Getting a good lot at a good price is often a matter of timing. The best locations in each price range usually go first. Most developers offer waiting lists for popular locations where houses are under construction. In deciding whether to take an okay lot in a section now being built or to wait and hope for a better location in the next section, consider the following:

- Salespeople who receive a full commission if you buy now—as opposed to a small cut if you put down a deposit on a house that won't be built for a while—will sometimes overpraise existing lots and emphasize possible difficulties and delays in connection with sections where future building will occur. If, however, you state that you'll buy in the yet-unbuilt area or not at all, these difficulties are likely to quickly evaporate.

- Developers often, but not always, build the more desirable sections of a tract first. This excites buyers' interest and moves in many people quickly, creating a positive atmosphere for later sales.

- In large developments where new sections open periodically, the longer you wait, the more choice you'll have. This strategy may cost you dearly, however, if the development is popular, because the developer may then mark up prices for newly built houses, and the resale price of existing houses will likely also increase.

- Sales in yet-to-be-completed sections of developments often fall through, and good houses may reappear on sales lists, sometimes just before closing. So, if you can commit quickly, you may save time and money by staying in touch with a developer and being ready to move fast when a good deal presents itself.

If you're buying a lot in an undeveloped area, be sure you get the developer's written confirmation of promised improvements, such as sidewalks and parks. If choosing between developments, favor the ones where the amenities have already been built.

Restrictions on the Use of Your Property: CC&Rs

Many new house developments and community associations such as condominiums include, as part of the deed to the property, a number of restrictions on how the property can be used and the responsibilities of the homeowners. These are called covenants, conditions, and restrictions (CC&Rs). CC&Rs commonly limit the color or colors you can paint your house (often brown or gray), the color of the curtains or blinds visible from the street (usually white), whether you can rent the place out if you move, and even the type of front yard landscaping you can do.

Some developments have so many restrictions that it's almost as if your house is part of a common park, over which you have little say. For example, with some CC&Rs, you don't have the right to cut your lawn, plant a tree, or tend flowers; instead, you pay a monthly fee to a gardening company that does the work. Typical CC&Rs in condos have additional restrictions such as limits on the placement of television satellite dishes and the banning of some home-based businesses.

CC&Rs in California may not, however, prohibit owners from keeping at least one pet—unless, however, the homeowners' association's bylaws were adopted before this law took effect in 2001. That leaves plenty of developments that prohibit pets or limit their number and poundage.

Getting relief from overly restrictive CC&Rs after you move in isn't usually easy. You'll likely have to submit an application (with fee) for a variance, get your neighbors' permission, and possibly go through a formal hearing at which you may not succeed. And if you want to make a structural change, such as enlarging a window, building a fence, or adding a room, you'll likely need formal permission from the association in addition to complying with city zoning rules.

Role of Homeowners' Associations

Some CC&Rs—especially with condos—put costly decision-making rights in the hands of a homeowners' association. These associations can assess mandatory fees for common property maintenance, which can get expensive in older housing developments requiring upkeep, or in upscale areas with a pool, golf course, or other recreational facilities. Many associations in housing developments let their boards raise regular assessments up to 20% per year and levy additional special assessments, for a new roof or other capital improvement, with no membership vote. Ask how much these assessments have been raised in recent years and whether any large new ones are being discussed.

In some housing developments, homeowners' associations are well run and enhance living conditions. Many residents, especially those who buy in an effort to build equity and move on, appreciate the fact that most associations are very sensitive to making decisions that will enhance the value of the properties.

Unfortunately, however, some associations are poorly run. Often the majority of residents aren't interested in management details, which can mean a small group of activists gains control and imposes restrictive and sometimes expensive rules and policies. These can lead to bitter squabbles, where neighbors fight each other, using the association as their arena, and splinter groups war with boards of directors. A mismanaged or underfinanced association can go bankrupt and lose assets such as cash reserves.

Avoiding Disputes With the Homeowners' Association

Foreclosure actions by homeowners' associations—the ultimate sign that the relationship between association and homeowner has collapsed—are not as uncommon as you'd expect in California. Worse yet, the amounts being foreclosed over tend to be relatively minor—under $5,000. These aren't cases where the homeowner has failed to pay the mortgage, but more often where they've failed or refused to make assessment payments and perhaps been punished with additional fines or collection costs.

Many disputes will simmer along without getting to a foreclosure action, and in many cases, it's the homeowner who sues the association. In fact, experts estimate that 75% of all California homeowners' associations are embroiled in some sort of legal dispute. To minimize lawsuits, state law requires homeowners' associations and their members to attempt arbitration or mediation when there is a dispute over who should do what according to the CC&Rs. (Civil Code § 1354.)

True Story

Steve and Catherine: Study Your CC&Rs

After burning out looking at overpriced quaint old houses, we decided to check out new ones. We found the ideal house in a beautiful development in Sonoma County. And the price was right, too. "What's wrong?" we asked ourselves.

We didn't have to wait long for the answer. "Here are your CC&Rs," the sales agent said as she handed us a package about an inch thick. Arrgg. No way will I live in a place governed by dozens of rules and a homeowners' association. Case closed.

But wait. Why did we like this house? It was near a school, and our son had about five years to go before he graduated from high school.

Then we could move to our dream rural hilltop. In truth, we were very interested in enhancing short-term property values. Suddenly, the CC&Rs looked quite different. By preserving the attractive character of the development, the CC&Rs might be our friend, not our enemy.

So, with some trepidation, we bought. Surprise! Over four years later, we're still happy with how the CC&Rs work. They provide a framework for resolving minor neighbor disputes and have set maintenance standards that keep our community looking spiffy. So far, we've not been set upon by power-hungry CC&R enforcers. And as we hoped, property values have done comparatively well.

Does the Association Have Adequate Reserves?

In condominiums, the money in reserves must cover repairs to all common spaces: roof, garage, and the like. While a $50 or $200 per month homeowner's fee may seem steep when added to your mortgage, insurance, and taxes, you are better off with a fee that's too high, not too low. Low fees often equal inadequate reserves. When something needs repair, and the reserves are too low, the owners must pay. Usually the association authorizes the repair and bills the owners through a special assessment. If your co-owner(s) don't have the money, you may have to pay their share or face a lawsuit or other collection efforts by whoever did the repairs.

How to Check Out a Development or Condo

While development or condo living is not for everyone, many people like the idea that rules govern the conduct of their neighbors and are happy to obey the rules themselves. If you now live in an area where people fix their cars in the driveway until midnight, and the house on one side of you hasn't been painted in 15 years and the one on the other side is bright purple, a little order may be welcome. If so, you'll want to investigate further. Here are some tips:

- **Get a copy of the CC&Rs and relevant documents.** Many listing agents selling condos will not give out CC&Rs until you have submitted an offer—with a contingency that the CC&Rs are okay, of course. But CC&Rs are public documents, which you can get by visiting the County Recorder's Office. It is harder to get bylaws and minutes of association meetings before making an offer. But after the offer is accepted, you should firmly ask for them, or ask to attend a board meeting. If anyone hesitates to hand them over, there may be information they don't want you to learn.

- **Read the CC&Rs carefully and decide whether the rules are compatible with your lifestyle.** If you don't understand something in the CC&Rs, ask for more information and seek legal advice if necessary.

- **Knock on a few doors.** If you find a friendly neighbor, politely ask what he or she likes the most and least about the community. Ask how long he or she has lived there, and whether there have been any arguments between the owners and the association during that time.

- **Check the membership fees and assessments and how easy it is for the board to increase these amounts.** Review past budgets and the history and amount of fee and assessment increases. Also, find out how much money is in the reserve account. If you know the roof needs to be replaced in one year for $500,000 and the association has only $100,000 in reserve, you could be facing a shocking special assessment soon after you buy. But the association must, by law, disclose to you before you buy whether there are plans for special assessments or whether they are contemplating any legal actions.

- **Ask about the parking situation.** Find out how much parking is available, whether there's an extra charge, and where and how parking spaces are assigned.

- **Make sure the association has adequate liability and property insurance.** Your mortgage lender or insurance agent may be willing to review the policy for you. But be aware the agent may have a financial interest in saying the insurance is inadequate and trying to sell you additional coverage for your own property or to cover the costs of unforeseen association expenses. Find out whether the development is involved in litigation. If the association is suing the developer, for example, you may have difficulty getting a loan.

- **Sniff out any financial or legal trouble.** Seek as much information as possible concerning the physical condition of the entire development, the financial position of the homeowners' association, and any pending litigation involving the development or association. State law requires associations and developments to give homeowners access to information about defects, along with a timeline for repairs. (Civil Code §§ 1375, 1375.1.) The law also compels sellers to inform buyers if the association is fighting a builder to make repairs and to provide a list of the association's demands. (Civil Code § 1368.) You should have a good general contractor (or an accountant, depending on the situation) review all disclosures. California requires that even small condo associations have financial reviews every few years, so be sure the condo association has complied with this law.

CAUTION

Don't expect your real estate agent to help with homeowner association disclosures. Real estate agents are not legally required to inspect areas off the site or public records regarding title to or use of the property. (*Padgett v. Phariss*, 54 Cal. App. 4th 1270 (1997).) (See Chapter 19 for more details on legally required disclosures.)

- **Think like a landlord.** If you ever plan to rent your house or condo, pay close attention to rules affecting tenants and your liability for their actions.

(See Clause 10 of our offer form in Chapter 16, which requires your review and approval of items such as CC&Rs and homeowners' association budgets.)

RESOURCE

CC&Rs and homeowners' associations. Many homeowners' associations belong to organizations that publish a wide variety of useful materials. These include:

- **Executive Council of Home Owners (ECHO),** 408-297-3246. www.echo-ca.org.
- **Community Associations Institute (CAI),** 703-548-8600. www.caionline.org.

CC&Rs and bylaws must conform to the California Corporations Code, §§ 5000 through 10014. (See "How to Find a California Statute Online" in Appendix B.)

Dealing With Delays

If you agree to buy a house that isn't finished (or even started), you'll be asked to sign a very one-sided contract. You'll be given numerous deadlines (to make deposits, agree to design changes, get loan approval, and more, while the developer will have great leeway—even up to a year from the target date—to deliver the house.

Do what you can to change this. Most importantly, you want to establish some reasonable date at which you can cancel the contract and get all of your money back if the developer doesn't deliver your house. At some point, you should be entitled to walk away or assign your contract to another buyer. Again, get it in writing.

Developer delays can cause serious problems, especially with your mortgage loan. As discussed in Chapter 13, Obtaining a Mortgage, lenders normally won't lock in (guarantee) a particular interest rate for more than about 30 days, although you can sometimes get an extension if you pay a higher fee up front. Thus, if the closing on your new house is delayed several months at a time when interest rates are rising, you'll end up paying a higher rate and, in volatile economies, may no longer be eligible for the loan. If you have to cancel your contract because interest rates have jumped so much that you can't afford the house, you'll most likely have to forfeit your deposits to the builder. In this situation, try (in writing) to have the deposits returned to you. Or insist that your contract with the developer contain a financial penalty if the house isn't ready in time.

If you're a current homeowner, you also face the problem of selling your existing house so you can move into your new one when it's ready. When you aren't sure exactly when a new house will be ready, your best bet is to sell the old one with a contingency that allows you to either delay the closing on your old house or to continue to live in it (and pay rent) for as long as possible. If you have a choice, it's possibly better to delay the closing, because mortgage interest is deductible but rent is not. Also, you will be paying rent based on the purchaser's monthly carrying costs, which will almost always be higher than yours.

The buyer of your old house will probably want some limitation (say 60, 90, or 120 days) on your right to remain living there. If you must accept this, realize that you may find yourself living in a motel if completion of your new house is seriously delayed.

If you rent, especially if you have a month-to-month tenancy, you're in a better position. When your new house is ready, give your landlord 30 days' written notice of when you plan to move out. Even if you have a lease of a year or more, you're probably in pretty good shape. Although you're liable to pay the rent for the entire lease, your landlord is legally responsible to try to rerent your place and to subtract the new tenant's rent from what you owe. See *California Tenants' Rights,* by Janet Portman and David Brown (Nolo), for steps to take to assure that your landlord rerents a place promptly.

Inspect the House Before Closing

The biggest complaint of people who live in newly built developments involves the developer's failure to do all the things promised in the purchase contract in a timely fashion—such as installing small items like shower heads, cabinet hardware, and closet fixtures; repairing or replacing malfunctioning appliances, heaters, or air conditioners; or completing promised landscaping. Sometimes more serious problems occur, such as shoddy construction or the omission of a room in the plan.

The best way to protect yourself is to include a contingency in your contract allowing you to conduct inspections during specific phases of construction as well as before escrow closes. (See Clause 9 of our offer form in Chapter 16). You can then refuse to close escrow until everything is complete and to your satisfaction. Otherwise, once escrow closes and you take occupancy, the developer pockets the money and has little incentive to finish anything quickly or correctly.

To make sure you're getting the best-quality construction, hire professionals experienced in checking out new homes to inspect the site at key points in the building process, such as during the framing of walls, doors, and floors. While it will cost you extra, hiring professional inspectors is the best way to assure quality construction. *Your New House,* by Alan and Denise Fields (Windsor Peak Press), includes an excellent discussion on scheduling inspections during home construction.

You'll also want to hire a professional home inspector during the entire construction process and definitely before closing. You should also do your own final inspection. Bring a tape measure, note pad, and pencil. Be as methodical as you can—open every cupboard door and window, turn on every faucet, and test every appliance.

Resist promises that if you'll close and move in now, the developer will fix all problems promptly. ("We'll install the washroom sinks the day they arrive, and start the landscaping as soon as the rainy season ends.") It's amazing how much work can be completed before closing, and how quickly "impossible to get" parts can appear if you refuse to close until everything is done.

But what if you're living in a motel (or will be soon) if you don't move in? If

---

Most Common New Home Defects

Buying a new home may help you avoid termites, corroded wiring, and other defects that aging homes commonly develop. However, new homes can present their own array of problems—some of them quite serious. In fact, a 2004 *Consumer Reports* article estimated that 15% of all new homes are seriously defective. Careless and hurried work, particularly by unskilled laborers, is often the cause. Here are the areas to make particularly sure your inspector checks on:

- **Foundation and drainage.** Some builders skimp on materials, fail to install drains, or don't let the concrete dry enough before continuing with construction. The result can be cracks that allow water into your basement or crawl space. The grading of the surface around your home is also critical to the health of the foundation.

- **Paint.** Some builders save money by thinning the paint or by not applying enough coats. Add to that the streaks and splatters that can result from hurried work, and you've got a potential problem worth examining.

- **Framing.** The bones of a house are its wood framing. The inspector will need to check not only that all the beams and joists are in the right places, but that the initial drying and settling of the wood hasn't caused cracks in the gypsum or plaster drywall or sagging floors.

- **Leakage.** Around the roof and windows, faulty flashing (gutter protection), improper installation, or badly placed shingles can leave cracks for rainwater to enter, causing mold, rot, and insect infestation. Inside the walls, pipes can leak if they're not joined correctly or have been damaged during construction.

significant and costly work remains, insist that the necessary funds be placed in a trust account after escrow closes. Then ask for a written agreement providing that if the work is performed on time, the money will be released to the developer; but if it isn't, the funds go to you to hire someone else to do the work. If the developer refuses, at the least make a list of what needs to be done, assign a new completion date to each, and have it signed by the developer (see the sample, below).

RESOURCE

New construction defects. *Home and Condo Defects: A Consumer Guide to Faulty Construction*, by Thomas E. Miller and Rachel M. Miller (Seven Locks Press).

Guarantees and Warranties

You've probably heard horror stories about new houses that began to disintegrate the day the buyer moved in. This shouldn't be a problem if you buy from a reputable developer. To protect yourself further, ask if the developer provides any guarantees. Even better is a new-house warranty provided by a third-party insurer.

Sample Agreement to Complete Work

Date: December 1, 2011

To: John Addison, Acme Development
From: Abigail Williams
Re: 11 Tulip Drive

On December 17, 2011, escrow is scheduled to close on the house I am planning to buy at 11 Tulip Drive. The price I am paying includes a high-quality sod lawn. In exchange for my promise to go ahead with the closing, Acme Development agrees to complete all yard grading and drainage work, and to install this lawn by March 15, 2012.

I'm sending you two signed copies of this memo. Please sign one on the "Agreed to by" line and return it to me by December 10, 2011.

Sincerely,

Abigail Williams

Abigail Williams

Agreed to by: _____
John Addison, Sales Manager
Acme Development

Developer guarantees. Most developers give a one-year guarantee on new houses. The better guarantees include all workmanship and materials. In addition, appliances will be new and will come with their own warranties. Get all model and serial numbers and a copy of each appliance warranty.

One problem with developer guarantees is that you have only the developer's promise that a problem will be fixed. If the developer goes out of business, as many do, you're out of luck. Also, most developer guarantees are worded vaguely, guaranteeing "acceptable standards of workmanship and material." This is hard to enforce if a developer doesn't voluntarily stand behind his or her work.

Consumer Action Lines Might Help With Contractor Complaints

If you can't get a developer to make good on a new home guarantee or warranty, take your problem to a consumer action line. Offered by many radio and TV stations and newspapers, the best have volunteers who will look into your problem and, if they're convinced you've got a legitimate beef, will go to bat for you against the developer. If this fails and the problem costs less than $7,500 to correct, consider suing the developer in small claims court. See *Everybody's Guide to Small Claims Court in California*, by Ralph Warner (Nolo).

Independent company warranties. Some developers purchase new-home warranty policies from independent companies, which are far better than developer guarantees. Typical policies cover workmanship and materials for one year; plumbing, electrical, heating, and air conditioning systems for two years. Less typically, but worth looking for, are policies that cover major structural defects for ten years. Definitions of defects in material and workmanship, and your rights, are spelled out in much more detail than in developer guarantees. And most third-party policies contain fair dispute resolution procedures if you're dissatisfied with the response to a claim.

If your developer doesn't—or won't—offer third-party warranty coverage, you can purchase your own house warranty. Be sure you're aware of all restrictions, deductible dollar limits of coverage, and dispute resolution procedures. (See Chapter 19 for more on home warranties.)

Financing Your House: An Overview

SKIP AHEAD

If you've already arranged to finance your house, skip ahead to Chapter 14.

Let's start with the bold truth— arranging to finance a house can be disheartening. To qualify, you must normally come up with a good-sized chunk of cash for the down payment. Then you need to borrow a huge sum of money and make monthly payments for what seems like the rest of your life. And, finally, if you don't want to end up with a lousy deal, you must understand seemingly endless details about the variety of mortgages with different interest rates, up-front costs, and fine print terms.

Chapters 8 through 13 provide the basic information necessary to sensibly finance the purchase of a house. If you carefully read all our material before making important decisions, you'll be equipped to obtain a good mortgage at a competitive price.

How Mortgage Lenders Think

The more money you have for a down payment, the higher your personal income, and the lower your debts, the better deal you're likely to get. You'll be a likely candidate for a favorable mortgage loan if:

- **You make a large down payment.** People rarely default on their loans when they have a large personal stake in the property.
- **You do well financially and have limited long-term debts.** The affluent usually repay their loans, sometimes ahead of time.

- **You have an excellent credit history.** People who have paid their bills on time for many years are likely to continue to do so. The reverse is also true.
- **The property is worth more than the loan amount.** The lender feels secure that if you default, the property can be sold for more than enough to repay the loan. Again, the reverse is also true.

Unfortunately, the less money you have to put down, the lower your income, and the greater your debts, the more likely you are to be stuck accepting a mortgage (if you can get one at all) with some undesirable features, such as a high interest rate, substantial points, or private mortgage insurance.

Who Lends Mortgage Money?

Many entities, including banks, credit unions, and savings and loans make home loans. Large lenders tend to work statewide, while smaller ones specialize in narrower geographical areas, types of housing, or types of mortgages. Fortunately, because mortgage rates are widely published and available online (see Chapter 13), and many types of loans are standardized no matter who the lender is, comparative shopping is not difficult. Government-guaranteed loans (see Chapter 11) offered by the Federal Housing Administration (FHA) and the U.S. Department of Veterans Affairs (VA) are also options.

As you sift through all the financing details in the next five chapters, remember this important truth: There's no one universally desirable mortgage, only one that will help you buy the house you want with maximum efficiency at a minimum cost.

TIP

Don't overlook private financing.
To bypass lender rules and restrictions, some home buyers borrow some or all mortgage money privately, that is, from parents, other relatives, and friends. (Chapter 12 covers private mortgages.)

Standardized Loans: Fannie Mae, Freddie Mac, and the Secondary Mortgage Market

Most financial institutions that lend money (banks, credit unions, savings and loans) don't keep most of the loans they make in their portfolio, but rather sell them to investors on the "secondary mortgage market." Several large institutions, including the Federal National Mortgage Association (FNMA or Fannie Mae) and Federal Home Loan Mortgage Corporation (FHLMC or Freddie Mac), buy a large portion of these mortgages.

But the secondary mortgage market buys only mortgages that conform to their financial qualification standards and rules regarding maximum size loan. (See Chapter 2.) The result is that most lenders follow these rules, and many mortgages are remarkably similar. For example, Fannie Mae and Freddie Mac buy no loans exceeding $417,000 in most areas (but up to $1 million or more in high-cost areas.) These limits change annually.

If you need a mortgage larger than the limit where you're buying you probably need what's called a "jumbo" loan, which typically has a slightly higher interest rate than Fannie Mae or Freddie Mac loans. These loans are becoming less common and more difficult to get as government regulation of the mortgage industry increases. If you need a loan for more than the conforming loan limit where you live, you'll almost certainly want to work with a mortgage broker, who can help you figure out the best option.

RESOURCE

Online mortgage resources. For information on Fannie Mae and Freddie Mac loan limits and programs, check their websites at www.fanniemae.com (click "Homebuyers") and www.freddiemac.com (select "About Home Ownership").

Mortgage Types

There are two basic types of mortgages, and a few permutations of these types.

Fixed Rate Mortgage. The interest rate and the amount you pay each month remain the same over the entire mortgage term. A number of variations are available, as explained in Chapter 9.

Adjustable Rate Mortgage (ARM). With an ARM, the interest rate is set for a fixed period, but then adjusts.

The traditional ARM offers an initial, "teaser" interest-rate, but it very soon becomes subject to monthly adjustments. You might also find a hybrid ARM, which starts out as a fixed loan for a certain period of time—usually three, five, or seven years— then turns into a traditional ARM.

CAUTION

Where have all the creative financing techniques gone? Although other, more creative strategies (like "interest-only loans") were commonly used just a few years ago, they're scarce now, due in part to the large number of borrowers who defaulted on them.

Comparing Fixed Rate and Adjustable Rate Mortgages

Before shopping for a mortgage, you'll probably want to decide whether a fixed rate or an adjustable rate mortgage (ARM) is a better fit for your financial situation.

With a fixed rate mortgage, your interest rate is fixed for the life of the loan. That means your monthly payment is always the same, which can be good for home buyers who want to minimize their financial risk and are happy with the current interest rate. But the downside is that you're paying a premium for that certainty. Fixed-rate loans usually have higher interest rates than adjustable rate loans. (The higher rate is because lenders build in a cushion against the possibility of interest rates increasing while they're stuck with charging you the same old rate.)

Also, if interest rates drop, you're stuck with your fixed interest rate, while home-buyers with ARMs may actually see their interest rates drop. Of course, refinancing may be an option for you, but every new loan costs money to set up, and those costs may eat into the gains that you acquire with your new, lower-interest mortgage.

With adjustable rate loans, on the other hand, you need to be ready for a less predictable series of payments. Some ARMs can change as early as the first month after your purchase, immediately increasing the interest rate. Most other ARMs protect you—and the lender—from wild ups and downs in interest rates by including percentage limits on these fluctuations, applied either every six months, yearly, or over the life of the loan. (These limits are somewhat misleadingly called "caps," even though they limit drops in your interest rates as well.) The classic ARM is attractive to people who need the initially low rate to afford a house and are prepared for the possibility of later rises in the interest rates.

Some ARMs let you start slowly, offering a rate that's fixed for the first three, five, or seven years and adjusts after that. These tend to start at lower interest rates than fixed rate mortgages. That makes them particularly attractive to borrowers who expect their personal or financial situation to change before the interest rate changes.

Rough-and-Ready Comparison of a Fixed Rate Mortgage and an Adjustable Rate Mortgage

Assume you're borrowing $250,000 for 30 years. Here's how the initial payments on a 4% adjustable rate mortgage and a 6.5% fixed rate compare:

6.5% Fixed	$ 1,580
4% ARM	1,194
	$ 386 difference each month

In this example, the fixed payment is 38% higher than the adjustable to start with. But this advantage won't last long. Assume the ARM is tied to a financial index that has an average interest rate of 4% over the next four years and that the lender collects a margin of 2.5% above this index interest rate. Assume also that the ARM can never increase more than six interest points (a life-of-the-loan cap). (Adjustable rate mortgage margins, indexes, and caps are all discussed in Chapter 10.) By the beginning of the second year, the interest rate on the ARM loan would be 6.5%, the same as the fixed rate.

If the index interest rate rises to the life-of-the-loan cap by the end of the four years (a full six interest points above the initial interest rate), the ARM owner would be paying 10% interest. A comparison would look like this:

6.5% Fixed	$ 1,580
10% ARM	$ 2,194

Nolo's website has a calculator to help you choose between a fixed or adjustable loan (look for "Which mortgage is better for me?") See www.nolo.com/legal-calculators.

In California a Mortgage Is Really a Deed of Trust

When you borrow money to buy a home, the lender records a legal instrument at a county office. That instrument is called a deed of trust, not a mortgage. We use the term mortgage in this book, however, because it's the word in common use. Here's the technical difference: A deed of trust gives the trustee (often a title company) the right to sell your property, with no court approval, if you fail to pay the lender on time (default). By contrast, a mortgage normally involves only a borrower and a lender, and often requires a more complicated judicial foreclosure proceeding if you default.

Here are common deed terms.

Beneficiary. Your lender is the beneficiary of the deed of trust; if you default and the trustee sells the house, it gets paid from the proceeds.

Promissory note. When you borrow, you sign this note promising to repay the loan over a set time period at certain terms. Normally, the note is secured by a deed of trust, in which you agree that the house itself is collateral (security) for repayment. If the note isn't repaid, the house can be sold and a portion of the proceeds used to pay off.

Trustee. If you default, the trustee's role is to sell the house and a portion of the proceeds used to pay what you still owe the lender.

Trustor. The trustor is the borrower—that's you. As trustor, you legally own the house but sign a deed of trust giving the trustee certain powers if you default on the loan.

Comparison of Adjustable Rate Mortgages and Fixed Rate Mortgages		
	Adjustable Rate Mortgages	**Fixed Rate Mortgages**
Advantages	• Initially lower interest rates. • Initially lower monthly payments. • Possibility that interest rates will go down (should interest rates drop). • Possibility that, over the life of the loan, you'll end up paying less interest than if you'd chosen a fixed rate loan. • May be easier to qualify for than a fixed rate loan, or you may qualify to borrow more money. • Comes with a lifetime rate cap (the rate can't exceed a predetermined interest rate). • Possibly assumable by a qualified purchaser when you sell.	• Monthly payments don't change, even if interest rates rise. • You get the peace of mind of knowing exactly how much your total mortgage will cost.
Disadvantages	• If interest rates go up, your monthly payments will rise. • If you chose the ARM because your finances are extremely tight, higher monthly payments may force you to sell the house or go into foreclosure.	• If interest rates go down, you may end up spending more than you would have over the life of the loan with an ARM (though the possibility of refinancing ameliorates this issue). • You'll be paying a premium on your interest rate to cover the lender's risk that interest rates will rise over the many years of the mortgage.

The Cost of Getting a Loan

Every mortgage comes with several fees. Here are the common ones.

- **General fees.** The lender typically charges loan application fees (around $650–$1,300) to cover the cost of processing, underwriting, administering, and drawing up documents for your loan. And, if you make a low down payment, you'll likely be required to purchase private mortgage insurance.

    The lender will also require that you pay fees to various third parties— including the appraiser who confirms the value of your house, the escrow company that acts as middleperson in the transaction, the title insurance company that figures out whether the seller has the right to sell you the property free and clear, credit reporting companies, and so on.

    These so-called closing costs typically add up to as much as 2%–5% of your purchase price. The fees can be added to your down payment money and paid at closing, or they can be folded into your mortgage. (See Chapter 18 for a full description of closing costs.)

- **Points.** Many lenders also charge a loan fee in the form of "points." Each point is 1% of the loan principal. Points, too, can add up fast—1% of a $100,000 is already $1,000. Lenders like to charge points because it's often their main source of profit on your loan, especially if they immediately turn around and resell on the secondary market.

Not all mortgages come with points. But by choosing to pay a point or more up front, you can usually "buy down" your interest rate, for an overall savings in the long term. For example, you might be offered a 30-year fixed rate loan of $500,000 with two points ($10,000) at 4.75% interest, or the same loan with no points at 5.25%. Let's run some numbers to see when paying points on this loan will start to save you money:

No points loan	5.25%	$2,993.52 monthly payment
Two points loan	4.75%	$2,840.74 monthly payment
Loan comparison		$152.78 monthly difference

As you can see, the loan at two points allows you to pay $152.78 less every month at mortgage-payment time. To find out how long it will take you to recoup your $10,000 investment, simply divide it by $152.78. You'll see that it will take approximately 65 months (five-plus years) until you've saved enough to equal your investment. After the 65 months, you're looking at pure savings.

So before comparing points to interest, factor in how long you plan to own your house. The longer you live in your house (or pay on the mortgage), the better off you'll be paying more points up front in return for a lower interest rate.

CAUTION

The APR isn't all it's cracked up to be. You may have heard that the way to compare loans and points between lenders is to look at the Annual Percentage Rate, or APR. Unfortunately, the APR tends to be misleading, because it's oversimplified. The APR is the cost of taking out a loan, expressed as a percentage spread out over the life of the loan. All the costs associated with obtaining the particular loan (lenders fees, credit report, appraisal fee, and so on) are factored in to arrive at the percentage. The oversimplification comes in because the calculation assumes that the loan will not be paid off until the loan term ends, usually 30 years. Most people don't keep their mortgages that long. Also, not all lenders use the same approach when calculating the costs that go into their loans, so it's very hard to arrive at an apples-to-apples comparison.

Refinancing: The Effect on Points and Interest Rates

Whether to opt for a loan with more points and a lower interest rate doesn't only depend on how long you'll own the house, but on how long you'll own the loan. Refinancing to get a better interest rate has the same effect as selling the house and buying another.

If interest rates are fairly high when you look for your initial loan, and you expect them to drop before long, you're a candidate to refinance soon. You'll want to shop for a loan with the fewest points, even if this means paying slightly higher interest.

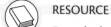

RESOURCE

For calculators to help make decisions on paying points or refinancing, see Nolo's website at www.nolo.com/legal-calculators.

Which Mortgage Is Best for You?

With careful thought and planning, you can choose the best mortgage for your own individual needs. For now, try to keep an open mind. As California mortgage broker Gwen Hoople advises, "Choose your mortgage only after all loan options available to you have been explained, and you've carefully weighed them against your own financial plans and needs." In the next five chapters, we'll give you lots of facts relevant to efficiently putting every piece in place. First, however, ask yourself the following five questions. The answers will help guide you as you read on.

Tax Deductibility of Points

Points on a mortgage are tax deductible. The IRS allows buyers to deduct points paid for them by the home sellers—in addition to points buyers themselves pay for a mortgage.

For more information on the tax deductibility of points, call the IRS at 800-TAX-FORM or check its website at www.irs.gov.

How Much House Can You Afford?

Deciding how much house you can afford is directly related to choosing a mortgage. The more you can easily afford a particular purchase (that is, your debt-to-income ratio is low), the more likely you can qualify for a good mortgage at a competitive interest rate. Chapter 2 gives detailed instructions on determining the maximum amount a lender will let you borrow to purchase a house, based on your income, down payment, and other factors. If you haven't yet done so, read Chapter 2 and complete the calculations.

Is Your Income Likely to Increase Soon?

If your income is modest now but likely to go up soon, you may be able to get a mortgage with smaller initial payments that will increase in the future. This will allow you to buy a more expensive house. One option is an ARM that is fixed for the first three, five, or seven years. This gives you short-term security and usually a lower interest rate, hopefully until your income increases. The downside is that if interest rates go way up later, when the loan becomes adjustable, your monthly payments could go higher than you had foreseen.

How Much Down Payment Can You Make?

The reality is that the less money you put down, the fewer lenders and loans you'll have to choose from, and the higher your mortgage payments will be. Loans with no down payment tend to charge higher interest rates than any other, and are extremely rare in any case. Most lenders will require at least a 3% down payment.

But it's most convenient if you can put down at least 20% of your loan. If not, you'll have to pay private mortgage insurance (PMI).

How Long Do You Plan to Own Your Home?

The length of time you plan to own your house is very relevant to choosing a mortgage. For example, if you intend to keep your home for five years, why not choose an ARM that is fixed for five years? That will give you a lower interest rate than a 30-year fixed rate loan, but you will still have the security of knowing exactly how much your payments will be for the next five years.

RESOURCE

Choosing a mortgage. See *The New Rules for Mortgages,* by Dale Robyn Siegel (Alpha); *Mortgage Ripoffs and Money Savers: An Industry Insider Explains How to Save Thousands on Your Mortgage or Re-Finance,* by Carolyn Warren (Wiley); and *All About Mortgages: Insider Tips to Finance the Home,* by Julie Garton-Good (Kaplan Publishing).

If inflation becomes more of a danger, however, interest rates are likely to increase. In this situation, ARM interest rates will surely go higher, perhaps much higher, than those for fixed rate mortgages.

RESOURCE

Several useful websites cover market trends and forecasts on mortgage interest rates. One especially good one is sponsored by HSH Associates at www.hsh.com. Also see www.bankrate.com.

Fixed Rate Mortgages

A generation ago, mortgage rules were simple—interest rates were always fixed in advance and repayable in equal monthly installments over a term of 15 to 30 years. The mortgage lender, usually a bank or savings and loan on a downtown corner, required the purchaser to make a down payment of 20% or more and have steady income and a good credit rating. The fixed rate mortgage is the one that most closely resembles this old system.

Today, new mortgage options come and go, including more affordable types of fixed rate mortgages.

Should You Choose a Fixed Rate Mortgage If You Can Afford One?

Many people ask whether they should get a fixed rate mortgage if they can afford one. The answer is a qualified yes; a fixed rate mortgage is the safest bet if you plan to own the house for an extended period. A fixed rate mortgage offers two main advantages:

- The amount you must pay is established in advance and does not increase.
- You may save on interest costs. Even though many Adjustable Rate Mortgages (ARMs) offer a lower initial interest rate, the total interest paid on a fixed rate mortgage may be less than on an ARM if interest rates go up substantially and stay up for an extended period. This is because the interest rate on ARMs increases over a few years' time to a current market rate. If market rates go up, so do the interest rates on ARMs.

Monthly Payments for a $100,000 Fixed Rate Mortgage	

This chart shows the variation among monthly payments for a 30-year, $100,000 fixed rate mortgage at different interest rates.

Interest Rate	Monthly Payment
4.5%	$507
5.0%	$537
5.5%	$568
6.0%	$600
6.5%	$632
7.0%	$665
7.5%	$699
8.0%	$734
8.5%	$769
9.0%	$805
9.5%	$841
10.0%	$878

You may want to forgo a fixed rate mortgage, however, if:

- **You'll be moving to another house or refinancing within three to four years.** If you're not planning on keeping your mortgage for a long time, you can usually find an ARM that will cost less in the short term. For example, if you plan to move within five years, a five-year hybrid ARM will have a low interest rate for five years, then adjust to a higher rate after that. You'll never pay the higher rate, because you'll move before it happens.

- **You believe that interest rates are likely to fall substantially (unlikely in the current market).** In this case, ARM rates will stay close to their initial level, or perhaps even drop. By contrast, if you have a fixed rate mortgage, you'll have to refinance to take advantage of lower rates.

Not All Fixed Rate Mortgages Are the Same: Down Payments, Points, Interest Rates, and Other Variables

Purchasing a good fixed rate mortgage involves comparing several features. In addition to interest rates, you need to consider:

- **Down payment.** In Chapter 4, we discussed the considerations in making a down payment within the generally required range of 5% to 20%. If you can readily put 20% down, doing so is advisable because it will eliminate the need to pay private mortgage insurance (PMI). If you can't put 20% down, then do the best you can. (See Chapter 4 for tips on scraping together cash.)

- **Private mortgage insurance.** Buyers are commonly required to purchase private mortgage insurance (PMI) when the lender supplies more than 80% of the financing. PMI protects the lender if you fail to make your mortgage payments. The cost of the insurance usually gets added to your monthly mortgage payment. We discuss PMI at greater length in Chapter 4.

- **Points and interest rates.** Points are up-front charges made by a lender as a condition of lending money. One point equals 1% of a loan. In Chapter 8, we discuss the relationship of points to interest rates and show you how to determine how many points, if any, you should pay.

- **Prepayment penalties.** If you can avoid it, don't take a loan that has a prepayment penalty—a financial penalty for paying off your mortgage early. At some point you may want to sell your home, refinance, or prepay the mortgage, and a penalty may limit your ability to do so. If you can't avoid a prepayment penalty, at least read the loan papers carefully so that you know the time period during which the lender may charge you a prepayment penalty (many loans penalize you only during the first few years of the loan; three years is the legal maximum for conforming loans under California's Finance Code § 4973. Also check on the maximum charge for prepaying your mortgage, and the periods, if any, when prepayment may be made without a penalty.

Mortgages' Lengths and Payment Schedules

Not all mortgages last for 30 years; 15-year terms are also available. (Ten-, and 20-year loans were once available but have now become rare.)

Short-Term Fixed Rate Mortgages Versus Prepaying Your Mortgage

Lenders commonly offer 15-year mortgages at more favorable interest rates than 30-year mortgages. That's because the faster the loan is paid off, the lower their risk of interest rates jumping (and eating up their profits) or buyers defaulting.

Even if the interest rate is low and you'll save money in the long run, the relatively large monthly payments of a shorter term mortgage will decrease your ability to take out other loans (for home improvements, a new car, and the like) or make other investments. You'll also be committed to high monthly payments, which may take quite a bite out of your income.

However, you will save significant interest over the long term. For example, with a $100,000 fixed rate loan at 5%, you'd have a higher monthly payment but pay nearly $51,000 less in interest with a 15-year mortgage. And that doesn't even account for the lower interest rate you're likely to pay.

But you can achieve the same savings and benefits by voluntarily paying more principal each month on a longer-term loan. The advantage of prepaying a long-term mortgage is its flexibility—you don't legally obligate yourself to the higher payment, so you can change your mind and pay less if need be.

Even prepaying a small amount per month makes a large difference in your total payments. For example, by paying an extra $50 per month on a 30-year, 6% fixed rate $100,000 mortgage, you'd repay the loan in 25 (not 30) years and save nearly $25,000 in

interest. If you don't want to pay a little extra each month, consider making a yearly lump sum payment—perhaps when you receive your tax refund.

CAUTION

If you plan to prepay a mortgage, remember this rule: No matter how much extra you pay in one month, you still must make at least the regular payment the next month.

RESOURCE

How to calculate savings from prepaying your mortgage. Go to Nolo's website at www.nolo.com/legal-calculators and choose "How much will I save by increasing my mortgage payments?".

Biweekly Mortgages

Some lenders offer fixed rate mortgages (and ARMs) that require biweekly (rather than monthly) payments. Others require an extra payment or two during each year. With these plans, you pay less interest over the life of the loan because the loan term is shortened and the lender gets the money sooner.

With biweekly mortgages, you make the equivalent of 13, not 12, monthly mortgage payments per year. On a regular 30-year, $100,000 fixed rate loan at 8%, your monthly payments would be $734 and the total cost of the mortgage is $264,240. With a biweekly mortgage, by contrast, you would pay $367 every two weeks and pay off your mortgage in a little less than 23 years at a cost of $217,998, saving over $46,000 in interest.

All this sounds good until you realize that most lenders charge an extra fee to handle this type of mortgage, which often cancels out any savings. (There are exceptions, though.) It's better to stick with a monthly payment plan, prepaying principal whenever you can. One simple yet effective strategy is to increase your monthly payment to the nearest round number by $100 to $200.

Most Fixed Rate Loans Aren't Assumable

Fixed rate loans in California (except government-guaranteed loans) are generally not assumable by a buyer. If you get a fixed rate loan and later sell your house, you must either pay it off and have the buyer take out a new loan or get the lender's permission for the buyer to assume yours. The latter rarely occurs, for obvious reasons: The buyer won't want the loan if it's above the current market rate, and the lender won't allow it to be assumed if it's below.

Adjustable Rate Mortgages

While adjustable rate mortgages, or "ARMs" may be a fine way to finance a home, especially if you're on a tight budget, they can be dangerous if you don't know exactly what you're getting. Fortunately, once ARM language is deciphered, obtaining a good one isn't too difficult. We'll show you how in this chapter, and in Chapter 13 we'll explain how to measure the true cost of a mortgage, adjusting for interest, margins, index, and finance charges.

When Should You Finance With an ARM?

Initial ARM interest rates are lower than fixed rate mortgages. However, the rate can change on a predetermined schedule such as monthly, semiannually, or annually. When it does, the new interest rate is tied to a current market rate (called an index) plus the lender's profit (called a margin). If market rates have increased since you first took out the loan, your loan payment will increase, too.

ARMs can be a good choice in either of the following cases:

- You need money for other purposes— say to start a small business—so having a lower initial monthly payment makes sense.
- You plan to move or refinance in the next three to five years. Because your initial ARM interest rate is lower than a fixed rate, an ARM is cheaper than a fixed rate loan for the first few years.

Don't Believe All the Ads

Many lenders heavily advertise low initial ARM rates—but before you get drawn in, realize that:

- The advertised start rates don't last long (usually six months).
- Discounted rates don't necessarily help with loan qualification, because your ability to handle the loan is usually analyzed using the first-year rate, not the discounted rate.
- The lender will probably get its money back by including less attractive ARM features in the fine print, such as higher periodic interest rate caps or negative amortization.

Loan and Payment Caps

The term "cap" sounds simple. If you have a 5% ARM with a 5% life-of-the-loan cap and a 2% one-year periodic cap, your mortgage can't go above 10% and can't increase to more than 7% after one year.

But caps aren't this straightforward. First, be aware that the "5% life-of-the-loan cap" refers to five percentage points, not a 5% increase. Five percentage points raise an interest rate of 5% to 10% during the life of a loan, a 100% increase.

Most ARMs also cap the maximum amount your interest rate can go up in a particular adjustment period (periodic caps) between one and two percentage points per year, often adjusted every six months.

ARM Terms Defined

Before getting an ARM, review the following mortgage terminology.

Adjustment period. The time that goes by before the interest rate or payment amount changes. Most loans have monthly, semiannual, or annual adjustment periods. Annual or semiannual are preferred; try to avoid monthly adjustment periods, if possible.

Caps. The term "cap" refers to two different concepts. One is how much your interest rate can go up or down over the term of your mortgage (life-of-the-loan cap). The other is how much it can go up or down at each adjustment period.

Life-of-the-loan cap (or overall cap). This is the maximum (usually five to six percentage points) that the interest rate can increase or decrease over the life of the loan. For example, if the interest rate starts at 4%, and the life-of-the-loan cap is six percentage points, your interest rate can never exceed 10%. (Although arithmetic dictates that your loan could decrease to –2%, ARM loans always include a floor provision, usually of 1%.)

Periodic cap. This limits the amount the interest rate of an ARM can change at each adjustment period. With a periodic cap, your interest rate might go up as much as 1% every six months or 2% annually—with your payments increasing accordingly.

Index. A market-sensitive financial yardstick to which ARM interest rates are linked. An index computed by averaging rates over a fairly long term (such as 26 or 52 weeks) will move up or down more slowly than one tied to daily or weekly rates.

Margin. The factor or percentage a lender adds to your index interest rate to arrive at the interest rate you pay. Most initial interest rates are set at, or below, the index interest rate (with no margin added). This means that, subject to the periodic or payment caps, ARM interest rates will automatically rise in the first several years to reach the market rate, unless the index interest rate falls substantially during this period.

Fully indexed rate. An ARM's true base interest rate after all initial discounts are filtered out. The fully indexed rate is calculated by adding the margin to the index. If your loan is based on the COFI with a 2.5% margin, your fully indexed rate is 7.5% when the COFI is 5%.

For a loan with an initial rate of 5%, a one percentage annual point cap means the rate can rise to 6% in one year.

> **TIP**
>
> **Don't be shy about asking for explanations.** In the words of Gwen Hoople, a loan consultant with Holmgren and Associates, "If you don't understand something that your lender or loan broker is telling you, it's not because you're dumb. Ask for a fuller explanation in plain English—and if you still don't understand, then their explanation wasn't good enough. Don't sign your loan papers until you fully understand the terms of your loan."

ARM Indexes and Margins

By now you understand that when interest rates go up, so do ARM payments. Different ARMs, however, are tied to different financial indexes, some of which fluctuate up or down more quickly than others.

Indexes that lenders often use include those tied to the rates paid on six-month or one-year U.S. Treasury Bills (called "T-bills"). Other common indexes use the rate at which U.S. T-bills are sold in Europe (LIBOR), and the Cost of Funds (COFI) of the 11th Federal Home Loan Bank District.

Lenders don't simply lend you money at the interest rate of the index, which is only slightly above what they pay their own CD depositors. Instead, lenders tack on two to three interest points (called a margin) to cover their costs and to make a profit.

So your payments don't jump too quickly, you want an ARM tied to a financial index that is likely to fluctuate slowly. Look for a loan where the lender computes interest rates based on an average of the index calculated over a number of weeks, because it will take a while before a quick spike in interest rates moves the average significantly higher. The most volatile indexes (and therefore the worst if interest rates spike up) are computed on a daily or weekly "spot basis." Sure, they can go down fast, too, but if you can't afford a big increase, they're not worth the risk. Historically, LIBOR rates have been the most volatile, while the COFI has been the least. T-bill rates have fallen in between.

Don't get so caught up in the index that you forget to look at the margin, the number added to the index to arrive at the interest rate you are charged. In the current market, we believe that a fair margin is 2.25% to 2.5%. This is because a small difference in the margin can translate into substantially higher loan costs. On a 30-year, $130,000 loan with a 2.5% margin and a 5% index, your interest rate will be 7.5% and your payments $909. With a 3% margin, your interest rate will be 8% and your payments $45 more per month and $19,440 more over the life of the loan.

Assumability

A few ARMs are written to allow creditworthy purchasers to assume them from the seller. After the interest rate discounts offered in the first few years are eliminated, ARMs track current interest rates, and lenders have nothing to lose by someone assuming your loan.

Should you make it a high priority to find an assumable loan? Most of the time, no. Many purchasers will want a fixed rate loan and won't want to assume your ARM. And even if they want an ARM, they will normally be able to get a new one at an initial rate lower than your current one. Only if interest rates skyrocket, as they did in the early 1980s, and you have an ARM with a fairly tight life-of-the-loan cap, will a subsequent purchaser want to assume it. This, of course, is because your ARM will then be cheaper than a new loan.

Prepayment Penalties

In California today, it's unusual to see prepayment penalties on loans. In fact, for conforming loans, California law prohibits lenders from assessing prepayment penalties after the first 36 months of the loan. (Finance Code § 4973.)

With no penalty, you can make an extra payment or increase your payment to reduce the amount of interest you pay. (Chapter 9 discusses the advantages of prepaying your mortgage.) Also, you can refinance your ARM without penalty.

Hybrid Adjustable Rate Mortgage

Some lenders offer a hybrid mortgage that features an initial fixed rate (often for three, five, seven, or even ten years) that later converts to an ARM. You get the security of fixed rate payments in the early years and

risk paying more later, when, hopefully, you'll have more income or can refinance.

This mortgage is especially popular with people who don't expect to own their houses beyond the point when the conversion to an ARM occurs. Because of life's unexpected happenings, however, look carefully to see that once the loan turns into an ARM, it's a good-quality one. Specifically, check the caps, the index and the margin used.

Summing Up—What Good ARMs Look Like

When it comes to ARMs, we recommend that you get the best margin and index you can, and be skeptical about initial discounted rates. Look for an ARM that conforms to these guidelines:

- A margin that is as low as possible, such as 2.25% points for a one-year ARM.
- An ARM tied to an index that will adjust for inflation relatively slowly, if you expect rates to increase. Again, historically, this has been most often the COFI. If possible (and it often isn't), avoid ARMs tied to much shorter periods.
- A periodic cap that limits interest rate increases to no more than two interest rate percentage points per year.
- A life-of-the-loan cap of five to six interest points.
- The right to prepay without penalty.

What to Ask When Choosing an ARM

If you're considering an ARM, here are the basic things you'll want to know before you commit:

- **Initial rate (start rate).** How long is your initial interest rate fixed for? For example, it may last one month, six months, one year, three years, five years, seven years, or ten years.
- **Index.** What index is your ARM's interest rate based on (for example, the LIBOR, COFI, or T-bill index)?
- **Margin.** What's the bank's profit margin—in other words, what percentage will your lender add to bring your interest rate above the index rate?
- **Periodic caps.** By how much could your interest rate go up or down, and how often does it adjust? (For example, it might change by 1%, 2%, or 5%, and this could happen every month, six months, or 12 months.)
- **Lifetime cap.** What is the lifetime maximum interest rate of your loan?

EXAMPLE: José and Sandra have a $200,000 loan with an initial interest rate of 5%, which is fixed for five years and then varies based on the LIBOR index plus a margin of 2.5%. The periodic cap is 5% for the first adjustment and 2% thereafter, occurring every 12 months. The lifetime cap is 5% above the initial start rate.

For the first five years, José and Sandra's monthly payment is $1,073.64. Then, their interest rate gets recalculated based on the latest LIBOR index, at 4.5%, to which the bank adds its 2.5% margin, bringing the interest rate for the next 12 months from 5% to 7%. Their monthly mortgage payments go up to $1,330.60.

José and Sandra know their interest rate will never go higher than 10% (the 5% initial rate plus the 5% lifetime cap) and it will never go lower than the margin plus the index at the time of adjustment. They can also expect that every 12 months, a new interest rate will be recalculated based on the current index plus the margin—but with a limit of 2% in any direction (the periodic cap). So, even if, after the index's initial jump from 4.5% to 7%, it went up by 3% to 7.5%, their interest rate for the next 12 months would be capped at 9% (7% plus the periodic cap of 2%). If the index fell by 3%, their interest rate would go down from 7% to 5% (again because of the 2% periodic cap).

Government-Assisted Loans

Four government-assisted mortgage programs (and some local financing programs) are available to help Californians buy homes. These are:

- U.S. Department of Veterans Affairs (VA)
- Federal Housing Administration (FHA)
- California Housing Finance Agency (CalHFA), and
- California Department of Veterans Affairs (Cal-Vet).

The CalHFA program primarily provides mortgage financing for first-time California house purchasers in designated areas, and for qualifying first-time buyers who wish to buy outside these areas. The Cal-Vet program provides low-down-payment mortgage loans to qualifying California veterans.

Veterans Affairs Loans

So-called "VA loans" are available to men and women who are now in the service and to veterans with an other-than-dishonorable discharge who meet specific eligibility rules, most of which relate to length of service. Certificates of Eligibility are available from a VA office, after you've submitted VA Form 26-1880, *Request For A Certificate of Eligibility For VA Home Loan Benefits.* The form is available on the VA website, www.va.gov.

However, the VA doesn't actually make mortgage loans, but guarantees part of the house loan you get from a bank, savings and loan, or other private lender. If you default, the VA pays the lender the amount guaranteed, and you in turn will owe the VA. The idea of VA loans is to give veterans home-financing opportunities with favorable loan terms and competitive rates of interest.

The VA itself doesn't set a maximum loan amount, but limits the amount of your loan that it will repay, as shown below.

Maximum VA Guarantees

Size of Loan	Maximum Guarantees
$45,000 or less	50% of loan
$45,000–$144,000	40% of loan, up to $36,000
$144,000 or more	25% of loan, up to the Freddie Mac conforming limit

Also, the loan amount may not exceed the VA's Certificate of Reasonable Value (CRV), based on the VA's appraisal of the property.

 RESOURCE

To find out whether your military service qualifies you for a VA loan, visit the VA website at www.homeloans.va.gov/elig2.htm.

In the following situations, the purchaser will need to come up with a cash down payment, in addition to the VA loan guarantee:

- The loan exceeds the guaranteed loan limit.
- The sales price of the house exceeds the VA's Certificate of Reasonable Value. All VA purchase contracts give the buyer the right to cancel the deal if the contract price exceeds the CRV.

The VA's guarantee effectively replaces the down payment. You still must repay the whole loan; the guarantee protects the lender against loss and makes it easier for veterans to get favorable loan terms. But you won't have to pay PMI.

Eligible VA borrowers must have a good credit history, prove that they've been employed for the last two years, and show that they've got enough cash to cover the down payment and closing costs. They must also demonstrate an ability to pay monthly carrying costs on the house, plus other monthly obligations, using approximately 41% or less of their monthly income. And, they must show that they plan to live in the house themselves (not rent it out, for example) within a reasonable period of time after closing the loan.

As a general rule, most mortgage companies make VA loans, but many banks and savings and loans don't. Contact a regional office of the VA for a list of lenders active in the program.

You must pay the VA an administrative fee for the loan, ranging from 1.25% to 3% of the total borrowed, depending upon the amount of the down payment; members of the Reserves and National Guard pay the highest fees. The interest rate is often slightly below the market rate, and the lender may try to compensate by requiring more points.

> **CAUTION**
>
> **Don't procrastinate in applying.** The VA warns that you should expect to wait four to six weeks for a decision on your application.

These loan benefits are reusable, though you have to pay off the first loan and sell the property to become newly eligible for full benefits. Even if you're buying a second property, however, you can take a second VA loan if you have any "leftover" from the first loan—that is, if you used only a portion of your earlier entitlement, or if the maximum loan amounts have risen since your last loan. You can also refinance with a new loan.

New Houses and VA Loans

For most loans for new houses, the VA inspects construction at various stages to ensure compliance with the approved plans. The builder must provide a one-year warranty that the house is built in conformity with the approved plans and specifications. If the builder provides an acceptable ten-year warranty, the VA may only require a final inspection. (See Chapter 7 for more on inspections of new houses.)

Assuming a VA Loan

You do not need to be a veteran to assume a VA loan on an existing house, as long as you are a creditworthy purchaser and meet VA standards. This means a fixed rate loan is assumable at its original interest rate, which can be a bargain if rates have increased.

The credit eligibility requirements for buyers seeking to assume VA loans are fairly strict. If a buyer assumes a VA loan, the veteran remains liable for the payments unless the VA approves the buyer and the assumption agreement and issues a release of liability. This release protects the seller in case the buyer (or any other future owner) defaults. The seller cannot, however, reuse the full eligibility until the old (now assumed) loan is fully paid off.

RESOURCE

The main VA phone number—which will lead you to a lot of prerecorded messages—is 800-827-1000. For general VA mortgage information, ask for VA Pamphlet 26-4, "VA-Guaranteed Home Loans for Veterans," and VA Pamphlet 26-6, "To the Homebuying Veteran." To get a Certificate of Eligibility, complete VA Form 26-1880, *Request for a Certificate of Eligibility*. Also ask for the list of participating lenders.

You can also check the VA's website (and download forms and pamphlets and get contact information for local VA offices) at www.va.gov. (Click "Veterans Services," then"Benefits," then "Home Loans.")

Federal Housing Administration Financing

The Federal Housing Administration (an agency of the Department of Housing and Urban Development) insures loans made to U.S. citizens, permanent residents, and other noncitizens who have Social Security numbers and permission to work in the United States. You must meet financial qualification rules and pay an annual premium. Under its most popular program, if the buyer defaults and the lender forecloses, the FHA pays 100% of the amount insured.

This loan insurance lets qualified people buy affordable houses. You can use it for both fixed and adjustable rate loans. The major attraction of an FHA-insured loan is that it requires a low down payment, usually about 3.5%–10%, depending on your credit score. (Below 580 means you'll have to put 10% down.) FHA also counts nontraditional sources of income when assessing your ability to make your monthly payments or down payment, including seasonal pay, regular overtime and bonus income, and money from a community savings club (a popular way of saving money in many minority communities). Qualified veterans may be eligible for a reduction in the minimum down payment.

The FHA loan limits vary by county and can go as high as $729,750 in some high-cost areas. Check with a regional FHA office or on the HUD website at www.hud.gov to find current rates in your area.

Like most government benefits, FHA loans have downsides:

- **Mortgage insurance.** If you'll be making a down payment of less than 20%, you'll probably have to pay for mortgage insurance (similar to, but not exactly the same as PMI). In 2010, you'll be charged an up-front premium of 2.25% of the loan amount, and a 0.5% annual fee thereafter.

- **Condition of the property.** Fixer-uppers and properties needing significant repair won't qualify for the standard FHA loan program. If you want to buy a house in need of repair, any work recommended by FHA appraisers or by a licensed pest control inspector must be done before the sale closes. Fixer-uppers might, however, qualify for the FHA's Rehabilitation Loan Program (Section 203(k)). The details of this program are beyond the scope of this book. Contact the FHA for more information.

- **Appraisals.** An FHA-approved appraiser must establish a fair market value for a house. FHA appraisers are strict, but reasonably fair. If the appraisal is less than what you pay for the house, the difference must be made up in cash, not by the FHA loan. A clause must be inserted in all sales contracts giving the buyer the right to cancel if the appraisal value is lower than the agreed-upon sales price.

- **General red tape.** It is often said that FHA loans are subject to inordinate bureaucratic snags and delays. But this isn't always true. In the hands of an experienced mortgage company or other FHA loan originator, FHA loans can be processed in about the same time as conventional loans.

- **Limits on seller-assisted down payments.** If buyers didn't have the requisite down payment for an FHA loan, they used to be able to turn to the seller for assistance. The seller could essentially donate the money to the buyer (often, increasing the purchase price to make up for the "donation"), who could then qualify for the loan. These programs are now eliminated.

> **RESOURCE**
>
> **You can also get information on FHA loans, or find a regional HUD office,** by calling the FHA Mortgage Hotline at 800-HUDSFHA or by checking the FHA website at www.hud.gov.

California Housing Finance Agency Programs

The California Housing Finance Agency (CalHFA) provides mortgage financing for first-time home buyers or people who haven't owned a home in three years. You must be a U.S. citizen, permanent resident, or other qualified alien.

CalHFA's offers a 30-year fixed rate loan at below-market interest rate. You can make a low down payment or none at all. The "first-time" requirement is waived if you are purchasing in a designated "target area." The program is available for both existing homes and newly constructed homes. CalHFA also offers down payment assistance programs.

Unlike the VA and FHA programs, CalHFA will help only if your income doesn't exceed certain limits established for the county where the house you want to buy is located. In fact, there are two levels of income limits: low income, which qualifies for a lower interest rate if you have had reasonable credit; and moderate income. For 2010, the low income limits range from $53,550 to $92,900 for a family of two buying an existing home, depending on what county you'll be living in—but check with CalHFA, as the limits change fairly often. Moderate income limits for a family of two range from $54,050 to $95,450 in the most expensive counties. Income limits are higher if you purchase in a "target area," and for families of three or more.

Because mortgage money comes from the sale of tax-exempt bonds, interest rates are lower than those offered by conventional lenders. Depending on the county, qualifying house prices are usually between $243,945 and $656,775, though they can go as high as $802,725 in targeted areas.

CalHFA requires that you have sufficient income to pay your closing costs and make payments. They recommend that you contact an approved CalHFA lender for an analysis of your personal situation.

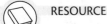

RESOURCE

For up-to-date information about the CalHFA program and a list of approved lenders, call 877-922-5432, or check the CalHFA website at www.calhfa.ca.gov.

Cal-Vet Loans

The California Department of Veterans Affairs, through the Cal-Vet Loans Program, provides loans to qualified veterans who purchase homes within the state. Cal-Vet home loans are direct loans funded from the sale of tax-exempt bonds. No taxpayer revenue is used to fund this program.

Cal-Vet loans work a little differently from ordinary mortgage loans: Cal-Vet buys the property you select, then immediately sells it to you using a contract of sale. You make monthly payments directly to the department. It is set up as a 30-year loan, though you can pay it off sooner with no penalty. The department holds title to the property until you have paid in full.

TIP

You don't have to be a current California resident to get a Cal-Vet loan. It's okay if you're simply planning to buy a house in California. You will, however, need to start living in the house within 60 days of buying it and make it your primary residence. Nearly all veterans purchasing homes in California are now eligible, including those who served during peacetime or are serving currently.

RESOURCE

If you are a veteran and would like to know whether your military service qualifies you for a Cal-Vet loan, visit the Cal-Vet website at www.cdva.ca.gov (search for "eligibility").

Many borrowers can qualify for a no down payment loan. Other Cal-Vet home loan programs offer down payment options as low as 2%–3% of the purchase price. Single-family homes, condominiums, and manufactured homes on private land are currently eligible for loans of up to $521,250. The maximum loan amount is tied to the Fannie Mae conforming loan limit and can be expected to adjust annually. And you can add up to $5,000 to the loan for the cost of any solar heating equipment. Before you make any decisions based on these figures, however, double-check them at one of the Cal-Vet Home Loans district offices or on their website.

RESOURCE

For more information, call the California Department of Veteran's Affairs at 800-952-5626, or check out their website: www.cdva.ca.gov. Click "Home Loans."

The interest rate on Cal-Vet home loans is based on the continuing cost of bonds sold to fund the program. The interest rates are variable, not fixed. However, the initial interest rate is set at the time you submit your application, and subsequent rate increases are limited to 0.5% over the life of the loan. Your initial interest rate will depend on the particular funding source. In 2010, the rate was around 6.2%

You will also be charged a loan origination fee, currently set at 1% of the loan amount. You will additionally need to pay a funding fee of 1.25%–3.30% of the loan amount (depending partly on the size of your down payment) to guaranty your loan.

What if the house you wish to buy costs more than the maximum Cal-Vet home loan (even after your down payment)? In this situation, you are free to seek a second mortgage from another lender to close the gap.

Cal-Vet also offers low down payment construction loans. The interest rate and terms will be the same as for a Cal-Vet loan on an existing home. You can use the loan both to buy the land and to build a home or to purchase a manufactured home to be placed on the land.

Municipal Financing Programs

Several California cities and counties offer various forms of financial assistance with down payments, primarily to first-time home buyers who are buying modestly priced properties. Often, these are the result of the city or county selling bonds for low "municipal rates" and passing the savings on to local purchasers. Call your city or county housing or planning office and inquire about any programs in your area. Programs come and go fairly quickly, because below-market-rate mortgage money tends to get committed very quickly.

RESOURCE

Looking for more information? The federal Housing and Urban Development office maintains a Web list of California cities offering first-time homebuyer assistance programs. See www.hud.gov (search for "California Assistance Programs").

Private Mortgages

Financial institutions and government programs are not the only sources for mortgage loans. A great deal of mortgage money is supplied by private sources—parents, other relatives, friends. Borrowing money privately is usually the most cost-efficient mortgage of all.

The three broad approaches to borrowing all or most of the money necessary to buy a house privately are:

- Borrow from friends or relatives.
- Borrow from the seller.
- Borrow from a noninstitutional private lender.

Advantages of Private Mortgages

The principal advantages of a private mortgage are:

- **Low interest.** Friends and relatives often charge far less than conventional lenders.
- **Flexible repayment structures.** Private lenders may let you pay interest only, or less, for a few years, or otherwise customize your payment schedule.
- **No points or loan fees.** Institutional lenders normally charge thousands of dollars in up-front points and fees. You avoid these costs by borrowing money privately.
- **Easier qualifying.** Private lenders don't insist on a great credit score.
- **Saving on private mortgage insurance.** By borrowing privately, you avoid paying PMI, which lenders require if you borrow 80% or more of the purchase price.
- **Minimal red tape.** To borrow from an institutional lender, you must fill out an application form, provide verifying documentation, and wait for approval. The process is much simpler when you borrow privately.
- **No lender-required approval of house's physical condition.** Private lenders don't usually require that a house's defects be repaired before closing, as institutional lenders do.

Get a Loan From Friends or Relatives

To consider whether private financing, either in whole or part, will work for you, ask yourself two questions:

- Can a parent, grandparent, other relative, close friend, or business acquaintance afford to lend the money?
- Does that person trust you?

If the answer to both of these is "yes," follow up with two more:

- Of those people who can help, who is most likely to do so?
- Of those who can help, who tends to make reasonably conservative investments, such as bank CDs and money market funds, not speculative investments, such as stocks, commodities, or commercial real estate?

This last question is important, because people who invest conservatively are more likely to be interested in lending mortgage money at an interest rate higher than they get now. By contrast, people who invest aggressively in an effort to achieve larger returns won't be as impressed by the prospect of getting an interest rate a little better than a bank would pay (though they may lend anyway, for personal reasons).

If a relative or friend has the ability to help you, don't assume that he or she will. The hardest part about borrowing money is convincing the lender that the investment is safe.

> **CAUTION**
>
> **Beware of imputed interest.** The IRS assumes that mortgage lenders receive reasonable interest on every loan and assesses taxes accordingly. This is true even if the lender charges no interest or low interest to a family member or friend. The "imputed" interest rate charged for loans of more than $10,000 changes, but generally is between 4% and 9%. So even if your generous friend or relative charges you less, the IRS requires him or her to report interest income at that rate. If your friend doesn't and is audited, and the IRS discovers the omission (a very unlikely scenario), the IRS will readjust his or her income using the imputed interest rate and charge the tax owed on the readjusted income plus a penalty.

Approaching Friends, Relatives, and Other Private Lenders

As you prepare to approach someone you know about borrowing, start with the idea that you're not asking for charity. You're offering a business proposition: a loan at a fair rate of interest, secured by a first mortgage. Understand that trust is the key to getting any business deal to work.

If your relative or friend has the money to lend and knows you're trustworthy, chances are he or she will make a loan. If your relative or friend doesn't trust you—you've racked up large credit card bills, bounced checks, or even forgotten to return a lawn mower—he or she will probably back off quickly.

So, are potential lenders likely to trust you? If you can unequivocally say "yes," terrific. If it's "no," or "maybe, with coaxing," consider what you can do to improve their view of your reliability. If you currently owe money to a relative or friend, pay it back in full before proposing a new loan. If you were wild in your younger years but are now staid and responsible, make sure your parents spread the word to wealthy Uncle Harry before you show up on his doorstep asking to borrow $280,000.

Once you decide whom to ask, think carefully about how to raise the subject. Never surprise a potential lender by blurting out a request at a social event or other inappropriate occasion. Make an appointment, even if you see the person regularly and the formality seems odd. Give the person a general idea of what you want to talk about, but save the details. For example, you might say, "Grandpa, I'm trying to buy a house and I'm reviewing a number of ways to finance it. Can we sit down and talk soon?" If Grandpa never seems to find the time, you have your answer. If he says "How about Tuesday?" be on time and prepared to make an effective presentation.

Mort: My Good Friend Helped Me

Several years ago, Mort found a house he wanted to buy. Although he had enough money to make a good-sized down payment, he needed much more to finance the entire purchase. Upon hearing about the new house plan, Babette, his good friend, volunteered to lend Mort $200,000, to be repaid over 20 years, at a very competitive interest rate, secured by a first mortgage.

Why would Babette make this generous, unsolicited offer? Certainly, the trust and good regard accumulated over a 20-year friendship was important. Financial factors were also important. Babette had just retired and was living off the interest from her investments, and she wanted a higher rate of return on her money than she currently received from CDs.

They quickly struck a bargain. Mort got a fixed rate, 20-year loan at 6.5% (about 1.5% points lower than the going rate at the time) and saved close to $10,000 on the fees, and $170,435 in interest over the life of the loan (assuming he would have taken out a 30-year fixed rate loan). He also saved the hassle and time of filling out a loan application.

But what was in it for Babette? She got a 6.5% interest rate on her money at a time when CDs were paying 5%. She also got a first mortgage on the house. Should Mort default, Babette could easily foreclose, have the house sold, and recover the balance of her loan, plus the costs of sale.

Making an Effective Loan Presentation

Before approaching anyone for a loan, put together a businesslike proposal explaining:

- **How much you wish to borrow.** Be as specific as you can if you don't have a particular house in mind yet.
- **The interest rate you propose to pay.** It should normally be higher than what financial institutions currently pay their investors, and lower than what you'd pay an institutional lender. Find out what CDs pay and what fixed rate mortgages cost. Propose paying around half the difference. For example, if fixed rate mortgages cost 6% and banks pay 4% on CDs, you might propose paying 5%.
- **The loan terms you propose.** This should include the length of the mortgage and the amount of the monthly payments. Use the amortization table in Chapter 2 or an online mortgage calculator to come up with exact figures.
- **A copy of the family financial statement you prepared in Chapter 2.** This lists your sources of income, existing debts, and other financial information.
- **A copy of a recent credit report from a credit reporting agency.** In Chapter 2 we discuss how to get one.

- **An estimate of the purchase price of the house you want to buy.** As explained, this won't be exact unless you've already made an offer and had it accepted, but do your homework. Be ready to show the potential lender your Ideal House Profile from Chapter 1 and a fairly tight estimate for such a house. If the potential lender wants to make sure the house you find will be worth what you want to pay, offer to get it appraised prior to purchase.
- **How much you have available for a down payment.** If it's 20% or more, point out that you're investing more than enough of your own money to guarantee that the lender will have little risk of loss, even if you default. (Chapter 4 discusses down payments.)
- **Your debt-to-income ratio.** As discussed in Chapter 2, financial institutions have found that it's safest to lend to people whose monthly carrying costs don't exceed 28%–36% of their monthly income. Even though a friend or relative probably won't insist on rigid qualification rules, it can be very important to demonstrate that you'll have enough income to comfortably make the payments.

When you meet with the potential lender, present your proposal in general terms first. This gives the other person a chance to back off gracefully, if desired. If you sense this happening, say, "Thanks for listening," and change the subject. Remember that people have many reasons for not lending money— don't take "no" as a personal rejection.

If the person shows some interest, briefly present the details. Give the potential lender ample time to ask questions, and don't expect a decision on the spot. Be prepared to leave photocopies of all documents.

How a Large Down Payment Minimizes the Lender's Risk

If you miss payments, the mortgage holder or lender has the legal right to have the property sold through foreclosure. Proceeds (after the costs of sale are subtracted) go to the first mortgage holder. If you have more than one mortgage, the mortgages are numbered in the order in which they were recorded at the county recorder's office. The lower the number (first being the lowest), the more likely the mortgage holder will be paid if you default.

If the sale price doesn't cover the mortgage debt, the mortgage holder doesn't get all that is owed. For this reason, lenders want the house to be worth considerably more than what they lend. Even allowing for the fact that houses usually sell for relatively low prices at foreclosure sales, most lenders feel safe in lending 80% of appraised value, with the buyer making a 20% down payment.

Responding to a Proposed Lender's Questions and Concerns

First, and most important, if you plan to approach a relative who doesn't have much business savvy, consider whether the loan makes sense for that person. For example, if Aunt Muriel's health is such that she may need most of her money in the next few years, don't borrow from her, even if she'll lend it. She's better off having access to her money, even at a lower interest rate.

Often, friends or relatives will be concerned about what happens to their investment should you become ill or disabled and unable to pay them back, or if you (or another breadwinner) die. The lender fears being caught needing the mortgage repaid and having to foreclose on a distressed family member or friend to get it.

One way to deal with this concern is to purchase both life and disability insurance on yourself and any other cobuyer, and to keep the insurance in force until the loan is repaid. Term life insurance for younger people, particularly, will cost little. (With a life insurance policy, you'd make the friend or relative the beneficiary.)

A good disability policy that will pay a large proportion of your monthly salary should you be unable to work is more expensive, but worth it. Make sure your policy pays at least 60% (more is better) of what you would have received had you been able to work.

Finalizing the Loan

If your presentation is successful, and your friend or relative agrees to lend you the needed money, you need to prepare the paperwork. You can do this yourself, although given what's at stake, this wouldn't be a bad time to hire an attorney. Here's what's needed:

- A promissory note for the amount of the loan, including the rate of interest and repayment and other terms. *101 Law Forms for Personal Use,* by Ralph Warner and Robin Leonard (Nolo), contains promissory notes, and Nolo also offers electronic promissory notes at www.nolo.com.

- A mortgage or, to use the technically correct term, a deed of trust. A tear-out one, with instructions for its use, is in *Deeds for California Real Estate,* by Mary Randolph (Nolo). Or, as part of the closing process on the house you buy, simply pay the title (or escrow) company a modest fee to prepare and record a deed for you.

 CAUTION

A promissory note is not enough. Some people skip the preparation and recording of a deed of trust, reasoning that a promissory note is enough. It isn't. The lender isn't fully protected— from either subsequent lenders or purchasers— unless a formal notice of the loan is recorded.

Shared Equity Transactions

If you're considering borrowing privately, you may also be open to purchasing a house with an investor. In this scenario, you ask a private investor to contribute toward the purchase and share equity in the house as a co-owner. When the house is ultimately sold, the investor will make a profit on his or her portion. For more information, see Chapter 3.

Second Mortgages— Financing by Sellers

In theory, if a seller has no immediate need for money, he or she can transfer the house to you and receive nothing in return but your promise to pay in the future, secured by a mortgage. In practice, however, because most sellers have no personal reason to help you, they will generally insist that your down payment and amount borrowed add up to the sales price. Still, some sellers will finance at least a portion of your purchase price themselves. In this situation, a conventional lender has usually agreed to lend you a substantial portion, and the seller provides a much smaller portion, say 10%, of the total secured by a second mortgage.

Here are some of the reasons a seller may provide a second mortgage:

- **To sell a house that has been on the market for a long time.** Taking back a second mortgage makes a house easier for a buyer to finance and, therefore, for the seller to sell.

EXAMPLE: You have $33,000 for a down payment on a house listed at $380,000, and qualify for a mortgage of $324,000 from an institutional lender, leaving $28,000 necessary to complete the deal (allowing $5,000 for closing costs). Your seller is retired and living off investments. He agrees to take back a second mortgage for the remaining $28,000, at a competitive interest rate.

- **For tax reasons.** If the seller doesn't qualify for the exclusion of capital gains, he or she will owe taxes for the year of sale. (See Chapter 14 for more on tax laws.) The seller may benefit by receiving a portion of these profits in future years, particularly if he or she is retiring and expects an income drop to a lower tax bracket.
- **For investment.** Because second mortgages are riskier than firsts, it's sometimes considered reasonable for the buyer to pay a fairly high rate of interest. A seller may take back a second mortgage if you'll pay a higher rate of interest than banks do on CDs, short-term U.S. government securities, and money market funds.

Second Mortgages: A Buyer's Wish List

- A reasonable interest rate
- Low initial payments so as to not jeopardize first mortgage financing
- No prepayment penalty
- No balloon payment for at least five years, and the automatic right to extend the loan if it's impossible to refinance to pay the balloon in full on the due date
- The right to have a subsequent credit-worthy buyer assume the second mortgage.

Seller financing can be as flexible as the buyer and seller agree. Many sellers will accept promissory notes with variable payment structures or interest rates. You can have low interest rates in the first year or two, with increases later. Or you can provide for fixed monthly payments with a floating interest rate.

A serious problem with second mortgages is that the monthly payments on the second are likely to be so large that you no longer qualify for a first mortgage under standard debt-to-income ratios. After all, if you weren't having affordability problems in the first place, you could borrow more on a first mortgage and wouldn't need a second.

Fortunately, second mortgages can be structured to deal with this problem. For example, you may make very low monthly payments on the second mortgage for several years, paying off the entire balance with a large balloon payment at a specific future date (often three to ten years after the sale). Under optimum circumstances, the house's value and your income will have risen before the balloon payment is due, so you can refinance the first mortgage, using a portion to pay off the second.

To allow for the possibility that your income and the house's value may increase more slowly than expected, institutional lenders usually require that at least five years of interest-only payments pass before the balloon payment is due on the second mortgage. You should also insist on an option to extend if you can't refinance the first mortgage.

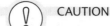 **CAUTION**

Don't overextend yourself. The need to arrange a second mortgage with a large balloon payment tells you that you're stretching your finances close to the breaking point and betting heavily on future property value appreciation to pull you through. Also, be aware that interest rates may increase substantially by the time the balloon payment is due and you need to refinance. Consider whether you're in danger of purchasing more house than you can reasonably afford.

CAUTION

Watch out for wraparound notes. In very rare cases, sellers will offer a wraparound note ("wrap"), also known as an All Inclusive Trust Deed (AITD). It "wraps around" existing financing; you pay the seller, and he or she pays the other note holder.

Be wary! You're usually much better off paying the first mortgage holder directly, rather than risking that the seller won't make the payment. A seller offers a wrap in order to receive a higher interest yield for the total loan than you would pay by negotiating the two mortgages separately.

Second Mortgages—Financing by Private Parties Other Than the Seller

Sellers aren't the only people who can provide second mortgages. Relatives and friends can make second loans, and some private investors will as well. Loan brokers can bring prospective borrowers and prospective second mortgage lenders together for a fee. Finally, many commercial lenders make second mortgage loans.

Preparing a Second Mortgage

Step 1: Determine the terms of the second, including the dollar amount, length of the loan, interest rate, and repayment terms. Make sure the second mortgage doesn't include a prepayment penalty.

Step 2: Be sure the lending institution that will provide the first mortgage knows and approves of the terms and conditions of the second.

Step 3: Prepare the necessary paperwork—the buyer's promissory note for the amount of the second mortgage, containing all mortgage terms. Nolo's *For Sale by Owner in California*, by George Devine, includes a promissory note for a second mortgage. Relatively straightforward arrangements can be handled by the title or escrow company that is doing the closing. For more complicated mortgages, including those with an adjustable interest rate, you may need the help of an experienced real estate lawyer. In addition, the title or escrow company should prepare and record a second mortgage (a "deed of trust") at the county recorder's office.

Step 4: Make sure your purchase contract contains all the terms and conditions of the second mortgage (required by Civil Code §§ 2956 through 2967).

Obtaining a Mortgage

The previous five chapters describe the kinds of mortgages available, and their pros and cons. You should have a good idea as to the type you want and can afford. Now it's time to actually get a mortgage, either on your own or with the help of a broker.

Assuming you're in decent financial shape (if you're not sure, refer back to Chapter 2), real money can be saved if you carefully shop for a mortgage. Everything else being equal, even a one-quarter percentage point difference in interest rates can mean savings of thousands of dollars over the life of a mortgage. To help you shop, this chapter will cover:

- where to get the latest information on mortgage rates and fees
- where to find useful information online
- how a good loan broker can help you
- how to work directly with mortgage lenders
- how to complete the loan application and get a speedy approval, and
- what to expect from the lender's home appraisal.

Gather Information on Mortgage Rates and Fees

Interest rates and mortgages change frequently—and often dramatically—and you need to be up-to-date. Fortunately, this need not be a daunting task, as mortgage interest tables are readily available online. Also look in the Sunday real estate section of your largest local paper. These tables include current mortgage interest rates and points and fees charged by various lenders for different mortgages.

Advertisements for mortgage loans will give you a feel for the market and an approximate idea of where your interest rate should be, but take them with a grain of salt. They always presume "best case scenarios" to arrive at the lowest possible rate. Also, remember that interest rates change daily, sometimes even twice or more a day. By the time you see an interest rate advertised in the newspaper, it may already be history.

While mortgage interest tables include only a small percentage of the total mortgages on the market, they can give you a feel for the current price range, especially if you ignore the mortgages with the lowest rates, which are usually lower than what most buyers will be offered and serve more as advertising to attract customers. And remember, just because a low-interest loan is available, there's no guarantee that you'll qualify for it or that it has all the features you want.

Researching Mortgages Online

Many online services provide mortgage rate information. While these sites don't list all the loans available, they offer a great way to get a sense of market rates and terms.

Individual lenders provide mortgage rate information online as well as all kinds of advice for buying a home—from choosing a mortgage to negotiating closing costs. Simply search for the name of a specific financial institution. However, realize that many of them present only their standard mortgage

How to Compare Mortgage Rates by APR

In an attempt to allow buyers to compare loans, federal law (Regulation Z) requires all lenders to state the Annual Percentage Rate (APR) and to include fees and points. When these fees are figured in, the APR is usually 0.25% to 0.30% higher than the advertised rate for 30-year loans.

Assume you're considering a $100,000 loan at 6% for 30 years. If there were no loan fees, the APR would be 6%. If there are two points, the APR would be 6.18%, because you'd receive only $98,000 after the $2,000 in points was subtracted.

But even APR comparisons aren't perfect. Depending on how lenders write loans, identical packages can end up with slightly different APRs. In addition, APR comparisons assume you'll pay off the loan over its entire term, and thus amortize the fees and points over this period. But most people move or refinance sooner, with the result that a loan with lots of points may be more expensive than one with fewer points (and a higher interest rate), even though the APR is the same. Also, APR comparisons don't take into consideration the tax deduction you get on mortgage interest and points. Your loan will cost you more or less depending on your tax bracket. (To compare points and interest rates, see "The Cost of Getting a Loan" in Chapter 8.) APR discussions also omit closing and transaction costs, which can vary slightly.

---

plans and deliberately provide only enough information to get you to personally contact the lender.

Sites such as HSH Associates, at www. hsh.com, publish mortgages and consumer loan information but do not make loans. The "Find the Best Mortgage Rates" area of hsh. com allows you to compare mortgage rates from financial institutions in a specific area. The site also includes all kinds of detailed mortgage information, including market forecasts and the latest ARM indexes.

Several websites have gone beyond providing basic mortgage rate information and actually allow you to compare rates from dozens of lenders, based on the amount, type, and length of mortgage you want. You can even prequalify and apply for a home loan online.

Other Internet mortgage loan sites include:

- www.bankrate.com
- www.eloan.com
- www.infoloan.com
- www.quickenloans.com
- www.interest.com
- www.realestate.msn.com
- www.lendingtree.com
- www.mortgagemarvel.com, and
- www.mortgage-net.com.

Work With a Loan Broker

Another approach to looking for a loan (after doing your own preliminary work) is to hire a loan broker, a person who specializes in matching house buyers and appropriate mortgage lenders. Assuming you qualify financially, a savvy loan broker can find you a competitively priced mortgage that meets your needs.

Loan brokers must have a real estate broker's license (although someone who works for a broker needs only a salesperson's license). They usually receive two types of compensation:

- A commission from the lender that is a portion of the points you pay on your loan. If there are no points, the lender pays the broker and recoups this payment by charging you a higher interest rate.
- A processing fee, ranging from $200 to $500. Brokers may charge this fee up front or at the close of escrow.

The broker is legally required to tell you both the amount and source of his or her compensation. Look for this information on the on the Good Faith Estimate (explained in Chapter 18).

Financial institutions accommodate loan brokers because lenders want more loan business and will pay a middleperson a commission to get it. In addition, because loan brokers do much of the paper preparation work, they often save lenders time in loan transactions.

Benefits. Working with a loan broker can make it much easier to find the cheapest rates. If you are a first-time home buyer or simply don't have the time to shop for mortgages, you'll appreciate the help a good loan broker can provide, such as:

- reviewing your financial profile and, if necessary, counseling you on steps to improve it before applying for a loan
- providing information about types of mortgages that meet your needs, comparing different mortgages, and translating difficult loan language
- identifying the financial institutions that offer the type of mortgage you want and are likely to qualify for
- helping you prepare the papers needed to apply for a loan (if you don't use a loan broker, you'll do this directly with the financial institution)
- acting as a buffer between you and the lender, clearing up problems such as an appraisal that's too low or a supporting document that's inappropriate before the lender ever sees them, and
- talking to the loan officers on your behalf, to anticipate and solve any problems.

Cautions. The potential downsides of using loan brokers include:

- You must be sure that the person you work with is knowledgeable and trustworthy.
- Not all loan brokers handle government loans or work with all lenders.
- A few loan brokers have been known to prefer financial institutions that treat them well (pass on more points or offer attractive prizes or gifts) but don't necessarily offer you the lowest or best rates.
- Some lenders keep their best loans in-house. That means they are available only if you contact the lender directly—these loans are not made available to loan brokers.

- A few loan brokers (like some banks) use bait-and-switch advertising to recruit customers—that is, they claim they can arrange better loans at lower rates than is actually possible. You can minimize your risk by checking out mortgage rates and features before contacting a broker.

California has thousands of loan brokers; some work alone, others in fair-sized companies. To find a good one, ask friends, relatives, acquaintances, and your real estate agent for a recommendation. Then make a few phone calls and check out the referrals. Some loan brokers are known on the local grapevine to be more helpful, creative, and trustworthy than others.

If you have a problem with a loan broker or a bank loan department, you can file a complaint with the Department of Real Estate. The DRE website is www.dre.ca.gov.

Mortgage brokers are required by law to publish their license number and a telephone number where you can verify their license status. (California Business and Professions Code §§ 10235.5, 10236.4, and 10236.5.)

Interview Lenders

An alternative to working with a loan broker is to comparison shop for a loan on your own. Even if you plan to work with a loan broker, doing your own research helps you get the best deal and educates you about market conditions so you can work more efficiently with the broker.

One good way to mortgage shop is to interview several lenders. Start by identifying lenders offering loans appropriate for you, based on newspaper or online listings or ads or recommendations from your real estate agent or a friend, relative, or employer. If you regularly do business with a bank or other financial institution, it makes sense to include that bank if it offers reasonably competitive loans. Obtain all written material describing available mortgages from lenders you have identified as possibilities. To the

---

True Story

Antonio and Gretel: Working With a Loan Broker

We'd made an offer on a house that several other people wanted. We knew that to be considered seriously we needed to show the sellers we could afford the purchase. We'd heard that a particular bank was a quick qualifier for adjustable rate mortgages and charged no application fee for ARMs.

Sure enough, within a few days, for no cost, we were told we qualified for a loan. This satisfied the sellers, who accepted our offer (rejecting another attractive one because the people couldn't secure financing).

Now we had time to shop for a good loan. We went back to the "quick qualifier" bank and pointed out that their rates seemed to be on the high side. They said take it or leave it; we left. On the recommendation of friends, we called a local loan broker. Though this took some time, we came out of it with an excellent fixed rate loan.

extent possible, gather all information on the same day, so you can do an accurate comparison.

After reviewing the lenders' written material, make an appointment to meet a residential real estate loan officer or to speak with one on the telephone. If you, or a relative or close friend, own a business and have an ongoing relationship with a bank, ask for an introduction to a real estate loan officer. You may get some extra personal time and attention this way.

When you call to schedule an appointment or obtain information, be sure to verify that the lender offers the type of loan you want, in terms of rates, fees, and points.

When you visit or speak to a lender, your goals are to review the following materials with the loan officer:

- The various mortgage plans available, including the required down payment, APR, interest rate, points, loan origination fees, credit check charges, and appraisal fees. If you've read the written material, what the loan officer tells you should come as little surprise.
- The family financial statement you prepared in Chapter 2. Based on this or an online mortgage calculator, the loan officer should be able to give you a good idea of the type of mortgage you qualify for.
- All details important to you. For example, if you plan to make a low down payment, find out whether private mortgage insurance (PMI) is required. If you're considering an ARM loan, ask about periodic caps, life-of-the-loan caps, and so forth.

Why Use a Loan Broker?

We asked Michael Cohen, a loan broker with Schnell Investment Company in Orinda, California, "Why use a loan broker?" Here's what he said:

"The main reasons are flexibility, service, and security. Any one lender has only a few products to offer. By contrast, a well-connected mortgage broker may place loans with 50–60 lenders, including large S&Ls, small local banks, or mortgage bankers representing insurance or pension fund investors.

"A loan broker has many program options, pricing trade-offs, and underwriting variations to offer. These may include access to swing loans, commercial and multifamily loans, and construction and 'rehab' loans. In addition, a good loan broker can counsel the borrower on loan qualification strategies and financing alternatives. The broker will also spot potential problems early on and suggest a way to resolve them. This may mean the difference between getting the loan or not.

"If one lender doesn't come through (despite the loan broker's advocacy efforts), the broker may be able to place the loan elsewhere. In these uncertain days when banks are combining into larger and more distant, faceless monoliths, working with an actual person may provide you with better service.

"One final word: The loan broker doesn't get paid by the lender unless the loan closes. Therefore, it's in the broker's enlightened self-interest to see that the loan is approved and the borrower is satisfied."

> ⓘ **CAUTION**
>
> **Shop around.** Keep in mind that the financial institution you talk to first—or even second—may not be the cheapest or best for you. If a loan officer tries to thrust a loan into your hands, politely state that you still want to look at other loans. Be sure to ask whether the loan officer is paid any commission for mortgage loans. Some loan officers make a commission based on the number or dollar amount of loans they make; this may affect what loans they recommend.

Apply For and Get a Loan

Once you've made an offer on a house and have identified what seems to be the best mortgage for you, it's time to apply for a loan. We're assuming that you applied for preapproval before you made an offer on the house. If not, your loan approval will involve a few more steps, as you'll have to fill out an application form and pull together basic supporting documentation such as W-2s, tax returns, pay stubs, bank statements, retirement statements, and the like. After you've been preapproved and are in contract to buy a house, the lender will additionally require the following:

- A copy of the purchase contract for the house you are buying. (If you're using a real estate agent, the agent will give this directly to the mortgage broker or lender.)
- Preliminary Title Report. (The title company will ordinarily give this to the broker or lender.)

- Property appraisal report. (The appraiser will ordinarily give this to the broker or lender.)
- If you are also selling a house, the listing agreement or sales contract or the final HUD1 statement if your house is already sold. (HUD1 Statements are final settlement statements prepared by the escrow company handling sales transactions.)
- The original, signed copy of your gift letter, if applicable.

Despite the ads that tout "overnight approval," you should allow a reasonable period for approval (or denial) after you complete a loan application. Before final loan approval (called funding the loan), the lender must verify all your financial, employment, and credit information; arrange an appraisal of the property; and prepare the necessary paperwork. Normally, this process takes about two to three weeks, unless you have a high income and plan to make a substantial down payment, in which case approval should be faster. And, in times of high volume, the process may take about a month.

The timeline at the end of this chapter shows all the steps involved from loan application to close of escrow.

Tips for Speeding Up Loan Approval

Here are some tips for faster loan approval.

Don't wait until the last minute to collect financial and other documents. Particularly if you haven't yet been preapproved, you don't want the process to be held up while you sift through piles of paperwork. Now's a good time to get your financial files in order, and save every pay stub or bank statement as it comes in.

Neatly complete every section of the application. Your broker may help you with this form. Don't leave any blanks! If some item doesn't apply, write "not applicable" or "N/A."

Tell the truth. Don't exaggerate your earnings or hide negative credit information—the lender will find out anyway. And, if so, this misrepresentation (or fraud) may automatically cancel your loan application.

Show you're creditworthy. If you're concerned that something on your application may work against you—for example, you have a job gap—write a simple letter of explanation.

Hand-deliver paperwork. To speed up the process, offer to hand-carry forms to your employer and banks, verifying your employment and deposit information.

Monitor the process. If you're under time pressure to close by a certain date, or have a limited time when interest rates are locked in, be sure to keep close tabs on the process. Make sure your loan officer has all the information needed to process your loan application. Keep in regular touch and document all phone and written communications with the lender.

Getting the Lender's Commitment

If a lender says that you qualify for a loan, ask for a "commitment" or "loan qualification" letter, stating the size and type of the loan and the interest rate you qualify for. The commitment letter may specify that certain conditions be met before final loan approval—for example, that you pay off a long-term debt or that the house appraises for at least the loan amount. As a precaution, don't remove financing contingencies from your offer (see Chapter 16) until these conditions have been met.

Locking in Interest Rates

It's important to understand that even a commitment letter isn't the same thing as a guarantee to borrow at a particular interest rate or particular terms. If interest rates go up, the lender will demand that you pay the higher amount, unless you've received a "lock-in" or "rate lock." If you haven't, and interest rates rise significantly, the lender could recalculate your debt-to-income ratio to see if you still qualify at the higher interest rate.

A rate lock is a guarantee by a lender to make a loan at a particular interest rate, even if the market changes. Most rate locks are good for about 21–30 days and usually apply to a specific house. (You can often arrange for a rate lock for longer, but you'll have to pay for it, usually in the form of higher points—as much as one-fifth to three-eighths of a point more.) One reason you'll have to pay more is that when a lender locks in a rate, it has made a commitment to deliver the loan to Freddie Mac, Fannie Mae, or another investor. If the lender doesn't deliver—that is, you don't buy the house—the lender still must pay a fee to the investor. Also, because of volatility in the market, Freddie Mac and Fannie Mae set a higher price on loans to be delivered later—for example, within 60 days versus ten days.

A rate lock is particularly valuable when the house is in escrow and you are on a tight budget, as it protects you from the possibility that a hike in interest rates will result in your no longer qualifying to make the purchase. If you are not worried about increasing rates, you'll probably want to skip obtaining a lock-in and hope rates go down so that you'll get the benefit of the lower rate.

> CAUTION
>
> **Beware of strategies unscrupulous lenders may use to avoid meeting a rate lock.** If your lender requires additional (and often very picky) documentation at the last minute—for example, details on a minor credit problem or more income data if you're self-employed—be leery. To avoid these kinds of delays, make sure all your information is complete when you apply for a loan. Get the rate lock agreement in writing. Keep in touch with the lender so you can head off any problems. Finally, file a complaint with a regulatory agency (see "Where to complain about problems with a loan application," below) if the deal threatens to come undone.

Get Your House Appraised

A few weeks after you apply for a loan, the lender will arrange for an appraisal of the property, to make sure it's worth the amount you want to borrow. The buyer typically pays a fee for the appraisal as part of the closing costs, usually $400 or more, depending upon the size and price of the house and property. Larger houses, houses with many units, and investment properties all tend to cost more to appraise. Some government loan programs, such as FHA, set their own appraisal procedures. (See Chapter 11.)

The appraiser may physically inspect the property inside and out and will estimate the value based on recent documented prices of comparable sales within a few blocks of the house, adjusting for differences in size and features among the properties.

If the appraisal comes in at or above the amount of money you need to borrow, and everything else checks out, your loan will be approved. There may be problems, however, if the appraisal comes in low. The lender doesn't want to risk a scenario in which it later forecloses on your property and comes up short because the property was worth less than its appraised amount. If the appraisal comes in below the asking price, make a list of the home's important features and gather together your research on recent sales prices of comparable homes, give copies of these to the appraiser, and ask for an amended report. If it still comes in too low, be sure to get a copy of the appraisal; if you pay for the appraisal, the lender is legally obligated to give you a copy. If you've collected your own comparable sales data before determining your offer price (see Chapter 15), you should be able to justify a higher appraisal price to the lender. Consider asking for a second appraisal.

If you can't get a higher appraisal, you can either back out of the deal (assuming financing contingencies in your contract allow this), come up with more money for a down payment, get the seller to lower the price or take back a second mortgage (discussed in Chapter 12), or look for another lender.

A Hypothetical Timeline: From Loan Application to Close of Escrow

Let's assume you submitted an offer to purchase a home to a seller and it was accepted on January 1. The application process should proceed roughly as follows. We assume here that you'll seek a loan directly from an institutional lender; if you instead work with a mortgage broker, he or she will perform many of the duties of the lender identified below.

Range of Possible Dates	Action
January 2–3	You submit loan application; lender runs credit check immediately and reviews with you any negative information.
January 3–4	Day after running credit check, you submit pay stubs and year-end tax documents to lender, in addition to six months' worth of bank statements.
January 2–5	Within 72 hours of when you submitted your application, lender must send you loan disclosures (annual percentage rate and other information) and good faith estimates of closing costs.
January 10–18	One to two weeks after lender arranges for appraisal of property, it's completed.
January 12–February 4	Lender assembles a loan package. Loan underwriter compares loan package to lender's guidelines. If it fits, underwriter sends package to supervisor and others for approval. If it doesn't fit, but is in the ballpark, underwriter sends package to others for second opinion. If it totally fails to fit guidelines, loan is rejected or lender specifies conditions for approval.
January 13–February 6	Lender loan committee gives final approval, sometimes with certain conditions (such as to pay off a long-term debt).
January 14–February 9	One to three days after loan approved (or condition removed), lender prepares loan papers.
January 15–February 10	One day after lender prepares loan papers, escrow holder prepares final closing papers for you and seller.
January 16–February 11	One day after escrow holder prepares final closing papers, you and seller go to escrow holder to sign all papers.
January 17–February 13	One to two days after you and seller sign escrow papers, loan package is sent to lender for final review and funding check.
January 18–February 15	One to two days after loan package is sent to lender for final review and funding, a check is sent to escrow holder or local bank. (Closing may be delayed until check is deposited into local bank or otherwise clears.)
January 19–February 16	Escrow closes! Congratulations.

RESOURCE

Where to complain about problems with a loan application. If you have a problem with how your loan application was handled and can't work things out with the lender, document your concerns and be prepared to file a complaint with a regulatory agency. Where you complain depends upon the type of financial institution—for example, whether it's a state-chartered bank or a savings and loan. To find out where to complain, start with the Department of Real Estate. The DRE website is www.dre.ca.gov. Also, contact the Department of Consumer Affairs (800-952-5210 or www.dca.ca.gov). If you feel the lender discriminated against you in the loan application process, contact the Department of Fair Employment and Housing at 800-233-3212 or www.dfeh.ca.gov.

Buying a House When You Already Own One

I f you already own a home and plan to sell it before buying another, questions of timing inevitably arise. Is it better to sell your old house before buying a new one? Or vice versa?

If you sell first, you'll be under time pressure to find another house quickly. This is stressful, and you may overpay in an anxious effort not to lose out to another purchaser.

But buying a new house first and then scrambling to sell your old one is no fun, either—especially if you're trading up substantially and need to sell your old house for top dollar to make the down payment on the new one. Being under time constraints to close on the new house, you may accept a lower-than-optimum price on your old house to make a quick sale.

This chapter gives you constructive steps to minimize the psychological and financial down side of selling one house while buying another.

SKIP AHEAD

If you are a first-time buyer or can afford to own two houses at once (even if for just a short period) you can skip this chapter.

RESOURCE

Nolo's book for home sellers. *For Sale by Owner in California,* by George Devine (a coauthor of this book), provides practical, easy-to-use forms and the legal, financial, and real estate knowledge needed to sell your house—on your own or with the help of a broker.

True Story

Mary Advises: Listen to Grandpa

In selling my house and buying another, I remembered my grandfather saying always, "Buy low and sell high." To accomplish this, he explained, you must get time on your side. People pay top dollar when they're pressed for time and get a bargain when they can be patient.

So the question became, how could I apply Grandpa's advice to my situation? To avoid selling my house in a hurry in order to pay for a new one, I called my dad and asked for a short-term loan. He helped some. Next I called my uncles and a college roommate who has a knack

with money. Together they agreed to advance me the rest of what I needed for a few months. Combined with my own savings, this let me make a very chunky down payment (55% of the purchase price) on a new house without the need to sell the old one. I then listed my existing house for sale at an aggressive price, perfectly prepared to have to wait for a while, and maybe even to take less. Instead, I immediately got a full price offer. I was so surprised, I almost forgot to say "yes." By preparing to be patient, I sold for about $25,000 more and bought for about $35,000 less than if I'd been in a hurry.

Check the Housing Market Carefully

Before you put your house on the market or commit to buying a new one, carefully investigate the sales prices of houses in the markets where you'll be selling and buying. Focus on whether the local market is "hot" (favors sellers) or "cold" (favors buyers). Judging the relative temperature of the market is important to buyers and sellers and is crucial for people who are both. Your dual position lets you adopt a strategy of protecting yourself in your weaker role while letting your stronger role take care of itself.

> ! CAUTION
>
> **Market conditions in California change frequently and vary by neighborhood.** Don't assume you know how to price your house, even if you bought it just last year or have been reading the real estate news.

Strategies in a Seller's Market

If sellers have the advantage in the communities where you both now own and plan to buy, selling your current house will likely be easier than buying a new one. Thus, you want to compete aggressively in purchasing a new house, while insisting on maximum flexibility as to the date you move out of your present house.

You can guarantee yourself this leeway by stipulating that the sale of your current house be contingent upon your finding and closing on a new one. When a buyer makes an offer on your house, include in your written counteroffer a provision spelling this out. Although few buyers will agree to an open-ended period, some will be so anxious to buy your house that they'll agree to delay the closing until you close on a new house or until a certain number of days pass, whichever comes first. In hot markets, buyers may even let the seller live rent-free in the home for two to four weeks.

Is the Market Hot or Cold?

Here's how to take the temperature of a particular housing market (see Chapter 15 for more details):

- If many more people want to buy than to sell, it's a hot, seller's market. Prices tend to rise (often quickly), and buyers must bid competitively (read: high) and have their financing lined up (and be preapproved) in advance.
- If sellers outnumber buyers the market is cold and favors buyers. Sellers often must court buyers by lowering prices and offering innovative financing packages. (See Chapter 12.) In new housing developments, sellers often offer to pay a portion of the buyer's monthly mortgage. (See Chapter 7.)

Because markets can change (sometimes very quickly), it's crucial to have current information. Pay careful attention to media reports on upward and downward trends in local real estate markets.

EXAMPLE: Roberta plans to sell her house. Both where she now lives and where she hopes to buy a home are hot (seller's) markets. She puts her current house on the market, making the sale contingent upon closing on her new house. A number of potential buyers surface, and the highest bidder is agreeable to waiting a reasonable time but balks at an open-ended contingency. Roberta agrees to move out either when she closes on another house or after 120 days pass from the closing on her present house, whichever occurs first.

Although she remains under a degree of time pressure, four months should be enough time to find a good new place, especially given that she got such a great price on the sale of her old one.

Strategies in a Buyer's Market

In a buyer's market, with lots of sellers, your position as a buyer is the stronger one. Consider protecting yourself by making your offer to buy contingent upon your selling your current house. A seller having a hard time finding a buyer is likely to accept this contingency, even though it means waiting.

Be ready for the seller to counter with a "wipe-out" or release clause. This lets the seller accept your offer, but keeps the house on the market, with the requirement that the seller give you written notice if he or she receives another offer and wants to accept it. Then, within 72 hours (or whatever length of time your agreement says), you must satisfy all contingencies and proceed with the purchase, or your offer is wiped out, and the seller can proceed with other offers.

In this situation, a wipe-out clause is not unreasonable, as the seller needs some way to get out of a deal if you never sell your house. We discuss wipe-out clauses in more detail in Chapter 18, After the Contract Is Signed.

EXAMPLE: Ronald and Phil would like to purchase a larger house than the one they already own, but houses are moving slowly. When they find a house they want to buy, they make their offer contingent upon their selling their old house. The seller accepts, but insists on including a 96-hour wipe-out clause, to take effect 30 days after the contract is signed. This means that once 30 days pass, the seller can accept other offers, contingent upon giving Ronald and Phil 96 hours' notice to satisfy (or eliminate) the requirement that they sell their existing house and go ahead with the deal.

Sometimes, the offer is made contingent upon arranging financing. This usually has the same effect as making your offer contingent on selling your present house. Unless you have large savings, a lender won't normally approve financing on a new purchase until the sale of the old house is made and the down payment money is in hand, or at least until the lender is confident that your present house is priced fairly and will sell soon.

Renting Your Own House

When you sell your house contingent upon moving into a new one, you have two options if you need more time to move.

Becoming a tenant. One option is to become a tenant in your old house. Here are a few hints on how to handle this:

- You and the new owner should sign a written rental agreement. A copy is available on the CD included with *The California Landlord's Law Book: Rights & Responsibilities*, by David Brown, Ralph Warner, and Janet Portman (Nolo). Modify the agreement to pay by the month but require only seven days' written notice to move, rather than the normal 30 days.

- Your daily rent should be the buyer's daily carrying costs (mortgage principal and interest, taxes, and insurance). This will be considerably higher than what you paid to live in that house (your old mortgage), but the interest you earn on the cash proceeds of the sale will offset this to a degree. In addition, it will probably be less than if you had to move to a temporary place, and it saves you the trouble of moving twice.

Delaying the closing. Another possible option is to put off the closing. As long as you are confident the buyer won't try to back out, this can make sense for two reasons. As an owner, you can deduct mortgage interest and property taxes; as a tenant, you can't. As a tenant, your rent will be figured at the new owner's higher costs. Of course, you will have a pile of money in the bank from the sale, but its true value won't equal your higher costs as a tenant.

Renting out your old house. Finally, if you're having a difficult time selling your house—and you must move into your new home right away—consider finding a tenant to rent your old house. Use the rent payments to cover your old mortgage and make your new purchase financially feasible. Try to make the rental temporary, and keep trying to sell your old house—assuming you anticipate a profit. Consult your tax adviser for tax consequences of renting out your old house. For advice on being a landlord, see *The California Landlord's Law Book: Rights & Responsibilities*, by David Brown, Ralph Warner, and Janet Portman (Nolo).

Save Money on Real Estate Commissions

If you're selling and buying in the same area, consider using the same real estate agent to sell your current house and buy a new one. If you do, you may well be able to save money on the typical 5%–7% commission sellers pay the listing agent, by negotiating a lower rate. Remember, even a 1% or 2% savings is a lot of money.

Bridge Financing: How to Briefly Own Two Houses

No matter how carefully you time things, you may not perfectly dovetail the sale of one house with the purchase of another. You may own no houses, in which case you'll have money in the bank and will need a temporary place to live, or you may own two houses at once. The following suggestions should help you pull this off:

- **Raise as much money as possible for the down payment on a new house.** If your savings, without the sale, put the second house within reach, maximize your cash, perhaps by charging living expenses or getting an advance from your employer. Although the interest on credit cards is high, you'll be able to pay bills off promptly when your existing house sells.

- **Borrow down payment money from family or friends.** Point out that you need help for only a short period, and offer a competitive interest rate. (In Chapters 4, Raising Money for Your Down Payment,

---

True Story

Jenny and Gregg: We Had to Act Fast

We found the house to buy so fast, we were late getting in gear to sell our existing house. We knew the sellers of the house we planned to buy wanted a quick, easy sale, and we would look good to them only as long as we appeared ready to close. If we tried to make the purchase contingent on our selling our existing house, they'd lose interest.

Instead, we agonized for a bit and said "yes." Immediately, we put our existing house on the market. Unfortunately, it was harder than we expected to sell at the high price we wanted. We faced the possibility of owning two houses at

once. Rather than panic and sell our existing house cheap, we lined up a bridge loan from a bank but held off making the final commitment, which would have cost a lot in fees. We then lowered our asking price slightly, to awaken buyer interest. It worked. The house sold at a still-very-good price, in time for us to make the closings simultaneous. We may have done better if we took the bridge loan and held out for a higher price, but with two kids and two jobs, the last thing we wanted to worry about was owning two houses.

and 12, Private Mortgages, we discuss borrowing from private sources.)

- **Get an equity line of credit in advance.** For a small application fee and annual fee, you may be able to arrange a line of credit to be ready if you need to draw on it. Home equity lines of credit are far less available than they used to be, but still possible for borrowers with excellent credit.

- **Get a bridge loan from a financial institution.** Unfortunately, borrowing money from a financial institution to "bridge" the period between when you close on your new house and when you get your money from the sale of your old one has become impossible. (And even when they were available, bridge loans were expensive, with a host of up-front points or fees for credit checks, appraisals, loan originations, and physical inspections.)

Tax Breaks for Selling Your Home

If you sell your home, you may exclude up to $250,000 of your capital gain from tax. Joint owners may divide their gain and exclude up to $250,000 per person. For married couples filing jointly, the exclusion is $500,000.

The law (I.R.C. (Title 26) § 121) applies to sales after May 6, 1997. To claim the whole exclusion, you must have owned and lived in your residence an aggregate of at least two of five years before the sale, and it must be your main home, not a vacation or second home (this rule is called the "ownership and use" test). You can claim the exclusion once every two years.

California Property Tax Relief

As a result of the California initiative of the mid-1970s, Proposition 13, property taxes are levied on the assessed value as of March 1, 1975, or the purchase price at any later transfer date, with exceptions for certain intrafamily transfers—for example, between spouses or between parents and children. For people who've owned homes for many years, their values are comparatively low. When they sell that house and purchase another, however, they pay property taxes on the price of the house being bought, which is likely to be higher than the one being sold.

To help older and disabled people deal with this, California law lets owners over age 55 (only one spouse of a married couple need qualify), or owners who are severely or permanently disabled, who sell one house and purchase another within two years in the same county, transfer their old tax assessment rate to the new house. (Revenue and Tax Code § 69.5.) Transferring the tax assessment intercounty is possible if you move to a county that participates in the statewide transfer system. The county tax assessor can tell you whether or not your county participates.

To qualify for this tax break, the new house must be of equal or lesser value than the old house. Check with your county tax assessor to see if the law applies when you contemplate your transaction.

For information on state taxes, contact the Franchise Tax Board at 800-852-5711, or check their website at www.ftb.ca.gov.

Even if you haven't lived in your home a total of two years out of the last five, you are still eligible for a partial exclusion of capital gains if you sold because of a change in employment, health, or unforeseen circumstances. You get a portion of the exclusion, based on the portion of the two-year period you lived there. To calculate it, take the number of months you lived there before the sale and divide it by 24.

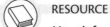

RESOURCE

More information on tax laws involving real estate transactions. Contact the IRS at 800-829-1040; or visit www.irs.gov. See IRS Publication 523, *Selling Your Home.*

What Will You Offer?

This chapter assumes that you've found a house you like and have the financial resources to buy it. Now you must decide how much to offer and what other terms to include in your offer.

How a Contract Is Formed

A contract to transfer ownership requires that one party make a specific, written, legal offer to buy or sell a particular piece of property and the other person legally accept it in writing.

The first legally binding offer in a California real estate sale is usually made in writing by the prospective buyer. Legally binding means that the offer is specific (lays out the price and other terms) and the seller has the opportunity to accept it in writing either before it is withdrawn or the time period for its acceptance runs out. The seller isn't obligated to accept, even if the offer is for the full asking price, as long as the refusal isn't motivated by an intent to discriminate. (He or she may be under pressure to sell with a full price offer, however, because the contract with the broker probably guarantees the broker a commission if the seller gets such an offer.)

Decide What You Will Offer

In putting together your actual offer, consider the following factors:
- the advertised price of the house
- what you can afford
- prices for comparable houses

- whether the local real estate market is hot or cold
- whether the house itself is hot or cold
- the seller's needs
- whether the house is uniquely valuable to you
- how much you're willing to pay
- making the final decision on price, and
- nonmonetary ways of making your offer attractive.

Let's consider each in brief.

What Is the Advertised Price?

A seller's advertised price should be treated as only a rough estimate of what the seller would like to receive. Some sellers deliberately overprice, others ask for pretty close to what they hope to get, and some underprice their houses in the hope of attracting a wide pool of visitors or creating a situation where potential buyers compete and overbid.

In considering the list price of a house you're serious about, take the time to learn about the seller's personality. Here are a few of the more common seller profiles.

Optimistic Charlie. Arrogant and optimistic, he tends to believe that his house is especially valuable and is likely to price it way above what comparable houses are selling for: as much as 30%–40% more, although 10%–25% is more typical. Unfortunately, some Optimistic Charlies are encouraged by brokers or agents so anxious to get the listing that they "romance" Charlie into believing that the house will fetch an inflated price. But FSBO (For Sale By Owner) sellers are also notoriously prone to this.

Straightforward William. William prices his house at exactly what he believes it's worth, not a dollar more, nor a dollar less. William may be stubborn if offered less than the asking price, but he may accommodate a buyer on other terms of the deal. For example, if a physical inspection turns up structural problems, William might agree to pay for $10,000 of needed work in the form of a credit in escrow if the buyer pays the asking price, rather than lower his asking price by $5,000. (Then again, if William is thinking clearly, he'll realize that lowering the house price will also lower the commission he owes to the agents.)

Canny Cynthia. Cynthia deliberately under-prices her house. Her plan is to excite a feeding frenzy among bargain hunters, who'll bid against each other so furiously that the winner will pay more than the house is worth. This strategy works best in hot real estate markets when competition is fierce. (See "Is the Local Real Estate Market Hot or Cold?" below.)

 TIP

Don't be suckered by too low a price. It's tough not to get excited when a house comes on the market with a "too good to be true" price. But keep in mind that loads of other aspiring purchasers will spot the same bargain. Don't get into a bidding war that only the seller will win.

Is Underpricing Ethical?

Why would a home seller (or a real estate agent) ask less for a home than it's really worth? To attract more lookers, create excitement, and generate a bidding war, of course.

Frustrated would-be buyers sometimes consult lawyers, hoping to find that sellers are obligated to accept the first offer at the full asking price. They're not.

The present consensus within the real estate community seems to be that pricing a tad under the market to attract a slightly larger pool of buyers is not a big deal; it's when a home is deliberately listed significantly below its true market value (say, a $500,000 home is listed at $399,000) that something is not right. We believe that it's unethical for sellers to put a house on the market at a price they'd never accept. (These sellers can often be identified by the listing comment "Seller reserves the right to refuse all offers.") Your best recourse, however, is to know the market and not waste your time bidding list price for a deliberately underpriced house.

How Much Can You Afford?

Chapter 2 focuses on how to determine how much house you can afford, based on your income, savings, and nonhousing long-term debts. Once you know your maximum, lower the number a little, to allow for the following additional expenses:

Closing costs. Your share will be about 2%–5% of the purchase price. (See Chapter 18 for details.)

Moving expenses. The amount depends on how much stuff you have to move, how far you're moving it, and how much you'll do yourself. If you plan on hiring a mover, get an estimate and add about 25%.

Redecorating. Keep a few dollars to redecorate with. If the house you buy hasn't had a facelift recently, you'll probably want to paint it, at least.

Two months' mortgage payments. The lender will probably want to see that you have two or three months of mortgage payments in the bank, as a cushion in case anything goes wrong like you losing your job.

What Are Prices of Comparable Houses?

Before making an offer, you should know the recent selling prices of comparable houses. If you've been looking for only a short time, or in other areas, you have some research to do. If you're working with an experienced agent, he or she should be able to provide you with the information, preferably laid out in a handy spreadsheet.

Real estate appraisers have developed the following sensible guidelines to distinguish comparable houses from others:

- A comparable sale should have occurred within the last three to six months (the more recent, the better). If prices are fluctuating quickly, comps should be on sales within the last 30 to 60 days. In extremely volatile markets, you'll need to compare prices of houses where sales are still pending.

- A comparable sale should be for a house quite similar to the one you're interested in. Look for houses of similar age, in comparable locations, and with a similar number of rooms, square feet, and similar yard size. In the real world, however, comparisons often must be made between houses that are somewhat different. A physically comparable house a few blocks away might be in a better school district or have a great view, which will raise the property's value. The more difference between houses, the less valuable the comparison.

- A comparable sale should be within six to ten blocks of the house you want to buy. The boundaries should be adjusted if the neighborhood changes significantly in a shorter radius, for example, if a major road or freeway marks a border between two different residential areas.

Realtors®' Comp Information

Usually, the best comparable sales data are in a Board of Realtors® database for the geographical area where you're looking (accessible by your agent). The database will list the sales price of houses that sold recently or are soon to close. We discuss the Multiple Listing Service, comp databases, and other services offered by local Boards of Realtors® in Chapter 5.

How to Analyze Prices of Current Listings and Pending Sales

Houses pending sale (still in escrow) are listed in the Realtors' Multiple Listing database and are noted in appraisal reports—but the actual sales price is not listed until the transaction closes. To find out the prices of houses pending sale, your real estate agent may need to call the broker who represents the seller of the pending sale you're interested in.

The asking prices of homes still on the market can also provide guidance. Despite the fact that asking prices don't tell you what a house will eventually sell for, they can give you some idea of the range of market values in your area, or trends upward or downward.

Comparable Sales Prices Available Online

Online services offer detailed—though not always up to date—comparable sales prices, based on information from county recorder's offices and property assessors, notably:

- Domania, www.domania.com
- Zillow, www.zillow.com
- SmartHomeBuy, www.smarthomebuy. com
- Trulia, at www.trulia.com, and
- www.homeradar.com.

Zillow and homeradar are free. By entering your prospective new home's address on both websites, you can collect a fair amount of information, including an estimate of that house's value (which you should take with a grain of salt, since the figure was generated without a live human seeing the place), each comparable house's address and location on an aerial photo, purchase price, year built, sales date, square footage, and numbers of bedrooms and bathrooms. In addition, SmartHomeBuy offers a free preliminary report that tells you your prospective home's assessed value and zoned use.

All of this information will help you decide which recently sold homes are truly comparable to the one in which you're interested, and how much a fair sales price would therefore be.

Checking Deeds at the County Recorder's Office

Comparable sales information is also available at the county recorder's office. You need to know the street name or the name of the buyer (grantee) or seller (grantor) of a particular property. If you don't know either, you can find out the seller's name at the county assessor's office. You then look up the deed in either the grantor or the grantee index.

When you find the deed, note the documentary transfer tax, located in the upper right-hand corner. The basic documentary transfer tax is $1.10 per $1,000 of price, except in cities and counties with local surtaxes. The sales price is figured from this transfer tax. You can use this technique to find out how much the current owner of the property originally paid and when he bought the house.

! CAUTION

The documentary transfer tax may not reflect the full price paid by the buyer. If the buyer assumed loans held by the seller, this amount won't be included.

Is the Local Real Estate Market Hot or Cold?

To know whether your market is hot or cold, closely follow the local residential real estate market for an extended period. (Even during the worst of the real estate slump, California has had some very hot local markets!) This involves visiting lots of houses and reading MLS and comparative sales listings. If you don't have time to get this "up to the elbows" sort of knowledge, consult with one or more experienced local real estate people.

To do your own temperature research, keep in mind these rules:

- If 25% or more of the houses sell within a week or ten days of being listed, the market is hot.
- If more than 40% of the houses listed sold for more than the listing price, the market is sizzling.
- If more than half of the houses were on the market a month or more before selling, and most sold for less than their listing price, the market is cool.
- If the supply of houses on the market is steadily increasing, sales are slow, and prices of the houses you're looking at have decreased more than once, the market is cold.

EXAMPLE: Thad falls in love with a house listed at $225,000, in a marginal neighborhood adjacent to a much nicer one. A comparable house in the upscale area sells for $375,000.

If houses are selling relatively slowly, and the house he wants has been on the market for a month or more, Thad can probably offer less, perhaps even much less, than the asking price. If houses are selling briskly, however, and the house he likes is new to the market (and reasonably priced, given the comparable sales data), he should offer close to the asking price. In a very hot market, he may even want to bid slightly more to preempt other offers and avoid a bidding war.

Another driver of a market's temperature is the level of current mortgage interest rates. As rates jump substantially (usually one percentage point or more), most housing markets begin to cool—although just as rates begin to rise, people may rush to buy, hoping to lock in before rates climb even higher. Conversely, as rates drop, more people can afford houses, and the market perks up.

Chapter 17 includes several strategies for bidding on houses in a competitive market.

Is the House Itself Hot or Cold?

At least as important as determining the local housing market temperature is figuring out the "temperature" of the particular house you want to buy. For many reasons, a particular house may be more or less attractive (hotter or colder) than those surrounding it. Here are some questions to ask:

- **How long has the house been on the market?** If it's more than 30 days, it's chilling fast, and you can probably buy it for less than the asking price.

- **Has the asking price dropped?** If it has been reduced once and it still hasn't sold (give it a month), the house is an icicle and may be ready for another reduction.

- **Does the house have serious structural problems requiring a hefty cash infusion?** If so, the house, even if otherwise attractive, may be hard to sell. If you have cash or can finance the purchase privately, the house may be yours. (See Chapter 3 for more on buying a house with structural problems.)

- **Has the seller, or perhaps the listing agent, tipped you off that a lower offer will be considered?** If you're told that the seller needs to sell quickly to close on a new house, because of a divorce or to move far away, you're almost surely being told to try a lower offer. Or, if a real estate agent says the seller "hopes to receive" a certain amount, the agent is saying that the seller is being unrealistic and that a lower offer will probably be accepted.

- **Has the seller set a cut-off date by which all offers must be made?** This can be a good indication that the house is hot, and you may have to bid aggressively to get it. But be careful—the seller and his agent may attempt to create a bidding war, or at least the appearance of one. A seller may state that "five offers will be made" (or that "many people are considering bidding"), when only one or two are serious.

- **Is the house an ugly duckling?** In a hot market, interest in an unattractive house is likely to be lukewarm; in a cool market, icy. If you find a dowdy place you know how to turn into a swan, keep your passion to yourself and bid relatively low. (Again, see Chapter 3 for more on buying a homely house.)

- **How eager is the seller to sell?** It's to your advantage to figure out where the seller is coming from. For example, if you see a house where the price has been reduced substantially after only one month on the market, chances are the owner is anxious to sell and may be willing to reduce the price further.

- **Is the house very expensive?** The biggest fluctuations in price occur at the luxury end of the market. Houses that sell for $3 million at the very top of a market can often be purchased for 30% to 50% less during the next recession. And, of course, the opposite is also true. The problem, of course, is that it's very difficult to accurately time economic cycles. As a general rule, avoid markets that have been going up for more than five years—but jump on those that have been going down for more than two.

What Are the Seller's Needs?

Historically, the real estate business is structured to keep buyer and seller at arm's length. Unfortunately, this tradition can work to your disadvantage. You want to be able to size up the seller and structure your offer and your negotiating strategy accordingly, but obviously you can't if you never meet.

Sometimes you can make friendly contact at an open house, if the seller is present. Follow up with a phone call (or a knock on the door) to ask a few questions that the agent wouldn't be expected to know the answer to. There's the danger that the seller will be annoyed. But if you're as pleasant as you are persistent, you may make contact and learn a lot.

Your agent may also be able to glean useful information by talking to the seller's agent, such as how much room there is to negotiate on price or other items. Also, you may gain valuable insights by chatting with the neighbors while legitimately checking out the neighborhood. If you have school-age children, talk to neighbors with kids about local schools. In casual conversation, they're likely to tell you why the seller is moving and lots of other useful information.

For example, sellers likely to want to close on the deal quickly, even if it means taking a lower price, include those who:
- have accepted a job in a different area
- have made an offer on another house contingent on selling the existing one
- are older people selling a long-time family home (sometimes with the help of a younger relative or friend)
- are families with small children, who have enough to think about without the disruptions of the home-marketing process

- are divorcing or going through other major life changes, such as a loss of a job or retirement
- have inherited a house they don't plan to live in, or
- need a new home because of an expanded family.

We are not advocating taking advantage of a seller in distress. But, nevertheless, it's only common sense to find out if a seller needs to close quickly. If so, you may find a good house for a very reasonable price.

Is the House Uniquely Valuable to You?

A house's worth on the market isn't necessarily the same as its worth to you. A modest house listed at a reasonable price, for example, may be a bargain if you have three kids, the house is in a city that has excellent public schools, and the lot is large enough to add on a couple of rooms. The same house, however, may be overpriced for a couple not planning to have children.

How Much Are You Willing to Pay?

Okay, now for the last and most important consideration. How much money do you really want to pay for the house? While tactical considerations (the temperature of the market, the seller's needs) are important, nothing should outweigh your own honest assessment of how much you are willing to fork over.

Don't Stretch Your Finances Too Far

Some real estate people urge buyers to plow every possible dollar into a house. This can be a mistake, especially if you can afford a nice house that meets your needs but instead choose to pour a lot of money into a fancier one. Once you invest money in a house, it's very difficult and costly to try to get it back out.

Why are we cautious? Anyone familiar with the California housing market knows that family problems are commonly traced to paying too much for houses, leaving inadequate money for other needs. A devastating illness or loss of work means a large house payment will be almost impossible to make. People who refuse to stretch their finances to the limit, however, have money for other uses, including paying for the kids' private school and taking an occasional vacation.

 **CAUTION**

Find out whether the house will be hard to insure before you bid high—or bid at all. Insuring a house with a history of problems, particularly from mold or water damage, has become surprisingly difficult. To find out what claims the seller and previous owner have made, request what's known as a "CLUE" report (Comprehensive Loss Underwriting Exchange) from the seller. These reports can also be obtained from www.propertyid.com (their website is difficult—best to call them, 800-626-0106), but you'll need the seller's written permission first.

Making the Final Price Decision

The moment of truth has arrived: It's time to look at the many personal and market factors we discussed and come up with a dollar amount that you think is appropriate. There's nothing scientific or absolute about these factors, and you'll ultimately have to decide

---

True Story

Art: I Got a Bargain Without Being Too Greedy

I was on a tight budget when house hunting, and excited when a bargain surfaced. An acquaintance was moving out of the country and needed to sell his two-bedroom bungalow quickly. After visiting the house, and based on looking at dozens of houses in the area, I guessed that it was worth close to $425,000. The seller indicated he'd take about $385,000 for a quick sale.

Then I heard that another person was ready to make an offer. My spirits fell. I spoke to my dad, who had worked in real estate years before. His advice was not to be too greedy. "Bid a few thousand more than $385,000." I agonized about the exact amount and bid $392,000. I beat the other bidder by $4,000 and got a super house for the price.

whether to err on the side of underpaying, at the risk of losing the house—or overpaying, at the risk of paying more than you had to.

> **EXAMPLE:** After a long search, Randy and Lee find a house that meets all their needs. It lists for $310,000 but needs about $28,000 in repairs and fix-up work. They check comparable prices and conclude that if the house were in tip-top shape, it would sell for about $350,000. Though the local market is cold, they believe that the house is competitively priced and will probably sell quickly.
>
> Randy and Lee first lean toward offering the full $310,000, in the hope of preempting other bids, but after looking at how many houses are on the market, they decide to start much lower. They offer $278,800. Although this increases the chance that someone else may get the house, they reason there's only a slight chance of this happening given the structural problems and figure if they can buy the house for between $290,000–$295,000, they have made a good deal. If not, they'll just keep looking.

Other Ways to Make Your Offer Attractive

Though price is usually the most important part of your offer, the seller will be considering other aspects of the deal as well. Some sellers have even been known to choose a lower-priced offer because it met their other needs. Below are some strategies for making the nonmonetary terms of your offer as appealing as possible; you'll learn more about some of these offer terms in subsequent chapters, which describe the offer contract in detail.

- **Schedule a speedy closing.** If you've got all your financing lined up and are prepared to throw yourself into following up on other parts of the deal such as inspections and appraisals, you may be able to offer a closing date that's a week or two earlier than the typical 30–45 days. That will be attractive to a seller who needs to get money out of the house quickly and move on. Realize, however, that getting final loan approval may require more time than you expect—talk to your mortgage broker before committing to an early date.
- **Give sellers ample time to move out.** Not all sellers want the deal to be tied up in a hurry. If, for example, your seller still needs to find a new home, you might offer a long closing period (60 days or more) or allow the seller to continue living in the home after the closing (for a low rent, or even free). If you offer a long closing period, however, make sure that your lender's commitment won't run out during this time.
- **Show good financing prospects.** You'll need to start by being clear about what type of loan you'll apply for and what interest rate you plan to pay, so that the seller can ascertain whether this is realistic in the current market.

In addition, a preapproval letter from a lender will help show the seller that your financing is likely to go through. And the higher your down payment, the more confidence the seller will have that your loan will go through. Offering a higher-than-normal earnest money deposit (discussed in Chapter 16) can also be used to show the sellers that you're serious about the deal and have the cash to follow through.

- **Offer to pay incidental expenses.** Aside from the cost of the house itself, every home sale requires someone to pay for various incidentals such as escrow fees, a title search, city transfer tax, and the like. These items can range from a few hundred dollars to several thousand. By tradition, the seller usually picks up some of these costs, and the buyer picks up others (discussed in detail in Chapter 16). You could offer to pay for costs traditionally borne by the seller.

- **Write a cover letter.** It has become almost commonplace for prospective buyers, especially if competing against other bidders, to include a cover letter summarizing the main points of their offer and saying a bit about themselves—in particular, why they like the house and that they will take good care of it. You could also mention that you're ready to be flexible about the various terms of the offer. But don't put the seller in a position of having to discriminate in accepting or rejecting your offer, by emphasizing your family composition (which might suggest

gender, sexual orientation, or marital status), religion, or ethnicity.

- **Show that you'll be easy to work with.** Chose an agent with a good reputation, or the seller's agent may advise, "Let's avoid this offer, or we'll spend all our time in hardball negotiations." Beyond this, try not to be too demanding in the initial offer. If the seller sees that you're insisting that he or she pay all the transaction fees, purchase a home warranty, and leave the curtains and basketball hoop behind as well, you might be shooting yourself in the foot.

- **Don't unreasonably limit the time by which the seller must accept.** Some buyers (usually egged on by aggressive agents) add a clause to their offer insisting that the seller accept (or reject) the offer "upon presentation" or within a few hours' time. Unfortunately, most sellers feel bullied. You can limit the time during which your offer remains open, but it's better to give the seller at least two or three days.

- **Don't waive the inspection contingencies.** Such a waiver would mean that you take the house without any inspections, or that, even if you conduct an inspection, you won't hold the seller responsible for any defects that are revealed. This is a risky proposition and most likely to be attractive to a seller who knows the home needs work. If you feel you must waive this contingency, ask to send in your own inspector *before* you make an offer.

- **Don't offer an open-ended amount.** Worried about being outbid, buyers have been known to resort to offers along the lines of, "We'll pay $5,000 more than your highest bidder." This is just plain foolhardy. If you are desperate enough to do this, at least put a cap on how high you'll go. Also add a provision giving you the right to review the other offer and preapproval letter to make sure it's legitimate.

(However, viewing another buyer's offer materials raises confidentiality issues, and you may have to settle for seeing documents with portions blacked out.)

In Chapters 16 and 17 we delve further into the nitty-gritty of presenting your offer and dealing with counteroffers from the seller.

Putting Your Offer in Writing

This chapter explains what should go into your written purchase offer. The next chapter discusses how to present it to the seller, and suggests good negotiating techniques. Read both chapters carefully even if your real estate agent is preparing the paperwork for you. Many important decisions are being made here, and it's essential that you know how to protect your interests—before signing your offer form. If anything in the offer form isn't clear to you, ask your real estate agent or attorney to explain it.

Although we've provided a sample offer form at the end of this chapter, we're going to assume that you'll use a standard form provided by your real estate agent and probably prepared by the California Association of Realtors® or by a company such as Realty Publications, Inc. or Professional Publishing. For that reason, this chapter will focus on all the topics that a real estate offer form normally covers. You should be able to use our discussion to evaluate any form that your agent uses, bearing in mind that the clauses won't necessarily appear in the same order.

What Makes an Offer Legally Valid

An offer to buy a house is legally useless unless it's in writing, has been delivered to the seller or the seller's agent, and contains specific financial and other terms so that if the seller says "yes," the deal can go through. The seller's acceptance, too, must be in writing.

Real estate offers almost always contain contingencies—events that must happen or else the deal won't become final. For example, your offer may be contingent on your qualifying for financing or the house passing certain physical inspections.

Most offers give the seller a certain period of time within which to accept. During this time, you may revoke (take back) your offer in writing so long as the seller hasn't yet communicated an acceptance to you or your agent. (See Chapter 17, Presenting Your Offer and Negotiating, for more on revoking.)

How Offers and Counteroffers Are Made

Before you look at your offer form, here are a few words on offer terminology and procedures in California. The exact same form may be called by different names, each with a different legal meaning, depending on when and by whom (buyer or seller) it's used.

- Making an *offer* is when you fill out a purchase agreement form and give it to the seller.
- A *counteroffer* is used by a seller who is willing to accept some of your terms but only if you'll agree to modify others. The seller may respond, for example, with a higher price or a shorter time for you to arrange financing. A counteroffer is sometimes (but not always) made using exactly the same form as the buyer's purchase offer, with the title changed to reflect that it's a counteroffer. You're not in contract yet—in fact, the more legally accurate way to think about your

position is that you've been rejected, but presented with a new offer.

- A *multiple counteroffer* is when the seller counters a number of offers simultaneously—though not always identically. The seller may submit a variety of counteroffers, including different prices, terms, or conditions, to different buyers. The seller will then ask for each buyer's "highest and best" offer in response. As if the seller wasn't already getting a good deal, the seller is likely to draft the counteroffers so as not to become obligated to accept any of the buyers' return offers. You're most likely to encounter this practice in Southern California.

- A *counter counteroffer* is when you state your willingness to accept some of the seller's counteroffer terms along with your wish to modify others. Again, you can do this using a redrafted version of the original offer form. (The back-and-forth dance can go on for a while with counter-counter counteroffers, and so forth.)

- The offer becomes a legally binding *contract* only when you and the seller agree on all the terms in the offer (or counteroffer, and so forth) and sign it. You can both sign an offer form, or a separate written document stating that all terms of the offer (or counteroffer) are accepted. Not only must you both sign the agreement, you must both also initial every page.

EXAMPLE 1: Mitch gives Patricia a written offer to purchase her house for $450,000, which includes seven days to accept. Two days later, Patricia accepts in writing. A contract has been formed.

EXAMPLE 2: Now assume the same offer from Mitch, but before Patricia says "yes," Mitch finds a house he likes better. He immediately calls Patricia's agent and withdraws his offer. While this revokes his offer, he puts his revocation in writing and drops it off at Patricia's agent's office so there can be no misunderstanding. Mitch's offer has now been withdrawn; Patricia can't call Mitch up and say, "I accept," because no contract can be formed between them unless one or the other makes a second offer and the other accepts it in writing.

What Your Purchase Agreement Should Cover

Below is a review of the clauses traditionally found in a California purchase agreement.

Opening section. Your offer form will start with the obvious stuff: your name and the property's address. If you're married but buying a house using only your separate property (property acquired before marriage, by gift or inheritance during marriage, or after permanent separation), enter only your name. Normally, however, some community property (property acquired by either spouse during marriage, except gifts or inheritances) is used toward the down payment or monthly payments, so your spouse's name should also appear on the offer. (For more on this subject, see Chapter 20, Legal Ownership: How to Take Title.)

The street number, city, county, and state are sufficient for the address—a formal legal description isn't required. If the property has no street address, do your best to describe it ("the ten-acre Norris Ranch on County Road 305, two miles south of Andersonville").

You'll also be asked early on to state the purchase price you're offering, both written out (such as "four hundred seventeen thousand") and numerically ($417,000).

Also specify how soon escrow will close after the seller accepts your offer (in other words, the date on which you'll finalize the deal and the house will become yours). Be sure to give yourself ample time to remove all contingencies, such as arranging financing and inspections. Chapter 18 contains details on opening and closing escrow and tips on choosing a closing date.

Financial terms. Time to talk money—not just what you're offering, but how you can get out of the deal if your intended financing doesn't come through. The agreement should cover:

- **Your deposit.** You'll normally accompany your offer with an "earnest money" deposit, the amount of which should be stated here. If the seller accepts your offer, he or she will bank the deposit and may be able to keep it as damages if you back out of the deal for a reason not allowed by the contract. The deposit is usually about 1%–3% of the purchase price or sometimes a flat $1,000–$2,000 for lower-priced houses. The seller may counteroffer and ask for more. We advise limiting your initial deposit to 1%–3% of the purchase price. Also indicate the form of the deposit (personal check is most common).

- **Any increase to your deposit.** Buyers commonly increase the amount of the deposit after the offer is accepted, typically after 17 days or after removing the inspection contingencies (covered elsewhere in the agreement). For example, you might make an initial deposit of 1% of the purchase price and increase it to 3% upon removal of inspection contingencies.

- **Terms of the loans you'll be seeking.** If you already have your financing lined up, this will be easy. If a paragraph doesn't apply, enter N/A (for not applicable) in the blank. If you're applying for a government loan, be ready to demonstrate to the seller that you're eligible.

- **Down payment.** Specify your proposed down payment balance—your total down payment less your deposit and deposit increase.

- **Total.** Your deposit, loans, and the down payment should total up to your offer price.

- **Financing time limits and contingencies.** For your and the seller's protection, you'll need to state the number of days within which you'll provide a copy of your loan approval (if you have to start from scratch, expect to spend several weeks getting this); provide verification that you can pay the down payment and closing costs; arrange your financing and remove the loan contingency; and get the property appraised and remove the appraisal contingency.

Rent and Eviction Control in California

Several California cities have ordinances that restrict the rent the owner can charge, as well as control the owner's ability to end a tenancy (known as "just cause" eviction protection). While this is most relevant with multiunit buildings, it can decrease the value of houses likely to be rented in the future. Even if you're not planning to rent your home now, your life may change. Rent control plus "just cause" cities include:

Berkeley	Hayward	San Francisco
Beverly Hills	Los Angeles	San Jose
Campbell*	Los Gatos	Santa Monica
East Palo Alto	Oakland	Thousand Oaks
Fremont*	Palm Springs	West Hollywood
Gardena*		

* Rent not actually controlled, but landlord must mediate any increases.

In addition, some cities impose just cause eviction protections, without rent control:

Glendale	Richmond*	San Diego
Maywood	Ridgecrest*	

* Following foreclosures only.

Occupancy. You'll need to indicate whether you intend to occupy the property as your primary residence. The seller is interested in this because if you plan to rent out the property, you may have a harder time getting a loan. The agreement may also cover situations where tenants already live in the property, in which case you may agree to allow them to continue living there or propose a time by which they must move out.

Note that you buy subject to the tenants' rights and existing rental agreements. Many tenants will move on their own when they find out the house is being sold. In rent control areas, however, a long-term tenant with low rent may resist. After escrow closes, you may have to bring an eviction action on the grounds that you intend to occupy the house yourself.

 RESOURCE

Buying property subject to tenants' rights or rental property? See *The California Landlord's Law Book: Rights & Responsibilities*, by David Brown (Nolo).

Although you'll probably want to take possession of the property on the day escrow closes, be prepared to give this up during your negotiations. Many sellers who are buying another house insist on not moving out until 60–90 days after escrow closes, normally in exchange for paying you rent. Some sellers who are renting new places won't want to move out until the first of the month when their lease begins—they, too, will pay you rent.

If you end up agreeing that the seller can stay on more than just a few days after closing, we suggest you and the seller sign a written rental agreement specifying a daily rent or security deposit, authorizing a final inspection, and indicating the rental term (length). (See Chapter 14 for resources on rental agreements.) Make sure your homeowners' insurance covers their stay; if

Who Pays for What		
Item	**Who usually pays**	**Comments**
Escrow fees	Buyer customarily pays in northern California, seller in southern California	Not uncommon for fees to be divided
Title search	Buyer customarily pays in northern California, seller in southern California	Buyer benefits—not unreasonable for buyer to pay
Title insurance for buyer/owner	Buyer customarily pays in northern California, seller in southern California	Buyer benefits—not unreasonable for buyer to pay
Title insurance for lender	Buyer	Buyer benefits—buyer should pay
Deed preparation fee	Buyer	Buyer benefits—buyer should pay
Notary fee	Buyer usually pays for grant and trust deeds; seller usually pays for reconveyance deed on the property	Grant and trust deeds help buyer purchase and finance property; seller receives reconveyance deed when paying off existing mortgage
Recording fee	Buyer usually pays for grant and trust deeds; seller usually pays for reconveyance deed on the property	Grant and trust deeds help buyer purchase and finance property; seller receives reconveyance deed when paying off existing mortgage
Attorney's fee (if attorney hired to clarify title)	Whoever hired attorney	
Documentary transfer tax	Seller usually pays except in probate sales, where buyer is usually required to pay by the terms of the notice of sale	
City transfer tax	Buyer and seller usually share the cost	
Pest control inspection report	Buyer usually picks inspector and pays for inspection in northern California; seller often has property inspected before listing it for sale in southern California	In southern California, lenders usually won't process buyer's loan application without termite inspection because termites are a serious problem; if seller didn't do inspection, buyer should pay to assure that report meets buyer's standard
General contractor report	Buyer usually picks inspector and pays for inspection	Buyer should pay to assure that report meets buyer's standard
Roof inspection report	Buyer usually picks inspector and pays	Buyer should pay to assure that report for inspection meets buyer's standard

Who Pays for What (continued)		
Item	**Who usually pays**	**Comments**
Other inspections	Buyer usually picks inspector and pays for inspection	Buyer should pay to assure that report meets buyer's standard
One-year home warranty	Seller	Sometimes seller offers to purchase a policy when listing the property—if seller doesn't, buyer can purchase one if desired or negotiate this as part of the contract
Real estate tax, Fire insurance, Bond liens (unless able to be paid off)	Buyer and seller usually prorate as of the date the deed is recorded (see these expenses listed in Clause 5)	Both parties benefit; should be prorated

not, you may need to buy short-term rental insurance. The agreement should also state that you expect a per-day charge of your prorated monthly carrying costs.

Who pays for what costs. Your offer should indicate those items you agree to pay for, those you want the seller to pay for, and those you propose to split. Don't feel compelled to pay for every item—a lot depends on the particular house and market.

Use the chart above, "Who Pays for What," as a guide to how expenses are commonly divided. It's quite all right for you and the seller to agree to a different arrangement from that shown on the chart.

Escrow. Escrow is a process in which a disinterested third party, usually a title or escrow company, transfers the funds and documents among the buyer, the seller, and their lenders, in accordance with instructions provided by the buyer and seller (or their agents). (Escrow is described more thoroughly in Chapter 18.)

The standard contract will give you a place to enter the name and address of the escrow holder you choose. It's wise to do some preliminary investigation beforehand, so that you'll have at least a tentative idea about which company you'll use. However, if the seller has already set up a "listing escrow" with a company (a preliminary step that some take to speed up the process by a week or so), the expectation is that you'll use that company. There's little reason to argue, unless you've heard something negative about the company the seller has chosen. But if you're buying and selling a house in the same area, you'll ideally want to use the same escrow holder for both properties, to coordinate the closings.

This section may also state the date upon which you intend escrow to close, usually within 30 to 90 days of the offer's acceptance. How much time you give yourself should depend both on your own needs and what you think will please the seller most, if you're competing against other offers. (The exact date may later need to be adjusted by a few days depending on how things go with removing contingencies and lining up your loan, but this isn't usually difficult to negotiate with the seller, who most likely wants the deal to go through as much as you do.)

Here are some money-saving tips for choosing the exact closing date:

- The later in the month your closing date, the less prorated interest you will owe in closing costs. If you close on the second of June, for example, you'll need to prepay interest from June 2 through the end of the month. If you close on June 28, you'll need to prepay interest for only a few days.

- Don't close escrow on a Monday (or a Tuesday following a three-day weekend). You may end up paying extra interest. Lenders must fund a loan, and start charging the buyer interest, the day before escrow closes. Closing on a Monday requires the lender to fund the loan on the previous Friday. This means you end up paying interest over the weekend, before you even own the property.

Disclosures. Some parts of the standard offer form don't need to be filled out—for example, clauses intended to alert you to the seller's obligation to give you various disclosure statements within a certain time. Some of these seller disclosure statements are generic (like a pamphlet on lead-paint hazards), while others are specific to the property (see the "Real Estate Transfer Disclosure Statement," in Chapter 19).

If you're buying a condo or a house in a planned development, the seller should provide you with all the rules and regulations, financial documents, and other pertinent paperwork. Study them carefully—you'll have an opportunity to cancel the agreement if you're not happy with them.

What Sellers Must Tell You About Registered Sex Offenders (Megan's Law)

Home sales contracts entered into after July 1, 1999 must include a notice, in eight-point type (at least), regarding the availability of a database maintained by law enforcement authorities on the location of registered sex offenders. (Civil Code § 2079.10a.)

The seller or broker is not required to provide additional information about the proximity of registered sex offenders. The law states, however, that it does not change the existing responsibilities of sellers and real estate brokers to make disclosures of "material facts" that would affect the "value and desirability" of a property. This arguably means that a seller or broker who knew for a fact that a registered sex offender lived nearby would be responsible for disclosing this "material" fact to the buyer. Since the law isn't clear, you should, if concerned, check the database yourself.

The California Department of Justice provides detailed information on Megan's Law and how to obtain information on sex offenders in your neighborhood (www. meganslaw.ca.gov).

Condition of property. Your offer contract should require the seller to keep the property in its current condition until you take possession. You will also require the seller to clear out all personal belongings and debris.

Fixtures included in the sale. Fixtures are items permanently attached to real property, like built-in appliances or bookshelves, chandeliers, and drapery rods (though usually not the drapes). If removing the item would cause damage, chances are it's a fixture. On the other hand, if the item is easily removed—like a refrigerator that can be unplugged and wheeled away—it's not a fixture, no matter how much it looks like a natural part of the house. Fixtures come with the house unless you and the seller agree that the seller can remove them.

Personal property included in the sale. Personal property doesn't come with the house unless the seller agrees in writing to include it. If the seller promises to include items such as rugs, beds, aboveground swimming pools, ladders, or appliances that aren't built in, list them in the agreement.

Title. This standard clause assures you that title to the house will be "clear" when you take possession. Someone will need to order a preliminary title report, either you or the seller (this differs based on local custom). If any clouds on the title are revealed in the preliminary report, and the seller is unable to clear up these difficulties before the close of escrow or you can't obtain a title insurance policy, you have the right to get out of the contract. We discuss checking out the title in Chapter 18.

Sale contingent on selling your property. Contingencies are conditions that either the seller or buyer must meet (or the other party must waive) before the deal will close. Once both of you have agreed that the other party has met all contingencies (that is, you've "removed" the contingency or, if you're no longer interested, "waived" it), you're legally bound to go forward with the purchase. The sale of your current home is perhaps the most common noninspection contingency.

Inspection contingencies and their removal. Your agreement will specify what inspections on the house you want and must approve before you complete the purchase (close escrow). You'll also note how soon after the acceptance of the offer the inspections must be done. Normally, 20 working days is reasonable. Most buyers request only a general contractor and a pest control report, unless the buyer or the general inspector suspects problems requiring an inspection by a specialist. As a very rough rule, you want to require more inspections when a house is older and expensive or vulnerable to special problems, such as being near an earthquake fault or a slide zone, or potentially containing toxic substances (lead, mold, or asbestos). With new houses, you should schedule inspections during key phases of construction, plus a final inspection. (See Chapter 7 regarding inspecting new houses.)

Other contingencies and their removal. The agreement will contain sections or allow space for you to specify other contingencies that must be met before you will close, and the dates by which you must agree to their removal:

- A title contingency is needed for all houses to make sure title is good, that is, no one has a lien on the house allowing them to foreclose, or claims an easement that might impact your use of the property. (See Chapter 18, After the Contract Is Signed, for a discussion of these terms and preliminary title reports.) In most cases, the buyer orders the preliminary title report within three days of acceptance.

Time Allowed for Removing Contingencies

Most offers call for the removal of all contingencies within 30–60 days after the seller's acceptance. You and the seller should decide depending on your time constraints and how long it will realistically take to remove each. If the house is in great physical shape, ten to 15 days should be adequate to remove all contingencies relating to its physical condition. Just don't hamper your ability to thoroughly check out the house in your eagerness to keep negotiations with the seller going smoothly.

A contingency based on your selling an existing house or obtaining a loan you haven't yet applied for will normally need 30–90 days for removal. If any contingencies aren't met in the specified time, the deal is over unless you and the seller agree in writing to extend the contingency release time.

Chapter 18 gives more detail on how to remove contingencies.

• You may request that the seller buy you a home warranty that will provide low-fee servicing repair, or replacement

How Clean Will It Be?

The sellers of the house are required to leave the premises vacant and undamaged, but not sparkling. Even if they have the house professionally cleaned before they leave (which some may do as a courtesy—feel free to ask), it may not look clean enough to you. After all, years of accumulated dirt and scuffs look invisible when they're in your own house but disgusting when created by someone else. As you plan your moving day, you might allow a day or two after the house is yours to tackle any cleaning tasks before your possessions arrive.

of certain items in the house. If so, be sure to also check "Seller" under the list of costs associated with the sale.

• California home buyers are finding it increasingly difficult to purchase hazard insurance with appropriate coverage (especially for earthquakes) at affordable rates. To protect yourself, you can make your purchase contingent upon your applying, and receiving a commitment in writing, for reasonably priced hazard insurance on the property as required by your lender. Ask for as much time as possible to remove this contingency, at least 30 days if possible, depending upon your particular situation.

Final walk-through. The agreement should let you have one last look at the property right before the close of escrow to make sure the seller (or tenant) didn't damage the place before moving out or leave an old stained sofa and other junk behind, and that all promised repairs have been done to your satisfaction.

Liquidated damages. If you refuse to go through with the sale because a contingency can't be fulfilled, the seller must return your deposit. But if you back out simply because you change your mind, or you don't try in good faith to fulfill a contingency (for example, you don't even apply for a loan), it's considered a default. Assuming you both agree to a liquidated damages provision, the seller need not return your deposit. Your deposit turns into "liquidated damages," which in legal terms means you and the seller have agreed in advance on the maximum amount of the damages if you default. By setting the maximum amount in the purchase contract, you and the seller can save both time and money by avoiding court or arbitration, and you are protected from the risk of a court or arbitrator awarding the seller a larger amount.

California law generally prohibits sellers from keeping more than 3% of the agreed-upon sale price as liquidated damages. (Civil Code § 1675.) But the seller generally must prove that the damages somehow relate to that amount. In some situations, where the seller immediately gets another acceptable offer, the damage is zero—and the seller won't be entitled to anything.

If your contract includes a liquidated damages provision, it must be in at least ten-point boldface type and signed or initialed by you and the seller.

Mediation of disputes. This clause lets you first try to settle any disputes that arise

under the contract by nonbinding mediation. Mediation is a process where you and the seller pick someone to help you reach a mutually agreeable decision. It is cheap, fast, and avoids the emotional drain and hostility of litigation.

Arbitration of disputes. You can choose to resolve your dispute by arbitration should your attempt to settle any dispute informally or by mediation not succeed. You give up your right to a court trial, but like mediation, it's cheaper, faster, and less hostile than litigation.

In arbitration, you submit your dispute to one or more arbitrators for a decision. In the standard provision, most agreements are governed by either the American Arbitration Association (AAA) or the Judicial Arbitration and Mediation Services, Inc. (JAMS), both of which provide that the parties may get a lawyer to represent them (but don't have to) and that the decision is final—neither party can appeal it to a court.

Property tax and insurance prorations; assessment bonds. This type of clause allocates payment of property taxes, insurance policies carried over from seller to buyer, rents, interests, and any homeowners' association (HOA) dues or regular assessments. Each owner pays only for the period of actual ownership during the year the house is sold.

This clause also provides that the buyer assumes certain bond liens to finance local improvements such as curbs, gutters, or street lights. The seller may not even know whether the house has any such bond liens, but they'll show up on the title report.

Often bonds must be paid off when a house is sold, but sometimes they can't be.

In that case, the buyer assumes responsibility to pay the lien, but the cost of doing so is credited by the seller to the buyer in escrow.

Attorney's fees. In any standard real estate purchase contract, the losing party in arbitration or litigation (you could wind up in litigation if you choose arbitration and the seller doesn't agree, or vice versa) is responsible for his or her own—and the other side's—attorneys' fees and court costs.

Time is of the essence. The statement that time is of the essence is standard contract language emphasizing the importance of the dates to which you and the seller agree. It means that a missed deadline by either party is considered a substantial breach of the contract, which can result in the other party being given money damages or being allowed to cancel the contract.

> **TIP**
>
> **Put away your stopwatch.** Despite this provision, many courts reject cries of "he breached the 'time is of the essence' clause" for a delay of a few hours or days, unless you can show that you have suffered, or will suffer, damages as a result.

Entire agreement. A standard contract will state that it is the entire and final agreement between you and the seller, and that all modifications to the contract must be in writing—in other words, that any other written or oral agreements floating around in the world don't count.

Agency disclosure and confirmation. Your offer contract must let you and the seller confirm your relationships with your agents. Long before you fill out this offer form,

if you are working with an agent, you will have completed a "Disclosure: Real Estate Agency Relationships" form, which should have told you whether the agent is representing you, the seller, or both. In the agreement, you acknowledge that you've received that form, and confirm some of the information in the form.

Broker compensation. The contract may also clarify who pays which broker, and how much. Your options are outlined in Chapter 5.

When offer expires. Your offer should give the seller a deadline to accept. If the seller doesn't accept by that time, your offer automatically expires unless you extend it in writing. (See Chapter 17 on how to extend an offer. Chapter 17 also covers revoking your offer before the seller accepts or the deadline expires.)

Buyer's signature. By signing and dating the purchase agreement form, you agree to make your offer a binding contract if it's accepted by the seller. All buyers must sign, including your spouse if you're using community property to make the purchase. If you have a broker, the broker (or agent) must sign too (sometimes your broker will be referred to as "Selling Firm").

Seller's acceptance of offer. If the seller signs, it means your offer has been accepted, and the seller promises that he or she owns the property and has the right to sell it to you. If the sellers are a married couple, they both must sign, even if one spouse claims the house is separate property. A title company won't want to get involved in the complexities of California community property law and will want to see both signatures.

Seller's rejection of offer. Your offer form may provide a place for the seller to formally reject your offer. It will definitely make your life easier to know whether and when your offer is no longer being considered by the seller. However, not all sellers will take the time to fill this in and return it to you.

Other advisories. Your offer form may also contain various clauses whose primary purpose is to advise you and the seller of your rights and responsibilities. Most of these are warnings that you, as the buyer, can't rely on every word that the seller or any broker says, and should be a cautious consumer and investigate matters on your own.

Addenda containing other terms and conditions. Standard contracts don't necessarily contain space for every term that you might want to include in your agreement. You can create supplementary documents that are part of the agreement, for example to cover such issues as:

- your acknowledgment that the property contains unremitted units

- details outlining a probate or foreclosure sale (get help from a real estate agent or attorney experienced in these matters), or

- specification of who will pay to pump and certify a septic system or connect a sewer.

Backup offer. If the seller has already accepted another offer and you'd like to make a backup offer, you will in most cases need to prepare an addendum explaining this. For example, the San Francisco Association of Realtors® provides a one-page form that simply references your original offer and gives the seller a space to sign upon deciding to elevate your offer to primary position. If the seller does this, you'll normally be given a certain amount of time to approve the deal in writing. This lets you make more than one backup offer without being obligated to purchase more than one house if your offers are simultaneously accepted.

Contract to Purchase Real Property

Property address, including county: _____

_____

Date: _____

(Buyer) _____ ,
makes this offer to purchase the property described above, for the sum of _____
_____ dollars ($_____). Buyer includes a deposit, in the amount of
_____ dollars ($_____),
evidenced by ☐ cash ☐ cashier's check ☐ personal check ☐ promissory note ☐ other.

1. Financial Terms

This offer is contingent upon Buyer securing financing as specified in Items D, E, F, and G below
within _____ days from acceptance of this offer.

$ _____ **A. DEPOSIT TO BE APPLIED TOWARD THE DOWN PAYMENT,** payable to
_____ (Payee), to be
held uncashed until the acceptance of this offer. If this offer is accepted, the
deposit shall be delivered to Payee and applied toward the down payment.

$ _____ **B. DOWN PAYMENT INCREASE,** to be paid into escrow ☐ within _____
calendar days of acceptance, or ☐ on or before _____ .

$ _____ **C. DOWN PAYMENT BALANCE,** to be paid into escrow on or before the close of
escrow.

$ _____ **D. FIRST LOAN—NEW LOAN.** Buyer shall obtain a new loan, amortized over not
fewer than _____ years. Buyer's financing shall be:

☐ Conventional (name of lender, if known) _____

☐ Private (name of lender, if known) _____

☐ Government (specify): ☐ VA ☐ FHA ☐ Cal-Vet ☐ CHFA

☐ Other: _____

Buyer's mortgage shall be

☐ at a maximum fixed rate of _____%

☐ an adjustable rate loan with a maximum beginning rate of _____%, or

☐ (fill in any other requirements here) _____

_____

$ _____ **E. FIRST LOAN—EXISTING LOAN.** Buyer shall ☐ assume ☐ buy subject to an existing loan under the same terms and conditions that Seller has with _____, the present lender. The approximate remaining balance is $ _____, at the current rate of interest of _____% on a ☐ fixed ☐ adjustable rate loan, for a remaining term of approximately _____ years, secured by a First Deed of Trust.

$ _____ **F. SECOND LOAN—NEW LOAN.** Buyer shall obtain a new loan, amortized over not fewer than _____ years. Buyer's financing shall be:

☐ Conventional (name of lender, if known) _____

☐ Private (name of lender, if known) _____

☐ Government (specify): ☐ VA ☐ FHA ☐ Cal-Vet ☐ CHFA

☐ Other: _____

Buyer's mortgage shall be

☐ at a maximum fixed rate of _____%

☐ an adjustable rate loan with a maximum beginning rate of _____%, or

☐ (fill in any other requirements here) _____

_____

_____

$ _____ **G. SECOND LOAN—EXISTING LOAN.** Buyer shall ☐ assume ☐ buy subject to an existing loan under the same terms and conditions that Seller has with _____, the present lender. The approximate remaining balance is $ _____, at the current rate of interest of _____% on a ☐ fixed ☐ adjustable rate loan, for a remaining term of approximately _____ years, secured by a Second Deed of Trust.

$ _____ **H. TOTAL PURCHASE PRICE, EXCLUDING EXPENSES OF SALE AND CLOSING COSTS.**

$ _____ **I. OTHER. (See Paragraph _____ of this contract for additional terms and conditions.)**

LOAN APPLICATION. Buyer shall submit complete loan application and financial statement to lender(s) within five days after acceptance. If Buyer, after making a good-faith effort, does not secure financing by the time specified, this contract shall become void, and all deposits shall be returned to Buyer.

GOVERNMENT FINANCING. In the event of FHA or VA financing, Buyer shall not be obligated to complete the purchase, nor shall Buyer forfeit the deposit, if the offer price exceeds the property's FHA or VA appraised value. Buyer shall, however, have the option of proceeding with the purchase from any above-named lender or a different lender without regard to the appraised value.

EXISTING LOAN. If Buyer is assuming any loans or purchasing the property subject to any loans, Seller shall, within seven days after acceptance, deliver to Buyer copies of all applicable notes and deeds of trust, loan balances, and current interest rates. Buyer's obligation under this contract is conditioned upon Buyer's written approval of the documents within seven days after receipt. If Buyer does not accept the documents, either party may terminate this contract.

SELLER FINANCING. The following terms apply only to financing extended by Seller.

1. The rate specified as the maximum interest rate in D or F, above, shall be the actual fixed interest rate for seller financing.

2. The loan documents shall be prepared in the form customarily used by Escrow Agent, identified in Clause 3.

3. The promissory note and deed of trust shall include the following:

   a. Request for Notice of Default on senior loans.

   b. Seller's right to have Buyer execute and pay for a Request for Notice of Delinquency.

   c. Acceleration clause making the loan due, at Seller's option, upon the sale or transfer of the property.

   d. Title insurance coverage insuring Seller's deed of trust interest in the property.

   e. Late charge of 6% of the amount of any installment received more than 10 days after the date it is due.

   f. Obligation of Buyer to maintain fire and extended insurance with Seller named as loss payee at least to cover lesser of replacement of improvements or the liens on the property.

4. Seller shall obtain at Buyer's expense a tax service to notify Seller in the event of a property tax delinquency by Buyer.

5. If the property contains 1–4 dwelling units, Buyer and Seller shall execute a Seller Financing Disclosure Statement as provided by the arranger of credit as soon as is practicable prior to the statements reflecting Buyer's financial condition in such detail as is customarily required by institutional lenders. Seller shall keep these documents confidential and use them only to approve Buyer's creditworthiness. Seller shall notify Buyer in writing within seven days after receipt of Seller's approval or disapproval of Buyer's credit.

6. Buyer shall notify Seller in writing within seven days after receipt of the Seller Financing Disclosure Statement of Buyer's approval or disapproval of the financing terms offered by Seller.

2. Occupancy

Buyer ☐ does ☐ does not intend to occupy the property as Buyer's primary residence.

3. Escrow

Buyer and Seller shall deliver signed escrow instructions to _____

_____, escrow agent

located at _____

_____, within a reasonable time

before the close of this sale. Escrow shall close within _____ days of acceptance of this offer.

4. Prepayment Penalty and Assumption Fee

Seller shall pay any prepayment penalty or other fees imposed by any existing lender who is paid off during escrow. Buyer shall pay any prepayment penalty, assumption fee, or other fee that becomes due after the close of escrow on any loans assumed from Seller.

5. Expenses of Sale

Expenses of sale, settlement costs, and closing costs shall be paid for as follows:

Buyer	Seller	Shared Equally	
A. ☐	☐	☐	Escrow fees
B. ☐	☐	☐	Title search
C. ☐	☐	☐	Title insurance for buyer/owner
D. ☐	☐	☐	Title insurance for buyer's lender
E. ☐	☐	☐	Deed preparation fee

	Buyer	Seller	Shared Equally	
F.	☐	☐	☐	Notary fee
G.	☐	☐	☐	Recording fee
H.	☐	☐	☐	Attorney's fee (if attorney hired to clarify title)
I.	☐	☐	☐	Documentary transfer tax
J.	☐	☐	☐	City transfer tax
K.	☐	☐	☐	Pest control inspection report
L.	☐	☐	☐	General contractor report
M.	☐	☐	☐	Roof inspection report
N.				Other inspections (specify): _____
1.	☐	☐	☐	_____
2.	☐	☐	☐	_____
3.	☐	☐	☐	_____
4.	☐	☐	☐	_____
O.	☐	☐	☐	One-year home warranty (specify covered items): _____
				_____
				_____
P.				Other (specify): _____
1.	☐	☐	☐	_____
2.	☐	☐	☐	_____
3.	☐	☐	☐	_____
4.	☐	☐	☐	_____

6. Property Tax and Insurance Prorations; Assessment Bonds

Seller shall be responsible for payment of Seller's prorated share of real estate taxes and assessments accrued until the deed transferring title to Buyer is recorded. Buyer understands that the property shall be reassessed upon change of ownership and that Buyer shall be sent a supplemental tax bill which may reflect an increase in taxes based on property value.

Any premiums on insurance carried over from Seller to Buyer and any homeowners' association dues and regular assessments, interests, and rents shall be prorated, that is, Seller shall pay the portion of the premiums and fees while title is in Seller's name and Buyer shall pay the portion of the premiums and fees while title is in Buyer's name.

Homeowners' association special assessments shall be ☐ paid current by Seller (payments not yet due shall be assumed by Buyer without credit toward the purchase price) or ☐ _____ .

Buyer agrees to assume those assessment bond liens that cannot be paid off by Seller as follows. _____ .

7. Fixtures

All fixtures and fittings that are permanently attached to the property or for which special openings have been made are included, free of liens, in the purchase price, including built-in appliances; electrical, plumbing, light and heating fixtures; garage door openers/remote controls; attached carpets and other floor coverings; screens; awnings; shutters; window shades; blinds; television antennas/satellite dishes and related equipment; private integrated phone systems; air coolers/conditioners; pool/spa equipment; water softeners (if owned by Seller); security systems/alarms (if owned by Seller); attached fireplace equipment; mailbox; in-ground landscaping including trees/shrubs, EXCEPT: _____

_____

_____

8. Personal Property

The following items of personal property, free of liens and without warranty of condition (unless otherwise provided), are INCLUDED in the sale:

☐ Stove   ☐ Oven   ☐ Refrigerator   ☐ Washer   ☐ Dryer   ☐ Freezer
☐ Trash Compactor   ☐ Dishwasher

_____

Seller shall, by the date of possession, remove any and all other items of personal property.

9. Inspection Contingencies

This offer is conditioned upon Buyer's written approval of the following inspection reports. All inspections shall be carried out within _____ days of acceptance of the offer. Buyer shall deliver written approval or disapproval to Seller within three days of receiving each report. If Buyer does not deliver a written disapproval within the time allowed, Buyer shall be deemed to approve of the report.

Seller is to provide reasonable access to the property to Buyer, his/her agent, all inspectors, and representatives of lending institutions to conduct appraisals.

☐ A. Pest control report, covering the main building and ☐ detached garage(s) or carport(s) ☐ the following other structures on the property: _____ _____ .

    Buyer may elect to pay for all, a portion, or none of the cost of the work recommended by the report.

☐ B. General contractor report as to the general physical condition of the property including, but not limited to, heating and plumbing, electrical systems, solar energy systems, roof, appliances, structural, soil, foundation, retaining walls, possible environmental hazards, location of property lines, size/square footage of the property, and water/utility restrictions.

☐ C. Plumbing contractor report.

☐ D. Soils engineer report.

☐ E. Energy conservation inspection report in accordance with local ordinances.

☐ F. Seismic safety report.

☐ G. Environmental hazards inspection reports including, but not limited to, asbestos, radon gas, lead-based paint, mold, underground storage tanks, and hazardous wastes.

☐ H. City or county inspection report.

☐ I. Roof inspection report.

☐ J. General contractor report at the following phases of construction (specify) _____ _____ _____ .

☐ K. Other (specify) _____ _____ .

If Buyer and Seller, after making a good-faith effort, cannot remove in writing the above contingencies by the time specified, this contract shall become void, and all deposits shall be returned to Buyer.

10. Other Contingencies

This offer is contingent upon the following:

☐ A. Buyer receiving and approving preliminary title report within _____ days of acceptance of this offer.

☐ B. Seller furnishing declaration of restrictions, CC&Rs, bylaws, articles of incorporation, rules and regulations currently in force, other governing documents, one year's homeowners' association minutes, financial statements of the owners' association for the past three years, a statement of reserves, assignment of parking spaces, within _____ days of acceptance.

☐ C. Sale of Buyer's current residence, the address of which is _____

_____, by _____ .

☐ D. Seller furnishing rental agreements within _____ days of acceptance.

☐ E. Seller providing Buyer with a home warranty to cover the following: _____

_____ .

☐ F. Buyer applying for insurance acceptable to Buyer and Lender so as to indemnify both in the event of casualty loss upon Buyer's taking title to the property, and Buyer receiving written commitment of said insurance within _____ days of acceptance of this offer. Seller to furnish Buyer with written disclosure of existing insurance policy and any previous claims within three business days of acceptance of this offer.

☐ G. Other: _____

_____

_____

_____

_____

_____ .

Buyer shall deliver written approval or disapproval to Seller within three days of receiving each report, statement, or warranty. If Buyer does not deliver a written disapproval within the time allowed, Buyer shall be deemed to approve of the report, statement, or warranty. If Buyer and Seller, after making a good-faith effort, cannot remove in writing the above contingencies, this offer shall become void, and all deposits shall be returned to Buyer.

11. Condition of Property

Seller represents that the roof, heating, plumbing, air conditioning, electrical, septic, drainage, sewers, gutters and downspouts, and sprinklers, as well as built-in appliances and other equipment and fixtures, are in working order. Seller agrees to maintain them in that condition, and to maintain all landscaping, grounds, and pools, until possession of the property is delivered to Buyer. Seller shall, by the date of possession, replace any cracked or broken glass and remove any trash or debris.

12. Foreign Investors

If Seller is a foreign person as defined in the Foreign Investment in Real Property Tax Act, Buyer shall, absent a specific exemption, have withheld in escrow ten percent (10%) of the gross sale price of the property. Buyer and Seller shall provide the escrow holder specified in Clause 3 above with all signed documentation required by the Act.

If Seller has a last known address outside of California or if Seller's proceeds will be paid to a financial intermediary of Seller, under California Revenue and Tax Code, Buyer, unless an exemption applies, must deduct and withhold 3⅓% of the gross sales price from Seller's proceeds and send it to the Franchise Tax Board.

13. Rent Control

The property ☐ is ☐ is not located in a city or county subject to local rent control. A rent control ordinance may restrict the rent that can be charged for this property, limit the right of the owner to evict the occupant for other than "just cause," and control the owner's rights and responsibilities.

14. Title

At close of escrow, title to the property is to be clear of all liens and encumbrances of record except those listed in the preliminary title report and agreed to be assumed by Buyer. Any such liens or encumbrances assumed by Buyer shall be credited toward the purchase price. If Seller cannot remove liens or encumbrances not assumed by Buyer, Buyer shall have the right to cancel this contract and be refunded his/her deposit and costs of inspection reports.

15. Possession

Buyer reserves the right to inspect the property three days before the close of escrow. Seller shall deliver physical possession of property, along with alarms, alarm codes, keys, garage door openers, and all other means to operate all property locks, to Buyer: ☐ at close of escrow ☐ no later than _____ days after the close of escrow.

If Buyer agrees to let Seller continue to occupy the property after close of escrow, Seller shall deposit into escrow for Buyer a prorated share of Buyer's monthly carrying costs (principal, interest, property taxes, and insurance) for each such day, subject to the terms of a written agreement, specifying rent or security deposit, authorizing a final inspection before Seller vacates, and indicating the length of tenancy, signed by both parties.

16. Agency Confirmation and Commission to Brokers

The following agency relationship(s) are confirmed for this transaction:

Listing agent: _____ is the agent of:

☐ a Seller exclusively   ☐ Buyer and Seller

Selling agent: _____ is the agent of:

☐ Buyer exclusively   ☐ Seller exclusively   ☐ Buyer and Seller

Notice: The amount or rate of real estate commissions is not fixed by law. They are set by each Broker individually and may be negotiable between the Seller and Broker.

Buyer and Seller shall each pay only those broker's commissions for which Buyer and Seller have separately contracted in writing with a broker licensed by the California Commissioner of Real Estate.

$_____ or_____% of selling price to be paid to _____

_____ by ☐ Seller ☐ Buyer.

$_____ or_____% of selling price to be paid to _____

_____ by ☐ Seller ☐ Buyer.

17. Advice

If Buyer or Seller wishes advice concerning the legal or tax aspects of this transaction, Buyer or Seller shall separately contract and pay for it.

18. Backup Offer

☐ This offer is being made as a backup offer. Should Seller accept this offer as a backup offer, the following terms and conditions apply:

If Seller accepts this offer as a primary offer, he/she must do so in writing. Until that time, Buyer's deposit check shall be held uncashed.

Buyer has 24 hours from receipt of Seller's written acceptance to ratify it in writing. If Buyer fails to do so, Buyer's offer shall be deemed withdrawn and any contractual relationship between Buyer and Seller terminated.

19. Duration of Offer

This offer is submitted to Seller by Buyer on _____, at _____ ☐ a.m.
☐ p.m. Pacific Time, and will be considered revoked unless a copy of this contract with Seller's signature accepting it is delivered in person, by mail, or by fax and personally received by Buyer or Buyer's real estate agent not later than _____ ☐ a.m. ☐ p.m. on _____ ,
or, if prior to Seller's acceptance of this offer, Buyer revokes this offer in writing.

20. Other Terms and Conditions

_____

_____

_____

_____

_____

21. Risk of Damage to Property

All risk of loss to the property that occurs after this offer is accepted shall be borne by Seller until title has been conveyed to Buyer. Any damage totaling _____% or less of the purchase price shall be repaired by Seller prior to the transfer of title. If the land or improvements are destroyed or material damaged in an amount exceeding _____% of the purchase price, Buyer shall have the option of either terminating this agreement and recovering all deposits made or purchasing the property in its then condition.

22. Liquidated Damages

If Seller accepts this offer, and Buyer later defaults on the contract, Seller shall be released from Seller's obligations under this contract. By signing their initials here, Buyer (_____) and Seller (_____) agree that if Buyer defaults, Seller shall keep no more than three percent (3%) of the purchase price stated above if the property is a dwelling with no more than four units, one of which Buyer intends to occupy as Buyer's residence.

Seller shall retain the right to proceed against Buyer for any other claim or remedy Seller may have, other than for breach of contract. In the event of a dispute, funds deposited into escrow are not released automatically and require mutual, signed release instructions from Buyer and Seller, a judicial decision, or an arbitration award.

23. Mediation of Disputes

If a dispute arises out of, or relates to, this agreement, Buyer and Seller ☐ agree ☐ do not agree to first try in good faith to settle the dispute by nonbinding mediation before resorting to court action or binding arbitration. Mediation is a process in which parties attempt to resolve a dispute by submitting it to an impartial, neutral mediator who is authorized to facilitate the resolution of the dispute but who is not empowered to impose a settlement on the Buyer and Seller.

To invoke mediation, one party shall notify the other of his/her intention to proceed with mediation and shall provide the name of a chosen mediator. The other party shall have seven days to respond. If he/she disagrees with the first person's chosen mediator, the parties shall ask the escrow holder to choose the mediator or to recommend someone to choose the mediator. The mediator shall conduct the mediation session or sessions within the next three weeks. Before the mediation begins, Buyer and Seller agree to sign a document limiting the admissibility in arbitration or a lawsuit of anything said or admitted, or any documents prepared, in the course of the mediation.

Costs of mediation shall be divided equally between Buyer and Seller.

_____ Buyer _____ Seller

_____ Buyer _____ Seller

24. Arbitration of Disputes

Any dispute or claim in law or equity between Buyer and Seller arising out of this contract or any resulting transaction that is not settled by mediation shall be decided by neutral, binding arbitration and not by court action except as provided by California law for judicial review of arbitration proceedings.

The arbitration shall be conducted in accordance with the rules of either the American Arbitration Association (AAA) or Judicial Arbitration and Mediation Services, Inc. (JAMS). The selection between AAA and JAMS rules shall be made by the claimant first filing for the arbitration. The parties to an arbitration may agree in writing to use different rules and/or arbitrator(s). In all other respects, the arbitration shall be conducted in accordance with Part III, Title 9, of the California Code of Civil Procedure.

Judgment upon the award rendered by the arbitrator(s) may be entered in any court having jurisdiction thereof. The parties shall have the right to discovery in accordance with Code of Civil Procedure § 1283.05. The following matters are excluded from arbitration hereunder: (a) a judicial or nonjudicial foreclosure or other action or proceeding to enforce a deed of trust, mortgage, or installment land sales contract as defined in Civil Code § 2985; (b) an unlawful detainer action; (c) the filing or enforcement of a mechanic's lien; (d) any matter which is within the jurisdiction of a probate or small claims court; and (e) an action for bodily injury or wrongful death, or for latent or patent defects, to which Code of Civil Procedure § 337.1 or § 337.15 applies. The filing of a judicial action to enable the recording of a notice of pending action, for order of attachment, receivership, injunction, or other provisional remedies, shall not constitute a waiver of the right to arbitrate under this provision.

Any dispute or claim by or against broker(s) and/or associate licensee(s) participating in this transaction shall be submitted to arbitration consistent with the provision above only if the broker(s) and/or associate licensee(s) making the claim or against whom the claim is made shall have agreed to submit it to arbitration consistent with this provision.

"NOTICE: BY INITIALING IN THE SPACE BELOW YOU ARE AGREEING TO HAVE ANY DISPUTE ARISING OUT OF THE MATTERS INCLUDED IN THE 'ARBITRATION OF DISPUTES' PROVISION DECIDED BY NEUTRAL ARBITRATION AS PROVIDED BY CALIFORNIA LAW, AND YOU ARE GIVING UP ANY RIGHTS YOU MIGHT POSSESS TO HAVE THE DISPUTE LITIGATED IN A COURT OR JURY TRIAL. BY INITIALING IN THE SPACE BELOW YOU ARE GIVING UP YOUR JUDICIAL RIGHTS TO DISCOVERY AND APPEAL, UNLESS THOSE RIGHTS ARE SPECIFICALLY INCLUDED IN THE 'ARBITRATION OF DISPUTES' PROVISION. IF YOU REFUSE TO SUBMIT TO ARBITRATION AFTER AGREEING TO THIS PROVISION, YOU MAY BE COMPELLED TO ARBITRATE UNDER THE AUTHORITY OF THE CALIFORNIA CODE OF CIVIL PROCEDURE. YOUR AGREEMENT TO THIS ARBITRATION PROVISION IS VOLUNTARY."

"WE HAVE READ AND UNDERSTAND THE FOREGOING AND AGREE TO SUBMIT DISPUTES ARISING OUT OF THE MATTERS INCLUDED IN THE 'ARBITRATION OF DISPUTES' PROVISION TO NEUTRAL ARBITRATION."

Buyer's(s') Initials _____/_____   Seller's(s') Initials _____/_____

25. Attorneys' Fees

If litigation or arbitration arises from this contract, the prevailing party shall be reimbursed by the other party for reasonable attorneys' fees and court or arbitration costs.

26. Entire Agreement

This document represents the entire agreement between Buyer and Seller. Any modifications or amendments to this contract shall be made in writing, signed and dated by both parties.

27. Time Is of the Essence

Time is of the essence in this transaction.

28. Disclosures

_____ By initialing here, Buyer requests a copy of the Real Estate Transfer Disclosure Statement.

_____ By initialing here, Buyer requests copies of the Natural Hazards Disclosure Statement.

_____ By initialing here, Buyer requests a copy of *The Homeowner's Guide to Earthquake Safety.*

_____ By initialing here, Buyer requests a copy of *Environmental Hazards: A Guide for Homeowners and Buyers.*

_____ By initialing here, Buyer requests a lead-based paint hazards disclosure.

_____ By initialing here, Buyer requests a copy of the following disclosures: (specify) _____

_____

29. Buyer's Signature

This constitutes an offer to purchase the above listed property.

Selling Broker _____   Buyer _____

By Selling Agent _____   Buyer _____

Broker's Address _____   Broker's Telephone _____

_____   Broker's Fax _____

_____   Broker's Email _____

Date _____

30. Seller's Acceptance

The undersigned Seller ☐ accepts ☐ accepts subject to the attached counteroffer the foregoing offer, and agrees to sell the property on the terms and conditions stated above.

Seller agrees to pay compensation for services as follows:

☐ _____% of the sales price or   ☐ $_____ to (Listing Broker) _____

_____

☐ _____% of the sales price or   ☐ $_____ to (Selling Broker) _____

_____

payable on recordation of the deed or other evidence of title. If the sale is prevented due to the default of Seller, the commission shall be paid at default. If the sale is prevented due to the default of Buyer, the commission shall be paid only if and when Seller collects damages from Buyer.

Listing Broker _____   Seller _____

By Listing Agent _____   Seller _____

Broker's Address _____   Broker's Telephone _____

_____   Broker's Fax _____

_____   Broker's Email _____

Date _____

Presenting Your Offer and Negotiating

This chapter discusses presenting your offer to the seller and, if necessary, negotiating the price and other terms. If you haven't done so already, read Chapter 16, Putting Your Offer in Writing.

 GO BACK

If you're looking to buy a new house. This chapter focuses on negotiating to purchase an existing house. We discuss negotiating with the developer to purchase a new house in Chapter 7.

Notify the Seller of Your Offer

Once you notify your agent that you are ready to make an offer and draw it up, your agent will contact the seller's agent (or the seller directly, if the house is for sale by owner). The seller or agent may respond by either:

- setting up an appointment to receive your offer (common in cold markets)
- telling you a date and time when offers will be accepted (common in hot markets, when sellers expect multiple offers), or
- stringing you along or coming up with a delaying strategy, if the seller thinks he or she may get a better deal by waiting.

No matter which strategy the seller employs, unless your offer is rejected outright, you should eventually be able to coordinate a meeting so your offer can be presented.

Don't Reveal Your Offer Too Early

If the seller asks questions about the terms of your offer, it's usually best to politely decline to answer until you can make a formal presentation. This is especially true if your offer is on the low side or contains a number of contingencies. Once you're in the same room, it's harder for the seller to dismiss your offer out of hand, and you can build rapport and ask for a counteroffer. On the other hand, an offer revealed prior to the formal presentation may be used by the seller or her agent to try to get you, and others, to bid higher.

Strategies in a Cold Market

When prices are dropping, you can bid less than the sellers' asking price. Assuming the sellers are anxious to close the deal, they will probably counter with a price somewhere between their most recent offering price and the amount you proposed. For example, let's say you bid $550,000 on a house offered at $625,000. The sellers counter by lowering their price to $595,000.

Your next step is to decide whether you want to raise your offer. Hide your eagerness to buy the house. Here are some ways to do this:

- Don't respond immediately. Instead, either wait until the sellers' deadline for a response or ask for a little more time.
- Make it clear, either directly or through your agent, that you are still looking at other properties.

- If you are willing to risk losing the property, consider breaking off negotiations for a week or two.

When you make a counteroffer, make it on the low side to get the best deal you can. You can raise your offer later if the seller says no.

Strategies in a Competitive Market

In real estate markets where demand is high, homes sell quickly—often above the asking price—as bidding wars erupt. If you're buying in a competitive market, it's crucial to develop a bidding strategy. For example, you might bid on several houses at once as discussed under "Bid on Two or More Houses," below.

Another option—for situations where your Realtor is preparing to present your offer without having received clear information on how many other offers will be on the table— is to prepare several bids at different prices. Present the lowest bid if you're the only one making an offer, the next highest if there are only one or two other people making offers, and your highest price if there are three or more bidders. (In most multiple-offer situations, however, your agent will simply keep in close touch with the seller's agent to find out how many people have made appointments to present offers, and you can plan accordingly.)

![icon] CAUTION

Think twice before you get caught up in a bidding war. When a number of people bid on a house, competitive juices begin to flow, and a

kind of "auction mentality" prevails. Be careful not to exceed your budget.

Remember, price alone is not the only consideration for sellers. Your ability to close the deal quickly—for example, by getting loan preapproval—is crucial in hot markets. Finally, your flexibility and sensitivity to the seller's needs—whether it's extending the closing date for a seller who can't move for a few months or paying for repairs—may make or break your offer.

What to Bring to the Offer Conference

Prepare the following materials for the offer conference:

1. A completed offer.
2. Proof that you can afford the purchase, such as, in order of effectiveness:
   - a preapproval letter
   - a credit report, or
   - a family financial statement (see Chapter 2).
3. A brief letter about you and why you love the house and will take great care of it yourself. Consider including a photo of you or your family.

Present Your Offer

Buyers don't usually accompany the agent to the offer presentation or subsequent negotiations. Most real estate people believe it's unwise for buyers to be there, fearing that you'll muck up the process or say something that the seller or agent could use against you. But it's your purchase, not the agent's, and you can call the shots if you want to.

If you are attending the conference, or representing yourself, you have two goals, in addition to presenting your offer:

- to fully understand the seller's needs so you can adjust your offer to meet them, without compromising your own objectives
- to convince the seller that you can afford to buy the house and are a reasonable person to work with.

Starting Off on the Right Foot

Don't overlook the basics when meeting with a seller to negotiate:

- Show up on time.
- Dress reasonably, but conservatively.
- If you don't own a decent car, borrow one (or ride with your agent).
- Leave your kids at home.

You want to convey to the seller that you are reasonably knowledgeable about the real estate market—though you don't want to come off like a know-it-all.

Approach the seller in a straightforward, friendly manner. As an opener, say something nice about an aspect of the house that reflects the owner's personal taste, such as the garden or artwork. But don't gush—you'll only drive up the price. On the other hand, don't criticize anything that reflects the seller's taste.

Bring a preapproval letter for an amount that shows you can afford the home. Another way to establish your economic bona fides is to casually mention your job, or jobs, such as, "One reason we like this house is that it's a convenient commute to both of our jobs—Sidney is a law librarian and works at the county courthouse, and I'm a nurse at the hospital, which is only about 20 minutes away."

Even though you have decided on the terms you need, it's not too late to glean some useful information from the seller. Encourage the seller to talk. If the seller needs to move quickly to close on another house, relocate before school starts, or cope with a divorce, you may be able to get a better price if you can close quickly.

 TIP

Need to regroup? If you get information from the seller that surprises you and you want to modify your offer, ask to speak privately with your agent. This may mean no more than walking around the block or it could mean recessing for hours or even days to get legal, tax, or other specialized advice.

Bid on Two or More Houses

If you are in a hot market where you may bid on multiple houses before an offer is accepted, or if you are in a cold market and want to aggressively pursue several options and give each the pressure of competing with others, you can bid on more than one house at a time without encountering any legal problems. Here's how:

- Make each formal written offer open to acceptance for a very short period of time, such as 24 or 48 hours. You can extend the time in writing if you want to.
- If you make a subsequent offer while your first offer is still outstanding, be sure at least one of the offers has enough contingencies so that you can avoid the multiple-acceptance trap—should both sellers accept your offers simultaneously. For example, if you're bidding on an older house that obviously has some problems, include a contingency that you approve, in writing, a structural pest control report and any other inspections and reports that you'd like to obtain.
- Make your offer contingent on your written ratification of the seller's acceptance of your offer. This is commonly done with backup offers, but can just as easily be done in your original offer.

Wouldn't a seller be less likely to accept this type of offer? Yes, but if you make your ratification time short (for example, six hours from the written notification), and yours is otherwise the best offer in terms of price and other conditions, a seller will probably give you a chance to say yes. And, of course, while you are doing so, be sure to formally revoke any outstanding offers.

The Seller's Response to Your Offer

The seller and his or her agent will read your offer and any others that are submitted. Sellers normally focus on price, financing, and contingencies:

- **Price.** If it's in the ballpark of what the seller expected, the negotiation process will likely begin. If your bid is way out of line, the seller may reject it or not bother to respond at all. If there are several bidders, the seller will normally

---

True Story

Li and Sam: How to Pursue Several Houses at Once

When they needed to move, Li and Sam discovered there was fierce competition for houses in their community and price range. After bidding on several houses and losing all of them, they tried something new.

In a weekend marathon of house hunting, the couple saw four houses they liked—and bid on all of them. Li and Sam's offer included a clause stating that the seller had to accept or reject the offer within two days. Also, if the seller accepted their offer, then the couple would be allowed six hours to ratify it or back out. On Wednesday morning, two of their offers were accepted almost simultaneously. They accepted the better one, and even though not legally bound to do so, immediately withdrew the other three offers in writing.

look at which is highest and then will focus on the quality of the offers— seeking, for example, a buyer who is preapproved by a mortgage lender, will make a substantial down payment, has few contingencies in the offer, and can close within a short period of time.

- **Financing.** The seller will look at your financing information and is likely to reject your offer on the spot if it seems unrealistic. If multiple offers come in at similar prices, a seller will probably prefer the buyer with the strongest financial profile.

- **Contingencies.** If the seller wants to sell fast, he or she will be particularly concerned with any difficult or time-

consuming contingency, such as your need to sell an existing house.

The Seller Accepts on the Spot

If the seller says "yes" to your entire offer, make sure he or she immediately follows up by putting it in writing. An oral acceptance is not legally enforceable.

The seller will ordinarily accept by completing the acceptance blank at the bottom of your Contract to Purchase Real Property form. If the seller accepts all but even one term, it technically isn't an acceptance, but a counteroffer, which you, in turn, can accept or reject. In fact, it is rare for a seller to say yes to all of the terms of an offer on the spot.

True Story

Chuck and Ming: Buying a Good House in a Bad Way

Chuck and Ming spot a house they like. Frederick, their agent, arranges with the sellers' agent, Shirley, to present the offer to the sellers, Mike and Gail, at 11:00 a.m. the next day. Frederick is 20 minutes late.

When he arrives he bursts in and slaps the offer on the table, barely saying hello. The offer is $15,000 less than the list price, but Chuck and Ming love the house and will meet the asking price, if necessary.

Shirley asks Chuck how they like the house. Ming interrupts, saying they really love it and adds that they're exhausted from looking at dozens of others.

Shirley, Mike and Gail excuse themselves. They're hardly out of the room when Chuck

and Ming criticize Frederick for being late; he, in turn, expresses anger at Ming for not letting a more knowledgeable person do the negotiating.

In the meantime, Shirley, Mike, and Gail are pleased; Ming and Chuck have offered a good price, they can obviously afford the purchase, and the only contingency is a routine inspection. The offer is so solid, Mike and Gail probably would have accepted it as is, but based on Ming's revelations about how they love the house, they counteroffer $13,000 higher than Chuck and Ming's offer. After some negotiating a deal is finally struck for $9,000 above the first offer. Ming and Chuck overpaid because they weren't prepared to negotiate properly.

The Seller Rejects on the Spot

If the seller rejects your offer, try to get it in writing. An oral rejection can cause problems if your original offer gives the seller additional time to accept. In theory, the seller could change his or her mind and accept your offer in writing two days later, when you may no longer want the house. If the seller refuses to go to the trouble of putting a rejection in writing, simply withdraw your offer using a written Revocation of Offer to Purchase Real Property form. (See "Revoking an Offer or Counteroffer," below.)

Normally, if the seller thinks a deal can be made, the seller will counter your offer, not reject it outright. Most outright rejections happen when the seller already has a better offer or thinks the buyer's offer is ridiculously low or otherwise weak. If you think you can make your offer more attractive—for example, by upping the price or getting rid of a contingency that you sell your current home—and you're willing to follow through, you can write another offer.

The Seller Asks for More Time

It's reasonable (although not required) to give the seller one to three days to decide whether to accept, reject, or counter your offer. If the seller wants more time than you have specified in your offer, and you are so anxious to get the house you decide to oblige, prepare an Extension of Offer to Purchase Real Property form. A sample is shown below.

If you make a take-it-or-leave-it offer to force a quick decision, you won't want to give the seller extra time. This preemptive bid strategy is a good one in a hot market, if you bid aggressively on a new listing (maybe even overbid the asking price) in an effort to grab the house fast. In addition, the strategy may be necessary if you're interested in more than one house and want to force a quick decision on one so you can bid on another if the first seller says no.

The Seller Is Waiting for Other Bids

If a seller is expecting other offers, he or she is unlikely to make a decision until all offers are in (unless the seller receives one too good to resist saying "yes" to). If you want the house, there's nothing you can do but wait, unless you want to force the matter by making an attractive offer that requires an immediate decision.

Concerned About Discrimination?

What are your rights if the seller refuses your offer and then promptly sells to another buyer at the same or a lower price, or on less favorable terms? If you think the seller's decision not to sell to you was based on your race, ethnic background, religion, sex, sexual orientation, marital status, age, family status, or disability, the seller may be violating laws prohibiting discrimination. Contact the California Department of Fair Employment and Housing at 800-233-3212, www.dfeh.ca.gov.

Extension of Offer to Purchase Real Property

(Buyer) _____

extends the offer made to purchase the real property at (address) _____

_____

_____

made on (date) _____ , until (time) _____ ☐ a.m. ☐ p.m.

on (date) _____ .

_____   _____
Offerer/Buyer   Date

_____   _____
Offerer/Buyer   Date

The Seller Has Received a Higher Bid

A seller may say that he or she has already received a higher offer and that you'll need to raise yours to be seriously considered. Ask to see the higher written offer, so you know what you're bidding against, and then ask the seller to give you a written counteroffer.

The seller is unlikely to show you the competing offer; even so, it doesn't hurt to ask.

If you're shown another offer contract, don't stop reading when you find out the amount offered. Check whether the financing is solid and whether there are any contingencies that make the offer chancy. If the offer has problems, the seller may accept your more solid, lower offer, or you may get another chance if the first deal falls through.

If the higher offer has real potential, and the seller counters your offer at, or above, the amount of the other offer, consider how much you can afford, how much you believe the house is worth, and your overall house purchase strategy.

Don't get so caught up in negotiating that you make a decision you'll regret later. If you do bid higher, take time away from the negotiating table to carefully consider each increase. A house you concluded was worth $600,000 on Sunday is unlikely to be worth $700,000 on Tuesday, just because another buyer wants it.

Your other option if you appear to be second in line is to accept a backup offer position, as discussed later in this chapter.

The Seller Responds With a Counteroffer

Typically, the seller responds with a written counteroffer accepting most of the offer terms but proposing certain changes. If the seller orally states a counteroffer, insist that it be put in writing before you consider or discuss it.

Major Provisions of a Typical Counteroffer

Most counteroffers correspond to these provisions of an offer:

- **Price.** Unless your offer meets or exceeds the asking price, the seller may ask for more money. If you decide to increase your initial bid (in a counter counteroffer or by accepting the counteroffer):
  - Make the increases small.
  - Try to get something in return for each increase. For example, ask the seller to pay for certain repairs.
  - Walk away if the price and the terms aren't right and you can't reasonably expect to come to agreement—for instance, if you want the seller to pay for expensive mold remediation, and he or she refuses.
- **Financing.** If the seller believes your financing is impractical, he or she will likely propose a change. Similarly, if you offer to put 10% down with the seller taking back a second mortgage, and the seller wants all of his or her equity in cash, he or she will counteroffer.
- **Occupancy.** The seller may want additional time to move out. Or, with so many deals falling apart lately due to

financing troubles, the seller may want to simply put off moving day until after you've successfully closed.
- **Your selling a current house.** If your offer is contingent on selling a current home, the seller may reject this in a counteroffer if the market is hot and the seller believes it will be easy to find another buyer. Or the seller may counteroffer with a wipe-out clause (see Chapter 18).
- **Inspections.** A seller's counteroffer for dealing with inspections may suggest a shorter period of time, eliminate one or more of your proposed inspections, or offer the house for sale "as is," meaning the seller won't pay for any defects the inspections turn up. Another possible scenario is for the seller to propose that the buyer be responsible for the first "X" dollars of any needed repairs. While it's reasonable for you to complete inspections in a timely manner, it's completely unreasonable (and a possible red flag indicating physical problems) for the seller to limit the type of inspections you can conduct or insist that you purchase "as is."

Sample Counteroffer

The sample counteroffer shown in this chapter may be used by either the seller or buyer when only limited changes are proposed in the counteroffer (or counter counteroffer). A seller can also counteroffer using a detailed offer form. Study any new form carefully—no two are the same. An experienced broker or real estate lawyer should review the paperwork. If one provision of the counteroffer is unacceptable and you no longer want the house, do nothing. A counteroffer not accepted by the deadline simply expires.

> **EXAMPLE:** Leili offers to buy Jorge and Jackie's house for $380,000, leaving the offer open for 48 hours. They counter-offer for $410,000 and permission to remove some built-in bookshelves. In addition, they require Leili to drop her contingency to sell her existing house first. Jorge and Jackie give Leili 12 hours to accept the counteroffer. Leili, who has found a house she likes better, does nothing, and the counteroffer simply expires.

Negotiate by Counteroffers

For many sales, the written offer acceptance process is completed relatively quickly: The buyer makes an offer, the seller suggests a few changes, the buyer agrees. Sometimes, however, the process drags on, with counter-offers, counter counteroffers, and counter counter counteroffers flying back and forth for days, or even weeks. This can work well, if you and the seller narrow your differences with each counteroffer. But don't get so caught up in negotiating that you pay more

than the house is worth, or otherwise make a bad deal.

If you participate in a counteroffer dance, make sure:

- All counteroffers are in writing.
- You and the seller meet all deadlines.
- All counteroffers contain a time limit by which responses must be accepted.
- You and the seller keep clear on what's being offered and what's being accepted. At some point, using short counteroffer forms that don't restate the entire offer will become confusing. Before that happens, use a new purchase agreement form. Retitle it "Counteroffer" (or "Counter Counteroffer" or whatever), state the terms you and the seller have agreed on, and make appropriate changes.

Multiple Counteroffers

Occasionally, the seller will counter several buyers' offers with a "multiple counteroffer." The terms of each offer need not be the same. Buyers who remain interested (some will drop out) must accept or counter the terms of the counteroffer. If you're really eager to get this house, you'll need to act strategically to set your offer apart from the competition. Consider bumping up your offer price a little or improving the offer's other terms. Multiple counteroffers are common in southern California, less so in northern California.

Counteroffer [Counter Counteroffer]

Date: _____   Time: _____ ☐ a.m. ☐ p.m.

In response to the offer [counteroffer] to purchase real property at (address) _____

_____ ,

dated _____ , _____

_____ , Buyer [Seller] submits the following counteroffer [counter counteroffer]:

_____

_____ .

All other terms of the offer [counteroffer] remain the same. This counteroffer [counter counteroffer] expires on _____ at (time) _____ ☐ a.m. ☐ p.m. unless Buyer [Seller] delivers a written acceptance to Seller [Buyer] or his/her agent before then.

_____   _____
Signature   Date

_____   _____
Signature   Date

Acceptance

The undersigned Buyer [Seller] ☐ accepts ☐ accepts subject to the attached counteroffer the foregoing offer and agrees to sell the property on the terms and conditions stated above.

Seller agrees to pay compensation for services as follows:

☐ ____% of the sales price or ☐ $ _____ to (Listing Broker) _____

☐ ____% of the sales price or ☐ $ _____ to (Selling Broker) _____

payable on recordation of the deed or other evidence of title. If the sale is prevented due to the default of Seller, the commission shall be paid at default. If the sale is prevented due to the default of Buyer, the commission shall be paid only if and when Seller collects damages from Buyer.

Buying [Listing] Broker _____

By Buying [Listing] Agent _____

Buyer [Seller] _____

Buyer [Seller] _____

Broker's Address _____

Broker's Telephone _____   Broker's Fax _____

Date: _____   Broker's Email _____

Christina: I'm Glad Our First Few Offers Fell Through

After eight years of renting a small apartment my husband and I decided we wanted a larger place with more grass and trees—someplace good to raise the kids we planned to have in a few years.

Our first weekend house hunting, we fell in love with a beautiful house in a nearby suburb, but it was $30,000 above our maximum price and needed some major structural work. The sellers were anxious to sell quickly for full price and "as is," because they had already bought a second house.

We made the classic mistake of thinking this house was the only one in the world; we counteroffered for days. Our real estate agent, who was anxious for a quick sale, fanned the flames. When this deal fell through, we repeated the same mistake with the next house. A few weeks later, we finally came to our senses and realized there were lots of houses out there. We got a new agent, slowed down our house search, and became more realistic—after all, we were in no real hurry to move. Once we relaxed, we found a lovely place—much nicer than the first one—for $15,000 less than we expected to pay. Now our advice to others is get out of the fast lane and enjoy the process.

An Offer Is Accepted—
A Contract Is Formed

A contract is formed when either the buyer or the seller accepts all of the terms of the other's offer or counteroffer in writing within the time allowed. After this happens:

- Make copies of the contract; keep one and make sure the seller has or gets one. If short-form counteroffers were used to change a long offer, all contract terms won't be stated in one document. It's best to retype all the accepted terms onto one form.
- Give the seller's agent a deposit check made out to an escrow or title company in the amount called for in the contract.

- Give copies of documents to any real estate agent, attorney, or tax adviser who's assisting you.
- Take steps to begin removing the contingencies—you usually have only a few days to act. At the least, you'll need to arrange inspections and apply for financing if you haven't already done so.

Revoking an Offer or Counteroffer

You may revoke (take back) your offer in writing any time before the seller accepts in writing. You needn't state a reason. If you want to revoke an offer (or counter counteroffer), do so immediately. Call the seller or her agent and say that you're revoking your offer; immediately follow up in writing. The best ways to do this are by email or fax (follow up by sending a signed original to the seller or agent), hand delivery, or overnight mail.

A sample Revocation of Offer to Purchase Real Property form is shown below.

Making a Backup Offer

If you locate a house you love, but end up losing out to another bidder, consider making a backup offer.

One way to do this by submitting a short addendum to your original purchase offer.

Your addenda should give you the right to say yes or no in writing within a certain number of hours should the seller inform you in writing that the primary offer has fallen through and the seller now wants to accept yours. You will, however, typically need to remove certain contingencies within those hours, including the financing and inspection contingencies.

Many cautious sellers are delighted to receive backup offers and accept desirable ones. If a seller accepts more than one, priority is set by the date and time of acceptance.

Revocation of Offer to Purchase Real Property

(Buyer) _____

hereby revokes the offer made to purchase the real property at (address) _____

_____ ,

made on (date) _____ .

_____   _____
Offerer/Buyer   Date

_____   _____
Offerer/Buyer   Date

After the Contract Is Signed: Escrow, Contingencies, and Insurance

Congratulations! Your offer to purchase a house has been accepted. But it's not yet time to buy a new doormat. Many tasks remain before the house is yours—opening an escrow account, removing contingencies, obtaining title insurance, and closing escrow—and all are discussed in this chapter.

The time it takes between the contract signing and the close of escrow (when you become the owner) depends on what deadline you and the seller agreed to, probably based on what remains to be done following the signing. If you have your financing lined up in advance and the house is in excellent condition, you shouldn't have any trouble meeting the standard 30- to 60-day closing date. If, however, your offer is contingent upon your selling an existing house, the inspections turn up lots of physical problems, or you need to arrange a complicated financing package, it could take several months or more. If your deadline is too soon, you and the seller can agree to extend it.

> **! CAUTION**
>
> **Understand escrow before you begin the process.** Opening and successfully closing escrow involves detailed, picky, and often overlapping steps. Read through your purchase contract and draw up a list, calendar, or flowchart that shows you who needs to perform what tasks, and when.

Open Escrow

In finalizing the purchase of your house, you and the seller need a neutral third party to hold onto, and then exchange, deeds and money, pay off existing loans, record deeds, prorate the property tax payments, and help with other transfer details.

To begin this process, you and the seller "open an escrow account" with a person or organization legally empowered to act as an escrow agent. Lawyers need not be involved with escrow in California, and usually aren't, unless an unusual problem arises (for example, the seller's title isn't clear)—in which case either buyer or seller may wish to consult an attorney.

By custom, escrow is done differently in northern and southern California. The common "dividing line" between northern and southern California escrow approaches is somewhere near the Tehachapi Mountains. Nevertheless, both escrow styles routinely appear in the middle of the state, and some northern California escrow agents are beginning to adopt southern California practices.

Northern California. An escrow account is normally opened with a title insurance company (often just called a title company) immediately after the purchase contract is signed. Title companies not only provide the necessary title insurance, but also handle financing arrangements such as collecting your down payment and funds for your lender, paying off the seller's lender, and preparing and recording a deed from the seller to you and a deed of trust for your lender.

Southern California. An escrow account is usually opened by the buyer and seller with an escrow company, which prepares the necessary papers and exchanges the seller's ownership interest for your money after

Escrow Terminology

Here are common real estate terms used during escrow.

Close of escrow or Closing. The final transfer of ownership of the house to the buyer. It occurs after both the buyer and seller have met all terms of the contract and the deed is recorded. "Closing" also refers to the time when the transfer will occur, such as, "The closing on my house will happen on January 27 at 10:00 a.m."

Closing costs. The expenses involved in the closing process, including broker commissions, title insurance, loan fees, lender's appraisal, inspection fees, private mortgage insurance, deed recording, and incidental fees charged by the escrow agent and lender.

Closing statement. A document prepared by the escrow holder containing a complete accounting of all funds, credits, and debts involved in the escrow process. Basically this amounts to a statement of the amount of cash the buyer and the buyer's lender have put into escrow, how much the seller has received, and how much money was used for other expenses.

Demand or Request for beneficiary statement. A letter from the seller's lender to the escrow holder telling how much the escrow holder must send the lender to pay the seller's existing mortgage in full. The lender sends it after being notified by the escrow holder that the seller is selling the house and expects to close escrow by a certain date. If the time between opening and closing escrow is reasonably short, the seller wants to receive the demand fast to include the calculations in the closing. If the time between opening and closing will take some time, however, the seller won't rush the demand. A demand is typically good for only 30 days; if it comes too soon, it will expire before escrow closes and the seller will have to request a second one.

Final title report or Final. Just before the close of escrow, the title company rechecks the condition of the title established in the preliminary title report. If it's the same (it usually is), the preliminary title report becomes the final report, and title insurance policies are issued.

Funding the loan. California law requires that checks and drafts be collected prior to disbursement. This means that to close escrow, funds must be deposited with the escrow holder one or more days prior to the close of escrow, except for cash and funds deposited by electronic transfer.

Good-faith estimate or Reg. Z Disclosure. Federal law requires the lender to disclose to you all the material terms of the loan (such as negative amortization, the annual percentage rate, and caps) you are applying for, on this form.

Legal description or Legal. The description of the parcel of land being sold that appears on the deed to the property. It has nothing to do with the buildings, but rather the land itself. The legal may specify Lot and Block numbers or metes and bounds (a complicated exercise in map reading), none of which should concern you. (If you want to know more about legally describing California real

Escrow Terminology (continued)

property, see *Deeds for California Real Estate,* by Mary Randolph (Nolo).)

Loan commitment. A written statement from a lender promising to lend you a certain sum of money on certain terms.

Opening escrow. Escrow is opened when you and the seller select an escrow agent to hold onto and transfer documents and money during the house purchase process.

Preliminary, Prelim, or Pre. The preliminary title report issued by a title company

soon after escrow opens. It shows current ownership information on the property (including any liens or encumbrances). If any problems are found, the seller can take steps to resolve them before escrow closes. The title insurance policy issued at the close of escrow is usually based on this report.

Taking title. Describes the transfer of ownership from seller to buyer. For example, "The buyer takes title [gets his or her name on the deed] next Tuesday."

---

deducting the amount needed to pay off the seller's existing mortgage, past taxes, and other liens. Title insurance is obtained from a title insurance company, which isn't usually otherwise involved in the escrow process.

Other escrow holders. Although it's unusual, escrow can be legally handled by someone other than a title or escrow company. The buyer or seller's attorney, a real estate broker who has a trust account for supervising escrows, or the escrow department of a bank are all legally empowered to do the job.

How to Open Escrow

When the seller accepts your offer, you'll normally give your agent a deposit check made out to the escrow holder. The deposit is taken to the title or escrow company, and an escrow account is opened. The deposit will be applied to the purchase price, or it

will be returned to you if you back out of the deal for a valid reason allowed by the contract—for example, a contingency can't be met.

 TIP

Consider getting a power of attorney. If you or a cobuyer will be traveling, consider filling out a power of attorney so the nontraveling buyer can sign the final papers. Ask your escrow company to draft the power of attorney.

How to Find an Escrow Holder

In your offer contract, you'll enter the name and address of the escrow holder you choose. In some situations, the seller may disagree and list his or her choice in the counteroffer. As the basic task to be accomplished and prices charged are similar, this should not be an issue to hold up the acceptance of an offer. Unless you feel very strongly about using "your" escrow agent or not using the seller's, give in.

How do you know which title company or escrow company to enter on the offer form? As with finding any service provider, it's best to get a recommendation from someone you trust, such as your agent. But be sure to confirm that your escrow officer won't be taking any long leaves or vacations during your escrow period.

If you are considering several recommended firms, you may be inclined to call around and compare prices. You may save a few dollars, but prices tend to be pretty similar. Because of the small potential savings involved, it normally makes more sense to concentrate on finding a company that offers superior service.

How to Work With the Escrow Holder

What happens after escrow opens depends to a considerable extent on your escrow agent, whether you're in northern or southern California, and your contract with the seller. If the contract contains contingencies, the escrow holder may do very little until you and the seller remove them, although many escrow holders in southern California routinely confer with agents, or with sellers and buyers without agents, to make sure steps are being taken to remove contingencies. Southern California escrow holders also frequently try to help resolve any title disputes. Even if your escrow holder is less involved, be sure the escrow holder gives you a list of what you

need to provide and the dates when you need to provide each item.

Your agent should help the escrow process go smoothly. If neither you nor the seller is working with an agent, however, you'll need to handle the details yourselves. Fortunately, it's not difficult. Make an initial appointment with the escrow agent. Bring the timeline from Chapter 13, Obtaining a Mortgage, and use it as your guide to ask questions. Check in regularly—about once a week—to be sure you're doing what's expected and that everything is on track.

If a dispute arises between you and the seller during escrow, don't look to the escrow holder to resolve it—or to transfer the money and deed. The escrow holder is a neutral party. You'll have to solve the problem (see Chapter 21, If Something Goes Wrong During Escrow); until you do, the escrow holder sits still. If the dispute drags on long enough, the escrow holder may get tired of being stuck in the middle and may initiate a lawsuit (called an "interpleader") to have the court resolve the dispute and direct the distribution of the deposited money.

Ordering Title Insurance

Ordering title insurance from a title insurance company (usually the same company handling the escrow in northern California) is the buyer's responsibility. The title company issues a preliminary title report and then, just before closing, a final title report and two title insurance policies. If you're represented by a real estate professional, he or she will be able to help you with this.

The Cost of Escrow

Closing costs are typically about 2%–5% of the purchase price, with the lion's share made up of loan points and fees. Escrow costs, which are considered part of closing costs, tend to be under 1% of the purchase price. (In southern California, the costs are divided between the escrow company and a title insurance company.) Included in the escrow costs are fees for the preliminary and final title reports, recording of the deed, notarization, the title company, the escrow company (if necessary), and two title insurance policies. One policy is for the buyer (CLTA policy), and one is for the lender (ALTA policy). (See "Obtain Title Report and Title Insurance," below, for more.)

No law specifies who pays escrow costs; you and the seller negotiate this as part of the forming of the contract. For our discussion on who *customarily* pays which fee, see Chapter 16.

Complying With IRS Foreign Investor Rules

The seller must complete a form, available from the escrow or title company or the IRS, stating whether he or she is a foreign investor as defined by law. (This is required by a federal law called FIRPTA, the Foreign Investment in Real Property Tax Act, Internal Revenue Code § 1445.) If the seller is a foreign investor, you must withhold in escrow 10% of the sale price of the house and fill out and file some papers with the IRS. The escrow agent can help you.

If the seller is located outside of California or the proceeds of the sale will be paid to an intermediary of the seller, you must withhold and send some money to the Franchise Tax Board (California's taxing authority). Again, the escrow agent can help you.

Remove Contingencies

If your contract contains contingencies, you must remove them in writing and let the escrow holder know they've been removed before the purchase becomes final. Removing the most common contingencies, and extending the time for doing so, is discussed below.

Inspection Contingencies

Most house purchase contracts give the buyer the right to have the house inspected by specified inspectors, and approve the results of their reports, before going through with the sale. This is an important part of the process, in which you'll learn a lot about your new house's foundation, structure, internal systems such as heating and electrical, and pest activity. You will normally hire one or more professional inspectors, including at a minimum a general contractor and a pest inspector.

Give each inspector a copy of the seller's Real Estate Transfer Disclosure Statement, Natural Hazard Disclosure Statement, and any other inspection reports and disclosures the seller provides you. The seller must let the inspectors have access to the house, although you may need authorization from a homeowners' association for the contractor to inspect common areas of a condominium. We suggest that you accompany the inspectors on their rounds. Chapter 19 discusses the seller's legally required disclosures and the house inspection system in detail.

Inspections often find problems. For example, the house may have termite damage, need new wiring, or require roof repairs. You have various options to deal with such problems:

- Ignore them. The inspector wouldn't be doing his or her job without alerting you to home defects of every scale, down to missing switchplates, cracked tiles, and so forth. Many of these are natural results of an aging house, and not worth making a big deal over in negotiations.
- If your offer is contingent on approving inspection reports, you can ask the seller to fix the problem before you go through with the purchase.
- If your offer is contingent upon your approving inspection reports, and a report indicates serious problems, you can back out of the deal.
- If the problem was disclosed before you made your offer, and you nevertheless offered to purchase the house "as is," you can't legally claim that it must be repaired at the seller's expense before you'll buy.

Assuming the house needs repairs and your offer wasn't "as is," your first question is, do you still want the house if it's repaired? If the problem is extremely serious (the house is in a hazardous slide zone or near an earthquake fault), you may say, "No." But

if you still want the house, you and the seller must negotiate over who pays for what.

Negotiating the Cost of Repairs

By the time an offer has been accepted and inspections have been done, neither you nor the seller wants to spend more money. At the same time, both of you have already invested considerable time and energy in the transaction and don't want to walk away and start over. If either of you needs the sale to go through to meet other commitments, time pressure (and, often, the other's leverage) can cause great stress and short tempers.

Who pays what usually comes down to who is perceived to have more negotiating clout. If the seller thinks he or she has agreed to sell at too low a price or can easily find another buyer, the seller will probably refuse to pay for all or most repairs. If you think the seller is right, you'd be smart to share modest repair costs. If, however, you believe you've offered top dollar for the house and don't think it's worth a penny more, you'll want to insist that the seller pay most or all of the repairs and refuse to finalize the deal otherwise.

Paying for Repairs

A seller willing to allow for the cost of repairs normally does so through either lowering the purchase price (which the agents won't like because it lowers their commissions) or by an "escrow credit." This means the seller agrees to leave money in escrow from the sale proceeds to cover the amount of the repairs. The exact amount the repairs will cost is normally agreed to by all parties based on contractors' bids. You want to be sure that the cost reflects all needed work using quality labor and materials.

If expensive repairs are needed, the lender often requires that work be done before escrow closes. Assuming the seller has agreed to cover the cost, a portion of the money placed in escrow can be paid to a contractor before the close of escrow, or held by the escrow holder after the sale closes, pending the contractor completing the work.

But if you've agreed to pay for a portion of the repairs, you must come up with the money. If this is difficult to do, explore having the seller mark up the price of the house by the amount of the repairs. This still results in your paying for the repairs through the higher price, but if the mortgage lender will go along, and if the appraisal value of the house justifies the higher price, it will help cover the extra expense. The seller who gets the artificially high price uses the extra money to pay for the repairs.

In some situations, especially where repairs aren't major, a lender will let escrow close without requiring the repairs to be made. In this situation, if the seller has agreed to pay a credit into escrow for the work, the buyer is free to use this money for other purposes, such as contributing to the down payment.

EXAMPLE: Mary agrees to sell her house to Albin for $581,000. Albin's offer is contingent upon his approval of a pest control and general contractor's inspection. The inspections turn up $30,000 worth of beetle damage and drainage problems. Albin refuses to go through with the sale unless Mary credits him $30,000 in escrow for the repairs. They negotiate and agree to share the costs, with Mary paying $24,000 and Albin $6,000. The compromise reflects the fact that Albin was ready to walk away from the deal if Mary didn't pay most of the cost. Mary, on the other hand, needed to move and didn't have time to find another buyer in a slow sales market.

True Story

Mitchell: How I Used an Escrow Credit to Reduce My Down Payment

I was going to offer $362,000 for a house I liked but changed my mind after reading an inspection report commissioned by another buyer. It identified leaks in an old roof and pest problems in the foundation. I offered $359,000 and asked for a $5,000 credit for roof work and a $12,000 credit for pest work. The seller agreed to install a new roof and give me $3,000 toward closing costs and $6,000 for pest work.

The pest problem was old and not getting worse, however, so the repair work wasn't immediately necessary, and I decided to hold off. I got to use $9,000 to reduce my out-of-pocket costs for closing and the down payment.

A problem remains, however. Albin doesn't have $6,000 to pay his share. This problem is solved when his lender agrees to let the price of the house be raised to $587,000, with Mary now paying for all repairs. The lender is willing to do this based on its appraisal, which concludes that once the $30,000 of repairs are made, $590,000 reflects a fair market value.

If the lender doesn't require that work be done, and you have enough cash to pay for the repairs yourself, consider asking the seller to reduce the asking price instead of giving you a credit in escrow. This saves you money because escrow and title fees, as well as annual property taxes, are based on the purchase price. The seller is often pleased, because the commission the sellers pay is based on the sale price. However, since the real estate commissions are reduced, the agents might not be excited about this arrangement.

Removing Inspection Contingencies

As you satisfy or waive an inspection contingency, you must remove it in writing. See "Releasing Contingencies," below, to learn how.

Financing Contingencies

In any standard purchase contract, the buyer makes the offer to buy contingent on arranging satisfactory financing. To remove (release) this contingency you should provide the seller written evidence that you have obtained financing sufficient to purchase the house, along with a contingency release form. Evidence of financing is usually a loan commitment letter from a lender or a bank confirmation if you arrange private financing. If you're assuming the seller's mortgage, order the assumption documents from the lender to start the process of taking over the loan.

Extending Time to Meet a Contingency

Buyers frequently need extra time to satisfy a contract contingency. Without the extra time, the contract ends (that is, the deal falls through) unless you and the seller agree to extend it. If the seller wants out, he or she won't extend the time. More commonly, however, the seller wants the deal to go through but needs reassurance that you're still serious about buying the house. The seller may demand that you increase your deposit in exchange. The amounts vary, but to extend a $300,000 offer for a few weeks, $1,000 or so is reasonable.

Any agreement to extend the time to meet a contingency (or to change any other term of the contract) must be in writing and signed. A sample is below.

> **EXAMPLE:** Julie agrees to buy Shawn's house for $600,000, contingent upon securing an adjustable rate mortgage at 4.8% or lower for 80% of the purchase price and selling her own house within 90 days. Julie arranges the financing easily but has trouble selling her house. She offers Shawn $3,000 cash to extend her time to purchase (to let her sell her existing house) for another 60 days. Shawn agrees.

Extending Time to Meet Contingencies

The material set out below is hereby made a part of the contract dated _____
between (Buyer) _____
and (Seller) _____
to purchase real property located at _____
_____ .

The final date for Buyer's removal of all contingencies set out in Clause _____ of the contract, is hereby extended until (month, day, year) _____ at (time) _____ ☐ a.m. ☐ p.m.

_____   _____
Signature of Buyer   Date

_____   _____
Signature of Buyer   Date

_____   _____
Signature of Seller   Date

_____   _____
Signature of Seller   Date

Releasing Contingencies

As you satisfy or abandon (waive) a contingency, you must remove (or release) it in writing. Don't wait until all contingencies are met to do this. Remove each one as it is satisfied or abandoned. You remove a contingency by executing a contingency release form such as the one below. Give the original to the seller and keep a copy for yourself.

If the seller has agreed to credit you for the cost of any repairs, add the following to the release, after the word "report":

"providing that by _____ ___.m. on _____ , Seller agrees in writing to extend to Buyer an escrow credit in the amount of $_____ against the purchase price to cover the cost of needed repair and rehabilitation work to be paid by Buyer."

Release Clauses (Wipe-Outs)

Some contracts let the seller demand in writing that you remove all contingencies within a certain time (usually between 24

Contingency Release

(Buyer) _____

of the property at (address) _____ ,

hereby removes the following contingency(ies) from the purchase contract dated _____ :

_____

_____

_____

_____

If this release is based on accepting any inspection report, a copy of the report, signed by Buyer, is attached, and Buyer releases Seller from liability for any physical defects disclosed by the attached report.

_____	_____
Signature of Buyer	Date
_____	_____
Signature of Buyer	Date
_____	_____
Signature of Seller	Date
_____	_____
Signature of Seller	Date

---

and 72 hours). This is sometimes called a "notice to perform" or a "72-hour release clause," and we call it a "Seller's Demand for Removal of Contingencies" in the sample below.

If you can't, the seller can give you written notice ending your contract (wiping it out) and go ahead with a backup offer. The seller can do this to you only if a wipe-out clause was included in the original contract. Wipe-out clauses are most common when an offer is contingent upon your selling an existing house or arranging financing that the seller believes may not come through.

When You Can't Fulfill a Contingency

If, after trying in good faith, you or the seller can't meet a contingency, the deal is over. The most common reasons sales fall through are:

- An inspection turns up expensive physical problems and you decide you no longer want the house, or you and the seller can't agree who will pay.
- You're unable to sell your existing house within the time provided.
- You can't secure adequate financing within the time provided.

Seller's Demand for Removal of Contingencies

Under the terms of the contract dated _____, between (Buyer)

_____ and (Seller)

_____ for the purchase of the real property at (address)

_____, Seller

hereby demands that Buyer remove the following contingency specified in Clause _____ of the contract:

_____

_____

_____

within ☐ ninety-six (96) hours from receipt of this demand if personally delivered.

☐ five (5) days from mailing this demand if mailed by certified mail.

If Buyer does not remove this contingency within the time specified, the contract shall become void. Seller shall promptly return Buyer's deposit upon Buyer's execution of a release, releasing Buyer and Seller from all obligations under the contract.

Signature of Seller _____ Date _____

Signature of Seller _____ Date _____

Personally delivered on: _____ Mailed by certified mail on: _____

You and the seller should sign a release canceling the contract and authorizing the return of your deposit. The seller has no right to keep your deposit if the deal falls through for failure to meet a contingency spelled out in the contract. If the seller refuses, or you refuse, to sign the release within 30 days following a written demand, the person who refuses to sign may be liable to the other for attorneys' fees and damages of three times the amount deposited in escrow, no more than $1,000 and no less than $100. (Civil Code § 1057.3.)

If an inspection turns up negligible problems and you refuse to go ahead with the purchase (or you refuse to proceed for another nonlegitimate reason), the seller can keep your deposit. A seller rarely keeps an entire deposit, however, because the seller will have trouble completing a subsequent sale until the escrow with you terminates; and termination of escrow normally can't happen until your deposit is released. Also, state law generally limits the amount sellers can keep if you default. (See Chapter 16 for our discussion of liquidated damages.)

Even if a buyer withdraws for a non-legitimate reason, it's common for the buyer and seller to compromise, with the seller keeping part of the deposit and some of it being returned to the buyer.

A sample release form is shown below.

Obtain Hazard Insurance

Before finalizing your loan, your lender will require that you purchase hazard coverage to pay the lender in the event your house is damaged or destroyed by fire, smoke, wind, hail, riot, vandalism, or another similar act. Don't balk at the insurance. You're going to want what's required, and probably more. And don't wait until right before escrow closes to start shopping for insurance—it's

---

Release of Real Estate Purchase Contract

(Buyer) _____

and (Seller) _____

hereby mutually release each other from any and all claims with respect to the real estate purchase

contract dated _____ for the property located at: _____

_____ .

It is the intent of this release to declare all rights and obligations arising out of the real estate purchase contract null and void.

☐ Buyer has received his/her deposit.

☐ Seller has directed the escrow holder to return Buyer's deposit.

Signature of Buyer	Date
Signature of Buyer	Date
Signature of Seller	Date
Signature of Seller	Date

getting harder and harder to find a good policy at a reasonable price, due to recent losses and clampdowns in the insurance industry.

Typical Coverage

Virtually all homeowners buy comprehensive homeowners' insurance, not just the minimum hazard insurance required by the lender. In addition to covering your house, homeowners' insurance protects other structures on the property (such as a pool or in-law unit) and your personal property, usually for 50% of the liability limit on your house, unless you pay extra.

A few valuable items, such as art, computer equipment, and antiques, are covered to a specific (low) amount; if you own more, you'll have to itemize them and pay extra. But this may not be the time to skimp—if everything you own is destroyed, say in a fire, being able to rebuild the bare house will be small comfort.

A comprehensive policy will also cover you for some types of personal liability—if the letter carrier trips over your kid's skate-board or a neighbor gets bitten by your dog, your policy will pay for expenses and other losses. In addition, if you injure someone off your property, you will likely be covered if the injury doesn't involve a motor vehicle or your business.

CAUTION

Beware of dogs raising your premiums. Most insurance companies are attaching canine exclusions for dog breeds that are particularly large or have bad reputations. While the various insurance companies are not consistent about which pooches they prohibit, owning an "ineligible" breed could impair your chances of purchasing a policy or result in your paying a policy surcharge.

How much insurance do you need? You should cover the full replacement value of your real property (not including the land) and your personal property. (At least 40%, and often more, of the value is the land itself, which will likely still be there even if your house is destroyed.) The coverage most people select is "extended replacement cost." This pays for replacement of your house up to a certain percentage (often 125%) of what the policy states is the house's value. Such coverage helps protect you if your house's stated value turns out to be less than what it would cost to replace it.

For added protection, you can also buy what's called an "inflation guard." This automatically amends your policy to raise the stated value of your house by a fixed percentage every year. You choose the percentage when you buy the inflation guard.

Fewer and fewer insurance companies write policies for "100% guaranteed replace-ment." This is because such a policy replaces your house at full value even if construction and labor costs have skyrocketed past the house's value as stated in the policy.

Special Insurance Concerns for Home-Based Businesses

If you run a home-based business, don't rely on the standard homeowners' policy to cover business-related losses. For example, many homeowners' policies don't cover damage to detached garages and storage sheds you were using to run a business out of (though storage of business goods is usually okay). If that's where your business will be located, you'll need to purchase extra coverage.

If you'll have business-related visitors, you should also consider buying liability coverage in case they're injured.

And even if your home is not your business's central location, inventory or equipment that you keep at home, particularly if it's worth more than $2,000, will not be covered by the standard homeowners' policy. Ask your insurance broker for more information.

Earthquakes and Floods

Two of the greatest risks facing California homeowners are not even covered in the standard homeowners' insurance policy: earthquakes and floods.

Because of the huge losses earthquakes have caused Californians in the past, the state of California now mandates that your insurance company offer you state-sponsored earthquake insurance, both when you first buy the policy and at every alternate renewal. The offered policy must cover loss or damage to the dwelling and its contents and living expenses for the occupants if the house is temporarily uninhabitable. (Insurance Code §§ 10081, 10089.). You actually have to sign something to decline this coverage.

Unfortunately, the state-sponsored coverage is not highly regarded, so you're better off looking for a private earthquake insurer. Whether you can find private coverage at a price you can afford will depend on where you live and when the last earthquake occurred (immediately after an earthquake, insurance companies stop selling earthquake coverage for a while).

Buying earthquake coverage typically costs at least a few hundred dollars per year. Houses near active faults or made of brick may be more expensive to insure. The problem with earthquake insurance is the high deductible—typically 10% to 15% of the policy amount. That means if you have a $200,000 policy, you won't get any benefits unless the damage is more than $20,000 (with a 10% deductible) or $30,000 (with a 15% deductible).

Another endorsement to consider, if you're one of the thousands of California residents buying a home in a flood zone, is flood coverage. Unfortunately, the extra coverage can be expensive and contain high deductibles. However, lenders require flood insurance for property in designated flood hazard areas. This is an irritant to property owners who live in designated flood areas but who haven't seen a real flood in years. If you're buying a house in such an area, you may be able to avoid buying flood insurance by having your property surveyed to show that it lies above the flood plain. (And, though it's many years away, once your house is paid off, the lender will have no say in whether you buy flood insurance!) Then again, no matter what the lender says, you may want to buy flood insurance if your own research shows a chance of flooding in your area—take a lesson from Hurricane Katrina, where many homeowners found themselves out of luck because their lenders hadn't mandated flood insurance, and they had relied on that in not purchasing insurance. Floods can happen for a myriad of reasons, from snow melt to being near a creek that's been disturbed due to a new housing development.

See Chapter 19 for a discussion of seller disclosures regarding flood, fire, and seismic hazards. Also, see Appendix A for information on the areas of California susceptible to earthquakes, fires, and floods.

Condominiums

If you are buying a condominium, a town house, or some other planned unit development property, consult the CC&Rs to determine what type of insurance protection you should or must buy. Often the homeowners' association buys insurance for all the buildings and the common areas. That leaves you responsible for buying coverage for your personal property (the contents of your unit) and personal liability (that is, claims made against you). But check carefully to see where the HOA insurance ends and yours should begin.

If you have any thoughts of replacing or improving the features of your unit, you should also invest in what's called "alterations and additions" coverage. For example, if

you were to replace the unit's existing cheap painted cabinetry with polished teak, and your unit burned, the association's homeowners' insurance would only cover the value of the cheap cabinets.

> ⓘ **CAUTION**
>
> **Be ready for CC&Rs that make you responsible for holes in the homeowners' association's insurance coverage.** For example, if the club house burns down and the association insurance won't cover the entire loss, a typical set of CC&Rs would allow the association to collect the shortfall from the unit owners. Insurance for this type of unhappy event, called "loss assessment" coverage, can be very cheaply included in your policy.

Shop Around for Insurance

Homeowners' insurance rates can vary up to 30% from company to company, so try to compare rates of several companies. Another way to save money is to opt for a larger-than-usual deductible. By increasing your deductible to $1,000 (or more), you may save 10% or more on your premiums.

Also, ask your insurance agent what discounts are available for new or remodeled houses, or houses with a security system or near a fire hydrant. Some companies also offer discounts if you buy more than one policy from them, for example, an auto as well as a home policy. And, if you're a retiree age 55 or over, you may qualify for a discount of up to 10% at some companies.

Price isn't the only factor to consider when choosing insurance. Some companies are better at processing claims fairly and quickly. If you live near an area where there was a severe fire, earthquake, or flood, ask community organizations which insurers were particularly responsive to consumers (and which ones to avoid).

And then there's the matter of convincing the insurance company that you qualify for insurance. Because the insurance industry in California has taken some economic hits recently, it has gotten skittish about doing the very thing it's supposed to do: sell insurance. You may be refused affordable coverage, or any coverage, based on your home's location, your credit score, your history of filing claims due to mold or water damage, or your history of filing other homeowners' insurance claims.

Your Home's Location

The insurance industry is not allowed to use outright discrimination (known as red-lining) when deciding which localities it will offer policies within. However, insurance underwriters come close to the wire, by following their home offices' guidelines stating that no insurance can be offered in certain "capacity exposure areas." When you apply for homeowners' insurance, the first thing the underwriter will do is to "map" the property. If you reside in a brush area, for example, the underwriter may turn down your application for insurance. If you promise to clear the brush away from your home, you may get a second chance, but woe unto you (and your coverage) if you fail to clear the brush or you allow it to grow back.

Soil instability in the area where your new home is located could also make the home difficult to insure. This seems especially odd given that most homeowner's policies do not even pay claims for earth movement, earthquakes, or soil slippage. However, some underwriters fear that our courts will be overly generous to a homeowner whose house has just been shaken into the mud, and they refuse to issue insurance policies in unstable soil areas.

Your Credit Score

Most insurance companies and their underwriters now order a copy of your credit report before they decide whether to sell you coverage. (That's why they'll ask you for your Social Security number.) Their theory is that if you have bad credit, you might turn in maintenance claims to the insurance company instead of taking care of the property yourself. They call this the "moral hazard."

Past Claims for Water Damage and Mold

The prospect of mushrooming mold claims makes the insurance industry very nervous—especially given the lack of medical information about which molds are dangerously toxic. If you have ever submitted a claim for water damage (in a past home), or if the home you are buying has had any history of water damage, expect difficulty in getting the underwriters to insure your property. Or, if they do agree to insure you, count on a complete mold exclusion or, at best, a pitifully low amount of coverage for any future mold claims, plus a large deductible for claims based on mold or water damage.

How to Make Sure Your Policy Gets Renewed

After making the important decision of which home insurance policy to buy, it's worth taking steps to hang onto it for more than a year. Try to:

- **Pay your premiums when they are due.** Don't allow your insurance policy to lapse or be cancelled due to late payments. Once you've had a policy cancelled for any reason, finding a replacement policy will be an uphill battle.
- **Think twice about turning in claims.** Unless your house has gone through major damage, any money that you realize by filing a claim may be wiped out by a resulting increase in your premium, or the cancellation of your insurance when it's time for renewal. With this in mind, ask your agent to increase your policy deductible—up to $2,500 to $5,000 is a safe amount, if your lender will allow it—and take advantage of the premium credit that will result. (Why have a low deductible if you won't be filing claims for these relatively low amounts, anyway?) Then save up money for home maintenance and fix those minor problems yourself, without even contacting your insurance company.
- **Cooperate with your insurance company.** If your insurance underwriter asks numerous questions during the application process, or sends you a questionnaire about you and your home at renewal time, call your agent. Find out what's going on and get back to the underwriter as soon as you can. Don't give the company an excuse to cancel your policy based on noncooperation.
- **Keep up with basic home maintenance.** Don't ignore little problems that could turn into big ones, such as leaking roofs and plumbing problems. If you aren't attuned to home repair issues, bring in a professional to assess your home's condition.
- **If you need additional help, get in touch with an experienced insurance broker.**

By the way, if you've got a decent insurance policy, hang onto it. Jumping from one insurance company to another in an effort to save a few dollars is not worth your time. Just when you get another policy, your new company is likely to institute a rate increase to catch up with the competition.

Other Past Claims

You might have thought that the purpose of insurance was to collect on it when you need to—but think again. To keep its risks low, insurance companies have recently been trying to insure only those homeowners who won't actually use the insurance! Your history of filing claims on the home you are leaving, as well as the seller's history of filing claims on the home you are buying, will all be taken into account. Yes, you heard right, even claims on your former home and claims that someone else made will be counted against you in the underwriting process. (Of course, if you are purchasing a brand new home or one in which you are the first owner, you'll have only your own past claims to contend with.)

Do You Need Life Insurance?

Some insurance companies will try to sell you life insurance or credit insurance so your heirs can pay off the mortgage if you die. Unless your survivors could not afford the monthly payments without you, don't bother. Even then, look for a policy that lets your survivors use the money as they wish, not just to pay off the mortgage. For this purpose, a term policy covering the period for which survivors (often small children) are vulnerable to losing the house if you die is far cheaper than a whole life policy, and just as good.

How Insurance Relates to the Closing

Once you arrange your insurance, have your insurance agent deliver your policy to the escrow holder before closing. Your lender will not approve your loan until your insurance takes effect. Many lenders will want you to prepay the first year of hazard insurance by the closing; ask if you can pay semiannually, quarterly, or monthly, if your budget is tight.

RESOURCE

Insurance information. For general information on homeowner's insurance, including premium comparisons among some of the state's larger companies, or to file a complaint about an insurance company, contact the Department of Insurance Consumer Hotline in Los Angeles, at 800-927-4357; www.insurance.ca.gov. Also, www.insure.com has a wide variety of useful information on homeowner's insurance. Check the websites of individual companies such as State Farm or Allstate as well.

CAUTION

After you find earthquake insurance, make sure your mortgage lender won't claim first dibs on the proceeds. Some mortgage agreements (deeds of trust) require that the lender be the primary payee of any earthquake insurance proceeds. The lender then collects amounts owing on the mortgage and dictates how whatever is left will be used for repairs. Worse yet, a California court has upheld this practice. (*Martin v. World Savings*, 92 Cal.App.4th 803 (2001).) Read your loan paperwork carefully.

Obtain Title Report and Title Insurance

Title insurance protects both you and your lender against unknown clouds on the legal title to the property. The title insurance company insures against the possibility of undisclosed legal challenges or liens against the property, such as an unrecorded deed, a forged deed, or an unrecorded easement— the right of someone else to use your property for a specific purpose (for example, the right the previous owner granted your neighbor to share your extra-wide driveway). If you think you might sell the house within the next two years, ask your title insurer about a "binder" policy that will give you a refund when you resell.

What Are Liens?

A lien is a claim for money, with property as security (collateral) for payment. Other common liens are for unpaid taxes and debts owed to contractors who worked on the property but were never paid (called a mechanic's lien).

Financial institutions require title insurance whenever they finance a house sale. As soon as you and the seller sign the house purchase contract, you should order a preliminary title report (also called a prelim or pre) on the property. Your offer should make your approval of a preliminary title report a contingency. (In northern California, the escrow holder—a title insurance company—will often order the policy itself.) This report is a statement summarizing the current condition of the title to the property, including liens; encumbrances; covenants, conditions, and restrictions (CC&Rs); and easements. You want the prelim early in escrow so that you, the seller, and the lender have time to address any problems that turn up.

The most common problems require the seller to pay off liens from the sale proceeds. These problems threaten your deal with the seller only if the seller disputes the lien and refuses to instruct the escrow holder to pay the lienholder. Other problems include a newly discovered easement, lawsuits disputing the boundary line or filed against the seller, an unknown heir (if the previous owner recently died), or an unexpected owner (such as a previous spouse). If any of these situations come up, the seller will likely need the help of a lawyer.

If problems arise with the title that the seller cannot quickly resolve, you can refuse to go through with the sale, give the seller an extension of time (if you think the extra time will help), or buy the house with less-than-perfect title. Deciding to do this is beyond the scope of this book; consult an experienced real estate lawyer.

If you pay all cash or borrow from Uncle Stanley, or if the seller takes back a second, you (or you and Uncle Stanley or you and the seller) must decide whether to buy title insurance. We recommend it, even if you search the title yourself at the county recorder's office and believe title is clear. In the future, you don't want any unpleasant surprises.

Financial institutions require a California Land Title Association (CLTA) policy and an American Land Title Association (ALTA) policy. The CLTA policy covers items in the public record, such as mortgage liens, trust deed liens, or judgment liens. The ALTA policy is more extensive, insuring against claims found both in the public record and by physically inspecting the house, such as unrecorded easements, boundary disputes, and physical encroachments.

The policies also differ regarding how much they cover and whom they benefit. The CLTA policy insures to the amount of the purchase price and benefits you. The ALTA policy insures to the amount of the loan and benefits the lender. If you'll occupy the house, the CLTA policy you receive will include the same extended coverage the lender gets on the ALTA policy. If you won't be occupying the house, you can buy the extended coverage for about 30% above the policy cost.

RESOURCE

CLTA and ALTA policies. For more information on CLTA policies, phone 916-444-2647 or check the CLTA website at www.clta.org.

For information on ALTA polices, phone 800-787-ALTA or check the ALTA website at www.alta.org.

Before closing, the title insurance company will check the public records for any changes since the prelim was issued. If all is the same (as is the usual case), the prelim becomes the final title report. If there are any changes, they'll be reported in a supplemental title report. You and your lender must decide whether to close or call the deal off.

Conduct Final Physical Inspection of Property

A few days before escrow closes, reinspect the property to make sure everything is in order. Your contract should give you the right to do so. You'll want to make sure:

- No damage has occurred to the house since you agreed to buy it.
- The fixtures and personal property the seller agreed to sell you are still in the house.
- Smoke detectors are installed in all sleeping rooms as required by state law. (Health and Safety Code §§ 13113.7 and 13113.8.)
- The water heater has been braced, anchored, or strapped to resist falling or displacement during an earthquake. (Health and Safety Code § 19211.)
- All agreed-upon work has been done to your satisfaction (this is especially important with new houses).
- The house is empty—that is, the seller (or tenant) has moved (unless your agreement lets him or her stay longer) and hasn't left piles of unwanted possessions behind.

If you discover a problem during this final inspection, you can:

- Insist that the closing be delayed until the seller fixes the problem.
- Insist that the seller credit you in escrow with a sum of money sufficient for you to remedy the problem—this means you pay that much less for the house.

- Conclude that the problem isn't significant and close anyway.

If you're at a real deadlock, consider mediation, as many standard real estate contracts require.

If you're buying a new house, be sure to reread Chapter 7 on dealing with final inspections, construction delays, and other problems.

TIP

Ask the sellers to accompany you during the final inspection or to give you a post-inspection "tour." Every house has its quirks and mysteries—how to light the old gas oven, the identity of garden plants, and more. If negotiations have remained friendly, going through the house with the sellers can yield a wealth of information. Prepare questions in advance. If you're happy with how the house has been maintained, ask for the names of the sellers' gardener, painter, and other servicepeople.

Closing Escrow

Until all contingencies in your offer are re-moved, no firm closing date can be set. Thus, during the early and middle stages of an escrow, the closing date is projected, not firm.

The paperwork necessary for closing escrow should be completed a minimum of four working days before the expected closing date. This allows for delays in the transmittal of the loan documents between the lender(s) and the escrow holder. The buyers and sellers usually sign closing docu-ments at different times, making separate visits to the escrow holder's office.

For safety's sake, it's also best to arrange to have any down payment money and other cash that will be part of your purchase arrive at the escrow office a day or two before the closing. Especially if you will use a nonlocal check, ask the escrow holder how many days in advance of closing your check must be submitted. Using a cashier's check is usually cheaper than arranging for a wire transfer from your bank to the escrow holder's bank.

Once the escrow officer has the necessary documents from both seller and you, along with your down payment and the loan proceeds, the officer will prepare a new deed, naming you as the owner. The escrow officer will send the new deed to the county recorder's office, which will record the deed the next day. The seller will receive his or her check late in the day that escrow closes. Others may also be paid out of the sale proceeds, for example, the seller's lender and any lienholders. (These procedures are very different from those in many other states, where the buyer, seller, and agents sit around the closing table, swap deeds and cashier's checks, and complete the sale the same day.)

The forms you'll be required to sign may include:

- Final escrow instructions. In northern California, the escrow holder prepares two slightly different sets of instruc-tions—one for the seller and one for the buyer—so read them carefully to be sure that you and the seller are in agreement; in southern California, the buyer and seller sign identical escrow instructions.
- Copy of the preliminary title report.

County Property Taxes and Exemptions

When real estate is sold in California, the county assesses the value of the property and imposes property taxes accordingly. This will be done shortly after you close on the sale.

Take a careful look at the assessment statement. If you will live in the house, most counties allow you to a yearly homeowner's property tax exemption of up to $7,000 on the assessed value of the property. If you move in after March 1, you are entitled to 80% of the full amount for the first year. If the assessment statement does not include the exemption, call your county tax assessor's office and find out how to file for it.

When a house sells for more than the previous assessed value, the county will issue a supplemental tax bill that accounts for the difference in price. The county issues this bill during the first year after you buy your home. If, for example, the house was previously assessed at $180,000, and you paid $540,000, you'll receive a supplementary tax bill representing the $360,000 difference—or, depending on the timing of your purchase, a portion of the difference. The bill will be prorated according to how far into the tax year you bought the house. Tax years run from July 1st to June 30th of the following year. So if you purchase your home on September 30, 2011, your tax bill will cover only the period from October 1, 2011 through June 30, 2012.

- Deed of trust (and other forms) from the lender.
- Copies of structural pest control and other inspection reports.
- FIRPTA (Foreign Investment in Real Property Tax Act) statement.
- Fund disbursement (or loan assumption) documents provided by the lender.
- Any rental agreement between you and the seller if the seller will live in the house for a while after the close.
- Settlement statement listing all costs, prepared by the escrow holder.
- Statements authorizing an impound account.
- A perjury statement where you attest to the truth of the information you provided.
- Statement showing your hazard insurance coverage.

If rehabilitation work must be done to repair damage or substandard conditions discovered in an inspection report, money may be held by the escrow holder after the sale closes to pay the contractor.

Chapter 21 covers what happens if there are delays or problems during escrow.

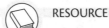 RESOURCE

Where to complain about an escrow or title insurance company. If you have any problem with your escrow company, contact the Department of Corporations at 800-275-2677, or check www.corp.ca.gov ("Consumer Complaints" area); this state agency regulates independent escrow companies. The Department of Insurance oversees title insurance companies and can be reached at 800-927-4357 or www.insurance.ca.gov.

Closing Costs and Loan Fees

Closing costs and loan fees usually add up to 2%–5% of your purchase price. Some fees are paid when you take out the loan, or at the same time you arrange inspection reports, but most are paid the day you close escrow. Not all lenders and escrow holders require all the fees (some are waived as part of special offers). When escrow closes, you'll receive a statement with an itemized list of the closing costs.

Here are typical closing costs and loan fees.

Appraisal fees. Charged by an appraiser hired by the lender to be sure the property is worth what you've agreed to pay. Fees usually run between $325 and $450 for a regular-sized single-family home, and somewhat more for a very large or multiple-unit building. (See Chapter 13 for more on appraisals.)

Lender fee. Loan application fees (typically $650 to $1,300) cover the lender's cost of processing your loan.

Assumption fee. Typically 1% of the loan balance to assume the seller's existing loan.

Attorneys' fees. If problems develop, such as the need to evaluate or clear title, you may need to hire an attorney, at around $200 per hour.

Credit report. Should cost around $20 to check your credit. While standard credit checks cost less, for home loans the lender checks at least two credit reporting agencies and the county records for judgment and tax liens.

Escrow company fees. An escrow company that is not a title insurance company may charge a nominal fee for doing the escrow work.

Junk fees. Real estate business slang for a number of small and unexpected fees,

including administrative, courier, and filing fees, which typically run from $150 to $250. You can negotiate to have the more ridiculous ones removed.

Loan fees. This includes points (one point is 1% of the loan principal) and an additional fee, usually between $100 and $450.

Physical inspection reports. May add several hundred dollars or more, depending on how many are requested. If you pay these at the time of the inspection directly to the inspectors, you can save a few dollars. Escrow companies will charge $25–$50 if they pay off your inspectors in escrow.

Prepaid homeowners' insurance. Amount as required by lenders, typically one year; depends on the house's value, level of coverage, and location.

Prepaid interest on the loan. You'll be asked to pay per diem interest in advance, from the date your loan is funded to the end of that month. The maximum you'll be charged is 30 days of interest.

Prepaid property taxes. Depends on tax assessment; covers the time period between closing and your first monthly mortgage payment. Some lenders have you prepay one or two months in addition.

Private mortgage insurance. As discussed in Chapter 4, if you make a down payment of less than 20%, most lenders will require private mortgage insurance, or PMI. You will probably need to pay a few months' worth of PMI premiums at the close of escrow. It's usually calculated at 0.52 of the loan amount, divided

Closing Costs and Loan Fees (continued)

by 12. On a $300,000 loan, that's $130 per month.

Recording and filing fees. The escrow holder will charge about $100 for drawing up, reviewing, and recording the deed of trust and other legal documents. The total escrow and title fees can amount to 0.5% of the loan.

Survey fee. May be needed to show plot measurements if house has easements; will run about $300.

Tax service fee. Issued to notify the lender if you default on your property taxes; usually costs about $75 to $80.

Title search and title insurance. Only in northern California does the buyer pay the title costs. Most lenders require title insurance for the face amount of their mortgage or for the value of their loan. Title insurance is a one-time premium that averages about $900.

Transfer tax. Tax assessed by the county when the property changes hands. Usually split with seller, in which case it costs about $1.10 per $1,000. Many cities also charge transfer tax; it varies city to city, but usually is not more than 1.5% of the purchase price.

Check Out a House's Condition

Before you finalize your house purchase, you'll want to check out its condition. If the house is in good shape, you can proceed knowing that you're getting what you paid for. But the few hundred dollars you spend may save you thousands later. If inspections discover problems, you can negotiate with the seller to pay for necessary repairs or back out of the deal, assuming your contract is written to allow that.

CAUTION

Don't rely solely on inspection reports from the seller. Sellers often commission a full set of inspections and provide buyers with a comprehensive "Disclosure Package" that can be over 100 pages long. Read these carefully, but don't rely on them solely. The seller's report may be from the most optimistic inspector they could find. Even if the inspector spots a problem, his or her analysis of what's needed to correct it may tend toward the low-cost solutions. What's more, the California Department of Real Estate reports that it is "not uncommon" for sellers who don't like the results of one report to commission a second one, and then present the more favorable-looking one to buyers.

Short History of California House Inspections

Until the mid-1980s, California houses, like houses in most states, were sold with a caveat emptor (buyer beware) approach. As long as the seller didn't fraudulently conceal defects, the buyer was responsible for discovering the physical problems. Not

surprisingly, with this system, buyers and their lenders were very concerned not to miss major defects in the house. Unfortunately, this usually only involved hiring a pest inspector—and pest inspectors rarely know about or checked the complex systems in the house (like electricity or plumbing) or structural defects unrelated to pests.

Sometimes, it later became obvious that the seller (and sometimes his agent) knew about a particular undiscovered defect but never said a word. California courts began to question this "find-it-if-you-can" system and started holding sellers and their agents financially liable for not disclosing known problems. Several state and local laws now require sellers to provide specific information on the condition of the house as well as disclose potential hazards like floods, earthquakes, and environmental hazards

The new statutes aren't the end of the story—California courts still require sellers to disclose any negative fact that could reasonably be expected to lower the value of the property. (See *Reed v. King*, 145 Cal. App.3d 261 (1983).) The sellers must even disclose any "psychological defects," or that the house is of "ill repute"—or else face liability. For example, in the *Reed* case, the sellers sold their house without revealing that it had been the site of a multiple murder ten years before—a fact that appraisers said brought the property's value down significantly. Courts in various states have looked to the *Reed* case to decide that sellers should have disclosed a previous suicide, neighborhood noise, groundwater contamination, and more.

Real Estate Transfer Disclosure Statement

State law requires sellers to tell you a lot about the condition of the house on a Real Estate Transfer Disclosure Statement form ("TDS" in real estate shorthand). (Civil Code § 1102.) The TDS includes three types of disclosures:

- items included in the property, such as a burglar alarm or trash compactor
- information on defects or malfunctions in the building's structure, such as the roof or windows
- a variety of special issues, such as the existence of a homeowners' association (and any covenants, conditions, and restrictions, or CC&Rs), environmental hazards like asbestos and lead-based paint, whether remodeling was done with permits and met local building codes, and neighborhood noise problems or nuisances.

We include a sample Real Estate Transfer Disclosure Statement (TDS) here. The TDS you'll be handed as part of your purchase should contain the identical language, as the disclosures are specified by state law. (Civil Code § 1102.6.)

 CAUTION

Exemptions from transfer disclosure statement. Certain properties, including foreclosures and probate sales and buildings with more than four units, are exempt from state disclosure laws. In these cases, be extra sure to get a professional home inspection before closing the deal.

Examining the Seller's Disclosure Statement

Sellers must provide you a copy of the Transfer Disclosure Statement "as soon as practicable before transfer of title." (Civil Code § 1102.3.) It's to your advantage to get a copy of the TDS as soon as possible; you don't want to invest the time and money in the house-buying process only to discover problems just before you close escrow.

Often, seller's disclosure forms are only cursorily filled out, and you'll need to ask questions for additional information. If the form you receive is sparse, you're confused about any of the seller's disclosures, or you simply want more details, make a written request for more information; send a copy to the seller's agent and keep a copy for yourself. Insist on a written response from the seller.

In your request, ask not only for elaboration on the Real Estate Transfer Disclosure Statement, but also for any other recent inspection reports the seller may have authorized, such as a pest inspection (especially if you're in southern California). In addition, ask for copies of any home insurance claims reports. The key here is not merely to discover previous damage, but to see how much insurance claim activity took place. As discussed in Chapter 18, a history of "too many" claims can lead to high premiums on your policy, or even to an uninsurable house. Be particularly concerned if you see any past claims for water damage, which make insurance companies skittish.

Real Estate Transfer Disclosure Statement
(California Civil Code § 1102.6)

THIS DISCLOSURE STATEMENT CONCERNS THE REAL PROPERTY SITUATED IN THE CITY OF _____, COUNTY OF _____, STATE OF CALIFORNIA, DESCRIBED AS _____ _____ . THIS STATEMENT IS A DISCLOSURE OF THE CONDITION OF THE ABOVE-DESCRIBED PROPERTY IN COMPLIANCE WITH SECTION 1102 OF THE CIVIL CODE AS OF _____, 20_____ . IT IS NOT A WARRANTY OF ANY KIND BY THE SELLER(S) OR ANY AGENT(S) REPRESENTING ANY PRINCIPAL(S) IN THIS TRANSACTION, AND IT IS NOT A SUBSTITUTE FOR ANY INSPECTIONS OR WARRANTIES THE PRINCIPAL(S) MAY WISH TO OBTAIN.

I
Coordination With Other Disclosure Forms

This Real Estate Transfer Disclosure Statement is made pursuant to Section 1102 of the Civil Code. Other statutes require disclosures, depending upon the details of the particular real estate transaction (for example: special study zone and purchase-money liens on residential property).

Substituted Disclosures: The following disclosures and other disclosures required by law, including the Natural Hazard Disclosure Report/Statement that may include airport annoyances, earthquake, fire, flood, or special assessment information, have been or will be made in connection with this real estate transfer, and are intended to satisfy the disclosure obligations on this form, where the subject matter is the same:

☐ Inspection reports completed pursuant to the contract of sale or receipt for deposit.

☐ Additional inspection reports or disclosures: _____ _____ _____

II
Seller's Information

The Seller discloses the following information with the knowledge that even though this is not a warranty, prospective Buyers may rely on this information in deciding whether and on what terms to purchase the subject property. Seller hereby authorizes any agent(s) representing any principal(s) in this transaction to provide a copy of this statement to any person or entity in connection with any actual or anticipated sale of the property.

THE FOLLOWING ARE REPRESENTATIONS MADE BY THE SELLER(S) AND ARE NOT THE REPRESENTATIONS OF THE AGENT(S), IF ANY. THIS INFORMATION IS A DISCLOSURE AND IT IS NOT INTENDED TO BE PART OF ANY CONTRACT BETWEEN THE BUYER AND SELLER.

Seller ☐ is ☐ is not occupying the property.

A. The subject property has the items checked below (read across):*

☐ Range	☐ Oven	☐ Microwave
☐ Dishwasher	☐ Trash Compactor	☐ Garbage Disposal
☐ Washer/Dryer Hookups	☐ Rain Gutters	☐ Carbon Monoxide Device(s)
☐ Burglar Alarms	☐ Smoke Detector(s)	☐ Fire Alarm
☐ TV Antenna	☐ Satellite Dish	☐ Intercom
☐ Central Heating	☐ Central Air Conditioning	☐ Evaporator Cooler(s)
☐ Wall/Window Air Conditioning	☐ Sprinklers	☐ Public Sewer System
☐ Septic Tank	☐ Sump Pump	☐ Water Softener
☐ Patio/Decking	☐ Built-in Barbecue	☐ Gazebo
☐ Sauna	☐ Hot Tub ☐ Locking Safety Cover	
☐ Pool ☐ Child-Resistant Barrier	☐ Spa ☐ Locking Safety Cover	
☐ Security Gate(s)	☐ Automatic Garage Door Opener(s)	☐ Number of Remote Controls
☐ Garage: ☐ Attached	☐ Not Attached	☐ Carport
☐ Pool/Spa Heater: ☐ Gas	☐ Solar	☐ Electric
☐ Water Heater: ☐ Gas	☐ Solar	
☐ Water Supply: ☐ City	☐ Well ☐ Bottled	☐ Private Utility or ☐ Other _____
☐ Gas Supply: ☐ Utility		
☐ Window Screens	☐ Window Security Bars ☐ Quick Release Mechanism on Bedroom Windows	
☐ Exhaust Fan(s) in	☐ 220 Volt Wiring in	☐ Fireplace(s) in
☐ Gas Starter _____	Roof(s): Type: _____	Age: (approx.) _____

Other: _____

Are there, to the best of your (Seller's) knowledge, any of the above that are not in operating condition? ☐ Yes ☐ No. If yes, then describe. (Attach additional sheets if necessary):

_____

* Installation of a listed appliance, device, or amenity is not a precondition of sale or transfer of the dwelling. The carbon monoxide device, garage door opener, or child-resistant pool barrier may not be in compliance with the safety standards relating to, respectively, carbon monoxide device standards of Chapter 8 (commencing with Section 13260) of Part 2 of Division 12 of, automatic reversing device stands of Chapter 12.5 (commencing with Section 19890) of Part 3 of Division 13 of, or with the pool safety standards of Article 2.5 (commencing with Section 115920) Chapter 5 of Part 10 of Division 104 of, the Health and Safety Code.

Window security bars may not have quick-release mechanisms in compliance with the 1995 Edition of the California Building Standards Code.

B. Are you (Seller) aware of any significant defects/malfunctions in any of the following?

☐ Yes ☐ No. If yes, check appropriate space(s) below.

☐ Interior Walls ☐ Ceilings ☐ Floors ☐ Exterior Walls ☐ Insulation

☐ Roof(s) ☐ Windows ☐ Doors ☐ Foundation ☐ Slab(s)

☐ Driveways ☐ Sidewalks ☐ Walls/Fences ☐ Electrical Systems ☐ Plumbing/Sewers/Septics

☐ Other Structural Components (describe): _____

If any of the above is checked, explain. (Attach additional sheets if necessary): _____

_____

_____

C. Are you (Seller) aware of any of the following?

☐ Yes ☐ No   1. Substances, materials, or products which may be an environmental hazard such as, but not limited to, asbestos, formaldehyde, radon gas, lead-based paint, mold, fuel or chemical storage tanks, and contaminated soil or water on the subject property.

☐ Yes ☐ No   2. Features of the property shared in common with adjoining landowners, such as walls, fences, and driveways, whose use or responsibility for maintenance may have an effect on the subject property.

☐ Yes ☐ No   3. Any encroachments, easements, or similar matters that may affect your interest in the subject property.

☐ Yes ☐ No   4. Room additions, structural modifications, or other alterations or repairs made without necessary permits.

☐ Yes ☐ No   5. Room additions, structural modifications, or other alterations or repairs not in compliance with building codes.

☐ Yes ☐ No   6. Fill (compacted or otherwise) on the property or any portion thereof.

☐ Yes ☐ No   7. Any settling from any cause, or slippage, sliding, or other soil problems.

☐ Yes ☐ No   8. Flooding, drainage, or grading problems.

☐ Yes ☐ No   9. Major damage to the property or any other structures from fire, earthquake, floods, or landslides.

☐ Yes ☐ No   10. Any zoning violations, nonconforming uses, or violations of "setback" requirements.

☐ Yes ☐ No   11. Neighborhood noise problems or other nuisances.

☐ Yes ☐ No   12. CC&Rs or other deed restrictions or obligations.

☐ Yes ☐ No   13. Homeowners' Association which has any authority over the subject property.

☐ Yes ☐ No   14. Any "common area" (facilities such as pools, tennis courts, walkways, or other areas co-owned in undivided interest with others).

☐ Yes ☐ No   15. Any notices of abatement or citations against the property.

☐ Yes ☐ No   16. Any lawsuits by or against the Seller threatening to or affecting this real property, including any lawsuits alleging a defect or deficiency in this real property or "common areas" (facilities such as pools, tennis courts, walkways, or other areas co-owned in undivided interest with others).

If the answer to any of these is yes, explain (attach additional sheets if necessary):_____

_____

_____

_____

D.

1. The Seller certifies that the property, as of the close of escrow, will be in compliance with Section 13113.8 of the Health and Safety Code by having operable smoke detectors(s) which are approved, listed, and installed in accordance with the State Fire Marshal's regulations and applicable local standards.

2. The Seller certifies that the property, as of the close of escrow, will be in compliance with Section 19211 of the Health and Safety Code by having the water heater tank(s) braced, anchored, or strapped in place in accordance with applicable law.

Seller certifies that the information herein is true and correct to the best of the Seller's knowledge as of the date signed by the Seller.

Seller _____   Date _____

Seller _____   Date _____

III
Agent's Inspection Disclosure (Listing Agent)

(To be completed only if the Seller is represented by an agent in this transaction.)

THE UNDERSIGNED, BASED ON THE ABOVE INQUIRY OF THE SELLER(S) AS TO THE CONDITION OF THE PROPERTY AND BASED ON REASONABLY COMPETENT AND DILIGENT VISUAL INSPECTION OF THE ACCESSIBLE AREAS OF THE PROPERTY IN CONJUNCTION WITH THAT INQUIRY, STATES THE FOLLOWING:

☐ Agent notes no items for disclosure.

☐ Agent notes the following items: _____

_____

_____

_____

_____

Agent (Broker obtaining the offer) _____

By _____
      (Associate Licensee or Broker Signature)

Date _____

IV
Agent's Inspection Disclosure

(To be completed only if the agent who has obtained the offer is other than the agent above.)

THE UNDERSIGNED, BASED ON A REASONABLY COMPETENT AND DILIGENT VISUAL INSPECTION OF THE ACCESSIBLE AREAS OF THE PROPERTY, STATES THE FOLLOWING:

☐ Agent notes no items for disclosure.

☐ Agent notes the following items: _____

Agent (Broker obtaining the offer) _____

By _____
      (Associate Licensee or Broker Signature)

Date _____

V

BUYER(S) AND SELLER(S) MAY WISH TO OBTAIN PROFESSIONAL ADVICE AND/OR INSPECTIONS OF THE PROPERTY AND TO PROVIDE FOR APPROPRIATE PROVISIONS IN A CONTRACT BETWEEN BUYER(S) AND SELLER(S) WITH RESPECT TO ANY ADVICE/INSPECTION/DEFECTS.

I/We acknowledge receipt of a copy of this statement.

Seller _____ Date _____

Seller _____ Date _____

Buyer _____ Date _____

Buyer _____ Date _____

Agent (Broker Representing Seller) _____

By _____
  (Associate Licensee or Broker Signature)

Date _____

Agent (Broker obtaining the offer) _____

By _____
  (Associate Licensee or Broker Signature)

Date _____

SECTION 1102.3 OF THE CIVIL CODE PROVIDES A BUYER WITH THE RIGHT TO RESCIND A PURCHASE CONTRACT FOR AT LEAST THREE DAYS AFTER THE DELIVERY OF THIS DISCLOSURE, IF DELIVERY OCCURS AFTER THE SIGNING OF AN OFFER TO PURCHASE. IF YOU WISH TO RESCIND THE CONTRACT, YOU MUST ACT WITHIN THE PRESCRIBED PERIOD.

A REAL ESTATE BROKER IS QUALIFIED TO ADVISE ON REAL ESTATE. IF YOU DESIRE LEGAL ADVICE, CONSULT YOUR ATTORNEY.

Sample Letter Requesting Further Seller's Disclosure

February 22, 20xx

Dear _____:

I have received your Real Estate Transfer Disclosure Statement, dated _____ .
In item _____, you indicate that _____ .
Please explain this condition more fully. Specifically, I would appreciate your letting me know in writing answers to the following questions:

1. _____

2. _____

3. _____

Also, please send me copies of any inspectors' reports that deal with any aspect of the physical condition of the property, and copies of all home insurance claim reports. Thank you for your cooperation.

Sincerely,

Also, be sure to carefully read the visual disclosures made by your agent and the seller's agent. The seller may not notice obvious defects he or she has lived with every day (such as cuts in linoleum or spots of mold on the walls). Therefore, the agent might be the only one to mention these issues.

Real Estate Agents' Disclosures

California law requires licensed real estate agents (brokers and salespeople) to conduct a "reasonably competent and diligent" visual inspection of property and to disclose to you anything that would affect the "value or desirability" of the property—that is, anything that would be likely to affect your decision to buy. (Civil Code §§ 2079, 2079.3.)

This obligation is on both your agent and the agent representing the seller. Agents do not have to inspect inaccessible areas (such as the sealed-off underside of the porch) or review public documents affecting title to or use of the property. Similarly, agents are not required to explain the legal ramifications of their disclosures.

When to Go Beyond the Real Estate Transfer Disclosure Statement

In addition to considering at face value the information disclosed, examine the disclosure statement for clues to other problems, and follow up with a professional inspection.

For example, if the seller says that several windows won't open, they may simply be painted shut. But it's also possible that the house has settled and the window frames are no longer properly aligned. Similarly, cracks in the dining room ceiling may mean no more than that the plaster is old, or they may be a clue to significant earth movement or to an otherwise unstable foundation. In either case, have the foundation checked extra carefully.

Handling Problems With the Transfer Disclosure Statement

The law specifically allows buyers, in deciding whether and on what terms to buy the house, to rely on a seller's disclosure statement. Even if your offer was not contingent upon your approving inspection reports, state law allows a person to terminate an offer to purchase real property three days after personal delivery of a Real Estate Transfer Disclosure Statement (five days from mailing). (Civil Code § 1102.3.) A buyer may alternatively decide to proceed with the sale and negotiate the cost of making repairs with the seller.

Although sellers and agents need disclose only defects within their personal knowledge, some sellers worry about being sued. They're afraid they won't be able to prove that they didn't know about a certain problem. In short, they now have a good reason to discover and disclose defects, just as do buyers.

A wise seller will disclose all possible (and sometimes even imagined) defects to protect against possible future lawsuits, often in a supplement to the TDS. On a supplementary form recommended by some San

Francisco real estate agents, for instance, sellers are asked to answer if they are aware of any problems, such as damages caused by animals, neighborhood animal problems, criminal activities on the property, or diseased trees on the property.

Disclosures Required With FHA Loans

The Department of Housing and Urban Development (HUD) requires disclosures regarding home inspections for borrowers seeking Federal Housing Administration (FHA) financing. All FHA borrowers must be given a form, "The Importance of a Home Inspection." This form must be signed and dated by the borrower before the execution of the sales contract. For more information on FHA loans, see Chapter 11.

Not all sellers and agents are savvy enough to provide detailed disclosures. Some still try to cover up serious problems, hoping that you and your inspector won't find them. The seller may be sued later, but some sellers don't think this far ahead. (For handling these types of legal problems, see Chapter 21.)

Natural Hazard Disclosure Statement

The Transfer Disclosure Statement discussed in the previous section includes information on many hazards affecting the house, some of which require additional disclosures. Many of these are made on the Natural

Hazard Disclosure Statement, which indicates whether the property is in one of the following hazard zones (Civil Code § 1103.2):

- a flood hazard zone designated by the Federal Emergency Management Agency (FEMA)
- an area of potential flooding due to failure of a dam as identified by the Office of Emergency Services on an "inundation map" (Government Code § 8589.5)
- a very high fire hazard severity zone designated by a local agency (Government Code §§ 51178, 51179)
- a state-designated wildland fire area zone (Public Resources Code § 4125)
- a delineated earthquake fault zone as identified by the California State Geologist (Public Resources Code § 2622)
- a seismic hazards zone (area where landslides and liquefaction are most likely to occur) as defined under Public Resources Code § 2696, or
- an airport annoyance area or one subject to special tax assessments (Civil Code § 1103.4).

These designations are often puzzling, at least to a layperson. For example, San Francisco is not within an earthquake fault zone. That's because the fault line isn't in San Francisco—although San Francisco has certainly experienced the ravages of earthquakes.

Also, sometimes the available maps and information are not of sufficient accuracy or scale for a seller to determine whether the property falls inside a designated hazard zone, such as a high fire hazard severity zone. In this case, the law requires the seller to mark "Yes" on the Natural Hazard Disclosure Statement—unless the seller has evidence, such as a report from a licensed engineer, that the property is not in the particular zone. (Civil Code § 1102.4.) More and more sellers, however, don't even fill this form out on their own, but instead pay a few hundred dollars to a company that generates a report based on the lot and block number of the home in question (or using the street address, to make it even easier). The reports carry explanatory language about how the various zones are set up legally and what their designations mean.

We include a sample Natural Hazard Disclosure Statement (NHDS) here so that you can familiarize yourself with this form. The NHDS you receive should contain identical language, as the disclosures are specified by state law (but it may contain extra language if prepared by an outside company). Examine the Natural Hazard Disclosure Statement and follow up on any questions or problems. Also, check with the local planning department for more information on earthquake hazards in the area. And see Appendix A, Welcome to California, which discusses areas of the state susceptible to various natural disasters and includes resources for more information on fires, floods, and earthquakes.

TIP

Alternative disclosure form. A seller may provide these disclosures on a Local Option Real Estate Disclosure Statement, described under "Local Disclosures," below.

Earthquake and Seismic Disclosures

To help buyers make earthquake-informed decisions, the seller must indicate on the Natural Hazard Disclosure Statement whether the property is in an earthquake fault zone or a seismic hazard zone. In addition, state law requires sellers to provide information on the safety of the house itself and its ability to resist earthquakes.

Residential Earthquake Hazards Report

The seller must tell you whether the property has any known seismic deficiencies, such as whether or not the house is bolted or anchored to the foundation and whether cripple walls, if any, are braced. (Government Code § 8897.) The seller is not required to hire anyone to help evaluate the house or to strengthen any weaknesses that exist. If the house was built in 1960 or later, oral disclosure is enough.

If the house was built before 1960, the seller must disclose in writing and sign the disclosure form, Residential Earthquake Hazards Report, included in a booklet called the *Homeowner's Guide to Earthquake Safety*. The seller must give the buyer a copy of this booklet and disclosure "as soon as practicable before the transfer." (Government Code § 8897.1.)

RESOURCE

The *Homeowner's Guide to Earthquake Safety* is available from the California Seismic Safety Commission (CSSC) at 916-263-5506, or www.seismic.ca.gov. This booklet provides

Natural Hazard Disclosure Statement

This statement applies to the following property: _____.

The transferor and his or her agent(s) or a third-party consultant disclose the following information with the knowledge that even though this is not a warranty, prospective transferees may rely on this information in deciding whether and on what terms to purchase the subject property. Transferor hereby authorizes any agent(s) representing any principal(s) in this action to provide a copy of this statement to any person or entity in connection with any actual or anticipated sale of the property.

The following are representations made by the transferor and his or her agent(s) based on their knowledge and maps drawn by the state and federal governments. This information is a disclosure and is not intended to be part of any contract between the transferee and the transferor.

THIS REAL PROPERTY LIES WITHIN THE FOLLOWING HAZARDOUS AREA(S):

A SPECIAL FLOOD HAZARD AREA (any type Zone "A" or "V") designated by the Federal Emergency Management Agency.
☐ Yes ☐ No ☐ Do not know and information not available from local jurisdiction

AN AREA OF POTENTIAL FLOODING shown on a dam failure inundation map pursuant to Section 8589.5 of the Government Code.
☐ Yes ☐ No ☐ Do not know and information not available from local jurisdiction

A VERY HIGH FIRE HAZARD SEVERITY ZONE pursuant to Section 51178 or 51179 of the Government Code. The owner of this property is subject to the maintenance requirements of Section 51182 of the Government Code.
☐ Yes ☐ No

A WILDLAND AREA THAT MAY CONTAIN SUBSTANTIAL FOREST FIRE RISKS AND HAZARDS pursuant to Section 4125 of the Public Resources Code. The owner of this property is subject to the maintenance requirements of Section 4291 of the Public Resources Code. Additionally, it is not the state's responsibility to provide fire protection services to any building or structure located within the wildlands unless the Department of Forestry and Fire Protection has entered into a cooperative agreement with a local agency for those purposes pursuant to Section 4142 of the Public Resources Code.
☐ Yes ☐ No

AN EARTHQUAKE FAULT ZONE pursuant to Section 2622 of the Public Resources Code.
☐ Yes ☐ No

A SEISMIC HAZARD ZONE pursuant to Section 2696 of the Public Resources Code.

☐ Yes (Landslide Zone) ☐ Yes (Liquefaction Zone) ☐ No ☐ Map not yet released by state

THESE HAZARDS MAY LIMIT YOUR ABILITY TO DEVELOP THE REAL PROPERTY, TO OBTAIN INSURANCE, OR TO RECEIVE ASSISTANCE AFTER A DISASTER.

THE MAPS ON WHICH THESE DISCLOSURES ARE BASED ESTIMATE WHERE NATURAL HAZARDS EXIST. THEY ARE NOT DEFINITIVE INDICATORS OF WHETHER OR NOT A PROPERTY WILL BE AFFECTED BY A NATURAL DISASTER. TRANSFEREE(S) AND TRANSFEROR(S) MAY WISH TO OBTAIN PROFESSIONAL ADVICE REGARDING THOSE HAZARDS AND OTHER HAZARDS THAT MAY AFFECT THE PROPERTY.

Signature of Transferor(s) _____ Date _____

Signature of Transferor(s) _____ Date _____

Agent(s) _____ Date _____

Agent(s) _____ Date _____

Check only one of the following:

☐ Transferor(s) and their agent(s) represent that the information herein is true and correct to the best of their knowledge as of the date signed by the transferor(s) and agent(s).

☐ Transferor(s) and their agent(s) acknowledge that they have exercised good faith in the selection of a third-party report provider as required in Civil Code Section 1103.7, and that the representations made in this Natural Hazard Disclosure Statement are based upon information provided by the independent third-party disclosure provider as a substituted disclosure pursuant to Civil Code Section 1103.4. Neither transferor(s) nor their agent(s) (1) has independently verified the information contained in this statement and report or (2) is personally aware of any errors or inaccuracies in the information contained on the statement. This statement was prepared by the provider below:

Third-Party Disclosure Provider(s) _____ Date _____

Transferee represents that he or she has read and understands this document. Pursuant to Civil Code Section 1103.8, the representations made in this Natural Hazard Disclosure Statement do not constitute all of the transferor's or agent's disclosure obligations in this transaction.

Signature of Transferee(s)_____ Date _____

Signature of Transferee(s)_____ Date _____

valuable information, including how to find and fix earthquake weaknesses and a detailed list of earthquake resources.

Water Heater Bracing

If the property you are buying has had a new or replacement water heater installed since January 1, 1991, it must be braced, anchored, or strapped to resist falling or displacement during an earthquake. (Health and Safety Code § 19211.) Anyone selling property with such a water heater must certify in writing that the heater complies with the law.

Environmental Hazards

Item C.1 on the Transfer Disclosure Statement asks the seller to identify environmental hazards on the property such as radon gas and contaminated soil. Mold was added to the hazard list in 2001. In addition, sellers should provide prospective home buyers a copy of *Residential Environmental Hazards: A Guide for Homeowners, Homebuyers, Landlords and Tenants*, which provides information on different environmental hazards that may be on or near the property, such as asbestos, formaldehyde, lead, and hazardous wastes.

Lead

HUD rules require that applicants for FHA mortgages be given a lead-based paint notice disclosure form before signing the final sales contract. Lead paint in homes financed by the FHA must be removed or repainted.

California law requires that a seller disclose lead-based paint hazards to prospective buyers on the Transfer Disclosure Statement. (Civil Code § 1102.6.) Furthermore, sellers of houses built before 1978 must comply with the Residential Lead-Based Paint Hazard Reduction Act of 1992 (42 U.S. Code § 4852d), also known as Title X [Ten]. Sellers must:

- disclose all known lead-based paint and paint hazards in the house
- give buyers a pamphlet prepared by the U.S. Environmental Protection Agency (EPA) called *Protect Your Family From Lead in Your Home*
- include certain warning language in the contract, as well as signed statements from all parties verifying that all requirements were completed
- keep signed acknowledgments for three years as proof of compliance, and
- give buyers a ten-day opportunity to test the housing for lead.

If a seller fails to comply with Title X requirements, you can sue the seller for triple the amount of your resulting damages.

 RESOURCE

Lead. The National Lead Information Center has extensive information on lead hazards, prevention, and disclosures. For more information, call the Center at 800-424-LEAD or check www.epa.gov/lead.

Disclosure of Deaths and/or AIDS

State law implies that the seller should disclose any death within the last three years that he or she knows occurred on the property. (Civil Code § 1710.2.) If a death occurred more than three years before, the seller need disclose it only if asked by the buyer—unless the circumstances of the death (for example, a multiple murder) would significantly lower the house's value. (*Reed v. King*, 145 Cal.App.3d 261 (1983).)

Disclosing Ghosts and Haunting

Do the sellers need to tell you if they think their house is haunted? Based on California's broad disclosure rules, most experts would say yes. You're not likely to see a seller boldly declare on the TDS form that the house is haunted—but if you see statements such as "dining room furniture tends to move around at night," "cats won't go near the attic stairs," or "unexplained vapors," you might want to ask further questions.

Despite *Reed*, a seller need not disclose that an owner had, or died from, AIDS, but the property owner or his agent should answer honestly any direct questions on this subject. (Civil Code § 1710.2.) The legislature didn't address any diseases other than AIDS—its concern was that the widespread fear and stigma around this disease would lead to sellers having to disclose their private health information.

Disclosure of Military Ordnance

Sellers who know of any former federal or state ordnance locations (once used for military training purposes and potentially containing explosive munitions) within one mile of the property must provide written disclosure to the buyer as soon as practicable before transfer of title. (Civil Code § 1102.15.)

Local Disclosures

Many cities and counties have local disclosure requirements. To make sure the seller complies, check with the local city or county planning or building department for any local requirements. For example:

- Many municipalities require sellers to upgrade insulation before selling and take specific energy-efficiency measures.
- Many coastal areas restrict owners from making structural modifications to their property without a permit.
- Some communities adjacent to agricultural or timber production zones require sellers to disclose agricultural nuisances such as noise, odors, and dust.
- Sellers of property in designated "community facilities" districts must disclose information on special taxes for police or fire departments, libraries, parks, and schools. (Civil Code § 1102.6b.)

Sellers in communities with local disclosure requirements passed after July 1990 may use a special form, the Local Option Real Estate Disclosure Statement. (Civil Code § 1102.6a.)

Inspecting the Property Yourself

At some point, you'll want to arrange professional inspections. Before you get this far, you should first conduct your own inspection—ideally, before you make a formal written offer so that you can save yourself the trouble should you find serious problems.

Various books can help you prepare for your preliminary home inspection, including *The Complete Book of Home Inspection,* or *Home Inspection Checklists*, both by Norman Becker (McGraw-Hill), as well as two good ones by Robert Irwin, *The Home Inspection Troubleshooter* (Dearborn Publishing) and *Home Buyer's Checklist* (McGraw-Hill). Books written for professional inspectors can also be excellent guides, such as *Inspecting a House,* by Rex Cauldwell (Taunton Press).

Make a list of areas you can check out without needing expertise or having to climb around in dangerous places. Focus on items of particular importance to you and your family. Bring along a note pad, tape measure, camera, and flashlight and a copy of the Ideal House Profile you prepared in Chapter 1. If you're buying a condo, be sure to visit the unit in the evening when neighbors are more likely to be home, to hear any loud noises.

CAUTION

Look hard at "do-it-yourself" home repair jobs. If you see signs that the previous owners took on major repairs or remodeling work without professional help, ask the inspector to take an especially hard look. Amateur home repair projects are notorious for violating codes and containing hidden—or not-so-hidden—defects. Be sure the work was done with permits, and that all the permits have been "finaled."

Arranging Professional Inspections

In addition to inspecting the house yourself and examining the seller's disclosure and inspection reports, you'll want to hire a general contractor to inspect the property and a licensed structural pest control inspector to check for pest damage. (A few inspectors are qualified to do both.) This is normally done after your written purchase offer has been accepted by the seller (which should be contingent upon your approving the results of one or more inspections). Make sure you have the seller's Transfer Disclosure Statement and Natural Hazard Disclosure Statement so that the inspectors can follow up on any problems identified therein. You may also want to arrange more specialized inspections after reviewing disclosure reports.

Even if you are an expert, such as an architect or investor, don't forgo the professional home inspection. The inspector may find defects that you missed—and his or her report of the cost of repairs will be given more weight than your own estimate. That means the cost of the inspection can be readily offset by negotiating price concessions or repairs by the seller.

If, on the other hand, the seller is not willing to negotiate on price, the inspection contingency gives you a ready opportunity to back out of the sale.

TIP

In a hot market, consider a professional inspection before you make an offer. This allows you to close the deal quickly, by waiving the inspection contingency, giving you an edge over the competition. Obviously, you'll need the seller's permission first to do a preoffer inspection (called a "preinspection"). And you may want to lower your offer price in light of what you find.

Request Copies of Utility and Water Bills

While sellers are not required to tell you how much they pay the gas and electric company every month, ask to see past bills, especially for the winter months. Gas and electric bills can vary a lot, depending on a house's location, size, and insulation, and the type and age of the furnace and hot water heater.

If utility bills are high, ask the local gas and electric company to conduct an energy check or audit. Many do it at no charge, identifying the problems, recommended solutions, and costs. If your utility company won't help or will take too long, ask for the names of private companies who conduct energy audits.

With water bills, look for any sudden increase in water usage. In older houses especially, this may be a tip-off that main pipes are leaking.

Structural Pest Control Inspection

An inspection by a licensed structural pest control inspector, covering infestation by termites and flying beetles, dry rot, and other fungal conditions, is almost always required by the lender. If you don't make it a condition of the contract, your lender may, particularly if you put down less than 20% of the purchase price.

If the seller had a pest report done before putting the house up for sale, you should still get your own done. Some inspectors are less picky than others, and the seller has a motive (wanting the deal to go through) to pick someone who won't be too fussy. Pest control reports are not costly, beginning at about $150 for a typical single-family dwelling. In a condo, you may need an authorization from the homeowners' association for the pest control inspector to look at common areas.

 RESOURCE

More information on pest control inspection. The Structural Pest Control Board keeps files of all pest control reports commissioned within the past two years and provides useful consumer information on pest control inspections and reports. The Board can provide complaint information on individual pest control companies and help mediate disputes. For more information, call 800-737-8188 or 916-561-8708, or go to www.pestboard.ca.gov.

General Inspection

A licensed inspector (usually with a background as a general contractor) inspects all major house systems, from top to bottom. The inspector will examine the general conditions of the site, such as drainage, retaining walls, fences (some skip the fences—remind them to look), and driveways; the integrity of the structure and the foundation; and the condition of the roof, exterior and interior paint, doors and windows, and plumbing, electrical, and heating systems. A growing number of inspectors test for lead in water or radiation exposure around a built-in microwave. And, starting in 2011, California law allows you to request that your inspection include an energy-efficiency audit. You might also want to arrange specialized inspections, such as for seismic safety or asbestos hazards (described below). If you're concerned about toxic mold, make sure the inspector has expertise in finding and assessing it.

How to Find a Good Inspector

A reliable personal recommendation is the best way to find a house inspector and structural pest control inspector. Remember, you want someone who will be thorough and tough. Ask your real estate agent for a referral to an inspector, but be sure to double-check any leads from your agent. Some agents are anxious that the deal go through and therefore may recommend an inspector not overly persnickety about identifying problems. The better agents, however, realize that referrals to tough inspectors work in everyone's interests— after all, most real estate lawsuits are filed by buyers against sellers as well as real estate agents, claiming that problems with the home weren't disclosed to them.

You can also get local referrals from two professional associations: the American Society of Home Inspectors (ASHI) or the California Real Estate Inspection Association (CREIA) (contact information below).

Get at least two or three specific proposals from recommended home inspectors and check the status of each individual's license and any outstanding complaints with the Contractor's State License Board or the Structural Pest Control Board (contact information below). Ask for references from customers who have owned their homes for a few years, so that any problems the inspector didn't discover have had a chance to pop up. Ask the inspector about his or her liability insurance coverage, including "errors and omissions" (E&O) or malpractice insurance to cover negligence.

Recognizing that there is an inherent conflict of interest in inspecting and bidding on the same job, state law prohibits this practice. Home inspectors may not perform any repairs to a house on which the inspector, or the inspector's company, has prepared a home inspection report in the past 12 months. (Business and Professions Code §§ 7195, 7197.) Note, however, that this law only covers home inspectors. There's nothing to stop you from asking a general contractor to examine your roof or foundation and then prepare a bid to do any necessary work.

 RESOURCE

Finding a good general inspector. A useful brochure, *What You Should Know Before You Hire a Contractor*, is available free from the Contractors State License Board by calling 800-321-CSLB or checking their website at www.cslb.ca.gov. There, you can also check a contractor's license and complaints. Or for referrals to local inspectors and information on buying a home in good shape, contact the American Society of Home Inspectors (ASHI), 800-743-2744, www.ashi.org, or the California Real Estate Inspection Association (CREIA), 800-848-7342, www.creia.org.

Inspections and Reports

The general inspection should take at least two to three hours, while the pest control inspection should take about an hour. Accompany the inspector during the examination. You will learn a lot and better understand the report the inspector will later write. You can also find out about the maintenance and preservation of the house and ask questions.

If a friend or relative has experience in any aspect of construction, bring him or her along. Another set of eyes that know what to look for is always a help. It's also a good idea to bring along a video camera to record the inspection—you may want to view it years later to remind yourself about maintenance issues.

Expect to receive the general inspector's report after a short time (a few days or up to a week), and the pest control report within about five days. Both reports should detail the condition of all major components of the house inspected or checked for infestation and estimated repair costs. The inspector should point out any problems and indicate which are truly important and which are minor, and give a rough estimate of the costs involved for repairs. The inspector may also recommend additional specialized inspections such as those listed below.

House inspection contractors often worry about their liability should they fail to discover a serious defect. While this encourages thoroughness, it can also result in overly defensive inspecting. Here's how to filter out inspector paranoia while reading an inspection report:

- Don't focus on the long-winded disclaimers written by lawyers. While this boilerplate language may sound scary, it's usually not a tip-off that all sorts of problems are lurking just out of sight.
- Pay attention to statements describing the tests the inspector didn't conduct or areas not inspected. If you have educated yourself by reading good house-inspection books, you'll be in a fairly decent position to determine whether any areas or systems were left out that shouldn't have been. (Sometimes, the seller will block off certain areas, for example by piling up boxes in the basement or attic, in which case you should insist that they be opened for reinspection.) Next, focus on what the inspector did discover. You'll have to decide whether the identified problems merit a specialized inspection (for example, by a structural engineer) and whether you still want to go through with the transaction, based on what the inspection revealed.
- Get a second opinion if a general contractor or pest control inspector discovers a potentially serious problem or doesn't inspect important areas. Arrange for the follow-up inspection to be conducted by a specialist.

Specialized Inspections Common in California

Here are some specialized inspections that may be necessary:

Asbestos. Exposure to airborne asbestos has been linked to an increased risk of cancer. Normally, a separate asbestos inspection is not necessary unless you suspect problems (generally not the case with homes built since the mid 1970s). A general contractor should tell you if the house contains asbestos insulation around heating systems, in ceilings, or in other areas.

Ira Serkes notes, "If a home has asbestos ducting, don't let that bother you. In many cases the asbestos can be removed for only a few thousand dollars."

RESOURCE

Information on asbestos inspections. Contact the Contractors State License Board, 800-321-2752, www.cslb.ca.gov, or the American Lung Association, 800-LUNG-USA, 548-8252, www.lungusa.org.

To check the license of an asbestos inspector, contact the California Department of Industrial Relations, Division of Occupational Safety and Health (Cal/OSHA), 916-574-2993, www.dir.ca.gov (search for "asbestos contractor").

Electrical. If you or a general contractor suspects problems (more likely if the house was built 25 years ago or more), have an electrician or an electrical engineer do a specialized electrical report. Many general contractors don't have enough knowledge of electrical codes to do an adequate job on a large older house. Be sure to replace any fuse boxes with circuit breakers.

Electromagnetic radiation. If you're considering a home near high-voltage electrical power lines, you may be worried about possible health hazards. Although links between electromagnetic radiation and diseases such as cancer have not been proven, you may still want to call the local utility company for a test and evaluation of the electromagnetic radiation levels. Some general contractors can test for this as well.

Foundation and structure. A general contractor can report on these; if the contractor suspects a problem, or you're concerned based upon the seller's disclosures, you'll want an expert to inspect the foundation and structure.

Lead. Exposure to lead-based paint and lead water pipes may lead to serious health problems, especially for children. For information on home testing for lead hazards and a list of state-certified lead inspectors and testing laboratories, contact the California Department of Health Services, 800-597-5323, www.dhs.ca.gov/childlead. For information on lead in drinking water, contact the EPA Safe Drinking Water Hotline at 800-426-4791, www.epa.gov/safewater. See the discussion, above, of state and federal disclosures regarding lead, including how to contact the National Lead Information Center.

Mold. Recent concerns about mold's effect on human health have brought it into the public spotlight. The concern is not with the relatively benign mold that appears on shower tiles—it's with the layers of mold that develop around leaky pipes or other major moisture problems. These villains are reputed to cause everything from allergic coughs to brain damage and death. Some people have major reactions to mold, while others have none at all.

Regardless of your sensitivity level, if the house you're hoping to buy has a mold problem, you'll want to know about it. Your first step is to look closely when you visit the house yourself. Look not only for visible signs, but also for unpleasant smells or areas of obvious moisture or water damage. Unfortunately, not all molds have a smell, and mold may hide in air ducts, crawl spaces or ceilings, and attics. For this reason, you should choose a home inspector who has experience in identifying mold problems. Many of them have been attending special trainings of late. For more information, see the website of the California Real Estate Inspection Association, www.creia.org, or call them at 800-848-7342.

To further protect home buyers, the California Legislature passed the Toxic Mold Protection Act of 2001. (Health & Safety Code §§ 26100 and following.) This requires sellers to disclose any significant known or suspected mold problems. However, sellers are not required to test for mold (reliable tests haven't yet been developed). It's entirely possible the sellers won't notice any mold on their own.

 RESOURCE

Mold. For information on the detection, removal, and prevention of mold, see the EPA website at www.epa.gov/iaq. By clicking "Mold," you'll find their document "A Brief Guide to Mold, Moisture, and Your Home." Additional publications are available from the California Department of Health Services at www.cal-iaq.org. This site includes many helpful links to other states'

health departments and to academic and scientific studies on the subject of mold.

Plumbing. If the general inspector's report indicates plumbing problems, get an in-depth report from a plumber. Your local water department may provide some useful information regarding water pressure and hardness or softness of water. If a house is more than 50 years old, the main sewer line to the street may need replacing before long. General contractors typically do not inspect wells and septic tanks; you'll need to hire a specialist if you want these checked out.

Radon. Radon is a naturally occurring radioactive gas associated with lung cancer that enters and can contaminate a house built on soil and rock with uranium deposits or through water from some private wells. Radon concentrations tend to be highest in newer buildings, whose tight sealing doesn't allow the gas to escape. It is not a problem in most of California, but if you're concerned, contact the National Safety Council (NSC) Radon Hotline at 800-767-7236 or visit www.nsc.org. The California Department of Health Services Radon Information Line can also provide information at 800-745-7236.

Subsoil. If earth movement, especially subsidence or slippage, is a problem or possibility (or if the house is on fill), contact your local building or planning department for any soil reports on file. For information sources on earthquake study zones and hazardous landslide and flood areas in California, see Appendix A, Welcome to California. In addition, you may want to consult a soils expert, who may recommend soil borings.

Which Inspections Do You Really Need?

Some very cautious buyers have different specialists check all major areas of the house, such as heating, plumbing, roof, and foundation. Involving specialists makes excellent sense if the house is old, large, expensive, or in obvious poor condition. But weigh the benefit against the cost. If you're buying a five-year-old house in apparently great shape, you have read up on inspections, and an experienced general inspector and pest control inspector have discovered no problems, spending any money on additional inspections is probably overkill. These guidelines should help you decide how many inspections you need:

- **Let your eyes be your first guide.** The poorer looking the house's condition, the more you should use a fine-tooth comb.
- **Age is a factor.** Houses deteriorate over time, and construction techniques (especially for foundations) weren't always the best years ago. So the older the house, the more it makes sense to examine it closely.
- **Mansions deserve a third look.** The more expensive the house, the more you want to be sure you're getting your money's worth.
- **In areas where the earth moves often, check the foundation and the subsoil carefully.** This is especially true for houses in landslide- or earthquake-vulnerable areas and houses built on landfill.
- **Look for evidence of seasonal problems.** If you buy a house in the middle of August, the roof won't be leaking or the basement flooding—but they may in December. So look carefully at ceilings, attic spaces, and basements for stains or water marks. If ceilings have recently been repainted, ask why. If you aren't satisfied with the answer, ask your inspector to check these areas extra carefully and the seller to state in writing that no problems have been covered up.
- **Question new construction.** If you have any questions about a room addition or any remodeling done on the house, check permits on file at the local planning department. Make sure that all the work was done with permits and that the final permits were issued.

EXAMPLE: Amy is making an offer on an older, two-story stucco house in the Berkeley hills. She read that pest control inspectors often fail to probe corners of buildings under inset gutters for hidden rot caused by overflowing and don't usually get behind the stucco. She also learned that in earthquake zone areas, like Berkeley, this is dangerous, because rotten wood at the corners can make buildings structurally unsafe. Sure enough, when she read the pest control report, no behind-the-stucco probing had been done. She hires another inspector who has a solid reputation. He probes the corners and discovers serious damage, which will cost $22,000 to repair. Fortunately, Amy gets the seller to lower the purchase price accordingly.

Thinking Green When Making Repairs or Replacements

Did your inspector recommend you replace your water heater? Do you need to repair the roof? Now's a great time to think green!

Consider replacing a 40 gallon water tank with a tankless unit. Instead of keeping 40-gallons of water hot all the time, the heater turns on only when you need hot water.

Or, if your new house will need a new roof, now's an excellent time to look into getting photovoltaic (PV) shingles, which generate solar power. The best time to install a PV system is when you're replacing or repairing the roof.

Coauthor Ira Serkes says, "I installed a 24-Panel PV system and now generate almost all the power we use up. I also installed two on-demand hot water heater units, which have greatly reduced our gas usage."

Who Pays for Inspections?

A general inspection typically costs about $500–$800 for a single-family home, and more for a multiple-unit dwelling. Structural pest control inspections cost about $150 for an average single-family house. Normally, the buyer pays for inspections required as part of the offer to purchase. This is custom, however, not law, and it's possible to negotiate an arrangement where the seller pays or shares in the cost of inspections. Just make sure that even if the seller pays, you choose the inspector.

Are the Repairs Really Needed?

If the inspection reports identify expensive repair needs, here are some questions to ask:

- **Should you get a second opinion?** Especially if the problem is serious or requires specialized knowledge, you might want one.
- **Has one inspector called for very different types of repairs from another?** If so, some work probably needs to be done, but you still need to figure out exactly what.
- **Is the problem real or potential?** Can the situation be monitored? Will less-expensive work solve the problem? Pest control inspectors must notify the person requesting the report that the information can be divided into two sections: corrective measures for damage from evident infestations and corrective measures for conditions deemed likely to lead to infestation and future problems. For potential problems, ask whether the expensive work needs to be done now.
- **Is the problem getting worse?** If so, it's an indicator that you'll probably have to take immediate steps to either repair it or at least prevent it from spreading.

Don't simply accept as gospel what the expert tells you. If the costs seem too high, get a second opinion from someone committed to helping you arrive at a less-expensive solution.

Why Some Inspectors Are Paranoid	**Earthquake Reinforcements**

In recent years, many buyers, discovering defects after the purchase, have sued the property inspector, claiming that the defects should have been discovered and disclosed. The possibility of being sued has made some inspectors ultracareful when it comes to emphasizing what's wrong with a house.

Who Pays for Defects?

If inspections turn up a laundry list of expensive defects, you and the seller will have to negotiate who pays what. If your offer is contingent upon your approving inspection reports, you have no obligation to proceed with the purchase until you approve of the plan to remedy the defects.

Ask for a Home Warranty

Several companies sell home repair warranty contracts. Typically, these service contracts cover the heating, air conditioning, plumbing, and electrical systems, as well as the water heater and built-in kitchen and laundry appliances. For an extra charge, the policy can also cover pools, spas, and even roofs.

Under standard home warranties, if one of these systems fails during the coverage period (usually one year), you call the warranty company, which sends out a repair person to fix or replace the item. You'll have to pay a fee of around $50 per visit,

Earthquakes in the late 1980s and 1990s have cast much new light on making houses earthquake safe. The time-tested advice to bolt a house to its foundation and install stiff plywood cripple walls in the basement proved to be helpful. These reinforcements typically cost only a few thousand dollars, won't trigger a reappraisal of your home for property tax purposes (Revenue and Tax Code § 74.5), and are frequently a condition of getting earthquake insurance.

Recent earthquakes have also focused attention on the possibility that vertical earth movements can make houses vulnerable to literally jumping off their foundations. To cope with this danger, it's best to secure the house to the foundation using steel ties, straps, and, in some cases, cables. You might also want the cripple walls strengthened with heavy-gauge metal fasteners and cross bracing. A thorough retrofit of this type typically costs $2,000–$8,000 or more, depending on the size and age of the house, but should be done only after an earthquake expert is consulted.

In addition, it's important to repair termite and other structural damage, or else earthquake retrofit work can actually make a house more susceptible to earthquake damage. Earthquake retrofit services are advertised heavily; many people sound convincing but actually know so little that they are apt to make the problem worse. For more information on earthquake-proofing your house, see the *Homeowner's Guide to Earthquake Safety*, discussed above.

depending upon the particular policy. In addition, there may be a modest deductible.

CAUTION

Buying a newly built home? It will normally come with a warranty between you and the builder, or purchased by the builder.

A growing number of sellers voluntarily include a year's service contract as part of the price of the house. If the seller doesn't offer you one, it doesn't hurt to ask. Depending on the size and age of the house, a home warranty contract might cost $300–$900. A seller may see this as a bargain if it clinches the sale. Sometimes a buyer's real estate agent will provide a buyer with a home warranty—again, as incentive for the deal to close. Around 90% of the houses sold in California now come with a home warranty.

If no one offers you a warranty, you can buy one yourself (but must do so now, as part of your purchase transaction). Although these contracts can be renewed indefinitely, having the coverage makes the most sense during the first year of ownership, when systems and appliances likely to give you trouble will probably do so. Coverage usually begins at the close of escrow.

Here are some keys to finding good coverage:

- Be sure the contract covers preexisting conditions that were not known to the seller or discovered in an inspection.
- Be sure you're aware of all restrictions and dollar limits of coverage. For example, while a home warranty might cover the cost of repairing a burst

pipe, secondary damage to furniture or carpeting typically won't be covered.

- Find out how disputes are handled and whether the warranty requires mediation or arbitration.
- If an appliance or system is still covered by its own warranty, don't bother including it in the home warranty unless the warranty that came with the appliance or system will expire shortly. Instead, ask for a fee reduction.

TIP

Don't worry—filing home warranty claims won't raise the price or availability of your homeowners' insurance coverage. Home warranty contracts are a different animal from regular homeowner's insurance. The offering companies don't even communicate with one another. And since home warranty claims don't tend to run into high dollar figures, the industry isn't paranoid about the number of claims you file per year—the current average per customer is two.

RESOURCE

Home warranties. For more information on home warranties, contact the Home Warranty Association of California at www.warrantyassn.com or 805-653-1648.

The California Department of Insurance licenses home warranty firms and can provide information on the current status of a particular company's license. Call them at 800-927-4357, or check their website at www.insurance.ca.gov.

For a discussion of developer's warranties on new homes, see Chapter 7.

Legal Ownership: How to Take Title

Before escrow closes on your new house, you'll need to choose how to take "title" (documented legal ownership). Title is evidenced by a deed recorded at the county recorder's office. The deed contains a description of the property and includes the name(s) of the seller(s) and buyer(s).

SKIP AHEAD

Owned a house before? If so, you may be familiar with your options and already know how you want to take title, and you can skip this chapter. If you're a first-time homeowner or new to California and its community property ownership system, however, read on carefully.

One Unmarried Person

If you're in this category, you simply take title in your own name. Many title companies may add "an unmarried man" or "an unmarried woman" to the deed. This isn't legally required, but it helps dispel any later questions about whether there's a spouse of yours out there with a community property interest in the house.

The name to put on the deed is the one that appears on your checks, driver's license, passport, and other similar documents. This need not be your birth name. If you use more than one name, list the name you most commonly use for business purposes first, followed by A.K.A. ("also known as") and the other name.

Two or More Unmarried People

Unmarried people who purchase a house together may take title in one of four ways:
- joint tenancy
- tenancy in common
- partnership, or
- if you've registered as domestic partners, as community property.

The overwhelming majority of unmarried couples or groups own property in joint tenancy or tenancy in common. Partnership is typically appropriate only if you already own a business together and purchase the house as a business asset, or if you buy the house as a business investment to fix up for resale.

Joint Tenancy

If you take title to real property as joint tenants, all buyers will share property ownership equally and have the right to use the entire property. The key feature of joint tenancy is "the right of survivorship." When one joint tenant dies, his or her share automatically goes to the survivor(s), even if the deceased attempted to leave a portion of the house to someone else by will or living trust.

The right of survivorship lets the survivor take the property right after the other's death, without the expense and trouble of probate. Property left in a will must go through formal probate court before being transferred to the new owner (although there is a simplified procedure for property left to a spouse). If, however, you're the property's primary owner and just adding someone's name to the title to avoid probate, consider

Forms of Real Property Co-Ownership

	Tenancy in Common	Joint Tenancy	Partnership	Community Property	Community Property With Right of Survivorship
Creation	Deed must transfer property to two or more persons "as tenants in common" or without specifying how title is to be held.	Deed must transfer property to two or more persons "as joint tenants" or "with right of survivorship."	Deed must transfer property to the name of the partnership, or partnership funds must be used to buy it.	Deed must transfer property to a married couple or to registered domestic partners "as community property."	Deed must transfer property to married couple as "community property with right of survivorship."
Shares of co-owners	May be unequal. (This is specified on the deed.)	All joint tenants must own equal shares.	Determined by partnership agreement or Uniform Partnership Act.	Each spouse owns half.	Each spouse owns half.
Survivorship	On co-owner's death, interest passes to heirs under intestate succession law or beneficiaries under will or living trust.	Deceased joint tenant's share automatically goes to surviving joint tenants.	Interests usually go to partner's heir or beneficiaries, but partnership agreement may limit this.	Spouse can leave his or her half to anyone; if nothing to the contrary, goes to surviving spouse.	When one spouse dies, survivor automatically owns entire property.
Probate	Interest left by will is subject to probate. Simplified procedure available if left to spouse.	No probate necessary to transfer title to surviving joint tenants.	Interest left by will is subject to probate.	Simplified probate procedure available to transfer title to surviving spouse.	No probate necessary to transfer title to surviving spouse.
Termination	Any co-owner may transfer his or her interest or get partition order from court. Co-owners can change the form of ownership by signing a new deed.	Joint tenant may transfer interest to him- or herself or another as tenants in common, or may get partition order from court.	Governed by partnership agreement or Uniform Partnership Act.	Both spouses must agree to transfers.	Both spouses must agree.

Source: *Deeds for California Real Estate,* by Mary Randolph (Nolo).

using a living trust instead; it allows you to change your mind later. See "Placing the Property in a Living Trust," below.

While the joint tenants are alive, any owner can end the joint tenancy by selling his or her share of the property, or by deeding it from him- or herself in joint tenancy to him- or herself in tenancy in common. (Civil Code § 683.2.) This ends the joint tenancy and, with it, the automatic right of survivorship.

Joint tenancy isn't a good choice for all unmarried couples or groups. First, it necessitates equal ownership shares, so if people want to own the house in unequal shares, joint tenancy won't work. Second, contrary to popular belief, joint tenancy won't necessarily protect a surviving owner from state tax authorities coming to reappraise the house's value after one owner dies. Although married couples and registered domestic partners are exempt from this reappraisal, unmarried couples are not. It's most appropriate for people in intimate, long-term relationships who wish to provide for each other after one dies.

Joint Tenants: What Your Deed Should Say

If you want to take title as joint tenants, the deed should specify that you hold title as joint tenants with right of survivorship. You need not use a form with "Joint Tenancy Deed" printed on it, though it's fine if you do. A "Grant Deed" or a "Quitclaim Deed" will also form a legal joint tenancy as long as the proper legal language is used.

Tenancy in Common

Tenancy in common ("TIC") is the appropriate way for many unmarried co-owners to take title to property, because co-owners need not own equal shares. For example, one person could own 70% of the property and the other person own 30%. If ownership is to be unequal, it's best to write a separate contract specifying each person's ownership percentage and what happens if one person wants to sell or dies. Two Nolo books—*Living Together: A Legal Guide for Unmarried Couples*, by Ralph Warner, Toni Ihara, and Frederick Hertz, and *A Legal Guide for Lesbian & Gay Couples,* by Denis Clifford, Frederick Hertz, and Emily Doskow—contain tenancy in common (and joint tenancy) contracts as well as lots of other useful information for unmarried couples buying together. Regardless of the percentages, however, each person owns an undivided portion of the entire house, not a particular part of it.

Tenancy in common has no right of survivorship—when a tenant in common dies, his or her share passes to the person named in a will or living trust, or by intestate succession (the laws that govern who gets your property if you fail to specify whom you want to receive it). If you're doing an equity share (described in Chapter 3), you must, unless there is some compelling reason against it, hold title as tenants in common.

If you wish to provide for the survivor without going through probate when the first partner dies, you can hold property as tenants in common and each put your share into a revocable living trust. Simply name each other as beneficiary to receive the owner's share on the owner's death. If you change your mind and decide not to leave your co-owner your share, simply change the trust beneficiary of the living trust.

Tenants in Common:
What Your Deed Should Say

In California, a transfer of real property to two or more persons automatically creates a tenancy in common unless the deed says otherwise. No special words are necessary.

Couple or Domestic Partners Owning Together

Married persons and registered domestic partners ("RDPs") who wish to co-own may take title as joint tenants, tenants in common, or as community property with right of survivorship. The last one is the choice we recommend for most married couples and RDPs.

 CAUTION

Get more details if you're in a registered domestic partnership or married to a person of the same sex. Because federal laws treat these statuses differently than state laws do, tax issues are considerably more complex. You'll want to consult an estate planning attorney before buying a house. For further information about related issues, contact Equality California (www.eqca.org, 415-581-0005) or the National Center for Lesbian Rights (NCLR) (www.nclrights.org, 415-392-6257).

Community Property With Right of Survivorship

 CAUTION

If you don't want to leave the property to your spouse or registered domestic partner, hold title a different way. If you and your spouse or partner own the property as "community property with right of survivorship," at your death your spouse or partner will inherit your half—even if your will contains instructions to the contrary. If you want the other advantages of community property without the automatic right of survivorship, you can hold title as plain "community property." Simply leave the words "with right of survivorship" off the deed. The deceased person's half of the property will then go to whoever is named in the will.

Taking title as community property with right of survivorship offers two advantages:
- avoiding formal probate when a spouse or partner dies, and
- easy qualification for a federal income tax break (for married couples only, not RDPs).

Probate Avoidance

When one spouse or partner dies, property held as community property with right of survivorship goes directly to the surviving person without formal probate. A surviving spouse or partner who inherits needs only to record a simple document with the county recorder. This can be done without a lawyer; the survivor avoids not only lengthy delays in transferring the property (and title), but also costly probate fees.

RESOURCE

The petition and instructions for completing and filing an affidavit with the probate court are included in *How to Probate an Estate in California*, by Julia Nissley (Nolo).

Tax Planning

Normally, if someone sells a house, taxable profits are determined by adding the price originally paid for the house to the cost of capital improvements, and then subtracting this total from the amount the house sells for less the costs of sale.

When title is held by a married, heterosexual couple as community property with right of survivorship, a surviving spouse who inherits the property automatically qualifies for a significant tax advantage. (One that's more difficult to achieve if the same property is held in tenancy in common or joint tenancy.) The cost basis of the entire property—the cost of the house and improvements—increases ("steps up") to the property's value at the deceased person's death. Because the higher the cost basis is, the lower the taxable profit will be, a stepped up basis can significantly reduce your overall tax liability if one spouse dies. If the property isn't community property, the basis of the survivor's share stays the same. Only the half inherited from the deceased spouse gets a stepped-up basis.

CAUTION

Domestic partners and couples in same sex marriages take note. Legal experts are doubtful about whether the IRS will permit registered domestic partners or couples in same sex marriages the same tax advantage. The issue is whether the step up in basis is available to anyone who can claim community property ownership, or whether the owners must also be a married, opposite-sex couple. The news is better when it comes to property reappraisal upon one owner's death: like opposite sex married couples, the surviving registered domestic partner or same sex spouse will be exempt from reappraisal by the California tax authorities.

Community Property With Right of Survivorship: What Your Deed Should Say

For a married couple and registered domestic partners, the deed need simply say, "Fred Parks hereby grants to Mabel Rivera and Albert Riviera, [either "spouses" or "registered domestic partners"] as community property with right of survivorship, [the legal description of the property]."

EXAMPLE: Carmen and Al brought a house in 1976. In tax lingo, what Carmen and Al originally paid for the house ($60,000), plus the cost of improvements ($40,000), is their "adjusted cost basis" in the property ($100,000). If they sell for $850,000, their taxable profit would be

$750,000: the selling price less the cost basis.

If instead Carmen dies, leaving everything to Al, and they owned their house as tenants in common, the cost basis on Carmen's half of the property would increase from $50,000 (half of the $100,000 adjusted cost basis) to $425,000 (half of the $850,000 value at the time of her death). The basis on Al's half remains $50,000; as owner of the entire property, his total cost basis becomes $475,000. If Al later sells the house for $975,000, his taxable profit will be $500,000.

But if Carmen and Al had taken title to the house as community property, Al would qualify for a 100% stepped-up federal cost basis, not just on the half of the house belonging to Carmen. Now, if Al sold the property for $975,000, he'd have no taxable profit from the sale, because his gain is less than $250,000.

It's possible to argue, even if you didn't hold title as community property, that the property was in fact community property, held in joint tenancy or tenancy in common "for convenience." But there are no draw-backs to holding title as community property, and you can save yourselves an argument with the IRS.

Joint Tenancy

What about holding co-owned property in joint tenancy? Some spouses need to do this, for example, because their bank or savings and loan insisted on it, for separate reasons.

Other than this type of situation, however, there is very little reason for a married couple to choose a joint tenancy. Community property with right of survivorship offers the same advantages and more.

What about qualifying for a stepped-up tax basis? Do you lose this big advantage if you hold title in joint tenancy? Not necessarily. If you want to put your co-owned property in joint tenancy and qualify for a stepped-up cost basis, too, you simply need to be able to convincingly document to the IRS that the property is community property. Some experts recommend that you place the words "community property held in joint tenancy" on the deed. Before taking property in joint tenancy, read the section above on joint tenancy for unmarried people.

Separate Versus Community Property

Separate property is property acquired by one spouse or registered domestic partner prior to marriage or registration, after permanent separation, or during marriage or registered partnership by gift or inheritance. If separate property is sold, and other property is bought with the proceeds, it, too, is separate property.

Community property is all money earned or otherwise acquired by either spouse or partner during the marriage or registered partnership (except for rents, dividends, interest, and the like earned on separate property). A spouse or partner can turn his or her separate property into community property by stating that intention in writing.

Tenants in Common

While married couples rarely hold property as tenants in common, it is occasionally done. If, for example, the house was bought with the separate property of the husband and the separate property of the wife, and they want to keep it in separate shares, tenancy in common makes sense.

Tenancy in common lets spouses own the property in unequal shares. The specific shares, however, must be identified in writing, and the document should be recorded with the county recorder. Otherwise, property held in tenancy in common is presumed to be community property if you die or divorce. Marital Property Agreement #1, below, is a sample agreement for spouses who hold unequal shares of their house as tenants in common. This is a tricky area of law; have a real estate lawyer look at any agreement you draft.

Married Person Owning Alone

If a married person wants to own a house separately, title should be in that person's name alone, and the couple should sign and record (with the deed) an agreement declaring their intention that one spouse owns the house as separate property. Otherwise, if the couple divorces and disagrees about ownership, a court will characterize the house as community or separate property depending on what funds (community or separate) paid for it, not whose name is on the deed. Because most couples mix and spend separate and community funds without regard to type, what property was used to pay the mortgage, insurance, improvements, and taxes won't always be clear.

CAUTION

A house that starts out as separate property may easily become a mix of separate and community. For example, if Jeff and Maida, a married couple, buy a house using Jeff's premarital earnings for the down payment and then use income earned during marriage for the insurance, taxes, mortgage payments, and improvements, everything but the down payment is community property, no matter what the deed says. Jeff and Maida can change this only by signing a written agreement. However, if Jeff had spent his separate property on a house that Maida owned before their marriage, not only would it not become community property, but he couldn't expect reimbursement in the event of their divorce. (See *In Re Marriage of Cross*, 94 Cal.App.4th 1143; 114 Cal. Rptr.2d 839 (2001).)

To put your understanding in writing, use an agreement like Marital Property Agreement #2, below.

CAUTION

Be careful if one spouse gives up property rights. If you or your spouse or partner gives up valuable property rights in the agreement, a court might later conclude that that person was unduly influenced by the other. The court could throw out the whole agreement. To be safe, consult a lawyer—who may recommend that you each see separate lawyers.

Marital Property Agreement #1

Diane Holst and James Kelvin, husband and wife, agree as follows:

1. We purchased the house at 9347 24th Street, Laguna Niguel, California, using as a down payment Diane's separate property plus a small amount of community property.

2. We hold title to the house as tenants in common.

3. Diane agrees to pay mortgage payments and taxes from her separate property, with only a small amount of community property being used for improvements.

4. As a result, Diane owns 80% of the equity in the house, and James owns 20%.

5. We intend this document to rebut the presumption of Civil Code § 4800.2 that, at dissolution, property held in joint title is community property. We do not wish the property to be treated as community property if we dissolve our marriage.

Diane Holst   9/30/11
Diane Holst   Date

James Kelvin   9/30/11
James Kelvin   Date

State of California

County of ___Orange___ }

On ___September 30___, 20 11 before me, ___Nora Public, Notary Public___,
personally appeared ___Diane Holst___ and
___James Kelvin___, personally known to
me (or proved to me on the basis of satisfactory evidence) to be the persons whose names are subscribed to the within instrument and acknowledged to me that they executed the same in their authorized capacities, and that by their signatures on the instrument the persons, or the entity upon behalf of which the persons acted, executed the instrument.

WITNESS my hand and official seal.

Signature ___Nora Public___

[SEAL]

Marital Property Agreement #2

We, Brian Morgan and Laura Stein, husband and wife, hereby agree that:

1. Brian Morgan holds title to a vacation cabin near Lake Tahoe, the address of which is 43566 Lake Tahoe Drive, Lake Tahoe, California, which he owned prior to our marriage as separate property.

2. Although the mortgage, maintenance, and improvements on the cabin have been, and will be, paid during our marriage with savings that are partially community property, we intend that Brian Morgan own the cabin as his separate property.

3. We make this agreement in light of the fact that Brian's earnings constitute a greater portion of our community savings, and that upon Brian's death, we both want the cabin to be inherited by Scott Morgan, Brian's son.

Brian Morgan   _9/30/11_
Brian Morgan   Date

Laura Stein   _9/30/11_
Laura Stein   Date

State of California

County of _Alameda_

On _September 30_ , 20 _11_ before me, _Jon Dough, Notary Public_ ,
personally appeared _Brian Morgan_ and
Laura Stein ,personally known to me (or proved to me on the basis of satisfactory evidence) to be the persons whose names are subscribed to the within instrument and acknowledged to me that they executed the same in their authorized capacities, and that by their signatures on the instrument the persons, or the entity upon behalf of which the persons acted, executed the instrument.

WITNESS my hand and official seal.

Signature _Jon Dough_

[SEAL]

Partnership

Partnership may be appropriate for people already in a business together who purchase a house as a business asset, or people buying a house purely as an investment to fix up and resell.

Property acquired with partnership funds is presumed to belong to the partnership, absent an agreement to the contrary. What the partners can do with the property once it's transferred to the partnership is governed either by their partnership agreement or, if they have no agreement, the Uniform Partnership Act. (Corp. Code §§ 16100 and following.)

RESOURCE

Partnership law. Home buyers don't usually form a partnership to purchase a house, so we do not discuss partnership rules in detail here. For more information on partnership law and written partnership agreements, see *Form a Partnership: The Complete Legal Guide*, by Denis Clifford and Ralph Warner (Nolo), and Nolo's *Quicken Legal Business Pro* (software), to create a partnership agreement.

Partnership: What Your Deed Should Say

When a partnership buys a house, the deed states the business name used by the partnership, or the partners' names themselves, such as, "Fred Parks hereby grants to the Stobert Partners, [the legal description of the property]."

Placing the Property in a Living Trust

Now is a good time to think about keeping the house from going through probate at your death. Probate is a long and expensive court process where assets are distributed by the terms of a will or, if there is no will, by the laws of the state.

TIP

Already taking title as joint tenants or as community property with right of survivorship? If so, the house will pass to the surviving spouse without probate anyway. Realize, however, that this doesn't cover you against all eventualities. You might, for example, want to think about avoiding probate in case both spouses die at once, or if you're both at a stage in life where you're planning who will inherit the house when you're gone.

Fortunately, avoiding probate is relatively easy. You set up a revocable living trust, name yourself as the trustee (which means you keep control over the property), and name a beneficiary to receive the property when you die. The beneficiary can be anyone: a spouse, lover, child, charity, or whoever. You prepare, sign, and record a deed transferring ownership from yourself to yourself as trustee of the living trust. When you die, the beneficiary takes title, usually in a few weeks, without probate.

Because you name yourself as trustee of your own living trust, you keep control over the property while you're alive. You can easily change the title to the house, sell the house, or change the trust beneficiary.

To create a living trust, you must prepare and sign the trust document papers. They appoint you as trustee and set out the terms of the trust, including how you are to manage the property, that the trust is revocable, and when ownership should be transferred to the beneficiary. We recommend Nolo's *Online Living Trust* or *Living Trust Maker* (software), which allow you to create a legally valid living trust tailored to your wishes and the laws of your state.

Before putting your house into a trust, however, check with the lender to see if changing title triggers any due-on-sale provision (requiring full payment when ownership changes) of your mortgage.

If you decide to create a living trust but don't have it ready when you buy your house, take title in your name or, if you own the house with someone else, in your name and the other person's name. After you create the trust, transfer title to the house (if you're the sole owner), or your share of the house, to yourself as trustee of the trust. If you are married, you'll need your spouse's consent to transfer your share of community property. This is simple to do; see *Deeds for California Real Estate,* by Mary Randolph (Nolo).

If Something Goes Wrong During Escrow

The likelihood of a major disaster befalling your purchase—such as the seller dying or an earthquake destroying the house—is slim. But it's possible that during escrow something will go wrong. A missing or incorrect loan document or last-minute title problems may simply delay closing a bit. More serious problems may jeopardize the whole deal. This chapter presents a brief overview of what may happen if your deal threatens to unravel. If you and the seller both agree to rescind the contract, there's no problem. Simply complete the Release of Real Estate Purchase Contract form in Chapter 18. If either of you wants to continue forward and close the deal, however, you'll need quick help from an experienced real estate lawyer.

The Seller Backs Out

Your purchase agreement probably gives both you and the seller a number of outs—that is, legal excuses to drop out of the deal, such as if the other person fails to comply with a time limit or other obligation. If the seller backs out for one of these justifiable excuses, there's no breach of contract, and you can't really complain, much less sue for damages. We're not going to get into the whole panoply of justifiable reasons for the seller to back out. Some of these might be highly technical, and need lawyers and courts to sort them out.

But suppose a seller backs out of the deal after you have met or waived all contingencies simply because he or she doesn't want to sell the house or gets another offer that looks better. Isn't that a clear breach of contract? Yes, and your remedy is normally to mediate or arbitrate (an option in many standard real estate contracts) or sue, demanding that the seller sell you the house and pay you damages based on your out-of-pocket costs.

The Seller Refuses to Move Out

In rare circumstances, the seller may refuse to move out, even though the house is legally yours. This is a particular problem in areas with rent or eviction controls. To force a "holdover" seller from your property, you must follow the same procedure as a landlord uses to evict a tenant—and file an unlawful detainer lawsuit in superior court. You can do this even if your purchase contract includes a mediation or arbitration clause, so long as unlawful detainers are listed as an exception to your dispute clause. See *The California Landlord's Law Book: Evictions,* by David Brown (Nolo), for step-by-step instructions and forms.

 CAUTION

If the seller has already moved out, keep an eye on the property. An obviously empty house can be a target for thieves and vandals. Now might be a good time to start getting to know your neighbors—ask them to watch for any suspicious activity. If you can, drive by the house regularly. Though chances are you won't catch a crime in progress, you might prevent one. You'll be making your presence felt and can deal with any obvious signs of your absence—such as a pizza flyer on the front door that would otherwise stay there for days.

You Back Out

If you refuse to go through with the deal without a good reason, the seller can pursue mediation, arbitration, or a lawsuit, requesting you pay damages. Damages aren't always easy to determine, however, because the seller has a duty to try to limit (mitigate, in legalese) losses by selling the house to someone else. To avoid arguing over the amount of the loss, most house purchase contracts provide a specific dollar figure (liquidated damages) for the seller's maximum damages if you breach the contract.

A liquidated damages clause means that the maximum amount the seller is entitled to is the stated amount. Disputes are often settled by the buyer and seller agreeing to allow the seller to keep part, but not all, of the deposit. Canny buyers know that sellers who are under pressure to find another buyer and transfer clear title want to get a deal-gone-bad behind them and are therefore often willing to compromise on the amount of the deposit they get to keep.

The Seller Dies

Technically, a contract to buy a house is enforceable even if the seller dies, because a deceased person's estate is responsible for fulfilling that person's lawful obligations. But in reality, the title insurance and/or escrow company will put on the brakes and call in their attorneys if the seller dies.

The executor of the seller's estate, and possibly the seller's inheritors, may want to get out of the deal. This could be a blessing in disguise, because after a seller dies, completing a house purchase transaction often becomes more complicated and time-consuming than when the seller was alive, especially if the house is part of an estate that must be probated. If the seller's inheritors do want out, insist that they reimburse you for any expenses you've thus far incurred.

If you and the inheritors want to proceed, be patient and sensitive. Try to determine whether the sale is likely to go through without difficulty. (Talking to an estate planning lawyer should help.) If settling the estate will be simple, the delay with the sale will probably be short. If settling the estate will be more complicated (for instance, the estate must be probated and 17 people claim the seller owed them money), consider discussing with the lawyer the best way to get out of the deal so that you can look for another house.

You Discover a Defect in the Property

If you feel that a seller knew about a defect—such as a basement that floods in a heavy rain—before the sale and failed to disclose it, contact the seller and the seller's broker and ask for money to correct the problem. If they turn down your request, and you can document that the defect was longstanding and should have been known to the seller, you have a good chance of going to court and recovering damages. You may sue both the seller and his or her broker in small claims court (up to $7,500). *Everybody's Guide to Small Claims Court in California*, by Ralph Warner (Nolo), shows how. If more money is involved or the situation is complicated, you'll need to obtain legal advice.

As long as the defect is disclosed, however, there is usually no legal liability. If the disclosure doesn't happen until late in escrow, however, you (the buyer) may have the right to get out of the deal or to be compensated. You may need to sue the seller or the title insurance company, depending on who was at fault. Again, you'll need legal advice for this type of situation.

The House Is Destroyed by Natural Disaster (Fire, Earthquake, Flood)

Destruction of the house is handled as follows: If you have either physical possession of, or legal title to, the property, you are responsible for its physical condition and insurance. Otherwise, the seller is responsible. Thus, the seller should make sure to have a homeowners' policy in force until the close of escrow, at which moment your policy goes into effect.

If the house is flooded three days before escrow closes, the seller can pay for the repairs and deliver the property in the condition it was in before the flood. If you want out of the deal, however, simply refuse to grant an extension to the seller to make the repairs.

House-Hungry Martians Take Possession of the House

While we don't expect your deal to be threatened by extraterrestrials, we include this heading to remind you that in this weird and wacky world of ours, all sorts of unexpected events can frustrate even the best plans. If you suddenly find your house purchase threatened from a totally unexpected angle (for example, the state announces that construction of a new freeway running through the house's kitchen will begin in a month), see an experienced real estate lawyer pronto.

Finding a Lawyer

This chapter points out a few instances when an attorney's advice or services may be useful. Finding a good, reasonably priced lawyer is not always an easy task. If you just pick a name out of the phone book, you may get a lawyer who's not qualified to deal with your particular problem, one who will charge too much, or both. If you use the attorney who drew up your family will, you may end up with someone who knows nothing about real estate law.

As a general rule, experience is most important. The best way to find a lawyer who specializes in real estate law is through a trusted person who has had a satisfactory experience with one. Your agent may have some suggestions (unless, of course, your legal problem involves your agent). Also check out Nolo's online Lawyer's Directory, where you can view extensive biographies of real estate lawyers in your area, including their photos and personal philosophy. Go to www.nolo.com

The worst referral sources are:

- heavily advertised legal clinics, which are less likely to offer competitive rates for competent representation in this specialized area, and
- referral panels set up by local bar associations, which sometimes refer people to inexperienced practitioners who don't have enough clients and use the panel as a way of generating needed business.

Once you get a good referral, call the law offices that have been recommended and state your problem. Find out the hourly fee and cost of an initial visit. Most lawyers charge $200 to $450 an hour. If you feel the lawyer is qualified to handle your problem, make an appointment to discuss your situation.

Here are some things to look for in your first meeting:

- Will the lawyer answer all your questions about his or her fees, experience in real estate matters, and your particular legal problem? Stay away from lawyers who make you feel uncomfortable asking questions.
- Is the lawyer willing to answer your specific questions over the phone and charge you only for the brief amount of time the conversation lasted? If the

lawyer won't give you any advice over the phone despite your invitation to bill you for it, find someone else.

- Does the lawyer represent sellers, too? Chances are that a lawyer who represents both buyers and sellers can advise you well on how to avoid many legal pitfalls of buying a house.

 CAUTION

Attorney fees clauses. If your contract has an attorney fees provision, you are entitled to recover your attorney fees if you win a lawsuit based on the terms of that agreement. There's no guarantee, however, that a judge will award attorney fees equal to your attorney's actual bill, or that you will ultimately be able to collect the money from the seller.

Getting Your Deposit Back

If the deal falls through, you and the seller should sign a Release of Real Estate Purchase Contract form (see Chapter 18 for a sample). If one of you refuses to sign within 30 days following a written demand to do so from the other, the person who refuses to sign may be liable to the other for attorney fees and damages of three times the amount deposited in escrow—no more than $1,000 and no less than $100. (Civil Code § 1057.3.)

True Story

Felicity and Melinda: Earthquake Jitters

We had contracts to buy one house and sell our existing one. The buyers of the house we were selling had the house inspected and signed off. Then a big earthquake hit. Our house suffered no damage, but the buyers wanted to pay less, claiming that the earthquake had generally lowered real estate values. After much haggling, we agreed to a small reduction in price, provided they increase their deposit to $4,000 and sign that it was nonrefundable.

Three weeks later, on the day the buyers got notice of their loan approval, they backed out.

The earthquake had scared them, and they changed their mind about living in California. Then they demanded that half of their nonrefundable deposit be refunded! A lawyer told us that going to binding arbitration or suing would be costly, risk clouding the title of the house, and prevent an easy sale to someone else. Nevertheless, we asked the lawyer to write a stiff letter demanding that we keep the full amount. As a result, the former buyers agreed to let us keep $3,000, which meant we ended up with $2,700 after our lawyer got his fee.

Welcome to California

This appendix is intended primarily for house purchasers who are new to California, moving from one part of the state to another, or first-time purchasers. There are a number of unique aspects to life on the Pacific coast—and to California in particular.

RESOURCE

California online. We list many California-specific websites throughout this section (and the entire book) on everything from home listings to crime to earthquake hazards to schools. Be sure to see Appendix B, Real Estate Websites, for a complete list organized by topic. We especially recommend the California Home Page at www. ca.gov.

Climate and Geography

Impressions of California are created by movie and television depictions of an endless summer. And why not? On New Year's Day, while you're snow-bound in the East or Midwest, the Rose Bowl is being broadcast from Pasadena, where the temperature is invariably 80 degrees. You're forgiven for your initial view of California.

But reality, even California-style, tends to come without a suntan in January. If you doubt this, trade your sunglasses for reading glasses and look at a map of the United States. Notice how far California stretches from top to bottom—a state of such varied latitude just can't be uniformly warm and sunny year-round. Sure, you might tan in January in San Diego on a particularly nice

day, but tanning is the last thing you'd do in Crescent City, near the Oregon border, which is as far north as Boston and gets significantly more wintertime precipitation.

The key to understanding California climate is in the word "variety." The state holds the U.S. records for highest and lowest summer temperatures and for greatest annual snowfall. Much of the San Francisco Bay Area (called "northern" California, but really part of the middle coast) has a Mediterranean climate—temperate, dry summers and relatively mild, wet winters. Summers along the coast are kept cool by the high fog that rolls in at night—thus the remark attributed to Mark Twain, "The coldest winter I ever spent was a summer in San Francisco." Twain could have found all the summer he ever wanted just a few miles inland, though, where 100 degree temperatures abound.

To the far north, the coast is practically a rain forest, where California's famous redwoods grow, and rainfall can exceed 100 inches a year. Inland, in the far north of the state, snow-capped Mount Shasta is often viewed as a symbol for the mountain regions of the state.

Most 14,000-foot peaks are in the Sierra Nevada mountain range, far to the south, and along the eastern side of the state. The Sierra not only is the source of much of the state's water, but also provides much of its power. Happily for all who love its spectacular natural beauty, it is within a reasonable drive of many of the state's population centers.

In southern California, the climate is semiarid; Los Angeles has dry, pleasant winters and warm summers, which attract flocks of people. Southeastern California is a desert (the best-known city is Palm Springs), inhabited by cacti and retired actors. It's within a few hours' drive of most of the southern part of the state.

More locally still, the weather within one city's limits can change considerably from neighborhood to neighborhood: Summer in San Francisco's Sunset District, for instance, is far cooler and foggier than in the warmest neighborhood, the Mission, just a few miles to the east.

How close your house is to the coast is a big factor in determining the weather you'll be enjoying—or complaining about. Hills and valleys are also important: West-facing slopes generally get more rain and lower temperatures than east-facing ones. So, however sunny a weather picture a real estate broker paints for you, listen with a drop of skepticism. If you can, ask a local resident what the weather is like.

Natural Hazards

California still seems to be getting more than its share of natural disasters. The four major natural hazards you'll find in California are earthquakes, fires, floods, and droughts.

Earthquake

There have been, and likely will continue to be, some devastating earthquakes as well as many smaller ones in the next 50 years. And in a state where faults underlie the land like a capillary system and the most populated

cities are on the coast, the area of highest fault activity, there are no areas where you are completely safe from earthquakes. (Take a look at the fault map on the following page.) While the odds of a quake shaking your home are unfortunately significant, you can take steps to minimize the risk of severe damage.

How Safe Is the Site?

Surprisingly, proximity to a major fault is not the primary factor that affects how well a house will hold up during an earthquake, according to seismic experts. Instead, other geologic and geographic factors should be examined, as should the structure of the house itself:

- **Avoid houses on unstable hillsides.** An unstable hillside is not a good place to be if an earthquake hits, because of the potential for landslides. In the San Francisco Bay Area, for example, experts predict that a sizable quake on the Hayward fault (one of the state's most dangerous), which runs through the Oakland and Berkeley hills on the east side of San Francisco Bay, will result in more homes being damaged from landslides than from shaking. The danger of a slide depends on the soil condition—rock is preferable to unconsolidated dirt. Flat, solid ground is even better.

- **The worst place for a house to be built is on fill.** Artificial fill is common along many California bays and rivers including, most notably, the San Francisco Bay. Some newer types of fill are sturdier than older ones. In a strong quake with a lot of vigorous shaking, older fill and bay mud may have a tendency to lose cohesiveness and liquefy. A house built on fill won't necessarily sink, but it could tilt.

- **Don't buy a house downstream from a dam.** Some dams in California will fail (leak or even break) in a really strong earthquake. This can sweep a whole town away in minutes.

A geologist or soils engineer can evaluate the site and give you an opinion on its safety. Seismic maps may also help you evaluate the earthquake hazards of a particular area. (See Resources: Earthquakes, below.)

How Safe Is the Structure?

Even more important than where a house is built is what it's made of. Wood frame houses are quite flexible and, if properly secured to their foundations, will shake but not break. Masonry houses are significantly less earthquake resistant than wood frame houses. An unreinforced brick house a few stories tall is considered extremely dangerous.

RESOURCE

Earthquakes. California Seismic Safety Commission publishes *The Homeowner's Guide to Earthquake Safety*, which includes the seismic disclosure form discussed in Chapter 19 of this book. The Commission's Sacramento office is at 916-263-5506, and their website is www.seismic.ca.gov.

California Department of Conservation, in particular the State Mining and Geology Board, publishes seismic hazard data and fault zone maps. Their Sacramento number is 916-322-1082, and their website is www.consrv.ca.gov/SMGB. Similar information may be available from your city or county planning department.

The California Emergency Management Agency provides local and regional earthquake maps and a wide variety of material on earthquake preparedness, including a do-it-yourself video on retrofitting wood frame houses and earthquake safety guides for businesses and schools. Check your phone book for the nearest regional Earthquake Preparedness Project, or contact its Sacramento office at 916-845-8510. The website is www.oes.ca.gov.

Peace of Mind in Earthquake Country, by Peter Yanev (Chronicle Books), is the best book around on earthquake preparedness.

The Building Education Center is a nonprofit organization that offers all-day seminars and publications on earthquake retrofitting. It's in Berkeley, CA at 510-525-7610, or www.bldgeductr.org.

Fire

The fires that pose the greatest threat to houses are grass and brush fires, most common in dry southern California, where large areas of parched brush and chaparral spark easily to flame. But these fires aren't limited to southern California. Fires begin in dry canyons all over the state. And once started, they can spread incredibly quickly, destroying thousands of homes, especially when fanned by hot winds that blow from the interior valleys toward the coast.

California Fault Map

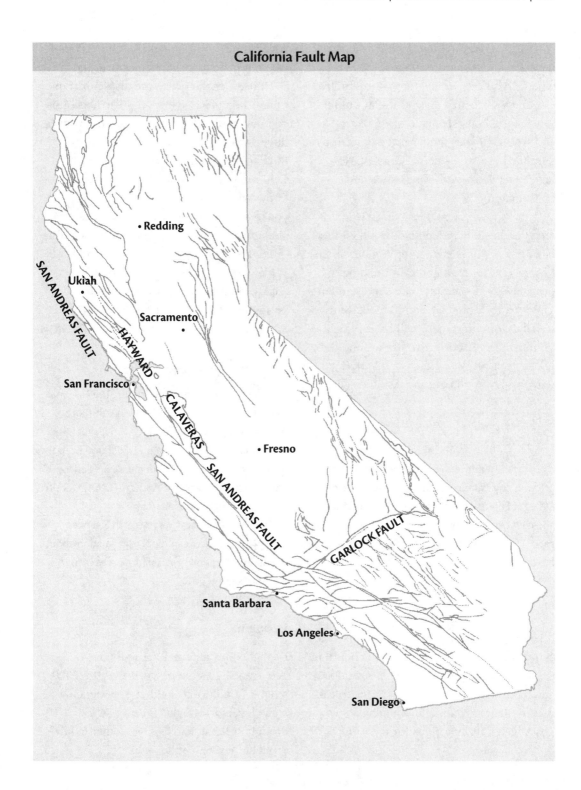

If you are considering buying a house near a wild canyon or hill area, look at whether you can reduce the risk of fire by clearing a wide area around it. Pay attention to what the house is made of; shake roofs and wood shingles are far more dangerous than tile roofs and stucco. Some cities have outlawed wood shingles for new construction.

If the house you're considering is in an area that has been identified as a high fire hazard zone, or is even a replacement house for one that burnt, any recent building probably had to comply with state standards. The roof, for example, should meet safety specifications, and there will have to be a minimum vegetation clearance around the house itself. (If the landscaping looks sparse, don't count on filling it in.) Ask the sellers for details.

RESOURCE

Wildfires. For fire safety information, call your city's fire department or the nearest Office of Emergency Management. Many cities and counties in high-risk areas have implemented special programs to reduce fire danger and improve fire department response to wildfires.

Flood

It hardly seems fair, but the same hills and canyons that make fires so hard to control in the summer are prone to dangerous floods and mudslides in the winter. The steep canyons in the San Gabriel mountains above Los Angeles are notorious for the torrents of water, mud, and boulders that have demolished many expensive homes over the years.

Houses by the ocean are also vulnerable to flood damage. Every year, Pacific storms combine with normal high tides to produce huge waves that roll over the beaches. The Russian and Sacramento rivers in northern California have flooded so often that locals know where the danger spots are. So, if you're considering buying a house near a stream or river, ask someone who has lived in the area for many years about floods. If you're told that the area flooded 40 years back or just last year, consider buying a bit higher up, because floods can recur at any time.

RESOURCE

Floods and landslides. The National Flood Insurance Program (NFIP) in Baltimore publishes hundreds of flood zone maps for California. For information on NFIP flood insurance policies, call 800-621-3362 or check the Federal Emergency Management Agency (FEMA) website at www.fema.gov/business/nfip.

The U.S. Geological Survey Earth Sciences Information Center can supply information about landslide susceptibility in California; see http://earthquake.usgs.gov.

Drought

Droughts in California are regular occurrences. As we proceed into the 2000s, much of California is either experiencing some level of drought or is at risk for drought. Climatologists say another multiyear drought may be on the way.

Rationing programs vary according to the severity of the drought. But they also vary depending on where you live—some water districts are harder hit than others.

For many homeowners, watering the landscaping is one of the first things that must go in a drought. Fortunately, California's native plants are accustomed to dry conditions. You may well want to lose the lawn as soon as you move in, and replace it with drought-tolerant, native options—many of which flower beautifully and attract hummingbirds and butterflies. For more information and lists of appropriate plants, see www.growingnative.com and www.californiagardens.com, or the book *Plants and Landscapes For Summer Dry Climates*, published by the East Bay Municipal Utility District, and available at bookstores and www.ebmud.com.

Pollution

Like any other state, California has its environmental problems. Some make a place unpleasant; others make it unhealthy, especially if you're particularly sensitive to environmental contaminants.

Water Pollution

Many towns and cities in California get drinking water good enough to bottle and sell. That's because it comes from mountain river reservoirs. Other parts of the state are not so lucky. Southern California, Los Angeles included, must import most of its water, often from as far away as the Colorado River. The water is not as pure as mountain water, and tastes bad, too.

"Where does it come from?" is the most important question to ask in determining the quality of a water supply. In general, water from aboveground sources is good water. Water pumped from ground aquifers can be just as good but can also be polluted with health-threatening substances such as toxic waste from industrial sources or agricultural chemicals. In a number of California areas, water quality isn't too different from that in developing countries. People who can afford to do so buy a filtration system or drink bottled water.

The key to determining water quality is to find out the source for a particular town. Often, one part of a county—Santa Clara, for example—will have excellent water piped in from the mountains, while a few miles away the water will be wretched.

 RESOURCE

Water quality and water pollution. Ask the local water district where the water comes from. If it's pumped from the ground or comes from a river, demand information on recent water-quality tests.

The best source for candid information on all pollution is private environmental groups, such as Communities for a Better Environment (CBE) (www.cbecal.org). They do their own studies and can tell you if a known pollution problem exists in your neighborhood. CBE has offices in Oakland, 510-302-0430, and Huntington Park, 323-826-9771.

Ask your regional office of the State Water Resources Control Board about pollution (www.swrcb.ca.gov). Or check http://water.

epa.gov/drink. These agencies, however, have limited information—they generally report only complaints received, unless a particular area has been tested recently. If so, ask for the results.

Toxic Waste

No one in his or her right mind would knowingly buy a house next door to a toxic waste dump. Unfortunately, the presence of toxic waste may not be obvious. Many toxic dumps are buried; other locations have yet to be disclosed. And some dumps may pose broader health threats if their contaminants leak into groundwater supplies.

A 1986 report by the California Legislature stated that all nine major toxic waste landfills in California leak, and that not one met state requirements to prevent leakage. Thousands of smaller waste landfills and underground storage tanks leak into the soil and water, resulting in almost 20% of California's major drinking water wells having been chemically polluted. Aquifers, which store water, are not naturally flushed. Once one becomes polluted, it stays that way. The situation is so bad that several communities in California whose aquifers became contaminated have been rendered uninhabitable.

RESOURCE

Toxic waste.
California Office of Environmental Protection, Department of Toxic Substance Control, 800-728-6942. This state agency maintains the Hazardous Waste and Substances Sites List of problem sites in California. (For more information, see www.dtsc. ca.gov.)

See also "Scorecard," a nonprofit website that provides information on toxic waste and environmental pollutants by community, at www.scorecard.org.

Air Pollution

The air quality in California varies about as much as the weather, as the two are closely related. Residents breathe easier near the coast, where the air circulates regularly, keeping the smog from ever getting really thick.

Unfortunately, if you enjoy hot weather, you'll have to learn to like polluted air. Anywhere the air sits still long enough to really warm up, pollution collects, particularly in the summer. Areas of the state east of the coastal range are blocked from the cleansing incursions of sea air. The Central Valley is often thick with smog, as are the San Gabriel and San Fernando valleys in southern California. Ditto the Livermore Valley, east of San Francisco.

Los Angeles has some of the most polluted air in the U.S. Despite efforts to convert to cleaner fuels, the situation is expected to worsen in coming years as more cars and industry fill the area. The Pacific winds blow much of L.A.'s smog inland to the rapidly developing Riverside and San Bernardino counties. L.A.'s coastal communities, such as Pacific Palisades, Santa Monica, Venice, and Palos Verdes, have relatively clean air, as well as the most expensive houses in the L.A. metropolitan area.

Many people consider air pollution more of a nuisance than a hazard, but recent studies show that airborne toxins pose a threat to anyone living near industry, including the "clean" computer industry. One survey linked exposure to air toxins with high cancer rates near Contra Costa County's petrochemical plants. If you're sensitive to air pollution, you'll want to move close to the coast or the Sierra foothills and avoid most areas in between, although there are still many rural parts of northern and central California where the air is relatively clean.

> **RESOURCE**
>
> **Air pollution.** Communities for a Better Environment (www.cbecal.org) can tell you if a known pollution problem exists in your neighborhood. Also see www.scorecard.org.
>
> A local or regional air quality district such as Bay Area Air Quality Management District (415-771-6000, www.baaqmd.gov) and www.sparetheair.org; South Coast Air Quality Management District (800-288-7664, www.aqmd.gov); or San Joaquin Valley Air Pollution Control District (209-557-6400 in Modesto, 559-230-6000 in Fresno, and 661-392-5500 in Bakersfield, www.valleyair.org) will tell you more about the air where you live. A city manager's or mayor's office should be able to refer you to a specific air quality district, or check the Air and Waste Management Association's website at www.awma.org for the nearest district.

Nuclear Plants

Atomically speaking, California is in better health than many other states. While four commercial nuclear power plants have been built, only two are operational—the Diablo Canyon plant in San Luis Obispo, 200 miles north of Los Angeles, and the San Onofre Nuclear Generating Station between Los Angeles and San Diego. Safety fears led to the close of the other two: the Humboldt Bay nuclear plant in Eureka and Rancho Seco near Sacramento. Many people believe it makes sense to avoid buying a house near any of the power plants, as serious safety questions have been raised about all four. These questions often center on whether the plants will withstand a strong earthquake, although operations problems (at the two up and working) also arise.

Even when a reactor is shut down, a hazard remains. At both of California's commercial nuclear power plants, spent fuel is stored in open containment ponds, awaiting the construction of a high-level waste repository. Should an earthquake occur before California gets around to building this repository, and should a containment pond crack and lose its water, the spent fuel could melt down and release radioactivity.

If you decide to live near a nuclear plant, a house to the north or west will be safer from possible releases of radioactivity than a house to the south or east, as winds in California blow toward the south and southeast 80% of the time.

> **RESOURCE**
>
> **Nuclear plants.** The Nuclear Information and Resource Service has helpful information at www.nirs.org.

Schools

California has many excellent public schools —the problem is finding them. The solution is to look yourself, not to simply ask your real estate agent, "How are the schools around here?"

Since California's Proposition 13 cut taxes, schools have had less money. Some schools are in worse shape than others, but all have had to cut back programs, usually in sports, art, music, languages, and drama. At some schools, where parent interest is high and financial resources available, parents pay to keep "nonessential" programs going.

Many people assume that the best schools are in the rich communities. This isn't always true. Money, by itself, doesn't guarantee good schools, although parents in prosperous areas (who themselves tend to have a relatively high level of education) usually take considerable interest in educating their children. But many middle class cities have excellent public schools too, because parents get involved.

To learn about average class size, course offerings, instructional practices, and available services, start by calling and visiting local schools and school districts. Obtain the *School Accountability Report Card* (or "SARC"), which each school must prepare annually. This report covers a range of important topics, including expenditures per student and types of services funded; class sizes and teaching loads; student achievement and progress toward meeting academic goals; and much more. Each school is required to post its report on its website, which you can link to from the Department of Education's website www.cde.ca.gov (click "Testing and Accountability," then "Accountability," then "School Accountability Report Card").

Arrange to visit schools you're considering. Observe the atmosphere by sitting in on classes and talking to some parents or teachers. And look for locally produced publications such as a school newsletter or parent handbook.

The State Department of Education in Sacramento can also provide useful information. Student performance in California is measured by a series of standardized tests, known as "STAR" tests (Standardized Testing and Reporting). For information about these tests and how California's students are scoring, see the following website put up by the Standards and Assessments Office of the Department of Education: http://star.cde.ca.gov.

The Educational Demographics Unit provides much data for schools and districts, including enrollment figures, racial and ethnic information, language census data, and even dropout rates. Call them in Sacramento at 916-327-0800. The Department of Education's website is www.cde.ca.gov.

Check out local resources at public libraries. Look under "Schools" in the index of local newspapers at a public library for articles on how active the district PTA is and how well attended parent open houses are. Local civic groups, such as the League of Women Voters or PTA, often publish ratings of local schools. Ask a reference librarian for help finding these. If you're interested in private schools, ask for information on local guides, such as *McCormack's Guides,* discussed below.

Contact EdSource, a nonprofit resource center that distributes impartial statewide information. EdSource publishes numerous impartial pamphlets discussing school budgets and finances, the ramifications of state education legislation, demographics, and bilingual education. If EdSource doesn't have what you need, they can help you find it. Contact them in Mountain View at 650-917-9481 or at www.edsource.org.

Additional online resources. Look in regional directories for a specific city or county, and then search the "schools" area for a particular school or district. Also, see The School Report, www.homefair.com (look in the left sidebar). This contains useful information on and maps of school districts throughout California. Another website offers detailed reports for a fee: School Match, www. schoolmatch.com. Also see the summaries of schools provided at www.greatschools.net (a nonprofit organization).

Traffic

In California cities, traffic has replaced weather as the favorite topic of conversation; as more people move here, traffic gets worse. In the San Francisco Bay Area, people in the North Bay and East Bay commonly arise before dawn and drive hours to reach major urban centers. Los Angeles has four of North America's five busiest freeways. Traffic typically crawls from morning to midnight.

Before you buy a house in California, figure out how you are going to get to work. Is driving reasonable? Will it still be in ten years? Don't assume you can jump in the car

and turn the key. Sometimes in California, you *can't* always get there from here (at least not before 9:00 a.m.).

Consider the availability of public transportation. As traffic continues to worsen, rapid transit may be the only alternative. And, of course, if you live near your job, you can avoid a commute altogether. If you work in the city, a house there may cost more, but this extra cost is increasingly likely to balance against your commuting (and sometimes parking) costs. This is a popular approach in L.A., where people are "rediscovering" downtown and the advantages of living close to work.

 RESOURCE

Transportation. Check the nearest office of the California Department of Transportation (Caltrans) for information on ride sharing and transportation planning, or call the state office. Call Caltrans at 916-654-5266, or check their website at www.dot.ca. gov. Also, city traffic departments may be of some help.

Crime

Crime always ranks high when people are asked about the social problems that most concern them. Indeed, in many areas neighbors are so concerned they have banded together to form crime prevention groups.

Picking an area that is reasonably safe is a major concern when purchasing a house, especially if you have children. Understand that a substantial percentage of the crime that occurs in any neighborhood is committed by people who live there—often teenagers and others who feel alienated, bored, or angry. There is no way to escape this type of crime except by taking home-security precautions and working with others as part of neighborhood groups designed to help local teenagers channel energy into healthier activities.

Still, it's sensible to be aware of a neighborhood's crime level when buying a house. Here are a few suggestions:

- Some cities have far less crime than others. The California Attorney General's Office publishes statewide statistics adjusted by population in *Crime in California*. It's available from the Criminal Justice Statistics Center in Sacramento at 916-227-3509 or online at http://ag.ca.gov/cjsc/pubs.htm.

- You can check on crime types and frequency with the local police department. Although they may not keep statistics on a block-by-block basis, you may be able to get numbers for the general neighborhood you are considering.

- Neighborhoods with active, effective neighborhood watch groups, where residents understand the importance of keeping their eyes on the street and maintaining good communication among neighbors, are usually much safer than those that remain unorganized.

- If you are seriously worried about crime, you may want to live in a community secured with walls and guards. But check with residents before you assume security is tight—some of these communities have become targets for burglars who easily evade lax security systems or unguarded front gates.

- Upscale suburban areas next to very poor ones are almost always targets for robbery and burglary. So before you buy, drive 20 blocks in every direction. Look for graffiti, broken windows, bars on doors, or boarded-up buildings. If you find yourself rolling up your window in your car, you'll likely need a burglar alarm and maybe bars on the windows at home.

- In California cities, neighborhood safety changes block to block, driven by many factors, most of which are invisible to newcomers. Ask long-time local residents in what areas they would feel safe walking the dog at 10:00 p.m. Then confirm what you hear by talking to patrol cops. Take any advice from a real estate agent with a grain of salt—they earn a commission regardless of how safe the neighborhood is.

Additional Information on California

For separate guides to many California counties, see *McCormack's Guides*. These annual publications provide a range of local information on schools (public and private), demographics, crime, weather, home prices, jobs, recreation, child and health care, and other topics of interest to newcomers, including profiles of individual cities. *McCormack's Guides* are available at many bookstores or via www.mccormacks.com.

California County Populations (as of January 2009)

In Alphabetical Order				In Order of Population			
County	Population	County	Population	County	Population	County	Population
Alameda	1,5556,657	Orange	3,139,017	Los Angeles	10,393,185	El Dorado	180,185
Alpine	1,201	Placer	339,577	San Diego	3,173,407	Imperial	179,254
Amador	38,080	Plumas	20,632	Orange	3,139,017	Kings	154,743
Butte	220,748	Riverside	2,107,653	Riverside	2,107,653	Madera	152,331
Calaveras	45,987	Sacramento	1,433,187	San Bernardino	2,060,950	Napa	137,571
Colusa	21,997	San Benito	58,016	Santa Clara	1,857,621	Humboldt	132,755
Contra Costa	1,060,435	San Bernardino	2,060,950	Alameda	1,556,657	Nevada	98,718
Del Norte	29,5547	San Diego	3,173,407	Sacramento	1,433,187	Sutter	96,554
El Dorado	180,185	San Francisco	845,559	Contra Costa	1,060,435	Mendocino	90,206
Fresno	942,298	San Joaquin	689,480	Fresno	942,298	Yuba	72,900
Glenn	29,239	San Luis Obispo	270,429	Ventura	836,080	Lake	64,025
Humboldt	132,755	San Mateo	745,858	San Francisco	845,559	Tehama	62,836
Imperial	179,254	Santa Barbara	431,312	Kern	827,173	San Benito	58,016
Inyo	18,049	Santa Clara	1,857,621	San Mateo	745,858	Tuolumne	56,335
Kern	827,173	Santa Cruz	268,637	San Joaquin	689,480	Calaveras	45,987
Kings	154,743	Shasta	183,023	Stanislaus	526,383	Siskiyou	45,971
Lake	64,025	Sierra	3,358	Sonoma	486,630	Amador	38,080
Lassen	35,550	Siskiyou	45,973	Tulare	441,481	Lassen	35,550
Los Angeles	10,393,185	Solano	426,729	Monterey	431,892	Del Norte	29,547
Madera	153,331	Sonoma	486,630	Solano	426,729	Glenn	29,239
Marin	258,618	Stanislaus	526,383	Santa Barbara	431,312	Colusa	21,997
Mariposa	18,306	Sutter	96,554	Placer	339,577	Plumas	20,632
Mendocino	90,206	Tehama	62,836	San Luis Obispo	270,429	Mariposa	18,306
Merced	256,450	Trinity	13,959	Santa Cruz	268,637	Inyo	18,049
Modoc	9,698	Tulare	441,481	Marin	258,618	Mono	13,504
Mono	13,504	Tuolumne	56,335	Merced	256,450	Trinity	13,959
Monterey	431,892	Ventura	836,080	Butte	220,748	Modoc	9,698
Napa	137,571	Yolo	200,709	Yolo	200,709	Sierra	3,358
Nevada	98,717	Yuba	72,900	Shasta	183,023	Alpine	1,201

Source: www.csac.counties.org

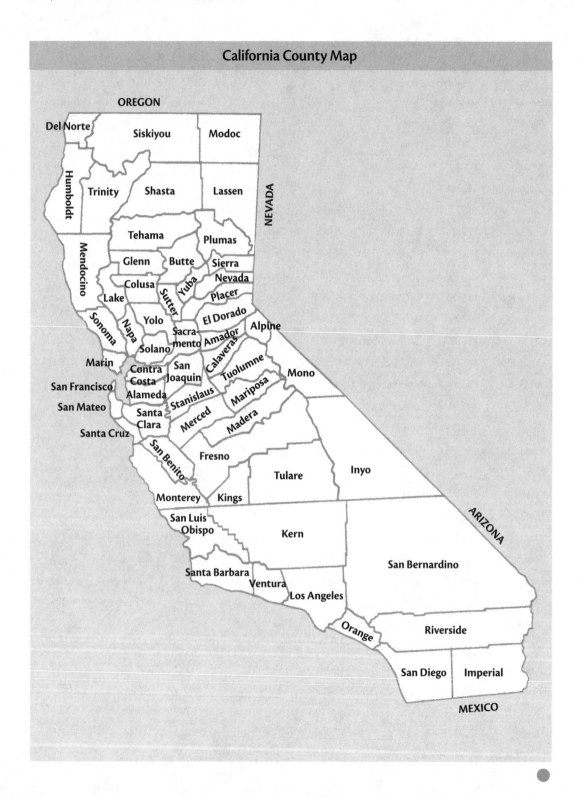

Real Estate Websites

There are hundreds of thousands of real-estate-related websites, with more added every day. That's a lot of surfing for home buyers! To make your online research easy, we've chosen the 100 or so websites of specific value to California homebuyers. Our list is organized in alphabetical order by topic, with reference to specific chapters for more information. This appendix also includes some general advice on doing real estate searches online, including how to find a California statute without setting foot in a law library.

Be sure to check Nolo's website at www.nolo.com for real estate calculators and other useful information and resources.

Top Real Estate Websites

From air pollution to title insurance, here are useful websites for California homebuyers.

Air Pollution (App. A)

Air and Waste Management Association: www.awma.org

Scorecard: www.scorecard.org

Asbestos Hazards and Inspections (Ch. 19)

American Lung Association: www.lungusa.org

California Department of Industrial Relations, Division of Occupational Safety and Health (Cal/OSHA): www.dir.ca.gov

Community and Relocation Information (Ch. 6)

California Home Page: www.ca.gov

HomeFair: www.homefair.com

National Association of Realtors: www.realtor.com

Sperling's Best Places: www.bestplaces.net

Comparable Sales Prices (Ch. 15)

Domania: www.domania.com

HomeRadar.com: www.homeradar.com

Smarthomebuy: www.smarthomebuy.com

National Association of Realtors: www.realtor.com

Trulia: www.trulia.com

Zillow: www.zillow.com

Contractors (Ch. 7 and 19)

Contractor's State License Board: www.cslb.ca.gov

Credit Bureaus and Reports (Ch. 2)

Equifax: www.equifax.com

Experian: www.experian.com

TransUnion: www.transunion.com

Annual Credit Report service: www.annualcreditreport.com

Credit Counseling (Ch. 2)

National Foundation for Credit Counseling: www.nfcc.org

National Consumer Law Center: www.nclc.org

Credit Scores (Ch. 2)

Fair Isaac: www.fairisaac.com or www.myfico.com

Crime (App. A)

California Attorney General's Office, Criminal Justice Statistics Center: http://ag.ca.gov/cjsc

Earthquakes and Seismic Hazards (Ch. 19 and App. A)

Seismic Safety Commission:
www.seismic.ca.gov

California Emergency Management Agency:
www.oes.ca.gov

California Department of Conservation, State Mining, and Geology Board:
www.consrv.ca.gov/SMGB

Escrow Companies (Ch. 18)

California Department of Corporations:
www.corp.ca.gov

Floods (Ch. 19 and App. A)

Federal Emergency Management Agency (FEMA):
www.fema.gov

U.S. Geological Survey: www.usgs.gov

Foreclosures (Ch. 3)

www.realtytrac.com

See **Government Loans** and websites of individual lenders.

Government Loans (Ch. 11)

Veterans Affairs (VA): www.va.gov

Federal Housing Administration (FHA):
www.hud.gov/buying

California Housing Finance Agency (CHFA):
www.calhfa.ca.gov

CalVet: www.cdva.ca.gov/newhome

Homes for Sale (Ch. 6 and 7)

California Living Network: http://ca.realtor.com

California Living Network's Spanish-language equivalent, Sucasa: www.sucasa.net

Fresno Bee: www.fresnobee.com/realestate

HomeBuilder: www.move.com

Los Angeles Times: www.latimes.com/classified/realestate

MSN Real Estate: www.realestate.msn.com

Owners' Network: www.owners.com

Press-Enterprise (Riverside):
www.pe.com/homes

Realtor.com: www.realtor.com

San Diego Union-Tribune: www.realestate.signsonsandiego.com

San Francisco Chronicle:
www.sfgate.com/classifieds/homes

San Jose Mercury News:
www.mercurynews.com/real

Also, see websites of local papers, individual real estate brokers, and mortgage lenders.

Home Inspections (Ch. 7 and 19)

American Society of Home Inspectors (ASHI):
www.ashi.org

Contractor's State License Board:
www.cslb.ca.gov

California Real Estate Inspection Association (CREIA): www.creia.org

Homeowners' Associations (Ch. 7)

Community Associations Institute:
www.caionline.org

Homeowners' Insurance (Ch. 18 and 19)

California Department of Insurance:
www.insurance.ca.gov

Insurance News Network: www.insure.com

Housing Discrimination (Ch. 6)

California Department of Fair Employment and Housing: www.dfeh.ca.gov

Lead Hazards, Inspections, and Disclosures (Ch. 19)

California Department of Health Services: www.dhs.ca.gov/childlead

National Lead Information Center: www.epa.gov/lead

Lenders (Complaints) (Ch. 13)

California Dept. of Real Estate: www.dre.ca.gov

California Dept. of Consumer Affairs: www.dca.ca.gov

Use a Web search engine such as Yahoo! to check out websites of individual lenders. Also see "Mortgage Rates, Loans, and Calculators," below, to find online mortgage lenders.

Mortgage and Financial Calculators (Ch. 2, 3, 8, 9, and 13)

Bankrate: www.bankrate.com

HomeFair: www.homefair.com

MortgageCalc: www.mortgagecalc.com

Nolo: www.nolo.com/legal-calculators

Yahoo! Real Estate: http://realestate.yahoo.com

Also, see websites listed under "Mortgage Rates, Loans, and Calculators," and "Rent Versus Buy Decisions," below.

Mortgage Rates, Loans, and Calculators (Ch. 2, 8, 9, and 13)

E-Loan: www.eloan.com

Interest.com: www.interest.com

The Mortgage Superstore: www.infoloan.com

QuickenMortgage: www.quickenloans.com

LendingTree: www.lendingtree.com

MSN Real Estate: www.realestate.msn.com

HSH Associates: www.hsh.com (rates only)

Mortgage Marvel: www.mortgagemarvel.com

Mortgage-Net: www.mortgage-net.com

Nolo: www.nolo.com/legal-calculators (calculators only)

Also, search for individual lenders, such as Bank of America, and see "Homes for Sale," above.

Moving Companies (Ch. 3 and App. C)

American Moving and Storage Association: www.moving.org

California Public Utilities Commission: www.cpuc.ca.gov

Moving.com: www.moving.com

New Homes (Ch. 7)

HomeBuilder: www.move.com

Homeowners Against Deficient Dwellings: www.hadd.com

Homeowners for Better Building: www.hobb.org

J.D. Power Consumer Center: www.jdpower.com

Nuclear Plants (App. A)

Nuclear Information and Resource Service: www.nirs.org

Pest Control Inspections (Ch. 19)

California Structural Pest Control Board: www.pestboard.ca.gov

Radon (Ch. 19)

California Department of Health Services: www.cdph.ca.gov (search for "radon")

National Safety Council: www.nsc.org

Real Estate Agents and Brokers (Ch. 5 and 13)

California Association of Realtors: www.car.org

California Department of Real Estate: www.dre.ca.gov

HomeGain: www.homegain.com

Ira Serkes: www.berkeleyhomes.com

Council of Residential Specialists: www.crs.com

Real Estate Buyer's Agent Council: www.rebac.net

National Association of Realtors: www.realtor.com

RealtyTimes: www.realtytimes.com

Real Estate Law (Ch. 5)

California Association of Realtors: www.car.org

California Department of Real Estate: www.dre.ca.gov

Refinancing Calculators (Ch. 9)

HomeFair: www.homefair.com

E-Loan: www.eloan.com

Nolo: www.nolo.com/legal-calculators

Remodeling (Ch. 3)

ImproveNet: www.improvenet.com

National Association of the Remodeling Industry: www.nari.org

Building Education Center: www.bldgeductr.org

Remodeling **Magazine:** www.remodeling.hw.net

Rent Versus Buy Decisions (Ch. 3)

HomeFair: www.homefair.com

E-Loan: www.eloan.com

Yahoo! Real Estate: http://realestate.yahoo.com

Also, see other websites listed under "Mortgage Rates, Loans, and Calculators," above.

Safe Drinking Water (App. A)

EPA Office of Ground Water and Safe Drinking Water: www.epa.gov/safewater

Communities for a Better Environment: www.cbecal.org

State Water Resources Control Board: www.swrcb.com

Schools (App. A)

Ed Source: www.edsource.org

The School Report: www.homefair.com/real-estate/school-reports

School Match: www.schoolmatch.com

Great Schools: www.greatschools.net

California State Department of Education: www.cde.ca.gov

Smart Home Buy: www.smarthomebuy.com

Also, see websites listed in "Community and Relocation Information," above.

Secondary Mortgage Market (Ch. 2 and 4)

Fannie Mae: www.fanniemae.com

Freddie Mac: www.freddiemac.com

Tax Information (Ch. 4, 8, and 14)

IRS: www.irs.gov

State Franchise Tax Board: www.ftb.ca.gov

Title Insurance (Ch. 18)

California Land Title Association (CLTA):
www.clta.org

American Land Title Association (ALTA):
www.alta.org

Toxic Waste (App. A)

California Office of Environmental Protection, Dept. of Toxic Substance Controls:
www.dtsc.ca.gov

Scorecard: www.scorecard.org

Transportation (App. A)

California Department of Transportation:
www.dot.ca.gov

Water Pollution (App. A)

Communities for a Better Environment:
www.cbecal.org

State Water Resources Control Board:
www.swrcb.ca.gov

California Online

We don't want you to miss two special sites that have a lot of useful information for California homebuyers.

California Home Page: www.ca.gov. Every California homebuyer, especially those new to the state, should bookmark this site. It provides information on the Golden State—from schools and jobs to business and environmental protection programs. It's especially useful for tapping into state and government agencies, programs, and laws.

The California Association of Realtors (CAR): www.car.org. This site provides useful consumer information, including updates on state and federal legislation; real estate listing information from nearly every Multiple Listing Service in California; median prices of California homes; and a directory of California Realtors®, including multilingual Realtors®.

General Real Estate Sites

If you can't find what you want on our top 100 list, here are some other useful suggestions for doing your online real estate search.

Realty Times: www.realtytimes.com. This is a great place to check out real estate information online. It has answers to common real estate questions, as does www.ourbroker.com, operated by real estate author Peter Miller.

The International Real Estate Digest (IRED): www.ired.com (provides links to 25,000 real estate websites throughout the world, primarily geared to real estate professionals).

For up-to-date real estate news, check out DeadlineNews.com by real estate writer Broderick Perkins, and *Inman News Features* at www.inman.com.

How to Find a California Statute Online

Using this book is a good way to educate yourself about the laws that affect the homebuying process. In some cases, you may want to read the exact California statute that we refer to in the text. This is easy to do online. Go to Nolo's home page at www.nolo.com. Click Site Map, then "State Law Resources," then "California," then "California Code." There you'll find a list of statutes, also called codes, grouped by subject matter into 29 Titles (for example, the Civil Code, Business and Professions Code, and so on).

There are two ways to find statutes; both are free:

- If you know the subject matter of the code (for example, real estate agents), you can enter these "keywords" into the search box and you'll get a list of codes that include this phrase.

- You can also "browse" the codes by asking to see a Table of Contents for each Title. As you look down the list, you may see the statute that interests you.

The state's Legislative Counsel also maintains a free Web page with current legislative information, www.leginfo.ca.gov. You can read the text of any pending bill, the analyses prepared by assembly and senate members, voting records, and lists of sponsors. You can also ask to be notified via email any time there is legislative action on a bill that you want to follow.

RESOURCE

Legal research. For more information, see *Legal Research: How to Find & Understand the Law*, by Stephen Elias (Nolo). This book gives easy-to use, step-by-step instructions on finding legal information.

Planning Your Move

I n terms of stress, studies show that moving ranks right up there behind divorce and the death of a loved one. But, with intelligent planning, you can at least minimize this stress. The following will help you plan your move.

Tax-Deductible Moving Expenses and Costs of Sale

You may deduct job-related moving expenses —such as travel, transportation, and storage costs—from your gross income on your federal tax return if all of the following are true:

- Your move is within one year of starting your new job.
- The distance from your old home to your new job is at least 50 miles more than the distance from your old home to your old job.
- The distance from your new home to your new job is less than the distance from your old home to your new job; this test need not be met if your employer said moving was a condition of your employment, or if you'll spend less time or money on your new commute.
- You were fully employed for 39 weeks out of the year following the move; and, if you're self-employed, you also worked for 78 weeks out of the two years following the move.

You may also deduct certain costs of selling and/or buying a home such as points and other loan fees.

RESOURCE
Tax-deductible expenses. For information on tax-deductible moving expenses, see IRS Publication 521, *Moving Expenses.*

For tax rules that apply when you sell a house, see IRS Publication 523, *Selling Your Home.*

These publications and related forms are available by calling the IRS at 800-829-1040 or visiting its website, www.irs.gov.

Moving Checklist: Two Weeks Before Moving

Not all items on this list will apply to you. If you're moving within the same town, you probably won't have to transfer your kids to a new school or have your car serviced for travel. Just focus on the applicable items.

- ☐ Check with your childrens' new school about what records and transcripts are needed, and arrange for their transfer.

- ☐ Close or transfer bank and safe deposit box accounts.

- ☐ Change your address for deliveries (newspaper, magazines (including alumni bulletins and nonprofit newsletters), diapers, laundry).

- ☐ Cancel utilities (gas, electric, cable, phone, water, garbage); transfer services (if possible) or arrange new services; request deposit refunds.

- ☐ Get recommendations for (or find in advance, especially if a medical condition needs regular attention) new doctors, dentist, and veterinarian; if possible, photocopy medical records to have with you.

☐ Get reference letters if you'll need to find a job.

☐ Cancel membership (and transfer membership, if relevant) in religious, civic, and athletic organizations.

☐ Have car serviced for travel.

☐ Buy travel insurance.

☐ Get maps.

☐ Line up storage facility.

☐ Arrange for moving pets, including a safe place for them to stay while the moving van is being loaded—a common time for animals to escape.

☐ Finalize arrangements with moving company. (Get bids and make preliminary arrangements weeks in advance.)

☐ Tell close friends and relatives your schedule and contact information.

RESOURCE

Moving companies. It's worth doing careful research before choosing a moving company. Complaints about them are skyrocketing. Customers report long delays, broken goods, and even having their possessions held "hostage" until an extra, unexpected cash payment is handed over. Ask friends for referrals, and get bids from at least three companies before choosing—while being wary of any exceptionally low bids. Also, check the state Public Utilities Commission's website, www.cpuc.ca.gov, for consumer information on choosing a moving company. Other good sources of information include the American Moving and Storage Association (a trade group, at www.moving.org) and the Web-based company Moving.com (www.moving.com).

Things to Remember While Packing

☐ Inventory your possessions before packing them, in case things get lost in the move. Take photos of the more valuable items.

☐ Label boxes on top and side—your name, new city, room of house, contents.

☐ Assemble moving kit—hammer, screwdriver, pliers, tape, nails, tape measure, scissors, flashlight, cleansers, cleaning cloths, rubber gloves, garbage bags, lightbulbs, extension cords, step stool, mop, broom, pail, vacuum cleaner.

☐ Keep the basics handy—comfortable clothes, toiletries, towels, battery-powered alarm clock, disposable plates, cups and utensils, can opener, one pot, one pan, sponge, paper towels, toilet paper, plastic containers, toys for kids.

☐ Carry jewelry, extremely fragile items, currency, and important documents.

☐ Make other arrangements if moving company won't move antiques, art collections, crystal, other valuables, or plants.

TIP
How to pack a truck like a pro. If you're handling your own move, minimize damage to your possessions—and your spine—by first placing extra-long items such as mattresses and framed art works along the walls of the truck, then putting in the heaviest objects (always keeping appliances upright), then piling the lighter objects on top. Use some rope to tie the doors on your appliances and dressers, and rent some blanket-style furniture pads to protect surfaces.

Who Should Get Changes of Address

- ☐ Friends and relatives.
- ☐ Subscriptions.
- ☐ Government agencies you regularly deal with—VA, IRS, Social Security Administration, and so on.
- ☐ Charge and credit accounts.
- ☐ Installment debt—such as student loan or car loan.
- ☐ Frequent flyer programs.
- ☐ Brokers and mutual funds.
- ☐ Insurance agent/companies.
- ☐ Medical providers—if you'll be able to use them after moving.
- ☐ Catalogs you want to keep receiving.

- ☐ Arts and theatre groups you wish to continue receiving information from.
- ☐ Charities you wish to continue donating to.
- ☐ Post office. (If you're trying to get off catalog and other direct mailing lists, only have first-class mail forwarded. Give your new address to those catalog companies on whose lists you want to remain, and tell them not to trade or sell your name.)

Things to Do After Moving In

- ☐ Open bank accounts and safe deposit box account.
- ☐ Begin deliveries: newspaper, diapers, laundry.
- ☐ Register to vote.
- ☐ Change (or get new) driver's license.
- ☐ Change auto registration.
- ☐ Install new batteries in existing smoke detectors (and install any additionally needed smoke detectors); buy fire extinguisher.
- ☐ Hold party for your house scouts and moving helpers, and take yourself out for a congratulatory dinner!

Worksheets

Explanations for the forms in this appendix can be found in Chapters 1 and 2.

Ideal House Profile

Upper price limit: _____

Maximum down payment: _____

Special financing needs: _____

	Must Have	Hope to Have
Neighborhood or location:		
_____	_____	_____
_____	_____	_____
School needs:	_____	_____
Desired neighborhood features:		
_____	_____	_____
_____	_____	_____
_____	_____	_____
_____	_____	_____
Length of commute:	_____	_____
Access to public transportation:	_____	_____
Size of house:	_____	_____
Number and type of rooms:		
_____	_____	_____
_____	_____	_____
_____	_____	_____
_____	_____	_____
Condition, age, and type of house:	_____	_____
Type of yard and grounds:		
_____	_____	_____
_____	_____	_____
_____	_____	_____
_____	_____	_____
Absolute no ways:		
_____		
_____		

House Priorities Worksheet

Date visited: _____ Price: $ _____

Address: _____

Contact: _____ Phone #: _____

Must have:

☐ _____

☐ _____

☐ _____

☐ _____

☐ _____

☐ _____

☐ _____

☐ _____

☐ _____

☐ _____

☐ _____

☐ _____

Hope to have:

☐ _____

☐ _____

☐ _____

☐ _____

☐ _____

☐ _____

☐ _____

☐ _____

Absolute no ways:

☐ _____

☐ _____

☐ _____

Comments about the particular house:

_____

_____

_____

House Comparison Worksheet

House 1 _____

House 2 _____

House 3 _____

House 4 _____

	1	2	3	4

Must have:

_____ __ __ __ __

_____ __ __ __ __

_____ __ __ __ __

_____ __ __ __ __

_____ __ __ __ __

_____ __ __ __ __

_____ __ __ __ __

_____ __ __ __ __

_____ __ __ __ __

_____ __ __ __ __

_____ __ __ __ __

_____ __ __ __ __

_____ __ __ __ __

_____ __ __ __ __

_____ __ __ __ __

Hope to have:

_____ __ __ __ __

_____ __ __ __ __

_____ __ __ __ __

_____ __ __ __ __

_____ __ __ __ __

_____ __ __ __ __

_____ __ __ __ __

_____ __ __ __ __

Absolute no ways:

_____ __ __ __ __

_____ __ __ __ __

_____ __ __ __ __

Family Financial Statement

	Borrower	Coborrower
Name and address:	_____	_____
Home phone number:	_____	_____
Email address:	_____	_____
Employer's name & address:	_____	_____
Work phone number:	_____	_____

WORKSHEET 1: INCOME AND EXPENSES

	Borrower ($)	Coborrower ($)	Total ($)
I. INCOME			
A. Monthly gross income			
1. Employment	_____	_____	_____
2. Public benefits	_____	_____	_____
3. Dividends	_____	_____	_____
4. Royalties	_____	_____	_____
5. Interest & other investment income	_____	_____	_____
6. Other (specify):	_____	_____	_____
B. Total monthly gross income	_____	_____	_____
II. MONTHLY EXPENSES	_____	_____	_____
A. Nonhousing	_____	_____	_____
1. Child care	_____	_____	_____
2. Clothing & personal expenses	_____	_____	_____
3. Food	_____	_____	_____
4. Insurance (auto, life, medical, & dental)	_____	_____	_____
5. Medical & dental care (not insurance)	_____	_____	_____
6. Taxes (nonhousing)	_____	_____	_____
7. Education	_____	_____	_____
8. Transportation	_____	_____	_____
9. Other (specify):	_____	_____	_____
B. Current housing	_____	_____	_____
1. Mortgage payment or rent	_____	_____	_____
2. Taxes	_____	_____	_____
3. Insurance	_____	_____	_____
4. Utilities	_____	_____	_____
C. Total monthly expenses	_____	_____	_____

WORKSHEET 2: ASSETS AND LIABILITIES

I. ASSETS (Cash or Market Value)	Borrower ($)	Coborrower ($)	Total ($)
A. Cash & cash equivalents			
1. Cash			
2. Deposits (list):			
B. Marketable securities			
1. Stocks & bonds (bid price)			
2. Other securities			
3. Mutual funds			
4. Life insurance			
5. Other (specify):			
C. Total cash & marketable securities			
D. Nonliquid assets			
1. Real estate			
2. Retirement funds			
3. Business			
4. Motor vehicles			
5. Other (specify):			
E. Total nonliquid assets			
F. Total all assets			
II. LIABILITIES			
A. Debts			
1. Real estate loans			
2. Student loans			
3. Motor vehicle loans			
4. Child or spousal support			
5. Personal loans			
6. Credit cards (specify):			
7. Other (specify):			
B. Total liabilities			
III. NET WORTH (Total assets minus total liabilities)			

Directions for Completing the Family Financial Statement

Top. Indicate the name(s), address(es), home phone number(s), email address(es), employer's name(s) and address(es), and work phone number(s) for yourself and any coborrower. A coborrower includes a spouse, partner, friend, or nonspouse relative with whom you are purchasing the house.

Worksheet 1: Income and Expenses

This worksheet shows you how much disposable income you have each month, a key fact in determining how big a mortgage you can realistically take on. In columns 1 and 2, you and any coborrower each list your monthly income and expenses. Total them in column 3.

IA. Monthly gross income. List your gross monthly income from all sources. Gross income means total income before amounts such as taxes, Social Security, or retirement contributions are withheld.

1. **Employment.** This is your base salary or wages plus any bonuses, tips, commissions, or overtime you regularly receive. If your income is irregular, take the average of the past 24 months. If you have more than one job, include your combined total.

2. **Public benefits.** Include income from Social Security, Disability, Temporary Assistance for Needy Families (TANF), Supplemental Security Income (SSI), and other public programs.

3. **Dividends.** Include all dividends from stocks, bonds, and similar investments.

4. **Royalties.** If you have continuing income from the sale (licensing) of books, music, software, inventions, or the like, list it here.

5. **Interest and other investment income.** Include interest received on savings or money market accounts, or as payments on rental property. If the source of the income has costs associated with it (such as the costs of owning rental property), include the net monthly profit received.

6. **Other.** Include payments from pensions, child or spousal support, or separate private maintenance income. Specify the source.

IB. Total monthly gross income. Total items 1–6. (This is the figure that lenders use to qualify you for mortgages.)

IIA. Monthly nonhousing expenses. List what you spend each month on items such as child care and clothing. These won't interest the lender as much as they are important to you in evaluating how much house you can afford. Here are some notes clarifying selected specific items:

2. **Clothing and personal expenses.** Include not only costs for your average monthly outlay on clothing, but your personal care (haircuts, shoe repairs, and toiletries) and personal fun (attending movies, buying DVDs and lottery tickets, and subscribing to newspapers). Also, include any regular personal loan payments.

3. **Food.** Include eating at restaurants, as well as at home.

7. **Education.** Include monthly payments for education loans here, plus educational payments such as your child's private school tuition.

8. **Transportation.** Include costs for both motor vehicle (include monthly car loan payments, but exclude insurance) and public transit. Include monthly upkeep for a vehicle and a reasonable amount for repairs.

9. **Other.** Specify such expenses as regular monthly credit card payments, charitable or religious donations, and savings deposits or child or spousal support payments.

IIB. Current housing expenses. If you currently own a home, list the mortgage and interest, taxes, and insurance. If you rent, include your monthly rent and renter's insurance (if any).

Also include utilities, such as gas, electricity, water, sewage, garbage, telephone, and cable or Internet access service.

IIC. Total monthly expenses. Here, total your nonhousing and housing expenses.

Worksheet 2: Assets and Liabilities

I. Assets. In columns 1 and 2, you and any coborrower write down the cash or market value of the assets listed. Total them up in column 3.

A. Cash and cash equivalents. List your cash and items easily converted into cash. Deposits include checking accounts, savings accounts, money market accounts, and certificates of deposit (even if there is a withdrawal penalty).

B. Marketable securities. Here you list items like stocks and bonds that are regularly traded and that you can normally turn into cash fairly readily. List the cash surrender value of any life insurance policy. Include items such as a short-term loan you made to a friend under the category "Other."

C. Total cash and marketable securities. Add up items A and B.

D. Nonliquid assets. These are items not easily converted into cash.

1. **Real estate.** List the market value: the amount the property would sell for.

2. **Retirement funds.** Include public or private pensions and self-directed accounts (IRAs, Keoghs, or 401(k) plans). List the amount vested in the plan.

3. **Business.** If you own a business, list your equity in it (market value less the debts on the business). Many small businesses are difficult to sell, and therefore difficult to value, but do your best to estimate accurately.

4. **Motor vehicles.** List the current market value of any car, truck, RV, or motorcycle, even if you're still making payments. Check used car guides for the information. The *Kelley Blue Book*'s used car values can be accessed online at www.kbb.com.

5. **Other.** Include nontangible assets such as copyrights, patents, and trademarks; the current value of

long-term loans you've made to others; and any really valuable personal property such as expensive jewelry or electronic gear.

E. **Total nonliquid assets.** Total up items D1–5.

F. **Total all assets.** Total up items IC and IE.

IIA. Liabilities—Debts. In columns 1 and 2, you and any coborrower write the total balances remaining for your outstanding loans under their respective categories.

Under "Other," don't include monthly insurance payments or medical (noninsurance) payments, as these go on Worksheet 1, Section IIA, Monthly Expenses—Nonhousing. Do include stock pledges, lawyer's and accountant's bills, and the like.

IIB. Total Liabilities. Total the monthly payments and balances remaining for items 1–7.

III. Net Worth. Total of all assets minus total liabilities.

Index

O

1 Go to Nolo.com/newsletters to sign up for free newsletters and discounts on Nolo products.

- **Nolo Briefs.** Our monthly email newsletter with great deals and free information.

- **Nolo's Special Offer.** A monthly newsletter with the biggest Nolo discounts around.

- **BizBriefs.** Tips and discounts on Nolo products for business owners and managers.

- **Landlord's Quarterly.** Deals and free tips just for landlords and property managers, too.

2 Don't forget to check for updates at **Nolo.com.** Under "Products," find this book and click "Legal Updates."

Let Us Hear From You

3 Register your Nolo product and give us your feedback at Nolo.com/book-registration.

- Once you've registered, you qualify for technical support if you have any trouble with a download or CD (though most folks don't).

- We'll also drop you an email when a new edition of your book is released—and we'll send you a coupon for 15% off your next Nolo.com order!

BHCA13

⚖ NOLO *Online Legal Forms*

Nolo offers a large library of legal solutions and forms, created by Nolo's in-house legal staff. These reliable documents can be prepared in minutes.

Create a Document

- **Incorporation.** Incorporate your business in any state.
- **LLC Formations.** Gain asset protection and pass-through tax status in any state.
- **Wills.** Nolo has helped people make over 2 million wills. Is it time to make or revise yours?
- **Living Trust (avoid probate).** Plan now to save your family the cost, delays, and hassle of probate.
- **Trademark.** Protect the name of your business or product.
- **Provisional Patent.** Preserve your rights under patent law and claim "patent pending" status.

Download a Legal Form

Nolo.com has hundreds of top quality legal forms available for download—bills of sale, promissory notes, nondisclosure agreements, LLC operating agreements, corporate minutes, commercial lease and sublease, motor vehicle bill of sale, consignment agreements and many, many more.

Review Your Documents

Many lawyers in Nolo's consumer-friendly lawyer directory will review Nolo documents for a very reasonable fee. Check their detailed profiles at **www.nolo.com/lawyers/index.html**.

EXPONENTIAL AND LOGARITHMIC FUNCTIONS

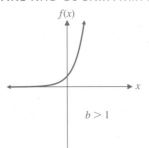

$b > 1$

Exponential function
$f(x) = b^x$

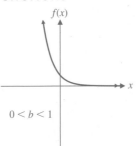

$0 < b < 1$

Exponential function
$f(x) = b^x$

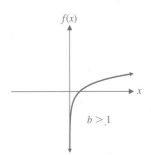

$b > 1$

Logarithmic function
$f(x) = \log_b x$

REPRESENTATIVE POLYNOMIAL FUNCTIONS (DEGREE > 2)

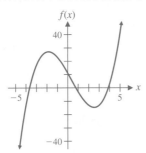

Third-degree polynomial
$f(x) = x^3 - x^2 - 14x + 11$

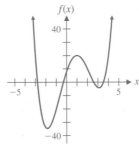

Fourth-degree polynomial
$f(x) = x^4 - 3x^3 - 9x^2 + 23x + 8$

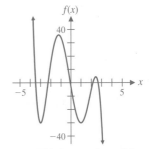

Fifth-degree polynomial
$f(x) = -x^5 - x^4 + 14x^3 + 6x^2 - 45x - 3$

REPRESENTATIVE RATIONAL FUNCTIONS

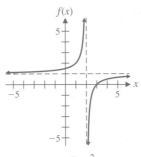

$$f(x) = \frac{x - 3}{x - 2}$$

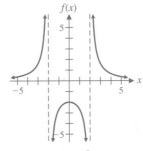

$$f(x) = \frac{8}{x^2 - 4}$$

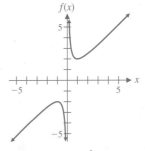

$$f(x) = x + \frac{1}{x}$$

GRAPH TRANSFORMATIONS

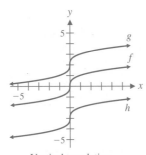

Vertical translation
$g(x) = f(x) + 2$
$h(x) = f(x) - 3$

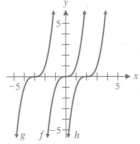

Horizontal translation
$g(x) = f(x + 3)$
$h(x) = f(x - 2)$

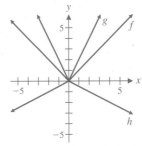

Expansion, contraction, and reflection
$g(x) = 2f(x)$
$h(x) = -0.5f(x)$

CALCULUS
FOR BUSINESS, ECONOMICS, LIFE SCIENCES, AND SOCIAL SCIENCES

CALCULUS

FOR BUSINESS, ECONOMICS, LIFE SCIENCES, AND SOCIAL SCIENCES

Tenth Edition

Raymond A. Barnett
Merritt College

Michael R. Ziegler
Marquette University

Karl E. Byleen
Marquette University

PEARSON

Prentice
Hall

Upper Saddle River, New Jersey 07458

Library of Congress Cataloging-in-Publication Data

Barnett, Raymond A.
  Calculus for business, economics, life sciences, and social sciences.—10th ed. /
Raymond A. Barnett, Michael R. Ziegler, Karl E. Byleen.
    p. cm.
  Includes indexes.
  ISBN 0-13-143261-3
  1. Calculus.   2. Social sciences—Mathematics.   3. Biomathematics.
I. Ziegler, Michael R.   II. Byleen, Karl.   III. Title.

QA303.2.B285 2005
515—dc22

2004044668

Executive Acquisitions Editor: Petra Recter
Editor in Chief: Sally Yagan
Project Manager: Jacquelyn Riotto Zupic
Vice President/Director of Production and Manufacturing: David W. Riccardi
Executive Managing Editor: Kathleen Schiaparelli
Senior Managing Editor: Linda Mihatov Behrens
Production Editor: Barbara Mack
Assistant Manufacturing Manager/Buyer: Michael Bell
Manufacturing Manager: Trudy Pisciotti
Marketing Manager: Krista M. Bettino
Marketing Assistant: Annett Uebel
Editorial Assistant/Print Supplements Editor: Joanne Wendelken
Art Director: Jonathan Boylan
Interior and Cover Designer: Geoffrey Cassar
Art Editor: Thomas Benfatti
Creative Director: Carole Anson
Director of Creative Services: Paul Belfanti
Manager, Cover Visual Research and Permissions: Karen Sanatar
Cover Photo: Alan Kearney/Taxi/Getty Images, Inc.
Art Studio: Scientific Illustrators
Composition: Interactive Composition Corporation
Part and Chapter Opening Photos: Getty Images, Inc.

© 2005, 2002, 1999, 1996, 1993, 1990, 1987,
1984, 1981, 1979 Pearson Education, Inc.
Pearson Prentice Hall
Pearson Education, Inc.
Upper Saddle River, New Jersey 07458

Pearson Prentice Hall® is a trademark of Pearson Education, Inc.

Printed in the United States of America

10 9 8 7 6 5 4 3 2 1

ISBN 0-13-143261-3

Pearson Education LTD., *London*
Pearson Education Australia PTY, Limited, *Sydney*
Pearson Education Singapore, Pte. Ltd
Pearson Education North Asia Ltd, *Hong Kong*
Pearson Education Canada, Ltd., *Toronto*
Pearson Educación de Mexico, S.A. de C.V.
Pearson Education—Japan, *Tokyo*
Pearson Education Malaysia, Pte. Ltd

CONTENTS

CHAPTER DEPENDENCIES

PART ONE A LIBRARY OF ELEMENTARY FUNCTIONS*

| 1 | A Beginning Library of Elementary Functions | → | 2 | Additional Elementary Functions |

PART TWO CALCULUS

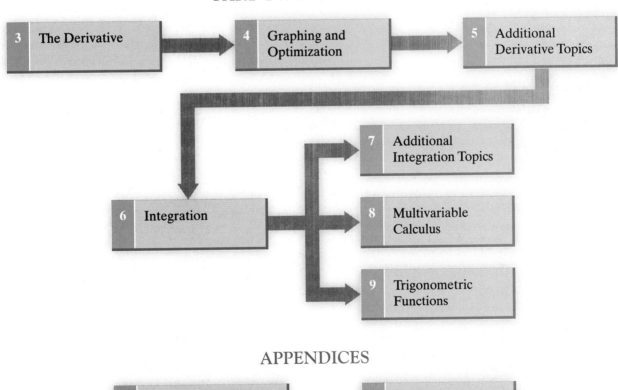

| 3 | The Derivative | → | 4 | Graphing and Optimization | → | 5 | Additional Derivative Topics |

| 6 | Integration |

| 7 | Additional Integration Topics |

| 8 | Multivariable Calculus |

| 9 | Trigonometric Functions |

APPENDICES

| A | Self-Test Basic Algebra Review |

| B | Special Topics |

* Selected topics from Part One may be referred to as needed in Part Two or reviewed systematically before starting Part Two.

PREFACE

The tenth edition of *Calculus for Business, Economics, Life Sciences, and Social Sciences* is designed for a one-term course in calculus and for students who have had $1\frac{1}{2}-2$ years of high school algebra or the equivalent. The choice and independence of topics make the text readily adaptable to a variety of courses (see the Chapter Dependency Chart on page ix). It is one of five books in the authors' college mathematics series.

Improvements in this edition evolved out of the generous response from a large number of users of the last and previous editions as well as survey results from instructors, mathematics departments, course outlines, and college catalogs. Fundamental to a book's growth and effectiveness is classroom use and feedback. Now in its tenth edition, *Calculus for Business, Economics, Life Sciences, and Social Sciences* has had the benefit of having a substantial amount of both.

Examples and Matched Problems

Over 290 completely worked examples, many of them updated for this edition, are used to introduce concepts and to demonstrate problem-solving techniques. Many examples have multiple parts, significantly increasing the total number of worked examples. The examples are **annotated** and the problem-solving steps are clearly identified. **Think Boxes** (dashed boxes) are used to enclose steps that are usually performed mentally (see Sections 1-1 and 1-4).

Each example is followed by a similar **matched problem** for the student to work while reading the material. This actively involves the student in the learning process. The answers to these matched problems are included at the end of each section for easy reference.

Exercise Sets

The book contains **over 4,000 carefully selected and graded exercises, and over 15% of these are new.** Many problems have multiple parts, significantly increasing the total number of exercises. Each exercise set is designed so that every student will experience success. Exercise sets are divided into A (routine, easy mechanics), B (more difficult mechanics), and C (difficult mechanics and some theory) levels.

Applications

A major objective of this book is to give the student substantial experience in modeling and solving real-world problems. Enough applications are included to convince even the most skeptical student that mathematics is really useful (see the Applications Index inside the back cover). Worked examples involving applications are identified by [icon].

Almost **every exercise set contains application problems**, usually divided into business and economics, life science, and social science groupings. An instructor with students from all three disciplines can let them choose applications from their own field of interest; if most students are from one of the three areas, then special emphasis can be placed there. Most of the applications are simplified versions of actual real-world problems taken from professional journals and books. No specialized experience is required to solve any of the applications.

Explore and Discuss

Every section contains **Explore–Discuss problems** interspersed at appropriate places to encourage the student to think about a relationship or process before a result is stated, or to investigate additional consequences of a development in the text. Verbalization of mathematical concepts, results, and processes is encouraged in these Explore–Discuss problems, as well as in some matched problems, and in some problems in almost every exercise set. This serves to foster critical thinking skills. The Explore–Discuss material also can be used as in-class or out-of-class group activities. In addition, at the end of every chapter, we have included two special chapter group activities that involve several of the concepts discussed in the chapter. Problems in the exercise sets that require verbalization are indicated by color problem numbers.

Technology

The generic term graphing utility is used to refer to any of the various graphing calculators or computer software packages that might be available to a student using this book. Although access to a graphing utility is not assumed, it is likely that many students will want to make use of one of these devices. To assist these students, optional graphing utility activities are included in appropriate places in the book. These include brief discussions in the text, examples or portions of examples solved on a graphing utility, exercises for the student to solve, and a group activity that involves the use of technology at the end of each chapter. In the group activity at the end of Chapter 1, and continuing through Chapter 2, linear regression on a graphing utility is used at appropriate points to illustrate mathematical modeling with real data. All the optional graphing utility material is clearly identified by either [icon] or [icon] and can be omitted without loss of continuity, if desired.

All **graphs** are computer-generated to ensure mathematical accuracy. Graphing utility screens displayed in the text are actual output from a graphing calculator.

Emphasis and Style

The text is written for student comprehension. Great care has been taken to write a book that is mathematically correct and accessible to students. Emphasis is on computational skills, ideas, and problem solving rather than mathematical theory. Most derivations and proofs are omitted except where their inclusion adds significant insight into a particular concept. General concepts and results are usually presented only after particular cases have been discussed.

Additional Pedagogical Features

Boxes are used to highlight important **definitions, results**, and **step-by-step processes** (see Sections 1-1 and 1-4). **Caution statements** appear throughout the text where student errors often occur (see Sections 3-1 and 3-7). An **insight feature,** new to this tenth edition and appearing in nearly every section, makes explicit connections with previous knowledge. **Functional use of color** improves the clarity of many illustrations, graphs, and developments, and guides students through certain critical steps (see Sections 1-1 and 3-1). **Boldface type** is used to introduce new terms and highlight important comments. **Chapter review sections** include a comprehensive summary of important terms, symbols, and concepts, followed by a comprehensive set of review exercises. **Answers to most review exercises,** keyed to appropriate sections, are included in the back of the book. Answers to all other odd-numbered problems are also in the back of the book. Answers to application problems in linear programming include both the mathematical model and the numeric answer.

Content

The text begins with the development of a library of elementary functions in Chapters 1 and 2, including their properties and uses. We encourage students to investigate mathematical ideas and processes graphically and numerically, as well as algebraically. This development lays a firm foundation for studying mathematics both in this book and in future endeavors. Depending on the syllabus for the course and the background of the students, some or all of this material can be covered at the beginning of a course, or selected portions can be referred to as needed later in the course.

The material in Part Two (Calculus) consists of differential calculus (Chapters 3–5), integral calculus (Chapters 6–7), multivariable calculus (Chapter 8), and a brief discussion of differentiation and integration of trigonometric functions (Chapter 9). In general, Chapters 3–6 must be covered in sequence; however, certain sections can be omitted or given brief treatments, as pointed out in the discussion that follows (see the Chapter Dependency Chart on page ix).

Chapter 3 introduces the derivative. The first two sections cover limits, continuity, and the limit properties that are essential to understanding the definition of the derivative in Section 3-3. The remaining sections of the chapter develop rules of differentiation (including the chain rule for power forms) and introduce applications of derivatives in business and economics. The interplay between graphical, numerical, and algebraic concepts is emphasized here and throughout the text.

Chapter 4 focuses on graphing and optimization. The first two sections cover first-derivative and second-derivative graph properties, while emphasizing polynomial graphing. Rational function graphing is covered in Section 4-3. In a course that does not include graphing rational functions, this section can be omitted or given a brief treatment. Optimization is covered in Sections 4-4 and 4-5, including examples and problems involving end-point solutions.

The first four sections of Chapter 5 extend the derivative concepts discussed in Chapters 3 and 4 to exponential and logarithmic functions (including the general form of the chain rule). This material is required for all the remaining chapters. Implicit differentiation is introduced in Section 5-5 and applied to related rates problems in Section 5-6. These topics are not referred to elsewhere in the text and can be omitted.

Chapter 6 introduces integration. The first two sections cover antidifferentiation techniques essential to the remainder of the text. Section 6-3 discusses some applications involving differential equations that can be omitted. The definite integral is defined in terms of Riemann sums in Section 6-4, and the fundamental theorem of calculus is discussed in Section 6-5. As before, the interplay between graphical, numeric, and algebraic properties is emphasized. These two sections also are required for the remaining chapters in the text.

Chapter 7 covers additional integration topics and is organized to provide maximum flexibility for the instructor. The first section extends the area concepts introduced in Chapter 6 to the area between two curves and related applications. Section 7-2 covers three more applications of integration, and Sections 7-3 and 7-4 deal with additional techniques of integration. Any or all of the topics in Chapter 7 can be omitted.

The first five sections of Chapter 8 deal with differential multivariable calculus and can be covered any time after Section 5-4 has been completed. Section 8-6 requires the integration concepts discussed in Chapter 6.

Chapter 9 provides brief coverage of trigonometric functions that can be incorporated into the course, if desired. Section 9-1 provides a review of basic trigonometric concepts. Section 9-2 can be covered any time after Section 5-3 has been completed. Section 9-3 requires the material in Chapter 6.

Appendix A contains a self-test and a concise review of basic algebra that also may be covered as part of the course or referred to as needed. As mentioned above, Appendix B contains additional topics that can be covered in conjunction with certain sections in the text, if desired.

Error Check

Because of the careful checking and proofing by a number of mathematics instructors (acting independently), the authors and publisher believe this book to be substantially error-free. For any errors remaining, the authors would be grateful if they were sent to: Karl E. Byleen, 9322 W. Garden Court, Hales Corners, WI 53130; or by e-mail, to: byleen@execpc.com

Acknowledgments

In addition to the authors, many others are involved in the successful publication of a book.

We wish to thank the following reviewers of the ninth edition:

Barbara Kenny, Boise State University
Charles G. Laws, Cleveland State Community College
Marna Mozeff, Drexel University
Julia Ledet, Louisiana State University
Phoebe Rouse, Louisiana State University
Carol A. Marinas, Barry University

We also wish to thank our colleagues who have provided input on previous editions:

Yasmine Akl, Chris Boldt, Bob Bradshaw, Celeste Carter, Bruce Chaffee, Robert Chaney, Dianne Clark, Charles E. Cleaver, Barbara Cohen,

Richard L. Conlon, Catherine Cron, Madhu Deshpande, John Dickerson, Kenneth A. Dodaro, Michael W. Ecker, Jerry R. Ehman, Lucina Gallagher, Martha Goshaw, Joel Haack, Martha M. Harvey, Sue Henderson, Lloyd R. Hicks, Louis F. Hoelzle, Paul Hutchins, K. Wayne James, Robert H. Johnston, Robert Krystock, James T. Loats, Frank Lopez, Roy H. Luke, Mel Mitchell, Michael Montano, Ann Pellegrino, Ronald Persky, Shala Petermans, Kenneth A. Peters, Jr., Lorenzo Pitts, Jr., Tom Plavchak, Bob Prielipp, Stephen Rodi, Arthur Rosenthal, Sheldon Rothman, Elaine Russell, Daniel E. Scanlon, George R. Schriro, Arnold L. Schroeder, Hari Shanker, Larry Small, Joan Smith, Steven Terry, Delores A. Williams, Caroline Woods, Charles W. Zimmerman, and Pat Zrolka.

We also express our thanks to:

Shala Petermans and Phoebe Rouse for many suggestions and exercises that have been incorporated in the tenth edition.

Hossein Hamedani and Caroline Woods for providing a careful and thorough check of all the mathematical calculations in the book.

Garret Etgen, Hossein Hamedani, David Schneider, and Mary Ann Teel for developing the supplemental manuals that are so important to the success of a text.

Jeanne Wallace for accurately and efficiently producing most of the manuals that supplement the text.

George Morris and his staff at Scientific Illustrators for their effective illustrations and accurate graphs.

All the people at Prentice Hall who contributed their efforts to the production of this book, especially Sally Yagan, editor in chief; Petra Recter, acquisitions editor; and Barbara Mack, production editor.

Producing this new edition with the help of all these extremely competent people has been a most satisfying experience.

R. A. Barnett
M. R. Ziegler
K. E. Byleen

STUDENT AND INSTRUCTOR RESOURCES

Student Resources

Student Study-Pack

Everything a student needs to succeed in one place. Free packaged with the book, or available for purchase stand-alone. Study-Pack contains:

➤ *Student Solutions Manual*
Fully worked solutions to odd-numbered exercises. This also contains a CD that contains:
 • *Math Anxiety Videos*
 • *Visual Calculus Software*
 Contains over twenty routines that provide additional insight into the topics discussed in the text.
➤ *Videos*
Cover a selection of applied calculus topics. Provide concepts explanations and skill examples.
➤ *Pearson Tutor Center*
Tutors provide one-on-one tutoring for any problem with an answer at the back of the book. Students access the Tutor Center via toll-free phone, fax, or e-mail.

Instructor Resources

Content Distribution Center

All instructor resources can be downloaded from a Website (URL and password can be obtained from your PH Sales Representative), or ordered individually:

➤ *Instructor Solutions Manual*
Fully worked solutions to all textbook exercises.
➤ *TestGen*
Test-generating software—create tests from textbook section objectives.
➤ *Test Item File*
A printed test bank derived from TestGen.
➤ *PowerPoint Lecture Slides*
Fully editable and printable slides that follow the textbook. Use during lecture or post to a Website in an online course.

MathXL® (Internet)

MathXL® is a powerful online homework, tutorial, and assessment system that accompanies your textbook. Instructors can create, edit, and assign online homework and tests using algorithmically generated exercises correlated at the objective level to the textbook. Student work is tracked in an online gradebook. Students can take chapter tests and receive personalized study plans based on their results. The study plan diagnoses weaknesses and links students to tutorial exercises for objectives they need to study. Students can also access video clips from selected exercises. MathXL is available to qualified adopters. For more information, visit our Website at www.mathxl.com, or contact your Prentice Hall sales representative for a demonstration.

MyMathLab (Internet)

MyMathLab is a text-specific, online course. MyMathLab contains MathXL (Internet) at its core, providing all of the tutorial, homework, testing, and diagnostic power of MathXL (described above). Beyond the power of MathXL, you also get access to

➤ *Course Management Tools* MyMathLab is a fully functioning course management system. Upload your own documents (i.e., syllabi, lecture notes, etc.), utilize communication tools (i.e., e-mail, chat rooms, virtual classroom), create and post assignments, and tailor the course to your liking.
➤ *Additional Resources for Instructors and Students* Access a multimedia textbook, online lecture videos, solutions manuals, online graphing calculator manuals, a video on overcoming math anxiety, PowerPoint lecture slides, and more.

Part One

A LIBRARY OF ELEMENTARY FUNCTIONS

OBJECTIVES

1. Sketch graphs and give domains and ranges of the identity, absolute value, square, cube, square root, and cube root functions.
2. Find formulas for functions whose graphs are translations, expansions, contractions, or reflections of the graph of a given function.
3. Write the equation of the line through two given points in slope-intercept and point-slope form.
4. Find the vertex and axis of symmetry of the graph of a given quadratic function.
5. Calculate break-even points using linear and quadratic functions to model cost, revenue, and profit.

CHAPTER PROBLEM

The owner of a house perched on the top of an ocean side cliff wants to add a deck to two sides of the house, but only if the railing for the deck is made of a rare Australian hardwood. The contractor who is building the deck can only locate enough rare hardwood to provide 60 feet of railing for the deck. Let x and y represent the width and length of the deck (see the figure).

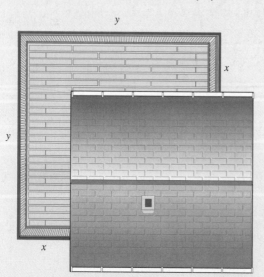

(A) Find the dimensions x and y if the deck has an area of 225 square feet.
(B) Find the dimensions x and y that will produce a deck with the maximum area.

A Beginning Library of Elementary Functions

INTRODUCTION

The function concept is one of the most important ideas in mathematics. The study of mathematics beyond the elementary level requires a firm understanding of a basic list of elementary functions, their properties, and their graphs. See the inside front cover of this book for a list of the functions that form our library of elementary functions. Most functions in the list will be introduced to you by the end of Chapter 2 and should become a part of your mathematical toolbox for use in this and most future courses or activities that involve mathematics. A few more elementary functions may be added to these in other courses, but the functions listed inside the front cover are more than sufficient for all the applications in this text.

Section 1-1 Functions

- ➤ Cartesian Coordinate System
- ➤ Graphing: Point by Point
- ➤ Definition of a Function
- ➤ Functions Specified by Equations
- ➤ Function Notation
- ➤ Applications

After a brief review of the Cartesian (rectangular) coordinate system in the plane and point-by-point graphing, we discuss the concept of function, one of the most important ideas in mathematics.

3

➤ Cartesian Coordinate System

Recall that to form a **Cartesian** or **rectangular coordinate system,** we select two real number lines, one horizontal and one vertical, and let them cross through their origins as indicated in Figure 1. Up and to the right are the usual choices for the positive directions. These two number lines are called the **horizontal axis** and the **vertical axis,** or, together, the **coordinate axes.** The horizontal axis is usually referred to as the *x* **axis** and the vertical axis as the *y* **axis,** and each is labeled accordingly. Other labels may be used in certain situations. The coordinate axes divide the plane into four parts called **quadrants,** which are numbered counterclockwise from I to IV (see Fig. 1).

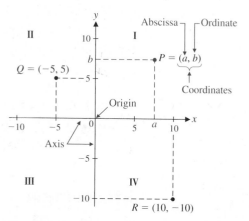

FIGURE 1   The Cartesian (rectangular) coordinate system

Now we want to assign *coordinates* to each point in the plane. Given an arbitrary point *P* in the plane, pass horizontal and vertical lines through the point (Fig. 1). The vertical line will intersect the horizontal axis at a point with coordinate *a*, and the horizontal line will intersect the vertical axis at a point with coordinate *b*. These two numbers written as the **ordered pair** (a, b) form the **coordinates** of the point *P*. The first coordinate, *a*, is called the **abscissa** of *P*; the second coordinate, *b*, is called the **ordinate** of *P*. The abscissa of *Q* in Figure 1 is −5, and the ordinate of *Q* is 5. The coordinates of a point can also be referenced in terms of the axis labels. The *x* **coordinate** of *R* in Figure 1 is 10, and the *y* **coordinate** of *R* is −10. The point with coordinates $(0, 0)$ is called the **origin.**

The procedure we have just described assigns to each point *P* in the plane a unique pair of real numbers (a, b). Conversely, if we are given an ordered pair of real numbers (a, b), then, reversing this procedure, we can determine a unique point *P* in the plane. Thus,

There is a one-to-one correspondence between the points in a plane and the elements in the set of all ordered pairs of real numbers.

This is often referred to as the **fundamental theorem of analytic geometry.**

➤ Graphing: Point by Point

The fundamental theorem of analytic geometry allows us to look at algebraic forms geometrically and to look at geometric forms algebraically. We begin by considering an algebraic form, an equation in two variables:

$$y = 9 - x^2 \tag{1}$$

A **solution** to equation (1) is an ordered pair of real numbers (a, b) such that

$$b = 9 - a^2$$

The **solution set** for equation (1) is the set of all these ordered pairs.

To find a solution to equation (1), we replace x with a number and calculate the value of y. For example, if $x = 2$, then $y = 9 - 2^2 = 5$, and the ordered pair $(2, 5)$ is a solution of equation (1). Similarly, if $x = -3$, then $y = 9 - (-3)^2 = 0$, and $(-3, 0)$ is a solution. Since any real number substituted for x in equation (1) will produce a solution, the solution set must have an infinite number of elements. We use a rectangular coordinate system to provide a geometric representation of this set.

The **graph of an equation** is the graph of all the ordered pairs in its solution set. To **sketch the graph of an equation,** we plot enough points from its solution set in a rectangular coordinate system so that the total graph is apparent and then connect these points with a smooth curve. This process is called **point-by-point plotting.**

EXAMPLE 1   **Point-by-Point Plotting**   Sketch a graph of $y = 9 - x^2$.

Solution   Make up a table of solutions—that is, ordered pairs of real numbers that satisfy the given equation. For easy mental calculation, choose integer values for x.

x	-4	-3	-2	-1	0	1	2	3	4
y	-7	0	5	8	9	8	5	0	-7

After plotting these solutions, if there are any portions of the graph that are unclear, plot additional points until the shape of the graph is apparent. Then join all the plotted points with a smooth curve as shown in Figure 2. Arrowheads are used to indicate that the graph continues beyond the portion shown here with no significant changes in shape.   ∎

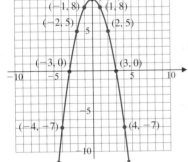

FIGURE 2

Matched Problem 1*   Sketch a graph of $y = x^2 - 4$ using point-by-point plotting.

EXPLORE & DISCUSS 1   To graph the equation $y = -x^3 + 3x$, we use point-by-point plotting to obtain

x	y
-1	-2
0	0
1	2

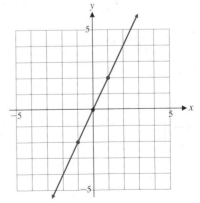

---

* Answers to matched problems are found near the end of each section, before the exercise set.

(A) Do you think this is the correct graph of the equation? If so, why? If not, why?

(B) Add points on the graph for $x = -2, -1.5, -0.5, 0.5, 1.5,$ and 2.

(C) Now, what do you think the graph looks like? Sketch your version of the graph, adding more points as necessary.

(D) Graph this equation on a graphing utility and compare it with your graph from part (C).

The icon in the margin is used throughout this book to identify optional graphing utility activities that are intended to give you additional insight into the concepts under discussion. You may have to consult the manual for your graphing utility for the details necessary to carry out these activities. For example, to graph the equation in Explore–Discuss 1 on most graphing utilities, you first have to enter the equation (Fig. 3A) and the window variables (Fig. 3B).

As Explore–Discuss 1 illustrates, the shape of a graph may not be "apparent" from your first choice of points on the graph. One of the objectives of this chapter is to provide you with a library of basic equations that will aid you in sketching graphs. For example, the curve in Figure 2 on page 5 is called a *parabola*. Notice that if we fold the paper along the y axis, the right side will match the left side. We say that the graph is *symmetric with respect to the y axis* and call the y axis the *axis of the parabola*. Later in this chapter, we will see that all parabolas have graphs with similar properties. Identifying a given equation as one whose graph will be a parabola simplifies graphing the equation by hand.

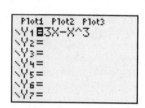

(A)

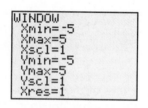

(B)

FIGURE 3

➤ Definition of a Function

Central to the concept of function is correspondence. You have already had experiences with correspondences in daily living. For example,

To each person there corresponds an annual income.

To each item in a supermarket there corresponds a price.

To each student there corresponds a grade-point average.

To each day there corresponds a maximum temperature.

For the manufacture of x items there corresponds a cost.

For the sale of x items there corresponds a revenue.

To each square there corresponds an area.

To each number there corresponds its cube.

One of the most important aspects of any science is the establishment of correspondences among various types of phenomena. Once a correspondence is known, predictions can be made. A cost analyst would like to predict costs for various levels of output in a manufacturing process; a medical researcher would like to know the correspondence between heart disease and obesity; a psychologist would like to predict the level of performance after a subject has repeated a task a given number of times; and so on.

What do all the examples above have in common? Each describes the matching of elements from one set with the elements in a second set. Consider the tables of the cube, square, and square root given in Tables 1–3.

Tables 1 and 2 specify functions, but Table 3 does not. Why not? The definition of the term *function* will explain.

TABLE 1	
Domain	**Range**
Number	*Cube*
−2 ⟶ −8	
−1 ⟶ −1	
0 ⟶ 0	
1 ⟶ 1	
2 ⟶ 8	

TABLE 2	
Domain	**Range**
Number	*Square*
−2	4
−1	
0	1
1	0
2	

TABLE 3	
Domain	**Range**
Number	*Square root*
0 ⟶ 0	
1	1
4	2
9	3

DEFINITION   Function

A **function** is a rule (process or method) that produces a correspondence between two sets of elements such that to each element in the first set there corresponds one and only one element in the second set.

The first set is called the **domain,** and the set of corresponding elements in the second set is called the **range.**

Tables 1 and 2 specify functions, since to each domain value there corresponds exactly one range value (for example, the cube of −2 is −8 and no other number). On the other hand, Table 3 does not specify a function, since to at least one domain value there corresponds more than one range value (for example, to the domain value 9 there corresponds −3 and 3, both square roots of 9).

EXPLORE & DISCUSS 2

Consider the set of students enrolled in a college and the set of faculty members of that college. Suppose we define a correspondence between the two sets by saying that a student corresponds to a faculty member if the student is currently enrolled in a course taught by that faculty member. Is this correspondence a function? Discuss.

➤ Functions Specified by Equations

Most of the domains and ranges included in this book will be (infinite) sets of real numbers, and the rules associating range values with domain values will be equations in two variables. Consider, for example, the equation for the area of a rectangle with width 1 inch less than its length (Fig. 4). If x is the length, then the area y is given by

$$y = x(x - 1) \qquad x \geq 1*$$

For each **input** x (length), we obtain an **output** y (area). For example,

If	$x = 5,$	then	$y = 5(5 - 1) = 5 \cdot 4 = 20.$
If	$x = 1,$	then	$y = 1(1 - 1) = 1 \cdot 0 = 0.$
If	$x = \sqrt{5},$	then	$y = \sqrt{5}(\sqrt{5} - 1) = 5 - \sqrt{5}$
			$\approx 2.7639.$

The input values are domain values, and the output values are range values. The equation (a rule) assigns each domain value x a range value y. The variable x is called an *independent variable* (since values can be "independently"

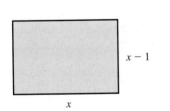

$x - 1$

x

FIGURE 4

* Inequalities are reviewed in Appendix A, Section A-7.

assigned to x from the domain), and y is called a *dependent variable* (since the value of y "depends" on the value assigned to x). In general, any variable used as a placeholder for domain values is called an **independent variable;** any variable that is used as a placeholder for range values is called a **dependent variable.**

When does an equation specify a function?

DEFINITION   Functions Defined by Equations

If in an equation in two variables, we get exactly one output (value for the dependent variable) for each input (value for the independent variable), then the equation defines a function.

If we get more than one output for a given input, the equation does not define a function.

EXAMPLE 2   **Functions and Equations** Determine which of the following equations specify functions with independent variable x.

(A) $4y - 3x = 8$, x a real number   (B) $y^2 - x^2 = 9$, x a real number

Solution   (A) Solving for the dependent variable y, we have

$$4y - 3x = 8$$
$$4y = 8 + 3x \tag{2}$$
$$y = 2 + \frac{3}{4}x$$

Since each input value x corresponds to exactly one output value $(y = 2 + \frac{3}{4}x)$, we see that equation (2) specifies a function.

(B) Solving for the dependent variable y, we have

$$y^2 - x^2 = 9$$
$$y^2 = 9 + x^2 \tag{3}$$
$$y = \pm\sqrt{9 + x^2}$$

Since $9 + x^2$ is always a positive real number for any real number x and since each positive real number has two square roots,* to each input value x there corresponds two output values $(y = -\sqrt{9 + x^2}$ and $y = \sqrt{9 + x^2})$. For example, if $x = 4$, then equation (3) is satisfied for $y = 5$ and for $y = -5$. Thus, equation (3) does not specify a function. ■

Matched Problem 2   Determine which of the following equations specify functions with independent variable x.

(A) $y^2 - x^4 = 9$, x a real number
(B) $3y - 2x = 3$, x a real number

Since the graph of an equation is the graph of all the ordered pairs that satisfy the equation, it is very easy to determine whether an equation specifies a function by examining its graph. The graphs of the two equations we considered in Example 2 are shown in Figure 5.

In Figure 5A notice that any vertical line will intersect the graph of the equation $4y - 3x = 8$ in exactly one point. This shows that to each x value

---

* Recall that each positive real number N has two square roots: $\sqrt{N}$, the principal square root, and $-\sqrt{N}$, the negative of the principal square root (see Appendix A, Section A-6).

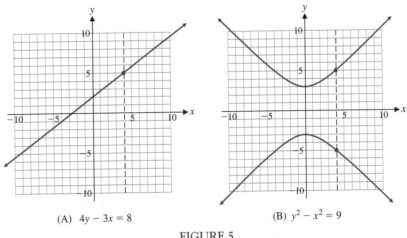

(A) $4y - 3x = 8$ (B) $y^2 - x^2 = 9$

FIGURE 5

there corresponds exactly one y value and confirms our conclusion that this equation specifies a function. On the other hand, Figure 5B shows that there exist vertical lines that intersect the graph of $y^2 - x^2 = 9$ in two points. This indicates that there exist x values to which there correspond two different y values and verifies our conclusion that this equation does not specify a function. These observations are generalized in Theorem 1.

THEOREM 1   Vertical-Line Test for a Function

An equation defines a function if each vertical line in the coordinate system passes through at most one point on the graph of the equation.

If any vertical line passes through two or more points on the graph of an equation, then the equation does not define a function.

The definition of a function specifies that to each element in the domain there corresponds one and only one element in the range.

(A) Give an example of a function such that to each element of the range there correspond exactly two elements of the domain.

(B) Give an example of a function such that to each element of the range there corresponds exactly one element of the domain.

In Example 2, the domains were explicitly stated along with the given equations. In many cases, this will not be done. Unless stated to the contrary, we shall adhere to the following convention regarding domains and ranges for functions specified by equations:

AGREEMENT   Domains and Ranges

If a function is specified by an equation and the domain is not indicated, then we assume that the domain is the set of all real number replacements of the independent variable (inputs) that produce real values for the dependent variable (outputs). The range is the set of all outputs corresponding to input values.

In many applied problems the domain is determined by practical considerations within the problem (see Example 7).

EXAMPLE 3   **Finding a Domain** Find the domain of the function specified by the equation $y = \sqrt{4 - x}$, assuming that x is the independent variable.

Solution   For y to be real, $4 - x$ must be greater than or equal to 0; that is,

$$4 - x \geq 0$$
$$-x \geq -4$$
$$x \leq 4 \quad \text{Sense of inequality reverses when both sides are divided by } -1.*$$

Thus,

Domain: $x \leq 4$ (inequality notation) or $(-\infty, 4]$ (interval notation)[†]   ■

Matched Problem 3   Find the domain of the function specified by the equation $y = \sqrt{x - 2}$, assuming x is the independent variable.

➤ Function Notation

We have just seen that a function involves two sets, a domain and a range, and a rule of correspondence that enables us to assign to each element in the domain exactly one element in the range. We use different letters to denote names for numbers; in essentially the same way, we will now use different letters to denote names for functions. For example, f and g may be used to name the functions specified by the equations $y = 2x + 1$ and $y = x^2 + 2x - 3$:

$$f: \quad y = 2x + 1$$
$$g: \quad y = x^2 + 2x - 3 \tag{4}$$

If x represents an element in the domain of a function f, then we frequently use the symbol

$$f(x)$$

in place of y to designate the number in the range of the function f to which x is paired (Fig. 6). This symbol does *not* represent the product of f and x. The symbol $f(x)$ is read as "f of x," "f at x," or "the value of f at x." Whenever we write $y = f(x)$, we assume that the variable x is an independent variable and that both y and $f(x)$ are dependent variables.

Using function notation, we can now write functions f and g in (4) in the form

$$f(x) = 2x + 1 \quad \text{and} \quad g(x) = x^2 + 2x - 3$$

Let us find $f(3)$ and $g(-5)$. To find $f(3)$, we replace x with 3 wherever x occurs in $f(x) = 2x + 1$ and evaluate the right side:

$$f(x) = 2x + 1$$
$$f(3) = 2 \cdot 3 + 1$$
$$= 6 + 1 = 7 \quad \text{For input 3, the output is 7.}$$

Thus,

$$f(3) = 7 \quad \text{The function } f \text{ assigns the range value 7 to the domain value 3.}$$

To find $g(-5)$, we replace each x by -5 in $g(x) = x^2 + 2x - 3$ and evaluate the right side:

$$g(x) = x^2 + 2x - 3$$
$$g(-5) = (-5)^2 + 2(-5) - 3$$
$$= 25 - 10 - 3 = 12 \quad \text{For input } -5, \text{ the output is 12.}$$

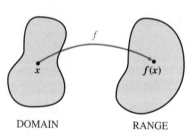

DOMAIN   RANGE

FIGURE 6

---

* Properties of inequalities are discussed in Appendix A, Section A-7.
† Interval notation is discussed in Appendix A, Section A-7.

Thus,

$$g(-5) = 12$$ The function g assigns the range value 12 to the domain value -5.

It is very important to understand and remember the definition of $f(x)$:

NOTATION   The Symbol $f(x)$

For any element x in the domain of the function f, the symbol $f(x)$ represents the element in the range of f corresponding to x in the domain of f. If x is an input value, then $f(x)$ is the corresponding output value. If x is an element that is not in the domain of f, then f is *not defined at x* and $f(x)$ *does not exist.*

EXAMPLE 4   **Function Evaluation** If

$$f(x) = \frac{12}{x - 2} \qquad g(x) = 1 - x^2 \qquad h(x) = \sqrt{x - 1}$$

then

(A) $f(6) = \dfrac{12}{6 - 2} \overset{*}{=} \dfrac{12}{4} = 3$

(B) $g(-2) = 1 - (-2)^2 = 1 - 4 = -3$

(C) $h(-2) = \sqrt{-2 - 1} = \sqrt{-3}$

But $\sqrt{-3}$ is not a real number. Since we have agreed to restrict the domain of a function to values of x that produce real values for the function, -2 is not in the domain of h and $h(-2)$ does not exist.

(D) $f(0) + g(1) - h(10) = \dfrac{12}{0 - 2} + (1 - 1^2) - \sqrt{10 - 1}$

$$= \dfrac{12}{-2} + 0 - \sqrt{9}$$

$$= -6 - 3 = -9$$

Matched Problem 4   Use the functions in Example 4 to find

(A) $f(-2)$ (B) $g(-1)$ (C) $h(-8)$ (D) $\dfrac{f(3)}{h(5)}$

EXAMPLE 5   **Finding Domains** Find the domains of functions f, g, and h:

$$f(x) = \frac{12}{x - 2} \qquad g(x) = 1 - x^2 \qquad h(x) = \sqrt{x - 1}$$

Solution   *Domain of f:* $12/(x - 2)$ represents a real number for all replacements of x by real numbers except for $x = 2$ (division by 0 is not defined). Thus, $f(2)$ does not exist, and the domain of f is the set of all real numbers except 2. We often indicate this by writing

$$f(x) = \frac{12}{x - 2} \qquad x \neq 2$$

---

*Dashed boxes are used throughout the book to represent steps that are usually performed mentally.

Domain of g: The domain is R, the set of all real numbers, since $1 - x^2$ represents a real number for all replacements of x by real numbers.

Domain of h: The domain is the set of all real numbers x such that $\sqrt{x - 1}$ is a real number—that is, such that

$$x - 1 \geq 0$$
$$x \geq 1 \quad \text{or} \quad [1, \infty)$$

Matched Problem 5   Find the domains of functions F, G, and H:

$$F(x) = x^2 - 3x + 1 \qquad G(x) = \frac{5}{x + 3} \qquad H(x) = \sqrt{2 - x}$$

In addition to evaluating functions at specific numbers, it is important to be able to evaluate functions at expressions that involve one or more variables. For example, the **difference quotient**

$$\frac{f(x + h) - f(x)}{h} \qquad \text{x and x + h in the domain of f, h} \neq 0$$

is studied extensively in calculus.

◉ Insight   In algebra, you learned to use parentheses for grouping variables. For example,

$$2(x + h) = 2x + 2h$$

Now we are using parentheses in the function symbol $f(x)$. For example, if $f(x) = x^2$, then

$$f(x + h) = (x + h)^2 = x^2 + 2xh + h^2$$

Note that $f(x) + f(h) = x^2 + h^2 \neq f(x + h)$. That is, the function name f does not distribute across the grouped variables $(x + h)$ as the "2" does in $2(x + h)$ (see Appendix A, Section A-2).   ●

EXPLORE & DISCUSS 4

Let x and h be real numbers.

(A) If $f(x) = 4x + 3$, which of the following is true?

(1) $f(x + h) = 4x + 3 + h$
(2) $f(x + h) = 4x + 4h + 3$
(3) $f(x + h) = 4x + 4h + 6$

(B) If $g(x) = x^2$, which of the following is true?

(1) $g(x + h) = x^2 + h$
(2) $g(x + h) = x^2 + h^2$
(3) $g(x + h) = x^2 + 2hx + h^2$

(C) If $M(x) = x^2 + 4x + 3$, describe the operations that must be performed to evaluate $M(x + h)$.

EXAMPLE 6   **Using Function Notation**   For $f(x) = x^2 - 2x + 7$, find

(A) $f(a)$ (B) $f(a + h)$ (C) $f(a + h) - f(a)$ (D) $\dfrac{f(a + h) - f(a)}{h}$

Solution (A) $f(a) = a^2 - 2a + 7$

(B) $f(a + h) = (a + h)^2 - 2(a + h) + 7 = a^2 + 2ah + h^2 - 2a - 2h + 7$

(C) $f(a + h) - f(a) = (a^2 + 2ah + h^2 - 2a - 2h + 7) - (a^2 - 2a + 7)$

$$= 2ah + h^2 - 2h$$

(D) $\dfrac{f(a + h) - f(a)}{h} = \dfrac{2ah + h^2 - 2h}{h} = \dfrac{h(2a + h - 2)}{h}$

$$= 2a + h - 2$$

Matched Problem 6 Repeat Example 6 for $f(x) = x^2 - 4x + 9$.

➤ Applications

We now turn to the important concepts of **break-even** and **profit–loss** analysis, which we will return to a number of times in this book. Any manufacturing company has **costs,** C, and **revenues,** R. The company will have a **loss** if $R < C$, will **break even** if $R = C$, and will have a **profit** if $R > C$. Costs include **fixed costs** such as plant overhead, product design, setup, and promotion; and **variable costs,** which are dependent on the number of items produced at a certain cost per item. In addition, **price–demand** functions, usually established by financial departments using historical data or sampling techniques, play an important part in profit–loss analysis. We will let x, the number of units manufactured and sold, represent the independent variable. Cost functions, revenue functions, profit functions, and price–demand functions are often stated in the following forms, where $a, b, m,$ and n are constants determined from the context of a particular problem:

Cost Function

$$C = (\text{fixed costs}) + (\text{variable costs})$$

$$= a + bx$$

Price–Demand Function

$$p = m - nx \quad x \text{ is the number of items that can be sold at \$p per item.}$$

Revenue Function

$$R = (\text{number of items sold}) \times (\text{price per item})$$

$$= xp = x(m - nx)$$

Profit Function

$$P = R - C$$

$$= x(m - nx) - (a + bx)$$

Example 7 and Matched Problem 7 explore the relationships among the algebraic definition of a function, the numerical values of the function, and the graphical representation of the function. The interplay among algebraic, numeric, and graphic viewpoints is an important aspect of our treatment of functions and their use. In Example 7, we also see how a function can be used to describe data from the real world, a process that is often referred to as *mathematical modeling.* The material in this example will be returned to in subsequent sections so that we can analyze it in greater detail and from different points of view.

EXAMPLE 7   **Price–Demand and Revenue Modeling** A manufacturer of a popular automatic camera wholesales the camera to retail outlets throughout the United States. Using statistical methods, the financial department in the company produced the price–demand data in Table 4, where p is the wholesale price per camera at which x million cameras are sold. Notice that as the price goes down, the number sold goes up.

TABLE 4 Price–Demand	
x **(Millions)**	p **($)**
2	87
5	68
8	53
12	37

Using special analytical techniques (regression analysis), an analyst arrived at the following price–demand function that models the Table 4 data:

$$p(x) = 94.8 - 5x \qquad 1 \le x \le 15 \tag{5}$$

TABLE 5 Revenue	
x **(Millions)**	$R(x)$ **(Million $)**
1	90
3	
6	
9	
12	
15	

(A) Plot the data in Table 4. Then sketch a graph of the price–demand function in the same coordinate system.

(B) What is the company's revenue function for this camera, and what is the domain of this function?

(C) Complete Table 5, computing revenues to the nearest million dollars.

(D) Plot the data in Table 5. Then sketch a graph of the revenue function using these points.

  (E) Plot the revenue function on a graphing utility.

Solution   (A)

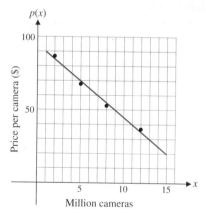

FIGURE 7 Price–demand

In Figure 7, notice that the model approximates the actual data in Table 4, and it is assumed that it gives realistic and useful results for all other values of x between 1 million and 15 million.

(B) $R(x) = xp(x) = x(94.8 - 5x)$ million dollars

Domain: $1 \leq x \leq 15$

[Same domain as the price–demand function, equation (5).]

(C)

TABLE 5 Revenue	
x (Millions)	R(x) (Million $)
1	90
3	239
6	389
9	448
12	418
15	297

(D)

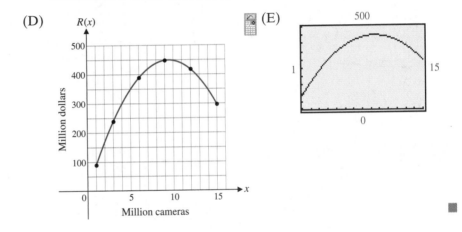

(E)

Matched Problem 7 The financial department in Example 7, using statistical techniques, produced the data in Table 6, where $C(x)$ is the cost in millions of dollars for manufacturing and selling x million cameras.

Using special analytical techniques (regression analysis), an analyst produced the following cost function to model the data:

$$C(x) = 156 + 19.7x \qquad 1 \leq x \leq 15 \qquad (6)$$

TABLE 6 Cost Data	
x (Millions)	C(x) (Million $)
1	175
5	260
8	305
12	395

(A) Plot the data in Table 6. Then sketch a graph of equation (6) in the same coordinate system.

(B) What is the company's profit function for this camera, and what is its domain?

(C) Complete Table 7, computing profits to the nearest million dollars.

TABLE 7 Profit	
x (Millions)	P(x) (Million $)
1	−86
3	
6	
9	
12	
15	

(D) Plot the points from part (C). Then sketch a graph of the profit function through these points.

(E) Plot the profit function on a graphing utility.

Answers to Matched Problems   **1.**

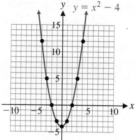

2. (A) Does not specify a function

(B) Specifies a function

3. $x \geq 2$ (inequality notation) or $[2, \infty)$ (interval notation)

4. (A) -3 (B) 0

(C) Does not exist   (D) 6

5. Domain of F: R; domain of G: all real numbers except -3;
domain of H: $x \leq 2$ (inequality notation) or $(-\infty, 2]$ (interval notation)

6. (A) $a^2 - 4a + 9$ (B) $a^2 + 2ah + h^2 - 4a - 4h + 9$

(C) $2ah + h^2 - 4h$ (D) $2a + h - 4$

7. (A)

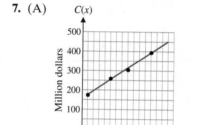

(B) $P(x) = R(x) - C(x) = x(94.8 - 5x) - (156 + 19.7x)$; domain: $1 \leq x \leq 15$

(C)

TABLE 7 Profit

x (Millions)	$P(x)$ (Million $)
1	-86
3	24
6	115
9	115
12	25
15	-155

(D)

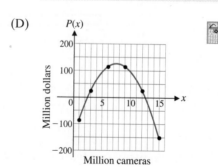

(E)

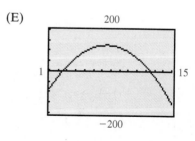

Exercise 1-1

A *Indicate whether each table in Problems 1–6 specifies a function.*

1.
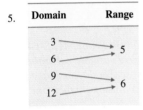

Domain	Range
3 ——→ 0	
5 ——→ 1	
7 ——→ 2	

2.
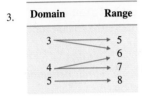

Domain	Range
−1 ——→ 5	
−2 ——→ 7	
−3 ——→ 9	

3.
Domain	Range
3	5
	6
4	7
5	8

4.
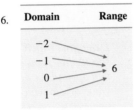

Domain	Range
8	0
9	1
	2
10	3

5.
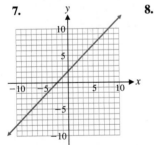

Domain	Range
3	
6	5
9	6
12	

6.
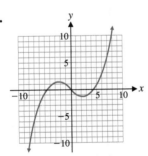

Domain	Range
−2	
−1	
0	6
1	

Indicate whether each graph in Problems 7–12 specifies a function.

7.
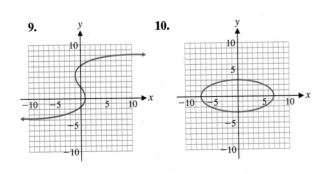

8.

9.

10.

11.
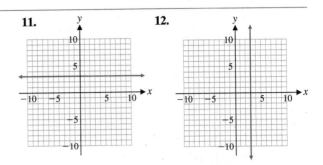

12.

In Problems 13 and 14, which of the indicated correspondences define functions? Explain.

13. Let P be the set of residents of Pennsylvania and let R and S be the set of members of the U.S. House of Representatives and the set of members of the U.S. Senate, respectively, elected by the residents of Pennsylvania.

   (A) A resident corresponds to the congress person representing the resident's congressional district.

   (B) A resident corresponds to the senator representing the resident's state.

14. Let P be the set of patients in a hospital, let D be the set of doctors on the hospital staff, and N be the set of nurses on the hospital staff.

   (A) A patient corresponds to the doctor if that doctor admitted the patient to the hospital.

   (B) A patient corresponds to the nurse if that nurse cares for the patient.

In Problems 15 and 16, the three points in the table are on the graph of the indicated function f. Do these three points provide sufficient information for you to sketch the graph of y = f(x)? Add more points to the table until you are satisfied that your sketch is a good representation of the graph of y = f(x) on the interval [−5, 5].

15.
x	−1	0	1
$f(x)$	−1	0	1

$$f(x) = \frac{2x}{x^2 + 1}$$

16.
x	0	1	2
$f(x)$	0	1	2

$$f(x) = \frac{3x^2}{x^2 + 2}$$

17. Let $f(x) = 100x - 5x^2$ and $g(x) = 150 + 20x$, $0 \le x \le 20$.

   (A) Evaluate $f(x), g(x)$, and $f(x) - g(x)$ for $x = 0, 5, 10, 15, 20$.

   (B) Graph $y = f(x), y = g(x)$, and $y = f(x) - g(x)$ on the interval $[0, 20]$.

18. Repeat Problem 17 for $f(x) = 200x - 10x^2$ and $g(x) = 200 + 50x$.

In Problems 19–26, use the following graph of a function f to determine x or y to the nearest integer, as indicated. Some problems may have more than one answer.

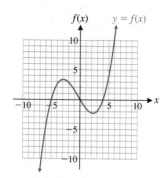

19. $y = f(-5)$ **20.** $y = f(4)$

21. $y = f(5)$ **22.** $y = f(-2)$

23. $0 = f(x)$ **24.** $3 = f(x), x < 0$

25. $-4 = f(x)$ **26.** $4 = f(x)$

If $f(x) = 2x - 3$ and $g(x) = x^2 + 2x$, find each of the expressions in Problems 27–38.

27. $f(2)$ **28.** $f(1)$

29. $f(-1)$ **30.** $g(1)$

31. $g(-3)$ **32.** $g(-2)$

33. $f(1) + g(2)$ **34.** $f(3) - g(3)$

35. $g(3) \cdot f(0)$ **36.** $g(0) \cdot f(-2)$

37. $\dfrac{g(-2)}{f(-2)}$ **38.** $\dfrac{g(-3)}{f(2)}$

B *In Problems 39–44, find the domain of each function.*

39. $F(x) = 2x^3 - x^2 + 3$ **40.** $H(x) = 7 - 2x^2 - x^4$

41. $f(x) = \dfrac{x - 2}{x + 4}$ **42.** $g(x) = \dfrac{x + 1}{x - 2}$

43. $g(x) = \sqrt{7 - x}$ **44.** $F(x) = \dfrac{1}{\sqrt{5 + x}}$

45. Two people are discussing the function

$$f(x) = \frac{x^2 - 4}{x^2 - 9}$$

and one says to the other, "$f(2)$ exists but $f(3)$ does not." Explain what they are talking about.

46. Referring to the function in Problem 45, do $f(-2)$ and $f(-3)$ exist? Explain.

The verbal statement "function f multiplies the square of the domain element by 3 and then subtracts 7 from

the result" and the algebraic statement "$f(x) = 3x^2 - 7$" define the same function. In Problems 47–50, translate each verbal definition of a function into an algebraic definition.

47. Function g subtracts 5 from twice the cube of the domain element.

48. Function f multiplies the domain element by -3 and adds 4 to the result.

49. Function G multiplies the square root of the domain element by 2 and subtracts the square of the domain element from the result.

50. Function F multiplies the cube of the domain element by -8 and adds 3 times the square root of 3 to the result.

In Problems 51–54, translate each algebraic definition of the function into a verbal definition.

51. $f(x) = 2x - 3$ **52.** $g(x) = -2x + 7$

53. $F(x) = 3x^3 - 2\sqrt{x}$ **54.** $G(x) = 4\sqrt{x} - x^2$

Determine which of the equations in Problems 55–64 specify functions with independent variable x. For those that do, find the domain. For those that do not, find a value of x to which there corresponds more than one value of y.

55. $4x - 5y = 20$ **56.** $3y - 7x = 15$

57. $x^2 - y = 1$ **58.** $x - y^2 = 1$

59. $x + y^2 = 10$ **60.** $x^2 + y = 10$

61. $xy - 4y = 1$ **62.** $xy + y - x = 5$

63. $x^2 + y^2 = 25$ **64.** $x^2 - y^2 = 16$

65. If $F(t) = 4t + 7$, find:
$$\frac{F(3 + h) - F(3)}{h}$$

66. If $G(r) = 3 - 5r$, find:
$$\frac{G(2 + h) - G(2)}{h}$$

67. If $Q(x) = x^2 - 5x + 1$, find:
$$\frac{Q(2 + h) - Q(2)}{h}$$

68. If $P(x) = 2x^2 - 3x - 7$, find:
$$\frac{P(3 + h) - P(3)}{h}$$

C *In Problems 69–74, find and simplify each of the following.*

(A) $f(x + h)$ (B) $f(x + h) - f(x)$

(C) $\dfrac{f(x + h) - f(x)}{h}$

69. $f(x) = 4x - 3$ **70.** $f(x) = -3x + 9$

71. $f(x) = 4x^2 - 7x + 6$ **72.** $f(x) = 3x^2 + 5x - 8$

73. $f(x) = x(20 - x)$ **74.** $f(x) = x(x + 40)$

Problems 75–78 refer to the area A and perimeter P of a rectangle with length l and width w (see the figure).

$A = lw$
$P = 2l + 2w$

w

l

75. The area of a rectangle is 25 square inches. Express the perimeter $P(w)$ as a function of the width w, and state the domain of this function.

76. The area of a rectangle is 81 square inches. Express the perimeter $P(l)$ as a function of the length l, and state the domain of this function.

77. The perimeter of a rectangle is 100 meters. Express the area $A(l)$ as a function of the length l, and state the domain of this function.

78. The perimeter of a rectangle is 160 meters. Express the area $A(w)$ as a function of the width w, and state the domain of this function.

Applications

Business & Economics

79. *Price–demand.* A company manufactures memory chips for microcomputers. Its marketing research department, using statistical techniques, collected the data shown in Table 8, where p is the wholesale price per chip at which x million chips can be sold. Using special analytical techniques (regression analysis), an analyst produced the following price–demand function to model the data:

$$p(x) = 75 - 3x \qquad 1 \le x \le 20$$

TABLE 8 Price–Demand

x (Millions)	p ($)
1	72
4	63
9	48
14	33
20	15

Plot the data points in Table 8, and sketch a graph of the price–demand function in the same coordinate system. What would be the estimated price per chip for a demand of 7 million chips? For a demand of 11 million chips?

80. *Price–demand.* A company manufactures "notebook" computers. Its marketing research department, using statistical techniques, collected the data shown in Table 9, where p is the wholesale price per computer at which x thousand computers can be

TABLE 9 Price–Demand

x (Thousands)	p ($)
1	1,940
8	1,520
16	1,040
21	740
25	500

sold. Using special analytical techniques (regression analysis), an analyst produced the following price–demand function to model the data:

$$p(x) = 2,000 - 60x \qquad 1 \le x \le 25$$

Plot the data points in Table 9, and sketch a graph of the price–demand function in the same coordinate system. What would be the estimated price per computer for a demand of 11 thousand computers? For a demand of 18 thousand computers?

81. *Revenue.*

(A) Using the price–demand function

$$p(x) = 75 - 3x \qquad 1 \le x \le 20$$

from Problem 79, write the company's revenue function and indicate its domain. $15x - 3x^2$

(B) Complete Table 10, computing revenues to the nearest million dollars.

TABLE 10 Revenue

x (Millions)	R (x) (Million $)
1	72
4	
8	
12	
16	
20	

(C) Plot the points from part (B) and sketch a graph of the revenue function through these points. Choose millions for the units on the horizontal and vertical axes.

82. *Revenue.*

(A) Using the price–demand function

$$p(x) = 2,000 - 60x \qquad 1 \le x \le 25$$

from Problem 80, write the company's revenue function and indicate its domain.

(B) Complete Table 11, computing revenues to the nearest thousand dollars.

TABLE 11 Revenue

x (Thousands)	$R(x)$ (Thousand $)
1	1,940
5	
10	
15	
20	
25	

(C) Plot the points from part (B) and sketch a graph of the revenue function through these points. Choose thousands for the units on the horizontal and vertical axes.

83. *Profit.* The financial department for the company in Problems 79 and 81 established the following cost function for producing and selling x million memory chips:

$$C(x) = 125 + 16x \text{ million dollars}$$

(A) Write a profit function for producing and selling x million memory chips, and indicate its domain.

(B) Complete Table 12, computing profits to the nearest million dollars.

[handwritten: $R - C$, $\frac{?}{-3x} - 125 - 16x$, $75x - 3x - 125 - 16x$, $-3x + 59x - 125$]

TABLE 12 Profit

x (Millions)	$P(x)$ (Million $)
1	−69
4	
8	
12	
16	
20	

(C) Plot the points in part (B) and sketch a graph of the profit function through these points.

84. *Profit.* The financial department for the company in Problems 80 and 82 established the following cost function for producing and selling x thousand "notebook" computers:

$$C(x) = 4,000 + 500x \text{ thousand dollars}$$

(A) Write a profit function for producing and selling x thousand "notebook" computers, and indicate the domain of this function.

(B) Complete Table 13, computing profits to the nearest thousand dollars.

TABLE 13 Profit

x (Thousands)	$P(x)$ (Thousand $)
1	−2,560
5	
10	
15	
20	
25	

(C) Plot the points in part (B) and sketch a graph of the profit function through these points.

85. *Packaging.* A candy box is to be made out of a piece of cardboard that measures 8 by 12 inches. Equal-sized squares x inches on a side will be cut out of each corner, and then the ends and sides will be folded up to form a rectangular box.

(A) Express the volume of the box $V(x)$ in terms of x.

(B) What is the domain of the function V (determined by the physical restrictions)?

(C) Complete Table 14.

TABLE 14 Volume

x	$V(x)$
1	
2	
3	

(D) Plot the points in part (C) and sketch a graph of the volume function through these points.

86. *Packaging.* Refer to Problem 85.

(A) Table 15 shows the volume of the box for some values of x between 1 and 2. Use these values to estimate to one decimal place the value of x between 1 and 2 that would produce a box with a volume of 65 cubic inches.

TABLE 15 Volume

x	$V(x)$
1.1	62.524
1.2	64.512
1.3	65.988
1.4	66.976
1.5	67.5
1.6	67.584
1.7	67.252

(B) Describe how you could refine this table to estimate x to two decimal places.

(C) Carry out the refinement you described in part (B) and approximate x to two decimal places.

87. *Packaging.* Refer to Problems 85 and 86.

(A) Examine the graph of $V(x)$ from Problem 85D and discuss the possible locations of other values of x that would produce a box with a volume of 65 cubic inches. Construct a table like Table 15 to estimate any such value to one decimal place.

(B) Refine the table you constructed in part (A) to provide an approximation to two decimal places.

88. *Packaging.* A parcel delivery service will only deliver packages with length plus girth (distance around) not exceeding 108 inches. A rectangular shipping box with square ends x inches on a side is to be used.

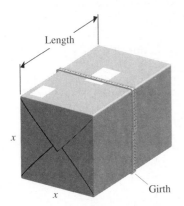

(A) If the full 108 inches is to be used, express the volume of the box $V(x)$ in terms of x.

(B) What is the domain of the function V (determined by the physical restrictions)?

(C) Complete Table 16.

TABLE 16 Volume	
x	$V(x)$
5	
10	
15	
20	
25	

(D) Plot the points in part (C) and sketch a graph of the volume function through these points.

Life Sciences

89. *Muscle contraction.* In a study of the speed of muscle contraction in frogs under various loads, noted British biophysicist and Nobel prize winner A.W. Hill determined that the weight w (in grams) placed on the muscle and the speed of contraction v (in centimeters per second) are approximately related by an equation of the form

$$(w + a)(v + b) = c$$

where a, b, and c are constants. Suppose that for a certain muscle, $a = 15$, $b = 1$, and $c = 90$. Express v as a function of w. Find the speed of contraction if a weight of 16 grams is placed on the muscle.

Social Sciences

90. *Politics.* The percentage s of seats in the House of Representatives won by Democrats and the percentage v of votes cast for Democrats (when expressed as decimal fractions) are related by the equation

$$5v - 2s = 1.4 \qquad 0 < s < 1, \quad 0.28 < v < 0.68$$

(A) Express v as a function of s, and find the percentage of votes required for the Democrats to win 51% of the seats.

(B) Express s as a function of v, and find the percentage of seats won if Democrats receive 51% of the votes.

Section 1-2 | Elementary Functions: Graphs and Transformations

- ➤ A Beginning Library of Elementary Functions
- ➤ Vertical and Horizontal Shifts
- ➤ Reflections, Expansions, and Contractions
- ➤ Piecewise-Defined Functions

The functions

$$g(x) = x^2 - 4 \qquad h(x) = (x - 4)^2 \qquad k(x) = -4x^2$$

all can be expressed in terms of the function $f(x) = x^2$ as follows:

$$g(x) = f(x) - 4 \qquad h(x) = f(x - 4) \qquad k(x) = -4f(x)$$

In this section we will see that the graphs of functions g, h, and k are closely related to the graph of function f. Insight gained by understanding these relationships will help us analyze and interpret the graphs of many different functions.

➤ A Beginning Library of Elementary Functions

As you progress through this book, and most any other mathematics course beyond this one, you will repeatedly encounter a relatively small list of elementary functions. We will identify these functions, study their basic properties, and include them in a library of elementary functions (see the inside front cover). This library will become an important addition to your mathematical toolbox and can be used in any course or activity where mathematics is applied.

We begin by placing six basic functions in our library.

DEFINITION   Basic Elementary Functions

$$f(x) = x \qquad \text{Identity function}$$

$$h(x) = x^2 \qquad \text{Square function}$$

$$m(x) = x^3 \qquad \text{Cube function}$$

$$n(x) = \sqrt{x} \qquad \text{Square root function}$$

$$p(x) = \sqrt[3]{x} \qquad \text{Cube root function}$$

$$g(x) = |x| \qquad \text{Absolute value function}$$

These elementary functions can be evaluated by hand for certain values of x and with a calculator for all values of x for which they are defined.

EXAMPLE 1   **Evaluating Basic Elementary Functions**   Evaluate each basic elementary function at

(A) $x = 64$ (B) $x = -12.75$

Round any approximate values to four decimal places.

Solution   (A) $f(64) = 64$

$h(64) = 64^2 = 4{,}096$ *Use a calculator.*

$m(64) = 64^3 = 262{,}144$ *Use a calculator.*

$n(64) = \sqrt{64} = 8$

$p(64) = \sqrt[3]{64} = 4$

$g(64) = |64| = 64$

(B) $f(-12.75) = -12.75$

$h(-12.75) = (-12.75)^2 = 162.5625$ *Use a calculator.*

$m(-12.75) = (-12.75)^3 \approx -2{,}072.6719$ *Use a calculator.*

$n(-12.75) = \sqrt{-12.75}$ *Not a real number.*

$p(-12.75) = \sqrt[3]{-12.75} \approx -2.3362$ *Use a calculator.*

$g(-12.75) = |-12.75| = 12.75$

Matched Problem 1   Evaluate each basic elementary function at

(A) $x = 729$ (B) $x = -5.25$

Round any approximate values to four decimal places.

Remark

Most computers and graphing calculators use ABS(x) to represent the absolute value function. The following representation can also be useful:

$$|x| = \sqrt{x^2}$$

Figure 1 shows the graph, range, and domain of each of the basic elementary functions.

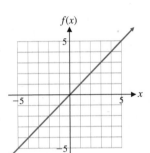

(A) **Identity function**
$f(x) = x$
Domain: R
Range: R

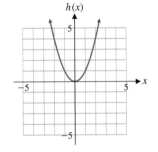

(B) **Square function**
$h(x) = x^2$
Domain: R
Range: $[0, \infty)$

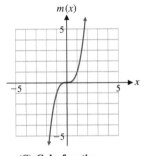

(C) **Cube function**
$m(x) = x^3$
Domain: R
Range: R

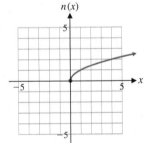

(D) **Square root function**
$n(x) = \sqrt{x}$
Domain: $[0, \infty)$
Range: $[0, \infty)$

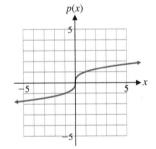

(E) **Cube root function**
$p(x) = \sqrt[3]{x}$
Domain: R
Range: R

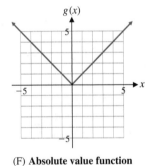

(F) **Absolute value function**
$g(x) = |x|$
Domain: R
Range: $[0, \infty)$

FIGURE 1 Some basic functions and their graphs
Note: Letters used to designate these functions may vary from context to context; R is the set of all real numbers.

Insight   **Absolute Value** In beginning algebra, absolute value is often interpreted as distance from the origin on a real number line (see Appendix A, Section A-1).

distance = 6 = −(−6)   distance = 5

If $x < 0$, then $-x$ is the *positive* distance from the origin to x and if $x > 0$, then x is the positive distance from the origin to x. Thus,

$$|x| = \begin{cases} -x & \text{if } x < 0 \\ x & \text{if } x \geq 0 \end{cases}$$

➤ Vertical and Horizontal Shifts

If a new function is formed by performing an operation on a given function, then the graph of the new function is called a **transformation** of the graph of the original function. For example, graphs of both $y = f(x) + k$ and $y = f(x + h)$ are transformations of the graph of $y = f(x)$.

Let $f(x) = x^2$.

(A) Graph $y = f(x) + k$ for $k = -4, 0,$ and 2 simultaneously in the same coordinate system. Describe the relationship between the graph of $y = f(x)$ and the graph of $y = f(x) + k$ for k any real number.

(B) Graph $y = f(x + h)$ for $h = -4, 0,$ and 2 simultaneously in the same coordinate system. Describe the relationship between the graph of $y = f(x)$ and the graph of $y = f(x + h)$ for h any real number.

EXAMPLE 2   **Vertical and Horizontal Shifts**

(A) How are the graphs of $y = |x| + 4$ and $y = |x| - 5$ related to the graph of $y = |x|$? Confirm your answer by graphing all three functions simultaneously in the same coordinate system.

(B) How are the graphs of $y = |x + 4|$ and $y = |x - 5|$ related to the graph of $y = |x|$? Confirm your answer by graphing all three functions simultaneously in the same coordinate system.

Solution   (A) The graph of $y = |x| + 4$ is the same as the graph of $y = |x|$ shifted upward 4 units, and the graph of $y = |x| - 5$ is the same as the graph of $y = |x|$ shifted downward 5 units. Figure 2 confirms these conclusions. [It appears that the graph of $y = f(x) + k$ is the graph of $y = f(x)$ shifted up if k is positive and down if k is negative.]

(B) The graph of $y = |x + 4|$ is the same as the graph of $y = |x|$ shifted to the left 4 units, and the graph of $y = |x - 5|$ is the same as the graph of $y = |x|$ shifted to the right 5 units. Figure 3 confirms these conclusions. [It appears that the graph of $y = f(x + h)$ is the graph of $y = f(x)$ shifted right if h is negative and left if h is positive—the opposite of what you might expect.]

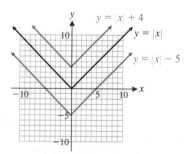

FIGURE 2   Vertical shifts

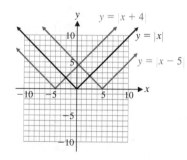

FIGURE 3   Horizontal shifts

Matched Problem 2

(A) How are the graphs of $y = \sqrt{x} + 5$ and $y = \sqrt{x} - 4$ related to the graph of $y = \sqrt{x}$? Confirm your answer by graphing all three functions simultaneously in the same coordinate system.

(B) How are the graphs of $y = \sqrt{x + 5}$ and $y = \sqrt{x - 4}$ related to the graph of $y = \sqrt{x}$? Confirm your answer by graphing all three functions simultaneously in the same coordinate system. ■

Comparing the graphs of $y = f(x) + k$ with the graph of $y = f(x)$, we see that the graph of $y = f(x) + k$ can be obtained from the graph of $y = f(x)$ by **vertically translating** (shifting) the graph of the latter upward k units if k is positive and downward $|k|$ units if k is negative. Comparing the graphs of $y = f(x + h)$ with the graph of $y = f(x)$, we see that the graph of $y = f(x + h)$ can be obtained from the graph of $y = f(x)$ by **horizontally translating** (shifting) the graph of the latter h units to the left if h is positive and $|h|$ units to the right if h is negative.

EXAMPLE 3 **Vertical and Horizontal Translations (Shifts)** The graphs in Figure 4 are either horizontal or vertical shifts of the graph of $f(x) = x^2$. Write appropriate equations for functions $H, G, M,$ and N in terms of f.

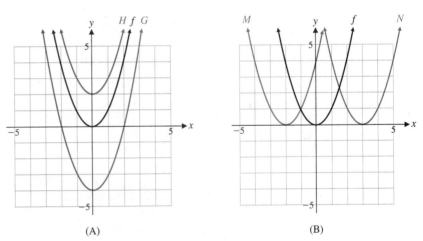

(A)   (B)

FIGURE 4 Vertical and horizontal shifts

Solution Functions H and G are vertical shifts given by

$$H(x) = x^2 + 2 \qquad G(x) = x^2 - 4$$

Functions M and N are horizontal shifts given by

$$M(x) = (x + 2)^2 \qquad N(x) = (x - 3)^2$$ ■

Matched Problem 3

The graphs in Figure 5 are either horizontal or vertical shifts of the graph of $f(x) = \sqrt[3]{x}$. Write appropriate equations for functions $H, G, M,$ and N in terms of f.

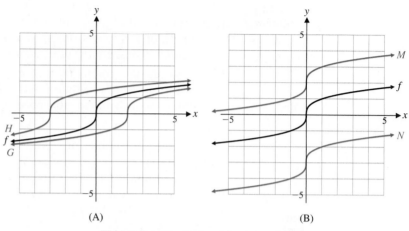

FIGURE 5 Vertical and horizontal shifts

▶ Reflections, Expansions, and Contractions

We now investigate how the graph of $y = Af(x)$ is related to the graph of $y = f(x)$ for different real numbers A.

(A) Graph $y = Ax^2$ for $A = 1, 4,$ and $\frac{1}{4}$ simultaneously in the same coordinate system.

(B) Graph $y = Ax^2$ for $A = -1, -4,$ and $-\frac{1}{4}$ simultaneously in the same coordinate system.

(C) Describe the relationship between the graph of $h(x) = x^2$ and the graph of $G(x) = Ax^2$ for A any real number.

Comparing $y = Af(x)$ to $y = f(x)$, we see that the graph of $y = Af(x)$ can be obtained from the graph of $y = f(x)$ by multiplying each ordinate value of the latter by A. The result is a **vertical expansion** of the graph of $y = f(x)$ if $A > 1$, a **vertical contraction** of the graph of $y = f(x)$ if $0 < A < 1$, and a **reflection in the x axis** if $A = -1$. If A is a negative number other than -1, then the result is a combination of a reflection in the x axis and either a vertical expansion or a vertical contraction.

EXAMPLE 4 **Reflections, Expansions, and Contractions**

(A) How are the graphs of $y = 2|x|$ and $y = 0.5|x|$ related to the graph of $y = |x|$? Confirm your answer by graphing all three functions simultaneously in the same coordinate system.

(B) How is the graph of $y = -2|x|$ related to the graph of $y = |x|$? Confirm your answer by graphing both functions simultaneously in the same coordinate system.

Solution (A) The graph of $y = 2|x|$ is a vertical expansion of the graph of $y = |x|$ by a factor of 2, and the graph of $y = 0.5|x|$ is a vertical contraction of the graph of $y = |x|$ by a factor of 0.5. Figure 6 confirms this conclusion.

(B) The graph of $y = -2|x|$ is a reflection in the x axis and a vertical expansion of the graph of $y = |x|$. Figure 7 confirms this conclusion.

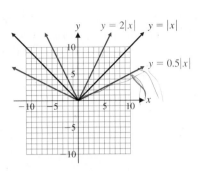

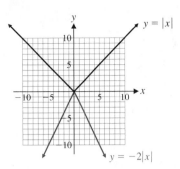

FIGURE 6 Vertical expansion
and contraction

FIGURE 7 Reflection and
vertical expansion

**Matched
Problem 4**

(A) How are the graphs of $y = 2x$ and $y = 0.5x$ related to the graph of
$y = x$? Confirm your answer by graphing all three functions simultaneously in the same coordinate system.

(B) How is the graph of $y = -0.5x$ related to the graph of $y = x$? Confirm
your answer by graphing both functions in the same coordinate system.

The various transformations considered above are summarized in the
following box for easy reference:

SUMMARY   Graph Transformations

Vertical Translation:

$$y = f(x) + k \quad \begin{cases} k > 0 & \text{Shift graph of } y = f(x) \text{ up } k \text{ units.} \\ k < 0 & \text{Shift graph of } y = f(x) \text{ down } |k| \text{ units.} \end{cases}$$

Horizontal Translation:

$$y = f(x + h) \quad \begin{cases} h > 0 & \text{Shift graph of } y = f(x) \text{ left } h \text{ units.} \\ h < 0 & \text{Shift graph of } y = f(x) \text{ right } |h| \text{ units.} \end{cases}$$

Reflection:

$$y = -f(x) \quad \text{Reflect the graph of } y = f(x) \text{ in the } x \text{ axis.}$$

Vertical Expansion and Contraction:

$$y = Af(x) \quad \begin{cases} A > 1 & \text{Expand graph of } y = f(x) \text{ vertically} \\ & \text{by multiplying each ordinate value by } A. \\ 0 < A < 1 & \text{Contract graph of } y = f(x) \text{ vertically} \\ & \text{by multiplying each ordinate value by } A. \end{cases}$$

> up

down

**EXPLORE
&DISCUSS
3**

Use a graphing utility to explore the graph of $y = A(x + h)^2 + k$ for various values of the constants A, h, and k. Discuss how the graph of
$y = A(x + h)^2 + k$ is related to the graph of $y = x^2$.

EXAMPLE 5   **Combining Graph Transformations** Discuss the relationship be-
tween the graphs of $y = -|x - 3| + 1$ and $y = |x|$. Confirm your answer by
graphing both functions simultaneously in the same coordinate system.

Solution   The graph of $y = -|x - 3| + 1$ is a reflection in the x axis, a horizontal translation of 3 units to the right, and a vertical translation of 1 unit upward of the graph of $y = |x|$. Figure 8 confirms this description.

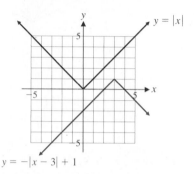

$$y = -|x - 3| + 1$$

FIGURE 8 Combined transformations

Matched Problem 5   The graph of $y = G(x)$ in Figure 9 involves a reflection and a translation of the graph of $y = x^3$. Describe how the graph of function G is related to the graph of $y = x^3$ and find an equation of the function G.

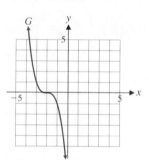

FIGURE 9 Combined transformations

➤ Piecewise-Defined Functions

Earlier we noted that the absolute value of a real number x can be defined as

$$|x| = \begin{cases} -x & \text{if } x < 0 \\ x & \text{if } x \geq 0 \end{cases}$$

Notice that this function is defined by different rules for different parts of its domain. Functions whose definitions involve more than one rule are called **piecewise-defined functions.** Graphing one of these functions involves graphing each rule over the appropriate portion of the domain (Fig. 10). In Figure 10C, notice that an open dot is used to show that the point $(0, -2)$ is not part of the graph and a solid dot is used to show that $(0, 2)$ is part of the graph.

As the next example illustrates, piecewise-defined functions occur naturally in many applications.

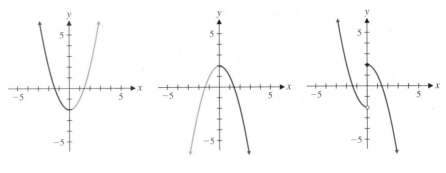

(A) $y = x^2 - 2$ (B) $y = 2 - x^2$ (C) $y = \begin{cases} x^2 - 2 & \text{if } x < 0 \\ 2 - x^2 & \text{if } x \geq 0 \end{cases}$

FIGURE 10 Graphing a piecewise-defined function

EXAMPLE 6

Natural Gas Rates Easton Utilities uses the rates shown in Table 1 to compute the monthly cost of natural gas for each customer. Write a piecewise definition for the cost of consuming x CCF (cubic hundred feet) of natural gas and graph the function.

TABLE 1 Charges per Month
\$0.7866 per CCF for the first 5 CCF
\$0.4601 per CCF for the next 35 CCF
\$0.2508 per CCF for all over 40 CCF

Solution   If $C(x)$ is the cost, in dollars, of using x CCF of natural gas in one month, then the first line of Table 1 implies that

$$C(x) = 0.7866x \quad \text{if } 0 \leq x \leq 5$$

Note that $C(5) = 3.933$ is the cost of 5 CCF. If $5 < x \leq 40$, then $x - 5$ represents the amount of gas that cost \$0.4601 per CCF, $0.4601(x - 5)$ represents the cost of this gas, and the total cost is

$$C(x) = 3.933 + 0.4601(x - 5)$$

If $x > 40$, then

$$C(x) = 20.0365 + 0.2508(x - 40)$$

where $20.0365 = C(40)$, the cost of the first 40 CCF. Combining all these equations, we have the following piecewise definition for $C(x)$:

$$C(x) = \begin{cases} 0.7866x & \text{if } 0 \leq x \leq 5 \\ 3.933 + 0.4601(x - 5) & \text{if } 5 < x \leq 40 \\ 20.0365 + 0.2508(x - 40) & \text{if } 40 < x \end{cases}$$

To graph C, first note that each rule in the definition of C represents a transformation of the identity function $f(x) = x$. Graphing each transformation over the indicated interval produces the graph of C shown in Figure 11.

$C(x)$

FIGURE 11 Cost of purchasing x CCF of natural gas

Matched Problem 6 *Natural Gas Rates* Trussville Utilities uses the rates shown in Table 2 to compute the monthly cost of natural gas for residential customers. Write a piecewise definition for the cost of consuming x CCF of natural gas and graph the function.

TABLE 2 Charges per Month
$0.7675 per CCF for the first 50 CCF
$0.6400 per CCF for the next 150 CCF
$0.6130 per CCF for all over 200 CCF

Answers to Matched Problems

1. (A) $f(729) = 729,\quad h(729) = 531{,}441,\quad m(729) = 387{,}420{,}489,$

   $n(729) = 27,\quad p(729) = 9,\quad g(729) = 729$

(B) $f(-5.25) = -5.25,\quad h(-5.25) = 27.5625,$

   $m(-5.25) = -144.7031,\quad n(-5.25)$ is not a real number,

   $p(-5.25) = -1.7380,\quad g(-5.25) = 5.25$

2. (A) The graph of $y = \sqrt{x} + 5$ is the same as the graph of $y = \sqrt{x}$ shifted upward 5 units, and the graph of $y = \sqrt{x} - 4$ is the same as the graph of $y = \sqrt{x}$ shifted downward 4 units. The figure confirms these conclusions.

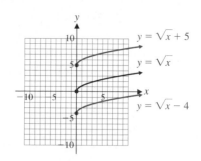

(B) The graph of $y = \sqrt{x + 5}$ is the same as the graph of $y = \sqrt{x}$ shifted to the left 5 units, and the graph of $y = \sqrt{x - 4}$ is the same as the graph of $y = \sqrt{x}$ shifted to the right 4 units. The figure on page 31 confirms these conclusions.

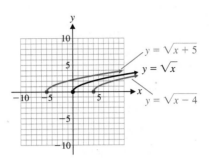

3. $H(x) = \sqrt[3]{x + 3}, G(x) = \sqrt[3]{x - 2}, M(x) = \sqrt[3]{x} + 2, N(x) = \sqrt[3]{x} - 3$

4. (A) The graph of $y = 2x$ is a vertical expansion of the graph of $y = x$, and the graph of $y = 0.5x$ is a vertical contraction of the graph of $y = x$. The figure confirms these conclusions.

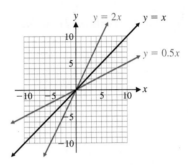

(B) The graph of $y = -0.5x$ is a vertical contraction and a reflection in the x axis of the graph of $y = x$. The figure confirms this conclusion.

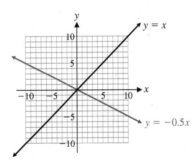

5. The graph of function G is a reflection in the x axis and a horizontal translation of 2 units to the left of the graph of $y = x^3$. An equation for G is $G(x) = -(x + 2)^3$.

6. $C(x) = \begin{cases} 0.7675x & \text{if } 0 \le x \le 50 \\ 38.375 + 0.64(x - 50) & \text{if } 50 < x \le 200 \\ 134.375 + 0.613(x - 200) & \text{if } 200 < x \end{cases}$

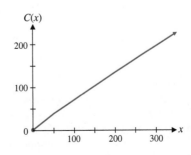

Exercise 1-2

A *Without looking back in the text, indicate the domain and range of each of the functions in Problems 1–8.*

1. $f(x) = 2x$ **2.** $g(x) = -0.3x$

3. $h(x) = -0.6\sqrt{x}$ **4.** $k(x) = 4\sqrt{x}$

5. $m(x) = 3|x|$ **6.** $n(x) = -0.1x^2$

7. $r(x) = -x^3$ **8.** $s(x) = 5\sqrt[3]{x}$

Graph each of the functions in Problems 9–20 using the graphs of functions f and g below.

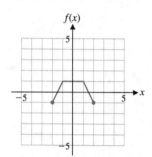

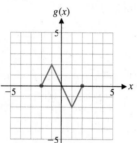

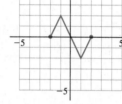

9. $y = f(x) + 2$ **10.** $y = g(x) - 1$

11. $y = f(x + 2)$ **12.** $y = g(x - 1)$

13. $y = g(x - 3)$ **14.** $y = f(x + 3)$

15. $y = g(x) - 3$ **16.** $y = f(x) + 3$

17. $y = -f(x)$ **18.** $y = -g(x)$

19. $y = 0.5g(x)$ **20.** $y = 2f(x)$

B *In Problems 21–28, indicate verbally how the graph of each function is related to the graph of one of the six basic functions in Figure 1 on page 23. Sketch a graph of each function.*

21. $g(x) = -|x + 3|$

22. $h(x) = -|x - 5|$

23. $f(x) = (x - 4)^2 - 3$

24. $m(x) = (x + 3)^2 + 4$

25. $f(x) = 7 - \sqrt{x}$

26. $g(x) = -6 + \sqrt[3]{x}$

27. $h(x) = -3|x|$

28. $m(x) = -0.4x^2$

Each graph in Problems 29–36 is the result of applying a sequence of transformations to the graph of one of the six basic functions in Figure 1 on page 23. Identify the basic function and describe the transformation verbally. Write an equation for the given graph.

29.

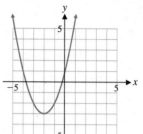

30.

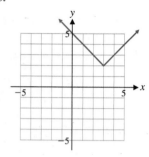

31.

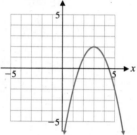

32.

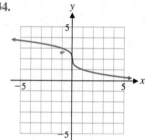

33.

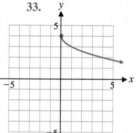

34.

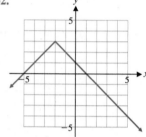

35.

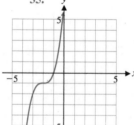

36.

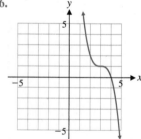

In Problems 37–42, the graph of the function g is formed by applying the indicated sequence of transformations to the given function f. Find an equation for the function g and graph g using $-5 \le x \le 5$ and $-5 \le y \le 5$.

37. The graph of $f(x) = \sqrt{x}$ is shifted 2 units to the right and 3 units down.

38. The graph of $f(x) = \sqrt[3]{x}$ is shifted 3 units to the left and 2 units up.

39. The graph of $f(x) = |x|$ is reflected in the x axis and shifted to the left 3 units.

40. The graph of $f(x) = |x|$ is reflected in the x axis and shifted to the right 1 unit.

41. The graph of $f(x) = x^3$ is reflected in the x axis and shifted 2 units to the right and down 1 unit.

42. The graph of $f(x) = x^2$ is reflected in the x axis and shifted to the left 2 units and up 4 units.

Graph each function in Problems 43–48.

43. $f(x) = \begin{cases} 2 - 2x & \text{if } x < 2 \\ x - 2 & \text{if } x \geq 2 \end{cases}$

44. $g(x) = \begin{cases} x + 1 & \text{if } x < -1 \\ 2 + 2x & \text{if } x \geq -1 \end{cases}$

45. $h(x) = \begin{cases} 5 + 0.5x & \text{if } 0 \leq x \leq 10 \\ -10 + 2x & \text{if } x > 10 \end{cases}$

46. $h(x) = \begin{cases} 10 + 2x & \text{if } 0 \leq x \leq 20 \\ 40 + 0.5x & \text{if } x > 20 \end{cases}$

47. $h(x) = \begin{cases} 2x & \text{if } 0 \leq x \leq 20 \\ x + 20 & \text{if } 20 < x \leq 40 \\ 0.5x + 45 & \text{if } x > 40 \end{cases}$

48. $h(x) = \begin{cases} 4x + 20 & \text{if } 0 \leq x \leq 20 \\ 2x + 60 & \text{if } 20 < x \leq 100 \\ -x + 360 & \text{if } x > 100 \end{cases}$

C *Each of the graphs in Problems 49–54 involves a reflection in the x axis and/or a vertical expansion or contraction of one of the basic functions in Figure 1 on page 23. Identify the basic function, and describe the transformation verbally. Write an equation for the given graph.*

49.
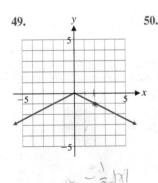

50.
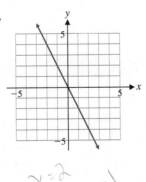

51.
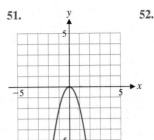

52.
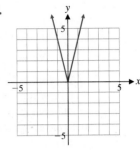

53.
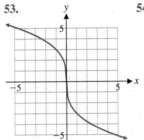

54.
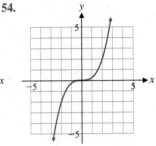

Changing the order in a sequence of transformations may change the final result. Investigate each pair of transformations in Problems 55–60 to determine if reversing their order can produce a different result. Support your conclusions with specific examples and/or mathematical arguments.

55. Vertical shift; horizontal shift

56. Vertical shift; reflection in y axis

57. Vertical shift; reflection in x axis

58. Vertical shift; vertical expansion

59. Horizontal shift; reflection in y axis

60. Horizontal shift; vertical contraction

Applications

Business & Economics

61. *Price–demand.* A retail chain sells CD players. The retail price $p(x)$ (in dollars) and the weekly demand x for a particular model are related by

$$p(x) = 115 - 4\sqrt{x} \qquad 9 \leq x \leq 289$$

(A) Describe how the graph of function p can be obtained from the graph of one of the basic functions in Figure 1 on page 23.

(B) Sketch a graph of function p using part (A) as an aid.

62. *Price–supply.* The manufacturers of the CD players in Problem 61 are willing to supply x players at a price of $p(x)$ as given by the equation

$$p(x) = 4\sqrt{x} \qquad 9 \le x \le 289$$

(A) Describe how the graph of function p can be obtained from the graph of one of the basic functions in Figure 1 on page 23.

(B) Sketch a graph of function p using part (A) as an aid.

63. *Hospital costs.* Using statistical methods, the financial department of a hospital arrived at the cost equation

$$C(x) = 0.00048(x - 500)^3 + 60,000 \qquad 100 \le x \le 1,000$$

where $C(x)$ is the cost in dollars for handling x cases per month.

(A) Describe how the graph of function C can be obtained from the graph of one of the basic functions in Figure 1 on page 23.

(B) Sketch a graph of function C using part (A) and a graphing utility as aids.

64. *Price–demand.* A company manufactures and sells in-line skates. Their financial department has established the price–demand function

$$p(x) = 190 - 0.013(x - 10)^2 \quad 10 \le x \le 100$$

where $p(x)$ is the price at which x thousand pairs of skates can be sold.

(A) Describe how the graph of function p can be obtained from the graph of one of the basic functions in Figure 1 on page 23.

(B) Sketch a graph of function p using part (A) and a graphing utility as aids.

65. *Electricity rates.* Table 3 shows the electricity rates charged by Monroe Utilities in the summer months. The base is a fixed monthly charge, independent of the kWh (kilowatthours) used during the month.

(A) Write a piecewise definition of the monthly charge $S(x)$ for a customer who uses x kWh in a summer month.

(B) Graph $S(x)$.

TABLE 3 Summer (July–October)
Base charge, $8.50
First 700 kWh or less at 0.0650/kWh
Over 700 kWh at 0.0900/kWh

66. *Electricity rates.* Table 4 shows the electricity rates charged by Monroe Utilities in the winter months.

(A) Write a piecewise definition of the monthly charge $W(x)$ for a customer who uses x kWh in a winter month.

TABLE 4 Winter (November–June)
Base charge, $8.50
First 700 kWh or less at 0.0650/kWh
Over 700 kWh at 0.0530/kWh

(B) Graph $W(x)$.

67. *State income tax.* Table 5 shows a recent state income tax schedule for married couples filing a joint return in the state of Kansas.

(A) Write a piecewise definition for the tax due $T(x)$ on an income of x dollars.

(B) Graph $T(x)$.

(C) Find the tax due on a taxable income of $40,000. Of $70,000.

TABLE 5 Kansas State Income Tax		
SCHEDULE I—MARRIED FILING JOINT		
If taxable income is		
Over	But Not Over	Tax Due Is
$0	$30,000	3.50% of taxable income
$30,000	$60,000	$1,050 plus 6.25% of excess over $30,000
$60,000		$2,925 plus 6.45% of excess over $60,000

68. *State income tax.* Table 6 shows a recent state income tax schedule for individuals filing a return in the state of Kansas.

(A) Write a piecewise definition for the tax due $T(x)$ on an income of x dollars.

(B) Graph $T(x)$.

(C) Find the tax due on a taxable income of $20,000. Of $35,000.

(D) Would it be better for a married couple in Kansas with two equal incomes to file jointly or separately? Discuss.

TABLE 6 Kansas State Income Tax		
SCHEDULE II—SINGLE, HEAD OF HOUSEHOLD, OR MARRIED FILING SEPARATE		
If taxable income is		
Over	But Not Over	Tax Due Is
$0	$15,000	3.50% of taxable income
$15,000	$30,000	$525 plus 6.25% of excess over $15,000
$30,000		$1,462.50 plus 6.45% of excess over $30,000

Life Sciences

69. *Physiology.* A good approximation of the normal weight of a person 60 inches or taller but not taller than 80 inches is given by $w(x) = 5.5x - 220$, where x is height in inches and $w(x)$ is weight in pounds.

(A) Describe how the graph of function w can be obtained from the graph of one of the basic functions in Figure 1, page 23.

(B) Sketch a graph of function w using part (A) as an aid.

70. *Physiology.* The average weight of a particular species of snake is given by $w(x) = 463x^3$, $0.2 \le x \le 0.8$, where x is length in meters and $w(x)$ is weight in grams.

(A) Describe how the graph of function w can be obtained from the graph of one of the basic functions in Figure 1, page 23.

(B) Sketch a graph of function w using part (A) as an aid.

Social Sciences

71. *Safety research.* Under ideal conditions, if a person driving a vehicle slams on the brakes and skids to a stop, the speed of the vehicle $v(x)$ (in miles per hour) is given approximately by $v(x) = C\sqrt{x}$, where x is the length of skid marks (in feet) and C is a constant that depends on the road conditions and the weight of the vehicle. For a particular vehicle, $v(x) = 7.08\sqrt{x}$ and $4 \le x \le 144$.

(A) Describe how the graph of function v can be obtained from the graph of one of the basic functions in Figure 1, page 23.

(B) Sketch a graph of function v using part (A) as an aid.

72. *Learning.* A production analyst has found that on the average it takes a new person $T(x)$ minutes to perform a particular assembly operation after x performances of the operation, where $T(x) = 10 - \sqrt[3]{x}, 0 \le x \le 125$.

(A) Describe how the graph of function T can be obtained from the graph of one of the basic functions in Figure 1, page 23.

(B) Sketch a graph of function T using part (A) as an aid.

Section **1-3** | Linear Functions and Straight Lines

- ➤ Intercepts
- ➤ Linear Functions, Equations, and Inequalities
- ➤ Graphs of $Ax + By = C$
- ➤ Slope of a Line
- ➤ Equations of Lines: Special Forms
- ➤ Applications

In this section we will add another important class of functions to our basic list of elementary functions. These functions are called *linear functions* and include the identity function $f(x) = x$ as a special case. We will investigate the relationship between linear functions and the solutions to linear equations and inequalities. (A detailed treatment of algebraic solutions to linear equations and inequalities can be found in Appendix A, Section A-7.) Finally, we will review the concept of slope and some of the standard equations of straight lines. These new tools will be applied to a variety of significant applications, including cost and price–demand functions.

➤ Intercepts

Figure 1 on page 36 illustrates the graphs of three functions f, g, and h.

If the graph of a function f crosses the x axis at a point with x coordinate a, then a is called an **x intercept** of f. If the graph of f crosses the y axis at a point with y coordinate b, then b is called the **y intercept.** It is common practice to

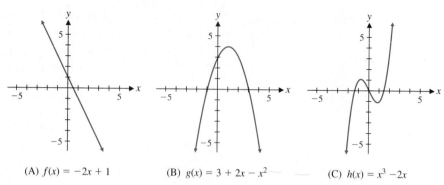

(A) $f(x) = -2x + 1$ (B) $g(x) = 3 + 2x - x^2$ (C) $h(x) = x^3 - 2x$

FIGURE 1 Graphs of several functions

refer to both the numbers a and b and the points $(a, 0)$ and $(0, b)$ as the x and y intercepts. If the y intercept exists, then 0 must be in the domain of f and the y intercept is simply $f(0)$. Thus, the graph of a function can have at most one y intercept. The x intercepts are all real solutions or roots of $f(x) = 0$, which may vary from none to an unlimited number. In Figure 1, function f has one y intercept and one x intercept; function g has one y intercept and two x intercepts; and function h has one y intercept and three x intercepts.

➤ Linear Functions, Equations, and Inequalities

In Figure 1, the graph of $f(x) = -2x + 1$ is a straight line, and because of this, we choose to call this type of function a *linear function*. In general,

DEFINITION   Linear and Constant Functions

A function f is a **linear function** if

$$f(x) = mx + b \qquad m \neq 0$$

where m and b are real numbers. The **domain** is the set of all real numbers, and the **range** is the set of all real numbers. If $m = 0$, then f is called a **constant function,**

$$f(x) = b$$

which has the set of all real numbers as its **domain** and the constant b as its **range.**

Since $mx + b, m \neq 0$, is a first-degree polynomial, linear functions are also called **first-degree functions.** Figure 2 shows the graphs of two linear functions f and g, and a constant function h.

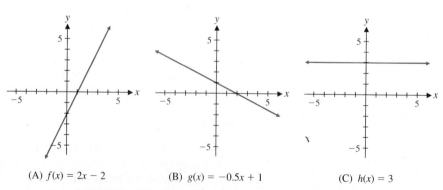

(A) $f(x) = 2x - 2$ (B) $g(x) = -0.5x + 1$ (C) $h(x) = 3$

FIGURE 2 Two linear functions and a constant function

◉ *Insight*   What do we know about the graph of a linear function $g(x) = mx + b$, $m \neq 0$? From Section 1-2, we know that the graph of $f(x) = x$ is a straight line. Using the transformations we studied in Section 1-2, we can see that the graph of g is obtained by reflecting the graph of f in the x axis (if m is negative), expanding or contracting by a factor of $|m|$, and then shifting up or down $|b|$ units. Theorems from plane geometry imply that the graph of g is always a line. If $m = 0$, then the graph of the constant function $g(x) = b$ is a horizontal line.   ●

What about vertical lines? Recall from Section 1-1 that the graph of a function cannot contain two points with the same x coordinate and different y coordinates. Since *all* points on a vertical line have the same x coordinate, the graph of a function can never be a vertical line. Later in this section we will discuss equations of vertical lines, but these equations never define functions.

EXPLORE
&DISCUSS
1

(A) Is it possible for a linear function to have two x intercepts? No x intercepts? If either of your answers is yes, give an example.

(B) Is it possible for a linear function to have two y intercepts? No y intercept? If either of your answers is yes, give an example.

(C) Discuss the possible number of x and y intercepts for a constant function.

EXAMPLE 1   Intercepts, Equations, and Inequalities

(A) Graph $f(x) = \frac{3}{2}x - 4$ in a rectangular coordinate system.

(B) Find the x and y intercepts algebraically to four decimal places.

(C) Graph $f(x) = \frac{3}{2}x - 4$ in a standard viewing window.

(D) Find the x and y intercepts to four decimal places using trace and the zero command on your graphing utility.

(E) Solve $\frac{3}{2}x - 4 \leq 0$ graphically to four decimal places using parts (A) and (B) or (C) and (D).

Solution   (A) Graph in a rectangular coordinate system:

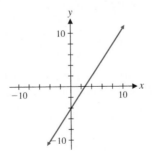

(B) Finding intercepts algebraically:

y intercept: $f(0) = \frac{3}{2}(0) - 4 = -4$

x intercept: $f(x) = 0$

$$\frac{3}{2}x - 4 = 0$$

$$\frac{3}{2}x = 4$$

$$x = \frac{8}{3} \approx 2.6667$$

(C) Graph in a graphing utility:

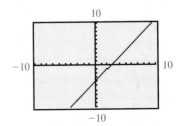

(D) Finding intercepts graphically in a graphing utility:

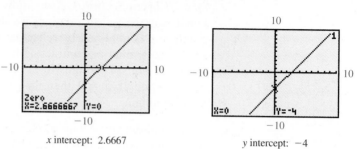

x intercept: 2.6667   y intercept: −4

(E) Solving $\frac{3}{2}x - 4 \leq 0$ graphically using parts (A) and (B) or (C) and (D): The linear inequality $\frac{3}{2}x - 4 \leq 0$ holds for those values of x for which the graph of $f(x) = \frac{3}{2}x - 4$ in the figure in part (A) or (C) is at or below the x axis. This happens for x less than or equal to the x intercept found in parts (B) or (D). Thus, the solution set for the linear inequality is $x \leq 2.6667$ or $(-\infty, 2.6667]$.

Matched Problem 1

(A) Graph $f(x) = -\frac{4}{3}x + 5$ in a rectangular coordinate system.

(B) Find the x and y intercepts algebraically to four decimal places.

(C) Graph $f(x) = -\frac{4}{3}x + 5$ in a standard viewing window.

(D) Find the x and y intercepts to four decimal places using trace and the zero command on your graphing utility.

(E) Solve $-\frac{4}{3}x + 5 \geq 0$ graphically to four decimal places using parts (A) and (B) or (C) and (D).

➤ Graphs of $Ax + By = C$

We now investigate graphs of linear, or first-degree, equations in two variables:

$$Ax + By = C \qquad (1)$$

where A and B are not both 0. Depending on the values of A and B, this equation defines a linear function, a constant function, or no function at all. If $A \neq 0$ and $B \neq 0$, then equation (1) can be written as

$$y = -\frac{A}{B}x + \frac{C}{B} \quad \text{Linear function (slanted line)} \qquad (2)$$

which is in the form $f(x) = mx + b, m \neq 0$, and hence is a linear function. If $A = 0$ and $B \neq 0$, then equation (1) can be written as

$$0x + By = C$$
$$y = \frac{C}{B} \quad \text{Constant function (horizontal line)} \qquad (3)$$

which is in the form $g(x) = b$, and hence is a constant function. If $A \neq 0$ and $B = 0$, then equation (1) can be written as

$$Ax + 0y = C$$
$$x = \frac{C}{A} \quad \text{Not a function (vertical line)} \qquad (4)$$

We can see that the graph of (4) is a vertical line, since the equation is satisfied for any value of y as long as x is the constant C/A. Hence, this form does not define a function.

The following theorem is a generalization of the preceding discussion:

THEOREM 1   Graph of a Linear Equation in Two Variables

In a Cartesian plane, the graph of any equation of the form

$$Ax + By = C \quad \text{Standard form} \tag{5}$$

where A, B, and C are real constants (A and B not both 0), is a straight line. Every straight line in a Cartesian plane coordinate system is the graph of an equation of this type.

Vertical and horizontal lines have particularly simple equations, which are special cases of equation (5):

Horizontal line with y intercept $C/B = b$: $y = b$

Vertical line with x intercept $C/A = a$: $x = a$

EXPLORE & DISCUSS 2

Graph the following three special cases of $Ax + By = C$ in the same coordinate system:

(A) $3x + 2y = 6$

(B) $0x - 3y = 12$

(C) $2x + 0y = 10$

Which cases define functions? Explain why, or why not.

   Graph each case in the same viewing window using a graphing utility. (Check your manual on how to graph vertical lines.)

Sketching the graphs of equations of either form

$$Ax + By = C \quad \text{or} \quad y = mx + b$$

is very easy, since the graph of each equation is a straight line. All that is necessary is to plot any two points from the solution set and use a straightedge to draw a line through these two points. The x and y intercepts are usually the easiest to find.

EXAMPLE 2   Sketching Graphs of Lines

(A) Graph $x = -4$ and $y = 6$ simultaneously in the same rectangular coordinate system. Also, graph in a graphing utility.

(B) Write the equations of the vertical and horizontal lines that pass through the point $(7, -5)$.

(C) Graph the equation $2x - 3y = 12$ by hand. Also, graph in a graphing utility.

Solution   (A) Graphing $x = -4$ and $y = 6$:

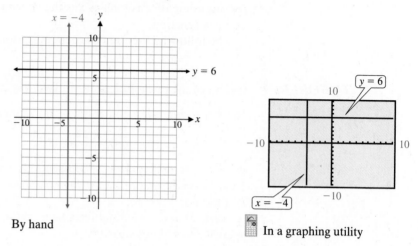

By hand   In a graphing utility

(B) Horizontal line through $(7, -5)$: $y = -5$
Vertical line through $(7, -5)$: $x = 7$

(C) Graphing $2x - 3y = 12$:   For the hand-drawn graph, find the intercepts by first letting $x = 0$ and solving for y and then letting $y = 0$ and solving for x. Then draw a line through the intercepts.   To graph in a graphing utility, solve the equation for y in terms of x and enter the result.

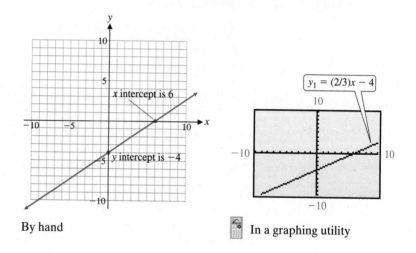

By hand   In a graphing utility

Matched Problem 2   (A) Graph $x = 5$ and $y = -3$ simultaneously in the same rectangular coordinate system.   Also, graph in a graphing utility.

(B) Write the equations of the vertical and horizontal lines that pass through the point $(-8, 2)$.

(C) Graph the equation $3x + 4y = 12$ by hand.   Also, graph in a graphing utility.

➤ **Slope of a Line**

If we take two points $P_1(x_1, y_1)$ and $P_2(x_2, y_2)$, on a line, then the ratio of the change in y to the change in x as the point moves from point P_1 to point P_2 is called the **slope** of the line. In a sense, slope provides a measure of the "steepness" of a line relative to the x axis. The change in x is often called the **run** and the change in y the **rise.**

DEFINITION   Slope of a Line

If a line passes through two distinct points $P_1(x_1, y_1)$ and $P_2(x_2, y_2)$, then its slope is given by the formula

$$m = \frac{y_2 - y_1}{x_2 - x_1} \qquad x_1 \neq x_2$$

$$= \frac{\text{vertical change (rise)}}{\text{horizontal change (run)}}$$

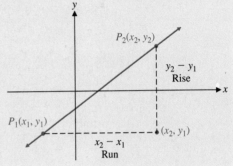

For a horizontal line, y does not change; hence, its slope is 0. For a vertical line, x does not change; hence, $x_1 = x_2$ and its slope is not defined. In general, the slope of a line may be positive, negative, 0, or not defined. Each case is illustrated geometrically in Table 1.

TABLE 1   Geometric Interpretation of Slope

Line	Rising as x moves from left to right	Falling as x moves from left to right	Horizontal	Vertical
Slope	Positive	Negative	0	Not defined
Example				

⊚ **Insight**   One property of real numbers discussed in Appendix A, Section A-1, is

$$\frac{-a}{-b} = -\frac{-a}{b} = -\frac{a}{-b} = \frac{a}{b}, \quad b \neq 0$$

This property implies that it does not matter which point we label as P_1 and which we label as P_2 in the slope formula. For example, if $A = (4, 3)$ and $B = (1, 2)$, then

$$B = P_2 = (1, 2) \qquad A = P_2 = (4, 3)$$
$$A = P_1 = (4, 3) \qquad B = P_1 = (1, 2)$$

$$m = \frac{2 - 3}{1 - 4} = \frac{-1}{-3} = \frac{1}{3} = \frac{3 - 2}{4 - 1}$$

A property of similar triangles (see Table II in Appendix C) ensures that the slope of a line is the same for any pair of distinct points on the line (Fig. 3).

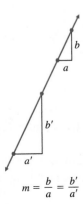

$$m = \frac{b}{a} = \frac{b'}{a'}$$

FIGURE 3

EXAMPLE 3 **Finding Slopes** Sketch a line through each pair of points, and find the slope of each line.

(A) $(-3, -2), (3, 4)$ (B) $(-1, 3), (2, -3)$

(C) $(-2, -3), (3, -3)$ (D) $(-2, 4), (-2, -2)$

Solution (A)

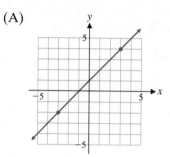

(B)

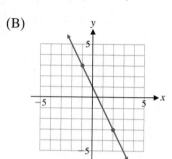

$$m = \frac{4 - (-2)}{3 - (-3)} = \frac{6}{6} = 1$$

$$m = \frac{-3 - 3}{2 - (-1)} = \frac{-6}{3} = -2$$

(C)

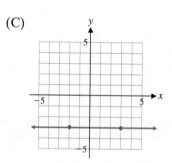

(D)

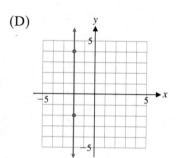

$$m = \frac{-3 - (-3)}{3 - (-2)} = \frac{0}{5} = 0$$

$$m = \frac{-2 - 4}{-2 - (-2)} = \frac{-6}{0}$$

Slope is not defined

Matched Problem 3 Find the slope of the line through each pair of points.

(A) $(-2, 4), (3, 4)$ (B) $(-2, 4), (0, -4)$

(C) $(-1, 5), (-1, -2)$ (D) $(-1, -2), (2, 1)$

➤ Equations of Lines: Special Forms

Let us start by investigating why $y = mx + b$ is called the *slope-intercept form* for a line.

EXPLORE & DISCUSS 3

(A) Graph $y = x + b$ for $b = -5, -3, 0, 3$, and 5 simultaneously in the same coordinate system. Verbally describe the geometric significance of b.

(B) Graph $y = mx - 1$ for $m = -2, -1, 0, 1$, and 2 simultaneously in the same coordinate system. Verbally describe the geometric significance of m.

(C) Using a graphing utility, explore the graph of $y = mx + b$ for different values of m and b.

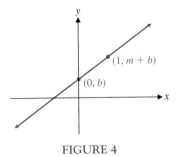

FIGURE 4

As you can see from the exploration before, constants m and b in $y = mx + b$ have special geometric significance, which we now explicitly state.

If we let $x = 0$, then $y = b$, and we observe that the graph of $y = mx + b$ crosses the y axis at $(0, b)$. The constant b is the y *intercept*. For example, the y intercept of the graph of $y = -4x - 1$ is -1.

To determine the geometric significance of m, we proceed as follows: If $y = mx + b$, then by setting $x = 0$ and $x = 1$, we conclude that $(0, b)$ and $(1, m + b)$ lie on its graph (Fig. 4). Hence, the slope of this line is given by:

$$\text{Slope} = \frac{y_2 - y_1}{x_2 - x_1} = \frac{(m + b) - b}{1 - 0} = m$$

Thus, m is the slope of the line given by $y = mx + b$.

DEFINITION   Slope-Intercept Form

The equation

$$y = mx + b \quad m = \text{Slope}, \ b = y \text{ intercept} \qquad (6)$$

is called the **slope-intercept form** of an equation of a line.

EXAMPLE 4   **Using the Slope-Intercept Form**

(A) Find the slope and y intercept, and graph $y = -\frac{2}{3}x - 3$.

(B) Write the equation of the line with slope $\frac{2}{3}$ and y intercept -2.

Solution   (A) Slope $= m = -\frac{2}{3}$ (B) $m = \frac{2}{3}$ and $b = -2$;

 y intercept $= b = -3$ thus, $y = \frac{2}{3}x - 2$

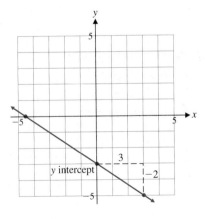

Matched Problem 4   Write the equation of the line with slope $\frac{1}{2}$ and y intercept -1. Graph.

Suppose that a line has slope m and passes through a fixed point (x_1, y_1). If the point (x, y) is any other point on the line (Fig. 5 on page 44), then

$$\frac{y - y_1}{x - x_1} = m$$

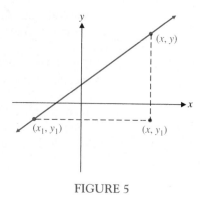

FIGURE 5

That is,

$$y - y_1 = m(x - x_1) \tag{7}$$

We now observe that (x_1, y_1) also satisfies equation (7) and conclude that equation (7) is an equation of a line with slope m that passes through (x_1, y_1).

> **DEFINITION** Point-Slope Form
>
> An equation of a line with slope m that passes through (x_1, y_1) is
>
> $$y - y_1 = m(x - x_1) \tag{7}$$
>
> which is called the **point-slope form** of an equation of a line.

The point-slope form is extremely useful, since it enables us to find an equation for a line if we know its slope and the coordinates of a point on the line or if we know the coordinates of two points on the line.

EXAMPLE 5 **Using the Point-Slope Form**

(A) Find an equation for the line that has slope $\frac{1}{2}$ and passes through $(-4, 3)$. Write the final answer in the form $Ax + By = C$.

(B) Find an equation for the line that passes through the two points $(-3, 2)$ and $(-4, 5)$. Write the resulting equation in the form $y = mx + b$.

Solution (A) Use $y - y_1 = m(x - x_1)$. Let $m = \frac{1}{2}$ and $(x_1, y_1) = (-4, 3)$. Then

$$y - 3 = \tfrac{1}{2}[x - (-4)]$$
$$y - 3 = \tfrac{1}{2}(x + 4) \qquad \text{Multiply by 2.}$$
$$2y - 6 = x + 4$$
$$-x + 2y = 10 \quad \text{or} \quad x - 2y = -10$$

(B) First, find the slope of the line by using the slope formula:

$$m = \frac{y_2 - y_1}{x_2 - x_1} = \frac{5 - 2}{-4 - (-3)} = \frac{3}{-1} = -3$$

Now use $y - y_1 = m(x - x_1)$ with $m = -3$ and $(x_1, y_1) = (-3, 2)$:

$$y - 2 = -3[x - (-3)]$$
$$y - 2 = -3(x + 3)$$
$$y - 2 = -3x - 9$$
$$y = -3x - 7$$

Matched Problem 5 (A) Find an equation for the line that has slope $\frac{2}{3}$ and passes through $(6, -2)$. Write the resulting equation in the form $Ax + By = C, A > 0$.

(B) Find an equation for the line that passes through $(2, -3)$ and $(4, 3)$. Write the resulting equation in the form $y = mx + b$.

The various forms of the equation of a line that we have discussed are summarized in Table 2 for convenient reference.

TABLE 2 Equations of a Line

Standard form	$Ax + By = C$	A and B not both 0
Slope-intercept form	$y = mx + b$	Slope: m; y intercept: b
Point-slope form	$y - y_1 = m(x - x_1)$	Slope: m; point: (x_1, y_1)
Horizontal line	$y = b$	Slope: 0
Vertical line	$x = a$	Slope: undefined

➤ Applications

We will now see how equations of lines occur in certain applications.

EXAMPLE 6   **Cost Equation** The management of a company that manufactures roller skates has fixed costs (costs at 0 output) of $300 per day and total costs of $4,300 per day at an output of 100 pairs of skates per day. Assume that cost C is linearly related to output x.

(A) Find the slope of the line joining the points associated with outputs of 0 and 100; that is, the line passing through $(0, 300)$ and $(100, 4,300)$.

(B) Find an equation of the line relating output to cost. Write the final answer in the form $C = mx + b$.

(C) Graph the cost equation from part (B) for $0 \le x \le 200$.

Solution (A) $m = \dfrac{y_2 - y_1}{x_2 - x_1}$

$$= \frac{4,300 - 300}{100 - 0}$$

$$= \frac{4,000}{100} = 40$$

(B) We must find an equation of the line that passes through $(0, 300)$ with slope 40. We use the slope-intercept form:

$$C = mx + b$$
$$C = 40x + 300$$

(C)

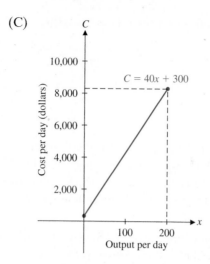

$$C = 40x + 300$$

In Example 6, the **fixed cost** of $300 per day covers plant cost, insurance, and so on. This cost is incurred whether or not there is any production. The **variable cost** is $40x$, which depends on the day's output. Since increasing production from x to $x + 1$ will increase the cost by $40 (from $40x + 300$ to $40x + 340$), the slope 40 can be interpreted as the **rate of change** of the cost function with respect to production x.

Matched Problem 6   Answer parts (A) and (B) in Example 6 for fixed costs of $250 per day and total costs of $3,450 per day at an output of 80 pairs of skates per day.

EXAMPLE 7   **Price–Demand** At the beginning of the twenty-first century, the world demand for crude oil was about 75 million barrels per day and the price of a barrel fluctuated between $20 and $40. Suppose that the daily demand for crude oil is 76.1 million barrels when the price is $25.52 per barrel and this demand drops to 74.9 million barrels when the price rises to $33.68. Assuming a linear relationship between the demand x and the price p, find a linear function in the form $p = ax + b$ that models the price–demand relationship for crude oil. Use this model to predict the demand if the price rises to $39.12 per barrel.

Solution   Find the equation of the line through (76.1, 25.52) and (74.9, 33.68). We first find the slope of the line:

$$m = \frac{33.68 - 25.52}{74.9 - 76.1}$$

$$= \frac{8.16}{-1.2} = -6.8$$

Use the point-slope form to find the equation of the line:

$$p - p_1 = m(x - x_1)$$
$$p - 25.52 = -6.8(x - 76.1)$$
$$p - 25.52 = -6.8x + 517.48$$
$$p = -6.8x + 543$$

To find the demand when the price is \$39.12 per barrel, we solve the equation $p = 39.12$ for x:

$$p = 39.12$$
$$-6.8x + 543 = 39.12$$
$$-6.8x = -503.88$$
$$x = \frac{-503.88}{-6.8} = 74.1 \text{ million barrels per day}$$

Matched Problem 7 The daily supply for crude oil also varies with the price. Suppose that the daily supply is 73.4 million barrels when the price is \$23.84 and this supply rises to 77.4 million barrels when the price rises to \$34.24. Assuming a linear relationship between the supply x and the price p, find a linear function in the form $p = ax + b$ that models the price–supply relationship for crude oil. Use this model to predict the supply if the price drops to \$20.98 per barrel.

Figure 6 shows the price–demand function from Example 7 and the price–supply function from Matched Problem 7 graphed on the same axes. In a free competitive market, the price of a product is determined by the relationship between supply and demand. The price tends to stabilize at the point of intersection of the demand and supply functions. This point is called the **equilibrium point,** the corresponding price is called the **equilibrium price,** and the common value of supply and demand is called the **equilibrium quantity.**

The equilibrium point for the supply and demand functions in Figure 6 is found as follows:

$$2.6x - 167 = -6.8x + 543$$
$$9.4x = 710$$
$$x = \frac{710}{9.4} = 75.532 \text{ million barrels} \qquad \textit{Equilibrium quantity}$$
$$p = 2.6(75.532) - 167 = \$29.38 \qquad \textit{Equilibrium price}$$
$$p = -6.8(75.532) + 543 = \$29.38 \qquad \textit{Check}$$

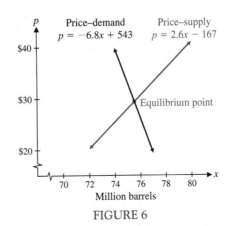

FIGURE 6

Answers to Matched Problems

1. (A)

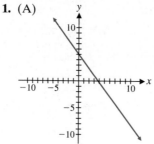

(B) *x* intercept: 3.75; *y* intercept: 5

(C)

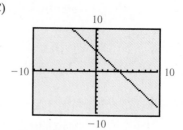

(D) *x* intercept: 3.75; *y* intercept: 5   (E) $x \leq 3.75$ or $(-\infty, 3.75]$

2. (A)

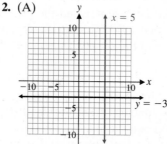

By hand

In graphing utility

(B) Horizontal line: $y = 2$; vertical line: $x = -8$

(C)

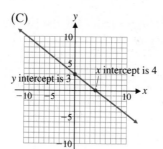

By hand

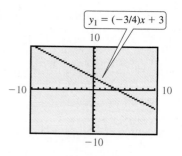

In graphing utility

3. (A) 0   (B) −4   (C) Not defined   (D) 1

4. $y = \frac{1}{2}x - 1$

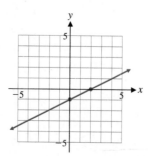

5. (A) $2x - 3y = 18$ (B) $y = 3x - 9$

6. (A) $m = 40$ (B) $C = 40x + 250$

7. $p(x) = 2.6x - 167$; 72.3 million barrels

Exercise 1-3

A *Problems 1–4 refer to graphs (A)–(D).*

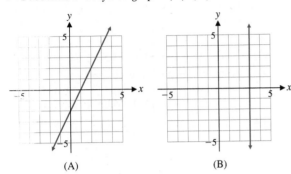

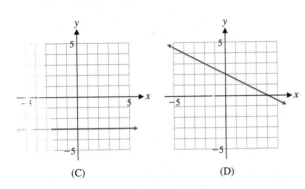

(A)   (B)

(C)   (D)

1. Identify the graph(s) of linear functions with a negative slope.

2. Identify the graph(s) of linear functions with a positive slope.

3. Identify the graph(s) of any constant functions. What is the slope of the graph?

4. Identify any graphs that are not the graphs of functions. What can you say about their slopes?

In Problems 5–8, sketch a graph of each equation in a rectangular coordinate system.

5. $y = 2x - 3$ 6. $y = \dfrac{x}{2} + 1$

7. $2x + 3y = 12$ 8. $8x - 3y = 24$

In Problems 9–12, find the slope and y intercept of the graph of each equation.

9. $y = 3x + 1$ 10. $y = \dfrac{x}{5} - 2$

11. $y = -\dfrac{3}{7}x - 6$ 12. $y = 0.7x + 5$

In Problems 13–16, write an equation of the line with the indicated slope and y intercept.

13. Slope $= -2$
    y intercept $= 3$

14. Slope $= \frac{3}{4}$
    y intercept $= -5$

15. Slope $= \frac{4}{3}$
    y intercept $= -4$

16. Slope $= -5$
    y intercept $= 9$

B *Sketch a graph of each equation or pair of equations in Problems 17–22 in a rectangular coordinate system.*

17. $y = -\frac{2}{3}x - 2$ 18. $y = -\frac{3}{2}x + 1$

19. $3x - 2y = 10$ 20. $5x - 6y = 15$

21. $x = 3; y = -2$ 22. $x = -3; y = 2$

In Problems 23–26, find the slope of the graph of each equation.

23. $4x + y = 3$ 24. $5x - y = -2$

25. $3x + 5y = 15$ 26. $2x - 3y = 18$

27. Given $Ax + By = 12$, graph each of the following three cases on the same coordinate axes.

   (A) $A = 2$ and $B = 0$
   (B) $A = 0$ and $B = 3$
   (C) $A = 3$ and $B = 4$

28. Given $Ax + By = 24$, graph each of the following three cases on the same coordinate axes.

   (A) $A = 6$ and $B = 0$
   (B) $A = 0$ and $B = 8$
   (C) $A = 2$ and $B = 3$

29. Graph $f(x) = 25x + 200, x \geq 0$.

30. Graph $g(x) = 40x + 160, x \geq 0$.

31. (A) Graph $f(x) = 1.2x - 4.2$ in a rectangular coordinate system.

   (B) Find the x and y intercepts algebraically to one decimal place.

    (C) Graph $f(x) = 1.2x - 4.2$ in a graphing utility.

   (D) Find the x and y intercepts to one decimal place using trace and the zero command on your graphing utility.

   (E) Using the results of parts (A) and (B) or (C) and (D), find the solution set for the linear inequality

   $$1.2x - 4.2 > 0$$

32. (A) Graph $f(x) = -0.8x + 5.2$ in a rectangular coordinate system.

   (B) Find the x and y intercepts algebraically to one decimal place.

    (C) Graph $f(x) = -0.8x + 5.2$ in a graphing utility.

   (D) Find the x and y intercepts to one decimal place using trace and the zero command on your graphing utility.

   (E) Using the results of parts (A) and (B) or (C) and (D), find the solution set for the linear inequality

   $$-0.8x + 5.2 < 0$$

In Problems 33–36, write the equations of the vertical and horizontal lines through each point.

33. $(4, -3)$ **34.** $(-5, 6)$

35. $(-1.5, -3.5)$ **36.** $(2.6, 3.8)$

In Problems 37–42, write the equation of the line through each indicated point with the indicated slope. Write the final answer in the form $y = mx + b$.

37. $m = -4; (2, -3)$ **38.** $m = -6; (-4, 1)$

39. $m = \frac{3}{2}; (-4, -5)$ **40.** $m = \frac{4}{3}; (-6, 2)$

41. $m = 0; (-1.5, 4.6)$ **42.** $m = 0; (3.1, -2.7)$

In Problems 43–50,

  (A) Find the slope of the line that passes through the given points.

  (B) Find the standard form of the equation of the line.

  (C) Indicate whether the equation defines a linear function, a constant function, or neither.

43. $(2, 5)$ and $(5, 7)$ **44.** $(1, 2)$ and $(3, 5)$

45. $(-2, -1)$ and $(2, -6)$ **46.** $(2, 3)$ and $(-3, 7)$

47. $(5, 3)$ and $(5, -3)$ **48.** $(1, 4)$ and $(0, 4)$

49. $(-2, 5)$ and $(3, 5)$ **50.** $(2, 0)$ and $(2, -3)$

51. Discuss the relationship among the graphs of the lines with equation $y = mx + 2$, where m is any real number.

52. Discuss the relationship among the graphs of the lines with equation $y = -0.5x + b$, where b is any real number.

C 53. (A) Graph the following equations in the same coordinate system:

$$3x + 2y = 6 \qquad 3x + 2y = 3$$
$$3x + 2y = -6 \qquad 3x + 2y = -3$$

  (B) From your observations in part (A), describe the family of lines obtained by varying C in $Ax + By = C$ while holding A and B fixed.

54. (A) Graph the following two equations in the same coordinate system:

$$3x + 4y = 12 \qquad 4x - 3y = 12$$

  (B) Graph the following two equations in the same coordinate system:

$$2x + 3y = 12 \qquad 3x - 2y = 12$$

  (C) From your observations in parts (A) and (B), describe the apparent relationship of the graphs of

$$Ax + By = C \quad \text{and} \quad Bx - Ay = C$$

55. Describe the relationship between the graphs of $f(x) = mx + b$ and $g(x) = |mx + b|, m \neq 0$, and illustrate with examples. Is $g(x)$ always, sometimes, or never a linear function?

56. Describe the relationship between the graphs of $f(x) = mx + b$ and $g(x) = m|x| + b, m \neq 0$, and illustrate with examples. Is $g(x)$ always, sometimes, or never a linear function?

Applications

Business & Economics

57. *Simple interest.* If P (the principal) is invested at an interest rate of r, then the amount A that is due after t years is given by

$$A = Prt + P$$

If $100 is invested at 6% ($r = 0.06$), then

$$A = 6t + 100, t \geq 0$$

  (A) What will $100 amount to after 5 years? After 20 years?

  (B) Sketch a graph of $A = 6t + 100$ for $0 \leq t \leq 20$.

  (C) Find the slope of the graph and interpret verbally.

58. *Simple interest.* Use the simple interest formula from Problem 57. If $1,000 is invested at 7.5% ($r = 0.075$), then $A = 75t + 1,000, t \geq 0$.

  (A) What will $1,000 amount to after 5 years? After 20 years?

  (B) Sketch a graph of $A = 75t + 1,000$ for $0 \leq t \leq 20$.

  (C) Find the slope of the graph and interpret verbally.

59. *Cost function.* The management of a company that manufactures surfboards has fixed costs (at 0 output) of $200 per day and total costs of $3,800 per day at a daily output of 20 boards.

  (A) Assuming the total cost per day, $C(x)$, is linearly related to the total output per day, x, write an equation for the cost function.

(B) What are the total costs for an output of 12 boards per day?

(C) Graph the cost function for $0 \leq x \leq 20$.

60. *Cost Function.* Repeat Problem 59 if the company has fixed costs of $300 per day and total costs per day at an output of 20 boards of $5,100.

61. *Price–demand function.* A manufacturing company is interested in introducing a new power mower. Its market research department gave the management the price–demand forecast listed in Table 3.

TABLE 3 Price–Demand

Demand x	Wholesale Price ($) $p(x)$
0	200
2,400	160
4,800	120
7,800	70

(A) Plot these points, letting $p(x)$ represent the price at which x number of mowers can be sold (demand). Label the horizontal axis x.

(B) Note that the points in part (A) lie along a straight line. Find an equation for the price–demand function.

(C) What would be the price for a demand of 3,000 units?

(D) Write a brief verbal interpretation of the slope of the line found in part (B).

62. *Depreciation.* Office equipment was purchased for $20,000 and is assumed to have a scrap value of $2,000 after 10 years. If its value is depreciated linearly (for tax purposes) from $20,000 to $2,000:

(A) Find the linear equation that relates value (V) in dollars to time (t) in years.

(B) What would be the value of the equipment after 6 years?

(C) Graph the equation for $0 \leq t \leq 10$.

(D) Write a brief verbal interpretation of the slope of the line found in part (A).

63. *Equilibrium point.* At a price of $2.50 per bushel, the annual U.S. supply and demand for corn are 8.5 and 9.8 million bushels, respectively. When the price rises to $3.30, the supply increases to 10.5 million bushels while the demand decreases to 7.8 million bushels.

(A) Assuming that the price–supply and the price–demand equations are linear, find equations for each.

(B) Find the equilibrium point for the U.S. corn market.

64. *Equilibrium point.* At a price of $5.50 per bushel, the annual U.S. supply and demand for soybeans are 2.4 and 2.9 million bushels, respectively. When the

price rises to $7.30, the supply increases to 2.8 million bushels while the demand decreases to 2.4 million bushels.

(A) Assuming that the price–supply and the price–demand equations are linear, find equations for each.

(B) Find the equilibrium point for the U.S. soybean market.

Merck & Co., Inc. is the world's largest pharmaceutical company. Problems 65 and 66 refer to the data in Table 4 taken from the company's annual reports.

TABLE 4 Selected Financial Data for Merck & Co., Inc. (Billion $)

	1995	1996	1997	1998	1999
Sales	16.7	19.8	23.6	26.9	32.7
Income	3.3	3.8	4.6	5.2	5.9

65. *Sales analysis.* A mathematical model for Merck's sales is given by

$$f(x) = 16.12 + 3.91x$$

where $x = 0$ corresponds to 1995.

(A) Complete the following table. Round values of $f(x)$ to one decimal place.

x	Sales	$f(x)$
0	16.7	
1	19.8	
2	23.6	
3	26.9	
4	32.7	

(B) Sketch the graph of f and the sales data on the same axes.

(C) Use the modeling equation to estimate the sales in 2005. In 2010.

(D) Write a brief verbal description of the company's sales from 1995 to 1999.

66. *Sales analysis.* A mathematical model for Merck's income is given by

$$f(x) = 3.24 + 0.66x$$

where $x = 0$ corresponds to 1995.

(A) Complete the following table. Round values of $f(x)$ to one decimal place.

x	Income	$f(x)$
0	3.3	
1	3.8	
2	4.6	
3	5.2	
4	5.9	

(B) Sketch the graph of f and the income data on the same axes.

(C) Use the modeling equation to estimate the income in 2005. In 2010.

(D) Write a brief verbal description of the company's income from 1995 to 1999.

67. *Energy consumption.* Analyzing data from the U.S. Energy Department for the period between 1920 and 1960 reveals that coal consumption as a percentage of all energy consumed (wood, coal, petroleum, natural gas, hydro, and nuclear) decreased almost linearly. Percentages for this period are given in the table.

Year	Consumption (%)
1920	72
1930	60
1940	50
1950	37
1960	22

(A) Let x represent the number of years since 1900. Find the equation of the linear function f satisfying $f(20) = 72$ and $f(60) = 22$. Graph the data and this function on the same axes. Does this function provide a good model for this data?

(B) Use $f(x)$ to estimate (to the nearest 1%) the percent of coal consumption in 1927. In 1953.

(C) If we assume that $f(x)$ continues to provide a good description of the percentage of coal consumption after 1960, when would $f(x)$ indicate that the percentage of coal consumption has reached 0? Did this really happen? (Consult some references if you are not certain.) If not, what are some reasons for the percentage of coal consumption to level off or even to increase at some point in time after 1960?

68. *Petroleum consumption.* Analyzing data from the U.S. Energy Department for the period between 1920 and 1960 reveals that petroleum consumption as a percentage of all energy consumed (wood, coal, petroleum, natural gas, hydro, and nuclear) increased almost linearly. Percentages for this period are given in the table.

Year	Consumption (%)
1920	11
1930	22
1940	29
1950	37
1960	44

(A) Let x represent the number of years since 1900. Find the equation of the linear function f

satisfying $f(20) = 11$ and $f(60) = 44$. Graph the data and this function on the same axes. Does this function provide a good model for this data?

(B) Use $f(x)$ to estimate (to the nearest 1%) the percent of petroleum consumption in 1932. In 1956.

(C) If we assume that $f(x)$ continues to provide a good description of the percentage of petroleum consumption after 1960, when would this percentage reach 100%? Is this likely to happen? Explain.

Life Sciences

69. *Nutrition.* In a nutrition experiment, a biologist wants to prepare a special diet for the experimental animals. Two food mixes, A and B, are available. If mix A contains 20% protein and mix B contains 10% protein, what combination of each mix will provide exactly 20 grams of protein? Let x be the amount of A used and let y be the amount of B used. Then write a linear equation relating x, y, and 20. Graph this equation for $x \geq 0$ and $y \geq 0$.

70. *Ecology.* As one descends into the ocean, pressure increases linearly. The pressure is 15 pounds per square inch on the surface and 30 pounds per square inch 33 feet below the surface.

(A) If p is the pressure in pounds per square inch and d is the depth below the surface in feet, write an equation that expresses p in terms of d. [*Hint:* Find an equation of the line that passes through $(0, 15)$ and $(33, 30)$.]

(B) What is the pressure at 12,540 feet (the average depth of the ocean)?

(C) Graph the equation for $0 \leq d \leq 12{,}540$.

(D) Write a brief verbal interpretation of the slope of the line found in part (A).

Social Sciences

71. *Psychology.* In an experiment on motivation, J. S. Brown trained a group of rats to run down a narrow passage in a cage to obtain food in a goal box. Using a harness, he then connected the rats to an overhead wire that was attached to a spring scale. A rat was placed at different distances d (in centimeters) from the goal box, and the pull p (in grams) of the rat toward the food was measured. Brown found that the relationship between these two variables was very close to being linear and could be approximated by the equation

$$p = -\tfrac{1}{5}d + 70 \qquad 30 \le d \le 175$$

(See J. S. Brown, *Journal of Comparative and Physiological Psychology*, 1948, 41:450–465.)

(A) What was the pull when $d = 30$? When $d = 175$?

(B) Graph the equation.

(C) What is the slope of the line?

Section 1-4 | Quadratic Functions

➤ Quadratic Functions, Equations, and Inequalities
➤ Properties of Quadratic Functions and Their Graphs
➤ Applications

If the degree of a linear function is increased by one, we obtain a *second-degree function,* usually called a *quadratic function,* another basic function that we will need in our library of elementary functions. We will investigate relationships between quadratic functions and the solutions to quadratic equations and inequalities. Other important properties of quadratic functions will also be investigated, including maximum and minimum properties. We will then be in a position to solve important practical problems such as finding production levels that will produce maximum revenue or maximum profit.

➤ Quadratic Functions, Equations, and Inequalities

The graph of the square function $h(x) = x^2$ is shown in Figure 1. Notice that the graph is symmetric with respect to the y axis and that $(0, 0)$ is the lowest point on the graph. Let's explore the effect of applying a sequence of basic transformations to the graph of h.

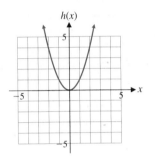

FIGURE 1 Square function $h(x) = x^2$

EXPLORE & DISCUSS 1

Indicate how the graph of each function is related to the graph of the function $h(x) = x^2$. Find the highest or lowest point, whichever exists, on each graph.

(A) $f(x) = (x - 3)^2 - 7 = x^2 - 6x + 2$

(B) $g(x) = 0.5(x + 2)^2 + 3 = 0.5x^2 + 2x + 5$

(C) $m(x) = -(x - 4)^2 + 8 = -x^2 + 8x - 8$

(D) $n(x) = -3(x + 1)^2 - 1 = -3x^2 - 6x - 4$

Graphing the functions in Explore–Discuss 1 produces figures similar in shape to the graph of the square function in Figure 1. These figures are called *parabolas.* The functions that produced these parabolas are examples of the important class of *quadratic functions,* which we now define.

DEFINITION   Quadratic Functions

If a, b, and c are real numbers with $a \ne 0$, then the function

$$f(x) = ax^2 + bx + c \quad \text{Standard form}$$

is a **quadratic function** and its graph is a **parabola.**

👁 *Insight*

If x is any real number, then $ax^2 + bx + c$ is also a real number. According to the agreement on domain and range in Section 1-1, the domain of a quadratic function is R, the set of real numbers.

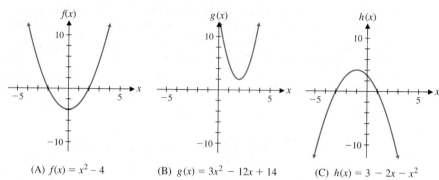

(A) $f(x) = x^2 - 4$ (B) $g(x) = 3x^2 - 12x + 14$ (C) $h(x) = 3 - 2x - x^2$

FIGURE 2 Graphs of quadratic functions

We will discuss methods for determining the range of a quadratic function later in this section. Typical graphs of quadratic functions are illustrated in Figure 2.

◉ Insight   The x intercepts of a linear function can be found by solving the linear equation $y = mx + b = 0$ for $x, m \neq 0$ (see Section 1-3). Similarly, the x intercepts of a quadratic function can be found by solving the quadratic equation $y = ax^2 + bx + c = 0$ for $x, a \neq 0$. Several methods for solving quadratic equations are discussed in Appendix A, Section A-8. The most popular of these is the **quadratic formula.**
    If $ax^2 + bx + c = 0, a \neq 0$, then

$$x = \frac{-b \pm \sqrt{b^2 - 4ac}}{2a}, \text{ provided } b^2 - 4ac \geq 0$$

EXAMPLE 1   **Intercepts, Equations, and Inequalities**

(A) Sketch a graph of $f(x) = -x^2 + 5x + 3$ in a rectangular coordinate system.
(B) Find x and y intercepts algebraically to four decimal places.
(C) Graph $f(x) = -x^2 + 5x + 3$ in a standard viewing window.
(D) Find the x and y intercepts to four decimal places using trace and the zero command on your graphing utility.
(E) Solve the quadratic inequality $-x^2 + 5x + 3 \geq 0$ graphically to four decimal places using the results of parts (A) and (B) or (C) and (D).
(F) Solve the equation $-x^2 + 5x + 3 = 4$ graphically to four decimal places using the intersection routine in your graphing utility.

Solution   (A) Hand-sketching a graph of f:

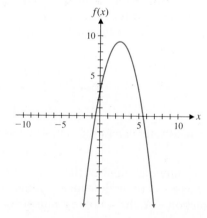

(B) Finding intercepts algebraically:

$$y \text{ intercept:} \quad f(0) = -(0)^2 + 5(0) + 3 = 3$$

$$x \text{ intercepts:} \quad f(x) = 0$$

$$-x^2 + 5x + 3 = 0 \quad \text{Quadratic equation}$$

$$x = \frac{-b \pm \sqrt{b^2 - 4ac}}{2a} \quad \text{Quadratic formula (see Appendix A-8)}$$

$$x = \frac{-(5) \pm \sqrt{5^2 - 4(-1)(3)}}{2(-1)}$$

$$= \frac{-5 \pm \sqrt{37}}{-2} = -0.5414 \quad \text{or} \quad 5.5414$$

(C) Graphing in a graphing utility:

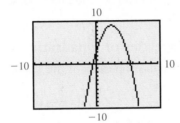

(D) Finding intercepts graphically using a graphing utility:

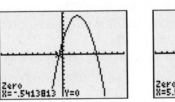 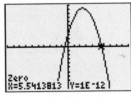 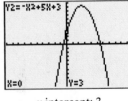

x intercept: -0.5414 x intercept: -0.5414 y intercept: 3

(E) Solving $-x^2 + 5x + 3 \geq 0$ graphically: The quadratic inequality

$$-x^2 + 5x + 3 \geq 0$$

holds for those values of x for which the graph of $f(x) = -x^2 + 5x + 3$ in the figures in parts (A) and (C) is at or above the x axis. This happens for x between the two x intercepts [found in part (B) or (D)], including the two x intercepts. Thus, the solution set for the quadratic inequality is $-0.5414 \leq x \leq 5.5414$ or $[-0.5414, 5.5414]$.

(F) Solving the equation $-x^2 + 5x + 3 = 4$ using a graphing utility:

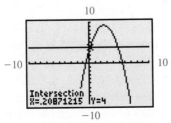 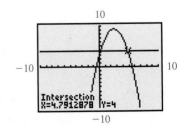

$-x^2 + 5x + 3 = 4$ at $x = 0.2087$ $-x^2 + 5x + 3 = 4$ at $x = 4.7913$

Matched Problem 1

(A) Sketch a graph of $g(x) = 2x^2 - 5x - 5$ in a rectangular coordinate system.

(B) Find x and y intercepts algebraically to four decimal places.

(C) Graph $g(x) = 2x^2 - 5x - 5$ in a standard viewing window.

(D) Find the x and y intercepts to four decimal places using trace and the zero command on your graphing utility.

(E) Solve $2x^2 - 5x - 5 \geq 0$ graphically to four decimal places using the results of parts (A) and (B) or (C) and (D).

(F) Solve the equation $2x^2 - 5x - 5 = -3$ graphically to four decimal places using trace and zoom or an appropriate built-in routine in your graphing utility.

EXPLORE &DISCUSS 2

How many x intercepts can the graph of a quadratic function have? How many y intercepts? Explain your reasoning.

➤ Properties of Quadratic Functions and Their Graphs

Many useful properties of the quadratic function can be uncovered by transforming

$$f(x) = ax^2 + bx + c \qquad a \neq 0$$

into the **vertex form***

$$f(x) = a(x - h)^2 + k$$

The process of *completing the square* (see Appendix A-8) is central to the transformation. We illustrate the process through a specific example and then generalize the results.

Consider the quadratic function given by

$$f(x) = -2x^2 + 16x - 24 \tag{1}$$

We use completing the square to transform this function into vertex form:

$$
\begin{aligned}
f(x) &= -2x^2 + 16x - 24 && \text{Factor the coefficient of } x^2 \text{ out of} \\
&= -2(x^2 - 8x) - 24 && \text{the first two terms.} \\
&= -2(x^2 - 8x + ?) - 24 && \\
&&& \text{Add 16 to complete the square in-} \\
&&& \text{side the parentheses. Because of} \\
&= -2(x^2 - 8x + 16) - 24 + 32 && \text{the } -2 \text{ outside the parentheses, we} \\
&&& \text{have actually added } -32, \text{ so we} \\
&&& \text{must add 32 to the outside.} \\
&= -2(x - 4)^2 + 8 && \text{The transformation is complete and} \\
&&& \text{can be checked by multiplying out.}
\end{aligned}
$$

Thus,

$$f(x) = -2(x - 4)^2 + 8 \tag{2}$$

If $x = 4$, then $-2(x - 4)^2 = 0$ and $f(4) = 8$. For any other value of x, the negative number $-2(x - 4)^2$ is added to 8, making it smaller. (Think about this.) Therefore,

$$f(4) = 8$$

is the *maximum value* of $f(x)$ for all x—a very important result! Furthermore, if we choose any two x values that are the same distance from 4, we will obtain

---

* This terminology is not universally agreed upon. Some call this the *standard form*.

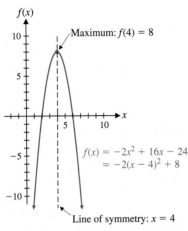

Maximum: $f(4) = 8$

$f(x) = -2x^2 + 16x - 24$
$= -2(x - 4)^2 + 8$

Line of symmetry: $x = 4$

FIGURE 3   Graph of a quadratic function

the same function value. For example, $x = 3$ and $x = 5$ are each one unit from $x = 4$ and their function values are

$$f(3) = -2(3 - 4)^2 + 8 = 6$$
$$f(5) = -2(5 - 4)^2 + 8 = 6$$

Thus, the vertical line $x = 4$ is a line of symmetry. That is, if the graph of equation (1) is drawn on a piece of paper and the paper is folded along the line $x = 4$, then the two sides of the parabola will match exactly. All these results are illustrated by graphing equations (1) and (2) and the line $x = 4$ simultaneously in the same coordinate system (Fig. 3).

From the preceding discussion, we see that as x moves from left to right, $f(x)$ is increasing on $(-\infty, 4]$, and decreasing on $[4, \infty)$, and that $f(x)$ can assume no value greater than 8. Thus,

$$\text{Range of } f: \quad y \le 8 \quad \text{or} \quad (-\infty, 8]$$

In general, the graph of a quadratic function is a parabola with line of symmetry parallel to the vertical axis. The lowest or highest point on the parabola, whichever exists, is called the **vertex.** The maximum or minimum value of a quadratic function always occurs at the vertex of the parabola. The line of symmetry through the vertex is called the **axis** of the parabola. In the example above, $x = 4$ is the axis of the parabola and $(4, 8)$ is its vertex.

◉ **Insight**   Applying the graph transformation properties discussed in Section 1-2 to the transformed equation,

$$f(x) = -2x^2 + 16x - 24$$
$$= -2(x - 4)^2 + 8$$

we see that the graph of $f(x) = -2x^2 + 16x - 24$ is the graph of $g(x) = x^2$ vertically expanded by a factor of 2, reflected in the x axis, and shifted to the right 4 units and up 8 units, as shown in Figure 4.

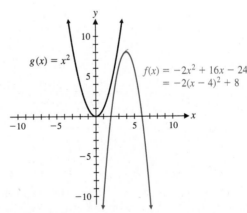

FIGURE 4   Graph of f is the graph of g transformed

Note the important results we have obtained from the vertex form of the quadratic function f:

► The vertex of the parabola
► The axis of the parabola
► The maximum value of $f(x)$

➤ The range of the function f

➤ The relationship between the graph of $g(x) = x^2$ and the graph of
$f(x) = -2x^2 + 16x - 24$

Now, let us explore the effects of changing the constants a, h, and k on the graph of $f(x) = a(x - h)^2 + k$.

EXPLORE &DISCUSS
3

(A) Let $a = 1$ and $h = 5$. Graph $f(x) = a(x - h)^2 + k$ for $k = -4, 0$, and 3 simultaneously in the same coordinate system. Explain the effect of changing k on the graph of f.

(B) Let $a = 1$ and $k = 2$. Graph $f(x) = a(x - h)^2 + k$ for $h = -4, 0$, and 5 simultaneously in the same coordinate system. Explain the effect of changing h on the graph of f.

(C) Let $h = 5$ and $k = -2$. Graph $f(x) = a(x - h)^2 + k$ for $a = 0.25, 1$, and 3 simultaneously in the same coordinate system. Graph function f for $a = 1, -1$, and -0.25 simultaneously in the same coordinate system. Explain the effect of changing a on the graph of f.

(D) Discuss parts (A)–(C) using a graphing utility and a standard viewing window.

The preceding discussion is generalized for all quadratic functions in the following box:

SUMMARY   **Properties of a Quadratic Function and Its Graph**

Given a quadratic function and the vertex form obtained by completing the square

$$f(x) = ax^2 + bx + c \qquad a \neq 0 \quad \text{Standard form}$$
$$= a(x - h)^2 + k \qquad\qquad \text{Vertex form}$$

we summarize general properties as follows:

1. The graph of f is a parabola:

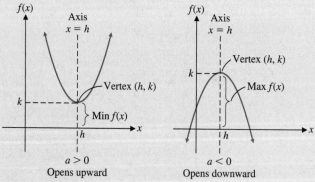

$a > 0$
Opens upward

$a < 0$
Opens downward

2. Vertex: (h, k) (parabola increases on one side of the vertex and decreases on the other)

3. Axis (of symmetry): $x = h$ (parallel to y axis)

4. $f(h) = k$ is the minimum if $a > 0$ and the maximum if $a < 0$

5. Domain: All real numbers

Range: $(-\infty, k]$ if $a < 0$ or $[k, \infty)$ if $a > 0$

6. The graph of f is the graph of $g(x) = ax^2$ translated horizontally h units and vertically k units.

EXAMPLE 2 **Analyzing a Quadratic Function** Given the quadratic function

$$f(x) = 0.5x^2 - 6x + 21$$

(A) Find the vertex form for f.

(B) Find the vertex and the maximum or minimum. State the range of f.

(C) Describe how the graph of function f can be obtained from the graph of $g(x) = x^2$ using transformations discussed in Section 1-2.

(D) Sketch a graph of function f in a rectangular coordinate system.

 (E) Graph function f using a suitable viewing window.

(F) Find the vertex and the maximum or minimum graphically using the minimum command. State the range of f.

Solution (A) Complete the square to find the vertex form:

$$\begin{aligned} f(x) &= 0.5x^2 - 6x + 21 \\ &= 0.5(x^2 - 12x + \textbf{?}) + 21 \\ &= 0.5(x^2 - 12x + 36) + 21 - 18 \\ &= 0.5(x - 6)^2 + 3 \end{aligned}$$

(B) From the vertex form, we see that $h = 6$ and $k = 3$. Thus, vertex: $(6, 3)$; minimum: $f(6) = 3$; range: $y \geq 3$ or $[3, \infty)$.

(C) The graph of $f(x) = 0.5(x - 6)^2 + 3$ is the same as the graph of $g(x) = x^2$ vertically contracted by a factor of 0.5, and shifted to the right 6 units and up 3 units.

(D) Graph in a rectangular coordinate system:

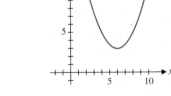

(E) Graph in a graphing utility:

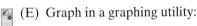

(F) Finding the vertex, minimum, and range graphically using a graphing utility:

Vertex: $(6, 3)$; minimum: $f(6) = 3$; range: $y \geq 3$ or $[3, \infty)$.

Matched Problem 2 Given the quadratic function $f(x) = -0.25x^2 - 2x + 2$

(A) Find the vertex form for f.

(B) Find the vertex and the maximum or minimum. State the range of f.

(C) Describe how the graph of function f can be obtained from the graph of $g(x) = x^2$ using transformations discussed in Section 1-2.

(D) Sketch a graph of function f in a rectangular coordinate system.

 (E) Graph function f using a suitable viewing window.

 (F) Find the vertex and the maximum or minimum graphically using the minimum command. State the range of f. _____

 ➤ **Applications**

EXAMPLE 3

Maximum Revenue This is a continuation of Example 7 in Section 1-1. Recall that the financial department in the company that produces an automatic camera arrived at the following price–demand function and the corresponding revenue function:

$$p(x) = 94.8 - 5x \qquad \text{Price–demand function}$$
$$R(x) = xp(x) = x(94.8 - 5x) \quad \text{Revenue function}$$

where $p(x)$ is the wholesale price per camera at which x million cameras can be sold and $R(x)$ is the corresponding revenue (in million dollars). Both functions have domain $1 \le x \le 15$.

(A) Find the output to the nearest thousand cameras that will produce the maximum revenue. What is the maximum revenue to the nearest thousand dollars? Solve the problem algebraically by completing the square.

(B) What is the wholesale price per camera (to the nearest dollar) that produces the maximum revenue?

 (C) Graph the revenue function using an appropriate viewing window.

(D) Find the output to the nearest thousand cameras that will produce the maximum revenue. What is the maximum revenue to the nearest thousand dollars? Solve the problem graphically using the maximum command.

Solution (A) Algebraic solution:

$$R(x) = x(94.8 - 5x)$$
$$= -5x^2 + 94.8x$$
$$= -5(x^2 - 18.96x + \text{?})$$
$$= -5(x^2 - 18.96x + 89.8704) + 449.352$$
$$= -5(x - 9.48)^2 + 449.352$$

The maximum revenue of 449.352 million dollars ($449,352,000) occurs when $x = 9.480$ million cameras (9,480,000 cameras).

(B) Finding the wholesale price per camera: Use the price–demand function for an output of 9.480 million cameras:

$$p(x) = 94.8 - 5x$$
$$p(9.480) = 94.8 - 5(9.480)$$
$$= \$47$$

(C) Graph in a graphing utility:

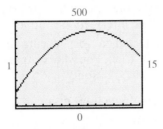

(D) Graphical solution using a graphing utility:

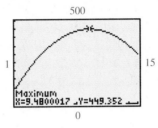

An output of 9.480 million cameras (9,480,000 cameras) will produce a maximum revenue of 449.352 million dollars ($449,352,000).   ■

Matched Problem 3   The financial department in Example 3, using statistical and analytical techniques (see Matched Problem 7 in Section 1-1), arrived at the cost function

$$C(x) = 156 + 19.7x \quad \textit{Cost function}$$

where $C(x)$ is the cost (in million dollars) for manufacturing and selling x million cameras.

(A) Using the revenue function from Example 3 and the preceding cost function, write an equation for the profit function.

(B) Find the output to the nearest thousand cameras that will produce the maximum profit. What is the maximum profit to the nearest thousand dollars? Solve the problem algebraically by completing the square.

(C) What is the wholesale price per camera (to the nearest dollar) that produces the maximum profit?

(D) Graph the profit function using an appropriate viewing window.

(E) Find the output to the nearest thousand cameras that will produce the maximum profit. What is the maximum profit to the nearest thousand dollars? Solve the problem graphically using the maximum routine.

EXAMPLE 4   Break-Even Analysis Use the revenue function from Example 3 and the cost function from Matched Problem 3:

$$R(x) = x(94.8 - 5x) \quad \textit{Revenue function}$$
$$C(x) = 156 + 19.7x \quad \textit{Cost function}$$

Both have domain $1 \le x \le 15$.

(A) Sketch the graphs of both functions in the same coordinate system.

(B) **Break-even points** are the production levels at which $R(x) = C(x)$. Find the break-even points algebraically to the nearest thousand cameras.

(C) Plot both functions simultaneously in the same viewing window.

(D) Find the break-even points graphically to the nearest thousand cameras using the intersection routine.

(E) Recall that a loss occurs if $R(x) < C(x)$ and a profit occurs if $R(x) > C(x)$. For what outputs (to the nearest thousand cameras) will a loss occur? A profit?

Solution   (A) Sketch of functions:

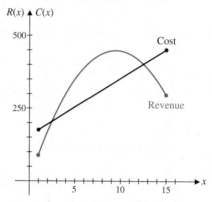

(B) Algebraic solution:

Find x such that $R(x) = C(x)$:

$$x(94.8 - 5x) = 156 + 19.7x$$

$$-5x^2 + 75.1x - 156 = 0$$

$$x = \frac{-75.1 \pm \sqrt{75.1^2 - 4(-5)(-156)}}{2(-5)}$$

$$= \frac{-75.1 \pm \sqrt{2,520.01}}{-10}$$

$$x = 2.490 \quad \text{or} \quad 12.530$$

The company breaks even at $x = 2.490$ and 12.530 million cameras.

(C) Graph in a graphing utility:

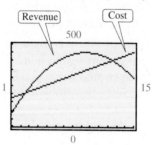

(D) Graphical solution:

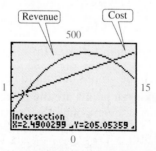

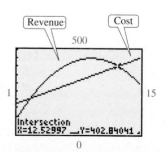

The company breaks even at $x = 2.490$ and 12.530 million cameras.
(E) Use the results from parts (A) and (B) or (C) and (D):

Loss: $1 \leq x < 2.490$ or $12.530 < x \leq 15$

Profit: $2.490 < x < 12.530$

Matched Problem 4

Use the profit equation from Matched Problem 3:

$$P(x) = R(x) - C(x)$$
$$= -5x^2 + 75.1x - 156 \quad \text{Profit function}$$

Domain: $1 \leq x \leq 15$

(A) Sketch a graph of the profit function in a rectangular coordinate system.
(B) Break-even points occur when $P(x) = 0$. Find the break-even points algebraically to the nearest thousand cameras.

(C) Plot the profit function in an appropriate viewing window.
(D) Find the break-even points graphically to the nearest thousand cameras.
(E) A loss occurs if $P(x) < 0$, and a profit occurs if $P(x) > 0$. For what outputs (to the nearest thousand cameras) will a loss occur? A profit?

Answers to Matched Problems **1.** (A)

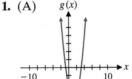

(B) x intercepts: $-0.7656, 3.2656$; y intercept: -5

(C)

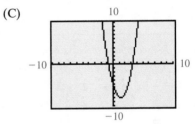

(D) x intercepts: $-0.7656, 3.2656$; y intercept: -5

(E) $x \leq -0.7656$ or $x \geq 3.2656$; or $(-\infty, -0.7656]$ or $[3.2656, \infty)$

(F) $x = -0.3508, 2.8508$

2. (A) $f(x) = -0.25(x + 4)^2 + 6$.

(B) Vertex: $(-4, 6)$; maximum: $f(-4) = 6$; range: $y \leq 6$ or $(-\infty, 6]$

(C) The graph of $f(x) = -0.25(x + 4)^2 + 6$ is the same as the graph of $g(x) = x^2$ vertically contracted by a factor of 0.25, reflected in the x axis, and shifted 4 units to the left and 6 units up.

(D)

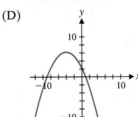

(E)

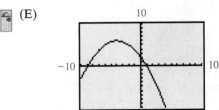

(F) Vertex: $(-4, 6)$; maximum: $f(-4) = 6$; range: $y \leq 6$ or $(-\infty, 6]$

3. (A) $P(x) = R(x) - C(x) = -5x^2 + 75.1x - 156$

(B) $P(x) = R(x) - C(x) = -5(x - 7.51)^2 + 126.0005$; output of 7.510 million cameras will produce a maximum profit of 126.001 million dollars.

(C) $p(7.510) = \$57$

(D)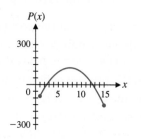

(E)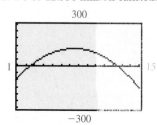

Maximum
X=7.5099984   Y=126.0005

An output of 7.51 million cameras will produce a maximum profit of 126.001 million dollars. (Notice that maximum profit does not occur at the same output where maximum revenue occurs.)

4. (A)

$P(x)$

(B) $x = 2.490$ or 12.530 million cameras

(C)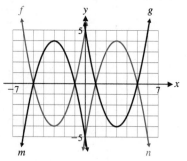

(D) $x = 2.490$ or 12.530 million cameras

(E) Loss: $1 \le x < 2.490$ or $12.530 < x \le 15$; profit: $2.490 < x < 12.530$

Exercise 1-4

A *In Problems 1–4, complete the square and find the standard form of each quadratic function.*

1. $f(x) = x^2 - 4x + 3$ **2.** $g(x) = x^2 - 2x - 5$

3. $m(x) = -x^2 + 6x - 4$ **4.** $n(x) = -x^2 + 8x - 9$

In Problems 5–8, write a brief verbal description of the relationship between the graph of the indicated function (from Problems 1–4) and the graph of $y = x^2$.

5. $f(x) = x^2 - 4x + 3$ **6.** $g(x) = x^2 - 2x - 5$

7. $m(x) = -x^2 + 6x - 4$ **8.** $n(x) = -x^2 + 8x - 9$

9. Match each equation with a graph of one of the functions f, g, m, or n in the figure.

(A) $y = -(x + 2)^2 + 1$ (B) $y = (x - 2)^2 - 1$
(C) $y = (x + 2)^2 - 1$ (D) $y = -(x - 2)^2 + 1$

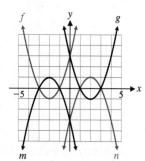

Figure for 9

10. Match each equation with a graph of one of the functions f, g, m, or n in the figure.

(A) $y = (x - 3)^2 - 4$ (B) $y = -(x + 3)^2 + 4$
(C) $y = -(x - 3)^2 + 4$ (D) $y = (x + 3)^2 - 4$

Figure for 10

For the functions indicated in Problems 11–14, find each of the following to the nearest integer by referring to the graphs for Problems 9 and 10.

(A) *Intercepts*   (B) *Vertex*
(C) *Maximum or minimum*   (D) *Range*
(E) *Increasing interval*   (F) *Decreasing interval*

11. Function n in the figure for Problem 9

12. Function m in the figure for Problem 10

13. Function f in the figure for Problem 9

14. Function g in the figure for Problem 10

In Problems 15–18, find each of the following:

(A) *Intercepts*   (B) *Vertex*

(C) *Maximum or minimum* (D) *Range*

15. $f(x) = -(x - 3)^2 + 2$

16. $g(x) = -(x + 2)^2 + 3$

17. $m(x) = (x + 1)^2 - 2$

18. $n(x) = (x - 4)^2 - 3$

B *In Problems 19–22, write an equation for each graph in the form $y = a(x - h)^2 + k$, where a is either 1 or −1 and h and k are integers.*

19.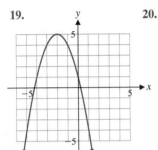

20.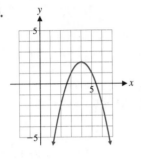

21.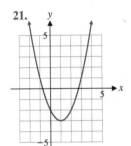

22.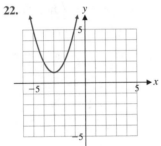

In Problems 23–28, find the vertex form for each quadratic function. Then find each of the following:

(A) *Intercepts*   (B) *Vertex*

(C) *Maximum or minimum* (D) *Range*

23. $f(x) = x^2 - 8x + 12$

24. $g(x) = x^2 - 6x + 5$

25. $r(x) = -4x^2 + 16x - 15$

26. $s(x) = -4x^2 - 8x - 3$

27. $u(x) = 0.5x^2 - 2x + 5$

28. $v(x) = 0.5x^2 + 4x + 10$

29. Let $f(x) = 0.3x^2 - x - 8$. Solve each equation graphically to four decimal places.

    (A) $f(x) = 4$ (B) $f(x) = -1$ (C) $f(x) = -9$

30. Let $g(x) = -0.6x^2 + 3x + 4$. Solve each equation graphically to four decimal places.

    (A) $g(x) = -2$ (B) $g(x) = 5$ (C) $g(x) = 8$

31. Let $f(x) = 125x - 6x^2$. Find the maximum value of f to four decimal places graphically.

32. Let $f(x) = 100x - 7x^2 - 10$. Find the maximum value of f to four decimal places graphically.

33. Explain under what graphical conditions a quadratic function has exactly one real zero.

34. Explain under what graphical conditions a quadratic function has no real zeros.

C *In Problems 35–38, first write each function in vertex form; then find each of the following (to four decimal places):*

(A) *Intercepts*

(B) *Vertex*

(C) *Maximum or minimum*

(D) *Range*

35. $g(x) = 0.25x^2 - 1.5x - 7$

36. $m(x) = 0.20x^2 - 1.6x - 1$

37. $f(x) = -0.12x^2 + 0.96x + 1.2$

38. $n(x) = -0.15x^2 - 0.90x + 3.3$

Solve Problems 39–44 graphically to two decimal places using a graphing utility.

39. $2 - 5x - x^2 = 0$

40. $7 + 3x - 2x^2 = 0$

41. $1.9x^2 - 1.5x - 5.6 < 0$

42. $3.4 + 2.9x - 1.1x^2 \geq 0$

43. $2.8 + 3.1x - 0.9x^2 \leq 0$

44. $1.8x^2 - 3.1x - 4.9 > 0$

45. Given that f is a quadratic function with minimum $f(x) = f(2) = 4$, find the axis, vertex, range, and x intercepts.

46. Given that f is a quadratic function with maximum $f(x) = f(-3) = -5$, find the axis, vertex, range, and x intercepts.

In Problems 47–50,

(A) *Graph f and g in the same coordinate system.*

(B) *Solve $f(x) = g(x)$ algebraically to two decimal places.*

(C) *Solve $f(x) > g(x)$ using parts (A) and (B).*

(D) *Solve $f(x) < g(x)$ using parts (A) and (B).*

47. $f(x) = -0.4x(x - 10)$
    $g(x) = 0.3x + 5$
    $0 \leq x \leq 10$

48. $f(x) = -0.7x(x - 7)$
    $g(x) = 0.5x + 3.5$
    $0 \leq x \leq 7$

49. $f(x) = -0.9x^2 + 7.2x$
    $g(x) = 1.2x + 5.5$
    $0 \leq x \leq 8$

50. $f(x) = -0.7x^2 + 6.3x$
$g(x) = 1.1x + 4.8$
$0 \le x \le 9$

51. Give a simple example of a quadratic function that has no real zeros. Explain how its graph is related to the x axis.

52. Give a simple example of a quadratic function that has exactly one real zero. Explain how its graph is related to the x axis.

Applications

 Solve each problem algebraically, then check on a graphing utility, using built-in zero and maximum/ minimum routines.

Business & Economics

53. *Tire mileage.* An automobile tire manufacturer collected the data in the table relating tire pressure x (in pounds per square inch) and mileage (in thousands of miles):

x	Mileage
28	45
30	52
32	55
34	51
36	47

A mathematical model for the data is given by

$$f(x) = -0.518x^2 + 33.3x - 481$$

(A) Complete the following table. Round values of $f(x)$ to one decimal place.

x	Mileage	$f(x)$
28	45	
30	52	
32	55	
34	51	
36	47	

(B) Sketch the graph of f and the mileage data in the same coordinate system.

(C) Use values of the modeling function rounded to two decimal places to estimate the mileage for a tire pressure of 31 pounds per square inch. For 35 pounds per square inch.

(D) Write a brief description of the relationship between tire pressure and mileage.

54. *Automobile production.* The table shows the retail market share of passenger cars from Ford Motor Company as a percentage of the U.S. market.

Year	Market Share
1975	23.6%
1980	17.2%
1985	18.8%
1990	20.0%
1995	20.7%

A mathematical model for this data is given by

$$f(x) = 0.04x^2 - 0.8x + 22$$

where $x = 0$ corresponds to 1975.

(A) Complete the following table.

x	Market Share	$f(x)$
0	23.6	
5	17.2	
10	18.8	
15	20.0	
20	20.7	

(B) Sketch the graph of f and the market share data in the same coordinate system.

(C) Use values of the modeling function f to estimate Ford's market share in 2000. In 2005.

(D) Write a brief verbal description of Ford's market share from 1975 to 1995.

55. *Revenue.* Refer to Problems 79 and 81, Exercise 1-1. We found that the marketing research department for the company that manufactures and sells memory chips for microcomputers established the following price–demand and revenue functions:

$p(x) = 75 - 3x$ *Price–demand function*
$R(x) = xp(x) = x(75 - 3x)$ *Revenue function*

where $p(x)$ is the wholesale price in dollars at which x million chips can be sold, and $R(x)$ is in millions of dollars. Both functions have domain $1 \le x \le 20$.

(A) Sketch a graph of the revenue function in a rectangular coordinate system.

(B) Find the output that will produce the maximum revenue. What is the maximum revenue?

(C) What is the wholesale price per chip (to the nearest dollar) that produces the maximum revenue?

56. *Revenue.* Refer to Problems 80 and 82, Exercise 1-1. We found that the marketing research department for the company that manufactures and sells "notebook" computers established the following price–demand and revenue functions:

$$p(x) = 2,000 - 60x \qquad \textit{Price–demand function}$$
$$R(x) = xp(x) \qquad \textit{Revenue function}$$
$$= x(2,000 - 60x)$$

where $p(x)$ is the wholesale price in dollars at which x thousand computers can be sold, and $R(x)$ is in thousands of dollars. Both functions have domain $1 \le x \le 25$.

(A) Sketch a graph of the revenue function in a rectangular coordinate system.

(B) Find the output (to the nearest hundred computers) that will produce the maximum revenue. What is the maximum revenue to the nearest thousand dollars?

(C) What is the wholesale price per computer (to the nearest dollar) that produces the maximum revenue?

57. *Break-even analysis.* Use the revenue function from Problem 55 in this exercise and the cost function from Problem 83, Exercise 1-1:

$$R(x) = x(75 - 3x) \quad \textit{Revenue function}$$
$$C(x) = 125 + 16x \quad \textit{Cost function}$$

where x is in millions of chips, and $R(x)$ and $C(x)$ are in millions of dollars. Both functions have domain $1 \le x \le 20$.

(A) Sketch a graph of both functions in the same rectangular coordinate system.

(B) Find the break-even points to the nearest thousand chips.

(C) For what outputs will a loss occur? A profit?

58. *Break-even analysis.* Use the revenue function from Problem 56, in this exercise and the cost function

from Problem 84, Exercise 1-1:

$$R(x) = x(2,000 - 60x) \quad \textit{Revenue function}$$
$$C(x) = 4,000 + 500x \quad \textit{Cost function}$$

where x is thousands of computers, and $C(x)$ and $R(x)$ are in thousands of dollars. Both functions have domain $1 \le x \le 25$.

(A) Sketch a graph of both functions in the same rectangular coordinate system.

(B) Find the break-even points.

(C) For what outputs will a loss occur? Will a profit occur?

59. *Profit–loss analysis.* Use the revenue function from Problem 55 in this exercise and the cost function from Problem 83, Exercise 1-1:

$$R(x) = x(75 - 3x) \quad \textit{Revenue function}$$
$$C(x) = 125 + 16x \quad \textit{Cost function}$$

where x is in millions of chips, and $R(x)$ and $C(x)$ are in millions of dollars. Both functions have domain $1 \le x \le 20$.

(A) Form a profit function P, and graph R, C, and P in the same rectangular coordinate system.

(B) Discuss the relationship between the intersection points of the graphs of R and C and the x intercepts of P.

(C) Find the x intercepts of P to the nearest thousand chips. Find the break-even points to the nearest thousand chips.

(D) Refer to the graph drawn in part (A). Does the maximum profit appear to occur at the same output level as the maximum revenue? Are the maximum profit and the maximum revenue equal? Explain.

(E) Verify your conclusion in part (D) by finding the output (to the nearest thousand chips) that produces the maximum profit. Find the maximum profit (to the nearest thousand dollars), and compare with Problem 55B.

60. *Profit–loss analysis.* Use the revenue function from Problem 56 in this exercise and the cost function from Problem 84, Exercise 1-1:

$$R(x) = x(2,000 - 60x) \quad \textit{Revenue function}$$
$$C(x) = 4,000 + 500x \quad \textit{Cost function}$$

where x is thousands of computers, and $R(x)$ and $C(x)$ are in thousands of dollars. Both functions have domain $1 \le x \le 25$.

(A) Form a profit function P, and graph R, C, and P in the same rectangular coordinate system.

(B) Discuss the relationship between the intersection points of the graphs of R and C and the x intercepts of P.

(C) Find the x intercepts of P to the nearest hundred computers. Find the break-even points.

(D) Refer to the graph drawn in part (A). Does the maximum profit appear to occur at the same output level as the maximum revenue? Are the maximum profit and the maximum revenue equal? Explain.

(E) Verify your conclusion in part (D) by finding the output that produces the maximum profit. Find the maximum profit and compare with Problem 56B.

Life Sciences

61. *Medicine.* The French physician Poiseuille was the first to discover that blood flows faster near the center of an artery than near the edge. Experimental evidence has shown that the rate of flow v (in centimeters per second) at a point x centimeters

from the center of an artery (see the figure) is given by

$$v = f(x) = 1,000(0.04 - x^2) \qquad 0 \le x \le 0.2$$

Find the distance from the center that the rate of flow is 20 centimeters per second. Round answer to two decimal places.

Figure for 59 and 60

62. *Medicine.* Refer to Problem 61. Find the distance from the center that the rate of flow is 30 centimeters per second. Round answer to two decimal places.

Chapter 1 Review

Important Terms, Symbols, and Concepts

1-1 Functions

- *Cartesian Coordinate System* A **Cartesian** or **rectangular coordinate system** is formed by the intersection of a horizontal real number line, usually called the **x axis,** and a vertical real number line, usually called the **y axis,** at their origins. The axes determine a plane and divide this plane into four **quadrants.** Each point in the plane corresponds to its **coordinates**—an **ordered pair** (a, b) determined by passing horizontal and vertical lines through the point. The **abscissa** or **x coordinate** a is the coordinate of the intersection of the vertical line and the x axis and the **ordinate** or **y coordinate** b is the coordinate of the intersection of the horizontal line and the y axis. The point with coordinates $(0, 0)$ is called the **origin.**

- *Point-by-Point Graphing* The **solution** to an equation is an ordered pair of real numbers that make the equation a true statement and the **solution set** is the set of all such ordered pairs. The **graph of an equation** is the graph of all the ordered pairs in the solution set. To **sketch the graph of an equation,** we use **point-by-point plotting** to plot sufficient points in the solution set to make the shape of the graph apparent and then connect these points with a curve.

- *Definition of a Function* A **function** is a rule (process or method) that produces a correspondence between two sets of elements such that to each element in the first set there corresponds one and only one element in the second set. The first set is called the **domain** and the set of corresponding elements in the second set is called the **range.** If x is a placeholder for the elements in the domain, x is called the **independent variable** or the **input.** If y is a placeholder for the elements in the range, y is called the

dependent variable or the **output.** If, in an equation in two variables, we get exactly one output for each input, then the equation defines a function.

> **Theorem 1 Vertical Line Test**
> An equation defines a function if each vertical line in the coordinate system passes through at most one point on the graph of the equation.

- *Functions Specified by Equations* If a **function is specified by an equation** and the domain is not indicated, we agree to assume that the domain is the set of all inputs that produce outputs that are real numbers.

- *Function Notation* The symbol $f(x)$ represents the element in the range of f corresponding to x in the domain of f. If x is an input value, then $f(x)$ is the corresponding output value. The **difference quotient** $(f(x + h) - f(x))/h$ is studied extensively in calculus.

- *Applications* **Break-even** and **profit–loss** analysis uses **costs,** C, and **revenues,** R, to determine when a company will have a **loss,** $R < C$, will **break even,** $R = C$, and will have a **profit,** $R > C$. Here are some typical functions used in this analysis, where x is the number of items manufactured and sold and $a, b, m,$ and n are constants determined from the context of a particular problem:

Cost Function	$C = $ (fixed costs) + (variable costs) $= a + bx$
Price–Demand Function	$p = m - nx$ x is the number items that can be sold at $\$p$ per item.
Revenue Function	$R = $ (number of items sold) $\times$ (price per item) $= xp = x(m - nx)$
Profit Function	$P = R - C = x(m - nx) - (a + bx)$

1-2 Elementary Functions: Graphs and Transformations

The six **basic elementary functions** are $f(x) = x$ (identity function), $h(x) = x^2$ (square function), $m(x) = x^3$ (cube function), $n(x) = \sqrt{x}$ (square root function), $p(x) = \sqrt[3]{x}$ (cube root function), and $g(x) = |x|$ (absolute value function). Performing an operation on a function produces a **transformation** of the graph of the function. The **basic transformations** are

Vertical Translation:

$$y = f(x) + k \begin{cases} k > 0 & \text{Shift graph of } y = f(x) \text{ up } k \text{ units} \\ k < 0 & \text{Shift graph of } y = f(x) \text{ down } |k| \text{ units} \end{cases}$$

Horizontal Translation:

$$y = f(x + h) \begin{cases} h > 0 & \text{Shift graph of } y = f(x) \text{ left } h \text{ units} \\ h < 0 & \text{Shift graph of } y = f(x) \text{ right } |h| \text{ units} \end{cases}$$

Vertical Expansion and Contraction:

$$y = Af(x) \begin{cases} A > 1 & \begin{array}{l}\text{Vertically expand the graph} \\ \text{of } y = f(x) \text{ by multiplying} \\ \text{each } y \text{ value by } A \end{array} \\ \\ 0 < A < 1 & \begin{array}{l}\text{Vertically contract the graph} \\ \text{of } y = f(x) \text{ by multiplying} \\ \text{each } y \text{ value by } A \end{array} \end{cases}$$

Reflection:

$$y = -f(x) \qquad \text{Reflect the graph of } y = f(x) \text{ in the } x \text{ axis}$$

A **piecewise-defined function** is a function whose definition involves more than one formula.

1-3 Linear Functions and Straight Lines

If the graph of a function f crosses the x axis at a point with x coordinate a, then both a and $(a, 0)$ are called an **x intercept** of f. If the graph of a function f crosses the y axis at a point with y coordinate b, then both b and $(0, b)$ are called the **y intercept** of f. The y intercept is $f(0)$, provided that 0 is in the domain of f, and the x intercepts are the real solutions of the equation $f(x) = 0$.

A function f is a **linear function** if $f(x) = mx + b, m \neq 0$, where m and b are real numbers. The **domain** is the set of all real numbers and the **range** is the set of all real numbers. If $m = 0$, then f is called a **constant function,** $f(x) = b$, which has the set of all real numbers as its **domain** and the constant b as its **range**. The **standard form** for the equation of a line is $Ax + By = C$, where $A, B,$ and C are real constants, A and B not both 0. Every straight line in a Cartesian coordinate system is the graph of an equation of this type. The **slope** of the line through the points (x_1, y_1) and (x_2, y_2) is the ratio of the change in y (the **rise**) to the change in x (the **run**) and is given by

$$m = \frac{y_2 - y_1}{x_2 - x_1} = \frac{\text{vertical change (rise)}}{\text{horizontal change (run)}} \qquad x_1 \neq x_2$$

The slope is not defined for a vertical line where $x_1 = x_2$.

Equations of a Line

Standard form	$Ax + By = C$	A and B not both 0
Slope-intercept form	$y = mx + b$	Slope: m; y intercept: b
Point-slope form	$y - y_1 = m(x - x_1)$	Slope: m; point: (x_1, y_1)
Horizontal line	$y = b$	Slope: 0
Vertical line	$x = a$	Slope: Undefined

If a price–demand function $p = D(x)$ and a price–supply function $p = S(x)$ intersect at a point (x_0, p_0), then this point is called the **equilibrium point,** p_0 is called the **equilibrium price,** and x_0 is called the **equilibrium quantity.**

1-4 Quadratic Functions

If $a, b,$ and c are real numbers with $a \neq 0$, then $f(x) = ax^2 + bx + c$ is a **quadratic function** in **standard form** and its graph is a **parabola.** The quadratic formula

$$x = \frac{-b \pm \sqrt{b^2 - 4ac}}{2a} \qquad b^2 - 4ac \geq 0$$

can be used to find the x intercepts of a quadratic function. Completing the square in the standard form of a quadratic function $f(x) = ax^2 + bx + c$ produces the **vertex form** $f(x) = a(x - h)^2 + k$ and the following properties:

1. The graph of f is a parabola:

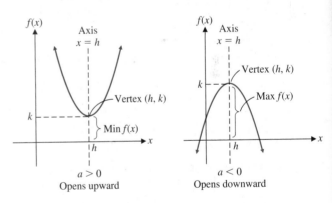

a > 0
Opens upward

a < 0
Opens downward

2. Vertex: (h, k) (parabola increases on one side of the vertex and decreases on the other)
3. Axis (of symmetry): $x = h$ (parallel to y axis)
4. $f(h) = k$ is the minimum if $a > 0$ and the maximum if $a < 0$.
5. Domain: All real numbers
   Range: $(-\infty, k]$ if $a < 0$ or $[k, \infty)$ if $a > 0$
6. The graph of f is the graph of $g(x) = ax^2$ translated horizontally h units and vertically k units.

If a revenue function $[y = R(x)]$ and a cost function $[y = C(x)]$ intersect at a point (x_0, y_0), then both this point and its x coordinate, x_0, are referred to as **break-even points.**

Review Exercise

Work through all the problems in this chapter review and check your answers in the back of the book. Answers to all review problems are there along with section numbers in italics to indicate where each type of problem is discussed. Where weaknesses show up, review appropriate sections in the text.

A

1. Use point-by-point plotting to sketch a graph of $y = 5 - x^2$. Use integer values for x from -3 to 3.

2. Indicate whether each graph specifies a function:

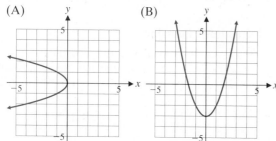

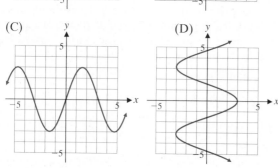

3. For $f(x) = 2x - 1$ and $g(x) = x^2 - 2x$, find:

(A) $f(-2) + g(-1)$ (B) $f(0) \cdot g(4)$

(C) $\dfrac{g(2)}{f(3)}$ (D) $\dfrac{f(3)}{g(2)}$

4. Use the graph of function f in the figure to determine (to the nearest integer) x or y as indicated.

(A) $y = f(0)$ (B) $4 = f(x)$

(C) $y = f(3)$ (D) $3 = f(x)$

(E) $y = f(-6)$ (F) $-1 = f(x)$

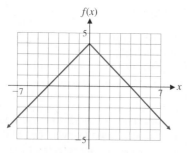

Figure for 4

5. Sketch a graph of each of the functions in parts (A)—(D) using the graph of function f in the figure below.

(A) $y = -f(x)$ (B) $y = f(x) + 4$

(C) $y = f(x - 2)$ (D) $y = -f(x + 3) - 3$

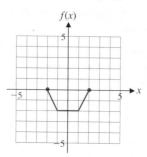

Figure for 5

6. Refer to the figure below.

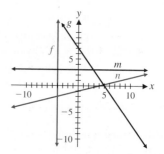

Figure for 6

(A) Identify the graphs of any linear functions with positive slopes.

(B) Identify the graphs of any linear functions with negative slopes.

(C) Identify the graphs of any constant functions. What are their slopes?

(D) Identify any graphs that are not graphs of functions. What can you say about their slopes?

7. Write an equation in the form $y = mx + b$ for a line with slope $-\frac{2}{3}$ and y intercept 6.

8. Write the equations of the vertical line and the horizontal line that pass through $(-6, 5)$.

9. Sketch a graph of $2x - 3y = 18$. What are the intercepts and slope of the line?

10. Complete the square and find the standard form for the quadratic function

$$f(x) = -x^2 + 4x$$

Then write a brief verbal description of the relationship between the graph of f and the graph of $y = x^2$.

11. Match each equation with a graph of one of the functions f, g, m, or n in the figure.

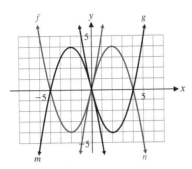

Figure for 11

(A) $y = (x - 2)^2 - 4$ (B) $y = -(x + 2)^2 + 4$

(C) $y = -(x - 2)^2 + 4$ (D) $y = (x + 2)^2 - 4$

12. Referring to the graph of function f in the figure for Problem 11 and using known properties of quadratic functions, find each of the following to the nearest integer:

(A) Intercepts   (B) Vertex

(C) Maximum or minimum   (D) Range

(E) Increasing interval   (F) Decreasing interval

13. Consider the set S of people living in the town of Newville. Which of the following correspondences specify a function? Explain.

(A) Each person in Newville (input) is paired with his or her mother (output).

(B) Each person in Newville (input) is paired with his or her children (output).

14. The three points in the table are on the graph of the indicated function f. Do these three points provide sufficient information for you to sketch the graph of $y = f(x)$? Add more points to the table until you are satisfied that your sketch is a good representation of the graph of $y = f(x)$ on the interval $[-5, 5]$.

x	-2	0	2
$f(x)$	-4	0	4

$f(x) = 6x - x^3$

15. Given $Ax + By = 30$, graph each of the following three cases on the same coordinate axes.

(A) $A = 5$ and $B = 0$ (B) $A = 0$ and $B = 6$

(C) $A = 6$ and $B = 5$

B

16. Indicate which of the following equations define a linear function or a constant function:

(A) $2x - 3y = 5$ (B) $x = -2$

(C) $y = 4 - 3x$ (D) $y = -5$

(E) $x = 3y + 5$ (F) $\dfrac{x}{2} - \dfrac{y}{3} = 1$

17. Find the domain of each function:

(A) $f(x) = \dfrac{2x - 5}{x^2 - x - 6}$ (B) $g(x) = \dfrac{3x}{\sqrt{5 - x}}$

18. The function g is defined by $g(x) = 2x - 3\sqrt{x}$. Translate into a verbal definition.

19. Find the vertex form for $f(x) = 4x^2 + 4x - 3$ and then find the intercepts, the vertex, the maximum or minimum, and the range.

20. Describe the graphs of $x = -3$ and $y = 2$. Graph both simultaneously in the same rectangular coordinate system.

21. Let $f(x) = 0.4x(x + 4)(2 - x)$.

(A) Sketch a graph of f on graph paper by first plotting points using odd integer values of x from -3 to 3. Then complete the graph using a graphing utility.

(B) Discuss the number of solutions of each of the following equations:

$$f(x) = 3 \qquad f(x) = 2 \qquad f(x) = 1$$

(C) Approximate the solutions of each equation in part (B) to three decimal places.

22. Let $f(x) = 3 - 2x$. Find

(A) $f(2)$ (B) $f(2 + h)$

(C) $f(2 + h) - f(2)$ (D) $\dfrac{f(2 + h) - f(2)}{h}$

23. Let $f(x) = x^2 - 3x + 1$. Find

(A) $f(a)$ (B) $f(a + h)$

(C) $f(a + h) - f(a)$ (D) $\dfrac{f(a + h) - f(a)}{h}$

24. Explain how the graph of $m(x) = -|x - 4|$ is related to the graph of $y = |x|$.

25. Explain how the graph of $g(x) = 0.3x^3 + 3$ is related to the graph of $y = x^3$.

26. The following graph is the result of applying a sequence of transformations to the graph of $y = x^2$. Describe the transformations verbally and write an equation for the graph.

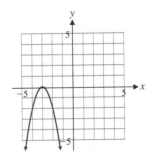

Figure for 26

27. The graph of a function f is formed by vertically expanding the graph of $y = \sqrt{x}$ by a factor of 2, and shifting it to the left 3 units and down 1 unit. Find an equation for function f and graph it for $-5 \le x \le 5$ and $-5 \le y \le 5$.

28. Sketch the graph of f for $x \geq 0$.

$$f(x) = \begin{cases} 9 + 0.3x & \text{if } 0 \leq x \leq 20 \\ 5 + 0.2x & \text{if } x > 20 \end{cases}$$

29. Sketch the graph of g for $x \geq 0$.

$$g(x) = \begin{cases} 0.5x + 5 & \text{if } 0 \leq x \leq 10 \\ 1.2x - 2 & \text{if } 10 < x \leq 30 \\ 2x - 26 & \text{if } x > 30 \end{cases}$$

30. Write the equation of a line through each indicated point with the indicated slope. Write the final answer in the form $y = mx + b$.

(A) $m = -\frac{2}{3}; (-3, 2)$ (B) $m = 0; (3, 3)$

31. Write the equation of the line through the two indicated points. Write the final answer in the form $Ax + By = C$.

(A) $(-3, 5), (1, -1)$

(B) $(-1, 5), (4, 5)$

(C) $(-2, 7), (-2, -2)$

32. Write an equation for the graph shown in the form $y = a(x - h)^2 + k$, where a is either -1 or $+1$ and h and k are integers.

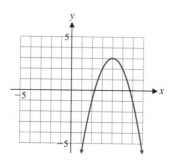

Figure for 32

33. Given $f(x) = -0.4x^2 + 3.2x + 1.2$, find the following algebraically (to three decimal places) without referring to a graph:

(A) Intercepts   (B) Vertex

(C) Maximum or minimum   (D) Range

34. Graph $f(x) = -0.4x^2 + 3.2x + 1.2$ in a graphing utility and find the following (to three decimal places) using trace and appropriate built-in commands:

(A) Intercepts   (B) Vertex

(C) Maximum or minimum   (D) Range

C

35. The following graph is the result of applying a sequence of transformations to the graph of $y = \sqrt[3]{x}$. Describe the transformations verbally, and write an equation for the graph.

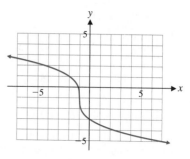

Figure for 35

36. Graph

$$y = mx + b \quad \text{and} \quad y = -\frac{1}{m}x + b$$

simultaneously in the same coordinate system for b fixed and several different values of m, $m \neq 0$. Describe the apparent relationship between the graphs of the two equations.

37. Given $G(x) = 0.3x^2 + 1.2x - 6.9$, find the following algebraically (to three decimal places) without the use of a graph:

(A) Intercepts

(B) Vertex

(C) Maximum or minimum

(D) Range

(E) Increasing and decreasing intervals

38. Graph $G(x) = 0.3x^2 + 1.2x - 6.9$ in a standard viewing window. Then find each of the following (to three decimal places) using appropriate commands.

(A) Intercepts

(B) Vertex

(C) Maximum or minimum

(D) Range

(E) Increasing and decreasing intervals

Applications

Business & Economics

39. *Linear depreciation.* A computer system was purchased by a small business for $12,000 and, for tax purposes, is assumed to have a salvage value of $2,000 after 8 years. If its value is depreciated linearly from $12,000 to $2,000:

  (A) Find the linear equation that relates the value V in dollars to the time t in years. Then graph the equation in a rectangular coordinate system.

  (B) What would be the value of the system after 5 years?

40. *Compound interest.* If $1,000 is invested at $100r\%$ compounded annually, at the end of 3 years it will grow to $A = 1,000(1 + r)^3$.

  (A) Graph the equation in a graphing utility for $0 \le r \le 0.25$; that is, for money invested at between 0% and 25% compounded annually.

  (B) At what rate of interest would $1,000 have to be invested to amount to $1,500 in 3 years? Solve for r graphically (to four decimal places) using an appropriate built-in command.

41. *Markup.* A sporting goods store sells a tennis racket that cost $130 for $208 and court shoes that cost $50 for $80.

  (A) If the markup policy of the store for items that cost over $10 is assumed to be linear and is reflected in the pricing of these two items, write an equation that relates retail price R to cost C.

  (B) What would be the retail price of a pair of in-line skates that cost $120?

  (C) What would be the cost of a pair of cross-country skis that had a retail price of $176?

  (D) What is the slope of the graph of the equation found in part (A)? Interpret the slope relative to the problem.

42. *Demand.* The table shows the annual per capita consumption of eggs in the United States.

Year	Number of Eggs
1980	271
1985	255
1990	233
1995	236
2000	256

A mathematical model for this data is given by

$$f(x) = 0.28x^2 - 6.5x + 274$$

where $x = 0$ corresponds to 1980.

  (A) Complete the following table.

x	Consumption	$f(x)$
0	271	
5	255	
10	233	
15	236	
20	256	

  (B) Graph $y = f(x)$ and the data in the same coordinate system.

  (C) Use the modeling function f to estimate the per capita egg consumption in 2005. In 2010.

  (D) Based on the information in the table, write a brief description of egg consumption from 1980 to 2000.

43. *Electricity rates.* The table shows the electricity rates charged by Easton Utilities in the summer months.

  (A) Write a piecewise definition of the monthly charge $S(x)$ (in dollars) for a customer who uses x kWh in a summer month.

  (B) Graph $S(x)$.

Energy Charge (June–September)
$3.00 for the first 20 kWh or less
5.70¢ per kWh for the next 180 kWh
3.46¢ per kWh for the next 800 kWh
2.17¢ per kWh for all over 1,000 kWh

44. *Equilibrium point.* At a price of $1.90 per bushel, the annual U.S. supply and demand for barley are 410 million bushels and 455 million bushels, respectively. When the price rises to $2.70 per bushel, the supply increases to 430 million bushels and the demand decreases to 415 million bushels.

  (A) Assuming that the price–supply and the price–demand equations are linear, find equations for each.

  (B) Find the equilibrium point for the U.S. barley market.

45. *Break-even analysis.* A video production company is planning to produce an instructional videotape. The producer estimates that it will cost $84,000 to shoot the video and $15 per unit to copy and distribute the tape. The wholesale price of the tape is $50 per unit.

  (A) Write cost and revenue equations, and graph both simultaneously in a rectangular coordinate system.

  (B) Determine algebraically when $R = C$. Then, with the aid of part (A), determine when $R < C$ and $R > C$.

  (C) Using a graphing utility, determine when $R = C$, $R < C$, and $R > C$.

46. *Break-even analysis.* The research department in a company that manufactures AM/FM clock radios established the following price–demand, cost, and revenue functions:

$$p(x) = 50 - 1.25x \quad \text{Price–demand function}$$

$$C(x) = 160 + 10x \quad \text{Cost function}$$

$$R(x) = xp(x)$$
$$\quad = x(50 - 1.25x) \quad \text{Revenue function}$$

where x is in thousands of units, and $C(x)$ and $R(x)$ are in thousands of dollars. All three functions have domain $1 \le x \le 40$.

(A) Graph the cost function and the revenue function simultaneously in the same coordinate system.

(B) Determine algebraically when $R = C$. Then, with the aid of part (A), determine when $R < C$ and $R > C$ to the nearest unit.

(C) Determine algebraically the maximum revenue (to the nearest thousand dollars) and the output (to the nearest unit) that produces the maximum revenue. What is the wholesale price of the radio (to the nearest dollar) at this output?

47. *Profit–loss analysis.* Use the cost and revenue functions from Problem 46.

(A) Write a profit function and graph it in a graphing utility.

(B) Determine graphically when $P = 0$, $P < 0$, and $P > 0$ to the nearest unit.

(C) Determine graphically the maximum profit (to the nearest thousand dollars) and the output (to the nearest unit) that produces the maximum profit. What is the wholesale price of the radio (to the nearest dollar) at this output? [Compare with Problem 46C.]

48. *Construction.* A construction company has 840 feet of chain-link fence that is used to enclose storage areas for equipment and materials at construction sites. The supervisor wants to set up two identical rectangular storage areas sharing a common fence (see the figure):

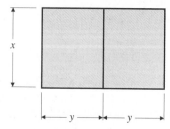

Figure for 48

Assuming that all fencing is used,

(A) Express the total area $A(x)$ enclosed by both pens as a function of x.

(B) From physical considerations, what is the domain of the function A?

(C) Graph function A in a rectangular coordinate system.

(D) Use the graph to discuss the number and approximate locations of values of x that would produce storage areas with a combined area of 25,000 square feet.

 (E) Approximate graphically (to the nearest foot) the values of x that would produce storage areas with a combined area of 25,000 square feet.

(F) Determine algebraically the dimensions of the storage areas that have the maximum total combined area. What is the maximum area?

Life Sciences

49. *Air pollution.* On an average summer day in a large city, the pollution index at 8:00 A.M. is 20 parts per million, and it increases linearly by 15 parts per million each hour until 3:00 P.M. Let $P(x)$ be the amount of pollutants in the air x hours after 8:00 A.M.

(A) Express $P(x)$ as a linear function of x.

(B) What is the air pollution index at 1:00 P.M.?

(C) Graph the function P for $0 \le x \le 7$.

(D) What is the slope of the graph? (The slope is the amount of increase in pollution for each additional hour of time.)

Social Sciences

50. *Psychology—sensory perception.* One of the oldest studies in psychology concerns the following question: Given a certain level of stimulation (light, sound, weight lifting, electric shock, and so on), how much should the stimulation be increased for a person to notice the difference? In the middle of the nineteenth century, E. H. Weber (a German physiologist) formulated a law that still carries his name: If Δs is the change in stimulus that will just be noticeable at a stimulus level s, then the ratio of Δs to s is a constant:

$$\frac{\Delta s}{s} = k$$

Hence, the amount of change that will be noticed is a linear function of the stimulus level, and we note that the greater the stimulus, the more it takes to notice a difference. In an experiment on weight lifting, the constant k for a given person was found to be $\frac{1}{30}$.

(A) Find Δs (the difference that is just noticeable) at the 30 pound level. At the 90 pound level.

(B) Graph $\Delta s = s/30$ for $0 \le s \le 120$.

(C) What is the slope of the graph?

Group Activity 1 *Introduction to Regression Analysis*

In real-world applications collected data may be assembled in table form and then examined to find a function to model the data. A very powerful mathematical tool called *regression analysis* is frequently used for this purpose. Several of the modeling functions stated in examples and exercises in Chapter 1 were constructed using *regression techniques* and a graphing utility.

Regression analysis is the process of fitting a function to a set of data points. This process is also referred to as **curve fitting.** In this group activity, we will restrict our attention to **linear regression**—that is, to fitting data with linear functions. Other types of regression analysis will be discussed in the next chapter.

At this time, we will not be interested in discussing the underlying mathematical methods used to construct a particular regression equation. Instead, we will concentrate on the mechanics of using a graphing utility to apply regression techniques to data sets.

In Example 7, Section 1-1, we were given the data in Table 1 and the corresponding modeling function

$$p(x) = 94.8 - 5x \tag{1}$$

where p is the wholesale price of a camera and x is the demand in millions.

Now we want to see how the function p was determined using linear regression on a graphing utility. On most graphing utilities, this process can be broken down into three steps:

Step 1. Enter the data set.

Step 2. Compute the desired regression equation.

Step 3. Graph the data set and the regression equation in the same viewing window.

The details for carrying out each step vary greatly from one graphing utility to another. Consult your manual.

Figure 1 shows the results of applying this process to the data in Table 1 on a graphing calculator, and Figure 2 on page 76 shows the same process on a spreadsheet.

Notice how well the line graphed in Figures 1 and 2 appears to fit this set of data. At this time, we will not discuss any mathematical techniques for determining how well a curve fits a given set of data. Instead, we will simply assume that, in some sense, the linear regression line for a given data set is the "best fit" for that data.

Most graphing utilities compute coefficients of regression equations to many more decimal places than we will need for our purposes. Normally, when a regression equation is written, the coefficients are rounded. For example, if we round each coefficient in Figure 1 or 2 to one decimal place, we

TABLE 1 Price–Demand	
x (Millions)	*p* ($)
2	87
5	68
8	53
12	37

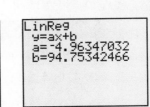
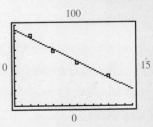

FIGURE 1   Linear regression on a graphing calculator

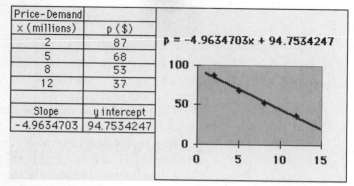

Price–Demand	
x (millions)	p ($)
2	87
5	68
8	53
12	37
Slope	y intercept
-4.9634703	94.7534247

$p = -4.9634703x + 94.7534247$

FIGURE 2   Linear regression on a spreadsheet

will obtain the modeling function f we used in Example 7, Section 1-1 [see equation (1)].

(A) If you have not already done so, carry out steps 1 to 3 for the data in Table 1. Write a brief summary of the details for performing these steps on your graphing utility and keep it for future reference. (Some of the optional exercises in subsequent chapters will require you to compute regression equations.)

(B) Each of the following examples and exercises from Chapter 1 contains a data set and an equation that models the data. In each case, use a graphing utility to compute a linear regression equation for the data. Plot the data and graph the equation in the same viewing rectangle. Discuss the difference between the graphing utility's regression equation and the modeling function stated in the problem.
   • Section 1-1, Matched Problem 7
   • Exercise 1-1, Problems 79 and 80
   • Exercise 1-3, Problems 65 and 66

Group Activity 2   *Mathematical Modeling in Business*

A company manufactures and sells mountain bikes. The management would like to have price–demand and cost functions for break-even and profit–loss analysis. Price–demand and cost functions are often established by collecting appropriate data at different levels of output, and then finding a model in the form of a basic elementary function (from our library of elementary functions) that "closely fits" the collected data. The financial department, using statistical techniques, arrived at the price–demand and cost data in Tables 1 and 2, where p is the wholesale price of a bike for a demand of x hundred bikes, $0 \le x \le 220$, and C is the cost (in hundreds of dollars) of producing and selling x bikes, $0 \le x \le 220$.

(A) *Building a Mathematical Model for Price–Demand.* Plot the data in Table 1 and observe that the relationship between p and x appears to be linear.

TABLE 1 Price–Demand	
x (Hundreds)	*p* ($)
0	525
64	370
125	270
185	130

TABLE 2 Cost	
x (Hundreds)	*C* (Hundred $)
0	8,470
30	13,510
120	19,140
180	22,580
220	28,490

1. If you have completed Group Activity 1, use your graphing utility to find the linear regression line for the data in Table 1. Graph the line and the data in the same viewing window.

2. The linear regression line found in part 1 is a mathematical model for price–demand and is given by

$$p(x) = -2.09x + 519 \quad \text{Price–demand equation}$$

Graph the data points from Table 1 and the price–demand equation in the same rectangular coordinate system.

3. The linear regression line defines a linear function. Interpret the slope of the line. Discuss its domain and range. Using the mathematical model, determine the price for a demand of 10,000 bikes. For a demand of 20,000 bikes.

(B) *Building a Mathematical Model for Cost.* Plot the data in Table 2 in a rectangular coordinate system. Which type of function appears to best fit the data?

1. If you have completed Group Activity 1, use your graphing utility to find the linear regression line for the data in Table 2. Graph the line and the data in the same viewing window.

2. The linear regression line found in part 1 is a mathematical model for cost and is given by

$$C(x) = 81x + 9,498 \quad \text{Cost equation}$$

Graph the data points from Table 2 and the cost equation in the same rectangular coordinate system.

3. Interpret the slope of the cost equation function. Discuss its domain and range. Using the mathematical model, determine the cost for an output and sales of 10,000 bikes. For an output and sales of 20,000 bikes.

(C) *Break-Even and Profit–Loss Analysis.* Refer to the price–demand equation in part (A) and the cost equation in part (B). Write an equation for the revenue function and state its domain. Write an equation for the profit function and state its domain.

1. Graph the revenue function and the cost function simultaneously in the same rectangular coordinate system. Determine algebraically at what outputs (to the nearest unit) the break-even points occur. Determine the outputs where costs exceed revenues and where revenues exceed costs.

2. Graph the revenue function and the cost function simultaneously in the same viewing window. Determine graphically at what outputs (to the nearest unit) break-even occurs, costs exceed revenues, and revenues exceed costs.

3. Graph the profit function in a rectangular coordinate system. Determine algebraically at what outputs (to the nearest unit) the break-even points occur. Determine where profits occur and where losses occur. At what output and price will a maximum profit occur? Does the maximum revenue and maximum profit occur for the same output? Discuss.

4. Graph the profit function in a graphing utility. Determine graphically at what outputs (to the nearest unit) break-even occurs, losses occur, and profits occur. At what output and price will a maximum profit occur? Does the maximum revenue and maximum profit occur for the same output? Discuss.

OBJECTIVES

1. Describe and distinguish, by graphical properties, the classes of polynomial, rational, exponential, and logarithmic functions.

2. Calculate compound interest and continuously compounded interest.

3. Solve problems in population growth, radioactive decay, and the spread of epidemics by using exponential functions as models.

4. Find the doubling time of an investment using logarithms.

5. Compute linear, quadratic, exponential, and logarithmic regression models for given data sets.

CHAPTER PROBLEM

The government agencies, the universities, and the electronic firms that maintain the World Wide Web are always trying to monitor the growth of the Internet so that they can anticipate future needs. One way to measure this growth is to consider the sales of computers, hard drives, printers, and so on. One firm, Internet Dynamics Corporation (IDC), reported that the worldwide hard drive capacity for the drives sold in 1998 was 695,000 terabytes (a terabyte is 1 trillion bytes) and for drives sold in 2000 was 3,222,000 terabytes.

(A) Use the data from IDC to find a compound growth model of the form $y = P(1 + r)^n$, where n is years since 1998. Express the annual compound rate r as a percentage correct to one decimal place.

(B) Use the data from IDC to find an exponential model of the form $y = ce^{rt}$, where t is years since 1998. Express the continuous compound rate r as a percentage correct to one decimal place.

(C) IDC projected that the hard drive capacity in 2004 will be 56,558,000 terabytes. What do the models you found in parts A and B project for 2004?

Additional Elementary Functions

2

INTRODUCTION

In this chapter we add the following four general classes of functions to the beginning library of elementary functions started in Chapter 1: polynomial, rational, exponential, and logarithmic. This expanded library of elementary functions contains most of the functions you will need in this and many other courses. The linear and quadratic functions studied in Chapter 1 are special cases of the more general class of functions called *polynomials*.

Section 2-1 | Polynomial and Rational Functions

➤ Polynomial Functions
➤ Polynomial Root Approximation
➤ Regression Polynomials
➤ Rational Functions
➤ Application

➤ Polynomial Functions

In Chapter 1 you were introduced to the basic functions

$$f(x) = b \qquad \text{Constant function}$$
$$f(x) = ax + b \qquad a \neq 0 \qquad \text{Linear function}$$
$$f(x) = ax^2 + bx + c \qquad a \neq 0 \qquad \text{Quadratic function}$$

as well as some special cases of

$$f(x) = ax^3 + bx^2 + cx + d \qquad a \neq 0 \qquad \text{Cubic function}$$

Most of the earlier applications we considered, including cost, revenue, profit, loss, and packaging applications, made use of these functions. Notice the evolving pattern going from the constant function to the cubic function—the terms in each equation are of the form ax^n, where n is a nonnegative integer and a is a real number. All these functions are special cases of the general class of functions called *polynomial functions*:

> **DEFINITION**   Polynomial Function
>
> A **polynomial function** is a function that can be written in the form
>
> $$f(x) = a_n x^n + a_{n-1} x^{n-1} + \cdots + a_1 x + a_0$$
>
> for n a nonnegative integer, called the **degree** of the polynomial. The coefficients $a_0, a_1, \ldots, a_n$ are real numbers with $a_n \neq 0$. The **domain** of a polynomial function is the set of all real numbers.

The shape of the graph of a polynomial function is connected to the degree of the polynomial. The shapes of odd-degree polynomial functions have something in common, and the shapes of even-degree polynomial functions have something in common. Figure 1 shows graphs of representative polynomial functions from degrees 1 to 6, and suggests some general properties of graphs of polynomial functions.

Notice that the odd-degree polynomial graphs start negative, end positive, and cross the x axis at least once. The even-degree polynomial graphs start positive, end positive, and may not cross the x axis at all. In all cases in Figure 1, the coefficient of the highest-degree term was chosen positive. If any leading coefficient had been chosen negative, then we would have a similar graph but reflected in the x axis.

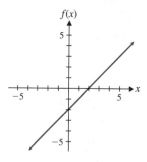

(A) $f(x) = x - 2$

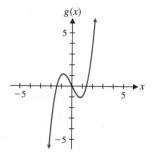

(B) $g(x) = x^3 - 2x$

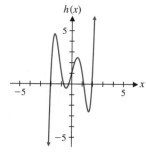

(C) $h(x) = x^5 - 5x^3 + 4x + 1$

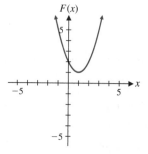

(D) $F(x) = x^2 - 2x + 2$

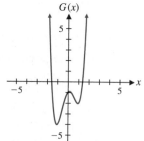

(E) $G(x) = 2x^4 - 4x^2 + x - 1$

(F) $H(x) = x^6 - 7x^4 + 14x^2 - x - 5$

FIGURE 1   Graphs of polynomial functions

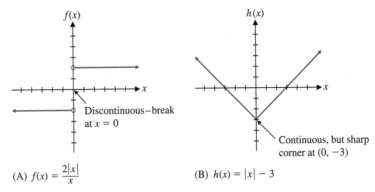

(A) $f(x) = \dfrac{2|x|}{x}$ (B) $h(x) = |x| - 3$

FIGURE 2   Discontinuous and sharp-corner functions

The graph of a polynomial function is **continuous,** with no holes or breaks. That is, the graph can be drawn without removing a pen from the paper. Also, the graph of a polynomial has no sharp corners. Figure 2 shows the graphs of two functions, one that is not continuous, and the other that is continuous, but with a sharp corner. Neither function is a polynomial.

Figure 1 gives examples of polynomial functions with graphs containing the maximum number of *turning points* possible for a polynomial of that degree. A **turning point** on a continuous graph is a point that separates an increasing* portion from a decreasing portion, or vice versa. Facts from algebra and calculus can be used to establish Theorem 1.

THEOREM 1   Turning Points and x Intercepts of Polynomials

The graph of a polynomial function of positive degree n can have at most $n - 1$ turning points and can cross the x axis at most n times.

EXPLORE
&DISCUSS
1

(A) What is the least number of turning points an odd-degree polynomial function can have? An even-degree polynomial function?

(B) What is the maximum number of x intercepts the graph of a polynomial function of degree n can have?

(C) What is the maximum number of real solutions an nth-degree polynomial equation can have?

(D) What is the least number of x intercepts the graph of a polynomial function of odd degree can have? Of even degree?

(E) What is the least number of real solutions a polynomial function of odd degree can have? Of even degree?

We now compare the graphs of two polynomial functions relative to points close to the origin and then "zoom out" to compare points distant from the origin. Compare the graphs in Figure 3 on page 82.

Figure 3 clearly shows that the highest-degree term in the polynomial dominates all other terms combined in the polynomial. As we "zoom out," the graph of $y = x^5 - 5x^3 + 4x + 1$ looks more and more like the graph of $y = x^5$. This is a general property of polynomial functions.

---

*Formally, we say that the function f is **increasing** on an interval (a, b) if $f(x_2) > f(x_1)$ whenever $a < x_1 < x_2 < b$; and f is **decreasing** on (a, b) if $f(x_2) < f(x_1)$ whenever $a < x_1 < x_2 < b$.

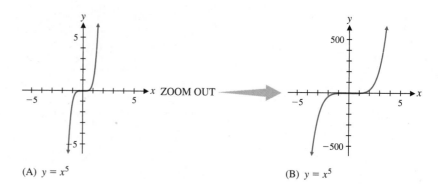

(A) $y = x^5$

ZOOM OUT

(B) $y = x^5$

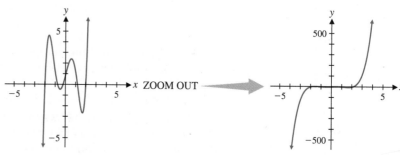

(C) $y = x^5 - 5x^3 + 4x + 1$

ZOOM OUT

(D) $y = x^5 - 5x^3 + 4x + 1$

FIGURE 3   Close and distant comparisons

EXPLORE
&DISCUSS
2

Compare the graphs of $y = x^6$ and $y = x^6 - 7x^4 + 14x^2 - x - 5$ in the following two viewing windows:

(A) $-5 \le x \le 5, -5 \le y \le 5$
(B) $-5 \le x \le 5, -500 \le y \le 500$

➤ Polynomial Root Approximation

An x intercept of a function f is also called a **zero*** or **root** of the function. Approximating the zeros of a function with a graphing utility is a simple matter, provided that we can find a window that shows where the graph of the function touches or crosses the x axis. But how can we be sure that a particular window shows all the zeros? For polynomial functions, Theorem 2 can be used to choose a window that contains all the zeros of the polynomial. Theorem 2 is due to A. L. Cauchy (1789–1857), a French mathematician who has many theorems and concepts associated with his name, and illustrates that classical mathematical results are often useful tools in modern applications.

THEOREM 2   Locating Zeros of a Polynomial

If r is a zero of the polynomial

$$P(x) = x^n + a_{n-1}x^{n-1} + a_{n-2}x^{n-2} + \cdots + a_1x + a_0$$

then[†]

$$|r| < 1 + \max\{|a_{n-1}|, |a_{n-2}|, \ldots, |a_1|, |a_0|\}$$

[†]Note: $\max\{|a_{n-1}|, |a_{n-2}|, \ldots, |a_1|, |a_0|\}$ is the largest number in the list $|a_{n-1}|, |a_{n-2}|, \ldots, |a_0|$.

---

* Only real numbers can be x intercepts. Functions may have complex zeros that are not real numbers, but such zeros, which are not x intercepts, will not be discussed in this book.

In a polynomial, the coefficient of the term containing the highest power of x is often referred to as the **leading coefficient.** Notice that Theorem 2 requires that this leading coefficient must be a 1.

EXAMPLE 1   **Approximating the Zeros of a Polynomial** Approximate (to four decimal places) the real zeros of

$$P(x) = 2x^4 - 5x^3 - 4x^2 + 3x + 6$$

Solution   Since the leading coefficient of $P(x)$ is 2, Theorem 2 cannot be applied to $P(x)$. But it can be applied to

$$Q(x) = \tfrac{1}{2}P(x) = \tfrac{1}{2}(2x^4 - 5x^3 - 4x^2 + 3x + 6)$$
$$= x^4 - \tfrac{5}{2}x^3 - 2x^2 + \tfrac{3}{2}x + 3$$

Since multiplying a function by a positive constant expands or contracts the graph vertically (see Section 1-2), but does not change the x intercepts, $P(x)$ and $Q(x)$ have the same zeros. Thus, Theorem 2 implies that any zero, r, of $P(x)$ must satisfy

$$|r| < 1 + \max\{|-\tfrac{5}{2}|, |-2|, |\tfrac{3}{2}|, |3|\} = 1 + 3 = 4$$

and all zeros of $P(x)$ must be between -4 and 4. Graphing $P(x)$ (Fig. 4A), we see two real zeros of $P(x)$ and we can be certain that there are no zeros outside this window. Using the zero command, the real zeros of $P(x)$ (to four decimal places) are 1.1539 (Fig. 4B) and 2.8881 (Fig. 4C). Note also that $P(x)$ has three turning points in this window, the maximum allowable for a fourth-degree polynomial. Thus, there cannot be any turning points outside this window.

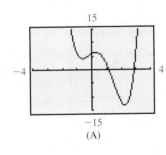
(A)

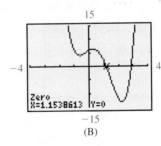
(B)

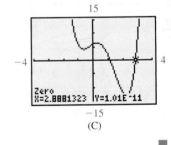
(C)

FIGURE 4

Matched Problem 1   Approximate (to two decimal places) the real zeros of

$$P(x) = 3x^3 + 12x^2 + 9x + 4$$

▶ Regression Polynomials

In Group Activity 1 at the end of Chapter 1, we saw that regression techniques can be used to fit a straight line to a set of data. Linear functions are not the only ones that can be applied in this manner. Most graphing utilities have the ability to fit a variety of curves to a given set of data. We will discuss polynomial regression models in this section and other types of regression models in later sections.

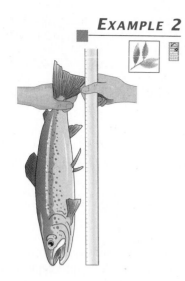

EXAMPLE 2   **Estimating the Weight of a Fish** Using the length of a fish to estimate its weight is of interest to both scientists and sport anglers. The data in Table 1 give the average weights of lake trout for certain lengths. Use the data and regression techniques to find a polynomial model that can be used to estimate the weight of a lake trout for any length. Estimate (to the nearest ounce) the weights of lake trout of lengths 39, 40, 41, 42, and 43 inches, respectively.

TABLE 1 Lake Trout

Length (in.)	Weight (oz)	Length (in.)	Weight (oz)
x	y	x	y
10	5	30	152
14	12	34	226
18	26	38	326
22	56	44	536
26	96		

Solution   The graph of the data in Table 1 (Fig. 5A) indicates that a linear regression model would not be appropriate in this case. And, in fact, we would not expect a linear relationship between length and weight. Instead, it is more likely that the weight would be related to the cube of the length. We use a cubic regression polynomial to model the data (Fig. 5B). (Consult your manual for the details of calculating regression polynomials on your graphing utility.) Figure 5C adds the graph of the polynomial model to the graph of the data. The graph in Figure 5C shows that this cubic polynomial does provide a good fit for the data. (We will have more to say about the choice of functions and the accuracy of the fit provided by regression analysis later in the book.) Figure 5D shows the estimated weights for the lengths requested.

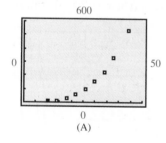
(A)

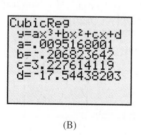
(B)

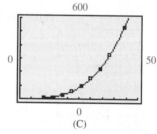
(C)

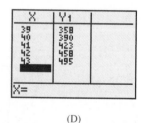
(D)

FIGURE 5

Matched Problem 2   The data in Table 2 give the average weights of pike for certain lengths. Use a cubic regression polynomial to model the data. Estimate (to the nearest ounce) the weights of pike of lengths 39, 40, 41, 42, and 43 inches, respectively.

TABLE 2 Pike

Length (in.)	Weight (oz)	Length (in.)	Weight (oz)
x	y	x	y
10	5	30	108
14	12	34	154
18	26	38	210
22	44	44	326
26	72	52	522

▶ Rational Functions

Just as rational numbers are defined in terms of quotients of integers, *rational functions* are defined in terms of quotients of polynomials. The following equations define rational functions:

$$f(x) = \frac{1}{x} \quad g(x) = \frac{x - 2}{x^2 - x - 6} \quad h(x) = \frac{x^3 - 8}{x}$$

$$p(x) = 3x^2 - 5x \quad q(x) = 7 \quad r(x) = 0$$

DEFINITION   Rational Function

A **rational function** is any function that can be written in the form

$$f(x) = \frac{n(x)}{d(x)} \quad d(x) \neq 0$$

where $n(x)$ and $d(x)$ are polynomials. The **domain** is the set of all real numbers such that $d(x) \neq 0$. We assume that $n(x)$ and $d(x)$ have no real zero in common.

EXAMPLE 3   **Domain and Intercepts** Find the domain and intercepts for the rational function

$$f(x) = \frac{x - 2}{x + 1}$$

Solution   *Domain:* The denominator is 0 at $x = -1$. Therefore, the domain is the set of all real numbers except -1. The graph of f cannot cross the vertical line $x = -1$.

x intercepts: Find x such that $f(x) = 0$. This happens only if $x - 2 = 0$, that is, at $x = 2$. Thus, 2 is the only x intercept.

y intercept: The y intercept is

$$f(0) = \frac{0 - 2}{0 + 1} = -2$$

Matched Problem 3   Find the domain and intercepts for the rational function: $g(x) = \dfrac{2x}{x - 2}$

In the next example we investigate the graph of $f(x) = (x - 2)/(x + 1)$ near the *point of discontinuity,* $x = -1$, and the behavior of the graph as x increases or decreases without bound. Using this information, we can complete a sketch of the graph of function f with little additional trouble. The investigation uncovers some characteristic features of graphs of rational functions.

EXAMPLE 4   **Graph of a Rational Function** Given function f from Example 3:

$$f(x) = \frac{x - 2}{x + 1}$$

(A) Investigate the graph of f near the point of discontinuity, $x = -1$.
(B) Investigate the graph of f as x increases or decreases without bound.
(C) Sketch a graph of function f.

Solution   (A) *Let x approach* −1 *from the left:*

x	f(x)
−2	4
−1.1	31
−1.01	301
−1.001	3,001
−1.0001	30,001
−1.00001	300,001

We see that $f(x)$ increases without bound as x approaches −1 from the left. Symbolically,

$$f(x) \to \infty \quad \text{as} \quad x \to -1^-$$

Let x approach −1 *from the right:*

x	f(x)
0	−2
−0.9	−29
−0.99	−299
−0.999	−2,999
−0.9999	−29,999
−0.99999	−299,999

We see that $f(x)$ decreases without bound as x approaches −1 from the right. Symbolically,

$$f(x) \to -\infty \quad \text{as} \quad x \to -1^+$$

The vertical line $x = -1$ is called a *vertical asymptote*. The graph of f gets closer to this line as x gets closer to −1. Sketching the vertical asymptote provides an aid to drawing the graph of f near the asymptote (Fig. 6).

(B) Divide each term in the numerator and denominator of $f(x)$ by x, the highest power of x to occur in $f(x)$:

$$f(x) = \frac{x - 2}{x + 1} = \frac{1 - \dfrac{2}{x}}{1 + \dfrac{1}{x}}$$

As x increases or decreases without bound, $2/x$ and $1/x$ approach 0 and $f(x)$ gets closer and closer to 1. The horizontal line $y = 1$ is called a *horizontal asymptote*. The graph of $y = f(x)$ gets closer to this line as x decreases or increases without bound. But how does the graph of $y = f(x)$ approach the horizontal line $y = 1$? Does it approach from above? From below? Or from both? To answer these questions we investigate table values as follows:

Let x approach ∞:

x	f(x)
10	0.72727
100	0.97030
1,000	0.99700
10,000	0.99970
100,000	0.99997

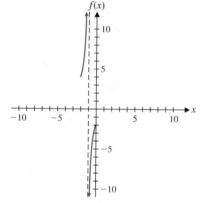

FIGURE 6 Graph near vertical asymptote $x = -1$

The graph of $y = f(x)$ approaches the line $y = 1$ from below as x increases without bound.

Let x approach $-\infty$:

x	$f(x)$
-10	1,33333
-100	1.03030
$-1,000$	1.00300
$-10,000$	1.00030
$-100,000$	1.00003

The graph of $y = f(x)$ approaches the line $y = 1$ from above as x decreases without bound.

Sketching the horizontal asymptote first provides an aid to drawing the graph of f as x moves away from the origin (Fig. 7).

(C) It is now easy to complete the sketch of the graph of f using the intercepts from Example 3 and filling in any points of uncertainty (Fig. 8).

x	$f(x)$
-4	2
-2	4
0	-2
2	0

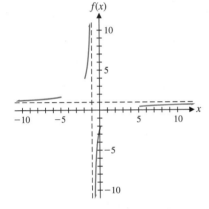

FIGURE 7 Graph of $y = f(x)$ near horizontal asymptote $y = 1$

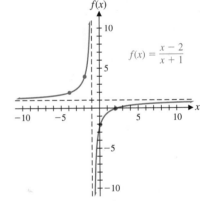

FIGURE 8 Sketch of the rational function f

Matched Problem 4 Given function g from Matched Problem 3, $g(x) = \dfrac{2x}{x - 2}$,

(A) Investigate the graph of g near the point of discontinuity, $x = 2$.

(B) Investigate the graph of g as x increases or decreases without bound.

(C) Sketch a graph of function g.

Graphing rational functions is considerably aided by locating vertical and horizontal asymptotes first, if they exist. The following general procedures are suggested by Example 4:

PROCEDURE Vertical and Horizontal Asymptotes and Rational Functions

Given the rational function

$$f(x) = \frac{n(x)}{d(x)}$$

where $n(x)$ and $d(x)$ are polynomials with no real zero in common:

1. If a is a real number such that $d(a) = 0$, then the line $x = a$ is a **vertical asymptote** of the graph of $y = f(x)$.

2. **Horizontal asymptotes**, if any exist, can be found by dividing each term of the numerator $n(x)$ and denominator $d(x)$ by the highest power of x that appears in $f(x)$, and then proceeding as in Example 4.

EXAMPLE 5   **Graphing Rational Functions** Given the rational function:

$$f(x) = \frac{3x}{x^2 - 4}$$

(A) Find intercepts and equations for any vertical and horizontal asymptotes.

(B) Using the information from part (A) and additional points as necessary, sketch a graph of f for $-7 \le x \le 7$ and $-7 \le y \le 7$.

Solution   (A) x *intercepts:* $f(x) = 0$ only if $3x = 0$, or $x = 0$. Thus, the only x intercept is 0.

y *intercept:*

$$f(0) = \frac{3 \cdot 0}{0^2 - 4} = \frac{0}{-4} = 0$$

Thus, the y intercept is 0.

Vertical asymptotes:

$$f(x) = \frac{3x}{x^2 - 4} = \frac{3x}{(x - 2)(x + 2)}$$

The denominator is 0 at $x = -2$ and $x = 2$; hence, $x = -2$ and $x = 2$ are vertical asymptotes.

Horizontal asymptotes: Divide each term in the numerator and denominator by x^2, the highest power of x in $f(x)$.

$$f(x) = \frac{3x}{x^2 - 4} = \frac{\dfrac{3x}{x^2}}{\dfrac{x^2}{x^2} - \dfrac{4}{x^2}} = \frac{\dfrac{3}{x}}{1 - \dfrac{4}{x^2}}$$

As x increases or decreases without bound, the numerator tends to 0 and the denominator tends to 1; thus, $f(x)$ tends to 0. The line $y = 0$ is a horizontal asymptote.

(B) Use the information from part (A) and plot additional points as necessary to complete the graph, as shown in Figure 9.

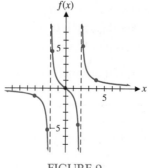

x	$f(x)$
-4	-1
-2.3	-5.3
-1.7	4.6
0	0
1.7	-4.6
2.3	5.3
4	1

FIGURE 9

Matched Problem 5   Given the rational function $g(x) = \dfrac{3x + 3}{x^2 - 9}$,

(A) Find all intercepts and equations for any vertical and horizontal asymptotes.

(B) Using the information from part (A) and additional points as necessary, sketch a graph of g for $-10 \le x \le 10$ and $-10 \le y \le 10$.

◉ Insight   The procedure for finding horizontal asymptotes, illustrated in Examples 4 and 5, reveals that **a rational function can have at most one horizontal asymptote.** Moreover, the graph of a rational function approaches the horizontal asymptote (when one exists) both as $x \to \infty$ and as $x \to -\infty$.   ●

➤ Application

Rational functions occur naturally in many types of applications.

EXAMPLE 6   **Employee Training** A company that manufactures computers has established that, on the average, a new employee can assemble $N(t)$ components per day after t days of on-the-job training, as given by

$$N(t) = \frac{50t}{t + 4} \quad t \geq 0$$

Sketch a graph of N, $0 \leq t \leq 100$, including any vertical or horizontal asymptotes. What does $N(t)$ approach as t increases without bound?

Solution   *Vertical asymptotes:* None for $t \geq 0$

Horizontal asymptote:

$$N(t) = \frac{50t}{t + 4} = \frac{50}{1 + \dfrac{4}{t}}$$

$N(t)$ approaches 50 as t increases without bound. Thus, $y = 50$ is a horizontal asymptote.

Sketch of graph: The graph is shown in the margin.

$N(t)$ approaches 50 as t increases without bound. It appears that 50 components per day would be the upper limit that an employee would be expected to assemble.   ■

$N(t)$

  Matched Problem 6   Repeat Example 6 for $N(t) = \dfrac{25t + 5}{t + 5} \quad t \geq 0$.

Answers to Matched Problems   **1.** -3.19

2.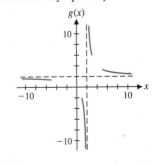

3. Domain: all real numbers except 2; x intercept: 0; y intercept: 0

4. (A) Vertical asymptote: $x = 2$ (B) Horizontal asymptote: $y = 2$

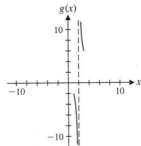

(C)

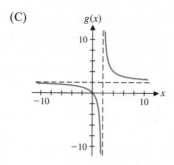

5. (A) x intercept: -1; y intercept; $-\frac{1}{3}$;
Vertical asymptotes: $x = -3$ and $x = 3$;
Horizontal asymptote: $y = 0$

(B)

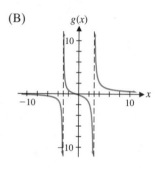

6. No vertical asymptotes for $t \geq 0$; $y = 25$ is a horizontal asymptote. $N(t)$ approaches 25 as t increases without bound. It appears that 25 components per day would be the upper limit that an employee would be expected to assemble.

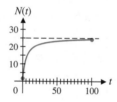

Exercise 2-1

A *In Problems 1–10, for each polynomial function find the following:*

(A) *Degree of the polynomial*

(B) *All x intercepts*

(C) *The y intercept*

1. $f(x) = 5x + 3$

2. $f(x) = 4 - 3x$

3. $f(x) = x^2 - 9$

4. $f(x) = 5x - x^2 - 6$

5. $f(x) = (x - 2)(x + 3)(x - 5)$

6. $f(x) = (x + 7)(x - 4)$

7. $f(x) = (2x - 9)(3x + 4)$

8. $f(x) = (2 - 5x)(x - 6)(x + 1)$

9. $f(x) = x^6 + 1$

10. $f(x) = (x^8 + 5)(x^{12} + 7)$

Each graph in Problems 11–18 is the graph of a polynomial function. Answer the following questions for each graph:

(A) *How many turning points are on the graph?*

(B) *What is the minimum degree of a polynomial function that could have the graph?*

(C) *Is the leading coefficient of the polynomial negative or positive?*

11.

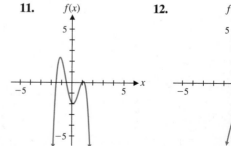

12.

13.

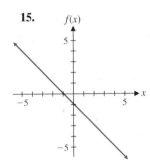

14.

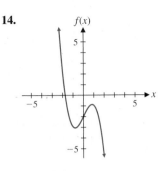

15.

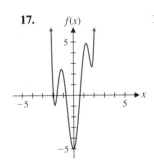

16.

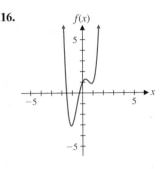

17.

18.

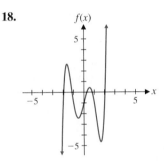

19. What is the maximum number of turning points that a polynomial of degree 8 can have?

20. What is the maximum number of turning points that a polynomial of degree 11 can have?

21. What is the maximum number of x intercepts that a polynomial of degree 10 can have?

22. What is the maximum number of x intercepts that a polynomial of degree 7 can have?

23. What is the minimum number of x intercepts that a polynomial of degree 9 can have? Explain.

24. What is the minimum number of x intercepts that a polynomial of degree 6 can have? Explain.

B *For each rational function in Problems 25–30,*

(A) *Find the intercepts for the graph.*

(B) *Determine the domain.*

(C) *Find any vertical or horizontal asymptotes for the graph.*

(D) *Sketch any asymptotes as dashed lines. Then sketch a graph of $y = f(x)$ for $-10 \le x \le 10$ and $-10 \le y \le 10$.*

(E) *Graph $y = f(x)$ in a standard viewing window using a graphing utility.*

25. $f(x) = \dfrac{x + 2}{x - 2}$

26. $f(x) = \dfrac{x - 3}{x + 3}$

27. $f(x) = \dfrac{3x}{x + 2}$

28. $f(x) = \dfrac{2x}{x - 3}$

29. $f(x) = \dfrac{4 - 2x}{x - 4}$

30. $f(x) = \dfrac{3 - 3x}{x - 2}$

31. How does the graph of $f(x) = 2x^4 - 5x^2 + x + 2$ compare to the graph of $y = 2x^4$ as we "zoom out" (see Fig. 3 on page 82)?

32. How does the graph of $f(x) = x^3 - 2x + 2$ compare to the graph of $y = x^3$ as we "zoom out"?

33. How does the graph of $f(x) = -x^5 + 4x^3 - 4x + 1$ compare to the graph of $y = -x^5$ as we "zoom out"?

34. How does the graph of $f(x) = -x^5 + 5x^3 + 4x - 1$ compare to the graph of $y = -x^5$ as we "zoom out"?

35. Compare the graph of $y = 2x^4$ to the graph of $y = 2x^4 - 5x^2 + x + 2$ in the following two viewing windows:

(A) $-5 \le x \le 5, -5 \le y \le 5$

(B) $-5 \le x \le 5, -500 \le y \le 500$

36. Compare the graph of $y = x^3$ to the graph of $y = x^3 - 2x + 2$ in the following two viewing windows:

(A) $-5 \le x \le 5, -5 \le y \le 5$

(B) $-5 \le x \le 5, -500 \le y \le 500$

37. Compare the graph of $y = -x^5$ to the graph of $y = -x^5 + 4x^3 - 4x + 1$ in the following two viewing windows:

(A) $-5 \le x \le 5, -5 \le y \le 5$

(B) $-5 \le x \le 5, -500 \le y \le 500$

38. Compare the graph of $y = -x^5$ to the graph of $y = -x^5 + 5x^3 - 5x + 2$ in the following two viewing windows:

(A) $-5 \le x \le 5, -5 \le y \le 5$

(B) $-5 \le x \le 5, -500 \le y \le 500$

In Problems 39–44, use Theorem 2 to find an interval on the x axis that must contain all the zeros of each polynomial. Then approximate each real zero to two decimal places.

39. $2x^3 - x^2 - 7x + 3$

40. $3x^3 + 10x^2 + 6x - 2$

41. $x^4 + 2x^3 - 3x^2 - 4x + 1$

42. $x^4 - 3x^3 - 4x^2 + 3x + 1$

43. $x^5 - 12x^4 + 7x^3 + 15$

44. $x^5 + 14x^4 - 10x^2 - 15$

45. Graph the line $y = 0.5x + 3$. Choose any two distinct points on this line and find the linear regression model for the data set consisting of the two points you chose. Experiment with other lines of your choice. Discuss the relationship between a linear regression model for two points and the line that goes through the two points.

46. Graph the parabola $y = x^2 - 5x$. Choose any three distinct points on this parabola and find the quadratic regression model for the data set consisting of the three points you chose. Experiment with other parabolas of your choice. Discuss the relationship between a quadratic regression model for three non-collinear points and the parabola that goes through the three points.

C *For each rational function in Problems 47–52,*

(A) *Find any intercepts for the graph.*

(B) *Find any vertical and horizontal asymptotes for the graph.*

(C) *Sketch any asymptotes as dashed lines. Then sketch a graph of f for $-10 \le x \le 10$ and $-10 \le y \le 10$.*

(D) *Graph the function in a standard viewing window using a graphing utility.*

47. $f(x) = \dfrac{2x^2}{x^2 - x - 6}$

48. $f(x) = \dfrac{3x^2}{x^2 + x - 6}$

49. $f(x) = \dfrac{6 - 2x^2}{x^2 - 9}$

50. $f(x) = \dfrac{3 - 3x^2}{x^2 - 4}$

51. $f(x) = \dfrac{-4x}{x^2 + x - 6}$

52. $f(x) = \dfrac{5x}{x^2 + x - 12}$

53. Write an equation for the lowest-degree polynomial function with the graph and intercepts shown in the figure.

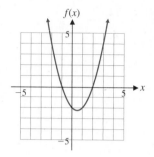

Figure for 53

54. Write an equation for the lowest-degree polynomial function with the graph and intercepts shown in the figure.

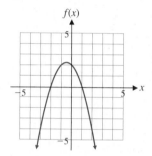

Figure for 54

55. Write an equation for the lowest-degree polynomial function with the graph and intercepts shown in the figure.

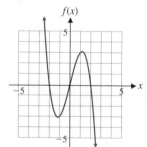

Figure for 55

56. Write an equation for the lowest-degree polynomial function with the graph and intercepts shown in the figure.

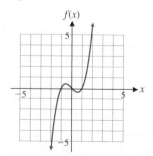

Figure for 56

Applications

Business & Economics

57. *Average cost.* A company manufacturing snow-boards has fixed costs of $200 per day and total costs of $3,800 per day at a daily output of 20 boards.

(A) Assuming that the total cost per day, $C(x)$, is linearly related to the total output per day, x, write an equation for the cost function.

(B) The average cost per board for an output of x boards is given by $\overline{C}(x) = C(x)/x$. Find the average cost function.

(C) Sketch a graph of the average cost function, including any asymptotes, for $1 \le x \le 30$.

(D) What does the average cost per board tend to as production increases?

58. *Average cost.* A company manufacturing surfboards has fixed costs of $300 per day and total costs of $5,100 per day at a daily output of 20 boards.

(A) Assuming that the total cost per day, $C(x)$, is linearly related to the total output per day, x, write an equation for the cost function.

(B) The average cost per board for an output of x boards is given by $\overline{C}(x) = C(x)/x$. Find the average cost function.

(C) Sketch a graph of the average cost function, including any asymptotes, for $1 \le x \le 30$.

(D) What does the average cost per board tend to as production increases?

59. *Replacement time.* An office copier has an initial price of $2,500. A service contract costs $200 for the first year and increases $50 per year thereafter. It can be shown that the total cost of the copier after n years is given by

$$C(n) = 2,500 + 175n + 25n^2$$

The average cost per year for n years is given by $\overline{C}(n) = C(n)/n$.

(A) Find the rational function $\overline{C}$.

(B) Sketch a graph of $\overline{C}$ for $2 \le n \le 20$.

(C) When is the average cost per year at a minimum, and what is the minimum average annual cost? [*Hint:* Refer to the sketch in part (B) and evaluate $\overline{C}(n)$ at appropriate integer values until a minimum value is found.] The time when the average cost is minimum is frequently referred to as the **replacement time** for the piece of equipment.

(D) Graph the average cost function $\overline{C}$ in a graphing utility and use an appropriate command to find when the average annual cost is at a minimum.

60. *Minimum average cost.* Financial analysts in a company that manufactures audio CD players arrived at the following daily cost equation for manufacturing x CD players per day:

$$C(x) = x^2 + 2x + 2,000$$

The average cost per unit at a production level of x players per day is $\overline{C}(x) = C(x)/x$.

(A) Find the rational function $\overline{C}$.

(B) Sketch a graph of $\overline{C}$ for $5 \le x \le 150$.

(C) For what daily production level (to the nearest integer) is the average cost per unit at a minimum, and what is the minimum average cost per player (to the nearest cent)? [*Hint:* Refer to the sketch in part (B) and evaluate $\overline{C}(x)$ at appropriate integer values until a minimum value is found.]

(D) Graph the average cost function $\overline{C}$ in a graphing utility and use an appropriate command to find the daily production level (to the nearest integer) at which the average cost per player is at a minimum. What is the minimum average cost to the nearest cent?

61. *Minimum average cost.* A consulting firm, using statistical methods, provided a veterinary clinic with the cost equation

$$C(x) = 0.00048(x - 500)^3 + 60,000$$

$$100 \le x \le 1,000$$

where $C(x)$ is the cost in dollars for handling x cases per month. The average cost per case is given by $\overline{C}(x) = C(x)/x$.

(A) Write the equation for the average cost function $\overline{C}$.

(B) Graph $\overline{C}$ on a graphing utility.

(C) Use an appropriate command to find the monthly caseload for the minimum average cost per case. What is the minimum average cost per case?

62. *Minimum average cost.* The financial department of a hospital, using statistical methods, arrived at the cost equation

$$C(x) = 20x^3 - 360x^2 + 2,300x - 1,000$$

$$1 \le x \le 12$$

where $C(x)$ is the cost in thousands of dollars for handling x thousand cases per month. The average cost per case is given by $\overline{C}(x) = C(x)/x$.

(A) Write the equation for the average cost function $\overline{C}$.

(B) Graph $\overline{C}$ on a graphing utility.

(C) Use an appropriate command to find the monthly caseload for the minimum average cost per case. What is the minimum average cost per case to the nearest dollar?

63. *Equilibrium point.* A particular CD is sold through a chain of stores in a city. A marketing company has established price–demand and price–supply tables for selected prices for this CD (Tables 3 and 4), where x is the daily number of CDs that people are willing to buy and the store is willing to sell at a price of p dollars per CD.

TABLE 3 Price–Demand

x	$p = D(x)$ ($)
25	19.50
100	14.25
175	10.00
250	8.25

TABLE 4 Price–Supply

x	$p = S(x)$ ($)
25	2.10
100	3.80
175	8.50
250	15.70

(A) Use a linear regression equation to model the data in Table 3 and a quadratic regression equation to model the data in Table 4.

(B) Find the point of intersection of the two equations from part (A). Write the equilibrium price to the nearest cent and the equilibrium quantity to the nearest unit.

64. *Equilibrium point.* Repeat Problem 63 with Tables 5 and 6, except use a quadratic regression model for the data in Table 5 and a linear regression model for the data in Table 6.

TABLE 5 Price–Demand

x	$p = D(x)$ ($)
0	24
40	23
65	20
115	11

TABLE 6 Price–Supply

x	$p = S(x)$ ($)
0	5
40	10
65	12
115	16

Life Sciences

65. *Diet.* Table 7 shows the per capita consumption of ice cream and eggs in the United States for selected years since 1980.

(A) Let x represent the number of years since 1980 and find a cubic regression polynomial for the per capita consumption of ice cream.

(B) Use the polynomial model from part (A) to estimate (to the nearest tenth of a pound) the per capita consumption of ice cream in 2010.

TABLE 7 Per Capita Consumption of Ice Cream and Eggs

Year	Ice Cream (pounds)	Eggs (number)
1980	17.5	271
1985	18.1	255
1990	15.8	234
1995	15.5	232
2000	16.5	250

66. *Diet.* Refer to Table 7.

(A) Let x represent the number of years since 1980 and find a cubic regression polynomial for the per capita consumption of eggs.

(B) Use the polynomial model from part (A) to estimate (to the nearest integer) the per capita consumption of eggs in 2010.

67. *Physiology.* In a study on the speed of muscle contraction in frogs under various loads, researchers W. O. Fems and J. Marsh found that the speed of contraction decreases with increasing loads. In particular, they found that the relationship between speed of contraction v (in centimeters per second) and load x (in grams) is given approximately by

$$v(x) = \frac{26 + 0.06x}{x} \qquad x \geq 5$$

(A) What does $v(x)$ approach as x increases?

(B) Sketch a graph of function v.

Social Sciences

68. *Learning theory.* In 1917, L. L. Thurstone, a pioneer in quantitative learning theory, proposed the rational function

$$f(x) = \frac{a(x + c)}{(x + c) + b}$$

to model the number of successful acts per unit time that a person could accomplish after x practice sessions. Suppose that for a particular person enrolled in a typing class,

$$f(x) = \frac{55(x + 1)}{(x + 8)} \quad x \geq 0$$

where $f(x)$ is the number of words per minute the person is able to type after x weeks of lessons.

(A) What does $f(x)$ approach as x increases?

(B) Sketch a graph of function f, including any vertical or horizontal asymptotes.

69. *Marriage.* Table 8 shows the marriage and divorce rates per 1,000 population for selected years since 1960.

(A) Let x represent the number of years since 1960 and find a cubic regression polynomial for the marriage rate.

TABLE 8 Marriages and Divorces (per 1,000 Population)		
Date	**Marriages**	**Divorces**
1960	8.5	2.2
1965	9.3	2.5
1970	10.6	3.5
1975	10.0	4.8
1980	10.6	5.2
1985	10.1	5.0
1990	9.8	4.7
1995	8.9	4.4
2000	8.5	4.1

(B) Use the polynomial model from part (A) to estimate the marriage rate (to one decimal place) for 2010.

70. *Divorce.* Refer to Table 8.

(A) Let x represent the number of years since 1950 and find a cubic regression polynomial for the divorce rate.

(B) Use the polynomial model from part (A) to estimate the divorce rate (to one decimal place) for 2010.

Section 2-2 | Exponential Functions

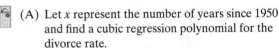

- ➤ Exponential Functions
- ➤ Base e Exponential Functions
- ➤ Growth and Decay Applications
- ➤ Compound Interest
- ➤ Continuous Compound Interest

This section introduces the important class of functions called *exponential functions*. These functions are used extensively in modeling and solving a wide variety of real-world problems, including growth of money at compound interest; growth of populations of people, animals, and bacteria; radioactive decay; and learning associated with the mastery of such devices as a new computer or an assembly process in a manufacturing plant.

➤ Exponential Functions

We start by noting that

$$f(x) = 2^x \quad \text{and} \quad g(x) = x^2$$

are not the same function. Whether a variable appears as an exponent with a constant base or as a base with a constant exponent makes a big difference. The function g is a quadratic function, which we have already discussed. The function f is a new type of function called an *exponential function*. In general,

DEFINITION   Exponential Function

The equation

$$f(x) = b^x \qquad b > 0, b \neq 1$$

defines an **exponential function** for each different constant b, called the **base.** The **domain** of f is the set of all real numbers, and the **range** of f is the set of all positive real numbers.

We require the base b to be positive to avoid imaginary numbers such as $(-2)^{1/2} = \sqrt{-2} = i\sqrt{2}$. We exclude $b = 1$ as a base, since $f(x) = 1^x = 1$ is a constant function, which we have already considered.

Asked to hand-sketch graphs of equations such as $y = 2^x$ or $y = 2^{-x}$, many students would not hesitate at all. [*Note:* $2^{-x} = 1/2^x = (1/2)^x$.] They would probably make up tables by assigning integers to x, plot the resulting points, and then join these points with a smooth curve as in Figure 1. The only catch is that we have not defined 2^x for all real numbers. From Appendix A, Section A-7, we know what $2^5, 2^{-3}, 2^{2/3}, 2^{-3/5}, 2^{1.4}$, and $2^{-3.14}$ mean (that is, 2^p, where p is a rational number), but what does

$$2^{\sqrt{2}}$$

mean? The question is not easy to answer at this time. In fact, a precise definition of $2^{\sqrt{2}}$ must wait for more advanced courses, where it is shown that

$$2^x$$

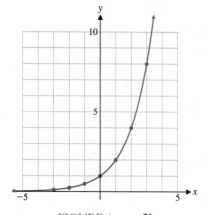

FIGURE 1 $y = 2^x$

names a positive real number for x any real number, and that the graph of $y = 2^x$ is indeed as indicated in Figure 1.

It is useful to compare the graphs of $y = 2^x$ and $y = 2^{-x}$ by plotting both on the same set of coordinate axes, as shown in Figure 2A. The graph of

$$f(x) = b^x \quad b > 1 \text{ (Fig. 2B)}$$

looks very much like the graph of $y = 2^x$, and the graph of

$$f(x) = b^x \quad 0 < b < 1 \text{ (Fig. 2B)}$$

looks very much like the graph of $y = 2^{-x}$. Note that in both cases the x axis is a horizontal asymptote for the graphs.

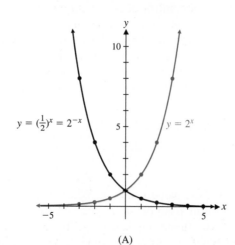

(A)

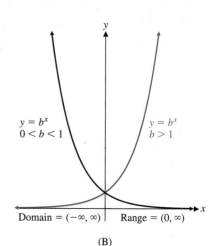

(B)

FIGURE 2 Exponential functions

The graphs in Figure 2 suggest the following important general properties of exponential functions, which we state without proof:

THEOREM 1　Basic Properties of the Graph of $f(x) = b^x, b > 0, b \neq 1$

1. All graphs will pass through the point $(0, 1)$.　$b^0 = 1$ for any permissible base b.

2. All graphs are continuous curves, with no holes or jumps.

3. The x axis is a horizontal asymptote.

4. If $b > 1$, then b^x increases as x increases.

5. If $0 < b < 1$, then b^x decreases as x increases.

☉ Insight　Recall that the graph of a rational function has at most one horizontal asymptote and that it approaches the horizontal asymptote (if one exists) both as $x \to \infty$ *and* as $x \to -\infty$ (see Section 2-1). The graph of an exponential function, on the other hand, approaches its horizontal asymptote as $x \to \infty$ *or* as $x \to -\infty$, but not both. In particular, there is no rational function that has the same graph as an exponential function.　●

The use of a calculator with the key $\boxed{y^x}$, or its equivalent, makes the graphing of exponential functions almost routine. Example 1 illustrates the process.

EXAMPLE 1　**Graphing Exponential Functions** Sketch a graph of $y = (\frac{1}{2})4^x$, $-2 \leq x \leq 2$.

Solution　Use a calculator to create the table of values shown. Plot these points, and then join them with a smooth curve as in Figure 3.

x	y
-2	0.031
-1	0.125
0	0.50
1	2.00
2	8.00

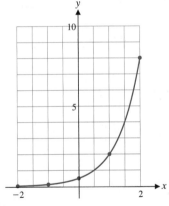

FIGURE 3　Graph of $y = (\frac{1}{2})4^x$

Matched Problem 1　Sketch a graph of $y = (\frac{1}{2})4^{-x}, -2 \leq x \leq 2$.

EXPLORE &DISCUSS 1　Graph the functions $f(x) = 2^x$ and $g(x) = 3^x$ on the same set of coordinate axes. At which values of x do the graphs intersect? For which values of x is the graph of f above the graph of g? Below the graph of g? Are the graphs close together as x increases without bound? Are the graphs close together as x decreases without bound? Discuss.

Exponential functions, whose domains include irrational numbers, obey the familiar laws of exponents discussed in Appendix A, Section A-7 for rational exponents. We summarize these exponent laws here and add two other important and useful properties.

THEOREM 2   Properties of Exponential Functions

For a and b positive, $a \neq 1$, $b \neq 1$, and x and y real,

1. Exponent laws:

$$a^x a^y = a^{x+y} \qquad \frac{a^x}{a^y} = a^{x-y} \qquad \frac{4^{2y}}{4^{5y}} = 4^{2y-5y} = 4^{-3y}$$

$$(a^x)^y = a^{xy} \qquad (ab)^x = a^x b^x \qquad \left(\frac{a}{b}\right)^x = \frac{a^x}{b^x}$$

2. $a^x = a^y$ if and only if $x = y$ If $7^{5t+1} = 7^{3t-3}$, then $5t + 1 = 3t - 3$, and $t = -2$.

3. For $x \neq 0$,

$a^x = b^x$ if and only if $a = b$ If $a^5 = 2^5$, then $a = 2$.

➤ Base e Exponential Functions

Of all the possible bases b we can use for the exponential function $y = b^x$, which ones are the most useful? If you look at the keys on a calculator, you will probably see $\boxed{10^x}$ and $\boxed{e^x}$. It is clear why base 10 would be important, because our number system is a base 10 system. But what is e, and why is it included as a base? It turns out that base e is used more frequently than all other bases combined. The reason for this is that certain formulas and the results of certain processes found in calculus and more advanced mathematics take on their simplest form if this base is used. This is why you will see e used extensively in expressions and formulas that model real-world phenomena. In fact, its use is so prevalent that you will often hear people refer to $y = e^x$ as the exponential function.

The base e is an irrational number, and like π, it cannot be represented exactly by any finite decimal fraction. However, e can be approximated as closely as we like by evaluating the expression

$$\left(1 + \frac{1}{x}\right)^x \tag{1}$$

for sufficiently large x. What happens to the value of expression (1) as x increases without bound? Think about this for a moment before proceeding. Maybe you guessed that the value approaches 1, because

$$1 + \frac{1}{x}$$

approaches 1, and 1 raised to any power is 1. Let us see if this reasoning is correct by actually calculating the value of the expression for larger and larger values of x. Table 1 summarizes the results.

TABLE 1	
x	$\left(1 + \dfrac{1}{x}\right)^{x}$
1	2
10	2.593 74 ...
100	2.704 81 ...
1,000	2.716 92 ...
10,000	2.718 14 ...
100,000	2.718 27 ...
1,000,000	2.718 28 ...
$\vdots$	$\vdots$

Interestingly, the value of expression (1) is never close to 1, but seems to be approaching a number close to 2.7183. In fact, as x increases without bound, the value of expression (1) approaches an irrational number that we call *e*. The irrational number *e* to 12 decimal places is

$$e = \mathbf{2.718\ 281\ 828\ 459}$$

Compare this value of *e* with the value of e^1 from a calculator. Exactly who discovered the constant *e* is still being debated. It is named after the great Swiss mathematician Leonhard Euler (1707–1783).

DEFINITION Exponential Function with Base *e*

Exponential functions with base *e* and base $1/e$, respectively, are defined by

$$y = e^x \quad \text{and} \quad y = e^{-x}$$

Domain: $(-\infty, \infty)$

Range: $(0, \infty)$

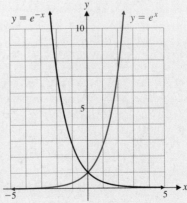

EXPLORE
&DISCUSS
2

Graph the functions $f(x) = e^x$, $g(x) = 2^x$, and $h(x) = 3^x$ on the same set of coordinate axes. At which values of x do the graphs intersect? For positive values of x, which of the three graphs lies above the other two? Below the other two? How does your answer change for negative values of x?

➤ Growth and Decay Applications

Most exponential growth and decay problems are modeled using base e exponential functions. We present two applications here and many more in Exercise 2-2.

EXAMPLE 2

Exponential Growth Cholera, an intestinal disease, is caused by a cholera bacterium that multiplies exponentially by cell division as given approximately by

$$N = N_0 e^{1.386t}$$

where N is the number of bacteria present after t hours and N_0 is the number of bacteria present at the start ($t = 0$). If we start with 25 bacteria, how many bacteria (to the nearest unit) will be present:

(A) In 0.6 hour?   (B) In 3.5 hours?

Solution   Substituting $N_0 = 25$ into the preceding equation, we obtain

$$N = 25e^{1.386t}$$ The graph is shown in Figure 4.

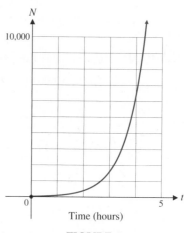

FIGURE 4

(A) Solve for N when $t = 0.6$:

$$N = 25e^{1.386(0.6)}$$ Use a calculator.
$$= 57 \text{ bacteria}$$

(B) Solve for N when $t = 3.5$:

$$N = 25e^{1.386(3.5)}$$ Use a calculator.
$$= 3{,}197 \text{ bacteria}$$

Matched Problem 2

Refer to the exponential growth model for cholera in Example 2. If we start with 55 bacteria, how many bacteria (to the nearest unit) will be present

(A) In 0.85 hour?   (B) In 7.25 hours?

EXAMPLE 3

Exponential Decay Cosmic-ray bombardment of the atmosphere produces neutrons, which in turn react with nitrogen to produce radioactive carbon-14 (^{14}C). Radioactive ^{14}C enters all living tissues through carbon dioxide, which is first absorbed by plants. As long as a plant or animal is alive, ^{14}C is maintained in the living organism at a constant level. Once the organism dies, however, ^{14}C decays according to the equation

$$A = A_0 e^{-0.000124t}$$

where A is the amount present after t years and A_0 is the amount present at time $t = 0$. If 500 milligrams of ^{14}C is present in a sample from a skull at the time of death, how many milligrams will be present in the sample in

(A) 15,000 years?   (B) 45,000 years?

Compute answers to two decimal places.

Solution   Substituting $A_0 = 500$ in the decay equation, we have

$$A = 500e^{-0.000124t} \quad \textit{See the graph in Figure 5.}$$

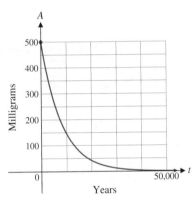

FIGURE 5

(A) Solve for A when $t = 15,000$:

$$A = 500e^{-0.000124(15,000)} \quad \textit{Use a calculator.}$$
$$= 77.84 \text{ milligrams}$$

(B) Solve for A when $t = 45,000$:

$$A = 500e^{-0.000124(45,000)} \quad \textit{Use a calculator.}$$
$$= 1.89 \text{ milligrams}$$

Matched Problem 3

Refer to the exponential decay model in Example 3. How many milligrams of ^{14}C would have to be present at the beginning in order to have 25 milligrams present after 18,000 years? Compute the answer to the nearest milligram.

EXPLORE &DISCUSS 3

(A) On the same set of coordinate axes, graph the three decay equations $A = A_0 e^{-0.35t}$, $t \geq 0$, for $A_0 = 10, 20$, and 30.

(B) Identify any asymptotes for the three graphs in part (A).

(C) Discuss the long-term behavior for the equations in part (A).

EXAMPLE 4   **Depreciation**   Table 2 gives the market value of a minivan (in dollars) x years after its purchase. Find an exponential regression model of the form $y = ab^x$ for this data set. Estimate the purchase price of the van. Estimate the value of the van 10 years after its purchase. Round answers to the nearest dollar.

TABLE 2	
x	Value ($)
1	12,575
2	9,455
3	8,115
4	6,845
5	5,225
6	4,485

Solution   Enter the data into a graphing utility (Fig. 6A) and find the exponential regression equation (Fig. 6B). The estimated purchase price is $y_1(0) = \$14,910$. The data set and the regression equation are graphed in Figure 6C. Using the trace feature, we see that the estimated value after 10 years is $1,959.

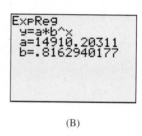

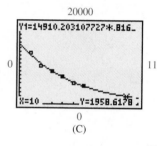

(A)   (B)   (C)

FIGURE 6

Matched Problem 4   Table 3 gives the market value of a luxury sedan (in dollars) x years after its purchase. Find an exponential regression model of the form $y = ab^x$ for this data set. Estimate the purchase price of the sedan. Estimate the value of the sedan 10 years after its purchase. Round answers to the nearest dollar.

TABLE 3	
x	Value ($)
1	23,125
2	19,050
3	15,625
4	11,875
5	9,450
6	7,125

➤ Compound Interest

We now turn to the growth of money at compound interest. The fee paid to use another's money is called **interest.** It is usually computed as a percent (called **interest rate**) of the principal over a given period of time. If, at the end of a payment period, the interest due is reinvested at the same rate, then the interest earned as well as the principal will earn interest during the next payment period. Interest paid on interest reinvested is called **compound interest,** and may be calculated using the following compound interest formula:

RESULT   Compound Interest

If a **principal P (present value)** is invested at an annual **rate r** (expressed as a decimal) compounded m times a year, then the **amount A (future value)** in the account at the end of t years is given by

$$A = P\left(1 + \frac{r}{m}\right)^{mt}$$

Note: P could be replaced by A_0, but convention dictates otherwise.

EXAMPLE 5 **Compound Growth** If $1,000 is invested in an account paying 10% compounded monthly, how much will be in the account at the end of 10 years? Compute the answer to the nearest cent.

Solution   We use the compound interest formula as follows:

$$A = P\left(1 + \frac{r}{m}\right)^{mt}$$

$$= 1,000\left(1 + \frac{0.10}{12}\right)^{(12)(10)} \quad \textit{Use a calculator.}$$

$$= \$2,707.04$$

The graph of

$$A = 1,000\left(1 + \frac{0.10}{12}\right)^{12t}$$

for $0 \le t \le 20$ is shown in Figure 7.

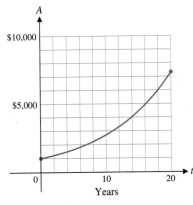

FIGURE 7

Matched Problem 5   If you deposit $5,000 in an account paying 9% compounded daily, how much will you have in the account in 5 years? Compute the answer to the nearest cent.

EXPLORE & DISCUSS 4   Suppose that $1,000 is deposited in a savings account at an annual rate of 5%. Guess the amount in the account at the end of 1 year if interest is compounded (1) quarterly, (2) monthly, (3) daily, (4) hourly. Use the compound interest formula to compute the amounts at the end of 1 year to the nearest cent. Discuss the accuracy of your initial guesses.

➤ Continuous Compound Interest

Returning to the compound interest formula,

$$A = P\left(1 + \frac{r}{m}\right)^{mt}$$

suppose that the principal P, the annual rate r, and the time t are held fixed, and the number of compounding periods per year m is increased without bound. Will the amount A increase without bound, or will it tend to some limiting value?

Starting with $P = \$100$, $r = 0.08$, and $t = 2$ years, we construct Table 4 for several values of m with the aid of a calculator. Notice that the largest gain appears in going from annual to semiannual compounding. Then, the gains slow down as m increases. It appears that A gets closer and closer to \$117.35 as m gets larger and larger.

TABLE 4

Compounding Frequency	m	$A = 100\left(1 + \dfrac{0.08}{m}\right)^{2m}$
Annually	1	\$116.6400
Semiannually	2	116.9859
Quarterly	4	117.1659
Weekly	52	117.3367
Daily	365	117.3490
Hourly	8,760	117.3510

It can be shown that

$$P\left(1 + \frac{r}{m}\right)^{mt}$$

gets closer and closer to Pe^{rt} as the number of compounding periods m gets larger and larger. The latter is referred to as the **continuous compound interest formula,** a formula that is widely used in business, banking, and economics.

RESULT Continuous Compound Interest Formula

If a principal P is invested at an annual rate r (expressed as a decimal) compounded continuously, then the amount A in the account at the end of t years is given by

$$A = Pe^{rt}$$

EXAMPLE 6 **Compounding Daily and Continuously** What amount will an account have after 2 years if \$5,000 is invested at an annual rate of 8%

(A) Compounded daily?   (B) Compounded continuously?

Compute answers to the nearest cent.

Solution (A) Use the compound interest formula

$$A = P\left(1 + \frac{r}{m}\right)^{mt}$$

with $P = 5,000$, $r = 0.08$, $m = 365$, and $t = 2$:

$$A = 5,000\left(1 + \frac{0.08}{365}\right)^{(365)(2)} \quad \textit{Use a calculator.}$$

$$= \$5,867.45$$

(B) Use the continuous compound interest formula

$$A = Pe^{rt}$$

with $P = 5,000$, $r = 0.08$, and $t = 2$:

$$A = 5,000e^{(0.08)(2)} \quad \textit{Use a calculator.}$$

$$= \$5,867.55 \qquad \blacksquare$$

Matched Problem 6 What amount will an account have after 1.5 years if \$8,000 is invested at an annual rate of 9%

(A) Compounded weekly?   (B) Compounded continuously?

Compute answers to the nearest cent. ——————————————— ∎

The formulas for simple interest, compound interest, and continuous compound interest are summarized in the box for convenient reference.

SUMMARY   Interest Formulas

Simple interest $A = P(1 + rt)$

Compound interest $A = P\left(1 + \dfrac{r}{m}\right)^{mt}$

Continous compound interest $A = Pe^{rt}$

Answers to Matched Problems **1.**

2. (A) 179 bacteria   (B) 1,271,659 bacteria

3. 233 mg   **4.** Purchase price: \$30,363; value after 10 yr: \$2,864

```
ExpReg
 y=a*b^x
 a=30363.17638
 b=.7896877851
```

5. \$7,841.13   **6.** (A) \$9,155.23   (B) \$9,156.29

Exercise 2-2

A

1. Match each equation with the graph of $f, g, h,$ or k in the figure.

(A) $y = 2^x$ 　　　　(B) $y = (0.2)^x$
(C) $y = 4^x$ 　　　　(D) $y = (\frac{1}{3})^x$

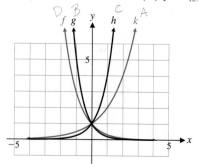

2. Match each equation with the graph of $f, g, h,$ or k in the figure.

(A) $y = (\frac{1}{4})^x$ 　　　　(B) $y = (0.5)^x$
(C) $y = 5^x$ 　　　　(D) $y = 3^x$

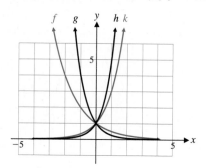

Graph each function in Problems 3–14 over the indicated interval.

3. $y = 5^x; [-2, 2]$ 　　　　**4.** $y = 3^x; [-3, 3]$
5. $y = (\frac{1}{5})^x = 5^{-x}; [-2, 2]$ 　**6.** $y = (\frac{1}{3})^x = 3^{-x}; [-3, 3]$
7. $f(x) = -5^x; [-2, 2]$ 　　**8.** $g(x) = -3^{-x}; [-3, 3]$
9. $y = -e^{-x}; [-3, 3]$ 　　**10.** $y = -e^x; [-3, 3]$
11. $y = 100e^{0.1x}; [-5, 5]$ 　**12.** $y = 10e^{0.2x}; [-10, 10]$
13. $g(t) = 10e^{-0.2t}; [-5, 5]$ 　**14.** $f(t) = 100e^{-0.1t}; [-5, 5]$

Simplify each expression in Problems 15–20.

15. $(4^{3x})^{2y}$ 　　**16.** $10^{3x-1}10^{4-x}$ 　　**17.** $\dfrac{e^{x-3}}{e^{x-4}}$

18. $\dfrac{e^x}{e^{1-x}}$ 　　**19.** $(2e^{1.2t})^3$ 　　**20.** $(3e^{-1.4x})^2$

B *In Problems 21–28, describe verbally the transformations that can be used to obtain the graph of g from the graph of f (see Section 1-2).*

21. $g(x) = -2^x; f(x) = 2^x$
22. $g(x) = 2^{x-2}; f(x) = 2^x$
23. $g(x) = 3^{x+1}; f(x) = 3^x$
24. $g(x) = -3^x; f(x) = 3^x$
25. $g(x) = e^x + 1; f(x) = e^x$
26. $g(x) = e^x - 2; f(x) = e^x$
27. $g(x) = 2e^{-(x+2)}; f(x) = e^{-x}$
28. $g(x) = 0.5e^{-(x-1)}; f(x) = e^{-x}$

29. Use the graph of f shown in the figure to sketch the graph of each of the following.

(A) $y = f(x) - 1$ 　　　　(B) $y = f(x + 2)$
(C) $y = 3f(x) - 2$ 　　　　(D) $y = 2 - f(x - 3)$

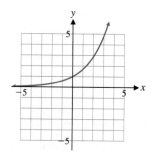

Figure for 29 and 30

30. Use the graph of f shown in the figure to sketch the graph of each of the following.

(A) $y = f(x) + 2$ 　　　　(B) $y = f(x - 3)$
(C) $y = 2f(x) - 4$ 　　　　(D) $y = 4 - f(x + 2)$

In Problems 31–40, graph each function over the indicated interval.

31. $f(t) = 2^{t/10}; [-30, 30]$
32. $G(t) = 3^{t/100}; [-200, 200]$
33. $y = -3 + e^{1+x}; [-4, 2]$
34. $y = 2 + e^{x-2}; [-1, 5]$
35. $y = e^{|x|}; [-3, 3]$
36. $y = e^{-|x|}; [-3, 3]$
37. $C(x) = \dfrac{e^x + e^{-x}}{2}; [-5, 5]$
38. $M(x) = e^{x/2} + e^{-x/2}; [-5, 5]$
39. $y = e^{-x^2}; [-3, 3]$
40. $y = 2^{-x^2}; [-3, 3]$

41. Find all real numbers a such that $a^2 = a^{-2}$. Explain why this does not violate the second exponential function property in Theorem 2 on page 98.

42. Find real numbers a and b such that $a \neq b$ but $a^4 = b^4$. Explain why this does not violate the third exponential function property in Theorem 2 on page 98.

Solve each equation in Problems 43–48 for x.

43. $10^{2-3x} = 10^{5x-6}$

44. $5^{3x} = 5^{4x-2}$

45. $4^{5x-x^2} = 4^{-6}$

46. $7^{x^2} = 7^{2x+3}$

47. $5^3 = (x + 2)^3$

48. $(1 - x)^5 = (2x - 1)^5$

C *Solve each equation in Problems 49–52 for x. (Remember:* $e^x \neq 0$ *and* $e^{-x} \neq 0$.)

49. $(x - 3)e^x = 0$

50. $2xe^{-x} = 0$

51. $3xe^{-x} + x^2e^{-x} = 0$

52. $x^2e^x - 5xe^x = 0$

Graph each function in Problems 53–56 over the indicated interval.

53. $h(x) = x(2^x)$; $[-5, 0]$

54. $m(x) = x(3^{-x})$; $[0, 3]$

55. $N = \dfrac{100}{1 + e^{-t}}$; $[0, 5]$

56. $N = \dfrac{200}{1 + 3e^{-t}}$; $[0, 5]$

 In Problems 57–60, approximate the real zeros of each function to two decimal places.

57. $f(x) = 4^x - 7$

58. $f(x) = 5 - 3^{-x}$

59. $f(x) = 2 + 3x + 10^x$

60. $f(x) = 7 - 2x^2 + 2^{-x}$

Applications

Business & Economics

61. *Finance.* Suppose that $2,500 is invested at 7% compounded quarterly. How much money will be in the account in

(A) $\frac{3}{4}$ year?   (B) 15 years?

Compute answers to the nearest cent.

62. *Finance.* Suppose that $4,000 is invested at 6% compounded weekly. How much money will be in the account in

(A) $\frac{1}{2}$ year?   (B) 10 years?

Compute answers to the nearest cent.

63. *Money growth.* If you invest $7,500 in an account paying 8.35% compounded continuously, how much money will be in the account at the end of

(A) 5.5 years?   (B) 12 years?

64. *Money growth.* If you invest $5,250 in an account paying 7.45% compounded continuously, how much money will be in the account at the end of

(A) 6.25 years?   (B) 17 years?

65. *Finance.* A person wishes to have $15,000 cash for a new car 5 years from now. How much should be placed in an account now, if the account pays 6.75% compounded weekly? Compute the answer to the nearest dollar.

66. *Finance.* A couple just had a baby. How much should they invest now at 5.5% compounded daily in order to have $40,000 for the child's education 17 years from now? Compute the answer to the nearest dollar.

67. *Money growth.* BanxQuote operates a network of Web sites providing real-time market data from leading financial providers. The following rates for 12-month certficates of deposit were taken from the Web sites:

(A) Stonebridge Bank, 2.15% compounded monthly

(B) DeepGreen Bank, 1.99% compounded daily

(C) Provident Bank, 1.95% compounded continuously

Compute the value of $10,000 invested in each account at the end of 1 year.

68. *Money growth.* Refer to Problem 67. The following rates for 60-month certificates of deposit were also taken from BanxQuote Web sites:

(A) Oriental Bank & Trust, 3.25% compounded quarterly

(B) BMW Bank of North America, 3.16% compounded monthly

(C) BankFirst Corporation, 2.97% compounded daily

Compute the value of $10,000 invested in each account at the end of 5 years.

69. *Present value.* A promissory note will pay $50,000 at maturity $5\frac{1}{2}$ years from now. How much should you be willing to pay for the note now if money is worth 8% compounded continuously?

70. *Present value.* A promissory note will pay $30,000 at maturity 10 years from now. How much should you be willing to pay for the note now if money is worth 7% compounded continuously?

71. *Advertising.* A company is trying to introduce a new product to as many people as possible through television advertising in a large metropolitan area with 2 million possible viewers. A model for the number of people N (in millions) who are aware of the product after t days of advertising was found to be

$$N = 2(1 - e^{-0.037t})$$

Graph this function for $0 \leq t \leq 50$. What value does N tend to as t increases without bound?

72. *Learning curve.* People assigned to assemble circuit boards for a computer manufacturing company undergo on-the-job training. From past experience it was found that the learning curve for the average employee is given by

$$N = 40(1 - e^{-0.12t})$$

where N is the number of boards assembled per day after t days of training. Graph this function for $0 \leq t \leq 30$. What is the maximum number of boards an average employee can be expected to produce in 1 day?

73. *Sports salaries.* Table 5 shows the average salaries for players in Major League Baseball (MLB) and the National Basketball Association (NBA) in selected years since 1990.

(A) Let x represent the number of years since 1990 and find an exponential regression model $(y = ab^x)$ for the average salary in MLB. Use the model to estimate the average salary (to the nearest thousand dollars) in 2010.

(B) The average salary in MLB in 2000 was 1.984 million. How does this compare with the value given by the model of part (A)? How would the inclusion of the year 2000 data affect the estimated average salary in 2010? Explain.

TABLE 5 Average Salary (thousand \$)		
Year	MLB	NBA
1990	589	750
1993	1,062	1,300
1996	1,101	2,000
1999	1,724	2,400
2002	2,300	4,500

74. *Sports salaries.* Refer to Table 5.

(A) Let x represent the number of years since 1990 and find an exponential regression model $(y = ab^x)$ for the average salary in the NBA. Use the model to estimate the average salary (to the nearest thousand dollars) in 2010.

(B) The average salary in the NBA in 1997 was \$2.2 million. How does this compare with the value given by the model of part (A)? How would the inclusion of the year 1997 data affect the estimated average salary in 2010? Explain.

Life Sciences

75. *Marine biology.* Marine life is dependent upon the microscopic plant life that exists in the photic zone, a zone that goes to a depth where about 1% of the surface light remains. In some waters with a great deal of sediment, the photic zone may go down only 15 to 20 feet. In some murky harbors, the intensity of light d feet below the surface is given approximately by

$$I = I_0 e^{-0.23d}$$

What percentage of the surface light will reach a depth of

(A) 10 feet?   (B) 20 feet?

76. *Marine biology.* Refer to Problem 75. Light intensity I relative to depth d (in feet) for one of the clearest bodies of water in the world, the Sargasso Sea in the West Indies, can be approximated by

$$I = I_0 e^{-0.00942d}$$

where I_0 is the intensity of light at the surface. What percentage of the surface light will reach a depth of

(A) 50 feet?   (B) 100 feet?

77. *HIV/AIDS epidemic.* The Joint United Nations Program on HIV/AIDS reported that HIV had infected 60 million people worldwide prior to 2002. Assume that number increases at an annual rate of 8% compounded continuously.

(A) Write an equation that models the worldwide spread of HIV, letting 2002 be year 0.

(B) Based on the model, how many people (to the nearest million) had been infected prior to 1999? How many would be infected prior to 2010?

(C) Sketch a graph of this growth equation from 2002 to 2010.

78. *HIV/AIDS epidemic.* The Joint United Nations Program on HIV/AIDS reported that 24.8 million people worldwide had died of AIDS prior to 2002. Assume that number increases at an annual rate of 19% compounded continuously.

(A) Write an equation that models total worldwide deaths from AIDS, letting 2002 be year 0.

(B) Based on the model, how many people (to the nearest million) had died from AIDS prior to 1999? How many would die from AIDS prior to 2010?

(C) Sketch a graph of this growth equation from 2002 to 2010.

Social Sciences

79. *World population growth.* It took from the dawn of humanity to 1830 for the population to grow to the first billion people, just 100 more years (by 1930) for the second billion, and 3 billion more were added in only 60 more years (by 1990). In 2002, the estimated world population was 6.2 billion with an annual growth rate of 1.25% compounded continuously.

(A) Write an equation that models the world population growth, letting 2002 be year 0.

(B) Based on the model, what is the expected world population (to the nearest hundred million) in 2010? In 2030?

(C) Sketch a graph of the equation found in part (A). Cover the years from 2002 through 2030.

80. *Population growth in Ethiopia.* In 2002, the estimated population in Ethiopia was 68 million people with an annual growth rate of 2.6% compounded continuously.

(A) Write an equation that models the population growth in Ethiopia, letting 2002 be year 0.

(B) Based on the model, what is the expected population in Ethiopia (to the nearest million) in 2010? In 2030?

(C) Sketch a graph of the equation found in part (A). Cover the years from 2002 through 2030.

 81. *Internet growth.* The number of Internet hosts grew very rapidly from 1994 to 2003 (Table 6).

(A) Let x represent the number of years since 1994. Find an exponential regression model ($y = ab^x$) for this data set and estimate the number of hosts in 2010 (to the nearest million).

(B) Discuss the implications of this model if the number of Internet hosts continues to grow at this rate.

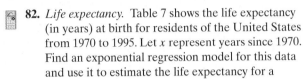

TABLE 6 Internet Hosts (Millions)	
Year	**Hosts**
1994	2.4
1997	16.1
2000	72.4
2003	171.6

Source: Internet Software Consortium

82. *Life expectancy.* Table 7 shows the life expectancy (in years) at birth for residents of the United States from 1970 to 1995. Let x represent years since 1970. Find an exponential regression model for this data and use it to estimate the life expectancy for a person born in 2010.

TABLE 7	
Year of Birth	**Life Expectancy**
1970	70.8
1975	72.6
1980	73.7
1985	74.7
1990	75.4
1995	75.9
2000	76.9

Section 2-3 | Logarithmic Functions

➤ Inverse Functions
➤ Logarithmic Functions
➤ Properties of Logarithmic Functions
➤ Calculator Evaluation of Logarithms
➤ Application

Find the exponential function keys $\boxed{10^x}$ and $\boxed{e^x}$ on your calculator. Close to these keys you will find $\boxed{\text{LOG}}$ and $\boxed{\text{LN}}$ keys. The latter represent *logarithmic functions,* and each is closely related to the exponential function it is near. In fact, the exponential function and the corresponding logarithmic function are said to be *inverses* of each other. In this section we will develop the concept of inverse functions and use it to define a logarithmic function as the inverse of an exponential function. We will then investigate basic properties of logarithmic functions, use a calculator to evaluate them for particular values of x, and apply them to real-world problems.

Logarithmic functions are used in modeling and solving many types of problems. For example, the decibel scale is a logarithmic scale used to measure sound intensity, and the Richter scale is a logarithmic scale used to measure the strength of the force of an earthquake. An important business application has to do with finding the time it takes money to double if it is invested at a certain rate compounded a given number of times a year or compounded continuously. This requires the solution of an exponential equation, and logarithms play a central role in the process.

➤ Inverse Functions

Look at the graphs of $f(x) = \dfrac{x}{2}$ and $g(x) = \dfrac{|x|}{2}$ in Figure 1:

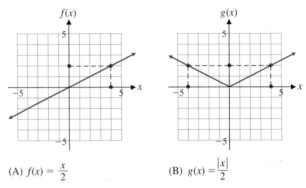

(A) $f(x) = \dfrac{x}{2}$ (B) $g(x) = \dfrac{|x|}{2}$

FIGURE 1

Because both f and g are functions, each domain value corresponds to exactly one range value. For which function does each range value correspond to exactly one domain value? This is the case only for function f. Note that for the range value 2, the corresponding domain value is 4. For function g the range value 2 corresponds to both -4 and 4. Function f is said to be *one-to-one*. In general,

DEFINITION   One-to-One Functions

A function f is said to be **one-to-one** if each range value corresponds to exactly one domain value.

It can be shown that any continuous function that is either increasing or decreasing for all domain values is one-to-one. If a continuous function increases for some domain values and decreases for others, it cannot be one-to-one. Figure 1 shows an example of each case.

 1   Graph $f(x) = 2^x$ and $g(x) = x^2$. For a range value of 4, what are the corresponding domain values for each function? Which of the two functions is one-to-one? Explain why.

Starting with a one-to-one function f, we can obtain a new function called the *inverse* of f as follows:

DEFINITION   Inverse of a Function

If f is a one-to-one function, then the **inverse** of f is the function formed by interchanging the independent and dependent variables for f. Thus, if (a, b) is a point on the graph of f, then (b, a) is a point on the graph of the inverse of f.

Note: If f is not one-to-one, then f **does not have an inverse.**

A number of important functions in any library of elementary functions are the inverses of other basic functions in the library. In this course, we are interested in the inverses of exponential functions, called *logarithmic functions.*

➤ Logarithmic Functions

If we start with the exponential function f defined by

$$y = 2^x \tag{1}$$

and interchange the variables, we obtain the inverse of f:

$$x = 2^y \tag{2}$$

We call the inverse the **logarithmic function with base 2,** and write

$$y = \log_2 x \quad \text{if and only if} \quad x = 2^y$$

We can graph $y = \log_2 x$ by graphing $x = 2^y$, since they are equivalent. Any ordered pair of numbers on the graph of the exponential function will be on the graph of the logarithmic function if we interchange the order of the components. For example, $(3, 8)$ satisfies equation (1) and $(8, 3)$ satisfies equation (2). The graphs of $y = 2^x$ and $y = \log_2 x$ are shown in Figure 2. Note that if we fold the paper along the dashed line $y = x$ in Figure 2, the two graphs match exactly. The line $y = x$ is a line of symmetry for the two graphs.

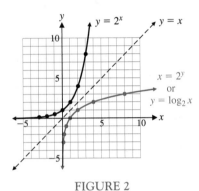

Exponential Function		Logarithmic Function	
x	$y = 2^x$	$x = 2^y$	y
-3	$\frac{1}{8}$	$\frac{1}{8}$	-3
-2	$\frac{1}{4}$	$\frac{1}{4}$	-2
-1	$\frac{1}{2}$	$\frac{1}{2}$	-1
0	1	1	0
1	2	2	1
2	4	4	2
3	8	8	3

FIGURE 2

$$\begin{bmatrix} \text{Ordered} \\ \text{pairs} \\ \text{reversed} \end{bmatrix}$$

In general, since the graphs of all exponential functions of the form $f(x) = b^x, b \neq 1, b > 0$, are either increasing or decreasing (see Section 2-2), exponential functions have inverses.

DEFINITION   Logarithmic Functions

The inverse of an exponential function is called a **logarithmic function.** For $b > 0$ and $b \neq 1$,

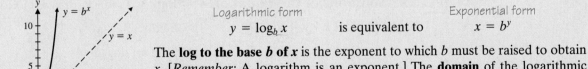

Logarithmic form		Exponential form
$y = \log_b x$	is equivalent to	$x = b^y$

The **log to the base b of x** is the exponent to which b must be raised to obtain x. [*Remember:* A logarithm is an exponent.] The **domain** of the logarithmic function is the set of all positive real numbers, which is also the range of the corresponding exponential function; and the **range** of the logarithmic function is the set of all real numbers, which is also the domain of the corresponding exponential function. Typical graphs of an exponential function and its inverse, a logarithmic function, are shown in the figure in the margin.

👁 *Insight* Because the domain of a logarithmic function consists of the positive real numbers, the entire graph of a logarithmic function lies to the right of the y axis. In contrast, the graphs of polynomial and exponential functions intersect every vertical line, and the graphs of rational functions intersect all but a finite number of vertical lines. ●

The following examples involve converting logarithmic forms to equivalent exponential forms, and vice versa.

EXAMPLE 1 **Logarithmic–Exponential Conversions** Change each logarithmic form to an equivalent exponential form:

(A) $\log_5 25 = 2$ (B) $\log_9 3 = \frac{1}{2}$ (C) $\log_2(\frac{1}{4}) = -2$

Solution (A) $\log_5 25 = 2$ is equivalent to $25 = 5^2$

(B) $\log_9 3 = \frac{1}{2}$ is equivalent to $3 = 9^{1/2}$

(C) $\log_2(\frac{1}{4}) = -2$ is equivalent to $\frac{1}{4} = 2^{-2}$ ∎

Matched Problem 1 Change each logarithmic form to an equivalent exponential form:

(A) $\log_3 9 = 2$ (B) $\log_4 2 = \frac{1}{2}$ (C) $\log_3(\frac{1}{9}) = -2$

EXAMPLE 2 **Exponential–Logarithmic Conversions** Change each exponential form to an equivalent logarithmic form:

(A) $64 = 4^3$ (B) $6 = \sqrt{36}$ (C) $\frac{1}{8} = 2^{-3}$

Solution (A) $64 = 4^3$ is equivalent to $\log_4 64 = 3$

(B) $6 = \sqrt{36}$ is equivalent to $\log_{36} 6 = \frac{1}{2}$

(C) $\frac{1}{8} = 2^{-3}$ is equivalent to $\log_2(\frac{1}{8}) = -3$ ∎

Matched Problem 2 Change each exponential form to an equivalent logarithmic form:

(A) $49 = 7^2$ (B) $3 = \sqrt{9}$ (C) $\frac{1}{3} = 3^{-1}$

To gain a little deeper understanding of logarithmic functions and their relationship to the exponential functions, we consider a few problems where we want to find x, b, or y in $y = \log_b x$, given the other two values. All values are chosen so that the problems can be solved exactly without a calculator.

EXAMPLE 3 **Solutions of the Equation $y = \log_b x$** Find y, b, or x, as indicated.

(A) Find y: $y = \log_4 16$ (B) Find x: $\log_2 x = -3$

(C) Find y: $y = \log_8 4$ (D) Find b: $\log_b 100 = 2$

Solution (A) $y = \log_4 16$ is equivalent to $16 = 4^y$. Thus,

$$y = 2$$

(B) $\log_2 x = -3$ is equivalent to $x = 2^{-3}$. Thus,

$$x = \frac{1}{2^3} = \frac{1}{8}$$

(C) $y = \log_8 4$ is equivalent to

$$4 = 8^y \quad \text{or} \quad 2^2 = 2^{3y}$$

Thus,

$$3y = 2$$
$$y = \tfrac{2}{3}$$

(D) $\log_b 100 = 2$ is equivalent to $100 = b^2$. Thus,

$$b = 10 \quad \textit{Recall that } b \textit{ cannot be negative.} \qquad \blacksquare$$

Matched Problem 3 Find $y, b,$ or x, as indicated.

(A) Find y: $y = \log_9 27$ (B) Find x: $\log_3 x = -1$
(C) Find b: $\log_b 1{,}000 = 3$

➤ **Properties of Logarithmic Functions**

Logarithmic functions have many powerful and useful properties. We list eight basic properties in Theorem 1.

THEOREM 1   Properties of Logarithmic Functions
If $b, M,$ and N are positive real numbers, $b \neq 1$, and p and x are real numbers, then

1. $\log_b 1 = 0$ 5. $\log_b MN = \log_b M + \log_b N$

2. $\log_b b = 1$ 6. $\log_b \dfrac{M}{N} = \log_b M - \log_b N$

3. $\log_b b^x = x$ 7. $\log_b M^p = p \log_b M$

4. $b^{\log_b x} = x, \quad x > 0$ 8. $\log_b M = \log_b N$ if and only if $M = N$

The first four properties in Theorem 1 follow directly from the definition of a logarithmic function. Here we will sketch a proof of property 5. The other properties are established in a similar way. Let

$$u = \log_b M \quad \text{and} \quad v = \log_b N$$

Or, in equivalent exponential form,

$$M = b^u \quad \text{and} \quad N = b^v$$

Now, see if you can provide reasons for each of the following steps:

$$\log_b MN = \log_b b^u b^v = \log_b b^{u+v} = u + v = \log_b M + \log_b N$$

EXAMPLE 4   **Using Logarithmic Properties**

(A) $\log_b \dfrac{wx}{yz}$ $= \log_b wx - \log_b yz$
$= \log_b w + \log_b x - (\log_b y + \log_b z)$
$= \log_b w + \log_b x - \log_b y - \log_b z$

(B) $\log_b(wx)^{3/5}$ $\boxed{= \frac{3}{5}\log_b wx}$ $= \frac{3}{5}(\log_b w + \log_b x)$

(C) $e^{x\log_e b} = e^{\log_e b^x} = b^x$

(D) $\dfrac{\log_e x}{\log_e b} = \dfrac{\log_e(b^{\log_b x})}{\log_e b} = \dfrac{(\log_b x)(\log_e b)}{\log_e b} = \log_b x$ ■

Matched Problem 4   Write in simpler forms, as in Example 4.

(A) $\log_b \dfrac{R}{ST}$ (B) $\log_b\left(\dfrac{R}{S}\right)^{2/3}$ (C) $2^{u\log_2 b}$ (D) $\dfrac{\log_2 x}{\log_2 b}$

The following examples and problems, although somewhat artificial, will give you additional practice in using basic logarithmic properties.

EXAMPLE 5   **Solving Logarithmic Equations**   Find x so that

$$\tfrac{3}{2}\log_b 4 - \tfrac{2}{3}\log_b 8 + \log_b 2 = \log_b x$$

Solution

$$\tfrac{3}{2}\log_b 4 - \tfrac{2}{3}\log_b 8 + \log_b 2 = \log_b x$$

$\log_b 4^{3/2} - \log_b 8^{2/3} + \log_b 2 = \log_b x$ Property 7

$$\log_b 8 - \log_b 4 + \log_b 2 = \log_b x$$

$$\log_b \frac{8 \cdot 2}{4} = \log_b x \quad \text{Properties 5 and 6}$$

$$\log_b 4 = \log_b x$$

$$x = 4 \qquad \text{Property 8}$$ ■

Matched Problem 5   Find x so that $3\log_b 2 + \tfrac{1}{2}\log_b 25 - \log_b 20 = \log_b x$.

EXAMPLE 6   **Solving Logarithmic Equations**   Solve: $\log_{10} x + \log_{10}(x + 1) = \log_{10} 6$.

Solution

$$\log_{10} x + \log_{10}(x + 1) = \log_{10} 6$$

$\log_{10}[x(x + 1)] = \log_{10} 6$ Property 5

$x(x + 1) = 6$ Property 8

$x^2 + x - 6 = 0$ Solve by factoring.

$$(x + 3)(x - 2) = 0$$

$$x = -3, 2$$

We must exclude $x = -3$, since the domain of the function $\log_{10}(x + 1)$ is $x > -1$ or $(-1, \infty)$; hence, $x = 2$ is the only solution.   ■

Matched Problem 6   Solve: $\log_3 x + \log_3(x - 3) = \log_3 10$.

EXPLORE
&DISCUSS
2

Discuss the relationship between each of the following pairs of expressions. If the two expressions are equivalent, explain why. If they are not, give an example.

(A) $\log_b M - \log_b N$; $\dfrac{\log_b M}{\log_b N}$

(B) $\log_b M - \log_b N$; $\log_b \dfrac{M}{N}$

(C) $\log_b M + \log_b N$; $\log_b MN$

(D) $\log_b M + \log_b N$; $\log_b(M + N)$

➤ Calculator Evaluation of Logarithms

Of all possible logarithmic bases, the base e and the base 10 are used almost exclusively. Before we can use logarithms in certain practical problems, we need to be able to approximate the logarithm of any positive number either to base 10 or to base e. And conversely, if we are given the logarithm of a number to base 10 or base e, we need to be able to approximate the number. Historically, tables were used for this purpose, but now calculators make computations faster and far more accurate.

Common logarithms (also called **Briggsian logarithms**) are logarithms with base 10. **Natural logarithms** (also called **Napierian logarithms**) are logarithms with base e. Most calculators have a key labeled "log" (or "LOG") and a key labeled "ln" (or "LN"). The former represents a common (base 10) logarithm and the latter a natural (base e) logarithm. In fact, "log" and "ln" are both used extensively in mathematical literature, and whenever you see either used in this book without a base indicated, they will be interpreted as follows:

NOTATION   Logarithmic Notation

Common logarithm: $\log x = \log_{10} x$

Natural logarithm: $\ln x = \log_e x$

Finding the common or natural logarithm using a calculator is very easy. On some calculators, you simply enter a number from the domain of the function and press LOG or LN. On other calculators, you press either LOG or LN, enter a number from the domain, and then press ENTER. Check the user's manual for your calculator.

EXAMPLE 7   **Calculator Evaluation of Logarithms**   Use a calculator to evaluate each to six decimal places:

(A) log 3,184   (B) ln 0.000 349   (C) log(−3.24)

Solution   (A) log 3,184 = 3.502 973   (B) ln 0.000 349 = −7.960 439

(C) log(−3.24) = Error*   −3.24 is not in the domain of the log function.   ■

---

* Some calculators use a more advanced definition of logarithms involving complex numbers and will display an ordered pair of real numbers as the value of log(−3.24). You should interpret such a result as an indication that the number entered is not in the domain of the logarithm function as we have defined it.

Matched Problem 7   Use a calculator to evaluate each to six decimal places:

(A) log 0.013 529   (B) ln 28.693 28   (C) ln(−0.438)

We now turn to the second problem mentioned previously: Given the logarithm of a number, find the number. We make direct use of the logarithmic–exponential relationships, which follow from the definition of logarithmic function given at the beginning of this section.

RESULT   **Logarithmic–Exponential Relationships**

$$\log x = y \quad \text{is equivalent to} \quad x = 10^y$$

$$\ln x = y \quad \text{is equivalent to} \quad x = e^y$$

EXAMPLE 8   **Solving $\log_b x = y$ for x**   Find x to four decimal places, given the indicated logarithm:

(A) $\log x = -2.315$ (B) $\ln x = 2.386$

Solution   (A) $\log x = -2.315$ *Change to equivalent exponential form.*
$\quad\quad\quad x = 10^{-2.315}$ *Evaluate with a calculator.*
$\quad\quad\quad\quad = 0.0048$

(B) $\ln x = 2.386$ *Change to equivalent exponential form.*
$\quad\quad x = e^{2.386}$ *Evaluate with a calculator.*
$\quad\quad\quad = 10.8699$

Matched Problem 8   Find x to four decimal places, given the indicated logarithm:

(A) $\ln x = -5.062$ (B) $\log x = 2.0821$

EXAMPLE 9   **Solving Exponential Equations**   Solve for x to four decimal places:

(A) $10^x = 2$ (B) $e^x = 3$ (C) $3^x = 4$

Solution   (A) $\quad 10^x = 2$ *Take common logarithms of both sides.*
$\quad\quad \log 10^x = \log 2$ *Property 3*
$\quad\quad\quad\quad x = \log 2$ *Use a calculator.*
$\quad\quad\quad\quad\quad = 0.3010$

(B) $\quad e^x = 3$ *Take natural logarithms of both sides.*
$\quad\quad \ln e^x = \ln 3$ *Property 3*
$\quad\quad\quad x = \ln 3$ *Use a calculator.*
$\quad\quad\quad\quad = 1.0986$

(C) $\quad 3^x = 4$ *Take either natural or common logarithms of both sides. (We choose commmon logarithms.)*
$\quad\quad \log 3^x = \log 4$ *Property 7*
$\quad\quad x \log 3 = \log 4$ *Solve for x.*
$\quad\quad\quad\quad x = \dfrac{\log 4}{\log 3}$ *Use a calculator.*
$\quad\quad\quad\quad\quad = 1.2619$

Exponential equations can also be solved graphically by graphing both sides of an equation and finding the points of intersection. Figure 3 illustrates this approach for the equations in Example 9.

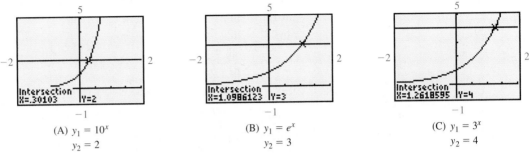

(A) $y_1 = 10^x$
    $y_2 = 2$

(B) $y_1 = e^x$
    $y_2 = 3$

(C) $y_1 = 3^x$
    $y_2 = 4$

FIGURE 3 Graphical solution of exponential equations

Matched Problem 9   Solve for x to four decimal places:

(A) $10^x = 7$ (B) $e^x = 6$ (C) $4^x = 5$

EXPLORE & DISCUSS 3   Discuss how you could find $y = \log_5 38.25$ using either natural or common logarithms on a calculator. [*Hint:* Start by rewriting the equation in exponential form.]

Remark

In the usual notation for natural logarithms, the simplifications of Example 4, parts (C) and (D) on page 114, become

$$e^{x \ln b} = b^x \quad \text{and} \quad \frac{\ln x}{\ln b} = \log_b x$$

With these formulas we can change an exponential function with base b, or a logarithmic function with base b, to expressions involving exponential or logarithmic functions, respectively, to the base e. Such **change-of-base formulas** are useful in calculus.

► Application

A convenient and easily understood way of comparing different investments is to use their **doubling times**—the length of time it takes the value of an investment to double. Logarithm properties, as you will see in Example 10, provide us with just the right tool for solving some doubling-time problems.

EXAMPLE 10   **Doubling Time for an Investment** How long (to the next whole year) will it take money to double if it is invested at 20% compounded annually?

Solution   We use the compound interest formula discussed in Section 2-2:

$$A = P\left(1 + \frac{r}{m}\right)^{mt} \quad \textit{Compound interest}$$

The problem is to find t, given $r = 0.20$, $m = 1$, and $A = 2p$; that is,

$$2P = P(1 + 0.2)^t$$
$$2 = 1.2^t$$
$$1.2^t = 2$$
$$\ln 1.2^t = \ln 2$$
$$t \ln 1.2 = \ln 2$$
$$t = \frac{\ln 2}{\ln 1.2}$$
$$= 3.8 \text{ years}$$
$$\approx 4 \text{ years}$$

Solve for t by taking the natural or common logarithm of both sides (we choose the natural logarithm).

Property 7

Use a calculator.

[Note: $(\ln 2)/(\ln 1.2) \neq \ln 2 - \ln 1.2$]

To the next whole year

When interest is paid at the end of 3 years, the money will not be doubled; when paid at the end of 4 years, the money will be slightly more than doubled. ∎

Example 10 can also be solved graphically by graphing both sides of the equation $2 = 1.2^t$, and finding the intersection point (Fig. 4).

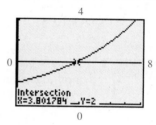

FIGURE 4 $y_1 = 1.2^x$, $y_2 = 2$

Matched Problem 10

How long (to the next whole year) will it take money to triple if it is invested at 13% compounded annually? _____∎

It is interesting and instructive to graph the doubling times for various rates compounded annually. We proceed as follows:

$$A = P(1 + r)^t$$
$$2P = P(1 + r)^t$$
$$2 = (1 + r)^t$$
$$(1 + r)^t = 2$$
$$\ln(1 + r)^t = \ln 2$$
$$t \ln(1 + r) = \ln 2$$
$$t = \frac{\ln 2}{\ln(1 + r)}$$

Figure 5 shows the graph of this equation (doubling time in years) for interest rates compounded annually from 1 to 70% (expressed as decimals). Note the dramatic change in doubling time as rates change from 1 to 20% (from 0.01 to 0.20).

FIGURE 5

Years (vertical axis: 10, 20, 30, 40, 50, 60, 70)

$t = \dfrac{\ln 2}{\ln(1 + r)}$

Rate compounded annually (horizontal axis: 0.20, 0.40, 0.60) — r

Answers to Matched Problems

1. (A) $9 = 3^2$ (B) $2 = 4^{1/2}$ (C) $\frac{1}{9} = 3^{-2}$

2. (A) $\log_7 49 = 2$ (B) $\log_9 3 = \frac{1}{2}$ (C) $\log_3(\frac{1}{3}) = -1$

3. (A) $y = \frac{3}{2}$ (B) $x = \frac{1}{3}$ (C) $b = 10$

4. (A) $\log_b R - \log_b S - \log_b T$ (B) $\frac{2}{3}(\log_b R - \log_b S)$ (C) b^u
    (D) $\log_b x$

5. $x = 2$ **6.** $x = 5$

7. (A) $-1.868\ 734$ (B) $3.356\ 663$ (C) Not defined

8. (A) 0.0063 (B) 120.8092

9. (A) 0.8451 (B) 1.7918 (C) 1.1610

10. 9 yr

Exercise 2-3

A *For Problems 1–6, rewrite in equivalent exponential form.*

1. $\log_3 27 = 3$ **2.** $\log_2 32 = 5$ **3.** $\log_{10} 1 = 0$

4. $\log_e 1 = 0$ **5.** $\log_4 8 = \frac{3}{2}$ **6.** $\log_9 27 = \frac{3}{2}$

For Problems 7–12, rewrite in equivalent logarithmic form.

7. $49 = 7^2$ **8.** $36 = 6^2$ **9.** $8 = 4^{3/2}$

10. $9 = 27^{2/3}$ **11.** $A = b^u$ **12.** $M = b^x$

For Problems 13–24, evaluate without a calculator.

13. $\log_{10} 1$ **14.** $\log_e 1$ **15.** $\log_e e$

16. $\log_{10} 10$ **17.** $\log_{0.2} 0.2$ **18.** $\log_{13} 13$

19. $\log_{10} 10^3$ **20.** $\log_{10} 10^{-5}$ **21.** $\log_2 2^{-3}$

22. $\log_3 3^5$ **23.** $\log_{10} 1{,}000$ **24.** $\log_6 36$

For Problems 25–30, write in terms of simpler forms, as in Example 4.

25. $\log_b \dfrac{P}{Q}$ **26.** $\log_b FG$ **27.** $\log_b L^5$

28. $\log_b w^{15}$ **29.** $3^{p \log_3 q}$ **30.** $\dfrac{\log_3 P}{\log_3 R}$

B *For Problems 31–42, find x, y, or b without a calculator.*

31. $\log_3 x = 2$ **32.** $\log_2 x = 2$

33. $\log_7 49 = y$ **34.** $\log_3 27 = y$

35. $\log_b 10^{-4} = -4$ **36.** $\log_b e^{-2} = -2$

37. $\log_4 x = \frac{1}{2}$ **38.** $\log_{25} x = \frac{1}{2}$

39. $\log_{1/3} 9 = y$ **40.** $\log_{49}(\frac{1}{7}) = y$

41. $\log_b 1{,}000 = \frac{3}{2}$ **42.** $\log_b 4 = \frac{2}{3}$

In Problems 43–52, discuss the validity of each statement. If the statement is always true, explain why. If not, give a counterexample.

43. Every polynomial function is one-to-one.

44. Every polynomial function of odd degree is one-to-one.

45. If g is the inverse of a function f, then g is one-to-one.

46. The graph of a one-to-one function intersects each vertical line exactly once.

47. The inverse of $f(x) = 2x$ is $g(x) = x/2$.

48. The inverse of $f(x) = x^2$ is $g(x) = \sqrt{x}$.

49. If $b > 0$ and $b \neq 1$, then the graph of $y = \log_b x$ is increasing.

50. If $b > 1$, then the graph of $y = \log_b x$ is increasing.

51. If f is one-to-one, then the domain of f is equal to the range of f.

52. If g is the inverse of a function f, then f is the inverse of g.

Find x in Problems 53–60.

53. $\log_b x = \frac{2}{3}\log_b 8 + \frac{1}{2}\log_b 9 - \log_b 6$

54. $\log_b x = \frac{2}{3}\log_b 27 + 2\log_b 2 - \log_b 3$

55. $\log_b x = \frac{3}{2}\log_b 4 - \frac{2}{3}\log_b 8 + 2\log_b 2$

56. $\log_b x = 3\log_b 2 + \frac{1}{2}\log_b 25 - \log_b 20$

57. $\log_b x + \log_b(x - 4) = \log_b 21$

58. $\log_b(x + 2) + \log_b x = \log_b 24$

59. $\log_{10}(x - 1) - \log_{10}(x + 1) = 1$

60. $\log_{10}(x + 6) - \log_{10}(x - 3) = 1$

Graph Problems 61 and 62 by converting to exponential form first.

61. $y = \log_2(x - 2)$ **62.** $y = \log_3(x + 2)$

63. Explain how the graph of the equation in Problem 61 can be obtained from the graph of $y = \log_2 x$ using a simple transformation (see Section 1-2).

64. Explain how the graph of the equation in Problem 62 can be obtained from the graph of $y = \log_3 x$ using a simple transformation (see Section 1-2).

65. What are the domain and range of the function defined by $y = 1 + \ln(x + 1)$?

66. What are the domain and range of the function defined by $y = \log(x - 1) - 1$?

For Problems 67 and 68, evaluate to five decimal places using a calculator.

67. (A) log 3,527.2   (B) log 0.006 913 2
       (C) ln 277.63   (D) ln 0.040 883

68. (A) log 72.604   (B) log 0.033 041
       (C) ln 40,257   (D) ln 0.005 926 3

For Problems 69 and 70, find x to four decimal places.

69. (A) $\log x = 1.1285$ (B) $\log x = -2.0497$
       (C) $\ln x = 2.7763$ (D) $\ln x = -1.8879$

70. (A) $\log x = 2.0832$ (B) $\log x = -1.1577$
       (C) $\ln x = 3.1336$ (D) $\ln x = -4.3281$

For Problems 71–78, solve each equation to four decimal places.

71. $10^x = 12$ **72.** $10^x = 153$

73. $e^x = 4.304$ **74.** $e^x = 0.3059$

75. $1.03^x = 2.475$ **76.** $1.075^x = 1.837$

77. $1.005^{12t} = 3$ **78.** $1.02^{4t} = 2$

Graph Problems 79–86 using a calculator and point-by-point plotting. Indicate increasing and decreasing intervals.

79. $y = \ln x$ **80.** $y = -\ln x$

81. $y = |\ln x|$ **82.** $y = \ln|x|$

83. $y = 2\ln(x + 2)$ **84.** $y = 2\ln x + 2$

85. $y = 4\ln x - 3$ **86.** $y = 4\ln(x - 3)$

C

87. Explain why the logarithm of 1 for any permissible base is 0.

88. Explain why 1 is not a suitable logarithmic base.

89. Write $\log_{10} y - \log_{10} c = 0.8x$ in an exponential form that is free of logarithms.

90. Write $\log_e x - \log_e 25 = 0.2t$ in an exponential form that is free of logarithms.

91. Let $p(x) = \ln x$, $q(x) = \sqrt{x}$, and $r(x) = x$. Use a graphing utility to draw graphs of all three functions in the same viewing window for $1 \le x \le 16$. Discuss what it means for one function to be larger than another on an interval, and then order the three functions from largest to smallest for $1 < x \le 16$.

92. Let $p(x) = \log x$, $q(x) = \sqrt[3]{x}$, and $r(x) = x$. Use a graphing utility to draw graphs of all three functions in the same viewing window for $1 \le x \le 16$. Discuss what it means for one function to be smaller than another on an interval, and then order the three functions from smallest to largest for $1 < x \le 16$.

Applications

Business & Economics

93. *Doubling time.* In its first 10 years the Gabelli Growth Fund produced an average annual return of 21.36%. Assume that money invested in this fund continues to earn 21.36% compounded annually. How long will it take money invested in this fund to double?

94. *Doubling time.* In its first 10 years the Janus Flexible Income Fund produced an average annual return of 9.58%. Assume that money invested in this fund continues to earn 9.58% compounded annually. How long will it take money invested in this fund to double?

95. *Investing.* How many years (to two decimal places) will it take $1,000 to grow to $1,800 if it is invested at 6% compounded quarterly? Compounded continuously?

96. *Investing.* How many years (to two decimal places) will it take $5,000 to grow to $7,500 if it is invested at 8% compounded semiannually? Compounded continuously?

97. *Investment.* A newly married couple wishes to have $30,000 in 6 years for the down payment on a house.

At what rate of interest compounded continuously (to three decimal places) must $20,000 be invested now to accomplish this goal?

98. *Investment.* The parents of a newborn child want to have $60,000 for the child's college education 17 years from now. At what rate of interest compounded continuously (to three decimal places) must a grandparent's gift of $20,000 be invested now to achieve this goal?

99. *Supply and demand.* A cordless screwdriver is sold through a national chain of discount stores. A marketing company established price–demand and price–supply tables (Tables 1 and 2), where x is the number of screwdrivers people are willing to buy and the store is willing to sell each month at a price of p dollars per screwdriver.

TABLE 1　Price–Demand	
x	$p = D(x)$ ($)
1,000	91
2,000	73
3,000	64
4,000	56
5,000	53

TABLE 2　Price–Supply	
x	$p = S(x)$ ($)
1,000	9
2,000	26
3,000	34
4,000	38
5,000	41

(A) Find a logarithmic regression model $(y = a + b \ln x)$ for the data in Table 1. Estimate the demand (to the nearest unit) at a price level of $50.

(B) Find a logarithmic regression model $(y = a + b \ln x)$ for the data in Table 2. Estimate the supply (to the nearest unit) at a price level of $50.

(C) Does a price level of $50 represent a stable condition, or is the price likely to increase or decrease? Explain.

100. *Equilibrium point.* Use the models constructed in Problem 99 to find the equilibrium point. Write the equilibrium price to the nearest cent and the equilibrium quantity to the nearest unit.

Life Sciences

101. *Sound intensity: decibels.* Because of the extraordinary range of sensitivity of the human ear (a range of over 1,000 million millions to 1), it is helpful to use a logarithmic scale, rather than an absolute scale, to measure sound intensity over this range. The unit of measure is called the *decibel,* after the inventor of the telephone, Alexander Graham Bell. If we let N be the number of decibels, I the power of the sound in question (in watts per square centimeter), and I_0 the power of sound just below the threshold of hearing (approximately 10^{-16} watt per square centimeter), then

$$I = I_0 10^{N/10}$$

Show that this formula can be written in the form

$$N = 10 \log \frac{I}{I_0}$$

102. *Sound intensity: decibels.* Use the formula in Problem 101 (with $I_0 = 10^{-16}$ W/cm^2) to find the decibel ratings of the following sounds:

(A) Whisper: 10^{-13} W/cm^2

(B) Normal conversation: 3.16×10^{-10} W/cm^2

(C) Heavy traffic: 10^{-8} W/cm^2

(D) Jet plane with afterburner: 10^{-1} W/cm^2

103. *Agriculture.* Table 3 shows the yield (in bushels per acre) and the total production (in millions of bushels) for corn in the United States for selected years since 1950. Let x represent years since 1900. Find a logarithmic regression model $(y = a + b \ln x)$ for the yield. Estimate (to one decimal place) the yield in 2010.

TABLE 3　United States Corn Production			
Year	x	Yield (bushels per acre)	Total Production (million bushels)
1950	50	37.6	2,782
1960	60	55.6	3,479
1970	70	81.4	4,802
1980	80	97.7	6,867
1990	90	115.6	7,802
2000	100	139.6	10,192

104. *Agriculture.* Refer to Table 3. Find a logarithmic regression model $(y = a + b \ln x)$ for the total production. Estimate (to the nearest million) the production in 2010.

Social Sciences

105. *World population.* If the world population is now 6.2 billion people and if it continues to grow at an annual rate of 1.25% compounded continuously, how long (to the nearest year) will it take before there is only 1 square yard of land per person? (The Earth contains approximately 1.68×10^{14} square yards of land.)

106. *Archaeology: carbon-14 dating.* The radioactive carbon-14 (^{14}C) in an organism at the time of its death decays according to the equation

$$A = A_0 e^{-0.000124t}$$

where t is time in years and A_0 is the amount of ^{14}C present at time $t = 0$. (See Example 3 in Section 2-2.) Estimate the age of a skull uncovered in an archaeological site if 10% of the original amount of ^{14}C is still present. [*Hint:* Find t such that $A = 0.1A_0$.]

Chapter 2 Review

Important Terms, Symbols, and Concepts

2-1 Polynomial and Rational Functions

• **Polynomial Functions**   A **polynomial function** is a function that can be written in the form $f(x) = a_n x^n + a_{n-1}x^{n-1} + \cdots + a_1 x + a_0$. The nonnegative integer n is the **degree** of the polynomial. The coefficients $a_0, a_1, \ldots, a_n$ are real numbers with $a_n \neq 0$. The **domain** of a polynomial function is the set of all real numbers. Graphs of polynomial functions are **continuous,** that is, have no holes or breaks. A **turning point** is a point on a continuous graph that separates an increasing portion from a decreasing portion, or vice versa. Graphs of polynomial functions of positive degree n can have at most $n - 1$ turning points and can cross the x axis at most n times.

  An x intercept of a function is also called a **zero** or **root** of the function. If r is a zero of a polynomial $P(x) = x^n + a_{n-1}x^{n-1} + \cdots + a_1 x + a_0$ that has **leading coefficient** a_n equal to 1, then $|r| < 1 + \max\{|a_{n-1}|, |a_{n-2}|, \ldots, |a_1|, |a_0|\}$.

  Regression techniques on a graphing utility can be used to fit a polynomial function to a data set.

• **Rational Functions**   A **rational function** is a function that can be written in the form $f(x) = n(x)/d(x)$, where $n(x)$ and $d(x)$ are polynomials. We assume that $n(x)$ and $d(x)$ have no real zero in common. The **domain** of a rational function is the set of all real numbers such that $d(x) \neq 0$. If a is a real number such that $d(a) = 0$, then the line $x = a$ is a **vertical asymptote** of the graph of $y = f(x)$. A rational function can have at most one **horizontal asymptote,** which can be found (when one exists) by analyzing the expression obtained by dividing each term of $n(x)$ and $d(x)$ by the highest power of x that appears in $f(x)$.

2-2 Exponential Functions

The function $f(x) = b^x$ is called an **exponential function,** where $b \neq 1$ is a positive constant called the **base.** The **domain** of f is the set of all real numbers, and the **range** of f is the set of all positive real numbers. The graph of an exponential function is continuous, passes through the point $(0, 1)$, and has the x axis as a horizontal asymptote. If $b > 1$, then b^x increases as x increases; if $0 < b < 1$, then b^x decreases as x increases. The base b that is used most frequently is the irrational number $e \approx 2.7183$.

• **Properties of Exponential Functions**   For a and b positive, $a \neq 1$, $b \neq 1$, and x and y real,

1. $a^x a^y = a^{x+y}$ $\dfrac{a^x}{a^y} = a^{x-y}$

   $(a^x)^y = a^{xy}$ $(ab)^x = a^x b^x$ $\left(\dfrac{a}{b}\right)^x = \dfrac{a^x}{b^x}$

2. $a^x = a^y$ if and only if $x = y$
3. For $x \neq 0$, $a^x = b^x$ if and only if $a = b$

  Exponential functions can be used to model population growth and radioactive decay. Exponential functions are also used in computations of **interest,** the fee paid to use another's money. If a **principal P** is invested at an annual **rate r** (expressed as a decimal) compounded m times a year, then the **amount A** in the account at the end of t years is given by

$$A = P\left(1 + \frac{r}{m}\right)^{mt} \quad \text{Compound interest formula}$$

If a principal P is invested at an annual rate r compounded continuously, then the amount A in the account at the end of t years is given by

$$A = Pe^{rt} \quad \text{Continuous compound interest formula}$$

2-3 Logarithmic Functions

A function is said to be **one-to-one** if each range value corresponds to exactly one domain value. If f is a one-to-one function, then the inverse of f is the function formed by interchanging the independent and dependent variables of f. That is, (a, b) is a point on the graph of f if and only if (b, a) is a point on the graph of the inverse of f. The inverse of the exponential function with base b is called the **logarithmic function with base b,** denoted $y = \log_b x$. The **domain** of $\log_b x$ is the set of all positive real numbers (which is the range of b^x), and the **range** of $\log_b x$ is the set of all real numbers (which is the domain of b^x). Because $\log_b x$ is the inverse of the function b^x,

Logarithmic form		Exponential form
$y = \log_b x$	is equivalent to	$x = b^y$

• **Properties of Logarithmic Functions**   If b, M, N are positive real numbers, $b \neq 1$, and p and x are real numbers, then

1. $\log_b 1 = 0$
2. $\log_b b = 1$
3. $\log_b b^x = x$
4. $b^{\log_b x} = x$
5. $\log_b MN = \log_b M + \log_b N$
6. $\log_b \dfrac{M}{N} = \log_b M - \log_b N$
7. $\log_b M^p = p \log_b M$
8. $\log_b M = \log_b N$ if and only if $M = N$

  Logarithms to the base 10 are called **common logarithms,** often denoted simply by $\log x$. Logarithms to the base e are called **natural logarithms,** often denoted by $\ln x$. Logarithms can be used to find an investment's **doubling time**—the length of time it takes the value of an investment to double.

Review Exercise

Work through all the problems in this chapter review and check your answers in the back of the book. Answers to all review problems are there along with section numbers in italics to indicate where each type of problem is discussed. Where weaknesses show up, review appropriate sections in the text.

A

1. Write in logarithmic form using base e: $u = e^v$.

2. Write in logarithmic form using base 10: $x = 10^y$.

3. Write in exponential form using base e: $\ln M = N$.

4. Write in exponential form using base 10: $\log u = v$.

Simplify Problems 5 and 6.

5. $\dfrac{5^{x+4}}{5^{4-x}}$

6. $\left(\dfrac{e^u}{e^{-u}}\right)^u$

Solve Problems 7–9 for x exactly without using a calculator.

7. $\log_3 x = 2$

8. $\log_x 36 = 2$

9. $\log_2 16 = x$

Solve Problems 10–12 for x to three decimal places.

10. $10^x = 143.7$

11. $e^x = 503{,}000$

12. $\log x = 3.105$

13. $\ln x = -1.147$

Each graph in Problems 14 and 15 is the graph of a polynomial function. Answer the following questions for each graph:

  (A) *How many turning points are on the graph?*

  (B) *What is the minimum degree of a polynomial function that could have the graph?*

  (C) *Is the leading coefficient of the polynomial negative or positive?*

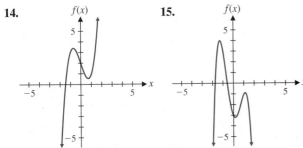

14. $f(x)$ **15.** $f(x)$

B *For each rational function in Problems 16 and 17,*

  (A) *Find the intercepts for the graph.*

  (B) *Determine the domain.*

  (C) *Find any vertical or horizontal asymptotes for the graph.*

  (D) *Sketch any asymptotes as dashed lines. Then sketch a graph of f for $-10 \leqslant x \leqslant 10$ and $-10 \leqslant y \leqslant 10$.*

  (E) *Graph $y = f(x)$ in a standard viewing window using a graphing utility.*

16. $f(x) = \dfrac{x + 4}{x - 2}$

17. $f(x) = \dfrac{3x - 4}{2 + x}$

Solve Problems 18–25 for x exactly without using a calculator.

18. $\log(x + 5) = \log(2x - 3)$

19. $2 \ln(x - 1) = \ln(x^2 - 5)$

20. $9^{x-1} = 3^{1+x}$

21. $e^{2x} = e^{x^2 - 3}$

22. $2x^2 e^x = 3xe^x$

23. $\log_{1/3} 9 = x$

24. $\log_x 8 = -3$

25. $\log_9 x = \frac{3}{2}$

Solve Problems 26–35 for x to four decimal places.

26. $x = 3(e^{1.49})$

27. $x = 230(10^{-0.161})$

28. $\log x = -2.0144$

29. $\ln x = 0.3618$

30. $35 = 7(3^x)$

31. $0.01 = e^{-0.05x}$

32. $8{,}000 = 4{,}000(1.08^x)$

33. $5^{2x-3} = 7.08$

34. $x = \log_2 7$

35. $x = \log_{0.2} 5.321$

36. How does the graph of $f(x) = x^4 - 4x^2 + 1$ compare to the graph of $y = x^4$ as we "zoom out"?

37. Compare the graphs of $y = x^4$ and $y = x^4 - 4x^2 + 1$ in the following two viewing windows:

  (A) $-5 \leqslant x \leqslant 5, -5 \leqslant y \leqslant 5$

  (B) $-5 \leqslant x \leqslant 5, -500 \leqslant y \leqslant 500$

38. Let $p(x) = 2x^4 - 11x^3 - 15x^2 - 14x - 16$. Approximate the real zeros of $p(x)$ to two decimal places.

39. Let $f(x) = e^x - 1$ and $g(x) = \ln(x + 2)$. Find all points of intersection for the graphs of f and g. Round answers to two decimal places.

In Problems 40–47, discuss the validity of each statement. If the statement is always true, explain why. If not, give a counterexample.

40. Every polynomial function is a rational function.

41. Every rational function is a polynomial function.

42. The graph of every rational function has at least one vertical asymptote.

43. The graph of every exponential function has a horizontal asymptote.

44. The graph of every logarithmic function has a vertical asymptote.

45. There exists a logarithmic function that has both a vertical and horizontal asymptote.

46. There exists a rational function that has both a vertical and horizontal asymptote.

47. There exists an exponential function that has both a vertical and horizontal asymptote.

Graph Problems 48–50 over the indicated interval. Indicate increasing and decreasing intervals.

48. $y = 2^{x-1}; [-2, 4]$

49. $f(t) = 10e^{-0.08t}; t \geq 0$

50. $y = \ln(x + 1); (-1, 10]$

C

51. Noting that $\pi = 3.141\,592\,654\ldots$ and $\sqrt{2} = 1.414\,213\,562\ldots$, explain why the calculator results shown here are obvious. Discuss similar connections between the natural logarithmic function and the exponential function with base e.

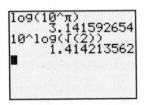

Solve Problems 52–55 exactly without using a calculator.

52. $\log x - \log 3 = \log 4 - \log(x + 4)$

53. $\ln(2x - 2) - \ln(x - 1) = \ln x$

54. $\ln(x + 3) - \ln x = 2 \ln 2$

55. $\log 3x^2 = 2 + \log 9x$

56. Write $\ln y = -5t + \ln c$ in an exponential form free of logarithms. Then solve for y in terms of the remaining variables.

57. Explain why 1 cannot be used as a logarithmic base.

Applications

Business & Economics

The two formulas below will be of use in some of the problems that follow:

$$A = P\left(1 + \frac{r}{m}\right)^{mt} \quad \text{Compound interest}$$

$$A = Pe^{rt} \quad \text{Continuous compound interest}$$

58. *Money growth.* Provident Bank of Cincinnati, Ohio recently offered a certificate of deposit that paid 3.55% compounded continuously. If a $5,000 CD earns this rate for 5 years, how much will it be worth?

59. *Money growth.* Capital One Bank of Glen Allen, Virginia recently offered a certificate of deposit that paid 3.62% compounded daily. If a $5,000 CD earns this rate for 5 years, how much will it be worth?

60. *Money growth.* How long will it take for money invested at 6.59% compounded continuously to triple?

61. *Money growth.* How long will it take for money invested at 6.58% compounded daily to double?

62. *Minimum average cost.* The financial department of a company that manufactures in-line skates has fixed costs of $300 per day and total costs of $4,300 per day at an output of 100 pairs of skates per day. Assume that the cost $C(x)$ is linearly related to output x.

(A) Find an expression for the cost function $C(x)$ and the average cost function $\overline{C}(x) = C(x)/x$.

(B) Sketch a graph of the average cost function for $5 \leq x \leq 200$.

(C) Identify any asymptotes.

(D) What does the average cost approach as production increases?

63. *Minimum average cost.* The cost $C(x)$ in thousands of dollars for operating a hospital for a year is given by

$$C(x) = 20x^3 - 360x^2 + 2,300x - 1,000$$

where x is the number of cases per year (in thousands). The average cost function $\overline{C}$ is given by $\overline{C}(x) = C(x)/x$.

(A) Write an equation for the average cost function.

(B) Graph the average cost function for $1 \leq x \leq 12$.

(C) Use an appropriate command to find the number of cases per year the hospital should handle to have the minimum average cost. What is the minimum average cost?

64. *Equilibrium point.* A company is planning to introduce a 10-piece set of nonstick cookware. A marketing company established price–demand and price–supply tables for selected prices (Tables 1 and 2), where *x* is the number of cookware sets people are willing to buy and the company is willing to sell each month at a price of *p* dollars per set.

TABLE 1 Price–Demand

x	$p = D(x)$ ($)
985	330
2,145	225
2,950	170
4,225	105
5,100	50

TABLE 2 Price–Supply

x	$p = S(x)$ ($)
985	30
2,145	75
2,950	110
4,225	155
5,100	190

(A) Find a quadratic regression model for the data in Table 1. Estimate the demand at a price level of $180.

(B) Find a linear regression model for the data in Table 2. Estimate the supply at a price level of $180.

(C) Does a price level of $180 represent a stable condition, or is the price likely to increase or decrease? Explain.

(D) Use the models in parts (A) and (B) to find the equilibrium point. Write the equilibrium price to the nearest cent and the equilibrium quantity to the nearest unit.

65. *Telecommunications.* According to the Telecommunications Industry Association, wireless telephone subscriptions grew from about 4 million in 1990 to over 143 million in 2002 (Table 3). Let *x* represent years since 1990.

TABLE 3 Wireless Telephone Subscribers

Year	Million Subscribers
1990	4
1993	13
1996	38
1999	76
2002	143

(A) Find an exponential regression model ($y = ab^x$) for this data. Estimate (to the nearest million) the number of subscribers in 2010.

(B) Some analysts estimate the number of wireless subscribers in 2006 to be 186 million. How does this compare with the prediction of the model of part (A)? Explain why the model will not give reliable predictions far into the future.

Life Sciences

66. *Medicine.* One leukemic cell injected into a healthy mouse will divide into 2 cells in about $\frac{1}{2}$ day. At the end of the day these 2 cells will divide into 4. This doubling continues until 1 billion cells are formed; then the animal dies with leukemic cells in every part of the body.

(A) Write an equation that will give the number *N* of leukemic cells at the end of *t* days.

(B) When, to the nearest day, will the mouse die?

67. *Marine biology.* The intensity of light entering water is reduced according to the exponential equation

$$I = I_0 e^{-kd}$$

where *I* is the intensity *d* feet below the surface, I_0 is the intensity at the surface, and *k* is the coefficient of extinction. Measurements in the Sargasso Sea in the West Indies have indicated that half of the surface light reaches a depth of 73.6 feet. Find *k* (to five decimal places), and find the depth (to the nearest foot) at which 1% of the surface light remains.

68. *Agriculture.* The number of dairy cows on farms in the United States is shown in Table 4 for selected years since 1950. Let 1940 be year 0.

TABLE 4 Dairy Cows on Farms in the United States

Year	Dairy Cows (thousands)
1950	23,853
1960	19,527
1970	12,091
1980	10,758
1990	10,015
2000	9,190

(A) Find a logarithmic regression model $(y = a + b \ln x)$ for the data. Estimate (to the nearest thousand) the number of dairy cows in 2010.

(B) Explain why it is not a good idea to let 1950 be year 0.

Social Sciences

69. *Population growth.* Many countries have a population growth rate of 3% (or more) per year. At this rate, how many years (to the nearest tenth of a year) will it take a population to double? Use the annual compounding growth model $P = P_0(1 + r)^t$.

70. *Population growth.* Repeat Problem 69 using the continuous compounding growth model $P = P_0 e^{rt}$.

71. *Medicare.* The annual expenditures for Medicare (in billions of dollars) by the U.S. government for

selected years since 1980 are shown in Table 5. Let x represent years since 1980.

TABLE 5 Medicare Expenditures	
Year	**Billion $**
1980	37
1985	72
1990	111
1995	181
2000	197

(A) Find an exponential regression model $(y = ab^x)$ for the data. Estimate (to the nearest billion) the total expenditures in 2010.

(B) When will the total expenditures reach 500 billion dollars?

Group Activity 1   Comparing the Growth of Exponential and Polynomial Functions, and Logarithmic and Root Functions

(A) An exponential function such as $f(x) = 2^x$ increases extremely rapidly for large values of x, more rapidly than any polynomial function. Show that the graphs of $f(x) = 2^x$ and $g(x) = x^2$ intersect three times. The intersection points divide the x axis into four regions. Describe which function is greater than the other relative to each region.

(B) A logarithmic function such as $r(x) = \ln x$ increases extremely slowly for large values of x, more slowly than a function like $s(x) = \sqrt[3]{x}$. Sketch graphs of both functions in the same coordinate system for $x > 0$, and determine how many times the two graphs intersect. Describe which function is greater than the other relative to the regions determined by the intersection points.

Group Activity 2   Comparing Regression Models

We have used polynomial, exponential, and logarithmic regression models to fit curves to data sets. And there are other equations that can be used for curve fitting. (The TI-83 Plus graphing calculator has 10 equations on its STAT-CALC menu.) How can we determine which equation provides the best fit for a given set of data? There are two principal ways to select models. The first is to use information about the type of data to help make a choice. For example, we expect the weight of a fish to be related to the cube of its length. And we expect most populations to grow exponentially, at least over the short term. The second method for choosing between equations involves developing a measure of how close an equation fits a given data set. This is best introduced through an example. Consider the data set in Figure 1, where L1 represents the x coordinates and L2 represents the y coordinates. The graph of this data set is shown in Figure 2. Suppose that we arbitrarily choose the equation $y_1 = 0.6x + 2$ to model the data (Fig. 3).

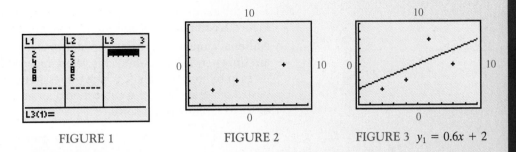

FIGURE 1   FIGURE 2   FIGURE 3 $y_1 = 0.6x + 2$

To measure how well the graph of y_1 fits the data, we examine the difference between the y coordinates in the data set and the corresponding y coordinates on the graph of y_1 (L3 in Figs. 4 and 5). Each of these differences is called a **residual.** The most commonly accepted measure of the fit provided by a given model is the **sum of the squares of the residuals (SSR).** Computing this quantity is a simple matter on a graphing calculator (Fig. 6) or a spreadsheet (Fig. 7).

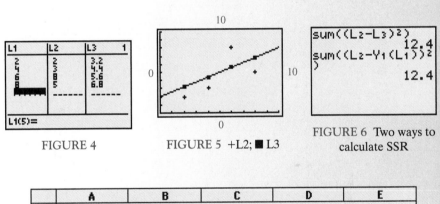

FIGURE 4   FIGURE 5 +L2; ■ L3   FIGURE 6 Two ways to
                                                      calculate SSR

	A	B	C	D	E
1		Data Set			
2	x	y	y1 = 0.6x + 2	Residual	Residual^2
3	2	2	3.2	-1.2	1.44
4	4	3	4.4	-1.4	1.96
5	6	8	5.6	2.4	5.76
6	8	5	6.8	-1.8	3.24
7				SSR	12.4

FIGURE 7

(A) Find the linear regression model for the data in Figure 1, compute the SSR for this equation, and compare it with the one we computed for y_1.

It turns out that among all possible linear polynomials, **the linear regression model minimizes the sum of the squares of the residuals.** For this reason, the linear regression model is often called the **least squares line.** A similar statement can be made for polynomials of any fixed degree. That is, the quadratic regression model minimizes the SSR over all quadratic polynomials, the cubic regression model minimizes the SSR over all cubic polynomials, and so on. The same statement cannot be made for exponential or logarithmic regression models. Nevertheless, the SSR can still be used to compare exponential, logarithmic, and polynomial models.

(B) Find the exponential and logarithmic regression models for the data in Figure 1, compute their SSRs, and compare with the linear model.

(C) National annual advertising expenditures for selected years since 1950 are shown in Table 1, where x is years since 1950 and y is total expenditures in billions of dollars. Which regression model would fit the data best: a quadratic model, a cubic model, or an exponential model? Use the SSRs to support your choice.

TABLE 1 Annual Advertising Expenditures, 1950–2000	
x (Years)	y (Billion $)
0	5.7
5	9.2
10	12.0
15	15.3
20	19.6
25	27.9
30	53.6
35	94.8
40	128.6
45	160.9
50	243.7

Part Two

CALCULUS

OBJECTIVES

1. Interpret limits and continuity utilizing graphical and algebraic techniques.
2. Use the definition of derivative to interpret the derivative of a function as velocity, slope, and, more generally, an instantaneous rate of change.
3. Use the rules and properties of differentiation in order to routinely differentiate a wide variety of functions, including any polynomial and any rational function.
4. Use marginal analysis to answer many important questions in economics.

CHAPTER PROBLEM

A New York publishing house recently brought out the autobiography of a former first lady. The total cost and revenue (in dollars) for printing and selling x copies of this book weekly are, respectively,

$$C(x) = 60,000 + 20x \qquad R(x) = 100x - 0.02x^2$$

(A) How many copies of the book should be printed weekly for the publisher to break even?

(B) How many copies of the book should be printed weekly in order for the publisher to realize the largest possible profit?

The Derivative

INTRODUCTION

How do algebra and calculus differ? The two words *static* and *dynamic* probably come as close as any in expressing the difference between the two disciplines. In algebra, we solve equations for a particular value of a variable—a static notion. In calculus, we are interested in how a change in one variable affects another variable—a dynamic notion.

Parts (A)–(C) of the figure on page 132 illustrate three basic problems in calculus. It may surprise you to learn that all three problems—as different as they appear—are related mathematically. The solutions to these problems and the discovery of their relationship required the creation of a new kind of mathematics. Isaac Newton (1642–1727) of England and Gottfried Wilhelm von Leibniz (1646–1716) of Germany, simultaneously and independently, developed this new mathematics, called **the calculus**—it was an idea whose time had come.

In addition to solving the problems described in the figure, calculus will enable us to solve many other important problems. Until fairly recently, calculus was used primarily in the physical sciences, but now people in many other disciplines are finding it a useful tool.

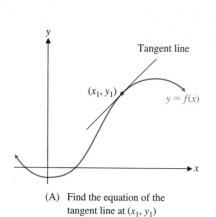

(A) Find the equation of the tangent line at (x_1, y_1) given $y = f(x)$

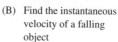

(B) Find the instantaneous velocity of a falling object

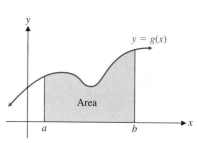

(C) Find the indicated area bounded by $y = g(x)$, $x = a$, $x = b$, and the x axis

Section **3-1** Introduction to Limits

> Functions and Graphs: Brief Review
> Limits—A Graphical Approach
> Limits—An Algebraic Approach
> Limits of Difference Quotients

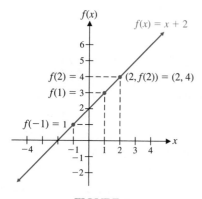

FIGURE 1

Basic to the study of calculus is the concept of *limit*. This concept helps us to describe, in a precise way, the behavior of $f(x)$ when x is close to but not equal to a particular value c. In this section we develop an intuitive and informal approach for evaluating limits. Our discussion concentrates on concept development and understanding rather than on formal mathematical detail.

> Functions and Graphs: Brief Review

The graph of the function $y = f(x) = x + 2$ is the graph of the set of all ordered pairs $(x, f(x))$. For example, if $x = 2$, then $f(2) = 4$ and $(2, f(2)) = (2, 4)$ is a point on the graph of f. Figure 1 shows $(-1, f(-1))$, $(1, f(1))$, and $(2, f(2))$ plotted on the graph of f. Notice that the domain values -1, 1, and 2 are associated with the x axis, and the range values $f(-1) = 1$, $f(1) = 3$, and $f(2) = 4$ are associated with the y axis.

Given x, it is sometimes useful to be able to read $f(x)$ directly from the graph of f. Example 1 reviews this process.

EXAMPLE 1 **Finding Values of a Function from Its Graph** Complete the following table using the given graph of the function g.

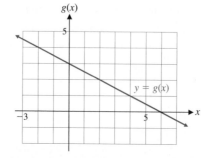

x	$g(x)$
-2	
1	
3	
4	

Solution   To determine $g(x)$, proceed vertically from the x value on the x axis to the graph of g, then horizontally to the corresponding y value, $g(x)$, on the y axis (as indicated by the dashed lines):

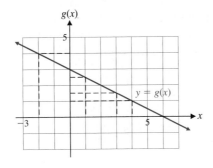

x	$g(x)$
-2	4.0
1	2.5
3	1.5
4	1.0

Matched Problem 1   Complete the following table using the given graph of the function h.

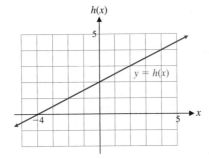

x	$h(x)$
-2	
-1	
0	
1	
2	
3	
4	

➤ Limits—A Graphical Approach

We introduce the important concept of *limit* through an example, which will lead to an intuitive definition of limit.

EXAMPLE 2   Analyzing a Limit   Let $f(x) = x + 2$. Discuss the behavior of the values of $f(x)$ when x is close to 2.

Solution   We begin by drawing a graph of f that includes the domain value $x = 2$ (Fig. 2).

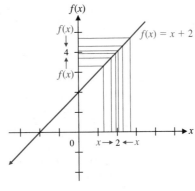

FIGURE 2

In Figure 2, we are using a static drawing to describe a dynamic process. This requires careful interpretation. The thin vertical lines in Figure 2 represent values of x that are close to 2. The corresponding horizontal lines identify the value of $f(x)$ associated with each value of x. [Example 1 dealt with the relationship between x and $f(x)$ on a graph.] The graph in Figure 2 indicates that as the values of x get closer and closer to 2, on either side of 2, the corresponding values of $f(x)$ get closer and closer to 4. Symbolically, we write

$$\lim_{x \to 2} f(x) = 4$$

This is read as "the limit of $f(x)$ as x approaches 2 is 4." Note that $f(2) = 4$. That is, the value of the function at 2 and the limit of the function as x approaches 2 are the same. This can be written as

$$\lim_{x \to 2} f(x) = f(2) = 4$$

Graphically, this means that there is no hole or break in the graph of f at $x = 2$.   ■

Matched Problem 2   Let $f(x) = x + 1$. Discuss the behavior of the values of $f(x)$ when x is close to 1.

We now present an informal definition of the important concept of limit. A precise definition is not needed for our discussion, but one is given in the footnote.*

DEFINITION   Limit

We write

$$\lim_{x \to c} f(x) = L \qquad \text{or} \qquad f(x) \to L \quad \text{as} \quad x \to c$$

if the functional value $f(x)$ is close to the single real number L whenever x is close to, but not equal to, c (on either side of c).

Note: The existence of a limit at c has nothing to do with the value of the function at c. In fact, c may not even be in the domain of f. However, the function must be defined on both sides of c.

The next example involves the **absolute value function:**

$$f(x) = |x| = \begin{cases} -x & \text{if } x < 0 \\ x & \text{if } x \geq 0 \end{cases} \qquad \begin{aligned} f(-2) &= |-2| = -(-2) = 2 \\ f(3) &= |3| = 3 \end{aligned}$$

The graph of f is shown in Figure 3.

---

* To make the informal definition of limit precise, the use of the word *close* must be made more precise. This is done as follows: We write $\lim_{x \to c} f(x) = L$ if for each $e > 0$, there exists a $d > 0$ such that $|f(x) - L| < e$ whenever $0 < |x - c| < d$. This definition is used to establish particular limits and to prove many useful properties of limits that will be helpful to us in finding particular limits. [Even though intuitive notions of limit existed for a long time, it was not until the nineteenth century that a precise definition was given by the German mathematician Karl Weierstrass (1815–1897).]

$$f(x)$$

FIGURE 3 $f(x) = |x|$

EXAMPLE 3 **Analyzing a Limit** Let $h(x) = |x|/x$. Explore the behavior of $h(x)$ for x near 0 but not equal to 0. Find $\lim_{x \to 0} h(x)$, if it exists.

Solution The function h is defined for all real numbers except 0. For example,

$$h(-2) = \frac{|-2|}{-2} = \frac{2}{-2} = -1$$

$$h(0) = \frac{|0|}{0} = \frac{0}{0} \qquad \textit{Not defined}$$

$$h(2) = \frac{|2|}{2} = \frac{2}{2} = 1$$

In general, $h(x)$ is -1 for all negative x and 1 for all positive x. Figure 4 illustrates the behavior of $h(x)$ for x near 0. Note that the absence of a solid dot on the vertical axis indicates that h is not defined when $x = 0$.

When x is near 0 (on either side of 0), is $h(x)$ near one specific number? The answer is "No," because $h(x)$ is -1 for $x < 0$ and 1 for $x > 0$. Consequently, we say that

$$\lim_{x \to 0} \frac{|x|}{x} \text{ does not exist}$$

Thus, neither $h(x)$ nor the limit of $h(x)$ exists at $x = 0$. However, the limit from the left and the limit from the right both exist at 0, but they are not equal. (We discuss this further later.)

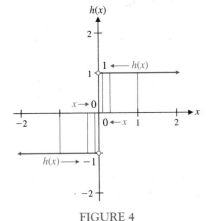

FIGURE 4

Matched Problem 3 Graph

$$h(x) = \frac{x - 2}{|x - 2|}$$

and find $\lim_{x \to 2} h(x)$, if it exists.

In Example 3 we saw that the values of the function $h(x)$ approached two different numbers, depending on the direction of approach, and it was natural to refer to these values as "the limit from the left" and "the limit from the right." These experiences suggest that the notion of **one-sided limits** will be very useful when discussing basic limit concepts.

DEFINITION   One-Sided Limits
We write

$$\lim_{x \to c^-} f(x) = K$$ $x \to c^-$ is read "x approaches c from
the left" and means $x \to c$ and $x < c$.

and call K the **limit from the left** or **left-hand limit** if $f(x)$ is close to K whenever x is close to c, but to the left of c, on the real number line. We write

$$\lim_{x \to c^+} f(x) = L$$ $x \to c^+$ is read "x approaches c from
the right" and means $x \to c$ and $x > c$.

and call L the **limit from the right** or **right-hand limit** if $f(x)$ is close to L whenever x is close to c, but to the right of c, on the real number line.

If no direction is specified in a limit statement, we will always assume that the limit is **two-sided** or **unrestricted.** Theorem 1 states an important relationship between one-sided limits and unrestricted limits.

THEOREM 1   On the Existence of a Limit
For a (two-sided) limit to exist, the limit from the left and the limit from the right must exist and be equal. That is,

$$\lim_{x \to c} f(x) = L \text{ if and only if } \lim_{x \to c^-} f(x) = \lim_{x \to c^+} f(x) = L$$

In Example 3,

$$\lim_{x \to 0^-} \frac{|x|}{x} = -1 \qquad \text{and} \qquad \lim_{x \to 0^+} \frac{|x|}{x} = 1$$

Since the left- and right-hand limits are not the same,

$$\lim_{x \to 0} \frac{|x|}{x} \text{ does not exist}$$

EXAMPLE 4   **Analyzing Limits Graphically** Given the graph of the function f shown in Figure 5, discuss the behavior of $f(x)$ for x near (A) -1, (B) 1, and (C) 2.

Solution   (A) Since we have only a graph to work with, we use vertical and horizontal lines to relate the values of x and the corresponding values of $f(x)$. For any x near -1 on either side of -1, we see that the corresponding value of $f(x)$, determined by a horizontal line, is close to 1.

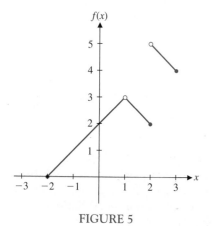

FIGURE 5

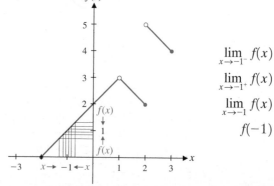

$$\lim_{x \to -1^-} f(x) = 1$$

$$\lim_{x \to -1^+} f(x) = 1$$

$$\lim_{x \to -1} f(x) = 1$$

$$f(-1) = 1$$

(B) Again, for any x near but not equal to 1, the vertical and horizontal lines indicate that the corresponding value of $f(x)$ is close to 3. The open dot at $(1, 3)$, together with the lack of a solid dot anywhere on the vertical line though $x = 1$, indicates that $f(1)$ is not defined.

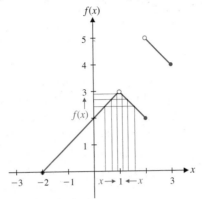

$$\lim_{x \to 1^-} f(x) = 3$$

$$\lim_{x \to 1^+} f(x) = 3$$

$$\lim_{x \to 1} f(x) = 3$$

$$f(1) \text{ not defined}$$

(C) The abrupt break in the graph at $x = 2$ indicates that the behavior near $x = 2$ is more complicated than in the two preceding cases. If x is close to 2 on the left side of 2, the corresponding horizontal line intersects the y axis at a point close to 2. If x is close to 2 on the right side of 2, the corresponding horizontal line intersects the y axis at a point close to 5. Thus, this is a case where the one-sided limits are different.

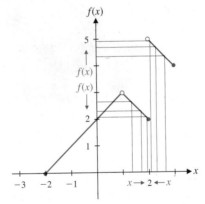

$$\lim_{x \to 2^-} f(x) = 2$$

$$\lim_{x \to 2^+} f(x) = 5$$

$$\lim_{x \to 2} f(x) \text{ does not exist}$$

$$f(2) = 2$$

Matched Problem 4   Given the graph of the function f shown in Figure 6, discuss the following, as we did in Example 4:

(A) Behavior of $f(x)$ for x near 0

(B) Behavior of $f(x)$ for x near 1

(C) Behavior of $f(x)$ for x near 3

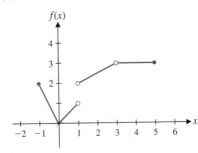

FIGURE 6

Insight   In Example 4B, note that $\lim\limits_{x \to 1} f(x)$ exists even though f is not defined at $x = 1$ and the graph has a hole at $x = 1$. In general, the value of a function at $x = c$ has no effect on the limit of the function as x approaches c.   ●

➤ Limits—An Algebraic Approach

Graphs are very useful tools for investigating limits, especially if something unusual happens at the point in question. However, many of the limits encountered in calculus are routine and can be evaluated quickly, using a little algebraic simplification, some intuition, and basic properties of limits. The following list of properties of limits forms the basis for this approach.

THEOREM 2   **Properties of Limits**

Let f and g be two functions, and assume that

$$\lim_{x \to c} f(x) = L \qquad \lim_{x \to c} g(x) = M$$

where L and M are real numbers (both limits exist). Then

1. $\lim\limits_{x \to c}[f(x) + g(x)] = \lim\limits_{x \to c} f(x) + \lim\limits_{x \to c} g(x) = L + M$

2. $\lim\limits_{x \to c}[f(x) - g(x)] = \lim\limits_{x \to c} f(x) - \lim\limits_{x \to c} g(x) = L - M$

3. $\lim\limits_{x \to c} kf(x) = k \lim\limits_{x \to c} f(x) = kL$ for any constant k

4. $\lim\limits_{x \to c}[f(x) \cdot g(x)] = [\lim\limits_{x \to c} f(x)][\lim\limits_{x \to c} g(x)] = LM$

5. $\lim\limits_{x \to c}\dfrac{f(x)}{g(x)} = \dfrac{\lim\limits_{x \to c} f(x)}{\lim\limits_{x \to c} g(x)} = \dfrac{L}{M}$ if $M \neq 0$

6. $\lim\limits_{x \to c}\sqrt[n]{f(x)} = \sqrt[n]{\lim\limits_{x \to c} f(x)} = \sqrt[n]{L}$ $L > 0$ for n even

Each property in Theorem 2 is also valid if $x \to c$ is replaced everywhere by $x \to c^-$ or replaced everywhere by $x \to c^+$.

EXPLORE & DISCUSS 1

The properties listed in Theorem 2 can be paraphrased in brief verbal statements. For example, property 1 simply states that *the limit of a sum is equal to the sum of the limits*. Write brief verbal statements for the remaining properties in Theorem 2.

EXAMPLE 5   **Using Limit Properties**   Find $\lim\limits_{x \to 3}(x^2 - 4x)$.

Solution   First, note the following obvious limit:

$$\lim_{x \to 3} x = 3$$

(All this says is that if x approaches 3, then x approaches 3.) Now we make use of this limit and the limit properties:

$$\lim_{x \to 3}(x^2 - 4x) = \lim_{x \to 3} x^2 - \lim_{x \to 3} 4x \qquad \text{Property 2}$$

$$= \left(\lim_{x \to 3} x\right) \cdot \left(\lim_{x \to 3} x\right) - 4\lim_{x \to 3} x \qquad \text{Properties 3 and 4}$$

$$= 3 \cdot 3 - 4 \cdot 3 = -3$$

With a little practice you will soon be able to omit the steps in the dashed boxes and simply write

$$\lim_{x \to 3}(x^2 - 4x) = 3 \cdot 3 - 4 \cdot 3 = -3$$ ▓

Matched Problem 5   Find $\lim_{x \to -2}(x^2 + 5x)$.

What happens if we try to evaluate a limit like the one in Example 5, but with x approaching an unspecified number, such as c? Proceeding as we did in Example 5, we have

$$\lim_{x \to c}(x^2 - 4x) = c \cdot c - 4 \cdot c = c^2 - 4c$$

If we let $f(x) = x^2 - 4x$, we have

$$\lim_{x \to c} f(x) = \lim_{x \to c}(x^2 - 4x) = c^2 - 4c = f(c)$$

That is, this limit can be evaluated simply by evaluating the function f at c. It would certainly simplify the process of evaluating limits if we could identify the functions for which

$$\lim_{x \to c} f(x) = f(c) \tag{1}$$

since we could use this fact to evaluate the limit. It turns out that there are many functions that satisfy equation (1). We postpone a detailed discussion of these functions until the next section. For now, we note that if

$$f(x) = a_n x^n + a_{n-1} x^{n-1} + \cdots + a_0$$

is a polynomial function, the properties in Theorem 1 imply that

$$\lim_{x \to c} f(x) = \lim_{x \to c}(a_n x^n + a_{n-1} x^{n-1} + \cdots + a_0)$$
$$= a_n c^n + a_{n-1} c^{n-1} + \cdots + a_0 = f(c)$$

And if

$$r(x) = \frac{n(x)}{d(x)}$$

is a rational function, where $n(x)$ and $d(x)$ are polynomials, $d(c) \neq 0$, then using property 5 and the fact that polynomials $n(x)$ and $d(x)$ satisfy equation (1), we have

$$\lim_{x \to c} r(x) = \lim_{x \to c} \frac{n(x)}{d(x)} = \frac{\lim_{x \to c} n(x)}{\lim_{x \to c} d(x)} = \frac{n(c)}{d(c)} = r(c)$$

These results are summarized in Theorem 3.

THEOREM 3   **Limits of Polynomial and Rational Functions**

1. $\lim_{x \to c} f(x) = f(c)$ f any polynomial function

2. $\lim_{x \to c} r(x) = r(c)$ r any rational function with a nonzero denominator at $x = c$

EXAMPLE 6   **Evaluating Limits**   Find each limit:

(A) $\lim_{x \to 2}(x^3 - 5x - 1)$ (B) $\lim_{x \to -1} \sqrt{2x^2 + 3}$ (C) $\lim_{x \to 4} \dfrac{2x}{3x + 1}$

Solution   (A) $\lim\limits_{x\to 2}(x^3 - 5x - 1) = 2^3 - 5\cdot 2 - 1 = -3$ Theorem 3

(B) $\lim\limits_{x\to -1}\sqrt{2x^2 + 3} = \sqrt{\lim\limits_{x\to -1}(2x^2 + 3)}$ Property 6

$= \sqrt{2(-1)^2 + 3}$ Theorem 3

$= \sqrt{5}$

(C) $\lim\limits_{x\to 4}\dfrac{2x}{3x + 1} = \dfrac{2\cdot 4}{3\cdot 4 + 1}$ Theorem 3

$= \dfrac{8}{13}$

Matched Problem 6   Find each limit:

(A) $\lim\limits_{x\to -1}(x^4 - 2x + 3)$ (B) $\lim\limits_{x\to 2}\sqrt{3x^2 - 6}$ (C) $\lim\limits_{x\to -2}\dfrac{x^2}{x^2 + 1}$

EXAMPLE 7   Evaluating Limits   Let

$$f(x) = \begin{cases} x^2 + 1 & \text{if } x < 2 \\ x - 1 & \text{if } x > 2 \end{cases}$$

Find

(A) $\lim\limits_{x\to 2^-} f(x)$ (B) $\lim\limits_{x\to 2^+} f(x)$ (C) $\lim\limits_{x\to 2} f(x)$ (D) $f(2)$

Solution   (A) $\lim\limits_{x\to 2^-} f(x) = \lim\limits_{x\to 2^-}(x^2 + 1)$ If $x < 2$, $f(x) = x^2 + 1$.

$= 2^2 + 1 = 5$

(B) $\lim\limits_{x\to 2^+} f(x) = \lim\limits_{x\to 2^+}(x - 1)$ If $x > 2$, $f(x) = x - 1$.

$= 2 - 1 = 1$

(C) Since the one-sided limits are not equal, $\lim\limits_{x\to 2} f(x)$ does not exist.

(D) Because the definition of f does not assign a value to f for $x = 2$, only for $x < 2$ and $x > 2$, $f(2)$ does not exist.

Matched Problem 7   Evaluating Limits

Let

$$f(x) = \begin{cases} 2x + 3 & \text{if } x < 5 \\ -x + 12 & \text{if } x > 5 \end{cases}$$

Find

(A) $\lim\limits_{x\to 5^-} f(x)$ (B) $\lim\limits_{x\to 5^+} f(x)$ (C) $\lim\limits_{x\to 5} f(x)$ (D) $f(5)$

It is important to note that there are restrictions on some of the limit properties. In particular, if

$$\lim_{x\to c} f(x) = 0 \quad\text{and}\quad \lim_{x\to c} g(x) = 0, \quad\text{then finding } \lim_{x\to c}\frac{f(x)}{g(x)}$$

may present some difficulties since limit property 5 (the limit of a quotient) does not apply when $\lim\limits_{x\to c} g(x) = 0$. The next example illustrates some techniques that can be useful in this situation.

EXAMPLE 8   **Evaluating Limits**   Find each limit:

(A) $\lim\limits_{x \to 2} \dfrac{x^2 - 4}{x - 2}$

(B) $\lim\limits_{x \to -1} \dfrac{x|x + 1|}{x + 1}$

Solution   (A) Algebraic simplification is often useful when the numerator and denominator are both approaching 0.

$$\lim_{x \to 2} \frac{x^2 - 4}{x - 2} = \lim_{x \to 2} \frac{(x - 2)(x + 2)}{x - 2} = \lim_{x \to 2}(x + 2) = 4$$

(B) One-sided limits are helpful for limits involving the absolute value function.

$$\lim_{x \to -1^+} \frac{x|x + 1|}{x + 1} = \lim_{x \to -1^+}(x) = -1 \quad \text{If } x > -1, \text{ then } \frac{|x + 1|}{x + 1} = 1.$$

$$\lim_{x \to -1^-} \frac{x|x + 1|}{x + 1} = \lim_{x \to -1^-}(-x) = 1 \quad \text{If } x < -1, \text{ then } \frac{|x + 1|}{x + 1} = -1.$$

Since the limit from the left and the limit from the right are not the same, we conclude that

$$\lim_{x \to -1} \frac{x|x + 1|}{x + 1} \quad \text{does not exist}$$

Matched Problem 8   Find each limit:

(A) $\lim\limits_{x \to -3} \dfrac{x^2 + 4x + 3}{x + 3}$ (B) $\lim\limits_{x \to 4} \dfrac{x^2 - 16}{|x - 4|}$

◉ Insight   In the solution for part A of Example 8, we used the following algebraic identity:

$$\frac{x^2 - 4}{x - 2} = \frac{(x - 2)(x + 2)}{x - 2} = x + 2 \qquad x \neq 2$$

The restriction $x \neq 2$ is necessary here because the first two expressions are not defined at $x = 2$. Why didn't we include this restriction in the solution in part A? When x approaches 2 in a limit problem, it is assumed that x is close to 2 but not equal to 2. It is important that you understand that both of the following statements are valid:

$$\lim_{x \to 2} \frac{x^2 - 4}{x - 2} = \lim_{x \to 2}(x + 2) \qquad \frac{x^2 - 4}{x - 2} = x + 2, \quad x \neq 2$$

Limits like those in Example 8 occur so frequently in calculus that they are given a special name.

DEFINITION   **Indeterminate Form**

If $\lim\limits_{x \to c} f(x) = 0$ and $\lim\limits_{x \to c} g(x) = 0$, then $\lim\limits_{x \to c} \dfrac{f(x)}{g(x)}$ is said to be **indeterminate,** or, more specifically, a **0/0 indeterminate form.**

The term *indeterminate* is used because the limit of an indeterminate form may or may not exist (see parts A and B of Example 8).

CAUTION The expression $0/0$ does not represent a real number and should never be used as the value of a limit. If a limit is a $0/0$ indeterminate form, further investigation is always required to determine whether the limit exists and to find its value, if it does exist.

If the denominator of a quotient approaches 0 and the numerator approaches a nonzero number, the limit of the quotient is not an indeterminate form. In fact, a limit of this form never exists, as Theorem 4 states.

THEOREM 4   **Limit of a Quotient**

If $\lim\limits_{x \to c} f(x) = L$, $L \neq 0$ and $\lim\limits_{x \to c} g(x) = 0$,

then

$$\lim\limits_{x \to c} \frac{f(x)}{g(x)} \qquad \text{does not exist.}$$

EXPLORE & DISCUSS 2

Use algebraic and/or graphical techniques to analyze each of the following indeterminate forms:

(A) $\lim\limits_{x \to 1} \dfrac{x - 1}{x^2 - 1}$ (B) $\lim\limits_{x \to 1} \dfrac{(x - 1)^2}{x^2 - 1}$ (C) $\lim\limits_{x \to 1} \dfrac{x^2 - 1}{(x - 1)^2}$

➤ Limits of Difference Quotients

Let the function f be defined in a open interval containing the number a. One of the most important limits in calculus is the limit of the **difference quotient:**

$$\lim\limits_{h \to 0} \frac{f(a + h) - f(a)}{h} \tag{3}$$

If

$$\lim\limits_{h \to 0} [f(a + h) - f(a)] = 0$$

as it often does, then limit (3) is an indeterminate form. The following examples illustrate some useful techniques for evaluating limits of difference quotients.

EXAMPLE 9   **Limit of a Difference Quotient**   Find the following limit for $f(x) = 4x - 5$.

$$\lim\limits_{h \to 0} \frac{f(3 + h) - f(3)}{h}$$

Solution

$$\lim\limits_{h \to 0} \frac{f(3 + h) - f(3)}{h} = \lim\limits_{h \to 0} \frac{[4(\mathbf{3 + h}) - 5] - [4(\mathbf{3}) - 5]}{h}$$

$$= \lim\limits_{h \to 0} \frac{12 + 4h - 5 - 12 + 5}{h}$$

$$= \lim\limits_{h \to 0} \frac{4h}{h} = \lim\limits_{h \to 0} 4 = 4$$

Since this is a $0/0$ indeterminate form and property 5 in Theorem 2 does not apply, we proceed with algebraic simplification.

Matched Problem 9   Find the following limit for $f(x) = 7 - 2x$: $\lim\limits_{h \to 0} \dfrac{f(4 + h) - f(4)}{h}$.

EXPLORE
&DISCUSS
3

The following is an incorrect solution to Example 9 with the invalid statements indicated by $\neq$. Explain why each $\neq$ is used.

$$\lim_{h \to 0} \frac{f(3 + h) - f(3)}{h} \neq \lim_{h \to 0} \frac{4(3 + h) - 5 - 4(3) - 5}{h}$$

$$= \lim_{h \to 0} \frac{-10 + 4h}{h}$$

$$\neq \lim_{h \to 0} \frac{-10 + 4}{1} = -6$$

EXAMPLE 10 **Limit of a Difference Quotient** Find the following limit for $f(x) = |x + 5|$.

$$\lim_{h \to 0} \frac{f(-5 + h) - f(-5)}{h}$$

Solution

$$\lim_{h \to 0} \frac{f(-5 + h) - f(-5)}{h} = \lim_{h \to 0} \frac{|(-5 + h) + 5| - |-5 + 5|}{h}$$

$$= \lim_{h \to 0} \frac{|h|}{h} \quad \text{does not exist}$$

Since this is a 0/0 indeterminate form and property 5 in Theorem 2 does not apply, we proceed with algebraic simplification.

Matched Problem 10 Find the following limit for $f(x) = |x - 1|$: $\lim_{h \to 0} \dfrac{f(1 + h) - f(1)}{h}$.

EXAMPLE 11 **Limit of a Difference Quotient** Find the following limit for $f(x) = \sqrt{x}$.

$$\lim_{h \to 0} \frac{f(2 + h) - f(2)}{h}$$

Solution

$$\lim_{h \to 0} \frac{f(2 + h) - f(2)}{h} = \lim_{h \to 0} \frac{\sqrt{2 + h} - \sqrt{2}}{h}$$

$$= \lim_{h \to 0} \frac{\sqrt{2 + h} - \sqrt{2}}{h} \cdot \frac{\sqrt{2 + h} + \sqrt{2}}{\sqrt{2 + h} + \sqrt{2}} \quad (A - B)(A + B) = A^2 - B^2$$

$$= \lim_{h \to 0} \frac{2 + h - 2}{h(\sqrt{2 + h} + \sqrt{2})}$$

$$= \lim_{h \to 0} \frac{1}{\sqrt{2 + h} + \sqrt{2}}$$

$$= \frac{1}{\sqrt{2} + \sqrt{2}} = \frac{1}{2\sqrt{2}}$$

This is 0/0 indeterminate form, so property 5 in Theorem 2 does not apply. Rationalizing the numerator will be of help.

Matched Problem 11 Find the following limit for $f(x) = \sqrt{x}$: $\lim_{h \to 0} \dfrac{f(3 + h) - f(3)}{h}$.

Answers to Matched Problems **1.**

x	-2	-1	0	1	2	3	4
$h(x)$	1.0	1.5	2.0	2.5	3.0	3.5	4.0

2. $\lim_{x \to 1} f(x) = 2$

3. $h(x)$

$h(x) = \dfrac{x-2}{|x-2|}$

$\lim_{x \to 2} \dfrac{x-2}{|x-2|}$ does not exist

4. (A) $\lim_{x \to 0^-} f(x) = 0$

$\lim_{x \to 0^+} f(x) = 0$

$\lim_{x \to 0} f(x) = 0$

$f(0) = 0$

(B) $\lim_{x \to 1^-} f(x) = 1$

$\lim_{x \to 1^+} f(x) = 2$

$\lim_{x \to 1} f(x)$ does not exist

$f(1)$ not defined

(C) $\lim_{x \to 3^-} f(x) = 3$

$\lim_{x \to 3^+} f(x) = 3$

$\lim_{x \to 3} f(x) = 3$

$f(3)$ not defined

5. -6

6. (A) 6
(B) $\sqrt{6}$
(C) $\frac{4}{5}$

7. (A) 13
(B) 7
(C) Does not exist
(D) Not defined

8. (A) -2
(B) Does not exist

9. -2 **10.** Does not exist   **11.** $1/(2\sqrt{3})$

Exercise 3-1

A *In Problems 1–4, use the graph of the function f shown below to estimate the indicated limits and function values.*

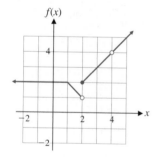

1. (A) $\lim_{x \to 0^-} f(x)$ (B) $\lim_{x \to 0^+} f(x)$

(C) $\lim_{x \to 0} f(x)$ (D) $f(0)$

2. (A) $\lim_{x \to 1^-} f(x)$ (B) $\lim_{x \to 1^+} f(x)$

(C) $\lim_{x \to 1} f(x)$ (D) $f(1)$

3. (A) $\lim_{x \to 2^-} f(x)$ (B) $\lim_{x \to 2^+} f(x)$

(C) $\lim_{x \to 2} f(x)$ (D) $f(2)$

(E) Is it possible to redefine $f(2)$ so that $\lim_{x \to 2} f(x) = f(2)$? Explain.

4. (A) $\lim_{x \to 4^-} f(x)$ (B) $\lim_{x \to 4^+} f(x)$

(C) $\lim_{x \to 4} f(x)$ (D) $f(4)$

(E) Is it possible to define $f(4)$ so that $\lim_{x \to 4} f(x) = f(4)$? Explain.

In Problems 5–8, use the graph of the function g shown below to estimate the indicated limits and function values.

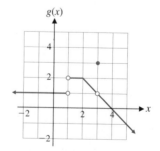

5. (A) $\lim_{x \to 1^-} g(x)$ (B) $\lim_{x \to 1^+} g(x)$

(C) $\lim_{x \to 1} g(x)$ (D) $g(1)$

(E) Is it possible to define $g(1)$ so that $\lim_{x \to 1} g(x) = g(1)$? Explain.

6. (A) $\lim\limits_{x\to2^-} g(x)$　(B) $\lim\limits_{x\to2^+} g(x)$

(C) $\lim\limits_{x\to2} g(x)$　(D) $g(2)$

7. (A) $\lim\limits_{x\to3^-} g(x)$　(B) $\lim\limits_{x\to3^+} g(x)$

(C) $\lim\limits_{x\to3} g(x)$　(D) $g(3)$

(E) Is it possible to redefine $g(3)$ so that $\lim\limits_{x\to3} g(x) = g(3)$? Explain.

8. (A) $\lim\limits_{x\to4^-} g(x)$　(B) $\lim\limits_{x\to4^+} g(x)$

(C) $\lim\limits_{x\to4} g(x)$　(D) $g(4)$

In Problems 9–12, use the graph of the function f shown below to estimate the indicated limits and function values.

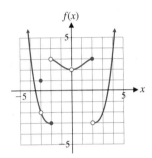

9. (A) $\lim\limits_{x\to-3^+} f(x)$　(B) $\lim\limits_{x\to-3^-} f(x)$

(C) $\lim\limits_{x\to-3} f(x)$　(D) $f(-3)$

(E) Is it possible to redefine $f(-3)$ so that $\lim\limits_{x\to-3} f(x) = f(-3)$? Explain.

10. (A) $\lim\limits_{x\to-2^+} f(x)$　(B) $\lim\limits_{x\to-2^-} f(x)$

(C) $\lim\limits_{x\to-2} f(x)$　(D) $f(-2)$

(E) Is it possible to define $f(-2)$ so that $\lim\limits_{x\to-2} f(x) = f(-2)$? Explain.

11. (A) $\lim\limits_{x\to0^+} f(x)$　(B) $\lim\limits_{x\to0^-} f(x)$

(C) $\lim\limits_{x\to0} f(x)$　(D) $f(0)$

(E) Is it possible to redefine $f(0)$ so that $\lim\limits_{x\to0} f(x) = f(0)$? Explain.

12. (A) $\lim\limits_{x\to2^+} f(x)$　(B) $\lim\limits_{x\to2^-} f(x)$

(C) $\lim\limits_{x\to2} f(x)$　(D) $f(2)$

(E) Is it possible to redefine $f(2)$ so that $\lim\limits_{x\to2} f(x) = f(2)$? Explain.

In Problems 13–22, find each limit, if it exists.

13. $\lim\limits_{x\to3} 4x$　**14.** $\lim\limits_{x\to-2} 3x$

15. $\lim\limits_{x\to-4} (x + 5)$　**16.** $\lim\limits_{x\to5} (x - 3)$

17. $\lim\limits_{x\to2} x(x - 4)$　**18.** $\lim\limits_{x\to-1} x(x + 3)$

19. $\lim\limits_{x\to-3} \dfrac{x}{x + 5}$　**20.** $\lim\limits_{x\to4} \dfrac{x - 2}{x}$

21. $\lim\limits_{x\to1} \sqrt{5x + 4}$　**22.** $\lim\limits_{x\to0} \sqrt{16 - 7x}$

Given $\lim\limits_{x\to1} f(x) = -5$ and $\lim\limits_{x\to1} g(x) = 4$, find the indicated limits in Problems 23–34.

23. $\lim\limits_{x\to1} (-3)f(x)$　**24.** $\lim\limits_{x\to1} 2g(x)$

25. $\lim\limits_{x\to1} [2f(x) + g(x)]$　**26.** $\lim\limits_{x\to1} [g(x) - 3f(x)]$

27. $\lim\limits_{x\to1} \dfrac{2 - f(x)}{x + g(x)}$　**28.** $\lim\limits_{x\to1} \dfrac{3 - f(x)}{1 - 4g(x)}$

29. $\lim\limits_{x\to1} f(x)[2 - g(x)]$　**30.** $\lim\limits_{x\to1} [f(x) - 7x]g(x)$

31. $\lim\limits_{x\to1} \sqrt{g(x) - f(x)}$　**32.** $\lim\limits_{x\to1} \sqrt[3]{2x + 2f(x)}$

16

$f^2 + 2f + 1$

33. $\lim\limits_{x\to1} [f(x) + 1]^2$　**34.** $\lim\limits_{x\to1} [2 - g(x)]^3$

In Problems 35–38, sketch a possible graph of a function that satisfies the given conditions.

35. $f(0) = 1$; $\lim\limits_{x\to0^-} f(x) = 3$; $\lim\limits_{x\to0^+} f(x) = 1$

36. $f(1) = -2$; $\lim\limits_{x\to1^-} f(x) = 2$; $\lim\limits_{x\to1^+} f(x) = -2$

37. $f(-2) = 2$; $\lim\limits_{x\to-2^-} f(x) = 1$; $\lim\limits_{x\to-2^+} f(x) = 1$

38. $f(0) = -1$; $\lim\limits_{x\to0^-} f(x) = 2$; $\lim\limits_{x\to0^+} f(x) = 2$

B *In Problems 39–54, find each indicated quantity, if it exists.*

39. Let $f(x) = \begin{cases} 1 - x^2 & \text{if } x \le 0 \\ 1 + x^2 & \text{if } x > 0 \end{cases}$. Find

(A) $\lim\limits_{x\to0^+} f(x)$　(B) $\lim\limits_{x\to0^-} f(x)$

(C) $\lim\limits_{x\to0} f(x)$　(D) $f(0)$

40. Let $f(x) = \begin{cases} 2 + x & \text{if } x \le 0 \\ 2 - x & \text{if } x > 0 \end{cases}$. Find

(A) $\lim\limits_{x\to0^+} f(x)$　(B) $\lim\limits_{x\to0^-} f(x)$

(C) $\lim\limits_{x\to0} f(x)$　(D) $f(0)$

41. Let $f(x) = \begin{cases} x^2 & \text{if } x < 1 \\ 2x & \text{if } x > 1 \end{cases}$. Find

(A) $\lim\limits_{x\to1^+} f(x)$　(B) $\lim\limits_{x\to1^-} f(x)$

(C) $\lim\limits_{x\to1} f(x)$　(D) $f(1)$

42. Let $f(x) = \begin{cases} x + 3 & \text{if } x < -2 \\ \sqrt{x + 2} & \text{if } x > -2 \end{cases}$. Find

(A) $\lim\limits_{x\to-2^+} f(x)$　(B) $\lim\limits_{x\to-2^-} f(x)$

(C) $\lim\limits_{x\to-2} f(x)$　(D) $f(-2)$

43. Let $f(x) = \begin{cases} \dfrac{x^2 - 9}{x + 3} & \text{if } x < 0 \\ \dfrac{x^2 - 9}{x - 3} & \text{if } x > 0 \end{cases}$. Find

(A) $\lim\limits_{x \to -3} f(x)$ (B) $\lim\limits_{x \to 0} f(x)$

(C) $\lim\limits_{x \to 3} f(x)$

44. Let $f(x) = \begin{cases} \dfrac{x}{x + 3} & \text{if } x < 0 \\ \dfrac{x}{x - 3} & \text{if } x > 0 \end{cases}$. Find

(A) $\lim\limits_{x \to -3} f(x)$ (B) $\lim\limits_{x \to 0} f(x)$

(C) $\lim\limits_{x \to 3} f(x)$

45. Let $f(x) = \dfrac{|x - 1|}{x - 1}$. Find

(A) $\lim\limits_{x \to 1^-} f(x)$ (B) $\lim\limits_{x \to 1^+} f(x)$

(C) $\lim\limits_{x \to 1} f(x)$ (D) $f(1)$

46. Let $f(x) = \dfrac{x - 3}{|x - 3|}$. Find

(A) $\lim\limits_{x \to 3^+} f(x)$ (B) $\lim\limits_{x \to 3^-} f(x)$

(C) $\lim\limits_{x \to 3} f(x)$ (D) $f(3)$

47. Let $f(x) = \dfrac{x - 2}{x^2 - 2x}$. Find

(A) $\lim\limits_{x \to 0} f(x)$ (B) $\lim\limits_{x \to 2} f(x)$

(C) $\lim\limits_{x \to 4} f(x)$

48. Let $f(x) = \dfrac{x + 3}{x^2 + 3x}$. Find

(A) $\lim\limits_{x \to -3} f(x)$ (B) $\lim\limits_{x \to 0} f(x)$

(C) $\lim\limits_{x \to 3} f(x)$

49. Let $f(x) = \dfrac{x^2 - x - 6}{x + 2}$. Find

(A) $\lim\limits_{x \to -2} f(x)$ (B) $\lim\limits_{x \to 0} f(x)$

(C) $\lim\limits_{x \to 3} f(x)$

50. Let $f(x) = \dfrac{x^2 + x - 6}{x + 3}$. Find

(A) $\lim\limits_{x \to -3} f(x)$ (B) $\lim\limits_{x \to 0} f(x)$

(C) $\lim\limits_{x \to 2} f(x)$

51. Let $f(x) = \dfrac{(x + 2)^2}{x^2 - 4}$. Find

(A) $\lim\limits_{x \to -2} f(x)$ (B) $\lim\limits_{x \to 0} f(x)$

(C) $\lim\limits_{x \to 2} f(x)$

52. Let $f(x) = \dfrac{x^2 - 1}{(x + 1)^2}$. Find

(A) $\lim\limits_{x \to -1} f(x)$ (B) $\lim\limits_{x \to 0} f(x)$

(C) $\lim\limits_{x \to 1} f(x)$

53. Let $f(x) = \dfrac{2x^2 - 3x - 2}{x^2 + x - 6}$. Find

(A) $\lim\limits_{x \to 2} f(x)$ (B) $\lim\limits_{x \to 0} f(x)$

(C) $\lim\limits_{x \to 1} f(x)$

54. Let $f(x) = \dfrac{3x^2 + 2x - 1}{x^2 + 3x + 2}$. Find

(A) $\lim\limits_{x \to -3} f(x)$ (B) $\lim\limits_{x \to -1} f(x)$

(C) $\lim\limits_{x \to 2} f(x)$

Compute the following limit for each function in Problems 55–64:

$$\lim_{h \to 0} \frac{f(2 + h) - f(2)}{h}$$

55. $f(x) = 3x + 1$ **56.** $f(x) = 5x - 1$

57. $f(x) = x^2 + 1$ **58.** $f(x) = x^2 - 2$

59. $f(x) = \sqrt{x} - 2$ **60.** $f(x) = 1 + \sqrt{x}$

61. $f(x) = |x - 2| - 3$ **62.** $f(x) = 2 + |x - 2|$

63. $f(x) = \dfrac{2}{x - 1}$ **64.** $f(x) = \dfrac{1}{x + 2}$

C

65. Let f be defined by

$$f(x) = \begin{cases} 1 + mx & \text{if } x \le 1 \\ 4 - mx & \text{if } x > 1 \end{cases}$$

where m is a constant.

(A) Graph f for $m = 1$, and find

$$\lim_{x \to 1^-} f(x) \quad \text{and} \quad \lim_{x \to 1^+} f(x)$$

(B) Graph f for $m = 2$, and find

$$\lim_{x \to 1^-} f(x) \quad \text{and} \quad \lim_{x \to 1^+} f(x)$$

(C) Find m so that

$$\lim_{x \to 1^-} f(x) = \lim_{x \to 1^+} f(x)$$

and graph f for this value of m.

(D) Write a brief verbal description of each graph. How does the graph in part (C) differ from the graphs in parts (A) and (B)?

66. Let f be defined by

$$f(x) = \begin{cases} -3m + 0.5x & \text{if } x \le 2 \\ 3m - x & \text{if } x > 2 \end{cases}$$

where m is a constant.

(A) Graph f for $m = 0$, and find

$$\lim_{x \to 2^-} f(x) \quad \text{and} \quad \lim_{x \to 2^+} f(x)$$

(B) Graph f for $m = 1$, and find

$$\lim_{x \to 2^-} f(x) \quad \text{and} \quad \lim_{x \to 2^+} f(x)$$

(C) Find m so that

$$\lim_{x \to 2^-} f(x) = \lim_{x \to 2^+} f(x)$$

and graph f for this value of m.

(D) Write a brief verbal description of each graph. How does the graph in part (C) differ from the graphs in parts (A) and (B)?

Find each limit in Problems 67–70, where a is a real constant.

67. $\lim_{h \to 0} \dfrac{(a + h)^2 - a^2}{h}$

68. $\lim_{h \to 0} \dfrac{[3(a + h) - 2] - (3a - 2)}{h}$

69. $\lim_{h \to 0} \dfrac{\sqrt{a + h} - \sqrt{a}}{h}, \quad a > 0$

70. $\lim_{h \to 0} \dfrac{\dfrac{1}{a + h} - \dfrac{1}{a}}{h}, \quad a \neq 0$

Applications

Business & Economics

71. *Telephone rates.* A 10-10 long-distance telephone service charges $0.99 for the first 20 minutes or less of a state-to-state call and $0.07 for each additional minute or fraction thereof.

(A) Write a piecewise definition of the charge $F(x)$ for a state-to-state long-distance call lasting x minutes.

(B) Graph $F(x)$ for $0 < x \leq 40$.

(C) Find $\lim_{x \to 20^-} F(x)$, $\lim_{x \to 20^+} F(x)$, and $\lim_{x \to 20} F(x)$, whichever exist.

72. *Telephone rates.* A second 10-10 long-distance telephone service charges $0.09 per minute or fraction thereof for calls lasting 10 minutes or more and $0.18 per minute or fraction thereof for calls lasting less than 10 minutes.

(A) Write a piecewise definition of the charge $G(x)$ for a state-to-state long-distance call lasting x minutes.

(B) Graph $G(x)$ for $0 < x \leq 40$.

(C) Find $\lim_{x \to 10^-} G(x)$, $\lim_{x \to 10^+} G(x)$, and $\lim_{x \to 10} G(x)$, whichever exist.

73. *Telephone rates.* Refer to Problems 71 and 72. Write a brief verbal comparison of these two services for calls lasting 20 minutes or less.

74. *Telephone rates.* Refer to Problems 71 and 72. Write a brief verbal comparison of these two services for calls lasting more than 20 minutes.

A company sells custom embroidered apparel and promotional products. The table shows the volume discounts offered by the company, where x is the volume of a purchase in dollars. Problems 75 and 76 deal with two different interpretations of this discount method.

Volume Discount (Excluding Tax)	
Volume ($x)	**Discount Amount**
$300 $\leq x <$ $1,000	3%
$1,000 $\leq x <$ $3,000	5%
$3,000 $\leq x <$ $5,000	7%
$5,000 $\leq x$	10%

75. *Volume discount.* Assume that the volume discounts in the table apply to the entire purchase. That is, if the volume x satisfies $300 \leq x < $1,000, the entire purchase is discounted 3%. If the volume x satisfies $1,000 \leq x < $3,000 the entire purchase is discounted 5% and so on.

(A) If x is the volume of a purchase before the discount is applied, write a piecewise definition for the discounted price $D(x)$ of this purchase.

(B) Use one-sided limits to investigate the limit of $D(x)$ as x approaches $1,000. As x approaches $3,000.

76. *Volume discount.* Assume that the volume discounts in the table apply only to that portion of the volume in each interval in the table. That is, the discounted price for a $4,000 purchase would be computed as follows:

$$300 + 0.97(700) + 0.95(2,000) + 0.93(1,000) = 3,809$$

(A) If x is the volume of a purchase before the discount is applied, write a piecewise definition for the discounted price $P(x)$ of this purchase.

(B) Use one-sided limits to investigate the limit of $P(x)$ as x approaches $1,000. As x approaches $3,000.

(C) Compare this discount method with the one in Problem 85. Does one always produce a lower price than the other? Discuss.

Life Sciences

77. *Pollution.* A state charges polluters an annual fee of $20 per ton for each ton of pollutant emitted into the atmosphere, up to a maximum of 4,000 tons. No fees are charged for emissions beyond the 4,000-ton limit. Write a piecewise definition of the fees $F(x)$ charged for the emission of x tons of pollutant in a year. What is the limit of $F(x)$ as x approaches 4,000 tons? As x approaches 8,000 tons?

78. *Pollution.* Refer to Problem 77. The fee per ton of pollution is given by $A(x) = F(x)/x$. Write a piecewise definition of $A(x)$. What is the limit of $A(x)$ as x approaches 4,000 tons? As x approaches 8,000 tons?

Social Sciences

79. *Voter turnout.* Statisticians often use piecewise-defined functions to predict outcomes of elections. For the functions f and g given next, find the limit of each function as x approaches 5 and as x approaches 10.

$$f(x) = \begin{cases} 0 & \text{if } x \leq 5 \\ 0.8 - 0.08x & \text{if } 5 < x < 10 \\ 0 & \text{if } 10 \leq x \end{cases}$$

$$g(x) = \begin{cases} 0 & \text{if } x \leq 5 \\ 0.8x - 0.04x^2 - 3 & \text{if } 5 < x < 10 \\ 1 & \text{if } 10 \leq x \end{cases}$$

Section 3-2 | Continuity

➤ Continuity
➤ Continuity Properties
➤ Solving Inequalities Using Continuity Properties

Theorem 3 in Section 3-1 states that if f is a polynomial function or a rational function with a nonzero denominator at $x = c$, then

$$\lim_{x \to c} f(x) = f(c) \qquad (1)$$

Functions that satisfy equation (1) are said to be *continuous* at $x = c$. A firm understanding of continuous functions is essential for sketching and analyzing graphs. We will also see that continuity properties provide a simple and efficient method for solving inequalities, a tool that we will use extensively in later sections.

➤ Continuity

Compare the graphs shown in Figure 1. Notice that two of the graphs are broken; that is, they cannot be drawn without lifting a pen off the paper. Informally, a function is *continuous over an interval* if its graph over the interval can be drawn without removing a pen from the paper. A function whose graph

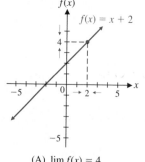

(A) $\lim_{x \to 2} f(x) = 4$
$f(2) = 4$

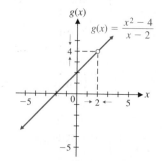

(B) $\lim_{x \to 2} g(x) = 4$
$g(2)$ is not defined

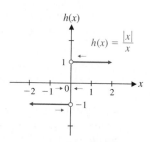

(C) $\lim_{x \to 0} h(x)$ does not exist
$h(0)$ is not defined

FIGURE 1

is broken (disconnected) at $x = c$ is said to be *discontinuous* at $x = c$. Function f (Fig. 1A) is continuous for all x. Function g (Fig. 1B) is discontinuous at $x = 2$, but is continuous over any interval that does not include 2. Function h (Fig. 1C) is discontinuous at $x = 0$, but is continuous over any interval that does not include 0.

Most graphs of natural phenomena are continuous, whereas many graphs in business and economics applications have discontinuities. Figure 2A illustrates temperature variation over a 24-hour period—a continuous phenomenon. Figure 2B illustrates warehouse inventory over a 1-week period—a discontinuous phenomenon.

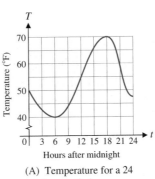

(A) Temperature for a 24 hour period

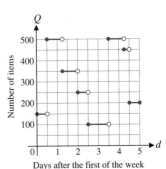

(B) Inventory in a warehouse during 1 week

FIGURE 2

EXPLORE & DISCUSS 1

(A) Write a brief verbal description of the temperature variation illustrated in Figure 2A, including estimates of the high and low temperatures during this period and the times at which they occurred.

(B) Write a brief verbal description of the changes in inventory illustrated in Figure 2B, including estimates of the changes in inventory and the times at which these changes occurred.

The preceding discussion leads to the following formal definition of continuity:

DEFINITION   Continuity

A function f is **continuous at the point $x = c$** if

1. $\lim\limits_{x \to c} f(x)$ exists   **2.** $f(c)$ exists   **3.** $\lim\limits_{x \to c} f(x) = f(c)$

A function is **continuous on the open interval* (a, b)** if it is continuous at each point on the interval.

---

* See Appendix A-7 for a review of interval notation.

If one or more of the three conditions in the definition fails, the function is **discontinuous** at $x = c$.

EXPLORE & DISCUSS 2

Sketch a graph of a function that is discontinuous at a point because it fails to satisfy condition 1 in the definition of continuity. Repeat for conditions 2 and 3.

EXAMPLE 1   **Continuity of a Function Defined by a Graph**   Use the definition of continuity to discuss the continuity of the function whose graph is shown in Figure 3.

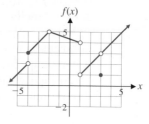

FIGURE 3

Solution   We begin by identifying the points of discontinuity. Examining the graph, we see breaks and/or holes in the graph at $x = -4, -2, 1,$ and 3. Now we must determine which conditions in the definition of continuity are not satisfied at each of these points. In each case, we find the value of the function and the limit of the function at the point in question.

Discontinuity at $x = -4$:
$$\lim_{x \to -4^-} f(x) = 2$$
$$\lim_{x \to -4^+} f(x) = 3$$

Since the one-sided limits are different, the limit does not exist (Section 3-1).

$$\lim_{x \to -4} f(x) \text{ does not exist}$$
$$f(-4) = 3$$

Thus, f is not continuous at $x = -4$ because condition 1 is not satisfied.

Discontinuity at $x = -2$:
$$\lim_{x \to -2^-} f(x) = 5$$
$$\lim_{x \to -2^+} f(x) = 5$$
$$\lim_{x \to -2} f(x) = 5$$

The hole at $(-2, 5)$ indicates that 5 is not the value of f at -2. Since there is no solid dot elsewhere on the vertical line $x = -2$, $f(-2)$ is not defined.

$$f(-2) \text{ does not exist}$$

Thus, f is not continuous at $x = -2$ because condition 2 is not satisfied.

Discontinuity at $x = 1$:
$$\lim_{x \to 1^-} f(x) = 4$$
$$\lim_{x \to 1^+} f(x) = 1$$
$$\lim_{x \to 1} f(x) \text{ does not exist}$$
$$f(1) \text{ does not exist}$$

This time, f is not continuous at $x = 1$ because both conditions 1 and 2 are not satisfied.

Discontinuity at $x = 3$:
$$\lim_{x \to 3^-} f(x) = 3$$
$$\lim_{x \to 3^+} f(x) = 3$$
$$\lim_{x \to 3} f(x) = 3$$

The solid dot at $(3, 1)$ indicates that $f(3) = 1$.

$$f(3) = 1$$

Conditions 1 and 2 are satisfied, but f is not continuous at $x = 3$ because condition 3 is not satisfied.

Having identified and discussed all points of discontinuity, we can now conclude that f is continuous except at $x = -4, -2, 1,$ and 3. ■

◉ **Insight**   Rather than list the points where a function is discontinuous, sometimes it is useful to state the intervals where the function is continuous. Using the set operation **union,** denoted by ∪, we can express the set of points where the function in Example 1 is continuous as follows:

$$(-\infty, -4) \cup (-4, -2) \cup (-2, 1) \cup (1, 3) \cup (3, \infty)$$ ●

Matched Problem 1   Use the definition of continuity to discuss the continuity of the function whose graph is shown in Figure 4.

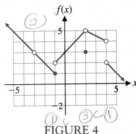

FIGURE 4

For functions defined by equations, it is also important to be able to locate points of discontinuity by examining the equation.

EXAMPLE 2   **Continuity of Functions Defined by Equations** Using the definition of continuity, discuss the continuity of each function at the indicated point (s).

(A) $f(x) = x + 2$ at $x = 2$ (B) $g(x) = \dfrac{x^2 - 4}{x - 2}$ at $x = 2$

(C) $h(x) = \dfrac{|x|}{x}$ at $x = 0$ and at $x = 1$

Solution   (A) f is continuous at $x = 2$, since

$$\lim_{x \to 2} f(x) = 4 = f(2)$$ See Figure 1A.

(B) g is not continuous at $x = 2$, since $g(2) = 0/0$ is not defined (see Fig. 1B).

(C) h is not continuous at $x = 0$, since $h(0) = |0|/0$ is not defined; also, $\lim_{x \to 0} h(x)$ does not exist.

h is continuous at $x = 1$, since

$$\lim_{x \to 1} \frac{|x|}{x} = 1 = h(1)$$ See Figure 1C.   ■

Matched Problem 2   Using the definition of continuity, discuss the continuity of each function at the indicated point (s).

(A) $f(x) = x + 1$ at $x = 1$ (B) $g(x) = \dfrac{x^2 - 1}{x - 1}$ at $x = 1$

(C) $h(x) = \dfrac{x - 2}{|x - 2|}$ at $x = 2$ and at $x = 0$

We can also talk about one-sided continuity, just as we talked about one-sided limits. For example, a function is said to be **continuous on the right** at $x = c$ if $\lim_{x \to c^+} f(x) = f(c)$ and **continuous on the left** at $x = c$ if $\lim_{x \to c^-} f(x) = f(c)$. A function is **continuous on the closed interval [a, b]** if it is continuous on the open interval (a, b) and is continuous on the right at a and continuous on the left at b.

Figure 5A illustrates a function that is continuous on the closed interval $[-1, 1]$. Figure 5B illustrates a function that is continuous on a half-closed interval $[0, \infty)$.

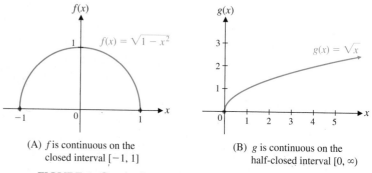

(A) f is continuous on the
closed interval $[-1, 1]$

(B) g is continuous on the
half-closed interval $[0, \infty)$

FIGURE 5 Continuity on closed and half-closed intervals

➤ Continuity Properties

Functions have some useful **general continuity properties:**

> **If two functions are continuous on the same interval, then their sum, difference, product, and quotient are continuous on the same interval, except for values of x that make a denominator 0.**

These properties, along with Theorem 1 below, enable us to determine intervals of continuity for some important classes of functions without having to look at their graphs or use the three conditions in the definition.

THEOREM 1 Continuity Properties of Some Specific Functions

(A) A constant function $f(x) = k$, where k is a constant, is continuous for all x.

$f(x) = 7$ is continuous for all x.

(B) For n a positive integer, $f(x) = x^n$ is continuous for all x.

$f(x) = x^5$ is continuous for all x.

(C) A polynomial function is continuous for all x.

$2x^3 - 3x^2 + x - 5$ is continuous for all x.

(D) A rational function is continuous for all x except those values that make a denominator 0.

$\dfrac{x^2 + 1}{x - 1}$ is continuous for all x except $x = 1$, a value that makes the denominator 0.

(E) For n an odd positive integer greater than 1, $\sqrt[n]{f(x)}$ is continuous wherever $f(x)$ is continuous.

$\sqrt[3]{x^2}$ is continuous for all x.

(F) For n an even positive integer, $\sqrt[n]{f(x)}$ is continuous wherever $f(x)$ is continuous and nonnegative.

$\sqrt[4]{x}$ is continuous on the interval $[0, \infty)$.

Parts C and D of Theorem 1 are the same as Theorem 3 in Section 3-1. They are repeated here to emphasize their importance.

EXAMPLE 3 **Using Continuity Properties** Using Theorem 1 and the general properties of continuity, determine where each function is continuous.

(A) $f(x) = x^2 - 2x + 1$ (B) $f(x) = \dfrac{x}{(x + 2)(x - 3)}$

(C) $f(x) = \sqrt[3]{x^2 - 4}$ (D) $f(x) = \sqrt{x - 2}$

Solution (A) Since f is a polynomial function, f is continuous for all x.

(B) Since f is a rational function, f is continuous for all x except -2 and 3 (values that make the denominator 0).

(C) The polynomial function $x^2 - 4$ is continuous for all x. Since $n = 3$ is odd, f is continuous for all x.

(D) The polynomial function $x - 2$ is continuous for all x and nonnegative for $x \geq 2$. Since $n = 2$ is even, f is continuous for $x \geq 2$, or on the interval $[2, \infty)$.

Matched Problem 3 Using Theorem 1 and the general properties of continuity, determine where each function is continuous.

(A) $f(x) = x^4 + 2x^2 + 1$ (B) $f(x) = \dfrac{x^2}{(x + 1)(x - 4)}$

(C) $f(x) = \sqrt{x - 4}$ (D) $f(x) = \sqrt[3]{x^3 + 1}$

➤ Solving Inequalities Using Continuity Properties

One of the basic tools for analyzing graphs in calculus is a special line graph called a *sign chart*. We will make extensive use of these charts in later sections. In the following discussion, we use continuity properties to develop a simple and efficient procedure for constructing sign charts.

Suppose that a function f is continuous over the interval $(1,8)$ and $f(x) \neq 0$ for any x in $(1,8)$. Also suppose that $f(2) = 5$, a positive number. Is it possible for $f(x)$ to be negative for any x in the interval $(1,8)$? The answer is "no." If $f(7)$ were -3, for example, as shown in Figure 6, how would it be possible to join the points $(2,5)$ and $(7,-3)$ with the graph of a continuous function without crossing the x axis between 1 and 8 at least once? [Crossing the x axis would violate our assumption that $f(x) \neq 0$ for any x in $(1,8)$.] Thus, we conclude that $f(x)$ must be positive for all x in $(1,8)$. If $f(2)$ were negative, then, using the same type of reasoning, $f(x)$ would have to be negative over the entire interval $(1,8)$.

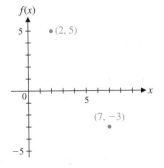

FIGURE 6

In general, **if f is continuous and $f(x) \neq 0$ on the interval (a, b), then $f(x)$ cannot change sign on (a, b).** This is the essence of Theorem 2.

THEOREM 2   Sign Properties on an Interval (a, b)

If f is continuous on (a, b) and $f(x) \neq 0$ for all x in (a, b), then either $f(x) > 0$ for all x in (a, b) or $f(x) < 0$ for all x in (a, b).

Theorem 2 provides the basis for an effective method of solving many types of inequalities. Example 4 illustrates the process.

EXAMPLE 4   **Solving an Inequality**   Solve: $\dfrac{x+1}{x-2} > 0$.

Solution   We start by using the left side of the inequality to form the function f:

$$f(x) = \frac{x+1}{x-2}$$

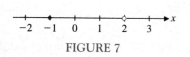

FIGURE 7

Test Numbers	
x	$f(x)$
-2	$\frac{1}{4}$ (+)
0	$-\frac{1}{2}$ (−)
3	4 (+)

The rational function f is discontinuous at $x = 2$, and $f(x) = 0$ for $x = -1$ (a fraction is 0 when the numerator is 0 and the denominator is not 0). We plot $x = 2$ and $x = -1$, which we call *partition numbers*, on a real number line (Fig. 7). (Note that the dot at 2 is open, because the function is not defined at $x = 2$.) The partition numbers 2 and -1 determine three open intervals: $(-\infty, -1)$, $(-1, 2)$, and $(2, \infty)$. The function f is continuous and nonzero on each of these intervals. From Theorem 2 we know that $f(x)$ does not change sign on any of these intervals. Thus, we can find the sign of $f(x)$ on each of these intervals by selecting a **test number** in each interval and evaluating $f(x)$ at that number. Since any number in each subinterval will do, we choose test numbers that are easy to evaluate: -2, 0, and 3. The table in the margin shows the results.

The sign of $f(x)$ at each test number is the same as the sign of $f(x)$ over the interval containing that test number. Using this information, we construct a **sign chart** for $f(x)$:

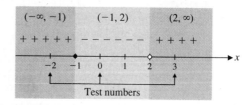

Now using the sign chart, we can easily write the solution for the given nonlinear inequality:

$$f(x) > 0 \quad \text{for} \quad \begin{array}{l} x < -1 \quad \text{or} \quad x > 2 \quad \text{\small Inequality notation} \\ (-\infty, -1) \cup (2, \infty) \quad \text{\small Interval notation} \end{array}$$

Most of the inequalities we encounter will involve strict inequalities ($>$ or $<$). If it is necessary to solve inequalities of the form $\geq$ or $\leq$, we simply include the endpoint x of any interval if f is defined at x and $f(x)$ satisfies the given inequality. For example, referring to the sign chart in Example 4, the solution of the inequality

$$\frac{x+1}{x-2} \geq 0 \quad \text{is} \quad \begin{array}{ll} x \leq -1 \quad \text{or} \quad x > 2 & \text{Inequality notation} \\ (-\infty, -1] \cup (2, \infty) & \text{Interval notation} \end{array}$$

In general, given a function f, a **partition number** is a value of x such that f is discontinuous at x or $f(x) = 0$. **Partition numbers determine open intervals where $f(x)$ does not change sign.** By using a test number from each interval, we can construct a sign chart for $f(x)$ on the real number line. It is then an easy matter to determine where $f(x) < 0$ or $f(x) > 0$; that is, to solve the inequality $f(x) < 0$ or $f(x) > 0$.

We summarize the procedure for constructing sign charts in the following box:

PROCEDURE   Constructing Sign Charts

Given a function f,

Step 1. Find all partition numbers. That is,

(A) Find all numbers where f is discontinuous. (Rational functions are discontinuous for values of x that make a denominator 0.)

(B) Find all numbers where $f(x) = 0$. (For a rational function, this occurs where the numerator is 0 and the denominator is not 0.)

Step 2. Plot the numbers found in step 1 on a real number line, dividing the number line into intervals.

Step 3. Select a test number in each open interval determined in step 2, and evaluate $f(x)$ at each test number to determine whether $f(x)$ is positive ($+$) or negative ($-$) in each interval.

Step 4. Construct a sign chart using the real number line in step 2. This will show the sign of $f(x)$ on each open interval.

Note: From the sign chart, it is easy to find the solution for the inequality $f(x) < 0$ or $f(x) > 0$.

Matched Problem 5   Solve: $\dfrac{x^2 - 1}{x - 3} < 0$.

Answers to Matched Problems   **1.** f is not continuous at $x = -3, -1, 2$, and 4.

$x = -3$: $\lim_{x \to -3} f(x) = 3$, but $f(-3)$ does not exist

$x = -1$: $f(-1) = 1$, but $\lim_{x \to -1} f(x)$ does not exist

$x = 2$: $\lim_{x \to 2} f(x) = 5$, but $f(2) = 3$

$x = 4$: $\lim_{x \to 4} f(x)$ does not exist, and $f(4)$ does not exist

2. (A) f is continuous at $x = 1$, since $\lim_{x \to 1} f(x) = 2 = f(1)$.

(B) g is not continuous at $x = 1$, since $g(1)$ is not defined.

(C) h is not continuous at $x = 2$ for two reasons: $h(2)$ does not exist and $\lim_{x \to 2} h(x)$ does not exist.

h is continuous at $x = 0$, since $\lim_{x \to 0} h(x) = -1 = h(0)$.

3. (A) Since f is a polynomial function, f is continuous for all x.

(B) Since f is a rational function, f is continuous for all x except -1 and 4 (values that make the denominator 0).

(C) The polynomial function $x - 4$ is continuous for all x and nonnegative for $x \geq 4$. Since $n = 2$ is even, f is continuous for $x \geq 4$, or on the interval $[4, \infty)$.

(D) The polynomial function $x^3 + 1$ is continuous for all x. Since $n = 3$ is odd, f is continuous for all x.

4. $-\infty < x < -1$ or $1 < x < 3$; $(-\infty, -1) \cup (1, 3)$

Exercise 3-2

A *In Problems 1–6, sketch a possible graph of a function that satisfies the given conditions at $x = 1$, and discuss the continuity of f at $x = 1$.*

1. $f(1) = 2$ and $\lim\limits_{x \to 1} f(x) = 2$

2. $f(1) = -2$ and $\lim\limits_{x \to 1} f(x) = 2$

3. $f(1) = 2$ and $\lim\limits_{x \to 1} f(x) = -2$

4. $f(1) = -2$ and $\lim\limits_{x \to 1} f(x) = -2$

5. $f(1) = -2$, $\lim\limits_{x \to 1^-} f(x) = 2$, and $\lim\limits_{x \to 1^+} f(x) = -2$

6. $f(1) = 2$, $\lim\limits_{x \to 1^-} f(x) = 2$, and $\lim\limits_{x \to 1^+} f(x) = -2$

Problems 7–10 refer to the function f shown in the figure. Use the graph to estimate the indicated quantities to the nearest integer.

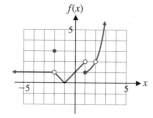

7. (A) $\lim\limits_{x \to 1^-} f(x)$ (B) $\lim\limits_{x \to 1^+} f(x)$

(C) $\lim\limits_{x \to 1} f(x)$ (D) $f(1)$

(E) Is f continuous at $x = 1$? Explain.

8. (A) $\lim\limits_{x \to 2^-} f(x)$ (B) $\lim\limits_{x \to 2^+} f(x)$

(C) $\lim\limits_{x \to 2} f(x)$ (D) $f(2)$

(E) Is f continuous at $x = 2$? Explain.

9. (A) $\lim\limits_{x \to -2^-} f(x)$ (B) $\lim\limits_{x \to -2^+} f(x)$

(C) $\lim\limits_{x \to -2} f(x)$ (D) $f(-2)$

(E) Is f continuous at $x = -2$? Explain.

10. (A) $\lim\limits_{x \to -1^-} f(x)$ (B) $\lim\limits_{x \to -1^+} f(x)$

(C) $\lim\limits_{x \to -1} f(x)$ (D) $f(-1)$

(E) Is f continuous at $x = -1$? Explain.

Problems 11–14 refer to the function g shown in the figure. Use the graph to estimate the indicated quantities to the nearest integer.

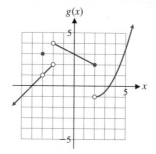

11. (A) $\lim\limits_{x \to -3^-} g(x)$ (B) $\lim\limits_{x \to -3^+} g(x)$

(C) $\lim\limits_{x \to -3} g(x)$ (D) $g(-3)$

(E) Is g continuous at $x = -3$? Explain.

12. (A) $\lim\limits_{x \to -2^-} g(x)$ (B) $\lim\limits_{x \to -2^+} g(x)$

(C) $\lim\limits_{x \to -2} g(x)$ (D) $g(-2)$

(E) Is g continuous at $x = -2$? Explain.

13. (A) $\lim\limits_{x \to 2^-} g(x)$ (B) $\lim\limits_{x \to 2^+} g(x)$

(C) $\lim\limits_{x \to 2} g(x)$ (D) $g(2)$

(E) Is g continuous at $x = 2$? Explain.

14. (A) $\lim\limits_{x \to 4^-} g(x)$ (B) $\lim\limits_{x \to 4^+} g(x)$

(C) $\lim\limits_{x \to 4} g(x)$ (D) $g(4)$

(E) Is g continuous at $x = 4$? Explain.

Use Theorem 1 to determine where each function in Problems 15–24 is continuous.

15. $f(x) = 3x - 4$ **16.** $h(x) = 4 - 2x$

17. $g(x) = \dfrac{3x}{x + 2}$ **18.** $k(x) = \dfrac{2x}{x - 4}$

19. $m(x) = \dfrac{x + 1}{(x - 1)(x + 4)}$

20. $n(x) = \dfrac{x - 2}{(x - 3)(x + 1)}$

21. $F(x) = \dfrac{2x}{x^2 + 9}$ **22.** $G(x) = \dfrac{1 - x^2}{x^2 + 1}$

23. $M(x) = \dfrac{x - 1}{4x^2 - 9}$ **24.** $N(X) = \dfrac{x^2 + 4}{4 - 25x^2}$

$x \neq \pm \dfrac{3}{2}$

B

25. Given the following function f,

$$f(x) = \begin{cases} 2 & \text{if } x \text{ is an integer} \\ 1 & \text{if } x \text{ is not an integer} \end{cases}$$

(A) Graph f.

(B) $\lim\limits_{x \to 2} f(x) = ?$

(C) $f(2) = ?$

(D) Is f continuous at $x = 2$?

(E) Where is f discontinuous?

26. Given the following function g,

$$g(x) = \begin{cases} -1 & \text{if } x \text{ is an even integer} \\ 1 & \text{if } x \text{ is not an even integer} \end{cases}$$

(A) Graph g.

(B) $\lim\limits_{x \to 1} g(x) = ?$

(C) $g(1) = ?$

(D) Is g continuous at $x = 1$?

(E) Where is g discontinuous?

In Problems 27–34, solve each inequality using a sign chart. Express answers in inequality and interval notation.

27. $x^2 - x - 12 < 0$ **28.** $x^2 - 2x - 8 < 0$

29. $x^2 + 21 > 10x$ **30.** $x^2 + 7x > -10$

31. $x^3 < 4x$ **32.** $x^4 - 9x^2 > 0$

33. $\dfrac{x^2 + 5x}{x - 3} > 0$ **34.** $\dfrac{x - 4}{x^2 + 2x} < 0$

35. Use the graph of f to determine where

(A) $f(x) > 0$ (B) $f(x) < 0$

Express answers in interval notation.

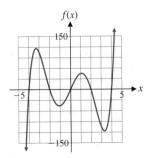

36. Use the graph of g to determine where

(A) $g(x) > 0$ (B) $g(x) < 0$

Express answers in interval notation.

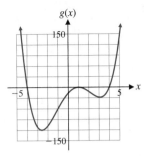

In Problems 37–40, use a graphing utility to approximate the partition numbers of each function $f(x)$ to four decimal places. Then solve the following inequalities:

(A) $f(x) > 0$ (B) $f(x) < 0$

Express answers in interval notation.

37. $f(x) = x^4 - 6x^2 + 3x + 5$

38. $f(x) = x^4 - 4x^2 - 2x + 2$

39. $f(x) = \dfrac{3 + 6x - x^3}{x^2 - 1}$

40. $f(x) = \dfrac{x^3 - 5x + 1}{x^2 - 1}$

Use Theorem 1 to determine where each function in Problems 41–48 is continuous. Express the answer in interval notation.

41. $\sqrt{x - 6}$ **42.** $\sqrt{7 - x}$

43. $\sqrt[3]{5 - x}$ **44.** $\sqrt[3]{x - 8}$

45. $\sqrt{x^2 - 9}$ **46.** $\sqrt{4 - x^2}$

47. $\sqrt{x^2 + 1}$ **48.** $\sqrt[3]{x^2 + 2}$

In Problems 49–54, graph f, locate all points of discontinuity, and discuss the behavior of f at these points.

49. $f(x) = \begin{cases} 1 + x & \text{if } x < 1 \\ 5 - x & \text{if } x \geq 1 \end{cases}$

50. $f(x) = \begin{cases} x^2 & \text{if } x \leq 1 \\ 2x & \text{if } x > 1 \end{cases}$

51. $f(x) = \begin{cases} 1 + x & \text{if } x \leq 2 \\ 5 - x & \text{if } x > 2 \end{cases}$

52. $f(x) = \begin{cases} x^2 & \text{if } x \leq 2 \\ 2x & \text{if } x > 2 \end{cases}$

53. $f(x) = \begin{cases} -x & \text{if } x < 0 \\ 1 & \text{if } x = 0 \\ x & \text{if } x > 0 \end{cases}$

54. $f(x) = \begin{cases} 1 & \text{if } x < 0 \\ 0 & \text{if } x = 0 \\ 1 + x & \text{if } x > 0 \end{cases}$

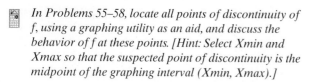

In Problems 55–58, locate all points of discontinuity of f, using a graphing utility as an aid, and discuss the behavior of f at these points. [Hint: Select Xmin and Xmax so that the suspected point of discontinuity is the midpoint of the graphing interval (Xmin, Xmax).]

55. $f(x) = x + \dfrac{|2x - 4|}{x - 2}$ **56.** $f(x) = x + \dfrac{|3x + 9|}{x + 3}$

57. $f(x) = \dfrac{x^2 - 1}{|x| - 1}$ **58.** $f(x) = \dfrac{x^3 - 8}{|x| - 2}$

C

59. Use the graph of the function g to answer the following questions:

(A) Is g continuous on the open interval $(-1, 2)$?

(B) Is g continuous from the right at $x = -1$? That is, does $\lim_{x \to -1^+} g(x) = g(-1)$?

(C) Is g continuous from the left at $x = 2$? That is, does $\lim_{x \to 2^-} g(x) = g(2)$?

(D) Is g continuous on the closed interval $[-1, 2]$?

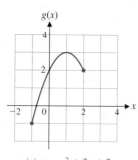

$$g(x) = -x^2 + 2x + 2$$

Figure for 59

60. Use the graph of the function f to answer the following questions:

(A) Is f continuous on the open interval $(0, 3)$?

(B) Is f continuous from the right at $x = 0$? That is, does $\lim_{x \to 0^+} f(x) = f(0)$?

(C) Is f continuous from the left at $x = 3$? That is, does $\lim_{x \to 3^-} f(x) = f(3)$?

(D) Is f continuous on the closed interval $[0, 3]$?

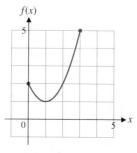

$$f(x) = x^2 - 2x + 2$$

Figure for 60

*Problems 61 and 62 refer to the **greatest integer function,** which is denoted by $[x]$ and is defined as follows:*

$$[x] = greatest\ integer \leq x$$

For example,

$$[-3.6] = greatest\ integer \leq -3.6 = -4$$
$$[2] = greatest\ integer \leq 2 = 2$$
$$[2.5] = greatest\ integer \leq 2.5 = 2$$

The graph of $f(x) = [x]$ is shown. There, we can see that

$$[x] = -2 \quad for \quad -2 \leq x < -1$$
$$[x] = -1 \quad for \quad -1 \leq x < 0$$
$$[x] = 0 \quad for \quad 0 \leq x < 1$$
$$[x] = 1 \quad for \quad 1 \leq x < 2$$
$$[x] = 2 \quad for \quad 2 \leq x < 3$$

and so on.

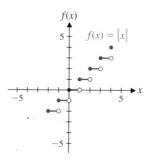

Figure for 61 and 62

61. (A) Is f continuous from the right at $x = 0$?

(B) Is f continuous from the left at $x = 0$?

(C) Is f continuous on the open interval $(0, 1)$?

(D) Is f continuous on the closed interval $[0, 1]$?

(E) Is f continuous on the half-closed interval $[0, 1)$?

62. (A) Is f continuous from the right at $x = 2$?

(B) Is f continuous from the left at $x = 2$?

(C) Is f continuous on the open interval $(1, 2)$?

(D) Is f continuous on the closed interval $[1, 2]$?

(E) Is f continuous on the half-closed interval $[1, 2)$?

In Problems 63–66, sketch a possible graph for a function f that is continuous for all real numbers and satisfies the given conditions. Find the x intercepts for f.

63. $f(x) < 0$ on $(-\infty, -5)$ and $(2, \infty)$; $f(x) > 0$ on $(-5, 2)$

64. $f(x) > 0$ on $(-\infty, -4)$ and $(3, \infty)$; $f(x) < 0$ on $(-4, 3)$

65. $f(x) < 0$ on $(-\infty, -6)$ and $(-1, 4)$; $f(x) > 0$ on $(-6, -1)$ and $(4, \infty)$

66. $f(x) > 0$ on $(-\infty, -3)$ and $(2, 7)$; $f(x) < 0$ on $(-3, 2)$ and $(7, \infty)$

67. The function $f(x) = 2/(1 - x)$ satisfies $f(0) = 2$ and $f(2) = -2$. Is f equal to 0 anywhere on the interval $(-1, 3)$? Does this contradict Theorem 2? Explain.

68. The function $f(x) = 6/(x - 4)$ satisfies $f(2) = -3$ and $f(7) = 2$. Is f equal to 0 anywhere on the interval $(0, 9)$? Does this contradict Theorem 2? Explain.

69. The function f is continuous and never 0 on the interval $(0, 4)$, and continuous and never 0 on the interval $(4, 8)$. Also, $f(2) = 3$ and $f(6) = -3$. Discuss the validity of the following statement and illustrate your conclusions with graphs: Either $f(4) = 0$ or f is discontinuous at $x = 4$.

70. The function f is continuous and never 0 on the interval $(-3, 1)$, and continuous and never 0 on the interval $(1, 4)$. Also, $f(-2) = -3$ and $f(3) = 4$. Discuss the validity of the following statement and illustrate your conclusions with graphs: Either $f(1) = 0$ or f is discontinuous at $x = 1$.

Applications

Business & Economics

71. *Postal rates.* First-class postage in 2004 was $0.37 for the first ounce (or any fraction thereof) and $0.23 for each additional ounce (or fraction thereof).

(A) Write a piecewise definition of the first-class postage $P(x)$ for a letter weighing x ounces.

(B) Graph $P(x)$ for $0 < x \le 5$.

(C) Is $P(x)$ continuous at $x = 4.5$? At $x = 4$? Explain.

72. *Telephone rates.* A long-distance telephone service charges $0.07 for the first minute (or any fraction thereof) and $0.05 for each additional minute (or fraction thereof).

(A) Write a piecewise definition of the charge $R(x)$ for a state-to-state long-distance call lasting x minutes.

(B) Graph $R(x)$ for $0 < x \le 6$

(C) Is $R(x)$ continuous at $x = 3.5$? At $x = 3$? Explain.

73. *Postal rates.* Discuss the differences between the function $Q(x) = 0.37 + 0.23[\![x]\!]$ and the function $P(x)$ defined in Problem 71.

74. *Telephone rates.* Discuss the differences between the function $S(x) = 0.07 + 0.05[\![x]\!]$ and the function $R(x)$ defined in Problem 72.

75. *Natural gas rates.* Table 1 shows the rates for natural gas charged by the Middle Tennessee Natural Gas Utility District during the summer months. The customer charge is a fixed monthly charge, independent of the amount of gas used during the month.

(A) Write a piecewise definition of the monthly charge $S(x)$ for a customer who uses x therms* in a summer month.

TABLE 1 Summer (May–September)	
Base charge	$5.00
First 50 therms	0.63 per therm
Over 50 therms	0.45 per therm

(B) Graph $S(x)$.

(C) Is $S(x)$ continuous at $x = 50$? Explain.

76. *Natural gas rates.* Table 2 shows the rates for natural gas charged by the Middle Tennessee Natural Gas Utility District during the winter months. The customer charge is a fixed monthly charge, independent of the amount of gas used during the month.

(A) Write a piecewise definition of the monthly charge $S(x)$ for a customer who uses x therms in a winter month.

(B) Graph $S(x)$.

(C) Is $S(x)$ continuous at $x = 5$? At $x = 50$? Explain.

TABLE 2 Winter (October– April)	
Base charge	$5.00
First 5 therms	0.69 per therm
Next 45 therms	0.65 per therm
Over 50 therms	0.63 per therm

---

*A British thermal unit (Btu) is the amount of heat required to raise the temperature of 1 pound of water 1 degree Fahrenheit and a therm is 100,000 Btu.

77. *Income.* A personal computer salesperson receives a base salary of $1,000 per month and a commission of 5% of all sales over $10,000 during the month. If the monthly sales are $20,000 or more, the salesperson is given an additional $500 bonus. Let $E(s)$ represent the person's earnings during the month as a function of the monthly sales s.

(A) Graph $E(s)$ for $0 \leq s \leq 30{,}000$.

(B) Find $\lim_{s \to 10{,}000} E(s)$ and $E(10{,}000)$.

(C) Find $\lim_{s \to 20{,}000} E(s)$ and $E(20{,}000)$.

(D) Is E continuous at $s = 10{,}000$? At $s = 20{,}000$?

78. *Equipment rental.* An office equipment rental and leasing company rents typewriters for $10 per day (and any fraction thereof) or for $50 per 7 day week. Let $C(x)$ be the cost of renting a typewriter for x days.

(A) Graph $C(x)$ for $0 \leq x \leq 10$.

(B) Find $\lim_{x \to 4.5} C(x)$ and $C(4.5)$.

(C) Find $\lim_{x \to 8} C(x)$ and $C(8)$.

(D) Is C continuous at $x = 4.5$? At $x = 8$?

Life Sciences

79. *Animal supply.* A medical laboratory raises its own rabbits. The number of rabbits $N(t)$ available at any time t depends on the number of births and deaths.

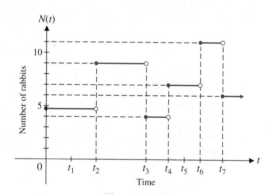

Figure for 79

When a birth or death occurs, the function N generally has a discontinuity, as shown in the figure.

(A) Where is the function N discontinuous?

(B) $\lim_{t \to t_5} N(t) = ?$; $N(t_5) = ?$

(C) $\lim_{t \to t_3} N(t) = ?$; $N(t_3) = ?$

Social Sciences

80. *Learning.* The graph might represent the history of a particular person learning the material on limits and continuity in this book. At time t_2, the student's mind goes blank during a quiz. At time t_4, the instructor explains a concept particularly well, and suddenly, a big jump in understanding takes place.

(A) Where is the function p discontinuous?

(B) $\lim_{t \to t_1} p(t) = ?$; $p(t_1) = ?$

(C) $\lim_{t \to t_2} p(t) = ?$; $p(t_2) = ?$

(D) $\lim_{t \to t_4} p(t) = ?$; $p(t_4) = ?$

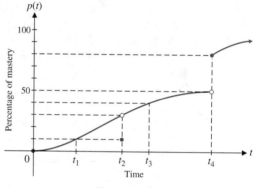

Figure for 80

Section 3-3 | The Derivative

➤ Rate of Change
➤ Slope of the Tangent Line
➤ The Derivative
➤ Nonexistence of the Derivative

We now use the concept of limit to solve the two important problems illustrated in Figure 1. The solution of these two apparently unrelated problems involves a common concept called *the derivative*.

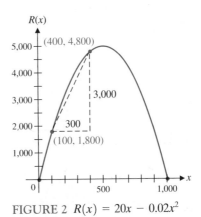

(A) Find the equation of the
tangent line at (x_1, y_1)
given $y = f(x)$

(B) Find the instantaneous
velocity of a falling
object

FIGURE 1 Two basic problems of calculus

➤ Rate of Change

Let us start by considering a simple example.

EXAMPLE 1   **Revenue Analysis** The revenue (in dollars) from the sale of x plastic planter boxes is given by

$$R(x) = 20x - 0.02x^2 \qquad 0 \le x \le 1,000$$

which is graphed in Figure 2.

FIGURE 2 $R(x) = 20x - 0.02x^2$

(A) What is the change in revenue if production is changed from 100 planters to 400 planters?

(B) What is the average change in revenue for this change in production?

Solution   (A) The change in revenue is given by

$$R(400) - R(100) = 20(400) - 0.02(400)^2 - [20(100) - 0.02(100)^2]$$
$$= 4,800 - 1,800 = \$3,000$$

Thus, increasing production from 100 planters to 400 planters will increase revenue by $3,000.

(B) To find the average change in revenue, we divide the change in revenue by the change in production:

$$\frac{R(400) - R(100)}{400 - 100} = \frac{3,000}{300} = \$10$$

Thus, the average change in revenue is $10 per planter when production is increased from 100 to 400 planters. ■

Matched Problem 1 Refer to the revenue function in Example 1.

(A) What is the change in revenue if production is changed from 600 planters to 800 planters?

(B) What is the average change in revenue for this change in production?

In general, if we are given a function $y = f(x)$ and if x is changed from a to $a + h$, then y will change from $f(a)$ to $f(a + h)$. The *average rate of change* is the ratio of the change in y to the change in x.

[handwritten note: increasing x values by h]

DEFINITION Average Rate of Change

For $y = f(x)$, the **average rate of change from $x = a$ to $x = a + h$** is

$$\frac{f(a + h) - f(a)}{(a + h) - a} = \frac{f(a + h) - f(a)}{h} \qquad h \neq 0 \qquad (1)$$

As we noted in Section 3-1, the mathematical expression (1) is called the **difference quotient.** The preceding discussion shows that the difference quotient can be interpreted as an average rate of change. The next example illustrates another interpretation of this quotient: velocity of a moving object.

EXAMPLE 2 **Velocity** A small steel ball dropped from a tower will fall a distance of y feet in x seconds, as given approximately by the formula (from physics)

$$y = f(x) = 16x^2$$

Figure 3 shows the position of the ball on a coordinate line (positive direction down) at the end of 0, 1, 2, and 3 seconds.

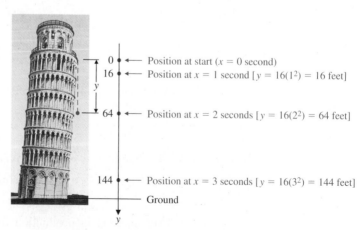

0 ← Position at start ($x = 0$ second)
16 ← Position at $x = 1$ second [$y = 16(1^2) = 16$ feet]
64 ← Position at $x = 2$ seconds [$y = 16(2^2) = 64$ feet]
144 ← Position at $x = 3$ seconds [$y = 16(3^2) = 144$ feet]
Ground

FIGURE 3 *Note:* Positive y direction is down.

(A) Find the average velocity from $x = 2$ seconds to $x = 3$ seconds.

(B) Find and simplify the average velocity from $x = 2$ seconds to $x = 2 + h$ seconds, $h \neq 0$.

(C) Find the limit of the expression from part B as $h \to 0$, if it exists.

(D) Discuss possible interpretations of the limit from part C.

Solution (A) Recall the formula $d = rt$, which can be written in the form

$$r = \frac{d}{t} = \frac{\text{Distance covered}}{\text{Elapsed time}} = \text{Average velocity}$$

For example, if a person drives from San Francisco to Los Angeles (a distance of about 420 miles) in 7 hours, then the average velocity is

$$r = \frac{d}{t} = \frac{420}{7} = 60 \text{ miles per hour}$$

Sometimes the person will be traveling faster and sometimes slower, but the average velocity is 60 miles per hour. In our present problem, the average velocity of the steel ball from $x = 2$ seconds to $x = 3$ seconds is

$$\begin{aligned}
\text{Average velocity} &= \frac{\text{Distance covered}}{\text{Elapsed time}} \\
&= \frac{f(3) - f(2)}{3 - 2} \\
&= \frac{16(3)^2 - 16(2)^2}{1} = 80 \text{ feet per second}
\end{aligned}$$

Thus, we see that if $y = f(x)$ is the position of the falling ball, then the average velocity is simply the average rate of change of $f(x)$ with respect to time x. And we have another interpretation of the difference quotient (1).

(B) Proceeding as in part A,

$$\begin{aligned}
\text{Average velocity} &= \frac{\text{Distance covered}}{\text{Elapsed time}} \\
&= \frac{f(2 + h) - f(2)}{h} \qquad \text{\textit{Difference quotient}} \\
&= \frac{16(2 + h)^2 - 16(2)^2}{h} \qquad \text{\textit{Simplify this 0/0}} \\
& \qquad\qquad\qquad\qquad\qquad \text{\textit{indeterminate form.}} \\
&= \frac{64 + 64h + 16h^2 - 64}{h} \\
&= \frac{h(64 + 16h)}{h} = 64 + 16h \qquad h \neq 0
\end{aligned}$$

Notice that if $h = 1$, the average velocity is 80 feet per second, our result in part A.

(C) The limit of the average velocity expression from part B as $h \to 0$ is

$$\begin{aligned}
\lim_{h \to 0} \frac{f(2 + h) - f(2)}{h} &= \lim_{h \to 0} (64 + 16h) \\
&= 64 \text{ feet per second}
\end{aligned}$$

(D) The average velocity over smaller and smaller time intervals approaches 64 feet per second. This limit can be interpreted as the velocity of the ball at the *instant* when the ball has been falling for exactly 2 seconds. Thus, 64 feet per second is referred to as the **instantaneous velocity** at $x = 2$ seconds. And we have solved the one of the basic problems of calculus (see Fig. 1B). ∎

Matched Problem 2   For the falling steel ball in Example 2, find

(A) The average velocity from $x = 1$ second to $x = 2$ seconds

(B) The average velocity (in simplified form) from $x = 1$ second to $x = 1 + h$ seconds, $h \neq 0$

(C) The instantaneous velocity at $x = 1$ second

EXPLORE & DISCUSS 1

Recall the revenue function in Example 1: $R(x) = 20x - 0.02x^2$. Find

$$\lim_{h\to 0} \frac{R(100 + h) - R(100)}{h}$$

Discuss possible interpretations of this limit.

The ideas introduced in Example 2 are not confined to average velocity but can be applied to the average rate of change of any function.

DEFINITION Instantaneous Rate of Change

For $y = f(x)$, the **instantaneous rate of change at $x = a$** is

$$\lim_{h\to 0} \frac{f(a + h) - f(a)}{h} \tag{2}$$

if the limit exists.

The adjective *instantaneous* is often omitted with the understanding that the phrase **rate of change** always refers to the instantaneous rate of change and not the average rate of change. Similarly, **velocity** always refers to the instantaneous rate of change of distance with respect to time.

▶ Slope of the Tangent Line

So far our interpretations of the difference quotient have been numerical in nature. Now we want to consider a geometric interpretation. A line through two points on the graph of a function is called a **secant line.** If $(a, f(a))$ and $(a + h, f(a + h))$ are two points on the graph of $y = f(x)$, we can use the slope formula from Section 1-3 to find the slope of the secant line through these points (see Fig. 4).

$$\textbf{Slope of secant line} = \frac{f(a + h) - f(a)}{(a + h) - a}$$
$$= \frac{f(a + h) - f(a)}{h} \quad \textit{Difference quotient}$$

Thus, the difference quotient can be interpreted as both the average rate of change and the slope of the secant line.

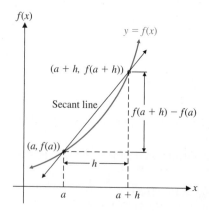

FIGURE 4   Secant line

◉ Insight   If (x_1, y_1) and (x_2, y_2) are two points in the plane with $x_1 \neq x_2$ and L is the line passing through these two points (see Section 1-3), then

Slope of L Point-slope form for L

$$m = \frac{y_2 - y_1}{x_2 - x_1} \qquad y - y_1 = m(x - x_1)$$

These formulas will be used extensively in the remainder of this chapter.   ●

EXAMPLE 3   **Slope of a Secant Line**   Given $f(x) = x^2$,

(A) Find the slope of the secant line for $a = 1$, and $h = 2$ and 1, respectively. Graph $y = f(x)$ and the two secant lines.

(B) Find and simplify the slope of the secant line for $a = 1$ and h any nonzero number.

(C) Find the limit of the expression in part B.

(D) Discuss possible interpretations of the limit in part C.

Solution   (A) For $a = 1$ and $h = 2$, the secant line goes through $(1, f(1)) = (1, 1)$ and $(3, f(3)) = (3, 9)$, and its slope is

$$\frac{f(1 + 2) - f(1)}{2} = \frac{3^2 - 1^2}{2} = 4$$

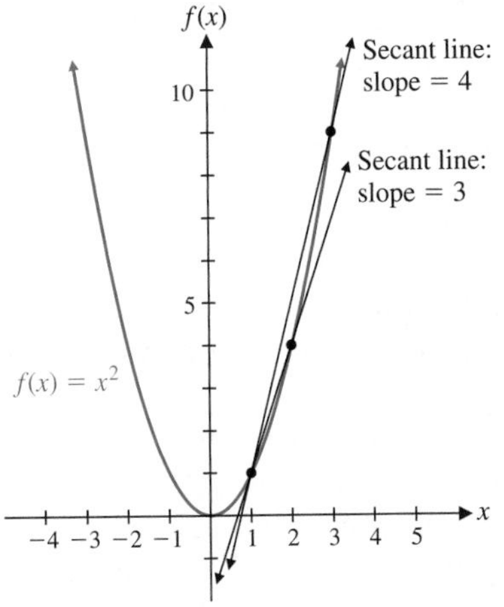

For $a = 1$ and $h = 1$, the secant line goes through $(1, f(1)) = (1, 1)$ and $(2, f(2)) = (2, 4)$, and its slope is

$$\frac{f(1 + 1) - f(1)}{1} = \frac{2^2 - 1^2}{1} = 3$$

The graphs of $y = f(x)$ and the two secant lines are shown in Figure 5.

(B) For $a = 1$ and h any nonzero number, the secant line goes through $(1, f(1)) = (1, 1)$ and $(1 + h, f(1 + h)) = (1 + h, (1 + h)^2)$, and its slope is

$$\frac{f(1 + h) - f(h)}{h} = \frac{(1 + h)^2 - 1^2}{h}$$

$$= \frac{1 + 2h + h^2 - 1}{h}$$

$$= \frac{h(2 + h)}{h}$$

$$= 2 + h \qquad h \neq 0$$

(C) The limit of the secant line slope from part B is

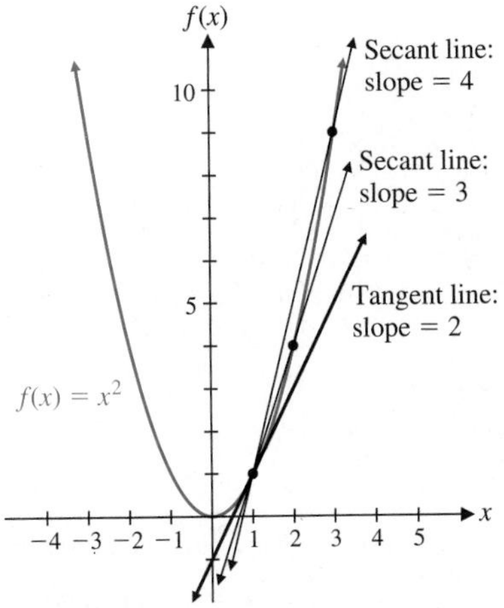

$$\lim_{h \to 0} \frac{f(1 + h) - f(h)}{h} = \lim_{h \to 0}(2 + h)$$

$$= 2$$

(D) In part C, we saw that the limit of the slopes of the secant lines through the point $(1, f(1))$ is 2. If we graph the line through $(1, f(1))$ with slope 2 (Fig. 6), this line appears to be the limit of the secant lines. The slope obtained from the limit of slopes of secant lines is called the *slope of the graph* at $x = 1$ and the line through the point $(1, f(1))$ with this slope is called the *tangent line*. And we have solved another basic problem of calculus (see Fig. 1A).

FIGURE 5 Secant lines

FIGURE 6 Tangent line

Matched Problem 3   Given $f(x) = x^2$,

(A) Find the slope of the secant line for $a = 2$, and $h = 2$ and 1, respectively.

(B) Find and simplify the slope of the secant line for $a = 2$ and h any nonzero number.

(C) Find the limit of the expression in part B.

(D) Find the slope of the graph and the slope of the tangent line at $a = 2$.

The ideas introduced in the preceding example are summarized in the following box.

DEFINITION   Slope of a Graph

Given $y = f(x)$, the **slope of the graph** at the point $(a, f(a))$ is given by

$$\lim_{h \to 0} \frac{f(a + h) - f(a)}{h} \tag{3}$$

provided that the limit exists. The slope of the graph is also the **slope of the tangent line** at the point $(a, f(a))$.

⦿ *Insight*   If the function f is continuous at a, then

$$\lim_{h \to 0} f(a + h) = f(a)$$

and limit (3) will be a 0/0 indeterminate form. As we saw in Examples 2 and 3, evaluation of this type of limit typically involves algebraic simplification.   ●

From plane geometry we know that a line tangent to a circle is a line that passes through one and only one point of the circle (see Fig. 7A). Although this definition cannot be extended to graphs of functions in general, the visual relationship between graphs of functions and their tangent lines is similar to the circle case (see Fig. 7B). Limit (3) provides both a mathematically sound definition for the concept of tangent line and a method for approximating the slope of the tangent line.

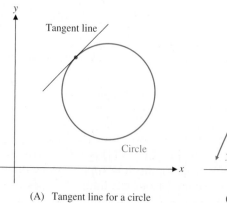

(A) Tangent line for a circle   (B) Tangent lines for the graph of a function

FIGURE 7

➤ The Derivative

We have seen that the limit of a difference quotient can be interpreted as a rate of change, as a velocity, or as the slope of a tangent line. In addition, this limit provides solutions to two of the three basic problems stated at the beginning of this chapter. We are now ready to introduce some terms that are used to refer to this limit. To follow customary practice, we use x in place of a and think of the difference quotient

$$\frac{f(x + h) - f(x)}{h}$$

as a function of h, with x held fixed as h tends to 0.

DEFINITION   The Derivative

For $y = f(x)$, we define the **derivative of f at x,** denoted by $f'(x)$, to be

$$f'(x) = \lim_{h \to 0} \frac{f(x + h) - f(x)}{h} \text{ if the limit exists}$$

If $f'(x)$ exists for each x in the open interval (a, b), then f is said to be **differentiable** over (a, b).

(Differentiability from the left or from the right is defined using $h \to 0^-$ or $h \to 0^+$, respectively, in place of $h \to 0$ in the definition above.)

The process of finding the derivative of a function is called **differentiation.** That is, the derivative of a function is obtained by **differentiating** the function.

SUMMARY   Interpretations of the Derivative

The derivative of a function f is a new function f'. The domain of f' is a subset of the domain of f. The derivative has various applications and interpretations, including the following:

1. *Slope of the tangent line.* For each x in the domain of f', $f'(x)$ is the slope of the line tangent to the graph of f at the point $(x, f(x))$.
2. *Instantaneous rate of change.* For each x in the domain of f', $f'(x)$ is the instantaneous rate of change of $y = f(x)$ with respect to x.
3. *Velocity.* If $f(x)$ is the position of a moving object at time x, then $v = f'(x)$ is the velocity of the object at that time.

Example 4 illustrates the **four-step process** that we use to find derivatives in this section. In subsequent sections, we develop rules for finding derivatives that do not involve limits. However, it is important that you master the limit process in order to fully comprehend and appreciate the various applications we will consider.

EXAMPLE 4   **Finding a Derivative** Find $f'(x)$, the derivative of f at x, for $f(x) = 4x - x^2$.

Solution   To find $f'(x)$, we use a four-step process.

Step 1. Find $f(x + h)$.

$$f(x + h) = 4(x + h) - (x + h)^2$$
$$= 4x + 4h - x^2 - 2xh - h^2$$

Step 2. Find $f(x + h) - f(x)$.

$$f(x + h) - f(x) = 4x + 4h - x^2 - 2xh - h^2 - (4x - x^2)$$
$$= 4h - 2xh - h^2$$

Step 3. Find $\dfrac{f(x + h) - f(x)}{h}$.

$$\frac{f(x + h) - f(x)}{h} = \frac{4h - 2xh - h^2}{h} = \frac{h(4 - 2x - h)}{h}$$
$$= 4 - 2x - h, \quad h \neq 0$$

Step 4. Find $f'(x) = \lim\limits_{h \to 0} \dfrac{f(x + h) - f(x)}{h}$.

$$f'(x) = \lim_{h \to 0} \frac{f(x + h) - f(x)}{h} = \lim_{h \to 0}(4 - 2x - h) = 4 - 2x$$

Thus, if $f(x) = 4x - x^2$, then $f'(x) = 4 - 2x$. The function f' is a new function derived from the function f.   ◼

Matched Problem 4   Find $f'(x)$, the derivative of f at x, for $f(x) = 8x - 2x^2$.

The four-step process used in Example 4 is summarized in the following box for easy reference.

PROCEDURE   The four-step process for finding the derivative of a function f.

Step 1. Find $f(x + h)$.

Step 2. Find $f(x + h) - f(x)$.

Step 3. Find $\dfrac{f(x + h) - f(x)}{h}$.

Step 4. Find $\lim\limits_{h \to 0} \dfrac{f(x + h) - f(x)}{h}$.

EXAMPLE 5   **Finding Tangent Line Slopes**   In Example 4 we started with the function specified by $f(x) = 4x - x^2$ and found the derivative of f at x to be $f'(x) = 4 - 2x$. Thus, the slope of a tangent line to the graph of f at any point $(x, f(x))$ on the graph is

$$m = f'(x) = 4 - 2x$$

(A) Find the slope of the graph of f at $x = 0$, $x = 2$, and $x = 3$.

(B) Graph $y = f(x) = 4x - x^2$, and use the slopes found in part (A) to make a rough sketch of the tangent lines to the graph at $x = 0$, $x = 2$, and $x = 3$.

Solution   (A) Using $f'(x) = 4 - 2x$, we have

$$f'(0) = 4 - 2(0) = 4 \quad \text{Slope at } x = 0$$
$$f'(2) = 4 - 2(2) = 0 \quad \text{Slope at } x = 2$$
$$f'(3) = 4 - 2(3) = -2 \quad \text{Slope at } x = 3$$

(B)

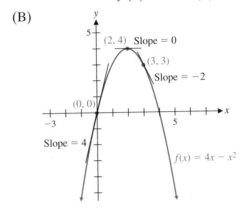

Matched Problem 5   In Matched Problem 4, we started with the function specified by $f(x) = 8x - 2x^2$. Using the derivative found there,

(A) Find the slope of the graph of f at $x = 1, x = 2$, and $x = 4$.

(B) Graph $y = f(x) = 8x - 2x^2$, and use the slopes from part (A) to make a rough sketch of the tangent lines to the graph at $x = 1, x = 2$, and $x = 4$.

EXPLORE & DISCUSS 2

In Example 4 we found that the derivative of $f(x) = 4x - x^2$ is $f'(x) = 4 - 2x$, and in Example 5 we graphed $f(x)$ and several tangent lines.

(A) Graph f and f' on the same set of axes.

(B) The graph of f' is a straight line. Is it a tangent line for the graph of f? Explain.

(C) Find the x intercept for the graph of f'. What is the slope of the line tangent to the graph of f for this value of x? Write a verbal description of the relationship between the slopes of the tangent lines of a function and the x intercepts of the derivative of the function.

EXAMPLE 6   **Finding a Derivative** Find $f'(x)$, the derivative of f at x, for $f(x) = \sqrt{x} + 2$.

Solution   We use the four-step process to find $f'(x)$.

Step 1. Find $f(x + h)$.

$$f(x + h) = \sqrt{x + h} + 2$$

Step 2. Find $f(x + h) - f(x)$.

$$f(x + h) - f(x) = \sqrt{x + h} + 2 - (\sqrt{x} + 2) = \sqrt{x + h} - \sqrt{x}$$

Step 3. Find $\dfrac{f(x + h) - f(x)}{h}$.

$$\dfrac{f(x + h) - f(x)}{h} = \dfrac{\sqrt{x + h} - \sqrt{x}}{h}$$

We rationalize the numerator (Appendix A, Section A-6) to change the form of this fraction.

$$= \dfrac{\sqrt{x + h} - \sqrt{x}}{h} \cdot \dfrac{\sqrt{x + h} + \sqrt{x}}{\sqrt{x + h} + \sqrt{x}}$$

$$= \dfrac{x + h - x}{h(\sqrt{x + h} + \sqrt{x})}$$

$$= \dfrac{h}{h(\sqrt{x + h} + \sqrt{x})}$$

$$= \dfrac{1}{\sqrt{x + h} + \sqrt{x}} \qquad h \neq 0$$

Step 4. Find $f'(x) = \lim\limits_{h \to 0} \dfrac{f(x + h) - f(x)}{h}$.

$$\lim_{h \to 0} \dfrac{f(x + h) - f(x)}{h} = \lim_{h \to 0} \dfrac{1}{\sqrt{x + h} + \sqrt{x}}$$

$$= \dfrac{1}{\sqrt{x} + \sqrt{x}} = \dfrac{1}{2\sqrt{x}} \qquad x > 0$$

Thus, the derivative of $f(x) = \sqrt{x} + 2$ is $f'(x) = 1/(2\sqrt{x})$, a new function. The domain of f is $[0, \infty)$. Since $f'(0)$ is not defined, the domain of f' is $(0, \infty)$, a subset of the domain of f.   ∎

Matched Problem 6   Find $f'(x)$ for $f(x) = \sqrt{x} + 4$.

EXAMPLE 7   **Sales Analysis**   The total sales of a company (in millions of dollars) t months from now are given by $S(t) = \sqrt{t} + 2$. Find $S(25)$ and $S'(25)$, and interpret. Use these results to estimate the total sales after 26 months and after 27 months.

Solution   The total sales function S has the same form as the function f in Example 6— only the letters used to represent the function and the independent variable have been changed. It follows that S' and f' also have the same form:

$$S(t) = \sqrt{t} + 2 \qquad f(x) = \sqrt{x} + 2$$

$$S'(t) = \dfrac{1}{2\sqrt{t}} \qquad f'(x) = \dfrac{1}{2\sqrt{x}}$$

Evaluating S and S' at $t = 25$, we have

$$S(25) = \sqrt{25} + 2 = 7 \qquad S'(25) = \dfrac{1}{2\sqrt{25}} = 0.1$$

Thus, 25 months from now the total sales are $7 million and are increasing at the rate of $0.1 million ($100,000) per month. If this instantaneous rate of change of sales remained constant, the sales would grow to $7.1 million after

26 months, $7.2 million after 27 months, and so on. Even though $S'(t)$ is not a constant function in this case, these values provide useful estimates of the total sales.   ■

Matched Problem 7

The total sales of a company (in millions of dollars) t months from now are given by $S(t) = \sqrt{t} + 4$. Find $S(12)$ and $S'(12)$, and interpret. Use these results to estimate the total sales after 13 months and after 14 months. (Use the derivative found in Matched Problem 6.)   ──────■

Refer to Example 7. It is instructive to compare the estimates of total sales obtained by using the derivative with the corresponding exact values of $S(t)$:

Exact values   Estimated values

$$S(26) = \sqrt{26} + 2 = 7.099\ldots \approx 7.1$$
$$S(27) = \sqrt{27} + 2 = 7.196\ldots \approx 7.2$$

For this function, the estimated values provide very good approximations to the exact values of $S(t)$. For other functions, the approximation might not be as accurate.

Using the instantaneous rate of change of a function at a point to estimate values of the function at nearby points is a simple but important application of the derivative.

➤ Nonexistence of the Derivative

The existence of a derivative at $x = a$ depends on the existence of a limit at $x = a$, that is, on the existence of

$$f'(a) = \lim_{h \to 0} \frac{f(a + h) - f(a)}{h} \tag{4}$$

If the limit does not exist at $x = a$, we say that the function f is **nondifferentiable at $x = a$, or $f'(a)$ does not exist.**

EXPLORE &DISCUSS 3

Let $f(x) = |x - 1|$.

(A) Graph f.

(B) Complete the following table:

h	-0.1	-0.01	$-0.001 \to 0 \leftarrow$		0.001	0.01	0.1
$\dfrac{f(1 + h) - f(1)}{h}$	?	?	?	$\to ? \leftarrow$	?	?	?

(C) Find the following limit, if it exists.

$$\lim_{h \to 0} \frac{f(1 + h) - f(1)}{h}$$

(D) Use the results of parts (A)–(C) to discuss the existence of $f'(1)$.

Repeat parts (A)–(D) for $g(x) = \sqrt[3]{x - 1}$.

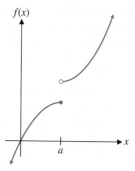

(A) Not continuous at
x = a

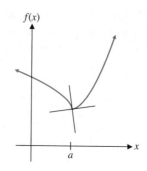

(B) Graph has sharp
corner at x = a

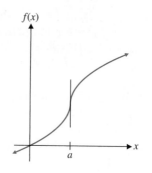

(C) Vertical tangent
at x = a

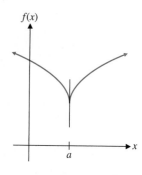

(D) Vertical tangent
at x = a

FIGURE 8 The function f is nondifferentiable at $x = a$.

How can we recognize the points on the graph of f where $f'(a)$ does not exist? It is impossible to describe all the ways that the limit of a difference quotient can fail to exist. However, we can illustrate some common situations where $f'(a)$ does fail to exist (see Fig. 8):

1. If the graph of f has a hole or a break at $x = a$, then $f'(a)$ does not exist (Fig. 8A).

2. If the graph of f has a sharp corner at $x = a$, then $f'(a)$ does not exist and the graph has no tangent line at $x = a$ (Fig. 8B). (In Fig. 8B, the left- and right-hand derivatives exist but are not equal.)

3. If the graph of f has a vertical tangent line at $x = a$, then $f'(a)$ does not exist (Fig. 8C and D).

Answers to Matched Problems

1. (A) $-\$1,600$ (B) $-\$8$ per planter

2. (A) 48 ft/s   (B) $32 + 16h$ (C) 32 ft/s

3. (A) 6, 5   (B) $4 + h$
   (C) 4   (D) Both are 4

4. $f'(x) = 8 - 4x$

5. (A) $f'(1) = 4, f'(2) = 0, f'(4) = -8$
   (B)

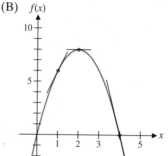

6. $f'(x) = 1/(2\sqrt{x + 4})$

7. $S(12) = 4, S'(12) = 0.125$; 12 months from now the total sales are $4 million and are increasing at the rate of $0.125 million ($125,000) per month. The estimated total sales are $4.125 million after 13 months and $4.25 million after 14 months.

Exercise 3-3

A *In Problems 1 and 2, find the indicated quantity for*
$y = f(x) = 5 - x^2$, and interpret in terms of the
following graph.

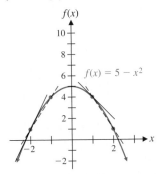

1. (A) $\dfrac{f(2) - f(1)}{2 - 1}$ (B) $\dfrac{f(1 + h) - f(1)}{h}$

(C) $\lim\limits_{h \to 0} \dfrac{f(1 + h) - f(1)}{h}$

2. (A) $\dfrac{f(-1) - f(-2)}{-1 - (-2)}$ (B) $\dfrac{f(-2 + h) - f(-2)}{h}$

(C) $\lim\limits_{h \to 0} \dfrac{f(-2 + h) - f(-2)}{h}$

3. Find the indicated quantities for $f(x) = 3x^2$.

(A) The average rate of change of $f(x)$ if x changes from 1 to 4.

(B) The slope of the secant line through the points $(1, f(1))$ and $(4, f(4))$ on the graph of $y = f(x)$.

(C) The slope of the secant line through the points $(1, f(1))$ and $(1 + h, f(1 + h))$, $h \neq 0$. Simplify your answer.

(D) The slope of the graph at $(1, f(1))$.

(E) The instantaneous rate of change of $y = f(x)$ with respect to x at $x = 1$.

(F) The slope of the tangent line at $(1, f(1))$.

(G) The equation of the tangent line at $(1, f(1))$.

4. Find the indicated quantities for $f(x) = 3x^2$.

(A) The average rate of change of $f(x)$ if x changes from 2 to 5.

(B) The slope of the secant line through the points $(2, f(2))$ and $(5, f(5))$ on the graph of $y = f(x)$.

(C) The slope of the secant line through the points $(2, f(2))$ and $(2 + h, f(2 + h))$, $h \neq 0$. Simplify your answer.

(D) The slope of the graph at $(2, f(2))$.

(E) The instantaneous rate of change of $y = f(x)$ with respect to x at $x = 2$.

(F) The slope of the tangent line at $(2, f(2))$.

(G) The equation of the tangent line at $(2, f(2))$.

In Problems 5–26, use the four-step process to find $f'(x)$
and then find $f'(1), f'(2),$ and $f'(3)$.

5. $f(x) = -5$ **6.** $f(x) = 9$

7. $f(x) = 3x - 7$ **8.** $f(x) = 4 - 6x$

9. $f(x) = 2 - 3x^2$ **10.** $f(x) = 2x^2 + 8$

11. $f(x) = x^2 + 6x - 10$ **12.** $f(x) = x^2 + 4x + 7$

13. $f(x) = 2x^2 - 7x + 3$ **14.** $f(x) = 2x^2 + 5x + 1$

15. $f(x) = -x^2 + 4x - 9$ **16.** $f(x) = -x^2 + 9x - 2$

17. $f(x) = 2x^3 + 1$ **18.** $f(x) = -2x^3 + 5$

19. $f(x) = 4 + \dfrac{4}{x}$ **20.** $f(x) = \dfrac{6}{x} - 2$

21. $f(x) = 5 + 3\sqrt{x}$ **22.** $f(x) = 3 - 7\sqrt{x}$

23. $f(x) = 10\sqrt{x} + 5$ **24.** $f(x) = 16\sqrt{x} + 9$

25. $f(x) = \dfrac{3x}{x + 2}$ **26.** $f(x) = \dfrac{5x}{3 + x}$

B *Problems 27 and 28 refer to the graph of*
$y = f(x) = x^2 + x$ shown.

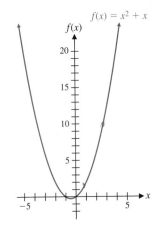

27. (A) Find the slope of the secant line joining $(1, f(1))$ and $(3, f(3))$.

(B) Find the slope of the secant line joining $(1, f(1))$ and $(1 + h, f(1 + h))$.

(C) Find the slope of the tangent line at $(1, f(1))$.

(D) Find the equation of the tangent line at $(1, f(1))$.

28. (A) Find the slope of the secant line joining $(2, f(2))$ and $(4, f(4))$.

(B) Find the slope of the secant line joining $(2, f(2))$ and $(2 + h, f(2 + h))$.

(C) Find the slope of the tangent line at $(2, f(2))$.

(D) Find the equation of the tangent line at $(2, f(2))$.

In Problems 29 and 30, suppose an object moves along the y axis so that its location is $y = f(x) = x^2 + x$ at time x (y is in meters and x is in seconds). Find

29. (A) The average velocity (the average rate of change of y with respect to x) for x changing from 1 to 3 seconds

(B) The average velocity for x changing from 1 to $1 + h$ seconds

(C) The instantaneous velocity at $x = 1$ second

30. (A) The average velocity (the average rate of change of y with respect to x) for x changing from 2 to 4 seconds

(B) The average velocity for x changing from 2 to $2 + h$ seconds

(C) The instantaneous velocity at $x = 2$ seconds

Problems 31–38 refer to the function F in the graph shown. Use the graph to determine whether $F'(x)$ exists at each indicated value of x.

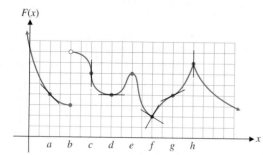

F(x)

31. $x = a$ **32.** $x = b$ ⁿᵒⁿ

33. $x = c$ Non   **34.** $x = d$

35. $x = e$ **36.** $x = f$ non

37. $x = g$ **38.** $x = h$ non

39. Given $f(x) = x^2 - 4x$,

(A) Find $f'(x)$.

(B) Find the slopes of the tangent lines to the graph of f at $x = 0, 2,$ and 4.

(C) Graph f, and sketch in the tangent lines at $x = 0, 2,$ and 4.

40. Given $f(x) = x^2 + 2x$,

(A) Find $f'(x)$.

(B) Find the slopes of the tangent lines to the graph of f at $x = -2, -1,$ and 1.

(C) Graph f, and sketch in the tangent lines at $x = -2, -1,$ and 1.

41. If an object moves along a line so that it is at $y = f(x) = 4x^2 - 2x$ at time x (in seconds), find the instantaneous velocity function $v = f'(x)$, and find the velocity at times $x = 1, 3,$ and 5 seconds (y is measured in feet).

42. Repeat Problem 41 with $f(x) = 8x^2 - 4x$.

43. Let $f(x) = x^2, g(x) = x^2 - 1,$ and $h(x) = x^2 + 2.$

(A) How are the graphs of these functions related? How would you expect the derivatives of these functions to be related?

(B) Use the four-step process to find the derivative of $m(x) = x^2 + C$, where C is any real number constant.

44. Let $f(x) = -x^2, g(x) = -x^2 - 1,$ and $h(x) = -x^2 + 2.$

(A) How are the graphs of these functions related? How would you expect the derivatives of these functions to be related?

(B) Use the four-step process to find the derivative of $m(x) = -x^2 + C$, where C is any real number constant.

45. (A) Give a geometric explanation of the following statement: If $f(x) = C$ is a constant function, then $f'(x) = 0$.

(B) Use the four-step process to verify the statement in part (A).

46. (A) Give a geometric explanation of the following statement: If $f(x) = mx + b$ is a linear function, then $f'(x) = m$.

(B) Use the four-step process to verify the statement in part (A).

C *In Problems 47–50, sketch the graph of f and determine where f is nondifferentiable.*

47. $f(x) = \begin{cases} 2x & \text{if } x < 1 \\ 2 & \text{if } x \geq 1 \end{cases}$

48. $f(x) = \begin{cases} 2x & \text{if } x < 2 \\ 6 - x & \text{if } x \geq 2 \end{cases}$

49. $f(x) = \begin{cases} x^2 + 1 & \text{if } x < 0 \\ 1 & \text{if } x \geq 0 \end{cases}$

50. $f(x) = \begin{cases} 2 - x^2 & \text{if } x \leq 0 \\ 2 & \text{if } x > 0 \end{cases}$

In Problems 51–56, determine whether f is differentiable at $x = 0$ by considering

$$\lim_{h \to 0} \frac{f(0 + h) - f(0)}{h}$$

51. $f(x) = |x|$ ⁿᵒ   **52.** $f(x) = 1 - |x|$

53. $f(x) = x^{1/3}$ ᵛ⁰   **54.** $f(x) = x^{2/3}$

55. $f(x) = \sqrt{1 - x^2}$ **56.** $f(x) = \sqrt{1 + x^2}$

57. A ball dropped from a balloon falls $y = 16x^2$ feet in x seconds. If the balloon is 576 feet above the ground when the ball is dropped, when does the ball hit the ground? What is the impact velocity of the ball at the instant it hits the ground?

58. Repeat Problem 57 if the balloon is 1,024 feet above the ground when the ball is dropped.

Applications

Business & Economics

59. *Revenue.* The revenue (in dollars) from the sale of x car seats for infants is given by

$$R(x) = 60x - 0.025x^2 \qquad 0 \le x \le 2,400$$

(A) Find the average change in revenue if production is changed from 1,000 car seats to 1,050 car seats.

(B) Use the four-step process to find $R'(x)$.

(C) Find the revenue and the instantaneous rate of change of revenue at a production level of 1,000 car seats and write a brief verbal interpretation of these results.

60. *Profit.* The profit (in dollars) from the sale of x car seats for infants is given by

$$P(x) = 45x - 0.025x^2 - 5,000 \qquad 0 \le x \le 2,400$$

(A) Find the average change in profit if production is changed from 800 car seats to 850 car seats.

(B) Use the four-step process to find $P'(x)$.

(C) Find the profit and the instantaneous rate of change of profit at a production level of 800 car seats and write a brief verbal interpretation of these results.

61. *Sales analysis.* The total sales of a company (in millions of dollars) t months from now are given by

$$S(t) = 2\sqrt{t} + 10$$

(A) Use the four-step process to find $S'(t)$.

(B) Find $S(15)$ and $S'(15)$. Write a brief verbal interpretation of these results.

(C) Use the results in part (B) to estimate the total sales after 16 months and after 17 months.

62. *Sales analysis.* The total sales of a company (in millions of dollars) t months from now are given by

$$S(t) = 2\sqrt{t} + 6$$

(A) Use the four-step process to find $S'(t)$.

(B) Find $S(10)$ and $S'(10)$. Write a brief verbal interpretation of these results.

(C) Use the results in part (B) to estimate the total sales after 11 months and after 12 months.

63. *Mineral production.* The U.S. production of zinc (in thousands of metric tons) is given approximately by

$$p(t) = 14t^2 - 6.6t + 602.4$$

where t is time in years and $t = 0$ corresponds to 1995.

(A) Use the four-step process to find $p'(t)$.

(B) Find the annual production in 2010, the instantaneous rate of change of production in 2010, and write a brief verbal interpretation of these results.

64. *Mineral consumption.* The U.S. consumption of copper (in thousands of metric tons) is given approximately by

$$p(t) = 27t^2 - 75t + 6,015$$

where t is time in years and $t = 0$ corresponds to 1990.

(A) Use the four-step process to find $p'(t)$.

(B) Find the annual production in 2010, the instantaneous rate of change of production in 2010, and write a brief verbal interpretation of these results.

Problems 65 and 66 require the use of quadratic regression on a graphing utility.

65. *Electricity consumption.* Table 1 gives the retail sales of electricity (in billion kilowatthours) for the residential and commercial sectors in the United States during the 1990s.

TABLE 1 Retail Electricity Sales		
Year	**Residential**	**Commercial**
1990	924	751
1991	955	766
1992	936	761
1993	995	795
1994	1,008	820
1995	1,043	863
1996	1,082	887
1997	1,075	928
1998	1,128	969
1999	1,146	983

(A) Let x represent time (in years) with $x = 0$ corresponding to 1990 and let y represent the corresponding residential sales. Enter the appropriate data set in a graphing utility and find a quadratic regression equation for the data.

(B) If $y = R(x)$ denotes the regression equation found in part (A) with coefficients rounded to four decimal places, find $R(20)$ and $R'(20)$, and write a brief verbal interpretation of these results. Round answers to the nearest tenth of a billion.

66. *Electricity consumption.* Refer to the data in Table 1.

(A) Let x represent time (in years) with $x = 0$ corresponding to 1990 and let y represent the corresponding commercial sales. Enter the appropriate data set in a graphing utility and find a quadratic regression equation for the data.

(B) If $y = C(x)$ denotes the regression equation found in part (A) with coefficients rounded to four decimal places, find $C(20)$ and $C'(20)$, and write a brief verbal interpretation of these results. Round answers to the nearest tenth of a billion.

Life Sciences

67. *Air pollution.* The ozone level (in parts per billion) on a summer day in a metropolitan area is given by

$$P(t) = 80 + 12t - t^2$$

where t is time in hours and $t = 0$ corresponds to 9 A.M.

(A) Use the four-step process to find $P'(t)$.

(B) Find $P(3)$ and $P'(3)$. Write a brief verbal interpretation of these results.

68. *Medicine.* The body temperature (in degrees Fahrenheit) of a patient t hours after being given a fever-reducing drug is given by

$$F(t) = 98 + \frac{4}{t + 1}$$

(A) Use the four-step process to find $F'(t)$.

(B) Find $F(3)$ and $F'(3)$. Write a brief verbal interpretation of these results.

Social Sciences

69. *Infant mortality.* The number of infant deaths per 100,000 births for males in the United States is given approximately by

$$f(t) = 0.011t^2 - t + 29.8$$

where t is time in years and $t = 0$ corresponds to 1960.

(A) Use the four-step process to find $f'(t)$.

(B) Find the number of male infant deaths in 2000, the instantaneous rate of change of the number of male infant deaths in 2000, and write a brief verbal interpretation of these results.

70. *Infant mortality.* The number of infant deaths per 100,000 births for females in the United States is given approximately by

$$f(t) = 0.008t^2 - 0.74t + 23$$

where t is time in years and $t = 0$ corresponds to 1960.

(A) Use the four-step process to find $f'(t)$.

(B) Find the number of female infant deaths in 2000, the instantaneous rate of change of the number of female infant deaths in 2000, and write a brief verbal interpretation of these results.

Section 3-4 | Power Rule and Basic Differentiation Properties

➤ Constant Function Rule
➤ Power Rule
➤ Constant Multiple Property
➤ Sum and Difference Properties
➤ Applications

In the preceding section, we defined the derivative of f at x as

$$f'(x) = \lim_{h \to 0} \frac{f(x + h) - f(x)}{h}$$

if the limit exists, and we used this definition and a four-step process to find the derivatives of several functions. In this and the next two sections, we develop some rules based on this definition that will enable us to determine the derivatives of a rather large class of functions without having to go through the four-step process each time.

Before starting on these rules, we list some symbols that are widely used to represent derivatives.

NOTATION   The Derivative

Given $y = f(x)$, then

$$f'(x) \qquad y' \qquad \frac{dy}{dx}$$

all represent the derivative of f at x.

Each of these symbols for the derivative has its particular advantage in certain situations. All of them will become familiar to you after a little experience.

➤ Constant Function Rule

If $f(x) = C$ is a constant function, then the four-step process can be used to show $f'(x) = 0$ (see Problem 45 in Exercise 3-3). Thus,

The derivative of any constant function is 0.

THEOREM 1   Constant Function Rule

If $y = f(x) = C$, then
$$f'(x) = 0$$

Also, $y' = 0$ and $dy/dx = 0$.

Note: When we write $C' = 0$ or $\dfrac{d}{dx}C = 0$, we mean that $y' = \dfrac{dy}{dx} = 0$ where $y = C$.

◉ *Insight*   The graph of $f(x) = C$ is a horizontal line with slope 0 (see Fig. 1), so we would expect $f'(x) = 0$.

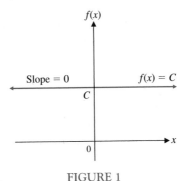

FIGURE 1

EXAMPLE 1   **Differentiating Constant Functions**

(A) If $f(x) = 3$,   then $f'(x) = 0$.   (B) If $y = -1.4$,   then $y' = 0$.

(C) If $y = \pi$,   then $\dfrac{dy}{dx} = 0$.   (D) $\dfrac{d}{dx}23 = 0$

Matched Problem 1   Find

(A) $f'(x)$ for $f(x) = -24$ (B) y' for $y = 12$

(C) $\dfrac{dy}{dx}$ for $y = -\sqrt{7}$ (D) $\dfrac{d}{dx}(-\pi)$

➤ Power Rule

A function of the form $f(x) = x^k$, where k is a real number, is called a **power function.** The elementary functions (see the inside front cover) listed below are examples of power functions:

$$f(x) = x \qquad h(x) = x^2 \qquad m(x) = x^3$$
$$n(x) = \sqrt{x} \qquad p(x) = \sqrt[3]{x} \tag{1}$$

EXPLORE
&DISCUSS
1

(A) It is clear that the functions f, h, and m in (1) are power functions. Explain why the functions n and p are also power functions.

(B) The domain of a power function depends on the power. Discuss the domain of each of the following power functions:

$$r(x) = x^4 \qquad s(x) = x^{-4} \qquad t(x) = x^{1/4}$$
$$u(x) = x^{-1/4} \qquad v(x) = x^{1/5} \qquad w(x) = x^{-1/5}$$

The definition of the derivative and the two-step process introduced in the preceding section can be used to find the derivatives of many power functions. For example, it can be shown that

$$\text{If} \quad f(x) = x^2, \quad \text{then} \quad f'(x) = 2x.$$
$$\text{If} \quad f(x) = x^3, \quad \text{then} \quad f'(x) = 3x^2.$$
$$\text{If} \quad f(x) = x^4, \quad \text{then} \quad f'(x) = 4x^3.$$
$$\text{If} \quad f(x) = x^5, \quad \text{then} \quad f'(x) = 5x^4.$$

Notice the pattern in these derivatives. In each case, the power in f becomes the coefficient in f' and the power in f' is 1 less than the power in f. In general, for any positive integer n:

$$\text{If} \quad f(x) = x^n, \quad \text{then} \quad f'(x) = nx^{n-1}. \tag{2}$$

In fact, more advanced techniques can be used to show that (2) holds for *any* real number n. We will assume this general result for the remainder of this book.

THEOREM 2   Power Rule

If $y = f(x) = x^n$, where n is a real number, then

$$f'(x) = nx^{n-1}$$

Also, $y' = nx^{n-1}$ and $dy/dx = nx^{n-1}$.

EXPLORE
&DISCUSS
2

(A) Write a verbal description of the power rule.

(B) If $f(x) = x$, what is $f'(x)$? Discuss how this derivative can be obtained from the power rule.

EXAMPLE 2   Differentiating Power Functions

(A) If $f(x) = x^5$, then $f'(x) = 5x^{5-1} = 5x^4$.

(B) If $y = x^{25}$, then $y' = 25x^{25-1} = 25x^{24}$.

(C) If $y = t^{-3}$, then $\dfrac{dy}{dt} = -3t^{-3-1} = -3t^{-4} = -\dfrac{3}{t^4}$.

(D) $\dfrac{d}{dx}x^{5/3} = \dfrac{5}{3}x^{(5/3)-1} = \dfrac{5}{3}x^{2/3}$.

Matched Problem 2   Find

(A) $f'(x)$ for $f(x) = x^6$ 　　　　(B) y' for $y = x^{30}$

(C) $\dfrac{dy}{dt}$ for $y = t^{-2}$ 　　　　(D) $\dfrac{d}{dx}x^{3/2}$

In some cases, properties of exponents must be used to rewrite an expression before the power rule is applied.

EXAMPLE 3 **Differentiating Power Functions**

(A) If $f(x) = 1/x^4$, we can write $f(x) = x^{-4}$ and

$$f'(x) = -4x^{-4-1} = -4x^{-5} \quad \text{or} \quad \frac{-4}{x^5}$$

(B) If $y = \sqrt{u}$, we can write $y = u^{1/2}$ and

$$y' = \frac{1}{2}u^{(1/2)-1} = \frac{1}{2}u^{-1/2} \quad \text{or} \quad \frac{1}{2\sqrt{u}}$$

(C) $\dfrac{d}{dx}\dfrac{1}{\sqrt[3]{x}} = \dfrac{d}{dx}x^{-1/3} = -\dfrac{1}{3}x^{(-1/3)-1} = -\dfrac{1}{3}x^{-4/3} \quad \text{or} \quad \dfrac{-1}{3\sqrt[3]{x^4}}$ ■

Matched Problem 3 Find

(A) $f'(x)$ for $f(x) = \dfrac{1}{x}$ (B) y' for $y = \sqrt[3]{u^2}$ (C) $\dfrac{d}{dx}\dfrac{1}{\sqrt{x}}$

➤ Constant Multiple Property

Let $f(x) = ku(x)$, where k is a constant and u is differentiable at x. Then, using the four-step process, we have the following:

Step 1. $f(x + h) = ku(x + h)$

Step 2. $f(x + h) - f(x) = ku(x + h) - ku(x) = k[u(x + h) - u(x)]$

Step 3. $\dfrac{f(x + h) - f(x)}{h} = \dfrac{k[u(x + h) - u(x)]}{h} = k\left[\dfrac{u(x + h) - u(x)}{h}\right]$

Step 4. $f'(x) = \lim\limits_{h \to 0} \dfrac{f(x + h) - f(x)}{h}$

$\qquad\qquad = \lim\limits_{h \to 0} k\left[\dfrac{u(x + h) - u(x)}{h}\right] \qquad \lim\limits_{x \to c} kg(x) = k \lim\limits_{x \to c} g(x)$

$\qquad\qquad = k \lim\limits_{h \to 0}\left[\dfrac{u(x + h) - u(x)}{h}\right] \qquad \text{Definition of } u'(x)$

$\qquad\qquad = ku'(x)$

Thus,

The derivative of a constant times a differentiable function is the constant times the derivative of the function.

THEOREM 3 Constant Multiple Property

If $y = f(x) = ku(x)$, then

$$f'(x) = ku'(x)$$

Also,

$$y' = ku' \qquad \frac{dy}{dx} = k\frac{du}{dx}$$

EXAMPLE 4 **Differentiating a Constant Times a Function**

(A) If $f(x) = 3x^2$, then $f'(x) = 3 \cdot 2x^{2-1} = 6x$.

(B) If $y = \dfrac{t^3}{6} = \dfrac{1}{6}t^3$, then $\dfrac{dy}{dt} = \dfrac{1}{6} \cdot 3t^{3-1} = \dfrac{1}{2}t^2$.

(C) If $y = \dfrac{1}{2x^4} = \dfrac{1}{2}x^{-4}$, then $y' = \dfrac{1}{2}(-4x^{-4-1}) = -2x^{-5}$ or $\dfrac{-2}{x^5}$.

(D) $\dfrac{d}{dx}\dfrac{0.4}{\sqrt{x^3}} = \dfrac{d}{dx}\dfrac{0.4}{x^{3/2}} = \dfrac{d}{dx}0.4x^{-3/2} = 0.4\left[-\dfrac{3}{2}x^{(-3/2)-1}\right]$

$$= -0.6x^{-5/2} \quad \text{or} \quad -\dfrac{0.6}{\sqrt{x^5}}$$

Matched Problem 4 Find

(A) $f'(x)$ for $f(x) = 4x^5$

(B) $\dfrac{dy}{dt}$ for $y = \dfrac{t^4}{12}$

(C) y' for $y = \dfrac{1}{3x^3}$

(D) $\dfrac{d}{dx}\dfrac{0.9}{\sqrt[3]{x}}$

➤ Sum and Difference Properties

Let $f(x) = u(x) + v(x)$, where $u'(x)$ and $v'(x)$ exist. Then, using the four-step process, we have the following:

Step 1. $f(x + h) = u(x + h) + v(x + h)$

Step 2. $f(x + h) - f(x) = u(x + h) - v(x + h) - [u(x) + v(x)]$
$$= u(x + h) - u(x) + v(x + h) - v(x)$$

Step 3. $\dfrac{f(x + h) - f(x)}{h} = \dfrac{u(x + h) - u(x) + v(x + h) - v(x)}{h}$

$$= \dfrac{u(x + h) - u(x)}{h} + \dfrac{v(x + h) - v(x)}{h}$$

Step 4. $f'(x) = \lim\limits_{h \to 0} \dfrac{f(x + h) - f(x)}{h}$

$$= \lim\limits_{h \to 0}\left[\dfrac{u(x + h) - u(x)}{h} + \dfrac{v(x + h) - v(x)}{h}\right]$$

$$\lim\limits_{x \to c}[g(x) + h(x)] = \lim\limits_{x \to c} g(x) + \lim\limits_{x \to c} h(x)$$

$$= \lim\limits_{h \to 0}\dfrac{u(x + h) - u(x)}{h} + \lim\limits_{h \to 0}\dfrac{v(x + h) - v(x)}{h}$$

$$= u'(x) + v'(x)$$

Thus,

> The derivative of the sum of two differentiable functions is the sum of the derivatives.

Similarly, we can show that

> The derivative of the difference of two differentiable functions is the difference of the derivatives.

Together, we then have the **sum and difference property** for differentiation:

THEOREM 4   Sum and Difference Property

If $y = f(x) = u(x) \pm v(x)$, then

$$f'(x) = u'(x) \pm v'(x)$$

Also,

$$y' = u' \pm v' \qquad \frac{dy}{dx} = \frac{du}{dx} \pm \frac{dv}{dx}$$

Note: This rule generalizes to the sum and difference of any given number of functions.

With this and the other rules stated previously, we will be able to compute the derivatives of all polynomials and a variety of other functions.

EXAMPLE 5   **Differentiating Sums and Differences**

(A) If $f(x) = 3x^2 + 2x$,   then

$$f'(x) \underset{\text{---}}{= (3x^2)' + (2x)' = 3(2x) + 2(1)} = 6x + 2$$

(B) If $y = 4 + 2x^3 - 3x^{-1}$,   then

$$y' \underset{\text{---}}{= (4)' + (2x^3)' - (3x^{-1})' = 0 + 2(3x^2) - 3(-1)x^{-2}} = 6x^2 + 3x^{-2}$$

(C) If $y = \sqrt[3]{w} - 3w$,   then

$$\frac{dy}{dw} = \frac{d}{dw}w^{1/3} - \frac{d}{dw}3w = \frac{1}{3}w^{-2/3} - 3 = \frac{1}{3w^{2/3}} - 3$$

(D) $\dfrac{d}{dx}\left(\dfrac{5}{3x^2} - \dfrac{2}{x^4} + \dfrac{x^3}{9}\right) \underset{\text{---}}{= \dfrac{d}{dx}\dfrac{5}{3}x^{-2} - \dfrac{d}{dx}2x^{-4} + \dfrac{d}{dx}\dfrac{1}{9}x^3}$

$$= \frac{5}{3}(-2)x^{-3} - 2(-4)x^{-5} + \frac{1}{9} \cdot 3x^2$$

$$= -\frac{10}{3x^3} + \frac{8}{x^5} + \frac{1}{3}x^2$$

Matched Problem 5   Find

(A) $f'(x)$ for $f(x) = 3x^4 - 2x^3 + x^2 - 5x + 7$

(B) y' for $y = 3 - 7x^{-2}$

(C) $\dfrac{dy}{dv}$ for $y = 5v^3 - \sqrt[4]{v}$

(D) $\dfrac{d}{dx}\left(-\dfrac{3}{4x} + \dfrac{4}{x^3} - \dfrac{x^4}{8}\right)$

 ➤ **Applications**

EXAMPLE 6   **Instantaneous Velocity**   An object moves along the y axis (marked in feet) so that its position at time x (in seconds) is

$$f(x) = x^3 - 6x^2 + 9x$$

(A) Find the instantaneous velocity function v.

(B) Find the velocity at $x = 2$ and $x = 5$ seconds.

(C) Find the time(s) when the velocity is 0.

Solution (A) $v = f'(x) \boxed{= (x^3)' - (6x^2)' + (9x)'} = 3x^2 - 12x + 9$

(B) $f'(2) = 3(2)^2 - 12(2) + 9 = -3$ feet per second

$f'(5) = 3(5)^2 - 12(5) + 9 = 24$ feet per second

(C) $v = f'(x) = 3x^2 - 12x + 9 = 0$

$$3(x^2 - 4x + 3) = 0$$
$$3(x - 1)(x - 3) = 0$$
$$x = 1, 3$$

Thus, $v = 0$ at $x = 1$ and $x = 3$ seconds. ∎

Matched Problem 6 Repeat Example 6 for $f(x) = x^3 - 15x^2 + 72x$.

EXAMPLE 7 **Tangents** Let $f(x) = x^4 - 6x^2 + 10$.

(A) Find $f'(x)$.

(B) Find the equation of the tangent line at $x = 1$.

(C) Find the values of x where the tangent line is horizontal.

Solution (A) $f'(x) \boxed{= (x^4)' - (6x^2)' + (10)'}$

$= 4x^3 - 12x$ $(1, 5)$

(B) $y - y_1 = m(x - x_1)$ $y_1 = f(x_1) = f(1) = (1)^4 - 6(1)^2 + 10 = 5$

$y - 5 = -8(x - 1)$ $m = f'(x_1) = f'(1) = 4(1)^3 - 12(1) = -8$

$y = -8x + 13$ Tangent line at $x = 1$

(C) Since a horizontal line has 0 slope, we must solve $f'(x) = 0$ for x:

$$f'(x) = 4x^3 - 12x = 0$$
$$4x(x^2 - 3) = 0$$
$$4x(x + \sqrt{3})(x - \sqrt{3}) = 0$$
$$x = 0, -\sqrt{3}, \sqrt{3}$$ ∎

Matched Problem 7 Repeat Example 7 for $f(x) = x^4 - 8x^3 + 7$.

Answers to Matched Problems   **1.** All are 0.

2. (A) $6x^5$ (B) $30x^{29}$ (C) $-2t^{-3} = -2/t^3$ (D) $\frac{3}{2}x^{1/2}$

3. (A) $-x^{-2}$, or $-1/x^2$ (B) $\frac{2}{3}u^{-1/3}$, or $2/(3\sqrt[3]{u})$ (C) $-\frac{1}{2}x^{-3/2}$, or $-1/(2\sqrt{x^3})$

4. (A) $20x^4$ (B) $t^3/3$ (C) $-x^{-4}$, or $-1/x^4$ (D) $-0.3x^{-4/3}$, or $-0.3/\sqrt[3]{x^4}$

5. (A) $12x^3 - 6x^2 + 2x - 5$

(B) $14x^{-3}$, or $14/x^3$

(C) $15v^2 - \frac{1}{4}v^{-3/4}$, or $15v^2 - 1/(4v^{3/4})$

(D) $3/(4x^2) - (12/x^4) - (x^3/2)$

6. (A) $v = 3x^2 - 30x + 72$
   (B) $f'(2) = 24$ ft/sec; $f'(5) = -3$ ft/sec
   (C) $x = 4$ and $x = 6$ sec

7. (A) $f'(x) = 4x^3 - 24x^2$
   (B) $y = -20x + 20$
   (C) $x = 0$ and $x = 6$

Exercise 3-4

A *Find the indicated derivatives in Problems 1–18.*

1. $f'(x)$ for $f(x) = 7$
2. $\dfrac{d}{dx} 3$
3. $\dfrac{dy}{dx}$ for $y = x^9$
4. y' for $y = x^6$
5. $\dfrac{d}{dx} x^3$
6. $g'(x)$ for $g(x) = x^5$
7. y' for $y = x^{-4}$
8. $\dfrac{dy}{dx}$ for $y = x^{-8}$
9. $g'(x)$ for $g(x) = x^{8/3}$
10. $f'(x)$ for $f(x) = x^{9/2}$
11. $\dfrac{dy}{dx}$ for $y = \dfrac{1}{x^{10}}$
12. y' for $y = \dfrac{1}{x^{12}}$
13. $f'(x)$ for $f(x) = 5x^2$
14. $\dfrac{d}{dx}(-2x^3)$
15. y' for $y = 0.4x^7$
16. $f'(x)$ for $f(x) = 0.8x^4$
17. $\dfrac{d}{dx}\left(\dfrac{x^3}{18}\right)$
18. $\dfrac{dy}{dx}$ for $y = \dfrac{x^5}{25}$

Problems 19–24 refer to functions f and g that satisfy $f'(2) = 3$ and $g'(2) = -1$. In each problem, find $h'(2)$ for the indicated function h.

19. $h(x) = 4f(x)$
20. $h(x) = 5g(x)$
21. $h(x) = f(x) + g(x)$
22. $h(x) = g(x) - f(x)$
23. $h(x) = 2f(x) - 3g(x) + 7$
24. $h(x) = -4f(x) + 5g(x) - 9$

B *Find the indicated derivatives in Problems 25–48.*

25. $\dfrac{d}{dx}(2x - 5)$
26. $\dfrac{d}{dx}(-4x + 9)$
27. $f'(t)$ if $f(t) = 2t^2 - 3t + 1$
28. $\dfrac{dy}{dt}$ if $y = 2 + 5t - 8t^3$

29. y' for $y = 5x^{-2} + 9x^{-1}$
30. $g'(x)$ if $g(x) = 5x^{-7} - 2x^{-4}$
31. $\dfrac{d}{du}(5u^{0.3} - 4u^{2.2})$
32. $\dfrac{d}{du}(2u^{4.5} - 3.1u + 13.2)$
33. $h'(t)$ if $h(t) = 2.1 + 0.5t - 1.1t^3$
34. $F'(t)$ if $F(t) = 0.2t^3 - 3.1t + 13.2$
35. y' if $y = \dfrac{2}{5x^4}$
36. w' if $w = \dfrac{7}{5u^2}$
37. $\dfrac{d}{dx}\left(\dfrac{3x^2}{2} - \dfrac{7}{5x^2}\right)$
38. $\dfrac{d}{dx}\left(\dfrac{5x^3}{4} - \dfrac{2}{5x^3}\right)$
39. $G'(w)$ if $G(w) = \dfrac{5}{9w^4} + 5\sqrt[3]{w}$
40. $H'(w)$ if $H(w) = \dfrac{5}{w^6} - 2\sqrt{w}$
41. $\dfrac{d}{du}(3u^{2/3} - 5u^{1/3})$
42. $\dfrac{d}{du}(8u^{3/4} + 4u^{-1/4})$
43. $h'(t)$ if $h(t) = \dfrac{3}{t^{3/5}} - \dfrac{6}{t^{1/2}}$
44. $F'(t)$ if $F(t) = \dfrac{5}{t^{1/5}} - \dfrac{8}{t^{3/2}}$
45. y' if $y = \dfrac{1}{\sqrt[3]{x}}$
46. w' if $w = \dfrac{10}{\sqrt[5]{u}}$
47. $\dfrac{d}{dx}\left(\dfrac{1.2}{\sqrt{x}} - 3.2x^{-2} + x\right)$
48. $\dfrac{d}{dx}\left(2.8x^{-3} - \dfrac{0.6}{\sqrt[3]{x^2}} + 7\right)$

For Problems 49–52, find

(A) $f'(x)$

(B) *The slope of the graph of f at x = 2 and x = 4*

(C) *The equations of the tangent lines at x = 2 and x = 4*

(D) *The value(s) of x where the tangent line is horizontal*

49. $f(x) = 6x - x^2$

50. $f(x) = 2x^2 + 8x$

51. $f(x) = 3x^4 - 6x^2 - 7$

52. $f(x) = x^4 - 32x^2 + 10$

If an object moves along the y axis (marked in feet) so that its position at time x (in seconds) is given by the indicated function in Problems 53–56, find

(A) *The instantaneous velocity function v = f'(x)*

(B) *The velocity when x = 0 and x = 3 seconds*

(C) *The time(s) when v = 0*

53. $f(x) = 176x - 16x^2$

54. $f(x) = 80x - 10x^2$

55. $f(x) = x^3 - 9x^2 + 15x$

56. $f(x) = x^3 - 9x^2 + 24x$

Problems 57–64 require the use of a graphing utility. For each problem, find f'(x) and approximate (to four decimal places) the value(s) of x where the graph of f has a horizontal tangent line.

57. $f(x) = x^2 - 3x - 4\sqrt{x}$

58. $f(x) = x^2 + x - 10\sqrt{x}$

59. $f(x) = 3\sqrt[3]{x^4} - 1.5x^2 - 3x$

60. $f(x) = 3\sqrt[3]{x^4} - 2x^2 + 4x$

61. $f(x) = 0.05x^4 + 0.1x^3 - 1.5x^2 - 1.6x + 3$

62. $f(x) = 0.02x^4 - 0.06x^3 - 0.78x^2 + 0.94x + 2.2$

63. $f(x) = 0.2x^4 - 3.12x^3 + 16.25x^2 - 28.25x + 7.5$

64. $f(x) = 0.25x^4 - 2.6x^3 + 8.1x^2 - 10x + 9$

65. Let $f(x) = ax^2 + bx + c, a \neq 0$. Recall that the graph of $y = f(x)$ is a parabola. Use the derivative $f'(x)$ to derive a formula for the x coordinate of the vertex of this parabola.

66. Now that you know how to find derivatives, explain why it is no longer necessary for you to memorize the formula for the x coordinate of the vertex of a parabola.

67. Give an example of a cubic polynomial function that has

(A) No horizontal tangents

(B) One horizontal tangent

(C) Two horizontal tangents

68. Can a cubic polynomial function have more than two horizontal tangents? Explain.

C *Find the indicated derivatives in Problems 69–76.*

69. $f'(x)$ if $f(x) = (2x - 1)^2$

70. y' if $y = (2x - 5)^2$

71. $\dfrac{d}{dx} \dfrac{10x + 20}{x}$

72. $\dfrac{dy}{dx}$ if $y = \dfrac{x^2 + 25}{x^2}$

73. $\dfrac{dy}{dx}$ if $y = \dfrac{3x - 4}{12x^2}$

74. $\dfrac{d}{dx} \dfrac{5x - 3}{15x^6}$

75. y' if $y = \dfrac{x^4 - 3x^3 + 5}{x^2}$

76. $f'(x)$ if $f(x) = \dfrac{2x^5 - 4x^3 + 2x}{x^3}$

In Problems 77 and 78, use the definition of the derivative and the four-step process to verify each statement.

77. $\dfrac{d}{dx}x^3 = 3x^2$ **78.** $\dfrac{d}{dx}x^4 = 4x^3$

79. The domain of the power function $f(x) = x^{1/3}$ is the set of all real numbers. Find the domain of the derivative $f'(x)$. Discuss the nature of the graph of $y = f(x)$ for any x values excluded from the domain of $f'(x)$.

80. The domain of the power function $f(x) = x^{2/3}$ is the set of all real numbers. Find the domain of the derivative $f'(x)$. Discuss the nature of the graph of $y = f(x)$ for any x values excluded from the domain of $f'(x)$.

Applications

Business & Economics

81. *Sales analysis.* The total sales of a company (in millions of dollars) t months from now are given by

$$S(t) = 0.03t^3 + 0.5t^2 + 2t + 3$$

(A) Find $S'(t)$.

(B) Find $S(5)$ and $S'(5)$ (to two decimal places). Write a brief verbal interpretation of these results.

(C) Find $S(10)$ and $S'(10)$ (to two decimal places). Write a brief verbal interpretation of these results.

82. *Sales analysis.* The total sales of a company (in millions of dollars) t months from now are given by

$$S(t) = 0.015t^4 + 0.4t^3 + 3.4t^2 + 10t - 3$$

(A) Find $S'(t)$.

(B) Find $S(4)$ and $S'(4)$ (to two decimal places). Write a brief verbal interpretation of these results.

(C) Find $S(8)$ and $S'(8)$ (to two decimal places). Write a brief verbal interpretation of these results.

83. *Advertising.* Using past records, it is estimated that a marine manufacturer will sell $N(x)$ power boats after spending x thousand on advertising, as given by

$$N(x) = 1,000 - \frac{3,780}{x} \qquad 5 \le x \le 30$$

See the figure.

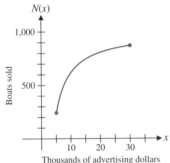

Figure for 83

(A) Find $N'(x)$.

(B) Find $N'(10)$ and $N'(20)$. Write a brief verbal interpretation of these results.

84. *Price–demand equation.* Suppose that in a given gourmet food store, people are willing to buy x pounds of chocolate candy per day at p per quarter pound, as given by the price–demand equation

$$x = 10 + \frac{180}{p} \qquad 2 \le p \le 10$$

This function is graphed in the figure. Find the demand and the instantaneous rate of change of demand with respect to price when the price is $5. Write a brief verbal interpretation of these results.

Figure for 84

85. *Motor vehicle production.* Annual limousine production in the United States for selected years is given in Table 1.

TABLE 1	
Year	Limousine Production
1980	2,500
1985	6,500
1990	4,400
1995	3,400
2000	5,700

(A) Let x represent time (in years) since 1980, and let y represent the corresponding U.S. production of limousines. Enter the data in a graphing utility and find a cubic regression equation for the data.

(B) If $y = L(x)$ denotes the regression equation found in part (A), find $L(12)$ and $L'(12)$ (to the nearest hundred), and write a brief verbal interpretation of these results.

(C) Repeat part (B) for $L(18)$ and $L'(18)$.

86. *Motor vehicle operation.* The total number of registered limousine operators in the United States for selected years is given in Table 2.

TABLE 2	
Year	Limousine Operators
1985	4,000
1990	7,000
1995	8,900
2000	11,000

(A) Let x represent time (in years) since 1980 and let y represent the corresponding number of registered limousine operators in the United States. Enter the data in a graphing utility and find a quadratic regression equation for the data.

(B) If $y = L(x)$ denotes the regression equation found in part (A), find $L(18)$ and $L'(18)$ (to the nearest hundred), and write a brief verbal interpretation of these results.

Life Sciences

87. *Medicine.* A person x inches tall has a pulse rate of y beats per minute, as given approximately by

$$y = 590x^{-1/2} \qquad 30 \le x \le 75$$

What is the instantaneous rate of change of pulse rate at the

(A) 36-inch level?

(B) 64-inch level?

88. *Ecology.* A coal-burning electrical generating plant emits sulfur dioxide into the surrounding air. The concentration $C(x)$, in parts per million, is given approximately by

$$C(x) = \frac{0.1}{x^2}$$

where x is the distance from the plant in miles. Find the instantaneous rate of change of concentration at

(A) $x = 1$ mile

(B) $x = 2$ miles

Social Sciences

89. *Learning.* Suppose that a person learns y items in x hours, as given by

$$y = 50\sqrt{x} \qquad 0 \leq x \leq 9$$

(see the figure). Find the rate of learning at the end of

(A) 1 hour   (B) 9 hours

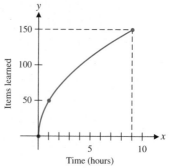

Figure for 89

90. *Learning.* If a person learns y items in x hours, as given by

$$y = 21\sqrt[3]{x^2} \qquad 0 \leq x \leq 8$$

find the rate of learning at the end of

(A) 1 hour   (B) 8 hours

Section 3-5 Derivatives of Products and Quotients

➤ Derivatives of Products
➤ Derivatives of Quotients

The derivative properties discussed in the preceding section added substantially to our ability to compute and apply derivatives to many practical problems. In this and the next sections we add a few more properties that will increase this ability even further.

➤ Derivatives of Products

In Section 3-4 we found that the derivative of a sum is the sum of the derivatives. Is the derivative of a product the product of the derivatives?

EXPLORE
&DISCUSS
1

Let $F(x) = x^2$, $S(x) = x^3$, and $f(x) = F(x)S(x) = x^5$. Which of the following is $f'(x)$?

(A) $F'(x)S'(x)$ $\longrightarrow$
(B) $F(x)S'(x)$
(C) $F'(x)S(x)$
(D) $F(x)S'(x) + F'(x)S(x)$

Comparing the various expressions computed in Explore–Discuss 1, we see that the derivative of a product is not the product of the derivatives, but appears to involve a slightly more complicated form.

Using the definition of the derivative and the two-step process, it can be shown that

The derivative of the product of two functions is the first function times the derivative of the second function plus the second function times the derivative of the first function.

That is,

THEOREM 1   Product Rule

If

$$y = f(x) = F(x)S(x)$$

and if $F'(x)$ and $S'(x)$ exist, then

$$f'(x) = F(x)S'(x) + S(x)F'(x)$$

Also,

$$y' = FS' + SF' \qquad \frac{dy}{dx} = F\frac{dS}{dx} + S\frac{dF}{dx}$$

EXAMPLE 1   **Differentiating a Product** Use two different methods to find $f'(x)$ for

$$f(x) = 2x^2(3x^4 - 2).$$

Solution   **Method 1.** Use the product rule:

$$\begin{aligned}
f'(x) &= 2x^2(3x^4 - 2)' + (3x^4 - 2)(2x^2)' \\
&= 2x^2(12x^3) + (3x^4 - 2)(4x) \\
&= 24x^5 + 12x^5 - 8x \\
&= 36x^5 - 8x
\end{aligned}$$

First times derivative of second plus second times derivative of first

Method 2. Multiply first; then take derivatives:

$$f(x) = 2x^2(3x^4 - 2) = 6x^6 - 4x^2$$
$$f'(x) = 36x^5 - 8x$$

■

Matched Problem 1   Use two different methods to find $f'(x)$ for $f(x) = 3x^3(2x^2 - 3x + 1)$.

At this point, all the products we encounter can be differentiated by either of the methods illustrated in Example 1. In the next and later sections we will see that there are situations where the product rule must be used. Unless instructed otherwise, you should use the product rule to differentiate all products in this section to gain experience with the use of this important differentiation rule.

EXAMPLE 2   **Tangent Lines** Let $f(x) = (2x - 9)(x^2 + 6)$.

(A) Find the equation of the line tangent to the graph of $f(x)$ at $x = 3$.

(B) Find the value(s) of x where the tangent line is horizontal.

Solution   (A) First, find $f'(x)$:

$$\begin{aligned}
f'(x) &= (2x - 9)(x^2 + 6)' + (x^2 + 6)(2x - 9)' \\
&= (2x - 9)(2x) + (x^2 + 6)(2)
\end{aligned}$$

Then, find $f(3)$ and $f'(3)$:

$$f(3) = [2(3) - 9](3^2 + 6) = (-3)(15) = -45$$
$$f'(3) = [2(3) - 9]2(3) + (3^2 + 6)(2) = -18 + 30 = 12$$

Now, find the equation of the tangent line at $x = 3$:

$$y - y_1 = m(x - x_1) \quad \text{$y_1 = f(x_1) = f(3) = -45$}$$
$$y - (-45) = 12(x - 3) \quad \text{$m = f'(x_1) = f'(3) = 12$}$$
$$y = 12x - 81 \quad \text{Tangent line at $x = 3$}$$

(B) The tangent line is horizontal at any value of x such that $f'(x) = 0$, so

$$f'(x) = (2x - 9)2x + (x^2 + 6)2 = 0$$
$$6x^2 - 18x + 12 = 0$$
$$x^2 - 3x + 2 = 0$$
$$(x - 1)(x - 2) = 0$$
$$x = 1, 2$$

The tangent line is horizontal at $x = 1$ and at $x = 2$. ■

Matched Problem 2   Repeat Example 2 for $f(x) = (2x + 9)(x^2 - 12)$. ────■

◉ Insight   As Example 2 illustrates, the way we write $f'(x)$ depends on what we want to do with it. If we are interested only in evaluating $f'(x)$ at specified values of x, the form in part (A) is sufficient. However, if we want to solve $f'(x) = 0$, we must multiply and collect like terms, as we did in part (B). ●

➤ Derivatives of Quotients

As is the case with a product, the derivative of a quotient of two functions is not the quotient of the derivatives of the two functions.

EXPLORE & DISCUSS 2

Let $T(x) = x^5$, $B(x) = x^2$, and

$$f(x) = \frac{T(x)}{B(x)} = \frac{x^5}{x^2} = x^3$$

Which of the following is $f'(x)$?

(A) $\dfrac{T'(x)}{B'(x)}$ (B) $\dfrac{T'(x)B(x)}{[B(x)]^2}$ (C) $\dfrac{T(x)B'(x)}{[B(x)]^2}$

(D) $\dfrac{T'(x)B(x)}{[B(x)]^2} - \dfrac{T(x)B'(x)}{[B(x)]^2} = \dfrac{T'(x)B(x) - T(x)B'(x)}{[B(x)]^2}$

The expressions in Explore–Discuss 2 suggest that the derivative of a quotient leads to a more complicated quotient than you might expect.

In general, if $T(x)$ and $B(x)$ are any two differentiable functions and

$$f(x) = \frac{T(x)}{B(x)}$$

it can be shown that

$$f'(x) = \frac{B(x)T'(x) - T(x)B'(x)}{[B(x)]^2}$$

Thus,

The derivative of the quotient of two functions is the bottom function times the derivative of the top function minus the top function times the derivative of the bottom function, all over the bottom function squared.

THEOREM 2   Quotient Rule

If

$$y = f(x) = \frac{T(x)}{B(x)}$$

and if $T'(x)$ and $B'(x)$ exist, then

$$f'(x) = \frac{B(x)T'(x) - T(x)B'(x)}{[B(x)]^2}$$

Also,

$$y' = \frac{BT' - TB'}{B^2} \qquad \frac{dy}{dx} = \frac{B\dfrac{dT}{dx} - T\dfrac{dB}{dx}}{B^2}$$

EXAMPLE 3   **Differentiating Quotients**

(A) If $f(x) = \dfrac{x^2}{2x - 1}$, find $f'(x)$.   (B) If $y = \dfrac{t^2 - t}{t^3 + 1}$, find y'.

(C) Find $\dfrac{d}{dx} \dfrac{x^2 - 3}{x^2}$ by using the quotient rule and also by splitting the fraction into two fractions.

Solution   (A) $f'(x) = \dfrac{(2x - 1)(x^2)' - x^2(2x - 1)'}{(2x - 1)^2}$ The bottom times the derivative of the top minus the top times the derivative of the bottom, all over the square of the bottom

$$= \frac{(2x - 1)(2x) - x^2(2)}{(2x - 1)^2}$$

$$= \frac{4x^2 - 2x - 2x^2}{(2x - 1)^2}$$

$$= \frac{2x^2 - 2x}{(2x - 1)^2}$$

(B) $y' = \dfrac{(t^3 + 1)(t^2 - t)' - (t^2 - t)(t^3 + 1)'}{(t^3 + 1)^2}$

$$= \frac{(t^3 + 1)(2t - 1) - (t^2 - t)(3t^2)}{(t^3 + 1)^2}$$

$$= \frac{2t^4 - t^3 + 2t - 1 - 3t^4 + 3t^3}{(t^3 + 1)^2}$$

$$= \frac{-t^4 + 2t^3 + 2t - 1}{(t^3 + 1)^2}$$

(C) **Method 1.** Use the quotient rule:

$$\frac{d}{dx}\frac{x^2-3}{x^2} = \frac{x^2\dfrac{d}{dx}(x^2-3) - (x^2-3)\dfrac{d}{dx}x^2}{(x^2)^2}$$

$$= \frac{x^2(2x) - (x^2-3)2x}{x^4}$$

$$= \frac{2x^3 - 2x^3 + 6x}{x^4} = \frac{6x}{x^4} = \frac{6}{x^3}$$

Method 2. Split into two fractions:

$$\frac{x^2-3}{x^2} = \frac{x^2}{x^2} - \frac{3}{x^2} = 1 - 3x^{-2}$$

$$\frac{d}{dx}(1 - 3x^{-2}) = 0 - 3(-2)x^{-3} = \frac{6}{x^3}$$

Comparing methods 1 and 2, we see that it often pays to change an expression algebraically before blindly using a differentiation formula. ∎

Matched Problem 3   Find

(A) $f'(x)$ for $f(x) = \dfrac{2x}{x^2+3}$

(B) y' for $y = \dfrac{t^3 - 3t}{t^2 - 4}$

(C) $\dfrac{d}{dx}\dfrac{2 + x^3}{x^3}$ two ways

EXPLORE & DISCUSS 3

Explain why $\neq$ is used below, and then find the correct derivative.

$$\frac{d}{dx}\frac{x^3}{x^2 + 3x + 4} \neq \frac{3x^2}{2x + 3}$$

EXAMPLE 4   **Sales Analysis**   The total sales S (in thousands of games) for a home video game t months after the game is introduced are given by

$$S(t) = \frac{125t^2}{t^2 + 100}$$

(A) Find $S'(t)$.

(B) Find $S(10)$ and $S'(10)$. Write a brief verbal interpretation of these results.

(C) Use the results from part (B) to estimate the total sales after 11 months.

Solution   (A) $S'(t) = \dfrac{(t^2 + 100)(125t^2)' - 125t^2(t^2 + 100)'}{(t^2 + 100)^2}$

$= \dfrac{(t^2 + 100)(250t) - 125t^2(2t)}{(t^2 + 100)^2}$

$= \dfrac{250t^3 + 25,000t - 250t^3}{(t^2 + 100)^2}$

$= \dfrac{25,000t}{(t^2 + 100)^2}$

(B) $S(10) = \dfrac{125(10)^2}{10^2 + 100} = 62.5$ and $S'(10) = \dfrac{25,000(10)}{(10^2 + 100)^2} = 6.25$

The total sales after 10 months are 62,500 games, and sales are increasing at the rate of 6,250 games per month.

(C) The total sales will increase by approximately 6,250 games during the next month. Thus, the estimated total sales after 11 months are $62,500 + 6,250 = 68,750$ games.   ∎

Matched Problem 4   Refer to Example 4. Suppose that the total sales S (in thousands of games) t months after the game is introduced are given by

$$S(t) = \frac{150t}{t + 3}$$

(A) Find $S'(t)$.

(B) Find $S(12)$ and $S'(12)$. Write a brief verbal interpretation of these results.

(C) Use the results from part (B) to estimate the total sales after 13 months.

Answers to Matched Problems   **1.** $30x^4 - 36x^3 + 9x^2$

2. (A) $y = 84x - 297$

(B) $x = -4, x = 1$

3. (A) $\dfrac{(x^2 + 3)2 - (2x)(2x)}{(x^2 + 3)^2} = \dfrac{6 - 2x^2}{(x^2 + 3)^2}$

(B) $\dfrac{(t^2 - 4)(3t^2 - 3) - (t^3 - 3t)(2t)}{(t^2 - 4)^2} = \dfrac{t^4 - 9t^2 + 12}{(t^2 - 4)^2}$

(C) $-\dfrac{6}{x^4}$

4. (A) $S'(t) = \dfrac{450}{(t + 3)^2}$

(B) $S(12) = 120; S'(12) = 2$. After 12 months, the total sales are 120,000 games, and sales are increasing at the rate of 2,000 games per month.

(C) 122,000 games

Exercise 3-5

The answers to most of the problems in this exercise set contain both an unsimplified form and a simplified form of the derivative. When checking your work, first check that you applied the rules correctly, and then check that you performed the algebraic simplification correctly. Unless instructed otherwise, when differentiating a product, use the product rule rather than performing the multiplication first.

A *In Problems 1–18, find $f'(x)$ and simplify.*

1. $f(x) = 2x^3(x^2 - 2)$

2. $f(x) = 5x^2(x^3 + 2)$

3. $f(x) = (x - 3)(2x - 1)$

4. $f(x) = (3x + 2)(4x - 5)$

5. $f(x) = \dfrac{x}{x - 3}$

6. $f(x) = \dfrac{3x}{2x + 1}$

7. $f(x) = \dfrac{2x + 3}{x - 2}$

8. $f(x) = \dfrac{3x - 4}{2x + 3}$

9. $f(x) = (x^2 + 1)(2x - 3)$

10. $f(x) = (3x + 5)(x^2 - 3)$

11. $f(x) = (0.4x + 2)(0.5x - 5)$

12. $f(x) = (0.5x - 4)(0.2x + 1)$

13. $f(x) = \dfrac{x^2 + 1}{2x - 3}$

14. $f(x) = \dfrac{3x + 5}{x^2 - 3}$

15. $f(x) = (x^2 + 2)(x^2 - 3)$

16. $f(x) = (x^2 - 4)(x^2 + 5)$

17. $f(x) = \dfrac{x^2 + 2}{x^2 - 3}$

18. $f(x) = \dfrac{x^2 - 4}{x^2 + 5}$

In Problems 19–26, find $h'(x)$, where $f(x)$ is an unspecified differentiable function.

19. $h(x) = xf(x)$

20. $h(x) = x^2 f(x)$

21. $h(x) = x^3 f(x)$

22. $h(x) = \dfrac{f(x)}{x}$

23. $h(x) = \dfrac{f(x)}{x^2}$

24. $h(x) = \dfrac{f(x)}{x^3}$

25. $h(x) = \dfrac{x}{f(x)}$

26. $h(x) = \dfrac{x^2}{f(x)}$

B *In Problems 27–34, find the indicated derivatives and simplify.*

27. $f'(x)$ for $f(x) = (2x + 1)(x^2 - 3x)$

28. y' for $y = (x^3 + 2x^2)(3x - 1)$

29. $\dfrac{dy}{dt}$ for $y = (2.5t - t^2)(4t + 1.4)$

30. $\dfrac{d}{dt}[(3 - 0.4t^3)(0.5t^2 - 2t)]$

31. y' for $y = \dfrac{5x - 3}{x^2 + 2x}$

32. $f'(x)$ for $f(x) = \dfrac{3x^2}{2x - 1}$

33. $\dfrac{d}{dw}\dfrac{w^2 - 3w + 1}{w^2 - 1}$

34. $\dfrac{dy}{dw}$ for $y = \dfrac{w^4 - w^3}{3w - 1}$

In Problems 35–38, find $f'(x)$ and find the equation of the line tangent to the graph of f at x = 2.

35. $f(x) = (1 + 3x)(5 - 2x)$

36. $f(x) = (7 - 3x)(1 + 2x)$

37. $f(x) = \dfrac{x - 8}{3x - 4}$

38. $f(x) = \dfrac{2x - 5}{2x - 3}$

In Problems 39–42, find $f'(x)$ and find the value(s) of x where $f'(x) = 0$.

39. $f(x) = (2x - 15)(x^2 + 18)$

40. $f(x) = (2x - 3)(x^2 - 6)$

41. $f(x) = \dfrac{x}{x^2 + 1}$

42. $f(x) = \dfrac{x}{x^2 + 9}$

In Problems 43–46, find $f'(x)$ two ways: by using the product or quotient rule and by simplifying first.

43. $f(x) = x^3(x^4 - 1)$ **44.** $f(x) = x^4(x^3 - 1)$

45. $f(x) = \dfrac{x^3 + 9}{x^3}$ **46.** $f(x) = \dfrac{x^4 + 4}{x^4}$

C *In Problems 47–60, find each indicated derivative and simplify.*

47. $f'(w)$ if $f(w) = (3w^2 - 1)^2$

48. $g'(w)$ if $g(w) = (5 - 2w^3)^2$

49. $\dfrac{d}{dx}\dfrac{3x^2 - 2x + 3}{4x^2 + 5x - 1}$

50. y' for $y = \dfrac{x^3 - 3x + 4}{2x^2 + 3x - 2}$

51. $\dfrac{dy}{dx}$ for $y = 9x^{1/3}(x^3 + 5)$

52. $\dfrac{d}{dx}\left[(4x^{1/2} - 1)(3x^{1/3} + 2)\right]$

53. $f'(x)$ for $f(x) = \dfrac{6\sqrt[3]{x}}{x^2 - 3}$

54. y' for $y = \dfrac{2\sqrt{x}}{x^2 - 3x + 1}$

55. $g'(t)$ if $g(t) = \dfrac{0.2t}{3t^2 - 1}$

56. $h'(t)$ if $h(t) = \dfrac{-0.05t^2}{2t + 1}$

57. $\dfrac{d}{dx}\dfrac{x^3 - 2x^2}{\sqrt[3]{x^2}}$

58. $\dfrac{dy}{dx}$ for $y = \dfrac{x^2 - 3x + 1}{\sqrt[4]{x}}$

59. $f'(x)$ for $f(x) = \dfrac{(2x^2 - 1)(x^2 + 3)}{x^2 + 1}$

60. y' for $y = \dfrac{2x - 1}{(x^3 + 2)(x^2 - 3)}$

In Problems 61–64, approximate (to four decimal places) the value (s) of x where the graph of f has a horizontal tangent line.

61. $f(x) = (x^2 + 4)(x^2 - 2x)$

62. $f(x) = (x^2 + 3)(x^2 + 4x)$

63. $f(x) = \dfrac{x^3 + 17x - 2}{x^2 + 1}$

64. $f(x) = \dfrac{x^3 + 15x - 1}{x^2 + 1}$

Applications

Business & Economics

65. *Sales analysis.* The total sales S (in thousands of CDs) for a compact disk are given by

$$S(t) = \dfrac{90t^2}{t^2 + 50}$$

where t is the number of months since the release of the CD.

(A) Find $S'(t)$.

(B) Find $S(10)$ and $S'(10)$. Write a brief verbal interpretation of these results.

(C) Use the results from part (B) to estimate the total sales after 11 months.

66. *Sales analysis.* A communications company has installed a cable television system in a city. The total number N (in thousands) of subscribers t months after the installation of the system is given by

$$N(t) = \dfrac{180t}{t + 4}$$

(A) Find $N'(t)$.

(B) Find $N(16)$ and $N'(16)$. Write a brief verbal interpretation of these results.

(C) Use the results from part (B) to estimate the total number of subscribers after 17 months.

67. *Price–demand equation.* According to classical economic theory, the demand x for a quantity in a free market decreases as the price p increases (see the figure). Suppose that the number x of CD players

people are willing to buy per week from a retail chain at a price of $\$p$ is given by

$$x = \dfrac{4{,}000}{0.1p + 1} \qquad 10 \le p \le 70$$

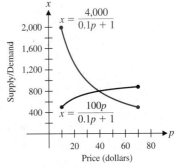

Figure for 67 and 68

(A) Find dx/dp.

(B) Find the demand and the instantaneous rate of change of demand with respect to price when the price is \$40. Write a brief verbal interpretation of these results.

(C) Use the results from part (B) to estimate the demand if the price is increased to \$41.

68. *Price–supply equation.* Also according to classical economic theory, the supply x for a quantity in a free market increases as the price p increases (see the figure). Suppose that the number x of CD players a retail chain is willing to sell per week at a price of p is given by

$$x = \frac{100p}{0.1p + 1} \qquad 10 \le p \le 70$$

(A) Find dx/dp.

(B) Find the supply and the instantaneous rate of change of supply with respect to price when the price is $40. Write a brief verbal interpretation of these results.

(C) Use the results from part (B) to estimate the supply if the price is increased to $41.

Life Sciences

69. *Medicine.* A drug is injected into the bloodstream of a patient through her right arm. The concentration of the drug (in milligrams per cubic centimeter) in the bloodstream of the left arm t hours after the injection is given by

$$C(t) = \frac{0.14t}{t^2 + 1}$$

(A) Find $C'(t)$.

(B) Find $C'(0.5)$ and $C'(3)$, and interpret the results.

70. *Drug sensitivity.* One hour after x milligrams of a particular drug are given to a person, the change in body temperature $T(x)$, in degrees Fahrenheit, is given approximately by

$$T(x) = x^2\left(1 - \frac{x}{9}\right) \qquad 0 \le x \le 7$$

The rate $T'(x)$ at which T changes with respect to the size of the dosage, x, is called the *sensitivity* of the body to the dosage.

(A) Find $T'(x)$ using the product rule.

(B) Find $T'(1)$, $T'(3)$, and $T'(6)$.

Social Sciences

71. *Learning.* In the early days of quantitative learning theory (around 1917), L. L. Thurstone found that a given person successfully accomplished $N(x)$ acts after x practice acts, as given by

$$N(x) = \frac{100x + 200}{x + 32}$$

(A) Find the instantaneous rate of change of learning, $N'(x)$, with respect to the number of practice acts x.

(B) Find $N'(4)$ and $N'(68)$.

Section 3-6 | General Power Rule (Chain Rule)

➤ Chain Rule: Power Rule
➤ Combining Rules of Differentiation

In this section we develop a rule for differentiating powers of functions—a special case of the very important *chain rule*, which we will return to in Chapter 5. Also, for the first time, we will encounter some product forms that cannot be simplified by multiplication and must be differentiated by the power rule.

➤ Chain Rule: Power Rule

We have already made extensive use of the power rule,

$$\frac{d}{dx}x^n = nx^{n-1} \tag{1}$$

Now we want to generalize this rule so that we can differentiate functions of the form $[u(x)]^n$, where $u(x)$ is a differentiable function. Is rule (1) still valid if we replace x with a function $u(x)$?

EXPLORE
&DISCUSS
1

Let $u(x) = 2x^2$ and $f(x) = [u(x)]^3 = 8x^6$. Which of the following is $f'(x)$?

(A) $3[u(x)]^2$

(B) $3[u'(x)]^2$

(C) $3[u(x)]^2u'(x)$

The calculations in Explore–Discuss 1 show that we cannot generalize the power rule simply by replacing x with $u(x)$ in equation (1).

How can we find a formula for the derivative of $[u(x)]^n$, where $u(x)$ is an arbitrary differentiable function? Let's begin by considering the derivatives of $[u(x)]^2$ and $[u(x)]^3$ to see if a general pattern emerges. Since $[u(x)]^2 = u(x)u(x)$, we use the product rule to write

$$\frac{d}{dx}[u(x)]^2 = \frac{d}{dx}[u(x)u(x)]$$
$$= u(x)u'(x) + u(x)u'(x)$$
$$= 2u(x)u'(x) \qquad (2)$$

Since $[u(x)]^3 = [u(x)]^2 u(x)$, we now use the product rule and the result in equation (2) to write

$$\frac{d}{dx}[u(x)]^3 = \frac{d}{dx}\{[u(x)]^2 u(x)\}$$
$$= [u(x)]^2 \frac{d}{dx}u(x) + u(x)\frac{d}{dx}[u(x)]^2$$
$$= [u(x)]^2 u'(x) + u(x)[2u(x)u'(x)]$$
$$= 3[u(x)]^2 u'(x)$$

Use equation (2) to substitute for $\frac{d}{dx}[u(x)]^2$.

Continuing in this fashion, it can be shown that

$$\frac{d}{dx}[u(x)]^n = n[u(x)]^{n-1}u'(x) \qquad n \text{ a positive integer} \qquad (3)$$

Using more advanced techniques, formula (3) can be established for all real numbers n. Thus, we have the **general power rule:**

THEOREM 1   General Power Rule

If $u(x)$ is a differentiable function, n is any real number, and

$$y = f(x) = [u(x)]^n$$

then

$$f'(x) = n[u(x)]^{n-1}u'(x)$$

This rule is often written more compactly as

$$y' = nu^{n-1}u' \qquad \text{or} \qquad \frac{d}{dx}u^n = nu^{n-1}\frac{du}{dx} \qquad \text{where } u = u(x)$$

The general power rule is a special case of a very important and useful differentiation rule called the **chain rule.** In essence, the chain rule will enable us to differentiate a composition form $f[g(x)]$ if we know how to differentiate $f(x)$ and $g(x)$. We defer a complete discussion of the chain rule until Chapter 5.

EXAMPLE 1   **Using the General Power Rule**   Find the indicated derivatives:

(A) $f'(x)$ if $f(x) = (3x + 1)^4$

(B) y' if $y = (x^3 + 4)^7$

(C) $\dfrac{d}{dt}\dfrac{1}{(t^2 + t + 4)^3}$

(D) $\dfrac{dh}{dw}$ if $h(w) = \sqrt{3 - w}$

Solution   (A) $f(x) = (3x + 1)^4$ Let $u = 3x + 1, n = 4$.

$f'(x) \boxed{= 4(3x + 1)^3(3x + 1)'}$ $nu^{n-1}\dfrac{du}{dx}$

$= 4(3x + 1)^3 \, 3$ $\dfrac{du}{dx} = 3$

$= 12(3x + 1)^3$

(B) $y = (x^3 + 4)^7$ Let $u = (x^3 + 4), n = 7$.

$y' \boxed{= 7(x^3 + 4)^6(x^3 + 4)'}$ $nu^{n-1}\dfrac{du}{dx}$

$= 7(x^3 + 4)^6 \, 3x^2$ $\dfrac{du}{dx} = 3x^2$

$= 21x^2(x^3 + 4)^6$

(C) $\dfrac{d}{dt}\dfrac{1}{(t^2 + t + 4)^3}$

$= \dfrac{d}{dt}(t^2 + t + 4)^{-3}$ Let $u = t^2 + t + 4, n = -3$

$\boxed{= -3(t^2 + t + 4)^{-4}(t^2 + t + 4)'}$ $nu^{n-1}\dfrac{du}{dt}$

$= -3(t^2 + t + 4)^{-4}(2t + 1)$ $\dfrac{du}{dt} = 2t + 1$

$= \dfrac{-3(2t + 1)}{(t^2 + t + 4)^4}$

(D) $h(w) = \sqrt{3 - w} = (3 - w)^{1/2}$ Let $u = 3 - w, n = \dfrac{1}{2}$

$\dfrac{dh}{dw} \boxed{= \dfrac{1}{2}(3 - w)^{-1/2}(3 - w)'}$ $nu^{n-1}\dfrac{du}{dw}$

$= \dfrac{1}{2}(3 - w)^{-1/2}(-1)$ $\dfrac{du}{dw} = -1$

$= -\dfrac{1}{2(3 - w)^{1/2}}$ or $-\dfrac{1}{2\sqrt{3 - w}}$ ■

Matched Problem 1   Find the indicated derivatives:

(A) $h'(x)$ if $h(x) = (5x + 2)^3$

(B) y' if $y = (x^4 - 5)^5$

(C) $\dfrac{d}{dt}\dfrac{1}{(t^2 + 4)^2}$ (D) $\dfrac{dg}{dw}$ if $g(w) = \sqrt{4 - w}$ ■

Notice that we used two steps to differentiate each function in Example 1. First, we applied the general power rule; then we found du/dx. As you gain experience with the general power rule, you may want to combine these two steps. If you do this, be certain to multiply by du/dx. For example,

$$\dfrac{d}{dx}(x^5 + 1)^4 = 4(x^5 + 1)^3 5x^4 \quad \text{Correct}$$

$$\dfrac{d}{dx}(x^5 + 1)^4 \neq 4(x^5 + 1)^3 \quad du/dx = 5x^4 \text{ is missing}$$

⊚ Insight   If we let $u(x) = x$, then $du/dx = 1$, and the general power rule reduces to the (ordinary) power rule discussed in Section 3-4. Compare the following:

$$\frac{d}{dx}x^n = nx^{n-1} \qquad \text{Yes—power rule}$$

$$\frac{d}{dx}u^n = nu^{n-1}\frac{du}{dx} \qquad \text{Yes—general power rule}$$

$$\frac{d}{dx}u^n \neq nu^{n-1} \qquad \text{Unless } u(x) = x + k \text{ so that } du/dx = 1$$

➤ **Combining Rules of Differentiation**

The following examples illustrate the use of the general power rule in combination with other rules of differentiation.

EXAMPLE 2   **Tangent Lines** Find the equation of the line tangent to the graph of f at $x = 2$ for $f(x) = x^2\sqrt{2x + 12}$.

Solution $f(x) = x^2\sqrt{2x + 12}$

$\qquad = x^2(2x + 12)^{1/2}$ Apply the product rule.

$f'(x) = x^2\dfrac{d}{dx}(2x + 12)^{1/2} + (2x + 12)^{1/2}\dfrac{d}{dx}x^2$ Use the general power rule to differentiate $(2x + 12)^{1/2}$ and the ordinary power rule to differentiate x^2.

$\qquad = x^2\left[\dfrac{1}{2}(2x + 12)^{-1/2}\right](2) + (2x + 12)^{1/2}(2x)$

$\qquad = \dfrac{x^2}{\sqrt{2x + 12}} + 2x\sqrt{2x + 12}$

$f'(2) = \dfrac{4}{\sqrt{16}} + 4\sqrt{16} = 1 + 16 = 17$

$f(2) = 4\sqrt{16} = 16$

$(x_1, y_1) = (2, f(2)) = (2, 16)$ Point

$m = f'(2) = 17$ Slope

$y - 16 = 17(x - 2)$ $y - y_1 = m(x - x_1)$

$\qquad y = 17x - 18$ Tangent line

Matched Problem 2   Find $f'(x)$ and the equation of the line tangent to the graph of f at $x = 3$ for $f(x) = x\sqrt{15 - 2x}$.

EXAMPLE 3   **Tangent Lines** Find the value(s) of x where the tangent line is horizontal for

$$f(x) = \frac{x^3}{(2 - 3x)^5}$$

Solution Use the quotient rule:

$$f'(x) = \frac{(2 - 3x)^5 \dfrac{d}{dx} x^3 - x^3 \dfrac{d}{dx}(2 - 3x)^5}{[(2 - 3x)^5]^2}$$

Use the ordinary power rule to differentiate x^3 and the general power rule to differentiate $(2 - 3x)^5$.

$$= \frac{(2 - 3x)^5 3x^2 - x^3 5(2 - 3x)^4(-3)}{(2 - 3x)^{10}}$$

$$= \frac{(2 - 3x)^4 3x^2[(2 - 3x) + 5x]}{(2 - 3x)^{10}}$$

$$= \frac{3x^2(2 + 2x)}{(2 - 3x)^6} = \frac{6x^2(x + 1)}{(2 - 3x)^6}$$

Since a fraction is 0 when the numerator is 0 and the denominator is not, we see that $f'(x) = 0$ at $x = -1$ and $x = 0$. Thus, the graph of f will have horizontal tangent lines at $x = -1$ and $x = 0$. ■

Matched Problem 3 Find the value(s) of x where the tangent line is horizontal for

$$f(x) = \frac{x^3}{(3x - 2)^2}$$

_____

EXAMPLE 4 **Combining Differentiation Rules** Starting with the function f in Example 3, write f as a product and then differentiate.

Solution

$$f(x) = \frac{x^3}{(2 - 3x)^5} = x^3(2 - 3x)^{-5}$$

$$f'(x) = x^3 \frac{d}{dx}(2 - 3x)^{-5} + (2 - 3x)^{-5} \frac{d}{dx} x^3$$

$$= x^3(-5)(2 - 3x)^{-6}(-3) + (2 - 3x)^{-5} 3x^2$$

$$= 15x^3(2 - 3x)^{-6} + 3x^2(2 - 3x)^{-5}$$

At this point, we have an unsimplified form for $f'(x)$. This may be satisfactory for some purposes, but not for others. For example, if we need to solve the equation $f'(x) = 0$, we must simplify algebraically:

$$f'(x) = \frac{15x^3}{(2 - 3x)^6} + \frac{3x^2}{(2 - 3x)^5} = \frac{15x^3}{(2 - 3x)^6} + \frac{3x^2(2 - 3x)}{(2 - 3x)^6}$$

$$= \frac{15x^3 + 3x^2(2 - 3x)}{(2 - 3x)^6} = \frac{3x^2(5x + 2 - 3x)}{(2 - 3x)^6}$$

$$= \frac{3x^2(2 + 2x)}{(2 - 3x)^6} = \frac{6x^2(1 + x)}{(2 - 3x)^6}$$

■

Matched Problem 4 Refer to the function f in Matched Problem 3. Write f as a product and then differentiate.

_____

Insight   As Example 4 illustrates, any quotient can be converted to a product and differentiated by the product rule. However, if the derivative must be simplified, it is usually easier to use the quotient rule. (Compare the algebraic simplifications in Example 4 with those in Example 3.) There is one special case where using negative exponents is the preferred method—a fraction whose numerator is a constant.

EXAMPLE 5   **Alternative Methods of Differentiation** Find $f'(x)$ two ways for

$$f(x) = \frac{4}{(x^2 + 9)^3}$$

Solution   **Method 1.** Use the quotient rule:

$$f'(x) = \frac{(x^2 + 9)^3 \dfrac{d}{dx}4 - 4\dfrac{d}{dx}(x^2 + 9)^3}{[(x^2 + 9)^3]^2}$$

$$= \frac{(x^2 + 9)^3(0) - 4[3(x^2 + 9)^2(2x)]}{(x^2 + 9)^6}$$

$$= \frac{-24x(x^2 + 9)^2}{(x^2 + 9)^6} = \frac{-24x}{(x^2 + 9)^4}$$

Method 2. Rewrite as a product, and use the general power rule:

$$f(x) = \frac{4}{(x^2 + 9)^3} = 4(x^2 + 9)^{-3}$$

$$f'(x) = 4(-3)(x^2 + 9)^{-4}(2x)$$

$$= \frac{-24x}{(x^2 + 9)^4}$$

Which method do you prefer?

Matched Problem 5   Find $f'(x)$ two ways for $f(x) = \dfrac{5}{(x^3 + 1)^2}$.

Answers to Matched Problems

1. (A) $15(5x + 2)^2$
   (B) $20x^3(x^4 - 5)^4$
   (C) $-4t/(t^2 + 4)^3$
   (D) $-1/(2\sqrt{4 - w})$

2. $f'(x) = \sqrt{15 - 2x} - \dfrac{x}{\sqrt{15 - 2x}}; y = 2x + 3$

3. $x = 0, x = 2$

4. $-6x^3(3x - 2)^{-3} + 3x^2(3x - 2)^{-2} = \dfrac{3x^2(x - 2)}{(3x - 2)^3}$

5. $\dfrac{-30x^2}{(x^3 + 1)^3}$

Exercise 3-6

The answers to many of the problems in this exercise set contain both an unsimplified form and a simplified form of a derivative. When checking your work, first check that you applied the rules correctly, and then check that you performed the algebraic simplification correctly.

A In Problems 1–6, replace the **?** with an expression that will make the indicated equation valid.

1. $\dfrac{d}{dx}(3x + 4)^4 = 4(3x + 4)^3$ **?**

2. $\dfrac{d}{dx}(5 - 2x)^6 = 6(5 - 2x)^5$ **?**

3. $\dfrac{d}{dx}(4 - 2x^2)^3 = 3(4 - 2x^2)^2$ **?**

4. $\dfrac{d}{dx}(3x^2 + 7)^5 = 5(3x^2 + 7)^4$ **?**

5. $\dfrac{d}{dx}(1 + 2x + 3x^2)^7 = 7(1 + 2x + 3x^2)^6$ **?**

6. $\dfrac{d}{dx}(4 - 3x - 2x^2)^8 = 8(4 - 3x - 2x^2)^7$ **?**

In Problems 7–20, find $f'(x)$ using the general power rule and simplify.

7. $f(x) = (2x + 5)^3$
8. $f(x) = (3x - 7)^5$
9. $f(x) = (5 - 2x)^4$
10. $f(x) = (9 - 5x)^2$
11. $f(x) = (4 + 0.2x)^5$
12. $f(x) = (6 - 0.5x)^4$
13. $f(x) = (3x^2 + 5)^5$
14. $f(x) = (5x^2 - 3)^6$
15. $f(x) = (x^3 - 2x^2 + 2)^8$
16. $f(x) = (2x^2 + x + 1)^7$
17. $f(x) = (2x - 5)^{1/2}$
18. $f(x) = (4x + 3)^{1/2}$
19. $f(x) = (x^4 + 1)^{-2}$
20. $f(x) = (x^5 + 2)^{-3}$

In Problems 21–24, find $f'(x)$ and the equation of the line tangent to the graph of f at the indicated value of x. Find the value(s) of x where the tangent line is horizontal.

21. $f(x) = (2x - 1)^3$; $x = 1$
22. $f(x) = (3x - 1)^4$; $x = 1$
23. $f(x) = (4x - 3)^{1/2}$; $x = 3$
24. $f(x) = (2x + 8)^{1/2}$; $x = 4$

B In Problems 25–44, use the general power rule to find the indicated derivative and simplify.

25. y' if $y = 3(x^2 - 2)^4$

26. y' if $y = 2(x^3 + 6)^5$

27. $\dfrac{d}{dt} 2(t^2 + 3t)^{-3}$

28. $\dfrac{d}{dt} 3(t^3 + t^2)^{-2}$

29. $\dfrac{dh}{dw}$ if $h(w) = \sqrt{w^2 + 8}$

30. $\dfrac{dg}{dw}$ if $g(w) = \sqrt[3]{3w - 7}$

31. $g'(x)$ if $g(x) = \sqrt[3]{3x + 4}$

32. $h'(x)$ if $h(x) = \sqrt{2x - 5}$

33. $\dfrac{d}{dx}\sqrt[4]{0.8x + 3.6}$

34. $\dfrac{d}{dx}\sqrt[5]{1.6x - 4.6}$

35. $F'(t)$ if $F(t) = (t^2 - 4t + 2)^{1/2}$

36. $G'(t)$ if $G(t) = (2t^2 + 2t - 3)^{1/2}$

37. y' if $y = \dfrac{1}{2x + 4}$

38. y' if $y = \dfrac{1}{3x - 7}$

39. $\dfrac{d}{dw} \dfrac{1}{(w^3 + 4)^5}$

40. $\dfrac{d}{dw} \dfrac{1}{(w^2 - 2)^6}$

41. $\dfrac{dy}{dx}$ if $y = (3\sqrt{x} - 1)^5$

42. $\dfrac{dy}{dx}$ if $y = \left(\dfrac{1}{x^2} - 5\right)^{-2}$

43. $f'(t)$ if $f(t) = \dfrac{4}{\sqrt{t^2 - 3t}}$

44. $g'(t)$ if $g(t) = \dfrac{3}{\sqrt[3]{t - t^2}}$

In Problems 45–50, find $f'(x)$, and find the equation of the line tangent to the graph of f at the indicated value of x.

45. $f(x) = x(4 - x)^3$; $x = 2$
46. $f(x) = x^2(1 - x)^4$; $x = 2$
47. $f(x) = \dfrac{x}{(2x - 5)^3}$; $x = 3$
48. $f(x) = \dfrac{x^4}{(3x - 8)^2}$; $x = 4$
49. $f(x) = x\sqrt{2x + 2}$; $x = 1$
50. $f(x) = x\sqrt{x - 6}$; $x = 7$

In Problems 51–56, find $f'(x)$, and find the value(s) of x where the tangent line is horizontal.

51. $f(x) = x^2(x - 5)^3$
52. $f(x) = x^3(x - 7)^4$

53. $f(x) = \dfrac{x}{(2x + 5)^2}$ **54.** $f(x) = \dfrac{x - 1}{(x - 3)^3}$

55. $f(x) = \sqrt{x^2 - 8x + 20}$

56. $f(x) = \sqrt{x^2 + 4x + 5}$

In Problems 57–62, approximate (to four decimal places) the value(s) of x where the graph of f has a horizontal tangent line.

57. $f(x) = x(x - 1)(x^2 - 5)$

58. $f(x) = x(x - 2)(x + 3)(x - 4)$

59. $f(x) = (x^3 - 2x^2)(x^2 + 1)$

60. $f(x) = (x^3 + 3x^2)(x^2 + 4)$

61. $f(x) = \sqrt{x^4 - 6x^2 + x + 12}$

62. $f(x) = \sqrt{x^4 - 4x^3 + 4x + 20}$

C *In Problems 63–74, find each derivative and simplify.*

63. $\dfrac{d}{dx}[3x(x^2 + 1)^3]$

64. $\dfrac{d}{dx}[2x^2(x^3 - 3)^4]$

65. $\dfrac{d}{dx}\dfrac{(x^3 - 7)^4}{2x^3}$

66. $\dfrac{d}{dx}\dfrac{3x^2}{(x^2 + 5)^3}$

67. $\dfrac{d}{dx}[(2x - 3)^2(2x^2 + 1)^3]$

68. $\dfrac{d}{dx}[(x^2 - 1)^3(x^2 - 2)^2]$

69. $\dfrac{d}{dx}(4x^2\sqrt{x^2 - 1})$

70. $\dfrac{d}{dx}(3x\sqrt{2x^2 + 3})$

71. $\dfrac{d}{dx}\dfrac{2x}{\sqrt{x - 3}}$

72. $\dfrac{d}{dx}\dfrac{x^2}{\sqrt{x^2 + 1}}$

73. $\dfrac{d}{dx}\sqrt{(2x - 1)^3(x^2 + 3)^4}$

74. $\dfrac{d}{dx}\sqrt{\dfrac{4x + 1}{2x^2 + 1}}$

Applications

Business & Economics

75. *Cost function.* The total cost (in hundreds of dollars) of producing x calculators per day is

$$C(x) = 10 + \sqrt{2x + 16} \qquad 0 \le x \le 50$$

(see the figure).

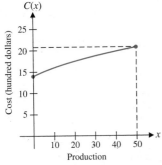

Figure for 75

(A) Find $C'(x)$.

(B) Find $C'(24)$ and $C'(42)$, and interpret the results.

76. *Cost function.* The total cost (in hundreds of dollars) of producing x cameras per week is

$$C(x) = 6 + \sqrt{4x + 4} \qquad 0 \le x \le 30$$

(A) Find $C'(x)$.

(B) Find $C'(15)$ and $C'(24)$, and interpret the results.

77. *Price–supply equation.* The number x of stereo speakers a retail chain is willing to sell per week at a price of $\$p$ is given by

$$x = 80\sqrt{p + 25} - 400 \qquad 20 \le p \le 100$$

(see the figure).

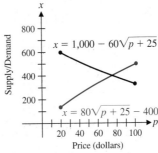

Figure for 77 and 78

(A) Find dx/dp.

(B) Find the supply and the instantaneous rate of change of supply with respect to price when the price is $\$75$. Write a brief verbal interpretation of these results.

78. *Price–demand equation.* The number x of stereo speakers people are willing to buy per week from a retail chain at a price of $\$p$ is given by

$$x = 1,000 - 60\sqrt{p + 25} \qquad 20 \le p \le 100$$

(see the previous figure).

(A) Find dx/dp.

(B) Find the demand and the instantaneous rate of change of demand with respect to price when the price is $75. Write a brief verbal interpretation of these results.

79. *Compound interest.* If $1,000 is invested at an annual interest rate r compounded monthly, the amount in the account at the end of 4 years is given by

$$A = 1,000\left(1 + \tfrac{1}{12}r\right)^{48}$$

Find the rate of change of the amount A with respect to the interest rate r.

80. *Compound interest.* If $100 is invested at an annual interest rate r compounded semiannually, the amount in the account at the end of 5 years is given by

$$A = 100\left(1 + \tfrac{1}{2}r\right)^{10}$$

Find the rate of change of the amount A with respect to the interest rate r.

Life Sciences

81. *Bacteria growth.* The number y of bacteria in a certain colony after x days is given approximately by

$$y = (3 \times 10^6)\left[1 - \frac{1}{\sqrt[3]{(x^2 - 1)^2}}\right]$$

Find dy/dx.

82. *Pollution.* A small lake in a resort area became contaminated with harmful bacteria because of excessive septic tank seepage. After treating the lake with a bactericide, the Department of Public Health estimated the bacteria concentration (number per cubic centimeter) after t days to be given by

$$C(t) = 500(8 - t)^2 \qquad 0 \le t \le 7$$

(A) Find $C'(t)$ using the general power rule.

(B) Find $C'(1)$ and $C'(6)$, and interpret the results.

Social Sciences

83. *Learning.* In 1930, L. L. Thurstone developed the following formula to indicate how learning time T depends on the length of a list n:

$$T = f(n) = \frac{c}{k}n\sqrt{n - a}$$

where a, c, and k are empirical constants. Suppose that for a particular person, time T (in minutes) for learning a list of length n is

$$T = f(n) = 2n\sqrt{n - 2}$$

(A) Find dT/dn.

(B) Find $f'(11)$ and $f'(27)$, and interpret the results.

Section 3-7 | Marginal Analysis in Business and Economics

- ➤ Marginal Cost, Revenue, and Profit
- ➤ Application
- ➤ Marginal Average Cost, Revenue, and Profit

➤ Marginal Cost, Revenue, and Profit

One important use of calculus in business and economics is in *marginal analysis.* In economics, the word *marginal* refers to a rate of change, that is, to a derivative. Thus, if $C(x)$ is the total cost of producing x items, then $C'(x)$ is called the *marginal cost* and represents the instantaneous rate of change of total cost with respect to the number of items produced. Similarly, the *marginal revenue* is the derivative of the total revenue function and the *marginal profit* is the derivative of the total profit function.

DEFINITION   Marginal Cost, Revenue, and Profit

If x is the number of units of a product produced in some time interval, then

$$\text{total cost} = C(x)$$
$$\textbf{marginal cost} = C'(x)$$
$$\text{total revenue} = R(x)$$
$$\textbf{marginal revenue} = R'(x)$$
$$\text{total profit} = P(x) = R(x) - C(x)$$
$$\textbf{marginal profit} = P'(x) = R'(x) - C'(x)$$
$$= (\text{marginal revenue}) - (\text{marginal cost})$$

Marginal cost (or revenue or profit) is the instantaneous rate of change of cost (or revenue or profit) relative to production at a given production level.

To begin our discussion, we consider a cost function $C(x)$. It is important to remember that $C(x)$ represents the *total* cost of producing x items, not the cost of producing a *single* item. To find the cost of producing a single item, we use the difference of two successive values of $C(x)$:

$$\text{Total cost of producing } x + 1 \text{ items} = C(x + 1)$$
$$\text{Total cost of producing } x \text{ items} = C(x)$$
$$\text{Exact cost of producing the } (x + 1)\text{st item} = C(x + 1) - C(x)$$

EXAMPLE 1   **Cost Analysis**   A company manufactures fuel tanks for automobiles. The total weekly cost (in dollars) of producing x tanks is given by

$$C(x) = 10,000 + 90x - 0.05x^2$$

(A) Find the marginal cost function.

(B) Find the marginal cost at a production level of 500 tanks per week and interpret the results.

(C) Find the exact cost of producing the 501st item.

Solution   (A) $C'(x) = 90 - 0.1x$

(B) $C'(500) = 90 - 0.1(500) = \$40$ Marginal cost

At a production level of 500 tanks per week, the total production costs are increasing at the rate of \$40 tank.

(C) $C(501) = 10,000 + 90(501) - 0.05(501)^2$

$\qquad = \$42,539.95$ Total cost of producing 501 tanks per week

$C(500) = 10,000 + 90(500) - 0.05(500)^2$

$\qquad = \$42,500.00$ Total cost of producing 500 tanks per week

$C(501) - C(500) = 42,539.95 - 42,500.00$

$\qquad\qquad = \$39.95$ Exact cost of producing the 501st tank   ■

Matched Problem 1   A company manufactures automatic transmissions for automobiles. The total weekly cost (in dollars) of producing x transmissions is given by

$$C(x) = 50,000 + 600x - 0.75x^2$$

(A) Find the marginal cost function.

(B) Find the marginal cost at a production level of 200 transmissions per week and interpret the results.

(C) Find the exact cost of producing the 201st transmission.

In Example 1, we found that the cost of the 501st tank and the marginal cost at a production level of 500 tanks differ by only a nickel. To explore this apparent relationship between marginal cost and cost of a single item, we return to the definition of the derivative. If $C(x)$ is any total cost function, then

$$C'(x) = \lim_{h \to 0} \frac{C(x + h) - C(x)}{h} \qquad \text{Marginal cost}$$

$$C'(x) \approx \frac{C(x + h) - C(x)}{h} \qquad h \neq 0$$

$$C'(x) \approx C(x + 1) - C(x) \qquad h = 1$$

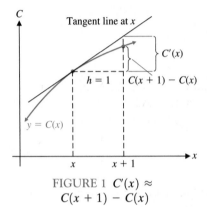

FIGURE 1 $C'(x) \approx$ $C(x + 1) - C(x)$

Thus, we see that the marginal cost $C'(x)$ approximates $C(x + 1) - C(x)$, the exact cost of producing the $(x + 1)$st item. These observations are summarized below and illustrated in Figure 1.

THEOREM 1   Marginal Cost and Exact Cost

If $C(x)$ is the total cost of producing x items, the marginal cost function approximates the exact cost of producing the $(x + 1)$st item:

$$\underset{\text{Marginal cost}}{} \quad \underset{\text{Exact cost}}{}$$
$$C'(x) \approx C(x + 1) - C(x)$$

Similar statements can be made for total revenue functions and total profit functions.

◉ **Insight**   Theorem 1 states that the marginal cost at a given production level x approximates the cost of producing the $(x + 1)$st or *next* item. In practice, the marginal cost is used more frequently than the exact cost. One reason for this is that the marginal cost is easily visualized when examining the graph of the total cost function. Figure 2 shows the graph of the cost function discussed in Example 1 with tangent lines added at $x = 200$ and $x = 500$. The graph clearly shows that as production increases, the slope of the tangent line decreases. Thus, the cost of producing the next tank also decreases, a desirable characteristic of a total cost function. We will have much more to say about graphical analysis in Chapter 4.

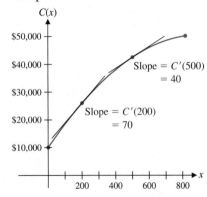

FIGURE 2 $C(x) = 10,000 + 90x - 0.05x^2$

► Application

We now want to discuss how price, demand, revenue, cost, and profit are tied together in typical applications. Although either price or demand can be used as the independent variable in a price–demand equation, it is common practice to use demand as the independent variable when marginal revenue, cost, and profit are also involved.

EXPLORE & DISCUSS

1

The market research department of a company used test marketing to determine the demand for a new radio (Table 1).

(A) Assuming that the relationship between price p and demand x is linear, find the price–demand equation and write the result in the form $x = f(p)$. Graph the equation and find the domain of f. Discuss the effect of price increases and decreases on demand.

(B) Solve the equation found in part (A) for p, obtaining an equation of the form $p = g(x)$. Graph this equation and find the domain of g. Discuss the effect of price increases and decreases on demand.

TABLE 1

Demand	Price
x	p
3,000	$7
6,000	$4

EXAMPLE 2

Production Strategy The market research department of a company recommends that the company manufacture and market a new transistor radio. After suitable test marketing, the research department presents the following **price–demand equation:**

$$x = 10,000 - 1,000p \quad \underline{x \text{ is demand at price } p.} \qquad (1)$$

Or, solving (1) for p,

$$p = 10 - 0.001x \qquad (2)$$

where x is the number of radios retailers are likely to buy at $\$p$ per radio.

The financial department provides the following **cost function:**

$$C(x) = 7,000 + 2x \qquad (3)$$

where $\$7,000$ is the estimate of fixed costs (tooling and overhead) and $\$2$ is the estimate of variable costs per radio (materials, labor, marketing, transportation, storage, etc.).

(A) Find the domain of the function defined by the price–demand equation (2).

(B) Find the marginal cost function $C'(x)$ and interpret.

(C) Find the revenue function as a function of x, and find its domain.

(D) Find the marginal revenue at $x = 2,000$, 5,000, and 7,000. Interpret these results.

(E) Graph the cost function and the revenue function in the same coordinate system, find the intersection points of these two graphs, and interpret the results.

(F) Find the profit function and its domain, and sketch its graph.

(G) Find the marginal profit at $x = 1,000$, 4,000, and 6,000. Interpret these results.

Solution (A) Since price p and demand x must be nonnegative, we have $x \geq 0$ and

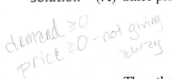

$$p = 10 - 0.001x \geq 0$$
$$10 \geq 0.001x$$
$$10,000 \geq x$$

Thus, the permissible values of x are $0 \leq x \leq 10,000$.

(B) The marginal cost is $C'(x) = 2$. Since this is a constant, it costs an additional \$2 to produce one more radio at any production level.

(C) The **revenue** is the amount of money R received by the company for manufacturing and selling x radios at \$$p$ per radio and is given by

$$R = (\text{number of radios sold})(\text{price per radio}) = xp$$

In general, the revenue R can be expressed as a function of p by using equation (1) or as a function of x by using equation (2). As we mentioned earlier, when using marginal functions, we will always use the number of items x as the independent variable. Thus, the **revenue function** is

$$R(x) = xp = x(10 - 0.001x) \quad \text{Using equation (2)} \tag{4}$$
$$= 10x - 0.001x^2$$

Since equation (2) is defined only for $0 \leq x \leq 10,000$, it follows that the domain of the revenue function is $0 \leq x \leq 10,000$.

(D) The **marginal revenue** is

$$R'(x) = 10 - 0.002x$$

For production levels of $x = 2,000, 5,000,$ and $7,000$, we have

$$R'(2,000) = 6 \qquad R'(5,000) = 0 \qquad R'(7,000) = -4$$

This means that at production levels of 2,000, 5,000, and 7,000, the respective approximate changes in revenue per unit change in production are \$6, \$0, and -\$4. That is, at the 2,000 output level, revenue increases as production increases; at the 5,000 output level, revenue does not change with a "small" change in production; and at the 7,000 output level, revenue decreases with an increase in production.

(E) When we graph $R(x)$ and $C(x)$ in the same coordinate system, we obtain Figure 3. The intersection points are called the **break-even points** because revenue equals cost at these production levels—the company neither makes nor loses money, but just breaks even. The break-even points are obtained as follows:

$$C(x) = R(x)$$
$$7,000 + 2x = 10x - 0.001x^2$$
$$0.001x^2 - 8x + 7,000 = 0 \quad \text{Solve using the quadratic formula}$$
$$x^2 - 8,000x + 7,000,000 = 0 \quad \text{(see Appendix A-8).}$$

$$x = \frac{8,000 \pm \sqrt{8,000^2 - 4(7,000,000)}}{2}$$

$$= \frac{8,000 \pm \sqrt{36,000,000}}{2}$$

$$= \frac{8,000 \pm 6,000}{2}$$

$$= 1,000, \quad 7,000$$

$$R(1,000) = 10(1,000) - 0.001(1,000)^2 = 9,000$$
$$C(1,000) = 7,000 + 2(1,000) = 9,000$$
$$R(7,000) = 10(7,000) - 0.001(7,000)^2 = 21,000$$
$$C(7,000) = 7,000 + 2(7,000) = 21,000$$

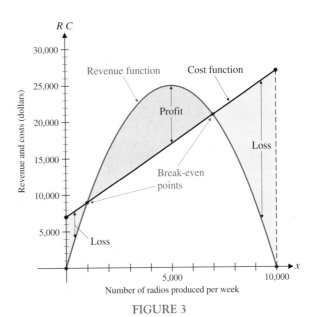

FIGURE 3

Thus, the break-even points are (1,000, 9,000) and (7,000, 21,000), as shown in Figure 3. Further examination of the figure shows that cost is greater than revenue for production levels between 0 and 1,000 and also between 7,000 and 10,000. Consequently, the company incurs a loss at these levels. On the other hand, for production levels between 1,000 and 7,000, revenue is greater than cost and the company makes a profit.

(F) The **profit function** is

$$P(x) = R(x) - C(x)$$
$$= (10x - 0.001x^2) - (7{,}000 + 2x)$$
$$= -0.001x^2 + 8x - 7{,}000$$

The domain of the cost function is $x \geq 0$ and the domain of the revenue function is $0 \leq x \leq 10{,}000$. Thus, the domain of the profit function is the set of x values for which both functions are defined; that is, $0 \leq x \leq 10{,}000$. The graph of the profit function is shown in Figure 4. Notice that the x coordinates of the break-even points in Figure 3 are the x intercepts of the profit function. Furthermore, the intervals where cost is greater than revenue and where revenue is greater than cost correspond, respectively, to the intervals where profit is negative and the intervals where profit is positive.

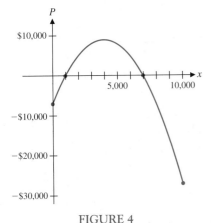

FIGURE 4

(G) The **marginal profit** is

$$P'(x) = -0.002x + 8$$

For production levels of 1,000, 4,000, and 6,000, we have

$$P'(1{,}000) = 6 \qquad P'(4{,}000) = 0 \qquad P'(6{,}000) = -4$$

This means that at production levels of 1,000, 4,000, and 6,000, the respective approximate changes in profit per unit change in production are $6, $0, and −$4. That is, at the 1,000 output level, profit will be increased if production is increased; at the 4,000 output level, profit does not change for "small" changes in production; and at the 6,000 output level, profits will decrease if production is increased. It seems the best production level to produce a maximum profit is 4,000.

Example 2 warrants careful study, since a number of important ideas in economics and calculus are involved. In the next chapter, we will develop a systematic procedure for finding the production level (and, using the demand equation, the selling price) that will maximize profit.

Matched Problem 2

Refer to the revenue and profit functions in Example 2.

(A) Find $R'(3,000)$ and $R'(6,000)$, and interpret the results.

(B) Find $P'(2,000)$ and $P'(7,000)$, and interpret the results.

EXPLORE & DISCUSS 2

Let

$$C(x) = 12,000 + 5x \quad \text{and} \quad R(x) = 9x - 0.002x^2$$

Explain why $\neq$ is used below. Then find the correct expression for the profit function.

$$P(x) = R(x) - C(x) \neq 9x - 0.002x^2 - 12,000 + 5x$$

➤ **Marginal Average Cost, Revenue, and Profit**

Sometimes, it is desirable to carry out marginal analysis relative to **average cost (cost per unit)**, **average revenue (revenue per unit)**, and **average profit (profit per unit)**. The relevant definitions are summarized in the following box:

DEFINITION   Marginal Average Cost, Revenue, and Profit

If x is the number of units of a product produced in some time interval, then

Cost per unit: average cost $= \overline{C}(x) = \dfrac{C(x)}{x}$

marginal average cost $= \overline{C}'(x) = \dfrac{d}{dx}\overline{C}(x)$

Revenue per unit: average revenue $= \overline{R}(x) = \dfrac{R(x)}{x}$

marginal average revenue $= \overline{R}'(x) = \dfrac{d}{dx}\overline{R}(x)$

Profit per unit: average profit $= \overline{P}(x) = \dfrac{P(x)}{x}$

marginal average profit $= \overline{P}'(x) = \dfrac{d}{dx}\overline{P}(x)$

EXAMPLE 3

Cost Analysis   A small machine shop manufactures drill bits used in the petroleum industry. The shop manager estimates that the total daily cost (in dollars) of producing x bits is

$$C(x) = 1,000 + 25x - 0.1x^2$$

(A) Find $\overline{C}(x)$ and $\overline{C}'(x)$.

(B) Find $\overline{C}(10)$ and $\overline{C}'(10)$, and interpret.

(C) Use the results in part (B) to estimate the average cost per bit at a production level of 11 bits per day.

Solution   (A) $\overline{C}(x) = \dfrac{C(x)}{x} = \dfrac{1{,}000 + 25x - 0.1x^2}{x}$

$\qquad\qquad = \dfrac{1{,}000}{x} + 25 - 0.1x \qquad\qquad$ *Average cost function*

$\qquad \overline{C}'(x) = \dfrac{d}{dx}\overline{C}(x) = -\dfrac{1{,}000}{x^2} - 0.1 \quad$ *Marginal average cost function*

(B) $\overline{C}(10) = \dfrac{1{,}000}{10} + 25 - 0.1(10) = \$124$

$\qquad \overline{C}'(10) = -\dfrac{1{,}000}{10^2} - 0.1 = -\$10.10$

At a production level of 10 bits per day, the average cost of producing a bit is \$124, and this cost is decreasing at the rate of \$10.10 per bit.

(C) If production is increased by 1 bit, then the average cost per bit will decrease by approximately \$10.10. Thus, the average cost per bit at a production level of 11 bits per day is approximately \$124 − \$10.10 = \$113.90. ■

Matched Problem 3   Consider the cost function for the production of radios from Example 2:

$$C(x) = 7{,}000 + 2x$$

(A) Find $\overline{C}(x)$ and $\overline{C}'(x)$.

(B) Find $\overline{C}(100)$ and $\overline{C}'(100)$, and interpret.

(C) Use the results in part (B) to estimate the average cost per radio at a production level of 101 radios. ————————————————■

EXPLORE & DISCUSS 3

A student produced the following solution to Matched Problem 3:

$$C(x) = 7{,}000 + 2x \quad \text{Cost}$$

$$C'(x) = 2 \qquad\qquad \text{Marginal cost}$$

$$\dfrac{C'(x)}{x} = \dfrac{2}{x} \qquad\qquad \text{"Average" of the marginal cost}$$

Explain why the last function is not the same as the marginal average cost function.

Caution

1. The marginal average cost function must be computed by first finding the average cost function and then finding its derivative. As Explore–Discuss 3 illustrates, reversing the order of these two steps produces a different function that does not have any useful economic interpretations.

2. Recall that the marginal cost function has two interpretations: the usual interpretation of any derivative as an instantaneous rate of change, and the special interpretation as an approximation to the exact cost of the $(x + 1)$st item. This special interpretation does not apply to the marginal average cost function. Referring to Example 3, it would be incorrect to interpret $\overline{C}'(10) = -\$10.10$ to mean that the average cost of the next bit is approximately −\$10.10. In fact, the phrase "average cost of the next bit" does not even make sense. Averaging is a concept applied to a collection of items, not to a single item.

These remarks also apply to revenue and profit functions.

Answers to Matched Problems   **1.** (A) $C'(x) = 600 - 1.5x$

(B) $C'(200) = 300$. At a production level of 200 transmissions, total costs are increasing at the rate of $300 per transmission.

(C) $C(201) - C(200) = \$299.25$.

2. (A) $R'(3,000) = 4$. At a production level of 3,000, a unit increase in production will increase revenue by approx. $4.

$R'(6,000) = -2$. At a production level of 6,000, a unit increase in production will decrease revenue by approx. $2.

(B) $P'(2,000) = 4$. At a production level of 2,000, a unit increase in production will increase profit by approx. $4.

$P'(7,000) = -6$. At a production level of 7,000, a unit increase in production will decrease profit by approx. $6.

3. (A) $\overline{C}(x) = \dfrac{7,000}{x} + 2;\ \overline{C}'(x) = -\dfrac{7,000}{x^2}$

(B) $\overline{C}(100) = \$72;\ \overline{C}'(100) = -\$0.70$. At a production level of 100 radios, the average cost per radio is $72, and this average cost is decreasing at a rate of $0.70 per radio.

(C) Approx. $71.30.

Exercise 3-7

Applications

Business & Economics

1. *Cost analysis.* The total cost (in dollars) of producing x food processors is

$$C(x) = 2,000 + 50x - 0.5x^2$$

(A) Find the exact cost of producing the 21st food processor.

(B) Use the marginal cost to approximate the cost of producing the 21st food processor.

2. *Cost analysis.* The total cost (in dollars) of producing x electric guitars is

$$C(x) = 1,000 + 100x - 0.25x^2$$

(A) Find the exact cost of producing the 51st guitar.

(B) Use the marginal cost to approximate the cost of producing the 51st guitar.

3. *Cost analysis.* The total cost (in dollars) of manufacturing x auto body frames is

$$C(x) = 60,000 + 300x$$

(A) Find the average cost per unit if 500 frames are produced.

(B) Find the marginal average cost at a production level of 500 units, and interpret the results.

(C) Use the results from parts (A) and (B) to estimate the average cost per frame if 501 frames are produced.

4. *Cost analysis.* The total cost (in dollars) of printing x dictionaries is

$$C(x) = 20,000 + 10x$$

(A) Find the average cost per unit if 1,000 dictionaries are produced.

(B) Find the marginal average cost at a production level of 1,000 units, and interpret the results.

(C) Use the results from parts (A) and (B) to estimate the average cost per dictionary if 1,001 dictionaries are produced.

5. *Profit analysis.* The total profit (in dollars) from the sale of x skateboards is

$$P(x) = 30x - 0.3x^2 - 250 \qquad 0 \le x \le 100$$

(A) Find the exact profit from the sale of the 26th skateboard.

(B) Use the marginal profit to approximate the profit from the sale of the 26th skateboard.

6. *Profit analysis.* The total profit (in dollars) from the sale of x portable stereos is

$$P(x) = 22x - 0.2x^2 - 400 \qquad 0 \le x \le 100$$

(A) Find the exact profit from the sale of the 41st stereo.

(B) Use the marginal profit to approximate the profit from the sale of the 41st stereo.

7. *Profit analysis.* The total profit (in dollars) from the sale of x video cassettes is

$$P(x) = 5x - 0.005x^2 - 450 \qquad 0 \le x \le 1,000$$

Evaluate the marginal profit at the given values of x, and interpret the results.

(A) $x = 450$ (B) $x = 750$

8. *Profit analysis.* The total profit (in dollars) from the sale of x cameras is

$$P(x) = 12x - 0.02x^2 - 1,000 \qquad 0 \le x \le 600$$

Evaluate the marginal profit at the given values of x, and interpret the results.

(A) $x = 200$ (B) $x = 350$

9. *Profit analysis.* The total profit (in dollars) from the sale of x lawn mowers is

$$P(x) = 30x - 0.03x^2 - 750 \qquad 0 \le x \le 1,000$$

(A) Find the average profit per mower if 50 mowers are produced.

(B) Find the marginal average profit at a production level of 50 mowers and interpret.

(C) Use the results from parts (A) and (B) to estimate the average profit per mower if 51 mowers are produced.

10. *Profit analysis.* The total profit (in dollars) from the sale of x charcoal grills is

$$P(x) = 20x - 0.02x^2 - 320 \qquad 0 \le x \le 1,000$$

(A) Find the average profit per grill if 40 grills are produced.

(B) Find the marginal average profit at a production level of 40 grills and interpret.

(C) Use the results from parts (A) and (B) to estimate the average profit per grill if 41 grills are produced.

11. *Revenue analysis.* The price p (in dollars) and the demand x for a particular clock radio are related by the equation

$$x = 4,000 - 40p$$

(A) Express the price p in terms of the demand x and find the domain of this function.

(B) Find the revenue $R(x)$ from the sale of x clock radios. What is the domain of R?

(C) Find the marginal revenue at a production level of 1,600 clock radios and interpret.

(D) Find the marginal revenue at a production level of 2,500 clock radios and interpret.

12. *Revenue analysis.* The price p (in dollars) and the demand x for a particular steam iron are related by the equation

$$x = 1,000 - 20p$$

(A) Express the price p in terms of the demand x and find the domain of this function.

(B) Find the revenue $R(x)$ from the sale of x clock radios. What is the domain of R?

(C) Find the marginal revenue at a production level of 400 steam irons and interpret.

(D) Find the marginal revenue at a production level of 650 steam irons and interpret.

13. *Revenue, cost and profit.* The price–demand equation and the cost function for the production of table saws are given, respectively, by

$$x = 6,000 - 30p \quad \text{and} \quad C(x) = 72,000 + 60x$$

where x is the number of saws that can be sold at a price of $\$p$ per saw and $C(x)$ is the total cost (in dollars) of producing x saws.

(A) Express the price p as a function of the demand x and find the domain of this function.

(B) Find the marginal cost.

(C) Find the revenue function and state its domain.

(D) Find the marginal revenue.

(E) Find $R'(1,500)$ and $R'(4,500)$, and interpret the results.

(F) Graph the cost function and the revenue function on the same coordinate system for $0 \le x \le 6,000$. Find the break-even points, and indicate regions of loss and profit.

(G) Find the profit function in terms of x.

(H) Find the marginal profit.

(I) Find $P'(1,500)$ and $P'(3,000)$, and interpret the results.

14. *Revenue, cost, and profit.* The price–demand equation and the cost function for the production of television sets are given, respectively, by

$$x = 9,000 - 30p \quad \text{and} \quad C(x) = 150,000 + 30x$$

where x is the number of sets that can be sold at a price of $\$p$ per set and $C(x)$ is the total cost (in dollars) of producing x sets.

(A) Express the price p as a function of the demand x and find the domain of this function.

(B) Find the marginal cost.

(C) Find the revenue function and state its domain.

(D) Find the marginal revenue.

(E) Find $R'(3,000)$ and $R'(6,000)$, and interpret the results.

(F) Graph the cost function and the revenue function on the same coordinate system for $0 \le x \le 9,000$. Find the break-even points, and indicate regions of loss and profit.

(G) Find the profit function in terms of x.

(H) Find the marginal profit.

(I) Find $P'(1,500)$ and $P'(4,500)$, and interpret the results.

15. *Revenue, cost, and profit.* A company is planning to manufacture and market a new two-slice electric toaster. After conducting extensive market surveys, the research department provides the following estimates: a weekly demand of 200 toasters at a price of $16 per toaster and a weekly demand of 300 toasters at a price of $14 per toaster. The financial department estimates that weekly fixed costs will be $1,400 and variable costs (cost per unit) will be $4.

(A) Assume that the relationship between the price p and the demand x is linear. Use the research department's estimates to express p as a function of x and find the domain of this function.

(B) Find the revenue function in terms of x and state its domain.

(C) Assume that the cost function is linear. Use the financial department's estimates to express the cost function in terms of x.

(D) Graph the cost function and the revenue function on the same coordinate system for $0 \le x \le 1,000$. Find the break-even points, and indicate regions of loss and profit.

(E) Find the profit function in terms of x.

(F) Evaluate the marginal profit at $x = 250$ and $x = 475$, and interpret the results.

16. *Revenue, cost, and profit.* The company in Problem 15 is also planning to manufacture and market a four-slice toaster. For this toaster, the research department's estimates are a weekly demand of 300 toasters at a price of $25 per toaster and a weekly demand of 400 toasters at a price of $20. The financial department's estimates are fixed weekly costs of $5,000 and variable costs of $5 per toaster.

(A) Assume that the relationship between the price p and the demand x is linear. Use the research department's estimates to express p as a function of x and find the domain of this function.

(B) Find the revenue function in terms of x and state its domain.

(C) Assume that the cost function is linear. Use the financial department's estimates to express the cost function in terms of x.

(D) Graph the cost function and the revenue function on the same coordinate system for $0 \le x \le 800$. Find the break-even points, and indicate regions of loss and profit.

(E) Find the profit function in terms of x.

(F) Evaluate the marginal profit at $x = 325$ and $x = 425$, and interpret the results.

17. *Revenue, cost, and profit.* The total cost and the total revenue (in dollars) for the production and sale of x ski jackets are given, respectively, by

$$C(x) = 24x + 21,900 \quad \text{and} \quad R(x) = 200x - 0.2x^2$$
$$0 \le x \le 1,000$$

(A) Find the value of x where the graph of $R(x)$ has a horizontal tangent line.

(B) Find the profit function $P(x)$.

(C) Find the value of x where the graph of $P(x)$ has a horizontal tangent line.

(D) Graph $C(x)$, $R(x)$, and $P(x)$ on the same coordinate system for $0 \le x \le 1,000$. Find the break-even points. Find the x intercepts for the graph of $P(x)$.

18. *Revenue, cost, and profit.* The total cost and the total revenue (in dollars) for the production and sale of x hair dryers are given, respectively, by

$$C(x) = 5x + 2,340 \quad \text{and} \quad R(x) = 40x - 0.1x^2$$
$$0 \le x \le 400$$

(A) Find the value of x where the graph of $R(x)$ has a horizontal tangent line.

(B) Find the profit function $P(x)$.

(C) Find the value of x where the graph of $P(x)$ has a horizontal tangent line.

(D) Graph $C(x)$, $R(x)$, and $P(x)$ on the same coordinate system for $0 \le x \le 400$. Find the break-even points. Find the x intercepts for the graph of $P(x)$.

19. *Break-even analysis.* The price–demand equation and the cost function for the production of garden hoses are given, respectively, by

$$p = 20 - \sqrt{x} \quad \text{and} \quad C(x) = 500 + 2x$$

where x is the number of garden hoses that can be sold at a price of p per unit and $C(x)$ is the total cost (in dollars) of producing x garden hoses.

(A) Express the revenue function in terms of x.

(B) Graph the cost function and the revenue function in the same viewing window for $0 \le x \le 400$. Use approximation techniques to find the break-even points correct to the nearest unit.

20. *Break-even analysis.* The price–demand equation and the cost function for the production of hand-woven silk scarves are given, respectively, by

$$p = 60 - 2\sqrt{x} \quad \text{and} \quad C(x) = 3{,}000 + 5x$$

where x is the number of scarves that can be sold at a price of $\$p$ per unit and $C(x)$ is the total cost (in dollars) of producing x scarves.

(A) Express the revenue function in terms of x.

(B) Graph the cost function and the revenue function in the same viewing window for $0 \le x \le 900$. Use approximation techniques to find the break-even points correct to the nearest unit.

21. *Break-even analysis.* Table 2 contains price–demand and total cost data for the production of overhead projectors, where p is the wholesale price (in dollars) of a projector for an annual demand of x projectors and C is the total cost (in dollars) of producing x projectors.

TABLE 2

x	$p(\$)$	$C(\$)$
3,190	581	1,130,000
4,570	405	1,241,000
5,740	181	1,410,000
7,330	85	1,620,000

(A) Find a quadratic regression equation for the price–demand data using x as the independent variable.

(B) Find a linear regression equation for the cost data using x as the independent variable. Use this equation to estimate the fixed costs and the variable costs per projector. Round answers to the nearest dollar.

(C) Find the break-even points. Round answers to the nearest integer.

(D) Find the price range for which the company will make a profit. Round answers to the nearest dollar.

22. *Break-even analysis.* Table 3 contains price–demand and total cost data for the production of treadmills, where p is the wholesale price (in dollars) of a treadmill for an annual demand of x treadmills and C is the total cost (in dollars) of producing x treadmills.

TABLE 3

x	$p(\$)$	$C(\$)$
2,910	1,435	3,650,000
3,415	1,280	3,870,000
4,645	1,125	4,190,000
5,330	910	4,380,000

(A) Find a linear regression equation for the price–demand data using x as the independent variable.

(B) Find a linear regression equation for the cost data using x as the independent variable. Use this equation to estimate the fixed costs and the variable costs per treadmill. Round answers to the nearest dollar.

(C) Find the break-even points. Round answers to the nearest integer.

(D) Find the price range for which the company will make a profit. Round answers to the nearest dollar.

Chapter 3 Review

Important Terms, Symbols, and Concepts

3-1 Introduction to Limits

We write $\lim_{x \to c} f(x) = L$ or $f(x) \to L$ as $x \to c$ if the functional value $f(x)$ is close to the single real number L whenever x is close to, but not equal to, c (on either side of c). The existence of a limit at c has nothing to do with the value of the function at c. In fact, c may not even be in the domain of f. However, the function must be defined on both sides of c.

We write $\lim_{x \to c^-} f(x) = K$ and call K the **limit from the left** or **left-hand limit** if $f(x)$ is close to K whenever x is close to c, but to the left of c, on the real number line.

We write

$$\lim_{x \to c^+} f(x) = L$$

and call L the **limit from the right** or **right-hand limit** if $f(x)$ is close to L whenever x is close to c, but to the right of c, on the real number line.

Theorem 1   On the Existence of a Limit

For a (two-sided) limit to exist, the limit from the left and the limit from the right must exist and be equal. That is,

$$\lim_{x \to c} f(x) = L \quad \text{if and only if} \quad \lim_{x \to c^-} f(x) = \lim_{x \to c^+} f(x) = L$$

Theorem 2   Properties of Limits

Let f and g be two functions, and assume that

$$\lim_{x \to c} f(x) = L \qquad \lim_{x \to c} g(x) = M$$

where L and M are real numbers (both limits exist). Then

1. $\lim\limits_{x \to c} [f(x) + g(x)] = \lim\limits_{x \to c} f(x) + \lim\limits_{x \to c} g(x) = L + M$

2. $\lim\limits_{x \to c} [f(x) - g(x)] = \lim\limits_{x \to c} f(x) - \lim\limits_{x \to c} g(x) = L - M$

3. $\lim\limits_{x \to c} kf(x) = k \lim\limits_{x \to c} f(x) = kL \qquad$ for any constant k

4. $\lim\limits_{x \to c} [f(x) \cdot g(x)] = [\lim\limits_{x \to c} f(x)][\lim\limits_{x \to c} g(x)] = LM$

5. $\lim\limits_{x \to c} \dfrac{f(x)}{g(x)} = \dfrac{\lim\limits_{x \to c} f(x)}{\lim\limits_{x \to c} g(x)} = \dfrac{L}{M} \qquad$ if $M \neq 0$

6. $\lim\limits_{x \to c} \sqrt[n]{f(x)} = \sqrt[n]{\lim\limits_{x \to c} f(x)} = \sqrt[n]{L} \qquad L > 0$ for n even

Theorem 3   Limits of Polynomial and Rational Functions

1. $\lim\limits_{x \to c} f(x) = f(c) \qquad$ f any polynomial function

2. $\lim\limits_{x \to c} r(x) = r(c) \qquad$ r any rational function with a nonzero denominator at $x = c$

If $\lim\limits_{x \to c} f(x) = 0$ and $\lim\limits_{x \to c} g(x) = 0$, then $\lim\limits_{x \to c} \dfrac{f(x)}{g(x)}$ is said to be **indeterminate,** or, more specifically, a **0/0 indeterminate form.**

Theorem 4   Limit of a Quotient

If $\lim\limits_{x \to c} f(x) = L$, $L \neq 0$ and $\lim\limits_{x \to c} g(x) = 0$, then $\lim\limits_{x \to c} \dfrac{f(x)}{g(x)}$ does not exist.

3-2   Continuity

A function f is **continuous at the point $x = c$** if

1. $\lim\limits_{x \to c} f(x)$ exists

2. $f(c)$ exists

3. $\lim\limits_{x \to c} f(x) = f(c)$

A function is **continuous on the open interval (a, b)** if it is continuous at each point in the interval. If one or more of the three conditions listed fails, the function is **discontinuous** at $x = c$. A function is **continuous on the right** at $x = c$ if $\lim\limits_{x \to c^+} f(x) = f(c)$ and **continuous on the left** at $x = c$ if $\lim\limits_{x \to c^-} f(x) = f(c)$. A function is **continuous on the closed interval $[a, b]$** if it is continuous on the open interval (a, b) and is continuous on the right at a and continuous on the left at b.

Theorem 1   Continuity Properties of Some Specific Functions

(A) A constant function $f(x) = k$, where k is a constant, is continuous for all x.

(B) For n a positive integer, $f(x) = x^n$ is continuous for all x.

(C) A polynomial function is continuous for all x.

(D) A rational function is continuous for all x except those values that make a denominator 0.

(E) For n an odd positive integer greater than 1, $\sqrt[n]{f(x)}$ is continuous wherever $f(x)$ is continuous.

(F) For n an even positive integer, $\sqrt[n]{f(x)}$ is continuous wherever $f(x)$ is continuous and nonnegative.

• **Constructing Sign Charts**   Given a function f,

Step 1. Find all **partition numbers.** That is,

(A) Find all numbers where f is discontinuous. (Rational functions are discontinuous for values of x that make a denominator 0.)

(B) Find all numbers where $f(x) = 0$. (For a rational function, this occurs where the numerator is 0 and the denominator is not 0.)

Step 2. Plot the numbers found in step 1 on a real number line, dividing the number line into intervals.

Step 3. Select a test number in each open interval determined in step 2, and evaluate $f(x)$ at each test number to determine whether $f(x)$ is positive $(+)$ or negative $(-)$ in each interval.

Step 4. Construct a sign chart using the real number line in step 2. This will show the sign of $f(x)$ on each open interval.

Note: From the sign chart, it is easy to find the solution for the inequality $f(x) < 0$ or $f(x) > 0$.

3-3   The Derivative

For $y = f(x)$, the **average rate of change from $x = a$ to $x = a + h$** is

$$\frac{f(a + h) - f(a)}{(a + h) - a} = \frac{f(a + h) - f(a)}{h} \qquad h \neq 0$$

This expression is called the **difference quotient.**

For $y = f(x)$, the **instantaneous rate of change at $x = a$** is

$$\lim_{h \to 0} \frac{f(a + h) - f(a)}{h}$$

The (instantaneous) rate of change of distance with respect to time is called the **velocity.**

A line through two points on a graph is called a **secant line.** The slope of the secant line through $(a, f(a))$ and $(a + h, f(a + h))$ is

$$\frac{f(a + h) - f(a)}{(a + h) - a} = \frac{f(a + h) - f(a)}{h} \qquad h \neq 0$$

Given $y = f(x)$, the **slope of the graph** at the point $(a, f(a))$ is given by

$$\lim_{h \to 0} \frac{f(a + h) - f(a)}{h}$$

provided that the limit exists. The slope of the graph is also the **slope of the tangent line** at the point $(a, f(a))$.

For $y = f(x)$, we define the **derivative of f at x,** denoted by $f'(x)$, to be

$$f'(x) = \lim_{h \to 0} \frac{f(x + h) - f(x)}{h} \quad \text{if the limit exists.}$$

If $f'(x)$ exists for each x in the open interval (a, b), then f is said to be **differentiable** over (a, b). The process of finding the derivative of a function is called **differentiation** and the derivative of a function is obtained by **differentiating** the function.

The **four-step process** for finding the derivative of a function f:

Step 1. Find $f(x + h)$.

Step 2. Find $f(x + h) - f(x)$.

Step 3. Find $\dfrac{f(x + h) - f(x)}{h}$.

Step 4. Find $\lim_{h \to 0} \dfrac{f(x + h) - f(x)}{h}$.

If $\lim_{h \to 0} \dfrac{f(a + h) - f(a)}{h}$ does not exist at $x = a$, then $f'(a)$ **does not exist** and f is **nondifferentiable at $x = a$.**

3-4 Power Rule and Basic Differentiation Properties

Given $y = f(x)$, then $f'(x)$, y', and $\dfrac{dy}{dx}$ all represent the derivative of f at x.

Theorem 1   Constant Function Rule
If $f(x) = C$, then $f'(x) = 0$.

Theorem 2   Power Rule
If $y = f(x) = x^n$, where n is a real number, then $f'(x) = nx^{n-1}$.

Theorem 3   Constant Multiple Property
If $y = f(x) = ku(x)$, then $f'(x) = ku'(x)$.

Theorem 4   Sum and Difference Property
If $y = f(x) = u(x) \pm v(x)$, then $f'(x) = u'(x) \pm v'(x)$.

3-5 Derivatives of Products and Quotients

Theorem 1   Product Rule
If $y = f(x) = F(x)S(x)$, then $f'(x) = F(x)S'(x) + S(x)F'(x)$, provided both $F'(x)$ and $S'(x)$ exist.

Theorem 2   Quotient Rule
If $y = f(x) = \dfrac{T(x)}{B(x)}$, then $f'(x) = \dfrac{B(x)T'(x) - T(x)B'(x)}{[B(x)]^2}$, provided both $T'(x)$ and $B'(x)$ exist.

3-6 General Power Rule (Chain Rule)

Theorem 1   General Power Rule
If $u(x)$ is a differentiable function, n is any real number, and $y = f(x) = [u(x)]^n$, then $f'(x) = n[u(x)]^{n-1}u'(x)$.

This is a special case of the **chain rule** that will be discussed later.

3-7 Marginal Analysis in Business & Economics

In economics, the word **marginal** refers to a rate of change, that is, to a derivative.

- *Marginal Cost, Revenue, and Profit* If x is the number of units of a product produced in some time interval, then

$$\text{total cost} = C(x)$$
$$\textbf{marginal cost} = C'(x)$$
$$\text{total revenue} = R(x)$$
$$\textbf{marginal revenue} = R'(x)$$
$$\text{total profit} = P(x) = R(x) - C(x)$$
$$\textbf{marginal profit} = P'(x) = R'(x) - C'(x)$$
$$= (\text{marginal revenue}) - (\text{marginal cost})$$

Marginal cost (or revenue or profit) is the instantaneous rate of change of cost (or revenue or profit) relative to production at a given production level.

Theorem 1   Marginal Cost and Exact Cost
If $C(x)$ is the total cost of producing x items, the marginal cost function approximates the exact cost of producing the $(x + 1)$st item. That is, $C'(x) \approx C(x + 1) - C(x)$.

If $C(x)$ and $R(x)$ are the total cost and total revenue functions, respectively, for producing and selling x items, then the intersection points of the graphs of $y = C(x)$ and $y = R(x)$ are called the **break-even points.**

If x is the number of units of a product produced in some time interval, then

Cost per unit: $\qquad \text{average cost} = \overline{C}(x) = \dfrac{C(x)}{x}$

$$\text{marginal average cost} = \overline{C}'(x) = \frac{d}{dx}\overline{C}(x)$$

Revenue per unit: average revenue $= \overline{R}(x) = \dfrac{R(x)}{x}$

marginal average revenue $= \overline{R}'(x) = \dfrac{d}{dx}\overline{R}(x)$

Profit per unit: average profit $= \overline{P}(x) = \dfrac{P(x)}{x}$

marginal average profit $= \overline{P}'(x) = \dfrac{d}{dx}\overline{P}(x)$

$\dfrac{d}{dx}kf(x) = kf'(x)$

$\dfrac{d}{dx}[u(x) \pm v(x)] = u'(x) \pm v'(x)$

$\dfrac{d}{dx}[F(x)S(x)] = F(x)S'(x) + S(x)F'(x)$

$\dfrac{d}{dx}\dfrac{T(x)}{B(x)} = \dfrac{B(x)T'(x) - T(x)B'(x)}{[B(x)]^2}$

$\dfrac{d}{dx}[u(x)]^n = n[u(x)]^{n-1}u'(x)$

• **Summary of Rules and Properties of Differentiation**

$\dfrac{d}{dx}k = 0$

$\dfrac{d}{dx}x^n = nx^{n-1}$

Review Exercise

Work through all the problems in this chapter review and check your answers in the back of the book. Answers to all review problems are there along with section numbers in italics to indicate where each type of problem is discussed. Where weaknesses show up, review appropriate sections in the text.

Many of the problems in this exercise set ask you to find a derivative. Most of the answers to these problems contain both an unsimplified form and a simplified form of the derivative. When checking your work, first check that you applied the rules correctly, and then check that you performed the algebraic simplification correctly.

A 1. Find the indicated quantities for
$y = f(x) = 2x^2 + 5$:

(A) The change in y if x changes from 1 to 3

(B) The average rate of change of y with respect to x if x changes from 1 to 3

(C) The slope of the secant line through the points $(1, f(1))$ and $(3, f(3))$ on the graph of $y = f(x)$

(D) The instantaneous rate of change of y with respect to x at $x = 1$

(E) The slope of the line tangent to the graph of $y = f(x)$ at $x = 1$

(F) $f'(1)$

2. Use the two-step limiting process to find $f'(x)$ for $f(x) = -3x + 2$.

3. If $\lim\limits_{x \to 1} f(x) = 2$ and $\lim\limits_{x \to 1} g(x) = 4$, find

(A) $\lim\limits_{x \to 1}(5f(x) + 3g(x))$

(B) $\lim\limits_{x \to 1}[f(x)g(x)]$

(C) $\lim\limits_{x \to 1}\dfrac{g(x)}{f(x)}$

(D) $\lim\limits_{x \to 1}[5 + 2x - 3g(x)]$

In Problems 4–6, use the graph of f shown below to estimate the indicated limits and function values.

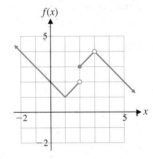

4. (A) $\lim\limits_{x \to 1^-} f(x)$

(B) $\lim\limits_{x \to 1^+} f(x)$

(C) $\lim\limits_{x \to 1} f(x)$

(D) $f(1)$

5. (A) $\lim\limits_{x \to 2^-} f(x)$

(B) $\lim\limits_{x \to 2^+} f(x)$

(C) $\lim\limits_{x \to 2} f(x)$

(D) $f(2)$

6. (A) $\lim\limits_{x \to 3^-} f(x)$

(B) $\lim\limits_{x \to 3^+} f(x)$

(C) $\lim\limits_{x \to 3} f(x)$

(D) $f(3)$

In Problems 7–9, use the graph of the function f shown in the figure to answer each question.

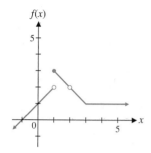

f(x)

7. (A) $\lim_{x \to 1} f(x) = ?$

(B) $f(1) = ?$

(C) Is f continuous at $x = 1$?

8. (A) $\lim_{x \to 2} f(x) = ?$

(B) $f(2) = ?$

(C) Is f continuous at $x = 2$?

9. (A) $\lim_{x \to 3} f(x) = ?$

(B) $f(3) = ?$

(C) Is f continuous at $x = 3$?

10. Use the four-step limiting process to find $f'(x)$ for $f(x) = 5x^2$.

11. If $f(5) = 4, f'(5) = -1, g(5) = 2$, and $g'(5) = -3$, find $h'(5)$ for each of the following functions:

(A) $h(x) = 2f(x) + 3g(x)$

(B) $h(x) = f(x)g(x)$

(C) $h(x) = \dfrac{f(x)}{g(x)}$

(D) $h(x) = [f(x)]^2$

(E) $h(x) = x^2 f(x)$

(F) $h(x) = \dfrac{g(x)}{x + 2}$

12. Replace the ? in the equation below with an expression that makes the equation valid.

$$\frac{d}{dx}(3x^2 + 4x + 1)^5 = 5(3x^2 + 4x + 1)^4 \underline{\ ?\ }$$

In Problems 13–24, find $f'(x)$ and simplify.

13. $f(x) = \dfrac{1}{3}x^3 - 5x^2 + 1$

14. $f(x) = 2x^{1/2} - 3x$

15. $f(x) = 5$

16. $f(x) = \dfrac{3}{2x} + \dfrac{5x^3}{4}$

17. $f(x) = \dfrac{0.5}{x^4} + 0.25x^4$

18. $f(x) = (2x - 1)(3x + 2)$

19. $f(x) = (x^2 - 1)(x^3 - 3)$

20. $f(x) = (0.2x - 1.5)(0.5x + 0.4)$

21. $f(x) = \dfrac{2x}{x^2 + 2}$

22. $f(x) = \dfrac{1}{3x + 2}$

23. $f(x) = (2x - 3)^3$

24. $f(x) = (x^2 + 2)^{-2}$

B Problems 25–27 refer to the function f in the figure.

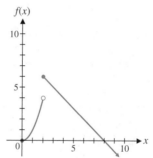

f(x)

Figure for 25–27: $f(x) = \begin{cases} x^2 & \text{if } 0 \le x < 2 \\ 8 - x & \text{if } x \ge 2 \end{cases}$

25. (A) $\lim_{x \to 2^-} f(x) = ?$

(B) $\lim_{x \to 2^+} f(x) = ?$

(C) $\lim_{x \to 2} f(x) = ?$

(D) $f(2) = ?$

(E) Is f continuous at $x = 2$?

26. (A) $\lim_{x \to 5^-} f(x) = ?$

(B) $\lim_{x \to 5^+} f(x) = ?$

(C) $\lim_{x \to 5} f(x) = ?$

(D) $f(5) = ?$

(E) Is f continuous at $x = 5$?

27. Solve each inequality. Express answers in interval notation.

(A) $f(x) < 0$

(B) $f(x) \ge 0$

In Problems 28–30, solve each inequality. Express the answer in interval notation. Use a graphing utility in Problem 30 to approximate partition numbers to four decimal places.

28. $x^2 - x < 12$

29. $\dfrac{x - 5}{x^2 + 3x} > 0$

30. $x^3 + x^2 - 4x - 2 > 0$

31. Let $f(x) = 0.5x^2 - 5$.

    (A) Find the slope of the secant line through $(2, f(2))$ and $(4, f(4))$.

    (B) Find the slope of the secant line through $(2, f(2))$ and $(2 + h, f(2 + h))$, $h \neq 0$.

    (C) Find the slope of the tangent line at $x = 2$.

In Problems 32–40, find the indicated derivative and simplify.

32. $\dfrac{dy}{dx}$ for $y = \dfrac{1}{3}x^{-3} - 5x^{-2} + 1$

33. y' for $y = (2x^2 - 3x + 2)(x^2 + 2x - 1)$

34. $f'(x)$ for $f(x) = \dfrac{2x - 3}{(x - 1)^2}$

35. y' for $y = \dfrac{3\sqrt{x}}{2} + \dfrac{5}{3\sqrt{x}}$

36. $g'(x)$ for $g(x) = 1.8\sqrt[3]{x} + \dfrac{0.9}{\sqrt[3]{x}}$

37. $\dfrac{d}{dx}[(x^2 - 1)(2x + 1)^2]$

38. $\dfrac{d}{dx}\sqrt[3]{x^3 - 5}$

39. $\dfrac{dy}{dx}$ for $y = \dfrac{2x^3 - 3}{5x^3}$

40. $\dfrac{d}{dx}\dfrac{(x^2 + 2)^4}{2x - 3}$

41. For $y = f(x) = x^2 + 4$, find

    (A) The slope of the graph at $x = 1$

    (B) The equation of the tangent line at $x = 1$ in the form $y = mx + b$

42. Repeat Problem 41 for $f(x) = x^3(x + 1)^2$.

In Problems 43–46, find the value(s) of x where the tangent line is horizontal.

43. $f(x) = 10x - x^2$

44. $f(x) = (x + 3)(x^2 - 45)$

45. $f(x) = \dfrac{x}{x^2 + 4}$

46. $f(x) = x^2(2x - 15)^3$

In Problems 47–49, approximate (to four decimal places) the value(s) of x where the graph of f has a horizontal tangent line.

47. $f(x) = x^4 - 2x^3 - 5x^2 + 7x$

48. $f(x) = \dfrac{x^3 - 5x + 10}{x^2 + 2}$

49. $f(x) = \dfrac{5x^4 - 40x^2}{(x^2 + 1)^2}$

50. If an object moves along the y axis (scale in feet) so that it is at $y = f(x) = 8x^2 - 4x + 1$ at time x (in seconds), find

    (A) The instantaneous velocity function

    (B) The velocity at time $x = 3$ seconds

51. An object moves along the y axis (scale in feet) so that at time x (in seconds) it is at $y = f(x) = -5x^2 + 16x + 3$. Find

    (A) The instantaneous velocity function

    (B) The time(s) when the velocity is 0

52. Let $f(x) = x^3$, $g(x) = (x - 4)^3$, and $h(x) = (x + 3)^3$.

    (A) How are the graphs of f, g, and h related? Illustrate your conclusion by graphing f, g, and h on the same coordinate axes.

    (B) How would you expect the graphs of the derivatives of these functions to be related? Illustrate your conclusion by graphing f', g', and h' on the same coordinate axes.

53. Let $f(x)$ be a differentiable function and let k be a nonzero constant. For each function g, write a brief verbal description of the relationship between the graphs of f and g. Do the same for the graphs of f' and g'.

    (A) $g(x) = f(x + k)$

    (B) $g(x) = f(x) + k$

In Problems 54–58, determine where f is continuous. Express the answer in interval notation.

54. $f(x) = x^2 - 4$

55. $f(x) = \dfrac{x + 1}{x - 2}$

56. $f(x) = \dfrac{x + 4}{x^2 + 3x - 4}$

57. $f(x) = \sqrt[3]{4 - x^2}$

58. $f(x) = \sqrt{4 - x^2}$

In Problems 59–65, evaluate the indicated limits if they exist.

59. Let $f(x) = \dfrac{2x}{x^2 - 3x}$. Find

   (A) $\lim\limits_{x \to 1} f(x)$ (B) $\lim\limits_{x \to 3} f(x)$ (C) $\lim\limits_{x \to 0} f(x)$

60. Let $f(x) = \dfrac{x + 1}{(3 - x)^2}$. Find

   (A) $\lim\limits_{x \to 1} f(x)$ (B) $\lim\limits_{x \to -1} f(x)$ (C) $\lim\limits_{x \to 3} f(x)$

61. Let $f(x) = \dfrac{|x - 4|}{x - 4}$. Find

   (A) $\lim\limits_{x \to 4^-} f(x)$ (B) $\lim\limits_{x \to 4^+} f(x)$ (C) $\lim\limits_{x \to 4} f(x)$

62. Let $f(x) = \dfrac{x - 3}{9 - x^2}$. Find

   (A) $\lim\limits_{x \to 3} f(x)$ (B) $\lim\limits_{x \to -3} f(x)$ (C) $\lim\limits_{x \to 0} f(x)$

63. Let $f(x) = \dfrac{x^2 - x - 2}{x^2 - 7x + 10}$. Find

   (A) $\lim\limits_{x \to -1} f(x)$ (B) $\lim\limits_{x \to 2} f(x)$ (C) $\lim\limits_{x \to 5} f(x)$

64. $\lim\limits_{h \to 0} \dfrac{f(2 + h) - f(2)}{h}$ for $f(x) = x^2 + 4$

65. $\lim\limits_{h \to 0} \dfrac{f(x + h) - f(x)}{h}$ for $f(x) = \dfrac{1}{x + 2}$

66. Let $f(x) = \dfrac{x^3 - 4x^2 - 4x + 16}{|x^2 - 4|}$

   Graph f and use zoom and trace to investigate the left- and right-hand limits at the indicated values of c.

   (A) $c = -2$ (B) $c = 0$ (C) $c = 2$

In Problems 67 and 68, use the definition of the derivative and the four-step process to find $f'(x)$.

67. $f(x) = x^2 - x$ **68.** $f(x) = \sqrt{x} - 3$

C *Problems 69–72 refer to the function f in the figure. Determine whether f is differentiable at the indicated value of x.*

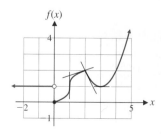

69. $x = 0$ **70.** $x = 1$ **71.** $x = 2$ **72.** $x = 3$

In Problems 73–77, find $f'(x)$ and simplify.

73. $f(x) = (x - 4)^4(x + 3)^3$

74. $f(x) = 5x^3(x^2 - 1)^2$ **75.** $f(x) = \dfrac{x^5}{(2x + 1)^4}$

76. $f(x) = \dfrac{\sqrt{x^2 - 1}}{x}$ **77.** $f(x) = \dfrac{x}{\sqrt{x^2 + 4}}$

78. The domain of the power function $f(x) = x^{1/5}$ is the set of all real numbers. Find the domain of the derivative $f'(x)$. Discuss the nature of the graph of $y = f(x)$ for any x values excluded from the domain of $f'(x)$.

79. Let f be defined by

$$f(x) = \begin{cases} x^2 - m & \text{if } x \le 1 \\ -x^2 + m & \text{if } x > 1 \end{cases}$$

   where m is a constant.

   (A) Graph f for $m = 0$, and find

$$\lim\limits_{x \to 1^-} f(x) \quad \text{and} \quad \lim\limits_{x \to 1^+} f(x)$$

   (B) Graph f for $m = 2$, and find

$$\lim\limits_{x \to 1^-} f(x) \quad \text{and} \quad \lim\limits_{x \to 1^+} f(x)$$

   (C) Find m so that

$$\lim\limits_{x \to 1^-} f(x) = \lim\limits_{x \to 1^+} f(x)$$

   and graph f for this value of m.

   (D) Write a brief verbal description of each graph. How does the graph in part (C) differ from the graphs in parts (A) and (B)?

80. Let $f(x) = 1 - |x - 1|, 0 \le x \le 2$ (see the figure).

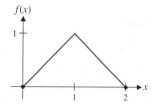

Figure for 80

   (A) $\lim\limits_{h \to 0^-} \dfrac{f(1 + h) - f(1)}{h} = \,?$

   (B) $\lim\limits_{h \to 0^+} \dfrac{f(1 + h) - f(1)}{h} = \,?$

   (C) $\lim\limits_{h \to 0} \dfrac{f(1 + h) - f(1)}{h} = \,?$

   (D) Does $f'(1)$ exist?

Applications

Business & Economics

81. *Natural gas rates.* The table shows the winter rates for natural gas charged by the Bay State Gas Company. The customer charge is a fixed monthly charge, independent of the amount of gas used during the month.

(A) Write a piecewise definition of the monthly charge $S(x)$ for a customer who uses x therms in a winter month.

(B) Graph $S(x)$.

(C) Is $S(x)$ continuous at $x = 90$? Explain.

Natural Gas Rates	
Monthly customer charge	$7.47
First 90 therms	$0.4000 per therm
All usage over 90 therms	$0.2076 per therm

82. *Cost analysis.* The total cost (in dollars) of producing x television sets is

$$C(x) = 10{,}000 + 200x - 0.1x^2$$

(A) Find the exact cost of producing the 101st television set.

(B) Use the marginal cost to approximate the cost of producing the 101st television set.

83. *Cost analysis.* The total cost (in dollars) of producing x bicycles is

$$C(x) = 5{,}000 + 40x + 0.05x^2$$

(A) Find the total cost and the marginal cost at a production level of 100 bicycles, and interpret the results.

(B) Find the average cost and the marginal average cost at a production level of 100 bicycles, and interpret the results.

84. *Cost analysis.* The total cost (in dollars) of producing x laser printers per week is shown in the figure. Which is greater, the approximate cost of producing the 201st printer or the approximate cost of producing the 601st printer? Does this graph represent a manufacturing process that is becoming more

efficient or less efficient as production levels increase? Explain.

85. *Cost analysis.* Let

$$p = 25 - 0.01x \quad \text{and} \quad C(x) = 2x + 9{,}000$$
$$0 \le x \le 2{,}500$$

be the price–demand equation and the cost function, respectively, for the manufacture of umbrellas.

(A) Find the marginal cost, average cost, and marginal average cost functions.

(B) Express the revenue in terms of x, and find the marginal revenue, average revenue, and marginal average revenue functions.

(C) Find the profit, marginal profit, average profit, and marginal average profit functions.

(D) Find the break-even point(s).

(E) Evaluate the marginal profit at $x = 1{,}000$, $1{,}150$, and $1{,}400$, and interpret the results.

(F) Graph $R = R(x)$ and $C = C(x)$ on the same coordinate system, and locate regions of profit and loss.

86. *Employee training.* A company producing computer components has established that on the average, a new employee can assemble $N(t)$ components per day after t days of on-the-job training, as given by

$$N(t) = \frac{40t}{t + 2}$$

(A) Find the average rate of change of $N(t)$ from 3 days to 6 days.

(B) Find the instantaneous rate of change of $N(t)$ at 3 days.

87. *Sales analysis.* Past sales records for a swimming pool manufacturer indicate that the total number of swimming pools, N (in thousands), sold during a year is given by

$$N(t) = t\sqrt{4 + t}$$

where t is the number of months since the beginning of the year. Find $N(5)$ and $N'(5)$, and interpret.

88. *Natural gas consumption.* The data in Table 1 give the U.S. consumption of natural gas in trillions of cubic feet.

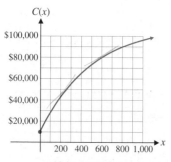

$C(x)$

Figure for 84

TABLE 1	
Year	Natural Gas Consumption
1960	12.0
1970	21.1
1980	19.9
1990	18.7
2000	21.9

(A) Let x represent time (in years), with $x = 0$ corresponding to 1960, and let y represent the corresponding U.S. consumption of natural gas. Enter the data set in a graphing utility and find a cubic regression equation for the data.

(B) If $y = N(x)$ denotes the regression equation found in part (A), find $N(50)$ and $N'(50)$, and write a brief verbal interpretation of these results.

89. *Break-even analysis.* Table 2 contains price–demand and total cost data from a bakery for the production of kringles (a Danish pastry), where p is the price (in dollars) of a kringle for a daily demand of x kringles and C is the total cost (in dollars) of producing x kringles.

TABLE 2

x	$p(\$)$	$C(\$)$
125	9	740
140	8	785
170	7	850
200	6	900

(A) Find a linear regression equation for the price–demand data using x as the independent variable.

(B) Find a linear regression equation for the cost data using x as the independent variable. Use this equation to estimate the fixed costs and the variable costs per kringle.

(C) Find the break-even points.

(D) Find the price range for which the bakery will make a profit.

In all answers, round dollar amounts to the nearest cent.

Life Sciences

90. *Pollution.* A sewage treatment plant disposes of its effluent through a pipeline that extends 1 mile toward the center of a large lake. The concentration of effluent $C(x)$, in parts per million, x meters from the end of the pipe is given approximately by

$$C(x) = 500(x + 1)^{-2}$$

What is the instantaneous rate of change of concentration at 9 meters? At 99 meters?

91. *Medicine.* The body temperature (in degrees Fahrenheit) of a patient t hours after being given a fever-reducing drug is given by

$$F(t) = 98 + \frac{4}{\sqrt{t + 1}}$$

Find $F(3)$ and $F'(3)$. Write a brief verbal interpretation of these results.

Social Sciences

92. *Learning.* If a person learns N items in t hours, as given by

$$N(t) = 20\sqrt{t}$$

find the rate of learning after

(A) 1 hour   (B) 4 hours

Group Activity 1   Minimal Average Cost

If $C(x)$ is the total cost of producing x items, the marginal cost function $C'(x)$ gives the approximate cost of the next item produced, while the average cost function $\overline{C}(x)$ gives the average cost per item for the items already produced. Thus, $C'(x)$ looks forward to the next item, while $\overline{C}(x)$ looks backward at all the items produced thus far. Given this difference in viewpoint, it is somewhat surprising that there is an important relationship between these two functions. As we will see, information gained from comparing the values of $C'(x)$ and $\overline{C}(x)$ can help determine the production level that minimizes average cost.

(A) The total cost (in dollars) of producing x items is given by

$$C(x) = 0.01x^2 + 40x + 3{,}600$$

Find $C'(x)$ and $\overline{C}(x)$, and complete Table 1.

(B) Repeat part (A) for

$$C(x) = 0.00016x^3 - 0.12x^2 + 30x + 10{,}000$$

TABLE 1

x	$\overline{C}(x)$	$C'(x)$
100		
200		
300		
400		
500		
600		
700		
800		
900		
1,000		

(C) Examine the values in the tables from parts (A) and (B), and write a brief verbal description of the behavior of each function. Does each average cost function appear to have a minimum value? What is the minimal value, and where does it occur? What relationship do you observe between the minimum average cost and the marginal cost at the production level that minimizes average cost?

(D) If you have access to a graphing utility, confirm your observations in part (C) by examining the graphs of $C'(x)$ and $\overline{C}(x)$.

(E) The following statements can help justify the relationship you observed in part (C). In each case, fill in the blank with "increase" or "decrease" and justify your choice.

1. If $C'(x) < \overline{C}(x)$ (that is, the cost of the next item is less than the average cost of the items already produced), then increasing production by 1 item will _____ the average cost.

2. If $C'(x) > \overline{C}(x)$ (that is, the cost of the next item is more than the average cost of the items already produced), then increasing production by 1 item will _____ the average cost.

(F) Discuss the validity of the following statement for an arbitrary cost function $C(x)$: If the minimum value of $\overline{C}(x)$ occurs at a production level x, then $C'(x) = \overline{C}(x)$ at that production level.

(G) We used a quadratic function and a cubic function in parts (A) and (B) to illustrate the relationship between $C'(x)$ and $\overline{C}(x)$. But linear cost functions are one of the most important types. To see why we did not choose a linear cost function, try to parallel the development for the cost function

$$C(x) = 30x + 12,000$$

Do any of your findings contradict the statements in parts (E) and (F)?

Group Activity 2   Numerical Differentiation on a Graphing Utility

Most graphing utilities have a built-in routine for approximating the derivative of a function, often denoted by nDeriv (check the manual for your graphing utility). For example, nDeriv(x^3, x, a) approximates the derivative of $y = x^3$ at a number a.

(A) Find nDeriv(x^3, x, a) on a graphing utility for $a = 1, 2, 3, 4,$ and 5, and compare with the corresponding values of

$$\frac{d}{dx}x^3 = 3x^2$$

(B) Enter $y_1 = x^3$, and $y_2 = 3x^2$, and $y_3 = $ nDeriv(y_1, x, x) in the equation editor of a graphing utility. Graph y_2 and y_3 for $-2 \le x \le 2, -2 \le y \le 2$, and discuss the relationship between these graphs. Use the trace feature or tables of values to support your conclusions.

Most graphing utilities use the following average of difference quotients with a fixed value of h to approximate a derivative:

$$\frac{1}{2}\left(\frac{f(x+h) - f(x)}{h} + \frac{f(x-h) - f(x)}{-h}\right) = \frac{f(x+h) - f(x-h)}{2h}$$

Thus, for a given number a and a fixed value of h,

$$\text{nDeriv}(f(x), x, a) = \frac{f(a + h) - f(a - h)}{2h} \qquad (1)$$

(C) Use equation (1) to find and simplify $\text{nDeriv}(f(x), x, a)$ for $f(x) = x^3$. Compare the values of the simplified form with the values of nDeriv you computed in part (A) to see if you can determine the fixed value of h for your graphing utility. Check your manual to see if you can change this value.

(D) Let $f(x) = |x|$. What is $\text{nDeriv}(f(x), x, 0)$? Is $f(x)$ differentiable at $x = 0$?

(E) Repeat part (D) for $f(x) = 1/x^2$.

(F) When using nDeriv to approximate the derivative of a function $f(x)$, why is it important to know in advance the location of any points where $f'(x)$ does not exist?

OBJECTIVES

1. Use the first derivative to analyze the graph of a function.

2. Use the first-derivative test to identify local maxima and minima.

3. Use the second derivative to identify concavity and inflection points.

4. Use the first and second derivative to sketch the graphs of polynomials and rational functions.

5. Find the absolute maximum value and the absolute minimum value of a function on an interval.

6. Use derivatives to solve a variety of applied optimization problems.

CHAPTER PROBLEM

A firm that sells sports memorabilia uses direct mail to market their products. They target a geographical area and continue to mail catalogs to potential customers in that area until the revenue reaches the point of diminishing returns. Then they move on to a different area. Analysis of past sales in a particular area indicates that the revenue (in dollars) generated by a mailing to x thousand customers is given by

$$R(x) = -0.25x^4 + 10x^3 \qquad 0 \le x \le 30$$

How many customers should be included in the next mailing in this area?

Graphing and Optimization

Section 4-1 | First Derivative and Graphs

➤ Increasing and Decreasing Functions
➤ Local Extrema
➤ First-Derivative Test
➤ Applications to Economics

Since the derivative is associated with the slope of the graph of a function at a point, we might expect that it is also associated with other properties of a graph. As we will see in this and the next section, the derivative can tell us a great deal about the shape of the graph of a function. In addition, this investigation will lead to methods for finding absolute maximum and minimum values for functions that do not require graphing. Manufacturing companies can use these methods to find production levels that will minimize cost or maximize profit. Pharmacologists can use them to find levels of drug dosages that will produce maximum sensitivity to a drug. And so on.

➤ Increasing and Decreasing Functions

EXPLORE & DISCUSS 1

Figure 1 on page 226 shows the graph of $y = f(x)$ and a sign chart for $f'(x)$, where

$$f(x) = x^3 - 3x$$

and

$$f'(x) = 3x^2 - 3 = 3(x + 1)(x - 1)$$

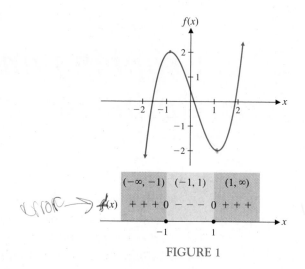

FIGURE 1

Discuss the relationship between the graph of f and the sign of $f'(x)$ over each interval where $f'(x)$ has a constant sign. Also, describe the behavior of the graph of f at each partition number for f'.

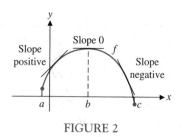

FIGURE 2

Graphs of functions generally have *rising* and *falling* sections as we scan graphs from left to right. Referring to the graph of $f(x) = x^3 - 3x$ in Figure 1, we see that on the interval $(-\infty, -1)$, the graph of f is *rising*, $f(x)$ is *increasing*,* and the slope of the graph is positive $[f'(x) > 0]$. On the other hand, on the interval $(-1, 1)$, the graph of f is *falling*, $f(x)$ is *decreasing*, and the slope of the graph is negative $[f'(x) < 0]$. Finally, on the interval $(1, \infty)$, once again the graph of f is rising, $f(x)$ is increasing, and $f'(x) > 0$. At $x = -1$ and $x = 1$, the slope of the graph is 0 $[f'(x) = 0]$ and the tangent lines are horizontal.

In general, if $f'(x) > 0$ (is positive) on the interval (a, b) (Fig. 2), then $f(x)$ increases ($\nearrow$) and the graph of f rises as we move from left to right over the interval; if $f'(x) < 0$ (is negative) on an interval (a, b), then $f(x)$ decreases ($\searrow$) and the graph of f falls as we move from left to right over the interval. We summarize these important results in Theorem 1.

THEOREM 1 Increasing and Decreasing Functions

For the interval (a, b),

$f'(x)$	$f(x)$	Graph of f	Examples
$+$	Increases $\nearrow$	Rises $\nearrow$	$\big)\,\big(\,\big/$
$-$	Decreases $\searrow$	Falls $\searrow$	$\big\backslash\,\big\backslash\,\big\backslash$

EXPLORE
&DISCUSS
2

The graphs of $f(x) = x^2$ and $g(x) = |x|$ are shown in Figure 3. Both functions change from decreasing to increasing at $x = 0$. Discuss the relationship between the graph of each function at $x = 0$ and the derivative of the function at $x = 0$.

---

* Formally, we say that the function f is **increasing** on an interval (a, b) if $f(x_2) > f(x_1)$ whenever $a < x_1 < x_2 < b$; and f is **decreasing** on (a, b) if $f(x_2) < f(x_1)$ whenever $a < x_1 < x_2 < b$.

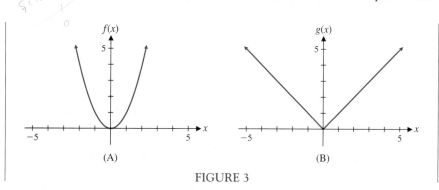

(A)   (B)

FIGURE 3

EXAMPLE 1 Finding Intervals Where a Function Is Increasing or Decreasing Given the function $f(x) = 8x - x^2$,

(A) Which values of x correspond to horizontal tangent lines?

(B) For which values of x is $f(x)$ increasing? Decreasing?

(C) Sketch a graph of f. Add any horizontal tangent lines.

Solution (A) $f'(x) = 8 - 2x = 0$

$$x = 4$$

Thus, a horizontal tangent line exists at $x = 4$ only.

(B) We will construct a sign chart for $f'(x)$ to determine which values of x make $f'(x) > 0$ and which values make $f'(x) < 0$. Recall from Section 3-2 that the partition numbers for a function are the points where the function is 0 or discontinuous. Thus, when constructing a sign chart for $f'(x)$, we must locate all points where $f'(x) = 0$ or $f'(x)$ is discontinuous. From part (A) we know that $f'(x) = 8 - 2x = 0$ at $x = 4$. Since $f'(x) = 8 - 2x$ is a polynomial, it is continuous for all x. Thus, 4 is the only partition number. We construct a sign chart for the intervals $(-\infty, 4)$ and $(4, \infty)$, using test numbers 3 and 5:

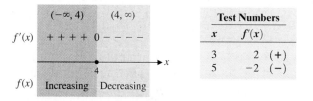

	Test Numbers
x	$f'(x)$
3	2 (+)
5	−2 (−)

Thus, $f(x)$ is increasing on $(-\infty, 4)$ and decreasing on $(4, \infty)$.

(C)

x	$f(x)$
0	0
2	12
4	16
6	12
8	0

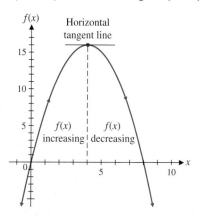

Matched Problem 1 Repeat Example 1 for $f(x) = x^2 - 6x + 10$.

As Example 1 illustrates, construction of a sign chart will play an important role in using the derivative to analyze and sketch the graph of a function f. The partition numbers for f' are central to the construction of these sign charts and also to the analysis of the graph of $y = f(x)$. We already know that if $f'(c) = 0$, the graph of $y = f(x)$ will have a horizontal tangent line at $x = c$. But the partition numbers for f' also include the numbers c where $f'(c)$ does not exist.* There are two possibilities at this type of number: $f(c)$ does not exist, or $f(c)$ exists, but the slope of the tangent line at $x = c$ is undefined.

DEFINITION Critical Values

The values of x in the domain of f where $f'(x) = 0$ or where $f'(x)$ does not exist are called the **critical values** of f.

👁 **Insight** The critical values of f are always in the domain of f and are also partition numbers for f', but f' may have partition numbers that are not critical values.
    If f is a polynomial, then both the partition numbers for f' and the critical values of f are the solutions of $f'(x) = 0$. ●

Example 2 will illustrate the relationship between critical values and partition numbers.

EXAMPLE 2 **Partition Numbers and Critical Values** For each function, find the partition numbers for f', the critical values for f, and determine the intervals where f is increasing and those where f is decreasing.

(A) $f(x) = 1 + x^3$ (B) $f(x) = (1 - x)^{1/3}$ (C) $f(x) = \dfrac{1}{x - 2}$

Solution (A) $f(x) = 1 + x^3$ $f'(x) = 3x^2 = 0$
$$x = 0$$

The only partition number for f' is $x = 0$. Since 0 is in the domain of f, $x = 0$ is also the only critical value for f.

Sign chart for $f'(x) = 3x^2$ (partition number is 0):

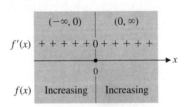

	$(-\infty, 0)$	$(0, \infty)$		**Test Numbers**	
$f'(x)$	$+ + + + + 0 + + + + +$			x	$f'(x)$
				-1	3 $(+)$
	0			1	3 $(+)$
$f(x)$	Increasing	Increasing			

The sign chart indicates that $f(x)$ is increasing on $(-\infty, 0)$ and $(0, \infty)$. Since f is continuous at $x = 0$, it follows that $f(x)$ is increasing for all x. The graph of f is shown in Figure 4.

FIGURE 4

$f(x)$ graph with axis labels 2, -1, 1.

---

* We are assuming that $f'(c)$ does not exist at any point of discontinuity of f'. There do exist functions where f' is discontinuous at $x = c$, yet $f'(c)$ exists. However, we do not consider such functions in this book.

(B) $f(x) = (1 - x)^{1/3}$ $f'(x) = -\dfrac{1}{3}(1 - x)^{-2/3} = \dfrac{-1}{3(1 - x)^{2/3}}$

To find partition numbers for f', we note that f' is continuous for all x except for values of x for which the denominator is 0; that is, $f'(1)$ does not exist and f' is discontinuous at $x = 1$. Since the numerator is the constant -1, $f'(x) \neq 0$ for any value of x. Thus, $x = 1$ is the only partition number for f'. Since 1 is in the domain of f, $x = 1$ is also the only critical value of f. When constructing the sign chart for f' we use the abbreviation ND to note the fact that $f'(x)$ is *not defined* at $x = 1$.

Sign chart for $f'(x) = -1/[3(1 - x)^{2/3}]$ (partition number is 1):

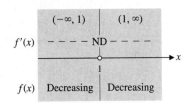

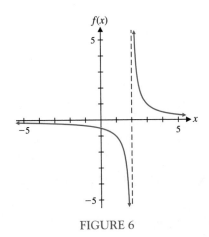

FIGURE 5

The sign chart indicates that f is decreasing on $(-\infty, 1)$ and $(1, \infty)$. Since f is continuous at $x = 1$, it follows that $f(x)$ is decreasing for all x. Thus, **a continuous function can be decreasing (or increasing) on an interval containing values of x where $f'(x)$ does not exist.** The graph of f is shown in Figure 5. Notice that the undefined derivative at $x = 1$ results in a vertical tangent line at $x = 1$. In general, **a vertical tangent will occur at $x = c$ if f is continuous at $x = c$ and $|f'(x)|$ becomes larger and larger as x approaches c.**

(C) $f(x) = \dfrac{1}{x - 2}$ $f'(x) = \dfrac{-1}{(x - 2)^2}$

To find the partition numbers for f', note that $f'(x) \neq 0$ for any x and f' is not defined at $x = 2$. Thus, $x = 2$ is the only partition number for f'. However, $x = 2$ is *not* in the domain of f. Consequently, $x = 2$ is not a critical value of f. This function has no critical values.

Sign chart for $f'(x) = -1/(x - 2)^2$ (partition number is 2):

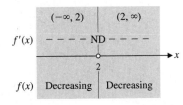

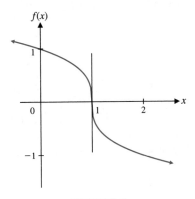

FIGURE 6

Thus, f is decreasing on $(-\infty, 2)$ and $(2, \infty)$. See the graph of f in Figure 6. ■

Matched Problem 2 For each function, find the partition numbers for f', the critical values for f, and determine the intervals where f is increasing and those where f is decreasing.

(A) $f(x) = 1 - x^3$ (B) $f(x) = (1 + x)^{1/3}$ (C) $f(x) = \dfrac{1}{x}$

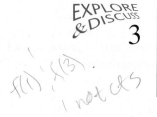

EXPLORE
&DISCUSS
3

A student examined the sign chart in Example 2C and concluded that $f(x) = 1/(x - 2)$ is decreasing for all x except $x = 2$. However, $f(1) = -1 < f(3) = 1$, which seems to indicate that f is increasing. Discuss the difference between the correct answer in Example 2C and the student's answer. Explain why the student's description of where f is decreasing is unacceptable.

◉ **Insight**   Example 2C illustrates two important ideas.

1. Do not assume that all partition numbers for the derivative f' are critical values of the function f. To be a critical value, a partition number must also be in the domain of f.
2. The values where a function is increasing or decreasing must always be expressed in terms of open intervals that are subsets of the domain of the function. ●

➤ Local Extrema

When the graph of a continuous function changes from rising to falling, a high point, or *local maximum,* occurs; and when the graph changes from falling to rising, a low point, or *local minimum,* occurs. In Figure 7, high points occur at c_3 and c_6, and low points occur at c_2 and c_4. In general, we call $f(c)$ a **local maximum** if there exists an interval (m, n) containing c such that

$$f(x) \leq f(c) \qquad \text{for all } x \text{ in } (m, n)$$

Note that this inequality need only hold for values of x near c, hence the use of the term *local.*

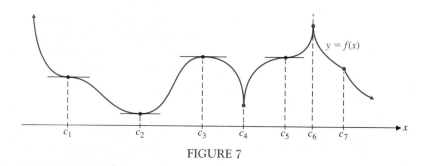

FIGURE 7

The quantity $f(c)$ is called a **local minimum** if there exists an interval (m, n) containing c such that

$$f(x) \geq f(c) \qquad \text{for all } x \text{ in } (m, n)$$

The quantity $f(c)$ is called a **local extremum** if it is either a local maximum or a local minimum. A point on a graph where a local extremum occurs is also called a **turning point.** Thus, in Figure 7 we see that local maxima occur at c_3 and c_6, local minima occur at c_2 and c_4, and all four values produce local extrema. Also note that the local maximum $f(c_3)$ is not the highest point on the graph in Figure 7. Later in this chapter we consider the problem of finding the highest and lowest points on a graph. For now, we are concerned only with locating local extrema.

EXAMPLE 3   **Analyzing a graph** Use the graph of f in Figure 8 to find the intervals where f is increasing, those where f is decreasing, any local maxima, and any local minima.

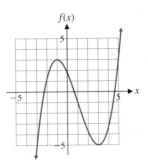

FIGURE 8

Solution   The function f is increasing (graph is rising) on $(-\infty, -1)$ and on $(3, \infty)$ and is decreasing (graph is falling) on $(-1, 3)$. Because the graph changes from rising to falling at $x = -1$, $f(-1) = 3$ is a local maximum. Because the graph changes from falling to rising at $x = 3$, $f(3) = -5$ is a local minimum. ∎

Matched Problem 3   Use the graph of g in Figure 9 to find the intervals where g is increasing, those where g is decreasing, any local maxima, and any local minima.

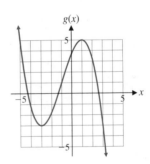

FIGURE 9

How can we locate local maxima and minima if we are given the equation for a function and not its graph? The key is to examine the critical values of the function. The local extrema of the function f in Figure 7 occur either at points where the derivative is 0 (c_2 and c_3) or at points where the derivative does not exist (c_4 and c_6). In other words, local extrema occur only at critical values of f. Theorem 2 shows that this is true in general.

THEOREM 2   **Existence of Local Extrema**

If f is continuous on the interval (a, b), c is a number in (a, b) and $f(c)$ is a local extremum, then either $f'(c) = 0$ or $f'(c)$ does not exist (is not defined).

Theorem 2 states that a local extremum can occur only at a critical value, but it does not imply that every critical value produces a local extremum. In Figure 7, c_1 and c_5 are critical values (the slope is 0), but the function does not have a local maximum or local minimum at either of these values.

Our strategy for finding local extrema is now clear. We find all critical values for f and test each one to see if it produces a local maximum, a local minimum, or neither.

➤ First-Derivative Test

If $f'(x)$ exists on both sides of a critical value c, the sign of $f'(x)$ can be used to determine whether the point $(c, f(c))$ is a local maximum, a local minimum, or neither. The various possibilities are summarized in the following box and illustrated in Figure 10.

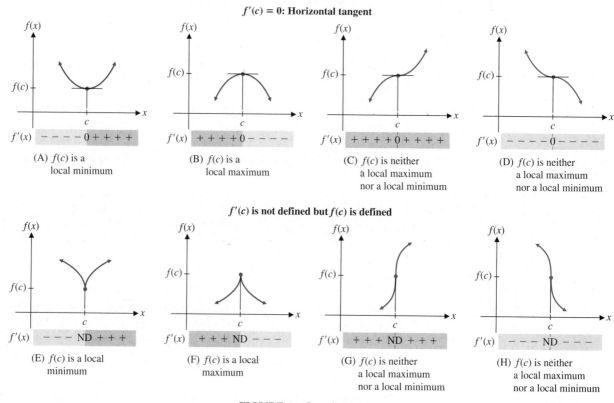

FIGURE 10 Local extrema

PROCEDURE   First-Derivative Test for Local Extrema

Let c be a critical value of f [$f(c)$ defined and either $f'(c) = 0$ or $f'(c)$ not defined]. Construct a sign chart for $f'(x)$ close to and on either side of c.

Sign Chart	$f(c)$
$f'(x)$ $---$ $+++$ m c n $f(x)$ Decreasing Increasing	$f(c)$ is local minimum. If $f'(x)$ changes from negative to positive at c, then $f(c)$ is a local minimum.
$f'(x)$ $+++$ $---$ m c n $f(x)$ Increasing Decreasing	$f(c)$ is local maximum. If $f'(x)$ changes from positive to negative at c, then $f(c)$ is a local maximum.

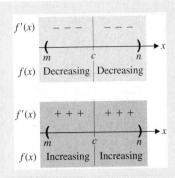

$f(c)$ is not a local extremum.
If $f'(x)$ does not change sign at c, then $f(c)$ is neither a local maximum nor a local minimum.

$f(c)$ is not a local extremum.
If $f'(x)$ does not change sign at c, then $f(c)$ is neither a local maximum nor a local minimum.

EXAMPLE 4   **Locating Local Extrema**   Given $f(x) = x^3 - 6x^2 + 9x + 1$,

(A) Find the critical values of f.

(B) Find the local maxima and minima.

(C) Sketch the graph of f.

Solution   (A) Find all numbers x in the domain of f where $f'(x) = 0$ or $f'(x)$ does not exist.

$$f'(x) = 3x^2 - 12x + 9 = 0$$
$$3(x^2 - 4x + 3) = 0$$
$$3(x - 1)(x - 3) = 0$$
$$x = 1 \quad \text{or} \quad x = 3$$

$f'(x)$ exists for all x; the critical values are $x = 1$ and $x = 3$.

(B) The easiest way to apply the first-derivative test for local maxima and minima is to construct a sign chart for $f'(x)$ for all x. Partition numbers for $f'(x)$ are $x = 1$ and $x = 3$ (which also happen to be critical values for f).

Sign chart for $f'(x) = 3(x - 1)(x - 3)$:

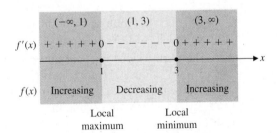

Test Numbers	
x	$f'(x)$
0	9 (+)
2	−3 (−)
4	9 (+)

The sign chart indicates that f increases on $(-\infty, 1)$, has a local maximum at $x = 1$, decreases on $(1, 3)$, has a local minimum at $x = 3$, and increases on $(3, \infty)$. These facts are summarized in the following table:

x	$f'(x)$	$f(x)$	Graph of f
$(-\infty, 1)$	+	Increasing	Rising
$x = 1$	0	Local maximum	Horizontal tangent
$(1, 3)$	−	Decreasing	Falling
$x = 3$	0	Local minimum	Horizontal tangent
$(3, \infty)$	+	Increasing	Rising

(C) We sketch a graph of *f* using the information from part (B) and point-by-point plotting.

x	f(x)
0	1
1	5
2	3
3	1
4	5

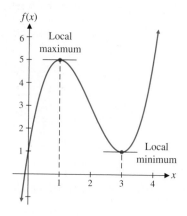

Matched Problem 4 Given $f(x) = x^3 - 9x^2 + 24x - 10$,

(A) Find the critical values of *f*.

(B) Find the local maxima and minima.

(C) Sketch a graph of *f*.

How can you tell if you have found all the local extrema for a function? In general, this can be a difficult question to answer. However, in the case of a polynomial function, there is an easily determined upper limit on the number of local extrema. Since the local extrema are the *x* intercepts of the derivative, this limit is a consequence of the number of *x* intercepts of a polynomial. The relevant information is summarized in the following theorem, which is stated without proof:

THEOREM 3 **Intercepts and Local Extrema for Polynomial Functions**

If $f(x) = a_n x^n + a_{n-1} x^{n-1} + \cdots + a_1 x + a_0, a_n \neq 0$, is an *n*th-degree polynomial, then *f* has at most *n* *x* intercepts and at most *n* − 1 local extrema.

Theorem 3 does not guarantee that every *n*th-degree polynomial has exactly *n* − 1 local extrema; it says only that there can never be more than *n* − 1 local extrema. For example, the third-degree polynomial in Example 4 has two local extrema, while the third-degree polynomial in Example 2A does not have any.

➤ **Applications to Economics**

In addition to providing information for hand-sketching graphs, the derivative is also an important tool for analyzing graphs and discussing the interplay between a function and its rate of change. The next two examples illustrate this process in the context of some applications to economics.

EXAMPLE 5 **Agricultural Exports and Imports** Over the past several decades, the United States has exported more agricultural products than it has imported, maintaining a positive balance of trade in this area. However, the trade balance fluctuated considerably during this period. The graph in Figure 11 approximates the rate of change of the trade balance over a 15-year period, where $B(t)$ is the trade balance (in billions of dollars) and t is time (in years).

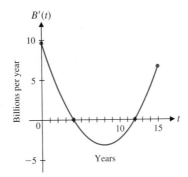

FIGURE 11 Rate of change of the balance of trade

(A) Write a brief verbal description of the graph of $y = B(t)$, including a discussion of any local extrema.

(B) Sketch a possible graph of $y = B(t)$.

Solution (A) The graph of the derivative $y = B'(t)$ contains the same essential information as a sign chart. That is, we see that $B'(t)$ is positive on $(0, 4)$, 0 at $t = 4$, negative on $(4, 12)$, 0 at $t = 12$, and positive on $(12, 15)$. Hence, the trade balance increases for the first 4 years to a local maximum, decreases for the next 8 years to a local minimum, and then increases for the final 3 years.

(B) Without additional information concerning the actual values of $y = B(t)$, we cannot produce an accurate graph. However, we can sketch a possible graph that illustrates the important features, as shown in Figure 12. The absence of a scale on the vertical axis is a consequence of the lack of information about the values of $B(t)$.

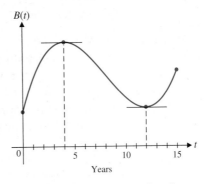

FIGURE 12 Balance of trade

Matched Problem 5   The graph in Figure 13 approximates the rate of change of the U.S. share of the total world production of motor vehicles over a 20-year period, where $S(t)$ is the U.S. share (as a percentage) and t is time (in years).

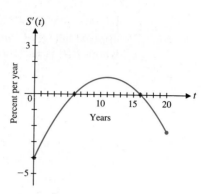

FIGURE 13

(A) Write a brief verbal description of the graph of $y = S(t)$, including a discussion of any local extrema.

(B) Sketch a possible graph of $y = S(t)$.

 EXAMPLE 6 **Revenue Analysis** The graph of the total revenue $R(x)$ (in dollars) from the sale of x bookcases is shown in Figure 14.

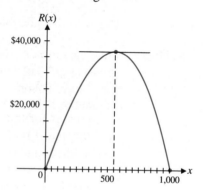

FIGURE 14 Revenue

(A) Write a brief verbal description of the graph of the marginal revenue function $y = R'(x)$, including a discussion of any x intercepts.

(B) Sketch a possible graph of $y = R'(x)$.

Solution (A) The graph of $y = R(x)$ indicates that $R(x)$ increases on $(0, 550)$, has a local maximum at $x = 550$, and decreases on $(550, 1,000)$. Consequently, the marginal revenue function $R'(x)$ must be positive on $(0, 550)$, 0 at $x = 550$, and negative on $(550, 1,000)$.

(B) A possible graph of $y = R'(x)$ illustrating the information summarized in part (A) is shown in Figure 15.

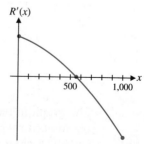

FIGURE 15 Marginal revenue

Matched Problem 6

The graph of the total revenue $R(x)$ (in dollars) from the sale of x desks is shown in Figure 16.

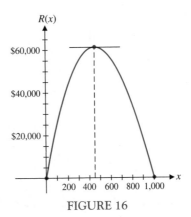

FIGURE 16

(A) Write a brief verbal description of the graph of the marginal revenue function $y = R'(x)$, including a discussion of any x intercepts.

(B) Sketch a possible graph of $y = R'(x)$.

Comparing Examples 5 and 6, we see that we were able to obtain more information about the function from the graph of its derivative (Example 5) than we were when the process was reversed (Example 6). In the next section we introduce some ideas that will enable us to extract additional information about the derivative from the graph of the function.

Answers to Matched Problems

1. (A) Horizontal tangent line at $x = 3$.

(B) Decreasing on $(-\infty, 3)$;
increasing on $(3, \infty)$

(C)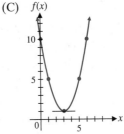

2. (A) Partition number: $x = 0$; critical value: $x = 0$; decreasing for all x

(B) Partition number: $x = -1$; critical value: $x = -1$; increasing for all x

(C) Partition number: $x = 0$; no critical values; decreasing on $(-\infty, 0)$ and $(0, \infty)$

3. Increasing on $(-3, 1)$; decreasing on $(-\infty, -3)$ and $(1, \infty)$; local maximum at $x = 1$; local minimum at $x = -3$

4. (A) Critical values: $x = 2, x = 4$

(B) Local maximum at $x = 2$;
local minimum at $x = 4$

(C)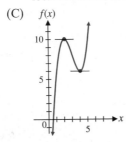

5. (A) The U.S. share of the world market decreases for 6 years to a local minimum, increases for the next 10 years to a local maximum, and then decreases for the final 4 years.

(B) S(t)

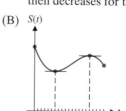

6. (A) The marginal revenue is positive on (0, 450), 0 at $x = 450$; and negative on (450, 1,000).

(B) R'(x)

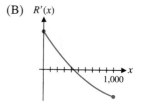

Exercise 4-1

A *Problems 1–8 refer to the graph of y = f(x) below.*

f(x)

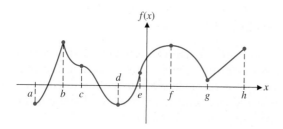

1. Identify the intervals over which $f(x)$ is increasing.

2. Identify the intervals over which $f(x)$ is decreasing.

3. Identify the intervals over which $f'(x) < 0$.

4. Identify the intervals over which $f'(x) > 0$.

5. Identify the x coordinates of the points where $f'(x) = 0$.

6. Identify the x coordinates of the points where $f'(x)$ does not exist.

7. Identify the x coordinates of the points where $f(x)$ has a local maximum.

8. Identify the x coordinates of the points where $f(x)$ has a local minimum.

In Problems 9 and 10, f(x) is continuous on $(-\infty, \infty)$ and has critical values at $x = a, b, c,$ and d. Use the sign chart for $f'(x)$ to determine whether f has a local maximum, a local minimum, or neither at each critical value.

9.

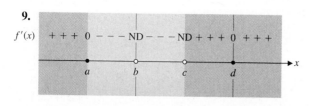

10.

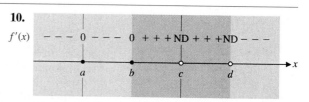

In Problems 11–18, match the graph of f with one of the sign charts a–h in the figure.

11.   f(x)

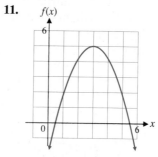

12.   f(x)

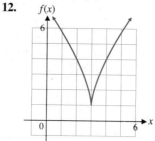

13.   f(x)

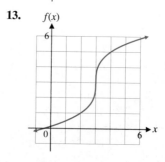

14.

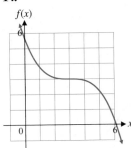

15.

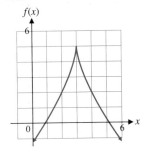

16.

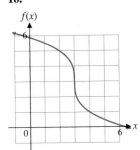

17.

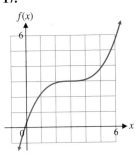

18.

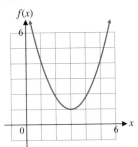

(a) $f'(x)$

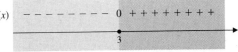

(b) $f'(x)$

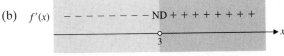

(c) $f'(x)$

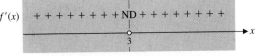

(d) $f'(x)$

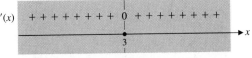

(e) $f'(x)$

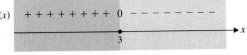

(f) $f'(x)$

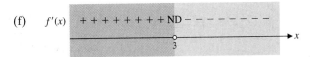

(g) $f'(x)$

(h) $f'(x)$

$$-------- \quad 0 \quad --------$$

Figure for 11–18

B *In Problems 19–32, find the intervals where $f(x)$ is increasing, the intervals where $f(x)$ is decreasing, and the local extrema.*

19. $f(x) = 2x^2 - 4x$

20. $f(x) = -3x^2 - 12x$

21. $f(x) = -2x^2 - 16x - 25$

22. $f(x) = -3x^2 + 12x - 5$

23. $f(x) = x^3 + 4x - 5$

24. $f(x) = -x^3 - 4x + 8$

25. $f(x) = x^3 - 6x^2 + 1$

26. $f(x) = -x^3 + 12x - 5$

27. $f(x) = 2x^3 - 3x^2 - 36x$

28. $f(x) = -2x^3 + 3x^2 + 120x$

29. $f(x) = 3x^4 - 4x^3 + 5$

30. $f(x) = x^4 + 2x^3 + 5$

31. $f(x) = -x^4 + 32x$

32. $f(x) = x^4 + 4x$

In Problems 33–38, use a graphing utility to approximate the critical values of $f(x)$ to two decimal places. Find the intervals where $f(x)$ is increasing, the intervals where $f(x)$ is decreasing, and the local extrema.

33. $f(x) = x^4 + x^2 + x$

34. $f(x) = x^4 + x^2 - 9x$

35. $f(x) = x^4 - 4x^3 + 9x$

36. $f(x) = x^4 + 5x^3 - 15x$

37. $f(x) = x^4 - 2x^3 - 5x^2 + 4x$

38. $f(x) = x^4 + 2x^3 - 4x^2 - 6x$

In Problems 39–46, find the intervals where $f(x)$ is increasing, the intervals where $f(x)$ is decreasing, and sketch the graph. Add horizontal tangent lines.

39. $f(x) = 4 + 8x - x^2$

40. $f(x) = 2x^2 - 8x + 9$

41. $f(x) = x^3 - 3x + 1$

42. $f(x) = x^3 - 12x + 2$

43. $f(x) = 10 - 12x + 6x^2 - x^3$

44. $f(x) = x^3 + 3x^2 + 3x$

45. $f(x) = x^4 - 18x^2$

46. $f(x) = -x^4 + 50x^2$

In Problems 47–54, $f(x)$ is continuous on $(-\infty, \infty)$. Use the given information to sketch the graph of f.

47.

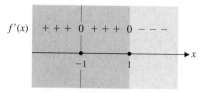

x	-2	-1	0	1	2
$f(x)$	-1	1	2	3	1

48.

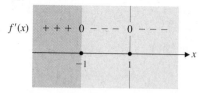

x	-2	-1	0	1	2
$f(x)$	1	3	2	1	-1

49.

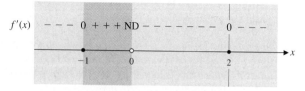

x	-2	-1	0	2	4
$f(x)$	2	1	2	1	0

50.

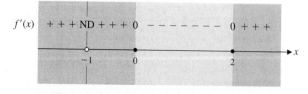

x	-2	-1	0	2	3
$f(x)$	-3	0	2	-1	0

51. $f(-2) = 4, f(0) = 0, f(2) = -4$;
$f'(-2) = 0, f'(0) = 0, f'(2) = 0$;
$f'(x) > 0$ on $(-\infty, -2)$ and $(2, \infty)$;
$f'(x) < 0$ on $(-2, 0)$ and $(0, 2)$

52. $f(-2) = -1, f(0) = 0, f(2) = 1$;
$f'(-2) = 0, f'(2) = 0$;
$f'(x) > 0$ on $(-\infty, -2), (-2, 2)$, and $(2, \infty)$

53. $f(-1) = 2, f(0) = 0, f(1) = -2$;
$f'(-1) = 0, f'(1) = 0, f'(0)$ is not defined;
$f'(x) > 0$ on $(-\infty, -1)$ and $(1, \infty)$;
$f'(x) < 0$ on $(-1, 0)$ and $(0, 1)$

54. $f(-1) = 2, f(0) = 0, f(1) = 2$;
$f'(-1) = 0, f'(1) = 0, f'(0)$ is not defined;
$f'(x) > 0$ on $(-\infty, -1)$ and $(0, 1)$;
$f'(x) < 0$ on $(-1, 0)$ and $(1, \infty)$

Problems 55–60 involve functions f_1–f_6 and their derivatives g_1–g_6. Use the graphs shown in figures (A) and (B) to match each function f_i with its derivative g_j.

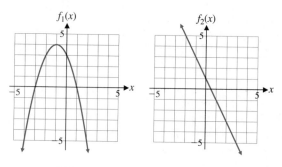

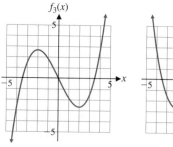

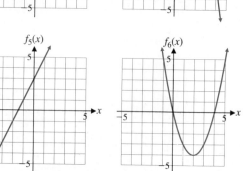

Figure (A) for 53–58

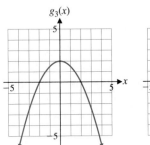

$g_1(x)$

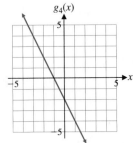

$g_2(x)$

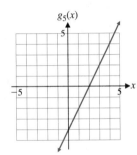

$g_3(x)$

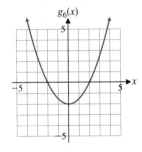

$g_4(x)$

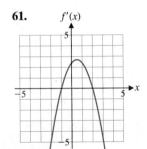

$g_5(x)$

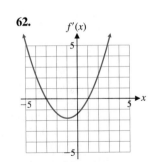

$g_6(x)$

Figure (B) for 55–60

55. f_1

56. f_2

57. f_3

58. f_4

59. f_5

60. f_6

In Problems 61–66, use the given graph of $y = f'(x)$ *to find the intervals where f is increasing, the intervals where f is decreasing, and the local extrema. Sketch a possible graph for* $y = f(x)$.

61.

$f'(x)$

62.

$f'(x)$

63.

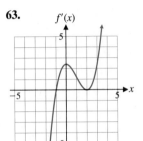

$f'(x)$

64.

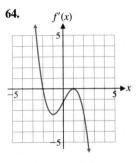

$f'(x)$

65.

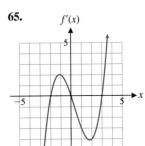

$f'(x)$

66.

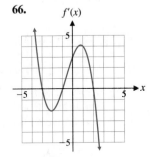

$f'(x)$

In Problems 67–70, use the given graph of $y = f(x)$ *to find the intervals where* $f'(x) > 0$, *the intervals where* $f'(x) < 0$, *and the values of x for which* $f'(x) = 0$. *Sketch a possible graph for* $y = f'(x)$.

67.

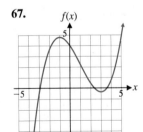

$f(x)$

68.

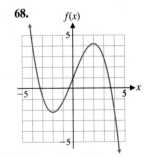

$f(x)$

69.

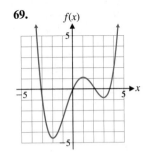

$f(x)$

70.

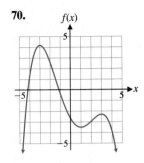

$f(x)$

C *In Problems 71–82, find the critical values, the intervals where* $f(x)$ *is increasing, the intervals where* $f(x)$ *is decreasing, and the local extrema. Do not graph.*

71. $f(x) = x + \dfrac{4}{x}$

72. $f(x) = \dfrac{9}{x} + x$

73. $f(x) = 1 + \dfrac{1}{x} + \dfrac{1}{x^2}$

74. $f(x) = 3 - \dfrac{4}{x} - \dfrac{2}{x^2}$

75. $f(x) = \dfrac{x^2}{x-2}$ 76. $f(x) = \dfrac{x^2}{x+1}$

77. $f(x) = x^4(x-6)^2$ 78. $f(x) = x^3(x-5)^2$

79. $f(x) = 3(x-2)^{2/3} + 4$

80. $f(x) = 6(4-x)^{2/3} + 4$

81. $f(x) = \dfrac{2x^2}{x^2+1}$ 82. $f(x) = \dfrac{-3x}{x^2+4}$

83. Let $f(x) = x^3 + kx$, where k is a constant. Discuss the number of local extrema and the shape of the graph of f if:

(A) $k > 0$ (B) $k < 0$ (C) $k = 0$

84. Let $f(x) = x^4 + kx^2$, where k is a constant. Discuss the number of local extrema and the shape of the graph of f if:

(A) $k > 0$ (B) $k < 0$ (C) $k = 0$

Applications

Business & Economics

85. *Profit analysis.* The graph of the total profit $P(x)$ (in dollars) from the sale of x cordless electric screwdrivers is shown in the figure.

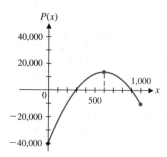

Figure for 85

(A) Write a brief verbal description of the graph of the marginal profit function $y = P'(x)$, including a discussion of any x intercepts.

(B) Sketch a possible graph of $y = P'(x)$.

86. *Revenue analysis.* The graph of the total revenue $R(x)$ (in dollars) from the sale of x cordless electric screwdrivers is shown in the figure.

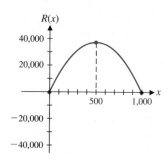

Figure for 86

(A) Write a brief verbal description of the graph of the marginal revenue function $y = R'(x)$, including a discussion of any x intercepts.

(B) Sketch a possible graph of $y = R'(x)$.

87. *Price analysis.* The graph in the figure approximates the rate of change of the price of bacon over a 70-month period, where $B(t)$ is the price of a pound of sliced bacon (in dollars) and t is time (in months).

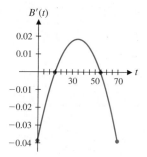

Figure for 87

(A) Write a brief verbal description of the graph of $y = B(t)$, including a discussion of any local extrema.

(B) Sketch a possible graph of $y = B(t)$.

88. *Price analysis.* The graph in the figure approximates the rate of change of the price of eggs over a 70-month period, where $E(t)$ is the price of a dozen eggs (in dollars) and t is time (in months).

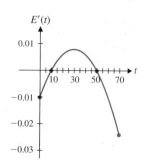

Figure for 88

(A) Write a brief verbal description of the graph of $y = E(t)$, including a discussion of any local extrema.

(B) Sketch a possible graph of $y = E(t)$.

89. *Average cost.* A manufacturer incurs the following costs in producing x toasters in one day for $0 < x < 150$: fixed costs, $320; unit production cost, $20 per toaster; equipment maintenance and repairs, $0.05x^2$ dollars. Thus, the cost of manufacturing x toasters in one day is given by

$$C(x) = 0.05x^2 + 20x + 320 \qquad 0 < x < 150$$

(A) What is the average cost, $\overline{C}(x)$, per toaster if x toasters are produced in one day?

(B) Find the critical values for $\overline{C}(x)$, the intervals where the average cost per toaster is decreasing, the intervals where the average cost per toaster is increasing, and the local extrema. Do not graph.

90. *Average cost.* A manufacturer incurs the following costs in producing x blenders in one day for $0 < x < 200$: fixed costs, $450; unit production cost, $30 per blender; equipment maintenance and repairs, $0.08x^2$ dollars.

(A) What is the average cost, $\overline{C}(x)$, per blender if x blenders are produced in one day?

(B) Find the critical values for $\overline{C}(x)$, the intervals where the average cost per blender is decreasing, the intervals where the average cost per blender is increasing, and the local extrema. Do not graph.

91. *Marginal analysis.* Show that profit will be increasing over production intervals (a, b) for which marginal revenue is greater than marginal cost. [*Hint:* $P(x) = R(x) - C(x)$]

92. *Marginal analysis.* Show that profit will be decreasing over production intervals (a, b) for which marginal revenue is less than marginal cost.

Life Sciences

93. *Medicine.* A drug is injected into the bloodstream of a patient through the right arm. The concentration of the drug in the bloodstream of the left arm t hours after the injection is approximated by

$$C(t) = \frac{0.28t}{t^2 + 4} \qquad 0 < t < 24$$

Find the critical values for $C(t)$, the intervals where the concentration of the drug is increasing, the intervals where the concentration of the drug is decreasing, and the local extrema. Do not graph.

94. *Medicine.* The concentration $C(t)$, in milligrams per cubic centimeter, of a particular drug in a patient's bloodstream is given by

$$C(t) = \frac{0.3t}{t^2 + 6t + 9} \qquad 0 < t < 12$$

where t is the number of hours after the drug is taken orally. Find the critical values for $C(t)$, the intervals where the concentration of the drug is increasing, the intervals where the concentration of the drug is decreasing, and the local extrema. Do not graph.

Social Sciences

95. *Politics.* Public awareness of a congressional candidate before and after a successful campaign was approximated by

$$P(t) = \frac{8.4t}{t^2 + 49} + 0.1 \qquad 0 < t < 24$$

where t is time (in months) after the campaign started and $P(t)$ is the fraction of people in the congressional district who could recall the candidate's (and later, congressman's) name. Find the critical values for $P(t)$, the time intervals where the fraction is increasing, the time intervals where the fraction is decreasing, and the local extrema. Do not graph.

Section **4-2** | Second Derivative and Graphs

➤ Concavity
➤ Inflection Points
➤ Analyzing Graphs
➤ A Graphing Strategy for Polynomials
➤ Point of Diminishing Returns

In Section 4-1 we saw that the derivative can be used to determine when a graph is rising and falling. Now we want to see what the *second derivative* (the derivative of the derivative) can tell us about the shape of a graph.

➤ Concavity

Consider the functions

$$f(x) = x^2 \quad \text{and} \quad g(x) = \sqrt{x}$$

for x in the interval $(0, \infty)$. Since

$$f'(x) = 2x > 0 \qquad \text{for } 0 < x < \infty$$

and

$$g'(x) = \frac{1}{2\sqrt{x}} > 0 \qquad \text{for } 0 < x < \infty$$

both functions are increasing on $(0, \infty)$.

EXPLORE
&DISCUSS
1

(A) Discuss the difference in the shapes of the graphs of f and g shown in Figure 1.

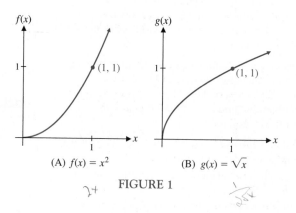

(A) $f(x) = x^2$ (B) $g(x) = \sqrt{x}$

FIGURE 1

(B) Complete the following table and discuss the relationship between the values of the derivatives of f and g and the shapes of their graphs.

x	0.25	0.5	0.75	1
$f'(x)$	$\frac{1}{2}$	1	1.5	2
$g'(x)$	1	.707	.3	5

We use the term *concave upward* to describe a graph that opens upward and *concave downward* to describe a graph that opens downward. Thus, the graph of f in Figure 1A is concave upward, and the graph of g in Figure 1B is concave downward. Finding a mathematical formulation of concavity will help us sketch and analyze graphs.

It will be instructive to examine the slopes of f and g at various points on their graphs (see Fig. 2). We can make two observations about each graph. Looking at the graph of f in Figure 2A, we see that $f'(x)$ (the slope of the tangent line) is *increasing* and that the graph lies *above* each tangent line. Looking at Figure 2B, we see that $g'(x)$ is *decreasing* and that the graph lies *below* each tangent line.

With these ideas in mind, we state the general definition of concavity.

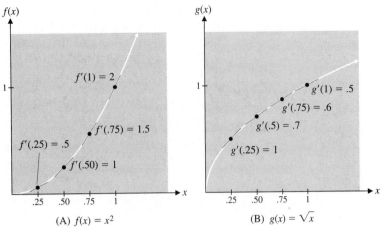

FIGURE 2

DEFINITION   Concavity

The graph of a function f is **concave upward** on the interval (a, b) if $f'(x)$ is *increasing* on (a, b) and is **concave downward** on the interval (a, b) if $f'(x)$ is *decreasing* on (a, b).

Geometrically, the graph is concave upward on (a, b) if it lies above its tangent lines in (a, b) and is concave downward on (a, b) if it lies below its tangent lines in (a, b).

How can we determine when $f'(x)$ is increasing or decreasing? In Section 4-1 we used the derivative of a function to determine when that function is increasing or decreasing. Thus, to determine when the function $f'(x)$ is increasing or decreasing, we use the derivative of $f'(x)$. The derivative of the derivative of a function is called the *second derivative* of the function. Various notations for the second derivative are given in the following box:

NOTATION   Second Derivative

For $y = f(x)$, the **second derivative** of f, provided that it exists, is

$$f''(x) = \frac{d}{dx}f'(x)$$

Other notations for $f''(x)$ are

$$\frac{d^2y}{dx^2} \qquad y''$$

Returning to the functions f and g discussed at the beginning of this section, we have

$$f(x) = x^2 \qquad\qquad g(x) = \sqrt{x} = x^{1/2}$$

$$f'(x) = 2x \qquad\qquad g'(x) = \frac{1}{2}x^{-1/2} = \frac{1}{2\sqrt{x}}$$

$$f''(x) = \frac{d}{dx}2x = 2 \qquad g''(x) = \frac{d}{dx}\frac{1}{2}x^{-1/2} = -\frac{1}{4}x^{-3/2} = -\frac{1}{4\sqrt{x^3}}$$

For $x > 0$, we see that $f''(x) > 0$; thus, $f'(x)$ is increasing and the graph of f is concave upward (see Fig. 2A). For $x > 0$, we also see that $g''(x) < 0$; thus, $g'(x)$ is decreasing and the graph of g is concave downward (see Fig. 2B). These ideas are summarized in the following box.

SUMMARY   Concavity

For the interval (a, b),

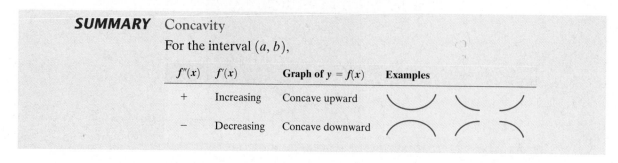

$f''(x)$	$f'(x)$	Graph of $y = f(x)$	Examples
+	Increasing	Concave upward	
−	Decreasing	Concave downward	

👁 **Insight**   Be careful not to confuse concavity with falling and rising. A graph that is concave upward on an interval may be falling, rising, or both falling and rising on that interval. A similar statement holds for a graph that is concave downward. See Figure 3.

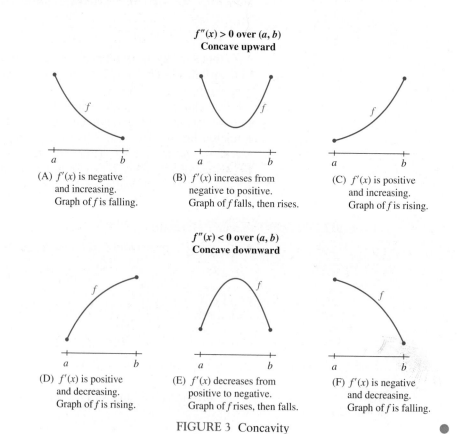

$f''(x) > 0$ over (a, b)
Concave upward

(A) $f'(x)$ is negative and increasing. Graph of f is falling.

(B) $f'(x)$ increases from negative to positive. Graph of f falls, then rises.

(C) $f'(x)$ is positive and increasing. Graph of f is rising.

$f''(x) < 0$ over (a, b)
Concave downward

(D) $f'(x)$ is positive and decreasing. Graph of f is rising.

(E) $f'(x)$ decreases from positive to negative. Graph of f rises, then falls.

(F) $f'(x)$ is negative and decreasing. Graph of f is falling.

FIGURE 3   Concavity

EXAMPLE 1   **Determining Concavity of a Graph**   Let $f(x) = x^3$. Find the intervals where the graph of f is concave upward and the intervals where the graph of f is concave downward. Sketch a graph of f.

Solution   To determine concavity, we must determine the sign of $f''(x)$.

$$f(x) = x^3 \qquad f'(x) = 3x^2 \qquad f''(x) = 6x$$

Sign chart for $f''(x) = 6x$ (partition number is 0):

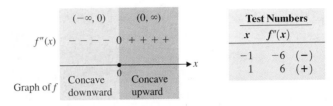

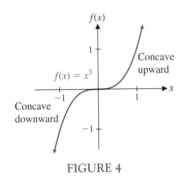

Thus, the graph of f is concave downward on $(-\infty, 0)$ and concave upward on $(0, \infty)$. The graph of f (without going through other graphing details) is shown in Figure 4.

FIGURE 4

 Matched Problem 1   Repeat Example 1 for $f(x) = 1 - x^3$.

The graph in Example 1 changes from concave downward to concave upward at the point $(0, 0)$. This point is called an *inflection point*.

➤ Inflection Points

EXPLORE & DISCUSS 2   Discuss the relationship between the change in concavity of each of the following functions at $x = 0$ and the second derivative at and near 0.

(A) $f(x) = x^3$ (B) $g(x) = x^{4/3}$ (C) $h(x) = x^4$

In general, an **inflection point** is a point on the graph of the function where the concavity changes (from upward to downward or from downward to upward). For the concavity to change at a point, $f''(x)$ must change sign at that point. But in Section 3-2 we saw that the partition numbers* identify the points where a function can change sign. Thus, we have the following theorem:

THEOREM 1   Inflection Points

If $y = f(x)$ is continuous on (a, b) and has an inflection point at $x = c$, then either $f''(c) = 0$ or $f''(c)$ does not exist.

Note that inflection points can occur only at partition numbers of f'', but not every partition number of f'' produces an inflection point. Two additional requirements must be satisfied for an inflection point:

A partition number c for f'' produces an inflection point for the graph of f only if

1. $f''(x)$ changes sign at c, and

2. c is in the domain of f.

Figure 5 illustrates several typical cases.

---

*As we did with the first derivative, we assume that if f'' is discontinuous at c, then $f''(c)$ does not exist.

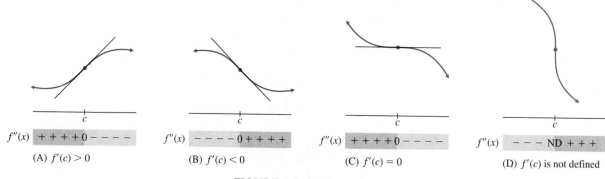

FIGURE 5 Inflection points

If $f'(c)$ exists and $f''(x)$ changes sign at $x = c$, the tangent line at an inflection point $(c, f(c))$ will always lie below the graph on the side that is concave upward and above the graph on the side that is concave downward (see Fig. 5A, B, and C).

EXAMPLE 2 **Locating Inflection Points** Find the inflection point(s) of

$$f(x) = x^3 - 6x^2 + 9x + 1$$

Solution Since inflection point(s) occur at values of x where $f''(x)$ changes sign, we construct a sign chart for $f''(x)$.

$$f(x) = x^3 - 6x^2 + 9x + 1$$
$$f'(x) = 3x^2 - 12x + 9$$
$$f''(x) = 6x - 12 = 6(x - 2)$$

Sign chart for $f''(x) = 6(x - 2)$ (partition number is 2):

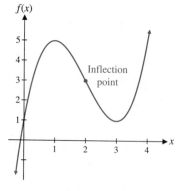

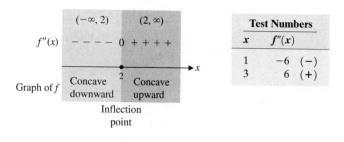

From the sign chart we see that the graph of f has an inflection point at $x = 2$. The graph of f is shown in Figure 6. (See also Example 4 in Section 4-1.)

FIGURE 6

Matched Problem 2 Find the inflection point(s) of $f(x) = x^3 - 9x^2 + 24x - 10$. (See the answer to Matched Problem 4 in Section 4-1 for the graph of f.)

👁 **Insight** It is important to remember that the partition numbers of f'' are only candidates for inflection points. The function f must be defined at $x = c$, and the second derivative must change sign at $x = c$ in order for the graph to have an inflection point at $x = c$. For example, consider

$$f(x) = x^4 \qquad g(x) = \frac{1}{x}$$

$$f'(x) = 4x^3 \qquad g'(x) = -\frac{1}{x^2}$$

$$f''(x) = 12x^2 \qquad g''(x) = \frac{2}{x^3}$$

In each case, $x = 0$ is a partition number for the second derivative, but neither graph has an inflection point at $x = 0$. Function f does not have an inflection point at $x = 0$ because $f''(x)$ does not change sign at $x = 0$ (see Fig. 7A). Function g does not have an inflection point at $x = 0$ because $g(0)$ is not defined (see Fig. 7B).

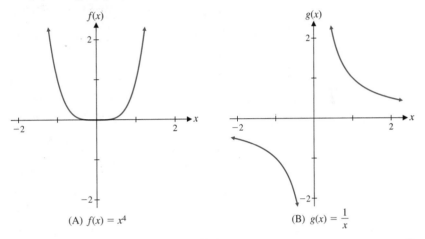

(A) $f(x) = x^4$ (B) $g(x) = \dfrac{1}{x}$

FIGURE 7

➤ Analyzing Graphs

In the next example we combine increasing/decreasing properties with concavity properties to analyze the graph of a function.

EXAMPLE 3   **Analyzing a Graph**   Figure 8 shows the graph of the derivative of a function f. Use this graph to discuss the graph of f. Include a sketch of a possible graph of f.

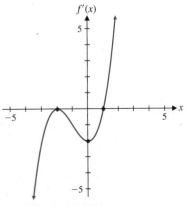

FIGURE 8

Solution The sign of the derivative determines where the original function is increasing and decreasing, and the increasing/decreasing properties of the derivative determine the concavity of the original function. The relevant information obtained from the graph of f' is summarized in Table 1, and a possible graph of f is shown in Figure 9.

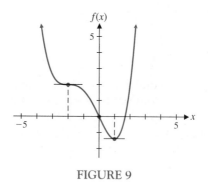

FIGURE 9

TABLE 1

x	$f'(x)$ (Fig. 10)	$f(x)$ (Fig. 11)
$-\infty < x < -2$	Negative and increasing	Decreasing and concave upward
$x = -2$	Local maximum	Inflection point
$-2 < x < 0$	Negative and decreasing	Decreasing and concave downward
$x = 0$	Local minimum	Inflection point
$0 < x < 1$	Negative and increasing	Decreasing and concave upward
$x = 1$	x intercept	Local minimum
$1 < x < \infty$	Positive and increasing	Increasing and concave upward

Matched Problem 3 Figure 10 shows the graph of the derivative of a function f. Use this graph to discuss the graph of f. Include a sketch of a possible graph of f.

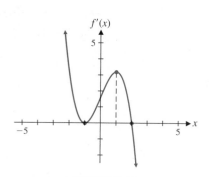

FIGURE 10

➤ A Graphing Strategy for Polynomial Functions

If $y = f(x)$ is a polynomial function, then $f(x)$, $f'(x)$, and $f''(x)$ exist for any real number x. The definitions of some of the concepts introduced in Sections 4-1 and 4-2 take simpler forms for polynomial functions. In particular, the critical values of $f(x)$, the partition numbers of $f'(x)$, and the zeros of $f'(x)$ all refer to the same set of x values. Similarly, the possible inflection points, the partition numbers for $f''(x)$, and the zeros of $f''(x)$ refer to the same set of x values. Keeping these relationships in mind, we summarize the graphing tools for polynomials in the next box.

PROCEDURE Strategy for Graphing a Polynomial $y = f(x)$

Step 1. *Analyze* $f(x)$. Find the intercepts. The x intercepts are the solutions to $f(x) = 0$, if they exist, and the y intercept is $f(0)$.

Step 2. *Analyze* $f'(x)$. Find the zeros of $f'(x)$. Construct a sign chart for $f'(x)$, determine the intervals where $f(x)$ is increasing and decreasing, and find local maxima and minima.

Step 3. *Analyze* $f''(x)$. Find the zeros of $f''(x)$. Construct a sign chart for $f''(x)$, determine where the graph of f is concave upward and concave downward, and find any inflection points.

Step 4. Sketch the graph of f.

An example will illustrate the use of this strategy.

EXAMPLE 4 **Using the Graphing Strategy** Analyze the function

$$f(x) = x^4 - 2x^3$$

following the graphing strategy. State all the pertinent information, and sketch the graph of f.

Solution **Step 1.** *Analyze* $f(x)$. $f(x) = x^4 - 2x^3$

x intercept: $f(x) = 0$

$$x^4 - 2x^3 = 0$$

$$x^3(x - 2) = 0$$

$$x = 0, 2$$

y intercept: $f(0) = 0$

Step 2. *Analyze* $f'(x)$. $f'(x) = 4x^3 - 6x^2 = 4x^2(x - \frac{3}{2})$

Zeros for $f'(x)$: 0 and $\frac{3}{2}$

Sign chart for $f'(x)$:

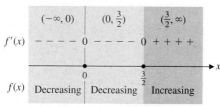

	Test Numbers	
x	$f'(x)$	
-1	-10	$(-)$
1	-2	$(-)$
2	8	$(+)$

Thus, $f(x)$ is decreasing on $(-\infty, \frac{3}{2})$, increasing on $(\frac{3}{2}, \infty)$, and has a local minimum at $x = \frac{3}{2}$.

Step 3. *Analyze* $f''(x)$. $f''(x) = 12x^2 - 12x = 12x(x - 1)$

Partition numbers for $f''(x)$: 0 and 1

Sign chart for $f''(x)$:

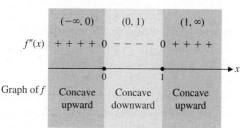

	Test Numbers	
x	$f''(x)$	
-1	24	$(+)$
$\frac{1}{2}$	-3	$(-)$
2	24	$(+)$

Thus, the graph of f is concave upward on $(-\infty, 0)$ and $(1, \infty)$, concave downward on $(0, 1)$, and has inflection points at $x = 0$ and $x = 1$.

Step 4. *Sketch the graph of f.*

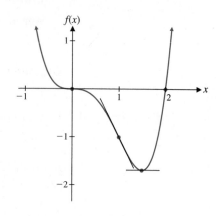

x	$f(x)$
0	0
1	-1
$\frac{3}{2}$	$-\frac{27}{16}$
2	0

Matched Problem 4　Analyze the function $f(x) = x^4 + 4x^3$ following the graphing strategy. State all the pertinent information, and sketch the graph of f.

◉ Insight　Refer to the solution for Example 4. Combining the sign charts for $f'(x)$ and $f''(x)$ (Fig. 11) partitions the real number line into intervals where neither $f'(x)$ nor $f''(x)$ change sign. On each of these intervals, the graph of $f(x)$ must have the shape of one of four basic shapes (see also Fig. 3, parts A, C, D, and F). This reduces sketching the graph of a polynomial to plotting the points identified in the graphing strategy and connecting them with one of these basic shapes.

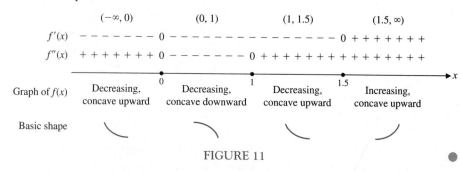

FIGURE 11

➤ Point of Diminishing Returns

If a company decides to increase spending on advertising, they would expect sales to increase. At first, sales will increase at an increasing rate and then increase at a decreasing rate. The value of x where the rate of change of sales changes from increasing to decreasing is called the **point of diminishing returns**. This is also the point where the rate of change has a maximum value. Money spent after this point may increase sales, but at a lower rate. The next example illustrates this concept.

EXAMPLE 5　**Maximum Rate of Change**　Currently, a discount appliance store is selling 200 large-screen television sets monthly. If the store invests $\$x$ thousand in an advertising campaign, the ad company estimates that sales will increase to

$$N(x) = 3x^3 - 0.25x^4 + 200 \qquad 0 \le x \le 9$$

When is rate of change of sales increasing and when is it decreasing? What is the point of diminishing returns and the maximum rate of change of sales? Graph N and N' on the same coordinate system.

Solution   The rate of change of sales with respect to advertising expenditures is

$$N'(x) = 9x^2 - x^3 = x^2(9 - x)$$

To determine when $N'(x)$ is increasing and decreasing, we find $N''(x)$, the derivative of $N'(x)$:

$$N''(x) = 18x - 3x^2 = 3x(6 - x)$$

The information obtained by analyzing the signs of $N'(x)$ and $N''(x)$ is summarized in Table 2 (sign charts are omitted).

TABLE 2				
x	$N''(x)$	$N'(x)$	$N'(x)$	$N(x)$
$0 < x < 6$	$+$	$+$	Increasing	Increasing, concave upward
$x = 6$	0	$+$	Local maximum	Inflection point
$6 < x < 9$	$-$	$+$	Decreasing	Increasing, concave downward

Examining Table 2, we see that $N'(x)$ is increasing on $(0, 6)$ and decreasing on $(6, 9)$. The point of diminishing returns is $x = 6$ and the maximum rate of change is $N'(6) = 108$. Note that $N'(x)$ has a local maximum and $N(x)$ has an inflection point at $x = 6$.

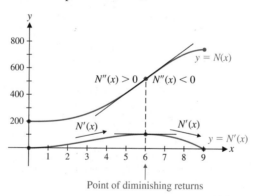

Matched Problem 5   Repeat Example 5 for

$$N(x) = 4x^3 - 0.25x^4 + 500 \qquad 0 \le x \le 12$$

Answers to Matched Problems   **1.** Concave upward on $(-\infty, 0)$
Concave downward on $(0, \infty)$

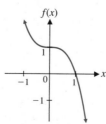

2. Inflection point at $x = 3$

3.

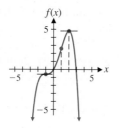

x	$f'(x)$	$f(x)$
$-\infty < x < -1$	Positive and decreasing	Increasing and concave downward
$x = -1$	Local minimum	Inflection point
$-1 < x < 1$	Positive and increasing	Increasing and concave upward
$x = 1$	Local maximum	Inflection point
$1 < x < 2$	Positive and decreasing	Increasing and concave downward
$x = 2$	x intercept	Local maximum
$2 < x < \infty$	Negative and decreasing	Decreasing and concave downward

4. x intercepts: $-4, 0$; y intercept: $f(0) = 0$
Decreasing on $(-\infty, -3)$; increasing on $(-3, \infty)$; local minimum at $x = -3$
Concave upward on $(-\infty, -2)$ and $(0, \infty)$; concave downward on $(-2, 0)$
Inflection points at $x = -2$ and $x = 0$

x	$f(x)$
-4	0
-3	-27
-2	-16
0	0

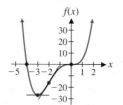

5. $N'(x)$ is increasing on $(0, 8)$ and decreasing on $(8, 12)$. The point of diminishing returns is $x = 8$ and the maximum rate of change is $N'(8) = 256$.

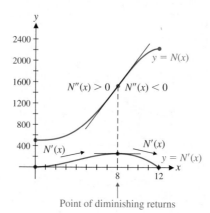

Point of diminishing returns

Exercise 4-2

A

1. Use the graph of $y = f(x)$ to identify

(A) Intervals over which the graph of f is concave upward

(B) Intervals over which the graph of f is concave downward

(C) Intervals over which $f''(x) < 0$

(D) Intervals over which $f''(x) > 0$

(E) Intervals over which $f'(x)$ is increasing

(F) Intervals over which $f'(x)$ is decreasing

(G) The x coordinates of inflection points

(H) The x coordinates of local extrema for $f'(x)$

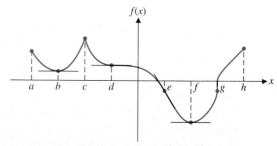

2. Use the graph of $y = g(x)$ to identify

(A) Intervals over which the graph of g is concave upward

(B) Intervals over which the graph of g is concave downward

(C) Intervals over which $g''(x) < 0$

(D) Intervals over which $g''(x) > 0$

(E) Intervals over which $g'(x)$ is increasing

(F) Intervals over which $g'(x)$ is decreasing

(G) The x coordinates of inflection points

(H) The x coordinates of local extrema for $g'(x)$

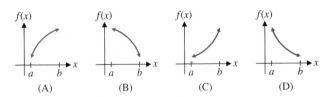

In Problems 3–6, match the indicated conditions with one of the graphs (A)–(D) shown in the figure.

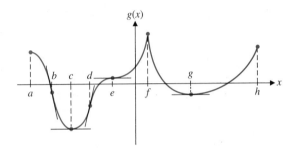

(A)   (B)   (C)   (D)

3. $f'(x) > 0$ and $f''(x) > 0$ on (a, b)

4. $f'(x) > 0$ and $f''(x) < 0$ on (a, b)

5. $f'(x) < 0$ and $f''(x) > 0$ on (a, b)

6. $f'(x) < 0$ and $f''(x) < 0$ on (a, b)

In Problems 7–14, find the indicated derivative for each function.

7. $f''(x)$ for $f(x) = 2x^3 - 4x^2 + 5x - 6$

8. $g''(x)$ for $g(x) = -x^3 + 2x^2 - 3x + 9$

9. $h''(x)$ for $h(x) = 2x^{-1} - 3x^{-2}$

10. $k''(x)$ for $k(x) = -6x^{-2} + 12x^{-3}$

11. d^2y/dx^2 for $y = x^2 - 18x^{1/2}$

12. d^2y/dx^2 for $y = x^3 - 24x^{1/3}$

13. y'' for $y = (x^2 + 9)^4$

14. y'' for $y = (x^2 - 16)^5$

In Problems 15–20, find the intervals where the graph of f is concave upward, the intervals where the graph of f is concave downward, and the inflection points.

15. $f(x) = x^4 + 6x^2$

16. $f(x) = x^4 + 6x$

17. $f(x) = x^3 - 4x^2 + 5x - 2$

18. $f(x) = -x^3 - 5x^2 + 4x - 3$

19. $f(x) = -x^4 + 12x^3 - 12x + 24$

20. $f(x) = x^4 - 2x^3 - 36x + 12$

In Problems 21–28, f(x) is continuous on $(-\infty, \infty)$. Use the given information to sketch the graph of f.

21.

x	-4	-2	-1	0	2	4
$f(x)$	0	3	1.5	0	-1	-3

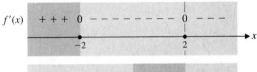

22.

x	-4	-2	-1	0	2	4
$f(x)$	0	-2	-1	0	1	3

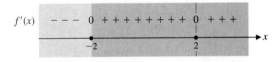

23.

x	-3	0	1	2	4	5
$f(x)$	-4	0	2	1	-1	0

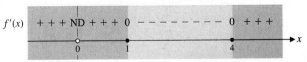

24.

x	-4	-2	0	2	4	6
$f(x)$	0	3	0	-2	0	3

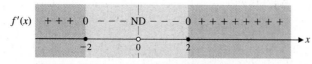

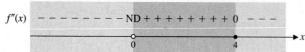

25. $f(0) = 2, f(1) = 0, f(2) = -2;$
$f'(0) = 0, f'(2) = 0;$
$f'(x) > 0$ on $(-\infty, 0)$ and $(2, \infty);$
$f'(x) < 0$ on $(0, 2);$
$f''(1) = 0;$
$f''(x) > 0$ on $(1, \infty);$
$f''(x) < 0$ on $(-\infty, 1)$

26. $f(-2) = -2, f(0) = 1, f(2) = 4;$
$f'(-2) = 0, f'(2) = 0;$
$f'(x) > 0$ on $(-2, 2);$
$f'(x) < 0$ on $(-\infty, -2)$ and $(2, \infty);$
$f''(0) = 0;$
$f''(x) > 0$ on $(-\infty, 0);$
$f''(x) < 0$ on $(0, \infty)$

27. $f(-1) = 0, f(0) = -2, f(1) = 0;$
$f'(0) = 0, f'(-1)$ and $f'(1)$ are not defined;
$f'(x) > 0$ on $(0, 1)$ and $(1, \infty);$
$f'(x) < 0$ on $(-\infty, -1)$ and $(-1, 0);$
$f''(-1)$ and $f''(1)$ are not defined;
$f''(x) > 0$ on $(-1, 1);$
$f''(x) < 0$ on $(-\infty, -1)$ and $(1, \infty)$

28. $f(0) = -2, f(1) = 0, f(2) = 4;$
$f'(0) = 0, f'(2) = 0, f'(1)$ is not defined;
$f'(x) > 0$ on $(0, 1)$ and $(1, 2);$
$f'(x) < 0$ on $(-\infty, 0)$ and $(2, \infty);$
$f''(1)$ is not defined;
$f''(x) > 0$ on $(-\infty, 1);$
$f''(x) < 0$ on $(1, \infty)$

B *In Problems 29–42, summarize the pertinent information obtained by applying the graphing strategy for polynomials and sketch the graph of $y = f(x)$.*

29. $f(x) = x^3 - 6x^2 + 16$

30. $f(x) = x^3 - 9x^2 + 15x + 10$

31. $f(x) = x^3 + x + 2$

32. $f(x) = 1 - 3x - x^3$

33. $f(x) = -0.25x^4 + x^3$

34. $f(x) = 0.25x^4 - 2x^3$

35. $f(x) = 16x(x - 1)^3$

36. $f(x) = -4x(x + 2)^3$

37. $f(x) = (x^2 + 3)(9 - x^2)$

38. $f(x) = (x^2 + 3)(x^2 - 1)$

39. $f(x) = (x^2 - 4)^2$

40. $f(x) = (x^2 - 1)(x^2 - 5)$

41. $f(x) = 2x^6 - 3x^5$ **42.** $f(x) = 3x^5 - 5x^4$

In Problems 43–46, use the graph of $y = f'(x)$ to discuss the graph of $y = f(x)$. Organize your conclusions in a table (see Example 4), and sketch a possible graph of $y = f(x)$.

43.
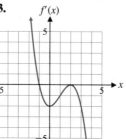

44.
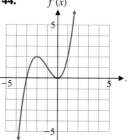

45.
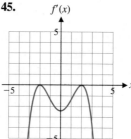

46.
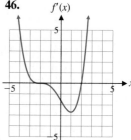

In Problems 47–54, apply steps 1–3 of the graphing strategy for polynomials to $f(x)$. Use a graphing utility to approximate (to two decimal places) x intercepts, critical values, and x coordinates of inflection points. Summarize all the pertinent information.

47. $f(x) = x^4 - 5x^3 + 3x^2 + 8x - 5$

48. $f(x) = x^4 + 2x^3 - 5x^2 - 4x + 4$

49. $f(x) = x^4 - 21x^3 + 100x^2 + 20x + 100$

50. $f(x) = x^4 - 12x^3 + 28x^2 + 76x - 50$

51. $f(x) = -x^4 - x^3 + 2x^2 - 2x + 3$

52. $f(x) = -x^4 + x^3 + x^2 + 6$

53. $f(x) = 0.1x^5 + 0.3x^4 - 4x^3 - 5x^2 + 40x + 30$

54. $f(x) = x^5 + 4x^4 - 7x^3 - 20x^2 + 20x - 20$

C *In Problems 55–58, assume that f is a polynomial.*

55. Explain how you can locate inflection points for the graph of $y = f(x)$ by examining the graph of $y = f'(x)$.

56. Explain how you can determine where $f'(x)$ is increasing or decreasing by examining the graph of $y = f(x)$.

57. Explain how you can locate local maxima and minima for the graph of $y = f'(x)$ by examining the graph of $y = f(x)$.

58. Explain how you can locate local maxima and minima for the graph of $y = f(x)$ by examining the graph of $y = f'(x)$.

Applications

Business & Economics

59. *Inflation.* One commonly used measure of inflation is the annual rate of change of the Consumer Price Index (CPI). A newspaper headline proclaims that the rate of change of inflation for consumer prices is increasing. What does this say about the shape of the graph of the CPI?

60. *Inflation.* Another commonly used measure of inflation is the annual rate of change of the Producers Price Index (PPI). A government report states that the rate of change of inflation for producer prices is decreasing. What does this say about the shape of the graph of the PPI?

61. *Cost analysis.* A company manufactures a variety of lighting fixtures at different locations. The total cost $C(x)$ (in dollars) of producing x desk lamps per week at plant A is shown in the figure. Discuss the shape of the graph of the marginal cost function $C'(x)$ and interpret in terms of the efficiency of the production process at this plant.

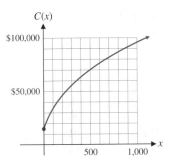

Figure for 61   Production costs at plant A

62. *Cost analysis.* The company in Problem 61 produces the same lamp at another plant. The total cost $C(x)$ (in dollars) of producing x desk lamps per week at

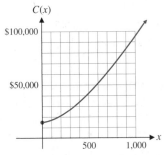

Figure for 62   Production costs at plant B

plant B is shown in the figure. Discuss the shape of the graph of the marginal cost function $C'(x)$ and interpret in terms of the efficiency of the production process at plant B. Compare the production processes at these two plants.

63. *Revenue.* The marketing research department for a computer company used a large city to test market their new product. They found that the relationship between price p (dollars per unit) and the demand x (units per week) was given approximately by

$$p = 1,296 - 0.12x^2 \qquad 0 < x < 80$$

Thus, the weekly revenue can be approximated by

$$R(x) = xp = 1,296x - 0.12x^3 \qquad 0 < x < 80$$

(A) Find the local extrema for the revenue function.

(B) Over which intervals is the graph of the revenue function concave upward? Concave downward?

64. *Profit.* Suppose that the cost equation for the company in Problem 63 is

$$C(x) = 830 + 396x$$

(A) Find the local extrema for the profit function.

(B) Over which intervals is the graph of the profit function concave upward? Concave downward?

65. *Production—point of diminishing returns.* A T-shirt manufacturer is planning to expand its work force. It estimates that the number of T-shirts produced by hiring x new workers is given by

$$T(x) = -0.25x^4 + 5x^3 \qquad 0 \le x \le 15$$

When is the rate of change of T-shirt production increasing and when is it decreasing? What is the point of diminishing returns and the maximum rate of change of T-shirt production? Graph T and T' on the same coordinate system.

66. *Production—point of diminishing returns.* A baseball cap manufacturer is planning to expand its work force. It estimates that the number of baseball caps produced by hiring x new workers is given by

$$T(x) = -0.25x^4 + 6x^3 \qquad 0 \le x \le 18$$

When is the rate of change of baseball cap production increasing and when is it decreasing? What is the point of diminishing returns and the maximum rate of change of baseball cap production? Graph T and T' on the same coordinate system.

67. *Advertising—point of diminishing returns.* A company estimates that it will sell $N(x)$ units of a product after spending $x thousand on advertising, as given by

$$N(x) = -0.25x^4 + 23x^3 - 540x^2 + 80,000 \qquad 24 \le x \le 45$$

When is the rate of change of sales increasing and when is it decreasing? What is the point of diminishing returns and the maximum rate of change of sales? Graph N and N' on the same coordinate system.

68. *Advertising—point of diminishing returns.* A company estimates that it will sell $N(x)$ units of a product after spending $x thousand on advertising, as given by

$$N(x) = -0.25x^4 + 13x^3 - 180x^2 + 10,000 \qquad 15 \le x \le 24$$

When is the rate of change of sales increasing and when is it decreasing? What is the point of diminishing returns and the maximum rate of change of sales? Graph N and N' on the same coordinate system.

69. *Advertising.* An automobile dealer uses television advertising to promote car sales. Using past records, the dealer arrived at the data in the table, where x is the number of ads placed monthly and y is the number of cars sold that month.

Number of Ads	Number of Cars
x	y
10	325
12	339
20	417
30	546
35	615
40	682
50	795

(A) Enter the data in a graphing utility and find a cubic regression equation for the number of cars sold monthly as a function of the number of ads.

(B) How many ads should the dealer place each month to maximize the rate of change of sales with respect to the number of ads, and how many cars can the dealer expect to sell with this number of ads? Round answers to the nearest integer.

70. *Advertising.* A music store uses radio advertising to promote sales of CDs. The store manager used past records to determine the data in the table, where x is the number of ads placed monthly and y is the number of CDs sold that month.

Number of Ads	Number of CDs
x	y
10	345
14	488
20	746
30	1,228
40	1,671
50	1,955

(A) Enter the data in a graphing utility and find a cubic regression equation for the number of CDs sold monthly as a function of the number of ads.

(B) How many ads should the store manager place each month to maximize the rate of change of sales with respect to the number of ads, and how many CDs can the manager expect to sell with this number of ads? Round answers to the nearest integer.

Life Sciences

71. *Population growth—bacteria.* A drug that stimulates reproduction is introduced into a colony of bacteria. After t minutes, the number of bacteria is given approximately by

$$N(t) = 1,000 + 30t^2 - t^3 \qquad 0 \le t \le 20$$

(A) When is the rate of growth $N'(t)$ increasing? Decreasing?

(B) Find the inflection points for the graph of N.

(C) Sketch the graphs of N and N' on the same coordinate system.

(D) What is the maximum rate of growth?

72. *Drug sensitivity.* One hour after x milligrams of a particular drug are given to a person, the change in body temperature $T(x)$, in degrees Fahrenheit, is given by

$$T(x) = x^2\left(1 - \frac{x}{9}\right) \qquad 0 \le x \le 6$$

The rate $T'(x)$ at which $T(x)$ changes with respect to the size of the dosage x is called the *sensitivity* of the body to the dosage.

(A) When is $T'(x)$ increasing? Decreasing?

(B) Where does the graph of T have inflection points?

(C) Sketch the graphs of T and T' on the same coordinate system.

(D) What is the maximum value of $T'(x)$?

Social Sciences

73. *Learning.* The time T (in minutes) it takes a person to learn a list of length n is

$$T(n) = 0.08n^3 - 1.2n^2 + 6n \qquad n \ge 0$$

(A) When is the rate of change of T with respect to the length of the list increasing? Decreasing?

(B) Where does the graph of T have inflection points? Graph T and T' on the same coordinate system.

(C) What is the minimum value of $T'(n)$?

Section 4-3 | Graphing Rational Functions

> ➤ Rational Functions
> ➤ Vertical Asymptotes
> ➤ Horizontal Asymptotes
> ➤ A Graphing Strategy for Rational Functions
> ➤ Rational Function Models—Average Cost

In Section 4-3, we will apply the graphing techniques discussed in Sections 4-1 and 4-2 to rational functions. Our goal is to develop a general graphing strategy that can be applied to any rational function. A brief review of Section 2-1 would be helpful at this point, but our discussion is complete and does not require that Section 2-1 be covered before studying Section 4-3.

➤ Rational Functions

Quotients of functions are often used for mathematical models. For example, if

$$C(x) = 500 + 0.1x^2$$

is the total cost of producing x units of a product, then

$$\overline{C}(x) = \frac{C(x)}{x} = \frac{500 + 0.1x^2}{x}$$

is the average cost per unit produced. Functions formed by taking the quotient of two polynomials are called *rational functions*, just as numbers formed by taking the quotient of two integers are called rational numbers.

DEFINITION   Rational Functions

A **rational function** is any function that can be written in the form

$$f(x) = \frac{n(x)}{d(x)} \qquad d(x) \neq 0$$

where $n(x)$ and $d(x)$ are polynomials. The **domain** of f is the set of all real numbers such that $d(x) \neq 0$.

➤ Vertical Asymptotes

What happens to the graph of a rational function near a number c where the denominator is 0? Consider the very simple rational function $f(x) = 1/x$. As x approaches 0 from the right, the values of $f(x)$ become larger and larger—that is, $f(x)$ increases without bound (see Table 1). We write this symbolically as

$$f(x) = \frac{1}{x} \to \infty \qquad \text{as} \qquad x \to 0^+$$

and say that the line $x = 0$ (the y axis) is a *vertical asymptote* for the graph of f.

TABLE 1 Behavior of $f(x) = 1/x$ as $x \to 0^+$

x	1	0.1	0.01	0.001	0.0001	0.000 001 … x approaches 0 from the right $(x \to 0^+)$
$1/x$	1	10	100	1,000	10,000	1,000,000 … $1/x$ increases without bound $(1/x \to \infty)$

If x approaches 0 from the left, the values of $f(x)$ are negative and become larger and larger in absolute value—that is, $f(x)$ decreases through negative values without bound (see Table 2). We write this symbolically as

$$f(x) = \frac{1}{x} \to -\infty \qquad \text{as} \qquad x \to 0^-$$

TABLE 2 Behavior of $f(x) = 1/x$ as $x \to 0^-$

x	-1	-0.1	-0.01	-0.001	-0.0001	$-0.000\,001$ ... x approaches 0 from the left ($x \to 0^-$)
$1/x$	-1	-10	-100	$-1,000$	$-10,000$	$-1,000,000$ ... $1/x$ decreases without bound ($1/x \to -\infty$)

EXPLORE & DISCUSS 1

Construct tables similar to Tables 1 and 2 for

$$g(x) = \frac{1}{x^2}$$

and discuss the behavior of the graph near $x = 0$.

The graphs of $f(x) = 1/x$ and $g(x) = 1/x^2$ are shown in Figure 1.

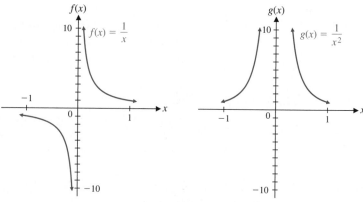

FIGURE 1

DEFINITION Vertical Asymptote

The vertical line $x = a$ is a **vertical asymptote** for the graph of $y = f(x)$ if

$$f(x) \to \infty \quad \text{or} \quad f(x) \to -\infty \quad \text{as} \quad x \to a^+ \quad \text{or} \quad x \to a^-$$

[that is, if $f(x)$ either increases or decreases without bound as x approaches a from the right or from the left].

THEOREM 1 Locating Vertical Asymptotes of Rational Functions

If $f(x) = n(x)/d(x)$ is a rational function, $d(c) = 0$ and $n(c) \neq 0$, then the line $x = c$ is a vertical asymptote of the graph of f.

If $f(x) = n(x)/d(x)$ and both $n(c) = 0$ and $d(c) = 0$, then the limit of $f(x)$ as x approaches c involves an indeterminate form and Theorem 1 does not apply:

$$\lim_{x \to c} f(x) = \lim_{x \to c} \frac{n(x)}{d(x)} \quad \frac{0}{0} \text{ indeterminate form}$$

Algebraic simplification is often useful in this situation.

EXAMPLE 1   **Locating Vertical Asymptotes** Find all vertical asymptotes for

$$f(x) = \frac{x^2 + x - 2}{x^2 - 1}$$

Solution   Let $n(x) = x^2 + x - 2$ and $d(x) = x^2 - 1$. Factoring the denominator, we see that

$$d(x) = x^2 - 1 = (x - 1)(x + 1)$$

Since $d(-1) = 0$ and $n(-1) = -2 \neq 0$, Theorem 1 tells us that the line $x = -1$ is a vertical asymptote. On the other hand, $d(1) = 0$ but $n(1) = 0$ also, so Theorem 1 does not apply at $x = 1$. We use algebraic simplification to investigate the behavior of the function at $x = 1$:

$$\lim_{x \to 1} f(x) = \lim_{x \to 1} \frac{x^2 + x - 2}{x^2 - 1} \qquad \frac{0}{0} \text{ indeterminate form}$$

$$= \lim_{x \to 1} \frac{(x - 1)(x + 2)}{(x - 1)(x + 1)}$$

$$= \lim_{x \to 1} \frac{x + 2}{x + 1} \qquad \text{Reduced to lowest terms (see Appendix A, Section A-4)}$$

$$= \frac{3}{2}$$

Since the limit exists as x approaches 1, f does not have a vertical asymptote at $x = 1$ (see Fig. 2).

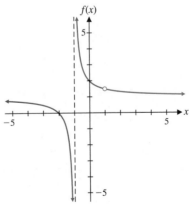

FIGURE 2 $f(x) = \dfrac{x^2 + x - 2}{x^2 - 1}$

Matched Problem 1   Find all vertical asymptotes for $f(x) = \dfrac{x - 3}{x^2 - 4x + 3}$.

👁 Insight   If $f(x) = n(x)/d(x)$, $d(c) = 0$, and $n(c) = 0$, then you must use limits to investigate the behavior of the graph of $f(x)$ at $x = c$, as we did in the solution for Example 1. Remember, the indeterminate form $0/0$ always requires further investigation.   ●

➤ Horizontal Asymptotes

We used the special symbol ∞ to indicate that the values of a function are increasing or decreasing without bound. Now we use this symbol to indicate that the independent variable x is increasing without bound ($x \to \infty$) or decreasing without bound ($x \to -\infty$). Figure 1 suggests that the values of $f(x) = 1/x$ and $g(x) = 1/x^2$ both approach 0 as $x \to \infty$ and as $x \to -\infty$. Limits involving x increasing without bound and x decreasing without bound are called *limits at infinity* and are used to identify *horizontal asymptotes*.

DEFINITION   Horizontal Asymptotes

The line $y = b$ is a **horizontal asymptote** for the graph of $y = f(x)$ if
$$\lim_{x \to \infty} f(x) = b \qquad \text{or} \qquad \lim_{x \to -\infty} f(x) = b$$

Referring to functions f and g in Figure 1, we can write
$$\lim_{x \to \infty} \frac{1}{x} = 0 \qquad \lim_{x \to -\infty} \frac{1}{x} = 0 \qquad \lim_{x \to \infty} \frac{1}{x^2} = 0 \qquad \lim_{x \to -\infty} \frac{1}{x^2} = 0$$

and conclude that the line $y = 0$ (the x axis) is a horizontal asymptote for each function. Theorem 2 extends these results to any positive power of x and provides an important tool for working with horizontal asymptotes.

THEOREM 2   Limits of Power Functions

If $p > 0$ and k is any constant, then
$$\lim_{x \to \infty} \frac{k}{x^p} = 0 \qquad \text{and} \qquad \lim_{x \to -\infty} \frac{k}{x^p} = 0$$

provided that x^p names a real number for negative values of x.

EXAMPLE 2   **Finding Horizontal Asymptotes**   Find any horizontal asymptotes for $f(x) = \dfrac{3x^2 - 5x + 9}{2x^2 + 7}$.

Solution   First we divide each term in the numerator and denominator of $f(x)$ by x^2, the highest power of x in $f(x)$:

$$\frac{3x^2 - 5x + 9}{2x^2 + 7} = \frac{\dfrac{3x^2}{x^2} - \dfrac{5x}{x^2} + \dfrac{9}{x^2}}{\dfrac{2x^2}{x^2} + \dfrac{7}{x^2}} = \frac{3 - \dfrac{5}{x} + \dfrac{9}{x^2}}{2 + \dfrac{7}{x^2}}$$

Using Theorem 2, we have

$$\lim_{x \to \infty} f(x) = \frac{3 - 0 + 0}{2 + 0} = \frac{3}{2} = 1.5 \qquad \lim_{x \to \infty} \frac{k}{x^p} = 0$$

and

$$\lim_{x \to -\infty} f(x) \boxed{= \frac{3 - 0 + 0}{2 + 0}} = \frac{3}{2} = 1.5 \qquad \lim_{x \to -\infty} \frac{k}{x^p} = 0$$

Thus, the line $y = 1.5$ is the only horizontal asymptote for $f(x)$. The graph of $y = f(x)$ is shown in Figure 3.

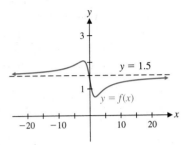

FIGURE 3 $f(x) = \dfrac{3x^2 - 5x + 9}{2x^2 + 7}$

Matched Problem 2   Find any horizontal asymptotes for

$$f(x) = \frac{3x^3 + 2x + 5}{7x^2 + 4}$$

Insight   Since $k/x^p \to 0$ as $x \to \infty$ and as $x \to -\infty$, the process used in the solution of Example 2 will never produce two different values for the limit of $f(x)$. That is, **a rational function can have at most one horizontal asymptote.**

If we apply Theorem 2 to the rational function

$$f(x) = \frac{a_m x^m + a_{m-1} x^{m-1} + \cdots + a_1 x + a_0}{b_n x^n + b_{n-1} x^{n-1} + \cdots + b_1 x + b_0} \qquad a_m \neq 0 \quad b_n \neq 0 \qquad (1)$$

it turns out that there are only three possible results.

THEOREM 3   Horizontal Asymptotes for Rational Functions
Let $f(x)$ be the rational function given in (1).

1. If $m < n$, then $y = 0$ (the x axis) is a horizontal asymptote for $f(x)$.
2. If $m = n$, then the line $y = a_m/b_n$ is a horizontal asymptote for $f(x)$.
3. If $m > n$, then $f(x)$ does not have a horizontal asymptote.

EXAMPLE 3   **Horizontal Asymptotes for Rational Functions**   Find all horizontal asymptotes for each function:

(A) $f(x) = \dfrac{5x^3 - 2x^2 + 1}{4x^3 + 2x - 7}$

(B) $f(x) = \dfrac{3x^4 - x^2 + 1}{8x^6 - 10}$

(C) $f(x) = \dfrac{2x^5 - x^3 - 1}{6x^3 + 2x^2 - 7}$

Solution   (A) Case 2 in Theorem 3 applies. The line $y = 5/4$ is a horizontal asymptote for the graph of f.

(B) Case 1 in Theorem 3 applies. The line $y = 0$ is a horizontal asymptote for the graph of f.

(C) Case 3 in Theorem 3 applies. This function does not have a horizontal asymptote. ∎

Matched Problem 3 Find all horizontal asymptotes for each function:

(A) $f(x) = \dfrac{4x^3 - 5x + 8}{2x^4 - 7}$

(B) $f(x) = \dfrac{5x^6 + 3x}{2x^5 - x - 5}$

(C) $f(x) = \dfrac{2x^3 - x + 7}{4x^3 + 3x^2 - 100}$

➤ A Graphing Strategy for Rational Functions

We can extend the graphing strategy for polynomials (Section 4-2) to rational functions by modifying the first step.

PROCEDURE   Strategy for Graphing a Rational Function $y = f(x)$

Step 1. *Analyze $f(x)$.*

(A) Find the domain of f.

(B) Find intercepts.

(C) Find asymptotes.

Step 2. *Analyze $f'(x)$.* Find the zeros of $f'(x)$. Construct a sign chart for $f'(x)$, determine the intervals where $f(x)$ is increasing and decreasing, and find local maxima and minima.

Step 3. *Analyze $f''(x)$.* Find the zeros of $f''(x)$. Construct a sign chart for $f''(x)$, determine where the graph of f is concave upward and concave downward, and find any inflection points.

Step 4. *Sketch the graph of f.* Draw asymptotes and locate intercepts, local maxima and minima, and inflection points. Sketch in what you know from steps 1–3. In regions of uncertainty, use point-by-point plotting to complete the graph.

EXAMPLE 4 **Using the Graphing Strategy** Use the graphing strategy to analyze the function $f(x) = (x - 1)/(x - 2)$. State all the pertinent information, and sketch the graph of f.

Solution Step 1. *Analyze $f(x)$.* $f(x) = \dfrac{x - 1}{x - 2}$

(A) Domain: All real x, except $x = 2$

(B) y intercept: $f(0) = \dfrac{0 - 1}{0 - 2} = \dfrac{1}{2}$

x intercepts: Since a fraction is 0 when its numerator is 0 and the denominator is not 0, the x intercept is $x = 1$.

(C)   Horizontal asymptote: $\dfrac{a_m x^m}{b_n x^n} = \dfrac{x}{x} = 1$

Thus, the line $y = 1$ is a horizontal asymptote.

Vertical asymptote: The denominator is 0 for $x = 2$, and the numerator is not 0 for this value. Therefore, the line $x = 2$ is a vertical asymptote.

Step 2. *Analyze $f'(x)$.* $f'(x) = \dfrac{(x - 2)(1) - (x - 1)(1)}{(x - 2)^2} = \dfrac{-1}{(x - 2)^2}$

Critical values for $f(x)$:   None

Partition number for $f'(x)$: $x = 2$

Sign chart for $f'(x)$:

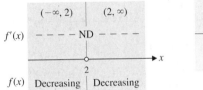

Test Numbers	
x	$f'(x)$
1	-1 $(-)$
3	-1 $(-)$

Thus, $f(x)$ is decreasing on $(-\infty, 2)$ and $(2, \infty)$. There are no local extrema.

Step 3. *Analyze $f''(x)$.* $f''(x) = \dfrac{2}{(x - 2)^3}$

Partition number for $f''(x)$: $x = 2$

Sign chart for $f''(x)$:

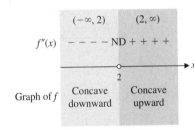

Test Numbers	
x	$f''(x)$
1	-2 $(-)$
3	2 $(+)$

Thus, the graph of f is concave downward on $(-\infty, 2)$ and concave upward on $(2, \infty)$. Since $f(2)$ is not defined, there is no inflection point at $x = 2$, even though $f''(x)$ changes sign at $x = 2$.

Step 4. *Sketch the graph of f.* Insert intercepts and asymptotes, and plot a few additional points (for functions with asymptotes, plotting additional points is often helpful). Then sketch the graph:

x	$f(x)$
-2	$\frac{3}{4}$
0	$\frac{1}{2}$
1	0
$\frac{3}{2}$	-1
$\frac{5}{2}$	3
3	2
4	$\frac{3}{2}$

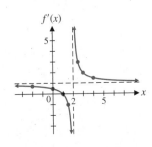

Matched Problem 4   Analyze the function $f(x) = 2x/(1 - x)$ following the graphing strategy. State all the pertinent information, and sketch the graph of f.

_____ ■

EXAMPLE 5   **Using the Graphing Strategy for Rational Functions** Use the graphing strategy to analyze the function

$$g(x) = \frac{2x - 1}{x^2}$$

State all pertinent information and sketch the graph of g.

Solution   **Step 1.** *Analyze* $g(x)$.

(A) Domain: All real x, except $x = 0$

(B) x intercept: $x = \dfrac{1}{2} = 0.5$

  y intercept: Since 0 is not in the domain of g, there is no y intercept.

(C) Horizontal asymptote: $y = 0$ (the x axis)

  Vertical asymptote: The denominator of $g(x)$ is 0 at $x = 0$ and the numerator is not. So the line $x = 0$ (the y axis) is a vertical asymptote.

Step 2. *Analyze* $g'(x)$.

$$g(x) = \frac{2x - 1}{x^2} = \frac{2}{x} - \frac{1}{x^2} = 2x^{-1} - x^{-2}$$

$$g'(x) = -2x^{-2} + 2x^{-3} = -\frac{2}{x^2} + \frac{2}{x^3} = \frac{-2x + 2}{x^3}$$

$$= \frac{2(1 - x)}{x^3}$$

Critical values for $g(x)$: $x = 1$

Partition numbers for $g'(x)$: $x = 0, x = 1$

Sign chart for $g'(x)$:

Function $f(x)$ is decreasing on $(-\infty, 0)$ and $(1, \infty)$, increasing on $(0, 1)$, and has a local maximum at $x = 1$.

Step 3. *Analyze* $g''(x)$.

$$g'(x) = -2x^{-2} + 2x^{-3}$$

$$g''(x) = 4x^{-3} - 6x^{-4} = \frac{4}{x^3} - \frac{6}{x^4} = \frac{4x - 6}{x^4} = \frac{2(2x - 3)}{x^4}$$

Partition numbers for $g''(x)$: $x = 0, x = \dfrac{3}{2} = 1.5$

Sign chart for $g''(x)$:

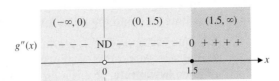

Function $g(x)$ is concave downward on $(-\infty, 0)$ and $(0, 1.5)$, concave upward on $(1.5, \infty)$, and has an inflection point at $x = 1.5$.

Step 4. *Sketch the graph of g.* Plot key points, note that the coordinate axes are asymptotes, and sketch the graph.

x	$g(x)$
-10	-0.21
-1	-3
0.5	0
1	1
1.5	0.89
10	0.19

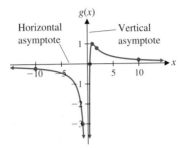

Matched Problem 5   Use the graphing strategy to analyze the function

$$h(x) = \frac{4x + 3}{x^2}$$

State all pertinent information and sketch the graph of h.

➤ **Rational Functions—Average Cost**

EXAMPLE 6   **Average Cost** Given the cost function $C(x) = 5{,}000 + 0.5x^2$, where x is the number of items produced, use the graphing strategy to analyze the graph of the average cost function. State all the pertinent information and sketch the graph of the average cost function. Find the marginal cost function and graph it on the same set of coordinate axes.

Solution   The average cost function is

$$\overline{C}(x) = \frac{5{,}000 + 0.5x^2}{x} = \frac{5{,}000}{x} + 0.5x$$

Step 1. *Analyze $\overline{C}(x)$.*

(A) Domain: Since negative values of x do not make sense and $\overline{C}(0)$ is not defined, the domain is the set of positive real numbers.

(B) Intercepts: None

(C) Horizontal asymptote: $\dfrac{a_m x^m}{b_n x^n} = \dfrac{0.5x^2}{x} = 0.5x$

Thus, there is no horizontal asymptote.

Vertical asymptote: The line $x = 0$ is a vertical asymptote since the denominator is 0 and the numerator is not 0 for $x = 0$.

Oblique asymptotes: If a graph approaches a line that is neither horizontal nor vertical as x approaches ∞ or $-\infty$, that line is called an **oblique asymptote.** If x is a large positive number, then $5,000/x$ is very small and

$$\overline{C}(x) = \frac{5,000}{x} + 0.5x \approx 0.5x$$

That is,

$$\lim_{x \to \infty} \left[\overline{C}(x) - 0.5x\right] = \lim_{x \to \infty} \frac{5,000}{x} = 0$$

This implies that the graph of $y = \overline{C}(x)$ approaches the line $y = 0.5x$ as x approaches ∞. This line is an oblique asymptote for the graph of $y = \overline{C}(x)$. [More generally, whenever $f(x) = n(x)/d(x)$ is a rational function for which the degree of $n(x)$ is 1 more than the degree of $d(x)$, we can use polynomial long division to write $f(x) = mx + b + r(x)/d(x)$ where the degree of $r(x)$ is less than the degree of $d(x)$. The line $y = mx + b$ is then an oblique asymptote for the graph of $y = f(x)$.]

Step 2. *Analyze $\overline{C}'(x)$.*

$$\overline{C}'(x) = -\frac{5,000}{x^2} + 0.5$$

$$= \frac{0.5x^2 - 5,000}{x^2}$$

$$= \frac{0.5(x - 100)(x + 100)}{x^2}$$

Critical value for $\overline{C}(x)$:   100

Partition numbers for $\overline{C}'(x)$:   0 and 100

Sign chart for $\overline{C}'(x)$:

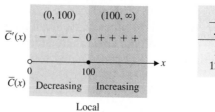

	Test Numbers	
x	$\overline{C}'(x)$	
50	-1.5	$(-)$
125	0.18	$(+)$

Thus, $\overline{C}(x)$ is decreasing on $(0, 100)$, increasing on $(100, \infty)$, and has a local minimum at $x = 100$.

Step 3. *Analyze $\overline{C}''(x)$:* $\overline{C}''(x) = \dfrac{10,000}{x^3}$.

$\overline{C}''(x)$ is positive for all positive x; therefore, the graph of $y = \overline{C}(x)$ is concave upward on $(0, \infty)$.

Step 4. *Sketch the graph of $\overline{C}$.* The graph of $\overline{C}$ is shown in Figure 4.

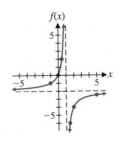

FIGURE 4

The marginal cost function is $C'(x) = x$. The graph of this linear function is also shown in Figure 4. ■

The graph in Figure 4 illustrates an important principle in economics:

The minimum average cost occurs when the average cost is equal to the marginal cost.

Matched Problem 6

Given the cost function $C(x) = 1,600 + 0.25x^2$, where x is the number of items produced,

(A) Use the graphing strategy to analyze the graph of the average cost function. State all the pertinent information and sketch the graph of the average cost function. Find the marginal cost function and graph it on the same set of coordinate axes. Include any oblique asymptotes.

(B) Find the minimum average cost.

Answers to Matched Problems

1. $x = 3$

2. No horizontal asymptote

3. (A) $y = 0$ (B) No horizontal asymptote   (C) $y = \dfrac{1}{2}$

4. Domain: All real x, except $x = 1$
y intercept: $f(0) = 0$;   x intercept: 0
Horizontal asymptote: $y = -2$;   vertical asymptote: $x = 1$
Increasing on $(-\infty, 1)$ and $(1, \infty)$
Concave upward on $(-\infty, 1)$; concave downward on $(1, \infty)$

x	$f(x)$
-1	-1
0	0
$\frac{1}{2}$	2
$\frac{3}{2}$	-6
2	-4
5	$-\frac{5}{2}$

5. Domain: All real x, except $x = 0$

x intercept: $= -\dfrac{3}{4} = -0.75$

$h(0)$ is not defined
Vertical asymptote: $x = 0$ (the y axis)
Horizontal asymptote: $y = 0$ (the x axis)
Increasing on $(-1.5, 0)$
Decreasing on $(-\infty, -1.5)$ and $(0, \infty)$
Local minimum at $x = 1.5$
Concave upward on $(-2.25, 0)$ and $(0, \infty)$
Concave downward on $(-\infty, -2.25)$
Inflection point at $x = -2.25$

x	$h(x)$
-10	-0.37
-2.25	-1.19
-1.5	-1.33
-0.75	0
2	2.75
10	0.43

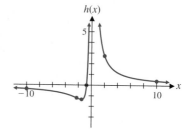

6. (A) Domain: $(0, \infty)$
Intercepts: None
Vertical asymptote: $x = 0$;   oblique asymptote: $y = 0.25x$
Decreasing on $(0, 80)$; increasing on $(80, \infty)$; local minimum at $x = 80$
Concave upward on $(0, \infty)$

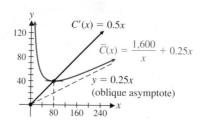

(B) Minimum average cost is 40 at $x = 80$.

Exercise 4-3

A

1. Use the graph of f shown below to identify

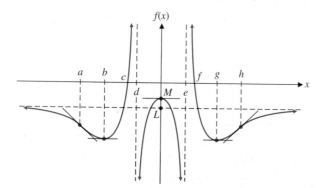

(A) the intervals over which $f'(x) < 0$
(B) the intervals over which $f'(x) > 0$
(C) the intervals over which $f(x)$ is increasing
(D) the intervals over which $f(x)$ is decreasing
(E) the x coordinate(s) of the point(s) where $f(x)$ has a local maximum
(F) the x coordinate(s) of the point(s) where $f(x)$ has a local minimum
(G) the intervals over which $f''(x) < 0$
(H) the intervals over which $f''(x) > 0$
(I) the intervals over which the graph of f is concave upward

(J)   the intervals over which the graph of *f* is concave downward

(K)   the *x* coordinate(s) of the inflection point(s)

(L)   the horizontal asymptote(s)

(M)   the vertical asymptote(s)

2. Repeat Problem 1 for the graph of *f* shown below.

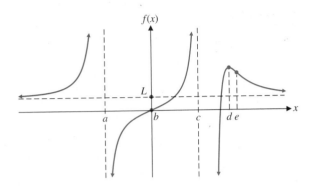

In Problems 3–14, find all horizontal and vertical asymptotes.

3. $f(x) = \dfrac{3x - 4}{x}$

4. $f(x) = \dfrac{3x}{x - 4}$

5. $f(x) = \dfrac{x^2 - 4}{x^2 + 4}$

6. $f(x) = \dfrac{x^2 + 9}{x^2 - 9}$

7. $f(x) = \dfrac{x}{x^2 - 1}$

8. $f(x) = \dfrac{x^3}{x^2 + 1}$

9. $f(x) = \dfrac{x^3}{x^2 - 16}$

10. $f(x) = \dfrac{3x}{x^2 + 3}$

11. $f(x) = \dfrac{2x^2 + x - 3}{x^2 - 2x + 1}$

12. $f(x) = \dfrac{5x^2 - 2x + 1}{2x^2 - 5x - 3}$

13. $f(x) = \dfrac{3x^2 + 2x + 5}{2x^2 + 3x - 20}$

14. $f(x) = \dfrac{2x^2 + x - 6}{x^2 + 4x + 4}$

In Problems 15–22, use the given information to sketch the graph of f. Assume that f is continuous on its domain and that all intercepts are included in the table of values.

15. Domain: All real *x*; $\lim\limits_{x \to \pm\infty} f(x) = 2$

x	−4	−2	0	2	4
f(x)	0	−2	0	−2	0

$f'(x)$ $-\ -\ -\ -\ -\ -\ -\ 0+\ +\ +\text{ND}-\ -\ -0+\ +\ +\ +\ +\ +\ +\ +$
            −2   0   2

$f''(x)$ $-\ -\ -\ 0\ +\ +\ +\ +\ +\ +\ \text{ND}\ +\ +\ +\ +\ +\ +\ 0\ -\ -\ -$
           −4   0   4

16. Domain: All real *x*; $\lim\limits_{x \to -\infty} f(x) = -3$; $\lim\limits_{x \to \infty} f(x) = 3$

x	−2	−1	0	1	2
f(x)	0	2	0	−2	0

$f'(x)$ $+\ +\ +\ +\ +\ +\ +0-\ -\ -\text{ND}-\ -\ -0+\ +\ +\ +\ +\ +\ +$
                    −1   0   1

$f''(x)$ $+\ +\ +\ 0\ -\ -\ -\ -\ -\ -\ -\ \text{ND}\ +\ +\ +\ +\ +\ +\ 0\ -\ -\ -$
                 −2   0   2

17. Domain: All real *x*, except $x = -2$; $\lim\limits_{x \to -2^-} f(x) = \infty$; $\lim\limits_{x \to -2^+} f(x) = -\infty$; $\lim\limits_{x \to \infty} f(x) = 1$

x	−4	0	4	6
f(x)	0	0	3	2

$f'(x)$ $+\ +\ +\ \text{ND}\ +\ +\ +\ 0\ -\ -\ -\ -\ -\ -\ -\ -\ -\ -$
                 −2   4

$f''(x)$ $+\ +\ +\ \text{ND}\ -\ -\ -\ -\ -\ -\ -\ -\ 0\ +\ +\ +$
                 −2   6

18. Domain: All real *x*, except $x = 1$; $\lim\limits_{x \to 1^-} f(x) = \infty$; $\lim\limits_{x \to 1^+} f(x) = \infty$; $\lim\limits_{x \to \infty} f(x) = -2$

x	−4	−2	0	2
f(x)	0	−2	0	0

$f'(x)$ $-\ -\ -\ 0\ +\ +\ +\ \text{ND}\ -\ -\ -$
              −2   1

$f''(x)$ $+\ +\ +\ +\ +\ +\ +\ +\ \text{ND}\ +\ +\ +$
                              1

19. Domain: All real *x*, except $x = -1$;
  $f(-3) = 2, f(-2) = 3, f(0) = -1, f(1) = 0$;
  $f'(x) > 0$ on $(-\infty, -1)$ and $(-1, \infty)$;
  $f''(x) > 0$ on $(-\infty, -1)$; $f''(x) < 0$ on $(-1, \infty)$;
  vertical asymptote: $x = -1$;
  horizontal asymptote: $y = 1$

20. Domain: All real x, except $x = 1$;
$f(0) = -2, f(2) = 0$;
$f'(x) < 0$ on $(-\infty, 1)$ and $(1, \infty)$;
$f''(x) < 0$ on $(-\infty, 1)$;
$f''(x) > 0$ on $(1, \infty)$;
vertical asymptote: $x = 1$;
horizontal asymptote: $y = -1$

21. Domain: All real x, except $x = -2$ and $x = 2$;
$f(-3) = -1, f(0) = 0, f(3) = 1$;
$f'(x) < 0$ on $(-\infty, -2)$ and $(2, \infty)$;
$f'(x) > 0$ on $(-2, 2)$;
$f''(x) < 0$ on $(-\infty, -2)$ and $(-2, 0)$;
$f''(x) > 0$ on $(0, 2)$ and $(2, \infty)$;
vertical asymptotes: $x = -2$ and $x = 2$;
horizontal asymptote: $y = 0$

22. Domain: All real x, except $x = -1$ and $x = 1$;
$f(-2) = 1, f(0) = 0, f(2) = 1$;
$f'(x) > 0$ on $(-\infty, -1)$ and $(0, 1)$;
$f'(x) < 0$ on $(-1, 0)$ and $(1, \infty)$;
$f''(x) > 0$ on $(-\infty, -1), (-1, 1)$, and $(1, \infty)$;
vertical asymptotes: $x = -1$ and $x = 1$;
horizontal asymptote: $y = 0$

B *In Problems 23–52, summarize the pertinent information obtained by applying the graphing strategy and sketch the graph of $y = f(x)$.*

23. $f(x) = \dfrac{x + 3}{x - 3}$

24. $f(x) = \dfrac{2x - 4}{x + 2}$

25. $f(x) = \dfrac{x}{x - 2}$

26. $f(x) = \dfrac{2 + x}{3 - x}$

27. $f(x) = \dfrac{x}{x^2 - 4}$

28. $f(x) = \dfrac{1}{x^2 - 4}$

29. $f(x) = \dfrac{1}{1 + x^2}$

30. $f(x) = \dfrac{x^2}{1 + x^2}$

31. $f(x) = \dfrac{2x}{1 - x^2}$

32. $f(x) = \dfrac{2x}{x^2 - 9}$

33. $f(x) = \dfrac{-5x}{(x - 1)^2}$

34. $f(x) = \dfrac{x}{(x - 2)^2}$

35. $f(x) = \dfrac{x^2 + 2}{x}$

36. $f(x) = \dfrac{3 - 2x}{x^2}$

37. $f(x) = \dfrac{x^2 + x - 2}{x^2}$

38. $f(x) = \dfrac{x^2 - 5x - 6}{x^2}$

39. $f(x) = \dfrac{x^2}{x - 1}$

40. $f(x) = \dfrac{x^2}{2 + x}$

41. $f(x) = \dfrac{3x^2 + 2}{x^2 - 9}$

42. $f(x) = \dfrac{2x^2 + 5}{4 - x^2}$

43. $f(x) = \dfrac{x^3}{x - 2}$

44. $f(x) = \dfrac{x^3}{4 - x}$

45. $f(x) = \dfrac{1}{x^2 + 2x - 8}$

46. $f(x) = \dfrac{1}{3 - 2x - x^2}$

47. $f(x) = \dfrac{x}{x^2 - 4}$

48. $f(x) = \dfrac{x}{x^2 - 36}$

49. $f(x) = \dfrac{x^3}{(x - 4)^2}$

50. $f(x) = \dfrac{x^3}{(x + 2)^2}$

51. $f(x) = \dfrac{x^3}{3 - x^2}$

52. $f(x) = \dfrac{x^3}{x^2 - 12}$

C *In Problems 53–60, show that the line $y = x$ is an oblique asymptote for the graph of $y = f(x)$, summarize all pertinent information obtained by applying the graphing strategy, and sketch the graph of $y = f(x)$.*

53. $f(x) = x + \dfrac{4}{x}$

54. $f(x) = x - \dfrac{9}{x}$

55. $f(x) = x - \dfrac{4}{x^2}$

56. $f(x) = x + \dfrac{32}{x^2}$

57. $f(x) = x - \dfrac{9}{x^3}$

58. $f(x) = x + \dfrac{27}{x^3}$

59. $f(x) = x + \dfrac{1}{x} + \dfrac{4}{x^3}$

60. $f(x) = x - \dfrac{16}{x^3}$

In Problems 61–68, summarize all pertinent information obtained by applying the graphing strategy, and sketch the graph of $y = f(x)$.
[Note: These rational functions are not reduced to lowest terms.]

61. $f(x) = \dfrac{x^2 + x - 6}{x^2 - 6x + 8}$

62. $f(x) = \dfrac{x^2 + x - 6}{x^2 - x - 12}$

63. $f(x) = \dfrac{2x^2 + x - 15}{x^2 - 9}$

64. $f(x) = \dfrac{2x^2 + 11x + 14}{x^2 - 4}$

65. $f(x) = \dfrac{x^3 - 5x^2 + 6x}{x^2 - x - 2}$

66. $f(x) = \dfrac{x^3 - 5x^2 - 6x}{x^2 + 3x + 2}$

67. $f(x) = \dfrac{x^2 + x - 2}{x^2 - 2x + 1}$

68. $f(x) = \dfrac{x^2 + x - 2}{x^2 + 4x + 4}$

Applications

Business & Economics

69. *Revenue.* The marketing research department for a computer company used a large city to test market their new product. They found that the relationship between price p (dollars per unit) and the demand x (units sold per week) was given approximately by

$$p = 1{,}296 - 0.12x^2 \qquad 0 \le x \le 80$$

Thus, the weekly revenue can be approximated by

$$R(x) = xp = 1{,}296x - 0.12x^3 \qquad 0 \le x \le 80$$

Graph the revenue function R.

70. *Profit.* Suppose that the cost function $C(x)$ (in dollars) for the company in Problem 69 is

$$C(x) = 830 + 396x$$

(A) Write an equation for the profit $P(x)$.

(B) Graph the profit function P.

71. *Pollution.* In Silicon Valley (California), a number of computer-related manufacturing firms were found to be contaminating underground water supplies with toxic chemicals stored in leaking underground containers. A water quality control agency ordered the companies to take immediate corrective action and to contribute to a monetary pool for testing and cleanup of the underground contamination. Suppose that the required monetary pool (in millions of dollars) for the testing and cleanup is estimated to be given by

$$P(x) = \dfrac{2x}{1 - x} \qquad 0 \le x < 1$$

where x is the percentage (expressed as a decimal fraction) of the total contaminant removed.

(A) Where is $P(x)$ increasing? Decreasing?

(B) Where is the graph of P concave upward? Downward?

(C) Find any horizontal and vertical asymptotes.

(D) Find the x and y intercepts.

(E) Sketch a graph of P.

72. *Employee training.* A company producing computer components has established that on the average a new employee can assemble $N(t)$ components per day after t days of on-the-job training, as given by

$$N(t) = \dfrac{100t}{t + 9} \qquad t \ge 0$$

(A) Where is $N(t)$ increasing? Decreasing?

(B) Where is the graph of N concave upward? Downward?

(C) Find any horizontal and vertical asymptotes.

(D) Find the intercepts.

(E) Sketch a graph of N.

73. *Replacement time.* An office copier has an initial price of $3,200. A maintenance/service contract costs $300 for the first year and increases $100 per year thereafter. It can be shown that the total cost of the copier (in dollars) after n years is given by

$$C(n) = 3{,}200 + 250n + 50n^2 \qquad n \ge 1$$

(A) Write an expression for the average cost per year, $\bar{C}(n)$, for n years.

(B) Graph the average cost function found in part (A).

(C) When is the average cost per year minimum? (This is frequently referred to as the **replacement time** for this piece of equipment.)

74. *Construction costs.* The management of a manufacturing plant wishes to add a fenced-in rectangular storage yard of 20,000 square feet, using the plant building as one side of the yard (see the figure). If x is the distance (in feet) from the building to the fence parallel to the building, show that the length of the fence required for the yard is given by

$$L(x) = 2x + \dfrac{20{,}000}{x} \qquad x > 0$$

Figure for 74

Number of Pizzas x	Total Costs y
50	595
100	755
150	1,110
200	1,380
250	1,875
300	2,410

(A) Graph L.

(B) What are the dimensions of the rectangle requiring the least amount of fencing?

75. *Average and marginal costs.* The total daily cost (in dollars) of producing x park benches is given by

$$C(x) = 1,000 + 5x + 0.1x^2$$

(A) Sketch the graphs of the average cost function and the marginal cost function on the same set of coordinate axes. Include any oblique asymptotes.

(B) Find the minimum average cost.

76. *Average and marginal costs.* The total daily cost (in dollars) of producing x picnic tables is given by

$$C(x) = 500 + 2x + 0.2x^2$$

(A) Sketch the graphs of the average cost function and the marginal cost function on the same set of coordinate axes. Include any oblique asymptotes.

(B) Find the minimum average cost.

77. *Minimizing average costs.* The data in the table give the total daily costs y (in dollars) of producing x pepperoni pizzas at various production levels.

Number of Pizzas x	Total Costs y
50	395
100	475
150	640
200	910
250	1,140
300	1,450

(A) Enter the data in a graphing utility and find a quadratic regression equation for the total costs.

(B) Use the regression equation from part (A) to find the minimum average cost (to the nearest cent) and the corresponding production level (to the nearest integer).

78. *Minimizing average costs.* The data in the table give the total daily costs y (in dollars) of producing x deluxe pizzas at various production levels.

(A) Enter the data in a graphing utility and find a quadratic regression equation for the total costs.

(B) Use the regression equation from part (A) to find the minimum average cost (to the nearest cent) and the corresponding production level (to the nearest integer).

Life Sciences

79. *Medicine.* A drug is injected into the bloodstream of a patient through her right arm. The concentration of the drug in the bloodstream of the left arm t hours after the injection is given by

$$C(t) = \frac{0.14t}{t^2 + 1}$$

Graph C.

80. *Physiology.* In a study on the speed of muscle contraction in frogs under various loads, researchers W. O. Fems and J. Marsh found that the speed of contraction decreases with increasing loads. More precisely, they found that the relationship between speed of contraction S (in centimeters per second) and load w (in grams) is given approximately by

$$S(w) = \frac{26 + 0.06w}{w} \qquad w \geq 5$$

Graph S.

Social Sciences

81. *Psychology: retention.* An experiment on retention is conducted in a psychology class. Each student in the class is given one day to memorize the same list of 30 special characters. The lists are turned in at the end of the day, and for each succeeding day for 30 days each student is asked to turn in a list of as many of the symbols as can be recalled. Averages are taken, and it is found that

$$N(t) = \frac{5t + 20}{t} \qquad t \geq 1$$

provides a good approximation of the average number of symbols $N(t)$ retained after t days. Graph N.

Section **4-4** | Absolute Maxima and Minima

➤ Absolute Maxima and Minima
➤ Second Derivative and Extrema

We are now ready to consider one of the most important applications of the derivative, namely, the use of derivatives to find the absolute maximum or minimum value of a function. An economist may be interested in the price or production level of a commodity that will bring a maximum profit; a doctor may be interested in the time it takes for a drug to reach its maximum concentration in the bloodstream after an injection; and a city planner might be interested in the location of heavy industry in a city to produce minimum pollution in residential and business areas. In this section, we develop the procedures needed to find the absolute maximum and absolute minimum values of a function.

➤ Absolute Maxima and Minima

Recall that $f(c)$ is a local maximum value if $f(x) \leq f(c)$ for x near c and a local minimum value if $f(x) \geq f(c)$ for x near c. Now we are interested in finding the largest and the smallest values of $f(x)$ throughout its domain.

DEFINITION Absolute Maxima and Minima

If $f(c) \geq f(x)$ for all x in the domain of f, then $f(c)$ is called the **absolute maximum value** of f.

If $f(c) \leq f(x)$ for all x in the domain of f, then $f(x)$ is called the **absolute minimum value** of f.

Figure 1 illustrates some typical examples.

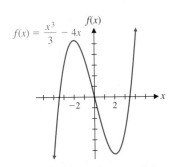

$f(x) = \dfrac{x^3}{3} - 4x$

(A) No absolute maximum or minimum
One local maximum at $x = -2$
One local minimum at $x = 2$

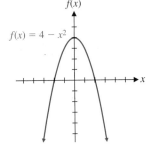

$f(x) = 4 - x^2$

(B) Absolute maximum at $x = 0$
No absolute minimum

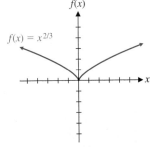

$f(x) = x^{2/3}$

(C) Absolute minimum at $x = 0$
No absolute maximum

FIGURE 1

◉ **Insight**   If $f(c)$ is the absolute maximum value of a function f, then $f(c)$ is obviously a "value" of f. It is common practice to omit "value" and to refer to $f(c)$ as the **absolute maximum** of f. In either usage, note that c is a value of x in the domain of f where the absolute maximum occurs. It is incorrect to refer to c as the absolute maximum. Collectively, the absolute maximum and the absolute minimum are referred to as **absolute extrema.**

EXPLORE
&DISCUSS
1

Functions f, g, and h, along with their graphs, are shown in Figure 2.

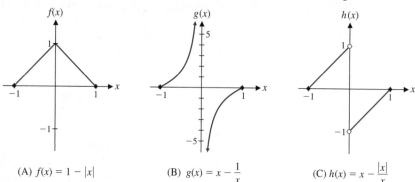

(A) $f(x) = 1 - |x|$ (B) $g(x) = x - \dfrac{1}{x}$ (C) $h(x) = x - \dfrac{|x|}{x}$

FIGURE 2

(A) Which of these functions are continuous on $[-1, 1]$?

(B) Find the absolute maximum and the absolute minimum of each function on $[-1, 1]$, if they exist, and the corresponding values of x that produce these absolute extrema.

(C) Suppose that a function p is continuous on $[-1, 1]$ and satisfies $p(-1) = 0$ and $p(1) = 0$. Sketch a possible graph for p. Does the function you graphed have an absolute maximum? An absolute minimum? Can you modify your sketch so that p does not have an absolute maximum or an absolute minimum on $[-1, 1]$?

In many practical problems, the domain of a function is restricted because of practical or physical considerations. If the domain is restricted to some closed interval, as is often the case, then Theorem 1 can be proved.

THEOREM 1   Extreme Value Theorem

A function f that is continuous on a closed interval $[a, b]$ has both an absolute maximum value and an absolute minimum value on that interval.

It is important to understand that the absolute maximum and minimum values depend on both the function f and the interval $[a, b]$. Figure 3 illustrates four cases.

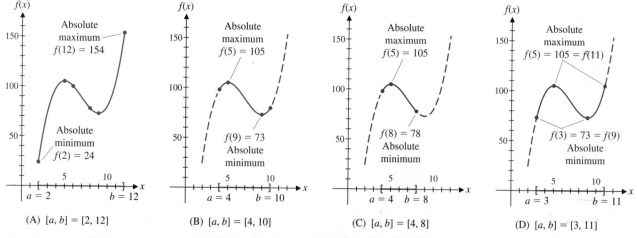

FIGURE 3   Absolute extrema for $f(x) = x^3 - 21x^2 + 135x - 170$ for various closed intervals

In all four cases illustrated in Figure 3, the absolute maximum value and absolute minimum value both occur at a critical value or an endpoint. Both the absolute maximum value and the absolute minimum value are unique, but each can occur at more than one point in the interval (Fig. 3D). In general,

THEOREM 2   Locating Absolute Extrema

Absolute extrema (if they exist) must always occur at critical values or at endpoints.

Thus, to find the absolute maximum or minimum value of a continuous function on a closed interval, we simply identify the endpoints and the critical values in the interval, evaluate the function at each, and then choose the largest and smallest values out of this group.

PROCEDURE   Finding Absolute Extrema on a Closed Interval

Step 1. Check to make certain that f is continuous over $[a, b]$.

Step 2. Find the critical values in the interval (a, b).

Step 3. Evaluate f at the endpoints a and b and at the critical values found in step 2.

Step 4. The absolute maximum $f(x)$ on $[a, b]$ is the largest of the values found in step 3.

Step 5. The absolute minimum $f(x)$ on $[a, b]$ is the smallest of the values found in step 3.

EXAMPLE 1   **Finding Absolute Extrema** Find the absolute maximum and absolute minimum values of

$$f(x) = x^3 + 3x^2 - 9x - 7$$

on each of the following intervals:

(A) $[-6, 4]$ (B) $[-4, 2]$ (C) $[-2, 2]$

Solution   (A) The function is continuous for all values of x.

$$f'(x) = 3x^2 + 6x - 9 = 3(x - 1)(x + 3)$$

Thus, $x = -3$ and $x = 1$ are critical values in the interval $(-6, 4)$. Evaluate f at the endpoints and critical values $(-6, -3, 1,$ and $4)$, and choose the maximum and minimum from these:

$$f(-6) = -61 \quad \text{Absolute minimum}$$
$$f(-3) = 20$$
$$f(1) = -12$$
$$f(4) = 69 \quad \text{Absolute maximum}$$

(B) Interval: $[-4, 2]$

x	$f(x)$	
-4	13	
-3	20	Absolute maximum
1	-12	Absolute minimum
2	-5	

(C) Interval: $[-2, 2]$

x	$f(x)$	
-2	15	Absolute maximum
1	-12	Absolute minimum
2	-5	

The critical value $x = -3$ is not included in this table, because it is not in the interval $[-2, 2]$.

■

Matched Problem 1 Find the absolute maximum and absolute minimum values of

$$f(x) = x^3 - 12x$$

on each of the following intervals:

(A) $[-5, 5]$ (B) $[-3, 3]$ (C) $[-3, 1]$ ───────────── ■

Now, suppose that we want to find the absolute maximum or minimum value of a function that is continuous on an interval that is not closed. Since Theorem 1 no longer applies, we cannot be certain that the absolute maximum or minimum value exists. Figure 4 illustrates several ways that functions can fail to have absolute extrema.

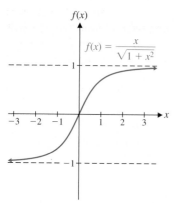

(A) No absolute extrema on $(-\infty, \infty)$:
$-1 < f(x) < 1$ for all x
$[f(x) \neq 1$ or -1 for any $x]$

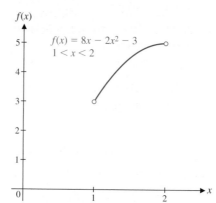

(B) No absolute extrema on $(1, 2)$:
$3 < f(x) < 5$ for $x \in (1, 2)$
$[f(x) \neq 3$ or 5 for any $x \in (1, 2)]$

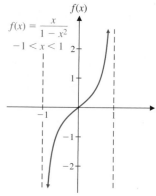

(C) No absolute extrema on $(-1, 1)$:
Graph has vertical asymptotes
at $x = -1$ and $x = 1$

FIGURE 4 Functions with no absolute extrema

In general, the best procedure to follow when searching for absolute extrema on an interval that is not of the form $[a, b]$ is to sketch a graph of the function. However, many applications can be solved using a new tool that does not require any graphing.

➤ Second Derivative and Extrema

The second derivative can be used to classify the local extrema of a function. Suppose that f is a function satisfying $f'(c) = 0$ and $f''(c) > 0$. First, note that if $f''(c) > 0$, it follows from the properties of limits* that $f''(x) > 0$ in some

*Actually, we are assuming that $f''(x)$ is continuous in an interval containing c. It is very unlikely that we will encounter a function for which $f''(c)$ exists but $f''(x)$ is not continuous in an interval containing c.

interval (m, n) containing c. Thus, the graph of f must be concave upward in this interval. But this implies that $f'(x)$ is increasing in this interval. Since $f'(c) = 0, f'(x)$ must change from negative to positive at $x = c$, and $f(c)$ is a local minimum (see Fig. 5). Reasoning in the same fashion, we conclude that if $f'(c) = 0$ and $f''(c) < 0$, then $f(c)$ is a local maximum. Of course, it is possible that both $f'(c) = 0$ and $f''(c) = 0$. In this case, the second derivative cannot be used to determine the shape of the graph around $x = c$; $f(c)$ may be a local minimum, a local maximum, or neither.

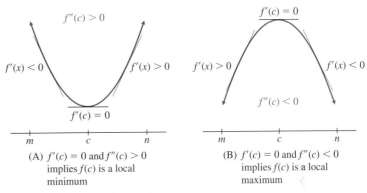

FIGURE 5 Second derivative and local extrema

The sign of the second derivative thus provides a simple test for identifying local maxima and minima. This test is most useful when we do not want to draw the graph of the function. If we are interested in drawing the graph and have already constructed the sign chart for $f'(x)$, the first-derivative test can be used to identify the local extrema.

RESULT Second-Derivative Test

Let c be a critical value for $f(x)$.

$f'(c)$	$f''(c)$	Graph of f is:	$f(c)$	Example
0	+	Concave upward	Local minimum	∪
0	−	Concave downward	Local maximum	∩
0	0	?	Test does not apply	

EXAMPLE 2 **Testing Local Extrema** Find the local maxima and minima for each function. Use the second-derivative test when it applies.

(A) $f(x) = x^3 - 6x^2 + 9x + 1$ (B) $f(x) = \frac{1}{6}x^6 - 4x^5 + 25x^4$

Solution (A) Take first and second derivatives and find critical values:

$$f(x) = x^3 - 6x^2 + 9x + 1$$
$$f'(x) = 3x^2 - 12x + 9 = 3(x - 1)(x - 3)$$
$$f''(x) = 6x - 12 = 6(x - 2)$$

Critical values are $x = 1$ and $x = 3$.

$$f''(1) = -6 < 0 \quad \text{f has a local maximum at $x = 1$.}$$
$$f''(3) = 6 > 0 \quad \text{f has a local minimum at $x = 3$.}$$

(B)
$$f(x) = \tfrac{1}{6}x^6 - 4x^5 + 25x^4$$
$$f'(x) = x^5 - 20x^4 + 100x^3 = x^3(x - 10)^2$$
$$f''(x) = 5x^4 - 80x^3 + 300x^2$$

Critical values are $x = 0$ and $x = 10$.

$f''(0) = 0$ The second-derivative test fails at both critical values, so

$f''(10) = 0$ the first-derivative test must be used.

Sign chart for $f'(x) = x^3(x - 10)^2$ (partition numbers are 0 and 10):

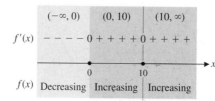

	Test Numbers	
x		$f'(x)$
-1		-121 $(-)$
1		81 $(+)$
11		$1{,}331$ $(+)$

From the sign chart we see that $f(x)$ has a local minimum at $x = 0$ and does not have a local extremum at $x = 10$. ∎

Matched Problem 2 Find the local maxima and minima for each function. Use the second-derivative test when it applies.

(A) $f(x) = x^3 - 9x^2 + 24x - 10$ (B) $f(x) = 10x^6 - 24x^5 + 15x^4$

◉ Insight The second-derivative test does not apply if $f''(c) = 0$ or if $f''(c)$ is not defined. As Example 3B illustrates, if $f''(c) = 0$, then $f(c)$ may or may not be a local extremum. Some other method, such as the first-derivative test, must be used when $f''(c) = 0$ or $f''(c)$ does not exist. ●

The solution of many optimization problems involves searching for an absolute extremum. If the function in question has only one critical value, then the second-derivative test not only classifies the local extremum but also guarantees that the local extremum is, in fact, the absolute extremum.

THEOREM 3 **Second-Derivative Test for Absolute Extremum**

Let f be continuous on an interval I with <u>only one critical value c in I.</u>

If $f'(c) = 0$ and $f''(c) > 0$, then $f(c)$ is the absolute minimum of f on I.

If $f'(c) = 0$ and $f''(c) < 0$, then $f(c)$ is the absolute maximum of f on I.

Since the second-derivative test cannot be applied when $f''(c) = 0$ or $f''(c)$ does not exist, Theorem 3 makes no mention of these cases.

EXAMPLE 3   **Finding an Absolute Extremum on an Open Interval** Find the absolute minimum value of

$$f(x) = x + \frac{4}{x}$$

on the interval $(0, \infty)$.

Solution $f'(x) = 1 - \frac{4}{x^2} = \frac{x^2 - 4}{x^2} = \frac{(x - 2)(x + 2)}{x^2}$ $f''(x) = \frac{8}{x^3}$

The only critical value in the interval $(0, \infty)$ is $x = 2$. Since $f''(2) = 1 > 0$, $f(2) = 4$ is the absolute minimum value of f on $(0, \infty)$.   ∎

Matched Problem 3   Find the absolute maximum value of

$$f(x) = 12 - x - \frac{9}{x}$$

on the interval $(0, \infty)$.

Answers to Matched Problems   **1.** (A) Absolute maximum: $f(5) = 65$; absolute minimum: $f(-5) = -65$
(B) Absolute maximum: $f(-2) = 16$; absolute minimum: $f(2) = -16$
(C) Absolute maximum: $f(-2) = 16$; absolute minimum: $f(1) = -11$

2. (A) $f(2)$ is a local maximum; $f(4)$ is a local minimum
(B) $f(0)$ is a local minimum; no local extremum at $x = 1$

3. $f(3) = 6$

Exercise 4-4

A *Problems 1–10 refer to the graph of $y = f(x)$ shown below. Find the absolute minimum and the absolute maximum over the indicated interval.*

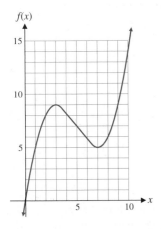

1. $[0, 10]$ **2.** $[2, 8]$ **3.** $[0, 8]$ **4.** $[2, 10]$

5. $[1, 10]$ **6.** $[0, 9]$ **7.** $[1, 9]$ **8.** $[0, 2]$

9. $[2, 5]$ **10.** $[5, 8]$

In Problems 11–26, find the absolute maximum and minimum, if either exists, for each function.

11. $f(x) = x^2 - 2x + 3$ **12.** $f(x) = x^2 + 4x - 3$

13. $f(x) = -x^2 - 6x + 9$ **14.** $f(x) = -x^2 + 2x + 4$

15. $f(x) = x^3 + x$ **16.** $f(x) = -x^3 - 2x$

17. $f(x) = 8x^3 - 2x^4$ **18.** $f(x) = x^4 - 4x^3$

19. $f(x) = x + \frac{16}{x}$ **20.** $f(x) = x + \frac{25}{x}$

21. $f(x) = \frac{x^2}{x^2 + 1}$ **22.** $f(x) = \frac{1}{x^2 + 1}$

23. $f(x) = \frac{2x}{x^2 + 1}$ **24.** $f(x) = \frac{-8x}{x^2 + 4}$

25. $f(x) = \frac{x^2 - 1}{x^2 + 1}$ **26.** $f(x) = \frac{9 - x^2}{x^2 + 4}$

B *In Problems 27–40, find the indicated extremum of each function on the given interval.*

27. Absolute minimum value on $[0, \infty)$ for

$$f(x) = 2x^2 - 8x + 6$$

28. Absolute maximum value on $[0, \infty)$ for
$$f(x) = 6x - x^2 + 4$$

29. Absolute maximum value on $[0, \infty)$ for
$$f(x) = 3x^2 - x^3$$

30. Absolute minimum value on $[0, \infty)$ for
$$f(x) = x^3 - 6x^2$$

31. Absolute minimum value on $[0, \infty)$ for
$$f(x) = (x + 4)(x - 2)^2$$

32. Absolute minimum value on $[0, \infty)$ for
$$f(x) = (2 - x)(x + 1)^2$$

33. Absolute maximum value on $(0, \infty)$ for
$$f(x) = 2x^4 - 8x^3$$

34. Absolute maximum value on $(0, \infty)$ for
$$f(x) = 4x^3 - 8x^4$$

35. Absolute maximum value on $(0, \infty)$ for
$$f(x) = 20 - 3x - \frac{12}{x}$$

36. Absolute minimum value on $(0, \infty)$ for
$$f(x) = 4 + x + \frac{9}{x}$$

37. Absolute maximum value on $(0, \infty)$ for
$$f(x) = 10 + 2x + \frac{64}{x^2}$$

38. Absolute maximum value on $(0, \infty)$ for
$$f(x) = 20 - 4x - \frac{250}{x^2}$$

39. Absolute minimum value on $(0, \infty)$ for
$$f(x) = x + \frac{1}{x} + \frac{30}{x^3}$$

40. Absolute minimum value on $(0, \infty)$ for
$$f(x) = 2x + \frac{5}{x} + \frac{4}{x^3}$$

In Problems 41–46, find the absolute maximum and minimum, if either exists, for each function on the indicated intervals.

41. $f(x) = x^3 - 6x^2 + 9x - 6$
(A) $[-1, 5]$ (B) $[-1, 3]$ (C) $[2, 5]$

42. $f(x) = 2x^3 - 3x^2 - 12x + 24$
(A) $[-3, 4]$ (B) $[-2, 3]$ (C) $[-2, 1]$

43. $f(x) = (x - 1)(x - 5)^3 + 1$
(A) $[0, 3]$ (B) $[1, 7]$ (C) $[3, 6]$

44. $f(x) = x^4 - 8x^2 + 16$
(A) $[-1, 3]$ (B) $[0, 2]$ (C) $[-3, 4]$

45. $f(x) = x^4 - 4x^3 + 5$
(A) $[-1, 2]$ (B) $[0, 4]$ (C) $[-1, 1]$

46. $f(x) = x^4 - 18x^2 + 32$
(A) $[-4, 4]$ (B) $[-1, 1]$ (C) $[1, 3]$

In Problems 47–54, describe the graph of f at the given point relative to the existence of a local maximum or minimum with one of the following phrases: "Local maximum," "Local minimum," "Neither," or "Unable to determine from the given information." Assume that $f(x)$ is continuous on $(-\infty, \infty)$.

47. $(2, f(2))$ if $f'(2) = 0$ and $f''(2) > 0$

48. $(4, f(4))$ if $f'(4) = 1$ and $f''(4) < 0$

49. $(-3, f(-3))$ if $f'(-3) = 0$ and $f''(-3) = 0$

50. $(-1, f(-1))$ if $f'(-1) = 0$ and $f''(-1) < 0$

51. $(6, f(6))$ if $f'(6) = 1$ and $f''(6)$ does not exist

52. $(5, f(5))$ if $f'(5) = 0$ and $f''(5)$ does not exist

53. $(-2, f(-2))$ if $f'(-2) = 0$ and $f''(-2) < 0$

54. $(1, f(1))$ if $f'(1) = 0$ and $f''(1) > 0$

Section 4-5 | Optimization

➤ Area and Perimeter
➤ Revenue and Profit
➤ Inventory Control

Now we want to use the calculus tools we have developed to solve **optimization problems**—that is, problems that involve finding the absolute maximum value or the absolute minimum value of a function. As you work through this section, note that the statement of the problem does not usually include the function that is to be optimized. Often, it is your responsibility to find the function and then to find its absolute extremum.

> ### Area and Perimeter

The techniques used to solve optimization problems are best illustrated through examples.

EXAMPLE 1   **Maximizing Area** A homeowner has \$320 to spend on building a fence around a rectangular garden. Three sides of the fence will be constructed with wire fencing at a cost of \$2 per linear foot. In order to provide a view block for a neighbor, the fourth side is to be constructed with wood fencing at a cost of \$6 per linear foot. Find the dimensions and the area of the largest garden that can be enclosed with \$320 worth of fencing.

Solution   To begin, we draw a figure (Fig. 1), introduce variables, and look for relationships among these variables.

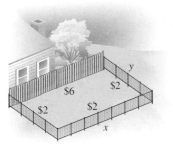

FIGURE 1

Since we don't know the dimensions of the garden, these lengths are represented by the variables x and y. The cost of each of the fencing materials is fixed, so these are represented by constants.

Now we look for relationships among the variables. The area of the garden is

$$A = xy$$

while the cost of the fencing is

$$C = 2y + 2x + 2y + 6x$$
$$= 8x + 4y$$

The problem states that the homeowner has \$320 to spend on fencing. We make the assumption that enclosing the largest area will use all of the money available for fencing. The problem has now been reduced to

Maximize $A = xy$ subject to $8x + 4y = 320$

Before we can use calculus techniques to find the maximum area A, we must express A as a function of a single variable. We use the cost equation to eliminate one of the variables in the expression for the area (we choose to eliminate y—either will work).

$$8x + 4y = 320$$
$$4y = 320 - 8x$$
$$y = 80 - 2x$$
$$A = xy = x(80 - 2x) = 80x - 2x^2$$

Now we consider the permissible values of x. Because x is one of the dimensions of a rectangle, x must satisfy

$$x \geq 0 \quad \text{Length is always nonnegative.}$$

And because $y = 80 - 2x$ is also a dimension of a rectangle, y must satisfy

$$y = 80 - 2x \geq 0 \quad \text{Width is always nonnegative.}$$
$$80 \geq 2x$$
$$40 \geq x \quad \text{or} \quad x \leq 40$$

We summarize the preceding discussion by stating the following model for this optimization problem:

Maximize $A(x) = 80x - 2x^2$ for $0 \leq x \leq 40$

Next, we find any critical values for A:

$$A'(x) = 80 - 4x = 0$$
$$80 = 4x$$
$$x = \frac{80}{4} = 20 \quad \text{Critical value}$$

$A''(20) = -4 \rightarrow 20 \text{ is máx val}$

Since $A(x)$ is continuous on $[0, 40]$, the absolute maximum value of A, if it exists, must occur at a critical value or an endpoint. Evaluating A at these values (Table 1), we see that the maximum area is 800 when

$$x = 20 \quad \text{and} \quad y = 80 - 2(20) = 40$$

Finally, we must answer the questions posed in the problem. The dimensions of the garden with the maximum area of 800 square feet are 20 feet by 40 feet with one 20-foot side with wood fencing. ■

TABLE 1

x	$A(x)$
0	0
20	800
40	0

Matched Problem 1 Repeat Example 1 if the wood fencing costs $8 per linear foot and all other information remains the same. ────────■

We summarize the steps we followed in the solution to Example 1 in the following box.

PROCEDURE Strategy for Solving Optimization Problems

Step 1. Introduce variables, look for relationships among these variables, and construct a mathematical model of the form

Maximize (or minimize) $f(x)$ on the interval I

Step 2. Find the critical values of $f(x)$.

Step 3. Use the procedures developed in Section 4-4 to find the absolute maximum (or minimum) value of $f(x)$ on the interval I and the value(s) of x where this occurs.

Step 4. Use the solution to the mathematical model to answer all the questions asked in the problem.

EXAMPLE 2 **Minimizing Perimeter** Refer to Example 1. The homeowner decides that an area of 800 square feet for the garden is too small and decides to increase the area to 1,250 square feet. What is the minimum cost of building a fence that will enclose a garden with area 1,250 square feet? What are the dimensions of this garden? Assume that the cost of fencing remains unchanged.

Solution Refer to Figure 1 in the solution for Example 1. This time we want to minimize the cost of the fencing that will enclose 1,250 square feet. This can be expressed as

Minimize $C = 8x + 4y$ subject to $xy = 1{,}250$

Since x and y represent distances, we know that $x \geq 0$ and $y \geq 0$. But neither variable can equal 0 because their product must be 1,250.

$$xy = 1{,}250 \qquad \text{Solve the area equation for } y.$$

$$y = \frac{1{,}250}{x}$$

$$C(x) = 8x + 4\frac{1{,}250}{x} \qquad \text{Substitute for } y \text{ in the cost equation.}$$

$$= 8x + \frac{5{,}000}{x} \qquad x > 0$$

The model for this problem is

$$\text{Minimize } C(x) = 8x + \frac{5{,}000}{x} \qquad \text{for } x > 0$$

$$= 8x + 5{,}000x^{-1}$$

$$C'(x) = 8 - 5{,}000x^{-2} = 8 - \frac{5{,}000}{x^2} = 0$$

$$8 = \frac{5{,}000}{x^2}$$

$$x^2 = \frac{5{,}000}{8} = 625$$

$$x = \sqrt{625} = 25 \quad \text{The negative square root is discarded since } x > 0.$$

We use the second derivative to determine the behavior at $x = 25$.

$$\boxed{C'(x) = 8 - 5{,}000x^{-2}}$$

$$C''(x) = 0 + 10{,}000x^{-3} = \frac{10{,}000}{x^3}$$

$$C''(25) = \frac{10{,}000}{25^3} = 0.64 > 0 \qquad C''(25)\ +$$

The second-derivative test shows that $C(x)$ has a local minimum at $x = 25$, and, since $x = 25$ is the only critical value for $x > 0$, $C(25)$ must be the absolute minimum value of $C(x)$ for $x > 0$. When $x = 25$, the cost is

$$C(25) = 8(25) + \frac{5{,}000}{25} = 200 + 200 = \$400$$

and

$$y = \frac{1{,}250}{25} = 50$$

The minimal cost for enclosing a 1,250-square-foot garden is $400 and the dimensions are 25 feet by 50 feet with one 25-foot side with wood fencing. ∎

Matched Problem 2 Repeat Example 2 if the homeowner wants to enclose an 1,800-square-foot garden and all other data remain unchanged.

👁 *Insight*   The restrictions on the variables in the solutions of Examples 1 and 2 are typical of problems involving areas or perimeters (or cost of the perimeter):

$$8x + 4y = 320 \quad \textit{Cost of fencing (Example 1)}$$
$$xy = 1{,}250 \qquad \textit{Area of garden (Example 2)}$$

The equation in Example 1 restricts the values of x to

$$0 \le x \le 40 \qquad \text{or} \qquad [0, 40]$$

The endpoints are included in the interval for our convenience (a closed interval is easier to work with than an open one). The area function is defined at each endpoint, so it does no harm to include them.

The equation in Example 2 restricts the values of x to

$$x > 0 \qquad \text{or} \qquad (0, \infty)$$

Neither endpoint can be included in this interval. We cannot include 0 because the area is not defined when $x = 0$ and we can never include ∞ as an endpoint. Remember, ∞ is not a number but a symbol that denotes that the interval is unbounded.   ●

➤ Maximizing Revenue and Profit

EXAMPLE 3   **Maximizing Revenue**   An office supply company sells x mechanical pencils per year at $\$p$ per pencil. The price demand equation for these pencils is $p = 10 - 0.001x$. What price should the company charge for these pencils to maximize their revenue? What is the maximum revenue?

Solution

$$\text{Revenue} = \text{price} \times \text{demand}$$
$$R(x) = (10 - 0.001x)x$$
$$= 10x - 0.001x^2$$

Both price and demand must nonnegative. So

$$x \ge 0 \quad \text{and} \quad p = 10 - 0.001x \ge 0$$
$$10 \ge 0.001x$$
$$10{,}000 \ge x$$

The mathematical model for this problem is

$$\text{Maximize} \quad R(x) = 10x - 0.001x^2 \qquad 0 \le x \le 10{,}000$$
$$R'(x) = 10 - 0.002x$$
$$10 - 0.002x = 0$$
$$10 = 0.002x$$
$$x = \frac{10}{0.002} = 5{,}000 \quad \textit{Critical value}$$

Use the second derivative test for absolute extrema:

$$R''(x) = -0.002 < 0 \quad \text{for all } x$$
$$\text{Max} \quad R(x) = R(5{,}000) = \$25{,}000$$

When the demand is $x = 5,000$, the price is

$$10 - 0.001(5,000) = \$5 \quad p = 10 - 0.001x$$

The company will realize a maximum revenue of $25,000 when the price of a pencil is $5. ∎

Matched Problem 3   An office supply company sells x heavy-duty paper shredders per year at $\$p$ per shredder. The price–demand equation for these shredders is

$$p = 300 - \frac{x}{30}$$

What price should the company charge for these shredders to maximize its revenue? What is the maximum revenue?   ——————∎

EXAMPLE 4   **Maximizing Profit**   The total annual cost of manufacturing x mechanical pencils for the office supply company in Example 3 is

$$C(x) = 5,000 + 2x$$

What is the company's maximum profit? What should the company charge for each pencil and how many pencils should be produced?

Solution   Using the revenue model in Example 3, we have

$$\text{Profit} = \text{Revenue} - \text{Cost}$$
$$P(x) = R(x) - C(x)$$
$$= 10x - 0.001x^2 - 5,000 - 2x$$
$$= 8x - 0.001x^2 - 5,000$$

The mathematical model for profit is

$$\text{Maximize} \quad P(x) = 8x - 0.001x^2 - 5,000 \qquad 0 \le x \le 10,000$$

(The restrictions on x come from the revenue model in Example 3.)

$$P'(x) = 8 - 0.002x = 0$$
$$8 = 0.002x$$
$$x = \frac{8}{0.002} = 4,000 \quad \text{Critical value}$$

$$P''(x) = -0.002 < 0 \quad \text{for all } x$$

Since $x = 4,000$ is the only critical value and $P''(x) < 0$,

$$\text{Max } P(x) = P(4,000) = \$11,000$$

Using the price–demand equation from Example 3 with $x = 4,000$, we find that

$$p = 10 - 0.001(4,000) = \$6 \quad p = 10 - 0.001x$$

Thus, a maximum profit of $11,000 is realized when 4,000 pencils are manufactured annually and sold for $6 each. ∎

The results in Examples 3 and 4 are illustrated in Figure 2.

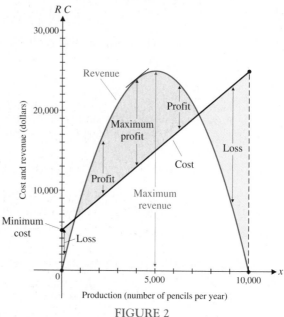

FIGURE 2

◉ **Insight**   In Figure 2, notice that the maximum revenue and the maximum profit occur at different production levels. The profit is maximum when

$$P'(x) = R'(x) - C'(x) = 0$$

that is, when the marginal revenue is equal to the marginal cost. Notice that the slopes of the revenue function and the cost function are the same at this production level.   ●

Matched Problem 4   The annual cost of manufacturing x paper shredders for the office supply company in Matched Problem 3 is $C(x) = 90,000 + 30x$. What is the company's maximum profit? What should it charge for each shredder, and how many shredders should it produce?   ■

EXAMPLE 5   **Maximizing Profit**   The government has decided to tax the company in Example 4 $2 for each pencil produced. Taking into account this additional cost, how many pencils should the company manufacture each week to maximize its weekly profit? What is the maximum weekly profit? How much should the company charge for the pencils to realize the maximum weekly profit?

Solution   The tax of $2 per unit changes the company's cost equation:

$$C(x) = \text{original cost} + \text{tax}$$
$$= 5,000 + 2x + 2x$$
$$= 5,000 + 4x$$

The new profit function is

$$P(x) = R(x) - C(x)$$
$$= 10x - 0.001x^2 - 5,000 - 4x$$
$$= 6x - 0.001x^2 - 5,000$$

Thus, we must solve the following:

$$\text{Maximize} \quad P(x) = 6x - 0.001x^2 - 5{,}000 \qquad 0 \le x \le 10{,}000$$
$$P'(x) = 6 - 0.002x$$
$$6 - 0.002x = 0$$
$$x = 3{,}000 \quad \text{Critical value}$$
$$P''(x) = -0.002 < 0 \quad \text{for all } x$$
$$\text{Max } P(x) = P(3{,}000) = \$4{,}000$$

Using the price–demand equation (Example 3) with $x = 3{,}000$, we find that

$$p = 10 - 0.001(3{,}000) = \$7 \quad p = 10 - 0.001x$$

Thus, the company's maximum profit is $4,000 when 3,000 pencils are produced and sold weekly at a price of $7.

Even though the tax caused the company's cost to increase by $2 per pencil, the price that the company should charge to maximize its profit increases by only $1. The company must absorb the other $1 with a resulting decrease of $7,000 in maximum profit. ■

Matched Problem 5 The government has decided to tax the office supply company in Matched Problem 4 $20 for each shredder produced. Taking into account this additional cost, how many shredders should the company manufacture each week to maximize its weekly profit? What is the maximum weekly profit? How much should the company charge for the shredders to realize the maximum weekly profit? ■

EXAMPLE 6 **Maximizing Revenue** When a management training company prices its seminar on management techniques at $400 per person, 1,000 people will attend the seminar. For each $5 reduction in the price, the company estimates an additional 20 people will attend the seminar. How much should the company charge for the seminar in order to maximize its revenue? What is the maximum revenue?

Solution Let x represent the number of $5 price reductions. Then

$$400 - 5x = \text{price per customer}$$
$$1{,}000 + 20x = \text{number of customers}$$
$$\text{Revenue} = (\text{price per customer})(\text{number of customers})$$
$$R(x) = (400 - 5x) \times (1{,}000 + 20x)$$

Since price cannot be negative, we have

$$400 - 5x \ge 0$$
$$400 \ge 5x$$
$$80 \ge x \quad \text{or} \quad x \le 80$$

A negative value of x would result in a price increase. Since the problem is stated in terms of price reductions, we must restrict x so that $x \ge 0$. Putting all this together, we have the following model:

$$\text{Maximize} \quad R(x) = (400 - 5x)(1{,}000 + 20x) \quad \text{for } 0 \le x \le 80$$
$$R(x) = 400{,}000 + 3{,}000x - 100x^2$$
$$R'(x) = 3{,}000 - 200x = 0$$
$$3{,}000 = 200x$$
$$x = 15 \quad \text{Critical value}$$

TABLE 2

x	$R(x)$
0	400,000
15	422,500
80	0

Since $R(x)$ is continuous on the interval $[0, 80]$, we can determine the behavior of the graph by constructing a table. Table 2 shows that $R(15) = \$422{,}500$ is the absolute maximum revenue. The price of attending the seminar at $x = 15$ is $400 - 5(15) = \$325$. The company should charge \$325 for the seminar in order to receive a maximum revenue of \$422,500. ∎

Matched Problem 6 A walnut grower estimates from past records that if 20 trees are planted per acre, each tree will average 60 pounds of nuts per year. If for each additional tree planted per acre the average yield per tree drops 2 pounds, how many trees should be planted to maximize the yield per acre? What is the maximum yield?

EXPLORE & DISCUSS 1

In Example 6, letting x be the number of \$5 price reductions produced a simple and direct solution to the problem. However, this is not the most obvious choice for a variable. Suppose that we proceed as follows:

Let x be the new price and let y be the attendance at this price level. Then the total revenue is given by xy.

(A) Find y when $x = 400$ and when $x = 395$. Find the equation of the line through these two points.

(B) Use the equation from part (A) to express the revenue in terms of either x or y, and use this expression to solve Example 6.

(C) Compare this method of solution to the one used in Example 6 with respect to ease of comprehension and ease of computation.

EXAMPLE 7 **Maximizing Revenue** After additional analysis, the management training company in Example 6 decides its estimate on attendance was too high. Its new estimate is that only 10 additional people will attend the seminar for each \$5 decrease in price. All other information remains the same. How much should the company charge for the seminar now in order to maximize revenue? What is the new maximum revenue?

Solution Under the new assumption, the model becomes

$$\text{Maximize} \quad R(x) = (400 - 5x)(1{,}000 + 10x) \qquad 0 \le x \le 80$$
$$= 400{,}000 - 1{,}000x - 50x^2$$
$$R'(x) = -1{,}000 - 100x = 0$$
$$-1{,}000 = 100x$$
$$x = -10 \quad \text{Critical value}$$

TABLE 3

x	$R(x)$
0	400,000
80	0

Note that $x = -10$ is not in the interval $[0, 80]$. Since $R(x)$ is continuous on $[0, 80]$, we can use a table to find the absolute maximum revenue. Table 3 shows that the maximum revenue is $R(0) = \$400{,}000$. The company should leave the price at \$400. Any \$5 decreases in price will lower the revenue. ∎

Matched Problem 7 After further analysis, the walnut grower in Example 7 determines that each additional tree planted will reduce the average yield by 4 pounds. All other information remains the same. How many additional trees per acre should the grower plant now in order to maximize the yield? What is the new maximum yield?

◉ Insight The solution in Example 7 is called an **endpoint solution** because the optimal value occurs at the endpoint of an interval rather than at a critical value in the interior of the interval. It is always important to verify that the optimal value has been found. ●

➤ Inventory Control

EXAMPLE 8

Inventory Control A recording company anticipates that there will be a demand for 20,000 copies of a certain compact disk (CD) during the following year. It costs the company $0.50 to store a CD for one year. Each time it must make additional CDs, it costs $200 to set up the equipment. How many CDs should the company make during each production run to minimize its total storage and setup costs?

Solution This type of problem is called an **inventory control problem.** One of the basic assumptions made in such problems is that the demand is uniform. For example, if there are 250 working days in a year, the daily demand would be $20,000 \div 250 = 80$ CDs. The company could decide to produce all 20,000 CDs at the beginning of the year. This would certainly minimize the setup costs but would result in very large storage costs. At the other extreme, it could produce 80 CDs each day. This would minimize the storage costs but would result in very large setup costs. Somewhere between these two extremes is the optimal solution that will minimize the total storage and setup costs. Let

x = number of CDs manufactured during each production run

y = number of production runs

It is easy to see that the total setup cost for the year is $200y$, but what is the total storage cost? If the demand is uniform, the number of CDs in storage between production runs will decrease from x to 0, and the average number in storage each day is $x/2$. This result is illustrated in Figure 3.

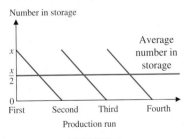

FIGURE 3

Since it costs $0.50 to store a CD for one year, the total storage cost is $0.5(x/2) = 0.25x$ and the total cost is

$$\text{total cost} = \text{setup cost} + \text{storage cost}$$

$$C = 200y + 0.25x$$

In order to write the total cost C as a function of one variable, we must find a relationship between x and y. If the company produces x CDs in each of y production runs, the total number of CDs produced is xy. Thus,

$$xy = 20{,}000$$

$$y = \frac{20{,}000}{x}$$

Certainly, x must be at least 1 and cannot exceed 20,000. Thus, we must solve the following:

$$\text{Minimize} \quad C(x) = 200\left(\frac{20{,}000}{x}\right) + 0.25x \qquad 1 \le x \le 20{,}000$$

$$C(x) = \frac{4{,}000{,}000}{x} + 0.25x$$

$$C'(x) = -\frac{4{,}000{,}000}{x^2} + 0.25$$

$$-\frac{4{,}000{,}000}{x^2} + 0.25 = 0$$

$$x^2 = \frac{4{,}000{,}000}{0.25}$$

$$x^2 = 16{,}000{,}000 \quad \text{\textit{−4,000 is not a critical value, since}}$$

$$x = 4{,}000 \qquad \text{\textit{1 ≤ x ≤ 20,000.}}$$

$$C''(x) = \frac{8{,}000{,}000}{x^3} > 0 \qquad \text{for } x \in (1, 20{,}000)$$

Thus,

$$\text{Min } C(x) = C(4{,}000) = 2{,}000$$

$$y = \frac{20{,}000}{4{,}000} = 5$$

The company will minimize its total cost by making 4,000 CDs five times during the year. ∎

Matched Problem 8

Repeat Example 8 if it costs $250 to set up a production run and $0.40 to store a CD for one year.

Answers to Matched Problems

1. The dimensions of the garden with the maximum area of 640 square feet are 16 feet by 40 feet with one 16-foot side with wood fencing.

2. The minimal cost for enclosing a 1,800-square-foot garden is $480 and the dimensions are 30 feet by 60 feet with one 30-foot side with wood fencing.

3. The company will realize a maximum revenue of $675,000 when the price of a shredder is $150.

4. A maximum profit of $456,750 is realized when 4,050 shredders are manufactured annually and sold for $165 each.

5. A maximum profit of $378,750 is realized when 3,075 shredders are manufactured annually and sold for $175 each.

6. The maximum yield is 1,250 pounds per acre when 5 additional trees are planted on each acre.

7. The maximum yield is 1,200 pounds when no additional trees are planted.

8. The company should produce 5,000 CDs four times a year.

Exercise 4-5

Preliminary word problems:

1. How would you divide a 10-inch line so that the product of the two lengths is a maximum?

2. What quantity should be added to 5 and subtracted from 5 to produce the maximum product of the results?

3. Find two numbers whose difference is 30 and whose product is a minimum.

4. Find two positive numbers whose sum is 60 and whose product is a maximum.

5. Find the dimensions of a rectangle with perimeter 100 centimeters that has maximum area. Find the maximum area.

6. Find the dimensions of a rectangle of area 225 square centimeters that has the least perimeter. What is the perimeter?

Problems 7–10 refer to a rectangular area enclosed by a fence that costs $B per foot. Discuss the existence of a solution and the economical implications of each optimization problem.

7. Given a fixed area, minimize the cost of the fencing.

8. Given a fixed area, maximize the cost of the fencing.

9. Given a fixed amount to spend on fencing, maximize the enclosed area.

10. Given a fixed amount to spend on fencing, minimize the enclosed area.

Business & Economics

11. *Maximum revenue and profit.* A company manufactures and sells x video phones per week. The weekly price–demand and cost equations are

$$p = 500 - 0.5x \quad \text{and} \quad C(x) = 20,000 + 135x$$

(A) What price should the company charge for the phones and how many phones should be produced to maximize the weekly revenue? What is the maximum weekly revenue?

(B) What is the maximum weekly profit? How much should the company charge for the phones and how many phones should be produced to realize the maximum weekly profit?

12. *Maximum revenue and profit.* A company manufactures and sells x digital cameras per week. The weekly price–demand and cost equations are

$$p = 400 - 0.4x \quad \text{and} \quad C(x) = 2,000 + 160x$$

(A) What price should the company charge for the cameras and how many cameras should be produced to maximize the weekly revenue? What is the maximum revenue?

(B) What is the maximum weekly profit? How much should the company charge for the cameras and how many cameras should be produced to realize the maximum weekly profit?

13. *Maximum revenue and profit.* A company manufactures and sells x television sets per month. The monthly cost and price–demand equations are

$$C(x) = 72,000 + 60x$$
$$p = 200 - \frac{x}{30} \quad 0 \le x \le 6,000$$

(A) Find the maximum revenue.

(B) Find the maximum profit, the production level that will realize the maximum profit, and the price the company should charge for each television set.

(C) If the government decides to tax the company $5 for each set it produces, how many sets should the company manufacture each month to maximize its profit? What is the maximum profit? What should the company charge for each set?

14. *Maximum revenue and profit.* Repeat Problem 13 for

$$C(x) = 60,000 + 60x$$
$$p = 200 - \frac{x}{50} \quad 0 \le x \le 10,000$$

15. *Maximum profit.* The table contains price–demand and total cost data for the production of radial arm saws, where p is the wholesale price (in dollars) of a saw for an annual demand of x saws and C is the total cost (in dollars) of producing x saws.

x	p	C
950	240	130,000
1,200	210	150,000
1,800	160	180,000
2,050	120	190,000

(A) Find a quadratic regression equation for the price–demand data using x as the independent variable.

(B) Find a linear regression equation for the cost data using x as the independent variable.

(C) What is the maximum profit? What is the wholesale price per saw that should be charged to realize the maximum profit? Round answers to the nearest dollar.

16. *Maximum profit.* The table contains price–demand and total cost data for the production of airbrushes, where p is the wholesale price (in dollars) of an airbrush for an annual demand of x airbrushes and C is the total cost (in dollars) of producing x airbrushes.

x	p	C
2,300	98	145,000
3,300	84	170,000
4,500	67	190,000
5,200	51	210,000

(A) Find a quadratic regression equation for the price–demand data using x as the independent variable.

(B) Find a linear regression equation for the cost data using x as the independent variable.

(C) What is the maximum profit? What is the wholesale price per airbrush that should be charged to realize the maximum profit? Round answers to the nearest dollar.

17. *Maximum revenue.* A deli sells 640 sandwiches per day at a price of $8 each.

(A) A market survey shows that for every $0.10 reduction in price 40 more sandwiches will be sold. How much should the deli charge for a sandwich in order to maximize its revenue?

(B) A different market survey shows that for every $0.20 reduction in the original $8 price 15 more sandwiches will be sold. Now how much should the deli charge for a sandwich in order to maximize its revenue?

18. *Maximum revenue.* A university student center sells 1,600 cups of coffee per day at a price of $2.40.

(A) A market survey shows that for every $0.05 reduction in price 50 more cups of coffee will be sold. How much should the student center charge for a cup of coffee in order to maximize its revenue?

(B) A different market survey shows that for every $0.10 reduction in the original $2.40 price 60 more cups of coffee will be sold. Now how much should the student center charge for a cup of coffee in order to maximize its revenue?

19. *Car rental.* A car rental agency rents 200 cars per day at a rate of $30 per day. For each $1 increase in rate, 5 fewer cars are rented. At what rate should the cars be rented to produce the maximum income? What is the maximum income?

20. *Rental income.* A 300-room hotel in Las Vegas is filled to capacity every night at $80 a room. For each $1 increase in rent, 3 fewer rooms are rented. If each rented room costs $10 to service per day, how much should the management charge for each room to maximize gross profit? What is the maximum gross profit?

21. *Agriculture.* A commercial cherry grower estimates from past records that if 30 trees are planted per acre, each tree will yield an average of 50 pounds of cherries per season. If for each additional tree planted per acre (up to 20), the average yield per tree is reduced by 1 pound, how many trees should be planted per acre to obtain the maximum yield per acre? What is the maximum yield?

22. *Agriculture.* A commercial pear grower must decide on the optimum time to have fruit picked and sold. If the pears are picked now, they will bring 30¢ per pound, with each tree yielding an average of 60 pounds of salable pears. If the average yield per tree increases 6 pounds per tree per week for the next 4 weeks, but the price drops 2¢ per pound per week, when should the pears be picked to realize the maximum return per tree? What is the maximum return?

23. *Manufacturing.* A candy box is to be made out of a piece of cardboard that measures 8 by 12 inches. Squares of equal size will be cut out of each corner, and then the ends and sides will be folded up to form a rectangular box. What size square should be cut from each corner to obtain a maximum volume?

24. *Packaging.* A parcel delivery service will deliver a package only if the length plus girth (distance around) does not exceed 108 inches.

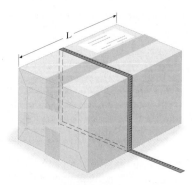

Figure for 24

(A) Find the dimensions of a rectangular box with square ends that satisfies the delivery service's restriction and has maximum volume. What is the maximum volume?

(B) Find the dimensions (radius and height) of a cylindrical container that meets the delivery service's requirement and has maximum volume. What is the maximum volume?

25. *Construction costs.* A fence is to be built to enclose a rectangular area of 800 square feet. The fence along three sides is to be made of material that costs $6 per foot. The material for the fourth side costs $18 per foot. Find the dimensions of the rectangle that will allow the most economical fence to be built.

26. *Construction costs.* The owner of a retail lumber store wants to construct a fence to enclose an outdoor storage area adjacent to the store, using all of the store as part of one side of the area (see the figure). Find the dimensions that will enclose the largest area if:

(A) 240 feet of fencing material are used.
(B) 400 feet of fencing material are used.

100 ft

Figure for 26

C(x) = 4

27. *Inventory control.* A paint manufacturer has a uniform annual demand for 16,000 cans of automobile primer. It costs $4 to store one can of paint for one year and $500 to set up the plant for production of the primer. How many times a year should the company produce this primer in order to minimize the total storage and setup costs?

28. *Inventory control.* A pharmacy has a uniform annual demand for 200 bottles of a certain antibiotic. It costs $10 to store one bottle for one year and $40 to place an order. How many times during the year should the pharmacy order the antibiotic in order to minimize the total storage and reorder costs?

29. *Inventory control.* A publishing company sells 50,000 copies of a certain book each year. It costs the company $1 to store a book for one year. Each time it must print additional copies, it costs the company $1,000 to set up the presses. How many books should the company produce during each printing in order to minimize its total storage and setup costs?

30. *Operational costs.* The cost per hour for fuel to run a train is $v^2/4$ dollars, where v is the speed of the train in miles per hour. (Note that the cost goes up as the square of the speed.) Other costs, including labor, are $300 per hour. How fast should the train travel

on a 360-mile trip to minimize the total cost for the trip?

31. *Construction costs.* A freshwater pipeline is to be run from a source on the edge of a lake to a small resort community on an island 5 miles offshore, as indicated in the figure.

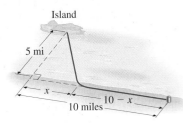

Island

5 mi

x

10 − x

10 miles

Figure for 31

(A) If it costs 1.4 times as much to lay the pipe in the lake as it does on land, what should x be (in miles) to minimize the total cost of the project?

(B) If it costs only 1.1 times as much to lay the pipe in the lake as it does on land, what should x be to minimize the total cost of the project? [*Note:* Compare with Problem 36.]

32. *Manufacturing costs.* A manufacturer wants to produce cans that will hold 12 ounces (approximately 22 cubic inches) in the form of a right circular cylinder. Find the dimensions (radius of an end and height) of the can that will use the smallest amount of material. Assume that the circular ends are cut out of squares, with the corner portions wasted, and the sides are made from rectangles, with no waste.

Life Sciences

33. *Bacteria control.* A recreational swimming lake is treated periodically to control harmful bacteria growth. Suppose that t days after a treatment, the concentration of bacteria per cubic centimeter is given by

$$C(t) = 30t^2 - 240t + 500 \qquad 0 \le t \le 8$$

How many days after a treatment will the concentration be minimal? What is the minimum concentration?

34. *Drug concentration.* The concentration $C(t)$, in milligrams per cubic centimeter, of a particular drug in a patient's bloodstream is given by

$$C(t) = \frac{0.16t}{t^2 + 4t + 4}$$

where t is the number of hours after the drug is taken. How many hours after the drug is given will the concentration be maximum? What is the maximum concentration?

35. *Laboratory management.* A laboratory uses 500 white mice each year for experimental purposes. It

costs $4 to feed a mouse for one year. Each time mice are ordered from a supplier, there is a service charge of $10 for processing the order. How many mice should be ordered each time to minimize the total cost of feeding the mice and of placing the orders for the mice?

36. *Bird flights.* Some birds tend to avoid flights over large bodies of water during daylight hours. (It is speculated that more energy is required to fly over water than land, because air generally rises over land and falls over water during the day.) Suppose that an adult bird with this tendency is taken from its nesting area on the edge of a large lake to an island 5 miles offshore and is then released (see the figure).

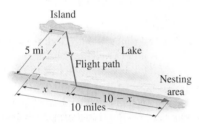

Figure for 36

(A) If it takes 1.4 times as much energy to fly over water as land, how far up-shore (x, in miles) should the bird head to minimize the total energy expended in returning to the nesting area?

(B) If it takes only 1.1 times as much energy to fly over water as land, how far up-shore should the bird head to minimize the total energy expended in returning to the nesting area? [*Note:* Compare with Problem 31.]

37. *Botany.* If it is known from past experiments that the height (in feet) of a given plant after t months is given approximately by

$$H(t) = 4t^{1/2} - 2t \qquad 0 \le t \le 2$$

how long, on the average, will it take a plant to reach its maximum height? What is the maximum height?

38. *Pollution.* Two heavy industrial areas are located 10 miles apart, as indicated in the figure. If the concentration of particulate matter (in parts per million) decreases as the reciprocal of the square of the distance from the source, and area A_1 emits eight times the particulate matter as A_2, the concentration of particulate matter at any point between the two areas is given by

$$C(x) = \frac{8k}{x^2} + \frac{k}{(10 - x)^2} \qquad 0.5 \le x \le 9.5, \quad k > 0$$

How far from A_1 will the concentration of particulate matter between the two areas be at a minimum?

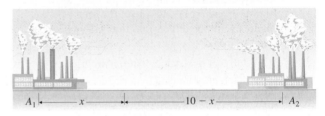

Figure for 38

Social Sciences

39. *Politics.* In a newly incorporated city, it is estimated that the voting population (in thousands) will increase according to

$$N(t) = 30 + 12t^2 - t^3 \qquad 0 \le t \le 8$$

where t is time in years. When will the rate of increase be most rapid?

40. *Learning.* A large grocery chain found that on the average, a checker can recall $P\%$ of a given price list x hours after starting work, as given approximately by

$$P(x) = 96x - 24x^2 \qquad 0 \le x \le 3$$

At what time x does the checker recall a maximum percentage? What is the maximum?

Chapter 4 Review

Important Terms, Symbols, and Concepts

4-1 First Derivative and Graphs

Theorem 1   Increasing and Decreasing Functions

For the interval (a, b),

$f'(x)$	$f(x)$	Graph of f	Examples
$+$	Increases ↗	Rises ↗	
$-$	Decreases ↘	Falls ↘	

The values of x in the domain of f where $f'(x) = 0$ or where $f'(x)$ does not exist are called the **critical values** of f.

We call $f(c)$ a **local maximum** if there exists an interval (m, n) containing c such that

$$f(x) \le f(c) \quad \text{for all } x \text{ in } (m, n)$$

and a **local minimum** if there exists an interval (m, n) containing x such that

$$f(x) \ge f(c) \quad \text{for all } x \text{ in } (m, n)$$

The quantity $f(c)$ is called a **local extremum** if it is either a local maximum or a local minimum. A point on a graph where a local extremum occurs is also called a **turning point.**

Theorem 2   Existence of Local Extrema
If f is continuous on the interval (a, b), c is a number in (a, b), and $f(c)$ is a local extremum, then either $f'(c) = 0$ or $f'(c)$ does not exist (is not defined).

Procedure   First-Derivative Test for Local Extrema
Let c be a critical value of f [$f(c)$ defined and either $f'(c) = 0$ or $f'(c)$ not defined]. Construct a sign chart for $f'(x)$ close to and on either side of c.

Sign Chart	$f(c)$
	$f(c)$ is local minimum. If $f'(x)$ changes from negative to positive at c, then $f(c)$ is a local minimum.
	$f(c)$ is local maximum. If $f'(x)$ changes from positive to negative at c, then $f(c)$ is a local maximum.
	$f(c)$ is not a local extremum. If $f'(x)$ does not change sign at c, then $f(c)$ is neither a local maximum nor a local minimum.
	$f(c)$ is not a local extremum. If $f'(x)$ does not change sign at c, then $f(c)$ is neither a local maximum nor a local minimum.

Theorem 3   Intercepts and Local Extrema for Polynomial Functions
If $f(x) = a_n x^n + a_{n-1} x^{n-1} + \cdots + a_1 x + a_0$, $a_n \neq 0$, is an nth-degree polynomial, then f has at most n intercepts and at most $n - 1$ local extrema.

4-2 Second Derivative and Graphs
The graph of a function f is **concave upward** on the interval (a, b) if $f'(x)$ is increasing on (a, b) and is **concave downward** on the interval (a, b) if $f'(x)$ is decreasing on (a, b).

Definition   Second Derivative
For $y = f(x)$, the **second derivative** of f, provided that it exists, is

$$f''(x) = \frac{d}{dx} f'(x)$$

Other notations for $f''(x)$ are

$$\frac{d^2 y}{dx^2} \qquad y''$$

An **inflection point** is a point on the graph of the function where the concavity changes (from upward to downward or from downward to upward). For the concavity to change at a point, $f''(x)$ must change sign at that point.

Theorem 1   Inflection Points
If $y = f(x)$ is continuous on (a, b) and has an inflection point at $x = c$, then either $f''(c) = 0$ or $f''(c)$ does not exist.

Procedure   Strategy for Graphing a Polynomial $y = f(x)$

Step 1. *Analyze $f(x)$.* Find the intercepts. The x intercepts are the solutions to $f(x) = 0$, if they exist, and the y intercept is $f(0)$.

Step 2. *Analyze $f'(x)$.* Find the zeros of $f'(x)$. Construct a sign chart for $f'(x)$, determine the intervals where $f(x)$ is increasing and decreasing, and find local maxima and minima.

Step 3. *Analyze $f''(x)$.* Find the zeros of $f''(x)$. Construct a sign chart for $f''(x)$, determine where the graph of f is concave upward and concave downward, and find any inflection points.

Step 4. *Sketch the graph of f.*

The value of x where the rate of change of sales changes from increasing to decreasing is called the **point of diminishing returns.** This is also the point where the rate of change has a maximum value.

4-3 Graphing Rational Functions
A **rational function** is any function that can be written in the form

$$f(x) = \frac{n(x)}{d(x)} \qquad d(x) \neq 0$$

where $n(x)$ and $d(x)$ are polynomials. The **domain** of f is the set of all real numbers such that $d(x) \neq 0$.

The vertical line $x = a$ is a **vertical asymptote** for the graph of $y = f(x)$ if

$$f(x) \to \infty \quad \text{or} \quad f(x) \to -\infty \quad \text{as} \quad x \to a^+ \quad \text{or} \quad x \to a^-$$

[that is, if $f(x)$ either increases or decreases without bound as x approaches a from the right or from the left].

Theorem 1   Locating Vertical Asymptotes

If $f(x) = n(x)/d(x)$, $d(c) = 0$ and $n(c) \neq 0$, then the line $x = c$ is a vertical asymptote of the graph of f.

The line $y = b$ is a **horizontal asymptote** for the graph of $y = f(x)$ if

$$\lim_{x \to \infty} f(x) = b \quad \text{or} \quad \lim_{x \to -\infty} f(x) = b$$

Theorem 2   Limits of Power Functions

If $p > 0$ and k is any constant, then

$$\lim_{x \to \infty} \frac{k}{x^p} = 0 \quad \text{and} \quad \lim_{x \to -\infty} \frac{k}{x^p} = 0$$

provided that x^p names a real number for negative values of x.

Theorem 3   Horizontal Asymptotes for Rational Functions

Let $f(x) = \dfrac{a_m x^m + a_{m-1} x^{m-1} + \cdots + a_1 x + a_0}{b_n x^n + b_{n-1} x^{n-1} + \cdots + b_1 x + b_0}$

$a_m \neq 0$ $b_n \neq 0$

1. If $m < n$, then $y = 0$ (the x axis) is a horizontal asymptote for $f(x)$.
2. If $m = n$, then the line $y = a_m/b_n$ is a horizontal asymptote for $f(x)$.
3. If $m > n$, then $f(x)$ does not have a horizontal asymptote.

Procedure   Strategy for Graphing a Rational Function $y = f(x)$

Step 1. *Analyze $f(x)$.*

(A) Find the domain of f.

(B) Find the intercepts.

(C) Find any asymptotes.

Step 2. *Analyze $f'(x)$.* Find the zeros of $f'(x)$. Construct a sign chart for $f'(x)$, determine the intervals where $f(x)$ is increasing and decreasing, and find local maxima and minima.

Step 3. *Analyze $f''(x)$.* Find the zeros of $f''(x)$. Construct a sign chart for $f''(x)$, determine where the graph of f is concave upward and concave downward, and find any inflection points.

Step 4. Sketch the graph of f.

If $\lim_{x \to \infty} [f(x) - (mx + b)] = 0$, then the line $y = mx + b$ is an **oblique asymptote** for the graph of f.

4-4 Absolute Maxima and Minima

If $f(c) \geq f(x)$ for all x in the domain of f, then $f(c)$ is called the **absolute maximum value** of f.

If $f(c) \leq f(x)$ for all x in the domain of f, then $f(x)$ is called the **absolute minimum value** of f.

Theorem 1   Extreme Value Theorem

A function f that is continuous on a closed interval $[a, b]$ has both an absolute maximum value and an absolute minimum value on that interval.

Theorem 2   Locating Absolute Extrema

Absolute extrema (if they exist) must always occur at critical values or at endpoints.

Procedure   Finding Absolute Extrema on a Closed Interval

Step 1. Check to make certain that f is continuous over $[a, b]$.

Step 2. Find the critical values in the interval (a, b).

Step 3. Evaluate f at the endpoints a and b and at the critical values found in step 2.

Step 4. The absolute maximum $f(x)$ on $[a, b]$ is the largest of the values found in step 3.

Step 5. The absolute minimum $f(x)$ on $[a, b]$ is the smallest of the values found in step 3.

Result   Second-Derivative Test

Let c be a critical value for $f(x)$.

$f'(c)$	$f''(c)$	Graph of f is:	$f(c)$	Example
0	+	Concave upward	Local minimum	$\smile$
0	−	Concave downward	Local maximum	$\frown$
0	0	?	Test does not apply	

Theorem 3   Second-Derivative Test for Absolute Extremum

Let f be continuous on an interval I with only one critical value c in I.

If $f'(c) = 0$ and $f''(c) > 0$, then $f(c)$ is the absolute minimum of f on I.

If $f'(c) = 0$ and $f''(c) < 0$, then $f(c)$ is the absolute maximum of f on I.

4-5 Optimization

An **optimization problem** is an application problem that can be solved by finding the absolute maximum value or the absolute minimum value of a function.

Procedure   Strategy for Solving Optimization Problems

Step 1. Introduce variables, look for relationships among these variables, and construct a mathematical model of the form

Maximize (or minimize) $f(x)$ on the interval I

Step 2. Find the critical values of $f(x)$.

Step 3. Use the procedures developed in Section 4-4 to find the absolute maximum (or minimum) value of $f(x)$ on the interval I and the value(s) of x where this occurs.

Step 4. Use the solution to the mathematical model to answer all the questions asked in the problem.

A solution to an optimization problem is called an **endpoint solution** if the optimal value occurs at the endpoint of an interval rather than at a critical value in the interior of the interval.

Review Exercise

Work through all the problems in this chapter review and check your answers in the back of the book. Answers to all review problems are there along with section numbers in italics to indicate where each type of problem is discussed. Where weaknesses show up, review appropriate sections in the text.

A *Problems 1–8 refer to the graph of $y = f(x)$ below. Identify the points or intervals on the x axis that produce the indicated behavior.*

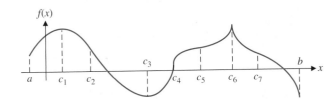

1. $f(x)$ is increasing
2. $f'(x) < 0$
3. Graph of f is concave downward
4. Local minima
5. Absolute maxima
6. $f'(x)$ appears to be 0
7. $f'(x)$ does not exist
8. Inflection points

In Problems 9 and 10, use the given information to sketch the graph of f. Assume that f is continuous on its domain and that all intercepts are included in the given information.

9. Domain: All real x

x	-3	-2	-1	0	2	3
$f(x)$	0	3	2	0	-3	0

f'(x) diagram: $+ + + \ 0 \ - - - - - - - - - \ 0 \ - - - \text{ND} + + +$ with marks at -2, 0, 2

f''(x) diagram: $- - - - - - - - - \ 0 \ + + + \ 0 \ - - - \text{ND} - - -$ with marks at -1, 0, 2

10. Domain: All real x;
$f(-2) = 1, f(0) = 0, f(2) = 1;$
$f'(0) = 0; f'(x) < 0$ on $(-\infty, 0);$
$f'(x) > 0$ on $(0, \infty);$
$f''(-2) = 0, f''(2) = 0;$
$f''(x) < 0$ on $(-\infty, -2)$ and $(2, \infty);$
$f''(x) > 0$ on $(-2, 2);$
$\lim_{x \to -\infty} f(x) = 2; \lim_{x \to \infty} f(x) = 2$

11. Find $f''(x)$ for $f(x) = x^4 + 5x^3$.

12. Find y'' for $y = 3x + \dfrac{4}{x}$.

B *In Problems 13–16, summarize all the pertinent information obtained by applying the graphing strategy for polynomials and sketch the graph of f.*

13. $f(x) = x^3 - 18x^2 + 81x$
14. $f(x) = (x + 4)(x - 2)^2$
15. $f(x) = 8x^3 - 2x^4$
16. $f(x) = (x - 1)^3(x + 3)$

In Problems 17–20, summarize all the pertinent information obtained by applying the graphing strategy for rational functions and sketch the graph of f.

17. $f(x) = \dfrac{3x}{x + 2}$

18. $f(x) = \dfrac{x^2}{x^2 + 27}$

19. $f(x) = \dfrac{x}{(x + 2)^2}$

20. $f(x) = \dfrac{x^3}{x^2 + 3}$

21. Use the graph of $y = f'(x)$ shown below to discuss the graph of $y = f(x)$. Organize your conclusions in a table (see Example 3, Section 4-2). Sketch a possible graph for $y = f(x)$.

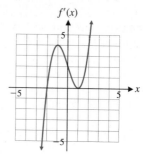

$f'(x)$

Figure for 21 and 22

22. Refer to the graph of $y = f'(x)$ above. Which of the following could be the graph of $y = f''(x)$?

(A)

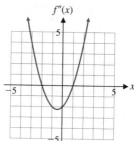

$f''(x)$

(B)

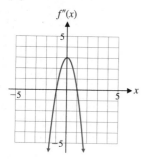

$f''(x)$

(C)

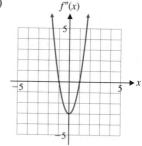

$f''(x)$

23. Use the second-derivative test to find any local extrema for
$$f(x) = x^3 - 6x^2 - 15x + 12$$

24. Find the absolute maximum and absolute minimum, if either exists, for
$$y = f(x) = x^3 - 12x + 12 \qquad -3 \le x \le 5$$

25. Find the absolute minimum, if it exists, for
$$y = f(x) = x^2 + \frac{16}{x^2} \qquad x > 0$$

26. Let $y = f(x)$ be a polynomial function with local minima at $x = a$ and $x = b$, $a < b$. Must f have at least one local maximum between a and b? Justify your answer.

27. The derivative of $f(x) = x^{-1}$ is $f'(x) = -x^{-2}$. Since $f'(x) < 0$ for $x \ne 0$, is it correct to say that $f(x)$ is decreasing for all x except $x = 0$? Explain.

28. Discuss the difference between a partition number for $f'(x)$ and a critical value for $f(x)$, and illustrate with examples.

C

29. Find the absolute maximum for $f'(x)$ if
$$f(x) = 6x^2 - x^3 + 8$$
Graph f and f' on the same coordinate system for $0 \le x \le 4$.

30. Find two positive numbers whose product is 400 and whose sum is a minimum. What is the minimum sum?

 In Problems 40 and 41, apply the graphing strategy for polynomials and summarize the pertinent information. Round any approximate values to two decimal places.

31. $f(x) = x^4 + x^3 - 4x^2 - 3x + 4$

32. $f(x) = 0.25x^4 - 5x^3 + 31x^2 - 70x$

Applications

Business & Economics

33. *Price analysis.* The graph in the figure approximates the rate of change of the price of tomatoes over a 60-month period, where $p(t)$ is the price of a pound of tomatoes and t is time (in months).

(A) Write a brief verbal description of the graph of $y = p(t)$, including a discussion of local extrema and inflection points.

(B) Sketch a possible graph of $y = p(t)$.

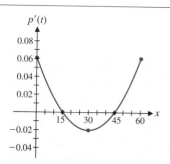

Figure for 33

34. *Maximum revenue and profit.* A company manufactures and sells x electric stoves per month. The monthly cost and price–demand equations are

$$C(x) = 350x + 50,000$$
$$p = 500 - 0.025x \qquad 0 \le x \le 20,000$$

(A) Find the maximum revenue.

(B) How many stoves should the company manufacture each month to maximize its profit? What is the maximum monthly profit? How much should the company charge for each stove?

(C) If the government decides to tax the company $20 for each stove it produces, how many stoves should the company manufacture each month to maximize its profit? What is the maximum monthly profit? How much should the company charge for each stove?

35. *Construction.* A fence is to be built to enclose a rectangular area. The fence along three sides is to be made of material that costs $5 per foot. The material for the fourth side costs $15 per foot.

(A) If the area is 5,000 square feet, find the dimensions of the rectangle that will allow the most economical fence to be built.

(B) If $3,000 is available for the fencing, find the dimensions of the rectangle that will enclose the most area.

36. *Rental income.* A 200-room hotel in Fresno is filled to capacity every night at a rate of $40 per room. For each $1 increase in the nightly rate, 4 fewer rooms are rented. If each rented room costs $8 a day to service, how much should the management charge per room in order to maximize gross profit? What is the maximum gross profit?

37. *Inventory control.* A computer store sells 7,200 boxes of floppy disks annually. It costs the store $0.20 to store a box of disks for one year. Each time it reorders disks, the store must pay a $5.00 service charge for processing the order. How many times during the year should the store order disks to minimize the total storage and reorder costs?

38. *Average cost.* The total cost of producing x garbage disposals per day is given by

$$C(x) = 4,000 + 10x + 0.1x^2$$

Find the minimum average cost. Graph the average cost and the marginal cost functions on the same coordinate system. Include any oblique asymptotes.

39. *Advertising—point of diminishing returns.* A company estimates that it will sell $N(x)$ units of a product after spending x thousand on advertising, as given by

$$N(x) = -0.25x^4 + 11x^3 - 108x^2 + 3,000 \qquad 9 \le x \le 24$$

When is the rate of change of sales increasing and when is it decreasing? What is the point of diminishing returns and the maximum rate of change of sales? Graph N and N' on the same coordinate system.

40. *Construction costs.* The ceiling supports in a new discount department store are 12 feet apart. Lights are to be hung from these supports by chains in the shape of a "Y." If the lights are 10 feet below the ceiling, what is the shortest length of chain that can be used to support these lights?

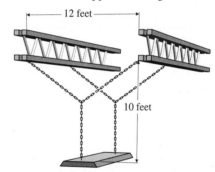

41. *Average cost.* The data in the table give the total daily cost y (in dollars) of producing x dozen chocolate chip cookies at various production levels.

Dozens of Cookies x	Total Cost y
50	119
100	187
150	248
200	382
250	505
300	695

(A) Enter the data in a graphing utility and find a quadratic regression equation for the total cost.

(B) Use the regression equation from part (A) to find the minimum average cost (to the nearest cent) and the corresponding production level (to the nearest integer).

42. *Advertising.* A chain of appliance stores uses television ads to promote the sales of refrigerators. Analyzing past records produced the data in the table, where x is the number of ads placed monthly and y is the number of refrigerators sold that month.

Number of Ads	Number of Refrigerators
x	y
10	271
20	427
25	526
30	629
45	887
48	917

(A) Enter the data in a graphing utility, set the utility to display two decimal places, and find a cubic regression equation for the number of refrigerators sold monthly as a function of the number of ads.

(B) How many ads should be placed each month to maximize the rate of change of sales with respect to the number of ads, and how many refrigerators can be expected to be sold with this number of ads? Round answers to the nearest integer.

Life Sciences

43. *Bacteria control.* If t days after a treatment, the bacteria count per cubic centimeter in a body of water is given by

$$C(t) = 20t^2 - 120t + 800 \qquad 0 \le t \le 9$$

in how many days will the count be a minimum?

Social Sciences

44. *Politics.* In a new suburb, it is estimated that the number of registered voters will grow according to

$$N = 10 + 6t^2 - t^3 \qquad 0 \le t \le 5$$

where t is time in years and N is in thousands. When will the rate of increase be maximum?

Group Activity 1   Maximizing Profit

A company manufactures and sells x air-conditioners per month. The monthly cost and price–demand equations are

$$C(x) = 180x + 20{,}000$$
$$p = 220 - 0.001x \qquad 0 \le x \le 100{,}000$$

(A) How many air-conditioners should the company manufacture each month to maximize its monthly profit? What is the maximum monthly profit, and what should the company charge for each air-conditioner to realize the maximum monthly profit?

(B) Repeat part (A) if the government decides to tax the company at the rate of $18 per air-conditioner produced. How much revenue will the government receive from the tax on these air-conditioners?

(C) Repeat part (A) if the government raises the tax to $23 per air-conditioner. Discuss the effect of this tax increase on the government's tax revenue.

(D) Repeat part (A) if the government sets the tax rate at $t per air-conditioner. What value of t will maximize the government's tax revenue? What is the government's maximum tax revenue?

Group Activity 2   Minimizing Construction Costs

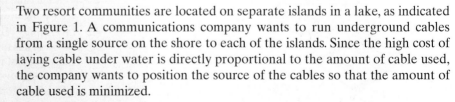

Two resort communities are located on separate islands in a lake, as indicated in Figure 1. A communications company wants to run underground cables from a single source on the shore to each of the islands. Since the high cost of laying cable under water is directly proportional to the amount of cable used, the company wants to position the source of the cables so that the amount of cable used is minimized.

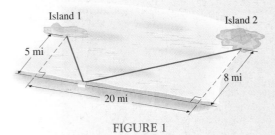

FIGURE 1

(A) Assume that the shoreline is straight and position a coordinate system as indicated in Figure 2. Let f be the function that represents the total length of cable used. Express f in terms of x (Fig. 2), graph f and f' (use the numerical derivative of f to graph f'), and find the value of x (in miles) that will minimize the total cable length.

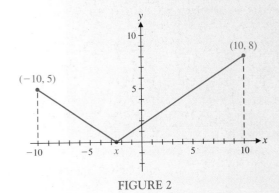

FIGURE 2

(B) Repeat part (A) under the assumption that the shoreline is in the shape of the parabola $y = 0.02x^2 - 2$ (Fig. 3).

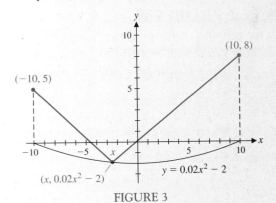

FIGURE 3

OBJECTIVES

1. Find the derivative of the exponential function and related exponential forms.
2. Find the derivative of the natural logarithm function and related logarithmic forms.
3. Find the logarithmic derivative of a function and study some of its applications.
4. Use elasticity of demand to determine if a price increase will increase or decrease revenue.
5. Find the derivative of a function defined implicitly by an equation.
6. Find relationships between the rates of change of quantities related by an equation.

CHAPTER PROBLEM

The daily demand x for a large pepperoni pizza at Pete's Pizzeria and the price $p are related by the following price–demand equation:

$$p = 30 - 5 \ln x \qquad 10 \le x \le 400$$

Pete's daily fixed costs are $200 and the cost of preparing a large pepperoni pizza is $1.50. Find the price $p that will produce the maximum profit for Pete.

Additional Derivative Topics

INTRODUCTION

In this chapter we complete our discussion of derivatives by first looking at the differentiation of exponential forms. Next we will consider the differentiation of logarithmic forms. Finally, we will consider some additional topics and applications involving all the different types of functions we have encountered thus far, including the general chain rule. You will probably find it helpful to review some of the important properties of the exponential and logarithmic functions given in Chapter 2 before proceeding further.

Section 5-1 | The Constant e and Continuous Compound Interest

➤ The Constant e
➤ Continuous Compound Interest

In Chapter 2, both the exponential function with base e and continuous compound interest were introduced informally. Now, with limit concepts at our disposal, we can give precise definitions of e and continuous compound interest.

➤ The Constant e

The special irrational number e is a particularly suitable base for both exponential and logarithmic functions. The reasons for choosing this number as a base will become clear as we develop differentiation formulas for the exponential function e^x and the natural logarithmic function $\ln x$.

In precalculus treatments (Chapter 2), the number e is informally defined as an irrational number that can be approximated by the expression $[1 + (1/n)]^n$ by taking n sufficiently large. Now we will use the limit concept to formally define e as either of the following two limits:

> **DEFINITION**   The Number e
>
> $$e = \lim_{n \to \infty} \left(1 + \frac{1}{n}\right)^n \qquad \text{or, alternatively,} \qquad e = \lim_{s \to 0}(1 + s)^{1/s}$$
>
> $$e = 2.718\,281\,828\,459\ldots$$

We will use both these limit forms. [*Note:* If $s = 1/n$, then as $n \to \infty, s \to 0$.]
The proof that the indicated limits exist and represent an irrational number between 2 and 3 is not easy and is omitted here.

👁 *Insight*   The two limits used to define e are unlike any we have encountered thus far. Some people reason (incorrectly) that the limits are 1, since "$1 + s \to 1$ as $s \to 0$ and 1 to any power is 1." A calculator experiment on an ordinary scientific calculator with a y^x key can convince you otherwise. Consider the following table of values for s and $f(s) = (1 + s)^{1/s}$ and the graph shown in Figure 1 for s close to 0.   ●

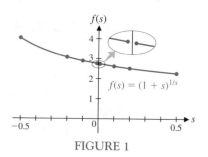

FIGURE 1

s approaches 0 from the left $\to$ 0 $\leftarrow$ s approaches 0 from the right

s	-0.5	-0.2	-0.1	$-0.01 \to$	0	$\leftarrow 0.01$	0.1	0.2	0.5
$(1 + s)^{1/s}$	4.0000	3.0518	2.8680	2.7320 $\to$	e	$\leftarrow$ 2.7048	2.5937	2.4883	2.2500

Compute some of the table values with a calculator yourself, and also try several values of s even closer to 0. Note that the function is discontinuous at $s = 0$.

Exactly who discovered e is still being debated. It is named after the great mathematician Leonhard Euler (1707–1783), who computed e to 23 decimal places using $[1 + (1/n)]^n$.

► Continuous Compound Interest

Now we will see how e appears quite naturally in the important application of compound interest. Let us start with simple interest, move on to compound interest, and then on to continuous compound interest.

If a principal P is borrowed at an annual rate of r,* then after t years at simple interest the borrower will owe the lender an amount A given by

$$A = P + Prt = P(1 + rt) \quad \text{Simple interest} \tag{1}$$

On the other hand, if interest is compounded n times a year, the borrower will owe the lender an amount A given by

$$A = P\left(1 + \frac{r}{n}\right)^{nt} \quad \text{Compound interest} \tag{2}$$

where r/n is the interest rate per compounding period and nt is the number of compounding periods. Suppose that P, r, and t in equation (2) are held fixed and n is increased. Will the amount A increase without bound, or will it tend to approach some limiting value?

Let us perform a calculator experiment before we attack the general limit problem. If $P = \$100$, $r = 0.06$, and $t = 2$ years, then

$$A = 100\left(1 + \frac{0.06}{n}\right)^{2n}$$

We compute A for several values of n in Table 1. The biggest gain appears in the first step; then the gains slow down as n increases. In fact, it appears that A might be tending to approach \$112.75 as n gets larger and larger.

TABLE 1

Compounding Frequency	n	$A = 100\left(1 + \dfrac{0.06}{n}\right)^{2n}$
Annually	1	\$112.3600
Semiannually	2	112.5509
Quarterly	4	112.6493
Monthly	12	112.7160
Weekly	52	112.7419
Daily	365	112.7486
Hourly	8,760	112.7496

EXPLORE & DISCUSS 1

(A) Suppose that \$1,000 is deposited in a savings account that earns 6% simple interest. How much will be in the account after 2 years?

(B) Suppose that \$1,000 is deposited in a savings account that earns compound interest at a rate of 6% per year. How much will be in the account after 2 years if interest is compounded annually? Semiannually? Quarterly? Weekly?

(C) How frequently must interest be compounded at the 6% rate in order to have \$1,150 in the account after 2 years?

Now we turn back to the general problem for a moment. Keeping P, r, and t fixed in equation (2), we compute the following limit and observe an interesting

---

* If r is the interest rate written as a decimal, then $100r\%$ is the rate using %. For example, if $r = 0.12$, we have $100r\% = 100(0.12)\% = 12\%$. The expressions 0.12 and 12% are therefore equivalent. Unless stated otherwise, all formulas in this book use r in decimal form.

and useful result:

$$\lim_{n \to \infty} P\left(1 + \frac{r}{n}\right)^{nt} = P \lim_{n \to \infty} \left(1 + \frac{r}{n}\right)^{(n/r)rt}$$

Insert r/r in the exponent and let $s = r/n$. Note that $n \to \infty$ implies $s \to 0$.

$$= P \lim_{s \to 0}[(1 + s)^{1/s}]^{rt}$$

Use the limit property given in the footnote below.*

$$= P[\lim_{s \to 0}(1 + s)^{1/s}]^{rt}$$

$\lim_{s \to 0}(1 + s)^{1/s} = e$

$$= Pe^{rt}$$

The resulting formula is called the **continuous compound interest formula,** a very important and widely used formula in business and economics.

RESULT   Continuous Compound Interest

$$A = Pe^{rt}$$

where

$P = $ principal

$r = $ annual nominal interest rate compounded continuously

$t = $ time in years

$A = $ amount at time t

EXAMPLE 1   **Computing Continuously Compounded Interest** If $100 is invested at 6% compounded continuously,[†] what amount will be in the account after 2 years? How much interest will be earned?

Solution
$$A = Pe^{rt}$$
$$= 100e^{(0.06)(2)}$$ 6% is equivalent to $r = 0.06$.
$$\approx \$112.7497$$

(Compare this result with the values calculated in Table 1.) The interest earned is $112.7497 − $100 = $12.7497.   ■

Matched Problem 1

What amount (to the nearest cent) will an account have after 5 years if $100 is invested at an annual nominal rate of 8% compounded annually? Semiannually? Continuously?

EXAMPLE 2   **Graphing the Growth of an Investment** Recently, Union Savings Bank offered a 5-year certificate of deposit (CD) that earned 5.75% compounded continuously. If $1,000 is invested in one of these CDs, graph the amount in the account relative to time for a period of 5 years.

---

* The following new limit property is used: If $\lim_{x \to c} f(x)$ exists, then $\lim_{x \to c}[f(x)]^p = [\lim_{x \to c} f(x)]^p$, provided that the last expression names a real number.

† Following common usage, we will often write "at 6% compounded continuously," understanding that this means "at an annual nominal rate of 6% compounded continuously."

Solution   We want to graph

$$A = 1,000e^{0.0575t} \qquad 0 \le t \le 5$$

We construct a table of values (Table 2) using a calculator, graph the points from the table, and join the points with a smooth curve (Fig. 2).

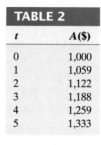

TABLE 2	
t	*A*($)
0	1,000
1	1,059
2	1,122
3	1,188
4	1,259
5	1,333

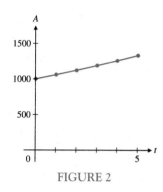

FIGURE 2

👁 ***Insight***   Depending on the domain, the graph of an exponential function can appear to be linear. Table 3 shows the slopes of the line segments connecting the dots in Figure 2. Since these slopes are not identical, this graph is not the graph of a straight line.

TABLE 3		
t	*A*	*m*
0	1,000	
		} 59
1	1,059	
		} 63
2	1,122	
		} 66
3	1,188	
		} 71
4	1,259	
		} 74
5	1,333	

Matched Problem 2   If $5,000 is invested in a Union Savings Bank 4-year CD that earns 5.61% compounded continuously, graph the amount in the account relative to time for a period of 4 years.

EXAMPLE 3   **Computing Growth Time**   How long will it take an investment of $5,000 to grow to $8,000 if it is invested at 5% compounded continuously?

Solution   Starting with the continuous compound interest formula $A = Pe^{rt}$, we must solve for t:

$$A = Pe^{rt}$$

$8{,}000 = 5{,}000e^{0.05t}$ Divide both sides by 5,000 and reverse the equation.

$e^{0.05t} = 1.6$ Take the natural logarithm of both sides—recall that $\log_b b^x = x$.

$\ln e^{0.05t} = \ln 1.6$

$0.05t = \ln 1.6$

$t = \dfrac{\ln 1.6}{0.05}$

$t \approx 9.4$ years

Figure 3 shows an alternative method for solving Example 3 on a graphing utility.

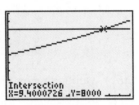

Intersection
X=9.4000726 Y=8000

FIGURE 3
$y_1 = 5{,}000e^{0.05x}$
$y_2 = 8{,}000$

Matched Problem 3   How long will it take an investment of $10,000 to grow to $15,000 if it is invested at 9% compounded continuously?

EXAMPLE 4   **Computing Doubling Time**   How long will it take money to double if it is invested at 6.5% compounded continuously?

Solution   Starting with the continuous compound interest formula $A = Pe^{rt}$, we must solve for t given $A = 2P$ and $r = 0.065$:

$2P = Pe^{0.065t}$ Divide both sides by P and reverse the equation.

$e^{0.065t} = 2$ Take the natural logarithm of both sides.

$\ln e^{0.065t} = \ln 2$

$0.065t = \ln 2$

$t = \dfrac{\ln 2}{0.065}$

$t \approx 10.66$ years

Matched Problem 4   How long will it take money to triple if it is invested at 5.5% compounded continuously?

EXPLORE & DISCUSS

2

You are considering three options for investing $10,000: at 7% compounded annually, at 6% compounded monthly, and at 5% compounded continuously.

(A) Which option would be the best for investing $10,000 for 8 years?

(B) How long would you need to invest your money for the third option to be the best?

Answers to Matched Problems

1. $146.93; $148.02; $149.18

2. $A = 5,000e^{0.0561t}$

3. 4.51 yr   **4.** 19.97 yr

t	$A(\$)$
0	5,000
1	5,289
2	5,594
3	5,916
4	6,258

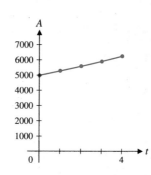

Exercise 5-1

A *Use a calculator to evaluate A to the nearest cent in Problems 1 and 2.*

1. $A = \$1,000e^{0.1t}$ for $t = 2, 5$, and 8

2. $A = \$5,000e^{0.08t}$ for $t = 1, 4$, and 10

3. If $6,000 is invested at 10% compounded continuously, graph the amount in the account relative to time for a period of 8 years.

4. If $4,000 is invested at 8% compounded continuously, graph the amount in the account relative to time for a period of 6 years.

B *In Problems 5–10, solve for t or r to two decimal places.*

5. $2 = e^{0.06t}$ **6.** $2 = e^{0.03t}$ **7.** $3 = e^{0.1r}$

8. $3 = e^{0.25t}$ **9.** $2 = e^{5r}$ **10.** $3 = e^{10r}$

C *In Problems 11 and 12, complete each table to five decimal places using a calculator.*

11.

n	$[1 + (1/n)]^n$
10	2.593 74
100	
1,000	
10,000	
100,000	
1,000,000	
10,000,000	
↓	↓
∞	$e = 2.718\ 281\ 828\ 459 \ldots$

12.

s	$(1 + s)^{1/s}$
0.01	2.704 81
−0.01	
0.001	
−0.001	
0.000 1	
−0.000 1	
0.000 01	
−0.000 01	
↓	↓
0	$e = 2.718\ 281\ 828\ 459 \ldots$

13. Use a calculator and a table of values to investigate
$$\lim_{n \to \infty} (1 + n)^{1/n}$$
Do you think this limit exists? If so, what do you think it is?

14. Use a calculator and a table of values to investigate
$$\lim_{s \to 0^+} \left(1 + \frac{1}{s}\right)^s$$
Do you think this limit exists? If so, what do you think it is?

15. It can be shown that the number *e* satisfies the inequality
$$\left(1 + \frac{1}{n}\right)^n < e < \left(1 + \frac{1}{n}\right)^{n+1} \qquad n \geq 1$$

Illustrate this graphically by graphing
$$y_1 = (1 + 1/n)^n$$
$$y_2 = 2.718\ 281\ 828 \approx e$$
$$y_3 = (1 + 1/n)^{n+1}$$
in the same viewing window for $1 \leq n \leq 20$.

16. It can be shown that

$$e^s = \lim_{n \to \infty} \left(1 + \frac{s}{n}\right)^n$$

for any real number s. Illustrate this graphically for $s = 2$ by graphing

$$y_1 = (1 + 2/n)^n$$
$$y_2 = 7.389\ 056\ 099 \approx e^2$$

in the same viewing window for $1 \le n \le 50$.

Applications

Business & Economics

17. *Continuous compound interest.* Recently, Provident Bank offered a 10-year CD that earns 5.51% compounded continuously.

(A) If $10,000 is invested in this CD, how much will it be worth in 10 years?

(B) How long will it take for the account to be worth $15,000?

18. *Continuous compound interest.* Provident Bank also offers a 3-year CD that earns 5.28% compounded continuously.

(A) If $10,000 is invested in this CD, how much will it be worth in 3 years?

(B) How long will it take for the account to be worth $11,000?

19. *Present value.* A note will pay $20,000 at maturity 10 years from now. How much should you be willing to pay for the note now if money is worth 5.2% compounded continuously?

20. *Present value.* A note will pay $50,000 at maturity 5 years from now. How much should you be willing to pay for the note now if money is worth 6.4% compounded continuously?

21. *Continuous compound interest.* An investor bought stock for $20,000. Five years later, the stock was sold for $30,000. If interest is compounded continuously, what annual nominal rate of interest did the original $20,000 investment earn?

22. *Continuous compound interest.* A family paid $40,000 cash for a house. Fifteen years later, they sold the house for $100,000. If interest is compounded continuously, what annual nominal rate of interest did the original $40,000 investment earn?

23. *Present value.* Solving $A = Pe^{rt}$ for P, we obtain

$$P = Ae^{-rt}$$

which is the present value of the amount A due in t years if money earns interest at an annual nominal rate r compounded continuously.

(A) Graph $P = 10,000e^{-0.08t}$, $0 \le t \le 50$.

(B) $\lim_{t \to \infty} 10,000e^{-0.08t} = ?$ [Guess, using part (A).]

[*Conclusion:* The longer the duration of time until the amount A is due, the smaller its present value, as we would expect.]

24. *Present value.* Referring to Problem 23, in how many years will the $10,000 have to be due in order for its present value to be $5,000?

25. *Doubling time.* How long will it take money to double if it is invested at 7% compounded continuously?

26. *Doubling time.* How long will it take money to double if it is invested at 5% compounded continuously?

27. *Doubling rate.* At what nominal rate compounded continuously must money be invested to double in 8 years?

28. *Doubling rate.* At what nominal rate compounded continuously must money be invested to double in 10 years?

29. *Growth time.* A man with $20,000 to invest decides to diversify his investments by placing $10,000 in an account that earns 7.2% compounded continuously and $10,000 in an account that earns 8.4% compounded annually. Use graphical approximation methods to determine how long it will take for his total investment in the two accounts to grow to $35,000.

30. *Growth time.* A woman invests $5,000 in an account that earns 8.8% compounded continuously and $7,000 in an account that earns 9.6% compounded annually. Use graphical approximation methods to determine how long it will take for her total investment in the two accounts to grow to $20,000.

31. *Doubling times*

(A) Show that the doubling time t (in years) at an annual rate r compounded continuously is given by

$$t = \frac{\ln 2}{r}$$

(B) Graph the doubling-time equation from part (A) for $0.02 \leq r \leq 0.30$. Are these restrictions on r reasonable? Explain.

(C) Determine the doubling times (in years, to two decimal places) for $r = 5\%, 10\%, 15\%, 20\%, 25\%$ and 30%.

32. *Doubling rates*

(A) Show that the rate r that doubles an investment at continuously compounded interest in t years is given by

$$r = \frac{\ln 2}{t}$$

(B) Graph the doubling-rate equation from part (A) for $1 \leq t \leq 20$. Are these restrictions on t reasonable? Explain.

(C) Determine the doubling rates for $t = 2, 4, 6, 8, 10,$ and 12 years.

Life Sciences

33. *Radioactive decay.* A mathematical model for the decay of radioactive substances is given by

$$Q = Q_0 e^{rt}$$

where

Q_0 = amount of the substance at time $t = 0$
r = continuous compound rate of decay
t = time in years
Q = amount of the substance at time t

If the continuous compound rate of decay of radium per year is $r = -0.000\ 433\ 2$, how long will it take a certain amount of radium to decay to half the original amount? (This period of time is the *half-life* of the substance.)

34. *Radioactive decay.* The continuous compound rate of decay of carbon-14 per year is $r = -0.000\ 123\ 8$. How long will it take a certain amount of carbon-14

to decay to half the original amount? (Use the radioactive decay model in Problem 33.)

35. *Radioactive decay.* A cesium isotope has a half-life of 30 years. What is the continuous compound rate of decay? (Use the radioactive decay model in Problem 33.)

36. *Radioactive decay.* A strontium isotope has a half-life of 90 years. What is the continuous compound rate of decay? (Use the radioactive decay model in Problem 33.)

Social Sciences

37. *World population.* A mathematical model for world population growth over short periods of time is given by

$$P = P_0 e^{rt}$$

where

P_0 = population at time $t = 0$
r = continuous compound rate of growth
t = time in years
P = population at time t

How long will it take the world population to double if it continues to grow at its current continuous compound rate of 1.3% per year?

38. *U.S. population.* How long will it take for the U.S. population to double if it continues to grow at a rate of 0.85% per year?

39. *Population growth.* Some underdeveloped nations have population doubling times of 50 years. At what continuous compound rate is the population growing? (Use the population growth model in Problem 37.)

40. *Population growth.* Some developed nations have population doubling times of 200 years. At what continuous compound rate is the population growing? (Use the population growth model in Problem 37.)

Section **5-2** | Exponential Functions and Their Derivatives

➤ Composite Functions
➤ The Derivative of e^x
➤ Graphing Techniques for Exponential Functions
➤ Application: Exponential Models

In this section we discuss the derivative of the exponential function $f(x) = e^x$ and other related exponential forms. Then we apply the tools of calculus developed in Chapters 3 and 4 to these new forms. To begin, we briefly review the concept of *composite functions*.

➤ **Composite Functions**

The function $m(x) = (x^2 + 4)^3$ is a combination of a quadratic function and a cubic function. To see this more clearly, let

$$y = f(u) = u^3 \quad \text{and} \quad u = g(x) = x^2 + 4$$

Then we can express y as a function of x as follows:

$$y = f(u) = f[g(x)] = [x^2 + 4]^3 = m(x)$$

The function m is said to be the *composite* of the two functions f and g. In general, we have the following:

DEFINITION Composite Functions

A function m is a **composite** of functions f and g if

$$m(x) = f[g(x)]$$

The domain of m is the set of all numbers x such that x is in the domain of g and $g(x)$ is in the domain of f.

EXAMPLE 1 **Composite Functions** Let $f(u) = e^u$ and $g(x) = -3x$. Find $f[g(x)]$ and $g[f(u)]$.

Solution
$$f[g(x)] = f(-3x) = e^{-3x}$$
$$g[f(u)] = g(e^u) = -3e^u$$

Matched Problem 1   Let $f(u) = 2u$ and $g(x) = e^x$. Find $f[g(x)]$ and $g[f(u)]$. ─────────────

EXAMPLE 2 **Composite Functions** Write each function as a composition of two simpler functions.

(A) $y = 100e^{0.04x}$

(B) $y = \sqrt{4 - x^2}$

Solution (A) Let
$$y = f(u) = 100e^u$$
$$u = g(x) = 0.04x$$

Check: $y = f[g(x)] = 100e^{g(x)} = 100e^{0.04x}$

(B) Let
$$y = f(u) = \sqrt{u}$$
$$u = g(x) = 4 - x^2$$

Check: $y = f[g(x)] = \sqrt{g(x)} = \sqrt{4 - x^2}$ ∎

Matched Problem 2   **Composite Functions** Write each function as a composition of two simpler functions.

(A) $y = 50e^{-2x}$ (B) $y = \sqrt[3]{1 + x^3}$

───────────────────────────────■

👁 **Insight**   There can be more than one way to express a function as a composition of simpler functions. Choosing $y = f(u) = 100u$ and $u = g(x) = e^{0.04x}$ in Example 2A produces the same result.

$$y = f[g(x)] = 100g(x) = 100e^{0.04x}$$

Since we will be using composition as a means to an end (finding a derivative), usually it will not matter what choices you make for the functions in the composition.   ●

> ### The Derivative of e^x

In the process of finding the derivative of e^x, we will use (without proof) the fact that

$$\lim_{h \to 0} \frac{e^h - 1}{h} = 1 \qquad\qquad (1)$$

EXPLORE & DISCUSS 1

Complete Table 1.

TABLE 1

h	-0.1	-0.01	-0.001	-0.0001	$\to 0^-$
$\dfrac{e^h - 1}{h}$					
h	0.1	0.01	0.001	0.0001	$\to 0^+$
$\dfrac{e^h - 1}{h}$					

Do your calculations make it reasonable to conclude that

$$\lim_{h \to 0} \frac{e^h - 1}{h} = 1?$$

Discuss.

We now apply the four-step process (Section 3-3) to the exponential function $f(x) = e^x$.

Step 1. Find $f(x + h)$.

$$f(x + h) = e^{x+h} = e^x e^h \quad \textit{See Section 2-2.}$$

Step 2. Find $f(x + h) - f(x)$.

$$f(x + h) - f(x) = e^x e^h - e^x \quad \textit{Factor out } e^x.$$
$$= e^x(e^h - 1)$$

Step 3. Find $\dfrac{f(x + h) - f(x)}{h}$.

$$\frac{f(x + h) - f(x)}{h} = \frac{e^x(e^h - 1)}{h} = e^x \left(\frac{e^h - 1}{h} \right)$$

Step 4. Find $f'(x) = \lim\limits_{h \to 0} \dfrac{f(x + h) - f(x)}{h}$.

$$\begin{aligned}
f'(x) &= \lim_{h \to 0} \frac{f(x + h) - f(x)}{h} \\
&= \lim_{h \to 0} e^x \left(\frac{e^h - 1}{h} \right) \\
&= e^x \lim_{h \to 0} \left(\frac{e^h - 1}{h} \right) \quad \text{Use the limit in (1).} \\
&= e^x \cdot 1 = e^x
\end{aligned}$$

Thus,

$$\frac{d}{dx} e^x = e^x \qquad \text{\textit{The derivative of the exponential}} \\ \text{\textit{function is the exponential function.}}$$

This new derivative formula can be combined with the rules of differentiation discussed in Chapter 3 to differentiate a variety of functions.

EXAMPLE 3   **Finding Derivatives** Find $f'(x)$ for

(A) $f(x) = (4x + 3e^x)^4$

(B) $f(x) = \dfrac{e^x}{x^3}$

Solution   (A) $f'(x) = \boxed{4(4x + 3e^x)^3 \dfrac{d}{dx}(4x + 3e^x)}$ *General power rule*

$$= 4(4x + 3e^x)^3(4 + 3e^x)$$
$$= (16 + 12e^x)(4x + 3e^x)^3$$

(B) $f'(x) = \boxed{\dfrac{x^3 \dfrac{d}{dx} e^x - e^x \dfrac{d}{dx} x^3}{(x^3)^2}}$ *Quotient rule*

$$= \frac{x^3 e^x - e^x 3x^2}{x^6}$$

$$= \frac{x^2 e^x (x - 3)}{x^6}$$

$$= \frac{e^x (x - 3)}{x^4}$$

Matched Problem 3   Find $f'(x)$ for

(A) $f(x) = (x^2 - 2e^x)^3$ (B) $f(x) = x^2 e^x$

Caution

$$\frac{d}{dx}e^x \neq xe^{x-1} \qquad \frac{d}{dx}e^x = e^x$$

The power rule cannot be used to differentiate the exponential function. The power rule applies to exponential forms x^n where the exponent is a constant and the base is a variable. In the exponential form e^x, the base is a constant and the exponent is a variable. ●

In Chapter 3, we used the chain rule to extend the power rule to the general power rule:

Power rule   General power rule

$$\frac{d}{dx}x^n = nx^{n-1} \qquad \frac{d}{dx}u^n = nu^{n-1}\frac{d}{dx}u, \quad \text{where } u = u(x)$$

The rule for the exponential function can be extended in a similar manner.

RESULT   **General Exponential Derivative Rule**
If $u = u(x)$ is a function of x, then

$$\frac{d}{dx}e^u = e^u\frac{d}{dx}u = e^{u(x)}u'(x)$$

EXAMPLE 4   **Finding Derivatives** Find $f'(x)$ for

(A) $f(x) = e^{x^2}$ (B) $f(x) = \sqrt{10 + 5e^{-2x}}$

Solution   (A) $f'(x) = \dfrac{d}{dx}e^{x^2} = e^{x^2}\dfrac{d}{dx}x^2 = e^{x^2}2x = 2xe^{x^2}$

(B) $f(x) = \sqrt{10 + 5e^{-2x}} = (10 + 5e^{-2x})^{1/2}$

$\qquad f'(x) = \dfrac{d}{dx}(10 + 5e^{-2x})^{1/2}$

$\qquad\qquad = \dfrac{1}{2}(10 + 5e^{-2x})^{-1/2}\dfrac{d}{dx}[10 + 5e^{-2x}]$

$\qquad\qquad = \dfrac{1}{2}(10 + 5e^{-2x})^{-1/2}\left[0 + 5e^{-2x}\dfrac{d}{dx}(-2x)\right]$

$\qquad\qquad = \dfrac{1}{2}(10 + 5e^{-2x})^{-1/2}5e^{-2x}(-2)$

$\qquad\qquad = -5e^{-2x}(10 + 5e^{-2x})^{-1/2}$ ∎

Matched Problem 4   Find $f'(x)$ for

(A) $f(x) = e^{-x^3}$ (B) $f(x) = \dfrac{e^{2x}}{1 + e^{2x}}$

➤ **Graphing Techniques**

The functions

$$f(x) = e^x \qquad \text{and} \qquad g(x) = e^{-x} = \frac{1}{e^x}$$

are continuous for $-\infty < x < \infty$ (Section 2-2). Now that we know how to differentiate these functions, we can use their first and second derivatives to provide more information about their graphs (Table 2).

TABLE 2

$f(x) = e^x > 0$	$g(x) = e^{-x} > 0$	$-\infty < x < \infty$
$f'(x) = e^x > 0$	$g'(x) = -e^{-x} < 0$	$-\infty < x < \infty$
$f''(x) = e^x > 0$	$g''(x) = e^{-x} > 0$	$-\infty < x < \infty$

From Table 2, we see that $f(x) = e^x$ is increasing and concave upward and $g(x) = e^{-x}$ is decreasing and concave upward.

EXPLORE & DISCUSS 2

Complete Tables 3 and 4 and estimate the limit of each function as $x \to \infty$ and as $x \to -\infty$.

TABLE 3

x	1	5	10	$\to \infty$
e^x				
e^{-x}				

TABLE 4

x	1	5	10	$\to \infty$
e^x				
e^{-x}				

Combining the information obtained from Tables 2–4, we graph $f(x) = e^x$ and $g(x) = e^{-x}$ in Figure 1.

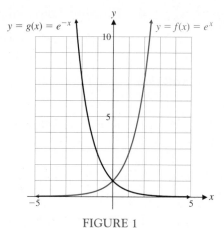

FIGURE 1

Insight Developing limit properties for exponential forms is time-consuming and, for our purposes, not really necessary. Tables like those in Explore–Discuss 1 and 2 will be sufficient to estimate the limits we will encounter. ●

EXAMPLE 5   **Graphing Strategy**   Analyze the function $f(x) = xe^x$ following the steps in the graphing strategy discussed in Section 4-3. State all the pertinent information and sketch the graph of f.

Solution   **Step 1.** Analyze $f(x)$: $f(x) = xe^x$.

   (A) Domain: All real numbers

   (B) y intercept: $f(0) = 0$

   x intercept: $xe^x = 0$ for $x = 0$ only, since $e^x > 0$ for all x (see Fig. 1).

(C)　Vertical asymptotes: None

Horizontal asymptotes: We use tables to determine the nature of the graph of f as $x \to \infty$ and $x \to -\infty$:

x	1	5	10	$\to \infty$
$f(x)$	2.72	742.07	220,264.66	$\to \infty$

x	-1	-5	-10	$\to -\infty$
$f(x)$	-0.37	-0.03	$-0.000\,45$	$\to 0$

Step 2. *Analyze $f'(x)$:*

$$f'(x) = \boxed{x\frac{d}{dx}e^x + e^x\frac{d}{dx}x}$$

$$= xe^x + e^x = e^x(x + 1)$$

Critical value for $f(x)$:　-1

Partition number for $f'(x)$:　-1

Sign chart for $f'(x)$:

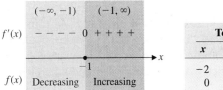

Test Numbers	
x	$f'(x)$
-2	$-e^{-2}$　$(-)$
0	1　$(+)$

Thus, $f(x)$ decreases on $(-\infty, -1)$, has a local minimum at $x = -1$, and increases on $(-1, \infty)$. (Since $e^x > 0$ for all x, we do not have to evaluate e^{-2} to conclude that $-e^{-2} < 0$ when using the test number -2.)

Step 3. *Analyze $f''(x)$:*

$$f''(x) = \boxed{e^x\frac{d}{dx}(x + 1) + (x + 1)\frac{d}{dx}e^x}$$

$$= e^x + (x + 1)e^x = e^x(x + 2)$$

Sign chart for $f''(x)$ (partition number is -2):

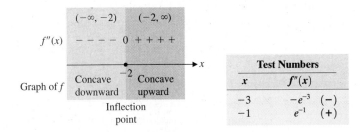

Test Numbers	
x	$f''(x)$
-3	$-e^{-3}$　$(-)$
-1	e^{-1}　$(+)$

Thus, the graph of f is concave downward on $(-\infty, -2)$, has an inflection point at $x = -2$, and is concave upward on $(-2, \infty)$.

Step 4. *Sketch the graph of f using the information from steps 1 to 3:*

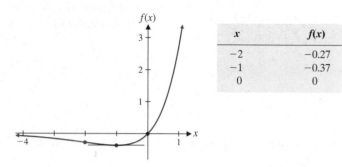

x	f(x)
−2	−0.27
−1	−0.37
0	0

Matched Problem 5   Analyze the function $f(x) = xe^{-0.5x}$. State all the pertinent information and sketch the graph of f.

◉ *Insight*   Remember, if p is any real number, then $e^p > 0$. The sign of the exponent p does not matter. This is a very useful fact when working with sign charts involving exponential forms.   ●

➤ Application: Exponential Models

EXAMPLE 6   **Price–Demand Model** An Internet store sells blankets made of the finest Australian wool. If the store sells x blankets at a price of $\$p$ per blanket, then the price–demand equation is $p = 350e^{-0.001x}$. Find the rate of change of price with respect to demand when the demand is 800 blankets and interpret.

Solution

$$\frac{dp}{dx} = \boxed{\frac{d}{dx}350e^{-0.001x}}$$

$$= 350e^{-0.001x}(-0.001) = -0.35e^{-0.001x}$$

If $x = 800$, then

$$\frac{dp}{dx} = -0.35e^{-0.8} = -0.157 \quad \text{or} \quad -\$0.16$$

When the demand is 800 blankets, the price is decreasing about $\$0.16$ per blanket.   ■

Matched Problem 6   The store in Example 6 also sells a reversible fleece blanket. If the price–demand equation for reversible fleece blankets is $p = 200e^{-0.002x}$, find the rate of change of price with respect to demand when the demand is 400 blankets and interpret.

EXAMPLE 7   **Maximizing Revenue** Refer to Example 6. How much should the store charge for Australian wool blankets in order to maximize revenue?

Solution

$$R(x) = xp = 350xe^{-0.001x}$$

Since $R(x)$ is defined for any nonnegative value of x, we have to solve the following:

$$\text{Maximize } R(x) = 350xe^{-0.001x} \quad \text{for} \quad x \geq 0$$

$$R'(x) = 350x\frac{d}{dx}e^{-0.001x} + e^{-0.001x}\frac{d}{dx}(350x)$$

$$= 350xe^{-0.001x}(-0.001) + e^{-0.001x}(350)$$

$$= e^{-0.001x}(350 - 0.35x) = 0 \qquad\qquad e^p > 0 \text{ for all}$$

$$350 - 0.35x = 0 \qquad\qquad\qquad\qquad \text{real numbers } p.$$

$$350 = 0.35x$$

$$x = \frac{350}{0.35}$$

$$= 1,000 \qquad\qquad \text{Critical value}$$

$$R''(x) = e^{-0.001x}\frac{d}{dx}(350 - 0.35x) + (350 - 0.35x)\frac{d}{dx}e^{-0.001x}$$

$$= e^{-0.001x}(-0.35) + (350 - 0.35x)e^{-0.001x}(-0.001)$$

$$= e^{-0.001x}(-0.35 - 0.35 + 0.00035x)$$

$$= e^{-0.001x}(0.00035x - 0.7)$$

$$R''(1,000) = e^{-1}(-0.35) < 0$$

Since $x = 1,000$ is the only critical value for R and since the graph of R is concave downward at $x = 1,000$, $R(1,000)$ is the absolute maximum value of the revenue. The corresponding price is

$$p = 350e^{-0.001(1,000)} = 350e^{-1} = 128.757 \quad \text{or} \quad \$128.76$$

The store should sell the blankets for $128.76 in order to maximize the revenue.   ■

Matched Problem 7

Refer to Matched Problem 6. How much should the store charge for reversible fleece blankets in order to maximize revenue?   ——————————■

Answers to Matched Problems

1. $f[g(x)] = 2e^x, \quad g[f(u)] = e^{2u}$

2. (A) $f(u) = 50e^u, \quad u = -2x$ (B) $f(u) = \sqrt[3]{u}, \quad u = 1 + x^3$
[*Note:* There are other correct answers.]

3. (A) $6(x - e^x)(x^2 - 2e^x)$ (B) $xe^x(x + 2)$ **4.** (A) $-3x^2e^{-x^3}$ (B) $\dfrac{2e^{2x}}{(1 + e^{2x})^2}$

5. Domain: $(-\infty, \infty)$
  y intercept: $f(0) = 0$
  x intercept: $x = 0$
  Horizontal asymptote: $y = 0$ (the x axis)
  Increasing on $(-\infty, 2)$
  Decreasing on $(2, \infty)$
  Local maximum at $x = 2$
  Concave downward on $(-\infty, 4)$
  Concave upward on $(4, \infty)$
  Inflection point at $x = 4$

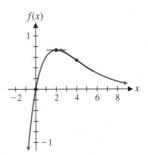

6. The price is decreasing at the rate of $0.18 per blanket.

7. Revenue is maximized when the price is $73.58.

Exercise 5-2

For many of the problems in this exercise set, the answers in the back of the book include both an unsimplified form and a simplified form. When checking your work, first check that you applied the rules correctly, and then check that you performed the algebraic simplification correctly.

A *In Problems 1–4, find f[g(x)].*

1. $f(u) = u^3$; $g(x) = 3x^2 + 2$

2. $f(u) = u^4$; $g(x) = 1 - 4x^3$

3. $f(u) = e^u$; $g(x) = -x^2$

4. $g(u) = e^u$; $g(x) = 3x^3$

In Problems 5–9, write each composite function in the form y = f(u) and u = g(x).

5. $y = (3x^2 - x + 5)^4$

6. $y = (2x^3 + x + 3)^5$

7. $y = e^{1+x+x^2}$

8. $y = e^{x^4+2x^2+5}$

In Problems 9–14, find the indicated derivative and simplify.

9. $f'(x)$ for $f(x) = 4x^3 + 5e^x$

10. $g'(x)$ for $g(x) = 3e^x - 5x^4$

11. $\dfrac{dy}{dx}$ for $y = 4e^x - 3e^e$

12. $\dfrac{dy}{dx}$ for $y = -7e^x + 9e^e$

13. y' for $y = -3e^{-x} + 2e^x$

14. y' for $y = 5e^{-x} - 6e^x$

B *In Problems 15–35, find f'(x) and simplify.*

15. $f(x) = x^3 e^x$ **16.** $f(x) = x^4 e^x$

17. $f(x) = 3e^{2x}$ **18.** $f(x) = 2e^{3x}$

19. $f(x) = 5e^{-3x}$ **20.** $f(x) = 6e^{-4x}$

21. $f(x) = 200e^{-0.5x}$ **22.** $f(x) = 300e^{0.1x}$

23. $f(x) = xe^{-2x}$ **24.** $f(x) = xe^{-4x}$

25. $f(x) = \dfrac{e^x}{x^2 + 9}$ **26.** $f(x) = \dfrac{e^x}{x^2 + 4}$

27. $f(x) = e^{3x^2-2x}$ **28.** $f(x) = e^{x^3-3x^2+1}$

29. $f(x) = (e^{2x} - 1)^4$ **30.** $f(x) = (e^x + 3)^5$

31. $f(x) = \dfrac{x^2 + 1}{e^x}$ **32.** $f(x) = \dfrac{x + 1}{e^x}$

33. $f(x) = (x^2 + 1)e^{-x}$ **34.** $f(x) = (1 - x)e^{2x}$

35. $f(x) = xe^x - e^{2x}$

36. $f(x) = x^2 e^x - 2xe^x + 2e^x$

37. A student claims that the tangent line to the graph of $f(x) = e^x$ at $x = 3$ passes through the point $(2, 0)$ (see the figure). Is she correct? Will the tangent line at $x = 4$ pass through $(3, 0)$? Explain.

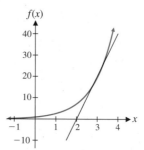

$f(x)$

Figure for 37

38. Does the tangent line to the graph of $f(x) = e^x$ at $x = 1$ pass through the origin? Are there any other tangent lines to the graph of f that pass through the origin? Explain.

C *In Problems 39–42, find the indicated extremum of each function for x > 0.*

39. Absolute minimum value of $f(x) = \dfrac{e^x}{x^2}$

40. Absolute maximum value of $f(x) = \dfrac{x^4}{e^x}$

41. Absolute maximum value of $f(x) = \dfrac{x^3}{e^x}$

42. Absolute minimum value of $f(x) = \dfrac{e^x}{x}$

In Problems 43–50, apply the graphing strategy discussed in Section 4-3 to f, summarize the pertinent information, and sketch the graph.

43. $f(x) = 1 - e^{-x}$ **44.** $f(x) = 2 - 3e^{-2x}$

45. $f(x) = 5 + 5e^{-0.1x}$ **46.** $f(x) = 3 + 7e^{-0.2x}$

47. $f(x) = 5xe^{-0.2x}$ **48.** $f(x) = 10xe^{-0.1x}$

49. $f(x) = (3 - x)e^x$ **50.** $f(x) = (x - 2)e^x$

51. $f(x) = e^{-0.5x^2}$ **52.** $f(x) = e^{-2x^2}$

Problems 53 and 54 require the use of a graphing utility. Approximate the critical values of f(x) to two decimal places and find the intervals where f(x) is increasing, the intervals where f(x) is decreasing, and the local extrema.

53. $f(x) = e^x - 2x^2$

54. $f(x) = e^x + x^2$

In Problems 55 and 56, use graphical approximation methods to find the points of intersection of f(x) and g(x) (to two decimal places).

55. $f(x) = e^x$; $g(x) = x^4$

[Note that there are three points of intersection and that e^x is greater than x^4 for large values of x.]

56. $f(x) = e^x$; $g(x) = x^5$

[Note that there are two points of intersection and that e^x is greater than x^5 for large values of x.]

Applications

Business & Economics

57. *Maximizing revenue.* A cosmetic company is planning the introduction and promotion of a new lipstick line. The marketing research department, after test marketing the new line in a carefully selected large city, found that the demand in that city is given approximately by

$$p = 10e^{-x} \qquad 0 \le x \le 2$$

where x thousand lipsticks were sold per week at a price of $\$p$ each.

(A) Find the rate of change of price with respect to demand when the weekly demand is 800 lipsticks and interpret.

(B) At what price will the weekly revenue $R(x) = xp$ be maximum? What is the maximum weekly revenue in the test city?

(C) Graph R for $0 \le x \le 2$.

58. *Maximizing revenue.* Repeat Problem 57 using the demand equation $p = 12e^{-x}, 0 \le x \le 2$.

59. *Maximum revenue.* Suppose the price–demand equation for x units of a commodity is determined from empirical data to be

$$p = 100e^{-0.05x}$$

where x units are sold per day at a price of $\$p$ each. Find the production level and price that maximize revenue. What is the maximum revenue?

60. *Maximum revenue.* Repeat Problem 59 using the price–demand equation

$$p = 10e^{-0.04x}$$

61. *Maximum profit.* Refer to Problem 59. If the daily fixed cost is $\$400$ and the cost per unit is $\$6$, use approximation techniques to find the production level and the price that maximize profit. What is the maximum profit? [*Hint:* Graph $y = P(x)$ and $y = P'(x)$ in the same viewing window.]

62. *Maximum profit.* Refer to Problem 60. If the daily fixed cost is $\$30$ and the cost per unit is $\$0.70$, use approximation techniques to find the production level and the price that maximize profit. What is the maximum profit? [*Hint:* Graph $y = P(x)$ and $y = P'(x)$ in the same viewing window.]

63. *Salvage value.* The salvage value S (in dollars) of a company airplane after t years is estimated to be given by

$$S(t) = 300,000e^{-0.1t}$$

What is the rate of depreciation (in dollars per year) after 1 year? 5 years? 10 years?

64. *Resale value.* The resale value R (in dollars) of a company car after t years is estimated to be given by

$$R(t) = 20,000e^{-0.15t}$$

What is the rate of depreciation (in dollars per year) after 1 year? 2 years? 3 years?

65. *Promotion and maximum profit.* A recording company has produced a new compact disk featuring a very popular recording group. Before launching a national sales campaign, the marketing research department chose to test market the CD in a bellwether city. Their interest is in determining the length of a sales campaign that will maximize total profits. From empirical data, the research department estimates that the proportion of a target group of 50,000 persons buying the CD after t days of television promotion is given by $1 - e^{-0.03t}$. If $\$4$ is received for each CD sold, the total revenue after t days of promotion will be approximated by

$$R(t) = (4)(50,000)(1 - e^{-0.03t}) \qquad t \ge 0$$

Television promotion costs are

$$C(t) = 4,000 + 3,000t \qquad t \ge 0$$

(A) How many days of television promotion should be used to maximize total profit? What is the maximum total profit? What percentage of the target market will have purchased the CD when the maximum profit is reached?

(B) Graph the profit function.

66. *Promotion and maximum profit.* Repeat Problem 65 using the revenue equation

$$R(t) = (3)(60,000)(1 - e^{-0.04t})$$

Life Sciences

67. *Drug concentration.* The concentration of a drug in the bloodstream t hours after injection is given approximately by

$$C(t) = 4.35e^{-t} \qquad 0 \le t \le 5$$

where $C(t)$ is concentration in milligrams per milliliter.

(A) What is the rate of change of concentration after 1 hour? After 4 hours?

(B) Graph C.

68. *Water pollution.* The use of iodine crystals is a popular way of making small quantities of nonpotable water safe to drink. Crystals placed in a 1-ounce bottle of water will dissolve until the solution is saturated. After saturation, half of this solution is poured into a quart container of non-potable water, and after about an hour, the water is usually safe to drink. The half-empty 1-ounce bottle is then refilled to be used again in the same way. Suppose that the concentration of iodine in the 1-ounce bottle t minutes after the crystals are introduced can be approximated by

$$C(t) = 250(1 - e^{-t}) \qquad t \ge 0$$

where $C(t)$ is the concentration of iodine in micro-grams per milliliter.

(A) What is the rate of change of the concentration after 1 minute? After 4 minutes?

(B) Graph C for $0 \le t \le 5$.

Social Sciences

69. *Sociology.* Daniel Lowenthal, a sociologist at Columbia University, made a 5-year study on the sale of popular records relative to their position in the top 20. He found that the average number of sales $N(n)$ of the nth-ranking record was given approximately by

$$N(n) = N_1 e^{-0.09(n-1)} \qquad 1 \le n \le 20$$

where N_1 was the number of sales of the top record on the list at a given time. Graph N for $N_1 = 1,000,000$ records.

70. *Political science.* Thomas W. Casstevens, a political scientist at Oakland University, has studied legislative turnover. He (with others) found that the number $N(t)$ of continuously serving members of an elected legislative body remaining t years after an election is given approximately by a function of the form

$$N(t) = N_0 e^{-ct}$$

In particular, for the 1965 election for the U.S. House of Representatives, it was found that

$$N(t) = 434e^{-0.0866t}$$

What is the rate of change after 2 years? After 10 years?

Section **5-3** | Logarithmic Functions and Their Derivatives

➤ Derivative Formulas for $\ln x$
➤ Other Logarithmic and Exponential Functions
➤ Graphing Techniques
➤ Applications: Logarithmic Models

Now that we know how to differentiate exponential functions, we turn our attention to logarithmic functions. A review of Section 2-3 would prove to be helpful at this point. We summarize some of the most important facts in the following box.

SUMMARY   Recall from Section 2-3 that the inverse of an exponential function is called a **logarithmic function.** For $b > 0$ and $b \ne 1$,

Logarithmic form		Exponential form
$y = \log_b x$	is equivalent to	$x = b^y$
Domain: $(0, \infty)$		Domain: $(-\infty, \infty)$
Range: $(-\infty, \infty)$		Range: $(0, \infty)$

The graphs of $y = \log_b x$ and $y = b^x$ are symmetric with respect to the line $y = x$. (See Figure 1.)

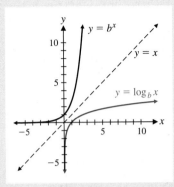

FIGURE 1

Of all the possible bases for logarithmic functions, the two most widely used are

$$\log x = \log_{10} x \quad \textit{Common logarithm (base 10)}$$
$$\ln x = \log_e x \quad \textit{Natural logarithm (base e)}$$

➤ Derivative Formulas for ln x

We are now ready to use the definition of derivative and the four-step process discussed in Section 3-3 to find a formula for the derivative of $\ln x$. Later we will extend this formula to include $\log_b x$ for any base b.

Let $f(x) = \ln x, x > 0$.

Step 1. Find $f(x + h)$.

$$f(x + h) = \ln(x + h) \quad \textit{ln(x + h) cannot be simplified.}$$

Step 2. Find $f(x + h) - f(x)$.

$$f(x + h) - f(x) = \ln(x + h) - \ln x \quad \textit{Use ln A} - \textit{ln B} = \textit{ln} \dfrac{A}{B}.$$
$$= \ln\frac{x + h}{x}$$

Step 3. Find $\dfrac{f(x + h) - f(x)}{h}$.

$$\frac{f(x + h) - f(x)}{h} = \frac{\ln(x + h) - \ln x}{h}$$
$$= \frac{1}{h}\ln\frac{x + h}{x} \quad \textit{Multiply by 1 = x/x to change form.}$$
$$= \frac{x}{x} \cdot \frac{1}{h}\ln\frac{x + h}{x}$$
$$= \frac{1}{x}\left[\frac{x}{h}\ln\left(1 + \frac{h}{x}\right)\right] \quad \textit{Use p ln A = ln A^p.}$$
$$= \frac{1}{x}\ln\left(1 + \frac{h}{x}\right)^{x/h}$$

Step 4. Find $f'(x) = \lim\limits_{h \to 0} \dfrac{f(x + h) - f(x)}{h}$.

$$f'(x) = \lim_{h \to 0} \frac{f(x + h) - f(x)}{h}$$

$$= \lim_{h \to 0} \left[\frac{1}{x} \ln \left(1 + \frac{h}{x} \right)^{x/h} \right] \qquad \text{Let } s = h/x. \text{ Note that } h \to 0 \text{ implies } s \to 0.$$

$$= \frac{1}{x} \lim_{s \to 0} \left[\ln(1 + s)^{1/s} \right] \qquad \text{Use the new limit property given in the footnote below.*}$$

$$= \frac{1}{x} \ln \left[\lim_{s \to 0} (1 + s)^{1/s} \right] \qquad \text{Use the definition of } e.$$

$$= \frac{1}{x} \ln e \qquad \ln e = \log_e e = 1$$

$$= \frac{1}{x}$$

Thus,

$$\frac{d}{dx} \ln x = \frac{1}{x}$$

◉ **Insight**　In the derivation of the derivative of $\ln x$, we used the following properties of logarithms:

$$\ln \frac{A}{B} = \ln A - \ln B \qquad \ln A^p = p \ln A$$

We also noted that there is no property that simplifies $\ln(A + B)$. See Theorem 1 in Section 2-3 for a list of properties of logarithms. ●

EXAMPLE 1　**Finding Derivatives**　Find the indicated derivatives:

(A) $f'(x)$ for $f(x) = (\ln x)^4$

(B) $\dfrac{dy}{dx}$ for $y = x^2 \ln x$

Solution　(A) $f'(x) = 4(\ln x)^3 \dfrac{d}{dx} \ln x$　General power rule

$$= 4(\ln x)^3 \left(\frac{1}{x} \right) = \frac{4(\ln x)^3}{x}$$

(B) $\dfrac{dy}{dx} = x^2 \dfrac{d}{dx}(\ln x) + (\ln x) \dfrac{d}{dx} x^2$　Product rule

$$= x^2 \left(\frac{1}{x} \right) + (\ln x)2x = x + 2x \ln x$$

Matched Problem 1　Find the indicated derivatives:

(A) $g'(x)$ for $g(x) = \dfrac{\ln x}{x^2}$　　　　(B) $\dfrac{dw}{dx}$ for $w = \sqrt{\ln x}$

---

* The following new limit property is used: If $\lim_{x \to c} f(x)$ exists and is positive, then $\lim_{x \to c}[\ln f(x)] = \ln[\lim_{x \to c} f(x)]$.

⊙ *Insight*   Use parentheses to avoid ambiguous expressions involving ln x. What is the correct interpretation for the product ln $x \cdot 2x$ (see Example 2B)?

$$\ln x \cdot 2x \overset{?}{=} \begin{cases} 2x \ln x & (1) \\ \ln(2x^2) & (2) \end{cases}$$

Expression (1) is the correct interpretation. Write the original product as $\ln(x \cdot 2x)$ if (2) is the intended interpretation.

What is the correct interpretation for the sum

$$\ln x + x^2 \overset{?}{=} \begin{cases} (\ln x) + x^2 & (3) \\ \ln(x + x^2) & (4) \end{cases}$$

Expression (3) is the correct interpretation. Parentheses must be used if (4) is the intended interpretation.   ●

In Section 5-2, we extended the rule for the derivative of e^x to a rule for $e^{f(x)}$. We now do the same for ln x.

RESULT   General Logarithmic Derivative Rule

If $u = u(x)$ is a function of x, then

$$\frac{d}{dx}\ln u = \frac{1}{u}\frac{d}{dx}u = \frac{1}{u(x)}u'(x) = \frac{u'(x)}{u(x)}$$

EXAMPLE 2   **Finding Derivatives**   Find the indicated derivatives:

(A) $g'(x)$ for $g(x) = \ln(1 + x^2)$

(B) y' for $y = \ln x^4$

Solution   (A) $g'(x) = \dfrac{1}{1 + x^2}\dfrac{d}{dx}(1 + x^2)$ *General logarithmic rule*

$$= \frac{1}{1 + x^2}2x = \frac{2x}{1 + x^2}$$

(B) $y' = \dfrac{1}{x^4}\dfrac{d}{dx}x^4$ *General logarithmic rule*

$$= \frac{1}{x^4}4x^3 = \frac{4x^3}{x^4} = \frac{4}{x}$$ ■

⊙ *Insight*   In Chapter 3, we found that sometimes it is easier to simplify a function first and then find the derivative. In Example 2B, we can simplify first as follows:

$$y = \ln x^4 = 4 \ln x \quad \text{\textit{Property of logarithms}}$$
$$y' = \frac{d}{dx}(4 \ln x) = 4\frac{1}{x} = \frac{4}{x}$$ ●

Matched Problem 2   Find the indicated derivatives:

(A) $g'(x)$ for $g(x) = \ln(1 + e^x)$

(B) y' for $y = \ln x^5$

➤ Other Logarithmic and Exponential Functions

In most applications involving logarithmic or exponential functions, the number e is the preferred base. However, there are situations where it is convenient to use a base other than e. Derivatives of $y = \log_b x$ and $y = b^x$ can be obtained by expressing these functions in terms of the natural logarithmic and exponential functions.

We begin by finding a relationship between $\log_b x$ and $\ln x$ for any base $b, b > 0$ and $b \neq 1$. Some of you may prefer to remember the process, and others the formula.

$$y = \log_b x \qquad \text{Change to exponential form.}$$
$$b^y = x \qquad \text{Take the natural logarithm of both sides.}$$
$$\ln b^y = \ln x \qquad \text{Recall that } \ln b^y = y \ln b.$$
$$y \ln b = \ln x \qquad \text{Solve for } y.$$
$$y = \frac{1}{\ln b} \ln x$$

Thus,

$$\log_b x = \frac{1}{\ln b} \ln x \quad \text{Change-of-base formula for logarithms*} \qquad (5)$$

Differentiating both sides of equation (5), we have

$$\frac{d}{dx} \log_b x = \frac{1}{\ln b} \frac{d}{dx} \ln x = \frac{1}{\ln b}\left(\frac{1}{x}\right)$$

(A) The graphs of $f(x) = \log_2 x$ and $g(x) = \log_4 x$ are shown in Figure 2. Which graph belongs to which function?

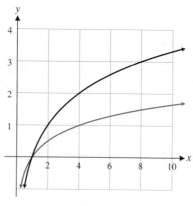

FIGURE 2

(B) Sketch graphs of $f'(x)$ and $g'(x)$.

(C) The function $f(x)$ is related to $g(x)$ in the same way that $f'(x)$ is related to $g'(x)$. What is that relationship?

---

* Equation (5) is a special case of the **general change-of-base formula** for logarithms (which can be derived in the same way): $\log_b x = (\log_a x)/(\log_a b)$.

EXAMPLE 3 **Differentiating Logarithmic Functions** Find $f'(x)$ for

(A) $f(x) = \log_2 x$

(B) $f(x) = \log(1 + x^3)$

Solution (A) $f(x) = \log_2 x = \dfrac{1}{\ln 2} \ln x$ *Using equation (5)*

$$f'(x) = \frac{1}{\ln 2}\left(\frac{1}{x}\right)$$

(B) $f(x) = \log(1 + x^3)$ *Recall that log $r = \log_{10} r$.*

$$= \frac{1}{\ln 10} \ln(1 + x^3)$$ *Using equation (5)*

$$f'(x) = \frac{1}{\ln 10}\left(\frac{1}{1 + x^3} 3x^2\right) = \frac{1}{\ln 10}\left(\frac{3x^2}{1 + x^3}\right)$$ ∎

Matched Problem 3 Find $f'(x)$ for

(A) $f(x) = \log x$ (B) $f(x) = \log_3(x + x^2)$

Now we want to find a relationship between b^x and e^x for any base $b, b > 0$ and $b \neq 1$.

$$y = b^x$$ *Take the natural logarithm of both sides.*

$$\ln y = \ln b^x$$

$$= x \ln b$$ *If ln $A = B$, then $A = e^B$.*

$$y = e^{x \ln b}$$

Thus,

$$b^x = e^{x \ln b}$$ *Change-of-base formula for exponential functions*   (6)

Differentiating both sides of equation (7), we have

$$\frac{d}{dx} b^x = e^{x \ln b} \ln b = b^x \ln b$$

EXAMPLE 4 **Differentiating Exponential Functions** Find $f'(x)$ for

(A) $f(x) = 2^x$ (B) $f(x) = 10^{x^5 + x}$

Solution (A) $f(x) = 2^x = e^{x \ln 2}$ *Using equation (6)*

$f'(x) = e^{x \ln 2} \ln 2 = 2^x \ln 2$

(B) $f(x) = 10^{x^5 + x} = e^{(x^5 + x) \ln 10}$ *Using equation (6)*

$f'(x) = e^{(x^5 + x) \ln 10}(5x^4 + 1) \ln 10$

$= 10^{x^5 + x}(5x^4 + 1) \ln 10$ ∎

Matched Problem 4 Find $f'(x)$ for

(A) $f(x) = 5^x$

(B) $f(x) = 4^{x^2 + 3x}$

👁 *Insight*   Using exponential regression on most graphing utilities produces a function of the form $y = a \cdot b^x$. Formula (6) enables you to change the base b (chosen by the graphing utility) to the more familiar base e:

$$y = a \cdot b^x = a \cdot e^{x \ln b}$$

➤ Graphing Techniques

Now that we can differentiate logarithmic functions, we can use our graphing tools to sketch their graphs.

EXAMPLE 5   **Graphing Strategy**   Let $f(x) = x^2 \ln x - 0.5x^2$. Analyze this function following the steps in the graphing strategy (Section 4-3). State all the pertinent information and sketch the graph of f.

Solution   **Step 1.** *Analyze* $f(x)$: $f(x) = x^2 \ln x - 0.5x^2 = x^2(\ln x - 0.5)$.

(A) Domain: $(0, \infty)$

(B) y intercept: None [$f(0)$ is not defined.]

x intercept: Solve $x^2(\ln x - 0.5) = 0$

$\ln x - 0.5 = 0$ or $x^2 = 0$ Discard since 0 is not in the domain of f.

$\ln x = 0.5$ In $x = a$ if and only if $x = e^a$.

$x = e^{0.5}$ x intercept

(C) Asymptotes: None. The following tables suggest the nature of the graph as $x \to 0^+$ and as $x \to \infty$.

x	0.1	0.01	0.001	$\to 0^+$
$f(x)$	-0.0280	-0.00051	-0.00007	$\to 0$

x	10	100	1,000	$\to \infty$
$f(x)$	180	41,000	6,400,000	$\to \infty$

Step 2. *Analyze* $f'(x)$:

$$f'(x) = x^2 \frac{d}{dx} \ln x + (\ln x) \frac{d}{dx} x^2 - 0.5 \frac{d}{dx} x^2$$

$$= x^2 \frac{1}{x} + (\ln x) 2x - 0.5(2x)$$

$$= x + 2x \ln x - x = 2x \ln x$$

Critical value for $f(x)$: 1

Partition number for $f'(x)$: 1

Sign chart for $f'(x)$:

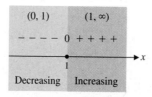

	Test Numbers	
x	$f'(x)$	
0.5	-0.2983	$(-)$
2	0.7726	$(+)$

The function $f(x)$ decreases on $(0, 1)$, has a local minimum at $x = 1$, and increases on $(1, \infty)$.

Step 3. *Analyze $f''(x)$:*

$$f''(x) \boxed{= 2x \frac{d}{dx}(\ln x) + (\ln x) \frac{d}{dx}(2x)}$$

$$= 2x \frac{1}{x} + (\ln x) 2 = 2 + 2 \ln x = 0$$

$$2 \ln x = -2$$

$$\ln x = -1$$

$$x = e^{-1} \approx 0.3679$$

Sign chart for $f'(x)$ (partition number is e^{-1}):

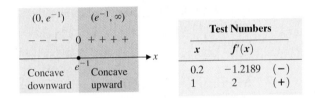

	Test Numbers	
x	$f'(x)$	
0.2	-1.2189	$(-)$
1	2	$(+)$

The graph of $f(x)$ is concave downward on $(0, e^{-1})$, has an inflection point at $x = e^{-1}$, and is concave upward on (e^{-1}, ∞).

Step 4. *Sketch the graph of f using the information from steps 1 to 3:*

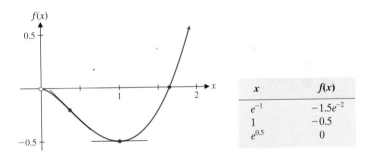

x	$f(x)$
e^{-1}	$-1.5e^{-2}$
1	-0.5
$e^{0.5}$	0

Matched Problem 5   Analyze the function $f(x) = x \ln x$. State all pertinent information and sketch the graph of f.

➤ Applications: Logarithmic Models

EXAMPLE 6   **Cable TV Subscribers** A statistician used data from the U.S. census to construct the following model:

$$S(t) = 21 \ln t + 2$$

where $S(t)$ is the number of cable TV subscribers (in millions) in year t ($t = 0$ corresponds to 1980). Use this model to estimate the number of cable TV subscribers in 2010 and the rate of change of the number of subscribers in 2010 (round both to the nearest tenth of a million). Interpret these results.

Solution   Since 2010 corresponds to $t = 30$, we must find $S(30)$ and $S'(30)$.

$$S(30) = 21 \ln 30 + 2 = 73.4 \text{ million}$$

$$S'(t) = 21 \frac{1}{t} = \frac{21}{t}$$

$$S'(30) = \frac{21}{30} = 0.7 \text{ million}$$

In 2010 there will be approximately 73.4 million subscribers and this number is growing at the rate of 0.7 million per year.   ∎

Matched Problem 6   Use the following model for newspaper circulation:

$$C(t) = 83 - 9 \ln t$$

where $C(t)$ is newspaper circulation (in millions) in year t ($t = 0$ corresponds to 1980). Use this model to estimate the circulation and the rate of change circulation in 2010 (round both to the nearest tenth of a million). Interpret these results.

─────────────────────────────── ∎

EXAMPLE 7   **Maximizing Profit**   The market research department of a chain of pet stores test marketed their aquarium pumps (as well as other items) in several of their stores in a test city. They found that the weekly demand for aquarium pumps is given approximately by

$$p = 12 - 2 \ln x \qquad 0 < x < 90$$

where x is the number of pumps sold each week and $\$p$ is the price of one pump. If each pump costs the chain $3, how should it be priced in order to maximize the weekly profit?

Solution   Although we want to find the price that maximizes the weekly profit, it will be easier first to find the number of pumps that will maximize the weekly profit. The revenue equation is

$$R(x) = xp = 12x - 2x \ln x$$

The cost equation is

$$C(x) = 3x$$

and the profit equation is

$$P(x) = R(x) - C(x)$$
$$= 12x - 2x \ln x - 3x$$
$$= 9x - 2x \ln x$$

Thus, we must solve the following:

$$\text{Maximize} \quad P(x) = 9x - 2x \ln x \qquad 0 < x < 90$$

$$P'(x) = 9 - 2x \left(\frac{1}{x} \right) - 2 \ln x$$

$$= 7 - 2 \ln x = 0$$

$$2 \ln x = 7$$

$$\ln x = 3.5$$

$$x = e^{3.5}$$

$$P''(x) = -2 \left(\frac{1}{x} \right) = -\frac{2}{x}$$

Since $x = e^{3.5}$ is the only critical value and $P''(e^{3.5}) < 0$, the maximum weekly profit occurs when $x = e^{3.5} \approx 33$ and $p = 12 - 2 \ln e^{3.5} = \$5$. ■

Matched Problem 7   Repeat Example 7 if each pump costs the chain $3.50. ──────── ■

Answers to Matched Problems

1. (A) $\dfrac{1 - 2 \ln x}{x^3}$ (B) $\dfrac{1}{2x\sqrt{\ln x}}$

2. (A) $\dfrac{e^x}{1 + e^x}$ (B) $\dfrac{5}{x}$

3. (A) $\dfrac{1}{\ln 10}\left(\dfrac{1}{x}\right)$ (B) $\dfrac{1}{\ln 3}\left(\dfrac{1 + 2x}{x + x^2}\right)$

4. (A) $5^x \ln 5$ (B) $4^{x^2+3x}(2x + 3) \ln 4$

5. Domain: $(0, \infty)$
   y intercept: None [$f(0)$ is not defined]
   x intercept: $x = 1$
   Increasing on (e^{-1}, ∞)
   Decreasing on $(0, e^{-1})$
   Local minimum at $x = e^{-1} \approx 0.368$
   Concave upward on $(0, \infty)$

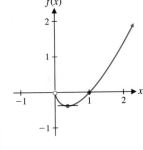

x	5	10	100	$\to \infty$
$f(x)$	8.05	23.03	460.52	$\to \infty$

x	0.1	0.01	0.001	0.000 1	$\to 0$
$f(x)$	-0.23	-0.046	$-0.006\ 9$	$-0.000\ 92$	$\to 0$

6. The circulation in 2010 is approximately 52.4 million and is decreasing at the rate of 0.3 million per year.

7. Maximum profit occurs for $x = e^{3.25} \approx 26$ and $p = \$5.50$.

Exercise 5-3

For many of the problems in this exercise set, the answers in the back of the book include both an unsimplified form and a simplified form. When checking your work, first check that you applied the rules correctly, and then check that you performed the algebraic simplification correctly.

A *In Problems 1–8, find the indicated derivative and simplify.*

1. f' for $f(x) = \ln(x - 3)$

2. g' for $g(x) = \ln(x + 100)$

3. $\dfrac{dy}{dt}$ for $y = \ln(3 - 2t)$

4. $\dfrac{dy}{dt}$ for $y = \ln(4 - 5t)$

5. y' for $y = \ln x^3$

6. y' for $y = (\ln x)^3$

7. $\dfrac{d}{dx}(\ln x)^6$

8. y' for $y = \ln x^6$

B *In Problems 9–34, find $f'(x)$ and simplify.*

9. $f(x) = x^4 \ln x$

10. $f(x) = x^3 \ln x$

11. $f(x) = \ln(x + 1)^4$

12. $f(x) = \ln(x + 1)^{-3}$

13. $f(x) = \dfrac{\ln x}{x^4}$

14. $f(x) = \dfrac{\ln x}{x^3}$

15. $f(x) = (x + 2)^3 \ln x$

16. $f(x) = (x - 1)^2 \ln x$

17. $f(x) = \ln(x^2 + 1)$

18. $f(x) = \ln(x^4 + 5)$

19. $f(x) = \ln(x^2 + 1)^{1/2}$

20. $f(x) = \ln(x^4 + 5)^{3/2}$

21. $f(x) = [\ln(x^2 + 1)]^{1/2}$

22. $f(x) = [\ln(x^4 + 5)]^{3/2}$

23. $f(x) = x(\ln x)^3$

24. $f(x) = x(\ln x)^2$

25. $f(x) = (1 + \ln x)^{1/2}$

26. $f(x) = (5 - \ln x)^4$

27. $f(x) = 2x^2 \ln x - x^2$

28. $f(x) = x \ln x - x$

29. $f(x) = e^{-x} \ln x$

30. $f(x) = \dfrac{\ln x}{e^x + 1}$

31. $f(x) = \dfrac{1}{\ln(1 + x^2)}$

32. $f(x) = \dfrac{1}{\ln(1 - x^3)}$

33. $f(x) = \sqrt[3]{\ln(1 - x^2)}$

34. $f(x) = \sqrt[5]{\ln(1 - x^5)}$

In Problems 35–38, find the equation of the line tangent to the graph of $y = f(x)$ at the indicated value of x.

35. $f(x) = \ln x$; $x = e$

36. $f(x) = \ln x$; $x = 1$

37. $f(x) = \ln(2 - x^2)$; $x = 1$

38. $f(x) = \ln(2 - \sqrt{x})$; $x = 1$

39. A student claims that the tangent line to the graph of $g(x) = \ln x$ at $x = 3$ passes through the origin (see the figure). Is he correct? Will the tangent line at $x = 4$ pass through the origin? Explain.

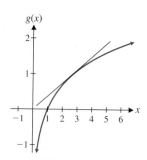

Figure for 39

40. Refer to Problem 39. Does the tangent line to the graph of $f(x) = \ln x$ at $x = e$ pass through the origin? Are there any other tangent lines to the graph of f that pass through the origin? Explain.

C In Problems 41–48, apply the graphing strategy discussed in Section 4-3 to f, summarize the pertinent information, and sketch the graph.

41. $f(x) = \ln(1 - x)$

42. $f(x) = \ln(2x + 4)$

43. $f(x) = x - \ln x$

44. $f(x) = \ln(x^2 + 4)$

45. $f(x) = x^2 \ln x$

46. $f(x) = \dfrac{\ln x}{x}$

47. $f(x) = (\ln x)^2$

48. $f(x) = \dfrac{x}{\ln x}$

In Problems 49–54, find the indicated extremum of each function for $x > 0$.

49. Absolute maximum value of

$$f(x) = 5x - 2x \ln x$$

50. Absolute minimum value of

$$f(x) = 4x \ln x - 7x$$

51. Absolute maximum value of

$$f(x) = x^2(3 - \ln x)$$

52. Absolute minimum value of

$$f(x) = x^3(\ln x - 2)$$

53. Absolute maximum value of

$$f(x) = \ln(xe^{-x})$$

54. Absolute maximum value of

$$f(x) = \ln(x^2 e^{-x})$$

In Problems 55–62, find each derivative.

55. $\dfrac{d}{dx}\log_2(3x^2 - 1)$

56. $\dfrac{d}{dx}\log(x^3 - 1)$

57. $\dfrac{d}{dx}10^{x^2+x}$

58. $\dfrac{d}{dx}8^{1-2x^2}$

59. $\dfrac{d}{dx}\log_3(4x^3 + 5x + 7)$

60. $\dfrac{d}{dx}\log_5(5^{x^2-1})$

61. $\dfrac{d}{dx}2^{x^3-x^2+4x+1}$

62. $\dfrac{d}{dx}10^{\ln x}$

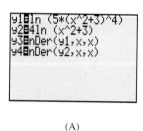 In Problems 63–66, use graphical approximation methods to find the points of intersection of f(x) and g(x) (to two decimal places).

63. $f(x) = (\ln x)^2$; $g(x) = x$

64. $f(x) = (\ln x)^3$; $g(x) = \sqrt{x}$

65. $f(x) = \ln x$; $g(x) = x^{1/5}$

66. $f(x) = \ln x$; $g(x) = x^{1/4}$

67. Suppose a student reasons that the functions $f(x) = \ln[5(x^2 + 3)^4]$ and $g(x) = 4 \ln(x^2 + 3)$ must have the same derivative, since he has entered $f(x)$, $g(x)$, $f'(x)$, and $g'(x)$ into a graphing utility, but only three graphs appear (see the figure). Is his reasoning correct? Are $f'(x)$ and $g'(x)$ the same function? Explain.

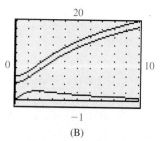

(A)   (B)

Figure for 67

68. Suppose a student reasons that the functions $f(x) = (x + 1) \ln(x + 1) - x$ and $g(x) = (x + 1)^{1/3}$ must have the same derivative, since she has entered $f(x), g(x), f'(x)$, and $g'(x)$ into a graphing utility, but only three graphs appear (see the figure). Is her reasoning correct? Are $f'(x)$ and $g'(x)$ the same function? Explain.

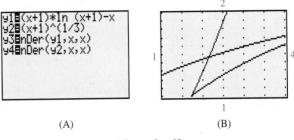

(A)   (B)

Figure for 68

Applications

Business & Economics

69. *Maximum profit.* A national food service runs food concessions for sporting events throughout the country. Their marketing research department chose a particular football stadium to test market a new jumbo hot dog. It was found that the demand for the new hot dog is given approximately by

$$p = 5 - \ln x \qquad 5 \le x \le 50$$

where x is the number of hot dogs (in thousands) that can be sold during one game at a price of $\$p$. If the concessionaire pays \$1 for each hot dog, how should the hot dogs be priced to maximize the profit per game?

70. *Maximum profit.* On a national tour of a rock band, the demand for T-shirts is given by

$$p = 15 - 4 \ln x \qquad 1 \le x \le 40$$

where x is the number of T-shirts (in thousands) that can be sold during a single concert at a price of $\$p$. If the shirts cost the band \$5 each, how should they be priced in order to maximize the profit per concert?

71. *Minimum average cost.* The cost of producing x units of a product is given by

$$C(x) = 600 + 100x - 100 \ln x \qquad x \ge 1$$

Find the minimum average cost.

72. *Minimum average cost.* The cost of producing x units of a product is given by

$$C(x) = 1,000 + 200x - 200 \ln x \qquad x \ge 1$$

Find the minimum average cost.

73. *Maximum profit.* A regional chain of department stores has collected the data in the table, showing weekly sales of a certain brand of jeans. The same jeans have been offered at various prices, ranging from the regular price of \$35.99 to the lowest sale price of \$23.99. Each pair of this brand costs the chain \$20.00. Use logarithmic regression ($p = a + b \ln x$) to find the price (to the nearest cent) that will maximize profit.

| Pairs of Jeans | Price per Pair (\$) |
x	p
21,543	23.99
14,029	25.99
12,130	27.99
9,169	29.99
6,964	31.99
5,506	33.99
4,187	35.99

74. *Maximum profit.* A mail-order company specializes in the sale of athletic shoes. Its market research team has determined the weekly demand shown in the table for a particular model of basketball shoe when priced at various levels. The company is able to purchase this model from the manufacturer for \$62 per pair. Use logarithmic regression ($p = a + b \ln x$) to find the price (to the nearest cent) that will maximize profit.

| Demand | Price per Pair (\$) |
x	p
4,312	74
3,064	79
2,499	84
2,047	89
1,823	94
1,781	99

75. *Maximum profit.* A mail-order company specializing in computer equipment has collected the data in the table, showing the weekly demand x for Data-Link modems at various prices p. The company purchases the modems from the manufacturer for $100 each. Use exponential regression ($p = ab^x$) to find the price (to the nearest cent) that will maximize the weekly profit.

Demand	Price per Modem ($)
x	p
412	169.95
488	149.95
575	139.95
722	129.95
786	119.95

76. *Maximum profit.* The mail-order company in Problem 75 also sells 100 megabyte disks. The data in the table show the weekly demand x for these disks at various price levels p. The company purchases the disks from the manufacturer for $6 each. Use exponential regression ($p = ab^x$) to find the price (to the nearest cent) that will maximize the weekly profit.

Demand	Price per Disk ($)
x	p
578	16.95
942	14.95
1,218	13.95
1,758	11.95
2,198	10.95

Life Sciences

77. *Blood pressure.* An experiment was set up to find a relationship between weight and systolic blood pressure in normal children. Using hospital records for 5,000 normal children, it was found that the systolic blood pressure was given approximately by

$$P(x) = 17.5(1 + \ln x) \qquad 10 \le x \le 100$$

where $P(x)$ is measured in millimeters of mercury and x is measured in pounds. What is the rate of change of blood pressure with respect to weight at the 40-pound weight level? At the 90-pound weight level?

78. *Blood pressure.* Graph the systolic blood pressure equation in Problem 77.

79. *Blood pressure and age.* A research group using hospital records developed the following approximate mathematical model relating systolic blood pressure and age:

$$P(x) = 40 + 25 \ln(x + 1) \qquad 0 \le x \le 65$$

where $P(x)$ is pressure measured in millimeters of mercury and x is age in years. What is the rate of change of pressure at the end of 10 years? At the end of 30 years? At the end of 60 years?

80. *Biology.* A yeast culture at room temperature ($68°F$) is placed in a refrigerator maintaining a constant temperature of $38°F$. After t hours, the temperature T of the culture is given approximately by

$$T = 30e^{-0.58t} + 38 \qquad t \ge 0$$

What is the rate of change of temperature of the culture at the end of 1 hour? At the end of 4 hours?

81. *Bacterial growth.* A single cholera bacterium divides every 0.5 hour to produce two complete cholera bacteria. If we start with a colony of 5,000 bacteria, after t hours there will be

$$A(t) = 5,000 \cdot 2^{2t}$$

bacteria. Find $A'(t)$, $A'(1)$, and $A'(5)$, and interpret the results.

82. *Bacterial growth.* Repeat Problem 81 for a starting colony of 1,000 bacteria where a single bacterium divides every 0.25 hour.

Social Sciences

83. *Psychology: stimulus/response.* In psychology, the Weber–Fechner law for stimulus response is

$$R = k \ln \frac{S}{S_0}$$

where R is the response, S is the stimulus, and S_0 is the lowest level of stimulus that can be detected. Find dR/dS.

84. *Psychology: learning.* A mathematical model for the average of a group of people learning to type is given by

$$N(t) = 10 + 6 \ln t \qquad t \ge 1$$

where $N(t)$ is the number of words per minute typed after t hours of instruction and practice (2 hours per day, 5 days per week). What is the rate of learning after 10 hours of instruction and practice? After 100 hours?

Section 5-4 | Chain Rule: Elasticity of Demand

- ➤ Chain Rule
- ➤ Relative Rate of Change
- ➤ Elasticity of Demand

The chain rule enabled us to generalize the derivative formulas for three basic functions: x^n, e^x, and $\ln x$. What happens if you encounter a different basic function? In this section, we discuss the general chain rule, which enables us to extend any basic derivative formula to a general rule. We also discuss some important applications of the derivative of the natural logarithm function.

➤ Chain Rule

The word *chain* in the name *chain rule* comes from the fact that a function formed by composition (such as those in Example 1) involves a chain of functions—that is, a function of a function. The *chain rule* will enable us to compute the derivative of a composite function in terms of the derivatives of the functions making up the composition.

EXPLORE & DISCUSS 1

The cost of bottling a soft drink depends on the number of bottles filled and the number of bottles filled depends on how long the bottling plant operates. If it costs $0.20 to fill one bottle and the plant can fill 10,000 bottles per hour of operation, then

$$y = C(x) = 0.2x \qquad \text{and} \qquad x = g(t) = 10,000t$$

where $C(x)$ is the cost, x is the number of bottles filled, and t is time in hours. What is the rate of change of cost with respect to time? How is this related to dy/dx and dx/dt?

Suppose that

$$y = m(x) = f[g(x)]$$

is a composite of f and g, where

$$y = f(u) \qquad \text{and} \qquad u = g(x)$$

We would like to express the derivative dy/dx in terms of the derivatives of f and g. From the definition of a derivative (see Section 3-3), we have

$$\frac{dy}{dx} = \lim_{h \to 0} \frac{m(x + h) - m(x)}{h} \qquad \text{Substitute } m(x + h) = f[g(x + h)] \text{ and } m(x) = f[g(x)].$$

$$= \lim_{h \to 0} \frac{f[g(x + h)] - f[g(x)]}{h} \qquad \text{Multiply by } 1 = \frac{g(x + h) - g(x)}{g(x + h) - g(x)}.$$

$$= \lim_{h \to 0} \left[\frac{f[g(x + h)] - f[g(x)]}{h} \cdot \frac{g(x + h) - g(x)}{g(x + h) - g(x)} \right]$$

$$= \lim_{h \to 0} \left[\frac{f[g(x + h)] - f[g(x)]}{g(x + h) - g(x)} \cdot \frac{g(x + h) - g(x)}{h} \right] \qquad (1)$$

We recognize the second factor in equation (1) as the difference quotient for $g(x)$. To interpret the first factor as the difference quotient for $f(u)$, we let

$k = g(x + h) - g(x)$. Since $u = g(x)$, we can write

$$u + k \boxed{= g(x) + g(x + h) - g(x)} = g(x + h)$$

Substituting in equation (1), we now have

$$\frac{dy}{dx} = \lim_{h \to 0} \left[\frac{f(u + k) - f(u)}{k} \cdot \frac{g(x + h) - g(x)}{h} \right] \qquad (2)$$

If we assume that $k = [g(x + h) - g(x)] \to 0$ as $h \to 0$, we can find the limit of each difference quotient in equation (2):

$$\frac{dy}{dx} = \left[\lim_{k \to 0} \frac{f(u + k) - f(u)}{k} \right]\left[\lim_{h \to 0} \frac{g(x + h) - g(x)}{h} \right]$$
$$= f'(u)g'(x)$$
$$= \frac{dy}{du}\frac{du}{dx}$$

This result is correct under rather general conditions, and is called the *chain rule,* but our "derivation" is superficial, because it ignores a number of hidden problems. Since a formal proof of the chain rule is beyond the scope of this book, we simply state it as follows:

DEFINITION   Chain Rule

If $y = f(u)$ and $u = g(x)$ define the composite function

$$y = m(x) = f[g(x)]$$

then

$$\frac{dy}{dx} = \frac{dy}{du}\frac{du}{dx} \qquad \text{provided that } \frac{dy}{du} \text{ and } \frac{du}{dx} \text{ exist}$$

or, equivalently,

$$m'(x) = f'[g(x)]g'(x) \qquad \text{provided that } f'[g(x)] \text{ and } g'(x) \text{ exist}$$

EXAMPLE 1   **Using the Chain Rule**   Find dy/du, du/dx, and dy/dx (express dy/dx as a function of x) for

(A) $y = u^{3/2}$ and $u = 3x^2 + 1$
(B) $y = e^u$ and $u = 2x^3 + 5$
(C) $y = \ln u$ and $u = x^2 - 4x + 2$

Solution   (A) $\dfrac{dy}{du} = \dfrac{3}{2}u^{1/2}$ and $\dfrac{du}{dx} = 6x$ *Basic derivative rules*

$$\frac{dy}{dx} = \frac{dy}{du}\frac{du}{dx} \qquad\qquad\qquad \textit{Chain rule}$$

$$= \frac{3}{2}u^{1/2}(6x) = 9x(3x^2 + 1)^{1/2} \qquad \textit{Since } u = 3x^2 + 1$$

(B) $\dfrac{dy}{du} = e^u$ and $\dfrac{du}{dx} = 6x^2$ Basic derivative rules

$\dfrac{dy}{dx} = \dfrac{dy}{du}\dfrac{du}{dx}$ Chain rule

$= e^u(6x^2) = 6x^2 e^{2x^3+5}$ Since $u = 2x^3 + 5$

(C) $\dfrac{dy}{du} = \dfrac{1}{u}$ and $\dfrac{du}{dx} = 2x - 4$ Basic derivative rules

$\dfrac{dy}{dx} = \dfrac{dy}{du}\dfrac{du}{dx}$ Chain rule

$= \dfrac{1}{u}(2x - 4) = \dfrac{2x - 4}{x^2 - 4x + 2}$ Since $u = x^2 - 4x + 2$ ■

Matched Problem 1 **Using the Chain Rule** Find dy/du, du/dx, and dy/dx (express dy/dx as a function of x) for

(A) $y = u^{-5}$ and $u = 2x^3 + 4$

(B) $y = e^u$ and $u = 3x^4 + 6$

(C) $y = \ln u$ and $u = x^2 + 9x + 4$ —————————— ■

EXPLORE & DISCUSS 2

Let $m(x) = f[g(x)]$. Use the chain rule and the graphs in Figures 1 and 2 to find

(A) $f(4)$ (B) $g(6)$ (C) $m(6)$

(D) $f'(4)$ (E) $g'(6)$ (F) $m'(6)$

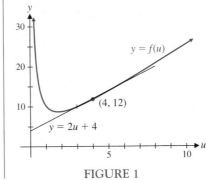

FIGURE 1

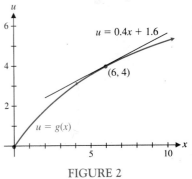

FIGURE 2

The chain rule can be extended to compositions of three or more functions. For example, if $y = f(w)$, $w = g(u)$, and $u = h(x)$, then

$$\frac{dy}{dx} = \frac{dy}{dw}\frac{dw}{du}\frac{du}{dx}$$

EXAMPLE 2 **Using the Chain Rule** For $y = h(x) = e^{1+(\ln x)^2}$, find dy/dx.

Solution   Note that h is of the form $y = e^w$, where $w = 1 + u^2$ and $u = \ln x$. Thus,

$$\frac{dy}{dx} = \frac{dy}{dw}\frac{dw}{du}\frac{du}{dx}$$

$$= e^w(2u)\left(\frac{1}{x}\right)$$

$$= e^{1+u^2}(2u)\left(\frac{1}{x}\right) \qquad \text{Since } w = 1 + u^2$$

$$= e^{1+(\ln x)^2}(2\ln x)\left(\frac{1}{x}\right) \qquad \text{Since } u = \ln x$$

$$= \frac{2}{x}(\ln x)e^{1+(\ln x)^2}$$

Matched Problem 2   For $y = h(x) = [\ln(1 + e^x)]^3$, find dy/dx.

The chain rule is the basis for extending basic derivative rules to general rules (see Sections 3-6, 5-2, and 5-3). We summarize the basic derivative rules here for convenient reference.

SUMMARY   General Derivative Rules

$$\frac{d}{dx}[f(x)]^n = n[f(x)]^{n-1}f'(x) \tag{3}$$

$$\frac{d}{dx}\ln[f(x)] = \frac{1}{f(x)}f'(x) \tag{4}$$

$$\frac{d}{dx}e^{f(x)} = e^{f(x)}f'(x) \tag{5}$$

Unless directed otherwise, you now have a choice between the chain rule and the general derivative rules. However, practicing with the chain rule will help prepare you for concepts that appear later in this text. Examples 1 and 2 illustrate the chain rule method and the next example reviews the general derivative rules method.

EXAMPLE 3   Using General Derivative Rules

(A) $\dfrac{d}{dx}e^{2x} = e^{2x}\dfrac{d}{dx}2x \qquad$ *Using equation (5)*

$\qquad = e^{2x}(2) = 2e^{2x}$

(B) $\dfrac{d}{dx}\ln(x^2 + 9) = \dfrac{1}{x^2 + 9}\dfrac{d}{dx}(x^2 + 9) \qquad$ *Using equation (4)*

$\qquad = \dfrac{1}{x^2 + 9}2x = \dfrac{2x}{x^2 + 9}$

(C) $\dfrac{d}{dx}(1 + e^{x^2})^3 = 3(1 + e^{x^2})^2 \dfrac{d}{dx}(1 + e^{x^2})$ Using equation (3)

$\qquad\qquad\qquad = 3(1 + e^{x^2})^2 e^{x^2} \dfrac{d}{dx}x^2$ Using equation (5)

$\qquad\qquad\qquad = 3(1 + e^{x^2})^2 e^{x^2}(2x)$

$\qquad\qquad\qquad = 6xe^{x^2}(1 + e^{x^2})^2$ ■

Matched Problem 3   Find

(A) $\dfrac{d}{dx}\ln(x^3 + 2x)$ (B) $\dfrac{d}{dx}e^{3x^2+2}$ (C) $\dfrac{d}{dx}(2 + e^{-x^2})^4$ —————

➤ Relative Rate of Change

EXPLORE & DISCUSS 3

A broker is trying to sell you two stocks, Biotech and Comstat. The broker estimates that Biotech's earnings will increase $2 per year over the next several years, while ComStat's earnings will increase only $1 per year. Is this sufficient information for you to choose between these two stocks? What other information might you request from the broker to help you decide?

Interpreting rates of change is a fundamental application of calculus. In Explore–Discuss 3, Biotech's earnings are increasing at twice the rate of Comstat's, but that does automatically make Biotech the better buy. The obvious information that is missing is the cost of each stock. If Biotech costs $100 a share and Comstat costs $25 share, then which stock is the better buy? To answer this question, we introduce two new concepts, *relative rate of change* and *percentage rate of change*.

DEFINITION   Relative and Percentage Rates of Change

The **relative rate of change** of a function $f(x)$ is $\dfrac{f'(x)}{f(x)}$.

The **percentage rate of change** is $100 \times \dfrac{f'(x)}{f(x)}$.

Since

$$\frac{d}{dx}\ln f(x) = \frac{f'(x)}{f(x)},$$

the relative rate of change of $f(x)$ is the derivative of the logarithm of $f(x)$. This is also referred to as the **logarithmic derivative** of $f(x)$. Returning to Explore–Discuss 3, we can now write

	Relative rate of change		Percentage rate of change
Biotech	$\dfrac{2}{100} = 0.02$	or	2%
Comstat	$\dfrac{1}{25} = 0.04$	or	4%

EXAMPLE 4 **Relative Rate of Change** Table 1 contains the real GDP (gross domestic product expressed in billions of 1996 dollars) and population of the United States from 1995 to 2002. A model for the GDP is

$$f(t) = 300t + 6,000$$

where t is years since 1990. Find and graph the percentage rate of change of $f(t)$ for $5 \leq t \leq 12$.

TABLE 1		
Year	Real GDP (billions of 1996 dollars)	Population (in millions)
1995	$7,540	262.765
1996	$7,810	265.19
1997	$8,150	267.744
1998	$8,500	270.299
1999	$8,850	272.82
2000	$9,190	275.306
2001	$9,210	277.803
2002	$9,440	280.306

Solution If $p(t)$ is the percentage rate of change of $f(t)$, then

$$p(t) = 100 \times \frac{d}{dx} \ln(300t + 6,000)$$

$$= \frac{30,000}{300t + 6,000}$$

$$= \frac{100}{t + 20}$$

The graph of $p(t)$ is shown in Figure 3 (graphing details omitted). Notice that $p(t)$ is decreasing, even though the GDP is increasing.

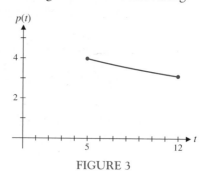

FIGURE 3

Matched Problem 4 A model for the population data in Table 1 is

$$f(t) = 2.5t + 250$$

where t is years since 1990. Find and graph $p(t)$, the percentage rate of change of $f(t)$ for $5 \leq t \leq 12$.

➤ Elasticity of Demand

Logarithmic derivatives and relative rates of change are used by economists to study the relationship among price changes, demand, and revenue. Suppose the price \$$p$ and the demand x for a certain product are related by the price–demand equation:

$$x + 500p = 10,000 \qquad (6)$$

In problems involving revenue, cost, and profit, it is customary to use the demand equation to express price as a function of demand. Since we are now interested in the effects that changes in price have on demand, it will be more convenient to express demand as a function of price. Solving (6) for x, we have

$$x = 10,000 - 500p$$
$$ = 500(20 - p) \qquad \text{Demand as a function of price}$$

or

$$x = f(p) = 500(20 - p) \qquad 0 \le p \le 20 \qquad (7)$$

Since x and p both represent nonnegative quantities, we must restrict p so that $0 \le p \le 20$. For most products, demand is assumed to be a decreasing function of price. That is, price increases result in lower demand and price decreases result in higher demand (see Figure 4).

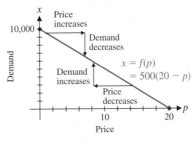

FIGURE 4

Economists use the *elasticity of demand* to study the relationship between changes in price and changes in demand. The **elasticity of demand** is the negative of the ratio of the relative rate of change of demand to the relative rate of change of price. If price and demand are related by a price–demand equation of the form $x = f(p)$, then the elasticity of demand can be expressed as

$$-\frac{\text{relative rate of change of demand}}{\text{relative rate of change of price}} = -\frac{\dfrac{d}{dp}\ln f(p)}{\dfrac{d}{dp}\ln p}$$

$$= -\frac{\dfrac{f'(p)}{f(p)}}{\dfrac{1}{p}}$$

$$= -\frac{pf'(p)}{f(p)} \qquad (8)$$

◉ Insight Since p and $f(p)$ are nonnegative and $f'(p)$ is negative (remember, demand is usually a decreasing function of price), the expression in (8) is always nonnegative. This is the reason that elasticity of demand was defined as the negative of a ratio. ●

Summarizing the preceding discussion, we have Theorem 1.

THEOREM 1   Elasticity of Demand

If price and demand are related by $x = f(p)$, then the elasticity of demand is given by

$$E(p) = -\frac{pf'(p)}{f(p)}$$

The next example illustrates interpretations of the elasticity of demand.

EXAMPLE 5   **Elasticity of Demand** Find $E(p)$ for the price–demand equation

$$x = f(p) = 500(20 - p)$$

Find and interpret each of the following:

(A) $E(4)$ (B) $E(16)$ (C) $E(10)$

Solution
$$E(p) = -\frac{pf'(p)}{f(p)} = -\frac{p(-500)}{500(20 - p)} = \frac{p}{20 - p}$$

In order to interpret values of $E(p)$, we must recall the definition of elasticity:

$$E(p) = -\frac{\text{relative rate of change of demand}}{\text{relative rate of change of price}}$$

or

$$-\left(\begin{array}{c}\text{relative rate of}\\\text{change of demand}\end{array}\right) \approx E(p)\left(\begin{array}{c}\text{relative rate of}\\\text{change of price}\end{array}\right)$$

(A) $E(4) = \frac{4}{16} = 0.25 < 1$. If the \$4 price changes by 10%, then the demand will change by approximately $0.25(10\%) = 2.5\%$.

(B) $E(16) = \frac{16}{4} = 4 > 1$. If the \$16 price changes by 10%, then the demand will change by approximately $4(10\%) = 40\%$.

(C) $E(10) = \frac{10}{10} = 1$. If the \$10 price changes by 10%, then the demand will also change by approximately 10%. ∎

◉ Insight   Do not be concerned with the omission of any negative signs in these interpretations. We already know that if price increases, then demand decreases and vice versa (Fig. 4). $E(p)$ is a measure of *how much* the demand changes for a given change in price. ●

Matched Problem 5   Find $E(p)$ for the price–demand equation

$$x = f(p) = 1,000(40 - p)$$

Find and interpret each of the following:

(A) $E(8)$ (B) $E(30)$ (C) $E(20)$

The three cases illustrated in the solution to Example 5 are referred to as **inelastic demand, elastic demand,** and **unit elasticity** as indicated in Table 2.

TABLE 2

$E(p)$	Demand	Interpretation
$0 < E(p) < 1$	Inelastic	Demand is not sensitive to changes in price. A change in price produces a smaller change in demand.
$E(p) > 1$	Elastic	Demand is sensitive to changes in price. A change in price produces a larger change in demand.
$E(p) = 1$	Unit	A change in price produces the same change in demand.

Now we want to see how revenue and elasticity are related. We have used the following model for revenue many times before:

$$\text{Revenue} = (\text{demand}) \times (\text{price})$$

Since we are looking for a connection between $E(p)$ and revenue, we will use a price–demand equation that has been written in the form $x = f(p)$, where x is demand and p is price.

$$R(p) = xp = pf(p) \qquad \textit{Revenue as a function of price}$$
$$R'(p) = pf'(p) + f(p)$$
$$= f(p)\left[\frac{pf'(p)}{f(p)} + 1\right] \qquad E(p) = -\frac{pf'(p)}{f(p)}$$
$$= f(p)[1 - E(p)] \qquad\qquad\qquad\qquad (9)$$

Since $x = f(p) > 0$, it follows from (9) that $R'(p)$ and $[1 - E(p)]$ always have the same sign (see Table 3).

TABLE 3 Revenue and Elasticity of Demand

All Are True or All Are False	All Are True or All Are False
$R'(p) > 0$	$R'(p) < 0$
$E(p) < 1$	$E(p) > 1$
Demand is inelastic	Demand is elastic

These facts are interpreted in the following summary and in Figure 5 on page 346.

Summary   **Revenue and Elasticity of Demand**

Demand is inelastic:

A price increase will increase revenue.
A price decrease will decrease revenue.

Demand is elastic:

A price increase will decrease revenue.
A price decrease will increase revenue.

◉ Insight   We know that a price increase will decrease demand at all price levels (Fig. 4). As Figure 5 illustrates, the effects of a price increase on revenue depends on the price level. If demand is elastic, a price increase decreases revenue. If demand is inelastic, a price increase increases revenue.

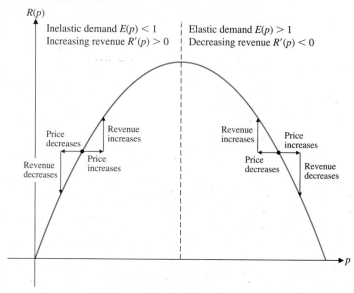

FIGURE 5   Revenue and elasticity

EXAMPLE 6   **Elasticity and Revenue**   A sunglass manufacturer currently sells one type of sunglasses for $4 a pair. The price p and the demand x for these glasses are related by

$$x = f(p) = 7{,}000 - 500p$$

If the current price is increased, will revenue increase or decrease?

Solution

$$E(p) = -\frac{pf'(p)}{f(p)}$$

$$= -\frac{p(-500)}{7{,}000 - 500p}$$

$$= \frac{p}{14 - p}$$

$$E(5) = \frac{4}{10} = 0.4$$

At the $5 price level, demand is inelastic and a price increase will increase revenue.   ■

Matched Problem 6   Repeat Example 6 if the current price for sunglasses is $10 a pair.

Answers to Matched Problems   **1.** (A) $\dfrac{dy}{dx} = -5u^{-4}, \dfrac{du}{dx} = 6x^2, \dfrac{dy}{dx} = -30x^2(2x^3 + 4)^{-6}$

(B) $\dfrac{dy}{du} = e^u, \dfrac{du}{dx} = 12x^3, \dfrac{dy}{dx} = 12x^3 e^{3x^4 + 6}$

(C) $\dfrac{dy}{du} = \dfrac{1}{u}, \dfrac{du}{dx} = 2x + 9, \dfrac{dy}{dx} = \dfrac{2x + 9}{x^2 + 9x + 4}$

2. $\dfrac{3e^x[\ln(1 + e^x)]^2}{1 + e^x}$

3. (A) $\dfrac{3x^2 + 2}{x^3 + 2x}$ (B) $6xe^{3x^2+2}$ (C) $-8xe^{-x^2}(2 + e^{-x^2})^3$

4. $p(t) = \dfrac{100}{t + 100}$

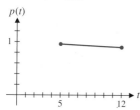

5. $E(p) = \dfrac{p}{20 - p}$

(A) $E(8) = 0.25$; demand is inelastic.

(B) $E(30) = 3$; demand is elastic.

(C) $E(20) = 1$; demand has unit elasticity

6. $E(10) = 2.5$; demand is elastic. Increasing price will decrease revenue.

Exercise 5-4

For some of the problems in this exercise set, the answers in the back of the book include both an unsimplified form and a simplified form. When checking your work, first check that you applied the rules correctly, and then check that you performed the algebraic simplification correctly.

A In Problems 1–6, find dy/du, du/dx, and dy/dx. Express dy/dx in terms of x.

1. $y = u^2; u = 2 + e^x$

2. $y = u^3; u = 3 - \ln x$

3. $y = e^u; u = 2 - x^4$

4. $y = e^u; u = x^6 + 5x^2$

5. $y = \ln u; u = 4x^5 - 7$

6. $y = \ln u; u = 2 + 3x^4$

In Problems 7–12, find dy/dw, dw/du, du/dx, and dy/dx. Express dy/dx in terms of x.

7. $y = 1 + w^2; w = \ln u; u = 2 + e^x$

8. $y = \ln w; w = 1 + e^u; u = x^2$

9. $y = \ln w; w = u^2 + 1; u = e^x$

10. $y = e^w; w = -u^2; u = \ln x$

11. $y = (w + 4)^2; w = \ln u; u = e^x$

12. $y = e^w; w = \sqrt{u}; u = \ln x$

In Problems 13–20, find the relative rate of change of f(x).

13. $f(x) = 10x + 500$

14. $f(x) = 5x + 200$

15. $f(x) = 100x - 0.5x^2$

16. $f(x) = 50x - 0.01x^2$

17. $f(x) = 4 + 2e^{-2x}$

18. $f(x) = 5 - 3e^{-x}$

19. $f(x) = 25x + 3x \ln x$

20. $f(x) = 15x + 2x \ln x$

B In Problems 21–24, use the price–demand equation to determine whether demand is elastic, inelastic, or has unit elasticity at the indicated values of p.

21. $x = f(p) = 12{,}000 - 10p^2$

(A) $p = 10$ (B) $p = 20$ (C) $p = 30$

22. $x = f(p) = 1{,}875 - p^2$

(A) $p = 15$ (B) $p = 25$ (C) $p = 40$

23. $x = f(p) = 950 - 2p - 0.1p^2$

(A) $p = 30$ (B) $p = 50$ (C) $p = 70$

24. $x = f(p) = 875 - p - 0.05p^2$

(A) $p = 50$ (B) $p = 70$ (C) $p = 100$

25. Given the price–demand equation

$$p + 0.005x = 30$$

(A) Express the demand x as a function of the price p.

(B) Find the elasticity of demand, $E(p)$.

(C) What is the elasticity of demand when $p = \$10$? If this price is increased by 10%, what is the approximate change in demand?

(D) What is the elasticity of demand when $p = \$25$? If this price is increased by 10%, what is the approximate change in demand?

(E) What is the elasticity of demand when $p = \$15$? If this price is increased by 10%, what is the approximate change in demand?

26. Given the price–demand equation

$$p + 0.01x = 50$$

(A) Express the demand x as a function of the price p.

(B) Find the elasticity of demand, $E(p)$.

(C) What is the elasticity of demand when $p = \$10$? If this price is decreased by 5%, what is the approximate change in demand?

(D) What is the elasticity of demand when $p = \$45$? If this price is decreased by 5%, what is the approximate change in demand?

(E) What is the elasticity of demand when $p = \$25$? If this price is decreased by 5%, what is the approximate change in demand?

27. Given the price–demand equation

$$0.02x + p = 60$$

(A) Express the demand x as a function of the price p.

(B) Express the revenue R as a function of the price p.

(C) Find the elasticity of demand, $E(p)$.

(D) For which values of p is demand elastic? Inelastic?

(E) For which values of p is revenue increasing? Decreasing?

(F) If $p = \$10$ and the price is decreased, will revenue increase or decrease?

(G) If $p = \$40$ and the price is decreased, will revenue increase or decrease?

28. Repeat Problem 27 for the price–demand equation

$$0.025x + p = 50$$

In 29–34, use the price–demand equation to find the values of p for which demand is elastic and the values for which demand is inelastic.

29. $x = f(p) = 10(p - 30)^2$

30. $x = f(p) = 5(p - 60)^2$

31. $x = f(p) = \sqrt{144 - 2p}$

32. $x = f(p) = \sqrt{324 - 2p}$

33. $x = f(p) = \sqrt{2{,}500 - 2p^2}$

34. $x = f(p) = \sqrt{3{,}600 - 2p^2}$

In Problems 35–40, use the demand equation to find the revenue function. Sketch the graph of the revenue function and indicate the regions of inelastic and elastic demand on the graph.

35. $x = f(p) = 20(10 - p)$

36. $x = f(p) = 10(16 - p)$

37. $x = f(p) = 40(p - 15)^2$

38. $x = f(p) = 10(p - 9)^2$

39. $x = f(p) = 30 - 10\sqrt{p}$

40. $x = f(p) = 30 - 5\sqrt{p}$

C *If a price–demand equation is solved for p, then price is expressed as $p = g(x)$ and x becomes the independent variable. In this case, it can be shown that the elasticity of demand is given by*

$$E(x) = -\frac{g(x)}{xg'(x)}$$

In Problems 41–44, use the price–demand equation to find $E(x)$ at the indicated value of x.

41. $p = g(x) = 50 - 0.1x, x = 200$

42. $p = g(x) = 30 - 0.05x, x = 400$

43. $p = g(x) = 50 - 2\sqrt{x}, x = 400$

44. $p = g(x) = 20 - \sqrt{x}, x = 100$

45. Find $E(p)$ for $x = f(p) = Ap^{-k}$, where A and k are positive constants.

46. Find $E(p)$ for $x = f(p) = Ae^{-kp}$, where A and k are positive constants.

Applications

47. *Rate of change of cost.* A fast food restaurant can produce a hamburger for $1.25. If the restaurant's daily sales are increasing at the rate of 20 hamburgers per day, how fast is their daily cost for hamburgers increasing?

48. *Rate of change of cost.* The fast food restaurant in Problem 47 can produce an order of fries for $0.40. If the restaurant's daily sales are increasing at the

rate of 15 per day, how fast is their daily cost for fries increasing?

49. *Revenue and elasticity.* The price–demand equation for hamburgers at a fast food restaurant is

$$x + 400p = 2{,}000$$

Currently, the price of a hamburger is $2.00. If the price is increased by 10%, will revenue increase or decrease?

50. *Revenue and elasticity.* Refer to Problem 49. If the current price of a hamburger is $3.00, will a 10% price increase cause the revenue to increase or decrease?

51. *Revenue and elasticity.* The price–demand equation for an order of fries at a fast food restaurant is

$$x + 1,000p = 1,000$$

Currently, the price of an order of fries is $0.30. If the price is decreased by 10%, will revenue increase or decrease?

52. *Revenue and elasticity.* Refer to Problem 51. If the current price of an order of fries is $0.60, will a 10% price decrease cause the revenue to increase or decrease?

53. *Maximum revenue.* Refer to Problem 49. What price will maximize the revenue from selling hamburgers?

54. *Maximum revenue.* Refer to Problem 51. What price will maximize the revenue from selling fries?

Life Sciences

55. *Population growth.* A model for Canada's population growth (Table 4) is

$$f(t) = 0.34t + 14.6$$

where t is years since 1950. Find and graph the percentage rate of change of $f(t)$ for $0 \le t \le 50$.

TABLE 4 Population Growth

Year	Canada (millions)	Mexico (millions)
1950	14	28
1960	18	39
1970	22	53
1980	25	68
1990	28	85
2000	31	100

56. *Population growth.* A model for Mexico's population growth (Table 4) is

$$f(t) = 1.47t + 25.5$$

where t is years since 1950. Find and graph the percentage rate of change of $f(t)$ for $0 \le t \le 50$.

Social Sciences

57. *Crime.* A model for the number of robberies in the United States (Table 5) is

$$r(t) = 11.3 - 3.6 \ln t$$

where t is years since 1990. Find the relative rate of change for robberies in 2002.

TABLE 5 Number of Victimizations per 1,000 Population Age 12 and Over

	Robbery	Aggravated Assault
1995	5.4	9.5
1996	5.2	8.8
1997	4.3	8.6
1998	4.0	7.5
1999	3.6	6.7
2000	3.2	5.7
2001	2.8	5.3
2002	2.2	4.3

58. *Crime.* A model for the number of assaults in the United States (Table 5) is

$$a(t) = 19.6 - 6.0 \ln t$$

where t is years since 1990. Find the relative rate of change for assaults in 2002.

Section 5-5 | Implicit Differentiation

➤ Special Function Notation
➤ Implicit Differentiation

➤ Special Function Notation

The equation

$$y = 2 - 3x^2 \tag{1}$$

defines a function f with y as a dependent variable and x as an independent variable. Using function notation, we would write

$$y = f(x) \quad \text{or} \quad f(x) = 2 - 3x^2$$

In order to reduce to a minimum the number of symbols involved in a discussion, we will often write equation (1) in the form

$$y = 2 - 3x^2 = y(x)$$

where y is *both* a dependent variable and a function symbol. This is a convenient notation, and no harm is done as long as one is aware of the double role of y. Other examples are

$$x = 2t^2 - 3t + 1 = x(t)$$
$$z = \sqrt{u^2 - 3u} = z(u)$$
$$r = \frac{1}{(s^2 - 3s)^{2/3}} = r(s)$$

This type of notation will simplify much of the discussion and work that follows.

Until now we have considered functions involving only one independent variable. There is no reason to stop there. The concept can be generalized to functions involving two or more independent variables, and this will be done in detail in Chapter 8. For now, we will "borrow" the notation for a function involving two independent variables. For example,

$$F(x, y) = x^2 - 2xy + 3y^2 - 5$$

specifies a function F involving two independent variables.

➤ Implicit Differentiation

Consider the equation

$$3x^2 + y - 2 = 0 \tag{2}$$

and the equation obtained by solving equation (2) for y in terms of x,

$$y = 2 - 3x^2 \tag{3}$$

Both equations define the same function using x as the independent variable and y as the dependent variable. For equation (3), we can write

$$y = f(x)$$

where

$$f(x) = 2 - 3x^2 \tag{4}$$

and we have an **explicit** (clearly stated) rule that enables us to determine y for each value of x. On the other hand, the y in equation (2) is the same y as in equation (3), and equation (2) **implicitly** gives (implies though does not plainly express) y as a function of x. Thus, we say that equations (3) and (4) define the function f explicitly, and equation (2) defines f implicitly.

The direct use of an equation that defines a function implicitly to find the derivative of the dependent variable with respect to the independent variable is called **implicit differentiation.** Let us differentiate equation (2) implicitly and equation (3) directly, and compare results.

Starting with

$$3x^2 + y - 2 = 0$$

we think of y as a function of x—that is, $y = y(x)$—and write

$$3x^2 + y(x) - 2 = 0$$

Then we differentiate both sides with respect to x:

$$\frac{d}{dx}[(3x^2 + y(x) - 2)] = \frac{d}{dx}0$$

Since y is a function of x, but is not
explicitly given, we simply write

$$\frac{d}{dx}3x^2 + \frac{d}{dx}y(x) - \frac{d}{dx}2 = 0$$

$\frac{d}{dx}y(x) = y'$ *to indicate its derivative.*

$$6x + y' - 0 = 0$$

Now, we solve for y':

$$y' = -6x$$

Note that we get the same result if we start with equation (3) and differentiate directly:

$$y = 2 - 3x^2$$
$$y' = -6x$$

Why are we interested in implicit differentiation? In general, why do we not solve for y in terms of x and differentiate directly? The answer is that there are many equations of the form

$$F(x, y) = 0 \tag{5}$$

that are either difficult or impossible to solve for y explicitly in terms of x (try it for $x^2y^5 - 3xy + 5 = 0$ or for $e^y - y = 3x$, for example). But it can be shown that, under fairly general conditions on F, equation (5) will define one or more functions where y is a dependent variable and x is an independent variable. To find y' under these conditions, we differentiate equation (5) implicitly.

(A) How many tangent lines are there to the graph in Figure 1 when $x = 0$? When $x = 1$? When $x = 2$? When $x = 4$? When $x = 6$?

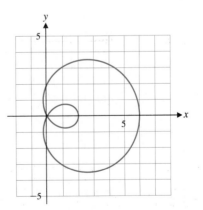

FIGURE 1

(B) Sketch the tangent lines referred to in part (A) and estimate each of their slopes.

(C) Explain why the graph in Figure 1 is not the graph of a function.

EXAMPLE 1   **Differentiating Implicitly** Given

$$F(x, y) = x^2 + y^2 - 25 = 0 \tag{6}$$

find y' and the slope of the graph at $x = 3$.

Solution   We start with the graph of $x^2 + y^2 - 25 = 0$ (a circle, as shown in Fig. 2) so that we can interpret our results geometrically. From the graph it is clear that equation (6) does not define a function. But with a suitable restriction on the variables, equation (6) can define two or more functions. For example, the upper half and the lower half of the circle each define a function. A point on each half-circle that corresponds to $x = 3$ is found by substituting $x = 3$ into equation (6) and solving for y:

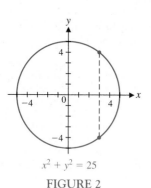

$$x^2 + y^2 - 25 = 0$$
$$(3)^2 + y^2 = 25$$
$$y^2 = 16$$
$$y = \pm 4$$

$x^2 + y^2 = 25$

FIGURE 2

Thus, the point $(3, 4)$ is on the upper half-circle, and the point $(3, -4)$ is on the lower half-circle. We will use these results in a moment. We now differentiate equation (6) implicitly, treating y as a function of x; that is, $y = y(x)$:

$$x^2 + y^2 - 25 = 0$$

$$x^2 + [y(x)]^2 - 25 = 0$$

$$\frac{d}{dx}\{x^2 + [y(x)]^2 - 25\} = \frac{d}{dx}0$$

$$\frac{d}{dx}x^2 + \frac{d}{dx}[y(x)]^2 - \frac{d}{dx}25 = 0 \qquad \text{Use the chain rule.}$$

$$2x + 2[y(x)]^{2-1}y'(x) - 0 = 0$$

$$2x + 2yy' = 0 \qquad \text{Solve for } y' \text{ in terms of } x \text{ and } y.$$

$$y' = -\frac{2x}{2y}$$

$$y' = -\frac{x}{y} \qquad \text{Leave the answer in terms of } x \text{ and } y.$$

We have found y' without first solving $x^2 + y^2 - 25 = 0$ for y in terms of x. And by leaving y' in terms of x and y, we can use $y' = -x/y$ to find y' for *any* point on the graph of $x^2 + y^2 - 25 = 0$ (except where $y = 0$). In particular, for $x = 3$, we found that $(3, 4)$ and $(3, -4)$ are on the graph; thus, the slope of the graph at $(3, 4)$ is

$$y'|_{(3, 4)} = -\tfrac{3}{4} \qquad \text{The slope of the graph at } (3, 4)$$

and the slope at $(3, -4)$ is

$$y'|_{(3, -4)} = -\tfrac{3}{-4} = \tfrac{3}{4} \qquad \text{The slope of the graph at } (3, -4)$$

The symbol

$$y'|_{(a, b)}$$

is used to indicate that we are evaluating y' at $x = a$ and $y = b$.

The results are interpreted geometrically on the original graph as shown in Figure 3. ∎

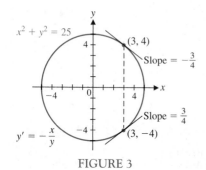

$x^2 + y^2 = 25$

$(3, 4)$

Slope $= -\tfrac{3}{4}$

Slope $= \tfrac{3}{4}$

$(3, -4)$

$y' = -\dfrac{x}{y}$

FIGURE 3

In Example 1, the fact that y' is given in terms of both x and y is not a great disadvantage. We have only to make certain that when we want **to evaluate y' for a particular value of x and y, say, (x_0, y_0), the ordered pair must satisfy the original equation.**

⊚ *Insight*   In the solution for Example 1, notice that the derivative of y^2 with respect to x is $2yy'$, not just $2y$. When first learning about implicit differentiation, it is a good idea to replace y with $y(x)$ in the original equation to emphasize that y is a function of x.
●

**Matched
Problem** 1   Graph $x^2 + y^2 - 169 = 0$, find y' by implicit differentiation, and find the slope of the graph when $x = 5$.
————————————■

EXAMPLE 2   **Differentiating Implicitly** Find the equation(s) of the tangent line(s) to the graph of

$$y - xy^2 + x^2 + 1 = 0 \qquad\qquad (7)$$

at the point(s) where $x = 1$.

Solution   We first find y when $x = 1$:

$$y - xy^2 + x^2 + 1 = 0$$
$$y - (1)y^2 + (1)^2 + 1 = 0$$
$$y - y^2 + 2 = 0$$
$$y^2 - y - 2 = 0$$
$$(y - 2)(y + 1) = 0$$
$$y = -1, 2$$

Thus, there are two points on the graph of (7) where $x = 1$; namely, $(1, -1)$ and $(1, 2)$. We next find the slope of the graph at these two points by differentiating equation (7) implicitly:

$$y - xy^2 + x^2 + 1 = 0 \qquad\qquad \text{Use the product rule and the}$$
$$\frac{d}{dx}y - \frac{d}{dx}xy^2 + \frac{d}{dx}x^2 + \frac{d}{dx}1 = \frac{d}{dx}0 \qquad \text{chain rule for } \frac{d}{dx}xy^2.$$
$$y' - (x \cdot 2yy' + y^2) + 2x = 0$$
$$y' - 2xyy' - y^2 + 2x = 0 \qquad \text{Solve for } y' \text{ by getting all}$$
$$y' - 2xyy' = y^2 - 2x \qquad \text{terms involving } y' \text{ on one side.}$$
$$(1 - 2xy)y' = y^2 - 2x$$
$$y' = \frac{y^2 - 2x}{1 - 2xy}$$

Now, find the slope at each point:

$$y'|_{(1,-1)} = \frac{(-1)^2 - 2(1)}{1 - 2(1)(-1)} = \frac{1 - 2}{1 + 2} = \frac{-1}{3} = -\frac{1}{3}$$

$$y'|_{(1,2)} = \frac{(2)^2 - 2(1)}{1 - 2(1)(2)} = \frac{4 - 2}{1 - 4} = \frac{2}{-3} = -\frac{2}{3}$$

Equation of tangent line at $(1, -1)$:   Equation of tangent line at $(1, 2)$:

$$y - y_1 = m(x - x_1) \qquad\qquad\qquad y - y_1 = m(x - x_1)$$
$$y + 1 = -\tfrac{1}{3}(x - 1) \qquad\qquad\qquad y - 2 = -\tfrac{2}{3}(x - 1)$$
$$y + 1 = -\tfrac{1}{3}x + \tfrac{1}{3} \qquad\qquad\qquad y - 2 = -\tfrac{2}{3}x + \tfrac{2}{3}$$
$$y = -\tfrac{1}{3}x - \tfrac{2}{3} \qquad\qquad\qquad\quad y = -\tfrac{2}{3}x + \tfrac{8}{3}$$
■

Matched Problem 2 Repeat Example 2 for $x^2 + y^2 - xy - 7 = 0$ at $x = 1$. ____

EXPLORE & DISCUSS 2

The slopes of the tangent lines to $y^2 + 3xy + 4x = 9$ when $x = 0$ can be found in either of the following ways: (1) by differentiating the equation implicitly; or (2) by solving for y explicitly in terms of x (using the quadratic formula), and then computing the derivative. Which of the two methods is more efficient? Explain.

EXAMPLE 3 **Differentiating Implicitly** Find x' for $x = x(t)$ defined implicitly by

$$t \ln x = xe^t - 1$$

and evaluate x' at $(t, x) = (0, 1)$.

Solution It is important to remember that x is the dependent variable and t is the independent variable. Therefore, we differentiate both sides of the equation with respect to t (using product and chain rules where appropriate), and then solve for x':

$$t \ln x = xe^t - 1 \qquad \text{Differentiate implicitly with respect to } t.$$

$$\frac{d}{dt}(t \ln x) = \frac{d}{dt}(xe^t) - \frac{d}{dt}1$$

$$t\frac{x'}{x} + \ln x = xe^t + x'e^t \qquad \text{Clear fractions.}$$

$$\boxed{x \cdot t\frac{x'}{x} + x \cdot \ln x = x \cdot xe^t + x \cdot e^t x'} \quad x \neq 0$$

$$tx' + x \ln x = x^2e^t + xe^tx' \qquad \text{Solve for } x'.$$

$$tx' - xe^tx' = x^2e^t - x \ln x \qquad \text{Factor out } x'.$$

$$(t - xe^t)x' = x^2e^t - x \ln x$$

$$x' = \frac{x^2e^t - x \ln x}{t - xe^t}$$

Now, we evaluate x' at $(t, x) = (0, 1)$, as requested:

$$x'|_{(0,1)} = \frac{(1)^2e^0 - 1 \ln 1}{0 - 1e^0}$$

$$= \frac{1}{-1} = -1$$

Matched Problem 3 Find x' for $x = x(t)$ defined implicitly by

$$1 + x \ln t = te^x$$

and evaluate x' at $(t, x) = (1, 0)$. ____

Answers to Matched Problems

1. $y' = -x/y$; when $x = 5$, $y = \pm 12$, thus, $y'|_{(5,12)} = -\frac{5}{12}$ and $y'|_{(5,-12)} = \frac{5}{12}$

2. $y' = \dfrac{y - 2x}{2y - x}$; $\quad y = \frac{4}{5}x - \frac{14}{5}$, $y = \frac{1}{5}x + \frac{14}{5}$

3. $x' = \dfrac{te^x - x}{t \ln t - t^2e^x}$; $x'|_{(1,0)} = -1$

Exercise 5-5

A *In Problems 1–4, find y′ two ways:*

(A) *Differentiate the given equation implicitly and then solve for y′.*

(B) *Solve the given equation for y and then differentiate directly.*

  1. $3x + 5y + 9 = 0$

  2. $-2x + 6y - 4 = 0$

  3. $3x^2 - 4y - 18 = 0$

  4. $2x^3 + 5y - 2 = 0$

In Problems 5–22, use implicit differentiation to find y′ and evaluate y′ at the indicated point.

  5. $y - 5x^2 + 3 = 0;\ (1, 2)$

  6. $5x^3 - y - 1 = 0;\ (1, 4)$

  7. $x^2 - y^3 - 3 = 0;\ (2, 1)$

  8. $y^2 + x^3 + 4 = 0;\ (-2, 2)$

  9. $y^2 + 2y + 3x = 0;\ (-1, 1)$

  10. $y^2 - y - 4x = 0;\ (0, 1)$

B

  11. $xy - 6 = 0;\ (2, 3)$

  12. $3xy - 2x - 2 = 0;\ (2, 1)$

  13. $2xy + y + 2 = 0;\ (-1, 2)$

  14. $2y + xy - 1 = 0;\ (-1, 1)$

  15. $x^2y - 3x^2 - 4 = 0;\ (2, 4)$

  16. $2x^3y - x^3 + 5 = 0;\ (-1, 3)$

  17. $e^y = x^2 + y^2;\ (1, 0)$

  18. $x^2 - y = 4e^y;\ (2, 0)$

  19. $x^3 - y = \ln y;\ (1, 1)$

  20. $\ln y = 2y^2 - x;\ (2, 1)$

  21. $x \ln y + 2y = 2x^3;\ (1, 1)$

  22. $xe^y - y = x^2 - 2;\ (2, 0)$

In Problems 23 and 24, find x′ for x = x(t) defined implicitly by the given equation. Evaluate x′ at the indicated point.

  23. $x^2 - t^2x + t^3 + 11 = 0;\ (-2, 1)$

  24. $x^3 - tx^2 - 4 = 0;\ (-3, -2)$

Problems 25 and 26 refer to the equation and graph shown in the figure.

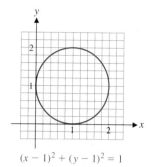

$(x - 1)^2 + (y - 1)^2 = 1$

25. Use implicit differentiation to find the slopes of the tangent lines at the points on the graph where $x = 1.6$. Check your answers by visually estimating the slopes on the graph in the figure.

26. Find the slopes of the tangent lines at the points on the graph where $x = 0.2$. Check your answers by visually estimating the slopes on the graph in the figure.

In Problems 27–30, find the equation(s) of the tangent line(s) to the graphs of the indicated equations at the point(s) with the given value of x.

  27. $xy - x - 4 = 0;\ x = 2$

  28. $3x + xy + 1 = 0;\ x = -1$

  29. $y^2 - xy - 6 = 0;\ x = 1$

  30. $xy^2 - y - 2 = 0;\ x = 1$

31. If $xe^y = 1$, find $y′$ in two ways: first by implicit differentiation, then by solving for y explicitly in terms of x. Which method do you prefer? Explain.

32. Explain the difficulty in solving $x^3 + y + xe^y = 1$ for y as an explicit function of x. Find the slope of the tangent line to the graph of the equation at the point $(0, 1)$.

C *In Problems 33–40, find y′ and the slope of the tangent line to the graph of each equation at the indicated point.*

  33. $(1 + y)^3 + y = x + 7;\ (2, 1)$

  34. $(y - 3)^4 - x = y;\ (-3, 4)$

  35. $(x - 2y)^3 = 2y^2 - 3;\ (1, 1)$

  36. $(2x - y)^4 - y^3 = 8;\ (-1, -2)$

  37. $\sqrt{7 + y^2} - x^3 + 4 = 0;\ (2, 3)$

  38. $6\sqrt{y^3 + 1} - 2x^{3/2} - 2 = 0;\ (4, 2)$

  39. $\ln(xy) = y^2 - 1;\ (1, 1)$

  40. $e^{xy} - 2x = y + 1;\ (0, 0)$

41. Find the equation(s) of the tangent line(s) at the point(s) on the graph of the equation

$$y^3 - xy - x^3 = 2$$

where $x = 1$. Round all approximate values to two decimal places.

42. Refer to the equation in Problem 41. Find the equation(s) of the tangent line(s) at the point(s) on the graph where $y = -1$. Round all approximate values to two decimal places.

Applications

Business & Economics

For the demand equations in Problems 43–46, find the rate of change of p with respect to x by differentiating implicitly (x is the number of items that can be sold at a price of $p.)

43. $x = p^2 - 2p + 1{,}000$

44. $x = p^3 - 3p^2 + 200$

45. $x = \sqrt{10{,}000 - p^2}$

46. $x = \sqrt[3]{1{,}500 - p^3}$

Life Sciences

47. *Biophysics.* In biophysics, the equation

$$(L + m)(V + n) = k$$

is called the *fundamental equation of muscle contraction*, where m, n, and k are constants, and V is the velocity of the shortening of muscle fibers for a muscle subjected to a load of L. Find dL/dV using implicit differentiation.

48. *Biophysics.* In Problem 47, find dV/dL using implicit differentiation.

Section 5-6 | Related Rates

The workers in a union are concerned that the rate at which wages are increasing is lagging behind the rate of increase in the company's profits. An automobile dealer wants to predict how badly an anticipated increase in interest rates will decrease his rate of sales. An investor is studying the connection between the rate of increase in the Dow Jones Average and the rate of increase in the Gross Domestic Product over the past 50 years.

In each of these situations there are two quantities—wages and profits in the first instance, for example—that are changing with respect to time. We would like to discover the precise relationship between the rates of increase (or decrease) of the two quantities. We will begin our discussion of such *related rates* by considering some familiar situations in which the two quantities are distances, and the two rates are velocities.

EXAMPLE 1   **Related Rates and Motion** A 26-foot ladder is placed against a wall (Fig. 1). If the top of the ladder is sliding down the wall at 2 feet per second, at what rate is the bottom of the ladder moving away from the wall when the bottom of the ladder is 10 feet away from the wall?

Solution   Many people reason that since the ladder is of constant length, the bottom of the ladder will move away from the wall at the same rate that the top of the ladder is moving down the wall. This is not the case, as we will see.

At any moment in time, let x be the distance of the bottom of the ladder from the wall, and let y be the distance of the top of the ladder on the wall (see Fig. 1). Both x and y are changing with respect to time and can be thought of

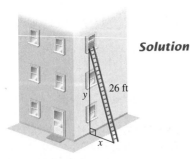

26 ft

FIGURE 1

as functions of time; that is, $x = x(t)$ and $y = y(t)$. Furthermore, x and y are related by the Pythagorean relationship:

$$x^2 + y^2 = 26^2 \qquad (1)$$

Differentiating equation (1) implicitly with respect to time t, and using the chain rule where appropriate, we obtain

$$2x\frac{dx}{dt} + 2y\frac{dy}{dt} = 0 \qquad (2)$$

The rates dx/dt and dy/dt are related by equation (2); hence, this type of problem is referred to as a **related rates problem.**

Now our problem is to find dx/dt when $x = 10$ feet, given that $dy/dt = -2$ (y is decreasing at a constant rate of 2 feet per second). We have all the quantities we need in equation (2) to solve for dx/dt, except y. When $x = 10$, y can be found using equation (1):

$$10^2 + y^2 = 26^2$$
$$y = \sqrt{26^2 - 10^2} = 24 \text{ feet}$$

Substitute $dy/dt = -2$, $x = 10$, and $y = 24$ into (2); then solve for dx/dt:

$$2(10)\frac{dx}{dt} + 2(24)(-2) = 0$$

$$\frac{dx}{dt} = \frac{-2(24)(-2)}{2(10)} = 4.8 \text{ feet per second}$$

Thus, the bottom of the ladder is moving away from the wall at a rate of 4.8 feet per second. ∎

◉ *Insight*   In the solution to Example 1, we used equation (1) two ways: first to find an equation relating dy/dt and dx/dt and second to find the value of y when $x = 10$. These steps must be done in this order. Substituting $x = 10$ and then differentiating does not produce any useful results:

$$x^2 + y^2 = 26^2 \quad \text{Substituting 10 for } x \text{ has the}$$
$$100 + y^2 = 26^2 \quad \text{effect of stopping the ladder.}$$
$$0 + 2yy' = 0 \quad \text{The rate of change of a stationary}$$
$$y' = 0 \quad \text{object is always 0, but that is not the}$$
$$\text{rate of change of the moving ladder.} \quad \bullet$$

Matched Problem 1   Again, a 26-foot ladder is placed against a wall (Fig. 1). If the bottom of the ladder is moving away from the wall at 3 feet per second, at what rate is the top moving down when the top of the ladder is 24 feet up the wall?

EXPLORE & DISCUSS 1   (A) For which values of x and y in Example 1 is dx/dt equal to 2 (that is, the same rate at which the ladder is sliding down the wall)?

(B) When is dx/dt greater than 2? Less than 2?

> **DEFINITION**   Suggestions for Solving Related Rates Problems
>
> **Step 1.** Sketch a figure if helpful.
>
> **Step 2.** Identify all relevant variables, including those whose rates are given and those whose rates are to be found.
>
> **Step 3.** Express all given rates and rates to be found as derivatives.
>
> **Step 4.** Find an equation connecting the variables in step 2.
>
> **Step 5.** Implicitly differentiate the equation found in step 4, using the chain rule where appropriate, and substitute in all given values.
>
> **Step 6.** Solve for the derivative that will give the unknown rate.

EXAMPLE 2   **Related Rates and Motion**   Suppose that two motorboats leave from the same point at the same time. If one travels north at 15 miles per hour and the other travels east at 20 miles per hour, how fast will the distance between them be changing after 2 hours?

Solution   First, draw a picture, as shown in Figure 2.

All variables, x, y, and z, are changing with time. Hence, they can be thought of as functions of time; $x = x(t)$, $y = y(t)$, and $z = z(t)$, given implicitly. It now makes sense to take derivatives of each variable with respect to time. From the Pythagorean theorem,

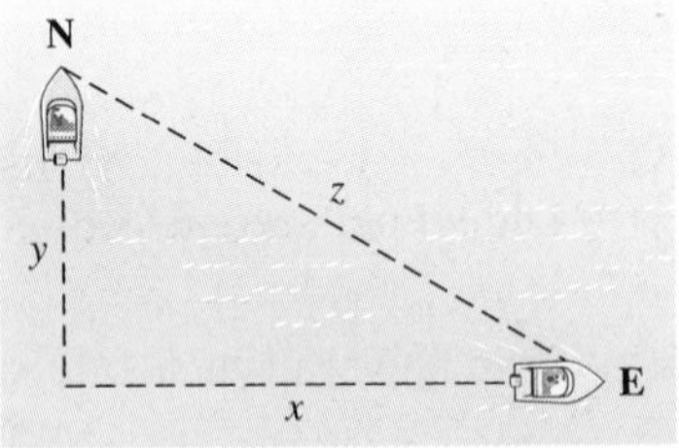

$$z^2 = x^2 + y^2 \tag{3}$$

We also know that

$$\frac{dx}{dt} = 20 \text{ miles per hour} \qquad \text{and} \qquad \frac{dy}{dt} = 15 \text{ miles per hour}$$

We would like to find dz/dt at the end of 2 hours; that is, when $x = 40$ miles and $y = 30$ miles. To do this, we differentiate both sides of equation (3) with respect to t and solve for dz/dt:

$$2z\frac{dz}{dt} = 2x\frac{dx}{dt} + 2y\frac{dy}{dt} \tag{4}$$

We have everything we need except z. When $x = 40$ and $y = 30$, we find z from equation (3) to be 50. Substituting the known quantities into equation (4), we obtain

$$2(50)\frac{dz}{dt} = 2(40)(20) + 2(30)(15)$$

$$\frac{dz}{dt} = 25 \text{ miles per hour}$$

Thus, the boats will be separating at a rate of 25 miles per hour.

FIGURE 2

Matched Problem 2   Repeat Example 2 for the situation at the end of 3 hours.

EXAMPLE 3   **Related Rates and Motion**   Suppose a point is moving along the graph of $x^2 + y^2 = 25$ (Fig. 3). When the point is at $(-3, 4)$, its x coordinate is increasing at the rate of 0.4 unit per second. How fast is the y coordinate changing at that moment?

Solution   Since both x and y are changing with respect to time, we can think of each as a function of time:

$$x = x(t) \qquad \text{and} \qquad y = y(t)$$

but restricted so that

$$x^2 + y^2 = 25 \qquad\qquad (5)$$

Our problem is now to find dy/dt, given $x = -3$, $y = 4$, and $dx/dt = 0.4$. Implicitly differentiating both sides of equation (5) with respect to t, we have

$$x^2 + y^2 = 25$$

$$2x\frac{dx}{dt} + 2y\frac{dy}{dt} = 0 \qquad\qquad \text{Divide both sides by 2.}$$

$$x\frac{dx}{dt} + y\frac{dy}{dt} = 0 \qquad\qquad \text{Substitute } x = -3, y = 4, \text{ and}$$
$$\qquad\qquad\qquad dx/dt = 0.4, \text{ and solve for}$$
$$(-3)(0.4) + 4\frac{dy}{dt} = 0 \qquad\qquad dy/dt.$$

$$\frac{dy}{dt} = 0.3 \text{ unit per second} \qquad\qquad \blacksquare$$

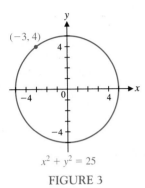

$x^2 + y^2 = 25$

FIGURE 3

Matched Problem 3   A point is moving on the graph of $y^3 = x^2$. When the point is at $(-8, 4)$, its y coordinate is decreasing at 2 units per second. How fast is the x coordinate changing at that moment? —————————— ∎

EXAMPLE 4   **Related Rates and Business** Suppose that for a company manufacturing transistor radios, the cost, revenue, and profit equations are given by

$$C = 5{,}000 + 2x \qquad \text{Cost equation}$$
$$R = 10x - 0.001x^2 \quad \text{Revenue equation}$$
$$P = R - C \qquad\qquad \text{Profit equation}$$

where the production output in 1 week is x radios. If production is increasing at the rate of 500 radios per week when production is 2,000 radios, find the rate of increase in

(A) Cost   (B) Revenue   (C) Profit

Solution   If production x is a function of time (it must be, since it is changing with respect to time), then C, R, and P must also be functions of time. These functions are implicitly (rather than explicitly) given. Letting t represent time in weeks, we differentiate both sides of each of the preceding three equations with respect to t, and then substitute $x = 2{,}000$ and $dx/dt = 500$ to find the desired rates.

(A) $C = 5{,}000 + 2x \qquad\qquad \text{Think: } C = C(t) \text{ and } x = x(t).$

$$\frac{dC}{dt} = \frac{d}{dt}(5{,}000) + \frac{d}{dt}(2x) \quad \text{Differentiate both sides with respect to } t.$$

$$\frac{dC}{dt} = 0 + 2\frac{dx}{dt} = 2\frac{dx}{dt}$$

Since $dx/dt = 500$ when $x = 2,000$,

$$\frac{dC}{dt} = 2(500) = \$1,000 \text{ per week}$$

Cost is increasing at a rate of $1,000 per week.

(B) $R = 10x - 0.001x^2$

$$\frac{dR}{dt} = \frac{d}{dt}(10x) - \frac{d}{dt}0.001x^2$$

$$\frac{dR}{dt} = 10\frac{dx}{dt} - 0.002x\frac{dx}{dt}$$

$$\frac{dR}{dt} = (10 - 0.002x)\frac{dx}{dt}$$

Since $dx/dt = 500$ when $x = 2,000$,

$$\frac{dR}{dt} = [10 - 0.002(2,000)](500) = \$3,000 \text{ per week}$$

Revenue is increasing at a rate of $3,000 per week.

(C) $P = R - C$

$$\frac{dP}{dt} = \frac{dR}{dt} - \frac{dC}{dt}$$

$$= \$3,000 - \$1,000 \quad \text{Results from parts (A) and (B)}$$

$$= \$2,000 \text{ per week}$$

Profit is increasing at a rate of $2,000 per week.

Matched Problem 4

Repeat Example 4 for a production level of 6,000 radios per week.

EXPLORE & DISCUSS 2

(A) In Example 4 suppose that $x(t) = 500t + 500$. Find the time and production level at which the profit is maximized.

(B) Suppose that $x(t) = t^2 + 492t + 16$. Find the time and production level at which the profit is maximized.

(C) Explain why it is unnecessary to know a formula for $x(t)$ in order to determine the production level at which the profit is maximized.

Answers to Matched Problems

1. $dy/dt = -1.25$ ft/sec

2. $dz/dt = 25$ mi/hr

3. $dx/dt = 6$ units/sec

4. (A) $dC/dt = \$1,000/\text{wk}$

   (B) $dR/dt = -\$1,000/\text{wk}$

   (C) $dP/dt = -\$2,000/\text{wk}$

Exercise 5-6

A *In Problems 1–6, assume that* $x = x(t)$ *and* $y = y(t)$.
Find the indicated rate, given the other information.

1. $y = x^2 + 2$; $dx/dt = 3$ when $x = 5$; find dy/dt

2. $y = x^3 - 3$; $dx/dt = -2$ when $x = 2$; find dy/dt

3. $x^2 + y^2 = 1$; $dy/dt = -4$ when $x = -0.6$ and $y = 0.8$; find dx/dt

4. $x^2 + y^2 = 4$; $dy/dt = 5$ when $x = 1.2$ and $y = -1.6$; find dx/dt

5. $x^2 + 3xy + y^2 = 11$; $dx/dt = 2$ when $x = 1$ and $y = 2$; find dy/dt

6. $x^2 - 2xy - y^2 = 7$; $dy/dt = -1$ when $x = 2$ and $y = -1$; find dx/dt

B

7. A point is moving on the graph of $xy = 36$. When the point is at $(4, 9)$, its x coordinate is increasing at 4 units per second. How fast is the y coordinate changing at that moment?

8. A point is moving on the graph of $4x^2 + 9y^2 = 36$. When the point is at $(3, 0)$, its y coordinate is decreasing at 2 units per second. How fast is its x coordinate changing at that moment?

9. A boat is being pulled toward a dock as indicated in the figure. If the rope is being pulled in at 3 feet per second, how fast is the distance between the dock and the boat decreasing when it is 30 feet from the dock?

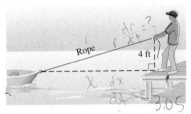

Figure for 9 and 10

10. Refer to Problem 9. Suppose that the distance between the boat and the dock is decreasing at 3.05 feet per second. How fast is the rope being pulled in when the boat is 10 feet from the dock?

11. A rock is thrown into a still pond and causes a circular ripple. If the radius of the ripple is increasing at 2 feet per second, how fast is the area changing when the radius is 10 feet? [Use $A = \pi R^2$, $\pi \approx 3.14$.]

12. Refer to Problem 11. How fast is the circumference of a circular ripple changing when the radius is 10 feet? [Use $C = 2\pi R$, $\pi \approx 3.14$.]

13. The radius of a spherical balloon is increasing at the rate of 3 centimeters per minute. How fast is the volume changing when the radius is 10 centimeters? [Use $V = \frac{4}{3}\pi R^3$, $\pi \approx 3.14$.]

14. Refer to Problem 13. How fast is the surface area of the sphere increasing when the radius is 10 centimeters? [Use $S = 4\pi R^2$, $\pi \approx 3.14$.]

15. Boyle's law for enclosed gases states that if the volume is kept constant, the pressure P and temperature T are related by the equation

$$\frac{P}{T} = k$$

where k is a constant. If the temperature is increasing at 3 kelvin per hour, what is the rate of change of pressure when the temperature is 250 kelvin and the pressure is 500 pounds per square inch?

16. Boyle's law for enclosed gases states that if the temperature is kept constant, the pressure P and volume V of the gas are related by the equation

$$VP = k$$

where k is a constant. If the volume is decreasing by 5 cubic inches per second, what is the rate of change of the pressure when the volume is 1,000 cubic inches and the pressure is 40 pounds per square inch?

17. A 10-foot ladder is placed against a vertical wall. Suppose the bottom slides away from the wall at a constant rate of 3 feet per second. How fast is the top sliding down the wall (negative rate) when the bottom is 6 feet from the wall? [*Hint:* Use the Pythagorean theorem: $a^2 + b^2 = c^2$, where c is the length of the hypotenuse of a right triangle and a and b are the lengths of the two shorter sides.]

18. A weather balloon is rising vertically at the rate of 5 meters per second. An observer is standing on the ground 300 meters from the point where the balloon was released. At what rate is the distance between the observer and the balloon changing when the balloon is 400 meters high?

C

19. A street light is on top of a 20-foot pole. A person who is 5 feet tall walks away from the pole at the rate of 5 feet per second. At what rate is the tip of the person's shadow moving away from the pole when he is 20 feet from the pole?

20. Refer to Problem 19. At what rate is the person's shadow growing when he is 20 feet from the pole?

21. Helium is pumped into a spherical balloon at a constant rate of 4 cubic feet per second. How fast is the

radius increasing after 1 minute? After 2 minutes? Is there any time at which the radius is increasing at a rate of 100 feet per second? Explain.

22. A point is moving along the x axis at a constant rate of 5 units per second. At which point is its distance from $(0, 1)$ increasing at a rate of 2 units per second? At 4 units per second? At 5 units per second? At 10 units per second? Explain.

23. A point is moving on the graph of $y = e^x + x + 1$ in such a way that its x coordinate is always increasing at a rate of 3 units per second. How fast is the y coordinate changing when the point crosses the x axis?

24. A point is moving on the graph of $x^3 + y^2 = 1$ in such a way that its y coordinate is always increasing at a rate of 2 units per second. At which point(s) is the x coordinate increasing at a rate of 1 unit per second?

Applications

Business & Economics

25. *Cost, revenue, and profit rates.* Suppose that for a company manufacturing calculators, the cost, revenue, and profit equations are given by

$$C = 90,000 + 30x \qquad R = 300x - \frac{x^3}{30}$$

$$P = R - C$$

where the production output in 1 week is x calculators. If production is increasing at a rate of 500 calculators per week when production output is 6,000 calculators, find the rate of increase (decrease) in

(A) Cost   (B) Revenue   (C) Profit

26. *Cost, revenue, and profit rates.* Repeat Problem 25 for

$$C = 72,000 + 60x \qquad R = 200x - \frac{x^2}{30}$$

$$P = R - C$$

where production is increasing at a rate of 500 calculators per week at a production level of 1,500 calculators.

27. *Advertising.* A retail store estimates that weekly sales s and weekly advertising costs x (both in dollars) are related by

$$s = 60,000 - 40,000e^{-0.0005x}$$

The current weekly advertising costs are $2,000, and these costs are increasing at the rate of $300 per week. Find the current rate of change of sales.

28. *Advertising.* Repeat Problem 27 for

$$s = 50,000 - 20,000e^{-0.0004x}$$

29. *Price–demand.* The price p (in dollars) and demand x for a product are related by

$$2x^2 + 5xp + 50p^2 = 80,000$$

(A) If the price is increasing at a rate of $2 per month when the price is $30, find the rate of change of the demand.

(B) If the demand is decreasing at a rate of 6 units per month when the demand is 150 units, find the rate of change of the price.

30. *Price–demand.* Repeat Problem 29 for

$$x^2 + 2xp + 25p^2 = 74,500$$

Life Sciences

31. *Pollution.* An oil tanker aground on a reef is leaking oil that forms a circular oil slick about 0.1 foot thick (see the figure). To estimate the rate dV/dt (in cubic feet per minute) at which the oil is leaking from the tanker, it was found that the radius of the slick was increasing at 0.32 foot per minute ($dR/dt = 0.32$) when the radius R was 500 feet. Find dV/dt, using $\pi \approx 3.14$.

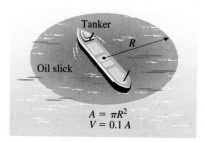

$$A = \pi R^2$$
$$V = 0.1 A$$

Figure for 31

Social Sciences

32. *Learning.* A person who is new on an assembly line performs an operation in T minutes after x performances of the operation, as given by

$$T = 6\left(1 + \frac{1}{\sqrt{x}}\right)$$

If $dx/dt = 6$ operations per hour, where t is time in hours, find dT/dt after 36 performances of the operation.

Chapter 5 Review

Important Terms, Symbols, and Concepts

5-1 The Constant e and Continuous Compound Interest

The number e is defined as

$$\lim_{x \to \infty}\left(1 + \frac{1}{n}\right)^n = \lim_{x \to 0}(1 + s)^{1/s} = 2.718\ 281\ 828\ 459\ldots$$

If the number of compounding periods in one year are increased without limit, we obtain the **compound interest formula**

$$A = Pe^{rt}$$

where

P = principal

r = annual nominal interest rate compounded continuously

t = time in years

A = amount at time t

5-2 Exponential Functions and Their Derivatives

A function m is a **composite** of functions f and g if

$$m(x) = f[g(x)]$$

The domain of m is the set of all numbers x such that x is in the domain of g and $g(x)$ is in the domain of f. **Derivative formulas for the exponential function** are

$$\frac{d}{dx}e^x = e^x \quad \text{and} \quad \frac{d}{dx}e^{u(x)} = e^{u(x)}u'(x)$$

5-3 Logarithmic Functions and Their Derivatives

The inverse of an exponential function is called a **logarithmic function.** For $b > 0$ and $b \neq 1$,

Logarithmic form		Exponential form
$y = \log_b x$	is equivalent to	$x = b^y$

Derivative formulas for logarithmic functions are

$$\frac{d}{dx}\ln x = \frac{1}{x} \quad \text{and} \quad \frac{d}{dx}\ln u(x) = \frac{u'(x)}{u(x)}$$

The **change-of-base formula,** $\log_b x = (1/\ln b)\ln x$, and other properties of logarithms and exponents produce derivative formulas for other bases ($b > 0, b \neq 1$):

$$\frac{d}{dx}\log_b x = \frac{1}{\ln b}\left(\frac{1}{x}\right) \quad \text{and} \quad \frac{d}{dx}b^x = b^x \ln b$$

5-4 Chain Rule: General Form

If $y = f(u)$ and $u = g(x)$ define the composite function $m(x) = f[g(x)]$, then the **chain rule** implies that $m'(x) = f'[g(x)]g'(x)$.

The **relative rate of change,** or the **logarithmic derivative,** of a function $f(x)$ is $f'(x)/f(x)$ and the **percentage rate of change** is $100 \times (f'(x)/f(x))$.

If price and demand are related by $x = f(p)$, then the **elasticity of demand** is given by

$$E(p) = -\frac{pf'(p)}{f(p)} = -\frac{\text{relative rate of change of demand}}{\text{relative rate of change of price}}$$

Demand is inelastic if $0 < E(p) < 1$. (Demand is not sensitive to changes in price. A change in price produces a smaller change in demand.) **Demand is elastic** if $E(p) > 1$. (Demand is sensitive to changes in price. A change in price produces a larger change in demand.) **Demand has unit elasticity** if $E(p) = 1$. (A change in price produces the same change in demand.)

If $R(p) = pf(p)$ is the revenue function, then $R'(p)$ and $[1 - E(p)]$ always have the same sign.

5-5 Implicit Differentiation

If $y = y(x)$ is a function defined by an equation like $F(x, y) = 0$, we use **implicit differentiation** to find an equation in x, y, and y'.

5-6 Related Rates

If x and y represent quantities that are changing with respect to time and are related by an equation like $F(x, y) = 0$, then implicit differentiation produces an equation that relates $x, y, dy/dt$ and dx/dt. Problems of this type are called **related rates problems.**

- *Suggestions for Solving Related Rates Problems*

  Step 1. Sketch a figure if helpful.

  Step 2. Identify all relevant variables, including those whose rates are given and those whose rates are to be found.

  Step 3. Express all given rates and rates to be found as derivatives.

  Step 4. Find an equation connecting the variables in step 2.

  Step 5. Implicitly differentiate the equation found in step 4, using the chain rule where appropriate, and substitute in all given values.

  Step 6. Solve for the derivative that will give the unknown rate.

Review Exercise

Work through all the problems in this chapter review and check your answers in the back of the book. Answers to all review problems are there along with section numbers in italics to indicate where each type of problem is discussed. Where weaknesses show up, review appropriate sections in the text.

A

1. Use a calculator to evaluate $A = 2{,}000e^{0.09t}$ to the nearest cent for $t = 5, 10,$ and 20.

Find the indicated derivatives in Problems 2–4.

2. $\dfrac{d}{dx}(2 \ln x + 3e^x)$ 3. $\dfrac{d}{dx}e^{2x-3}$

4. y' for $y = \ln(2x + 7)$

5. Let $y = \ln u$ and $u = 3 + e^x$.

   (A) Express y in terms of x.

   (B) Use the chain rule to find dy/dx, and then express dy/dx in terms of x.

6. Find y' for $y = y(x)$ defined implicitly by the equation $2y^2 - 3x^3 - 5 = 0$, and evaluate at $(x, y) = (1, 2)$.

7. For $y = 3x^2 - 5$, where $x = x(t)$ and $y = y(t)$, find dy/dt if $dx/dt = 3$ when $x = 12$.

8. Given the demand equation $25p + x = 1{,}000$:

   (A) Express the demand x as a function of the price p.

   (B) Find the elasticity of demand, $E(p)$.

   (C) Find $E(15)$ and interpret.

   (D) Express the revenue function as a function of price p.

   (E) If $p = \$25$, what is the effect of a price cut on revenue?

B

9. Graph $y = 100e^{-0.1x}$.

10. Use a calculator and a table of values to investigate

$$\lim_{n \to \infty} \left(1 + \frac{2}{n}\right)^n$$

Do you think the limit exists? If so, what do you think it is?

Find the indicated derivatives in Problems 11–16.

11. $\dfrac{d}{dz}[(\ln z)^7 + \ln z^7]$ 12. $\dfrac{d}{dx}(x^6 \ln x)$

13. $\dfrac{d}{dx} \dfrac{e^x}{x^6}$

14. y' for $y = \ln(2x^3 - 3x)$

15. $f'(x)$ for $f(x) = e^{x^3 - x^2}$

16. dy/dx for $y = e^{-2x} \ln 5x$

17. Find the equation of the line tangent to the graph of $y = f(x) = 1 + e^{-x}$ at $x = 0$. At $x = -1$.

18. Find y' for $y = y(x)$ defined implicitly by the equation $x^2 - 3xy + 4y^2 = 23$, and find the slope of the graph at $(-1, 2)$.

19. Find x' for $x = x(t)$ defined implicitly by $x^3 - 2t^2x + 8 = 0$, and evaluate at $(t, x) = (-2, 2)$.

20. Find y' for $y = y(x)$ defined implicitly by $x - y^2 = e^y$, and evaluate at $(1, 0)$.

21. Find y' for $y = y(x)$ defined implicitly by $\ln y = x^2 - y^2$, and evaluate at $(1, 1)$.

22. A point is moving on the graph of $y^2 - 4x^2 = 12$ so that its x coordinate is decreasing at 2 units per second when $(x, y) = (1, 4)$. Find the rate of change of the y coordinate.

23. A 17-foot ladder is placed against a wall. If the foot of the ladder is pushed toward the wall at 0.5 foot per second, how fast is the top rising when the foot of the ladder is 8 feet from the wall?

24. Water from a water heater is leaking onto a floor. A circular pool is created whose area is increasing at the rate of 24 square inches per minute. How fast is the radius R of the pool increasing when the radius is 12 inches? $[A = \pi R^2]$

25. Find the values of p for which demand is elastic and the values for which demand is inelastic if the price–demand equation is
$$x = f(p) = 20(p - 15)^2 \qquad 0 \le p \le 15$$

26. Graph the revenue function and indicate the regions of inelastic and elastic demand of the graph if the price–demand equation is
$$x = f(p) = 5(20 - p) \qquad 0 \le p \le 20$$

C *In Problems 27–30, find the absolute maximum value of $f(x)$ for $x > 0$.*

27. $f(x) = 11x - 2x \ln x$

28. $f(x) = 10xe^{-2x}$

29. $f(x) = 3x - x^2 + e^{-x}$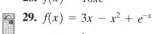

30. $f(x) = \dfrac{\ln x}{e^x}$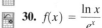

In Problems 31 and 32, apply the graphing strategy discussed in Section 4-4 to f, summarize the pertinent information, and sketch the graph.

31. $f(x) = 5 - 5e^{-x}$ 32. $f(x) = x^3 \ln x$

33. Let $y = w^3$, $w = \ln u$, and $u = 4 - e^x$.

(A) Express y in terms of x.

(B) Use the chain rule to find dy/dx, and then express dy/dx in terms of x.

Find the indicated derivatives in Problems 34–36.

34. y' for $y = 5^{x^2-1}$

35. $\dfrac{d}{dx} \log_5(x^2 - x)$

36. $\dfrac{d}{dx} \sqrt{\ln(x^2 + x)}$

37. Find y' for $y = y(x)$ defined implicitly by the equation $e^{xy} = x^2 + y + 1$, and evaluate at $(0, 0)$.

38. A rock is thrown into a still pond and causes a circular ripple. Suppose the radius is increasing at a constant rate of 3 feet per second. Show that the area does not increase at a constant rate. When is the rate of increase of the area the smallest? The largest? Explain.

39. A point moves along the graph of $y = x^3$ in such a way that its y coordinate is increasing at a constant rate of 5 units per second. Does the x coordinate ever increase at a faster rate than the y coordinate? Explain.

Applications

Business & Economics

40. *Doubling time.* How long will it take money to double if it is invested at 5% interest compounded

(A) Annually?   (B) Continuously?

41. *Continuous compound interest.* If $100 is invested at 10% interest compounded continuously, the amount (in dollars) at the end of t years is given by

$$A = 100e^{0.1t}$$

Find $A'(t)$, $A'(1)$, and $A'(10)$.

42. *Marginal analysis.* The price–demand equation for 14-cubic foot refrigerators at an appliance store is

$$p(x) = 1{,}000e^{-0.02x}$$

where x is the monthly demand and p is the price in dollars. Find the marginal revenue equation.

43. *Maximum revenue.* For the price–demand equation in Problem 42, find the production level and price per unit that produces the maximum revenue. What is the maximum revenue?

44. *Maximum revenue.* Graph the revenue function from Problems 42 and 43 for $0 \le x \le 100$.

45. *Maximum profit.* Refer to Problem 42. If the refrigerators cost the store $220 each, find the price (to the nearest cent) that maximizes the profit. What is the maximum profit (to the nearest dollar)?

46. *Maximum profit.* The data in the table show the daily demand x for cream puffs at a state fair at various price levels p. If it costs $1 to make a cream puff, use logarithmic regression ($p = a + b \ln x$) to find the price (to the nearest cent) that maximizes profit.

Demand	Price per Cream Puff ($)
x	p
3,125	1.99
3,879	1.89
5,263	1.79
5,792	1.69
6,748	1.59
8,120	1.49

47. *Minimum average cost.* The cost of producing x units of a product is given by

$$C(x) = 200 + 50x - 50 \ln x \qquad x \ge 1$$

Find the minimum average cost.

48. *Demand equation.* Given the demand equation

$$x = \sqrt{5{,}000 - 2p^3}$$

find the rate of change of p with respect to x by implicit differentiation (x is the number of items that can be sold at a price of p per item).

49. *Rate of change of revenue.* A company is manufacturing a new video game and can sell all that it manufactures. The revenue (in dollars) is given by

$$R = 36x - \frac{x^2}{20}$$

where the production output in 1 day is x games. If production is increasing at 10 games per day when production is 250 games per day, find the rate of increase in revenue.

50. *Revenue and elasticity.* The price–demand equation for home-delivered 12-inch pizzas is

$$p = 16.8 - 0.002x$$

where x is the number of pizzas delivered weekly. The current price of one pizza is $8. In order to generate additional revenue from the sale of 12-inch pizzas, would you recommend a price increase or a price decrease?

51. *Average income.* A model for the average income per household before taxes are paid is

$$f(t) = 1,700t + 20,500$$

where t is years since 1980. Find the relative rate of change of household income in 2010.

Life Sciences

52. *Drug concentration.* The concentration of a drug in the bloodstream t hours after injection is given approximately by

$$C(t) = 5e^{-0.3t}$$

where $C(t)$ is concentration in milligrams per milliliter. What is the rate of change of concentration after 1 hour? After 5 hours?

53. *Wound healing.* A circular wound on an arm is healing at the rate of 45 square millimeters per day (the area of the wound is decreasing at this rate). How

fast is the radius R of the wound decreasing when $R = 15$ millimeters? $[A = \pi R^2]$

Social Sciences

54. *Psychology: learning.* In a computer assembly plant, a new employee, on the average, is able to assemble

$$N(t) = 10(1 - e^{-0.4t})$$

units after t days of on-the-job training.

(A) What is the rate of learning after 1 day? After 5 days?

(B) Graph N for $0 \le t \le 10$.

55. *Learning.* A new worker on the production line performs an operation in T minutes after x performances of the operation, as given by

$$T = 2\left(1 + \frac{1}{x^{3/2}}\right)$$

If, after performing the operation 9 times, the rate of improvement is $dx/dt = 3$ operations per hour, find the rate of improvement in time dT/dt in performing each operation.

Group Activity 1   *Increasing Production of Cellular Phones*

A manufacturer of cellular phones is formulating plans to increase production from the current level of 5,000 phones per week. The marketing research department has determined the price–demand equation to be

$$p = -0.5e^{0.0005x} + 0.003x + 75 \qquad \text{for } 5,000 \le x \le 10,000$$

where x is the weekly demand and p is the price per phone (in dollars).

(A) If the demand is increasing at a rate of 400 phones per week when the demand is 6,000 phones per week, find the rate of change of the price.

(B) Assume the cost function is $C(x) = 300,000 + 25x$. Determine the production level that maximizes profit. Graph and interpret the cost function, the revenue function, and the profit function for $5,000 \le x \le 10,000$.

(C) Suppose the manufacturer decides to increase production from 5,000 phones per week to 7,500 phones per week over a 10-week period. If the rate of increase in production is constant over the 10-week period, find functions that represent production, cost, revenue, and profit, all as functions of time for $0 \le t \le 10$. Graph and interpret each of these four functions of time.

(D) Repeat part (C), assuming the manufacturer adopts a strategy whereby production increases slowly at the beginning of the 10-week period and more rapidly near the end, in accordance with the production function

$$x = 5,000 + 25t^2 \text{ for } 0 \le t \le 10$$

Group Activity 2   *Point of Diminishing Returns**

Table 1 shows the total number of copies of a new spreadsheet for personal computers that have been sold x months after the product has been introduced. The **point of diminishing returns** occurs at the value of x where the rate of change of sales assumes its maximum value. In Section 4-3 we saw that a cubic polynomial model can be used to describe this situation.

TABLE 1

Month x	Total Sales (thousands of copies)
4	71
8	182
12	305
16	405
20	450

(A) Find a cubic regression model $P(x)$ for the data in Table 1, and find the point of diminishing returns (correct to two decimal places).

The cubic polynomial model provides a good description of the data for $4 \leq x \leq 20$, but not for $x > 20$. A more sophisticated model that can be used to predict the behavior for $x > 20$ is provided by a **logistic growth function** of the form

$$L(x) = \frac{c}{1 + ae^{-bx}} \tag{1}$$

(B) Find a logistic regression model $L(x)$ for the data in Table 1, and find the point of diminishing returns (correct to two decimal places) for this model.

(C) Graph $P(x)$ and $L(x)$ for Xmin = 4, Xmax = 20, Ymin = 0, and Ymax = 500. Are there any significant differences in the descriptions of the data provided by these two functions?

(D) Repeat part (C) with Xmax increased to 30.

(E) Find $\lim_{x \to \infty} L(x)$ (correct to the nearest integer). The value of this limit is called the **carrying capacity** of the model. Compare the carrying capacity with the value of $L(x)$ at the point of diminishing returns found in part (B).

TABLE 2

Month x	Total Sales (thousands of copies)
4	151
8	204
12	327
16	480
20	530

(F) Sales data for a new word processor are given in Table 2. Find a logistic regression model for the data, the point of diminishing returns (correct to two decimal places), and the carrying capacity (correct to the nearest integer).

(G) For any function of the form in equation (1), show that the carrying capacity is c, the point of diminishing returns is $(\ln a)/b$, and the value of the function at the point of diminishing returns is $c/2$.

*This group activity requires a graphing utility that supports logistic regression.

OBJECTIVES

1. Find antiderivatives of basic functions.
2. Find indefinite integrals using the method of substitution.
3. Use solutions of differential equations to solve problems in population growth, radioactive decay, continuous compound interest, advertising, blood pressure, and epidemiology.
4. Approximate areas by summing the areas of rectangles.
5. Evaluate definite integrals using the Fundamental Theorem of Calculus.
6. Use the definite integral to determine the average value of a continuous function over a closed interval.

CHAPTER PROBLEM

The total accumulated costs $C(t)$ and revenues $R(t)$ (in millions of dollars) for an oil well satisfy

$$C'(t) = 9 \quad \text{and} \quad R'(t) = 20e^{-0.05t} \quad 0 \le t \le 30$$

(A) Find the useful life of the well and the total profit accumulated during the useful life.

(B) To encourage a longer production time, the tax laws are changed so that C' becomes

$$C'(t) = 7 \qquad 0 \le t \le 30$$

What is the useful life of the well now?

Integration

INTRODUCTION

The preceding three chapters dealt with differential calculus. We now begin the development of the second main part of calculus, called *integral calculus*. Two types of integrals are introduced, the *indefinite integral* and the *definite integral*, each quite different from the other. But through the remarkable *fundamental theorem of calculus*, we show that not only are the two integral forms intimately related, but both are intimately related to differentiation.

Section 6-1 | Antiderivatives and Indefinite Integrals

➤ Antiderivatives
➤ Indefinite Integrals: Formulas and Properties
➤ Applications

Many operations in mathematics have reverses—compare addition and subtraction, multiplication and division, and powers and roots. We now know how to find the derivatives of many functions. The reverse operation, *antidifferentiation* (the reconstruction of a function from its derivative) will receive our attention in this and the next two sections. A function F is an **antiderivative** of a function f if $F'(x) = f(x)$. We develop special antiderivative formulas in much the same way as we developed derivative formulas.

➤ Antiderivatives

(A) Find three antiderivatives of $2x$.

(B) How many antiderivatives of $2x$ exist, and how are they related to each other?

(C) What notation would you use to represent all antiderivatives of $2x$?

The function $F(x) = \dfrac{x^3}{3}$ is an antiderivative of the function $f(x) = x^2$ because

$$\frac{d}{dx}\left(\frac{x^3}{3}\right) = x^2$$

However, $F(x)$ is not the only antiderivative of x^2. Note also that

$$\frac{d}{dx}\left(\frac{x^3}{3} + 2\right) = x^2 \qquad \frac{d}{dx}\left(\frac{x^3}{3} - \pi\right) = x^2 \qquad \frac{d}{dx}\left(\frac{x^3}{3} + \sqrt{5}\right) = x^2$$

Therefore,

$$\frac{x^3}{3} + 2 \qquad \frac{x^3}{3} - \pi \qquad \frac{x^3}{3} + \sqrt{5}$$

are also antiderivatives of x^2, because each has x^2 as a derivative. In fact, it appears that

$$\frac{x^3}{3} + C \qquad \text{for any real number } C$$

is an antiderivative of x^2, because

$$\frac{d}{dx}\left(\frac{x^3}{3} + C\right) = x^2$$

Antidifferentiation of a given function does not lead to a unique function, but to an entire family of functions.

Does the expression

$$\frac{x^3}{3} + C \qquad \text{with } C \text{ any real number}$$

include all antiderivatives of x^2? Theorem 1 (which we state without proof) indicates that the answer is yes.

THEOREM 1   On Antiderivatives

If the derivatives of two functions are equal on an open interval (a, b), then the functions differ by at most a constant. Symbolically: If F and G are differentiable functions on the interval (a, b) and $F'(x) = G'(x)$ for all x in (a, b), then $F(x) = G(x) + k$ for some constant k.

◉ Insight   Suppose that $F(x)$ is an antiderivative of $f(x)$. If $G(x)$ is any other antiderivative of $f(x)$, then, by Theorem 1, the graph of $G(x)$ is a vertical translation of the graph of $F(x)$ (see Section 1-2).   ●

EXAMPLE 1   **A Family of Antiderivatives**   Note that

$$\frac{d}{dx}\left(\frac{x^2}{2}\right) = x$$

(A) Find all antiderivatives of $f(x) = x$.

(B) Graph the antiderivative of $f(x) = x$ that passes through the point $(0, 0)$; through the point $(0, 1)$; through the point $(0, 2)$.

(C) How are the graphs of the three antiderivatives in part (B) related?

Solution   (A) By Theorem 1, any antiderivative of $f(x)$ has the form

$$F(x) = \frac{x^2}{2} + k$$

where k is a real number.

(B) Because $F(0) = (0^2/2) + k = k$, the functions

$$F_0(x) = \frac{x^2}{2}, \quad F_1(x) = \frac{x^2}{2} + 1, \quad \text{and} \quad F_2(x) = \frac{x^2}{2} + 2$$

pass through the points $(0, 0)$, $(0, 1)$, and $(0, 2)$, respectively (see Fig. 1).

(C) The graphs of the three antiderivatives are vertical translations of each other.

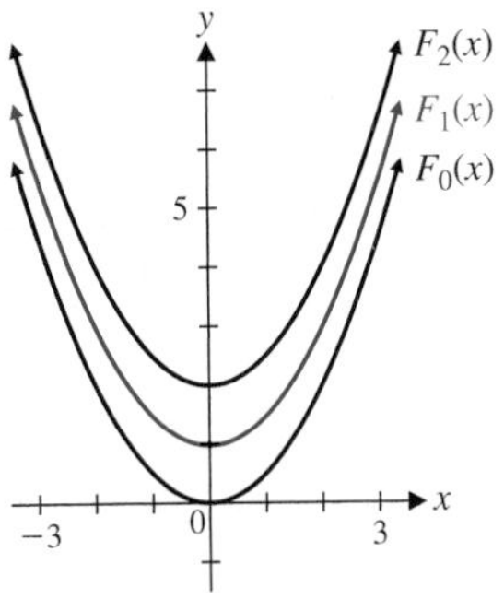

FIGURE 1

Matched Problem 1   Note that

$$\frac{d}{dx}(x^3) = 3x^2$$

(A) Find all antiderivatives of $f(x) = 3x^2$.

(B) Graph the antiderivative of $f(x) = 3x^2$ that passes through the point $(0, 0)$; through the point $(0, 1)$; through the point $(0, 2)$.

(C) How are the graphs of the three antiderivatives in part (B) related?

▶ Indefinite Integrals: Formulas and Properties

Theorem 1 states that if the derivatives of two functions are equal, then the functions differ by at most a constant. We use the symbol

$$\int f(x)\, dx$$

called the **indefinite integral,** to represent the family of all antiderivatives of $f(x)$, and write

$$\int f(x)\, dx = F(x) + C \quad \text{if} \quad F'(x) = f(x)$$

The symbol $\int$ is called an **integral sign,** and the function $f(x)$ is called the **integrand.** The symbol dx indicates that the antidifferentiation is performed with respect to the variable x. (We will have more to say about the symbols $\int$ and dx later in this chapter.) The arbitrary constant C is called the **constant of integration.** Referring to the preceding discussion, we can write

$$\int x^2\, dx = \frac{x^3}{3} + C \quad \text{since} \quad \frac{d}{dx}\left(\frac{x^3}{3} + C\right) = x^2$$

Of course, variables other than x can be used in indefinite integrals. For example,

$$\int t^2 \, dt = \frac{t^3}{3} + C \qquad \text{since} \qquad \frac{d}{dt}\left(\frac{t^3}{3} + C\right) = t^2$$

or

$$\int u^2 \, du = \frac{u^3}{3} + C \qquad \text{since} \qquad \frac{d}{du}\left(\frac{u^3}{3} + C\right) = u^2$$

The fact that indefinite integration and differentiation are reverse operations, except for the addition of the constant of integration, can be expressed symbolically as

$$\frac{d}{dx}\left[\int f(x) \, dx\right] = f(x) \quad \text{\textit{The derivative of the indefinite integral of f(x) is f(x).}}$$

and

$$\int F'(x) \, dx = F(x) + C \quad \text{\textit{The indefinite integral of the derivative of F(x) is F(x) + C.}}$$

We can develop formulas for the indefinite integrals of certain basic functions from the formulas for derivatives that were established in Chapters 3 and 5.

FORMULAS   **Indefinite Integrals of Basic Functions**

For C a constant:

1. $\displaystyle\int x^n \, dx = \frac{x^{n+1}}{n + 1} + C, \qquad n \neq -1$

2. $\displaystyle\int e^x \, dx = e^x + C$

3. $\displaystyle\int \frac{1}{x} \, dx = \ln|x| + C, \qquad x \neq 0$

Each formula can be justified by showing that the derivative of the right-hand side is the integrand of the left-hand side (see Problems 93–96 in Exercise 6-1). Note that formula 1 does not give the antiderivative of x^{-1} (because $x^{n+1}/(n + 1)$ is undefined when $n = -1$), but formula 3 does.

Formulas 1, 2, and 3 do *not* provide a formula for the indefinite integral of the function $\ln x$. Show, however, assuming $x > 0$, that

$$\int \ln x \, dx = x \ln x - x + C$$

by differentiating the right-hand side. [We will discuss a technique for deriving such indefinite integral formulas in Section 7-3.]

We can obtain properties of the indefinite integral from properties of the derivative that were established in Chapter 3.

PROPERTIES　Of Indefinite Integrals

For k a constant:

4. $\displaystyle\int kf(x)\,dx = k\int f(x)\,dx$

5. $\displaystyle\int [f(x) \pm g(x)]\,dx = \int f(x)\,dx \pm \int g(x)\,dx$

Property 4 states that

> **The indefinite integral of a constant times a function is the constant times the indefinite integral of the function.**

Property 5 states that

> **The indefinite integral of the sum of two functions is the sum of the indefinite integrals, and the indefinite integral of the difference of two functions is the difference of the indefinite integrals.**

To establish property 4, let F be a function such that $F'(x) = f(x)$. Then

$$k\int f(x)\,dx = k\int F'(x)\,dx = k[F(x) + C_1] = kF(x) + kC_1$$

and since $[kF(x)]' = kF'(x) = kf(x)$, we have

$$\int kf(x)\,dx = \int kF'(x)\,dx = kF(x) + C_2$$

But $kF(x) + kC_1$ and $kF(x) + C_2$ describe the same set of functions, since C_1 and C_2 are arbitrary real numbers. Thus, property 4 is established. Property 5 can be established in a similar manner (see Problems 97–98 in Exercise 6-1).

Caution

It is important to remember that property 4 states that **a constant factor can be moved across an integral sign. A variable factor cannot be moved across an integral sign:**

CONSTANT FACTOR	VARIABLE FACTOR
$\displaystyle\int 5x^{1/2}\,dx = 5\int x^{1/2}\,dx$	$\displaystyle\int xx^{1/2}\,dx \neq x\int x^{1/2}\,dx$

Indefinite integral formulas and properties can be used together to find indefinite integrals for many frequently encountered functions. For **example**, formula 1, for $n = 0$, gives

$$\int dx = x + C$$

Therefore, by property 4,

$$\int k\,dx = k(x + C) = kx + kC$$

Because kC is a constant, it is customary to replace it by a single symbol that denotes an arbitrary constant (usually C), so we write

$$\int k\,dx = kx + C$$

In words,

> **The indefinite integral of a constant function with value k is $kx + C$.**

Similarly, using property 5, and then formulas 2 and 3,

$$\int \left(e^x + \frac{1}{x} \right) dx = \int e^x \, dx + \int \frac{1}{x} \, dx$$

$$= e^x + C_1 + \ln|x| + C_2$$

Because $C_1 + C_2$ is a constant, it is usually replaced by the symbol C, and we write

$$\int \left(e^x + \frac{1}{x} \right) dx = e^x + \ln|x| + C$$

EXAMPLE 2 **Using Indefinite Integral Properties and Formulas**

(A) $\displaystyle\int 5 \, dx = 5x + C$

(B) $\displaystyle\int 9e^x \, dx = 9 \int e^x \, dx = 9e^x + C$

(C) $\displaystyle\int 5t^7 \, dt = 5 \int t^7 \, dt = 5\frac{t^8}{8} + C = \frac{5}{8}t^8 + C$

(D) $\displaystyle\int (4x^3 + 2x - 1) \, dx = \int 4x^3 \, dx + \int 2x \, dx - \int dx$ Property 4 can be extended to the sum and difference of an arbitrary number of functions.

$$= 4 \int x^3 \, dx + 2 \int x \, dx - \int dx$$

$$= \frac{4x^4}{4} + \frac{2x^2}{2} - x + C$$

$$= x^4 + x^2 - x + C$$

(E) $\displaystyle\int \left(2e^x + \frac{3}{x} \right) dx = 2 \int e^x \, dx + 3 \int \frac{1}{x} \, dx$

$$= 2e^x + 3 \ln|x| + C$$

To check any of the results in Example 2, we differentiate the final result to obtain the integrand in the original indefinite integral. When you evaluate an indefinite integral, do not forget to include the arbitrary constant C.

Matched Problem 2   Find each indefinite integral:

(A) $\displaystyle\int 2 \, dx$

(B) $\displaystyle\int 16e^t \, dt$

(C) $\displaystyle\int 3x^4 \, dx$

(D) $\displaystyle\int (2x^5 - 3x^2 + 1) \, dx$

(E) $\displaystyle\int \left(\frac{5}{x} - 4e^x \right) dx$

EXAMPLE 3   **Using Indefinite Integral Properties and Formulas**

(A) $\displaystyle\int \frac{4}{x^3}\, dx = \int 4x^{-3}\, dx = \frac{4x^{-3+1}}{-3+1} + C = -2x^{-2} + C$

(B) $\displaystyle\int 5\sqrt[3]{u^2}\, du = 5\int u^{2/3}\, du = 5\frac{u^{(2/3)+1}}{\frac{2}{3}+1} + C$

$$= 5\frac{u^{5/3}}{\frac{5}{3}} + C = 3u^{5/3} + C$$

(C) $\displaystyle\int \frac{x^3 - 3}{x^2}\, dx = \int \left(\frac{x^3}{x^2} - \frac{3}{x^2}\right) dx$

$$= \int (x - 3x^{-2})\, dx$$

$$= \int x\, dx - 3\int x^{-2}\, dx$$

$$= \frac{x^{1+1}}{1+1} - 3\frac{x^{-2+1}}{-2+1} + C$$

$$= \tfrac{1}{2}x^2 + 3x^{-1} + C$$

(D) $\displaystyle\int \left(\frac{2}{\sqrt[3]{x}} - 6\sqrt{x}\right) dx = \int (2x^{-1/3} - 6x^{1/2})\, dx$

$$= 2\int x^{-1/3}\, dx - 6\int x^{1/2}\, dx$$

$$= 2\frac{x^{(-1/3)+1}}{-\frac{1}{3}+1} - 6\frac{x^{(1/2)+1}}{\frac{1}{2}+1} + C$$

$$= 2\frac{x^{2/3}}{\frac{2}{3}} - 6\frac{x^{3/2}}{\frac{3}{2}} + C$$

$$= 3x^{2/3} - 4x^{3/2} + C$$

(E) $\displaystyle\int x(x^2 + 2)\, dx = \int (x^3 + 2x)\, dx = \frac{x^4}{4} + x^2 + C$

Matched Problem 3   Find each indefinite integral:

(A) $\displaystyle\int \left(2x^{2/3} - \frac{3}{x^4}\right) dx$

(B) $\displaystyle\int 4\sqrt[5]{w^3}\, dw$

(C) $\displaystyle\int \frac{x^4 - 8x^3}{x^2}\, dx$

(D) $\displaystyle\int \left(8\sqrt[3]{x} - \frac{6}{\sqrt{x}}\right) dx$

(E) $\displaystyle\int (x^2 - 2)(x + 3)\, dx$

Caution

1. Note from Example 3(*E*) that

$$\int x(x^2 + 2)\, dx \neq \frac{x^2}{2}\left(\frac{x^3}{3} + 2x\right) + C$$

In general, the **indefinite integral of a product is not the product of the indefinite integrals** (this is to be expected, because the derivative of a product is not the product of the derivatives).

2.
$$\int e^x\, dx \neq \frac{e^{x+1}}{x + 1} + C$$

The power rule applies only to power functions of the form x^n, where the exponent n is a real constant not equal to -1 and the base x is the variable. The function e^x is an exponential function with variable exponent x and constant base e. The correct form is

$$\int e^x\, dx = e^x + C$$

3. Not all elementary functions have elementary antiderivatives. It is impossible, for example, to give a formula for the antiderivative of $f(x) = e^{x^2}$ in terms of elementary functions. Nevertheless, finding such a formula when it exists can markedly simplify the solution of certain problems.

➤ Applications

Let us now consider some applications of the indefinite integral to see why we are interested in finding antiderivatives of functions.

EXAMPLE 4 **Curves** Find the equation of the curve that passes through $(2, 5)$ if its slope is given by $dy/dx = 2x$ at any point x.

Solution We are interested in finding a function $y = f(x)$ such that

$$\frac{dy}{dx} = 2x \tag{1}$$

and

$$y = 5 \qquad \text{when} \qquad x = 2 \tag{2}$$

If $dy/dx = 2x$, then

$$y = \int 2x\, dx$$
$$= x^2 + C \tag{3}$$

Since $y = 5$ when $x = 2$, we determine the *particular value of C* so that

$$5 = 2^2 + C$$

Thus, $C = 1$, and

$$y = x^2 + 1$$

is the *particular antiderivative* out of all those possible from equation (3) that satisfies both equations (1) and (2) (see Fig. 2). ∎

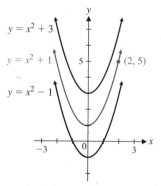

FIGURE 2 $y = x^2 + C$

Matched Problem 4 Find the equation of the curve that passes through $(2, 6)$ if its slope is given by $dy/dx = 3x^2$ at any point x.

In certain situations, it is easier to determine the rate at which something happens than how much of it has happened in a given length of time (for example, population growth rates, business growth rates, rate of healing of a wound, rates of learning or forgetting). If a rate function (derivative) is given and we know the value of the dependent variable for a given value of the independent variable, then—if the rate function is not too complicated—we can often find the original function by integration.

EXAMPLE 5

Cost Function If the marginal cost of producing x units is given by

$$C'(x) = 0.3x^2 + 2x$$

and the fixed cost is $2,000, find the cost function $C(x)$ and the cost of producing 20 units.

Solution Recall that marginal cost is the derivative of the cost function and that fixed cost is cost at a 0 production level. Thus, the mathematical problem is to find $C(x)$ given

$$C'(x) = 0.3x^2 + 2x \qquad C(0) = 2,000$$

We now find the indefinite integral of $0.3x^2 + 2x$ and determine the arbitrary integration constant using $C(0) = 2,000$:

$$C'(x) = 0.3x^2 + 2x$$
$$C(x) = \int (0.3x^2 + 2x)\, dx$$
$$= 0.1x^3 + x^2 + K \qquad \text{\small\textit{Since C represents the cost, we}}$$
$$\text{\small\textit{use K for the constant of integration.}}$$

But

$$C(0) = (0.1)0^3 + 0^2 + K = 2,000$$

Thus, $K = 2,000$, and the particular cost function is

$$C(x) = 0.1x^3 + x^2 + 2,000$$

We now find $C(20)$, the cost of producing 20 units:

$$C(20) = (0.1)20^3 + 20^2 + 2,000$$
$$= \$3,200$$

See Figure 3 for a geometric representation.

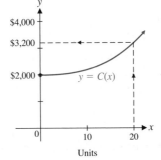

FIGURE 3

Matched Problem 5

Find the revenue function $R(x)$ when the marginal revenue is

$$R'(x) = 400 - 0.4x$$

and no revenue results at a 0 production level. What is the revenue at a production level of 1,000 units?

EXAMPLE 6

Advertising An FM radio station is launching an aggressive advertising campaign in order to increase the number of daily listeners. The station currently has 27,000 daily listeners, and management expects the number of daily listeners, $S(t)$, to grow at the rate of

$$S'(t) = 60t^{1/2}$$

listeners per day, where t is the number of days since the campaign began. How long should the campaign last if the station wants the number of daily listeners to grow to 41,000?

Solution   We must solve the equation $S(t) = 41,000$ for t, given that

$$S'(t) = 60t^{1/2} \quad \text{and} \quad S(0) = 27,000$$

First, we use integration to find $S(t)$:

$$S(t) = 60t^{1/2} \, dt$$

$$= 60 \frac{t^{3/2}}{\frac{3}{2}} + C$$

$$= 40t^{3/2} + C$$

Since

$$S(0) = 40(0)^{3/2} + C = 27,000$$

we have $C = 27,000$, and

$$S(t) = 40t^{3/2} + 27,000$$

Now we solve the equation $S(t) = 41,000$ for t:

$$40t^{3/2} + 27,000 = 41,000$$
$$40t^{3/2} = 14,000$$
$$t^{3/2} = 350$$
$$t = 350^{2/3} \qquad \textit{Use a calculator.}$$
$$= 49.664\,419\ldots$$

Thus, the advertising campaign should last approximately 50 days. ∎

Matched Problem 6   The current monthly circulation of the magazine *Computing News* is 640,000 copies. Due to competition from a new magazine in the same field, the monthly circulation of *Computing News*, $C(t)$, is expected to decrease at the rate of

$$C'(t) = -6,000t^{1/3}$$

copies per month, where t is the time in months since the new magazine began publication. How long will it take for the circulation of *Computing News* to decrease to 460,000 copies per month?

Answers to Matched Problems   **1.** (A) $x^3 + C$
(B)

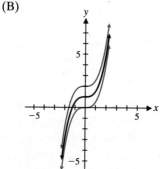

(C) The graphs are vertical translations of each other.

2. (A) $2x + C$ (B) $16e^t + C$ (C) $\frac{3}{5}x^5 + C$
   (D) $\frac{1}{3}x^6 - x^3 + x + C$ (E) $5\ln|x| - 4e^x + C$

3. (A) $\frac{6}{5}x^{5/3} + x^{-3} + C$ (B) $\frac{5}{2}w^{8/5} + C$ (C) $\frac{1}{3}x^3 - 4x^2 + C$
   (D) $6x^{4/3} - 12x^{1/2} + C$ (E) $\frac{1}{4}x^4 + x^3 - x^2 - 6x + C$

4. $y = x^3 - 2$

5. $R(x) = 400x - 0.2x^2$; $R(1,000) = \$200,000$

6. $t = (40)^{3/4} \approx 16$ mo

Exercise 6-1

A *In Problems 1–22, find each indefinite integral. (Check by differentiating.)*

1. $\int x^2 \, dx$

2. $\int x^5 \, dx$

3. $\int x^7 \, dx$

4. $\int x^{-4} \, dx$

5. $\int 2 \, dx$

6. $\int -10 \, dx$

7. $\int 5t^{-3} \, dt$

8. $\int 3u^6 \, du$

9. $\int \pi^2 \, dx$

10. $\int e^3 \, dx$

11. $\int (6t + 3) \, dt$

12. $\int (5 - 4t) \, dt$

13. $\int 3e^t \, dt$

14. $\int 12e^t \, dt$

15. $\int \frac{6}{x} \, dx$

16. $\int 4z^{-1} \, dz$

17. $\int 15x^{1/2} \, dx$

18. $\int 8t^{2/3} \, dt$

19. $\int 7t^{-4/3} \, dt$

20. $\int 2x^{-5/2} \, dx$

21. $\int (x - \sqrt{x}) \, dx$

22. $\int (3\sqrt{x} - x^{-1}) \, dx$

In Problems 23–32, find all the antiderivatives for each derivative.

23. $\frac{dy}{dx} = 200x^4$

24. $\frac{dx}{dt} = 42t^5$

25. $\frac{dP}{dx} = 24 - 6x$

26. $\frac{dy}{dx} = 3x^2 - 4x^3$

27. $\frac{dy}{du} = 2u^5 - 3u^2 - 1$

28. $\frac{dA}{dt} = 3 - 12t^3 - 9t^5$

29. $\frac{dy}{dx} = e^x + 3$

30. $\frac{dy}{dx} = x - e^x$

31. $\frac{dx}{dt} = 5t^{-1} + 1$

32. $\frac{du}{dv} = \frac{4}{v} + \frac{v}{4}$

B *In Problems 33 and 34, discuss the validity of each statement. If the statement is always true, explain why. If not, give a counterexample.*

33. (A) If n is an integer, then $x^{n+1}/(n + 1)$ is an antiderivative of x^n.
    (B) The function $f(x) = \pi$ is an antiderivative of the function $g(x) = 0$.

34. (A) $\int \frac{d}{dx}(x^4 + x^2) \, dx = x^4 + x^2 + C$
    (B) $\frac{d}{dx}\left(\int x^2 \, dx\right) = x^2 + C$

In Problems 35–38, could the three graphs be antiderivatives of the same function? Explain.

35.
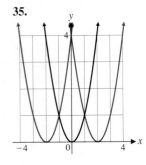

36.
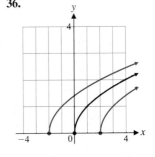

37.
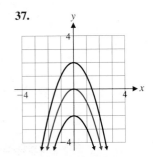

38.
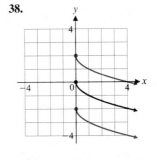

In Problems 39–64, find each indefinite integral. (Check by differentiation.)

39. $\int 5x(1-x)\,dx$

40. $\int x^2(1+x^3)\,dx$

41. $\int (2+x^2)(3+x^2)\,dx$

42. $\int (1+x)(1-x)\,dx$

43. $\int \dfrac{du}{\sqrt{u}}$

44. $\int \dfrac{dt}{\sqrt[3]{t}}$

45. $\int \dfrac{dx}{4x^3}$

46. $\int \dfrac{6\,dm}{m^2}$

47. $\int \dfrac{4+u}{u}\,du$

48. $\int \dfrac{1-y^2}{3y}\,dy$

49. $\int (5e^z + 4)\,dz$

50. $\int \dfrac{e^t - t}{2}\,dt$

51. $\int \left(3x^2 - \dfrac{2}{x^2}\right)dx$

52. $\int \left(4x^3 + \dfrac{2}{x^3}\right)dx$

53. $\int \left(10x^4 - \dfrac{8}{x^5} - 2\right)dx$

54. $\int \left(\dfrac{6}{x^4} - \dfrac{2}{x^3} + 1\right)dx$

55. $\int \left(3\sqrt{x} + \dfrac{2}{\sqrt{x}}\right)dx$

56. $\int \left(\dfrac{2}{\sqrt[3]{x}} - \sqrt[3]{x^2}\right)dx$

57. $\int \left(\sqrt[3]{x^2} - \dfrac{4}{x^3}\right)dx$

58. $\int \left(\dfrac{12}{x^5} - \dfrac{1}{\sqrt[3]{x^2}}\right)dx$

59. $\int \dfrac{e^x - 3x}{4}\,dx$

60. $\int \dfrac{e^x - 3x^2}{2}\,dx$

61. $\int \dfrac{12 + 5z - 3z^3}{z^4}\,dz$

62. $\int \dfrac{(1+z^2)^2}{z}\,dz$

63. $\int \left(\dfrac{6x^2}{5} - \dfrac{2}{3x}\right)dx$

64. $\int \left(\dfrac{2}{3x^2} - \dfrac{5}{4x^3}\right)dx$

In Problems 65–74, find the particular antiderivative of each derivative that satisfies the given condition.

65. $\dfrac{dy}{dx} = 2x - 3;\ y(0) = 5$

66. $\dfrac{dy}{dx} = 5 - 4x;\ y(0) = 20$

67. $C'(x) = 6x^2 - 4x;\ C(0) = 3{,}000$

68. $R'(x) = 600 - 0.6x;\ R(0) = 0$

69. $\dfrac{dx}{dt} = \dfrac{20}{\sqrt{t}};\ x(1) = 40$

70. $\dfrac{dR}{dt} = \dfrac{100}{t^2};\ R(1) = 400$

71. $\dfrac{dy}{dx} = 2x^{-2} + 3x^{-1} - 1;\ y(1) = 0$

72. $\dfrac{dy}{dx} = 3x^{-1} + x^{-2};\ y(1) = 1$

73. $\dfrac{dx}{dt} = 4e^t - 2;\ x(0) = 1$

74. $\dfrac{dy}{dt} = 5e^t - 4;\ y(0) = -1$

75. Find the equation of the curve that passes through $(2, 3)$ if its slope is given by

$$\dfrac{dy}{dx} = 4x - 3$$

for each x.

76. Find the equation of the curve that passes through $(1, 3)$ if its slope is given by

$$\dfrac{dy}{dx} = 12x^2 - 12x$$

for each x.

C *In Problems 77–82, find each indefinite integral.*

77. $\int \dfrac{2x^4 - x}{x^3}\,dx$

78. $\int \dfrac{x^{-1} - x^4}{x^2}\,dx$

79. $\int \dfrac{x^5 - 2x}{x^4}\,dx$

80. $\int \dfrac{1 - 3x^4}{x^2}\,dx$

81. $\int \dfrac{x^2 e^x - 2x}{x^2}\,dx$

82. $\int \dfrac{1 - xe^x}{x}\,dx$

For each derivative in Problems 83–88, find an antiderivative that satisfies the given condition.

83. $\dfrac{dM}{dt} = \dfrac{t^2 - 1}{t^2};\ M(4) = 5$

84. $\dfrac{dR}{dx} = \dfrac{1 - x^4}{x^3};\ R(1) = 4$

85. $\dfrac{dy}{dx} = \dfrac{5x + 2}{\sqrt[3]{x}};\ y(1) = 0$

86. $\dfrac{dx}{dt} = \dfrac{\sqrt{t^3} - t}{\sqrt{t^3}};\ x(9) = 4$

87. $p'(x) = -\dfrac{10}{x^2};\ p(1) = 20$

88. $p'(x) = \dfrac{10}{x^3};\ p(1) = 15$

In Problems 89–92, find the derivative or indefinite integral as indicated.

89. $\dfrac{d}{dx}\left(\int x^3\,dx\right)$

90. $\dfrac{d}{dt}\left(\int \dfrac{\ln t}{t}\,dt\right)$

91. $\int \dfrac{d}{dx}(x^4 + 3x^2 + 1)\,dx$

92. $\int \dfrac{d}{du}(e^{u^2})\,du$

93. Use differentiation to justify the formula

$$\int x^n \, dx = \frac{x^{n+1}}{n+1} + C$$

provided $n \neq -1$.

94. Use differentiation to justify the formula

$$\int e^x \, dx = e^x + C$$

95. Assuming $x > 0$, use differentiation to justify the formula

$$\int \frac{1}{x} \, dx = \ln|x| + C$$

96. Assuming $x < 0$, use differentiation to justify the formula

$$\int \frac{1}{x} \, dx = \ln|x| + C$$

97. Show that the indefinite integral of the sum of two functions is the sum of the indefinite integrals. [*Hint:* Assume that $\int f(x) \, dx = F(x) + C_1$ and $\int g(x) \, dx = G(x) + C_2$. Using differentiation, show that $F(x) + C_1 + G(x) + C_2$ is the indefinite integral of the function $s(x) = f(x) + g(x)$.]

98. Show that the indefinite integral of the difference of two functions is the difference of the indefinite integrals.

Applications

Business & Economics

99. *Cost function.* The marginal average cost for producing x digital sports watches is given by

$$\overline{C}'(x) = -\frac{1,000}{x^2} \qquad \overline{C}(100) = 25$$

where $\overline{C}(x)$ is the average cost in dollars. Find the average cost function and the cost function. What are the fixed costs?

100. *Renewable energy.* In 1998 the U.S. consumption of renewable energy was 6.98 quadrillion Btu (that is, 6.98×10^{15} Btu). Since 1960, consumption has been growing at a rate given by

$$f'(t) = 0.004t + 0.062$$

where t is years after 1960. Find $f(t)$ and estimate the U.S. consumption of renewable energy in 2020.

101. *Manufacturing costs.* The graph of the marginal cost function from the manufacturing of x thousand watches per month [where cost $C(x)$ is in thousands of dollars per month] is given in the figure.

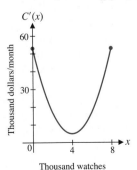

Figure for 101

(A) Using the graph shown, verbally describe the shape of the graph of the cost function $C(x)$ as x increases from 0 to 8,000 watches per month.

(B) Given the equation of the marginal cost function,

$$C'(x) = 3x^2 - 24x + 53$$

find the cost function if monthly fixed costs at 0 output are $30,000. What is the cost for manufacturing 4,000 watches per month? 8,000 watches per month?

(C) Graph the cost function for $0 \leq x \leq 8$. [Check the shape of the graph relative to the analysis in part (A).]

(D) Why do you think that the graph of the cost function is steeper at both ends than in the middle?

102. *Revenue.* The graph of the marginal revenue function from the sale of x digital sports watches is given in the figure.

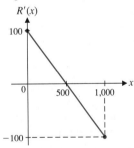

Figure for 102

(A) Using the graph shown, verbally describe the shape of the graph of the revenue function $R(x)$ as x increases from 0 to 1,000.

(B) Find the equation of the marginal revenue function (the linear function shown in the figure).

(C) Find the equation of the revenue function that satisfies $R(0) = 0$. Graph the revenue function over the interval $[0, 1,000]$. [Check the shape of the graph relative to the analysis in part (A).]

(D) Find the price–demand equation and determine the price when the demand is 700 units.

103. *Sales analysis.* The monthly sales of a particular personal computer are expected to decline at the rate of

$$S'(t) = -25t^{2/3}$$

computers per month, where t is time in months and $S(t)$ is the number of computers sold each month. The company plans to stop manufacturing this computer when the monthly sales reach 800 computers. If the monthly sales now ($t = 0$) are 2,000 computers, find $S(t)$. How long will the company continue to manufacture this computer?

104. *Sales analysis.* The rate of change of the monthly sales of a new home video game cartridge is given by

$$S'(t) = 500t^{1/4} \qquad S(0) = 0$$

where t is the number of months since the game was released and $S(t)$ is the number of cartridges sold each month. Find $S(t)$. When will the monthly sales reach 20,000 cartridges?

105. *Sales analysis.* Repeat Problem 103 if $S'(t) = -25t^{2/3} - 70$ and all other information remains the same. Use a graphing utility to approximate the solution to the equation $S(t) = 800$ to two decimal places.

106. *Sales analysis.* Repeat Problem 104 if $S'(t) = 500t^{1/4} + 300$ and all other information remains the same. Use a graphing utility to approximate the solution to the equation $S(t) = 20,000$ to two decimal places.

107. *Labor costs and learning.* A defense contractor is starting production on a new missile control system. On the basis of data collected while assembling the first 16 control systems, the production manager obtained the following function describing the rate of labor use:

$$g(x) = 2,400x^{-1/2}$$

where $g(x)$ is the number of labor-hours required to assemble the xth unit of the control system. For example, after assembling 16 units, the rate of assembly is 600 labor-hours per unit, and after assembling 25 units, the rate of assembly is 480 labor-hours per unit. The more units assembled, the more efficient the process because of learning. If 19,200 labor-hours are required to assemble the first 16 units, how many labor-hours, $L(x)$, will be required to assemble the first x units? The first 25 units?

108. *Labor costs and learning.* If the rate of labor use in Problem 107 is

$$g(x) = 2,000x^{-1/3}$$

and if the first 8 control units require 12,000 labor-hours, how many labor-hours, $L(x)$, will be required for the first x control units? The first 27 control units?

Life Sciences

109. *Weight–height.* For an average person, the rate of change of weight W (in pounds) with respect to height h (in inches) is given approximately by

$$\frac{dW}{dh} = 0.0015h^2$$

Find $W(h)$ if $W(60) = 108$ pounds. Also, find the weight for a person who is 5 feet 10 inches tall.

110. *Wound healing.* If the area A of a healing wound changes at a rate given approximately by

$$\frac{dA}{dt} = -4t^{-3} \qquad 1 \le t \le 10$$

where t is time in days and $A(1) = 2$ square centimeters, what will the area of the wound be in 10 days?

Social Sciences

111. *Urban growth.* The rate of growth of the population, $N(t)$, of a newly incorporated city t years after incorporation is estimated to be

$$\frac{dN}{dt} = 400 + 600\sqrt{t} \qquad 0 \le t \le 9$$

If the population was 5,000 at the time of incorporation, find the population 9 years later.

112. *Learning.* A beginning high school language class was chosen for an experiment in learning. Using a list of 50 words, the experiment involved measuring the rate of vocabulary memorization at different times during a continuous 5-hour study session. It was found that the average rate of learning for the entire class was inversely proportional to the time spent studying and was given approximately by

$$V'(t) = \frac{15}{t} \qquad 1 \le t \le 5$$

If the average number of words memorized after 1 hour of study was 15 words, what was the average number of words learned after t hours of study for $1 \le t \le 5$? After 4 hours of study? (Round answer to the nearest whole number.)

Section 6-2 | Integration by Substitution

➤ Reversing the Chain Rule
➤ Integration by Substitution
➤ Additional Substitution Techniques
➤ Application

Many of the indefinite integral formulas introduced in the preceding section are based on corresponding derivative formulas studied earlier. We now consider indefinite integral formulas and procedures based on the chain rule for differentiation.

➤ Reversing the Chain Rule

Recall the chain rule:

$$\frac{d}{dx} f[g(x)] = f'[g(x)]g'(x)$$

The expression on the right is formed by taking the derivative of the outside function f and multiplying it by the derivative of the inside function g. If we recognize an integrand as a chain-rule form $f'[g(x)]g'(x)$, we can easily find an antiderivative and its indefinite integral:

RESULT Reversing the Chain Rule

$$\int f'[g(x)]g'(x)\, dx = f[g(x)] + C \tag{1}$$

(A) Which of the following has e^{x^3-1} as an antiderivative?

$$x^2 e^{x^3-1} \qquad 3x^2 e^{x^3-1} \qquad 3x e^{x^3-1}$$

(B) Which of the following would have e^{x^3-1} as an antiderivative if it were multiplied by a constant factor? A variable factor?

$$3x e^{x^3-1} \qquad x^2 e^{x^3-1}$$

We are interested in finding the indefinite integral:

$$\int 3x^2 e^{x^3-1}\, dx \tag{2}$$

The integrand appears to be the chain-rule form $e^{g(x)}g'(x)$, which is the derivative of $e^{g(x)}$. Since

$$\frac{d}{dx} e^{x^3-1} = 3x^2 e^{x^3-1}$$

it follows that

$$\int 3x^2 e^{x^3-1}\, dx = e^{x^3-1} + C \tag{3}$$

How does the following indefinite integral differ from integral (2)?

$$\int x^2 e^{x^3-1}\, dx \tag{4}$$

It is missing the constant factor 3. That is, $x^2 e^{x^3-1}$ is within a constant factor of being the derivative of e^{x^3-1}. But because a constant factor can be moved across the integral sign, this causes us little trouble in finding the indefinite integral of $x^2 e^{x^3-1}$. We introduce the constant factor 3, and at the same time multiply by $\frac{1}{3}$ and move the $\frac{1}{3}$ factor outside the integral sign. This is equivalent to multiplying the integrand in integral (4) by 1.

$$\int x^2 e^{x^3-1}\, dx \boxed{= \int \frac{3}{3} x^2 e^{x^3-1}\, dx}$$

$$= \frac{1}{3}\int 3x^2 e^{x^3-1}\, dx = \frac{1}{3} e^{x^3-1} + C \tag{5}$$

The derivative of the right side of equation (5) is the integrand of the indefinite integral (4). You should check this.

How does the following indefinite integral differ from integral (2)?

$$\int 3x e^{x^3-1}\, dx \tag{6}$$

It is missing a variable factor x. This is more serious. As tempting as it might be, we *cannot* adjust integral (6) by introducing the variable factor x and moving $1/x$ outside the integral sign, as we did with the constant 3 in equation (5). If we could move $1/x$ across the integral sign, what would stop us from moving the entire integrand across the integral sign? Then, indefinite integration would become a trivial exercise and would not give us the results we want—antiderivatives of the integrand.

Summary of the Preceding Integral Forms

$$\int 3x^2 e^{x^3-1}\, dx = e^{x^3-1} + C \qquad \text{Integrand is a chain-rule form.}$$

$$\int x^2 e^{x^3-1}\, dx = \frac{1}{3} e^{x^3-1} + C \qquad \text{Integrand can be adjusted to a chain-rule form.}$$

$$\int 3x e^{x^3-1}\, dx = \text{?} \qquad \text{Integrand cannot be adjusted to be a chain-rule form.}$$

Caution

A constant factor can be moved across an integral sign, but a variable factor cannot.

There is nothing wrong with educated guessing when looking for an antiderivative of a given function, and you are encouraged to do so. You have only to check the result by differentiation. If you are right, you go on your way; if you are wrong, you simply try another approach.

In Section 5-4, we saw that the chain rule extends the derivative formulas for x^n, e^x, and $\ln x$ to derivative formulas for $[f(x)]^n$, $e^{f(x)}$, and $\ln[f(x)]$. The chain rule can also be used to extend the indefinite integral formulas discussed in Section 6-1. Some general formulas are summarized in the following box:

FORMULAS   General Indefinite Integral Formulas

1. $\int [f(x)]^n f'(x)\, dx = \dfrac{[f(x)]^{n+1}}{n+1} + C, n \ne -1$

2. $\int e^{f(x)} f'(x)\, dx = e^{f(x)} + C$

3. $\int \dfrac{1}{f(x)} f'(x)\, dx = \ln|f(x)| + C$

Each formula can be verified by using the chain rule to show that the derivative of the function on the right is the integrand on the left. For example,

$$\frac{d}{dx}\left[e^{f(x)} + C \right] = e^{f(x)} f'(x)$$

verifies formula 2.

EXAMPLE 1   **Reversing the Chain Rule**

(A) $\displaystyle\int (3x + 4)^{10}(3)\, dx = \dfrac{(3x+4)^{11}}{11} + C$ Formula 1 with $f(x) = 3x + 4$ and $f'(x) = 3$

Check: $\dfrac{d}{dx}\dfrac{(3x+4)^{11}}{11} = 11\dfrac{(3x+4)^{10}}{11}\dfrac{d}{dx}(3x+4) = (3x+4)^{10}(3)$

(B) $\displaystyle\int e^{x^2}(2x)\, dx = e^{x^2} + C$ Formula 2 with $f(x) = x^2$ and $f'(x) = 2x$

Check: $\dfrac{d}{dx}e^{x^2} = e^{x^2}\dfrac{d}{dx}x^2 = e^{x^2}(2x)$

(C) $\displaystyle\int \dfrac{1}{1+x^3}3x^2\, dx = \ln|1 + x^3| + C$ Formula 3 with $f(x) = 1 + x^3$ and $f'(x) = 3x^2$

Check: $\dfrac{d}{dx}\ln|1 + x^3| = \dfrac{1}{1+x^3}\dfrac{d}{dx}(1 + x^3) = \dfrac{1}{1+x^3}3x^2$

Matched Problem 1   Find each indefinite integral.

(A) $\displaystyle\int (2x^3 - 3)^{20}(6x^2)\, dx$ (B) $\displaystyle\int e^{5x}(5)\, dx$

(C) $\displaystyle\int \dfrac{1}{4+x^2}2x\, dx$

▶ **Integration by Substitution**

The key step in using formulas 1, 2, and 3 is recognizing the form of the integrand. Some people find it difficult to identify $f(x)$ and $f'(x)$ in these formulas and prefer to use a *substitution* to simplify the integrand. The *method of substitution,* which we now discuss, becomes increasingly useful as one progresses in studies of integration.

We start by introducing the idea of the *differential.* We represented the derivative by the symbol dy/dx taken as a whole. We now define dy and dx as two separate quantities with the property that their ratio is still equal to $f'(x)$:

DEFINITION   Differentials

If $y = f(x)$ defines a differentiable function, then

1. The **differential** dx of the independent variable x is an arbitrary real number.

2. The **differential** dy of the dependent variable y is defined as the product of $f'(x)$ and dx—that is, as

$$dy = f'(x)\, dx$$

Differentials involve mathematical subtleties that are treated carefully in advanced mathematics courses. Here, we are interested in them mainly as a bookkeeping device to aid in the process of finding indefinite integrals. We can always check the results by differentiating.

EXAMPLE 2   **Differentials**

(A) If $y = f(x) = x^2$, then
$$dy = f'(x)\, dx = 2x\, dx$$

(B) If $u = g(x) = e^{3x}$, then
$$du = g'(x)\, dx = 3e^{3x}\, dx$$

(C) If $w = h(t) = \ln(4 + 5t)$, then
$$dw = h'(t)\, dt = \frac{5}{4 + 5t}\, dt$$

Matched Problem 2   (A) Find dy for $y = f(x) = x^3$.
(B) Find du for $u = h(x) = \ln(2 + x^2)$.
(C) Find dv for $v = g(t) = e^{-5t}$.

The **method of substitution** is developed through the following examples.

EXAMPLE 3   **Using Substitution**   Find $\int (x^2 + 2x + 5)^5(2x + 2)\, dx$.

Solution   If
$$u = x^2 + 2x + 5$$

then the differential of u is
$$du = (2x + 2)\, dx$$

Notice that du is one of the factors in the integrand. Substitute u for $x^2 + 2x + 5$ and du for $(2x + 2)\,dx$ to obtain

$$\int (x^2 + 2x + 5)^5 (2x + 2)\,dx = \int u^5\,du$$

$$= \frac{u^6}{6} + C$$

$$= \frac{1}{6}(x^2 + 2x + 5)^6 + C \quad \begin{array}{l} Since \\ u = x^2 + 2x + 5 \end{array}$$

Check: $\dfrac{d}{dx} \dfrac{1}{6}(x^2 + 2x + 5)^6 = \dfrac{1}{6}(6)(x^2 + 2x + 5)^5 \dfrac{d}{dx}(x^2 + 2x + 5)$

$$= (x^2 + 2x + 5)^5 (2x + 2) \qquad ■$$

Matched Problem 3 Find $\int (x^2 - 3x + 7)^4 (2x - 3)\,dx$ by substitution. ————————— ■

The substitution method is also called the **change-of-variable method**, since u replaces the variable x in the process. Substituting $u = f(x)$ and $du = f'(x)\,dx$ in formulas 1, 2, and 3 produces the general indefinite integral formulas in the following box:

FORMULAS   General Indefinite Integral Formulas

4. $\displaystyle\int u^n\,du = \frac{u^{n+1}}{n+1} + C, \qquad n \neq -1$

5. $\displaystyle\int e^u\,du = e^u + C$

6. $\displaystyle\int \frac{1}{u}\,du = \ln|u| + C$

These formulas are valid if u is an independent variable or if u is a function of another variable and du is its differential with respect to that variable.

The substitution method for evaluating certain indefinite integrals is outlined in the following box:

PROCEDURE   Integration by Substitution

Step 1. Select a substitution that appears to simplify the integrand. In particular, try to select u so that du is a factor in the integrand.

Step 2. Express the integrand entirely in terms of u and du, completely eliminating the original variable and its differential.

Step 3. Evaluate the new integral, if possible.

Step 4. Express the antiderivative found in step 3 in terms of the original variable.

EXAMPLE 4   **Using Substitution**   Use a substitution to find the following:

(A) $\displaystyle\int (3x + 4)^6 (3)\,dx$ (B) $\displaystyle\int e^{t^2}(2t)\,dt$

Solution   (A) If we let $u = 3x + 4$, then $du = 3\,dx$, and

$$\int (3x+4)^6(3)\,dx = \int u^6\,du \qquad \text{Use formula 4.}$$

$$= \frac{u^7}{7} + C$$

$$= \frac{(3x+4)^7}{7} + C \quad \text{Since } u = 3x + 4$$

Check: $\dfrac{d}{dx}\dfrac{(3x+4)^7}{7} = \dfrac{7(3x+4)^6}{7}\dfrac{d}{dx}(3x+4) = (3x+4)^6(3)$

(B) If we let $u = t^2$, then $du = 2t\,dt$, and

$$e^{t^2}(2t)\,dt = e^u\,du \qquad \text{Use formula 5.}$$

$$= e^u + C$$

$$= e^{t^2} + C \quad \text{Since } u = t^2$$

Check: $\dfrac{d}{dt}e^{t^2} = e^{t^2}\dfrac{d}{dt}t^2 = e^{t^2}(2t)$ ∎

Matched Problem 4   Use a substitution to find each indefinite integral.

(A) $\displaystyle\int (2x^3 - 3)^4(6x^2)\,dx$

(B) $\displaystyle\int e^{5w}(5)\,dw$

➤ Additional Substitution Techniques

In order to use the substitution method, **the integrand must be expressed entirely in terms of u and du.** In some cases, the integrand will have to be modified before making a substitution and using one of the integration formulas. Example 5 illustrates this process.

EXAMPLE 5   **Substitution Techniques**   Integrate:

(A) $\displaystyle\int \frac{1}{4x+7}\,dx$ (B) $\displaystyle\int te^{-t^2}\,dt$ (C) $\displaystyle\int 4x^2\sqrt{x^3+5}\,dx$

Solution   (A) If $u = 4x + 7$, then $du = 4\,dx$. We are missing a factor of 4 in the integrand to match formula 6 exactly. Recalling that a constant factor can be moved across an integral sign, we proceed as follows:

$$\int \frac{1}{4x+7}\,dx = \int \frac{1}{4x+7}\frac{4}{4}\,dx$$

$$= \frac{1}{4}\int \frac{1}{4x+7}4\,dx \quad \text{Substitute } u = 4x+7 \text{ and } du = 4\,dx.$$

$$= \frac{1}{4}\int \frac{1}{u}\,du \qquad \text{Use formula 6.}$$

$$= \tfrac{1}{4}\ln|u| + C$$

$$= \tfrac{1}{4}\ln|4x+7| + C \quad \text{Since } u = 4x+7$$

Check: $\dfrac{d}{dx}\dfrac{1}{4}\ln|4x + 7| = \dfrac{1}{4}\dfrac{1}{4x + 7}\dfrac{d}{dx}(4x + 7) = \dfrac{1}{4}\dfrac{1}{4x + 7}4 = \dfrac{1}{4x + 7}$

(B) If $u = -t^2$, then $du = -2t\,dt$. Proceed as in part (A):

$$\int te^{-t^2}\,dt = \int e^{-t^2}\dfrac{-2}{-2}t\,dt$$

$$= -\dfrac{1}{2}\int e^{-t^2}(-2t)\,dt \quad \text{Substitute } u = -t^2 \text{ and } du = -2t\,dt.$$

$$= -\dfrac{1}{2}\int e^{u}\,du \qquad\qquad \text{Use formula 5.}$$

$$= -\tfrac{1}{2}e^{u} + C$$

$$= -\tfrac{1}{2}e^{-t^2} + C \qquad\qquad \text{Since } u = -t^2$$

Check: $\dfrac{d}{dt}\left(-\tfrac{1}{2}e^{-t^2}\right) = -\tfrac{1}{2}e^{-t^2}\dfrac{d}{dt}(-t^2) = -\tfrac{1}{2}e^{-t^2}(-2t) = te^{-t^2}$

(C) $\displaystyle\int 4x^2\sqrt{x^3 + 5}\,dx = 4\int \sqrt{x^3 + 5}(x^2)\,dx$ Move the 4 across the
integral sign and proceed as
before.

$$= 4\int \sqrt{x^3 + 5}\dfrac{3}{3}(x^2)\,dx$$

$$= \dfrac{4}{3}\int \sqrt{x^3 + 5}(3x^2)\,dx \quad \text{Substitute } u = x^3 + 5 \text{ and } du = 3x^2\,dx.$$

$$= \dfrac{4}{3}\int \sqrt{u}\,du$$

$$= \dfrac{4}{3}\int u^{1/2}\,du \qquad\qquad \text{Use formula 4.}$$

$$= \dfrac{4}{3}\dfrac{u^{3/2}}{\frac{3}{2}} + C$$

$$= \tfrac{8}{9}u^{3/2} + C$$

$$= \tfrac{8}{9}(x^3 + 5)^{3/2} + C \qquad\qquad \text{Since } u = x^3 + 5$$

Check: $\dfrac{d}{dx}\left[\tfrac{8}{9}(x^3 + 5)^{3/2}\right] = \tfrac{4}{3}(x^3 + 5)^{1/2}\dfrac{d}{dx}(x^3 + 5)$

$$= \tfrac{4}{3}(x^3 + 5)^{1/2}(3x^2) = 4x^2\sqrt{x^3 + 5}$$

Matched Problem 5   Integrate:

(A) $\displaystyle\int e^{-3x}\,dx$

(B) $\displaystyle\int \dfrac{x}{x^2 - 9}\,dx$

(C) $\displaystyle\int 5t^2(t^3 + 4)^{-2}\,dt$

Even if it is not possible to find a substitution that makes an integrand match one of the integration formulas exactly, a substitution may sufficiently simplify the integrand so that other techniques can be used.

EXAMPLE 6   **Substitution Techniques**   Find: $\displaystyle\int \frac{x}{\sqrt{x+2}}\,dx$

Solution   Proceeding as before, if we let $u = x + 2$, then $du = dx$ and

$$\int \frac{x}{\sqrt{x+2}}\,dx = \int \frac{x}{\sqrt{u}}\,du$$

Notice that this substitution is not yet complete, because we have not expressed the integrand entirely in terms of u and du. As we noted earlier, only a constant factor can be moved across an integral sign, so we cannot move x outside the integral sign (as much as we would like to). Instead, we must return to the original substitution, solve for x in terms of u, and use the resulting equation to complete the substitution:

$$u = x + 2 \qquad \text{Solve for } x \text{ in terms of } u.$$
$$u - 2 = x \qquad \text{Substitute this expression for } x.$$

Thus,

$$\int \frac{x}{\sqrt{x+2}}\,dx = \int \frac{u-2}{\sqrt{u}}\,du \qquad \text{Simplify the integrand.}$$

$$= \int \frac{u-2}{u^{1/2}}\,du$$

$$= \int (u^{1/2} - 2u^{-1/2})\,du$$

$$\boxed{= \int u^{1/2}\,du - 2\int u^{-1/2}\,du}$$

$$= \frac{u^{3/2}}{\frac{3}{2}} - 2\frac{u^{1/2}}{\frac{1}{2}} + C$$

$$= \tfrac{2}{3}(x+2)^{3/2} - 4(x+2)^{1/2} + C \qquad \text{Since } u = x + 2$$

Check: $\dfrac{d}{dx}\left[\tfrac{2}{3}(x+2)^{3/2} - 4(x+2)^{1/2}\right] = (x+2)^{1/2} - 2(x+2)^{-1/2}$

$$= \frac{x+2}{(x+2)^{1/2}} - \frac{2}{(x+2)^{1/2}}$$

$$= \frac{x}{(x+2)^{1/2}} \qquad \blacksquare$$

Matched Problem 6   Find: $\int x\sqrt{x+1}\,dx$

◉ **Insight**   We can find the indefinite integral of some functions in more than one way. For example, we can employ substitution to find

$$\int x(1+x^2)^2\,dx$$

by letting $u = 1 + x^2$. As a second approach, we can expand the integrand, obtaining

$$\int (x + 2x^3 + x^5)\, dx$$

for which we can easily calculate an antiderivative. In such a case, use the approach that you prefer.

There are also some functions for which substitution is not an effective approach to finding the indefinite integral. For example, substitution is not helpful in finding

$$\int e^{x^2}\, dx \quad\text{or}\quad \int \ln x\, dx$$

➤ Application

EXAMPLE 7   **Price–Demand**   The market research department for a supermarket chain has determined that for one store the marginal price $p'(x)$ at x tubes per week for a certain brand of toothpaste is given by

$$p'(x) = -0.015e^{-0.01x}$$

Find the price–demand equation if the weekly demand is 50 tubes when the price of a tube is $2.35. Find the weekly demand when the price of a tube is $1.89.

Solution

$$p(x) = \int -0.015e^{-0.01x}\, dx$$

$$= -0.015 \int e^{-0.01x}\, dx$$

$$= -0.015 \int e^{-0.01x} \frac{-0.01}{-0.01}\, dx$$

$$= \frac{-0.015}{-0.01} \int e^{-0.01x}(-0.01)\, dx \qquad \text{Substitute } u = -0.01x \text{ and } du = -0.01\, dx.$$

$$= 1.5 \int e^u\, du$$

$$= 1.5e^u + C$$

$$= 1.5e^{-0.01x} + C \qquad\qquad \text{Since } u = -0.01x$$

We find C by noting that

$$p(50) = 1.5e^{-0.01(50)} + C = \$2.35$$

$$C = \$2.35 - 1.5e^{-0.5} \quad \text{Use a calculator.}$$

$$= \$2.35 - 0.91$$

$$= \$1.44$$

Thus,

$$p(x) = 1.5e^{-0.01x} + 1.44$$

To find the demand when the price is $1.89, we solve $p(x) = \$1.89$ for x:

$$1.5e^{-0.01x} + 1.44 = 1.89$$

$$1.5e^{-0.01x} = 0.45$$

$$e^{-0.01x} = 0.3$$

$$-0.01x = \ln 0.3$$

$$x = -100 \ln 0.3 \approx 120 \text{ tubes}$$

Matched Problem 7   The marginal price $p'(x)$ at a supply level of x tubes per week for a certain brand of toothpaste is given by

$$p'(x) = 0.001e^{0.01x}$$

Find the price–supply equation if the supplier is willing to supply 100 tubes per week at a price of $1.65 each. How many tubes would the supplier be willing to supply at a price of $1.98 each?

EXPLORE & DISCUSS 2   In each of the following examples explain why $\neq$ is used; then work the problem correctly using either an appropriate substitution or another method.

1. $$\int (x^2 + 3)^2 \, dx = \int (x^2 + 3)^2 \frac{2x}{2x} \, dx$$

$$\neq \frac{1}{2x} \int (x^2 + 3)^2 (2x) \, dx$$

2. $$\int \frac{1}{10x + 3} \, dx = \int \frac{1}{u} \, dx \qquad u = 10x + 3$$

$$\neq \ln|u| + C$$

We conclude with two final cautions (the first was stated earlier, but is worth repeating):

Caution

1. A variable cannot be moved across an integral sign!
2. An integral must be expressed entirely in terms of u and du before applying integration formulas 4, 5, and 6.

Answers to Matched Problems

1. (A) $\frac{1}{21}(2x^3 - 3)^{21} + C$ (B) $e^{5x} + C$
   (C) $\ln|4 + x^2| + C$ or $\ln(4 + x^2) + C$, since $4 + x^2 > 0$

2. (A) $dy = 3x^2 \, dx$ (B) $du = \frac{2x}{2 + x^2} \, dx$ (C) $dv = -5e^{-5t} \, dt$

3. $\frac{1}{5}(x^2 - 3x + 7)^5 + C$

4. (A) $\frac{1}{5}(2x^3 - 3)^5 + C$ (B) $e^{5w} + C$

5. (A) $-\frac{1}{3}e^{-3x} + C$ (B) $\frac{1}{2}\ln|x^2 - 9| + C$ (C) $-\frac{5}{3}(t^3 + 4)^{-1} + C$

6. $\frac{2}{5}(x + 1)^{5/2} - \frac{2}{3}(x + 1)^{3/2} + C$

7. $p(x) = 0.1e^{0.01x} + 1.38$; 179 tubes

Exercise 6-2

A *In Problems 1–40, find each indefinite integral, and check the result by differentiating.*

1. $\displaystyle\int (3x + 5)^2(3) \, dx$

2. $\displaystyle\int (6x - 1)^3(6) \, dx$

3. $\displaystyle\int (x^2 - 1)^5(2x) \, dx$

4. $\displaystyle\int (x^6 + 1)^4(6x^5) \, dx$

5. $\displaystyle\int (5x^3 + 1)^{-3}(15x^2) \, dx$

6. $\displaystyle\int (4x^2 - 3)^{-6}(8x) \, dx$

7. $\displaystyle\int e^{5x}(5) \, dx$

8. $\displaystyle\int e^{x^3}(3x^2) \, dx$

9. $\displaystyle\int \frac{1}{1 + x^2}(2x) \, dx$

10. $\displaystyle\int \frac{1}{5x - 7}(5) \, dx$

11. $\int \sqrt{1 + x^4}\,(4x^3)\,dx$ **12.** $\int (x^2 + 9)^{-1/2}(2x)\,dx$

B

13. $\int (x + 3)^{10}\,dx$ **14.** $\int (x - 3)^{-4}\,dx$

15. $\int (6t - 7)^{-2}\,dt$ **16.** $\int (5t + 1)^3\,dt$

17. $\int (t^2 + 1)^5\,t\,dt$ **18.** $\int (t^3 + 4)^{-2}\,t^2\,dt$

19. $\int xe^{x^2}\,dx$ **20.** $\int e^{-0.01x}\,dx$

21. $\int \dfrac{1}{5x + 4}\,dx$ **22.** $\int \dfrac{x}{1 + x^2}\,dx$

23. $\int e^{1-t}\,dt$ **24.** $\int \dfrac{3}{2 - t}\,dt$

25. $\int \dfrac{t}{(3t^2 + 1)^4}\,dt$ **26.** $\int \dfrac{t^2}{(t^3 - 2)^5}\,dt$

27. $\int \dfrac{x^2}{(4 - x^3)^2}\,dx$ **28.** $\int \dfrac{x}{(5 - 2x^2)^5}\,dx$

29. $\int x\sqrt{x + 4}\,dx$ **30.** $\int x\sqrt{x - 9}\,dx$

31. $\int \dfrac{x}{\sqrt{x - 3}}\,dx$ **32.** $\int \dfrac{x}{\sqrt{x + 5}}\,dx$

33. $\int x(x - 4)^9\,dx$ **34.** $\int x(x + 6)^8\,dx$

35. $\int e^{2x}(1 + e^{2x})^3\,dx$ **36.** $\int e^{-x}(1 - e^{-x})^4\,dx$

37. $\int \dfrac{1 + x}{4 + 2x + x^2}\,dx$ **38.** $\int \dfrac{x^2 - 1}{x^3 - 3x + 7}\,dx$

39. $\int \dfrac{x^3 + x}{(x^4 + 2x^2 + 1)^4}\,dx$ **40.** $\int \dfrac{x^2 - 1}{(x^3 - 3x + 7)^2}\,dx$

In Problems 41–46, imagine that the indicated "solutions" were given to you by a student whom you are tutoring in this class.

(A) How would you have the student check each solution?

(B) Is the solution right or wrong? If the solution is wrong, explain what is wrong and how it can be corrected.

(C) Show a correct solution for each incorrect solution, and check the result by differentiation.

41. $\int \dfrac{1}{2x - 3}\,dx = \ln|2x - 3| + C$

42. $\int \dfrac{x}{x^2 + 5}\,dx = \ln|x^2 + 5| + C$

43. $\int x^3 e^{x^4}\,dx = e^{x^4} + C$

44. $\int e^{4x-5}\,dx = e^{4x-5} + C$

45. $\int 2(x^2 - 2)^2\,dx = \dfrac{(x^2 - 2)^2}{3x} + C$

46. $\int (-10x)(x^2 - 3)^{-4}\,dx = (x^2 - 3)^{-5} + C$

C *In Problems 47–58, find each indefinite integral, and check the result by differentiating.*

47. $\int x\sqrt{3x^2 + 7}\,dx$ **48.** $\int x^2\sqrt{2x^3 + 1}\,dx$

49. $\int x(x^3 + 2)^2\,dx$ **50.** $\int x(x^2 + 2)^2\,dx$

51. $\int x^2(x^3 + 2)^2\,dx$ **52.** $\int (x^2 + 2)^2\,dx$

53. $\int \dfrac{x^3}{\sqrt{2x^4 + 3}}\,dx$ **54.** $\int \dfrac{x^2}{\sqrt{4x^3 - 1}}\,dx$

55. $\int \dfrac{(\ln x)^3}{x}\,dx$ **56.** $\int \dfrac{e^x}{1 + e^x}\,dx$

57. $\int \dfrac{1}{x^2}e^{-1/x}\,dx$ **58.** $\int \dfrac{1}{x \ln x}\,dx$

In Problems 59–64, find the antiderivative of each derivative.

59. $\dfrac{dx}{dt} = 7t^2(t^3 + 5)^6$

60. $\dfrac{dm}{dn} = 10n(n^2 - 8)^7$

61. $\dfrac{dy}{dt} = \dfrac{3t}{\sqrt{t^2 - 4}}$

62. $\dfrac{dy}{dx} = \dfrac{5x^2}{(x^3 - 7)^4}$

63. $\dfrac{dp}{dx} = \dfrac{e^x + e^{-x}}{(e^x - e^{-x})^2}$

64. $\dfrac{dm}{dt} = \dfrac{\ln(t - 5)}{t - 5}$

Use substitution techniques to derive the integration formulas in Problems 65 and 66. Then check your work by differentiation.

65. $\int e^{au}\,du = \dfrac{1}{a}e^{au} + C, \qquad a \neq 0$

66. $\int \dfrac{1}{au + b}\,du = \dfrac{1}{a}\ln|au + b| + C, \qquad a \neq 0$

Applications

Business & Economics

67. *Price–demand equation.* The marginal price for a weekly demand of x bottles of baby shampoo in a drug store is given by

$$p'(x) = \frac{-6,000}{(3x + 50)^2}$$

Find the price–demand equation if the weekly demand is 150 when the price of a bottle of shampoo is $4. What is the weekly demand when the price is $2.50?

68. *Price–supply equation.* The marginal price at a supply level of x bottles of baby shampoo per week is given by

$$p'(x) = \frac{300}{(3x + 25)^2}$$

Find the price–supply equation if the distributor of the shampoo is willing to supply 75 bottles a week at a price of $1.60 per bottle. How many bottles would the supplier be willing to supply at a price of $1.75 per bottle?

69. *Cost function.* The weekly marginal cost of producing x pairs of tennis shoes is given by

$$C'(x) = 12 + \frac{500}{x + 1}$$

where C(x) is cost in dollars. If the fixed costs are $2,000 per week, find the cost function. What is the average cost per pair of shoes if 1,000 pairs of shoes are produced each week?

70. *Revenue function.* The weekly marginal revenue from the sale of x pairs of tennis shoes is given by

$$R'(x) = 40 - 0.02x + \frac{200}{x + 1} \qquad R(0) = 0$$

where R(x) is revenue in dollars. Find the revenue function. Find the revenue from the sale of 1,000 pairs of shoes.

71. *Marketing.* An automobile company is ready to introduce a new line of cars with a national sales campaign. After test marketing the line in a carefully selected city, the marketing research department estimates that sales (in millions of dollars) will increase at the monthly rate of

$$S'(t) = 10 - 10e^{-0.1t} \qquad 0 \le t \le 24$$

t months after the national campaign has started.

(A) What will be the total sales, S(t), t months after the beginning of the national campaign if we assume 0 sales at the beginning of the campaign?

(B) What are the estimated total sales for the first 12 months of the campaign?

(C) When will the estimated total sales reach $100 million? Use a graphing utility to approximate the answer to two decimal places.

72. *Marketing.* Repeat Problem 71 if the monthly rate of increase in sales is found to be approximated by

$$S'(t) = 20 - 20e^{-0.05t} \qquad 0 \le t \le 24$$

73. *Oil production.* Using data from the first 3 years of production as well as geological studies, the management of an oil company estimates that oil will be pumped from a producing field at a rate given by

$$R(t) = \frac{100}{t + 1} + 5 \qquad 0 \le t \le 20$$

where R(t) is the rate of production (in thousands of barrels per year) t years after pumping begins. How many barrels of oil, Q(t), will the field produce the first t years if Q(0) = 0? How many barrels will be produced the first 9 years?

74. *Oil production.* Assume that the rate in Problem 73 is found to be

$$R(t) = \frac{120t}{t^2 + 1} + 3 \qquad 0 \le t \le 20$$

(A) When is the rate of production greatest?

(B) How many barrels of oil, Q(t), will the field produce the first t years if Q(0) = 0? How many barrels will be produced the first 5 years?

(C) How long (to the nearest tenth of a year) will it take to produce a total of a quarter of a million barrels of oil?

Life Sciences

75. *Biology.* A yeast culture is growing at the rate of $W'(t) = 0.2e^{0.1t}$ grams per hour. If the starting culture weighs 2 grams, what will be the weight of the culture, W(t), after t hours? After 8 hours?

76. *Medicine.* The rate of healing for a skin wound (in square centimeters per day) is approximated by $A'(t) = -0.9e^{-0.1t}$. If the initial wound has an area of 9 square centimeters, what will its area, A(t), be after t days? After 5 days?

77. *Pollution.* A contaminated lake is treated with a bactericide. The rate of increase in harmful bacteria t days after the treatment is given by

$$\frac{dN}{dt} = -\frac{2,000t}{1 + t^2} \qquad 0 \le t \le 10$$

where N(t) is the number of bacteria per milliliter of water (since dN/dt is negative, the count of harmful bacteria is decreasing).

(A) Find the minimum value of dN/dt.

(B) If the initial count was 5,000 bacteria per milliliter, find $N(t)$ and then find the bacteria count after 10 days.

(C) When (to two decimal places) is the bacteria count 1,000 bacteria per milliliter?

78. *Pollution.* An oil tanker aground on a reef is losing oil and producing an oil slick that is radiating outward at a rate given approximately by

$$\frac{dR}{dt} = \frac{60}{\sqrt{t + 9}} \qquad t \geq 0$$

where R is the radius (in feet) of the circular slick after t minutes. Find the radius of the slick after 16 minutes if the radius is 0 when $t = 0$.

Social Sciences

79. *Learning.* In a particular business college, it was found that an average student enrolled in an advanced typing class progressed at a rate of $N'(t) = 6e^{-0.1t}$ words per minute per week, t weeks after enrolling in a 15-week course. If at the

beginning of the course a student could type 40 words per minute, how many words per minute, $N(t)$, would the student be expected to type t weeks into the course? After completing the course?

80. *Learning.* In the same business college, it was also found that an average student enrolled in a beginning shorthand class progressed at a rate of $N'(t) = 12e^{-0.06t}$ words per minute per week, t weeks after enrolling in a 15-week course. If at the beginning of the course a student could take dictation in shorthand at 0 words per minute, how many words per minute, $N(t)$, would the student be expected to handle t weeks into the course? After completing the course?

81. *College enrollment.* The projected rate of increase in enrollment in a new college is estimated by

$$\frac{dE}{dt} = 5,000(t + 1)^{-3/2} \qquad t \geq 0$$

where $E(t)$ is the projected enrollment in t years. If enrollment is 2,000 now ($t = 0$), find the projected enrollment 15 years from now.

Section **6-3** | Differential Equations; Growth and Decay

- ➤ Differential Equations and Slope Fields
- ➤ Continuous Compound Interest Revisited
- ➤ Exponential Growth Law
- ➤ Population Growth, Radioactive Decay, and Learning
- ➤ Comparison of Exponential Growth Phenomena

In the preceding section we considered equations of the form

$$\frac{dy}{dx} = 6x^2 - 4x \qquad p'(x) = -400e^{-0.04x}$$

These are examples of *differential equations*. In general, an equation is a **differential equation** if it involves an unknown function and one or more of its derivatives. Other examples of differential equations are

$$\frac{dy}{dx} = ky \qquad y'' - xy' + x^2 = 5 \qquad \frac{dy}{dx} = 2xy$$

The first and third equations are called **first-order** equations because each involves a first derivative, but no higher derivative. The second equation is called a **second-order** equation because it involves a second derivative, and no higher derivatives. Finding solutions to different types of differential equations (functions that satisfy the equation) is the subject matter for entire books and courses on this topic. Here, we consider only a few very special but very important first-order equations that have immediate and significant applications.

We start by looking at some first-order equations geometrically, in terms of *slope fields*. We then reconsider continuous compound interest as modeled by a first-order differential equation, and from this we will be able to generalize the approach to a wide variety of other types of growth phenomena.

➤ Differential Equations and Slope Fields

We introduce the concept of *slope field* through an example. Suppose that we are given the first-order differential equation

$$\frac{dy}{dx} = 0.2y \tag{1}$$

A function f is a solution of equation (1) if $y = f(x)$ satisfies equation (1) for all values of x in the domain of f. Geometrically interpreted, equation (1) gives us the slope of a solution curve that passes through the point (x, y). For example, if $y = f(x)$ is a solution of equation (1) that passes through the point $(0, 2)$, then the slope of f at $(0, 2)$ is given by

$$\frac{dy}{dx} = 0.2(2) = 0.4$$

We indicate this by drawing a short segment of the tangent line at the point $(0, 2)$, as shown in Figure 1A. This procedure is repeated for points $(-3, 1)$ and $(2, 3)$, as also shown in Figure 1A. Assuming that the graph of f passes through all three points, we sketch an approximate graph of f in Figure 1B.

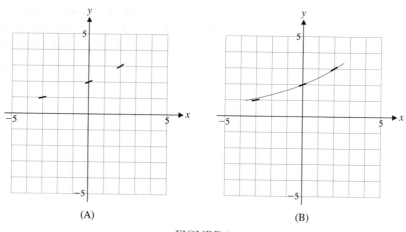

(A)

(B)

FIGURE 1

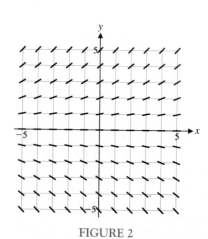

FIGURE 2

If we continue the process of drawing tangent line segments at each point in the grid in Figure 1—a task easily handled by computers but not by hand—we obtain a *slope field*. A slope field for differential equation (1), drawn by a computer, is shown in Figure 2. In general, a **slope field** for a first-order differential equation is obtained by drawing tangent line segments determined by the equation at each point in a grid. In a more advanced treatment of the subject, one can find out a lot about the shape and behavior of solution curves of first-order differential equations by looking at slope fields. Our interests are more modest here.

(A) In Figure 1A (or a copy), draw tangent line segments for a solution curve of differential equation (1) that passes through $(-3, -1)$, $(0, -2)$, and $(2, -3)$.

(B) In Figure 1B (or a copy), sketch an approximate graph of the solution curve that passes through these three points. (Repeat the tangent line segments first.)

(C) Of all the elementary functions discussed in the first two chapters, make a conjecture as to what type of function appears to be a solution to differential equation (1).

In Explore–Discuss 1, if you guessed that solutions to equation (1) are exponential functions, you are to be congratulated. We now show that

$$y = Ce^{0.2x} \tag{2}$$

is a solution to equation (1) for any real number C. [Later in this section we show how to find equation (2) directly from equation (1).] To do this, we substitute $y = Ce^{0.2x}$ into equation (1) to see if the left side is equal to the right side for all real x:

$$\frac{dy}{dx} = 0.2y$$

$$\text{Left side:} \quad \frac{dy}{dx} = \frac{d}{dx}(Ce^{0.2x}) = 0.2Ce^{0.2x}$$

$$\text{Right side:} \quad 0.2y = 0.2Ce^{0.2x}$$

Thus, equation (2) is a solution of equation (1) for C any real number. Which values of C will produce solution curves that pass through $(0, 2)$ and $(0, -2)$, respectively? Substituting the coordinates of each point into equation (2) and solving for C (a task left the reader), we obtain

$$y = 2e^{0.2x} \quad \text{and} \quad y = -2e^{0.2x} \tag{3}$$

as can easily be checked. The graphs of equations (3) are shown in Figure 3 and confirm the results in Figure 1B.

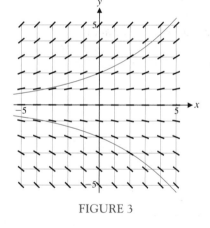

FIGURE 3

(A) In Figure 3 (or a copy), sketch in an approximate solution curve that passes through $(0, 3)$ and one that passes through $(0, -3)$.

(B) Use a graphing utility to graph $y = Ce^{0.2x}$ for $C = -4, -3, -2, 2, 3, 4$, all in the same viewing window. Notice how these solution curves follow the flow of the tangent line segments in the slope field in Figure 2.

◉ **Insight**   For a complicated first-order differential equation, say

$$\frac{dy}{dx} = \frac{3 + \sqrt{xy}}{x^2 - 5y^4}$$

it may be impossible to find a formula analogous to (2) for its solutions. Nevertheless, it is routine to evaluate the right hand side at each point in a grid. The resulting slope field provides a graphical representation of the solutions to the differential equation.   ●

As indicated, drawing slope fields by hand is not a task for human beings—a 20 by 20 grid would require drawing 400 tangent line segments! Repetitive tasks of this type are what computers are for. A few problems in Exercise 6-3 involve interpreting slope fields, not drawing them.

➤ Continuous Compound Interest Revisited

Let P be the initial amount of money deposited in an account, and let A be the amount in the account at any time t. Instead of assuming that the money in the account earns a particular rate of interest, suppose we say that the rate of growth of the amount of money in the account at any time t is proportional to the amount present at that time. Since dA/dt is the rate of growth of A with respect to t, we have

$$\frac{dA}{dt} = rA \qquad A(0) = P \qquad A, P > 0 \tag{4}$$

where r is an appropriate constant. We would like to find a function $A = A(t)$ that satisfies these conditions. Multiplying both sides of equation (4) by $1/A$, we obtain

$$\frac{1}{A}\frac{dA}{dt} = r$$

Now we integrate each side with respect to t:

$$\int \frac{1}{A}\frac{dA}{dt}\,dt = \int r\,dt \qquad \frac{dA}{dt}dt = A'(t)dt = dA$$

$$\int \frac{1}{A}\,dA = \int r\,dt$$

$$\ln|A| = rt + C \quad |A| = A, \text{ since } A > 0$$

$$\ln A = rt + C$$

We convert this last equation into the equivalent exponential form

$$A = e^{rt+C} \quad \text{Definition of logarithmic function:}$$
$$y = \ln x \text{ if and only if } x = e^y$$
$$= e^C e^{rt} \quad \text{Property of exponents: } b^m b^n = b^{m+n}$$

Since $A(0) = P$, we evaluate $A(t) = e^C e^{rt}$ at $t = 0$ and set it equal to P:

$$A(0) = e^C e^0 = e^C = P$$

Hence, $e^C = P$, and we can rewrite $A = e^C e^{rt}$ in the form

$$A = Pe^{rt}$$

This is the same continuous compound interest formula obtained in Section 5-1, where the principal P is invested at an annual nominal rate r compounded continuously for t years.

➤ Exponential Growth Law

In general, if the rate of change with respect to time of a quantity Q is proportional to the amount present and $Q(0) = Q_0$, then proceeding in exactly the same way as above, we obtain the following:

RESULT Exponential Growth Law

If $\dfrac{dQ}{dt} = rQ$ and $Q(0) = Q_0$, then $Q = Q_0 e^{rt}$,

where

$$Q_0 = \text{amount at } t = 0$$

$$r = \text{continuous compound growth rate (expressed as a decimal)}$$

$$t = \text{time}$$

$$Q = \text{quantity at time } t$$

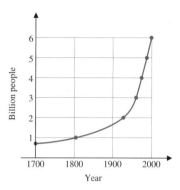

FIGURE 4 World population growth

The constant r in the exponential growth law is sometimes called the **growth constant,** or the **growth rate.** The last term can be misleading, since the rate of growth of Q with respect to time is dQ/dt, not r. Notice that if $r < 0$, then $dQ/dt < 0$ and Q is decreasing. This type of growth is called **exponential decay.**

Once we know that the rate of growth of something is proportional to the amount present, we know that it has exponential growth and we can use the results summarized in the box without having to solve the differential equation each time. The exponential growth law applies not only to money invested at interest compounded continuously, but also to many other types of problems—population growth, radioactive decay, natural resource depletion, and so on.

 ➤ Population Growth, Radioactive Decay, and Learning

The world population passed 1 billion in 1804, 2 billion in 1927, 3 billion in 1960, 4 billion in 1974, 5 billion in 1987, and 6 billion in 1999, as illustrated in Figure 4. **Population growth** over certain periods of time often can be approximated by the exponential growth law described previously.

EXAMPLE 1 **Population Growth** India had a population of about 1.0 billion in 2000 ($t = 0$). Let P represent the population (in billions) t years after 2000, and assume a growth rate of 1.3% compounded continuously.

(A) Find an equation that represents India's population growth after 2000, assuming that the 1.3% growth rate continues.

(B) What is the estimated population (to the nearest tenth of a billion) for India in the year 2030?

(C) Graph the equation found in part (A) from 2000 to 2030.

Solution (A) The exponential growth law applies, and we have

$$\frac{dP}{dt} = 0.013P \qquad P(0) = 1.0$$

Thus,

$$P = 1.0e^{0.013t} \tag{5}$$

(B) Using equation (5), we can estimate the population in India in 2030 ($t = 30$):

$$P = 1.0e^{0.013(30)} = 1.5 \text{ billion people}$$

(C) The graph is shown in Figure 5.

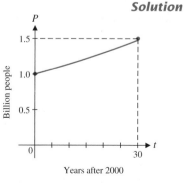

FIGURE 5 Population of India

Matched Problem 1   Assuming the same continuous compound growth rate as in Example 1, what will India's population be (to the nearest tenth of a billion) in the year 2015?

EXAMPLE 2   **Population Growth**   If the exponential growth law applies to Canada's population growth, at what continuous compound growth rate will the population double over the next 100 years?

Solution   The problem is to find r, given $P = 2P_0$ and $t = 100$:

$$P = P_0 e^{rt}$$
$$2P_0 = P_0 e^{100r}$$
$$2 = e^{100r} \qquad \text{Take the natural logarithm of both sides}$$
$$100r = \ln 2 \qquad \text{and reverse the equation.}$$
$$r = \frac{\ln 2}{100}$$
$$\approx 0.0069 \quad \text{or} \quad 0.69\%$$

Matched Problem 2   If the exponential growth law applies to population growth in Nigeria, find the doubling time (to the nearest year) of the population if it grows at 2.1% per year compounded continuously.

We now turn to another type of exponential growth—**radioactive decay.** In 1946, Willard Libby (who later received a Nobel Prize in chemistry) found that as long as a plant or animal is alive, radioactive carbon-14 is maintained at a constant level in its tissues. Once the plant or animal is dead, however, the radioactive carbon-14 diminishes by radioactive decay at a rate proportional to the amount present. Thus,

$$\frac{dQ}{dt} = rQ \qquad Q(0) = Q_0$$

and we have another example of the exponential growth law. The continuous compound rate of decay for radioactive carbon-14 has been found to be 0.000 123 8; thus, $r = -0.000\ 123\ 8$, since decay implies a negative continuous compound growth rate.

EXAMPLE 3   **Archaeology**   A piece of human bone was found at an archaeological site in Africa. If 10% of the original amount of radioactive carbon-14 was present, estimate the age of the bone (to the nearest 100 years).

Solution   Using the exponential growth law for

$$\frac{dQ}{dt} = -0.000\ 123\ 8Q \qquad Q(0) = Q_0$$

we find that

$$Q = Q_0 e^{-0.0001238t}$$

and our problem is to find t so that $Q = 0.1Q_0$ (since the amount of carbon-14 present now is 10% of the amount present, Q_0, at the death of the person).

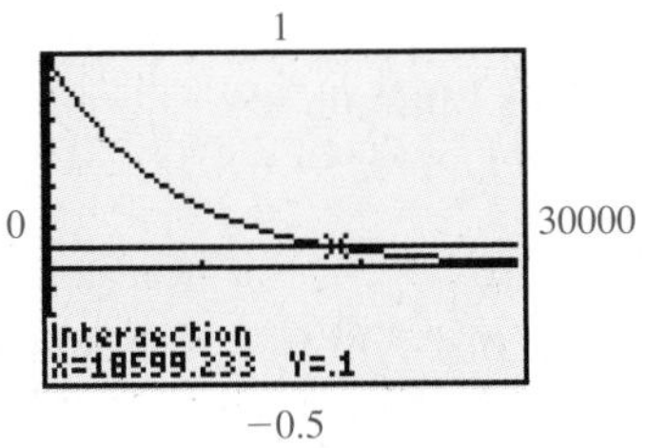

Thus,

$$0.1Q_0 = Q_0 e^{-0.0001238t}$$

$$0.1 = e^{-0.0001238t}$$

$$\ln 0.1 = \ln e^{-0.0001238t}$$

$$t = \frac{\ln 0.1}{-0.000\ 123\ 8} \approx 18{,}600 \text{ years}$$ ■

See Figure 6 for a graphical solution to Example 3.

FIGURE 6
$y_1 = e^{-0.0001238x}$; $y_2 = 0.1$

Matched Problem 3

Estimate the age of the bone in Example 3 (to the nearest 100 years) if 50% of the original amount of carbon-14 is present. ————————■

In learning certain skills such as typing and swimming, a mathematical model often used is one that assumes there is a maximum skill attainable, say, M, and the rate of improving is proportional to the difference between that achieved, y, and that attainable, M. Mathematically,

$$\frac{dy}{dt} = k(M - y) \qquad y(0) = 0$$

We solve this type of problem using the same technique that was used to obtain the exponential growth law. First, multiply both sides of the first equation by $1/(M - y)$ to obtain

$$\frac{1}{M - y} \frac{dy}{dt} = k$$

and then integrate each side with respect to t:

$$\int \frac{1}{M - y} \frac{dy}{dt} dt = \int k\, dt$$

$$-\int \frac{1}{M - y} \left(-\frac{dy}{dt}\right) dt = \int k\, dt \qquad \text{Substitute } u = M - y \text{ and}$$

$$-\int \frac{1}{u} du = \int k\, dt \qquad du = -dy = -\frac{dy}{dt} dt.$$

$$-\ln|u| = kt + C \qquad \text{Substitute } M - y = u.$$

$$-\ln(M - y) = kt + C \qquad \text{Absolute value signs are not required.}$$

$$\ln(M - y) = -kt - C \quad \text{(Why?)}$$

Change this last equation to equivalent exponential form:

$$M - y = e^{-kt - C}$$

$$M - y = e^{-C} e^{-kt}$$

$$y = M - e^{-C} e^{-kt}$$

Now, $y(0) = 0$; hence,

$$y(0) = M - e^{-C} e^0 = 0$$

Solving for e^{-C}, we obtain

$$e^{-C} = M$$

and our final solution is

$$y = M - M e^{-kt} = M(1 - e^{-kt})$$

EXAMPLE 4   **Learning** For a particular person who is learning to swim, it is found that the distance y (in feet) the person is able to swim in 1 minute after t hours of practice is given approximately by

$$y = 50(1 - e^{-0.04t})$$

What is the rate of improvement (to two decimal places) after 10 hours of practice?

Solution

$$y = 50 - 50e^{-0.04t}$$
$$y'(t) = 2e^{-0.04t}$$
$$y'(10) = 2e^{-0.04(10)} \approx 1.34 \text{ feet per hour of practice}$$

Matched Problem 4   In Example 4, what is the rate of improvement (to two decimal places) after 50 hours of practice?

➤ Comparison of Exponential Growth Phenomena

The graphs and equations given in Table 1 compare several widely used growth models. These are divided basically into two groups: unlimited growth and limited growth. Following each equation and graph is a short (and necessarily incomplete) list of areas in which the models are used. This only touches

TABLE 1 Exponential Growth

Description	Model	Solution	Graph	Uses
Unlimited growth: Rate of growth is proportional to the amount present	$\dfrac{dy}{dt} = ky$ $k, t > 0$ $y(0) = c$	$y = ce^{kt}$		• Short-term population growth (people, bacteria, etc.) • Growth of money at continuous compound interest • Price–supply curves
Exponential decay: Rate of growth is proportional to the amount present	$\dfrac{dy}{dt} = -ky$ $k, t > 0$ $y(0) = c$	$y = ce^{-kt}$		• Depletion of natural resources • Radioactive decay • Light absorption in water • Price–demand curves • Atmospheric pressure (t is altitude)
Limited growth: Rate of growth is proportional to the difference between the amount present and a fixed limit	$\dfrac{dy}{dt} = k(M - y)$ $k, t > 0$ $y(0) = 0$	$y = M(1 - e^{-kt})$		• Sales fads (for example, skateboards) • Depreciation of equipment • Company growth • Learning
Logistic growth: Rate of growth is proportional to the amount present and to the difference between the amount present and a fixed limit	$\dfrac{dy}{dt} = ky(M - y)$ $k, t > 0$ $y(0) = \dfrac{M}{1 + c}$	$y = \dfrac{M}{1 + ce^{-kMt}}$		• Long-term population growth • Epidemics • Sales of new products • Rumor spread • Company growth

on a subject that has been extensively developed and which you are likely to encounter in greater depth in the future.

Answers to Matched Problems   **1.** 1.2 billion people   **2.** 33 yr   **3.** 5,600 yr   **4.** 0.27 ft/hr

Exercise 6-3

A *In Problems 1–12, find the general or particular solution, as indicated, for each differential equation.*

1. $\dfrac{dy}{dx} = 6x$

2. $\dfrac{dy}{dx} = 3x^{-2}$

3. $\dfrac{dy}{dx} = \dfrac{7}{x}$

4. $\dfrac{dy}{dx} = e^{0.1x}$

5. $\dfrac{dy}{dx} = e^{0.02x}$

6. $\dfrac{dy}{dx} = 8x^{-1}$

7. $\dfrac{dy}{dx} = x^2 - x;\ y(0) = 0$

8. $\dfrac{dy}{dx} = \sqrt{x};\ y(0) = 0$

9. $\dfrac{dy}{dx} = -2xe^{-x^2};\ y(0) = 3$

10. $\dfrac{dy}{dx} = e^{x-3};\ y(3) = -5$

11. $\dfrac{dy}{dx} = \dfrac{2}{1 + x};\ y(0) = 5$

12. $\dfrac{dy}{dx} = \dfrac{1}{4(3 - x)};\ y(0) = 1$

B *Problems 13–18 refer to the following slope fields:*

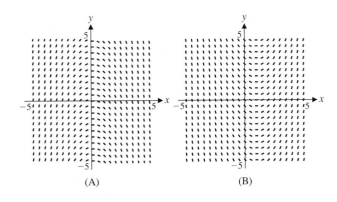

(A)   (B)

13. Which slope field is associated with the differential equation $dy/dx = x - 1$? Briefly justify your answer.

14. Which slope field is associated with the differential equation $dy/dx = -x$? Briefly justify your answer.

15. Solve the differential equation $dy/dx = x - 1$, and find the particular solution that passes through $(0, -2)$.

16. Solve the differential equation $dy/dx = -x$, and find the particular solution that passes through $(0, 3)$.

17. Graph the particular solution found in Problem 15 in the appropriate figure above (or a copy).

18. Graph the particular solution found in Problem 16 in the appropriate figure above (or a copy).

In Problems 19–26, find the general or particular solution, as indicated, for each differential equation.

19. $\dfrac{dy}{dt} = 2y$

20. $\dfrac{dy}{dt} = -3y$

21. $\dfrac{dy}{dx} = -0.5y;\ y(0) = 100$

22. $\dfrac{dy}{dx} = 0.1y;\ y(0) = -2.5$

23. $\dfrac{dx}{dt} = -5x$

24. $\dfrac{dx}{dt} = 4t$

25. $\dfrac{dx}{dt} = -5t$

26. $\dfrac{dx}{dt} = 4x$

C *Problems 27–34 refer to the following slope fields:*

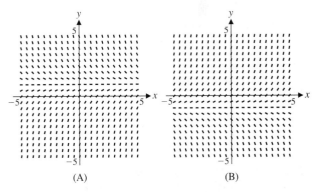

(A)   (B)

27. Which slope field is associated with the differential equation $dy/dx = 1 - y$? Briefly justify your answer.

28. Which slope field is associated with the differential equation $dy/dx = y + 1$? Briefly justify your answer.

29. Show that $y = 1 - Ce^{-x}$ is a solution of the differential equation $dy/dx = 1 - y$ for any real number C. Find the particular solution that passes through $(0, 0)$.

30. Show that $y = Ce^x - 1$ is a solution of the differential equation $dy/dx = y + 1$ for any real number C. Find the particular solution that passes through $(0, 0)$.

31. Graph the particular solution found in Problem 29 in the appropriate figure above (or a copy).

32. Graph the particular solution found in Problem 30 in the appropriate figure above (or a copy).

33. Use a graphing utility to graph $y = 1 - Ce^{-x}$ for $C = -2, -1, 1,$ and 2 for $-5 \le x \le 5, -5 \le y \le 5,$ all in the same viewing window. Observe how the solution curves go with the flow of the tangent line segments in the corresponding slope field shown above.

34. Use a graphing utility to graph $y = Ce^x - 1$ for $C = -2, -1, 1,$ and 2 for $-5 \le x \le 5, -5 \le y \le 5,$ all in the same viewing window. Observe how the solution curves go with the flow of the tangent line segments in the corresponding slope field shown above.

In Problems 35–42, use a graphing utility to graph the given examples of the various cases in Table 1.

35. Unlimited growth:
$y = 1,000e^{0.08t}$
$0 \le t \le 15$
$0 \le y \le 3,500$

36. Unlimited growth:
$y = 5,250e^{0.12t}$
$0 \le t \le 10$
$0 \le y \le 20,000$

37. Exponential decay:
$p = 100e^{-0.05x}$
$0 \le x \le 30$
$0 \le p \le 100$

38. Exponential decay:
$p = 1,000e^{-0.08x}$
$0 \le x \le 40$
$0 \le p \le 1,000$

39. Limited growth:
$N = 100(1 - e^{-0.05t})$
$0 \le t \le 100$
$0 \le N \le 100$

40. Limited growth:
$N = 1,000(1 - e^{-0.07t})$
$0 \le t \le 70$
$0 \le N \le 1,000$

41. Logistic growth:
$$N = \frac{1,000}{1 + 999e^{-0.4t}}$$
$0 \le t \le 40$
$0 \le N \le 1,000$

42. Logistic growth:
$$N = \frac{400}{1 + 99e^{-0.4t}}$$
$0 \le t \le 30$
$0 \le N \le 400$

43. Show that the rate of logistic growth, $dy/dt = ky(M - y)$, has its maximum value when $y = M/2$.

44. Find the value of t for which the logistic function
$$y = \frac{M}{1 + ce^{-kMt}}$$
is equal to $M/2$.

45. Let $Q(t)$ denote the population of the world at time t. In 1967 the world population was 3.5 billion and increasing at 2.0% per year; in 1999 it was 6.0 billion and increasing at 1.3% per year. In which year, 1967 or 1999, was dQ/dt (the rate of growth of Q with respect to t) greater? Explain.

46. Refer to Problem 45. Explain why the world population function $Q(t)$ does not satisfy an exponential growth law.

Applications

Business & Economics

47. *Continuous compound interest.* Find the amount A in an account after t years if
$$\frac{dA}{dt} = 0.08A \quad \text{and} \quad A(0) = 1,000$$

48. *Continuous compound interest.* Find the amount A in an account after t years if
$$\frac{dA}{dt} = 0.12A \quad \text{and} \quad A(0) = 5,250$$

49. *Continuous compound interest.* Find the amount A in an account after t years if
$$\frac{dA}{dt} = rA \quad A(0) = 8,000 \quad A(2) = 9,020$$

50. *Continuous compound interest.* Find the amount A in an account after t years if
$$\frac{dA}{dt} = rA \quad A(0) = 5,000 \quad A(5) = 7,460$$

51. *Price–demand.* The marginal price dp/dx at x units of demand per week is proportional to the price p. There is no weekly demand at a price of $100 per unit $[p(0) = 100]$, and there is a weekly demand of 5 units at a price of $77.88 per unit $[p(5) = 77.88]$.

(A) Find the price–demand equation.

(B) At a demand of 10 units per week, what is the price?

(C) Graph the price–demand equation for $0 \le x \le 25$.

52. *Price–supply.* The marginal price dp/dx at x units of supply per day is proportional to the price p. There is no supply at a price of $10 per unit $[p(0) = 10]$, and there is a daily supply of 50 units at a price of $12.84 per unit $[p(50) = 12.84]$.

(A) Find the price–supply equation.

(B) At a supply of 100 units per day, what is the price?

(C) Graph the price–supply equation for $0 \le x \le 250$.

53. *Advertising.* A company is trying to expose a new product to as many people as possible through television advertising. Suppose that the rate of exposure to new people is proportional to the number of those who have not seen the product out of L possible viewers. No one is aware of the product at the start of the campaign, and after 10 days 40% of L are aware of the product. Mathematically,

$$\frac{dN}{dt} = k(L - N) \quad N(0) = 0 \quad N(10) = 0.4L$$

(A) Solve the differential equation.

(B) What percent of L will have been exposed after 5 days of the campaign?

(C) How many days will it take to expose 80% of L?

(D) Graph the solution found in part (A) for $0 \le t \le 90$.

54. *Advertising.* Suppose that the differential equation for Problem 53 is

$$\frac{dN}{dt} = k(L - N) \quad N(0) = 0 \quad N(10) = 0.1L$$

(A) Interpret $N(10) = 0.1L$ verbally.

(B) Solve the differential equation.

(C) How many days will it take to expose 50% of L?

(D) Graph the solution found in part (B) for $0 \le t \le 300$.

Life Sciences

55. *Biology.* For relatively clear bodies of water, light intensity is reduced according to

$$\frac{dI}{dx} = -kI \quad I(0) = I_0$$

where I is the intensity of light at x feet below the surface. For the Sargasso Sea off the West Indies, $k = 0.00942$. Find I in terms of x, and find the depth at which the light is reduced to half of that at the surface.

56. *Blood pressure.* It can be shown under certain assumptions that blood pressure P in the largest artery in the human body (the aorta) changes between beats with respect to time t according to

$$\frac{dP}{dt} = -aP \quad P(0) = P_0$$

where a is a constant. Find $P = P(t)$ that satisfies both conditions.

57. *Drug concentration.* A single injection of a drug is administered to a patient. The amount Q in the body

then decreases at a rate proportional to the amount present, and for a particular drug the rate is 4% per hour. Thus,

$$\frac{dQ}{dt} = -0.04Q \quad Q(0) = Q_0$$

where t is time in hours.

(A) If the initial injection is 3 milliliters $[Q(0) = 3]$, find $Q = Q(t)$ satisfying both conditions.

(B) How many milliliters (to two decimal places) are in the body after 10 hours?

(C) How many hours (to two decimal places) will it take for only 1 milliliter of the drug to be left in the body?

(D) Graph the solution found in part (A).

58. *Simple epidemic.* A community of 1,000 people is assumed to be homogeneously mixed. One person who has just returned from another community has influenza. Assume that the home community has not had influenza shots and all are susceptible. One mathematical model for an influenza epidemic assumes that influenza tends to spread at a rate in direct proportion to the number who have it, N, and to the number who have not yet contracted it—in this case, $1,000 - N$. Mathematically,

$$\frac{dN}{dt} = kN(1,000 - N) \quad N(0) = 1$$

where N is the number of people who have contracted influenza after t days. For $k = 0.0004$, it can be shown that $N(t)$ is given by

$$N(t) = \frac{1,000}{1 + 999e^{-0.4t}}$$

(A) How many people have contracted influenza after 10 days? After 20 days?

(B) How many days will it take until half the community has contracted influenza?

(C) Find $\lim_{t \to \infty} N(t)$.

(D) Graph $N = N(t)$ for $0 \le t \le 30$.

59. *Nuclear accident.* One of the dangerous radioactive isotopes detected after the Chernobyl nuclear accident in 1986 was cesium-137. If 93.3% of the cesium-137 emitted during the accident is still present 3 years later, find the continuous compound rate of decay of this isotope.

60. *Insecticides.* Many countries have banned the use of the insecticide DDT because of its long-term adverse effects. Five years after a particular country stopped using DDT, the amount of DDT in the ecosystem had declined to 75% of the amount present at the time of the ban. Find the continuous compound rate of decay of DDT.

Social Sciences

61. *Archaeology.* A skull from an ancient tomb was discovered and was found to have 5% of the original amount of radioactive carbon-14 present. Estimate the age of the skull. (See Example 3.)

62. *Learning.* For a particular person learning to type, it was found that the number of words per minute, N, the person was able to type after t hours of practice was given approximately by

$$N = 100(1 - e^{-0.02t})$$

See Table 1 (limited growth) for a characteristic graph. What is the rate of improvement after 10 hours of practice? After 40 hours of practice?

63. *Small group analysis.* In a study on small group dynamics, sociologists Stephan and Mischler found that when the members of a discussion group of 10 were ranked according to the number of times each participated, the number of times $N(k)$ the kth-ranked person participated was given approximately by

$$N(k) = N_1 e^{-0.11(k-1)}   1 \le k \le 10$$

where N_1 is the number of times the first-ranked person participated in the discussion. If, in a particular discussion group of 10 people, $N_1 = 180$, estimate how many times the sixth-ranked person participated. The 10th-ranked person.

64. *Perception.* One of the oldest laws in mathematical psychology is the Weber–Fechner law (discovered in the middle of the nineteenth century). It concerns a person's sensed perception of various strengths of stimulation involving weights, sound, light, shock, taste, and so on. One form of the law states that the rate of change of sensed sensation S with respect to stimulus R is inversely proportional to the strength of the stimulus R. Thus,

$$\frac{dS}{dR} = \frac{k}{R}$$

where k is a constant. If we let R_0 be the threshold level at which the stimulus R can be detected (the least amount of sound, light, weight, and so on, that can be detected), it is appropriate to write

$$S(R_0) = 0$$

Find a function S in terms of R that satisfies the preceding conditions.

65. *Rumor spread.* A group of 400 parents, relatives, and friends are waiting anxiously at Kennedy Airport for a student charter flight to return after a year in Europe. It is stormy and the plane is late. A particular parent thought he had heard that the plane's radio had gone out and related this news to some friends, who in turn passed it on to others, and so on. Sociologists have studied rumor propagation and have found that a rumor tends to spread at a rate in direct proportion to the number who have heard it, x, and to the number who have not, $P - x$, where P is the total population. Mathematically, for our case, $P = 400$ and

$$\frac{dx}{dt} = 0.001x(400 - x)   x(0) = 1$$

where t is time (in minutes). From this, it can be shown that

$$x(t) = \frac{400}{1 + 399e^{-0.4t}}$$

See Table 1 (logistic growth) for a characteristic graph.

(A) How many people have heard the rumor after 5 minutes? 20 minutes?

(B) Find $\lim_{t \to \infty} x(t)$.

 (C) Graph $x = x(t)$ for $0 \le t \le 30$.

66. *Rumor spread.* In Problem 65, how long (to the nearest minute) will it take for half of the group of 400 to have heard the rumor?

Section **6-4** | The Definite Integral

> Approximating Areas by Left and Right Sums
> The Definite Integral as a Limit of Sums
> Properties of the Definite Integral

The first three sections of this chapter focused on the *indefinite integral*. In this section we introduce the *definite integral*. The definite integral is used to compute areas, probabilities, average values of functions, future values of continuous income streams, and many other quantities. Initially, the concept of the definite integral may appear to be unrelated to the notion of the indefinite integral. There is, however, a close connection between the two integrals. The fundamental theorem of calculus, discussed in Section 6-5, makes that connection precise.

➤ Approximating Areas by Left and Right Sums

How do we find the shaded area in Figure 1? That is, how do we find the area bounded by the graph of $f(x) = 0.25x^2 + 1$, the x axis, and the vertical lines $x = 1$ and $x = 5$? [This cumbersome description is usually shortened to "the area under the graph of $f(x) = 0.25x^2 + 1$ from $x = 1$ to $x = 5$."] Our standard geometric area formulas do not apply directly, but the formula for the area of a rectangle can be used indirectly. To see how, we look at a method of approximating the area under the graph by using rectangles. This method will give us any accuracy desired, which is quite different from finding the area exactly. Our first area approximation is made by dividing the interval $[1, 5]$ on the x axis into four equal parts of length

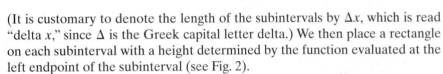

$$\Delta x = \frac{5 - 1}{4} = 1$$

(It is customary to denote the length of the subintervals by Δx, which is read "delta x," since Δ is the Greek capital letter delta.) We then place a rectangle on each subinterval with a height determined by the function evaluated at the left endpoint of the subinterval (see Fig. 2).

Summing the areas of the rectangles in Figure 2, we obtain a **left sum** of four rectangles, denoted by L_4, as follows:

$$L_4 = f(1) \cdot 1 + f(2) \cdot 1 + f(3) \cdot 1 + f(4) \cdot 1$$
$$= 1.25 + 2.00 + 3.25 + 5 = 11.5$$

From Figure 3, since $f(x)$ is increasing, it is clear that the left sum L_4 underestimates the area, and we can write

$$11.5 = L_4 < \text{Area}$$

FIGURE 1   What is the shaded area?

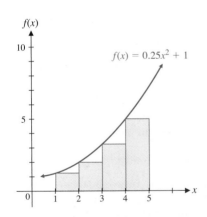

FIGURE 2   Left rectangles

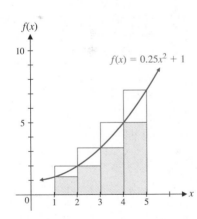

FIGURE 3   Left and right rectangles

EXPLORE & DISCUSS 1

If $f(x)$ were decreasing over the interval $[1, 5]$, would the left sum L_4 over- or underestimate the actual area under the curve? Explain.

Now suppose that we use the right endpoint of each subinterval to obtain the height of the rectangle placed on top of it. Superimposing this result on top of Figure 2, we obtain Figure 3.

Summing the areas of the higher rectangles in Figure 3, we obtain the **right sum** of the four rectangles, denoted by R_4, as follows (compare R_4 with L_4 and note that R_4 can be obtained from L_4 by deleting one rectangular area and adding one more):

$$R_4 = f(2) \cdot 1 + f(3) \cdot 1 + f(4) \cdot 1 + f(5) \cdot 1$$
$$= 2.00 + 3.25 + 5.00 + 7.25 = 17.5$$

From Figure 3, since $f(x)$ is increasing, it is clear that the right sum R_4 overestimates the area, and we conclude that the actual area is between 11.5 and 17.5. That is,

$$11.5 = L_4 < \text{Area} < R_4 = 17.5$$

If $f(x)$ in Figure 3 were decreasing over the interval $[1, 5]$, would the right sum R_4 over- or underestimate the actual area under the curve? Explain.

The first approximation of the area under the curve in (1) is fairly coarse, but the method outlined can be continued with increasingly accurate results by dividing the interval $[1, 5]$ into more and more equal subintervals. Of course, this is not a job for hand calculation but a job that computers are designed to do.* Figure 4 shows left and right rectangle approximations for 16 equal subdivisions.

For this case,

$$\Delta x = \frac{5 - 1}{16} = 0.25$$

$$L_{16} = f(1) \cdot \Delta x + f(1.25) \cdot \Delta x + \cdots + f(4.75) \cdot \Delta x$$
$$= 13.59$$

$$R_{16} = f(1.25) \cdot \Delta x + f(1.50) \cdot \Delta x + \cdots + f(5) \cdot \Delta x$$
$$= 15.09$$

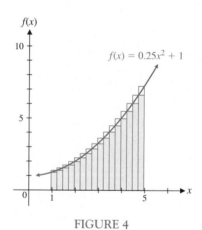

$f(x) = 0.25x^2 + 1$

FIGURE 4

Thus, we now know that the area under the curve is between 13.59 and 15.09. That is,

$$13.59 = L_{16} < \text{Area} < R_{16} = 15.09$$

For 100 equal subdivisions, computer calculations give us

$$14.214 = L_{100} < \text{Area} < R_{100} = 14.454$$

The **error in an approximation** is the absolute value of the difference between the approximation and the actual value. In general, neither the actual value nor the error in an approximation is known. However, it is often possible to calculate an **error bound,** a positive number such that the error is guaranteed to be less than or equal to that number.

The error in the approximation of the area under the graph of f from $x = 1$ to $x = 5$ by the left sum L_{16} (or the right sum R_{16}) is less than the sum of the areas of the small rectangles in Figure 4. By stacking those rectangles (see Fig. 5), we see that

$$\text{Error} = |\text{Area} - L_{16}| < |f(5) - f(1)| \cdot \Delta x = 1.5$$

---

* The computer software that accompanies this book will perform these calculations (see the Preface).

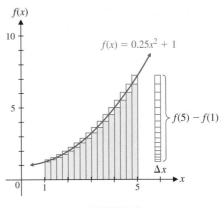

FIGURE 5

Therefore, 1.5 is an error bound for the approximation of the area under f by L_{16}. We can apply the same stacking argument to any positive function that is increasing on $[a, b]$ or decreasing on $[a, b]$, to obtain the error bound in Theorem 1.

THEOREM 1   **Error Bounds for Approximations of Area by Left or Right Sums**

If $f(x) > 0$ and is either increasing on $[a, b]$ or decreasing on $[a, b]$, then

$$|f(b) - f(a)| \cdot \frac{b - a}{n}$$

is an error bound for the approximation of the area between the graph of f and the x axis, from $x = a$ to $x = b$, by L_n or R_n.

Because the error bound of Theorem 1 approaches 0 as $n \to \infty$, it can be shown that left and right sums, for certain functions, approach the same limit as $n \to \infty$.

THEOREM 2   **Limits of Left and Right Sums**

If $f(x) > 0$ and is either increasing on $[a, b]$ or decreasing on $[a, b]$, then its left and right sums approach the same real number as $n \to \infty$.

The number approached as $n \to \infty$ by the left and right sums in Theorem 2 is the area between the graph of f and the x axis from $x = a$ to $x = b$.

EXAMPLE 1   **Approximating Areas** Given the function $f(x) = 9 - 0.25x^2$, we are interested in approximating the area under $y = f(x)$ from $x = 2$ to $x = 5$.

(A) Graph the function over the interval $[0, 6]$; then draw left and right rectangles for the interval $[2, 5]$ with $n = 6$.

(B) Calculate L_6, R_6, and error bounds for each.

(C) How large should n be chosen for the approximation of the area by L_n or R_n to be within 0.05 of the true value?

Solution   (A) $\Delta x = 0.5$:

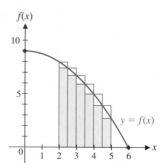

(B) $L_6 = f(2) \cdot \Delta x + f(2.5) \cdot \Delta x + f(3) \cdot \Delta x + f(3.5) \cdot \Delta x + f(4) \cdot \Delta x$
$\quad\quad + f(4.5) \cdot \Delta x = 18.53$

$\quad R_6 = f(2.5) \cdot \Delta x + f(3) \cdot \Delta x + f(3.5) \cdot \Delta x + f(4) \cdot \Delta x$
$\quad\quad + f(4.5) \cdot \Delta x + f(5) \cdot \Delta x = 15.91$

Error bound for L_6 and R_6:

$$\text{error} \le |f(5) - f(2)| \frac{5 - 2}{6} = |2.75 - 8|(0.5) = 2.625$$

(C) For L_n and R_n, find n such that error ≤ 0.05:

$$|f(b) - f(a)| \frac{b - a}{n} \le 0.05$$

$$|2.75 - 8| \frac{3}{n} \le 0.05$$

$$15.75 \le 0.05n$$

$$n \ge \frac{15.75}{0.05} = 315$$

∎

Matched Problem 1   Given the function $f(x) = 8 - 0.5x^2$, we are interested in approximating the area under $y = f(x)$ from $x = 1$ to $x = 3$.

(A) Graph the function over the interval $[0, 4]$; then draw left and right rectangles for the interval $[1, 3]$ with $n = 4$.

(B) Calculate L_4, R_4, and error bounds for each.

(C) How large should n be chosen for the approximation of the area by L_n or R_n to be within 0.5 of the true value?

◉ Insight   Note from Example 1(C) that a relatively large value of n ($n = 315$) is required to approximate the area by L_n or R_n to within 0.05. In other words, 315 rectangles must be used, and 315 terms must be summed, to guarantee that the error does not exceed 0.05. We can obtain a more efficient approximation of the area (in the sense that fewer terms must be summed to achieve a given accuracy) by replacing rectangles by trapezoids. The resulting **trapezoidal rule,** and other methods for approximating areas, are discussed in Group Activity 1.   ●

➤ The Definite Integral as a Limit of Sums

Left and right sums are special cases of more general sums, called *Riemann sums* [named after the German mathematician Georg Riemann (1826–1866)], that are used to approximate areas using rectangles.

Let f be a function defined on the interval $[a, b]$. We partition $[a, b]$ into n subintervals of equal length $\Delta x = (b - a)/n$ with endpoints

$$a = x_0 < x_1 < x_2 < \cdots < x_n = b$$

Then, using **summation notation** (see Appendix B-1),

Left sum: $L_n = f(x_0)\Delta x + f(x_1)\Delta x + \cdots + f(x_{n-1})\Delta x = \displaystyle\sum_{k=1}^{n} f(x_{k-1})\Delta x$

Right sum: $R_n = f(x_1)\Delta x + f(x_2)\Delta x + \cdots + f(x_n)\Delta x = \displaystyle\sum_{k=1}^{n} f(x_k)\Delta x$

Riemann sum: $S_n = f(c_1)\Delta x + f(c_2)\Delta x + \cdots + f(c_n)\Delta x = \displaystyle\sum_{k=1}^{n} f(c_k)\Delta x$

In a **Riemann sum,*** each c_k is required to belong to the subinterval $[x_{k-1}, x_k]$. Left and right sums are the special cases of Riemann sums in which c_k is the left endpoint or right endpoint, respectively, of the subinterval. If $f(x) > 0$, then each term of a Riemann sum S_n represents the area of a rectangle having height $f(c_k)$ and width Δx (see Fig. 6). If $f(x)$ has both positive and negative values, then some terms of S_n represent areas of rectangles, and others represent the negatives of areas of rectangles, depending on the sign of $f(c_k)$ (see Fig. 7).

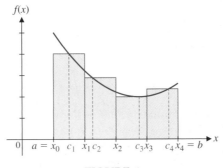

FIGURE 6

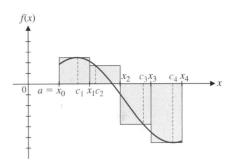

FIGURE 7

EXAMPLE 2   **Riemann Sums**   Consider the function $f(x) = 15 - x^2$ on $[1, 5]$. Partition the interval $[1, 5]$ into four subintervals of equal length. For each subinterval $[x_{k-1}, x_k]$, let c_k be the midpoint. Calculate the corresponding Riemann sum S_4. (Riemann sums for which the c_k are the midpoints of the subintervals are called **midpoint sums.**)

Solution
$$\Delta x = \frac{5 - 1}{4} = 1$$
$$\begin{aligned}
S_4 &= f(c_1) \cdot \Delta x + f(c_2) \cdot \Delta x + f(c_3) \cdot \Delta x + f(c_4) \cdot \Delta x \\
&= f(1.5) \cdot 1 + f(2.5) \cdot 1 + f(3.5) \cdot 1 + f(4.5) \cdot 1 \\
&= 12.75 + 8.75 + 2.75 - 5.25 = 19
\end{aligned}$$

---

* The term *Riemann sum* is often applied to more general sums in which the subintervals $[x_{k-1}, x_k]$ are not required to have the same length. Such sums are not considered in this book.

Matched Problem 2   Consider the function $f(x) = x^2 - 2x - 10$ on $[2, 8]$. Partition the interval $[2, 8]$ into three subintervals of equal length. For each subinterval $[x_{k-1}, x_k]$, let c_k be the midpoint. Calculate the corresponding Riemann sum S_3.

By analyzing properties of a continuous function on a closed interval, it can be shown that the conclusion of Theorem 2 is valid if f is continuous. Moreover, not just left and right sums, but Riemann sums have the same limit as $n \to \infty$.

THEOREM 3   Limit of Riemann Sums

If f is a continuous function on $[a, b]$, then the Riemann sums for f on $[a, b]$ approach a real number limit I as $n \to \infty$.*

DEFINITION   Definite Integral

Let f be a continuous function on $[a, b]$. The limit I of Riemann sums for f on $[a, b]$, guaranteed by Theorem 2, is called the **definite integral** of f from a to b, denoted

$$\int_a^b f(x)\, dx$$

The **integrand** is $f(x)$, the **lower limit of integration** is a, and the **upper limit of integration** is b.

Because area is a positive quantity, the definite integral has the following geometric interpretation:

$$\int_a^b f(x)\, dx$$

represents the cumulative sum of the signed areas between the graph of f and the x axis from $x = a$ to $x = b$, where the areas above the x axis are counted positively, and the areas below the x axis are counted negatively (see Fig. 8, where A and B are the actual areas of the indicated regions).

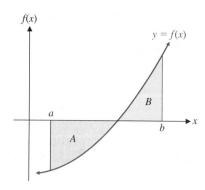

FIGURE 8 $\displaystyle\int_a^b f(x)\, dx = -A + B$

---

* The precise meaning of this limit statement is as follows: For each $e > 0$ there exists some $d > 0$ such that $|S_n - I| < e$ whenever S_n is a Riemann sum for f on $[a, b]$ for which $\Delta x < d$.

EXAMPLE 3  **Definite Integrals** Calculate the definite integrals by referring to Figure 9 with the indicated areas.

(A) $\displaystyle\int_a^b f(x)\,dx$

(B) $\displaystyle\int_a^c f(x)\,dx$

(C) $\displaystyle\int_b^c f(x)\,dx$

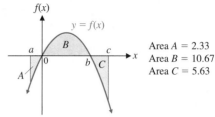

Area $A = 2.33$
Area $B = 10.67$
Area $C = 5.63$

FIGURE 9

Solution (A) $\displaystyle\int_a^b f(x)\,dx = -2.33 + 10.67 = 8.34$

(B) $\displaystyle\int_a^c f(x)\,dx = -2.33 + 10.67 - 5.63 = 2.71$

(C) $\displaystyle\int_b^c f(x)\,dx = -5.63$

Matched Problem 3 Referring to the figure for Example 3, calculate the definite integrals.

(A) $\displaystyle\int_a^0 f(x)\,dx$ (B) $\displaystyle\int_0^c f(x)\,dx$ (C) $\displaystyle\int_0^b f(x)\,dx$

➤ Properties of the Definite Integral

Because the definite integral is defined as the limit of Riemann sums, many properties of sums are also properties of the definite integral. Note that Properties 3 and 4 parallel properties given in Section 6-1 for indefinite integrals.

PROPERTIES Properties of Definite Integrals

1. $\displaystyle\int_a^a f(x)\,dx = 0$

2. $\displaystyle\int_a^b f(x)\,dx = -\int_b^a f(x)\,dx$

3. $\displaystyle\int_a^b kf(x)\,dx = k\int_a^b f(x)\,dx,\quad k \text{ a constant}$

4. $\displaystyle\int_a^b [f(x) \pm g(x)]\,dx = \int_a^b f(x)\,dx \pm \int_a^b g(x)\,dx$

5. $\displaystyle\int_a^b f(x)\,dx = \int_a^c f(x)\,dx + \int_c^b f(x)\,dx$

Example 4 illustrates how properties of definite integrals can be used.

EXAMPLE 4 **Using Properties of the Definite Integral** If

$$\int_0^2 x\,dx = 2 \qquad \int_0^2 x^2\,dx = \frac{8}{3} \qquad \int_2^3 x^2\,dx = \frac{19}{3}$$

then

(A) $\displaystyle\int_0^2 12x^2\,dx = 12\int_0^2 x^2\,dx = 12\left(\frac{8}{3}\right) = 32$

(B) $\displaystyle\int_0^2 (2x - 6x^2)\,dx = 2\int_0^2 x\,dx - 6\int_0^2 x^2\,dx = 2(2) - 6\left(\frac{8}{3}\right) = -12$

(C) $\displaystyle\int_3^2 x^2\,dx = -\int_2^3 x^2\,dx = -\frac{19}{3}$

(D) $\displaystyle\int_5^5 3x^2\,dx = 0$

(E) $\displaystyle\int_0^3 3x^2\,dx = 3\int_0^2 x^2\,dx + 3\int_2^3 x^2\,dx = 3\left(\frac{8}{3}\right) + 3\left(\frac{19}{3}\right) = 27$ ■

Matched Problem 4 Using the same integral values given in Example 4, find

(A) $\displaystyle\int_2^3 6x^2\,dx$ (B) $\displaystyle\int_0^2 (9x^2 - 4x)\,dx$ (C) $\displaystyle\int_2^0 3x\,dx$

(D) $\displaystyle\int_{-2}^{-2} 3x\,dx$ (E) $\displaystyle\int_0^3 12x^2\,dx$ ■

Answers to Matched Problems   **1.** (A) $\Delta x = 0.5$:

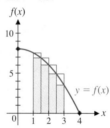

$f(x)$

(B) $L_4 = 12.625$, $R_4 = 10.625$; error for L_4 and $R_4 = 2$
(C) $n > 16$ for L_n and R_n

2. $S_3 = 46$

3. (A) -2.33 (B) 5.04 (C) 10.67

4. (A) 38 (B) 16 (C) -6
       (D) 0 (E) 108

Exercise 6-4

A *Problems 1–10 involve estimating the area under the curves in Figures A–D from $x = 1$ to $x = 4$. For each figure, divide the interval $[1, 4]$ into three equal subintervals.*

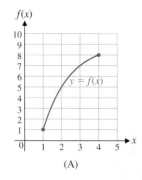

(A)

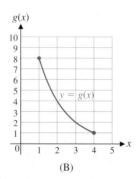

(B)

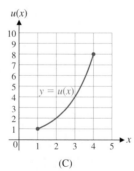

(C)

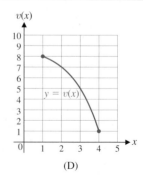

(D)

1. Draw in left and right rectangles for Figures A and B.

2. Draw in left and right rectangles for Figures C and D.

3. Using the results of Problem 1, compute L_3 and R_3 for Figure A and for Figure B.

4. Using the results of Problem 2, compute L_3 and R_3 for Figure C and for Figure D.

5. Replace the question marks with L_3 and R_3 as appropriate. Explain your choice.

$$? \le \int_1^4 f(x)\,dx \le ? \qquad ? \le \int_1^4 g(x)\,dx \le ?$$

6. Replace the question marks with L_3 and R_3 as appropriate. Explain your choice.

$$? \le \int_1^4 u(x)\,dx \le ? \qquad ? \le \int_1^4 v(x)\,dx \le ?$$

7. Compute error bounds for L_3 and R_3 found in Problem 3 for both figures.

8. Compute error bounds for L_3 and R_3 found in Problem 4 for both figures.

In Problems 9–12, calculate the indicated Riemann sum S_n for the function $f(x) = 25 - 3x^2$.

9. Partition $[-2, 8]$ into five subintervals of equal length, and for each subinterval $[x_{k-1}, x_k]$ let $c_k = (x_{k-1} + x_k)/2$.

10. Partition $[0, 12]$ into four subintervals of equal length, and for each subinterval $[x_{k-1}, x_k]$ let $c_k = (x_{k-1} + 2x_k)/3$.

11. Partition $[0, 12]$ into four subintervals of equal length, and for each subinterval $[x_{k-1}, x_k]$ let $c_k = (2x_{k-1} + x_k)/3$.

12. Partition $[-5, 5]$ into five subintervals of equal length, and for each subinterval $[x_{k-1}, x_k]$ let $c_k = (x_{k-1} + x_k)/2$.

In Problems 13–16, calculate the indicated Riemann sum S_n for the function $f(x) = x^2 - 5x - 6$.

13. Partition $[0, 3]$ into three subintervals of equal length, and let $c_1 = 0.7, c_2 = 1.8, c_3 = 2.4$.

14. Partition $[0, 3]$ into three subintervals of equal length, and let $c_1 = 0.2, c_2 = 1.5, c_3 = 2.8$.

15. Partition $[1, 7]$ into six subintervals of equal length, and let $c_1 = 1, c_2 = 3, c_3 = 3, c_4 = 5, c_5 = 5, c_6 = 7$.

16. Partition $[1, 7]$ into six subintervals of equal length, and let $c_1 = 2, c_2 = 2, c_3 = 4, c_4 = 4, c_5 = 6, c_6 = 6$.

In Problems 17–28, calculate the definite integral by referring to the figure with the indicated areas.

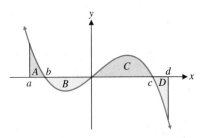

Area $A = 1.408$
Area $B = 2.475$
Area $C = 5.333$
Area $D = 1.792$

17. $\displaystyle\int_b^0 f(x)\,dx$

18. $\displaystyle\int_0^c f(x)\,dx$

19. $\displaystyle\int_a^c f(x)\,dx$

20. $\displaystyle\int_b^d f(x)\,dx$

21. $\displaystyle\int_a^d f(x)\,dx$

22. $\displaystyle\int_0^d f(x)\,dx$

23. $\displaystyle\int_c^0 f(x)\,dx$

24. $\displaystyle\int_d^a f(x)\,dx$

25. $\displaystyle\int_0^a f(x)\,dx$

26. $\displaystyle\int_c^a f(x)\,dx$

27. $\displaystyle\int_d^b f(x)\,dx$

28. $\displaystyle\int_c^b f(x)\,dx$

In Problems 29–40, calculate the definite integral given that

$$\int_1^4 x\,dx = 7.5 \qquad \int_1^4 x^2\,dx = 21 \qquad \int_4^5 x^2\,dx = \frac{61}{3}$$

29. $\displaystyle\int_1^4 2x\,dx$

30. $\displaystyle\int_1^4 3x^2\,dx$

31. $\displaystyle\int_1^4 (5x + x^2)\,dx$

32. $\displaystyle\int_1^4 (7x - 2x^2)\,dx$

33. $\displaystyle\int_1^4 (x^2 - 10x)\,dx$

34. $\displaystyle\int_1^4 (4x^2 - 9x)\,dx$

35. $\displaystyle\int_1^5 6x^2\,dx$

36. $\displaystyle\int_1^5 -4x^2\,dx$

37. $\displaystyle\int_4^4 (7x - 2)^2\,dx$

38. $\displaystyle\int_5^5 (10 - 7x + x^2)\,dx$

39. $\displaystyle\int_5^4 9x^2\,dx$

40. $\displaystyle\int_4^1 x(1 - x)\,dx$

B *In Problems 41 and 42, discuss the validity of each statement. If the statement is always true, explain why. If not, give a counterexample.*

41. (A) The function $f(x) = x^2 - 2x$ is increasing over $[0, 2]$.

(B) The function $f(x) = x^2 - 2x$ is increasing over $[1, 3]$.

42. (A) If f is a decreasing function on $[a, b]$, then the area under the graph of $f(x)$ is greater than the left sum L_n and less than the right sum R_n for any positive integer n.

   (B) If the area under the graph of $f(x)$ on $[a, b]$ is equal to both the left sum L_n and the right sum R_n for some positive integer n, then f is a constant function.

Problems 43 and 44 refer to the figure below showing two parcels of land along a river.

43. You are interested in purchasing both parcels of land shown in the figure and wish to make a quick check on their combined area. There is no equation for the river frontage, so you use the average of the left and right sums of rectangles covering the area. The 1,000-foot baseline is divided into 10 equal parts. At the end of each subinterval, a measurement is made from the baseline to the river, and the results are tabulated. Let x be the distance from the left end of the baseline and let $h(x)$ be the distance from the baseline to the river at x. Estimate the combined area of both parcels using L_{10}, and calculate an error bound for this estimate. How many subdivisions of the baseline would be required so that the error in using L_n would not exceed 2,500 square feet?

x	0	100	200	300	400	500
$h(x)$	0	183	235	245	260	286

x	600	700	800	900	1,000
$h(x)$	322	388	453	489	500

44. Refer to Problem 43. Estimate the combined area of both parcels using R_{10}, and calculate an error bound for this estimate. How many subdivisions of the baseline would be required so that the error in using R_n would not exceed 1,000 square feet?

C *Problems 45 and 46 refer to the following figure.*

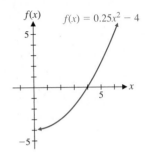

45. Approximate $\int_2^5 (0.25x^2 - 4)\, dx$ using L_6 and R_6. Compute error bounds for each. (Round answers to two decimal places.) Describe in geometric terms what the definite integral over the interval $[2, 5]$ represents.

46. Approximate $\int_1^6 (0.25x^2 - 4)\, dx$ using L_5 and R_5. Compute error bounds for each. (Round answers to two decimal places.) Describe in geometric terms what the definite integral over the interval $[1, 6]$ represents.

For Problems 47–50, use a graphing utility to determine the intervals on which each function is increasing or decreasing.

47. $f(x) = e^{-x^2}$

48. $f(x) = \dfrac{3}{1 + 2e^{-x}}$

49. $f(x) = x^4 - 2x^2 + 3$

50. $f(x) = e^{x^2}$

In Problems 51–54, the left sum L_n or the right sum R_n is used to approximate the definite integral to the indicated accuracy. How large must n be chosen in each case? (Each function is increasing over the indicated interval.)

51. $\displaystyle\int_1^3 \ln x \, dx = R_n \pm 0.1$

52. $\displaystyle\int_0^{10} \ln(x^2 + 1)\, dx = L_n \pm 0.5$

53. $\displaystyle\int_1^3 x^x \, dx = L_n \pm 0.5$

54. $\displaystyle\int_1^4 x^x \, dx = R_n \pm 0.5$

Applications

Business & Economics

55. *Employee training.* A company producing computer components has established that, on the average, a new employee can assemble $N(t)$ components per day after t days of on-the-job training, as indicated in the following table (a new employee's productivity increases continuously with time on the job):

t	0	20	40	60	80	100	120
$N(t)$	10	51	68	76	81	84	86

Use left and right sums to estimate the area under the graph of $N(t)$ from $t = 0$ to $t = 60$. Use three equal subintervals for each. Calculate an error bound for each estimate.

56. *Employee training.* For a new employee in Problem 55, use left and right sums to estimate the area under the graph of $N(t)$ from $t = 20$ to $t = 100$. Use four equal subintervals for each. Replace the question marks with the values of L_4 or R_4 as appropriate:

$$? \le \int_{20}^{100} N(t)\, dt \le ?$$

Life Sciences

57. *Medicine.* The rate of healing $A'(t)$ (in square centimeters per day) for a certain type of abrasive skin wound is given approximately by the following table:

t	0	1	2	3	4	5
$A'(t)$	0.90	0.81	0.74	0.67	0.60	0.55

t	6	7	8	9	10
$A'(t)$	0.49	0.45	0.40	0.36	0.33

(A) Approximate the area under the graph of $A'(t)$ from $t = 0$ to $t = 5$ using left and right sums over five equal subintervals.

(B) Replace the question marks with values of L_5 and R_5 as appropriate:

$$? \le \int_0^5 A'(t)\, dt \le ?$$

58. *Medicine.* Refer to Problem 57. Approximate the area under the graph of $A'(t)$ from $t = 5$ to $t = 10$ using left and right sums over five equal subintervals. Calculate an error bound for this estimate.

Social Sciences

59. *Learning.* During a special study on learning, a psychologist found that, on the average, the rate of learning a list of special symbols in a code, $N'(x)$, after x days of practice was given approximately by the following table values:

x	0	2	4	6	8	10	12
$N'(x)$	29	26	23	21	19	17	15

Approximate the area under the graph of $N'(x)$ from $x = 6$ to $x = 12$ using left and right sums over three equal subintervals. Calculate an error bound for this estimate.

60. *Learning.* For the data in Problem 59, approximate the area under the graph of $N'(x)$ from $x = 0$ to $x = 6$ using left and right sums over three equal subintervals. Replace the question marks with values of L_3 and R_3 as appropriate:

$$? \le \int_0^6 N'(x)\, dx \le ?$$

Section **6-5** The Fundamental Theorem of Calculus

➤ Evaluating Definite Integrals
➤ Recognizing a Definite Integral: Average Value

The definite integral of a function f on an interval $[a, b]$ is a number, the area (if $f(x) > 0$) between the graph of f and the x axis from $x = a$ to $x = b$. The indefinite integral of a function is a family of antiderivatives. In this section we explain the connection between these two integrals, a connection that is made precise by the fundamental theorem of calculus.

Suppose that the daily cost function for a small manufacturing firm is given (in dollars) by

$$C(x) = 180x + 200 \qquad 0 \le x \le 20$$

Then the marginal cost function is given (in dollars per unit) by

$$C'(x) = 180$$

What is the change in cost as production is increased from $x = 5$ units to $x = 10$ units? That change is equal to

$$C(10) - C(5) = (180 \cdot 10 + 200) - (180 \cdot 5 + 200)$$
$$= 180(10 - 5)$$
$$= \$900$$

Notice that $180(10 - 5)$ is equal to the area between the graph of $C'(x)$ and the x axis from $x = 5$ to $x = 10$. Therefore,

$$C(10) - C(5) = \int_5^{10} 180\, dx$$

In other words, the change in cost from $x = 5$ to $x = 10$ is equal to the area between the marginal cost function and the x axis from $x = 5$ to $x = 10$ (see Fig. 1).

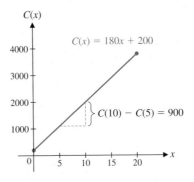

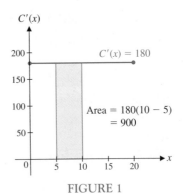

FIGURE 1

◎ Insight   Consider the formula for the slope of a line:

$$m = \frac{y_2 - y_1}{x_2 - x_1}$$

Multiplying both sides of the equation by $x_2 - x_1$ gives

$$y_2 - y_1 = m(x_2 - x_1)$$

The right-hand side, $m(x_2 - x_1)$, is equal to the area of a rectangle of height m and width $x_2 - x_1$. So the change in y coordinates is equal to the area under the constant function with value m from $x = x_1$ to $x = x_2$.   ●

EXAMPLE 1   **Change in Cost vs Area under Marginal Cost** The daily cost function for a company (in dollars) is given by

$$C(x) = -5x^2 + 210x + 400 \qquad 0 \le x \le 20$$

(A) Graph $C(x)$ for $0 \le x \le 20$, calculate the change in cost from $x = 5$ to $x = 10$, and indicate that change in cost on the graph.

(B) Graph the marginal cost function $C'(x)$ for $0 \le x \le 20$, and use geometric formulas (see Appendix C) to calculate the area between $C'(x)$ and the x axis from $x = 5$ to $x = 10$.

(C) Compare the results of the calculations in parts (A) and (B).

Solution   (A) $C(10) - C(5) = 2{,}000 - 1{,}325 = 675$, and this change in cost is indicated in Figure 2A.

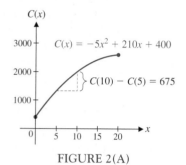

FIGURE 2(A)

(B) $C'(x) = -10x + 210$, so the area between $C'(x)$ and the x axis from $x = 5$ to $x = 10$ (see Fig. 2B) is the area of a trapezoid (geometric formulas are given in Appendix C):

$$\text{Area} = \frac{C(5) + C(10)}{2}(10 - 5) = \frac{160 + 110}{2}(5) = 675$$

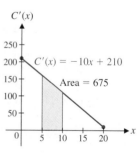

FIGURE 2(B)

(C) The change in cost from $x = 5$ to $x = 10$ is equal to the area between the marginal cost function and the x axis from $x = 5$ to $x = 10$.   ■

Matched Problem 1   Repeat Example 1 for the daily cost function

$$C(x) = -7.5x^2 + 305x + 625$$

The connection illustrated in Example 1, between the change in a function from $x = a$ to $x = b$ and the area under its derivative, provides the link between antiderivatives (or indefinite integrals) and the definite integral. It is known as the fundamental theorem of calculus. (See Problems 59 and 60 in Exercise 6-5 for an outline of its proof.)

THEOREM 1   Fundamental Theorem of Calculus
If f is a continuous function on $[a, b]$, and F is any antiderivative of f, then

$$\int_a^b f(x)\, dx = F(b) - F(a)$$

◉ Insight   Because a definite integral is the limit of Riemann sums, we expect it would be difficult to calculate definite integrals exactly. The fundamental theorem, however, gives us an easy method for evaluating definite integrals, *provided we can find an antiderivative $F(x)$ of $f(x)$:* Simply calculate the difference $F(b) - F(a)$. What if we are unable to find an antiderivative of $f(x)$? In that case, we must resort to left sums, right sums, or other approximation methods to approximate the definite integral. But it is often useful to remember that such an approximation is also an estimate of the change $F(b) - F(a)$.   ●

➤ Evaluating Definite Integrals

By the fundamental theorem, we can evaluate $\int_a^b f(x)\, dx$ easily and exactly whenever we can find an antiderivative $F(x)$ for $f(x)$. We simply calculate the difference $F(b) - F(a)$.

Now you know why we studied techniques of indefinite integration before this section—so we would have methods of finding antiderivatives of large classes of elementary functions for use with the fundamental theorem. It is important to remember that

Any antiderivative of $f(x)$ can be used in the fundamental theorem. One generally chooses the simplest antiderivative by letting $C = 0$, since any other value of C will drop out when computing the difference $F(b) - F(a)$.

In evaluating definite integrals by the fundamental theorem it is convenient to use the notation $F(x)\big|_a^b$, which represents the change in $F(x)$ from $x = a$ to $x = b$, as an intermediate step in the calculation. The technique is illustrated in the following examples.

EXAMPLE 2   **Evaluating Definite Integrals**   Evaluate: $\displaystyle\int_1^2 \left(2x + 3e^x - \frac{4}{x} \right) dx$

Solution $\displaystyle\int_1^2 \left(2x + 3e^x - \frac{4}{x} \right) dx = 2\int_1^2 x\, dx + 3\int_1^2 e^x\, dx - 4\int_1^2 \frac{1}{x}\, dx$

$$= 2\frac{x^2}{2}\bigg|_1^2 + 3e^x\bigg|_1^2 - 4\ln|x|\big|_1^2$$

$$= (2^2 - 1^2) + (3e^2 - 3e^1) - (4\ln 2 - 4\ln 1)$$

$$= 3 + 3e^2 - 3e - 4\ln 2 \approx 14.24$$ ■

Matched Problem 2   Evaluate: $\displaystyle\int_1^3 \left(4x - 2e^x + \frac{5}{x} \right) dx$

The evaluation of a definite integral is a two-step process: First, find an antiderivative, then find the change in that antiderivative. If *substitution techniques* are required to find the antiderivative, there are two different ways to proceed. The next example illustrates both methods.

EXAMPLE 3 **Definite Integrals and Substitution Techniques** Evaluate:

$$\int_0^5 \frac{x}{x^2 + 10}\,dx$$

Solution We will solve this problem using substitution in two different ways:

Method 1. Use substitution in an indefinite integral to find an antiderivative as a function of x; then evaluate the definite integral:

$$\int \frac{x}{x^2 + 10}\,dx = \frac{1}{2}\int \frac{1}{x^2 + 10}2x\,dx \quad \text{Substitute } u = x^2 + 10 \text{ and}$$
$$\qquad\qquad\qquad\qquad\qquad\qquad du = 2x\,dx.$$

$$= \frac{1}{2}\int \frac{1}{u}\,du$$

$$= \tfrac{1}{2}\ln|u| + C$$

$$= \tfrac{1}{2}\ln(x^2 + 10) + C \quad \text{Since } u = x^2 + 10 > 0$$

We choose $C = 0$ and use the antiderivative $\tfrac{1}{2}\ln(x^2 + 10)$ to evaluate the definite integral:

$$\int_0^5 \frac{x}{x^2 + 10}\,dx = \frac{1}{2}\ln(x^2 + 10)\Big|_0^5$$

$$= \tfrac{1}{2}\ln 35 - \tfrac{1}{2}\ln 10 \approx 0.626$$

Method 2. Substitute directly in the definite integral, changing both the variable of integration and the limits of integration: In the definite integral

$$\int_0^5 \frac{x}{x^2 + 10}\,dx$$

the upper limit is $x = 5$ and the lower limit is $x = 0$. When we make the substitution $u = x^2 + 10$ in this definite integral, we must change the limits of integration to the corresponding values of u:

$$x = 5 \qquad \text{implies} \qquad u = 5^2 + 10 = 35 \quad \text{New upper limit}$$
$$x = 0 \qquad \text{implies} \qquad u = 0^2 + 10 = 10 \quad \text{New lower limit}$$

Thus, we have

$$\int_0^5 \frac{x}{x^2 + 10}\,dx = \frac{1}{2}\int_0^5 \frac{1}{x^2 + 10}2x\,dx$$

$$= \frac{1}{2}\int_{10}^{35} \frac{1}{u}\,du$$

$$= \frac{1}{2}\left(\ln|u|\Big|_{10}^{35}\right)$$

$$= \tfrac{1}{2}(\ln 35 - \ln 10) \approx 0.626 \qquad\blacksquare$$

Matched Problem 3   Use both methods described in Example 4 to evaluate: $\displaystyle\int_0^1 \frac{1}{2x+4}\,dx$

EXAMPLE 4   **Definite Integrals and Substitution**   Use method 2 described in Example 3 to evaluate

$$\int_{-4}^1 \sqrt{5-t}\,dt$$

Solution   If $u = 5 - t$, then $du = -dt$, and

$t = 1$	implies	$u = 5 - 1 = 4$
$t = -4$	implies	$u = 5 - (-4) = 9$

New upper limit
New lower limit

Notice that the lower limit for u is larger than the upper limit. Be careful not to reverse these two values when substituting in the definite integral.

$$\int_{-4}^1 \sqrt{5-t}\,dt = -\int_{-4}^1 \sqrt{5-t}\,(-dt)$$

$$= -\int_9^4 \sqrt{u}\,du$$

$$= -\int_9^4 u^{1/2}\,du$$

$$= -\left(\frac{u^{3/2}}{\frac{3}{2}}\Big|_9^4\right)$$

$$= -\left[\tfrac{2}{3}(4)^{3/2} - \tfrac{2}{3}(9)^{3/2}\right]$$

$$= -\left[\tfrac{16}{3} - \tfrac{54}{3}\right] = \tfrac{38}{3} \approx 12.667$$

Matched Problem 4   Use method 2 described in Example 4 to evaluate: $\displaystyle\int_2^5 \frac{1}{\sqrt{6-t}}\,dt$

EXPLORE & DISCUSS 1

Explain why $\neq$ is used in each and finish each correctly:

1. $\displaystyle\int_0^2 e^x\,dx = e^x\big|_0^2 \neq e^2$

2. $\displaystyle\int_2^5 \frac{1}{2x+3}\,dx \neq \frac{1}{2}\int_2^5 \frac{1}{u}\,du \qquad u = 2x+3, \qquad du = 2\,dx$

EXAMPLE 5   **Change in Profit**   A company manufactures x television sets per month. The monthly marginal profit (in dollars) is given by

$$P'(x) = 165 - 0.1x \qquad 0 \le x \le 4{,}000$$

The company is currently manufacturing 1,500 sets per month, but is planning to increase production. Find the change in the monthly profit if monthly production is increased to 1,600 sets.

Solution

$$P(1,600) - P(1,500) = \int_{1,500}^{1,600} (165 - 0.1x)\, dx$$

$$= (165x - 0.05x^2)\big|_{1,500}^{1,600}$$

$$= [165(1,600) - 0.05(1,600)^2]$$
$$\quad - [165(1,500) - 0.05(1,500)^2]$$

$$= 136,000 - 135,000$$

$$= 1,000$$

Thus, increasing monthly production from 1,500 units to 1,600 units will increase the monthly profit by $1,000. ∎

Matched Problem 5

Repeat Example 5 if

$$P'(x) = 300 - 0.2x \qquad 0 \le x \le 3,000$$

and monthly production is increased from 1,400 sets to 1,500 sets.

[handwritten annotations in margin:]
$$\int_{1400}^{1500} 300 - 0.2x$$
$$300x - 0.1x^2 \Big|_{1400}^{1500}$$
$$3000$$

EXAMPLE 6

Useful Life An amusement company maintains records for each video game it installs in an arcade. Suppose that $C(t)$ and $R(t)$ represent the total accumulated costs and revenues (in thousands of dollars), respectively, t years after a particular game has been installed and that

$$C'(t) = 2 \qquad R'(t) = 9e^{-0.5t}$$

The value of t for which $C'(t) = R'(t)$ is called the **useful life** of the game.

(A) Find the useful life of the game to the nearest year.
(B) Find the total profit accumulated during the useful life of the game.

Solution (A) $R'(t) = C'(t)$

$$9e^{-0.5t} = 2$$

$$e^{-0.5t} = \tfrac{2}{9} \qquad\qquad \textit{Convert to equivalent logarithmic form.}$$

$$-0.5t = \ln \tfrac{2}{9}$$

$$t = -2 \ln \tfrac{2}{9} \approx 3 \text{ years}$$

Thus, the game has a useful life of 3 years. This is illustrated graphically in Figure 3.

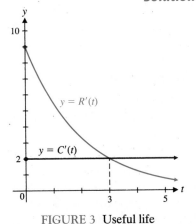

FIGURE 3 Useful life

(B) The total profit accumulated during the useful life of the game is

$$P(3) - P(0) = \int_0^3 P'(t)\, dt$$

$$= \int_0^3 [R'(t) - C'(t)]\, dt$$

$$= \int_0^3 (9e^{-0.5t} - 2)\, dt$$

$$= \left(\frac{9}{-0.5} e^{-0.5t} - 2t \right)\Big|_0^3 \quad \text{Recall: } \int e^{ax}\, dx = \frac{1}{a} e^{ax} + C$$

$$= (-18e^{-0.5t} - 2t)\big|_0^3$$

$$= (-18e^{-1.5} - 6) - (-18e^0 - 0)$$

$$= 12 - 18e^{-1.5} \approx 7.984 \quad \text{or} \quad \$7{,}984 \qquad \blacksquare$$

Matched Problem 6   Repeat Example 6 if $C'(t) = 1$ and $R'(t) = 7.5e^{-0.5t}$. ────────

EXAMPLE 7   **Numerical Integration on a Graphing Utility**   Evaluate (to three decimal places): $\int_{-1}^2 e^{-x^2}\, dx$

Solution   The integrand e^{-x^2} does not have an elementary antiderivative, so we are unable to use the fundamental theorem to evaluate the definite integral. Instead, we use a numerical integration routine that has been preprogrammed in a graphing utility (consult your user's manual for specific details). Such a routine is an approximation algorithm, more powerful than the left sum and right sum methods discussed in Section 6-4. From Figure 4,

$$\int_{-1}^2 e^{-x^2}\, dx = 1.629 \qquad \blacksquare$$

```
fnInt(e^(-X²),X,
-1,2)
          1.628905524
```

FIGURE 4

Matched Problem 7   Evaluate (to three decimal places): $\int_{1.5}^{4.3} \frac{x}{\ln x}\, dx$ ────────

➤ **Recognizing a Definite Integral: Average Value**

Recall that the derivative of a function f was defined in Section 3-3 by

$$f'(x) = \lim_{h \to 0} \frac{f(x + h) - f(x)}{h}$$

This form is generally not easy to compute directly, but it is easy to recognize it in certain practical problems (slope, instantaneous velocity, rates of change, and so on). Once we know that we are dealing with a derivative, we then proceed to try to compute the derivative using derivative formulas and rules.

Similarly, evaluating a definite integral using the definition

$$\int_a^b f(x)\,dx = \lim_{n \to \infty} [f(c_1)\Delta x_1 + f(c_2)\Delta x_2 + \cdots + f(c_n)\Delta x_n] \qquad (1)$$

is generally not easy; but the form on the right occurs naturally in many practical problems. We can use the fundamental theorem to evaluate the definite integral (once it is recognized) if an antiderivative can be found; otherwise, we will approximate it using a rectangle sum. We will now illustrate these points by finding the *average value* of a continuous function.

Suppose that the temperature F (in degrees Fahrenheit) in the middle of a small shallow lake from 8 AM ($t = 0$) to 6 PM ($t = 10$) during the month of May is given approximately as shown in Figure 5.

How can we compute the average temperature from 8 AM to 6 PM? We know that the average of a finite number of values $a_1, a_2, \ldots, a_n$ is given by

$$\text{average} = \frac{a_1 + a_2 + \cdots + a_n}{n}$$

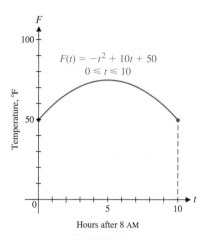

$F(t) = -t^2 + 10t + 50$
$0 \le t \le 10$

Hours after 8 AM

FIGURE 5

But how can we handle a continuous function with infinitely many values? It would seem reasonable to divide the time interval $[0, 10]$ into n equal subintervals, compute the temperature at a point in each subinterval, and then use the average of these values as an approximation of the average value of the continuous function $F = F(t)$ over $[0, 10]$. We would expect the approximations to improve as n increases. In fact, we would be inclined to define the limit of the average of n values as $n \to \infty$ as the *average value of F over* $[0, 10]$, if the limit exists. This is exactly what we will do:

$$\left(\begin{array}{c}\text{average temperature}\\ \text{for } n \text{ values}\end{array}\right) = \frac{1}{n}[F(t_1) + F(t_2) + \cdots + F(t_n)] \qquad (2)$$

where t_k is a point in the kth subinterval. We will call the limit of equation (2) as $n \to \infty$ the *average temperature over the time interval* $[0, 10]$.

Form (2) looks sort of like form (1), but we are missing the Δt_k. We take care of this by multiplying equation (2) by $(b - a)/(b - a)$, which will change the form of equation (2) without changing its value:

$$\frac{b-a}{b-a} \cdot \frac{1}{n}[F(t_1) + F(t_2) + \cdots + F(t_n)] = \frac{1}{b-a} \cdot \frac{b-a}{n}[F(t_1) + F(t_2) + \cdots + F(t_n)]$$

$$= \frac{1}{b-a}\left[F(t_1)\frac{b-a}{n} + F(t_2)\frac{b-a}{n} + \cdots + F(t_n)\frac{b-a}{n}\right]$$

$$= \frac{1}{b-a}[F(t_1)\Delta t + F(t_2)\Delta t + \cdots + F(t_n)\Delta t]$$

Thus,

$$\left(\begin{array}{c}\text{average temperature}\\ \text{over } [a, b] = [0, 10]\end{array}\right) = \lim_{n \to \infty}\left\{\frac{1}{b-a}[F(t_1)\Delta t + F(t_2)\Delta t + \cdots + F(t_n)\Delta t]\right\}$$

$$= \frac{1}{b-a}\left\{\lim_{n \to \infty}[F(t_1)\,\Delta t + F(t_2)\,\Delta t + \cdots + F(t_n)\,\Delta t]\right\}$$

Now the limit inside the braces is of form (1)—that is, a definite integral. Thus,

$$\left(\begin{array}{l} \text{average temperature} \\ \text{over } [a, b] = [0, 10] \end{array} \right) = \frac{1}{b - a} \int_a^b F(t) \, dt$$

$$= \frac{1}{10 - 0} \int_0^{10} (-t^2 + 10t + 50) \, dt$$

$$= \frac{1}{10} \left(-\frac{t^3}{3} + 5t^2 + 50t \right) \Big|_0^{10}$$

$$= \frac{200}{3} \approx 67°F$$

We now evaluate the definite integral using the fundamental theorem.

In general, proceeding as above for an arbitrary continuous function f over an interval $[a, b]$, we obtain the following general formula:

DEFINITION   Average Value of a Continuous Function f over $[a, b]$

$$\frac{1}{b - a} \int_a^b f(x) \, dx$$

EXPLORE &DISCUSS 2

In Figure 6 the rectangle has the same area as the area under the graph of $y = f(x)$ from $x = a$ to $x = b$. Explain how the average value of $f(x)$ over the interval $[a, b]$ is related to the height of the rectangle.

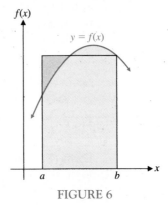

FIGURE 6

EXAMPLE 8   **Average Value of a Function** Find the average value of $f(x) = x - 3x^2$ over the interval $[-1, 2]$.

Solution

$$\frac{1}{b - a} \int_a^b f(x) \, dx = \frac{1}{2 - (-1)} \int_{-1}^2 (x - 3x^2) \, dx$$

$$= \frac{1}{3} \left(\frac{x^2}{2} - x^3 \right) \Big|_{-1}^2 = -\frac{5}{2}$$

Matched Problem 8   Find the average value of $g(t) = 6t^2 - 2t$ over the interval $[-2, 3]$.

EXAMPLE 9   **Average Price** Given the demand function

$$p = D(x) = 100e^{-0.05x}$$

find the average price (in dollars) over the demand interval $[40, 60]$.

Solution

$$\text{Average price} = \frac{1}{b-a}\int_a^b D(x)\,dx$$

$$= \frac{1}{60-40}\int_{40}^{60} 100e^{-0.05x}\,dx$$

$$= \frac{100}{20}\int_{40}^{60} e^{-0.05x}\,dx \quad \text{Use } \int e^{ax}\,dx = \frac{1}{a}e^{ax}, a \neq 0.$$

$$= -\frac{5}{0.05}e^{-0.05x}\Big|_{40}^{60}$$

$$= 100(e^{-2} - e^{-3}) \approx \$8.55$$

Matched Problem 9

Given the supply equation

$$p = S(x) = 10e^{0.05x}$$

find the average price (in dollars) over the supply interval [20, 30].

Answers to Matched Problems

1. (A)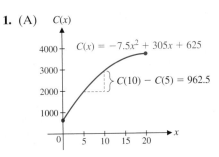

   (B)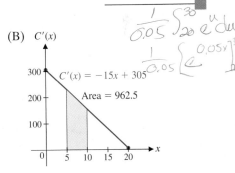

   (C) The change in cost from $x = 5$ to $x = 10$ is equal to the area between the marginal cost function and the x axis from $x = 5$ to $x = 10$.

2. $16 + 2e - 2e^3 + 5\ln 3 \approx -13.241$ 3. $\frac{1}{2}(\ln 6 - \ln 4) \approx 0.203$

4. 2   5. $1,000

6. (A) $-2\ln\frac{2}{15} \approx 4$ yr
   (B) $11 - 15e^{-2} \approx 8.970$ or $8,970

7. 8.017   8. 13   9. $35.27

Exercise 6-5

A *In Problems 1–4,*

(A) *Calculate the change in $F(x)$ from $x = 10$ to $x = 15$.*

(B) *Graph $F'(x)$ and use geometric formulas (see Appendix C) to calculate the area between the graph of $F'(x)$ and the x axis from $x = 10$ to $x = 15$.*

(C) *Verify that your answers to (A) and (B) are equal, as guaranteed by the fundamental theorem of calculus.*

1. $F(x) = 3x^2 + 160$ 2. $F(x) = 9x + 120$

3. $F(x) = -x^2 + 42x + 240$

4. $F(x) = x^2 + 30x + 210$

Evaluate the integrals in Problems 5–22.

5. $\int_2^3 2x\,dx$ 6. $\int_1^2 3x^2\,dx$

7. $\int_3^4 5\,dx$ 8. $\int_{12}^{20} dx$

9. $\int_1^3 (2x - 3)\,dx$ 10. $\int_1^3 (6x + 5)\,dx$

11. $\int_{-3}^4 (4 - x^2)\,dx$ 12. $\int_{-1}^2 (x^2 - 4x)\,dx$

13. $\int_0^1 24x^{11}\, dx$

14. $\int_0^2 30x^5\, dx$

15. $\int_0^1 e^{2x}\, dx$

16. $\int_{-1}^1 e^{5x}\, dx$

17. $\int_1^{3.5} 2x^{-1}\, dx$

18. $\int_1^2 \dfrac{dx}{x}$

19. $\int_1^2 \dfrac{2}{x^3}\, dx$

20. $\int_2^5 3x^{-2}\, dx$

21. $\int_1^4 6x^{-1/2}\, dx$

22. $\int_0^4 9x^{1/2}\, dx$

B *Evaluate the integrals in Problems 23–40.*

23. $\int_1^2 (2x^{-2} - 3)\, dx$

24. $\int_1^2 (5 - 16x^{-3})\, dx$

25. $\int_1^4 3\sqrt{x}\, dx$

26. $\int_4^{25} \dfrac{2}{\sqrt{x}}\, dx$

27. $\int_2^3 12(x^2 - 4)^5 x\, dx$

28. $\int_0^1 32(x^2 + 1)^7 x\, dx$

29. $\int_3^9 \dfrac{1}{x - 1}\, dx$

30. $\int_2^8 \dfrac{1}{x + 1}\, dx$

31. $\int_{-5}^{10} e^{-0.05x}\, dx$

32. $\int_{-10}^{25} e^{-0.01x}\, dx$

33. $\int_1^e \dfrac{\ln t}{t}\, dt$

34. $\int_e^{e^2} \dfrac{(\ln t)^2}{t}\, dt$

35. $\int_0^2 x\sqrt{4 - x^2}\, dx$

36. $\int_0^4 x\sqrt{4 - x}\, dx$

37. $\int_0^1 xe^{-x^2}\, dx$

38. $\int_0^1 xe^{x^2}\, dx$

39. $\int_{-2}^{-1} \dfrac{x^2 + 1}{x}\, dx$

40. $\int_{-2}^{-1} \dfrac{x}{x^2 + 1}\, dx$

In Problems 41–48,

(A) *Find the average value of each function over the indicated interval.*

(B) *Use a graphing utility to graph the function and its average value over the indicated interval in the same viewing window.*

41. $f(x) = 500 - 50x;\ [0, 10]$

42. $g(x) = 2x + 7;\ [0, 5]$

43. $f(t) = 3t^2 - 2t;\ [-1, 2]$

44. $g(t) = 4t - 3t^2;\ [-2, 2]$

45. $f(x) = \sqrt[3]{x};\ [1, 8]$

46. $g(x) = \sqrt{x + 1};\ [3, 8]$

47. $f(x) = 4e^{-0.2x};\ [0, 10]$

48. $f(x) = 64e^{0.08x};\ [0, 10]$

C *Evaluate the integrals in Problems 49–54.*

49. $\int_2^3 x\sqrt{2x^2 - 3}\, dx$

50. $\int_0^1 x\sqrt{3x^2 + 2}\, dx$

51. $\int_0^1 \dfrac{x - 1}{x^2 - 2x + 3}\, dx$

52. $\int_1^2 \dfrac{x + 1}{2x^2 + 4x + 4}\, dx$

53. $\int_{-1}^1 \dfrac{e^{-x} - e^x}{(e^{-x} + e^x)^2}\, dx$

54. $\int_6^7 \dfrac{\ln(t - 5)}{t - 5}\, dt$

Evaluate each definite integral in Problems 55–58 (to three decimal places) using a numerical integration routine.

55. $\int_{1.7}^{3.5} x \ln x\, dx$

56. $\int_{-1}^1 e^{x^2}\, dx$

57. $\int_{-2}^2 \dfrac{1}{1 + x^2}\, dx$

58. $\int_0^3 \sqrt{9 - x^2}\, dx$

59. The **mean value theorem** states that if $F(x)$ is a differentiable function on the interval $[a, b]$, then there exists some number c between a and b such that

$$F'(c) = \frac{F(b) - F(a)}{b - a}$$

Explain why the mean value theorem implies that if a car averages 60 miles per hour in some 10-minute interval, then the car's instantaneous velocity is 60 miles per hour at least once in that time interval.

60. The fundamental theorem of calculus can be proved by showing that for every positive integer n, there is a Riemann sum for f on $[a, b]$ that is equal to $F(b) - F(a)$. By the mean value theorem (see Problem 59), within each subinterval $[x_{k-1}, x_k]$ that belongs to a partition of $[a, b]$, there is some c_k such that

$$f(c_k) = F'(c_k) = \frac{F(x_k) - F(x_{k-1})}{x_k - x_{k-1}}$$

Multiplying by the denominator $x_k - x_{k-1}$, we get

$$f(c_k)(x_k - x_{k-1}) = F(x_k) - F(x_{k-1})$$

Show that the Riemann sum

$$S_n = \sum_{k=1}^n f(c_k)(x_k - x_{k-1})$$

is equal to $F(b) - F(a)$.

Applications

Business & Economics

61. *Cost.* A company manufactures mountain bikes. The research department produced the following marginal cost function:

$$C'(x) = 500 - \frac{x}{3} \qquad 0 \le x \le 900$$

where $C'(x)$ is in dollars and x is the number of bikes produced per month. Compute the increase in cost going from a production level of 300 bikes per month to 900 bikes per month. Set up a definite integral and evaluate.

62. *Cost.* Referring to Problem 61, compute the increase in cost going from a production level of 0 bikes per month to 600 bikes per month. Set up a definite integral and evaluate.

63. *Salvage value.* A new piece of industrial equipment will depreciate in value rapidly at first, then less rapidly as time goes on. Suppose that the rate (in dollars per year) at which the book value of a new milling machine changes is given approximately by

$$V'(t) = f(t) = 500(t - 12) \qquad 0 \le t \le 10$$

where $V(t)$ is the value of the machine after t years. What is the total loss in value of the machine in the first 5 years? In the second 5 years? Set up appropriate integrals and solve.

64. *Maintenance costs.* Maintenance costs for an apartment house generally increase as the building gets older. From past records, a managerial service determines that the rate of increase in maintenance costs (in dollars per year) for a particular apartment complex is given approximately by

$$M'(x) = f(x) = 90x^2 + 5,000$$

where x is the age of the apartment complex in years and $M(x)$ is the total (accumulated) cost of maintenance for x years. Write a definite integral that will give the total maintenance costs from the end of the second year to the end of the seventh year after the apartment complex was built, and evaluate it.

65. *Employee training.* A company producing computer components has established that, on the average, a new employee can assemble $N(t)$ components per day after t days of on-the-job training, as indicated in the table (a new employee's productivity usually increases with time on the job up to a leveling-off point):

t	0	20	40	60	80	100	120
$N(t)$	10	51	68	76	81	84	85

(A) Find a quadratic regression equation for the data, and graph it and the data set in the same viewing window.

(B) Use the regression equation and a numerical integration routine on a graphing utility to approximate the number of units assembled by a new employee during the first 100 days on the job.

66. *Employee training.* Refer to Problem 65.

(A) Find a cubic regression equation for the data, and graph it and the data set in the same viewing window.

(B) Use the regression equation and a numerical integration routine on a graphing utility to approximate the number of units assembled by a new employee during the second 60 days on the job.

67. *Useful life.* The total accumulated costs $C(t)$ and revenues $R(t)$ (in thousands of dollars), respectively, for a coin-operated photocopying machine satisfy

$$C'(t) = \tfrac{1}{11}t \qquad \text{and} \qquad R'(t) = 5te^{-t^2}$$

where t is time in years. Find the useful life of the machine to the nearest year. What is the total profit accumulated during the useful life of the machine?

68. *Useful life.* The total accumulated costs $C(t)$ and revenues $R(t)$ (in thousands of dollars), respectively, for a coal mine satisfy

$$C'(t) = 3 \qquad \text{and} \qquad R'(t) = 15e^{-0.1t}$$

where t is the number of years the mine has been in operation. Find the useful life of the mine to the nearest year. What is the total profit accumulated during the useful life of the mine?

69. *Average cost.* The total cost (in dollars) of manufacturing x auto body frames is $C(x) = 60,000 + 300x$.

(A) Find the average cost per unit if 500 frames are produced. [*Hint:* Recall that $\overline{C}(x)$ is the average cost per unit.]

(B) Find the average value of the cost function over the interval $[0, 500]$.

(C) Discuss the difference between parts (A) and (B).

70. *Average cost.* The total cost (in dollars) of printing x dictionaries is $C(x) = 20,000 + 10x$.

(A) Find the average cost per unit if 1,000 dictionaries are produced.

(B) Find the average value of the cost function over the interval $[0, 1,000]$.

(C) Discuss the difference between parts (A) and (B).

71. *Cost.* The marginal cost at various levels of output per month for a company that manufactures watches is shown in the table. The output x is given in thousands of units per month, and $C(x)$ is given in thousands of dollars per month.

x	0	1	2	3	4	5	6	7	8
$C'(x)$	58	30	18	9	5	7	17	33	51

(A) Find a quadratic regression equation for the data, and graph it and the data set in the same viewing window.

(B) Use the regression equation and a numerical integration routine on a graphing utility to approximate (to the nearest dollar) the increased cost in going from a production level of 2 thousand watches per month to 8 thousand watches per month.

72. *Cost.* Refer to Problem 71.

(A) Find a cubic regression equation for the data, and graph it and the data set in the same viewing window.

(B) Use the regression equation and a numerical integration routine on a graphing utility to approximate (to the nearest dollar) the increased cost in going from a production level of 1 thousand watches per month to 7 thousand watches per month.

73. *Supply function.* Given the supply function

$$p = S(x) = 10(e^{0.02x} - 1)$$

find the average price (in dollars) over the supply interval $[20, 30]$.

74. *Demand function.* Given the demand function

$$p = D(x) = \frac{1,000}{x}$$

find the average price (in dollars) over the demand interval $[400, 600]$.

75. *Labor costs and learning.* A defense contractor is starting production on a new missile control system. On the basis of data collected while assembling the first 16 control systems, the production manager obtained the following function for rate of labor use:

$$g(x) = 2,400x^{-1/2}$$

where $g(x)$ is the number of labor-hours required to assemble the xth unit of a control system. Approximately how many labor-hours will be required to assemble the 17th through the 25th control units? [*Hint*: Let $a = 16$ and $b = 25$.]

76. *Labor costs and learning.* If the rate of labor use in Problem 91 is

$$g(x) = 2,000x^{-1/3}$$

approximately how many labor-hours will be required to assemble the 9th through the 27th control units? [*Hint*: Let $a = 8$ and $b = 27$.]

77. *Inventory.* A store orders 600 units of a product every 3 months. If the product is steadily depleted to 0 by the end of each 3 months, the inventory on hand, I, at any time t during the year is illustrated as shown in the figure.

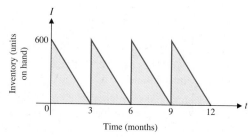

Figure for 77

(A) Write an inventory function (assume that it is continuous) for the first 3 months. [The graph is a straight line joining $(0, 600)$ and $(3, 0)$.]

(B) What is the average number of units on hand for a 3-month period?

78. Repeat Problem 77 with an order of 1,200 units every 4 months.

79. *Oil production.* Using data from the first 3 years of production as well as geological studies, the management of an oil company estimates that oil will be pumped from a producing field at a rate given by

$$R(t) = \frac{100}{t + 1} + 5 \qquad 0 \le t \le 20$$

where $R(t)$ is the rate of production (in thousands of barrels per year) t years after pumping begins. Approximately how many barrels of oil will the field produce during the first 10 years of production? From the end of the 10th year to the end of the 20th year of production?

80. *Oil production.* In Problem 79, if the rate is found to be

$$R(t) = \frac{120t}{t^2 + 1} + 3 \qquad 0 \le t \le 20$$

approximately how many barrels of oil will the field produce during the first 5 years of production? The second 5 years of production?

Life Sciences

81. *Biology.* A yeast culture weighing 2 grams is removed from a refrigerator unit and is expected to grow at the rate of $W'(t) = 0.2e^{0.1t}$ grams per hour at a higher controlled temperature. How much will the weight of the culture increase during the first 8 hours of growth? How much will the weight of the culture increase from the end of the 8th hour to the end of the 16th hour of growth?

82. *Medicine.* The rate of healing for a skin wound (in square centimeters per day) is given approximately by $A'(t) = -0.9e^{-0.1t}$. The initial wound has an area of 9 square centimeters. How much will the area change during the first 5 days? The second 5 days?

83. *Temperature.* If the temperature $C(t)$ in an aquarium is made to change according to

$$C(t) = t^3 - 2t + 10 \qquad 0 \le t \le 2$$

(in degrees Celsius) over a 2-hour period, what is the average temperature over this period?

84. *Medicine.* A drug is injected into the bloodstream of a patient through her right arm. The concentration of the drug in the bloodstream of the left arm t hours after the injection is given by

$$C(t) = \frac{0.14t}{t^2 + 1}$$

What is the average concentration of the drug in the bloodstream of the left arm during the first hour after the injection? During the first 2 hours after the injection?

Social Sciences

85. *Politics.* Public awareness of a congressional candidate before and after a successful campaign was approximated by

$$P(t) = \frac{8.4t}{t^2 + 49} + 0.1 \qquad 0 \le t \le 24$$

where t is time in months after the campaign started and $P(t)$ is the fraction of people in the congressional district who could recall the candidate's name. What is the average fraction of people who could recall the candidate's name during the first 7 months after the campaign began? During the first 2 years after the campaign began?

86. *Population composition.* Because of various factors (such as birth rate expansion, then contraction; family flights from urban areas; and so on), the number of children in a large city was found to increase and then decrease rather drastically. If the number of children over a 6-year period was found to be given approximately by

$$N(t) = -\tfrac{1}{4}t^2 + t + 4 \qquad 0 \le t \le 6$$

what was the average number of children in the city over the 6-year time period? [Assume $N = N(t)$ is continuous.]

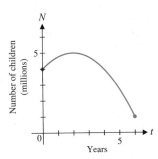

Figure for 86

Chapter 6 Review

Important Terms, Symbols, and Concepts

6-1 Antiderivatives and Indefinite Integrals

A function F is an **antiderivative** of a function f if $F'(x) = f(x)$. If F and G are both antiderivatives of f, then F and G differ by a constant; that is, $F(x) = G(x) + k$ for some constant k. We use the symbol $\int f(x)\, dx$, called an **indefinite integral,** to represent the family of all antiderivatives of f, and we write

$$\int f(x)\, dx = F(x) + C$$

The symbol $\int$ is called an **integral sign,** $f(x)$ is the **integrand,** and C is the **constant of integration.**

• *Indefinite Integrals of Basic Functions* For C a constant:

1. $\displaystyle\int x^n\, dx = \frac{x^{n+1}}{n+1} + C, \qquad n \ne -1$

2. $\displaystyle\int e^x\, dx = e^x + C$

3. $\displaystyle\int \frac{1}{x}\, dx = \ln|x| + C, \qquad x \ne 0$

• *Properties of Indefinite Integrals* For k a constant:

4. $\displaystyle\int kf(x)\, dx = k\int f(x)\, dx$

5. $\displaystyle\int [f(x) \pm g(x)]\, dx = \int f(x)\, dx \pm \int g(x)\, dx$

By property 4, a constant factor can be moved across an integral sign. However, a variable factor *cannot* be moved across an integral sign.

6-2 Integration by Substitution

The **method of substitution** (also called the **change-of-variable method**) is a technique for finding indefinite integrals. It is based on the following formula, which is obtained by reversing the chain rule:

$$\int f'[g(x)]g'(x)\,dx = f[g(x)] + C$$

This formula implies the following general indefinite integral formulas:

1. $\int [f(x)]^n f'(x)\,dx = \dfrac{[f(x)]^{n+1}}{n+1} + C, \qquad n \neq 1$

2. $\int e^{f(x)} f'(x)\,dx = e^{f(x)} + C$

3. $\int \dfrac{1}{f(x)} f'(x)\,dx = \ln|f(x)| + C$

In using the method of substitution it is helpful to employ differentials as a bookkeeping device:

1. The **differential dx** of the independent variable x is an arbitrary real number.
2. The **differential dy** of the dependent variable y is defined by $dy = f'(x)\,dx$.

The following steps serve as guidelines for the substitution method:

Step 1. Select a substitution that appears to simplify the integrand. In particular, try to select u so that du is a factor in the integrand.

Step 2. Express the integrand entirely in terms of u and du, completely eliminating the original variable and its differential.

Step 3. Evaluate the new integral, if possible.

Step 4. Express the antiderivative found in step 3 in terms of the original variable.

6-3 Differential Equations; Growth and Decay

An equation is a **differential equation** if it involves an unknown function and one or more of its derivatives. The equation

$$\frac{dy}{dx} = 3x(1 + xy^2)$$

is a **first-order** differential equation because it involves the first derivative of the unknown function y, but no second or higher-order derivative. A **slope field** can be constructed for the equation above by drawing a tangent line segment with slope $3x(1 + xy^2)$ at each point (x, y) of a grid. The slope field gives a graphical representation of the functions that are solutions of the differential equation.

The differential equation

$$\frac{dQ}{dt} = rQ$$

(in words, the rate at which the unknown function Q increases is proportional to Q) is called the **exponential growth law.** The constant r is called the **growth constant.** The solutions to the exponential growth law are the

functions

$$Q(t) = Q_0 e^{rt}$$

where Q_0 denotes $Q(0)$, the amount present at time $t = 0$. These functions can be used to solve problems in population growth, continuous compound interest, radioactive decay, blood pressure, and light absorption.

The first-order equations

$$\frac{dy}{dt} = k(M - y) \qquad \text{and} \qquad \frac{dy}{dt} = ky(M - y)$$

have solutions of the form

$$y = M(1 - e^{-kt}) \qquad \text{and} \qquad y = \frac{M}{1 + ce^{-kMt}}$$

respectively. These functions can be used to model the limited or logistic growth of epidemics, sales, and corporations.

6-4 The Definite Integral

If the function f is positive on $[a, b]$, then the area between the graph of f and the x axis, from $x = a$ to $x = b$, can be approximated by partitioning $[a, b]$ into n subintervals $[x_{k-1}, x_k]$ of equal length $\Delta x = (b - a)/n$, and summing the areas of n rectangles. This can be accomplished by **left sums, right sums,** or, more generally, by **Riemann sums:**

Left sum: $\qquad L_n = \displaystyle\sum_{k=1}^{n} f(x_{k-1})\Delta x$

Right sum: $\qquad R_n = \displaystyle\sum_{k=1}^{n} f(x_k)\Delta x$

Riemann sum: $\quad S_n = \displaystyle\sum_{k=1}^{n} f(c_k)\Delta x$

In a Riemann sum, each c_k is required to belong to the subinterval $[x_{k-1}, x_k]$. Left sums and right sums are the special cases of Riemann sums in which c_k is the left endpoint or right endpoint, respectively, of the subinterval.

The **error in an approximation** is the absolute value of the difference between the approximation and the actual value. An **error bound** is a positive number such that the error is guaranteed to be less than or equal to that number.

Theorem 1   Error Bounds for Approximations of Area by Left or Right Sums

If $f(x) > 0$ and is either increasing on $[a, b]$ or decreasing on $[a, b]$, then

$$|f(b) - f(a)| \cdot \frac{b - a}{n}$$

is an error bound for the approximation of the area between the graph of f and the x axis, from $x = a$ to $x = b$, by L_n or R_n.

Theorem 2   Limits of Left and Right Sums

If $f(x) > 0$ and is either increasing on $[a, b]$ or decreasing on $[a, b]$, then its left and right sums approach the same real number as $n \to \infty$.

Theorem 3   Limit of Riemann Sums
If f is a continuous function on $[a, b]$, then the Riemann sums for f on $[a, b]$ approach a real number limit I as $n \to \infty$.

Let f be a continuous function on $[a, b]$. The limit I of Riemann sums for f on $[a, b]$, guaranteed by Theorem 3, is called the **definite integral** of f from a to b, denoted

$$\int_a^b f(x)\, dx$$

The **integrand** is $f(x)$, the **lower limit of integration** is a, and the **upper limit of integration** is b.

Geometrically, the definite integral

$$\int_a^b f(x)\, dx$$

represents the cumulative sum of the signed areas between the graph of f and the x axis from $x = a$ to $x = b$.

• **Properties of Definite Integrals**

1. $\displaystyle \int_a^a f(x)\, dx = 0$

2. $\displaystyle \int_a^b f(x)\, dx = -\int_b^a f(x)\, dx$

3. $\displaystyle \int_a^b kf(x)\, dx = k \int_a^b f(x)\, dx,\ k$ a constant

4. $\displaystyle \int_a^b [f(x) \pm g(x)]\, dx = \int_a^b f(x)\, dx \pm \int_a^b g(x)\, dx$

5. $\displaystyle \int_a^b f(x)\, dx = \int_a^c f(x)\, dx + \int_c^b f(x)\, dx$

6-5 The Fundamental Theorem of Calculus

• **Fundamental Theorem of Calculus** If f is a continuous function on $[a, b]$ and F is any antiderivative of f, then

$$\int_a^b f(x)\, dx = F(b) - F(a)$$

The fundamental theorem gives an easy and exact method for evaluating definite integrals, provided we can find an antiderivative $F(x)$ of $f(x)$. In practice, we first find an antiderivative $F(x)$ (when possible), using techniques for computing indefinite integrals, then we calculate the difference $F(b) - F(a)$. If it is impossible to find an antiderivative, we must resort to left or right sums, or other approximation methods, to evaluate the definite integral. Graphing calculators have a built-in numerical approximation routine, more powerful than left or right sum methods, for this purpose.

If f is a continuous function on $[a, b]$, then the **average value of f over $[a, b]$** is defined to be

$$\frac{1}{b - a} \int_a^b f(x)\, dx$$

Review Exercise

Work through all the problems in this chapter review and check your answers in the back of the book. Answers to all review problems are there along with section numbers in italics to indicate where each type of problem is discussed. Where weaknesses show up, review appropriate sections in the text.

A *Find each integral in Problems 1–6.*

1. $\displaystyle \int (6x + 3)\, dx$

2. $\displaystyle \int_{10}^{20} 5\, dx$

3. $\displaystyle \int_0^9 (4 - t^2)\, dt$

4. $\displaystyle \int (1 - t^2)^3 t\, dt$

5. $\displaystyle \int \frac{1 + u^4}{u}\, du$

6. $\displaystyle \int_0^1 xe^{-2x^2}\, dx$

In Problems 7 and 8, find the derivative or indefinite integral as indicated.

7. $\displaystyle \frac{d}{dx}\left(\int e^{-x^2}\, dx \right)$

8. $\displaystyle \int \frac{d}{dx}(\sqrt{4 + 5x})\, dx$

9. Find a function $y = f(x)$ that satisfies both conditions:

$$\frac{dy}{dx} = 3x^2 - 2 \qquad f(0) = 4$$

10. Find all antiderivatives of:

(A) $\displaystyle \frac{dy}{dx} = 8x^3 - 4x - 1$

(B) $\displaystyle \frac{dx}{dt} = e^t - 4t^{-1}$

11. Approximate $\int_1^5(x^2 + 1)\,dx$ using a right sum with $n = 2$. Calculate an error bound for this approximation.

12. Evaluate the integral in Problem 11 using the fundamental theorem of calculus, and calculate the actual error $|I - R_2|$ produced in using R_2.

13. Use the table of values below and a left sum with $n = 4$ to approximate $\int_1^{17} f(x)\,dx$.

x	1	5	9	13	17
$f(x)$	1.2	3.4	2.6	0.5	0.1

14. Find the average value of $f(x) = 6x^2 + 2x$ over the interval $[-1, 2]$.

15. Describe a rectangle that would have the same area as the area under the graph of $f(x) = 6x^2 + 2x$ from $x = -1$ to $x = 2$ (see Problem 14).

In Problems 16 and 17, calculate the indicated Riemann sum S_n for the function $f(x) = 100 - x^2$.

16. Partition $[3, 11]$ into four subintervals of equal length, and for each subinterval $[x_{i-1}, x_i]$, let $c_i = (x_{i-1} + x_i)/2$.

17. Partition $[-5, 5]$ into five subintervals of equal length and let $c_1 = -4, c_2 = -1, c_3 = 1, c_4 = 2, c_5 = 5$.

B *Use the graph and actual areas of the indicated regions in the figure to evaluate the integrals in Problems 18–25:*

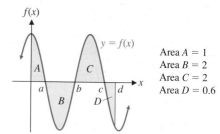

Area A = 1
Area B = 2
Area C = 2
Area D = 0.6

18. $\int_a^b 5f(x)\,dx$

19. $\int_b^c \dfrac{f(x)}{5}\,dx$

20. $\int_b^d f(x)\,dx$

21. $\int_a^c f(x)\,dx$

22. $\int_0^d f(x)\,dx$

23. $\int_b^a f(x)\,dx$

24. $\int_c^b f(x)\,dx$

25. $\int_d^0 f(x)\,dx$

Problems 26–31 refer to the slope field shown in the figure:

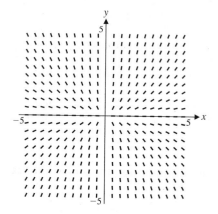

26. (A) For $dy/dx = (2y)/x$, what is the slope of a solution curve at $(2, 1)$? At $(-2, -1)$?

 (B) For $dy/dx = (2x)/y$, what is the slope of a solution curve at $(2, 1)$? At $(-2, -1)$?

27. Is the slope field shown in the figure for $dy/dx = (2x)/y$ or for $dy/dx = (2y)/x$? Explain.

28. Show that $y = Cx^2$ is a solution of $dy/dx = (2y)/x$ for any real number C.

29. Referring to Problem 28, find the particular solution of $dy/dx = (2y)/x$ that passes through $(2, 1)$. Through $(-2, -1)$.

30. Graph the two particular solutions found in Problem 29 in the slope field shown above (or a copy).

31. Use a graphing utility to graph in the same viewing window graphs of $y = Cx^2$ for $C = -2, -1, 1,$ and 2 for $-5 \le x \le 5$ and $-5 \le y \le 5$.

Find each integral in Problems 32–42.

32. $\int_{-1}^{1} \sqrt{1 + x}\,dx$

33. $\int_{-1}^{0} x^2(x^3 + 2)^{-2}\,dx$

34. $\int 5e^{-t}\,dt$

35. $\int_1^e \dfrac{1 + t^2}{t}\,dt$

36. $\int xe^{3x^2}\,dx$

37. $\displaystyle\int_{-3}^{1} \frac{1}{\sqrt{2-x}}\, dx$

38. $\displaystyle\int_{0}^{3} \frac{x}{1+x^2}\, dx$

39. $\displaystyle\int_{0}^{3} \frac{x}{(1+x^2)^2}\, dx$

40. $\displaystyle\int x^3(2x^4+5)^5\, dx$

41. $\displaystyle\int \frac{e^{-x}}{e^{-x}+3}\, dx$

42. $\displaystyle\int \frac{e^x}{(e^x+2)^2}\, dx$

43. Find a function $y = f(x)$ that satisfies both conditions:

$$\frac{dy}{dx} = 3x^{-1} - x^{-2} \qquad f(1) = 5$$

44. Find the equation of the curve that passes through $(2, 10)$ if its slope is given by

$$\frac{dy}{dx} = 6x + 1$$

for each x.

45. (A) Find the average value of $f(x) = 3\sqrt{x}$ over the interval $[1, 9]$.

   (B) Graph $f(x) = 3\sqrt{x}$ and its average over the interval $[1, 9]$ in the same coordinate system.

C *Find each integral in Problems 46–50.*

46. $\displaystyle\int \frac{(\ln x)^2}{x}\, dx$

47. $\displaystyle\int x(x^3 - 1)^2\, dx$

48. $\displaystyle\int \frac{x}{\sqrt{6-x}}\, dx$

49. $\displaystyle\int_{0}^{7} x\sqrt{16-x}\, dx$

50. $\displaystyle\int_{-1}^{1} x(x+1)^4\, dx$

51. Find a function $y = f(x)$ that satisfies both conditions:

$$\frac{dy}{dx} = 9x^2 e^{x^3} \qquad f(0) = 2$$

52. Solve the differential equation:

$$\frac{dN}{dt} = 0.06N \qquad N(0) = 800 \qquad N > 0$$

Graph Problems 53–56 on a graphing utility and identify each as unlimited growth, exponential decay, limited growth, or logistic growth:

53. $N = 50(1 - e^{-0.07t}); \ 0 \le t \le 80, 0 \le N \le 60$

54. $p = 500e^{-0.03x}; \ 0 \le x \le 100, 0 \le p \le 500$

55. $A = 200e^{0.08t}; \ 0 \le t \le 20, 0 \le A \le 1{,}000$

56. $N = \dfrac{100}{1+9e^{-0.3t}}; \ 0 \le t \le 25, 0 \le N \le 100$

Evaluate each definite integral in Problems 57–59 (to three decimal places) using a numerical integration routine.

57. $\displaystyle\int_{-0.5}^{0.6} \frac{1}{\sqrt{1-x^2}}\, dx$

58. $\displaystyle\int_{-2}^{3} x^2 e^x\, dx$

59. $\displaystyle\int_{0.5}^{2.5} \frac{\ln x}{x^2}\, dx$

Applications

Business & Economics

60. *Cost.* A company manufactures downhill skis. The research department produced the marginal cost graph shown in the figure, where $C'(x)$ is in dollars and x is the number of pairs of skis produced per week. Estimate the increase in cost going from a production level of 200 to 600 pairs of skis per week. Use left and right sums over two equal subintervals. Replace the question marks with the values of L_2 and R_2 as appropriate:

$$? \le \int_{200}^{600} C'(x)\, dx \le ?$$

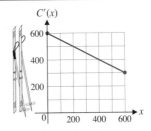

Figure for 60

61. *Cost.* Assuming that the marginal cost function in Problem 60 is linear, find its equation and write a definite integral that represents the increase in costs going from a production level of 200 to 600 pairs of skis per week. Evaluate the definite integral.

62. *Profit and production.* The weekly marginal profit for an output of x units is given approximately by

$$P'(x) = 150 - \frac{x}{10} \qquad 0 \le x \le 40$$

What is the total change in profit for a production change from 10 units per week to 40 units? Set up a definite integral and evaluate it.

63. *Profit function.* If the marginal profit for producing x units per day is given by

$$P'(x) = 100 - 0.02x \qquad P(0) = 0$$

where $P(x)$ is the profit in dollars, find the profit function P and the profit on 10 units of production per day.

64. *Resource depletion.* An oil well starts out producing oil at the rate of 60,000 barrels of oil per year, but the production rate is expected to decrease by 4,000 barrels per year. Thus, if $P(t)$ is the total production (in thousands of barrels) in t years, then

$$P'(t) = f(t) = 60 - 4t \qquad 0 \le t \le 15$$

Write a definite integral that will give the total production after 15 years of operation and evaluate it.

65. *Inventory.* Suppose that the inventory of a certain item t months after the first of the year is given approximately by

$$I(t) = 10 + 36t - 3t^2 \qquad 0 \le t \le 12$$

What is the average inventory for the second quarter of the year?

66. *Price–supply.* Given the price–supply function

$$p = S(x) = 8(e^{0.05x} - 1)$$

find the average price (in dollars) over the supply interval $[40, 50]$.

67. *Useful life.* The total accumulated costs $C(t)$ and revenues $R(t)$ (in thousands of dollars), respectively, for a coal mine satisfy

$$C'(t) = 3 \qquad \text{and} \qquad R'(t) = 20e^{-0.1t}$$

where t is the number of years the mine has been in operation. Find the useful life of the mine to the nearest year. What is the total profit accumulated during the useful life of the mine?

68. *Marketing.* The market research department for an automobile company estimates that the sales (in millions of dollars) of a new automobile will increase at the monthly rate of

$$S'(t) = 4e^{-0.08t} \qquad 0 \le t \le 24$$

t months after the introduction of the automobile. What will be the total sales $S(t)$, t months after the automobile is introduced if we assume that there were 0 sales at the time the automobile entered the marketplace? What are the estimated total sales during the first 12 months after the introduction of the automobile? How long will it take for the total sales to reach \$40 million?

Life Sciences

69. *Wound healing.* The area of a small, healing surface wound changes at a rate given approximately by

$$\frac{dA}{dt} = -5t^{-2} \qquad 1 \le t \le 5$$

where t is time in days and $A(1) = 5$ square centimeters. What will the area of the wound be in 5 days?

70. *Pollution.* An environmental protection agency estimates that the rate of seepage of toxic chemicals from a waste dump (in gallons per year) is given by

$$R(t) = \frac{1,000}{(1 + t)^2}$$

where t is time in years since the discovery of the seepage. Find the total amount of toxic chemicals that seep from the dump during the first 4 years after the seepage is discovered.

71. *Population.* The population of Mexico was 100 million in 2000 and was growing at a rate of 1.5% per year compounded continuously.

(A) Assuming that the population continues to grow at this rate, estimate the population of Mexico in the year 2025.

(B) At the growth rate indicated, how long will it take the population of Mexico to double?

Social Sciences

72. *Archaeology.* The continuous compound rate of decay for carbon-14 is $r = -0.000\ 123\ 8$. A piece of animal bone found at an archaeological site contains 4% of the original amount of carbon-14. Estimate the age of the bone.

73. *Learning.* In a particular business college, it was found that an average student enrolled in a typing class progressed at a rate of $N'(t) = 7e^{-0.1t}$ words per minute t weeks after enrolling in a 15-week course. If at the beginning of the course a student could type 25 words per minute, how many words per minute, $N(t)$, would the student be expected to type t weeks into the course? After completing the course?

Group Activity 1   *Simpson's Rule*

Introduction to Simpson's Rule

The left sum L_n, right sum R_n, average A_n of left and right sums, and midpoint sum M_n can all be used as numerical integration devices to approximate definite integrals. If a function f is increasing, the right sum overestimates and the left sum underestimates the definite integral (Fig. 1).

$$L_n \leq \int_a^b f(x)\, dx \leq R_n$$

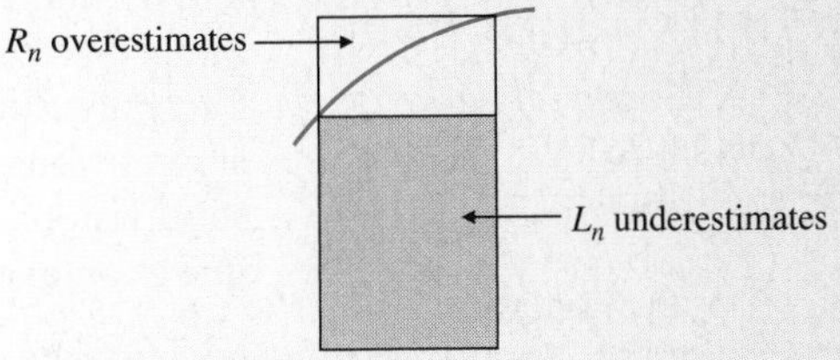

R_n overestimates

L_n underestimates

FIGURE 1

A function is **monotone** on $[a, b]$ if it is increasing on $[a, b]$ or decreasing on $[a, b]$. The average A_n of left and right sums is a better estimate for the definite integral of a monotone function than either L_n or R_n. It is often called a *trapezoidal sum,* and denoted by T_n, since the average area of a left rectangle and right rectangle is the area of a trapezoid (the smaller, shaded trapezoid in Fig. 2). Adding the following expressions for L_n and R_n and dividing by 2 gives the expression for $T_n = A_n$ called the **trapezoidal rule.** The midpoint sum M_n, like T_n, is also a better estimate for the definite integral of a monotone function than either the left or right sum.

$$L_n = [f(x_0) + f(x_1) + \cdots + f(x_{n-1})]\Delta x \qquad \text{Left sum}$$

$$R_n = [f(x_1) + f(x_2) + \cdots + f(x_n)]\Delta x \qquad \text{Right sum}$$

$$T_n = [f(x_0) + 2f(x_1) + \cdots + 2f(x_{n-1}) + f(x_n)]\frac{\Delta x}{2} \qquad \text{Trapezoidal rule}$$

$$M_n = \left[f\left(\frac{x_0 + x_1}{2}\right) + f\left(\frac{x_1 + x_2}{2}\right) + \cdots + f\left(\frac{x_{n-1} + x_n}{2}\right)\right]\Delta x \quad \text{Midpoint sum}$$

A midpoint sum rectangle has the same area as the corresponding tangent line trapezoid (the larger trapezoid in Fig. 2). It appears from Figure 2, and can be proved in general, that the trapezoidal sum error is about double the midpoint sum error when the graph of the function is concave up or concave down.

$$T_n \leq \int_a^b f(x)\, dx \leq M_n$$

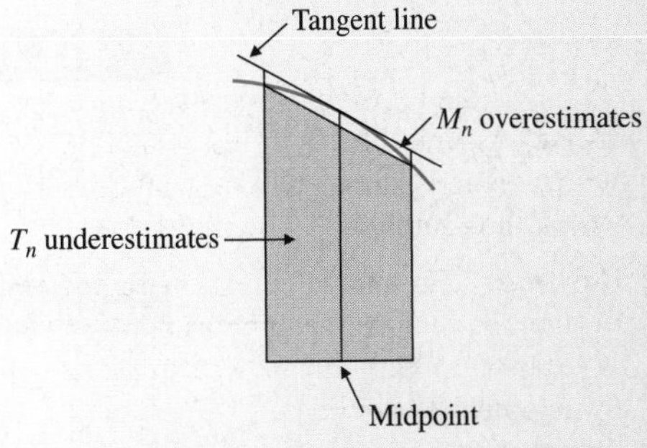

Tangent line

M_n overestimates

T_n underestimates

Midpoint

FIGURE 2

This suggests that a weighted average of the two estimates, with the midpoint sum being counted double the trapezoidal sum, might be an even better estimate than either separately. This weighted average is called **Simpson's rule,** and is given symbolically as follows:

$$S_{2n} = \frac{2M_n + T_n}{3} \quad \text{Simpson's rule} \tag{1}$$

The trapezoidal rule involves integrand values at $n + 1$ points (including a and b), and the midpoint sum involves integrand values at the n midpoints. So Simpson's rule involves integrand values at $2n + 1$ points (including a and b). To apply Simpson's rule, we divide the interval $[a, b]$ into $2n$ equal subdivisions, evaluate the integrand at each subdivision point, and then use n equal subdivisions for each of the sums M_n and T_n. Thus, **Simpson's rule always requires an even number of equal subdivisions of [a, b].**

(A) For $\Delta x = (b - a)/4$, show, starting with equation (1) in the form

$$S_4 = \frac{2M_2 + T_2}{3}$$

that

$$S_4 = [f(x_0) + 4f(x_1) + 2f(x_2) + 4f(x_3) + f(x_4)]\frac{\Delta x}{3}$$

Error Comparisons

One way to compare the effectiveness of a numerical integration technique is to find the error produced for a given value of n and to see what happens to the error as n is increased. We do this for the five sums discussed above, $L_n, R_n, M_n, T_n,$ and S_{2n}, by using these sums to approximate a definite integral of known value and looking at the corresponding errors.

(B) Given the definite integral

$$I = \int_4^{12} \frac{dx}{x} = 1.099 \quad \text{To three decimal places}$$

use the values of the integrand in Table 1 to complete Table 2. Round all answers to three decimal places.

TABLE 1 Integrand Values

x	4	5	6	7	8	9	10	11	12
$1/x$	0.250	0.200	0.167	0.143	0.125	0.111	0.100	0.091	0.083

TABLE 2 Error

	$L_n - I$	$R_n - I$	$M_n - I$	$T_n - I$	$S_{2n} - I$
$n = 2$	0.401				0.002
$n = 4$			−0.009		

Table 2 suggests that the relationships between error and the change in n shown in Table 3 exist. This can be confirmed in general.

TABLE 3 Error and Change in n

Change in n	L_n, R_n		M_n, T_n		S_{2n}	
	Factor by Which Error Is Changed					
$2n$	$\dfrac{1}{2}$		$\dfrac{1}{4}$		$\dfrac{1}{16}$	
$10n$	$\dfrac{1}{10}$	Adds one more digit of accuracy	$\dfrac{1}{10^2}$	Adds two more digits of accuracy	$\dfrac{1}{10^4}$	Adds four more digits of accuracy

We have already noted that L_n and R_n give exact results if the integrand is a constant function. Also, M_n and T_n give exact results for constant and linear functions. What about Simpson's rule? Simpson's rule gives exact results if the integrand is any polynomial of degree 3 or less. It should now be clear why Simpson's rule is so popular. However, Simpson's rule is generally not used in numerical integration routines. More powerful algorithms exist. For example, the Gauss–Kronrod algorithm is used in a number of popular graphing utilities and gives exact results for polynomials of degree 5 or less.

(C) Use Simpson's rule to approximate the definite integral

$$I = \int_2^{10} \frac{x}{\ln x}\,dx$$

for $2n = 4$ and for $2n = 8$. Compute S_{2n} to three decimal places.

(D) Using more powerful algorithms, it is known that $I = 27.159$ to three decimal places. Compute the error $|I - S_{2n}|$ for the two estimates in part (C).

Application

We now turn to an example where Simpson's rule is used to estimate cost. (Note that it is not necessary to find a regression equation, as we would in order to use a numerical integration routine on a graphing utility.)

A company manufactures and wholesales a popular brand of sunglasses. Their financial research department collected the data in Table 4, showing marginal cost $C'(x)$ (in dollars) at selected production levels of x pairs of sunglasses per hour.

TABLE 4 Marginal Costs

t	50	100	150	200	250	300	350	400	450
$C'(x)$	21.80	16.95	15.31	14.50	14.00	13.66	13.42	13.25	13.11

(E) If the company is now producing 50 pairs of sunglasses per hour and increases production to 450 pairs per hour, estimate the total increase in costs per hour using L_n and R_n with an appropriate value of n. How are L_n and R_n related to the actual increase in cost?

(F) Use Simpson's rule to estimate the increase in cost in part (E).

Group Activity 2 Bell-Shaped Curves

One of the most important functions in probability and statistics is the **normal probability density function** and its bell-shaped graph or **normal curve,** as shown in Figure 1.

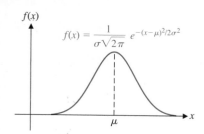

$$f(x) = \frac{1}{\sigma\sqrt{2\pi}} \, e^{-(x-\mu)^2/2\sigma^2}$$

FIGURE 1 Normal curve

It can be shown that the total area under the curve from $-\infty$ to ∞, for μ any real number and σ any positive real number, is always 1. Thus, the area under the curve over an interval $[a, b]$ is the percentage of the total area that is under the curve between a and b. We will interpret the normal probability density function through an example.

A manufacturer of 100-watt light bulbs tests a large sample and finds that the average life of these bulbs is 5 hundred hours ($\mu = 5$) with a *standard deviation* of 1 hundred hours ($\sigma = 1$). (Standard deviation measures the dispersion of the normal probability density function about the mean or average. A small standard deviation is associated with a tall, narrow normal curve, and a large standard deviation is related to a low, flat normal curve. You will see this below.) For $\mu = 5$ and $\sigma = 1$, the probability density function and corresponding normal curve are shown in Figure 2. The area under the curve between 5 hundred hours and 6 hundred hours represents the percentage of light bulbs in the manufacturing process that will have a life between 5 and 6 hundred hours; that is, the probability of a light bulb drawn at random having a life between 5 and 6 hundred hours.

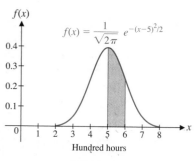

$$f(x) = \frac{1}{\sqrt{2\pi}} \, e^{-(x-5)^2/2}$$

Hundred hours

FIGURE 2

(A) Write a definite integral that represents the probability of a light bulb drawn at random having a life between 5 and 6 hundred hours.

(B) Approximate the definite integral in part (A) with a midpoint sum using five equal subintervals. Explain what the result means relative to the original problem.

(C) Compute $f''(x)$. Use a graphing utility to graph $y = |f''(x)|$ over the interval $[5, 6]$, and use the graph to show that 0.4 is an upper bound for $|f''(x)|$ on this interval.

(D) Calculate an error bound for the estimate M_5 in part (B) using the result from part (C).

(E) Using the result from part (C), how large should n be chosen so that the error in using M_n is no greater than 0.00005?

(F) If the area under the normal curve from 5 to ∞ is 0.5, what is the probability of selecting a light bulb at random that has a life greater than 600 hours? Explain how you arrived at your answer.

(G) What is the probability of selecting a light bulb at random that has a life less than 500 hours? Explain how you arrived at your answer.

(H) Use a numerical integration routine on a graphing utility to find the probability of selecting a light bulb at random that has a life between 450 and 550 hours. That has a life between 350 and 650 hours.

(I) Graph normal probability density functions with $\mu = 8$ and $\sigma = 1, 2$, and 3, in the same viewing window. What effect does changing σ have on the shape of the curve?

OBJECTIVES

1. Calculate the area between two curves.
2. Compute the Gini index to measure the income concentration of income distributions given by Lorenz curves.
3. Use the definite integral to find probabilities associated with continuous random variables.
4. Calculate the total income and future value of continuous income streams.
5. Given price–demand and price–supply equations, determine the equilibrium price and the consumers' surplus and producers' surplus at the equilibrium price level.
6. Find indefinite integrals using integration by parts.
7. Use a table of integrals to compute indefinite and definite integrals.

CHAPTER PROBLEM

A toy company markets an inflatable jumbo beach ball. The price-demand and price-supply equations for this ball are

$$p = D(x) = \frac{6,000}{600 + x}$$

and

$$p = S(x) = \frac{6x}{120 + x}$$

Find the equilibrium price and find both the consumers' and the producers' surplus at the equilibrium price level.

Additional Integration Topics

INTRODUCTION

This chapter contains additional topics on integration. Since they are essentially independent of one another, they may be taken up in any order, and certain sections may be omitted if desired.

Section 7-1 | Area Between Curves

➤ Area Between Two Curves
➤ Application: Income Distribution

In Chapter 6 we found that the definite integral $\int_a^b f(x)\,dx$ represents the sum of the signed areas between the graph of $y = f(x)$ and the x axis from $x = a$ to $x = b$, where the areas above the x axis are counted positively and the areas below the x axis are counted negatively (see Fig. 1). In this section we are interested in using the definite integral to find the actual area between a curve and the x axis or the actual area between two curves. These areas are always nonnegative quantities—**area measure is never negative.**

➤ Area Between Two Curves

Consider the area bounded by $y = f(x)$ and $y = g(x)$, where $f(x) \geq g(x) \geq 0$, for $a \leq x \leq b$, as indicated in Figure 2.

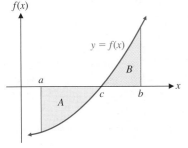

$$\begin{pmatrix} \text{Area } A \text{ between} \\ f(x) \text{ and } g(x) \end{pmatrix} = \begin{pmatrix} \text{area} \\ \text{under } f(x) \end{pmatrix} - \begin{pmatrix} \text{area} \\ \text{under } g(x) \end{pmatrix}$$

Areas are from $x = a$ to $x = b$ above the x axis.

$$= \int_a^b f(x)\,dx - \int_a^b g(x)\,dx$$

Use definite integral property 4 (Section 6-4).

$$= \int_a^b [f(x) - g(x)]\,dx$$

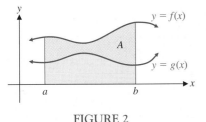

FIGURE 1

$$\int_a^b f(x)\,dx = -A + B$$

FIGURE 2

It can be shown that the preceding result does not require $f(x)$ or $g(x)$ to remain positive over the interval $[a, b]$. A more general result is stated in the box:

THEOREM 1   Area Between Two Curves

If f and g are continuous and $f(x) \geq g(x)$ over the interval $[a, b]$, then the area bounded by $y = f(x)$ and $y = g(x)$ for $a \leq x \leq b$ is given exactly by

$$A = \int_a^b [f(x) - g(x)]\, dx$$

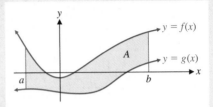

◉ **Insight**   Theorem 1 requires the graph of f to be *above* (or equal to) the graph of g throughout $[a, b]$, but f and g can be either positive or negative or 0. In Section 6-4 we considered the special cases of Theorem 1 in which (1) f is positive, g is the zero function on $[a, b]$; and (2) f is the zero function, g is negative on $[a, b]$:

Special case 1. If f is continuous and positive over $[a, b]$, then the area bounded by the graph of f and the x axis for $a \leq x \leq b$ is given exactly by

$$\int_a^b f(x)\, dx$$

Special case 2. If g is continous and negative over $[a, b]$, then the area bounded by the graph of g and the x axis for $a \leq x \leq b$ is given exactly by

$$\int_a^b -g(x)\, dx$$ ●

EXPLORE & DISCUSS 1

A Riemann sum for the integral representing the area between the graphs of $y = f(x)$ and $y = g(x)$ in Theorem 1 has the form

$$\sum_{k=1}^{n} [f(c_k) - g(c_k)]\, \Delta x_k$$

Each term in this sum represents the area of a rectangle with height $f(c_k) - g(c_k)$ and width Δx. Discuss the relationship between these rectangles and the area between the graphs of $y = f(x)$ and $y = g(x)$.

EXAMPLE 1   **Area Between a Curve and the x Axis** Find the area bounded by $f(x) = 6x - x^2$ and $y = 0$ for $1 \leq x \leq 4$.

Solution   We sketch a graph of the region first (Fig. 3). (The solution of every area problem should begin with a sketch.) Since $f(x) \geq 0$ on $[1, 4]$,

$$A = \int_1^4 (6x - x^2)\, dx = \left(3x^2 - \frac{x^3}{3} \right)\Big|_1^4$$

$$= \left[3(4)^2 - \frac{(4)^3}{3} \right] - \left[3(1)^2 - \frac{(1)^3}{3} \right]$$

$$= 48 - \frac{64}{3} - 3 + \frac{1}{3}$$

$$= 48 - 21 - 3$$

$$= 24$$

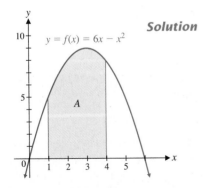

FIGURE 3

Matched Problem 1   Find the area bounded by $f(x) = x^2 + 1$ and $y = 0$ for $-1 \le x \le 3$.

EXAMPLE 2   **Area Between a Curve and the x Axis** Find the area between the graph of $f(x) = x^2 - 2x$ and the x axis over the indicated intervals:

(A) $[1, 2]$

(B) $[-1, 1]$

Solution   We begin by sketching the graph of f, as shown in Figure 4.

(A) From the graph, we see that $f(x) \le 0$ for $1 \le x \le 2$, so we integrate $-f(x)$:

$$A_1 = \int_1^2 [-f(x)]\, dx$$

$$= \int_1^2 (2x - x^2)\, dx$$

$$= \left(x^2 - \frac{x^3}{3} \right)\Big|_1^2$$

$$= \left[(2)^2 - \frac{(2)^3}{3} \right] - \left[(1)^2 - \frac{(1)^3}{3} \right]$$

$$\boxed{= 4 - \tfrac{8}{3} - 1 + \tfrac{1}{3}} = \tfrac{2}{3} \approx 0.667$$

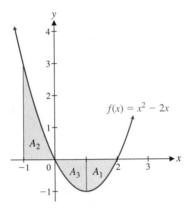

FIGURE 4

(B) Since the graph shows that $f(x) \ge 0$ on $[-1, 0]$ and $f(x) \le 0$ on $[0, 1]$, the computation of this area will require two integrals:

$$A = A_2 + A_3$$

$$= \int_{-1}^0 f(x)\, dx + \int_0^1 [-f(x)]\, dx$$

$$= \int_{-1}^0 (x^2 - 2x)\, dx + \int_0^1 (2x - x^2)\, dx$$

$$= \left(\frac{x^3}{3} - x^2 \right)\Big|_{-1}^0 + \left(x^2 - \frac{x^3}{3} \right)\Big|_0^1$$

$$\boxed{= \tfrac{4}{3} + \tfrac{2}{3}} = 2$$

Matched Problem 2   Find the area between the graph of $f(x) = x^2 - 9$ and the x axis over the indicated intervals:

(A) $[0, 2]$

(B) $[2, 4]$

EXAMPLE 3   **Area Between Two Curves** Find the area bounded by the graphs of $f(x) = \frac{1}{2}x + 3$, $g(x) = -x^2 + 1$, $x = -2$, and $x = 1$.

Solution   We first sketch the area (Fig. 5), and then set up and evaluate an appropriate definite integral. We observe from the graph that $f(x) \geq g(x)$ for $-2 \leq x \leq 1$, so

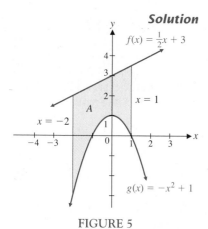

$$A = \int_{-2}^{1} [f(x) - g(x)]\, dx = \int_{-2}^{1}\left[\left(\frac{x}{2} + 3\right) - (-x^2 + 1)\right] dx$$

$$= \int_{-2}^{1}\left(x^2 + \frac{x}{2} + 2\right) dx$$

$$= \left(\frac{x^3}{3} + \frac{x^2}{4} + 2x\right)\Big|_{-2}^{1}$$

$$= \left(\frac{1}{3} + \frac{1}{4} + 2\right) - \left(\frac{-8}{3} + \frac{4}{4} - 4\right) = \frac{33}{4} = 8.25$$ ∎

FIGURE 5

Matched Problem 3   Find the area bounded by $f(x) = x^2 - 1$, $g(x) = -\frac{1}{2}x - 3$, $x = -1$, and $x = 2$.

EXAMPLE 4   **Area Between Two Curves** Find the area bounded by $f(x) = 5 - x^2$ and $g(x) = 2 - 2x$.

Solution   First, graph f and g on the same coordinate system, as shown in Figure 6. Since the statement of the problem does not include any limits on the values of x, we must determine the appropriate values from the graph. The graph of f is a parabola and the graph of g is a line, as shown. The area bounded by these two graphs extends from the intersection point on the left to the intersection point on the right. To find these intersection points, we solve the equation $f(x) = g(x)$ for x:

$$f(x) = g(x)$$
$$5 - x^2 = 2 - 2x$$
$$x^2 - 2x - 3 = 0$$
$$x = -1, 3$$

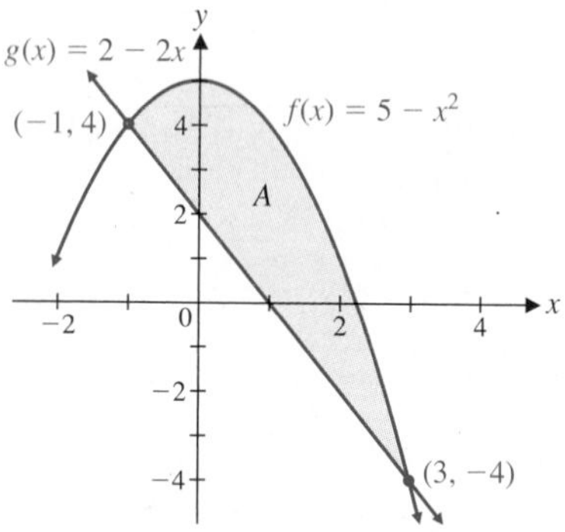

FIGURE 6

You should check these values in the original equations. (Note that the area between the graphs for $x < -1$ is unbounded on the left, and the area between the graphs for $x > 3$ is unbounded on the right.) Figure 6 shows that $f(x) \geq g(x)$ over the interval $[-1, 3]$, so we have

$$A = \int_{-1}^{3} [f(x) - g(x)]\, dx = \int_{-1}^{3} [5 - x^2 - (2 - 2x)]\, dx$$

$$= \int_{-1}^{3} (3 + 2x - x^2)\, dx$$

$$= \left(3x + x^2 - \frac{x^3}{3}\right)\Big|_{-1}^{3}$$

$$= \left[3(3) + (3)^2 - \frac{(3)^3}{3}\right] - \left[3(-1) + (-1)^2 - \frac{(-1)^3}{3}\right] = \frac{32}{3} \approx 10.667$$ ∎

Matched Problem 4   Find the area bounded by $f(x) = 6 - x^2$ and $g(x) = x$.

EXAMPLE 5   **Area Between Two Curves** Find the area bounded by $f(x) = x^2 - x$ and $g(x) = 2x$ for $-2 \le x \le 3$.

Solution   The graphs of f and g are shown in Figure 7. Examining the graph, we see that $f(x) \ge g(x)$ on the interval $[-2, 0]$, but $g(x) \ge f(x)$ on the interval $[0, 3]$. Thus, two integrals are required to compute this area:

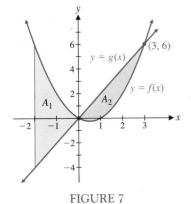

FIGURE 7

$$A_1 = \int_{-2}^{0} [f(x) - g(x)]\, dx \quad f(x) \ge g(x) \text{ on } [-2, 0]$$

$$= \int_{-2}^{0} [x^2 - x - 2x]\, dx$$

$$= \int_{-2}^{0} (x^2 - 3x)\, dx$$

$$= \left(\frac{x^3}{3} - \frac{3}{2}x^2 \right) \Big|_{-2}^{0}$$

$$= (0) - \left[\frac{(-2)^3}{3} - \frac{3}{2}(-2)^2 \right] = \frac{26}{3} \approx 8.667$$

$$A_2 = \int_{0}^{3} [g(x) - f(x)]\, dx \quad g(x) \ge f(x) \text{ on } [0, 3]$$

$$= \int_{0}^{3} [2x - (x^2 - x)]\, dx$$

$$= \int_{0}^{3} (3x - x^2)\, dx$$

$$= \left(\frac{3}{2}x^2 - \frac{x^3}{3} \right) \Big|_{0}^{3}$$

$$= \left[\frac{3}{2}(3)^2 - \frac{(3)^3}{3} \right] - (0) = \frac{9}{2} = 4.5$$

The total area between the two graphs is

$$A = A_1 + A_2 = \tfrac{26}{3} + \tfrac{9}{2} = \tfrac{79}{6} \approx 13.167$$

Matched Problem 5   Find the area bounded by $f(x) = 2x^2$ and $g(x) = 4 - 2x$ for $-2 \le x \le 2$.

EXAMPLE 6   **Computing Areas Using a Numerical Integration Routine** Find the area (to three decimal places) bounded by $f(x) = e^{-x^2}$ and $g(x) = x^2 - 1$.

Solution   First, we use a graphing utility to graph the functions f and g and find their intersection points (see Fig. 8A). We see that the graph of f is bell shaped and the graph of g is a parabola, and note that $f(x) \ge g(x)$ on the interval $[-1.131, 1.131]$. Now we compute the area A by a numerical integration routine (see Fig. 8B):

$$A = \int_{-1.131}^{1.131} [e^{-x^2} - (x^2 - 1)]\, dx = 2.876$$

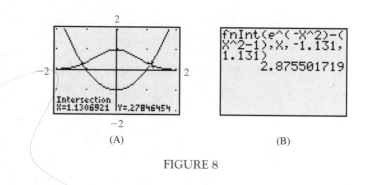

(A)   (B)

FIGURE 8

Matched Problem 6

Find the area (to three decimal places) bounded by the graphs of $f(x) = x^2 \ln x$ and $g(x) = 3x - 3$.

➤ Application: Income Distribution

The U.S. Bureau of the Census compiles and analyzes a great deal of data having to do with the distribution of income among families in the United States. For 1997 the Bureau reported that the lowest 20% of families received 4% of all family income, and the top 20% received 47%. Table 1 and Figure 9 give a detailed picture of the distribution of family income in 1997.

The graph of $y = f(x)$ in Figure 9 is called a **Lorenz curve** and is generally found using *regression analysis,* a technique of fitting a particular elementary function to a data set over a given interval. The variable **x represents the cumulative percentage of families at or below a given income level** and **y represents the cumulative percentage of total family income received.** For example, data point (0.40, 0.14) in Table 1 indicates that the bottom 40% of families (those with incomes under \$36,000) receive 14% of the total income for all families; data point (0.60, 0.30) indicates that the bottom 60% of families receive 30% of the total income for all families; and so on.

Absolute equality of income would occur if the area between the Lorenz curve and $y = x$ were 0. In this case, the Lorenz curve would be $y = x$ and all families would receive equal shares of the total income. That is, 5% of the families would receive 5% of the income, 20% of the families would receive 20%

TABLE 1 Family Income Distribution in the United States, 1997		
Income Level	x	y
Under \$21,000	0.20	0.04
Under \$36,000	0.40	0.14
Under \$54,000	0.60	0.30
Under \$80,000	0.80	0.53

Source: U.S. Bureau of the Census

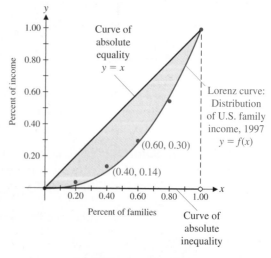

FIGURE 9   Lorenz chart

of the income, 65% of the families would receive 65% of the income, and so on. The maximum possible area between a Lorenz curve and $y = x$ is $\frac{1}{2}$, the area of the triangle below $y = x$. In this case, we would have **absolute inequality**—all the income would be in the hands of one family and the rest would have none. In actuality, Lorenz curves lie between these two extremes. But as the shaded area increases, the greater the inequality of income distribution.

We use a single number, the **Gini index** [named after the Italian sociologist Corrado Gini (1884–1965)], to measure income concentration. The Gini index is the ratio of two areas: the area between $y = x$ and the Lorenz curve, and the area between $y = x$ and the x axis, from $x = 0$ to $x = 1$. The first area equals $\int_0^1 [x - f(x)]\, dx$ and the second (triangular) area equals $\frac{1}{2}$, giving the following definition.

DEFINITION   Gini Index of Income Concentration
If $y = f(x)$ is the equation of a Lorenz curve, then

$$\textbf{Gini index} = 2 \int_0^1 [x - f(x)]\, dx$$

The Gini index is always a number between 0 and 1:

A measure of 0 indicates absolute equality—all people share equally in the income. A measure of 1 indicates absolute inequality—one person has all the income and the rest have none.

The closer the index is to 0, the closer the income is to being equally distributed. The closer the index is to 1, the closer the income is to being concentrated in a few hands. The Gini index of income concentration is used to compare income distributions at various points in time, between different groups of people, before and after taxes are paid, between different countries, and so on.

EXAMPLE 7 **Distribution of Income** The Lorenz curve for the distribution of income in a certain country in 2000 is given by $f(x) = x^{2.6}$. Economists predict that the Lorenz curve for the country in the year 2020 will be given by $g(x) = x^{1.8}$. Find the Gini index of income concentration for each curve, and interpret the results.

Solution   The Lorenz curves are shown in Figure 10.

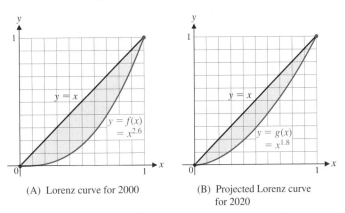

(A) Lorenz curve for 2000

(B) Projected Lorenz curve for 2020

FIGURE 10

The Gini index in 2000 is (see Fig. 10A)

$$2 \int_0^1 [x - f(x)] \, dx = 2 \int_0^1 [x - x^{2.6}] \, dx = 2 \left(\frac{1}{2} x^2 - \frac{1}{3.6} x^{3.6} \right) \Big|_0^1$$

$$= 2 \left(\frac{1}{2} - \frac{1}{3.6} \right) \approx 0.444$$

The projected Gini index in 2020 is (see Fig. 10B)

$$2 \int_0^1 [x - g(x)] \, dx = 2 \int_0^1 [x - x^{1.8}] \, dx = 2 \left(\frac{1}{2} x^2 - \frac{1}{2.8} x^{2.8} \right) \Big|_0^1$$

$$= 2 \left(\frac{1}{2} - \frac{1}{2.8} \right) \approx 0.286$$

If this projection is correct, the Gini index will decrease, and income will be more equally distributed in the year 2020 than in 2000. ∎

Matched Problem 7   Repeat Example 7 if the projected Lorenz curve in the year 2020 is given by $g(x) = x^{3.8}$.

EXPLORE & DISCUSS 2   Do you agree or disagree with each of the following statements? Explain your answers by making reference to the data in Table 2.

(A) In countries with a low Gini index, there is little incentive for individuals to strive for success, and therefore productivity is low.

(B) In countries with a high Gini index, it is almost impossible to rise out of poverty, and therefore productivity is low.

TABLE 2

Country	Gini Index	Per Capita Gross Domestic Product
Brazil	0.60	$6,500
China	0.40	3,600
France	0.33	24,400
Germany	0.30	23,400
Japan	0.25	24,900
Jordan	0.36	3,500
Mexico	0.54	9,100
Russia	0.50	7,700
Sweden	0.25	22,200
United States	0.41	36,200

Source: The World Bank

Answers to Matched Problems   **1.** $A = \int_{-1}^3 (x^2 + 1) \, dx = \frac{40}{3} \approx 13.333$

2. (A) $A = \int_0^2 (9 - x^2) \, dx = \frac{46}{3} \approx 15.333$

(B) $A = \int_2^3 (9 - x^2) \, dx + \int_3^4 (x^2 - 9) \, dx = 6$

3. $A = \int_{-1}^2 \left[(x^2 - 1) - \left(-\frac{x}{2} - 3 \right) \right] dx = \frac{39}{4} = 9.75$

4. $A = \int_{-3}^2 [(6 - x^2) - x] \, dx = \frac{125}{6} \approx 20.833$

5. $A = \int_{-2}^{1}[(4 - 2x) - 2x^2]\, dx + \int_{1}^{2}[2x^2 - (4 - 2x)]\, dx = \frac{38}{3} \approx 12.667$

6. 0.443

7. Gini index of income concentration ≈ 0.583; income will be less equally distributed in 2020.

Exercise 7-1

A *Problems 1–6 refer to Figures A–D. Set up definite integrals in Problems 1–4 that represent the indicated shaded area.*

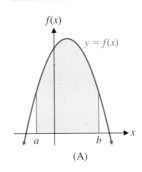

(A)

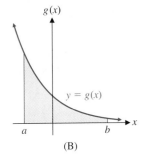

(B)

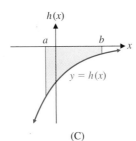

(C)

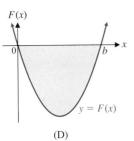

(D)

1. Shaded area in Figure B

2. Shaded area in Figure A

3. Shaded area in Figure C

4. Shaded area in Figure D

5. Explain why $\int_{a}^{b} h(x)\, dx$ does not represent the area between the graph of $y = h(x)$ and the x axis from $x = a$ to $x = b$ in Figure C.

6. Explain why $\int_{a}^{b}[-h(x)]\, dx$ represents the area between the graph of $y = h(x)$ and the x axis from $x = a$ to $x = b$ in Figure C.

In Problems 7–16, find the area bounded by the graphs of the indicated equations over the given intervals. Compute answers to three decimal places.

7. $y = -2x - 1; y = 0, 0 \le x \le 4$

8. $y = 2x - 4; y = 0, -2 \le x \le 1$

9. $y = x^2 + 2; y = 0, -1 \le x \le 0$

10. $y = 3x^2 + 1; y = 0, -2 \le x \le 0$

11. $y = x^3 + 1; y = 0, 0 \le x \le 2$

12. $y = -x^3 + 2; y = 0, -2 \le x \le 1$

13. $y = e^x; y = 0, -1 \le x \le 2$

14. $y = e^{-x}; y = 0, -2 \le x \le 1$

15. $y = -1/t; y = 0, 0.5 \le t \le 1$

16. $y = -1/t; y = 0, 0.1 \le t \le 1$

B *Problems 17–26 refer to Figures A and B. Set up definite integrals in Problems 17–24 that represent the indicated shaded areas over the given intervals.*

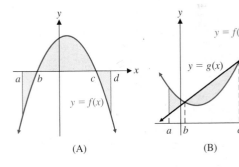

(A)   (B)

17. Over interval $[a, b]$ in Figure A

18. Over interval $[c, d]$ in Figure A

19. Over interval $[b, d]$ in Figure A

20. Over interval $[a, c]$ in Figure A

21. Over interval $[c, d]$ in Figure B

22. Over interval $[a, b]$ in Figure B

23. Over interval $[a, c]$ in Figure B

24. Over interval $[b, d]$ in Figure B

25. Referring to Figure B, explain how you would use definite integrals and the functions f and g to find the area bounded by the two functions from $x = a$ to $x = d$.

26. Referring to Figure A, explain how you would use definite integrals to find the area between the graph of $y = f(x)$ and the x axis from $x = a$ to $x = d$.

In Problems 27–42, find the area bounded by the graphs of the indicated equations over the given intervals (when stated). Compute answers to three decimal places.

27. $y = -x; y = 0, -2 \le x \le 1$

28. $y = -x + 1; y = 0, -1 \le x \le 2$

29. $y = x^2 - 4; y = 0, 0 \le x \le 3$

30. $y = 4 - x^2; y = 0, 0 \le x \le 4$

31. $y = x^2 - 3x; y = 0, -2 \le x \le 2$

32. $y = -x^2 - 2x; y = 0, -2 \le x \le 1$

33. $y = -2x + 8; y = 12; -1 \le x \le 2$

34. $y = 2x + 6; y = 3; -1 \le x \le 2$

35. $y = 3x^2; y = 12$

36. $y = x^2; y = 9$

37. $y = 4 - x^2; y = -5$

38. $y = x^2 - 1; y = 3$

39. $y = x^2 + 1; y = 2x - 2; -1 \le x \le 2$

40. $y = x^2 - 1; y = x - 2; -2 \le x \le 1$

41. $y = e^{0.5x}; y = -\dfrac{1}{x}; 1 \le x \le 2$

42. $y = \dfrac{1}{x}; y = -e^x; 0.5 \le x \le 1$

In Problems 43–46, use a graphing utility to graph the equations and find relevant intersection points. Then find the area bounded by the curves. Compute answers to three decimal places.

43. $y = 3 - 5x - 2x^2; y = 2x^2 + 3x - 2$

44. $y = 3 - 2x^2; y = 2x^2 - 4x$

45. $y = -0.5x + 2.25; y = \dfrac{1}{x}$

46. $y = x - 4.25; y = -\dfrac{1}{x}$

C In Problems 47–54, find the area bounded by the graphs of the indicated equations over the given intervals (when stated). Compute answers to three decimal places.

47. $y = e^x; y = e^{-x}; 0 \le x \le 4$

48. $y = e^x; y = -e^{-x}; 1 \le x \le 2$

49. $y = x^3; y = 4x$

50. $y = x^3 + 1; y = x + 1$

51. $y = x^3 - 3x^2 - 9x + 12; y = x + 12$

52. $y = x^3 - 6x^2 + 9x; y = x$

53. $y = x^4 - 4x^2 + 1; y = x^2 - 3$

54. $y = x^4 - 6x^2; y = 4x^2 - 9$

In Problems 55–60, use a graphing utility to graph the equations and find relevant intersection points. Then find the area bounded by the curves. Compute answers to three decimal places.

55. $y = x^3 - x^2 + 2; y = -x^3 + 8x - 2$

56. $y = 2x^3 + 2x^2 - x; y = -2x^3 - 2x^2 + 2x$

57. $y = e^{-x}; y = 3 - 2x$

58. $y = 2 - (x + 1)^2; y = e^{x+1}$

59. $y = e^x; y = 5x - x^3$

60. $y = 2 - e^x; y = x^3 + 3x^2$

In Problems 61–64, use a numerical integration routine on a graphing utility to find the area bounded by the graphs of the indicated equations over the given interval (when stated). Compute answers to three decimal places.

61. $y = e^{-x}; y = \sqrt{\ln x}; 2 \le x \le 5$

62. $y = x^2 + 3x + 1; y = e^{e^x}; -3 \le x \le 0$

63. $y = e^{x^2}; y = x + 2$

64. $y = \ln(\ln x); y = 0.01x$

Applications

In the following applications it is helpful to sketch graphs to get a clearer understanding of each problem and to interpret results. A graphing utility will prove useful if you have one, but it is not necessary.

Business & Economics

65. *Oil production.* Using data from the first 3 years of production as well as geological studies, the management of an oil company estimates that oil will be pumped from a producing field at a rate given by

$$R(t) = \frac{100}{t + 10} + 10 \qquad 0 \le t \le 15$$

where $R(t)$ is the rate of production (in thousands of barrels per year) t years after pumping begins. Find the area between the graph of R and the t axis over the interval [5, 10] and interpret the results.

66. *Oil production.* In Problem 65, if the rate is found to be

$$R(t) = \frac{100t}{t^2 + 25} + 4 \qquad 0 \le t \le 25$$

find the area between the graph of R and the t axis over the interval [5, 15] and interpret the results.

67. *Useful life.* An amusement company maintains records for each video game it installs in an arcade.

Suppose that $C(t)$ and $R(t)$ represent the total accumulated costs and revenues (in thousands of dollars), respectively, t years after a particular game has been installed. If

$$C'(t) = 2 \quad \text{and} \quad R'(t) = 9e^{-0.3t}$$

find the area between the graphs of C' and R' over the interval on the t axis from 0 to the useful life of the game and interpret the results.

68. *Useful life.* Repeat Problem 67 if

$$C'(t) = 2t \quad \text{and} \quad R'(t) = 5te^{-0.1t^2}$$

69. *Income distribution.* As part of a study of the effects of World War II on the economy of the United States, an economist used data from the U.S. Bureau of the Census to produce the following Lorenz curves for distribution of income in the United States in 1935 and in 1947:

$$f(x) = x^{2.4} \quad \text{Lorenz curve for 1935}$$
$$g(x) = x^{1.6} \quad \text{Lorenz curve for 1947}$$

Find the Gini index of income concentration for each Lorenz curve and interpret the results.

70. *Income distribution.* Using data from the U.S. Bureau of the Census, an economist produced the following Lorenz curves for distribution of income in the United States in 1962 and in 1972:

$$f(x) = \tfrac{3}{10}x + \tfrac{7}{10}x^2 \quad \text{Lorenz curve for 1962}$$
$$g(x) = \tfrac{1}{2}x + \tfrac{1}{2}x^2 \quad \text{Lorenz curve for 1972}$$

Find the Gini index of income concentration for each Lorenz curve and interpret the results.

71. *Distribution of wealth.* Lorenz curves also can be used to provide a relative measure of the distribution of the total assets of a country. Using data in a report by the U.S. Congressional Joint Economic Committee, an economist produced the following Lorenz curves for the distribution of total assets in the United States in 1963 and in 1983:

$$f(x) = x^{10} \quad \text{Lorenz curve for 1963}$$
$$g(x) = x^{12} \quad \text{Lorenz curve for 1983}$$

Find the Gini index of income concentration for each Lorenz curve and interpret the results.

72. *Income distribution.* The government of a small country is planning sweeping changes in the tax structure in order to provide a more equitable distribution of income. The Lorenz curves for the current income distribution and for the projected income distribution after enactment of the tax changes are given below. Find the Gini index of income concentration for each Lorenz curve. Will the proposed changes provide a more equitable income distribution? Explain.

$$f(x) = x^{2.3} \quad \text{Current Lorenz curve}$$
$$g(x) = 0.4x + 0.6x^2 \quad \text{Projected Lorenz curve after changes in tax laws}$$

73. *Distribution of wealth.* The data in the table describe the distribution of wealth in a country:

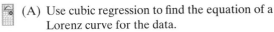

x	0	0.20	0.40	0.60	0.80	1
y	0	0.12	0.31	0.54	0.78	1

(A) Use quadratic regression to find the equation of a Lorenz curve for the data.

(B) Use the regression equation and a numerical integration routine to approximate the Gini index of income concentration.

74. *Distribution of wealth.* Refer to Problem 73.

(A) Use cubic regression to find the equation of a Lorenz curve for the data.

(B) Use the cubic regression equation and a numerical integration routine to approximate the Gini index of income concentration.

Life Sciences

75. *Biology.* A yeast culture is growing at a rate of $W'(t) = 0.3e^{0.1t}$ grams per hour. Find the area between the graph of W' and the t axis over the interval $[0, 10]$ and interpret the results.

76. *Natural resource depletion.* The instantaneous rate of change of the demand for lumber in the United States since 1970 ($t = 0$) in billions of cubic feet per year is estimated to be given by

$$Q'(t) = 12 + 0.006t^2 \quad 0 \le t \le 50$$

Find the area between the graph of Q' and the t axis over the interval $[15, 20]$ and interpret the results.

Social Sciences

77. *Learning.* A beginning high school language class was chosen for an experiment on learning. Using a list of 50 words, the experiment involved measuring the rate of vocabulary memorization at different times during a continuous 5-hour study session. It was found that the average rate of learning for the entire class was inversely proportional to the time spent studying and was given approximately by

$$V'(t) = \frac{15}{t} \quad 1 \le t \le 5$$

Find the area between the graph of V' and the t axis over the interval $[2, 4]$ and interpret the results.

78. *Learning.* Repeat Problem 77 if $V'(t) = 13/t^{1/2}$ and the interval is changed to $[1, 4]$.

Section 7-2 | Applications in Business and Economics

➤ Probability Density Functions
➤ Continuous Income Stream
➤ Future Value of a Continuous Income Stream
➤ Consumers' and Producers' Surplus

This section contains a number of important applications of the definite integral from business and economics. Included are three independent topics: probability density functions, continuous income streams, and consumers' and producers' surplus. Any of the three may be covered as time and interests dictate, and in any order.

➤ Probability Density Functions

We now take a brief look at the use of the definite integral to determine probabilities. Our approach will be intuitive and informal. A more formal treatment of the subject requires use of the special "improper" integral form $\int_{-\infty}^{\infty} f(x)\,dx$, which we have not defined or discussed at this point.

Suppose that an experiment is designed in such a way that any real number x on the interval $[c, d]$ is a possible outcome. For example, x may represent an IQ score, the height of a person in inches, or the life of a light bulb in hours. Technically, we refer to x as a *continuous random variable*.

In certain situations it is possible to find a function f with x as an independent variable such that the function f can be used to determine the probability that the outcome x of an experiment will be in the interval $[c, d]$. Such a function, called a **probability density function,** must satisfy the following three conditions (see Fig. 1):

1. $f(x) \geq 0$ for all real x

2. The area under the graph of $f(x)$ over the interval $(-\infty, \infty)$ is exactly 1.

3. If $[c, d]$ is a subinterval of $(-\infty, \infty)$, then

$$\text{Probability } (c \leq x \leq d) = \int_c^d f(x)\,dx$$

$y = f(x) \geq 0$ \qquad $\int_c^d f(x)\,dx = \text{Probability}(c \leq x \leq d)$

Area = 1

(A) \qquad\qquad (B)

FIGURE 1 Probability density function

EXPLORE & DISCUSS 1

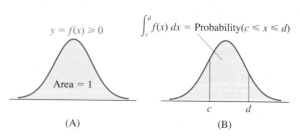

Let $f(x) = \begin{cases} \frac{1}{4}e^{-x/4} & \text{if } x \geq 0 \\ 0 & \text{otherwise} \end{cases}$

(A) Explain why $f(x) \geq 0$ over the interval $(-\infty, \infty)$.

(B) Find $\int_0^{10} f(x)\,dx$, $\int_0^{20} f(x)\,dx$, and $\int_0^{30} f(x)\,dx$.

(C) On the basis of part (B), what would you conjecture the area under the graph of $f(x)$ over the interval $(-\infty, \infty)$ to be equal to?

EXAMPLE 1

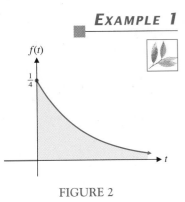

$f(t)$

$\frac{1}{4}$

FIGURE 2

Duration of Telephone Calls Suppose that the length of telephone calls (in minutes) in a public telephone booth is a continuous random variable with probability density function shown in Figure 2.

$$f(t) = \begin{cases} \frac{1}{4}e^{-t/4} & \text{if } t \geq 0 \\ 0 & \text{otherwise} \end{cases}$$

(A) Determine the probability that a call selected at random will last between 2 and 3 minutes.

(B) Find b (to two decimal places) so that the probability of a call selected at random lasting between 2 and b minutes is .5.

Solution (A) Probability $(2 \leq t \leq 3) = \displaystyle\int_2^3 \frac{1}{4}e^{-t/4}\,dt$

$$= (-e^{-t/4})\big|_2^3$$

$$= -e^{-3/4} + e^{-1/2} \approx .13$$

(B) We want to find b such that Probability $(2 \leq t \leq b) = .5$.

$$\int_2^b \frac{1}{4}e^{-t/4}\,dt = .5$$

$$-e^{-b/4} + e^{-1/2} = .5 \qquad \text{Solve for } b.$$

$$e^{-b/4} = e^{-.5} - .5$$

$$-\frac{b}{4} = \ln(e^{-.5} - .5)$$

$$b = 8.96 \text{ minutes}$$

Thus, the probability of a call selected at random lasting from 2 to 8.96 minutes is .5.

Matched Problem 1

(A) In Example 1, find the probability that a call selected at random will last 4 minutes or less.

(B) Find b (to two decimal places) so that the probability of a call selected at random lasting b minutes or less is .9

◉ Insight The probability that a phone call in Example 1 lasts exactly 2 minutes (not 1.999 minutes, not 1.999 999 minutes) is given by

$$\text{Probability } (2 \leq t \leq 2) = \int_2^2 \frac{1}{4}e^{-t/4}\,dt \quad \text{Use Property 1, Section 6-4}$$

$$= 0$$

In fact, for any *continuous* random variable x with probability density function $f(x)$, the probability that x is exactly equal to a constant c is equal to 0:

$$\text{Probability } (c \leq x \leq c) = \int_c^c f(x)\,dx \quad \text{Use Property 1, Section 6-4}$$

$$= 0$$

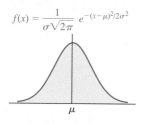

$$f(x) = \frac{1}{\sigma\sqrt{2\pi}}\, e^{-(x-\mu)^2/2\sigma^2}$$

FIGURE 3   Normal curve

In this respect, a *continuous* random variable differs from a *discrete* random variable. If x, for example, is the discrete random variable that represents the number of dots that appear on the top face when a fair die is rolled, then

$$\text{Probability } (2 \leq x \leq 2) = \tfrac{1}{6}$$

●

Group Activity 2 at the end of Chapter 6 investigated one of the most important probability density functions, the **normal probability density function** defined as follows and graphed in Figure 3.

$$f(x) = \frac{1}{\sigma\sqrt{2\pi}}\, e^{-(x-\mu)^2/2\sigma^2} \qquad \begin{array}{l}\mu \text{ is the mean.}\\ \sigma \text{ is the standard deviation.}\end{array}$$

It can be shown (but not easily) that the area under the normal curve in Figure 3 over the interval $(-\infty, \infty)$ is exactly 1. Since $\int e^{-x^2}\,dx$ is nonintegrable in terms of elementary functions (that is, the antiderivative cannot be expressed as a finite combination of simple functions), probabilities such as

$$\text{Probability } (c \leq x \leq d) = \frac{1}{\sigma\sqrt{2\pi}} \int_c^d e^{-(x-\mu)^2/2\sigma^2}\,dx$$

are generally determined by making an appropriate substitution in the integrand and then using a table of areas under the standard normal curve (that is, the normal curve with $\mu = 0$ and $\sigma = 1$). Such tables are readily available in most mathematical handbooks. A table can be constructed by using a rectangle rule, as discussed in Section 6-5; however, computers that employ refined techniques are generally used for this purpose. Some calculators have the capability of computing normal curve areas directly.

➤ Continuous Income Stream

We start with a simple example having an obvious solution and generalize the concept to examples having less obvious solutions.

Suppose an aunt has established a trust that pays you $2,000 a year for 10 years. What is the total amount you will receive from the trust by the end of the 10th year? Since there are 10 payments of $2,000 each, you will receive

$$10 \times \$2,000 = \$20,000$$

We now look at the same problem from a different point of view, a point of view that will be useful in more complex problems. Let us assume that the income stream is continuous at a rate of $2,000 per year. In Figure 4 the area under the graph of $f(t) = 2,000$ from 0 to t represents the income accumulated t years after the start. For example, for $t = \frac{1}{4}$ year, the income would be $\frac{1}{4}(2,000) = \$500$; for $t = \frac{1}{2}$ year, the income would be $\frac{1}{2}(2,000) = \$1,000$; for $t = 1$ year, the income would be $1(2,000) = \$2,000$; for $t = 5.3$ years, the

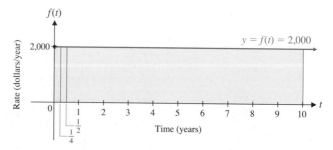

FIGURE 4   Continuous income stream

income would be $5.3(2,000) = \$10,600$; and for $t = 10$ years, the income would be $10(2,000) = \$20,000$. The total income over a 10-year period—that is, the area under the graph of $f(t) = 2,000$ from 0 to 10—is also given by the definite integral

$$\int_0^{10} 2,000\,dt = 2,000t\Big|_0^{10} = 2,000(10) - 2,000(0) = \$20,000$$

We now apply the idea of a continuous income stream to a less obvious problem.

EXAMPLE 2 **Continuous Income Stream** The rate of change of the income produced by a vending machine located at an airport is given by

$$f(t) = 5,000e^{0.04t}$$

where t is time in years since the installation of the machine. Find the total income produced by the machine during the first 5 years of operation.

Solution The area under the graph of the rate of change function from 0 to 5 represents the total change in income over the first 5 years (Fig. 5), and hence is given by a definite integral:

$$\text{Total income} = \int_0^5 5,000e^{0.04t}\,dt$$

$$= 125,000e^{0.04t}\Big|_0^5$$

$$= 125,000e^{0.04(5)} - 125,000e^{0.04(0)}$$

$$= 152,675 - 125,000$$

$$= \$27,675 \quad \textit{Rounded to the nearest dollar}$$

Thus, the vending machine produces a total income of \$27,675 during the first 5 years of operation.

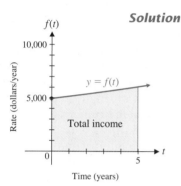

FIGURE 5 Continuous income stream

Matched Problem 2 Referring to Example 2, find the total income produced (to the nearest dollar) during the second 5 years of operation.

In reality, income from a vending machine is not usually received as a single payment at the end of each year, even though the rate is given as a yearly rate. Income is usually collected on a daily or weekly basis. In problems of this type it is convenient to assume that income is actually received in a **continuous stream;** that is, we assume that the rate at which income is received is a continuous function of time. The rate of change is called the **rate of flow** of the continuous income stream. In general, we have the following:

DEFINITION   Total Income for a Continuous Income Stream

If $f(t)$ is the rate of flow of a continuous income stream, the **total income** produced during the time period from $t = a$ to $t = b$ is

$$\text{Total income} = \int_a^b f(t)\,dt$$

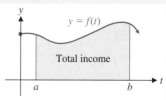

➤ Future Value of a Continuous Income Stream

In Section 5-1 we discussed the continuous compound interest formula

$$A = Pe^{rt}$$

where P is the principal (or present value), A is the amount (or future value), r is the annual rate of continuous compounding (expressed as a decimal), and t is time in years. For example, if money is worth 12% compounded continuously, then the future value of a $10,000 investment in 5 years is (to the nearest dollar)

$$A = 10,000e^{0.12(5)} = \$18,221$$

Now we want to apply the future value concept to the income produced by a continuous income stream. Suppose that $f(t)$ is the rate of flow of a continuous income stream, and the income produced by this continuous income stream is invested as soon as it is received at a rate r, compounded continuously. We already know how to find the total income produced after T years, but how can we find the total of the income produced and the interest earned by this income? Since the income is received in a continuous flow, we cannot just use the formula $A = Pe^{rt}$. This formula is valid only for a single deposit P, not for a continuous flow of income. Instead, we use a Riemann sum approach that will allow us to apply the formula $A = Pe^{rt}$ repeatedly. To begin, we divide the time interval $[0, T]$ into n equal subintervals of length Δt and choose an arbitrary point c_k in each subinterval, as illustrated in Figure 6.

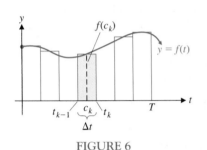

FIGURE 6

The total income produced during the time period from $t = t_{k-1}$ to $t = t_k$ is equal to the area under the graph of $f(t)$ over this subinterval and is approximately equal to $f(c_k)\,\Delta t$, the area of the shaded rectangle in Figure 6. The income received during this time period will earn interest for approximately $T - c_k$ years. Thus, using the future value formula $A = Pe^{rt}$ with $P = f(c_k)\,\Delta t$ and $t = T - c_k$, the future value of the income produced during the time period from $t = t_{k-1}$ to $t = t_k$ is approximately equal to

$$f(c_k)\,\Delta t\, e^{(T-c_k)r}$$

The total of these approximate future values over n subintervals is then

$$f(c_1)\,\Delta t\, e^{(T-c_1)r} + f(c_2)\,\Delta t\, e^{(T-c_2)r} + \cdots + f(c_n)\,\Delta t\, e^{(T-c_n)r} = \sum_{k=1}^{n} f(c_k) e^{r(T-c_k)}\,\Delta t$$

This has the form of a Riemann sum, and the limit of this sum is a definite integral. (See the definition of the definite integral in Section 6-4.) Thus, the *future value, FV*, of the income produced by the continuous income stream is given by

$$FV = \int_0^T f(t)e^{r(T-t)}\,dt$$

Since r and T are constants, we also can write

$$FV = \int_0^T f(t)e^{rT}e^{-rt}\,dt = e^{rT}\int_0^T f(t)e^{-rt}\,dt \tag{1}$$

This last form is preferable, since the integral is usually easier to evaluate than the first form.

DEFINITION   Future Value of a Continuous Income Stream

If $f(t)$ is the rate of flow of a continuous income stream, $0 \le t \le T$, and if the income is continuously invested at a rate r compounded continuously, then the **future value, FV,** at the end of T years is given by

$$FV = \int_0^T f(t)e^{r(T-t)}\,dt = e^{rT}\int_0^T f(t)e^{-rt}\,dt$$

The future value of a continuous income stream is the total value of all money produced by the continuous income stream (income and interest) at the end of T years.

We return to the trust set up for you by your aunt. Suppose that the $2,000 per year you receive from the trust is invested as soon as it is received at 8% compounded continuously. We consider the trust income a continuous income stream with a flow rate of $2,000 per year. What is its future value (to the nearest dollar) by the end of the 10th year? Using the definite integral for future value from the box, we have

$$FV = e^{rT}\int_0^T f(t)e^{-rt}\,dt$$

$$FV = e^{0.08(10)}\int_0^{10} 2{,}000e^{-0.08t}\,dt \quad r = 0.08,\ T = 10,\ f(t) = 2{,}000$$

$$= 2{,}000e^{0.8}\int_0^{10} e^{-0.08t}\,dt$$

$$= 2{,}000e^{0.8}\left[\frac{e^{-0.08t}}{-0.08}\right]\Bigg|_0^{10}$$

$$= -25{,}000e^{0.8}\left[e^{-0.08(10)} - e^{-0.08(0)}\right] = \$30{,}639$$

Thus, at the end of 10 years you will have received $30,639, including interest. How much is interest? Since you received $20,000 in income from the trust, the interest is the difference between the future value and income. Thus,

$$\$30{,}639 - \$20{,}000 = \$10{,}639$$

is the interest earned by the income received from the trust over the 10-year period.

EXPLORE & DISCUSS 2   Suppose that a trust fund is set up to pay you $2,000 per year for 20 years with the continuous income stream invested at 8% compounded continuously. When will its future value be equal to $50,000?

We now apply the same analysis to Example 2, the slightly more involved vending machine problem.

EXAMPLE 3   **Future Value of a Continuous Income Stream**   Using the continuous income rate of flow for the vending machine in Example 2,

$$f(t) = 5{,}000e^{0.04t}$$

find the future value of this income stream at 12% compounded continuously for 5 years, and find the total interest earned. Compute answers to the nearest dollar.

Solution   Using the formula

$$FV = e^{rT} \int_0^T f(t)e^{-rt}\, dt$$

with $r = 0.12$, $T = 5$, and $f(t) = 5{,}000e^{0.04t}$, we have

$$FV = e^{0.12(5)} \int_0^5 5{,}000e^{0.04t}e^{-0.12t}\, dt$$

$$= 5{,}000e^{0.6} \int_0^5 e^{-0.08t}\, dt$$

$$= 5{,}000e^{0.6}\left(\frac{e^{-0.08t}}{-0.08}\right)\Big|_0^5$$

$$= 5{,}000e^{0.6}(-12.5e^{-0.4} + 12.5)$$

$$= \$37{,}545 \quad \textit{Rounded to the nearest dollar}$$

Thus, the future value of the income stream at 12% compounded continuously at the end of 5 years is $37,545.

In Example 2, we saw that the total income produced by this vending machine over a 5-year period was $27,675. The difference between the future value and income is interest. Thus,

$$\$37{,}545 - \$27{,}675 = \$9{,}870$$

is the interest earned by the income produced by the vending machine during the 5-year period.   ■

Matched Problem 3   Repeat Example 3 if the interest rate is 9% compounded continuously.

➤ Consumers' and Producers' Surplus

Let $p = D(x)$ be the price–demand equation for a product, where x is the number of units of the product that consumers will purchase at a price of $\$p$ per unit. Suppose that $\bar{p}$ is the current price and $\bar{x}$ is the number of units that can be sold at that price. The price–demand curve in Figure 7 shows that if the price is higher than $\bar{p}$, the demand x is less than $\bar{x}$, but some consumers are still willing to pay the higher price. Consumers who are willing to pay more than $\bar{p}$ but are still able to buy the product at $\bar{p}$ have saved money. We want to determine the total amount saved by all the consumers who are willing to pay a price higher than $\bar{p}$ for this product.

To do this, consider the interval $[c_k, c_k + \Delta x]$, where $c_k + \Delta x < \bar{x}$. If the price remained constant over this interval, the savings on each unit would be the difference between $D(c_k)$, the price consumers are willing to pay, and $\bar{p}$, the price they actually pay. Since Δx represents the number of units purchased by consumers over the interval, the total savings to consumers over this interval is approximately equal to

$$[D(c_k) - \bar{p}]\,\Delta x \quad \text{(savings per unit)} \times \text{(number of units)}$$

which is the area of the shaded rectangle shown in Figure 7. If we divide the interval $[0, \bar{x}]$ into n equal subintervals, the total savings to consumers is approximately equal to

$$[D(c_1) - \bar{p}]\,\Delta x + [D(c_2) - \bar{p}]\,\Delta x + \cdots + [D(c_n) - \bar{p}]\,\Delta x = \sum_{k=1}^{n}[D(c_k) - \bar{p}]\,\Delta x$$

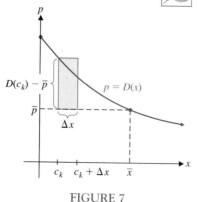

FIGURE 7

which we recognize as a Riemann sum for the following integral:

$$\int_0^{\bar{x}} [D(x) - \bar{p}]\, dx$$

Thus, we define the *consumers' surplus* to be this integral.

DEFINITION   Consumers' Surplus

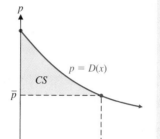

If $(\bar{x}, \bar{p})$ is a point on the graph of the price–demand equation $p = D(x)$ for a particular product, then the **consumers' surplus, CS,** at a price level of $\bar{p}$ is

$$CS = \int_0^{\bar{x}} [D(x) - \bar{p}]\, dx$$

which is the area between $p = \bar{p}$ and $p = D(x)$ from $x = 0$ to $x = \bar{x}$, as shown in the margin.

The consumers' surplus represents the total savings to consumers who are willing to pay more than $\bar{p}$ for the product but are still able to buy the product for $\bar{p}$.

EXAMPLE 4   **Consumers' Surplus**   Find the consumers' surplus at a price level of $8 for the price–demand equation

$$p = D(x) = 20 - 0.05x$$

Solution   **Step 1.** Find $\bar{x}$, the demand when the price is $\bar{p} = 8$:

$$\bar{p} = 20 - 0.05\bar{x}$$
$$8 = 20 - 0.05\bar{x}$$
$$0.05\bar{x} = 12$$
$$\bar{x} = 240$$

Step 2. Sketch a graph, as shown in Figure 8.

Step 3. Find the consumers' surplus (the shaded area in the graph):

$$CS = \int_0^{\bar{x}} [D(x) - \bar{p}]\, dx$$

$$= \int_0^{240} (20 - 0.05x - 8)\, dx$$

$$= \int_0^{240} (12 - 0.05x)\, dx$$

$$= (12x - 0.025x^2)\Big|_0^{240}$$

$$= 2{,}880 - 1{,}440 = \$1{,}440$$

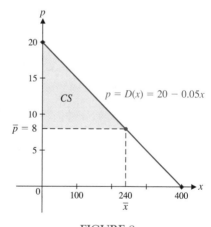

FIGURE 8

Thus, the total savings to consumers who are willing to pay a higher price for the product is $1,440.   ∎

Matched Problem 4   Repeat Example 4 for a price level of $4.

If $p = S(x)$ is the price–supply equation for a product, $\bar{p}$ is the current price, and $\bar{x}$ is the current supply, some suppliers are still willing to supply some units at a lower price than $\bar{p}$. The additional money that these suppliers gain from the higher price is called the *producers' surplus* and can be expressed in terms of a definite integral (proceeding as we did for the consumers' surplus).

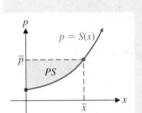

DEFINITION   Producers' Surplus

If $(\bar{x}, \bar{p})$ is a point on the graph of the price–supply equation $p = S(x)$, then the **producers' surplus, PS,** at a price level of $\bar{p}$ is

$$PS = \int_0^{\bar{x}} [\bar{p} - S(x)] \, dx$$

which is the area between $p = \bar{p}$ and $p = S(x)$ from $x = 0$ to $x = \bar{x}$, as shown in the margin.

The producers' surplus represents the total gain to producers who are willing to supply units at a lower price than $\bar{p}$ but are still able to supply units at $\bar{p}$.

EXAMPLE 5 **Producers' Surplus** Find the producers' surplus at a price level of $20 for the price–supply equation

$$p = S(x) = 2 + 0.0002x^2$$

Solution   **Step 1.** Find $\bar{x}$, the supply when the price is $\bar{p} = 20$:

$$\bar{p} = 2 + 0.0002\bar{x}^2$$
$$20 = 2 + 0.0002\bar{x}^2$$
$$0.0002\bar{x}^2 = 18$$
$$\bar{x}^2 = 90,000$$
$$\bar{x} = 300 \qquad \text{There is only one solution since } \bar{x} \geq 0.$$

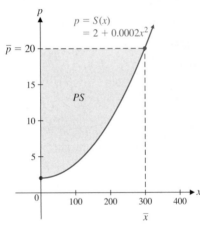

FIGURE 9

Step 2. Sketch a graph, as shown in Figure 9.

Step 3. Find the producers' surplus (the shaded area in the graph):

$$PS = \int_0^{\bar{x}} [\bar{p} - S(x)] \, dx = \int_0^{300} [20 - (2 + 0.0002x^2)] \, dx$$

$$= \int_0^{300} (18 - 0.0002x^2) \, dx = \left(18x - 0.0002\frac{x^3}{3} \right)\Big|_0^{300}$$

$$= 5,400 - 1,800 = \$3,600$$

Thus, the total gain to producers who are willing to supply units at a lower price is $3,600.

Matched Problem 5   Repeat Example 5 for a price level of $4.

In a free competitive market, the price of a product is determined by the relationship between supply and demand. If $p = D(x)$ and $p = S(x)$ are the price–demand and price–supply equations, respectively, for a product and if $(\bar{x}, \bar{p})$ is the point of intersection of these equations, $\bar{p}$ is called the **equilibrium price** and $\bar{x}$ is called the **equilibrium quantity.** If the price stabilizes at the equilibrium price $\bar{p}$, this is the price level that will determine both the consumers' surplus and the producers' surplus.

EXAMPLE 6 **Equilibrium Price and Consumers' and Producers' Surplus**
Find the equilibrium price and then find the consumers' surplus and producers' surplus at the equilibrium price level if

$$p = D(x) = 20 - 0.05x \quad \text{and} \quad p = S(x) = 2 + 0.0002x^2$$

Solution   **Step 1.** Find the equilibrium point. Set $D(x)$ equal to $S(x)$ and solve:

$$D(x) = S(x)$$
$$20 - 0.05x = 2 + 0.0002x^2$$
$$0.0002x^2 + 0.05x - 18 = 0$$
$$x^2 + 250x - 90{,}000 = 0$$
$$x = 200, -450$$

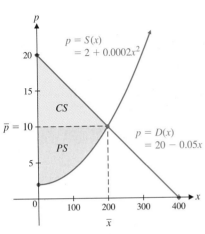

FIGURE 10

Since x cannot be negative, the only solution is $x = 200$. The equilibrium price can be determined by using $D(x)$ or $S(x)$. We will use both to check our work:

$$\bar{p} = D(200) \qquad\qquad \bar{p} = S(200)$$
$$= 20 - 0.05(200) = 10 \qquad = 2 + 0.0002(200)^2 = 10$$

Thus, the equilibrium price is $\bar{p} = 10$, and the equilibrium quantity is $\bar{x} = 200$.

Step 2. Sketch a graph, as shown in Figure 10.

Step 3. Find the consumers' surplus:

$$CS = \int_0^{\bar{x}} [D(x) - \bar{p}] \, dx$$
$$= \int_0^{200} (20 - 0.05x - 10) \, dx$$
$$= \int_0^{200} (10 - 0.05x) \, dx$$
$$= (10x - 0.025x^2)\big|_0^{200}$$
$$= 2{,}000 - 1{,}000 = \$1{,}000$$

Step 4. Find the producers' surplus:

$$PS = \int_0^{\bar{x}} [\bar{p} - S(x)] \, dx$$
$$= \int_0^{200} [10 - (2 + 0.0002x^2)] \, dx$$
$$= \int_0^{200} (8 - 0.0002x^2) \, dx$$
$$= \left(8x - 0.0002\frac{x^3}{3}\right)\Big|_0^{200}$$
$$= 1{,}600 - \tfrac{1{,}600}{3} \approx \$1{,}067 \quad \textit{Rounded to the nearest dollar}$$

A graphing utility offers an alternative approach to finding the equilibrium point for Example 6 (Fig. 11A). A numerical integration routine can then be used to find the consumers' and producers' surplus (Fig. 11B).

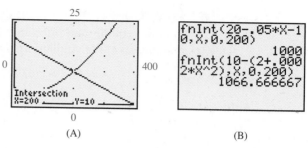

FIGURE 11

Matched Problem 6   Repeat Example 6 for

$$p = D(x) = 25 - 0.001x^2 \quad \text{and} \quad p = S(x) = 5 + 0.1x$$

Answers to Matched Problems   **1.** (A) .63   (B) 9.21 min   **2.** $33,803   **3.** FV = $34,691; interest = $7,016
4. $2,560   **5.** $133   **6.** $\bar{p}$ = 15; CS = $667; PS = $500

Exercise 7-2

A *In Problems 1–4, evaluate each definite integral to two decimal places.*

1. $\int_0^5 e^{-0.08t}\, dt$

2. $\int_0^5 e^{0.08(5-t)}\, dt$

3. $\int_0^{30} e^{0.06t} e^{0.12(30-t)}\, dt$

4. $\int_0^{20} 1,000 e^{0.03t} e^{0.15(20-t)}\, dt$

5. (A) $\int_0^8 e^{0.07(8-t)}\, dt$ (B) $\int_0^8 (e^{0.56} - e^{0.07t})\, dt$

(C) $e^{0.56} \int_0^8 e^{-0.07t}\, dt$

6. (A) $\int_0^{10} 2,000 e^{0.05t} e^{0.12(10-t)}\, dt$

(B) $2,000 e^{1.2} \int_0^{10} e^{-0.07t}\, dt$

(C) $2,000 e^{0.05} \int_0^{10} e^{0.12(10-t)}\, dt$

B *In Problems 5 and 6, explain which of (A), (B), and (C) are equal before evaluating the expressions. Then evaluate each expression to two decimal places.*

Applications

Business & Economics

Unless stated to the contrary, compute all monetary answers to the nearest dollar.

7. The life expectancy (in years) of a certain brand of clock radio is a continuous random variable with probability density function

$$f(x) = \begin{cases} 2/(x+2)^2 & \text{if } x \ge 0 \\ 0 & \text{otherwise} \end{cases}$$

(A) Find the probability that a randomly selected clock radio lasts at most 6 years.

(B) Find the probability that a randomly selected clock radio lasts from 6 to 12 years.

(C) Graph $y = f(x)$ for [0, 12] and show the shaded region for part (A).

8. The shelf life (in years) of a certain brand of flashlight batteries is a continuous random variable with probability density function

$$f(x) = \begin{cases} 1/(x+1)^2 & \text{if } x \ge 0 \\ 0 & \text{otherwise} \end{cases}$$

(A) Find the probability that a randomly selected battery has a shelf life of 3 years or less.

(B) Find the probability that a randomly selected battery has a shelf life of from 3 to 9 years.

(C) Graph $y = f(x)$ for [0, 10] and show the shaded region for part (A).

9. In Problem 7, find d so that the probability of a randomly selected clock radio lasting d years or less is .8.

10. In Problem 8, find d so that the probability of a randomly selected battery lasting d years or less is .5.

11. A manufacturer guarantees a product for 1 year. The time to failure of the product after it is sold is given by the probability density function

$$f(t) = \begin{cases} .01e^{-.01t} & \text{if } t \geq 0 \\ 0 & \text{otherwise} \end{cases}$$

where t is time in months. What is the probability that a buyer chosen at random will have a product failure:

(A) During the warranty period?

(B) During the second year after purchase?

12. In a certain city, the daily use of water (in hundreds of gallons) per household is a continuous random variable with probability density function

$$f(x) = \begin{cases} .15e^{-.15x} & \text{if } x \geq 0 \\ 0 & \text{otherwise} \end{cases}$$

Find the probability that a household chosen at random will use:

(A) At most 400 gallons of water per day

(B) Between 300 and 600 gallons of water per day

13. In Problem 11, what is the probability that the product will last at least 1 year? [*Hint:*   Recall that the total area under the probability density function curve is 1.]

14. In Problem 12, what is the probability that a household will use more than 400 gallons of water per day? [See the hint in Problem 13.]

15. Find the total income produced by a continuous income stream in the first 5 years if the rate of flow is $f(t) = 2,500$.

16. Find the total income produced by a continuous income stream in the first 10 years if the rate of flow is $f(t) = 3,000$.

17. Interpret the results in Problem 15 with both a graph and a verbal description of the graph.

18. Interpret the results in Problem 16 with both a graph and a verbal description of the graph.

19. Find the total income produced by a continuous income stream in the first 3 years if the rate of flow is $f(t) = 400e^{0.05t}$.

20. Find the total income produced by a continuous income stream in the first 2 years if the rate of flow is $f(t) = 600e^{0.06t}$.

21. Interpret the results in Problem 19 with both a graph and a verbal description of the graph.

22. Interpret the results in Problem 20 with both a graph and a verbal description of the graph.

23. Starting at age 25, you deposit $2,000 a year into an IRA account for retirement. Treat the yearly deposits into the account as a continuous income stream. If money in the account earns 5% compounded continuously, how much will be in the account 40 years later when you retire at age 65? How much of the final amount is interest?

24. Suppose in Problem 23 that you start the IRA deposits at age 30, but the account earns 6% compounded continuously. Treat the yearly deposits into the account as a continuous income stream. How much will be in the account 35 years later when you retire at age 65? How much of the final amount is interest?

25. Find the future value at 6.25% interest compounded continuously for 4 years for the continuous income stream with rate of flow $f(t) = 1,650e^{-0.02t}$.

26. Find the future value at 5.75% interest compounded continuously for 6 years for the continuous income stream with rate of flow $f(t) = 2,000e^{0.06t}$.

27. Compute the interest earned in Problem 25.

28. Compute the interest earned in Problem 26.

29. An investor is presented with a choice of two investments, an established clothing store and a new computer store. Each choice requires the same initial investment and each produces a continuous income stream of 10% compounded continuously. The rate of flow of income from the clothing store is $f(t) = 12,000$, and the rate of flow of income from the computer store is expected to be $g(t) = 10,000e^{0.05t}$. Compare the future values of these investments to determine which is the better choice over the next 5 years.

30. Refer to Problem 29. Which investment is the better choice over the next 10 years?

31. An investor has $10,000 to invest in either a bond that matures in 5 years or a business that will produce a continuous stream of income over the next 5 years with rate of flow $f(t) = 2,000$. If both the bond and the continuous income stream earn 8% compounded continuously, which is the better investment?

32. Refer to Problem 31. Which is the better investment if the rate of the income from the business is $f(t) = 3,000$?

33. A business is planning to purchase a piece of equipment that will produce a continuous stream of income for 8 years with rate of flow $f(t) = 9,000$. If the continuous income stream earns 6.95% compounded continuously, what single deposit into an account earning the same interest rate will produce the same future value as the continuous income stream? (This deposit is called the **present value** of the continuous income stream.)

34. Refer to Problem 33. Find the present value of a continuous income stream at 7.65% compounded continuously for 12 years if the rate of flow is $f(t) = 1{,}000e^{0.03t}$.

35. Find the future value at a rate r compounded continuously for T years for a continuous income stream with rate of flow $f(t) = k$, where k is a constant.

36. Find the future value at a rate r compounded continuously for T years for a continuous income stream with rate of flow $f(t) = ke^{ct}$, where c and k are constants, $c \neq r$.

37. Find the consumers' surplus at a price level of $\bar{p} = \$150$ for the price–demand equation

$$p = D(x) = 400 - 0.05x$$

38. Find the consumers' surplus at a price level of $\bar{p} = \$120$ for the price–demand equation

$$p = D(x) = 200 - 0.02x$$

39. Interpret the results in Problem 37 with both a graph and a verbal description of the graph.

40. Interpret the results in Problem 38 with both a graph and a verbal description of the graph.

41. Find the producers' surplus at a price level of $\bar{p} = \$67$ for the price–supply equation

$$p = S(x) = 10 + 0.1x + 0.0003x^2$$

42. Find the producers' surplus at a price level of $\bar{p} = \$55$ for the price–supply equation

$$p = S(x) = 15 + 0.1x + 0.003x^2$$

43. Interpret the results in Problem 41 with both a graph and a verbal description of the graph.

44. Interpret the results in Problem 42 with both a graph and a verbal description of the graph.

In Problems 45–52, find the consumers' surplus and the producers' surplus at the equilibrium price level for the given price–demand and price–supply equations. Include a graph that identifies the consumers' surplus

and the producers' surplus. Round all values to the nearest integer.

45. $p = D(x) = 50 - 0.1x; p = S(x) = 11 + 0.05x$

46. $p = D(x) = 25 - 0.004x^2; p = S(x) = 5 + 0.004x^2$

47. $p = D(x) = 80e^{-0.001x}; p = S(x) = 30e^{0.001x}$

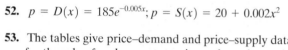

48. $p = D(x) = 185e^{-0.005x}; p = S(x) = 25e^{0.005x}$

49. $p = D(x) = 80 - 0.04x; p = S(x) = 30e^{0.001x}$

50. $p = D(x) = 190 - 0.2x; p = S(x) = 25e^{0.005x}$

51. $p = D(x) = 80e^{-0.001x}; p = S(x) = 15 + 0.0001x^2$

52. $p = D(x) = 185e^{-0.005x}; p = S(x) = 20 + 0.002x^2$

53. The tables give price–demand and price–supply data for the sale of soybeans at a grain market, where x is the number of bushels of soybeans (in thousands of bushels) and p is the price per bushel (in dollars):

Price–Demand		Price–Supply	
x	$p = D(x)$	x	$p = S(x)$
0	6.70	0	6.43
10	6.59	10	6.45
20	6.52	20	6.48
30	6.47	30	6.53
40	6.45	40	6.62

Use quadratic regression to model the price–demand data and linear regression to model the price–supply data.

(A) Find the equilibrium quantity (to three decimal places) and equilibrium price (to the nearest cent).

(B) Use a numerical integration routine to find the consumers' surplus and producers' surplus at the equilibrium price level.

54. Repeat Problem 53 using quadratic regression to model both sets of data.

Section 7-3   Integration by Parts

In Section 6-1 we said we would return later to the indefinite integral

$$\int \ln x \, dx$$

since none of the integration techniques considered up to that time could be used to find an antiderivative for $\ln x$. We now develop a very useful technique, called *integration by parts,* that will enable us to find not only the preceding integral, but also many others, including integrals such as

$$\int x \ln x \, dx \qquad \text{and} \qquad \int xe^x \, dx$$

The technique of integration by parts is also used to derive many integration formulas that are tabulated in mathematical handbooks. Some of these handbook formulas are discussed in the next section.

The method of integration by parts is based on the product formula for derivatives. If f and g are differentiable functions, then

$$\frac{d}{dx}[f(x)g(x)] = f(x)g'(x) + g(x)f'(x)$$

which can be written in the equivalent form

$$f(x)g'(x) = \frac{d}{dx}[f(x)g(x)] - g(x)f'(x)$$

Integrating both sides, we obtain

$$\int f(x)g'(x)\, dx = \int \frac{d}{dx}[f(x)g(x)]\, dx - \int g(x)f'(x)\, dx$$

The first integral to the right of the equal sign is $f(x)g(x) + C$. (Why?) We will leave out the constant of integration for now, since we can add it after integrating the second integral to the right of the equal sign. So we have

$$\int f(x)g'(x)\, dx = f(x)g(x) - \int g(x)f'(x)\, dx$$

This equation can be transformed into a more convenient form by letting $u = f(x)$ and $v = g(x)$; then $du = f'(x)\, dx$ and $dv = g'(x)\, dx$. Making these substitutions, we obtain the **integration by parts formula:**

FORMULA   Integration by Parts

$$\int u\, dv = uv - \int v\, du$$

This formula can be very useful when the integral on the left is difficult or impossible to integrate using standard formulas. If u and dv are chosen with care—this is the crucial part of the process—then the integral on the right side may be easier to integrate than the one on the left. The formula provides us with another tool that is helpful in many, but not all, cases. We are able to easily check the results by differentiating to get the original integrand, a good habit to develop. Several examples will demonstrate the use of the formula.

EXAMPLE 1   **Integration by Parts**   Find $\int xe^x\, dx$ using integration by parts and check the result.

Solution   First, write the integration by parts formula:

$$\int u\, dv = uv - \int v\, du \qquad (1)$$

Now try to identify u and dv in $\int xe^x\, dx$ so that the integral $\int v\, du$ on the right side of (1) is easier to integrate than $\int u\, dv = \int xe^x\, dx$ on the left side. There are essentially two reasonable choices in selecting u and dv in $\int xe^x\,dx$:

$$
\begin{array}{cc}
\text{Choice 1} & \text{Choice 2} \\
\overset{u}{\frown}\overset{dv}{\frown} & \overset{u}{\frown}\overset{dv}{\frown} \\
\int x\,e^x\,dx & \int e^x\,x\,dx
\end{array}
$$

We pursue choice 1 and leave choice 2 for you to explore (see Explore–Discuss 1 following this example).

From choice 1, $u = x$ and $dv = e^x\,dx$. Looking at formula (1), we need du and v to complete the right side. It is convenient to proceed with the following arrangement: Let

$$u = x \qquad dv = e^x\,dx$$

Then

$$du = dx \qquad \int dv = \int e^x\,dx$$
$$v = e^x$$

Any constant may be added to v, but we will always choose 0 for simplicity. The general arbitrary constant of integration will be added at the end of the process.

Substituting these results in formula (1), we obtain

$$\int u\,dv = uv - \int v\,du$$

$$\int xe^x\,dx = xe^x - \int e^x\,dx \quad \text{The right integral is easy to integrate.}$$

$$= xe^x - e^x + C \quad \text{Now add the arbitrary constant C.}$$

Check: $\dfrac{d}{dx}(xe^x - e^x + C) = xe^x + e^x - e^x = xe^x$ ■

EXPLORE & DISCUSS 1

Pursue choice 2 in Example 1 using the integration by parts formula, and explain why this choice does not work out.

Matched Problem 1   Find: $\int xe^{2x}\,dx$ ———————■

EXAMPLE 2   **Integration by Parts**   Find: $\int x \ln x\,dx$

Solution   As before, we have essentially two choices in choosing u and dv:

$$
\begin{array}{cc}
\text{Choice 1} & \text{Choice 2} \\
\overset{u}{\frown}\overset{dv}{\frown} & \overset{u}{\frown}\overset{dv}{\frown} \\
\int x \ln x\,dx & \int \ln x\,x\,dx
\end{array}
$$

Choice 1 is rejected, since we do not yet know how to find an antiderivative of $\ln x$. So we move to choice 2 and choose $u = \ln x$ and $dv = x\,dx$; then proceed as in Example 1. Let

$$u = \ln x \qquad dv = x\,dx$$

Then

$$du = \frac{1}{x}dx \qquad \int dv = \int x\,dx$$

$$v = \frac{x^2}{2}$$

Substitute these results into the integration by parts formula:

$$\int u\,dv = uv - \int v\,du$$

$$\int x \ln x\,dx = (\ln x)\left(\frac{x^2}{2}\right) - \int \left(\frac{x^2}{2}\right)\left(\frac{1}{x}\right)dx$$

$$= \frac{x^2}{2}\ln x - \int \frac{x}{2}dx \quad \text{An easy integral to evaluate}$$

$$= \frac{x^2}{2}\ln x - \frac{x^2}{4} + C$$

Check: $\dfrac{d}{dx}\left(\dfrac{x^2}{2}\ln x - \dfrac{x^2}{4} + C\right) = x \ln x + \left(\dfrac{x^2}{2}\cdot\dfrac{1}{x}\right) - \dfrac{x}{2} = x \ln x$ ∎

Matched Problem 2 Find: $\int x \ln 2x\,dx$

◎ Insight As you should have discovered in Explore–Discuss 1, some choices for u and dv will lead to integrals that are more complicated than the original integral. This does not mean that there is an error in the calculations or the integration by parts formula. It simply means that the particular choice of u and dv does not change the problem into one we can solve. When this happens, we must look for a different choice of u and dv. In some problems, it is possible that no choice will work.   ●

Guidelines for selecting u and dv for integration by parts are summarized in the following box.

SUMMARY **Integration by Parts: Selection of u and dv**

For $\int u\,dv = uv - \int v\,du$,

1. The product $u\,dv$ must equal the original integrand.
2. It must be possible to integrate dv (preferably by using standard formulas or simple substitutions).
3. The new integral $\int v\,du$ should not be more complicated than the original integral $\int u\,dv$.
4. For integrals involving $x^p e^{ax}$, try

$$u = x^p \qquad \text{and} \qquad dv = e^{ax}\,dx$$

5. For integrals involving $x^p(\ln x)^q$, try

$$u = (\ln x)^q \qquad \text{and} \qquad dv = x^p\,dx$$

In some cases, repeated use of the integration by parts formula will lead to the evaluation of the original integral. The next example provides an illustration of such a case.

EXAMPLE 3 **Repeated Use of Integration by Parts** Find: $\int x^2 e^{-x}\, dx$

Solution Following suggestion 4 in the box, we choose

$$u = x^2 \qquad dv = e^{-x}\, dx$$

Then

$$du = 2x\, dx \qquad v = -e^{-x}$$

and

$$x^2 e^{-x}\, dx = x^2(-e^{-x}) - (-e^{-x})2x\, dx$$
$$= -x^2 e^{-x} + 2xe^{-x}\, dx \qquad\qquad (2)$$

The new integral is not one we can evaluate by standard formulas, but it is simpler than the original integral. Applying the integration by parts formula to it will produce an even simpler integral. For the integral $\int xe^{-x}\, dx$, we choose

$$u = x \qquad dv = e^{-x}\, dx$$

Then

$$du = dx \qquad v = -e^{-x}$$

and

$$\int xe^{-x}\, dx = x(-e^{-x}) - \int (-e^{-x})\, dx$$

$$= -xe^{-x} + \int e^{-x}\, dx$$

$$= -xe^{-x} - e^{-x} \quad \textit{Choose 0 for the constant.} \qquad (3)$$

Substituting equation (3) into equation (2), we have

$$\int x^2 e^{-x}\, dx = -x^2 e^{-x} + 2(-xe^{-x} - e^{-x}) + C \quad \begin{array}{l}\textit{Add an arbitrary}\\ \textit{constant here.}\end{array}$$
$$= -x^2 e^{-x} - 2xe^{-x} - 2e^{-x} + C$$

Check: $\dfrac{d}{dx}(-x^2 e^{-x} - 2xe^{-x} - 2e^{-x} + C) = x^2 e^{-x} - 2xe^{-x} + 2xe^{-x} - 2e^{-x} + 2e^{-x}$

$$= x^2 e^{-x} \qquad\qquad \blacksquare$$

Matched Problem 3 Find: $\int x^2 e^{2x}\, dx$

EXAMPLE 4 **Using Integration by Parts** Find $\int_1^e \ln x\, dx$ and interpret geometrically.

Solution First, we will find $\int \ln x\, dx$, and then return to the definite integral. Following suggestion 5 in the box (with $p = 0$), we choose

$$u = \ln x \qquad dv = dx$$

Then

$$du = \frac{1}{x}\, dx \qquad v = x$$

Hence,

$$\int \ln x \, dx = (\ln x)(x) - \int (x)\frac{1}{x} dx$$

$$= x \ln x - x + C$$

Note that this is the important result we mentioned at the beginning of this section. Now, we have

$$\int_1^e \ln x \, dx = (x \ln x - x)\Big|_1^e$$

$$= (e \ln e - e) - (1 \ln 1 - 1)$$

$$= (e - e) - (0 - 1)$$

$$= 1$$

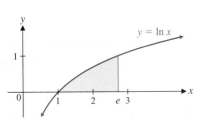

y = ln x

FIGURE 1

The integral represents the area under the curve $y = \ln x$ from $x = 1$ to $x = e$, as shown in Figure 1. ■

Matched Problem 4 Find: $\int_1^2 \ln 3x \, dx$ ──────────■

EXPLORE
&DISCUSS
2

Try using the integration by parts formula for $\int e^{x^2} dx$ and explain why it does not solve the problem.

Answers to Matched Problems   **1.** $\dfrac{x}{2}e^{2x} - \dfrac{1}{4}e^{2x} + C$ **2.** $\dfrac{x^2}{2}\ln 2x - \dfrac{x^2}{4} + C$

3. $\dfrac{x^2}{2}e^{2x} - \dfrac{x}{2}e^{2x} + \dfrac{1}{4}e^{2x} + C$ **4.** $2 \ln 6 - \ln 3 - 1 \approx 1.4849$

Exercise 7-3

A *In Problems 1–4, integrate using the method of integration by parts. Assume that x > 0 whenever the natural logarithm function is involved.*

1. $\displaystyle\int xe^{3x} \, dx$ **2.** $\displaystyle\int xe^{4x} \, dx$

3. $\displaystyle\int x^2 \ln x \, dx$ **4.** $\displaystyle\int x^3 \ln x \, dx$

B

5. If you want to use integration by parts to find $\int (x + 1)^5(x + 2) \, dx$, which is the better choice for u: $u = (x + 1)^5$ or $u = x + 2$? Explain your choice, and then integrate.

6. If you want to use integration by parts to find $\int (5x - 7)(x - 1)^4 \, dx$, which is the better choice for u: $u = 5x - 7$ or $u = (x - 1)^4$? Explain your choice, and then integrate.

Problems 7–20 are mixed—some require integration by parts and others can be solved using techniques we have considered earlier. Integrate as indicated, assuming x > 0 whenever the natural logarithm function is involved.

7. $\displaystyle\int xe^{-x} \, dx$

8. $\displaystyle\int (x - 1)e^{-x} \, dx$

9. $\displaystyle\int xe^{x^2} \, dx$

10. $\displaystyle\int xe^{-x^2} \, dx$

11. $\displaystyle\int_0^1 (x - 3)e^x \, dx$

12. $\displaystyle\int_0^1 (x + 1)e^x \, dx$

13. $\displaystyle\int_1^3 \ln 2x \, dx$

14. $\displaystyle\int_1^2 \ln\left(\frac{x}{2}\right) dx$

15. $\displaystyle\int \frac{2x}{x^2 + 1} dx$

16. $\displaystyle\int \frac{x^2}{x^3 + 5} dx$

17. $\displaystyle\int \frac{\ln x}{x} dx$

18. $\displaystyle\int \frac{e^x}{e^x + 1} dx$

19. $\displaystyle\int \sqrt{x} \ln x \, dx$

20. $\displaystyle\int \frac{\ln x}{\sqrt{x}} dx$

In Problems 21–24, illustrate each integral graphically and describe what the integral represents in terms of areas.

21. Problem 11

22. Problem 12

23. Problem 13

24. Problem 14

C

Problems 25–42 are mixed—some may require use of the integration by parts formula along with techniques we have considered earlier; others may require repeated use of the integration by parts formula. Assume that $g(x) > 0$ whenever $\ln g(x)$ is involved.

25. $\displaystyle\int x^2 e^x \, dx$

26. $\displaystyle\int x^3 e^x \, dx$

27. $\displaystyle\int x e^{ax} \, dx, a \neq 0$

28. $\displaystyle\int \ln(ax) \, dx, a > 0$

29. $\displaystyle\int_1^e \frac{\ln x}{x^2} \, dx$

30. $\displaystyle\int_1^2 x^3 e^{x^2} \, dx$

31. $\displaystyle\int_0^2 \ln(x + 4) \, dx$

32. $\displaystyle\int_0^2 \ln(4 - x) \, dx$

33. $\displaystyle\int x e^{x-2} \, dx$

34. $\displaystyle\int x e^{x+1} \, dx$

35. $\displaystyle\int x \ln(1 + x^2) \, dx$

36. $\displaystyle\int x \ln(1 + x) \, dx$

37. $\displaystyle\int e^x \ln(1 + e^x) \, dx$

38. $\displaystyle\int \frac{\ln(1 + \sqrt{x})}{\sqrt{x}} \, dx$

39. $\displaystyle\int (\ln x)^2 \, dx$

40. $\displaystyle\int x(\ln x)^2 \, dx$

41. $\displaystyle\int (\ln x)^3 \, dx$

42. $\displaystyle\int x(\ln x)^3 \, dx$

In Problems 43–46, use a graphing utility to graph each equation over the indicated interval, and find the area between the curve and the x axis over that interval. Find answers to two decimal places.

43. $y = x - 2 - \ln x; 1 \leq x \leq 4$

44. $y = 6 - x^2 - \ln x; 1 \leq x \leq 4$

45. $y = 5 - x e^x; 0 \leq x \leq 3$

46. $y = x e^x + x - 6; 0 \leq x \leq 3$

Applications

Business & Economics

47. *Profit.* If the marginal profit (in millions of dollars per year) is given by

$$P'(t) = 2t - t e^{-t}$$

find the total profit earned over the first 5 years of operation (to the nearest million dollars) by use of an appropriate definite integral.

48. *Production.* An oil field is estimated to produce oil at a rate of $R(t)$ thousand barrels per month t months from now, as given by

$$R(t) = 10t e^{-0.1t}$$

Find the total production in the first year of operation (to the nearest thousand barrels) by use of an appropriate definite integral.

49. *Profit.* Interpret the results in Problem 47 with both a graph and a verbal description of the graph.

50. *Production.* Interpret the results in Problem 48 with both a graph and a verbal description of the graph.

51. *Continuous income stream.* Find the future value at 8% compounded continuously for 5 years of a continuous income stream with a rate of flow of

$$f(t) = 1,000 - 200t$$

52. *Continuous income stream.* Find the interest earned at 10% compounded continuously for 4 years for a continuous income stream with a rate of flow of

$$f(t) = 1,000 - 250t$$

53. *Income distribution.* Find the Gini index of income concentration for the Lorenz curve with equation

$$y = x e^{x-1}$$

54. *Income distribution.* Find the Gini index of income concentration for the Lorenz curve with equation

$$y = x^2 e^{x-1}$$

55. *Income distribution.* Interpret the results in Problem 53 with both a graph and a verbal description of the graph.

56. *Income distribution.* Interpret the results in Problem 54 with both a graph and a verbal description of the graph.

57. *Sales analysis.* The monthly sales of a particular personal computer are expected to decline at the rate of

$$S'(t) = -4t e^{0.1t}$$

computers per month, where t is time in months and $S(t)$ is the number of computers sold each month. The company plans to stop manufacturing this computer when the monthly sales reach 800 computers. If the monthly sales now ($t = 0$) are 2,000 computers, find $S(t)$. How long, to the nearest month, will the company continue to manufacture this computer?

58. *Sales analysis.* The rate of change of the monthly sales of a new home video game cartridge is given by

$$S'(t) = 350 \ln(t + 1) \qquad S(0) = 0$$

where t is the number of months since the game was released and $S(t)$ is the number of cartridges sold each month. Find $S(t)$. When, to the nearest month, will the monthly sales reach 15,000 cartridges?

59. *Consumers' surplus.* Find the consumers' surplus (to the nearest dollar) at a price level of $\overline{p} = \$2.089$ for the price–demand equation

$$p = D(x) = 9 - \ln(x + 4)$$

Use $\overline{x}$ computed to the nearest higher unit.

60. *Producers' surplus.* Find the producers' surplus (to the nearest dollar) at a price level of $\overline{p} = \$26$ for the price–supply equation

$$p = S(x) = 5 \ln(x + 1)$$

Use $\overline{x}$ computed to the nearest higher unit.

61. *Consumers' surplus.* Interpret the results in Problem 59 with both a graph and a verbal description of the graph.

62. *Producers' surplus.* Interpret the results in Problem 60 with both a graph and a verbal description of the graph.

Life Sciences

63. *Pollution.* The concentration of particulate matter (in parts per million) t hours after a factory ceases operation for the day is given by

$$C(t) = \frac{20 \ln(t + 1)}{(t + 1)^2}$$

Find the average concentration for the time period from $t = 0$ to $t = 5$.

64. *Medicine.* After a person takes a pill, the drug contained in the pill is assimilated into the bloodstream. The rate of assimilation t minutes after taking the pill is

$$R(t) = te^{-0.2t}$$

Find the total amount of the drug that is assimilated into the bloodstream during the first 10 minutes after the pill is taken.

Social Sciences

65. *Learning.* In a particular business college, it was found that an average student enrolled in an advanced typing class progressed at a rate of

$$N'(t) = (t + 6)e^{-0.25t}$$

words per minute per week, t weeks after enrolling in a 15-week course. If at the beginning of the course a student could type 40 words per minute, how many words per minute, $N(t)$, would the student be expected to type t weeks into the course? How long, to the nearest week, should it take the student to achieve the 70-word per minute level? How many words per minute should the student be able to type by the end of the course?

66. *Learning.* In the same business college, it was also found that an average student enrolled in a beginning shorthand class progressed at a rate of

$$N'(t) = (t + 10)e^{-0.1t}$$

words per minute per week, t weeks after enrolling in a 15-week course. If at the beginning of the course a student had no knowledge of shorthand (that is, could take dictation in shorthand at 0 words per minute), how many words per minute, $N(t)$, would the student be expected to handle t weeks into the course? How long, to the nearest week, should it take the student to achieve 90 words per minute? How many words per minute should the student be able to handle by the end of the course?

67. *Politics.* The number of voters (in thousands) in a certain city is given by

$$N(t) = 20 + 4t - 5te^{-0.1t}$$

where t is time in years. Find the average number of voters during the time period from $t = 0$ to $t = 5$.

Section **7-4**   **Integration Using Tables**

➤ Using a Table of Integrals
➤ Substitution and Integral Tables
➤ Reduction Formulas
➤ Application

A **table of integrals** is a list of integration formulas used to evaluate integrals. People who frequently evaluate complex integrals may refer to tables that contain hundreds of formulas. Tables of this type are included in mathematical handbooks available in most college bookstores. Table II of Appendix C contains a short list of integral formulas illustrating the types found in more extensive tables. Some of these formulas can be derived using the integration techniques discussed earlier, while others require techniques we have not considered. However, it is possible to verify each formula by differentiating the right side.

➤ Using a Table of Integrals

The formulas in Table II (and in larger integral tables) are organized by categories, such as "Integrals Involving $a + bu$," "Integrals Involving $\sqrt{u^2 - a^2}$," and so on. The variable u is the variable of integration. All other symbols represent constants. To use a table to evaluate an integral, you must first find the category that most closely agrees with the form of the integrand and then find a formula in that category that can be made to match the integrand exactly by assigning values to the constants in the formula. The following examples illustrate this process.

EXAMPLE 1 **Integration Using Tables** Use Table II to find

$$\int \frac{x}{(5 + 2x)(4 - 3x)}\, dx$$

Solution Since the integrand

$$f(x) = \frac{x}{(5 + 2x)(4 - 3x)}$$

is a rational function involving terms of the form $a + bu$ and $c + du$, we examine formulas 15 to 20 in Table II to see if any of the integrands in these formulas can be made to match $f(x)$ exactly. Comparing the integrand in formula 16 with $f(x)$, we see that this integrand will match $f(x)$ if we let $a = 5, b = 2, c = 4$, and $d = -3$. Letting $u = x$ and substituting for a, b, c, and d in formula 16, we have

$$\int \frac{u}{(a + bu)(c + du)}\, du = \frac{1}{ad - bc}\left(\frac{a}{b}\ln|a + bu| - \frac{c}{d}\ln|c + du|\right) \quad \text{Formula 16}$$

$$\int \frac{x}{(5 + 2x)(4 - 3x)}\, dx = \frac{1}{5\cdot(-3) - 2\cdot 4}\left(\frac{5}{2}\ln|5 + 2x| - \frac{4}{-3}\ln|4 - 3x|\right) + C$$

$$\quad a \quad b \quad c \quad d \qquad\qquad a\cdot d - b\cdot c = 5\cdot(-3) - 2\cdot 4 = -23$$

$$= -\tfrac{5}{46}\ln|5 + 2x| - \tfrac{4}{69}\ln|4 - 3x| + C$$

Notice that the constant of integration C is not included in any of the formulas in Table II. However, you must still include C in all antiderivatives. ■

Matched Problem 1 Use Table II to find $\displaystyle\int \frac{1}{(5 + 3x)^2(1 + x)}\, dx$

EXAMPLE 2 **Integration Using Tables** Evaluate: $\displaystyle\int_3^4 \frac{1}{x\sqrt{25 - x^2}}\, dx$

Solution First, we use Table II to find

$$\int \frac{1}{x\sqrt{25 - x^2}}\,dx$$

Since the integrand involves the expression $\sqrt{25 - x^2}$, we examine formulas 29 to 31 and select formula 29 with $a^2 = 25$ and $a = 5$:

$$\int \frac{1}{u\sqrt{a^2 - u^2}}\,du = -\frac{1}{a}\ln\left|\frac{a + \sqrt{a^2 - u^2}}{u}\right| \qquad \text{Formula 29}$$

$$\int \frac{1}{x\sqrt{25 - x^2}}\,dx = -\frac{1}{5}\ln\left|\frac{5 + \sqrt{25 - x^2}}{x}\right| + C$$

Thus,

$$\int_3^4 \frac{1}{x\sqrt{25 - x^2}}\,dx = -\frac{1}{5}\ln\left|\frac{5 + \sqrt{25 - x^2}}{x}\right|\Big|_3^4$$

$$= -\frac{1}{5}\ln\left|\frac{5 + 3}{4}\right| + \frac{1}{5}\ln\left|\frac{5 + 4}{3}\right|$$

$$= -\tfrac{1}{5}\ln 2 + \tfrac{1}{5}\ln 3 = \tfrac{1}{5}\ln 1.5 \approx 0.0811 \qquad \blacksquare$$

Matched Problem 2 Evaluate: $\displaystyle\int_6^8 \frac{1}{x^2\sqrt{100 - x^2}}\,dx$ _____■

➤ Substitution and Integral Tables

As Examples 1 and 2 illustrate, if the integral we want to evaluate can be made to match one in the table exactly, evaluating the indefinite integral consists of simply substituting the correct values of the constants into the formula. What happens if we cannot match an integral with one of the formulas in the table? In many cases, a substitution will change the given integral into one that corresponds to a table entry. The following examples illustrate several frequently used substitutions.

EXAMPLE 3 **Integration Using Substitution and Tables** Find: $\displaystyle\int \frac{x^2}{\sqrt{16x^2 - 25}}\,dx$

Solution In order to relate this integral to one of the formulas involving $\sqrt{u^2 - a^2}$ (formulas 40 to 45), we observe that if $u = 4x$, then

$$u^2 = 16x^2 \qquad \text{and} \qquad \sqrt{16x^2 - 25} = \sqrt{u^2 - 25}$$

Thus, we will use the substitution $u = 4x$ to change this integral into one that appears in the table:

$$\int \frac{x^2}{\sqrt{16x^2 - 25}}\,dx = \frac{1}{4}\int \frac{\frac{1}{16}u^2}{\sqrt{u^2 - 25}}\,du \qquad \begin{array}{l}\text{Substitution:}\\ u = 4x,\ du = 4\,dx,\ x = \tfrac{1}{4}u\end{array}$$

$$= \frac{1}{64}\int \frac{u^2}{\sqrt{u^2 - 25}}\,du$$

This last integral can be evaluated by using formula 44 with $a = 5$:

$$\int \frac{u^2}{\sqrt{u^2 - a^2}}\, du = \frac{1}{2}\left(u\sqrt{u^2 - a^2} + a^2 \ln|u + \sqrt{u^2 - a^2}|\right) \qquad \text{Formula 44}$$

$$\begin{aligned}
\int \frac{x^2}{\sqrt{16x^2 - 25}}\, dx &= \frac{1}{64}\int \frac{u^2}{\sqrt{u^2 - 25}}\, du & \text{Use formula 44 with } a = 5. \\
&= \tfrac{1}{128}\left(u\sqrt{u^2 - 25} + 25 \ln|u + \sqrt{u^2 - 25}|\right) + C & \text{Substitute } u = 4x. \\
&= \tfrac{1}{128}\left(4x\sqrt{16x^2 - 25} + 25 \ln|4x + \sqrt{16x^2 - 25}|\right) + C & \blacksquare
\end{aligned}$$

Matched Problem 3 Find: $\int \sqrt{9x^2 - 16}\, dx$

EXAMPLE 4 **Integration Using Substitution and Tables** Find: $\int \frac{x}{\sqrt{x^4 + 1}}\, dx$

Solution None of the formulas in the table involve fourth powers; however, if we let $u = x^2$, then

$$\sqrt{x^4 + 1} = \sqrt{u^2 + 1}$$

and this form does appear in formulas 32 to 39. Thus, we substitute $u = x^2$:

$$\int \frac{1}{\sqrt{x^4 + 1}} x\, dx = \frac{1}{2}\int \frac{1}{\sqrt{u^2 + 1}}\, du \qquad \begin{array}{l} \text{Substitution:} \\ u = x^2, du = 2x\, dx \end{array}$$

We recognize the last integral as formula 36 with $a = 1$:

$$\int \frac{1}{\sqrt{u^2 + a^2}}\, du = \ln|u + \sqrt{u^2 + a^2}| \qquad \text{Formula 36}$$

$$\begin{aligned}
\int \frac{x}{\sqrt{x^4 + 1}}\, dx &= \frac{1}{2}\int \frac{1}{\sqrt{u^2 + 1}}\, du & \text{Use formula 36 with } a = 1. \\
&= \tfrac{1}{2}\ln|u + \sqrt{u^2 + 1}| + C & \text{Substitute } u = x^2. \\
&= \tfrac{1}{2}\ln|x^2 + \sqrt{x^4 + 1}| + C & \blacksquare
\end{aligned}$$

Matched Problem 4 Find: $\int x\sqrt{x^4 + 1}\, dx$

➤ **Reduction Formulas**

EXAMPLE 5 **Using Reduction Formulas** Use Table II to find $\int x^2 e^{3x}\, dx$

Solution Since the integrand involves the function e^{3x}, we examine formulas 46–48 and conclude that formula 47 can be used for this problem. Letting $u = x, n = 2$, and $a = 3$ in formula 47, we have

$$\int u^n e^{au}\, du = \frac{u^n e^{au}}{a} - \frac{n}{a}\int u^{n-1} e^{au}\, du \qquad \text{Formula 47}$$

$$\int x^2 e^{3x}\, dx = \frac{x^2 e^{3x}}{3} - \frac{2}{3}\int xe^{3x}\, dx$$

Notice that the expression on the right still contains an integral, but the exponent of x has been reduced by 1. Formulas of this type are called **reduction formulas** and are designed to be applied repeatedly until an integral that can be evaluated is obtained. Applying formula 47 to $\int xe^{3x}\,dx$ with $n = 1$, we have

$$\int x^2 e^{3x}\,dx = \frac{x^2 e^{3x}}{3} - \frac{2}{3}\left(\frac{xe^{3x}}{3} - \frac{1}{3}\int e^{3x}\,dx\right)$$

$$= \frac{x^2 e^{3x}}{3} - \frac{2xe^{3x}}{9} + \frac{2}{9}\int e^{3x}\,dx$$

This last expression contains an integral that is easy to evaluate:

$$\int e^{3x}\,dx = \tfrac{1}{3}e^{3x}$$

After making a final substitution and adding a constant of integration, we have

$$\int x^2 e^{3x}\,dx = \frac{x^2 e^{3x}}{3} - \frac{2xe^{3x}}{9} + \frac{2}{27}e^{3x} + C$$

Matched Problem 5   Use Table II to find $\int (\ln x)^2\,dx$

➤ **Application**

EXAMPLE 6   **Producers' Surplus**   Find the producers' surplus at a price level of $20 for the price–supply equation

$$p = S(x) = \frac{5x}{500 - x}$$

Solution   **Step 1.** Find $\bar{x}$, the supply when the price is $\bar{p} = 20$:

$$\bar{p} = \frac{5\bar{x}}{500 - \bar{x}}$$

$$20 = \frac{5\bar{x}}{500 - \bar{x}}$$

$$10{,}000 - 20\bar{x} = 5\bar{x}$$

$$10{,}000 = 25\bar{x}$$

$$\bar{x} = 400$$

Step 2. Sketch a graph, as shown in Figure 1.

Step 3. Find the producers' surplus (the shaded area in the graph):

$$PS = \int_0^{\bar{x}} [\bar{p} - S(x)]\,dx$$

$$= \int_0^{400} \left(20 - \frac{5x}{500 - x}\right) dx$$

$$= \int_0^{400} \frac{10{,}000 - 25x}{500 - x}\,dx$$

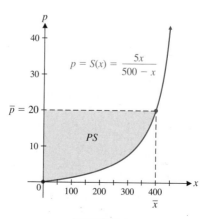

FIGURE 1

Use formula 20 with $a = 10{,}000$, $b = -25$, $c = 500$, and $d = -1$:

$$\int \frac{a + bu}{c + du}\, du = \frac{bu}{d} + \frac{ad - bc}{d^2}\, \ln|c + du| \quad \text{Formula 20}$$

$$PS = (25x + 2{,}500 \ln|500 - x|)\big|_0^{400}$$

$$= 10{,}000 + 2{,}500 \ln|100| - 2{,}500 \ln|500|$$

$$\approx \$5{,}976$$

Matched Problem 6 Find the consumers' surplus at a price level of $10 for the price–demand equation

$$p = D(x) = \frac{20x - 8{,}000}{x - 500}$$

EXPLORE &DISCUSS 1

Use algebraic manipulation, including algebraic long division, on the integrand in Example 6 to show that

$$\frac{5x}{500 - x} = \frac{-5x}{x - 500} = -5 - \frac{2{,}500}{x - 500}$$

Use this result to find the indefinite integral in Example 6 without resorting to table formulas.

Answers to Matched Problems

1. $\dfrac{1}{2}\left(\dfrac{1}{5 + 3x}\right) + \dfrac{1}{4}\ln\left|\dfrac{1 + x}{5 + 3x}\right| + C$

2. $\frac{7}{1{,}200} \approx 0.0058$

3. $\frac{1}{6}(3x\sqrt{9x^2 - 16} - 16\ln|3x + \sqrt{9x^2 - 16}|) + C$

4. $\frac{1}{4}(x^2\sqrt{x^4 + 1} + \ln|x^2 + \sqrt{x^4 + 1}|) + C$

5. $x(\ln x)^2 - 2x\ln x + 2x + C$

6. $3{,}000 + 2{,}000 \ln 200 - 2{,}000 \ln 500 \approx \$1{,}167$

Exercise 7-4

A *Use Table II to find each indefinite integral in Problems 1–14.*

1. $\displaystyle\int \frac{1}{x(1 + x)}\, dx$

2. $\displaystyle\int \frac{1}{x^2(1 + x)}\, dx$

3. $\displaystyle\int \frac{1}{(3 + x)^2(5 + 2x)}\, dx$

4. $\displaystyle\int \frac{x}{(5 + 2x)^2(2 + x)}\, dx$

5. $\displaystyle\int \frac{x}{\sqrt{16 + x}}\, dx$

6. $\displaystyle\int \frac{1}{x\sqrt{16 + x}}\, dx$

7. $\displaystyle\int \frac{1}{x\sqrt{1 - x^2}}\, dx$

8. $\displaystyle\int \frac{\sqrt{9 - x^2}}{x}\, dx$

9. $\displaystyle\int \frac{1}{x\sqrt{x^2 + 4}}\, dx$

10. $\displaystyle\int \frac{1}{x^2\sqrt{x^2 - 16}}\, dx$

11. $\displaystyle\int x^2 \ln x\, dx$

12. $\int x^3 \ln x \, dx$

13. $\int \dfrac{1}{1 + e^x} \, dx$

14. $\int \dfrac{1}{5 + 2e^{3x}} \, dx$

Evaluate each definite integral in Problems 15–20. Use Table II to find the antiderivative.

15. $\int_1^3 \dfrac{x^2}{3 + x} \, dx$

16. $\int_2^6 \dfrac{x}{(6 + x)^2} \, dx$

17. $\int_0^7 \dfrac{1}{(3 + x)(1 + x)} \, dx$

18. $\int_0^7 \dfrac{x}{(3 + x)(1 + x)} \, dx$

19. $\int_0^4 \dfrac{1}{\sqrt{x^2 + 9}} \, dx$

20. $\int_4^5 \sqrt{x^2 - 16} \, dx$

B *In Problems 21–32, use substitution techniques and Table II to find each indefinite integral.*

21. $\int \dfrac{\sqrt{4x^2 + 1}}{x^2} \, dx$

22. $\int x^2 \sqrt{9x^2 - 1} \, dx$

23. $\int \dfrac{x}{\sqrt{x^4 - 16}} \, dx$

24. $\int x \sqrt{x^4 - 16} \, dx$

25. $\int x^2 \sqrt{x^6 + 4} \, dx$

26. $\int \dfrac{x^2}{\sqrt{x^6 + 4}} \, dx$

27. $\int \dfrac{1}{x^3 \sqrt{4 - x^4}} \, dx$

28. $\int \dfrac{\sqrt{x^4 + 4}}{x} \, dx$

29. $\int \dfrac{e^x}{(2 + e^x)(3 + 4e^x)} \, dx$

30. $\int \dfrac{e^x}{(4 + e^x)^2(2 + e^x)} \, dx$

31. $\int \dfrac{\ln x}{x\sqrt{4 + \ln x}} \, dx$

32. $\int \dfrac{1}{x \ln x \sqrt{4 + \ln x}} \, dx$

C *In Problems 33–38, use Table II to find each indefinite integral.*

33. $\int x^2 e^{5x} \, dx$

34. $\int x^2 e^{-4x} \, dx$

35. $\int x^3 e^{-x} \, dx$

36. $\int x^3 e^{2x} \, dx$

37. $\int (\ln x)^3 \, dx$

38. $\int (\ln x)^4 \, dx$

Problems 39–46 are mixed—some require the use of Table II and others can be solved using techniques we considered earlier.

39. $\int_3^5 x \sqrt{x^2 - 9} \, dx$

40. $\int_3^5 x^2 \sqrt{x^2 - 9} \, dx$

41. $\int_2^4 \dfrac{1}{x^2 - 1} \, dx$

42. $\int_2^4 \dfrac{x}{(x^2 - 1)^2} \, dx$

43. $\int \dfrac{\ln x}{x^2} \, dx$

44. $\int \dfrac{(\ln x)^2}{x} \, dx$

45. $\int \dfrac{x}{\sqrt{x^2 - 1}} \, dx$

46. $\int \dfrac{x^2}{\sqrt{x^2 - 1}} \, dx$

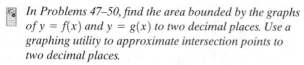

In Problems 47–50, find the area bounded by the graphs of $y = f(x)$ and $y = g(x)$ to two decimal places. Use a graphing utility to approximate intersection points to two decimal places.

47. $f(x) = \dfrac{10}{\sqrt{x^2 + 1}}; g(x) = x^2 + 3x$

48. $f(x) = \sqrt{1 + x^2}; g(x) = 5x - x^2$

49. $f(x) = x\sqrt{4 + x}; g(x) = 1 + x$

50. $f(x) = \dfrac{x}{\sqrt{x + 4}}; g(x) = x - 2$

Applications

Use Table II to evaluate all integrals involved in any solutions of Problems 51–74.

Business & Economics

51. *Consumers' surplus.* Find the consumers' surplus at a price level of $\bar{p} = \$15$ for the price–demand equation

$$p = D(x) = \frac{7{,}500 - 30x}{300 - x}$$

52. *Producers' surplus.* Find the producers' surplus at a price level of $\bar{p} = \$20$ for the price–supply equation

$$p = S(x) = \frac{10x}{300 - x}$$

53. *Consumers' surplus.* For Problem 51, graph the price–demand equation and the price level equation $\bar{p} = 15$ in the same coordinate system. What region represents the consumers' surplus?

54. *Producers' surplus.* For Problem 52, graph the price–supply equation and the price level equation $\bar{p} = 20$ in the same coordinate system. What region represents the producers' surplus?

55. *Cost.* A company manufactures downhill skis. It has fixed costs of $\$25{,}000$ and a marginal cost given by

$$C'(x) = \frac{250 + 10x}{1 + 0.05x}$$

where $C(x)$ is the total cost at an output of x pairs of skis. Find the cost function $C(x)$ and determine the production level (to the nearest unit) that produces a cost of $\$150{,}000$. What is the cost (to the nearest dollar) for a production level of 850 pairs of skis?

56. *Cost.* A company manufactures a portable CD player. It has fixed costs of $\$11{,}000$ per week and a marginal cost given by

$$C'(x) = \frac{65 + 20x}{1 + 0.4x}$$

where $C(x)$ is the total cost per week at an output of x players per week. Find the cost function $C(x)$ and determine the production level (to the nearest unit) that produces a cost of $\$52{,}000$ per week. What is the cost (to the nearest dollar) for a production level of 700 players per week?

57. *Continuous income stream.* Find the future value at 10% compounded continuously for 10 years for the

continuous income stream with rate of flow $f(t) = 50t^2$.

58. *Continuous income stream.* Find the interest earned at 8% compounded continuously for 5 years for the continuous income stream with rate of flow $f(t) = 200t$.

59. *Income distribution.* Find the Gini index of income concentration for the Lorenz curve with equation

$$y = \tfrac{1}{2}x\sqrt{1 + 3x}$$

60. *Income distribution.* Find the Gini index of income concentration for the Lorenz curve with equation

$$y = \tfrac{1}{2}x^2\sqrt{1 + 3x}$$

61. *Income distribution.* For Problem 59, graph $y = x$ and the Lorenz curve over the interval $[0, 1]$. Discuss the effect of the area bounded by $y = x$ and the Lorenz curve getting smaller relative to the equitable distribution of income.

62. *Income distribution.* For Problem 60, graph $y = x$ and the Lorenz curve over the interval $[0, 1]$. Discuss the effect of the area bounded by $y = x$ and the Lorenz curve getting larger relative to the equitable distribution of income.

63. *Marketing.* After test marketing a new high-fiber cereal, the market research department of a major food producer estimates that monthly sales (in millions of dollars) will grow at the monthly rate of

$$S'(t) = \frac{t^2}{(1 + t)^2}$$

t months after the cereal is introduced. If we assume 0 sales at the time the cereal is introduced, find the total sales, $S(t)$, t months after the cereal is introduced. Find the total sales during the first 2 years this cereal is on the market.

64. *Average price.* At a discount department store, the price–demand equation for premium motor oil is given by

$$p = D(x) = \frac{50}{\sqrt{100 + 6x}}$$

where x is the number of cans of oil that can be sold at a price of $\$p$. Find the average price over the demand interval $[50, 250]$.

65. *Marketing.* In Problem 63, show the sales over the first 2 years geometrically, and verbally describe the geometric representation.

66. *Price–demand.* In Problem 64, graph the price–demand equation and the line representing the average price in the same coordinate system over the interval $[50, 250]$. Describe how the areas under the two curves over the interval $[50, 250]$ are related.

67. *Profit.* The marginal profit for a small car agency that sells x cars per week is given by

$$P'(x) = x\sqrt{2 + 3x}$$

where $P(x)$ is the profit in dollars. The agency's profit on the sale of only 1 car per week is $-\$2,000$. Find the profit function and the number of cars that must be sold (to the nearest unit) to produce a profit of $\$13,000$ per week. How much weekly profit (to the nearest dollar) will the agency have if 80 cars are sold per week?

68. *Revenue.* The marginal revenue for a company that manufactures and sells x solar-powered calculators per week is given by

$$R'(x) = \frac{x}{\sqrt{1 + 2x}} \qquad R(0) = 0$$

where $R(x)$ is the revenue in dollars. Find the revenue function and the number of calculators that must be sold (to the nearest unit) to produce $\$10,000$ in revenue per week. How much weekly revenue (to the nearest dollar) will the company have if 1,000 calculators are sold per week?

Life Sciences

69. *Pollution.* An oil tanker aground on a reef is losing oil and producing an oil slick that is radiating outward at a rate given approximately by

$$\frac{dR}{dt} = \frac{100}{\sqrt{t^2 + 9}} \qquad t \geq 0$$

where R is the radius (in feet) of the circular slick after t minutes. Find the radius of the slick after 4 minutes if the radius is 0 when $t = 0$.

70. *Pollution.* The concentration of particulate matter (in parts per million) during a 24-hour period is given approximately by

$$C(t) = t\sqrt{24 - t} \qquad 0 \leq t \leq 24$$

where t is time in hours. Find the average concentration during the time period from $t = 0$ to $t = 24$.

Social Sciences

71. *Learning.* A person learns N items at a rate given approximately by

$$N'(t) = \frac{60}{\sqrt{t^2 + 25}} \qquad t \geq 0$$

where t is the number of hours of continuous study. Determine the total number of items learned in the first 12 hours of continuous study.

72. *Politics.* The number of voters (in thousands) in a metropolitan area is given approximately by

$$f(t) = \frac{500}{2 + 3e^{-t}} \qquad t \geq 0$$

where t is time in years. Find the average number of voters during the time period from $t = 0$ to $t = 10$.

73. *Learning.* Interpret Problem 71 geometrically. Verbally describe the geometric interpretation.

74. *Politics.* In Problem 72, graph $y = f(t)$ and the line representing the average number of voters over the interval $[0, 10]$ in the same coordinate system. Describe how the areas under the two curves over the interval $[0, 10]$ are related.

Chapter 7 Review

Important Terms, Symbols, and Concepts

7-1 Area Between Curves

If f and g are continuous and $f(x) \geq g(x)$ over the interval $[a, b]$, then the area bounded by $y = f(x)$ and $y = g(x)$ for $a \leq x \leq b$ is given exactly by

$$A = \int_a^b [f(x) - g(x)]\, dx$$

A graphical representation of the distribution of income among a population can be obtained by plotting data points (x, y), where **x represents the cumulative percentage of families at or below a given income level** and **y represents the cumulative percentage of total family income received.** Regression analysis can be used to find a particular function $y = f(x)$, called a **Lorenz curve,** that best fits the data. A single number, the **Gini index,** measures index concentration:

$$\text{Gini index} = 2 \int_0^1 [x - f(x)]\, dx$$

A Gini index of 0 indicates **absolute equality**—all families share equally in the income. A Gini index of 1 indicates **absolute inequality**—one family has all of the income and the rest have none.

7-2 Applications in Business and Economics

- **Probability Density Functions.**   If any real number x in an interval is a possible outcome of an experiment, then x is said to be a **continuous random variable.** The probability distribution of a continuous random variable is described by a **probability density function** f that satisfies

  1. $f(x) \geq 0$ for all real x.
  2. The area under the graph of $f(x)$ over the interval $(-\infty, \infty)$ is exactly 1.
  3. If $[c, d]$ is a subinterval of $(-\infty, \infty)$, then

  $$\text{Probability } (c \leq x \leq d) = \int_c^d f(x)\, dx$$

- **Continuous Income Stream**   If the rate at which income is received—its **rate of flow**—is a continuous function $f(t)$ of time, then the income is said to be a **continuous income stream.** The **total income** produced by a continuous income stream from $t = a$ to $t = b$ is

  $$\text{Total income} = \int_a^b f(t)\, dt$$

  The **future value** of a continuous income stream that is invested at rate r, compounded continuously, for $0 \leq t \leq T$, is

  $$FV = \int_0^T f(t) e^{r(T-t)}\, dt$$

- **Consumers' and Producers' Surplus**   If $(\bar{x}, \bar{p})$ is a point on the graph of a price–demand equation $p = D(x)$, then the **consumers' surplus** at a price level of $\bar{p}$ is

  $$CS = \int_0^{\bar{x}} [D(x) - \bar{p}]\, dx$$

  The consumers' surplus represents the total savings to consumers who are willing to pay more than $\bar{p}$ but are still able to buy the product for $\bar{p}$.

  Similarly, for a point $(\bar{x}, \bar{p})$ on the graph of a price–supply equation $p = S(x)$, the **producers' surplus** at a price level of $\bar{p}$ is

  $$PS = \int_0^{\bar{x}} [\bar{p} - S(x)]\, dx$$

  The producers' surplus represents the total gain to producers who are willing to supply units at a lower price $\bar{p}$ but are still able to supply units at $\bar{p}$.

  If $(\bar{x}, \bar{p})$ is the intersection point of a price–demand equation $p = D(x)$ and a price–supply equation $p = S(x)$, then $\bar{p}$ is called the **equilibrium price** and $\bar{x}$ is called the **equilibrium quantity.**

7-3 Integration by Parts

Some indefinite integrals, but not all, can be found by means of the **integration by parts formula**

$$\int u\, dv = uv - \int v\, du$$

Select u and dv with the help of the following guidelines:

1. The product $u\, dv$ must equal the original integrand.
2. It must be possible to integrate dv (preferably by using standard formulas or simple substitutions).
3. The new integral $\int v\, du$ should not be more complicated than the original integral $\int u\, dv$.
4. For integrals involving $x^p e^{ax}$, try

   $$u = x^p \quad \text{and} \quad dv = e^{ax}\, dx$$

5. For integrals involving $x^p (\ln x)^q$, try

   $$u = (\ln x)^q \quad \text{and} \quad dv = x^p\, dx$$

7-4 Integration Using Tables

A **table of integrals** is a list of integration formulas that can be used to find indefinite or definite integrals of frequently encountered functions. Such a list appears in Table II of Appendix C.

Review Exercise

Work through all the problems in this chapter review and check your answers in the back of the book. Answers to all review problems are there along with section numbers in italics to indicate where each type of problem is discussed. Where weaknesses show up, review appropriate sections in the text.

Compute all numerical answers to three decimal places unless directed otherwise.

A *In Problems 1–3, set up definite integrals that represent the shaded areas in the figure over the indicated intervals.*

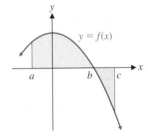

1. Interval $[a, b]$

2. Interval $[b, c]$

3. Interval $[a, c]$

4. Sketch a graph of the area between the graphs of $y = \ln x$ and $y = 0$ over the interval $[0.5, e]$, and find the area.

In Problems 5–10, evaluate each integral.

5. $\displaystyle\int xe^{4x}\, dx$

6. $\displaystyle\int x \ln x\, dx$

7. $\displaystyle\int \frac{\ln x}{x}\, dx$

8. $\displaystyle\int \frac{x}{1 + x^2}\, dx$

9. $\displaystyle\int \frac{1}{x(1 + x)^2}\, dx$

10. $\displaystyle\int \frac{1}{x^2\sqrt{1 + x}}\, dx$

B *In Problems 11–14, set up definite integrals that represent the shaded areas in the figure over the indicated intervals.*

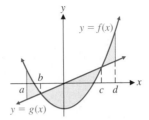

11. Interval $[a, b]$

12. Interval $[b, c]$

13. Interval $[b, d]$

14. Interval $[a, d]$

15. Sketch a graph of the area bounded by the graphs of $y = x^2 - 6x + 9$ and $y = 9 - x$, and find the area.

In Problems 16–21, evaluate each integral.

16. $\displaystyle\int_0^1 xe^x\, dx$

17. $\displaystyle\int_0^3 \frac{x^2}{\sqrt{x^2 + 16}}\, dx$

18. $\displaystyle\int \sqrt{9x^2 - 49}\, dx$

19. $\displaystyle\int te^{-0.5t}\, dt$

20. $\displaystyle\int x^2 \ln x\, dx$

21. $\displaystyle\int \frac{1}{1 + 2e^x}\, dx$

22. Sketch a graph of the area bounded by the indicated graphs and find the area. In part (B), approximate intersection points and area to two decimal places.

   (A) $y = x^3 - 6x^2 + 9x;\ y = x$

   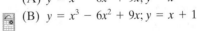 (B) $y = x^3 - 6x^2 + 9x;\ y = x + 1$

C *In Problems 23–30, evaluate each integral.*

23. $\displaystyle\int \frac{(\ln x)^2}{x}\, dx$

24. $\displaystyle\int x(\ln x)^2\, dx$

25. $\displaystyle\int \frac{x}{\sqrt{x^2 - 36}}\, dx$

26. $\displaystyle\int \frac{x}{\sqrt{x^4 - 36}}\, dx$

27. $\displaystyle\int_0^4 x \ln(10 - x)\, dx$

28. $\int (\ln x)^2 \, dx$

29. $\int x e^{-2x^2} \, dx$

30. $\int x^2 e^{-2x} \, dx$

31. Use a numerical integration routine on a graphing utility to find the area (to three decimal places) in the first quadrant that is below the graph of

$$y = \frac{6}{2 + 5e^{-x}}$$

and above the graph of $y = 0.2x + 1.6$.

Applications

Business & Economics

32. *Product warranty.* A manufacturer warrants a product for parts and labor for 1 year, and for parts only for a second year. The time to a failure of the product after it is sold is given by the probability density function

$$f(t) = \begin{cases} 0.21e^{-0.21t} & \text{if } t \geq 0 \\ 0 & \text{otherwise} \end{cases}$$

What is the probability that a buyer chosen at random will have a product failure

(A) During the first year of warranty?

(B) During the second year of warranty?

33. *Product warranty.* Graph the probability density function for Problem 32 over the interval $[0, 3]$, interpret part (B) of Problem 32 geometrically, and verbally describe the geometric representation.

34. *Revenue function.* The weekly marginal revenue from the sale of x hair dryers is given by

$$R'(x) = 65 - 6\ln(x + 1) \qquad R(0) = 0$$

where $R(x)$ is the revenue in dollars. Find the revenue function and the production level (to the nearest unit) for a revenue of $20,000 per week. What is the weekly revenue (to the nearest dollar) at a production level of 1,000 hair dryers per week?

35. *Continuous income stream.* The rate of flow (in dollars per year) of a continuous income stream for a 5-year period is given by

$$f(t) = 2{,}500e^{0.05t} \qquad 0 \leq t \leq 5$$

(A) Graph $y = f(t)$ over $[0, 5]$ and shade in the area that represents the total income received from the end of the first year to the end of the fourth year.

(B) Find the total income received, to the nearest dollar, from the end of the first year to the end of the fourth year.

36. *Future value of a continuous income stream.* The continuous income stream in Problem 35 is invested as it is received at 15% compounded continuously.

(A) Find the future value (to the nearest dollar) at the end of the 5-year period.

(B) Find the interest earned (to the nearest dollar) during this 5-year period.

37. *Income distribution.* An economist produced the following Lorenz curves for the current income distribution and the projected income distribution 10 years from now in a certain country:

$$f(x) = 0.1x + 0.9x^2 \quad \text{Current Lorenz curve}$$
$$g(x) = x^{1.5} \qquad\qquad \text{Projected Lorenz curve}$$

(A) Graph $y = x$ and the current Lorenz curve on one set of coordinate axes for $[0, 1]$, and graph $y = x$ and the projected Lorenz curve on another set of coordinate axes over the same interval.

(B) Looking at the areas bounded by the Lorenz curves and $y = x$, can you say that the income will be more or less equitably distributed 10 years from now?

(C) Compute the Gini index of income concentration (to one decimal place) for the current and projected curves. Now what can you say about the distribution of income 10 years from now? More equitable or less?

38. *Consumers' and producers' surplus.* Find the consumers' surplus and the producers' surplus at the equilibrium price level for each pair of price–demand and price–supply equations. Include a graph that identifies the consumers' surplus and the producers' surplus. Round all values to the nearest integer.

(A) $p = D(x) = 70 - 0.2x$;
$p = S(x) = 13 + 0.0012x^2$

(B) $p = D(x) = 70 - 0.2x$; $p = S(x) = 13e^{0.006x}$

39. *Producers' surplus.* The following table gives price–supply data for the sale of hogs at a livestock market, where x is the number of pounds (in thousands) and p is the price per pound (in cents).

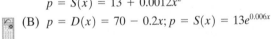

Price–Supply	
x	$p = S(x)$
0	43.50
10	46.74
20	50.05
30	54.72
40	59.18

(A) Using quadratic regression to model the data, find the demand at a price of 52.50 cents per pound.

(B) Use a numerical integration routine to find the producers' surplus (to the nearest dollar) at a price level of 52.50 cents per pound.

Life Sciences

40. *Drug assimilation.* The rate at which the body eliminates a drug (in milliliters per hour) is given by

$$R(t) = \frac{60t}{(t + 1)^2(t + 2)}$$

where t is the number of hours since the drug was administered. How much of the drug is eliminated during the first hour after it was administered? During the fourth hour?

41. With the aid of a graphing utility, illustrate Problem 40 geometrically.

42. *Medicine.* For a particular doctor, the length of time (in hours) spent with a patient per office visit has the probability density function

$$f(t) = \begin{cases} \dfrac{\frac{4}{3}}{(t + 1)^2} & \text{if } 0 \le t \le 3 \\ 0 & \text{otherwise} \end{cases}$$

(A) What is the probability that this doctor will spend less than 1 hour with a randomly selected patient?

(B) What is the probability that this doctor will spend more than 1 hour with a randomly selected patient?

43. *Medicine.* Illustrate part (B) in Problem 42 geometrically. Describe the geometric interpretation verbally.

Social Sciences

44. *Politics.* The rate of change of the voting population of a city with respect to time t (in years) is estimated to be

$$N'(t) = \frac{100t}{(1 + t^2)^2}$$

where $N(t)$ is in thousands. If $N(0)$ is the current voting population, how much will this population increase during the next 3 years?

45. *Psychology.* Rats were trained to go through a maze by rewarding them with a food pellet upon successful completion. After the seventh successful run, it was found that the probability density function for length of time (in minutes) until success on the eighth trial is given by

$$f(t) = \begin{cases} .5e^{-.5t} & \text{if } t \ge 0 \\ 0 & \text{otherwise} \end{cases}$$

What is the probability that a rat selected at random after seven successful runs will take 2 or more minutes to complete the eighth run successfully? [Recall that the area under a probability density function curve from $-\infty$ to ∞ is 1.]

Group Activity 1   *Analysis of Income Concentration from Raw Data*

This group activity may be done without the use of a graphing utility, but additional insight into mathematical modeling will be gained if one is available.

We start with raw data on income distribution supplied in table form by the U.S. Bureau of the Census (Table 1). From the raw data in the table, we wish to compare income distribution among whites and income distribution among blacks in the United States in 1997. The approach will be numeric, geometric, and symbolic. We will first organize in table form the data that correspond to data points for a Lorenz curve. We will then find Lorenz curves of the form $f(x) = x^p$ for each set of data points. We will interpret the income distribution geometrically by graphing the Lorenz curves and $y = x$ for both sets of data. Finally, we compute the Gini index of income concentration for blacks and for whites, and interpret the results. (See the discussion of Lorenz curves in Section 7-1 for relevant background material.)

TABLE 1 Income Distribution by Population Fifths

Families, 1997	Upper Limit of Each Fifth*				
Race	Lowest	Second	Third	Fourth	Top 5%[†]
Total	$20,586	$36,000	$53,616	$80,000	$137,080
White	22,576	38,258	55,783	82,442	142,400
Black	11,396	21,875	36,052	57,000	95,684

Families, 1997	Percentage Distribution of Total Income					
Race	Lowest Fifth	Second Fifth	Third Fifth	Fourth Fifth	Highest Fifth	Top 5%
Total	4.2	9.9	15.7	23.0	47.2	20.7
White	4.6	10.2	15.7	22.8	46.8	20.7
Black	3.4	9.1	15.6	25.1	46.8	17.6

*The highest fifth does not have an upper limit.
[†] Lower limit for top 5%.

Source: U.S. Bureau of the Census, U.S. Department of Commerce

TABLE 2 Black Family Income Distribution, 1997

Income Level	x	y
Under $11,000	0.20	0.03
Under		0.13
Under		
Under $57,000	0.80	

TABLE 3 White Family Income Distribution, 1997

Income Level	x	y
Under $23,000	0.20	0.05
Under		0.15
Under		
Under $82,000	0.80	

Part 1.   *Numeric analysis.* Complete Tables 2 and 3 using the data in Table 1. Round income levels to the nearest thousand dollars and represent percents in decimal form to two decimal places. Remember that x represents the cumulative percentage of families in a given category and y represents the corresponding cumulative percentage of income received by these families. Verbally describe the meaning of the last two lines in Tables 2 and 3 after they are completed.

Part 2.   *Geometric analysis*

(A) Sketch separate graphs on suitable graph paper for each table by plotting the data points from the x and y columns in Tables 2 and 3. Also, graph the line $y = x$ over the interval $[0, 1]$ in each graph.

(B) Find p (to one decimal place) so that the graph of the function $f(x) = x^p$ goes through the point $(0.20, 0.03)$ in Table 2. Plot this curve on the corresponding graph, $0 \le x \le 1$. Also, find q (to one decimal place) so that the function $g(x) = x^q$ goes through the point $(0.20, 0.05)$ in Table 3. Plot this curve on the corresponding graph, $0 \le x \le 1$. Repeat this process for each of the remaining points in each table. Compare all the graphs based on Table 2 and select the value of p that best fits the data (by eye). Do the same for all the graphs based on Table 3.

(C) From the final graphs chosen in part (B) can you draw any conclusions about whether income is distributed more equitably among blacks or whites? Verbally support your conclusions.

Part 3.   *Symbolic analysis.* Use the values of p and q you determined in part 2B to compute the Gini index of income concentration for blacks and for whites, and interpret.

Group Activity 2   *Grain Exchange*

The following tables give price–demand and price–supply data for the sale of wheat at a grain market, where x is the number of bushels of wheat (in thousands) and p is the price per bushel (in cents).

Price–Demand		Price–Supply	
x	$p = D(x)$	x	$p = S(x)$
20	345	20	311
25	336	25	312
30	323	30	321
35	320	35	323
40	318	40	326
45	307	45	338

(A) Find quadratic, logarithmic, and exponential regression models for each set of data.

(B) Use the sum of squares of the residuals (see Group Activity 2 in Chapter 2) to compare the models from part (A).

(C) Using the models that best fit the data, approximate the supply and demand supported by a price of $3.50 per bushel; by a price of $3.25 per bushel; by a price of $3.00 per bushel.

(D) Using the models that best fit the data, find the equilibrium quantity and equilibrium price.

(E) Use a numerical integration routine to find the consumers' surplus and the producers' surplus at the equilibrium price level.

OBJECTIVES

1. Compute values of functions of several variables.
2. Calculate partial derivatives of functions of several variables.
3. Find local extrema for functions of two variables using an analogue of the second derivative test.
4. Use the method of Lagrange multipliers to find local extrema of functions of several variables.
5. Calculate regression curves by minimizing appropriate functions of several variables.
6. Determine the average value of a function of two variables by calculating a double integral.
7. Calculate volumes using double integrals.

CHAPTER PROBLEM

A national shipping company classifies a package weighing less than 50 lb and measuring more than 108 inches in combined length and girth as an Oversize 2 (OS2) package. What are the dimensions of the largest (in volume) shipping carton that can be classified as an OS2 package?

Multivariable Calculus

8

Section 8-1 | Functions of Several Variables

➤ Functions of Two or More Independent Variables
➤ Examples of Functions of Several Variables
➤ Three-Dimensional Coordinate Systems

➤ Functions of Two or More Independent Variables

In Section 1-1 we introduced the concept of a function with one independent variable. Now we broaden the concept to include functions with more than one independent variable. We start with an example.

A small manufacturing company produces a standard type of surfboard and no other products. If fixed costs are \$500 per week and variable costs are \$70 per board produced, the weekly cost function is given by

$$C(x) = 500 + 70x \tag{1}$$

where x is the number of boards produced per week. The cost function is a function of a single independent variable x. For each value of x from the domain of C there exists exactly one value of $C(x)$ in the range of C.

Now, suppose that the company decides to add a high-performance competition board to its line. If the fixed costs for the competition board are \$200 per week and the variable costs are \$100 per board, the cost function (1) must be modified to

$$C(x, y) = 700 + 70x + 100y \tag{2}$$

where $C(x, y)$ is the cost for weekly output of x standard boards and y competition boards. Equation (2) is an example of a function with two independent

489

variables, x and y. Of course, as the company expands its product line even further, its weekly cost function must be modified to include more and more independent variables, one for each new product produced.

In general, an equation of the form

$$z = f(x, y)$$

describes a **function of two independent variables** if for each permissible ordered pair (x, y), there is one and only one value of z determined by $f(x, y)$. The variables x and y are **independent variables,** and the variable z is a **dependent variable.** The set of all ordered pairs of permissible values of x and y is the **domain** of the function, and the set of all corresponding values $f(x, y)$ is the **range** of the function. Unless otherwise stated, we will assume that the domain of a function specified by an equation of the form $z = f(x, y)$ is the set of all ordered pairs of real numbers (x, y) such that $f(x, y)$ is also a real number. It should be noted, however, that certain conditions in practical problems often lead to further restrictions of the domain of a function.

We can similarly define functions of three independent variables, $w = f(x, y, z)$; of four independent variables, $u = f(w, x, y, z)$; and so on. In this chapter we concern ourselves primarily with functions of two independent variables.

EXAMPLE 1

Evaluating a Function of Two Independent Variables For the cost function $C(x, y) = 700 + 70x + 100y$ described earlier, find $C(10, 5)$.

Solution
$$C(10, 5) = 700 + 70(10) + 100(5)$$
$$= \$1,900$$

Matched Problem 1   Find $C(20, 10)$ for the cost function in Example 1.

EXAMPLE 2

Evaluating a Function of Three Independent Variables For the function $f(x, y, z) = 2x^2 - 3xy + 3z + 1$, find $f(3, 0, -1)$.

Solution
$$f(3, 0, -1) = 2(3)^2 - 3(3)(0) + 3(-1) + 1$$
$$= 18 - 0 - 3 + 1 = 16$$

Matched Problem 2   Find $f(-2, 2, 3)$ for f in Example 2.

EXAMPLE 3

Revenue, Cost, and Profit Functions The surfboard company discussed at the beginning of this section has determined that the demand equations for the two types of boards they produce are given by

$$p = 210 - 4x + y$$
$$q = 300 + x - 12y$$

where p is the price of the standard board, q is the price of the competition board, x is the weekly demand for standard boards, and y is the weekly demand for competition boards.

(A) Find the weekly revenue function $R(x, y)$, and evaluate $R(20, 10)$.

(B) If the weekly cost function is

$$C(x, y) = 700 + 70x + 100y$$

find the weekly profit function $P(x, y)$, and evaluate $P(20, 10)$.

Solution   (A)

$$\text{Revenue} = \begin{pmatrix} \text{demand for} \\ \text{standard} \\ \text{boards} \end{pmatrix} \times \begin{pmatrix} \text{price of a} \\ \text{standard} \\ \text{board} \end{pmatrix} + \begin{pmatrix} \text{demand for} \\ \text{competition} \\ \text{boards} \end{pmatrix} \times \begin{pmatrix} \text{price of a} \\ \text{competition} \\ \text{board} \end{pmatrix}$$

$$\begin{aligned}
R(x, y) &= xp + yq \\
&= x(210 - 4x + y) + y(300 + x - 12y) \\
&= 210x + 300y - 4x^2 + 2xy - 12y^2 \\
R(20, 10) &= 210(20) + 300(10) - 4(20)^2 + 2(20)(10) - 12(10)^2 \\
&= \$4,800
\end{aligned}$$

(B) $\text{Profit} = \text{revenue} - \text{cost}$

$$\begin{aligned}
P(x, y) &= R(x, y) - C(x, y) \\
&= 210x + 300y - 4x^2 + 2xy - 12y^2 - 700 - 70x - 100y \\
&= 140x + 200y - 4x^2 + 2xy - 12y^2 - 700 \\
P(20, 10) &= 140(20) + 200(10) - 4(20)^2 + 2(20)(10) - 12(10)^2 - 700 \\
&= \$1,700
\end{aligned}$$

Matched Problem 3

Repeat Example 3 if the demand and cost equations are given by

$$p = 220 - 6x + y$$
$$q = 300 + 3x - 10y$$
$$C(x, y) = 40x + 80y + 1,000$$

➤ Examples of Functions of Several Variables

A number of concepts we have already considered can be thought of in terms of functions of two or more variables. We list a few of these below.

Area of a rectangle $A(x, y) = xy$

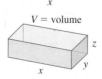

Volume of a box $V(x, y, z) = xyz$

Volume of a right
circular cylinder $V(r, h) = \pi r^2 h$

Simple interest $A(P, r, t) = P(1 + rt)$

$A = \text{amount}$
$P = \text{principal}$
$r = \text{annual rate}$
$t = \text{time in years}$

Compound interest $A(P, r, t, n) = P\left(1 + \dfrac{r}{n}\right)^{nt}$ A = amount
P = principal
r = annual rate
t = time in years
n = compound periods
          per year

IQ $Q(M, C) = \dfrac{M}{C}(100)$ Q = IQ = intelligence
                   quotient
M = MA = mental age
C = CA
      = chronological age

Resistance for $R(L, r) = k\dfrac{L}{r^4}$ R = resistance
blood flow L = length of vessel
in a vessel r = radius of vessel
(Poiseuille's law) k = constant

EXAMPLE 4   **Package Design** A company uses a box with a square base and an open top for one of its products (see the figure). If x is the length (in inches) of each side of the base and y is the height (in inches), find the total amount of material $M(x, y)$ required to construct one of these boxes, and evaluate $M(5, 10)$.

Solution

$$\text{Area of base} = x^2$$
$$\text{Area of one side} = xy$$
$$\text{Total material} = (\text{area of base}) + 4(\text{area of one side})$$
$$M(x, y) = x^2 + 4xy$$
$$M(5, 10) = (5)^2 + 4(5)(10)$$
$$= 225 \text{ square inches}$$

Matched Problem 4   For the box in Example 4, find the volume $V(x, y)$, and evaluate $V(5, 10)$.

The next example concerns the **Cobb–Douglas production function,**

$$f(x, y) = kx^m y^n$$

where k, m, and n are positive constants with $m + n = 1$. Economists use this function to describe the number of units $f(x, y)$ produced from the utilization of x units of labor and y units of capital (for equipment such as tools, machinery, buildings, and so on). Cobb–Douglas production functions are also used to describe the productivity of a single industry, of a group of industries producing the same product, or even of an entire country.

EXAMPLE 5   **Productivity** The productivity of a steel manufacturing company is given approximately by the function

$$f(x, y) = 10x^{0.2}y^{0.8}$$

with the utilization of x units of labor and y units of capital. If the company uses 3,000 units of labor and 1,000 units of capital, how many units of steel will be produced?

Solution   The number of units of steel produced is given by

$$f(3{,}000, 1{,}000) = 10(3{,}000)^{0.2}(1{,}000)^{0.8}$$ *Use a calculator.*

$$\approx 12{,}457 \text{ units}$$ ■

Matched Problem 5   Refer to Example 5. Find the steel production if the company uses 1,000 units of labor and 2,000 units of capital.   ────────■

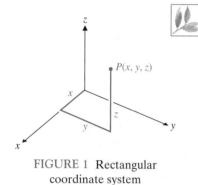

FIGURE 1 Rectangular coordinate system

➤ Three-Dimensional Coordinate Systems

We now take a brief look at some graphs of functions of two independent variables. Since functions of the form $z = f(x, y)$ involve two independent variables, x and y, and one dependent variable, z, we need a *three-dimensional coordinate system* for their graphs. A **three-dimensional coordinate system** is formed by three mutually perpendicular number lines intersecting at their origins (see Fig. 1). In such a system, every ordered **triplet of numbers** (x, y, z) can be associated with a unique point, and conversely.

EXAMPLE 6   **Three-Dimensional Coordinates** Locate $(-3, 5, 2)$ in a rectangular coordinate system.

Solution

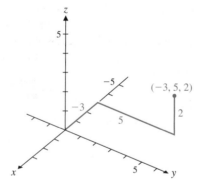

■

Matched Problem 6   Find the coordinates of the corners A, C, G, and D of the rectangular box shown in the figure.

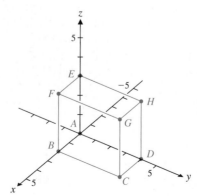

────────■

EXPLORE & DISCUSS 1

Imagine that you are facing the front of a classroom whose rectangular walls meet at right angles. Suppose that the point of intersection of the floor, front wall, and left side wall is the origin of a three-dimensional coordinate system in which every point in the room has nonnegative coordinates. Then the plane $z = 0$ (or, equivalently, the xy plane) can be described as "the floor," and the plane $z = 2$ can be described as "the plane parallel to, but 2 units above, the floor." Give similar descriptions of the following planes:

(A) $x = 0$ (B) $x = 3$ (C) $y = 0$
(D) $y = 4$ (E) $x = -1$

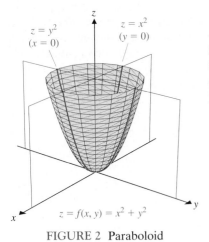

FIGURE 2 Paraboloid

$z = y^2$ $(x = 0)$

$z = x^2$ $(y = 0)$

$z = f(x, y) = x^2 + y^2$

What does the graph of $z = x^2 + y^2$ look like? If we let $x = 0$ and graph $z = 0^2 + y^2 = y^2$ in the yz plane, we obtain a parabola; if we let $y = 0$ and graph $z = x^2 + 0^2 = x^2$ in the xz plane, we obtain another parabola. It can be shown that the graph of $z = x^2 + y^2$ is either one of these parabolas rotated around the z axis (see Fig. 2). This cup-shaped figure is a *surface* and is called a **paraboloid.**

In general, the graph of any function of the form $z = f(x, y)$ is called a **surface.** The graph of such a function is the graph of all ordered triplets of numbers (x, y, z) that satisfy the equation. Graphing functions of two independent variables is often a very difficult task, and the general process will not be dealt with in this book. We present only a few simple graphs to suggest extensions of earlier geometric interpretations of the derivative and local maxima and minima to functions of two variables. Note that $z = f(x, y) = x^2 + y^2$ appears (see Fig. 2) to have a local minimum at $(x, y) = (0, 0)$. Figure 3 shows a local maximum at $(x, y) = (0, 0)$.

Figure 4 shows a point at $(x, y) = (0, 0)$, called a **saddle point,** which is neither a local minimum nor a local maximum. Note that if $x = 0$, the saddle point is a local minimum, and if $y = 0$, the saddle point is a local maximum. More will be said about local maxima and minima in Section 8-3.

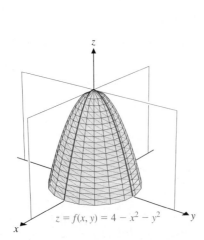

$z = f(x, y) = 4 - x^2 - y^2$

FIGURE 3 Local maximum: $f(0, 0) = 4$

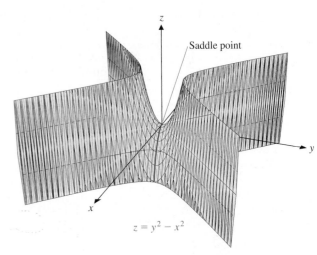

Saddle point

$z = y^2 - x^2$

FIGURE 4 Saddle point at $(0, 0, 0)$

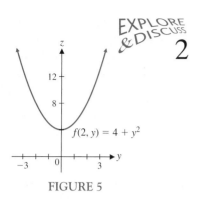

FIGURE 5

EXPLORE &DISCUSS 2

(A) Let $f(x, y) = x^2 + y^2$. The cross section of the surface $z = f(x, y)$ by the plane $x = 2$ is the graph of $z = f(2, y) = 4 + y^2$, which is a parabola (see Fig. 5). Explain why each cross section of $z = f(x, y)$ by a plane parallel to the yz plane is a parabola that opens upward. Explain why each cross section of $z = f(x, y)$ by a plane parallel to the xz plane is a parabola that opens upward.

(B) Let $g(x, y) = y^2 - x^2$. Explain why each cross section of $z = g(x, y)$ by a plane parallel to the yz plane is a parabola that opens upward (see Fig. 4). Explain why each cross section of $z = f(x, y)$ by a plane parallel to the xz plane is a parabola that opens downward.

Some graphing utilities are designed to draw graphs (like those of Figs. 2, 3, and 4) of functions of two independent variables. Others, like the graphing calculator used for the displays in this book, are designed to draw graphs of functions of just a single independent variable. When using the latter type of calculator, we can graph cross sections by planes parallel to the xz plane or yz plane to gain insight into the graph of a function of two independent variables.

EXAMPLE 7   Graphing Cross Sections

(A) Describe the cross sections of $f(x, y) = 2x^2 + y^2$ in the planes $y = 0$, $y = 1$, $y = 2$, $y = 3$, and $y = 4$.

(B) Describe the cross sections of $f(x, y) = 2x^2 + y^2$ in the planes $x = 0$, $x = 1$, $x = 2$, $x = 3$, and $x = 4$.

Solution (A) The cross section of $f(x, y) = 2x^2 + y^2$ by the plane $y = 0$ is the graph of the function $f(x, 0) = 2x^2$ in this plane. We can examine the shape of this cross section by graphing $y_1 = 2x^2$ on a graphing utility (Fig. 6). Similarly, the graphs of $y_2 = f(x, 1) = 2x^2 + 1$, $y_3 = f(x, 2) = 2x^2 + 4$, $y_4 = f(x, 3) = 2x^2 + 9$, and $y_5 = f(x, 4) = 2x^2 + 16$ show the shapes of the other four cross sections (see Fig. 6). Each of these is a parabola that opens upward. Note the correspondence between the graphs in Figure 6 and the actual cross sections of $f(x, y) = 2x^2 + y^2$ shown in Figure 7.

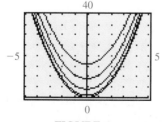

FIGURE 6
$y_1 = 2x^2$ $y_4 = 2x^2 + 9$
$y_2 = 2x^2 + 1$ $y_5 = 2x^2 + 16$
$y_3 = 2x^2 + 4$

FIGURE 7

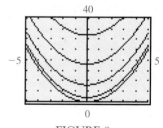

FIGURE 8
$y_1 = x^2$ $y_4 = 18 + x^2$
$y_2 = 2 + x^2$ $y_5 = 32 + x^2$
$y_3 = 8 + x^2$

(B) The five cross sections are represented by the graphs of the functions $f(0, y) = y^2$, $f(1, y) = 2 + y^2$, $f(2, y) = 8 + y^2$, $f(3, y) = 18 + y^2$, and $f(4, y) = 32 + y^2$. These five functions are graphed in Figure 8. (Note that changing the name of the independent variable from y to x for graphing purposes does not affect the graph displayed.) Each of the five cross sections is a parabola that opens upward.

Matched Problem 7   (A) Describe the cross sections of $g(x, y) = y^2 - x^2$ in the planes $y = 0$, $y = 1, y = 2, y = 3$, and $y = 4$.

(B) Describe the cross sections of $g(x, y) = y^2 - x^2$ in the planes $x = 0$, $x = 1, x = 2, x = 3$, and $x = 4$.

⊙ **Insight**   The graph of the *equation*

$$x^2 + y^2 + z^2 = 4 \tag{3}$$

is the graph of all ordered triplets of numbers (x, y, z) that satisfy the equation. The Pythagorean theorem can be used to show that the distance from the point (x, y, z) to the origin $(0, 0, 0)$ is equal to

$$\sqrt{x^2 + y^2 + z^2}$$

Therefore, the graph of (3) consists of all points that are a distance 2 from the origin; that is, all points on the sphere of radius 2 with center the origin. Recall that a circle in the plane is *not* the graph of a function $y = f(x)$ because it fails the vertical line test (Section 1-1). Similarly, a sphere is *not* the graph of a *function $z = f(x, y)$* of two variables.   ●

Answers to Matched Problems   **1.** $3,100   **2.** 30

3. (A) $R(x, y) = 220x + 300y - 6x^2 + 4xy - 10y^2; R(20, 10) = \$4,800$
(B) $P(x, y) = 180x + 220y - 6x^2 + 4xy - 10y^2 - 1,000; P(20, 10) = \$2,200$

4. $V(x, y) = x^2y; V(5, 10) = 250$ in.^{3} **5.** 17,411 units

6. $A(0, 0, 0); C(2, 4, 0); G(2, 4, 3); D(0, 4, 0)$

7. (A) Each cross section is a parabola that opens downward.
(B) Each cross section is a parabola that opens upward.

Exercise 8-1

A *In Problems 1–10, find the indicated values of the functions*

$$f(x, y) = 2x + 7y - 5 \quad \text{and} \quad g(x, y) = \frac{88}{x^2 + 3y}$$

1. $f(4, -1)$ **2.** $f(0, 10)$

3. $f(8, 0)$ **4.** $f(5, 6)$

5. $g(1, 7)$ **6.** $g(-2, 0)$

7. $g(3, -3)$ **8.** $g(0, 0)$

9. $3f(-2, 2) + 5g(-2, 2)$

10. $2f(10, -4) - 7g(10, -4)$

In Problems 11–14, find the indicated values of

$$f(x, y, z) = 2x - 3y^2 + 5z^3 - 1$$

11. $f(0, 0, 0)$ **12.** $f(0, 0, 2)$

13. $f(6, -5, 0)$ **14.** $f(-10, 4, -3)$

B

15. $V(2, 4)$ for $V(r, h) = \pi r^2 h$

16. $S(4, 2)$ for $S(x, y) = 5x^2y^3$

17. $R(1, 2)$ for
$R(x, y) = -5x^2 + 6xy - 4y^2 + 200x + 300y$

18. $P(2, 2)$ for
$P(x, y) = -x^2 + 2xy - 2y^2 - 4x + 12y + 5$

19. $R(6, 0.5)$ for $R(L, r) = 0.002\dfrac{L}{r^4}$

20. $L(2,000, 50)$ for $L(w, v) = (1.25 \times 10^{-5})wv^2$

21. $A(100, 0.06, 3)$ for $A(P, r, t) = P + Prt$

22. $A(10, 0.04, 3, 2)$ for $A(P, r, t, n) = P\left(1 + \dfrac{r}{n}\right)^{tn}$

23. $P(0.05, 12)$ for $P(r, T) = \displaystyle\int_0^T 4,000e^{-rt}\, dt$

24. $F(0.07, 10)$ for $F(r, T) = \displaystyle\int_0^T 4{,}000e^{r(T-t)}\, dt$

 25. Let $F(x, y) = x^2 + e^x y - y^2$. Find all values of x such that $F(x, 2) = 0$.

 26. Let $G(a, b, c) = a^3 + b^3 + c^3 - (ab + ac + bc) - 6$. Find all values of b such that $G(2, b, 1) = 0$.

C

27. For the function $f(x, y) = x^2 + 2y^2$, find
$$\frac{f(x + h, y) - f(x, y)}{h}$$

28. For the function $f(x, y) = x^2 + 2y^2$, find
$$\frac{f(x, y + k) - f(x, y)}{k}$$

29. For the function $f(x, y) = 2xy^2$, find
$$\frac{f(x + h, y) - f(x, y)}{h}$$

30. For the function $f(x, y) = 2xy^2$, find
$$\frac{f(x, y + k) - f(x, y)}{k}$$

31. Find the coordinates of E and F in the figure for Matched Problem 6 (in the text).

32. Find the coordinates of B and H in the figure for Matched Problem 6 (in the text).

 In Problems 33–38, use a graphing utility as necessary to explore the graphs of the indicated cross sections.

33. Let $f(x, y) = x^2$.

 (A) Explain why the cross sections of the surface $z = f(x, y)$ by planes parallel to $y = 0$ are parabolas.

 (B) Describe the cross sections of the surface by the planes $x = 0$, $x = 1$, and $x = 2$.

 (C) Describe the surface $z = f(x, y)$.

34. Let $f(x, y) = \sqrt{4 - y^2}$.

 (A) Explain why the cross sections of the surface $z = f(x, y)$ by planes parallel to $x = 0$ are semi-circles of radius 2.

 (B) Describe the cross sections of the surface by the planes $y = 0$, $y = 2$, and $y = 3$.

 (C) Describe the surface $z = f(x, y)$.

35. Let $f(x, y) = \sqrt{36 - x^2 - y^2}$.

 (A) Describe the cross sections of the surface $z = f(x, y)$ by the planes $y = 1$, $y = 2$, $y = 3$, $y = 4$, and $y = 5$.

 (B) Describe the cross sections of the surface by the planes $x = 0$, $x = 1$, $x = 2$, $x = 3$, $x = 4$, and $x = 5$.

 (C) Describe the surface $z = f(x, y)$.

36. Let $f(x, y) = 100 + 10x + 25y - x^2 - 5y^2$.

 (A) Describe the cross sections of the surface $z = f(x, y)$ by the planes $y = 0$, $y = 1$, $y = 2$, and $y = 3$.

 (B) Describe the cross sections of the surface by the planes $x = 0$, $x = 1$, $x = 2$, and $x = 3$.

 (C) Describe the surface $z = f(x, y)$.

37. Let $f(x, y) = e^{-(x^2 + y^2)}$.

 (A) Explain why $f(a, b) = f(c, d)$ whenever (a, b) and (c, d) are points on the same circle centered at the origin in the xy plane.

 (B) Describe the cross sections of the surface $z = f(x, y)$ by the planes $x = 0$, $y = 0$, and $x = y$.

 (C) Describe the surface $z = f(x, y)$.

38. Let $f(x, y) = 4 - \sqrt{x^2 + y^2}$.

 (A) Explain why $f(a, b) = f(c, d)$ whenever (a, b) and (c, d) are points on the same circle with center at the origin in the xy plane.

 (B) Describe the cross sections of the surface $z = f(x, y)$ by the planes $x = 0$, $y = 0$, and $x = y$.

 (C) Describe the surface $z = f(x, y)$.

Applications

Business & Economics

39. *Cost function.* A small manufacturing company produces two models of a surfboard: a standard model and a competition model. If the standard model is produced at a variable cost of $70 each, the competition model at a variable cost of $100 each, and the total fixed costs per month are $2,000, the monthly cost function is given by

$$C(x, y) = 2{,}000 + 70x + 100y$$

where x and y are the numbers of standard and competition models produced per month, respectively. Find $C(20, 10)$, $C(50, 5)$, and $C(30, 30)$.

40. *Advertising and sales.* A company spends $x thousand per week on newspaper advertising and $y thousand per week on television advertising. Its weekly sales are found to be given by

$$S(x, y) = 5x^2y^3$$

Find $S(3, 2)$ and $S(2, 3)$.

41. *Revenue function.* A supermarket sells two brands of coffee: brand A at $p per pound and brand B at $q per pound. The daily demand equations for brands A and B are, respectively,

$$x = 200 - 5p + 4q$$
$$y = 300 + 2p - 4q$$

(both in pounds). Find the daily revenue function $R(p, q)$. Evaluate $R(2, 3)$ and $R(3, 2)$.

42. *Revenue, cost, and profit functions.* A company manufactures ten- and three-speed bicycles. The weekly demand and cost equations are

$$p = 230 - 9x + y$$
$$q = 130 + x - 4y$$
$$C(x, y) = 200 + 80x + 30y$$

where $p is the price of a ten-speed bicycle, $q is the price of a three-speed bicycle, x is the weekly demand for ten-speed bicycles, y is the weekly demand for three-speed bicycles, and $C(x, y)$ is the cost function. Find the weekly revenue function $R(x, y)$ and the weekly profit function $P(x, y)$. Evaluate $R(10, 15)$ and $P(10, 15)$.

43. *Productivity.* The Cobb–Douglas production function for a petroleum company is given by

$$f(x, y) = 20x^{0.4}y^{0.6}$$

where x is the utilization of labor and y is the utilization of capital. If the company uses 1,250 units of labor and 1,700 units of capital, how many units of petroleum will be produced?

44. *Productivity.* The petroleum company in Problem 43 is taken over by another company that decides to double both the units of labor and the units of capital utilized in the production of petroleum. Use the Cobb–Douglas production function given in Problem 43 to find the amount of petroleum that will be produced by this increased utilization of labor and capital. What is the effect on productivity of doubling both the units of labor and the units of capital?

45. *Future value.* At the end of each year, $2,000 is invested into an IRA earning 9% compounded annually.

(A) How much will be in the account at the end of 30 years? Use the annuity formula

$$F(P, i, n) = P\frac{(1 + i)^n - 1}{i}$$

where

$$P = \text{periodic payment}$$
$$i = \text{rate per period}$$
$$n = \text{number of payments (periods)}$$
$$F = FV = \text{future value}$$

(B) Use graphical approximation methods to determine the rate of interest that would produce $500,000 in the account at the end of 30 years.

46. *Package design.* The packaging department in a company has been asked to design a rectangular box with no top and a partition down the middle (see the figure). Let x, y, and z be the dimensions (in inches).

Figure for 46

(A) Find the total amount of material $M(x, y, z)$ used in constructing one of these boxes, and evaluate $M(10, 12, 6)$.

(B) Suppose that the box is to have a square base and a volume of 720 cubic inches. Use graphical approximation methods to determine the dimensions that require the least amount of material.

Life Sciences

47. *Marine biology.* In using scuba diving gear, a marine biologist estimates the time of a dive according to the equation

$$T(V, x) = \frac{33V}{x + 33}$$

where

$$T = \text{time of dive in minutes}$$
$$V = \text{volume of air, at sea level pressure,}$$
$$\quad \text{compressed into tanks}$$
$$x = \text{depth of dive in feet}$$

Find $T(70, 47)$ and $T(60, 27)$.

48. *Blood flow.* Poiseuille's law states that the resistance, R, for blood flowing in a blood vessel varies directly as the length of the vessel, L, and inversely as the fourth power of its radius, r. Stated as an equation,

$$R(L, r) = k\frac{L}{r^4} \qquad k \text{ a constant}$$

Find $R(8, 1)$ and $R(4, 0.2)$.

49. *Physical anthropology.* Anthropologists, in their study of race and human genetic groupings, often use an index called the *cephalic index*. The cephalic index, C, varies directly as the width W, of the head, and inversely as the length, L, of the head (both viewed from the top). In terms of an equation,

$$C(W, L) = 100\frac{W}{L}$$

where

$$W = \text{width in inches}$$
$$L = \text{length in inches}$$

Find $C(6, 8)$ and $C(8.1, 9)$

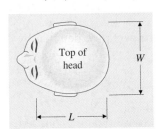

Social Sciences

50. *Safety research.* Under ideal conditions, if a person driving a car slams on the brakes and skids to a stop, the length of the skid marks (in feet) is given by the formula

$$L(w, v) = kwv^2$$

where

$$k = \text{constant}$$
$$w = \text{weight of car in pounds}$$
$$v = \text{speed of car in miles per hour}$$

For $k = 0.000\,013\,3$, find $L(2,000, 40)$ and $L(3,000, 60)$.

51. *Psychology.* The intelligence quotient (IQ) is defined to be the ratio of mental age (MA), as determined by certain tests, and chronological age (CA), multiplied by 100. Stated as an equation,

$$Q(M, C) = \frac{M}{C} \cdot 100$$

where

$$Q = \text{IQ} \qquad M = \text{MA} \qquad C = \text{CA}$$

Find $Q(12, 10)$ and $Q(10, 12)$.

Section 8-2 | Partial Derivatives

➤ Partial Derivatives
➤ Second-Order Partial Derivatives

➤ Partial Derivatives

We know how to differentiate many kinds of functions of one independent variable and how to interpret the results. What about functions with two or more independent variables? Let us return to the surfboard example considered at the beginning of the chapter.

For the company producing only the standard board, the cost function was

$$C(x) = 500 + 70x$$

Differentiating with respect to x, we obtain the marginal cost function

$$C'(x) = 70$$

Since the marginal cost is constant, $70 is the change in cost for a 1-unit increase in production at any output level.

For the company producing two types of boards, a standard model and a competition model, the cost function was

$$C(x, y) = 700 + 70x + 100y$$

Now suppose that we differentiate with respect to x, holding y fixed, and denote this by $C_x(x, y)$; or suppose we differentiate with respect to y, holding x fixed, and denote this by $C_y(x, y)$. Differentiating in this way, we obtain

$$C_x(x, y) = 70 \qquad C_y(x, y) = 100$$

Each of these is called a **partial derivative,** and, in this example, each represents marginal cost. The first is the change in cost due to a 1-unit increase in production of the standard board with the production of the competition model held fixed. The second is the change in cost due to a 1-unit increase in production of the competition board with the production of the standard board held fixed.

In general, if $z = f(x, y)$, then the **partial derivative of f with respect to x,** denoted by $\partial z/\partial x$, f_x, or $f_x(x, y)$, is defined by

$$\frac{\partial z}{\partial x} = \lim_{h \to 0} \frac{f(x + h, y) - f(x, y)}{h}$$

provided that the limit exists. We recognize this as the ordinary derivative of f with respect to x, holding y constant. Thus, we are able to continue to use all the derivative rules and properties discussed in Chapters 3 to 5 for partial derivatives.

Similarly, the **partial derivative of f with respect to y,** denoted by $\partial z/\partial y$, f_y, or $f_y(x, y)$, is defined by

$$\frac{\partial z}{\partial y} = \lim_{k \to 0} \frac{f(x, y + k) - f(x, y)}{k}$$

which is the ordinary derivative with respect to y, holding x constant.

Parallel definitions and interpretations hold for functions with three or more independent variables.

EXAMPLE 1   **Partial Derivatives** For $z = f(x, y) = 2x^2 - 3x^2y + 5y + 1$, find

(A) $\partial z/\partial x$ (B) $f_x(2, 3)$

Solution   (A) $z = 2x^2 - 3x^2y + 5y + 1$

Differentiating with respect to x, holding y constant (that is, treating y as a constant), we obtain

$$\frac{\partial z}{\partial x} = 4x - 6xy$$

(B) $f(x, y) = 2x^2 - 3x^2y + 5y + 1$

First, differentiate with respect to x. From part (A) we have

$$f_x(x, y) = 4x - 6xy$$

Then evaluate at $(2, 3)$:

$$f_x(2, 3) = 4(2) - 6(2)(3) = -28$$

In Example 1B, an alternative approach would be to substitute $y = 3$ into $f(x, y)$ and graph the function $f(x, 3) = -7x^2 + 16$, which represents the cross section of the surface $z = f(x, y)$ by the plane $y = 3$. Then determine the slope of the tangent line when $x = 2$. Again, we conclude that $f_x(2, 3) = -28$ (see Fig. 1).

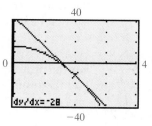

FIGURE 1 $y_1 = -7x^2 + 16$

Matched Problem 1 For f in Example 1, find

(A) $\partial z/\partial y$ (B) $f_y(2, 3)$

EXAMPLE 2 **Partial Derivatives Using the Chain Rule** For $z = f(x, y) = e^{x^2 + y^2}$, find

(A) $\partial z/\partial x$ (B) $f_y(2, 1)$

Solution (A) Using the chain rule [thinking of $z = e^u$, $u = u(x)$; y is held constant], we obtain

$$\frac{\partial z}{\partial x} = e^{x^2 + y^2} \frac{\partial(x^2 + y^2)}{\partial x}$$

$$= 2xe^{x^2 + y^2}$$

(B)
$$f_y(x, y) = e^{x^2 + y^2} \frac{\partial(x^2 + y^2)}{\partial y} = 2ye^{x^2 + y^2}$$

$$f_y(2, 1) = 2(1)e^{(2)^2 + (1)^2}$$

$$= 2e^5$$

Matched Problem 2 For $z = f(x, y) = (x^2 + 2xy)^5$, find

$5(x^2 + 2xy)^4 \cdot 2x$

(A) $\partial z/\partial y$ (B) $f_x(1, 0)$

EXAMPLE 3 **Profit** The profit function for the surfboard company in Example 3 in Section 8-1 was

$$P(x, y) = 140x + 200y - 4x^2 + 2xy - 12y^2 - 700$$

Find $P_x(15, 10)$ and $P_x(30, 10)$, and interpret the results.

Solution
$$P_x(x, y) = 140 - 8x + 2y$$

$$P_x(15, 10) = 140 - 8(15) + 2(10) = 40$$

$$P_x(30, 10) = 140 - 8(30) + 2(10) = -80$$

At a production level of 15 standard and 10 competition boards per week, increasing the production of standard boards by 1 unit and holding the production of competition boards fixed at 10 will increase profit by approximately $40. At a production level of 30 standard and 10 competition boards per week, increasing the production of standard boards by 1 unit and holding the production of competition boards fixed at 10 will decrease profit by approximately $80.   ▪

Matched Problem 3

For the profit function in Example 3, find $P_y(25, 10)$ and $P_y(25, 15)$, and interpret the results.   ▪

EXPLORE & DISCUSS 1

Let $P(x, y)$ be the profit function of Example 3 and Matched Problem 3.

(A) Assume that the production of competition boards remains fixed at 10. Which production level of standard boards will yield a maximum profit? Calculate that maximum profit.

(B) Assume that the production of standard boards remains fixed at 25. Which production level of competition boards will yield a maximum profit? Calculate that maximum profit.

EXAMPLE 4   **Productivity**   The productivity of a major computer manufacturer is given approximately by the Cobb–Douglas production function

$$f(x, y) = 15x^{0.4}y^{0.6}$$

with the utilization of x units of labor and y units of capital. The partial derivative $f_x(x, y)$ represents the rate of change of productivity with respect to labor and is called the **marginal productivity of labor.** The partial derivative $f_y(x, y)$ represents the rate of change of productivity with respect to capital and is called the **marginal productivity of capital.** If the company is currently utilizing 4,000 units of labor and 2,500 units of capital, find the marginal productivity of labor and the marginal productivity of capital. For the greatest increase in productivity, should the management of the company encourage increased use of labor or increased use of capital?

Solution

$$f_x(x, y) = 6x^{-0.6}y^{0.6}$$
$$f_x(4,000, 2,500) = 6(4,000)^{-0.6}(2,500)^{0.6}$$
$$\approx 4.53 \qquad \text{Marginal productivity of labor}$$

$$f_y(x, y) = 9x^{0.4}y^{-0.4}$$
$$f_y(4,000, 2,500) = 9(4,000)^{0.4}(2,500)^{-0.4}$$
$$\approx 10.86 \qquad \text{Marginal productivity of capital}$$

At the current level of utilization of 4,000 units of labor and 2,500 units of capital, each 1-unit increase in labor utilization (keeping capital utilization fixed at 2,500 units) will increase production by approximately 4.53 units, and each 1-unit increase in capital utilization (keeping labor utilization fixed at 4,000 units) will increase production by approximately 10.86 units. Thus, the management of the company should encourage increased use of capital.   ▪

Matched Problem 4

The productivity of an airplane manufacturing company is given approximately by the Cobb–Douglas production function

$$f(x, y) = 40x^{0.3}y^{0.7}$$

(A) Find $f_x(x, y)$ and $f_y(x, y)$.

(B) If the company is currently using 1,500 units of labor and 4,500 units of capital, find the marginal productivity of labor and the marginal productivity of capital.

(C) For the greatest increase in productivity, should the management of the company encourage increased use of labor or increased use of capital?

Partial derivatives have simple geometric interpretations, as indicated in Figure 2. If we hold x fixed, say, $x = a$, then $f_y(a, y)$ is the slope of the curve obtained by intersecting the plane $x = a$ with the surface $z = f(x, y)$. A similar interpretation is given to $f_x(x, b)$.

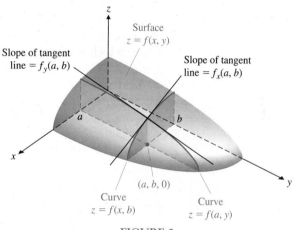

FIGURE 2

Let $f(x, y) = x^2y - 2xy^2 + 3$ and consider the surface $z = f(x, y)$.

(A) The cross section of the surface by the plane $x = 2$ is the graph of $f(2, y) = 4y - 4y^2 + 3$, which is a parabola. Use an ordinary derivative to find the slope of the tangent line to this parabola when $y = \frac{1}{2}$.

(B) Use partial derivatives to confirm your answer to part (A).

(C) Explain why the cross section of the surface by the plane $y = 1$ is also a parabola. Use an ordinary derivative to find the slope of the tangent line to this parabola when $x = 3$.

(D) Use partial derivatives to confirm your answer to part (C).

➤ Second-Order Partial Derivatives

The function

$$z = f(x, y) = x^4y^7$$

has two **first-order partial derivatives,**

$$\frac{\partial z}{\partial x} = f_x = f_x(x, y) = 4x^3y^7 \qquad \text{and} \qquad \frac{\partial z}{\partial y} = f_y = f_y(x, y) = 7x^4y^6$$

Each of these partial derivatives, in turn, has two partial derivatives called **second-order partial derivatives** of $z = f(x, y)$. Generalizing the various notations we have for first-order partial derivatives, the four second-order partial derivatives of $z = f(x, y) = x^4y^7$ are written as

Equivalent notations

$$f_{xx} = f_{xx}(x, y) = \frac{\partial^2 z}{\partial x^2} = \frac{\partial}{\partial x}\left(\frac{\partial z}{\partial x}\right) = \frac{\partial}{\partial x}(4x^3y^7) = 12x^2y^7$$

$$f_{xy} = f_{xy}(x, y) = \frac{\partial^2 z}{\partial y\,\partial x} = \frac{\partial}{\partial y}\left(\frac{\partial z}{\partial x}\right) = \frac{\partial}{\partial y}(4x^3y^7) = 28x^3y^6$$

$$f_{yx} = f_{yx}(x, y) = \frac{\partial^2 z}{\partial x\,\partial y} = \frac{\partial}{\partial x}\left(\frac{\partial z}{\partial y}\right) = \frac{\partial}{\partial x}(7x^4y^6) = 28x^3y^6$$

$$f_{yy} = f_{yy}(x, y) = \frac{\partial^2 z}{\partial y^2} = \frac{\partial}{\partial y}\left(\frac{\partial z}{\partial y}\right) = \frac{\partial}{\partial y}(7x^4y^6) = 42x^4y^5$$

In the mixed partial derivative $\partial^2 z/\partial y\,\partial x = f_{xy}$, we started with $z = f(x, y)$ and first differentiated with respect to x (holding y constant). Then we differentiated with respect to y (holding x constant). In the other mixed partial derivative, $\partial^2 z/\partial x\,\partial y = f_{yx}$, the order of differentiation was reversed; however, the final result was the same—that is, $f_{xy} = f_{yx}$. Although it is possible to find functions for which $f_{xy} \neq f_{yx}$, such functions rarely occur in applications involving partial derivatives. Thus, for all the functions in this book, we will assume that $f_{xy} = f_{yx}$.

In general, we have the following definitions:

DEFINITION Second-Order Partial Derivatives

If $z = f(x, y)$, then

$$f_{xx} = f_{xx}(x, y) = \frac{\partial^2 z}{\partial x^2} = \frac{\partial}{\partial x}\left(\frac{\partial z}{\partial x}\right)$$

$$f_{xy} = f_{xy}(x, y) = \frac{\partial^2 z}{\partial y\,\partial x} = \frac{\partial}{\partial y}\left(\frac{\partial z}{\partial x}\right)$$

$$f_{yx} = f_{yx}(x, y) = \frac{\partial^2 z}{\partial x\,\partial y} = \frac{\partial}{\partial x}\left(\frac{\partial z}{\partial y}\right)$$

$$f_{yy} = f_{yy}(x, y) = \frac{\partial^2 z}{\partial y^2} = \frac{\partial}{\partial y}\left(\frac{\partial z}{\partial y}\right)$$

EXAMPLE 5 **Second-Order Partial Derivatives** For $z = f(x, y) = 3x^2 - 2xy^3 + 1$, find

(A) $\dfrac{\partial^2 z}{\partial x\,\partial y}, \dfrac{\partial^2 z}{\partial y\,\partial x}$ (B) $\dfrac{\partial^2 z}{\partial x^2}$ (C) $f_{yx}(2, 1)$

Solution (A) First differentiate with respect to y and then with respect to x:

$$\frac{\partial z}{\partial y} = -6xy^2 \qquad \frac{\partial^2 z}{\partial x\,\partial y} = \frac{\partial}{\partial x}\left(\frac{\partial z}{\partial y}\right) = \frac{\partial}{\partial x}(-6xy^2) = -6y^2$$

First differentiate with respect to x and then with respect to y:

$$\frac{\partial z}{\partial x} = 6x - 2y^3 \qquad \frac{\partial^2 z}{\partial y\,\partial x} = \frac{\partial}{\partial y}\left(\frac{\partial z}{\partial x}\right) = \frac{\partial}{\partial y}(6x - 2y^3) = -6y^2$$

(B) Differentiate with respect to x twice:

$$\frac{\partial z}{\partial x} = 6x - 2y^3 \qquad \frac{\partial^2 z}{\partial x^2} = \frac{\partial}{\partial x}\left(\frac{\partial z}{\partial x}\right) = 6$$

(C) First find $f_{yx}(x, y)$; then evaluate at (2, 1). Again, remember that f_{yx} means to differentiate with respect to y first and then with respect to x. Thus,

$$f_y(x, y) = -6xy^2 \qquad f_{yx}(x, y) = -6y^2$$

and

$$f_{yx}(2, 1) = -6(1)^2 = -6$$

∎

Matched Problem 5 For $z = f(x, y) = x^3y - 2y^4 + 3$, find

(A) $\dfrac{\partial^2 z}{\partial y\, \partial x}$ (B) $\dfrac{\partial^2 z}{\partial y^2}$

(C) $f_{xy}(2, 3)$ (D) $f_{yx}(2, 3)$

◉ Insight Although the mixed second-order partial derivatives f_{xy} and f_{yx} are equal for all functions considered in this book, it is a good idea to compute both of them, as in Example 5(A), as a check on your work. On the other hand, the other two second-order partial derivatives, f_{xx} and f_{yy}, are generally not equal to each other. For example, for the function

$$f(x, y) = 3x^2 - 2xy^3 + 1$$

of Example 5,

$$f_{xx} = 6 \qquad \text{and} \qquad f_{yy} = -12xy$$

●

Answers to Matched Problems

1. (A) $\partial z/\partial y = -3x^2 + 5$ (B) $f_y(2, 3) = -7$
2. (A) $10x(x^2 + 2xy)^4$ (B) 10
3. $P_y(25, 10) = 10$: at a production level of $x = 25$ and $y = 10$, increasing y by 1 unit and holding x fixed at 25 will increase profit by approx. \$10; $P_y(25, 15) = -110$: at a production level of $x = 25$ and $y = 15$, increasing y by 1 unit and holding x fixed at 25 will decrease profit by approx. \$110
4. (A) $f_x(x, y) = 12x^{-0.7}y^{0.7}$; $f_y(x, y) = 28x^{0.3}y^{-0.3}$
   (B) Marginal productivity of labor ≈ 25.89;
       marginal productivity of capital ≈ 20.14
   (C) Labor
5. (A) $3x^2$ (B) $-24y^2$ (C) 12   (D) 12

Exercise 8-2

A *In Problems 1–4, let $z = f(x, y) = 3 + 4x - 5y^2$ and find the indicated function or value.*

1. $\partial z/\partial x$ 2. $\partial z/\partial y$

3. $f_y(1, 2)$ 4. $f_x(1, 2)$

In Problems 5–10, let $z = f(x, y) = 8x + 6y^3 - 3xy^2$ and find the indicated function or value.

5. $\partial z/\partial y$ 6. $\partial z/\partial x$

7. $\dfrac{\partial^2 z}{\partial y^2}$ 8. $\dfrac{\partial^2 z}{\partial x^2}$

9. $f_x(2, 3)$ 10. $f_y(2, 3)$

In Problems 11–18, find the indicated function or value if $C(x, y) = -7x^2 + 10xy + 4y^2 - 9x + 8y + 12$.

11. $C_x(x, y)$ 12. $C_y(x, y)$

13. $C_x(2, 2)$ 14. $C_y(2, 2)$

15. $C_{xy}(x, y)$ **16.** $C_{yx}(x, y)$

17. $C_{xx}(x, y)$ **18.** $C_{yy}(x, y)$

In Problems 19–24, let $S(x, y) = 2y^3e^x + 5x^4 \ln y$ and find the indicated function or value.

19. $S_x(x, y)$ **20.** $S_y(x, y)$

21. $S_y(2, 1)$ **22.** $S_x(2, 1)$

23. $S_{xy}(x, y)$ **24.** $S_{yx}(x, y)$

In Problems 25–32, let $z = f(x, y) = e^{4x^2 + 5y}$ and find the indicated function or value.

25. $\dfrac{\partial z}{\partial x}$ **26.** $\dfrac{\partial z}{\partial y}$

27. $\dfrac{\partial^2 z}{\partial x \, \partial y}$ **28.** $\dfrac{\partial^2 z}{\partial y \, \partial x}$

29. $f_{xy}(1, 0)$ **30.** $f_{yx}(0, 1)$

31. $f_{xx}(0, 1)$ **32.** $f_{yy}(1, 0)$

In Problems 33–42, find $f_x(x, y)$ and $f_y(x, y)$ for each function f.

33. $f(x, y) = (x^2 - y^3)^3$ **34.** $f(x, y) = \sqrt{2x - y^2}$

35. $f(x, y) = (3x^2y - 1)^4$ **36.** $f(x, y) = (3 + 2xy^2)^3$

37. $f(x, y) = \ln(x^2 + y^2)$ **38.** $f(x, y) = \ln(2x - 3y)$

39. $f(x, y) = y^2e^{xy^2}$ **40.** $f(x, y) = x^3e^{x^2y}$

41. $f(x, y) = \dfrac{x^2 - y^2}{x^2 + y^2}$ **42.** $f(x, y) = \dfrac{2x^2y}{x^2 + y^2}$

43. (A) Let $f(x, y) = y^3 + 4y^2 - 5y + 3$. Show that $\partial f / \partial x = 0$.

  (B) Explain why there are an infinite number of functions $g(x, y)$ such that $\partial g / \partial x = 0$.

44. (A) Find an example of a function $f(x, y)$ such that $\partial f / \partial x = 3$ and $\partial f / \partial y = 2$.

  (B) How many such functions are there? Explain.

In Problems 45–50, find $f_{xx}(x, y), f_{xy}(x, y), f_{yx}(x, y),$ and $f_{yy}(x, y)$ for each function f.

45. $f(x, y) = x^2y^2 + x^3 + y$

46. $f(x, y) = x^3y^3 + x + y^2$

47. $f(x, y) = \dfrac{x}{y} - \dfrac{y}{x}$

48. $f(x, y) = \dfrac{x^2}{y} - \dfrac{y^2}{x}$

49. $f(x, y) = xe^{xy}$

50. $f(x, y) = x \ln(xy)$

C

51. For

$$P(x, y) = -x^2 + 2xy - 2y^2 - 4x + 12y - 5$$

find all values of x and y such that

$$P_x(x, y) = 0 \quad \text{and} \quad P_y(x, y) = 0$$

simultaneously.

52. For

$$C(x, y) = 2x^2 + 2xy + 3y^2 - 16x - 18y + 54$$

find all values of x and y such that

$$C_x(x, y) = 0 \quad \text{and} \quad C_y(x, y) = 0$$

simultaneously.

53. For

$$F(x, y) = x^3 - 2x^2y^2 - 2x - 4y + 10$$

find all values of x and y such that

$$F_x(x, y) = 0 \quad \text{and} \quad F_y(x, y) = 0$$

simultaneously.

54. For

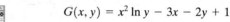

$$G(x, y) = x^2 \ln y - 3x - 2y + 1$$

find all values of x and y such that

$$G_x(x, y) = 0 \quad \text{and} \quad G_y(x, y) = 0$$

simultaneously.

55. Let $f(x, y) = 3x^2 + y^2 - 4x - 6y + 2$.

  (A) Find the minimum value of $f(x, y)$ when $y = 1$.

  (B) Explain why the answer to part (A) is not the minimum value of the function $f(x, y)$.

56. Let $f(x, y) = 5 - 2x + 4y - 3x^2 - y^2$.

  (A) Find the maximum value of $f(x, y)$ when $x = 2$.

  (B) Explain why the answer to part (A) is not the maximum value of the function $f(x, y)$.

57. Let $f(x, y) = 4 - x^4y + 3xy^2 + y^5$.

  (A) Use graphical approximation methods to find c (to three decimal places) such that $f(c, 2)$ is the maximum value of $f(x, y)$ when $y = 2$.

  (B) Find $f_x(c, 2)$ and $f_y(c, 2)$.

58. Let $f(x, y) = e^x + 2e^y + 3xy^2 + 1$.

  (A) Use graphical approximation methods to find d (to three decimal places) such that $f(1, d)$ is the minimum value of $f(x, y)$ when $x = 1$.

  (B) Find $f_x(1, d)$ and $f_y(1, d)$.

In Problems 59 and 60, show that the function f satisfies $f_{xx}(x, y) + f_{yy}(x, y) = 0$.

59. $f(x, y) = \ln(x^2 + y^2)$

60. $f(x, y) = x^3 - 3xy^2$

61. For $f(x, y) = x^2 + 2y^2$, find

(A) $\displaystyle\lim_{h \to 0} \frac{f(x + h, y) - f(x, y)}{h}$

(B) $\displaystyle\lim_{k \to 0} \frac{f(x, y + k) - f(x, y)}{k}$

62. For $f(x, y) = 2xy^2$, find

(A) $\displaystyle\lim_{h \to 0} \frac{f(x + h, y) - f(x, y)}{h}$

(B) $\displaystyle\lim_{k \to 0} \frac{f(x, y + k) - f(x, y)}{k}$

Applications

Business & Economics

63. *Profit function.* A firm produces two types of calculators, x of type A and y of type B each week. The weekly revenue and cost functions (in dollars) are

$$R(x, y) = 80x + 90y + 0.04xy - 0.05x^2 - 0.05y^2$$
$$C(x, y) = 8x + 6y + 20,000$$

Find $P_x(1,200, 1,800)$ and $P_y(1,200, 1,800)$, and interpret the results.

64. *Advertising and sales.* A company spends $\$x$ per week on newspaper advertising and $\$y$ per week on television advertising. Its weekly sales were found to be given by

$$S(x, y) = 10x^{0.4}y^{0.8}$$

Find $S_x(3,000, 2,000)$ and $S_y(3,000, 2,000)$, and interpret the results.

65. *Demand equations.* A supermarket sells two brands of coffee, brand A at $\$p$ per pound and brand B at $\$q$ per pound. The daily demands x and y (in pounds) for brands A and B, respectively, are given by

$$x = 200 - 5p + 4q$$
$$y = 300 + 2p - 4q$$

Find $\partial x / \partial p$ and $\partial y / \partial p$, and interpret the results.

66. *Revenue and profit functions.* A company manufactures ten- and three-speed bicycles. The weekly demand and cost functions are

$$p = 230 - 9x + y$$
$$q = 130 + x - 4y$$
$$C(x, y) = 200 + 80x + 30y$$

where $\$p$ is the price of a ten-speed bicycle, $\$q$ is the price of a three-speed bicycle, x is the weekly demand for ten-speed bicycles, y is the weekly demand for three-speed bicycles, and $C(x, y)$ is the cost function. Find $R_x(10, 5)$ and $P_x(10, 5)$, and interpret the results.

67. *Productivity.* The productivity of a certain third-world country is given approximately by the function

$$f(x, y) = 10x^{0.75}y^{0.25}$$

with the utilization of x units of labor and y units of capital.

(A) Find $f_x(x, y)$ and $f_y(x, y)$.

(B) If the country is now using 600 units of labor and 100 units of capital, find the marginal productivity of labor and the marginal productivity of capital.

(C) For the greatest increase in the country's productivity, should the government encourage increased use of labor or increased use of capital?

68. *Productivity.* The productivity of an automobile manufacturing company is given approximately by the function

$$f(x, y) = 50\sqrt{xy} = 50x^{0.5}y^{0.5}$$

with the utilization of x units of labor and y units of capital.

(A) Find $f_x(x, y)$ and $f_y(x, y)$.

(B) If the company is now using 250 units of labor and 125 units of capital, find the marginal productivity of labor and the marginal productivity of capital.

(C) For the greatest increase in the company's productivity, should the management encourage increased use of labor or increased use of capital?

Problems 69–72 refer to the following: If a decrease in demand for one product results in an increase in demand for another product, the two products are said to be **competitive, or substitute, products.** *(Real whipping cream and imitation whipping cream are examples of competitive, or substitute, products.) If a decrease in demand for one product results in a decrease in demand for another product, the two products are said to be* **complementary products.** *(Fishing boats and outboard motors are examples of complementary products.) Partial derivatives can be used to test whether two products are competitive, complementary, or neither. We start with demand functions for two products where the demand for either depends on the prices for both:*

$$x = f(p, q) \quad \text{Demand function for product } A$$
$$y = g(p, q) \quad \text{Demand function for product } B$$

The variables x and y represent the number of units demanded of products A and B, respectively, at a price p for 1 unit of product A and a price q for 1 unit of product B. Normally, if the price of A increases while the price of B is held constant, then the demand for A will decrease; that is, $f_p(p, q) < 0$. Then, if A and B are competitive products, the demand for B will increase; that is, $g_p(p, q) > 0$. Similarly, if the price of B increases while the price of A is held constant, the demand for B will decrease; that is, $g_q(p, q) < 0$. And if A and B are competitive products, the demand for A will increase; that is, $f_q(p, q) > 0$. Reasoning similarly for complementary products, we arrive at the following test:

Test for Competitive and Complementary Products

Partial Derivatives	Products A and B
$f_q(p, q) > 0$ and $g_p(p, q) > 0$	Competitive (substitute)
$f_q(p, q) < 0$ and $g_p(p, q) < 0$	Complementary
$f_q(p, q) \geq 0$ and $g_p(p, q) \leq 0$	Neither
$f_q(p, q) \leq 0$ and $g_p(p, q) \geq 0$	Neither

Use this test in Problems 69–72 to determine whether the indicated products are competitive, complementary, or neither.

69. Product demand. The weekly demand equations for the sale of butter and margarine in a supermarket are

$x = f(p, q) = 8,000 - 0.09p^2 + 0.08q^2$ Butter

$y = g(p, q) = 15,000 + 0.04p^2 - 0.3q^2$ Margarine

70. Product demand. The daily demand equations for the sale of brand A coffee and brand B coffee in a supermarket are

$x = f(p, q) = 200 - 5p + 4q$ Brand A coffee

$y = g(p, q) = 300 + 2p - 4q$ Brand B coffee

71. Product demand. The monthly demand equations for the sale of skis and ski boots in a sporting goods store are

$x = f(p, q) = 800 - 0.004p^2 - 0.003q^2$ Skis

$y = g(p, q) = 600 - 0.003p^2 - 0.002q^2$ Ski boots

72. Product demand. The monthly demand equations for the sale of tennis rackets and tennis balls in a sporting goods store are

$x = f(p, q) = 500 - 0.5p - q^2$ Tennis rackets

$y = g(p, q) = 10,000 - 8p - 100q^2$ Tennis balls (cans)

Life Sciences

73. Medicine. The following empirical formula relates the surface area A (in square inches) of an average human body to its weight w (in pounds) and its height h (in inches):

$$A = f(w, h) = 15.64w^{0.425}h^{0.725}$$

Knowing the surface area of a human body is useful, for example, in studies pertaining to hypothermia (heat loss due to exposure).

(A) Find $f_w(w, h)$ and $f_h(w, h)$.

(B) For a 65-pound child who is 57 inches tall, find $f_w(65, 57)$ and $f_h(65, 57)$, and interpret the results.

74. Blood flow. Poiseuille's law states that the resistance, R, for blood flowing in a blood vessel varies directly as the length of the vessel, L, and inversely as the fourth power of its radius, r. Stated as an equation,

$$R(L, r) = k\frac{L}{r^4}   \quad k \text{ a constant}$$

Find $R_L(4, 0.2)$ and $R_r(4, 0.2)$, and interpret the results.

Social Sciences

75. Physical anthropology. Anthropologists, in their study of race and human genetic groupings, often use the cephalic index, C, which varies directly as the width, W, of the head, and inversely as the length, L, of the head (both viewed from the top). In terms of an equation,

$$C(W, L) = 100\frac{W}{L}$$

where

W = width in inches L = length in inches

Find $C_W(6, 8)$ and $C_L(6, 8)$, and interpret the results.

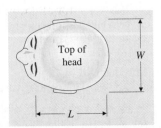

76. *Safety research.* Under ideal conditions, if a person driving a car slams on the brakes and skids to a stop, the length of the skid marks (in feet) is given by the formula

$$L(w, v) = kwv^2$$

where

k = constant
w = weight of car in pounds
v = speed of car in miles per hour

For $k = 0.000\ 013\ 3$, find $L_w(2{,}500, 60)$ and $L_v(2{,}500, 60)$, and interpret the results.

Section 8-3 | Maxima and Minima

We are now ready to undertake a brief but useful analysis of local maxima and minima for functions of the type $z = f(x, y)$. Basically, we are going to extend the second-derivative test developed for functions of a single independent variable. To start, we assume that all second-order partial derivatives exist for the function f in some circular region in the xy plane. This guarantees that the surface $z = f(x, y)$ has no sharp points, breaks, or ruptures. In other words, we are dealing only with smooth surfaces with no edges (like the edge of a box); or breaks (like an earthquake fault); or sharp points (like the bottom point of a golf tee). See Figure 1.

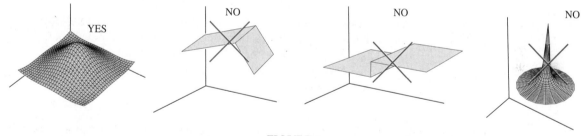

FIGURE 1

In addition, we will not concern ourselves with boundary points or absolute maxima–minima theory. Despite these restrictions, the procedure we are now going to describe will help us solve a large number of useful problems.

What does it mean for $f(a, b)$ to be a local maximum or a local minimum? We say that **$f(a, b)$ is a local maximum** if there exists a circular region in the domain of f with (a, b) as the center, such that

$$f(a, b) \geq f(x, y)$$

for all (x, y) in the region. Similarly, we say that **$f(a, b)$ is a local minimum** if there exists a circular region in the domain of f with (a, b) as the center, such that

$$f(a, b) \leq f(x, y)$$

for all (x, y) in the region. Figure 2A illustrates a local maximum, Figure 2B a local minimum, and Figure 2C a **saddle point,** which is neither a local maximum nor a local minimum.

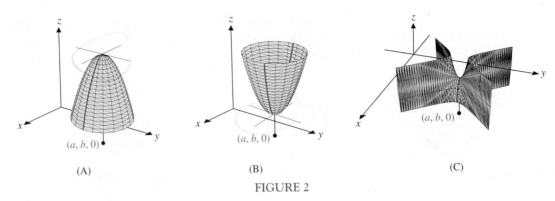

(A)   (B)   (C)

FIGURE 2

What happens to $f_x(a, b)$ and $f_y(a, b)$ if $f(a, b)$ is a local minimum or a local maximum and the partial derivatives of f exist in a circular region containing (a, b)? Figure 2 suggests that $f_x(a, b) = 0$ and $f_y(a, b) = 0$, since the tangent lines to the given curves are horizontal. Theorem 1 indicates that our intuitive reasoning is correct.

THEOREM 1   Local Extrema and Partial Derivatives

Let $f(a, b)$ be a local extremum (a local maximum or a local minimum) for the function f. If both f_x and f_y exist at (a, b) then

$$f_x(a, b) = 0 \quad \text{and} \quad f_y(a, b) = 0 \tag{1}$$

The converse of this theorem is false. That is, if $f_x(a, b) = 0$ and $f_y(a, b) = 0$, then $f(a, b)$ may or may not be a local extremum; for example, the point $(a, b, f(a, b))$ may be a saddle point (see Fig. 2C).

Theorem 1 gives us *necessary* (but not *sufficient*) conditions for $f(a, b)$ to be a local extremum. We thus find all points (a, b) such that $f_x(a, b) = 0$ and $f_y(a, b) = 0$ and test these further to determine whether $f(a, b)$ is a local extremum or a saddle point. Points (a, b) such that conditions (1) hold are called **critical points.**

1

(A) Let $f(x, y) = y^2 + 1$. Explain why $f(x, y)$ has a local minimum at every point on the x axis. Verify that every point on the x axis is a critical point. Explain why the graph of $z = f(x, y)$ could be described as a "trough."

(B) Let $g(x, y) = x^3$. Show that every point on the y axis is a critical point. Explain why no point on the y axis is a local extremum. Explain why the graph of $z = g(x, y)$ could be described as a "slide."

The next theorem, using second-derivative tests, gives us *sufficient* conditions for a critical point to produce a local extremum or a saddle point. (As was the case with Theorem 1, we state this theorem without proof.)

THEOREM 2   Second-Derivative Test for Local Extrema

Given

1. $z = f(x, y)$

2. $f_x(a, b) = 0$ and $f_y(a, b) = 0$ [(a, b) is a critical point]

3. All second-order partial derivatives of f exist in some circular region containing (a, b) as a center.

4. $A = f_{xx}(a, b)$, $B = f_{xy}(a, b)$, $C = f_{yy}(a, b)$

Then

Case 1. If $AC - B^2 > 0$ and $A < 0$, then $f(a, b)$ is a local maximum.

Case 2. If $AC - B^2 > 0$ and $A > 0$, then $f(a, b)$ is a local minimum.

Case 3. If $AC - B^2 < 0$, then f has a saddle point at (a, b).

Case 4. If $AC - B^2 = 0$, the test fails.

◉ **Insight**   The condition $A = f_{xx}(a, b) < 0$ in Case 1 of Theorem 2 is analogous to the condition $f''(c) < 0$ in the second-derivative test for a function of one variable (Section 4-4), which implies that the function is concave downward and therefore has a local maximum. Similarly, the condition $A = f_{xx}(a, b) > 0$ in Case 2 is analogous to the condition $f''(c) > 0$ in the earlier second-derivative test, which implies that the function is concave upward and therefore has a local minimum.   ●

FIGURE 3

To illustrate the use of Theorem 2, we will first find the local extremum for a very simple function whose solution is almost obvious: $z = f(x, y) = x^2 + y^2 + 2$. From the function f itself and its graph (Fig. 3), it is clear that a local minimum is found at $(0, 0)$. Let us see how Theorem 2 confirms this observation.

Step 1. Find critical points: Find (x, y) such that $f_x(x, y) = 0$ and $f_y(x, y) = 0$ simultaneously:

$$f_x(x, y) = 2x = 0 \qquad f_y(x, y) = 2y = 0$$
$$x = 0 \qquad\qquad y = 0$$

The only critical point is $(a, b) = (0, 0)$.

Step 2. Compute $A = f_{xx}(0, 0)$, $B = f_{xy}(0, 0)$, and $C = f_{yy}(0, 0)$:

$$f_{xx}(x, y) = 2 \qquad \text{thus} \qquad A = f_{xx}(0, 0) = 2$$
$$f_{xy}(x, y) = 0 \qquad \text{thus} \qquad B = f_{xy}(0, 0) = 0$$
$$f_{yy}(x, y) = 2 \qquad \text{thus} \qquad C = f_{yy}(0, 0) = 2$$

Step 3. Evaluate $AC - B^2$ and try to classify the critical point $(0, 0)$ using Theorem 2:

$$AC - B^2 = (2)(2) - (0)^2 = 4 > 0 \qquad \text{and} \qquad A = 2 > 0$$

Therefore, case 2 in Theorem 2 holds. That is, $f(0, 0) = 2$ is a local minimum.

We will now use Theorem 2 in the following examples to analyze extrema without the aid of graphs.

EXAMPLE 1   **Finding Local Extrema** Use Theorem 2 to find local extrema for

$$f(x, y) = -x^2 - y^2 + 6x + 8y - 21$$

Solution   **Step 1.** Find critical points: Find (x, y) such that $f_x(x, y) = 0$ and $f_y(x, y) = 0$ simultaneously:

$$f_x(x, y) = -2x + 6 = 0 \qquad f_y(x, y) = -2y + 8 = 0$$
$$x = 3 \qquad\qquad\qquad y = 4$$

The only critical point is $(a, b) = (3, 4)$.

Step 2. Compute $A = f_{xx}(3, 4)$, $B = f_{xy}(3, 4)$, and $C = f_{yy}(3, 4)$:

$$f_{xx}(x, y) = -2 \qquad \text{thus} \qquad A = f_{xx}(3, 4) = -2$$
$$f_{xy}(x, y) = 0 \qquad \text{thus} \qquad B = f_{xy}(3, 4) = 0$$
$$f_{yy}(x, y) = -2 \qquad \text{thus} \qquad C = f_{yy}(3, 4) = -2$$

Step 3. Evaluate $AC - B^2$ and try to classify the critical point $(3, 4)$ using Theorem 2:

$$AC - B^2 = (-2)(-2) - (0)^2 = 4 > 0 \qquad \text{and} \qquad A = -2 < 0$$

Therefore, case 1 in Theorem 2 holds. That is, $f(3, 4) = 4$ is a local maximum.

$\blacksquare$

Matched Problem 1   Use Theorem 2 to find local extrema for

$$f(x, y) = x^2 + y^2 - 10x - 2y + 36$$ _____

EXAMPLE 2   **Finding Local Extrema: Multiple Critical Points**   Use Theorem 2 to find local extrema for

$$f(x, y) = x^3 + y^3 - 6xy$$

Solution   **Step 1.** Find critical points for $f(x, y) = x^3 + y^3 - 6xy$:

$$f_x(x, y) = 3x^2 - 6y = 0 \qquad \text{Solve for } y.$$
$$6y = 3x^2$$
$$y = \tfrac{1}{2}x^2 \qquad\qquad\qquad\qquad (2)$$

$$f_y(x, y) = 3y^2 - 6x = 0$$
$$3y^2 = 6x \qquad \text{Use equation (2) to eliminate } y.$$
$$3(\tfrac{1}{2}x^2)^2 = 6x$$
$$\tfrac{3}{4}x^4 = 6x \qquad \text{Solve for } x.$$
$$3x^4 - 24x = 0$$
$$3x(x^3 - 8) = 0$$
$$x = 0 \quad \text{or} \quad x = 2$$
$$y = 0 \qquad\qquad y = \tfrac{1}{2}(2)^2 = 2$$

The critical points are $(0, 0)$ and $(2, 2)$.

Since there are two critical points, steps 2 and 3 must be performed twice.

Test (0, 0)   **Step 2.** Compute $A = f_{xx}(0, 0)$, $B = f_{xy}(0, 0)$, and $C = f_{yy}(0, 0)$:

$$f_{xx}(x, y) = 6x \qquad \text{thus} \qquad A = f_{xx}(0, 0) = 0$$
$$f_{xy}(x, y) = -6 \qquad \text{thus} \qquad B = f_{xy}(0, 0) = -6$$
$$f_{yy}(x, y) = 6y \qquad \text{thus} \qquad C = f_{yy}(0, 0) = 0$$

Step 3. Evaluate $AC - B^2$ and try to classify the critical point $(0, 0)$ using Theorem 2:

$$AC - B^2 = (0)(0) - (-6)^2 = -36 < 0$$

Therefore, case 3 in Theorem 2 applies. That is, f has a saddle point at $(0, 0)$.
Now we will consider the second critical point, $(2, 2)$.

Test (2, 2)   **Step 2.** Compute $A = f_{xx}(2, 2)$, $B = f_{xy}(2, 2)$, and $C = f_{yy}(2, 2)$:

$$
\begin{aligned}
f_{xx}(x, y) &= 6x &\text{thus} &\quad A = f_{xx}(2, 2) = 12 \\
f_{xy}(x, y) &= -6 &\text{thus} &\quad B = f_{xy}(2, 2) = -6 \\
f_{yy}(x, y) &= 6y &\text{thus} &\quad C = f_{yy}(2, 2) = 12
\end{aligned}
$$

Step 3. Evaluate $AC - B^2$ and try to classify the critical point $(2, 2)$ using Theorem 2:

$$AC - B^2 = (12)(12) - (-6)^2 = 108 > 0 \quad \text{and} \quad A = 12 > 0$$

Thus, case 2 in Theorem 2 applies, and $f(2, 2) = -8$ is a local minimum.   ∎

Our conclusions in Example 2 may be confirmed geometrically by graphing cross sections of the function f. The cross sections of f by the planes $y = 0$, $x = 0$, $y = x$, and $y = -x$ [each of these planes contains $(0, 0)$] are represented by the graphs of the functions $f(x, 0) = x^3$, $f(0, y) = y^3$, $f(x, x) = 2x^3 - 6x^2$, and $f(x, -x) = 6x^2$, respectively, as shown in Figure 4A (note that the first two functions have the same graph). The cross sections of f by the planes $y = 2, x = 2, y = x$, and $y = 4 - x$ [each of these planes contains $(2, 2)$] are represented by the graphs of the functions $f(x, 2) = x^3 - 12x + 8$, $f(2, y) = y^3 - 12y + 8$, $f(x, x) = 2x^3 - 6x^2$, and $f(x, 4 - x) = x^3 + (4 - x)^3 + 6x^2 - 24x$, respectively, as shown in Figure 4B (the first two functions have the same graph). Figure 4B illustrates the fact that since f has a local minimum at $(2, 2)$, each of the cross sections of f through $(2, 2)$ has a local minimum of -8 at $(2, 2)$. Figure 4A, on the other hand, indicates that some cross sections of f through $(0, 0)$ have a local minimum, some a local maximum, and some neither one, at $(0, 0)$.

(A) $y_1 = x^3$
$y_2 = 2x^3 - 6x^2$
$y_3 = 6x^2$

(B) $y_1 = x^3 - 12x + 8$
$y_2 = 2x^3 - 6x^2$
$y_3 = x^3 + (4 - x)^3 + 6x^2 - 24x$

FIGURE 4

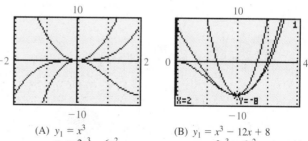

Matched Problem 2   Use Theorem 2 to find local extrema for $f(x, y) = x^3 + y^2 - 6xy$.

EXPLORE
&DISCUSS
2

Let $f(x, y) = x^4 + y^2 + 3$, $g(x, y) = 10 - x^2 - y^4$, and $h(x, y) = x^3 + y^2$.

(A) Show that each function has only $(0, 0)$ as a critical point.

(B) Explain why $f(x, y)$ has a minimum at $(0, 0)$, $g(x, y)$ has a maximum at $(0, 0)$, and $h(x, y)$ has neither a minimum nor a maximum at $(0, 0)$.

(C) Are the results of part (B) consequences of Theorem 2? Explain.

EXAMPLE 3   **Profit** Suppose that the surfboard company discussed earlier has developed the yearly profit equation

$$P(x, y) = -22x^2 + 22xy - 11y^2 + 110x - 44y - 23$$

where x is the number (in thousands) of standard surfboards produced per year, y is the number (in thousands) of competition surfboards produced per year, and P is profit (in thousands of dollars). How many of each type of board should be produced per year to realize a maximum profit? What is the maximum profit?

Solution **Step 1.** Find critical points:

$$P_x(x, y) = -44x + 22y + 110 = 0$$
$$P_y(x, y) = 22x - 22y - 44 = 0$$

Solving this system, we obtain $(3, 1)$ as the only critical point.

Step 2. Compute $A = P_{xx}(3, 1)$, $B = P_{xy}(3, 1)$, and $C = P_{yy}(3, 1)$:

$$P_{xx}(x, y) = -44 \quad \text{thus} \quad A = P_{xx}(3, 1) = -44$$
$$P_{xy}(x, y) = 22 \quad \text{thus} \quad B = P_{xy}(3, 1) = 22$$
$$P_{yy}(x, y) = -22 \quad \text{thus} \quad C = P_{yy}(3, 1) = -22$$

Step 3. Evaluate $AC - B^2$ and try to classify the critical point $(3, 1)$ using Theorem 2:

$$AC - B^2 = (-44)(-22) - 22^2 = 484 > 0 \quad \text{and} \quad A = -44 < 0$$

Therefore, case 1 in Theorem 2 applies. That is, $P(3, 1) = 120$ is a local maximum. A maximum profit of $120,000 is obtained by producing and selling 3,000 standard boards and 1,000 competition boards per year.

Matched Problem 3   Repeat Example 3 with

$$P(x, y) = -66x^2 + 132xy - 99y^2 + 132x - 66y - 19$$

EXAMPLE 4   **Package Design** The packaging department in a company has been asked to design a rectangular box with no top and a partition down the middle. The box must have a volume of 48 cubic inches. Find the dimensions that will minimize the amount of material used to construct the box.

Solution Refer to Figure 5. The amount of material used in constructing this box is

$$\underset{\substack{\text{Base}}}{} \underset{\substack{\text{Front,} \\ \text{back}}}{} \underset{\substack{\text{Sides,} \\ \text{partition}}}{}$$

$$M = xy + 2xz + 3yz \qquad (3)$$

FIGURE 5

The volume of the box is

$$V = xyz = 48 \qquad (4)$$

Since Theorem 2 applies only to functions with two independent variables, we must use equation (4) to eliminate one of the variables in equation (3):

$$M = xy + 2xz + 3yz \qquad \text{Substitute } z = 48/xy.$$

$$= xy + 2x\left(\frac{48}{xy}\right) + 3y\left(\frac{48}{xy}\right)$$

$$= xy + \frac{96}{y} + \frac{144}{x}$$

Thus, we must find the minimum value of

$$M(x, y) = xy + \frac{96}{y} + \frac{144}{x} \qquad x > 0 \qquad \text{and} \qquad y > 0$$

Step 1. Find critical points:

$$M_x(x, y) = y - \frac{144}{x^2} = 0$$

$$y = \frac{144}{x^2} \qquad (5)$$

$$M_y(x, y) = x - \frac{96}{y^2} = 0$$

$$x = \frac{96}{y^2} \qquad \text{Solve for } y^2.$$

$$y^2 = \frac{96}{x} \qquad \text{Use equation (5) to eliminate } y \text{ and solve for } x.$$

$$\left(\frac{144}{x^2}\right)^2 = \frac{96}{x}$$

$$\frac{20{,}736}{x^4} = \frac{96}{x} \qquad \text{Multiply both sides by } x^4/96 \text{ (recall, } x > 0\text{).}$$

$$x^3 = \frac{20{,}736}{96} = 216$$

$$x = 6 \qquad \text{Use equation (5) to find } y.$$

$$y = \frac{144}{36} = 4$$

Thus, $(6, 4)$ is the only critical point.

Step 2. Compute $A = M_{xx}(6, 4)$, $B = M_{xy}(6, 4)$, and $C = M_{yy}(6, 4)$:

$$M_{xx}(x, y) = \frac{288}{x^3} \qquad \text{thus} \qquad A = M_{xx}(6, 4) = \tfrac{288}{216} = \tfrac{4}{3}$$

$$M_{xy}(x, y) = 1 \qquad \text{thus} \qquad B = M_{xy}(6, 4) = 1$$

$$M_{yy}(x, y) = \frac{192}{y^3} \qquad \text{thus} \qquad C = M_{yy}(6, 4) = \tfrac{192}{64} = 3$$

Step 3. Evaluate $AC - B^2$ and try to classify the critical point $(6, 4)$ using Theorem 2:

$$AC - B^2 = \left(\tfrac{4}{3}\right)(3) - (1)^2 = 3 > 0 \qquad \text{and} \qquad A = \tfrac{4}{3} > 0$$

Therefore, case 2 in Theorem 2 applies; $M(x, y)$ has a local minimum at $(6, 4)$. If $x = 6$ and $y = 4$, then

$$z = \frac{48}{xy} = \frac{48}{(6)(4)} = 2$$

Thus, the dimensions that will require the minimum amount of material are 6 inches by 4 inches by 2 inches. ■

Matched Problem 4 If the box in Example 4 must have a volume of 384 cubic inches, find the dimensions that will require the least amount of material. ──────────■

Answers to Matched Problems   **1.** $f(5, 1) = 10$ is a local minimum

2. f has a saddle point at $(0, 0)$; $f(6, 18) = -108$ is a local minimum

3. Local maximum for $x = 2$ and $y = 1$; $P(2, 1) = 80$; a maximum profit of \$80,000 is obtained by producing and selling 2,000 standard boards and 1,000 competition boards

4. 12 in. by 8 in. by 4 in.

Exercise 8-3

A *In Problems 1–4, find $f_x(x, y)$ and $f_y(x, y)$ and explain, using Theorem 1, why $f(x, y)$ has no local extrema.*

1. $f(x, y) = 4x + 5y - 6$

2. $f(x, y) = 10 - 2x - 3y + x^2$

3. $f(x, y) = 3.7 - 1.2x + 6.8y + 0.2y^3 + x^4$

4. $f(x, y) = x^3 - y^2 + 7x + 3y + 1$

Find local extrema in Problems 5–24 using Theorem 2.

5. $f(x, y) = 6 - x^2 - 4x - y^2$

6. $f(x, y) = 3 - x^2 - y^2 + 6y$

7. $f(x, y) = x^2 + y^2 + 2x - 6y + 14$

8. $f(x, y) = x^2 + y^2 - 4x + 6y + 23$

B

9. $f(x, y) = xy + 2x - 3y - 2$

10. $f(x, y) = x^2 - y^2 + 2x + 6y - 4$

11. $f(x, y) = -3x^2 + 2xy - 2y^2 + 14x + 2y + 10$

12. $f(x, y) = -x^2 + xy - 2y^2 + x + 10y - 5$

13. $f(x, y) = 2x^2 - 2xy + 3y^2 - 4x - 8y + 20$

14. $f(x, y) = 2x^2 - xy + y^2 - x - 5y + 8$

C

15. $f(x, y) = e^{xy}$

16. $f(x, y) = x^2y - xy^2$

17. $f(x, y) = x^3 + y^3 - 3xy$

18. $f(x, y) = 2y^3 - 6xy - x^2$

19. $f(x, y) = 2x^4 + y^2 - 12xy$

20. $f(x, y) = 16xy - x^4 - 2y^2$

21. $f(x, y) = x^3 - 3xy^2 + 6y^2$

22. $f(x, y) = 2x^2 - 2x^2y + 6y^3$

23. $f(x, y) = y^3 + 2x^2y^2 - 3x - 2y + 8$

24. $f(x, y) = x \ln y + x^2 - 4x - 5y + 3$

25. Explain why $f(x, y) = x^2$ has an infinite number of local extrema.

26. (A) Find the local extrema of the functions $f(x, y) = x + y$, $g(x, y) = x^2 + y^2$, and $h(x, y) = x^3 + y^3$.

(B) Discuss the local extrema of the function $k(x, y) = x^n + y^n$, where n is a positive integer.

27. (A) Show that $(0, 0)$ is a critical point for the function $f(x, y) = x^4e^y + x^2y^4 + 1$, but that the second-derivative test for local extrema fails.

(B) Use cross sections, as in Example 2, to decide whether f has a local maximum, a local minimum, or a saddle point at $(0, 0)$.

28. (A) Show that $(0, 0)$ is a critical point for the function $g(x, y) = e^{xy^2} + x^2y^3 + 2$, but that the second-derivative test for local extrema fails.

(B) Use cross sections, as in Example 2, to decide whether g has a local maximum, a local minimum, or a saddle point at $(0, 0)$.

Applications

Business & Economics

29. *Product mix for maximum profit.* A firm produces two types of calculators, x thousand of type A and y thousand of type B per year. If the revenue and cost equations for the year are (in millions of dollars)

$$R(x, y) = 2x + 3y$$
$$C(x, y) = x^2 - 2xy + 2y^2 + 6x - 9y + 5$$

determine how many of each type of calculator should be produced per year to maximize profit. What is the maximum profit?

30. *Automation–labor mix for minimum cost.* The annual labor and automated equipment cost (in millions of dollars) for a company's production of television sets is given by

$$C(x, y) = 2x^2 + 2xy + 3y^2 - 16x - 18y + 54$$

where x is the amount spent per year on labor and y is the amount spent per year on automated equipment (both in millions of dollars). Determine how much should be spent on each per year to minimize this cost. What is the minimum cost?

31. *Maximizing profit.* A department store sells two brands of inexpensive calculators. The store pays \$6 for each brand A calculator and \$8 for each brand B calculator. The research department has estimated the following weekly demand equations for these two competitive products:

$x = 116 - 30p + 20q$ *Demand equation for brand A*
$y = 144 + 16p - 24q$ *Demand equation for brand B*

where p is the selling price for brand A and q is the selling price for brand B.

(A) Determine the demands x and y when $p = \$10$ and $q = \$12$; when $p = \$11$ and $q = \$11$.

(B) How should the store price each calculator to maximize weekly profits? What is the maximum weekly profit? [*Hint:* $C = 6x + 8y$, $R = px + qy$, and $P = R - C$.]

32. *Maximizing profit.* A store sells two brands of color print film. The store pays \$2 for each roll of brand A film and \$3 for each roll of brand B film. A consulting firm has estimated the following daily demand equations for these two competitive products:

$x = 75 - 40p + 25q$ *Demand equation for brand A*
$y = 80 + 20p - 30q$ *Demand equation for brand B*

where p is the selling price for brand A and q is the selling price for brand B.

(A) Determine the demands x and y when $p = \$4$ and $q = \$5$; when $p = \$4$ and $q = \$4$.

(B) How should the store price each brand of film to maximize daily profits? What is the

maximum daily profit? [*Hint:* $C = 2x + 3y$, $R = px + qy$, and $P = R - C$.]

33. *Minimizing cost.* A satellite television reception station is to be located at $P(x, y)$ so that the sum of the squares of the distances from P to the three towns A, B, and C is minimum (see the figure). Find the coordinates of P. This location will minimize the cost of providing satellite cable television for all three towns.

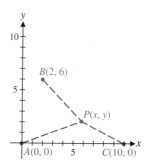

Figure for 33

34. *Minimizing cost.* Repeat Problem 33, replacing the coordinates of B with $B(6, 9)$ and the coordinates of C with $C(9, 0)$.

35. *Minimum material.* A rectangular box with no top and two parallel partitions (see the figure) is to be made to hold a volume of 64 cubic inches. Find the dimensions that will require the least amount of material.

Figure for 35

36. *Minimum material.* A rectangular box with no top and two intersecting partitions (see the figure) is to be made to hold a volume of 72 cubic inches. What should its dimensions be in order to use the least amount of material in its construction?

Figure for 36

37. *Maximum volume.* A mailing service states that a rectangular package shall have the sum of the length and girth not to exceed 120 inches (see the figure). What are the dimensions of the largest (in volume) mailing carton that can be constructed meeting these restrictions?

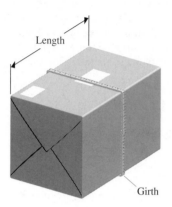

Figure for 37

38. *Maximum shipping volume.* A shipping box is to be reinforced with steel bands in all three directions, as indicated in the figure. A total of 150 inches of steel tape is to be used, with 6 inches of waste because of a 2-inch overlap in each direction. Find the dimensions of the box with maximum volume that can be taped as indicated.

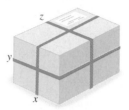

Figure for 38

Section 8-4 | Maxima and Minima Using Lagrange Multipliers

➤ Functions of Two Independent Variables
➤ Functions of Three Independent Variables

➤ Functions of Two Independent Variables

We will now consider a particularly powerful method of solving a certain class of maxima–minima problems. The method is due to Joseph Louis Lagrange (1736–1813), an eminent eighteenth-century French mathematician, and it is called the **method of Lagrange multipliers.** We introduce the method through an example; then we formalize the discussion in the form of a theorem.

A rancher wants to construct two feeding pens of the same size along an existing fence (see Fig. 1). If the rancher has 720 feet of fencing materials available, how long should x and y be in order to obtain the maximum total area? What is the maximum area?

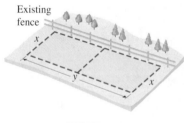

FIGURE 1

The total area is given by

$$f(x, y) = xy$$

which can be made as large as we like, provided that there are no restrictions on x and y. But there are restrictions on x and y, since we have only 720 feet of fencing. That is, x and y must be chosen so that

$$3x + y = 720$$

This restriction on x and y, called a **constraint,** leads to the following maxima–minima problem:

$$\text{Maximize} \quad f(x, y) = xy \tag{1}$$
$$\text{subject to} \quad 3x + y = 720 \quad \text{or} \quad 3x + y - 720 = 0 \tag{2}$$

This problem is a special case of a general class of problems of the form

$$\text{Maximize (or minimize)} \quad z = f(x, y) \tag{3}$$
$$\text{subject to} \quad g(x, y) = 0 \tag{4}$$

Of course, we could try to solve equation (4) for y in terms of x, or for x in terms of y, then substitute the result into equation (3), and use methods developed in Section 4-4 for functions of a single variable. But what if equation (4) were more complicated than equation (2), and solving for one variable in terms of the other was either very difficult or impossible? In the method of Lagrange multipliers, we will work with $g(x, y)$ directly and avoid having to solve equation (4) for one variable in terms of the other. In addition, the method generalizes to functions of arbitrarily many variables subject to one or more constraints.

Now, to the method. We form a new function F, using functions f and g in equations (3) and (4), as follows:

$$F(x, y, \lambda) = f(x, y) + \lambda g(x, y) \tag{5}$$

where λ (the Greek lowercase letter lambda) is called a **Lagrange multiplier.** Theorem 1 gives the basis for the method.

THEOREM 1   Method of Lagrange Multipliers for Functions of Two Variables

Any local maxima or minima of the function $z = f(x, y)$ subject to the constraint $g(x, y) = 0$ will be among those points (x_0, y_0) for which (x_0, y_0, λ_0) is a solution to the system

$$F_x(x, y, \lambda) = 0$$
$$F_y(x, y, \lambda) = 0$$
$$F_\lambda(x, y, \lambda) = 0$$

where $F(x, y, \lambda) = f(x, y) + \lambda g(x, y)$, provided that all the partial derivatives exist.

We now solve the fence problem using the method of Lagrange multipliers.

Step 1. Formulate the problem in the form of equations (3) and (4):

$$\text{Maximize} \quad f(x, y) = xy$$
$$\text{subject to} \quad g(x, y) = 3x + y - 720 = 0$$

Step 2. Form the function F, introducing the Lagrange multiplier λ:

$$F(x, y, \lambda) = f(x, y) + \lambda g(x, y)$$
$$= xy + \lambda(3x + y - 720)$$

Step 3. Solve the system $F_x = 0, F_y = 0, F_\lambda = 0$. (The solutions are called **critical points** for F.)

$$F_x = y + 3\lambda = 0$$
$$F_y = x + \lambda = 0$$
$$F_\lambda = 3x + y - 720 = 0$$

From the first two equations, we see that

$$y = -3\lambda$$
$$x = -\lambda$$

Substitute these values for x and y into the third equation and solve for λ:

$$-3\lambda - 3\lambda = 720$$
$$-6\lambda = 720$$
$$\lambda = -120$$

Thus,

$$y = -3(-120) = 360 \text{ feet}$$
$$x = -(-120) = 120 \text{ feet}$$

and $(x_0, y_0, \lambda_0) = (120, 360, -120)$ is the only critical point for F.

Step 4. According to Theorem 1, if the function $f(x, y)$, subject to the constraint $g(x, y) = 0$, has a local maximum or minimum, it must occur at $x = 120$, $y = 360$. Although it is possible to develop a test similar to Theorem 2 in Section 8-3 to determine the nature of this local extremum, we will not do so. [Note that Theorem 2 cannot be applied to $f(x, y)$ at $(120, 360)$, since this point is not a critical point of the unconstrained function $f(x, y)$.] We simply assume that the maximum value of $f(x, y)$ must occur for $x = 120$, $y = 360$. Thus,

$$\text{Max } f(x, y) = f(120, 360)$$
$$= (120)(360) = 43{,}200 \text{ square feet}$$

The key steps in applying the method of Lagrange multipliers are listed in the following box:

PROCEDURE   **Method of Lagrange Multipliers: Key Steps**

Step 1. Formulate the problem in the form

$$\text{Maximize (or minimize)} \quad z = f(x, y)$$
$$\text{subject to} \qquad\qquad g(x, y) = 0$$

Step 2. Form the function F:

$$F(x, y, \lambda) = f(x, y) + \lambda g(x, y)$$

Step 3. Find the critical points for F, that is, solve the system

$$F_x(x, y, \lambda) = 0$$
$$F_y(x, y, \lambda) = 0$$
$$F_\lambda(x, y, \lambda) = 0$$

Step 4. If (x_0, y_0, λ_0) is the only critical point of F, we assume that (x_0, y_0) will always produce the solution to the problems we consider. If F has more than one critical point, we evaluate $z = f(x, y)$ at (x_0, y_0) for each critical point (x_0, y_0, λ_0) of F. For the problems we consider, we assume that the largest of these values is the maximum value of $f(x, y)$, subject to the constraint $g(x, y) = 0$, and the smallest is the minimum value of $f(x, y)$, subject to the constraint $g(x, y) = 0$.

EXAMPLE 1   **Minimization Subject to a Constraint** Minimize $f(x, y) = x^2 + y^2$ subject to $x + y = 10$.

Solution   **Step 1.**   Minimize $f(x, y) = x^2 + y^2$
$$\text{subject to} \quad g(x, y) = x + y - 10 = 0$$

Step 2.
$$F(x, y, \lambda) = x^2 + y^2 + \lambda(x + y - 10)$$

Step 3.
$$F_x = 2x + \lambda = 0$$
$$F_y = 2y + \lambda = 0$$
$$F_\lambda = x + y - 10 = 0$$

From the first two equations, $x = -\lambda/2$ and $y = -\lambda/2$. Substituting these into the third equation, we obtain

$$-\frac{\lambda}{2} - \frac{\lambda}{2} = 10$$
$$-\lambda = 10$$
$$\lambda = -10$$

The only critical point is $(x_0, y_0, \lambda_0) = (5, 5, -10)$.

Step 4. Since $(5, 5, -10)$ is the only critical point for F, we conclude that (see step 4 in the box)

$$\text{Min } f(x, y) = f(5, 5) = (5)^2 + (5)^2 = 50 \qquad \blacksquare$$

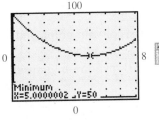

FIGURE 2 $h(x) = x^2 + (10 - x)^2$

Since $g(x, y)$ in Example 1 has a relatively simple form, an alternative to the method of Lagrange multipliers is to solve $g(x, y) = 0$ for y, and then substitute into $f(x, y)$ to obtain the function $h(x) = f(x, 10 - x) = x^2 + (10 - x)^2$ in the single variable x. Then minimize h (see Fig. 2). Again, we conclude that Min $f(x, y) = f(5, 5) = 50$. This technique depends on being able to solve the constraint for one of the two variables, and thus is not always available as an alternative to the method of Lagrange multipliers.

Matched Problem 1   Maximize $f(x, y) = 25 - x^2 - y^2$ subject to $x + y = 4$.

Figures 3 and 4 illustrate the results obtained in Example 1 and Matched Problem 1, respectively.

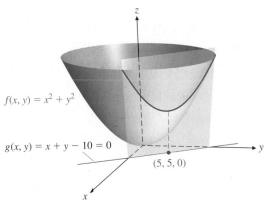

FIGURE 3

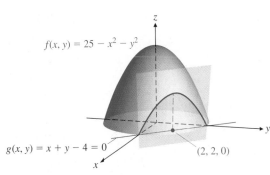

FIGURE 4

Consider the problem of minimizing $f(x, y) = 3x^2 + 5y^2$ subject to the constraint $g(x, y) = 2x + 3y - 6 = 0$.

(A) Compute the value of $f(x, y)$ when x and y are integers, $0 \le x \le 3$, $0 \le y \le 2$. Record your answers next to the points (x, y) in Figure 5.

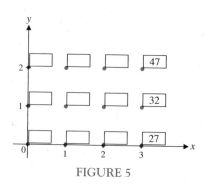

FIGURE 5

(B) Graph the constraint $g(x, y) = 0$.
(C) Estimate the minimum value of f on the basis of your graph and the computations from part (A).
(D) Use the method of Lagrange multipliers to solve the minimization problem.

EXAMPLE 2 **Productivity** The Cobb–Douglas production function for a new product is given by

$$N(x, y) = 16x^{0.25}y^{0.75}$$

where x is the number of units of labor and y is the number of units of capital required to produce $N(x, y)$ units of the product. Each unit of labor costs \$50 and each unit of capital costs \$100. If \$500,000 has been budgeted for the production of this product, how should this amount be allocated between labor and capital in order to maximize production? What is the maximum number of units that can be produced?

Solution The total cost of using x units of labor and y units of capital is $50x + 100y$. Thus, the constraint imposed by the \$500,000 budget is

$$50x + 100y = 500,000$$

Step 1. Maximize $N(x, y) = 16x^{0.25}y^{0.75}$

subject to $g(x, y) = 50x + 100y - 500,000 = 0$

Step 2. $F(x, y, \lambda) = 16x^{0.25}y^{0.75} + \lambda(50x + 100y - 500,000)$

Step 3. $F_x = 4x^{-0.75}y^{0.75} + 50\lambda = 0$

$F_y = 12x^{0.25}y^{-0.25} + 100\lambda = 0$

$F_\lambda = 50x + 100y - 500,000 = 0$

From the first two equations,

$$\lambda = -\tfrac{2}{25}x^{-0.75}y^{0.75} \qquad \text{and} \qquad \lambda = -\tfrac{3}{25}x^{0.25}y^{-0.25}$$

Thus,

$$-\tfrac{2}{25}x^{-0.75}y^{0.75} = -\tfrac{3}{25}x^{0.25}y^{-0.25} \quad \text{Multiply both sides by } x^{0.75}y^{0.25}.$$

$$-\tfrac{2}{25}y = -\tfrac{3}{25}x \qquad \text{(We can assume that } x \neq 0 \text{ and } y \neq 0.)$$

$$y = \tfrac{3}{2}x$$

Now, substitute for y in the third equation and solve for x:

$$50x + 100(\tfrac{3}{2}x) - 500{,}000 = 0$$

$$200x = 500{,}000$$

$$x = 2{,}500$$

Thus,

$$y = \tfrac{3}{2}(2{,}500) = 3{,}750$$

and

$$\lambda = -\tfrac{2}{25}(2{,}500)^{-0.75}(3{,}750)^{0.75} \approx -0.1084$$

The only critical point of F is $(2{,}500, 3{,}750, -0.1084)$.

Step 4. Since F has only one critical point, we conclude that maximum productivity occurs when 2,500 units of labor and 3,750 units of capital are used (see step 4 in the method of Lagrange multipliers). Thus,

$$\text{Max } N(x, y) = N(2{,}500, 3{,}750)$$

$$= 16(2{,}500)^{0.25}(3{,}750)^{0.75}$$

$$\approx 54{,}216 \text{ units} \qquad \blacksquare$$

The negative of the value of the Lagrange multiplier found in step 3 is called the **marginal productivity of money** and gives the approximate increase in production for each additional dollar spent on production. In Example 2, increasing the production budget from $500,000 to $600,000 would result in an approximate increase in production of

$$0.1084(100{,}000) = 10{,}840 \text{ units}$$

Note that simplifying the constraint equation

$$50x + 100y - 500{,}000 = 0$$

to

$$x + 2y - 10{,}000 = 0$$

before forming the function $F(x, y, \lambda)$ would make it difficult to interpret $-\lambda$ correctly. Thus, **in marginal productivity problems, the constraint equation should not be simplified.**

Matched Problem 2

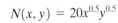

The Cobb–Douglas production function for a new product is given by

$$N(x, y) = 20x^{0.5}y^{0.5}$$

where x is the number of units of labor and y is the number of units of capital required to produce $N(x, y)$ units of the product. Each unit of labor costs $40 and each unit of capital costs $120.

(A) If $300,000 has been budgeted for the production of this product, how should this amount be allocated in order to maximize production? What is the maximum production?

(B) Find the marginal productivity of money in this case, and estimate the increase in production if an additional $40,000 is budgeted for production.

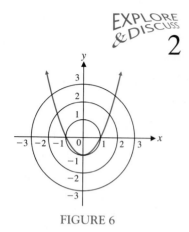

FIGURE 6

EXPLORE
&DISCUSS
2

Consider the problem of maximizing $f(x, y) = 4 - x^2 - y^2$ subject to the constraint $g(x, y) = y - x^2 + 1 = 0$.

(A) Explain why $f(x, y) = 3$ whenever (x, y) is a point on the circle of radius 1 centered at the origin. What is the value of $f(x, y)$ when (x, y) is a point on the circle of radius 2 centered at the origin? On the circle of radius 3 centered at the origin? (See Fig. 6.)

(B) Explain why some points on the parabola $y - x^2 + 1 = 0$ lie inside the circle $x^2 + y^2 = 1$.

(C) In light of part (B), would you guess that the maximum value of $f(x, y)$ subject to the constraint is greater than 3? Explain.

(D) Use Lagrange multipliers to solve the maximization problem.

➤ Functions of Three Independent Variables

We have indicated that the method of Lagrange multipliers can be extended to functions with arbitrarily many independent variables with one or more constraints. We now state a theorem for functions with three independent variables and one constraint, and consider an example that will demonstrate the advantage of the method of Lagrange multipliers over the method used in Section 8-3.

THEOREM 1 **Method of Lagrange Multipliers for Functions of Three Variables**

Any local maxima or minima of the function $w = f(x, y, z)$ subject to the constraint $g(x, y, z) = 0$ will be among the set of points (x_0, y_0, z_0) for which $(x_0, y_0, z_0, \lambda_0)$ is a solution to the system

$$F_x(x, y, z, \lambda) = 0$$
$$F_y(x, y, z, \lambda) = 0$$
$$F_z(x, y, z, \lambda) = 0$$
$$F_\lambda(x, y, z, \lambda) = 0$$

where $F(x, y, z, \lambda) = f(x, y, z) + \lambda g(x, y, z)$, provided that all the partial derivatives exist.

EXAMPLE 3 **Package Design** A rectangular box with an open top and one partition is to be constructed from 162 square inches of cardboard (Fig. 7). Find the dimensions that will result in a box with the largest possible volume.

Solution We must maximize

$$V(x, y, z) = xyz$$

subject to the constraint that the amount of material used is 162 square inches. Thus, x, y, and z must satisfy

$$xy + 2xz + 3yz = 162$$

Step 1. Maximize $V(x, y, z) = xyz$
subject to $g(x, y, z) = xy + 2xz + 3yz - 162 = 0$

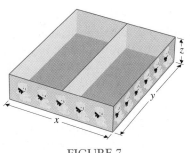

FIGURE 7

Step 2.
$$F(x, y, z, \lambda) = xyz + \lambda(xy + 2xz + 3yz - 162)$$

Step 3.
$$F_x = yz + \lambda(y + 2z) = 0$$
$$F_y = xz + \lambda(x + 3z) = 0$$
$$F_z = xy + \lambda(2x + 3y) = 0$$
$$F_\lambda = xy + 2xz + 3yz - 162 = 0$$

From the first two equations, we can write

$$\lambda = \frac{-yz}{y + 2z} \qquad \lambda = \frac{-xz}{x + 3z}$$

Eliminating λ, we have

$$\frac{-yz}{y + 2z} = \frac{-xz}{x + 3z}$$
$$-xyz - 3yz^2 = -xyz - 2xz^2 \qquad \textit{We can assume that } z \neq 0.$$
$$3yz^2 = 2xz^2$$
$$3y = 2x$$
$$x = \tfrac{3}{2}y$$

From the second and third equations,

$$\lambda = \frac{-xz}{x + 3z} \qquad \lambda = \frac{-xy}{2x + 3y}$$

Eliminating λ, we have

$$\frac{-xz}{x + 3z} = \frac{-xy}{2x + 3y}$$
$$-2x^2z - 3xyz = -x^2y - 3xyz \qquad \textit{We can assume that } x \neq 0.$$
$$2x^2z = x^2y$$
$$2z = y$$
$$z = \tfrac{1}{2}y$$

Substituting $x = \tfrac{3}{2}y$ and $z = \tfrac{1}{2}y$ in the fourth equation, we have

$$\left(\tfrac{3}{2}y\right)y + 2\left(\tfrac{3}{2}y\right)\left(\tfrac{1}{2}y\right) + 3y\left(\tfrac{1}{2}y\right) - 162 = 0$$

$$\tfrac{3}{2}y^2 + \tfrac{3}{2}y^2 + \tfrac{3}{2}y^2 = 162$$
$$y^2 = 36 \qquad \textit{We can assume that } y > 0.$$
$$y = 6$$
$$x = \tfrac{3}{2}(6) = 9 \quad \textit{Using } x = \tfrac{3}{2}y$$
$$z = \tfrac{1}{2}(6) = 3 \quad \textit{Using } z = \tfrac{1}{2}y$$

and finally,

$$\lambda = \frac{-(6)(3)}{6 + 2(3)} = -\frac{3}{2} \quad \textit{Using } \lambda = \frac{-yz}{y + 2z}$$

Thus, the only critical point of F with x, y, and z all positive is $(9, 6, 3, -\tfrac{3}{2})$.

Step 4. The box with maximum volume has dimensions 9 inches by 6 inches by 3 inches.

Matched Problem 3 A box of the same type as described in Example 3 is to be constructed from 288 square inches of cardboard. Find the dimensions that will result in a box with the largest possible volume.

Insight An alternative to the method of Lagrange multipliers would be to solve Example 3 by means of Theorem 2 (The Second Derivative Test for Local Extrema) of Section 8-3. That approach would involve solving the material constraint for one of the variables, say z:

$$z = \frac{162 - xy}{2x + 3y}$$

Then we would eliminate z in the volume function to obtain a function of two variables:

$$V(x, y) = xy\frac{162 - xy}{2x + 3y}$$

The method of Lagrange multipliers allows us to avoid the formidable tasks of calculating the partial derivatives of V and finding the critical points of V in order to apply Theorem 2.

Answers to Matched Problems

1. Max $f(x, y) = f(2, 2) = 17$ (see Fig. 4)

2. (A) 3,750 units of labor and 1,250 units of capital;
   Max $N(x, y) = N(3,750, 1,250) \approx 43,301$ units
   (B) Marginal productivity of money ≈ 0.1443; increase in production $\approx 5,774$ units

3. 12 in. by 8 in. by 4 in.

Exercise 8-4

A *Use the method of Lagrange multipliers in Problems 1–4.*

1. Maximize $f(x, y) = 2xy$
   subject to $x + y = 6$

2. Minimize $f(x, y) = 6xy$
   subject to $y - x = 6$

3. Minimize $f(x, y) = x^2 + y^2$
   subject to $3x + 4y = 25$

4. Maximize $f(x, y) = 25 - x^2 - y^2$
   subject to $2x + y = 10$

B *In Problems 5 and 6, use Theorem 1 to explain why no maxima or minima exist.*

5. Minimize $f(x, y) = 4y - 3x$
   subject to $2x + 5y = 3$

6. Maximize $f(x, y) = 6x + 5y + 24$
   subject to $3x + 2y = 4$

Use the method of Lagrange multipliers in Problems 7–16.

7. Find the maximum and minimum of $f(x, y) = 2xy$ subject to $x^2 + y^2 = 18$.

8. Find the maximum and minimum of $f(x, y) = x^2 - y^2$ subject to $x^2 + y^2 = 25$.

9. Maximize the product of two numbers if their sum must be 10.

10. Minimize the product of two numbers if their difference must be 10.

C

11. Minimize $f(x, y, z) = x^2 + y^2 + z^2$
   subject to $2x - y + 3z = -28$

12. Maximize $f(x, y, z) = xyz$
   subject to $2x + y + 2z = 120$

13. Maximize and minimize $f(x, y, z) = x + y + z$
   subject to $x^2 + y^2 + z^2 = 12$

14. Maximize and minimize $f(x, y, z) = 2x + 4y + 4z$
subject to $x^2 + y^2 + z^2 = 9$

15. Maximize $f(x, y) = y + xy^2$
subject to $x + y^2 = 1$

16. Maximize and minimize $f(x, y) = x + e^y$
subject to $x^2 + y^2 = 1$

In Problems 17 and 18, use Theorem 1 to explain why no maxima or minima exist.

17. Maximize $f(x, y) = e^x + 3e^y$
subject to $x - 2y = 6$

18. Minimize $f(x, y) = x^3 + 2y^3$
subject to $6x - 2y = 1$

19. Consider the problem of maximizing $f(x, y)$ subject to $g(x, y) = 0$, where $g(x, y) = y - 5$. Explain how the maximization problem can be solved without using the method of Lagrange multipliers.

20. Consider the problem of minimizing $f(x, y)$ subject to $g(x, y) = 0$, where $g(x, y) = 4x - y + 3$. Explain how the minimization problem can be solved without using the method of Lagrange multipliers.

21. Consider the problem of maximizing $f(x, y) = e^{-(x^2+y^2)}$ subject to the constraint $g(x, y) = x^2 + y - 1 = 0$.

(A) Solve the constraint equation for y, and then substitute into $f(x, y)$ to obtain a function $h(x)$ of the single variable x. Graph h and solve the original maximization problem by maximizing h (round answers to three decimal places).

(B) Confirm your answer using the method of Lagrange multipliers.

22. Consider the problem of minimizing
$$f(x, y) = x^2 + 2y^2$$
subject to the constraint $g(x, y) = ye^{x^2} - 1 = 0$.

(A) Solve the constraint equation for y, and then substitute into $f(x, y)$ to obtain a function $h(x)$ of the single variable x. Graph h and solve the original minimization problem by minimizing h (round answers to three decimal places).

(B) Confirm your answer using the method of Lagrange multipliers.

Applications

Business & Economics

23. *Budgeting for least cost.* A manufacturing company produces two models of a television set, x units of model A and y units of model B per week, at a cost (in dollars) of
$$C(x, y) = 6x^2 + 12y^2$$
If it is necessary (because of shipping considerations) that
$$x + y = 90$$
how many of each type of set should be manufactured per week to minimize cost? What is the minimum cost?

24. *Budgeting for maximum production.* A manufacturing firm has budgeted \$60,000 per month for labor and materials. If \$$x$ thousand is spent on labor and \$$y$ thousand is spent on materials, and if the monthly output (in units) is given by
$$N(x, y) = 4xy - 8x$$
how should the \$60,000 be allocated to labor and materials in order to maximize N? What is the maximum N?

25. *Productivity.* A consulting firm for a manufacturing company arrived at the following Cobb–Douglas production function for a particular product:
$$N(x, y) = 50x^{0.8}y^{0.2}$$

where x is the number of units of labor and y is the number of units of capital required to produce $N(x, y)$ units of the product. Each unit of labor costs \$40 and each unit of capital costs \$80.

(A) If \$400,000 is budgeted for production of the product, determine how this amount should be allocated to maximize production, and find the maximum production.

(B) Find the marginal productivity of money in this case, and estimate the increase in production if an additional \$50,000 is budgeted for the production of this product.

26. *Productivity.* The research department for a manufacturing company arrived at the following Cobb–Douglas production function for a particular product:
$$N(x, y) = 10x^{0.6}y^{0.4}$$

where x is the number of units of labor and y is the number of units of capital required to produce $N(x, y)$ units of the product. Each unit of labor costs \$30 and each unit of capital costs \$60.

(A) If \$300,000 is budgeted for production of the product, determine how this amount should be allocated to maximize production, and find the maximum production.

(B) Find the marginal productivity of money in this case, and estimate the increase in production if an additional $80,000 is budgeted for the production of this product.

27. *Maximum volume.* A rectangular box with no top and two intersecting partitions is to be constructed from 192 square inches of cardboard (see the figure). Find the dimensions that will maximize the volume.

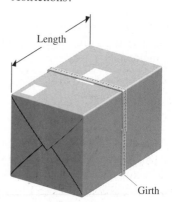

Figure for 27

28. *Maximum volume.* A mailing service states that a rectangular package shall have the sum of the length and girth not to exceed 120 inches (see the figure). What are the dimensions of the largest (in volume) mailing carton that can be constructed meeting these restrictions?

Figure for 28

Life Sciences

29. *Agriculture.* Three pens of the same size are to be built along an existing fence (see the figure). If 400 feet of fencing is available, what length should x and y be to produce the maximum total area? What is the maximum area?

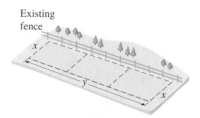

Figure for 29

30. *Diet and minimum cost.* A group of guinea pigs is to receive 25,600 calories per week. Two available foods produce $200xy$ calories for a mixture of x kilograms of type M food and y kilograms of type N food. If type M costs $1 per kilogram and type N costs $2 per kilogram, how much of each type of food should be used to minimize weekly food costs? What is the minimum cost?

Note: $x \geq 0$, $y \geq 0$

Section 8-5 | Method of Least Squares

➤ Least Squares Approximation
➤ Applications

➤ Least Squares Approximation

Regression analysis is the process of fitting an elementary function to a set of data points using the **method of least squares.** The mechanics of using regression techniques were introduced in Chapter 2. Now, using the optimization techniques of Section 8-3, we are able to develop and explain the mathematical foundation of the method of least squares. We begin with **linear regression,** the process of finding the equation of the line that is the "best" approximation to a set of data points.

A manufacturer wants to approximate the cost function for a product. The value of the cost function has been determined for certain levels of production, as listed in Table 1. Although these points do not all lie on a line (see Fig. 1), they are very close to being linear. The manufacturer would like to approximate

TABLE 1	
Number of Units	**Cost**
x (hundreds)	*y (thousand $)*
2	4
5	6
6	7
9	8

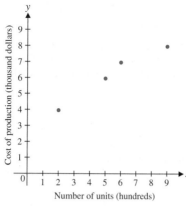

Number of units (hundreds)

FIGURE 1

the cost function by a linear function, that is, determine values a and b so that the line

$$y = ax + b$$

is, in some sense, the "best" approximation to the cost function.

What do we mean by "best"? Since the line $y = ax + b$ will not go through all four points, it is reasonable to examine the differences between the y coordinates of the points listed in the table and the y coordinates of the corresponding points on the line. Each of these differences is called the **residual** at that point (see Fig. 2). For example, at $x = 2$, the point from Table 1 is $(2, 4)$ and the point on the line is $(2, 2a + b)$, so the residual is

$$4 - (2a + b) = 4 - 2a - b$$

All the residuals are listed in Table 2.

TABLE 2

x	y	$ax + b$	Residual
2	4	$2a + b$	$4 - 2a - b$
5	6	$5a + b$	$6 - 5a - b$
6	7	$6a + b$	$7 - 6a - b$
9	8	$9a + b$	$8 - 9a - b$

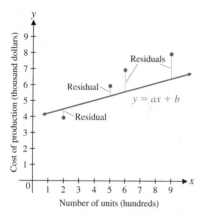

Number of units (hundreds)

FIGURE 2

Our criterion for the "best" approximation is the following: Determine the values of a and b that *minimize the sum of the squares* of the residuals. The resulting line is called the **least squares line,** or the **regression line.** To this end, we minimize

$$F(a, b) = (4 - 2a - b)^2 + (6 - 5a - b)^2 + (7 - 6a - b)^2 + (8 - 9a - b)^2$$

Step 1. Find critical points:

$$\begin{aligned}
F_a(a, b) &= 2(4 - 2a - b)(-2) + 2(6 - 5a - b)(-5) \\
&\quad + 2(7 - 6a - b)(-6) + 2(8 - 9a - b)(-9) \\
&= -304 + 292a + 44b = 0 \\
F_b(a, b) &= 2(4 - 2a - b)(-1) + 2(6 - 5a - b)(-1) \\
&\quad + 2(7 - 6a - b)(-1) + 2(8 - 9a - b)(-1) \\
&= -50 + 44a + 8b = 0
\end{aligned}$$

After dividing each equation by 2, we solve the system

$$146a + 22b = 152$$
$$22a + 4b = 25$$

obtaining $(a, b) = (0.58, 3.06)$ as the only critical point.

Step 2. Compute $A = F_{aa}(a, b), B = F_{ab}(a, b),$ and $C = F_{bb}(a, b)$:

$$\begin{aligned}
F_{aa}(a, b) &= 292 & \text{thus} && A &= F_{aa}(0.58, 3.06) = 292 \\
F_{ab}(a, b) &= 44 & \text{thus} && B &= F_{ab}(0.58, 3.06) = 44 \\
F_{bb}(a, b) &= 8 & \text{thus} && C &= F_{bb}(0.58, 3.06) = 8
\end{aligned}$$

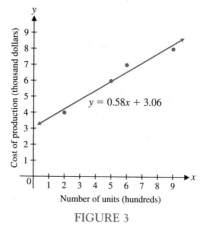

y = 0.58x + 3.06

FIGURE 3

Step 3. Evaluate $AC - B^2$ and try to classify the critical point (a, b) using Theorem 2 in Section 8-3:

$$AC - B^2 = (292)(8) - (44)^2 = 400 > 0 \qquad \text{and} \qquad A = 292 > 0$$

Therefore, case 2 in Theorem 2 applies, and $F(a, b)$ has a local minimum at the critical point $(0.58, 3.06)$.

Thus, the least squares line for the given data is

$$y = 0.58x + 3.06 \qquad \text{Least squares line}$$

The sum of the squares of the residuals is minimized for this choice of a and b (see Fig. 3).

This linear function can now be used by the manufacturer to estimate any of the quantities normally associated with the cost function—such as costs, marginal costs, average costs, and so on. For example, the cost of producing 2,000 units is approximately

$$y = (0.58)(20) + 3.06 = 14.66 \qquad \text{or} \qquad \$14,660$$

The marginal cost function is

$$\frac{dy}{dx} = 0.58$$

The average cost function is

$$\bar{y} = \frac{0.58x + 3.06}{x}$$

In general, if we are given a set of n points $(x_1, y_1), (x_2, y_2), \ldots, (x_n, y_n)$, we want to determine the line $y = ax + b$ for which the sum of the squares of the residuals is minimized. Using summation notation, the sum of the squares of the residuals is given by

$$F(a, b) = \sum_{k=1}^{n} (y_k - ax_k - b)^2$$

Note that in this expression the variables are a and b, and the x_k and y_k are all known values. To minimize $F(a, b)$, we thus compute the partial derivatives with respect to a and b and set them equal to 0:

$$F_b(a, b) = \sum_{k=1}^{n} 2(y_k - ax_k - b)(-x_k) = 0$$

$$F_b(a, b) = \sum_{k=1}^{n} 2(y_k - ax_k - b)(-1) = 0$$

Dividing each equation by 2 and simplifying, we see that the coefficients a and b of the least squares line $y = ax + b$ must satisfy the following system of *normal equations*:

$$\left(\sum_{k=1}^{n} x_k^2 \right) a + \left(\sum_{k=1}^{n} x_k \right) b = \sum_{k=1}^{n} x_k y_k$$

$$\left(\sum_{k=1}^{n} x_k \right) a + nb = \sum_{k=1}^{n} y_k$$

Solving this system for a and b produces the formulas given in the box.

FORMULAS   Least Squares Approximation

For a set of n points $(x_1, y_1), (x_2, y_2), \ldots, (x_n, y_n)$, the coefficients of the least squares line $y = ax + b$ are the solutions of the system of **normal equations**

$$\left(\sum_{k=1}^{n} x_k^2 \right) a + \left(\sum_{k=1}^{n} x_k \right) b = \sum_{k=1}^{n} x_k y_k \tag{1}$$

$$\left(\sum_{k=1}^{n} x_k \right) a + nb = \sum_{k=1}^{n} y_k$$

and are given by the formulas

$$a = \frac{n\left(\sum_{k=1}^{n} x_k y_k \right) - \left(\sum_{k=1}^{n} x_k \right)\left(\sum_{k=1}^{n} y_k \right)}{n\left(\sum_{k=1}^{n} x_k^2 \right) - \left(\sum_{k=1}^{n} x_k \right)^2} \tag{2}$$

$$b = \frac{\sum_{k=1}^{n} y_k - a\left(\sum_{k=1}^{n} x_k \right)}{n} \tag{3}$$

Now we return to the data in Table 1 and tabulate the sums required for the normal equations and their solution in Table 3.

The normal equations (1) are then

$$146a + 22b = 152$$
$$22a + 4b = 25$$

The solution to the normal equations given by equations (2) and (3) is

$$a = \frac{4(152) - (22)(25)}{4(146) - (22)^2} = 0.58$$

$$b = \frac{25 - 0.58(22)}{4} = 3.06$$

TABLE 3

	x_k	y_k	$x_k y_k$	x_k^2
	2	4	8	4
	5	6	30	25
	6	7	42	36
	9	8	72	81
Totals	22	25	152	146

Compare these results with step 1 on page 529. Note that Table 3 provides a convenient format for the computation of step 1 in the preceding list.

Many graphing utilities have a linear regression feature that solves the system of normal equations obtained by setting the partial derivatives of the sum of squares of the residuals equal to 0. Therefore, in practice, we simply enter the given data points and use the linear regression feature to determine the line $y = ax + b$ that best fits the data (see Fig. 4). There is no need to compute partial derivatives, or even to tabulate sums (as in Table 3).

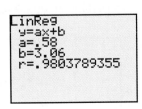

(A)   (B)

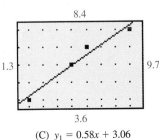

(C) $y_1 = 0.58x + 3.06$

FIGURE 4

EXPLORE
&DISCUSS
1

(A) Plot the four points $(0, 0), (0, 1), (10, 0)$, and $(10, 1)$. Which line would you guess "best" fits these four points? Use formulas (2) and (3) to test your conjecture.

(B) Plot the four points $(0, 0), (0, 10), (1, 0)$ and $(1, 10)$. Which line would you guess "best" fits these four points? Use formulas (2) and (3) to test your conjecture.

(C) If either of your conjectures was wrong, explain how your reasoning was mistaken.

◉ **Insight**   Formula (2) for a is undefined if the denominator equals 0. When can this happen? Suppose $n = 3$. Then

$$n\left(\sum_{k=1}^{n} x_k^2\right) - \left(\sum_{k=1}^{n} x_k\right)^2 = 3(x_1^2 + x_2^2 + x_3^2) - (x_1 + x_2 + x_3)^2$$

$$= 3(x_1^2 + x_2^2 + x_3^2) - (x_1^2 + x_2^2 + x_3^2 + 2x_1x_2 + 2x_1x_3 + 2x_2x_3)$$
$$= 2(x_1^2 + x_2^2 + x_3^2) - (2x_1x_2 + 2x_1x_3 + 2x_2x_3)$$
$$= (x_1^2 + x_2^2) + (x_1^2 + x_3^2) + (x_2^2 + x_3^2) - (2x_1x_2 + 2x_1x_3 + 2x_2x_3)$$
$$= (x_1^2 - 2x_1x_2 + x_2^2) + (x_1^2 - 2x_1x_3 + x_3^2) + (x_2^2 - 2x_2x_3 + x_3^2)$$
$$= (x_1 - x_2)^2 + (x_1 - x_3)^2 + (x_2 - x_3)^2$$

and the last expression is equal to 0 if and only if $x_1 = x_2 = x_3$ (that is, if and only if the three points all lie on the same vertical line). A similar algebraic manipulation works for any integer $n > 1$, showing that, in formula (2) for a, the denominator equals 0 if and only if all n points lie on the same vertical line.   ●

The method of least squares can also be applied to find the quadratic equation $y = ax^2 + bx + c$ that best fits a set of data points. In this case, the sum of the squares of the residuals is a function of three variables:

$$F(a, b, c) = \sum_{k=1}^{n} (y_k - ax_k^2 - bx_k - c)^2$$

There are now three partial derivatives to compute and set equal to 0:

$$F_a(a, b, c) = \sum_{k=1}^{n} 2(y_k - ax_k^2 - bx_k - c)(-x_k^2) = 0$$

$$F_b(a, b, c) = \sum_{k=1}^{n} 2(y_k - ax_k^2 - bx_k - c)(-x_k) = 0$$

$$F_c(a, b, c) = \sum_{k=1}^{n} 2(y_k - ax_k^2 - bx_k - c)(-1) = 0$$

The resulting set of three linear equations in the three variables a, b, and c is called the *set of normal equations for quadratic regression*.

A quadratic regression feature on a calculator is designed to solve such normal equations after the given set of points has been entered. Figure 5 illustrates the computation for the data of Table 1.

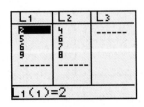

(A)

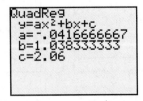

(B)

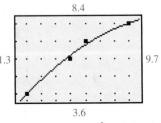

(C) $y_1 = -0.0417x^2 + 1.0383x + 2.06$

FIGURE 5

EXPLORE
&DISCUSS
2

(A) Use the graphs in Figures 4 and 5 to predict which technique, linear regression or quadratic regression, yields the smaller sum of squares of the residuals for the data of Table 1. Explain.

(B) Confirm your prediction by computing the sum of squares of the residuals in each case.

The method of least squares can also be applied to other regression equations—for example, cubic, quartic, logarithmic, exponential, and power regression models. Details are explored in some of the exercises at the end of this section.

➤ Applications

EXAMPLE 1 **Educational Testing** Table 4 lists the midterm and final examination scores for 10 students in a calculus course.

TABLE 4			
Midterm	Final	Midterm	Final
49	61	78	77
53	47	83	81
67	72	85	79
71	76	91	93
74	68	99	99

(A) Use formulas (1), (2), and (3) to find the normal equations and the least squares line for the data given in Table 4.

(B) Use the linear regression feature on a graphing utility to find and graph the least squares line.

(C) Use the least squares line to predict the final examination score for a student who scored 95 on the midterm examination.

Solution (A) Table 5 shows a convenient way to compute all the sums in the formulas for a and b.

TABLE 5			
	x_k	y_k	$x_k y_k$	x_k^2
	49	61	2,989	2,401
	53	47	2,491	2,809
	67	72	4,824	4,489
	71	76	5,396	5,041
	74	68	5,032	5,476
	78	77	6,006	6,084
	83	81	6,723	6,889
	85	79	6,715	7,225
	91	93	8,463	8,281
	99	99	9,801	9,801
Totals	750	753	58,440	58,496

From the last line in Table 5, we have

$$\sum_{k=1}^{10} x_k = 750 \qquad \sum_{k=1}^{10} y_k = 753 \qquad \sum_{k=1}^{10} x_k y_k = 58,440 \qquad \sum_{k=1}^{10} x_k^2 = 58,496$$

and the normal equations are

$$58,496a + 750b = 58,440$$
$$750a + 10b = 753$$

Using formulas (2) and (3),

$$a = \frac{10(58{,}440) - (750)(753)}{10(58{,}496) - (750)^2} = \frac{19{,}650}{22{,}460} \approx 0.875$$

$$b = \frac{753 - 0.875(750)}{10} = 9.675$$

The least squares line is given (approximately) by

$$y = 0.875x + 9.675$$

(B) We enter the data and use the linear regression feature, as shown in Figure 6. [The discrepancy between values of a and b in the preceding and those in Figure 6B is due to rounding in part (A).]

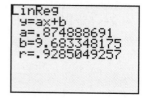

(A)   (B)   (C)

FIGURE 6

(C) If $x = 95$, then $y = 0.875(95) + 9.675 \approx 92.8$ is the predicted score on the final exam. This is also indicated in Figure 6C. If we assume that the exam score must be an integer, we would predict a score of 93. ∎

Matched Problem 1

Repeat Example 1 for the scores listed in Table 6.

TABLE 6

Midterm	Final	Midterm	Final
54	50	84	80
60	66	88	95
75	80	89	85
76	68	97	94
78	71	99	86

EXAMPLE 2

Energy Consumption The use of fuel oil for home heating in the United States has declined steadily for several decades. Table 7 lists the percentage of occupied housing units in the United States that were heated by fuel oil for various years between 1960 and 1991. Use the data in the table and linear regression to predict the percentage of occupied housing units in the United States that will be heated by fuel oil in the year 2010.

TABLE 7 Occupied Housing Units Heated by Fuel Oil

Year	Percent	Year	Percent
1960	32.4	1985	14.1
1970	26.0	1989	13.3
1975	22.5	1993	12.9
1980	18.1	1997	10.9

Solution   We enter the data, with $x = 0$ representing 1960, $x = 10$ representing 1970, and so on, and use the linear regression feature, as shown in Figure 7.

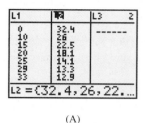

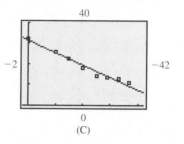

(A)   (B)   (C)

FIGURE 7

Figure 7 indicates that the least squares line is $y = -0.60x + 31.43$. The estimated percentage of occupied housing units heated by fuel oil in the year 2010 (corresponding to $x = 50$) is thus $-0.60(50) + 31.43 = 1.43\%$. ■

Matched Problem 2

In 1950, coal was still a major source of fuel for home energy consumption, and the percentage of occupied housing units heated by fuel oil was only 22.1. Add the data for 1950 to the data for Example 2, and compute the new least squares line and the new estimate for the percentage of occupied housing units heated by fuel oil in the year 2010. Discuss the discrepancy between the two estimates. ────────────■

EXPLORE & DISCUSS 3

The data in Table 8 give the amount A (in milligrams) of the radioactive isotope gallium-67, used in the diagnosis of malignant tumors, at time t (in hours).

TABLE 8

t (hours)	A (milligrams)
0	50.0
5	46.4
10	43.1
15	39.9
20	37.1

(A) Since the data describe radioactive decay, we would expect the relationship between A and t to be exponential—that is, $A = ae^{bt}$ for some constants a and b. Show that if $A = ae^{bt}$, the relationship between $\ln A$ and t is linear.

(B) Compute $\ln A$ for each data point and find the line that "best" fits the data $(t, \ln A)$.

(C) Determine the "best" values of a and b.

(D) Confirm your results by using the exponential regression feature on a graphing utility.

Answers to Matched Problems   **1.** (A) $y = 0.85x + 9.47$

(B)

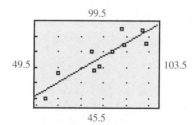

(C) 90.3

2. $y = -0.38x + 25.87$; 6.87%

Exercise 8-5

A *In Problems 1–6, find the least squares line. Graph the data and the least squares line.*

1.

x	y
1	1
2	3
3	4
4	3

2.

x	y
1	-2
2	-1
3	3
4	5

3.

x	y
1	8
2	5
3	4
4	0

4.

x	y
1	20
2	14
3	11
4	3

5.

x	y
1	3
2	4
3	5
4	6

6.

x	y
1	2
2	3
3	3
4	2

B *In Problems 7–14, find the least squares line and use it to estimate y for the indicated value of x. Round answers to two decimal places.*

7.

x	y
1	3
2	1
2	2
3	0

Estimate y when x = 2.5.

8.

x	y
1	0
3	1
3	6
3	4

Estimate y when x = 3.

9.

x	y
0	10
5	22
10	31
15	46
20	51

Estimate y when x = 25.

10.

x	y
-5	60
0	50
5	30
10	20
15	15

Estimate y when x = 20.

11.

x	y
-1	14
1	12
3	8
5	6
7	5

Estimate y when x = 2.

12.

x	y
2	-4
6	0
10	8
14	12
18	14

Estimate y when x = 15.

13.

x	y	x	y
0.5	25	9.5	12
2	22	11	11
3.5	21	12.5	8
5	21	14	5
6.5	18	15.5	1

Estimate y when x = 8.

14.

x	y	x	y
0	-15	12	11
2	-9	14	13
4	-7	16	19
6	-7	18	25
8	-1	20	33

Estimate y when x = 10.

C

15. To find the coefficients of the parabola

$$y = ax^2 + bx + c$$

that is the "best" fit for the points $(1, 2), (2, 1), (3, 1),$ and $(4, 3)$, minimize the sum of the squares of the residuals

$$\begin{aligned} F(a, b, c) = {} & (a + b + c - 2)^2 \\ & + (4a + 2b + c - 1)^2 \\ & + (9a + 3b + c - 1)^2 \\ & + (16a + 4b + c - 3)^2 \end{aligned}$$

by solving the system of normal equations

$$F_a(a, b, c) = 0 \qquad F_b(a, b, c) = 0 \qquad F_c(a, b, c) = 0$$

for $a, b,$ and c. Graph the points and the parabola.

16. Repeat Problem 15 for the points $(-1, -2), (0, 1),$ $(1, 2),$ and $(2, 0)$.

Problems 17 and 18 refer to the system of normal equations and the formulas for a and b given in the text.

17. Verify formulas (2) and (3) by solving the system of normal equations (1) for a and b.

18. If

$$\bar{x} = \frac{1}{n} \sum_{k=1}^{n} x_k \qquad \text{and} \qquad \bar{y} = \frac{1}{n} \sum_{k=1}^{n} y_k$$

are the averages of the x and y coordinates, respectively, show that the point $(\bar{x}, \bar{y})$ satisfies the equation of the least squares line $y = ax + b$.

19. (A) Suppose that $n = 5$ and that the x coordinates of the data points $(x_1, y_1), (x_2, y_2), \ldots, (x_n, y_n)$ are $-2, -1, 0, 1, 2$. Show that system (1) implies that

$$a = \frac{\sum x_k y_k}{\sum x_k^2}$$

and that b is equal to the average of the values of y_k.

(B) Show that the conclusion of part (A) holds whenever the average of the x coordinates of the data points is 0.

20. (A) Give an example of a set of six data points such that half of the points lie above the least squares line and half lie below.

(B) Give an example of a set of six data points such that just one of the points lies above the least squares line and five lie below.

21. (A) Find the linear and quadratic functions that best fit the data points $(0, 1.3), (1, 0.6), (2, 1.5),$ $(3, 3.6)$ and $(4, 7.4)$. (Round coefficients to two decimal places.)

(B) Which of the two functions best fits the data? Explain.

22. (A) Find the linear, quadratic, and logarithmic functions that best fit the data points $(1, 3.2)$, $(2, 4.2)$, $(3, 4.7)$, $(4, 5.0)$, and $(5, 5.3)$. (Round coefficients to two decimal places.)

(B) Which of the three functions best fits the data? Explain.

23. Describe the normal equations for cubic regression. How many equations are there? What are the variables? What techniques could be used to solve them?

24. Describe the normal equations for quartic regression. How many equations are there? What are the variables? What techniques could be used to solve them?

Applications

Business & Economics

25. *Motor vehicle production.* Data for motor vehicle production in Canada for the years 1990 to 1999 is given in the table.

Motor Vehicle Production in Canada			
Year	Thousands	Year	Thousands
1990	1,928	1995	2,408
1991	1,888	1996	2,397
1992	1,961	1997	2,571
1993	2,246	1998	2,568
1994	2,321	1999	3,026

(A) Find the least squares line for the data using $x = 0$ for 1990.

(B) Use the least squares line to estimate the annual production of motor vehicles in Canada in 2010.

26. *Beef production.* Data for U.S. production of beef for the years 1990 to 1999 is given in the table.

U.S. Beef Production			
Year	Million Pounds	Year	Million Pounds
1990	22,743	1995	25,222
1991	22,917	1996	25,525
1992	23,086	1997	25,490
1993	23,049	1998	25,760
1994	24,386	1999	26,493

(A) Find the least squares line for the data using $x = 0$ for 1990.

(B) Use the least squares line to estimate the annual production of beef in the United States in 2012.

27. *Maximizing profit.* The market research department for a drugstore chain chose two summer resort areas to test market a new sunscreen lotion packaged in 4-ounce plastic bottles. After a summer of varying the selling price and recording the monthly demand, the research department arrived at the demand table given below, where y is the number of bottles purchased per month (in thousands) at x dollars per bottle.

x	y
5.0	2.0
5.5	1.8
6.0	1.4
6.5	1.2
7.0	1.1

(A) Find a demand equation using the method of least squares.

(B) If each bottle of sunscreen costs the drugstore chain \$4, how should it be priced to achieve a maximum monthly profit? [*Hint:* Use the result of part (A), with $C = 4y$, $R = xy$, and $P = R - C$.]

28. *Maximizing profit.* A market research consultant for a supermarket chain chose a large city to test market a new brand of mixed nuts packaged in 8-ounce cans. After a year of varying the selling price and recording the monthly demand, the consultant arrived at the demand table given below, where y is the number of cans purchased per month (in thousands) at x dollars per can.

x	y
4.0	4.2
4.5	3.5
5.0	2.7
5.5	1.5
6.0	0.7

(A) Find a demand equation using the method of least squares.

(B) If each can of nuts costs the supermarket chain \$3, how should it be priced to achieve a maximum monthly profit?

Life Sciences

29. *Medicine.* If a person dives into cold water, a neural reflex response automatically shuts off blood circulation to the skin and muscles and reduces the pulse rate. A medical research team conducted an experiment using a group of ten 2-year-olds. A child's face was placed momentarily in cold water, and the corresponding reduction in pulse rate was recorded. The data for the average reduction in heart rate for each temperature is summarized in the table.

Water Temperature (°F)	Pulse Rate Reduction
50	15
55	13
60	10
65	6
70	2

(A) If T is water temperature (in degrees Fahrenheit) and P is pulse rate reduction (in beats per minute), use the method of least squares to find a linear equation relating T and P.

(B) Use the equation found in part (A) to find P when $T = 57$.

30. *Biology.* In biology there is an approximate rule, called the *bioclimatic rule for temperate climates,* that has been known for a couple of hundred years. This rule states that in spring and early summer, periodic phenomena such as blossoming of flowers, appearance of insects, and ripening of fruit usually come about 4 days later for each 500 feet of altitude. Stated as a formula,

$$d = 8h \qquad 0 \le h \le 4$$

where d is the change in days and h is the altitude (in thousands of feet). To test this rule, an experiment was set up to record the difference in blossoming time of the same type of apple tree at different altitudes. A summary of the results is given in the table.

h	d
0	0
1	7
2	18
3	28
4	33

(A) Use the method of least squares to find a linear equation relating h and d. Does the bioclimatic rule, $d = 8h$, appear to be approximately correct?

(B) How much longer will it take this type of apple tree to blossom at 3.5 thousand feet than at sea level? [Use the linear equation found in part (A).]

31. *Global warming.* Average global temperatures from 1885 to 1995 are given in the table.

Average Global Temperatures			
Year	°F	Year	°F
1885	56.65	1945	57.13
1895	56.64	1955	57.06
1905	56.52	1965	57.05
1915	56.57	1975	57.04
1925	56.74	1985	57.36
1935	57.00	1995	57.64

(A) Find the least squares line for the data using $x = 0$ for 1885.

(B) Use the least squares line to estimate the average global temperature in 2085.

32. *Air pollution.* Data for emissions of air pollutants in the United States for the years 1989 to 1998 is given in the table.

Emissions of Air Pollutants in the United States			
Year	Million Short Tons	Year	Million Short Tons
1989	179.6	1994	174.6
1990	170.5	1995	161.4
1991	172.5	1996	160.9
1992	169.0	1997	160.6
1993	169.6	1998	154.3

(A) Find the least squares line for the data using $x = 0$ for 1989.

(B) Use the least squares line to estimate the emissions of air pollutants in the United States in 2015.

Social Sciences

33. *Political science.* Association of economic class and party affiliation did not start with Roosevelt's New Deal; it goes back to the time of Andrew Jackson (1767–1845). Paul Lazarsfeld of Columbia University published an article in the November 1950 issue of *Scientific American* in which he discusses statistical investigations of the relationships between economic class and party affiliation. The data in the table is taken from this article.

(A) If A represents the average assessed value per person in a given ward in 1836 and D represents the percentage of people in that ward voting Democratic in 1836, use the method of least squares to find a linear equation relating A and D.

| Political Affiliations, 1836 | | |
Ward	Average Assessed Value per Person (Hundred $)	Democratic Votes (%)
12	1.7	51
3	2.1	49
1	2.3	53
5	2.4	36
2	3.6	65
11	3.7	35
10	4.7	29
4	6.2	40
6	7.1	34
9	7.4	29
8	8.7	20
7	11.9	23

(B) If the average assessed value per person in a ward had been $300, what is the predicted percentage of people in that ward that would have voted Democratic?

34. *Education.* The table lists the high school grade-point averages (GPAs) of 10 students, along with their grade-point averages after one semester of college.

High School GPA	College GPA	High School GPA	College GPA
2.0	1.5	3.0	2.3
2.2	1.5	3.1	2.5
2.4	1.6	3.3	2.9
2.7	1.8	3.4	3.2
2.9	2.1	3.7	3.5

(A) Find the least squares line for the data.

(B) Estimate the college GPA for a student with a high school GPA of 3.5.

(C) Estimate the high school GPA necessary for a college GPA of 2.7.

35. *Olympic Games.* The table gives the winning heights in the pole vault in the Olympic Games from 1896 to 2000.

Olympic Pole Vault Winning Height			
Year	Height (ft)	Year	Height (ft)
1896	10.81	1956	14.96
1900	10.82	1960	15.43
1904	11.50	1964	16.73
1906	11.60	1968	17.71
1908	12.17	1972	18.04
1912	12.96	1976	18.04
1920	13.46	1980	18.96
1924	12.96	1984	18.85
1928	13.78	1988	19.35
1932	14.16	1992	19.02
1936	14.27	1996	19.42
1948	14.10	2000	19.35
1952	14.93		

(A) Use a graphing utility to find the least squares line for the data using $x = 0$ for 1896.

(B) Estimate the winning height in the pole vault in the Olympic Games of 2016.

Section 8-6 | Double Integrals over Rectangular Regions

➤ Introduction
➤ Definition of the Double Integral
➤ Average Value over Rectangular Regions
➤ Volume and Double Integrals

➤ Introduction

We have generalized the concept of differentiation to functions with two or more independent variables. How can we do the same with integration, and how can we interpret the results? Let us first look at the operation of antidifferentiation. We can antidifferentiate a function of two or more variables with respect to one of the variables by treating all the other variables as though they were constants. Thus, this operation is the reverse operation of partial differentiation, just as ordinary antidifferentiation is the reverse operation of ordinary differentiation. We write $\int f(x, y)\, dx$ to indicate that we are to antidifferentiate $f(x, y)$ with respect to x, holding y fixed; we write $\int f(x, y)\, dy$ to indicate that we are to antidifferentiate $f(x, y)$ with respect to y, holding x fixed.

EXAMPLE 1   **Partial Antidifferentiation**   Evaluate:

(A) $\displaystyle\int (6xy^2 + 3x^2)\, dy$ (B) $\displaystyle\int (6xy^2 + 3x^2)\, dx$

Solution   (A) Treating x as a constant and using the properties of antidifferentiation from Section 6-1, we have

$$\int (6xy^2 + 3x^2)\, dy = \int 6xy^2\, dy + \int 3x^2\, dy$$

$$= 6x \int y^2\, dy + 3x^2 \int dy$$

$$= 6x \left(\frac{y^3}{3}\right) + 3x^2(y) + C(x)$$

$$= 2xy^3 + 3x^2y + C(x)$$

The dy tells us we are looking for the anti-derivative of $6xy^2 + 3x^2$ with respect to y only, holding x constant.

Notice that the constant of integration actually can be *any function of x alone,* since for any such function

$$\frac{\partial}{\partial y} C(x) = 0$$

Check: We can verify that our answer is correct by using partial differentiation:

$$\frac{\partial}{\partial y}[2xy^3 + 3x^2y + C(x)] = 6xy^2 + 3x^2 + 0$$

$$= 6xy^2 + 3x^2$$

(B) Now we treat y as a constant:

$$\int (6xy^2 + 3x^2)\, dx = \int 6xy^2\, dx + \int 3x^2\, dx$$

$$= 6y^2 \int x\, dx + 3 \int x^2\, dx$$

$$= 6y^2 \left(\frac{x^2}{2}\right) + 3\left(\frac{x^3}{3}\right) + E(y)$$

$$= 3x^2y^2 + x^3 + E(y)$$

This time, the antiderivative contains an arbitrary function $E(y)$ of y alone.

Check: $\dfrac{\partial}{\partial x}[3x^2y^2 + x^3 + E(y)] = 6xy^2 + 3x^2 + 0$

$$= 6xy^2 + 3x^2$$

Matched Problem 1   Evaluate: (A) $\displaystyle\int (4xy + 12x^2y^3)\, dy$ (B) $\displaystyle\int (4xy + 12x^2y^3)\, dx$

Now that we have extended the concept of antidifferentiation to functions with two variables, we also can evaluate definite integrals of the form

$$\int_a^b f(x, y) \, dx \qquad \text{or} \qquad \int_c^d f(x, y) \, dy$$

EXAMPLE 2 **Evaluating a Partial Antiderivative** Evaluate, substituting the limits of integration in y if dy is used and in x if dx is used:

(A) $\displaystyle\int_0^2 (6xy^2 + 3x^2) \, dy$ (B) $\displaystyle\int_0^1 (6xy^2 + 3x^2) \, dx$

Solution (A) From Example 1A, we know that

$$\int (6xy^2 + 3x^2) \, dy = 2xy^3 + 3x^2y + C(x)$$

According to properties of the definite integral for a function of one variable, we can use any antiderivative to evaluate the definite integral. Thus, choosing $C(x) = 0$, we have

$$\int_0^2 (6xy^2 + 3x^2) \, dy = (2xy^3 + 3x^2y)\big|_{y=0}^{y=2}$$
$$= [2x(2)^3 + 3x^2(2)] - [2x(0)^3 + 3x^2(0)]$$
$$= 16x + 6x^2$$

(B) From Example 1B, we know that

$$\int (6xy^2 + 3x^2) \, dx = 3x^2y^2 + x^3 + E(y)$$

Thus, choosing $E(y) = 0$, we have

$$\int_0^1 (6xy^2 + 3x^2) \, dx = (3x^2y^2 + x^3)\big|_{x=0}^{x=1}$$
$$= [3y^2(1)^2 + (1)^3] - [3y^2(0)^2 + (0)^3]$$
$$= 3y^2 + 1$$ ■

Matched Problem 2 Evaluate:

(A) $\displaystyle\int_0^1 (4xy + 12x^2y^3) \, dy$ (B) $\displaystyle\int_0^3 (4xy + 12x^2y^3) \, dx$

Notice that integrating and evaluating a definite integral with integrand $f(x, y)$ with respect to y produces a function of x alone (or a constant). Likewise, integrating and evaluating a definite integral with integrand $f(x, y)$ with respect to x produces a function of y alone (or a constant). Each of these results, involving at most one variable, can now be used as an integrand in a second definite integral.

EXAMPLE 3 **Evaluating Iterated Integrals** Evaluate:

(A) $\displaystyle\int_0^1 \left[\int_0^2 (6xy^2 + 3x^2) \, dy \right] dx$ (B) $\displaystyle\int_0^2 \left[\int_0^1 (6xy^2 + 3x^2) \, dx \right] dy$

Solution   (A) Example 2A showed that

$$\int_0^2 (6xy^2 + 3x^2)\, dy = 16x + 6x^2$$

Thus,

$$\int_0^1 \left[\int_0^2 (6xy^2 + 3x^2)\, dy \right] dx = \int_0^1 (16x + 6x^2)\, dx$$

$$= (8x^2 + 2x^3)\big|_{x=0}^{x=1}$$

$$= [8(1)^2 + 2(1)^3] - [8(0)^2 + 2(0)^3] = 10$$

(B) Example 2B showed that

$$\int_0^1 (6xy^2 + 3x^2)\, dx = 3y^2 + 1$$

Thus,

$$\int_0^2 \left[\int_0^1 (6xy^2 + 3x^2)\, dx \right] dy = \int_0^2 (3y^2 + 1)\, dy$$

$$= (y^3 + y)\big|_{y=0}^{y=2}$$

$$= [(2)^3 + 2] - [(0)^3 + 0] = 10 \qquad ∎$$

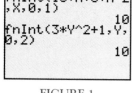

FIGURE 1

A numerical integration routine can be used as an alternative to the fundamental theorem of calculus to evaluate the last integrals in Examples 3A and 3B, $\int_0^1 (16x + 6x^2)\, dx$ and $\int_0^2 (3y^2 + 1)\, dy$, since the integrand in each case is a function of a single variable (see Fig. 1).

Matched Problem 3   Evaluate:

(A) $\displaystyle \int_0^3 \left[\int_0^1 (4xy + 12x^2y^3)\, dy \right] dx$

(B) $\displaystyle \int_0^1 \left[\int_0^3 (4xy + 12x^2y^3)\, dx \right] dy$

➤ **Definition of the Double Integral**

Notice that the answers in Examples 3A and 3B are identical. This is not an accident. In fact, it is this property that enables us to define the *double integral*, as follows:

DEFINITION   Double Integral

The **double integral** of a function $f(x, y)$ over a rectangle

$$R = \{(x, y)\,|\,a \le x \le b, \quad c \le y \le d\}$$

is

$$\iint_R f(x, y)\, dA = \int_a^b \left[\int_c^d f(x, y)\, dy \right] dx$$

$$= \int_c^d \left[\int_a^b f(x, y)\, dx \right] dy$$

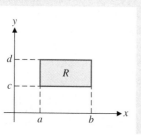

In the double integral $\iint_R f(x, y)\, dA$, $f(x, y)$ is called the **integrand** and R is called the **region of integration**. The expression dA indicates that this is an integral over a two-dimensional region. The integrals

$$\int_a^b \left[\int_c^d f(x, y)\, dy \right] dx \qquad \text{and} \qquad \int_c^d \left[\int_a^b f(x, y)\, dx \right] dy$$

are referred to as **iterated integrals** (the brackets are often omitted), and the order in which dx and dy are written indicates the order of integration. This is not the most general definition of the double integral over a rectangular region; however, it is equivalent to the general definition for all the functions we will consider.

EXAMPLE 4   **Evaluating a Double Integral**   Evaluate:

$$\iint_R (x + y)\, dA \qquad \text{over} \qquad R = \{(x, y)\,|\,1 \le x \le 3, \ -1 \le y \le 2\}$$

Solution   Region R is illustrated in Figure 2. We can choose either order of iteration. As a check, we will evaluate the integral both ways:

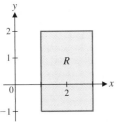

FIGURE 2

$$\iint_R (x + y)\, dA = \int_1^3 \int_{-1}^2 (x + y)\, dy\, dx$$

$$= \int_1^3 \left[\left(xy + \frac{y^2}{2} \right)\Big|_{y=-1}^{y=2} \right] dx$$

$$= \int_1^3 \left[(2x + 2) - \left(-x + \tfrac{1}{2} \right) \right] dx$$

$$= \int_1^3 \left(3x + \tfrac{3}{2} \right) dx$$

$$= \left(\tfrac{3}{2}x^2 + \tfrac{3}{2}x \right)\Big|_{x=1}^{x=3}$$

$$= \left(\tfrac{27}{2} + \tfrac{9}{2} \right) - \left(\tfrac{3}{2} + \tfrac{3}{2} \right) = 18 - 3 = 15$$

$$\iint_R (x + y)\, dA = \int_{-1}^2 \int_1^3 (x + y)\, dx\, dy$$

$$= \int_{-1}^2 \left[\left(\frac{x^2}{2} + xy \right)\Big|_{x=1}^{x=3} \right] dy$$

$$= \int_{-1}^2 \left[\left(\tfrac{9}{2} + 3y \right) - \left(\tfrac{1}{2} + y \right) \right] dy$$

$$= \int_{-1}^2 (4 + 2y)\, dy$$

$$= (4y + y^2)\Big|_{y=-1}^{y=2}$$

$$= (8 + 4) - (-4 + 1) = 12 - (-3) = 15 \qquad \blacksquare$$

Matched Problem 4   Evaluate both ways:

$$\iint_R (2x - y)\, dA \qquad \text{over} \qquad R = \{(x, y)\,|\,-1 \le x \le 5, \ 2 \le y \le 4\}$$

EXAMPLE 5   **Double Integral of an Exponential Function**   Evaluate:

$$\iint_R 2xe^{x^2+y}\, dA \qquad \text{over} \qquad R = \{(x, y)\,|\,0 \le x \le 1,\ -1 \le y \le 1\}$$

Solution   Region R is illustrated in Figure 3.

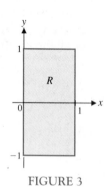

FIGURE 3

$$\iint_R 2xe^{x^2+y}\, dA = \int_{-1}^{1} \int_0^1 2xe^{x^2+y}\, dx\, dy$$

$$= \int_{-1}^{1} \left[(e^{x^2+y}) \Big|_{x=0}^{x=1} \right] dy$$

$$= \int_{-1}^{1} (e^{1+y} - e^y)\, dy$$

$$= (e^{1+y} - e^y)\big|_{y=-1}^{y=1}$$

$$= (e^2 - e) - (e^0 - e^{-1})$$

$$= e^2 - e - 1 + e^{-1} \qquad\blacksquare$$

Matched Problem 5   Evaluate: $\displaystyle\iint_R \frac{x}{y^2} e^{x/y}\, dA$ over $R = \{(x, y)\,|\,0 \le x \le 1,\ 1 \le y \le 2\}$

➤ Average Value over Rectangular Regions

In Section 6-5, the average value of a function $f(x)$ over an interval $[a, b]$ was defined as

$$\frac{1}{b-a} \int_a^b f(x)\, dx$$

This definition is easily extended to functions of two variables over rectangular regions, as shown in the box. Notice that the denominator in the expression given in the box, $(b-a)(d-c)$, is simply the area of the rectangle R.

DEFINITION   Average Value over Rectangular Regions

The **average value** of the function $f(x, y)$ over the rectangle

$$R = \{(x, y)\,|\,a \le x \le b,\ c \le y \le d\}$$

is

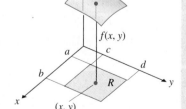

$$\frac{1}{(b-a)(d-c)} \iint_R f(x, y)\, dA$$

EXAMPLE 6   **Average Value**   Find the average value of $f(x, y) = 4 - \frac{1}{2}x - \frac{1}{2}y$ over the rectangle $R = \{(x, y)\,|\,0 \le x \le 2,\ 0 \le y \le 2\}$.

Solution   Region R is illustrated in Figure 4.

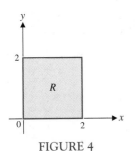

FIGURE 4

$$\frac{1}{(b-a)(d-c)}\iint_R f(x,y)\,dA = \frac{1}{(2-0)(2-0)}\iint_R \left(4 - \frac{1}{2}x - \frac{1}{2}y\right)dA$$

$$= \frac{1}{4}\int_0^2\int_0^2 \left(4 - \frac{1}{2}x - \frac{1}{2}y\right)dy\,dx$$

$$= \frac{1}{4}\int_0^2 \left[\left(4y - \frac{1}{2}xy - \frac{1}{4}y^2\right)\Big|_{y=0}^{y=2}\right]dx$$

$$= \frac{1}{4}\int_0^2 (7 - x)\,dx$$

$$= \frac{1}{4}(7x - \frac{1}{2}x^2)\Big|_{x=0}^{x=2}$$

$$= \frac{1}{4}(12) = 3$$

Figure 5 illustrates the surface $z = f(x, y)$, and our calculations show that 3 is the average of the z values over the region R.

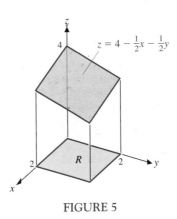

FIGURE 5

Matched Problem 6   Find the average value of $f(x, y) = x + 2y$ over the rectangle
$$R = \{(x, y)\,|\,0 \le x \le 2, \quad 0 \le y \le 1\}$$

EXPLORE & DISCUSS 1

(A) Which of the functions, $f(x, y) = 4 - x^2 - y^2$ or $g(x, y) = 4 - x - y$, would you guess has the greater average value over the rectangle $R = \{(x, y)\,|\,0 \le x \le 1, \quad 0 \le y \le 1\}$? Explain.

(B) Use double integrals to check the correctness of your guess in part (A).

➤ Volume and Double Integrals

One application of the definite integral of a function with one variable is the calculation of areas, so it is not surprising that the definite integral of a function of two variables can be used to calculate volumes of solids.

RESULT   Volume under a Surface

If $f(x, y) \geq 0$ over a rectangle $R = \{(x, y) \mid a \leq x \leq b, \quad c \leq y \leq d\}$, then the volume of the solid formed by graphing f over the rectangle R is given by

$$V = \iint_R f(x, y) \, dA$$

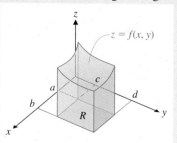

A proof of the statement in the box is left to a more advanced text.

EXAMPLE 7   **Volume** Find the volume of the solid under the graph of $f(x, y) = 1 + x^2 + y^2$ over the rectangle $R = \{(x, y) \mid 0 \leq x \leq 1, \quad 0 \leq y \leq 1\}$.

Solution   Figure 6 shows the region R, and Figure 7 illustrates the volume under consideration.

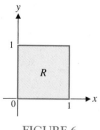

FIGURE 6

$$V = \iint_R (1 + x^2 + y^2) \, dA$$

$$= \int_0^1 \int_0^1 (1 + x^2 + y^2) \, dx \, dy$$

$$= \int_0^1 \left[\left(x + \tfrac{1}{3}x^3 + xy^2 \right) \Big|_{x=0}^{x=1} \right] dy$$

$$= \int_0^1 \left(\tfrac{4}{3} + y^2 \right) dy$$

$$= \left(\tfrac{4}{3}y + \tfrac{1}{3}y^3 \right) \Big|_{y=0}^{y=1} = \tfrac{5}{3} \text{ cubic units}$$

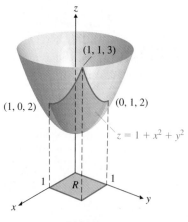

FIGURE 7

Matched Problem 7   Find the volume of the solid under the graph of $f(x, y) = 1 + x + y$ over the rectangle $R = \{(x, y) \mid 0 \leq x \leq 1, \quad 0 \leq y \leq 2\}$.

EXPLORE
&DISCUSS
2

Consider the solid under the graph of $f(x, y) = 4 - y^2$ and above the rectangle $R = \{(x, y)\,|\,0 \le x \le 3, \quad 0 \le y \le 2\}$.

(A) Explain why each cross section of the solid by a plane parallel to the yz plane has the same area, and compute that area.

(B) Compute the areas of the cross sections of the solid by the planes $y = 0, y = \frac{1}{2}$, and $y = 1$.

(C) Compute the volume of the solid in two different ways.

◎ **Insight**   Double integrals can be defined over regions that are more general than rectangles. For example, let $R > 0$. The function $f(x, y) = \sqrt{R^2 - (x^2 + y^2)}$ can be integrated over the *circular* region $C = \{(x, y)\,|\,x^2 + y^2 \le R^2\}$. In fact, it can be shown that

$$\iint\limits_{C} \sqrt{R^2 - (x^2 + y^2)}\, dx\, dy = \frac{2\pi R^3}{3}$$

Because $x^2 + y^2 + z^2 = R^2$ is the equation of a sphere of radius R centered at the origin, the double integral over C represents the volume of the upper hemisphere. Therefore, the volume of a sphere of radius R is given by

$$V = \frac{4\pi R^3}{3} \quad \textit{Volume of sphere of radius } R$$

Double integrals can also be used to obtain volume formulas for other geometric figures (see Table 1, Appendix C).   ●

Answers to Matched Problems   **1.** (A) $2xy^2 + 3x^2y^4 + C(x)$ (B) $2x^2y + 4x^3y^3 + E(y)$

2. (A) $2x + 3x^2$ (B) $18y + 108y^3$ **3.** (A) 36   (B) 36

4. 12   **5.** $e - 2e^{1/2} + 1$ **6.** 2   **7.** 5 cubic units

Exercise 8-6

A *In Problems 1–8, find each antiderivative. Then use the antiderivative to evaluate the definite integral.*

1. (A) $\displaystyle\int 12x^2y^3\, dy$ (B) $\displaystyle\int_0^1 12x^2y^3\, dy$

2. (A) $\displaystyle\int 12x^2y^3\, dx$ (B) $\displaystyle\int_{-1}^2 12x^2y^3\, dx$

3. (A) $\displaystyle\int (4x + 6y + 5)\, dx$

(B) $\displaystyle\int_{-2}^3 (4x + 6y + 5)\, dx$

4. (A) $\displaystyle\int (4x + 6y + 5)\, dy$

(B) $\displaystyle\int_1^4 (4x + 6y + 5)\, dy$

5. (A) $\displaystyle\int \frac{x}{\sqrt{y + x^2}}\, dx$ (B) $\displaystyle\int_0^2 \frac{x}{\sqrt{y + x^2}}\, dx$

6. (A) $\displaystyle\int \frac{x}{\sqrt{y + x^2}}\, dy$ (B) $\displaystyle\int_1^5 \frac{x}{\sqrt{y + x^2}}\, dy$

7. (A) $\displaystyle\int \frac{\ln x}{xy}\, dy$ (B) $\displaystyle\int_1^{e^2} \frac{\ln x}{xy}\, dy$

8. (A) $\displaystyle\int \frac{\ln x}{xy}\, dx$ (B) $\displaystyle\int_1^e \frac{\ln x}{xy}\, dx$

B *In Problems 9–16, evaluate each iterated integral. (See the indicated problem for the evaluation of the inner integral.)*

9. $\displaystyle\int_{-1}^2 \int_0^1 12x^2y^3\, dy\, dx$ **10.** $\displaystyle\int_0^1 \int_{-1}^2 12x^2y^3\, dx\, dy$

(See Problem 1.)   (See Problem 2.)

11. $\int_{1}^{4} \int_{-2}^{3} (4x + 6y + 5) \, dx \, dy$

(See Problem 3.)

12. $\int_{-2}^{3} \int_{1}^{4} (4x + 6y + 5) \, dy \, dx$

(See Problem 4.)

13. $\int_{1}^{5} \int_{0}^{2} \frac{x}{\sqrt{y + x^2}} \, dx \, dy$

(See Problem 5.)

14. $\int_{0}^{2} \int_{1}^{5} \frac{x}{\sqrt{y + x^2}} \, dy \, dx$

(See Problem 6.)

15. $\int_{1}^{e} \int_{1}^{e^2} \frac{\ln x}{xy} \, dy \, dx$

(See Problem 7.)

16. $\int_{1}^{e^2} \int_{1}^{e} \frac{\ln x}{xy} \, dx \, dy$

(See Problem 8.)

Use both orders of iteration to evaluate each double integral in Problems 17–20.

17. $\iint_{R} xy \, dA; R = \{(x, y) \,|\, 0 \le x \le 2, \quad 0 \le y \le 4\}$

18. $\iint_{R} \sqrt{xy} \, dA; R = \{(x, y) \,|\, 1 \le x \le 4, \quad 1 \le y \le 9\}$

19. $\iint_{R} (x + y)^5 \, dA;$

$R = \{(x, y) \,|\, -1 \le x \le 1, \quad 1 \le y \le 2\}$

20. $\iint_{R} xe^y \, dA; R = \{(x, y) \,|\, -2 \le x \le 3, \quad 0 \le y \le 2\}$

In Problems 21–24, find the average value of each function over the given rectangle.

21. $f(x, y) = (x + y)^2;$

$R = \{(x, y) \,|\, 1 \le x \le 5, \quad -1 \le y \le 1\}$

22. $f(x, y) = x^2 + y^2;$

$R = \{(x, y) \,|\, -1 \le x \le 2, \quad 1 \le y \le 4\}$

23. $f(x, y) = x/y; R = \{(x, y) \,|\, 1 \le x \le 4, \quad 2 \le y \le 7\}$

24. $f(x, y) = x^2 y^3;$

$R = \{(x, y) \,|\, -1 \le x \le 1, \quad 0 \le y \le 2\}$

In Problems 25–28, find the volume of the solid under the graph of each function over the given rectangle.

25. $f(x, y) = 2 - x^2 - y^2;$

$R = \{(x, y) \,|\, 0 \le x \le 1, \quad 0 \le y \le 1\}$

26. $f(x, y) = 5 - x;$

$R = \{(x, y) \,|\, 0 \le x \le 5, \quad 0 \le y \le 5\}$

27. $f(x, y) = 4 - y^2;$

$R = \{(x, y) \,|\, 0 \le x \le 2, \quad 0 \le y \le 2\}$

28. $f(x, y) = e^{-x-y};$

$R = \{(x, y) \,|\, 0 \le x \le 1, \quad 0 \le y \le 1\}$

C *Evaluate each double integral in Problems 29–32. Select the order of integration carefully—each problem is easy to do one way and difficult the other.*

29. $\iint_{R} xe^{xy} \, dA; R = \{(x, y) \,|\, 0 \le x \le 1, \quad 1 \le y \le 2\}$

30. $\iint_{R} xye^{x^2y} \, dA; R = \{(x, y) \,|\, 0 \le x \le 1, \quad 1 \le y \le 2\}$

31. $\iint_{R} \frac{2y + 3xy^2}{1 + x^2} \, dA;$

$R = \{(x, y) \,|\, 0 \le x \le 1, \quad -1 \le y \le 1\}$

32. $\iint_{R} \frac{2x + 2y}{1 + 4y + y^2} \, dA;$

$R = \{(x, y) \,|\, 1 \le x \le 3, \quad 0 \le y \le 1\}$

33. Show that $\int_{0}^{2} \int_{0}^{2} (1 - y) \, dx \, dy = 0$. Does the double integral represent the volume of a solid? Explain.

34. (A) Find the average values of the functions

$f(x, y) = x + y, g(x, y) = x^2 + y^2$, and

$h(x, y) = x^3 + y^3$ over the rectangle

$R = \{(x, y) \,|\, 0 \le x \le 1, \quad 0 \le y \le 1\}$

(B) Does the average value of $k(x, y) = x^n + y^n$ over the rectangle

$R_1 = \{(x, y) \,|\, 0 \le x \le 1, \quad 0 \le y \le 1\}$

increase or decrease as n increases? Explain.

(C) Does the average value of $k(x, y) = x^n + y^n$ over the rectangle

$R_2 = \{(x, y) \,|\, 0 \le x \le 2, \quad 0 \le y \le 2\}$

increase or decrease as n increases? Explain.

35. Let $f(x, y) = x^3 + y^2 - e^{-x} - 1$.

(A) Find the average value of $f(x, y)$ over the rectangle $R = \{(x, y) \,|\, -2 \le x \le 2, \quad -2 \le y \le 2\}$.

(B) Graph the set of all points (x, y) in R for which $f(x, y) = 0$.

(C) For which points (x, y) in R is $f(x, y)$ greater than 0? Less than 0? Explain.

36. Find the dimensions of the square S centered at the origin for which the average value of $f(x, y) = x^2 e^y$ over S is equal to 100.

Applications

Business & Economics

37. *Multiplier principle.* Suppose that Congress enacts a one-time-only 10% tax rebate that is expected to infuse $y billion, $5 \leq y \leq 7$, into the economy. If every person and every corporation is expected to spend a proportion x, $0.6 \leq x \leq 0.8$, of each dollar received, then by the **multiplier principle** in economics, the total amount of spending S (in billions of dollars) generated by this tax rebate is given by

$$S(x, y) = \frac{y}{1 - x}$$

What is the average total amount of spending for the indicated ranges of the values of x and y? Set up a double integral and evaluate.

38. *Multiplier principle.* Repeat Problem 37 if $6 \leq y \leq 10$ and $0.7 \leq x \leq 0.9$.

39. *Cobb–Douglas production function.* If an industry invests x thousand labor-hours, $10 \leq x \leq 20$, and $y million, $1 \leq y \leq 2$, in the production of N thousand units of a certain item, then N is given by

$$N(x, y) = x^{0.75}y^{0.25}$$

What is the average number of units produced for the indicated ranges of x and y? Set up a double integral and evaluate.

40. *Cobb–Douglas production function.* Repeat Problem 39 for

$$N(x, y) = x^{0.5}y^{0.5}$$

where $10 \leq x \leq 30$ and $1 \leq y \leq 3$.

Life Sciences

41. *Population distribution.* In order to study the population distribution of a certain species of insects, a biologist has constructed an artificial habitat in the shape of a rectangle 16 feet long and 12 feet wide. The only food available to the insects in this habitat is located at its center. The biologist has determined that the concentration C of insects per square foot at a point d units from the food supply (see the figure) is given approximately by

$$C = 10 - \tfrac{1}{10}d^2$$

What is the average concentration of insects throughout the habitat? Express C as a function of x and y, set up a double integral, and evaluate.

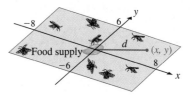

Figure for 41

42. *Population distribution.* Repeat Problem 41 for a square habitat that measures 12 feet on each side, where the insect concentration is given by

$$C = 8 - \tfrac{1}{10}d^2$$

43. *Pollution.* A heavy industrial plant located in the center of a small town emits particulate matter into the atmosphere. Suppose that the concentration of particulate matter (in parts per million) at a point d miles from the plant (see the figure) is given by

$$C = 100 - 15d^2$$

If the boundaries of the town form a rectangle 4 miles long and 2 miles wide, what is the average concentration of particulate matter throughout the city? Express C as a function of x and y, set up a double integral, and evaluate.

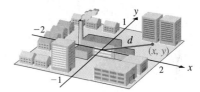

Figure for 43

44. *Pollution.* Repeat Problem 43 if the boundaries of the town form a rectangle 8 miles long and 4 miles wide and the concentration of particulate matter is given by

$$C = 100 - 3d^2$$

Social Sciences

45. *Safety research.* Under ideal conditions, if a person driving a car slams on the brakes and skids to a stop, the length of the skid marks (in feet) is given by the formula

$$L = 0.000\ 013\ 3xy^2$$

where x is the weight of the car (in pounds) and y is the speed of the car (in miles per hour). What is the average length of the skid marks for cars weighing between 2,000 and 3,000 pounds and traveling at speeds between 50 and 60 miles per hour? Set up a double integral and evaluate.

46. *Safety research.* Repeat Problem 45 for cars weighing between 2,000 and 2,500 pounds and traveling at speeds between 40 and 50 miles per hour.

47. *Psychology.* The intelligence quotient Q for a person with mental age x and chronological age y is given by

$$Q(x, y) = 100\frac{x}{y}$$

In a group of sixth-graders, the mental age varies between 8 and 16 years and the chronological age varies between 10 and 12 years. What is the average intelligence quotient for this group? Set up a double integral and evaluate.

48. *Psychology.* Repeat Problem 47 for a group with mental ages between 6 and 14 years and chronological ages between 8 and 10 years.

Chapter 8 Review

Important Terms, Symbols, and Concepts

8-1 Functions of Several Variables

An equation of the form $z = f(x, y)$ describes a **function of two independent variables** if for each permissible ordered pair (x, y) there is one and only one value of z determined by $f(x, y)$. The variables x and y are **independent variables,** and z is a **dependent variable.** The set of all ordered pairs of permissible values of x and y is the **domain** of the function, and the set of all corresponding values $f(x, y)$ is the **range.** Functions of more than two independent variables are defined similarly.

The graph of $z = f(x, y)$ consists of all triples (x, y, z) in a **three-dimensional coordinate system** that satisfy the equation. The graphs of the functions $z = f(x, y) = x^2 + y^2$ and $z = g(x, y) = x^2 - y^2$, for example, are **surfaces;** the first has a local minimum and the second has a **saddle point** at $(0, 0)$.

8-2 Partial Derivatives

If $z = f(x, y)$, then the **partial derivative of f with respect to x,** denoted by $\partial z/\partial x$, f_x, or $f_x(x, y)$, is

$$\frac{\partial z}{\partial x} = \lim_{h \to 0} \frac{f(x + h, y) - f(x, y)}{h}$$

Similarly, the **partial derivative of f with respect to y,** denoted by $\partial z/\partial y$, f_y, or $f_y(x, y)$, is

$$\frac{\partial z}{\partial y} = \lim_{k \to 0} \frac{f(x, y + k) - f(x, y)}{k}$$

The partial derivatives $\partial z/\partial x$ and $\partial z/\partial y$ are said to be **first-order partial derivatives.** The **second-order partial derivatives** of $z = f(x, y)$ are

$$f_{xx} = f_{xx}(x, y) = \frac{\partial^2 z}{\partial x^2} = \frac{\partial}{\partial x}\left(\frac{\partial z}{\partial x}\right)$$

$$f_{xy} = f_{xy}(x, y) = \frac{\partial^2 z}{\partial y\, \partial x} = \frac{\partial}{\partial y}\left(\frac{\partial z}{\partial x}\right)$$

$$f_{yx} = f_{yx}(x, y) = \frac{\partial^2 z}{\partial x\, \partial y} = \frac{\partial}{\partial x}\left(\frac{\partial z}{\partial y}\right)$$

$$f_{yy} = f_{yy}(x, y) = \frac{\partial^2 z}{\partial y^2} = \frac{\partial}{\partial y}\left(\frac{\partial z}{\partial y}\right)$$

8-3 Maxima and Minima

If $f(a, b) \geq f(x, y)$ for all (x, y) in a circular region in the domain of f with (a, b) as center, then $f(a, b)$ is a **local maximum.** If $f(a, b) \leq f(x, y)$ for all (x, y) in such a region, then $f(a, b)$ is a **local minimum.**

Theorem 1

If $f(a, b)$ is a local extremum (a local maximum or local minimum) of f and both f_x and f_y exist at (a, b), then $f_x(a, b) = 0$ and $f_y(a, b) = 0$.

Theorem 2   Second Derivative Test for Local Extrema

Given

1. $z = f(x, y)$
2. $f_x(a, b) = 0$ and $f_y(a, b) = 0$ [(a, b) is a critical point]
3. All second-order partial derivatives of f exist in some circular region containing (a, b) as a center.
4. $A = f_{xx}(a, b)$, $B = f_{xy}(a, b)$, $C = f_{yy}(a, b)$

Then

Case 1. If $AC - B^2 > 0$ and $A < 0$, then $f(a, b)$ is a local maximum.

Case 2. If $AC - B^2 > 0$ and $A > 0$, then $f(a, b)$ is a local minimum.

Case 3. If $AC - B^2 < 0$, then f has a saddle point at (a, b).

Case 4. If $AC - B^2 = 0$, the test fails.

8-4 Maxima and Minima Using Lagrange Multipliers

Theorem 1 Method of Lagrange Multipliers for Functions of Two Variables

Any local maxima or minima of the function $z = f(x, y)$ subject to the constraint $g(x, y) = 0$ will be among those points (x_0, y_0) for which (x_0, y_0, λ_0) is a solution to the system

$$F_x(x, y, \lambda) = 0$$
$$F_y(x, y, \lambda) = 0$$
$$F_\lambda(x, y, \lambda) = 0$$

where $F(x, y, \lambda) = f(x, y) + \lambda g(x, y)$, provided that all the partial derivatives exist. [λ is called a **Lagrange multiplier.**]

Theorem 2 Method of Lagrange Multipliers for Functions of Three Variables

Any local maxima or minima of the function $w = f(x, y, z)$ subject to the constraint $g(x, y, z) = 0$ will be among the set of points (x_0, y_0, z_0) for which $(x_0, y_0, z_0, \lambda_0)$ is a solution to the system

$$F_x(x, y, z, \lambda) = 0$$
$$F_y(x, y, z, \lambda) = 0$$
$$F_z(x, y, z, \lambda) = 0$$
$$F_\lambda(x, y, z, \lambda) = 0$$

where $F(x, y, z, \lambda) = f(x, y, z) + \lambda g(x, y, z)$, provided that all the partial derivatives exist.

8-5 Method of Least Squares

Linear regression is the process of fitting a line $y = ax + b$ to a set of data points $(x_1, y_1), (x_2, y_2), \ldots, (x_n, y_n)$ using the **method of least squares.** We minimize

$$F(a, b) = \sum_{k=1}^{n} (y_k - ax_k - b)^2,$$ the **sum of the squares of**

the residuals, by computing the first-order partial derivatives of F and setting them equal to 0. Solving for a and b gives the formulas

$$a = \frac{n\left(\sum_{k=1}^{n} x_k y_k\right) - \left(\sum_{k=1}^{n} x_k\right)\left(\sum_{k=1}^{n} y_k\right)}{n\left(\sum_{k=1}^{n} x_k^2\right) - \left(\sum_{k=1}^{n} x_k\right)^2}$$

$$b = \frac{\sum_{k=1}^{n} y_k - a\left(\sum_{k=1}^{n} x_k\right)}{n}$$

Graphing calculators have built-in routines to calculate linear—as well as quadratic, cubic, quartic, logarithmic, exponential, power, and trigonometric—regression equations.

8-6 Double Integrals over Rectangular Regions

The **double integral** of a function $f(x, y)$ over a rectangle

$$R = \{(x, y) | a \le x \le b, \quad c \le y \le d\}$$

is

$$\iint\limits_{R} f(x, y)\, dA = \int_a^b \left[\int_c^d f(x, y)\, dy \right] dx$$

$$= \int_c^d \left[\int_a^b f(x, y)\, dx \right] dy$$

In the double integral $\iint_R f(x, y)\, dA$, $f(x, y)$ is called the **integrand** and R is called the **region of integration.** The expression dA indicates that this is an integral over a two-dimensional region. The integrals

$$\int_a^b \left[\int_c^d f(x, y)\, dy \right] dx \quad \text{and} \quad \int_c^d \left[\int_a^b f(x, y)\, dx \right] dy$$

are referred to as **iterated integrals** (the brackets are often omitted), and the order in which dx and dy are written indicates the order of integration.

The **average value** of the function $f(x, y)$ over the rectangle

$$R = \{(x, y) | a \le x \le b, \quad c \le y \le d\}$$

is

$$\frac{1}{(b - a)(d - c)} \iint\limits_{R} f(x, y)\, dA$$

If $f(x, y) \ge 0$ over a rectangle $R = \{(x, y) | a \le x \le b, c \le y \le d\}$, then the volume of the solid formed by graphing f over the rectangle R is given by

$$V = \iint\limits_{R} f(x, y)\, dA$$

Review Exercise

Work through all the problems in this chapter review and check your answers in the back of the book. Answers to all review problems are there along with section numbers in italics to indicate where each type of problem is discussed. Where weaknesses show up, review appropriate sections in the text.

A

1. For $f(x, y) = 2,000 + 40x + 70y$, find $f(5, 10)$, $f_x(x, y)$, and $f_y(x, y)$.

2. For $z = x^3y^2$, find $\partial^2 z/\partial x^2$ and $\partial^2 z/\partial x\, \partial y$.

3. Evaluate: $\int (6xy^2 + 4y)\, dy$

4. Evaluate: $\int (6xy^2 + 4y)\, dx$

5. Evaluate: $\int_0^1 \int_0^1 4xy\, dy\, dx$

6. For $f(x, y) = 6 + 5x - 2y + 3x^2 + x^3$, find $f_x(x, y)$ and $f_y(x, y)$, and explain why $f(x, y)$ has no local extrema.

B

7. For $f(x, y) = 3x^2 - 2xy + y^2 - 2x + 3y - 7$, find $f(2, 3), f_y(x, y)$, and $f_y(2, 3)$.

8. For $f(x, y) = -4x^2 + 4xy - 3y^2 + 4x + 10y + 81$, find $[f_{xx}(2, 3)][f_{yy}(2, 3)] - [f_{xy}(2, 3)]^2$

9. If $f(x, y) = x + 3y$ and $g(x, y) = x^2 + y^2 - 10$, find the critical points of $F(x, y, \lambda) = f(x, y) + \lambda g(x, y)$.

10. Use the least squares line for the data in the table to estimate y when $x = 10$.

x	y
2	12
4	10
6	7
8	3

11. For $R = \{(x, y)\,|-1 \le x \le 1;\ \ 1 \le y \le 2\}$, evaluate the following in two ways:

$$\iint_R (4x + 6y)\, dA$$

C

12. For $f(x, y) = e^{x^2 + 2y}$, find f_x, f_y, and f_{xy}.

13. For $f(x, y) = (x^2 + y^2)^5$, find f_x and f_{xy}.

14. Find all critical points and test for extrema for

$$f(x, y) = x^3 - 12x + y^2 - 6y$$

15. Use Lagrange multipliers to maximize $f(x, y) = xy$ subject to $2x + 3y = 24$.

16. Use Lagrange multipliers to minimize $f(x, y, z) = x^2 + y^2 + z^2$ subject to $2x + y + 2z = 9$.

17. Find the least squares line for the data in the table.

x	y	x	y
10	50	60	80
20	45	70	85
30	50	80	90
40	55	90	90
50	65	100	110

18. Find the average value of $f(x, y) = x^{2/3}y^{1/3}$ over the rectangle

$$R = \{(x, y)\,|-8 \le x \le 8,\ \ 0 \le y \le 27\}$$

19. Find the volume of the solid under the graph of $z = 3x^2 + 3y^2$ over the rectangle

$$R = \{(x, y)\,|0 \le x \le 1,\ \ -1 \le y \le 1\}$$

20. Without doing any computation, predict the average value of $f(x, y) = x + y$ over the rectangle $R = \{(x, y)\,|-10 \le x \le 10,\ \ -10 \le y \le 10\}$. Then check the correctness of your prediction by evaluating a double integral.

21. (A) Find the dimensions of the square S centered at the origin such that the average value of

$$f(x, y) = \frac{e^x}{y + 10}$$

over S is equal to 5.

(B) Is there a square centered at the origin over which

$$f(x, y) = \frac{e^x}{y + 10}$$

has average value 0.05? Explain.

22. Explain why the function $f(x, y) = 4x^3 - 5y^3$, subject to the constraint $3x + 2y = 7$, has no maxima or minima.

Applications

Business & Economics

23. *Maximizing profit.* A company produces x units of product A and y units of product B (both in hundreds per month). The monthly profit equation (in thousands of dollars) is found to be

$$P(x, y) = -4x^2 + 4xy - 3y^2 + 4x + 10y + 81$$

(A) Find $P_x(1, 3)$ and interpret the results.

(B) How many of each product should be produced each month to maximize profit? What is the maximum profit?

24. *Minimizing material.* A rectangular box with no top and six compartments (see the figure) is to have a volume of 96 cubic inches. Find the dimensions that will require the least amount of material.

Figure for 24

25. *Profit.* A company's annual profits (in millions of dollars) over a 5-year period are given in the table. Use the least squares line to estimate the profit for the sixth year.

Year	Profit
1	2
2	2.5
3	3.1
4	4.2
5	4.3

26. *Productivity.* The Cobb–Douglas production function for a product is

$$N(x, y) = 10x^{0.8}y^{0.2}$$

where x is the number of units of labor and y is the number of units of capital required to produce N units of the product.

(A) Find the marginal productivity of labor and the marginal productivity of capital at $x = 40$ and $y = 50$. For the greatest increase in productivity, should management encourage increased use of labor or increased use of capital?

(B) If each unit of labor costs $100, each unit of capital costs $50, and $10,000 is budgeted for production of this product, use the method of Lagrange multipliers to determine the allocations of labor and capital that will maximize the number of units produced and find the maximum production. Find the marginal productivity of money and approximate the increase in production that would result from an increase of $2,000 in the amount budgeted for production.

(C) If $50 \le x \le 100$ and $20 \le y \le 40$, find the average number of units produced. Set up a definite integral and evaluate.

Life Sciences

27. *Marine biology.* The function used for timing dives with scuba gear is

$$T(V, x) = \frac{33V}{x + 33}$$

where T is the time of the dive in minutes, V is the volume of air (in cubic feet, at sea level pressure) compressed into tanks, and x is the depth of the dive in feet. Find $T_x(70, 17)$ and interpret the results.

28. *Pollution.* A heavy industrial plant located in the center of a small town emits particulate matter into the atmosphere. Suppose that the concentration of particulate matter (in parts per million) at a point d miles from the plant is given by

$$C = 100 - 24d^2$$

If the boundaries of the town form a square 4 miles long and 4 miles wide, what is the average concentration of particulate matter throughout the town? Express C as a function of x and y, set up a double integral, and evaluate.

Social Sciences

29. *Sociology.* Joseph Cavanaugh, a sociologist, found that the number of long-distance telephone calls, n, between two cities in a given period of time varied (approximately) jointly as the populations P_1 and P_2 of the two cities, and varied inversely as the distance, d, between the two cities. In terms of an equation for a time period of 1 week,

$$n(P_1, P_2, d) = 0.001 \frac{P_1 P_2}{d}$$

Find $n(100{,}000, 50{,}000, 100)$.

30. *Education.* At the beginning of the semester, students in a foreign language course are given a proficiency exam. The same exam is given at the end of the semester. The results for 5 students are given in the table. Use the least squares line to estimate the score on the second exam for a student who scored 40 on the first exam.

First Exam	Second Exam
30	60
50	75
60	80
70	85
90	90

31. *Population density.* The table gives the population per square mile in the United States for the years 1900–2000.

U.S. Population Density			
Year	Population (Per Square Mile)	Year	Population (Per Square Mile)
1900	25.6	1960	50.6
1910	31.0	1970	57.4
1920	35.6	1980	64.0
1930	41.2	1990	70.4
1940	44.2	2000	77.8
1950	50.7		

(A) Find the least squares line for the data using $x = 0$ for 1900.

(B) Use linear regression to estimate the population density in the United States in the year 2020.

(C) Use quadratic regression and exponential regression to make the estimate of part (B).

32. *Life expectancy.* The table gives life expectancies for males and females in a sample of Central and South American countries.

Life Expectancies for Central and South American Countries			
Males	Females	Males	Females
62.30	67.50	70.15	74.10
68.05	75.05	62.93	66.58
72.40	77.04	68.43	74.88
63.39	67.59	66.68	72.80
55.11	59.43		

(A) Find the least squares line for the data.

(B) Use linear regression to estimate the life expectancy of a female in a Central or South American country in which the life expectancy for males is 60 years.

(C) Use quadratic and logarithmic regression to make the estimate of part (B).

33. *Women in the workforce.* It is reasonable to conjecture from the data given in the table that many Japanese women tend to leave the workforce to marry and have children, but then reenter the workforce when the children are grown.

Women in the Workforce in Japan, 1997			
Age	Percentage of Women Employed	Age	Percentage of Women Employed
22	73	47	72
27	65	52	68
32	56	57	59
37	63	62	42
42	71		

(A) Explain why you might expect cubic regression to provide a better fit to the data than linear or quadratic regression.

(B) Investigate your expectation by plotting the data points and graphing the curve of best fit using linear, quadratic, and cubic regression.

Group Activity 1   City Planning

A city planning commission is seeking to identify prime locations for a new zoo and a new hospital. The city's economy is heavily dependent on two industrial plants located relatively near the city center. Both emit particulate matter into the atmosphere, and the resulting air pollution is of concern to the commission and will influence its decisions. The consensus of the commission is that the new zoo should be built in the least polluted area within the city limits, and the new hospital should be built in the least polluted location within 2 miles of the city center.

The boundaries of the city form a rectangle 10 miles from east to west and 6 miles from north to south. When a coordinate system is chosen with the origin at the center of the rectangle (the city center), industrial plant 1 has coordinates $(-1, 1)$ and industrial plant 2 has coordinates $(1, 0)$. At a point (x, y), the concentration of particulate matter (in parts per million) due to emissions from plant 1 is given by $C_1 = 200 - 3(d_1)^2$, where d_1 is the distance from (x, y) to plant 1. Similarly, the concentration due to emissions from plant 2 is given by $C_2 = 200 - 3(d_2)^2$, where d_2 is the distance from (x, y) to plant 2.

(A) Find the point within the city limits that has the greatest concentration of particulate matter.

(B) Find the points on the city boundaries that have the greatest and least concentrations of particulate matter.

(C) Find the average concentration of particulate matter throughout the city.

(D) Find the points on the circle of radius 2 miles, centered at the origin, that have the greatest and least concentrations of particulate matter.

(E) Determine the optimal locations for the city's new zoo and new hospital.

Group Activity 2   Numerical Integration of Multivariable Functions

A definite integral $\int_a^b f(x)\, dx$ is a limit of Riemann sums of the form

$$\sum_{k=1}^n f(c_k)\, \Delta x_k$$

(see Section 6-4). Analogously, a double integral $\iint_R f(x, y)\, dx\, dy$ over a rectangle $R = \{(x, y) \,|\, a \le x \le b, \quad c \le x \le d\}$ is a limit of sums of the form

$$\sum_{j=1}^m \sum_{k=1}^n f(c_j, d_k)\, \Delta x_j\, \Delta y_k$$

where $a = x_0 < x_1 < x_2 < \cdots < x_m = b, c = y_0 < y_1 < y_2 < \cdots < y_n = d$, $x_{j-1} \le c_j \le x_j$ for $j = 1, 2, \ldots, m$, and $y_{k-1} \le d_k \le y_k$ for $k = 1, 2, \ldots, n$.

It follows that numerical integration methods such as Simpson's rule (see Group Activity 1 in Chapter 6) can also be used to approximate double integrals. We illustrate with an example.

EXAMPLE 1   **Using Simpson's Rule to Approximate Double Integrals** Use Simpson's rule to approximate

$$\int_0^4 \int_0^6 (x^2 y + 2y^2 + 3x + 1) \, dy \, dx$$

by partitioning $[0, 4]$ into four equal subintervals and $[0, 6]$ into six equal subintervals.

Solution   We evaluate the function $f(x, y) = x^2 y + 2y^2 + 3x + 1$ at each of the 35 intersection points of the grid determined by the two partitions (see Table 1).

TABLE 1							
	$y = 0$	1	2	3	4	5	6	R_j
$x = 0$	1	3	9	19	33	51	73	150
1	4	7	14	25	40	59	82	186
2	7	13	23	37	55	77	103	258
3	10	21	36	55	78	105	136	366
4	13	31	53	79	109	143	181	510

Then we apply Simpson's rule for six equal subdivisions of an interval to each row of the table to compute the entries in the column labeled R_j. For example, letting $g(y) = f(x_0, y)$, we have

$$R_0 = [g(y_0) + 4g(y_1) + 2g(y_2) + 4g(y_3) + 2g(y_4) + 4g(y_5) + g(y_6)] \frac{\Delta y}{3}$$

$$= [(1) + 4(3) + 2(9) + 4(19) + 2(33) + 4(51) + 1(73)] \tfrac{1}{3}$$

$$= 150$$

Finally, we apply Simpson's rule for four equal subdivisions of an interval to the values R_0, R_1, R_2, R_3, R_4:

$$S = [R_0 + 4R_1 + 2R_2 + 4R_3 + R_4] \frac{\Delta x}{3}$$

$$= [150 + 4(186) + 2(258) + 4(366) + 510] \tfrac{1}{3}$$

$$= 1,128$$

Therefore, the value of the double integral $\int_0^4 \int_0^6 (x^2 y + 2y^2 + 3x + 1) \, dy \, dx$ is approximately 1,128.   ∎

In Example 1, the double integral can be evaluated as an iterated integral. The exact value of the double integral is also 1,128. This is not surprising since Simpson's rule gives exact results for polynomials of degree 3 or less. But the technique illustrated above can also be applied when it is impossible to find antiderivatives, or when we have only a table of values (and not a formula) for $f(x, y)$.

(A) Evaluate the double integral of Example 1 as an iterated integral.

(B) Show that the sum S in Example 1 may also be found by applying Simpson's rule to each column of Table 1, obtaining $C_0, C_1, \ldots, C_6$ and then applying Simpson's rule to $C_0, C_1, \ldots, C_6$.

(C) Approximate

$$\int_0^3 \int_0^3 e^{-(x^2+y^2)} \, dx \, dy$$

by partitioning each of the intervals $[0, 3]$ into six equal subintervals, evaluating the function $f(x, y) = e^{-(x^2+y^2)}$ (to four decimal places) at each of the 49 intersection points of the grid determined by the two partitions, and applying Simpson's rule.

(D) Repeat part (C), but use a numerical integration routine on a graphing utility, rather than Simpson's rule, to approximate the R_j.

(E) It can be shown that the volume under the graph of $f(x, y) = e^{-(x^2+y^2)}$ and above the entire first quadrant is $\pi/4$. Compare your answers to parts (C) and (D) with this value and explain any discrepancy.

OBJECTIVES

1. Find the values of the trigonometric functions for angles measured in degrees or radians.

2. Calculate derivatives and antiderivatives of trigonometric functions.

3. Apply optimization methods and the definite integral to trigonometric models in order to solve problems involving periodic phenomena.

CHAPTER PROBLEM

A statistician determines that the revenues (in millions of dollars) for a soft drink company are given approximately by

$$R(t) = 2.8 + 0.05t - 1.9 \cos\frac{\pi t}{6} \qquad 0 \le t \le 60$$

where t is time in months. Use a definite integral to approximate the total revenue from t = 48 to t = 60.

Trigonometric Functions

9

INTRODUCTION

Until now we have restricted our attention to algebraic, logarithmic, and exponential functions. These functions were used to model many real-life situations from business, economics, and the life and social sciences. Now we turn our attention to another important class of functions, called the *trigonometric functions*. These functions are particularly useful in describing periodic phenomena—that is, phenomena that repeat in cycles. Consider the sunrise times for a 2-year period starting January 1, as pictured in the figure. We see that the cycle repeats after 1 year. Business cycles, blood pressure in the aorta, seasonal growth, water waves, and amounts of pollution in the atmosphere are often periodic and can be modeled with similar types of graphs.

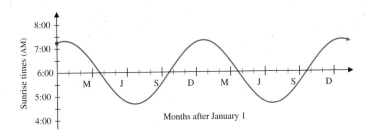

We assume that the reader has had a course in trigonometry. In Section 9-1 we provide a brief review of the topics that are most important for our purposes.

Section **9-1** | Trigonometric Functions Review

➤ Angles: Degree–Radian Measure
➤ Trigonometric Functions
➤ Graphs of the Sine and Cosine Functions
➤ Four Other Trigonometric Functions

➤ Angles: Degree–Radian Measure

An **angle** is formed by rotating (in a plane) a ray, m, called the **initial side** of the angle, around its endpoint until it coincides with a ray, n, called the **terminal side** of the angle. The common endpoint P of m and n is called the **vertex** (see Fig. 1).

There is no restriction on the amount or direction of rotation. A counter-clockwise rotation produces a **positive** angle (Fig. 2A), and a clockwise rotation produces a **negative** angle (Fig. 2B). Two different angles may have the same initial and terminal sides, as shown in Figure 2C. Such angles are said to be **coterminal.**

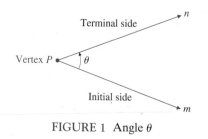

FIGURE 1 Angle θ

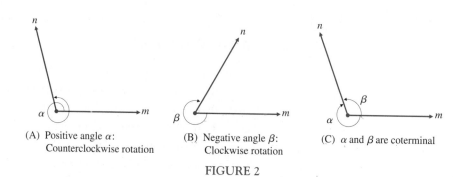

(A) Positive angle α:
Counterclockwise rotation

(B) Negative angle β:
Clockwise rotation

(C) α and β are coterminal

FIGURE 2

There are two widely used measures of angles—the *degree* and the *radian*. A central angle of a circle subtended by an arc $\frac{1}{360}$ of the circumference of the circle is said to have **degree measure 1,** written **1°** (see Fig. 3A). It follows that a central angle subtended by an arc $\frac{1}{4}$ the circumference has degree measure 90; $\frac{1}{2}$ the circumference has degree measure 180; and the whole circumference of a circle has degree measure 360.

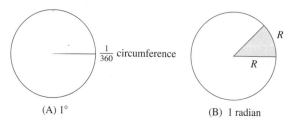

(A) 1°

(B) 1 radian

FIGURE 3 Degree and radian measure

The other measure of angles, which we use extensively in the next two sections, is radian measure. A central angle subtended by an arc of length equal to the radius (R) of the circle is said to have **radian measure 1,** written **1 radian** or

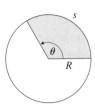

FIGURE 4

1 rad (see Fig. 3B). In general, a central angle subtended by an arc of length s has radian measure determined as follows:

$$\theta_{\text{rad}} = \text{radian measure of } \theta = \frac{\text{arc length}}{\text{radius}} = \frac{s}{R}$$

See Figure 4. [*Note:* If $R = 1$, then $\theta_{\text{rad}} = s$.]

What is the radian measure of an angle of 180°? A central angle of 180° is subtended by an arc of $\frac{1}{2}$ the circumference of a circle. Thus,

$$s = \frac{C}{2} = \frac{2\pi R}{2} = \pi R \qquad \text{and} \qquad \theta_{\text{rad}} = \frac{s}{R} = \frac{\pi R}{R} = \pi \text{ rad}$$

The following proportion can be used to convert degree measure to radian measure, and vice versa:

FORMULA   Degree–Radian Conversion

$$\frac{\theta_{\text{deg}}}{180°} = \frac{\theta_{\text{rad}}}{\pi \text{ rad}}$$

EXAMPLE 1   **From Degrees to Radians** Find the radian measure of 1°.

Solution
$$\frac{1°}{180°} = \frac{\theta_{\text{rad}}}{\pi \text{ rad}}$$

$$\theta_{\text{rad}} = \frac{\pi}{180} \text{rad} \approx 0.0175 \text{ rad}$$

Matched Problem 1   Find the degree measure of 1 rad.

A comparison of degree and radian measure for a few important angles is given in the following table:

Radian	0	$\pi/6$	$\pi/4$	$\pi/3$	$\pi/2$	π	2π
Degree	0	30°	45°	60°	90°	180°	360°

An angle in a rectangular coordinate system is said to be in **standard position** if its vertex is at the origin and its initial side is on the positive x axis. Figure 5 shows three angles in standard position.

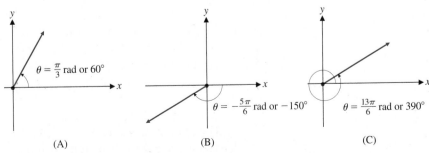

FIGURE 5 Angles in standard position

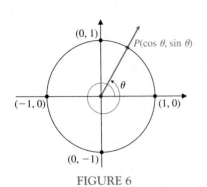

FIGURE 6

➤ Trigonometric Functions

Let us locate a unit circle (radius 1) in a coordinate system with center at the origin (Fig. 6). The terminal side of any angle in standard position will pass through this circle at some point P. The abscissa of this point P is called the **cosine of θ** (abbreviated **cos θ**), and the ordinate of the point is the **sine of θ** (abbreviated **sin θ**). Thus, the set of all ordered pairs of the form $(\theta, \cos \theta)$, and the set of all ordered pairs of the form $(\theta, \sin \theta)$ constitute, respectively, the **cosine** and **sine functions**. The **domain** of these two functions is the set of all angles, positive or negative, with measure either in degrees or radians. The **range** is a subset of the set of real numbers.

It is desirable, and necessary for our work in calculus, to define these two trigonometric functions in terms of real number domains. This is easily done as follows:

DEFINITION   Sine and Cosine Functions with Real Number Domains

For any real number x,

$$\sin x = \sin(x \text{ radians}) \qquad \cos x = \cos(x \text{ radians})$$

EXAMPLE 2   **Evaluating Sine and Cosine Functions** Referring to Figure 6, find

(A) $\cos 90°$ (B) $\sin(-\pi/2 \text{ rad})$ (C) $\cos \pi$

Solution   (A) The terminal side of an angle of degree measure 90 passes through $(0, 1)$ on the unit circle. This point has abscissa 0. Thus,

$$\cos 90° = 0$$

(B) The terminal side of an angle of radian measure $-\pi/2$ $(-90°)$ passes through $(0, -1)$ on the unit circle. This point has ordinate -1. Thus,

$$\sin\left(-\frac{\pi}{2} \text{ rad}\right) = -1$$

(C) $\cos \pi = \cos(\pi \text{ rad}) = -1$, since the terminal side of an angle of radian measure $\pi (180°)$ passes through $(-1, 0)$ on the unit circle and this point has abscissa -1.

Matched Problem 2   Referring to Figure 6, find

(A) $\sin 180°$ (B) $\cos(2\pi \text{ rad})$ (C) $\sin(-\pi)$

EXPLORE & DISCUSS 1

(A) For the sine and cosine functions with angle domains, discuss the range for each function by referring to Figure 6.

(B) For the sine and cosine functions with real number domains, discuss the range for each function by referring to Figure 6.

To find the value of either the sine or the cosine function for any angle or any real number by direct use of the definition is not easy. Calculators with $\boxed{\text{sin}}$ and $\boxed{\text{cos}}$ keys are used. Calculators generally have degree and radian options, so we can use a calculator to evaluate these functions for most of the real numbers in which we might have an interest. The following table includes a few values produced by a calculator in the radian mode.

x	1	-7	35.26	-105.9
$\sin x$	0.8415	-0.6570	-0.6461	0.7920
$\cos x$	0.5403	0.7539	-0.7632	0.6105

EXPLORE & DISCUSS 2

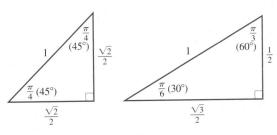

Many errors in trigonometry can be traced to having the calculator in the wrong mode, radian instead of degree, or vice versa, when performing calculations. The window display from a calculator shown here gives two different values for cos 30. Experiment with your calculator and explain the discrepancy.

Exact values of the sine and cosine functions can be obtained for multiples of the special angles shown in the triangles in Figure 7, because these triangles can be used to find the coordinate of the intersection of the terminal side of each angle with the unit circle.

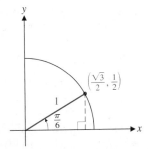

FIGURE 7

Remark

We now drop the word *radian* after $\pi/4$ and interpret $\pi/4$ as the radian measure of an angle or simply as a real number, depending on the context.

EXAMPLE 3   **Finding Exact Values for Special "Angles"**   Find the exact value of each of the following using Figure 7:

(A) $\cos\dfrac{\pi}{4}$ (B) $\sin\dfrac{\pi}{6}$ (C) $\sin\left(-\dfrac{\pi}{6}\right)$

Solution   (A) $\cos\dfrac{\pi}{4} = \dfrac{\sqrt{2}}{2}$ (B) $\sin\dfrac{\pi}{6} = \dfrac{1}{2}$

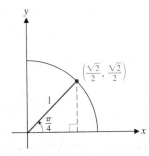

(C) $\sin\left(-\dfrac{\pi}{6}\right) = -\dfrac{1}{2}$

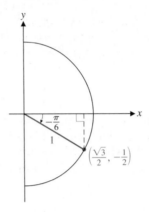

Matched Problem 3   Find the exact value of each of the following using Figure 7 on the preceding page:

(A) $\sin\dfrac{\pi}{4}$ (B) $\cos\dfrac{\pi}{3}$ (C) $\cos\left(-\dfrac{\pi}{3}\right)$ ─────────────■

➤ **Graphs of the Sine and Cosine Functions**

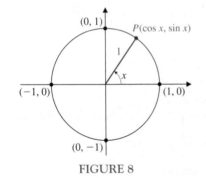

FIGURE 8

To graph $y = \sin x$ or $y = \cos x$ for x a real number, we could use a calculator to produce a table, and then plot the ordered pairs from the table in a coordinate system. However, we can speed up the process by returning to basic definitions. Referring to Figure 8, since $\cos x$ and $\sin x$ are the coordinates of a point on the unit circle, we see that

$$-1 \le \sin x \le 1 \quad \text{and} \quad -1 \le \cos x \le 1$$

for all real numbers x. Furthermore, as x increases and P moves around the unit circle in a counterclockwise (positive) direction, both $\sin x$ and $\cos x$ behave in uniform ways, as indicated in the table:

As x Increases from	$y = \sin x$	$y = \cos x$
0 to $\pi/2$	Increases from 0 to 1	Decreases from 1 to 0
$\pi/2$ to π	Decreases from 1 to 0	Decreases from 0 to -1
π to $3\pi/2$	Decreases from 0 to -1	Increases from -1 to 0
$3\pi/2$ to 2π	Increases from -1 to 0	Increases from 0 to 1

Note that P has completed one revolution and is back at its starting place. If we let x continue to increase, the second and third columns in the table will be repeated every 2π units. In general, it can be shown that

$$\sin(x + 2\pi) = \sin x \qquad \cos(x + 2\pi) = \cos x$$

for all real numbers x. Functions such that

$$f(x + p) = f(x)$$

for some positive constant p and all real numbers x for which the functions are defined are said to be **periodic**. The smallest such value of p is called the

period of the function. Thus, both the sine and cosine functions are periodic (a very important property) with period 2π.

Putting all this information together, and, perhaps adding a few values obtained from a calculator or Figure 7, we obtain the graphs of the sine and cosine functions illustrated in Figure 9. Notice that these curves are continuous. It can be shown that **the sine and cosine functions are continuous for all real numbers.**

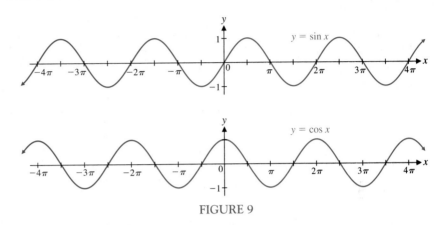

FIGURE 9

➤ Four Other Trigonometric Functions

The sine and cosine functions are only two of six trigonometric functions. They are, however, the most important of the six for many applications. We define the other four trigonometric functions in the box. Problems involving these functions may be found in the exercise set that follows.

DEFINITION   Four Other Trigonometric Functions

$$\tan x = \frac{\sin x}{\cos x} \quad \cos x \neq 0 \qquad \sec x = \frac{1}{\cos x} \quad \cos x \neq 0$$

$$\cot x = \frac{\cos x}{\sin x} \quad \sin x \neq 0 \qquad \csc x = \frac{1}{\sin x} \quad \sin x \neq 0$$

◉ Insight   The functions $\sin x$ and $\cos x$ are periodic with period 2π, so

$$\tan(x + 2\pi) = \frac{\sin(x + 2\pi)}{\cos(x + 2\pi)} = \frac{\sin x}{\cos x} = \tan x$$

One might therefore guess that $\tan x$ is periodic with period 2π. However, 2π is not the *smallest* positive constant p such that $\tan(x + p) = \tan x$. Because the points $(\cos x, \sin x)$ and $(\cos(x + \pi), \sin(x + \pi))$ are diametrically opposed on the unit circle,

$$\sin(x + \pi) = -\sin x \qquad \text{and} \qquad \cos(x + \pi) = -\cos x$$

Therefore,

$$\tan(x + \pi) = \frac{\sin(x + \pi)}{\cos(x + \pi)} = \frac{-\sin x}{-\cos x} = \tan x$$

It follows that the functions $\tan x$ and $\cot x$ have period π. The other four trigonometric functions, $\sin x$, $\cos x$, $\sec x$, and $\csc x$, all have period 2π.   ●

Exercise 9–1

A *Recall that 180° corresponds to π radians. Mentally convert each degree measure given in Problems 1–6 to radian measure in terms of π.*

1. 18°   **2.** 60°   **3.** 90°

4. 135°   **5.** 540°   **6.** 360°

In Problems 7–12, indicate the quadrant in which the terminal side of each angle lies.

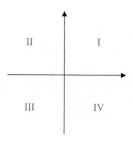

7. 85°   **8.** −105°   **9.** −210°

10. 175°   **11.** 4 rad   **12.** −6 rad

Use Figure 6 to find the exact value of each expression in Problems 13–18.

13. $\sin(-90°)$ **14.** $\cos 180°$ **15.** $\cos\left(\dfrac{\pi}{2}\right)$

16. $\sin\left(\dfrac{-3\pi}{2}\right)$ **17.** $\sin 540°$ **18.** $\cos 360°$

B *Recall that π rad corresponds to 180° Mentally convert each radian measure given in Problems 19–24 to degree measure.*

19. $2\pi/3$ rad   **20.** $\pi/4$ rad   **21.** 2π rad

22. 3π rad   **23.** $3\pi/4$ rad **24.** $5\pi/3$ rad

Use Figure 7 to find the exact value of each expression in Problems 25–30.

25. $\cos 60°$ **26.** $\sin 45°$ **27.** $\sin(-30°)$

28. $\cos\left(-\dfrac{\pi}{6}\right)$ **29.** $\cos\left(\dfrac{3\pi}{4}\right)$ **30.** $\sin\left(\dfrac{5\pi}{6}\right)$

Use a calculator (set in radian mode) to find the value (to four decimal places) of each expression in Problems 31–36.

31. $\sin 3$ **32.** $\cos 13$ **33.** $\cos 33.74$

34. $\sin 325.9$ **35.** $\sin(-43.06)$ **36.** $\cos(-502.3)$

C *In Problems 37 and 38, convert to radian measure.*

37. 27°   **38.** 18°

In Problems 39 and 40, convert to degree measure.

39. $\pi/12$ rad   **40.** $\pi/60$ rad

Use Figure 7 to find the exact value of each expression in Problems 41–46.

41. $\tan 45°$ **42.** $\cot 45°$ **43.** $\sec\dfrac{\pi}{3}$

44. $\csc\dfrac{\pi}{6}$ **45.** $\cot\dfrac{\pi}{3}$ **46.** $\tan\dfrac{\pi}{6}$

47. Refer to Figure 6 and use the Pythagorean theorem to show that

$$(\sin x)^2 + (\cos x)^2 = 1$$

for all x.

48. Use the results of Problem 47 and basic definitions to show that

(A) $(\tan x)^2 + 1 = (\sec x)^2$

(B) $1 + (\cot x)^2 = (\csc x)^2$

In Problems 49–52, graph each trigonometric form using a graphing utility set in radian mode.

49. $y = 2\sin \pi x; 0 \le x \le 2, -2 \le y \le 2$

50. $y = -0.5\cos 2x; 0 \le x \le 2\pi, -0.5 \le y \le 0.5$

51. $y = 4 - 4\cos\dfrac{\pi x}{2}; 0 \le x \le 8, 0 \le y \le 8$

52. $y = 6 + 6\sin\dfrac{\pi x}{26}; 0 \le x \le 104, 0 \le y \le 12$

Applications

Business & Economics

53. *Seasonal business cycle.* Suppose that profits on the sale of swimming suits in a department store over a 2-year period are given approximately by

$$P(t) = 5 - 5 \cos \frac{\pi t}{26} \qquad 0 \le t \le 104$$

where P is profit (in hundreds of dollars) for a week of sales t weeks after January 1. The graph of the profit function is shown in the figure.

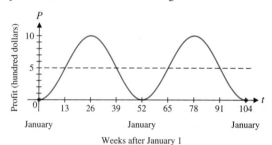

Figure for 53

(A) Find the exact values of $P(13)$, $P(26)$, $P(39)$, and $P(52)$ without using a calculator.

(B) Use a calculator to find $P(30)$ and $P(100)$. Interpret the results verbally.

(C) Use a graphing utility to confirm the graph shown here for $y = P(t)$.

54. *Seasonal business cycle.* A soft drink company has revenues from sales over a 2-year period as given approximately by

$$R(t) = 4 - 3 \cos \frac{\pi t}{6} \qquad 0 \le t \le 24$$

where $R(t)$ is revenue (in millions of dollars) for a month of sales t months after February 1. The graph of the revenue function is shown in the figure.

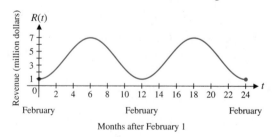

Figure for 54

(A) Find the exact values of $R(0)$, $R(2)$, $R(3)$, and $R(18)$ without using a calculator.

(B) Use a calculator to find $R(5)$ and $R(23)$. Interpret the results verbally.

(C) Use a graphing utility to confirm the graph shown here for $y = R(t)$.

Life Sciences

55. *Physiology.* A normal seated adult breathes in and exhales about 0.8 liter of air every 4 seconds. The volume of air $V(t)$ in the lungs t seconds after exhaling is given approximately by

$$V(t) = 0.45 - 0.35 \cos \frac{\pi t}{2} \qquad 0 \le t \le 8$$

The graph for two complete respirations is shown in the figure.

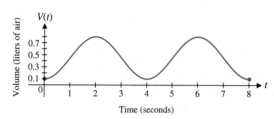

Figure for 55

(A) Find the exact value of $V(0)$, $V(1)$, $V(2)$, $V(3)$, and $V(7)$ without using a calculator.

(B) Use a calculator to find $V(3.5)$ and $V(5.7)$. Interpret the results verbally.

(C) Use a graphing utility to confirm the graph shown here for $y = V(t)$.

56. *Pollution.* In a large city, the amount of sulfur dioxide pollutant released into the atmosphere due to the burning of coal and oil for heating purposes varies seasonally. Suppose that the number of tons of pollutant released into the atmosphere during the nth week after January 1 is given approximately by

$$P(n) = 1 + \cos \frac{\pi n}{26} \qquad 0 \le n \le 104$$

The graph of the pollution function is shown in the figure.

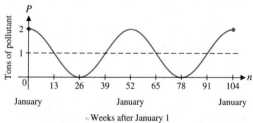

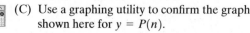

Figure for 56

(A) Find the exact values of $P(0)$, $P(39)$, $P(52)$, and $P(65)$ without using a calculator.

(B) Use a calculator to find $P(10)$ and $P(95)$. Interpret the results verbally.

(C) Use a graphing utility to confirm the graph shown here for $y = P(n)$.

Social Sciences

57. *Psychology: perception.* An important area of study in psychology is perception. Individuals perceive objects differently in different settings. Consider the well-known illusions shown in Figure A. Lines that appear parallel in one setting may appear to be curved in another (the two vertical lines are actually parallel). Lines of the same length may appear to be of different lengths in two different settings (the two horizontal lines are actually the same length). An interesting experiment in visual perception was conducted by psychologists Berliner and Berliner (*American Journal of Psychology,* 1952, 65:271–277). They reported that when subjects were presented with a large tilted field of parallel lines and were asked to estimate the position of a horizontal line in the field, most of the subjects were consistently off. They found that the difference in degrees, d, between the estimates and the actual horizontal could be approximated by the equation

$$d = a + b \sin 4\theta$$

where a and b are constants associated with a particular person and θ is the angle of tilt of the visual field (in degrees). Suppose that for a given person, $a = -2.1$ and $b = -4$. Find d if

(A) $\theta = 30°$ (B) $\theta = 10°$

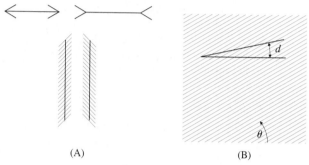

(A)   (B)

Figure for 57

Section 9-2 | Derivatives of Trigonometric Functions

> ➤ Derivative Formulas
> ➤ Application

➤ Derivative Formulas

In this section we discuss derivative formulas for the sine and cosine functions. Once we have these formulas, we automatically have integral formulas for the same functions, which we discuss in the next section.

From the definition of the derivative (Section 3-3),

$$\frac{d}{dx} \sin x = \lim_{h \to 0} \frac{\sin(x + h) - \sin x}{h}$$

Using trigonometric identities and some special trigonometric limits, it can be shown that the limit on the right is $\cos x$. Similarly, it can be shown that

$$\frac{d}{dx} \cos x = -\sin x$$

We now add the following important derivative formulas to our list of derivative formulas:

FORMULAS   Derivative of Sine and Cosine

Basic Form

$$\frac{d}{dx} \sin x = \cos x \qquad \frac{d}{dx} \cos x = -\sin x$$

Generalized Form

For $u = u(x)$,

$$\frac{d}{dx}\sin u = \cos u \frac{du}{dx} \qquad \frac{d}{dx}\cos u = -\sin u \frac{du}{dx}$$

⊚ **Insight**   The derivative formula for the function $y = \sin x$ implies that each tangent line to its graph has a slope between -1 and 1. Furthermore, the slope of the tangent line to $y = \sin x$ is equal to 1 if and only if $\cos x = 1$, that is, at $x = 0, \pm 2\pi, \pm 4\pi, \dots$. Similarly, the derivative formula for $y = \cos x$ implies that each tangent line to its graph has a slope between -1 and 1. Furthermore, the slope of the tangent line is equal to 1 if and only if $-\sin x = 1$, that is, at $x = 3\pi/2, (3\pi/2) \pm 2\pi, (3\pi/2) \pm 4\pi, \dots$. Note that these observations are consistent with the graphs of $y = \sin x$ and $y = \cos x$ shown in Figure 9, Section 9-1.   ●

EXAMPLE 1   **Derivatives Involving Sine and Cosine**

(A) $\dfrac{d}{dx}\sin x^2 = (\cos x^2)\dfrac{d}{dx}x^2 = (\cos x^2)2x = 2x \cos x^2$

(B) $\dfrac{d}{dx}\cos(2x - 5) = -\sin(2x - 5)\dfrac{d}{dx}(2x - 5) = -2\sin(2x - 5)$

(C) $\dfrac{d}{dx}(3x^2 - x)\cos x = (3x^2 - x)\dfrac{d}{dx}\cos x + (\cos x)\dfrac{d}{dx}(3x^2 - x)$

$\qquad\qquad = -(3x^2 - x)\sin x + (6x - 1)\cos x$

$\qquad\qquad = (x - 3x^2)\sin x + (6x - 1)\cos x$ ■

Matched Problem 1   Find each of the following derivatives:

(A) $\dfrac{d}{dx}\cos x^3$ (B) $\dfrac{d}{dx}\sin(5 - 3x)$ (C) $\dfrac{d}{dx}\dfrac{\sin x}{x}$

EXAMPLE 2   **Slope**   Find the slope of the graph of $f(x) = \sin x$ at $(\pi/2, 1)$, and sketch in the tangent line to the graph at this point.

Solution   Slope at $(\pi/2, 1) = f'(\pi/2) = \cos(\pi/2) = 0$.

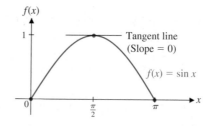

Matched Problem 2   Find the slope of the graph of $f(x) = \cos x$ at $(\pi/6, \sqrt{3}/2)$

EXPLORE
&DISCUSS
1

From the graph of $y = f'(x)$ shown in Figure 1, describe the shape of the graph of $y = f(x)$ relative to increasing, decreasing, concavity, and local maxima and minima. Make a sketch of a possible graph of $y = f(x)$, $0 \le x \le 2\pi$, given that it has x intercepts at $(0, 0)$, $(\pi, 0)$, and $(2\pi, 0)$. Can you identify $f(x)$ and $f'(x)$ in terms of sine or cosine functions?

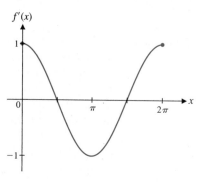

FIGURE 1

EXAMPLE 3 **Derivative of Secant** Find: $\dfrac{d}{dx}\sec x$

Solution

$$\frac{d}{dx}\sec x = \frac{d}{dx}\frac{1}{\cos x} = \frac{d}{dx}(\cos x)^{-1} \qquad \text{Since } \sec x = \frac{1}{\cos x}$$

$$= -(\cos x)^{-2}\frac{d}{dx}\cos x$$

$$= -(\cos x)^{-2}(-\sin x)$$

$$= \frac{\sin x}{(\cos x)^2} = \left(\frac{\sin x}{\cos x}\right)\left(\frac{1}{\cos x}\right)$$

$$= \tan x \sec x \qquad \text{Since } \tan x = \frac{\sin x}{\cos x}$$

Matched Problem 3   Find: $\dfrac{d}{dx}\csc x$

➤ **Application**

EXAMPLE 4   **Revenue** A sporting goods store has revenues from the sale of ski jackets that are given approximately by

$$R(t) = 1.55 + 1.45\cos\frac{\pi t}{26} \qquad 0 \le t \le 104$$

where $R(t)$ is revenue (in thousands of dollars) for a week of sales t weeks after January 1.

(A) What is the rate of change of revenue t weeks after the first of the year?

(B) What is the rate of change of revenue 10 weeks after the first of the year? 26 weeks after the first of the year? 40 weeks after the first of the year?

(C) Find all local maxima and minima for $0 < t < 104$.

(D) Find the absolute maximum and minimum for $0 \le t \le 104$.

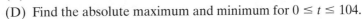

(E) Illustrate the results from parts (A)–(D) by sketching a graph of $y = R(t)$ with the aid of a graphing utility.

Solution (A) $R'(t) = -\dfrac{1.45\pi}{26} \sin \dfrac{\pi t}{26}$ $0 \le t \le 104$

(B) $R'(10) \approx -\$0.164$ thousand   or $-\$164$ per week

$R'(26) = \$0$ per week

$R'(40) \approx \$0.174$ thousand   or $\$174$ per week

(C) Find the critical points:

$$R'(t) = -\dfrac{1.45\pi}{26} \sin \dfrac{\pi t}{26} = 0 \quad 0 < t < 104$$

$$\sin \dfrac{\pi t}{26} = 0$$

$$\dfrac{\pi t}{26} = \pi, 2\pi, 3\pi \quad \text{Note: } 0 < t < 104 \text{ implies that } 0 < \dfrac{\pi t}{26} < 4\pi.$$

$$t = 26, 52, 78$$

Use the second-derivative test to get the results shown in Table 1.

$$R''(t) = -\dfrac{1.45\pi^2}{26^2} \cos \dfrac{\pi t}{26}$$

(D) Evaluate $R(t)$ at endpoints $t = 0$ and $t = 104$ and at the critical points found in part (C), as listed in Table 2.

TABLE 1

t	$R''(t)$	Graph of R
26	+	Local minimum
52	−	Local maximum
78	+	Local minimum

TABLE 2

t	$R(t)$	
0	$3,000	Absolute maximum
26	$100	Absolute minimum
52	$3,000	Absolute maximum
78	$100	Absolute minimum
104	$3,000	Absolute maximum

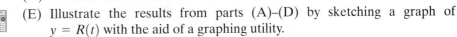

(E) The results from parts (A)–(D) can be visualized as shown in the graph of $y = R(t)$ in Figure 2.

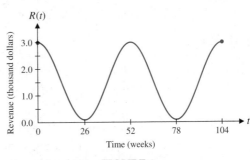

FIGURE 2

**Matched
Problem 4**

Suppose that in Example 4 revenues from the sale of ski jackets are given approximately by

$$R(t) = 6.2 + 5.8 \cos \frac{\pi t}{6} \qquad 0 \le t \le 24$$

where $R(t)$ is revenue (in thousands of dollars) for a month of sales t months after January 1.

(A) What is the rate of change of revenue t months after the first of the year?

(B) What is the rate of change of revenue 2 months after the first of the year? 12 months after the first of the year? 23 months after the first of the year?

(C) Find all local maxima and minima for $0 < t < 24$.

(D) Find the absolute maximum and minimum for $0 \le t \le 24$.

(E) Illustrate the results from parts (A) to (D) by sketching a graph of $y = R(t)$ with the aid of a graphing utility.

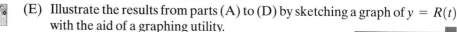

Answers to Matched Problems   **1.** (A) $-3x^2 \sin x^3$ (B) $-3 \cos(5 - 3x)$ (C) $\dfrac{x \cos x - \sin x}{x^2}$

2. $-\frac{1}{2}$ **3.** $-\cot x \csc x$

4. (A) $R'(t) = -\dfrac{5.8\pi}{6} \sin \dfrac{\pi t}{6}, 0 < t < 24$

(B) $R'(2) \approx -\$2.630$ thousand or $-\$2,630/$month; $R'(12) = \$0/$month; $R'(23) \approx \$1.518$ thousand or $\$1,518/$month

(C) Local minima at $t = 6$ and $t = 18$; local maximum at $t = 12$

(D)

	t	$R(t)$	
Endpoint	0	$12,000	Absolute maximum
	6	$400	Absolute minimum
	12	$12,000	Absolute maximum
	18	$400	Absolute minimum
Endpoint	24	$12,000	Absolute maximum

(E)

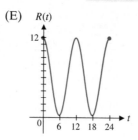

Exercise 9-2

Find the indicated derivatives in Problems 1–14.

A

1. $\dfrac{d}{dt} \cos t$

2. $\dfrac{d}{dw} \sin w$

3. $\dfrac{d}{dx} \sin x^3$

4. $\dfrac{d}{dx} \cos(x^2 - 1)$

B

5. $\dfrac{d}{dt} t \sin t$

6. $\dfrac{d}{du} u \cos u$

7. $\dfrac{d}{dx} \sin x \cos x$

8. $\dfrac{d}{dx} \dfrac{\sin x}{\cos x}$

9. $\dfrac{d}{dx}(\sin x)^5$

10. $\dfrac{d}{dx}(\cos x)^8$

11. $\dfrac{d}{dx}\sqrt{\sin x}$

12. $\dfrac{d}{dx}\sqrt{\cos x}$

13. $\dfrac{d}{dx}\cos\sqrt{x}$

14. $\dfrac{d}{dx}\sin\sqrt{x}$

15. Find the slope of the graph of $f(x) = \sin x$ at $x = \pi/6$.

16. Find the slope of the graph of $f(x) = \cos x$ at $x = \pi/4$.

17. From the graph of $y = f'(x)$ shown here, describe the shape of the graph of $y = f(x)$ relative to increasing, decreasing, concavity, and local maxima and minima. Make a sketch of a possible graph of $y = f(x)$, $-\pi \le x \le \pi$, given it has x intercepts at $(-\pi/2, 0)$ and $(\pi/2, 0)$. Identify $f(x)$ and $f'(x)$ as particular trigonometric functions.

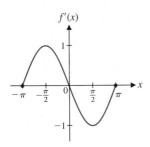

Figure for 17

18. From the graph of $y = f'(x)$ shown here, describe the shape of the graph of $y = f(x)$ relative to increasing, decreasing, concavity, and local maxima and minima. Make a sketch of a possible graph of $y = f(x)$, $-\pi \le x \le \pi$, given it has x intercepts at $(-\pi/2, 0)$ and $(\pi/2, 0)$.

Identify $f(x)$ and $f'(x)$ as particular trigonometric functions.

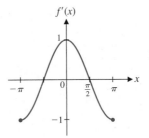

Figure for 18

C *Find the indicated derivatives in Problems 19–22.*

19. $\dfrac{d}{dx}\tan x$

20. $\dfrac{d}{dx}\cot x$

21. $\dfrac{d}{dx}\sin\sqrt{x^2 - 1}$

22. $\dfrac{d}{dx}\cos\sqrt{x^4 - 1}$

In Problems 23 and 24, find $f''(x)$.

23. $f(x) = e^x \sin x$

24. $f(x) = e^x \cos x$

 In Problems 25–30, graph each function on a graphing utility.

25. $y = x \sin \pi x; 0 \le x \le 9, -9 \le y \le 9$

26. $y = -x \cos \pi x; 0 \le x \le 9, -9 \le y \le 9$

27. $y = \dfrac{\cos \pi x}{x}; 0 \le x \le 8, -2 \le y \le 3$

28. $y = \dfrac{\sin \pi x}{0.5x}; 0 \le x \le 8, -2 \le y \le 3$

29. $y = e^{-0.3x} \sin \pi x; 0 \le x \le 10, -1 \le y \le 1$

30. $y = e^{-0.2x} \cos \pi x; 0 \le x \le 10, -1 \le y \le 1$

Applications

Business & Economics

31. *Profit.* Suppose that profits on the sale of swimming suits in a department store are given approximately by

$$P(t) = 5 - 5\cos\frac{\pi t}{26} \qquad 0 \le t \le 104$$

where $P(t)$ is profit (in hundreds of dollars) for a week of sales t weeks after January 1.

(A) What is the rate of change of profit t weeks after the first of the year?

(B) What is the rate of change of profit 8 weeks after the first of the year? 26 weeks after the first of the year? 50 weeks after the first of the year?

(C) Find all local maxima and minima for $0 < t < 104$.

(D) Find the absolute maximum and minimum for $0 \le t \le 104$.

 (E) Repeat part (C) using a graphing utility.

32. *Revenue.* A soft drink company has revenues from sales over a 2-year period as given

approximately by

$$R(t) = 4 - 3 \cos \frac{\pi t}{6} \qquad 0 \le t \le 24$$

where $R(t)$ is revenue (in millions of dollars) for a month of sales t months after February 1.

(A) What is the rate of change of revenue t months after February 1?

(B) What is the rate of change of revenue 1 month after February 1? 6 months after February 1? 11 months after February 1?

(C) Find all local maxima and minima for $0 < t < 24$.

(D) Find the absolute maximum and minimum for $0 \le t \le 24$.

 (E) Repeat part (C) using a graphing utility.

Life Sciences

33. *Physiology.* A normal seated adult breathes in and exhales about 0.8 liter of air every 4 seconds. The volume of air $V(t)$ in the lungs t seconds after exhaling is given approximately by

$$V(t) = 0.45 - 0.35 \cos \frac{\pi t}{2} \qquad 0 \le t \le 8$$

(A) What is the rate of flow of air t seconds after exhaling?

(B) What is the rate of flow of air 3 seconds after exhaling? 4 seconds after exhaling? 5 seconds after exhaling?

(C) Find all local maxima and minima for $0 < t < 8$.

(D) Find the absolute maximum and minimum for $0 \le t \le 8$.

 (E) Repeat part (C) using a graphing utility.

34. *Pollution.* In a large city, the amount of sulfur dioxide pollutant released into the atmosphere due to the burning of coal and oil for heating purposes varies seasonally. Suppose that the number of tons of pollutant released into the atmosphere during the nth week after January 1 is given approximately by

$$P(n) = 1 + \cos \frac{\pi n}{26} \qquad 0 \le n \le 104$$

(A) What is the rate of change of pollutant n weeks after the first of the year?

(B) What is the rate of change of pollutant 13 weeks after the first of the year? 26 weeks after the first of the year? 30 weeks after the first of the year?

(C) Find all local maxima and minima for $0 < t < 104$.

(D) Find the absolute maximum and minimum for $0 \le t \le 104$.

 (E) Repeat part (C) using a graphing utility.

Section 9-3 | Integration of Trigonometric Functions

➤ Integral Formulas
➤ Application

➤ Integral Formulas

Now that we know the derivative formulas

$$\frac{d}{dx} \sin x = \cos x \qquad \text{and} \qquad \frac{d}{dx} \cos x = -\sin x$$

from the definition of the indefinite integral of a function (Section 6-1), we automatically have the two integral formulas

$$\int \cos x \, dx = \sin x + C \qquad \text{and} \qquad \int \sin x \, dx = -\cos x + C$$

EXAMPLE 1   **Area under a Sine Curve**   Find the area under the sine curve $y = \sin x$ from 0 to π.

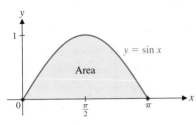

Solution
$$\text{Area} = \int_0^\pi \sin x \, dx = -\cos x \Big|_0^\pi$$
$$= (-\cos \pi) - (-\cos 0)$$
$$= [-(-1)] - [-(1)] = 2$$

Matched Problem 1   Find the area under the cosine curve $y = \cos x$ from 0 to $\pi/2$.

EXPLORE & DISCUSS 1   From the graph of $y = \sin x$, $0 \le x \le 2\pi$, guess the value for $\int_0^{2\pi} \sin x \, dx$ and explain the reasoning behind your guess. Confirm the guess by direct evaluation of the definite integral.

From the general derivative formulas
$$\frac{d}{dx} \sin u = \cos u \frac{du}{dx} \quad \text{and} \quad \frac{d}{dx} \cos u = -\sin u \frac{du}{dx}$$
we obtain the general integral formulas below.

FORMULAS   Indefinite Integrals of Sine and Cosine
For $u = u(x)$,
$$\int \sin u \, du = -\cos u + C \quad \text{and} \quad \int \cos u \, du = \sin u + C$$

EXAMPLE 2   **Indefinite Integrals and Trigonometric Functions**   Find: $\int x \sin x^2 \, dx$

Solution
$$\int x \sin x^2 \, dx = \frac{1}{2} \int 2x \sin x^2 \, dx$$
$$= \frac{1}{2} \int (\sin x^2) 2x \, dx \quad \text{Let } u = x^2; \text{ then } du = 2x \, dx.$$
$$= \frac{1}{2} \int \sin u \, du$$
$$= -\frac{1}{2} \cos u + C$$
$$= -\frac{1}{2} \cos x^2 + C \quad \text{Since } u = x^2$$

Check: To check, we differentiate the result to obtain the original integrand:

$$\frac{d}{dx}\left(-\frac{1}{2}\cos x^2\right) = -\frac{1}{2}\frac{d}{dx}\cos x^2$$

$$= -\frac{1}{2}(-\sin x^2)\frac{d}{dx}x^2$$

$$= -\frac{1}{2}(-\sin x^2)(2x)$$

$$= x \sin x^2$$

Matched Problem 2   Find: $\int \cos 20\pi t\, dt$

EXAMPLE 3   Indefinite Integrals and Trigonometric Functions

Find: $\int (\sin x)^5 \cos x\, dx$

Solution   This is of the form $\int u^p\, du$, where $u = \sin x$ and $du = \cos x\, dx$. Thus,

$$\int (\sin x)^5 \cos x\, dx = \frac{(\sin x)^6}{6} + C$$

Matched Problem 3   Find: $\int \sqrt{\sin x}\cos x\, dx$

EXAMPLE 4   Definite Integrals and Trigonometric Functions

Evaluate: $\int_2^{3.5} \cos x\, dx$

Solution

$$\int_2^{3.5} \cos x\, dx = \sin x\Big|_2^{3.5}$$

$$= \sin 3.5 - \sin 2 \qquad \textit{Use a calculator in radian mode.}$$

$$= -0.3508 - 0.9093$$

$$= -1.2601$$

Matched Problem 4   Use a calculator to evaluate: $\int_1^{1.5} \sin x\, dx$

◉ Insight   Recall that $y = \sin x$ is a periodic function with period 2π, and let c be any real number. Then

$$\int_c^{c+2\pi} \cos x\, dx = \sin x\Big|_c^{c+2\pi} = \sin(c + 2\pi) - \sin c = 0$$

In other words, over any interval of the form $[c, c + 2\pi]$, the area that is above the x axis but below the graph of $y = \cos x$ is equal to the area that is below the x axis but above the graph of $y = \cos x$ (see Figure 9, Section 9-1). Similarly, for any real number c,

$$\int_c^{c+2\pi} \sin x\, dx = 0$$

➤ Application

EXAMPLE 5

Total Revenue In Example 4 (Section 9-2), we were given the following revenue equation from the sale of ski jackets:

$$R(t) = 1.55 + 1.45 \cos\frac{\pi t}{26} \qquad 0 \le t \le 104$$

where $R(t)$ is revenue (in thousands of dollars) for a week of sales t weeks after January 1.

(A) Find the total revenue taken in over the 2-year period—that is, from $t = 0$ to $t = 104$.

(B) Find the total revenue taken in from $t = 39$ to $t = 65$.

Solution (A) The area under the graph of the revenue equation for the 2-year period approximates the total revenue taken in for that period:

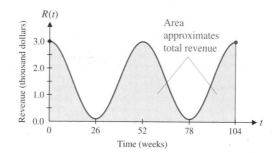

This area (and total revenue) is given by the following definite integral:

$$\text{total revenue} \approx \int_0^{104} \left(1.55 + 1.45 \cos\frac{\pi t}{26}\right) dt$$

$$= \left[1.55t + 1.45\left(\frac{26}{\pi}\right)\sin\frac{\pi t}{26}\right]\Big|_0^{104}$$

$$= \$161.200 \text{ thousand} \quad \text{or} \quad \$161,200$$

(B) The total revenue from $t = 39$ to $t = 65$ is approximated by the area under the curve from $t = 39$ to $t = 65$:

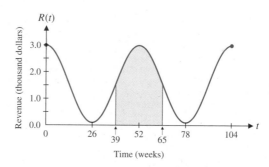

$$\text{Total revenue} \approx \int_{39}^{65} \left(1.55 + 1.45 \cos\frac{\pi t}{26}\right) dt$$

$$= \left[1.55t + 1.45\left(\frac{26}{\pi}\right)\sin\frac{\pi t}{26}\right]\Big|_{39}^{65}$$

$$= \$64.301 \text{ thousand} \quad \text{or} \quad \$64,301$$

Matched Problem 5

Suppose that in Example 5 revenues from the sale of ski jackets are given approximately by

$$R(t) = 6.2 + 5.8 \cos \frac{\pi t}{6} \qquad 0 \le t \le 24$$

where $R(t)$ is revenue (in thousands of dollars) for a month of sales t months after January 1.

(A) Find the total revenue taken in over the 2 year period—that is, from $t = 0$ to $t = 24$.

(B) Find the total revenue taken in from $t = 4$ to $t = 8$. ──────────■

Answers to Matched Problems   **1.** 1   **2.** $\frac{1}{20\pi} \sin 20\pi t + C$ **3.** $\frac{2}{3}(\sin x)^{3/2} + C$ **4.** 0.4696

5. (A) $148.8 thousand or $148,800   (B) $5.614 thousand or $5,614

Exercise 9-3

Find each of the indefinite integrals in Problems 1–10.

A

1. $\int \sin t \, dt$

2. $\int \cos w \, dw$

3. $\int \cos 3x \, dx$

4. $\int \sin 2x \, dx$

5. $\int (\sin x)^{12} \cos x \, dx$

6. $\int \sin x \cos x \, dx$

B

7. $\int \sqrt[3]{\cos x} \sin x \, dx$

8. $\int \frac{\cos x}{\sqrt{\sin x}} \, dx$

9. $\int x^2 \cos x^3 \, dx$

10. $\int (x + 1) \sin(x^2 + 2x) \, dx$

Evaluate each of the definite integrals in Problems 11–14.

11. $\int_0^{\pi/2} \cos x \, dx$

12. $\int_0^{\pi/4} \cos x \, dx$

13. $\int_{\pi/2}^{\pi} \sin x \, dx$

14. $\int_{\pi/6}^{\pi/3} \sin x \, dx$

15. Find the shaded area under the cosine curve in the figure:

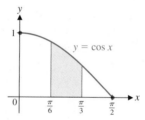

16. Find the shaded area under the sine curve in the figure:

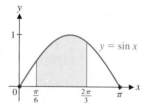

Use a calculator to evaluate the definite integrals in Problems 17–20 after performing the indefinite integration. (Remember that the limits are real numbers, so the radian mode must be used on the calculator.)

17. $\int_0^2 \sin x \, dx$

18. $\int_0^{0.5} \cos x \, dx$

19. $\int_1^2 \cos x \, dx$

20. $\int_1^3 \sin x \, dx$

C *Find each of the indefinite integrals in Problems 21–26.*

21. $\int e^{\sin x} \cos x \, dx$

22. $\int e^{\cos x} \sin x \, dx$

23. $\int \frac{\cos x}{\sin x} \, dx$

24. $\int \frac{\sin x}{\cos x} \, dx$

25. $\int \tan x \, dx$ **26.** $\int \cot x \, dx$

27. Given the definite integral

$$I = \int_0^3 e^{-x} \sin x \, dx$$

(A) Graph the integrand $f(x) = e^{-x} \sin x$ over $[0, 3]$.

(B) Approximate I using the left sum L_6 (see Section 6-5).

28. Given the definite integral

$$I = \int_0^3 e^{-x} \cos x \, dx$$

(A) Graph the integrand $f(x) = e^{-x} \cos x$ over $[0, 3]$.

(B) Approximate I using the right sum R_6 (see Section 6-5).

Applications

Business & Economics

29. *Seasonal business cycle.* Suppose that profits on the sale of swimming suits in a department store are given approximately by

$$P(t) = 5 - 5 \cos \frac{\pi t}{26} \qquad 0 \le t \le 104$$

where $P(t)$ is profit (in hundreds of dollars) for a week of sales t weeks after January 1. Use definite integrals to approximate:

(A) The total profit earned during the 2-year period

(B) The total profit earned from $t = 13$ to $t = 26$

 (C) Illustrate part (B) graphically with an appropriate shaded region representing the total profit earned.

30. *Seasonal business cycle.* A soft drink company has revenues from sales over a 2-year period as given approximately by

$$R(t) = 4 - 3 \cos \frac{\pi t}{6} \qquad 0 \le t \le 24$$

where $R(t)$ is revenue (in millions of dollars) for a month of sales t months after February 1. Use

definite integrals to approximate:

(A) Total revenues taken in over the 2-year period

(B) Total revenues taken in from $t = 8$ to $t = 14$

 (C) Illustrate part (B) graphically with an appropriate shaded region representing the total revenues taken in.

Life Sciences

31. *Pollution.* In a large city, the amount of sulfur dioxide pollutant released into the atmosphere due to the burning of coal and oil for heating purposes is given approximately by

$$P(n) = 1 + \cos \frac{\pi n}{26} \qquad 0 \le n \le 104$$

where $P(n)$ is the amount of sulfur dioxide (in tons) released during the nth week after January 1.

(A) How many tons of pollutants were emitted into the atmosphere over the 2-year period?

(B) How many tons of pollutants were emitted into the atmosphere from $n = 13$ to $n = 52$?

(C) Illustrate part (B) graphically with an appropriate shaded region representing the total tons of pollutants emitted into the atmosphere.

Chapter 9 Review

Important Terms, Symbols, and Concepts

9-1 Trigonometric Functions Review

An **angle** is formed by rotating (in a plane) a ray, m, called the **initial side** of the angle, around its endpoint until it coincides with a ray, n, called the **terminal side** of the angle. The common endpoint P of m and n is called the **vertex**. A counterclockwise rotation produces a **positive** angle, and a clockwise rotation produces a **negative** angle. Two angles with the same initial and terminal sides are said to be **coterminal**. An angle of **degree measure 1** is $\frac{1}{360}$ of a complete rotation. An angle of **radian measure 1** is the central angle of a circle

subtended by an arc having the same length as the radius. Degree measure can be converted to radian measure, and vice versa, by the proportion

$$\frac{\theta_{\deg}}{180°} = \frac{\theta_{\text{rad}}}{\pi \text{ rad}}$$

An angle in a rectangular coordinate system is in **standard position** if its vertex is at the origin and its initial side is on the positive x axis.

If θ is an angle in standard position, its terminal side intersects the unit circle at a point P. We denote the coordinates of P by $(\cos \theta, \sin \theta)$.

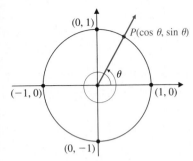

The set of all ordered pairs of the form $(\theta, \sin\theta)$ is the **sine function,** and the set of all ordered pairs of the form $(\theta, \cos\theta)$ is the **cosine function.** For work in calculus, we define these functions for angles measured in radians; that is, for any real number x,

$$\sin x = \sin(x \text{ radians}) \qquad \cos x = \cos(x \text{ radians})$$

A function f is **periodic** if $f(x + p) = f(x)$ for some constant p and all real numbers x for which $f(x)$ is defined. The smallest such constant p is called the **period.** Both $\sin x$ and $\cos x$ are periodic continuous functions with period 2π.

Four additional trigonometric functions are defined in terms of $\sin x$ and $\cos x$:

$$\tan x = \frac{\sin x}{\cos x} \quad \cos x \neq 0 \qquad \sec x = \frac{1}{\cos x} \quad \cos x \neq 0$$

$$\cot x = \frac{\cos x}{\sin x} \quad \sin x \neq 0 \qquad \csc x = \frac{1}{\sin x} \quad \sin x \neq 0$$

9-2 Derivatives of Trigonometric Functions

The derivatives of the functions $\sin x$ and $\cos x$ are

$$\frac{d}{dx}\sin x = \cos x \qquad \frac{d}{dx}\cos x = -\sin x$$

For $u = u(x)$,

$$\frac{d}{dx}\sin u = \cos u\frac{du}{dx} \qquad \frac{d}{du}\cos u = -\sin u\frac{du}{dx}$$

9-3 Integration of Trigonometric Functions

Indefinite integrals of the functions $\sin x$ and $\cos x$ are

$$\int \sin u \, du = -\cos u + C \qquad \int \cos u \, du = \sin u + C$$

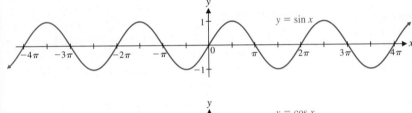

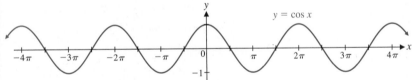

Review Exercise

Work through all the problems in this chapter review and check your answers in the back of the book. Answers to all review problems are there along with section numbers in italics to indicate where each type of problem is discussed. Where weaknesses show up, review appropriate sections in the text.

A

1. Convert to radian measure in terms of π:

   (A) 30°   (B) 45°   (C) 60°   (D) 90°

2. Evaluate without using a calculator:

   (A) $\cos\pi$ (B) $\sin 0$ (C) $\sin\dfrac{\pi}{2}$

In Problems 3–6, find each derivative or integral.

3. $\dfrac{d}{dm}\cos m$ 4. $\dfrac{d}{du}\sin u$

5. $\dfrac{d}{dx}\sin(x^2 - 2x + 1)$ 6. $\displaystyle\int \sin 3t \, dt$

B

7. Convert to degree measure:

   (A) $\pi/6$ (B) $\pi/4$ (C) $\pi/3$ (D) $\pi/2$

8. Evaluate without using a calculator:

   (A) $\sin\dfrac{\pi}{6}$ (B) $\cos\dfrac{\pi}{4}$ (C) $\sin\dfrac{\pi}{3}$

9. Evaluate using a calculator:

   (A) $\cos 33.7$ (B) $\sin(-118.4)$

In Problems 10–16, find each derivative or integral.

10. $\dfrac{d}{dx}(x^2 - 1)\sin x$ 11. $\dfrac{d}{dx}(\sin x)^6$

12. $\dfrac{d}{dx}\sqrt[3]{\sin x}$ 13. $\displaystyle\int t\cos(t^2 - 1)\,dt$

14. $\displaystyle\int_0^\pi \sin u \, du$ 15. $\displaystyle\int_0^{\pi/3} \cos x \, dx$ 16. $\displaystyle\int_1^{2.5} \cos x \, dx$

17. Find the slope of the cosine curve $y = \cos x$ at $x = \pi/4$.

18. Find the area under the sine curve $y = \sin x$ from $x = \pi/4$ to $x = 3\pi/4$.

19. Given the definite integral

$$I = \int_1^5 \frac{\sin x}{x}\, dx$$

(A) Graph the integrand

$$f(x) = \frac{\sin x}{x}$$

over $[1, 5]$.

(B) Approximate I using the right sum R_4.

C

20. Convert $15°$ to radian measure.

21. Evaluate without using a calculator:

(A) $\sin\dfrac{3\pi}{2}$ (B) $\cos\dfrac{5\pi}{6}$ (C) $\sin\left(\dfrac{-\pi}{6}\right)$

In Problems 22–26, find each derivative or integral.

22. $\dfrac{d}{du}\tan u$ **23.** $\dfrac{d}{dx}e^{\cos x^2}$ **24.** $\displaystyle\int e^{\sin x}\cos x\, dx$

25. $\displaystyle\int \tan x\, dx$ **26.** $\displaystyle\int_2^5 (5 + 2\cos 2x)\, dx$

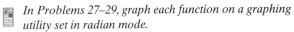 *In Problems 27–29, graph each function on a graphing utility set in radian mode.*

27. $y = \dfrac{\sin \pi x}{0.2x}; 1 \le x \le 8, -4 \le y \le 4$

28. $y = 0.5x\cos \pi x; 0 \le x \le 8, -5 \le y \le 5$

29. $y = 3 - 2\cos \pi x; 0 \le x \le 6, 0 \le y \le 5$

Applications

Business & Economics

Problems 30–32 refer to the following: Revenues from sweater sales in a sportswear chain are given approximately by

$$R(t) = 3 + 2\cos\frac{\pi t}{6} \qquad 0 \le t \le 24$$

where $R(t)$ is the revenue (in thousands of dollars) for a month of sales t months after January 1.

30. (A) Find the exact values of $R(0)$, $R(2)$, $R(3)$, and $R(6)$ without using a calculator.

(B) Use a calculator to find $R(1)$ and $R(22)$. Interpret the results verbally.

31. (A) What is the rate of change of revenue t months after January 1?

(B) What is the rate of change of revenue 3 months after January 1? 10 months after January 1? 18 months after January 1?

(C) Find all local maxima and minima for $0 < t < 24$.

(D) Find the absolute maximum and minimum for $0 \le t \le 24$.

 (E) Repeat part (C) using a graphing utility.

32. (A) Find the total revenues taken in over the 2-year period.

(B) Find the total revenues taken in from $t = 5$ to $t = 9$.

(C) Illustrate part (B) graphically with an appropriate shaded region representing the total revenue taken in.

Group Activity 1   *Seasonal Business Cycles*

A large soft drink company's profits are seasonal, with the greatest profits occurring during the warm part of the year and the least profits occurring during the cold part of the year. Table 1 gives the profit for a month of sales (profit per month) t months after February 1 over a 2-year period.

TABLE 1 Profit t Months After February 1 (Million Dollars)

t	$P(t)$	t	$P(t)$	t	$P(t)$	t	$P(t)$
0	1.551						
1	1.082	7	10.447	13	0.932	19	9.578
2	1.804	8	10.353	14	1.785	20	9.116
3	4.255	9	8.662	15	3.461	21	8.533
4	5.692	10	5.960	16	7.011	22	5.506
5	8.137	11	2.847	17	8.245	23	3.725
6	9.907	12	1.158	18	9.137	24	1.879

(A) Plot the data points from Table 1 on graph paper.

(B) Estimate the total profit from $t = 1$ to $t = 13$ using the average of the left and right sums (see Section 6-4) and estimate the error.
[*Hint:* Break the problem into two parts where $P(t)$ is monotonic in each.]

(C) Sketch a graph of

$$P(t) = 5.682 - 4.425 \cos\left(\frac{\pi t}{6} - 0.43\right)$$

on top of the plot from part (A) over the interval $[1, 13]$. [The equation $y = P(t)$ provides a reasonable model for the data in Table 1.]

(D) With an appropriate use of a definite integral involving the profit function in part (C), estimate the total profit earned from $t = 1$ to $t = 13$.

Group Activity 2   Heating Degree Days

Estimating the energy demand for heating and cooling homes is an important activity for government agencies, local utilities, oil companies, and other energy suppliers. **Heating degree days** are used to estimate the amount of energy required for residential space heating. If the average temperature T on a given day is less than 65°F, the number of heating degree days for that day is $65 - T$. If $T \geq 65$, the number of heating degree days is 0. The sum of the heating degree days over the entire year is used to predict the annual heating demand.

Table 1 gives the average monthly temperature $T(x)$ for Tulsa, Oklahoma, where x is days after January 1.

TABLE 1 Average Monthly Temperatures for Tulsa (°F)

Month	Jan.	Feb.	Mar.	Apr.	May	June	July	Aug.	Sept.	Oct.	Nov.	Dec.
x	15	45	75	105	135	165	195	225	255	285	315	345
$T(x)$	35	40	51	61	69	78	83	82	73	62	50	39

(A) To construct a model that uses monthly average temperatures to approximate the annual heating demand in Tulsa, we assume that each month has exactly 30 days. Enter x, the midpoint of each month, and the corresponding temperature $T(x)$ in the statistics editor of a graphing utility. If your graphing utility supports sinusoidal regression, find a model of the form $T(x) = a \sin(bx + c) + d$. Otherwise, find a fourth-degree polynomial model for $T(x)$.

(B) Graph $T(x)$ and the line $y = 65$ for $0 \leq x \leq 360$, and describe the region whose area would approximate the annual heating demand.

(C) Express the area from part (B) in terms of one or more definite integrals, and use numerical integration to approximate this area.
In a similar manner, **cooling degree days** are defined to be the difference between the average daily temperature T and 65 if $T > 65$, and 0 otherwise.

(D) Describe the region on the graph in part (B) that would approximate the annual cooling demand.

(E) Express the area from part (D) in terms of one or more definite integrals, and use numerical integration to approximate this area.

APPENDIX A

BASIC ALGEBRA REVIEW

Self-Test on Basic Algebra
A-1 *Algebra and Real Numbers*
A-2 *Operations on Polynomials*
A-3 *Factoring Polynomials*
A-4 *Operations on Rational Expressions*
A-5 *Integer Exponents and Scientific Notation*
A-6 *Rational Exponents and Radicals*
A-7 *Linear Equations and Inequalities in One Variable*
A-8 *Quadratic Equations*

INTRODUCTION

Appendix A reviews some important basic algebra concepts usually studied in earlier courses. The material may be studied systematically before beginning the rest of the book or reviewed as needed. The Self-Test on Basic Algebra that precedes Section A-1 may be taken to locate areas of weakness. All the answers to the self-test are in the answer section in the back of the book and are keyed to the sections in Appendix A where the related topics are discussed.

Self-Test on Basic Algebra

Work through all the problems in this self-test and check your answers in the back of the book. All answers are there and are keyed to relevant sections in Appendix A. Where weaknesses show up, review appropriate sections in the appendix.

1. Replace each question mark with an appropriate expression that will illustrate the use of the indicated real number property:

   (A) Commutative $(\cdot)$: $x(y + z) = ?$
   (B) Associative $(+)$: $2 + (x + y) = ?$
   (C) Distributive: $(2 + 3)x = ?$

Problems 2–6 refer to the following polynomials:

   (A) $3x - 4$
   (B) $x + 2$
   (C) $2 - 3x^2$
   (D) $x^3 + 8$

2. Add all four.

3. Subtract the sum of (A) and (C) from the sum of (B) and (D).

4. Multiply (C) and (D).

5. What is the degree of each polynomial?

6. What is the leading coefficient of each polynomial?

In Problems 7–12, perform the indicated operations and simplify.

7. $5x^2 - 3x[4 - 3(x - 2)]$

8. $(2x + y)(3x - 4y)$

9. $(2a - 3b)^2$

10. $(2x - y)(2x + y) - (2x - y)^2$

11. $(3x^3 - 2y)^2$

12. $(x - 2y)^3$

583

13. Write in scientific notation:

(A) 4,065,000,000,000

(B) 0.0073

14. Write in standard decimal form:

(A) 2.55×10^8

(B) 4.06×10^{-4}

15. Indicate true (T) or false (F):

(A) A natural number is a rational number.

(B) A number with a repeating decimal expansion is an irrational number.

16. Give an example of an integer that is not a natural number.

Simplify Problems 17–25 and write answers using positive exponents only. All variables represent positive real numbers.

17. $6(xy^3)^5$

18. $\dfrac{9u^8v^6}{3u^4v^8}$

19. $(2 \times 10^5)(3 \times 10^{-3})$

20. $(x^{-3}y^2)^{-2}$

21. $u^{5/3}u^{2/3}$

22. $(9a^4b^{-2})^{1/2}$

23. $\dfrac{5^0}{3^2} + \dfrac{3^{-2}}{2^{-2}}$

24. $(x^{1/2} + y^{1/2})^2$

25. $(3x^{1/2} - y^{1/2})(2x^{1/2} + 3y^{1/2})$

Write Problems 26–31 in completely factored form relative to the integers. If a polynomial cannot be factored further relative to the integers, say so.

26. $12x^2 + 5x - 3$

27. $8x^2 - 18xy + 9y^2$

28. $t^2 - 4t - 6$

29. $6n^3 - 9n^2 - 15n$

30. $(4x - y)^2 - 9x^2$

31. $6x(2x + 1)^2 - 15x^2(2x + 1)$

In Problems 32–37, perform the indicated operations and reduce to lowest terms. Represent all compound fractions as simple fractions reduced to lowest terms.

32. $\dfrac{2}{5b} - \dfrac{4}{3a^3} - \dfrac{1}{6a^2b^2}$

33. $\dfrac{3x}{3x^2 - 12x} + \dfrac{1}{6x}$

34. $\dfrac{x}{x^2 - 16} - \dfrac{x + 4}{x^2 - 4x}$

35. $\dfrac{(x + y)^2 - x^2}{y}$

36. $\dfrac{\dfrac{1}{7 + h} - \dfrac{1}{7}}{h}$

37. $\dfrac{x^{-1} + y^{-1}}{x^{-2} - y^{-2}}$

38. Each statement illustrates the use of one of the following real number properties or definitions. Indicate which one.

Commutative $(+, \cdot)$ Associative $(+, \cdot)$ Distributive

Identity $(+, \cdot)$ Inverse $(+, \cdot)$ Subtraction

Division   Negatives   Zero

(A) $(-7) - (-5) = (-7) + [-(-5)]$

(B) $5u + (3v + 2) = (3v + 2) + 5u$

(C) $(5m - 2)(2m + 3) =$
$(5m - 2)2m + (5m - 2)3$

(D) $9 \cdot (4y) = (9 \cdot 4)y$

(E) $\dfrac{u}{-(v - w)} = -\dfrac{u}{v - w}$

(F) $(x - y) + 0 = (x - y)$

39. Change to rational exponent form:
$$6\sqrt[5]{x^2} - 7\sqrt[4]{(x - 1)^3}$$

40. Change to radical form: $2x^{1/2} - 3x^{2/3}$

41. Write in the form $ax^p + bx^q$, where a and b are real numbers and p and q are rational numbers:
$$\dfrac{4\sqrt{x} - 3}{2\sqrt{x}}$$

In Problems 42 and 43, rationalize the denominator.

42. $\dfrac{3x}{\sqrt{3x}}$

43. $\dfrac{x - 5}{\sqrt{x} - \sqrt{5}}$

In Problems 44 and 45, rationalize the numerator.

44. $\dfrac{\sqrt{x} - 5}{x - 5}$

45. $\dfrac{\sqrt{u + h} - \sqrt{u}}{h}$

Solve Problems 46–50 for x.

46. $\dfrac{x}{12} - \dfrac{x - 3}{3} = \dfrac{1}{2}$

47. $x^2 = 5x$

48. $3x^2 - 21 = 0$

49. $x^2 - x - 20 = 0$

50. $-6x^2 + 7x - 1 = 0$

In Problems 51–53, solve and graph on a real number line.

51. $2(x + 4) > 5x - 4$

52. $1 - \dfrac{x - 3}{3} \le \dfrac{1}{2}$

53. $-1 < -2x + 5 \le 3$

In Problems 54 and 55, solve for y in terms of x.

54. $2x - 3y = 6$

55. $3xy - 2x = y$

Applications

56. *Economics.* If the gross domestic product (GDP) was $8,511,000,000,000 for the United States in 1998 and the population was 270,300,000, determine the GDP per person using scientific notation. Express the answer in scientific notation and in standard decimal form to the nearest dollar.

57. *Investment.* An investor has $60,000 to invest. If part is invested at 8% and the rest at 14%, how much

should be invested at each rate to yield 12% on the total amount?

58. *Break-even analysis.* A producer of educational videos is producing an instructional video. The producer estimates that it will cost $72,000 to shoot the video and $12 per unit to copy and distribute the tape. If the wholesale price of the tape is $30, how many tapes must be sold for the producer to break even?

Section **A-1** | Algebra and Real Numbers

> Set of Real Numbers
> Real Number Line
> Basic Real Number Properties
> Further Properties
> Fraction Properties

The rules for manipulating and reasoning with symbols in algebra depend, in large measure, on properties of the real numbers. In this section we look at some of the important properties of this number system. To make our discussions here and elsewhere in the book clearer and more precise, we occasionally make use of simple *set* concepts and notation.

➤ Set of Real Numbers

What number system have you been using most of your life? The *real number system.* Informally, a **real number** is any number that has a decimal representation. Table 1 describes the set of real numbers and some of its important subsets. Figure 1 on page 586 illustrates how these sets of numbers are related.

The set of integers contains all the natural numbers and something else—their negatives and 0. The set of rational numbers contains all the integers and something else—noninteger ratios of integers. And the set of real numbers contains all the rational numbers and something else—irrational numbers.

TABLE 1	**Set of Real Numbers**		
Symbol	**Name**	**Description**	**Examples**
N	Natural numbers	Counting numbers (also called positive integers)	$1, 2, 3, \ldots$
Z	Integers	Natural numbers, their negatives, and 0	$\ldots, -2, -1, 0, 1, 2, \ldots$
Q	Rational numbers	Numbers that can be represented as a/b, where a and b are integers and $b \neq 0$; decimal representations are repeating or terminating	$-4, 0, 1, 25, \frac{-3}{5}, \frac{2}{3}, 3.67, -0.33\overline{3}, 5.272\,7\overline{27}$*
I	Irrational numbers	Numbers that can be represented as nonrepeating and nonterminating decimal numbers	$\sqrt{2}, \pi, \sqrt[3]{7}, 1.414\,213\ldots, 2.718\,281\,82\ldots$
R	Real numbers	Rational and irrational numbers	

* The overbar indicates that the number (or block of numbers) repeats indefinitely. The space after every third digit is used to help keep track of the number of decimal places.

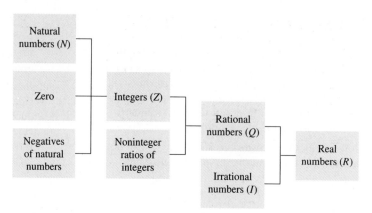

FIGURE 1 Real numbers and important subsets

➤ Real Number Line

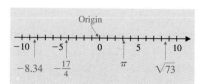

FIGURE 2 Real number line

A one-to-one correspondence exists between the set of real numbers and the set of points on a line. That is, each real number corresponds to exactly one point, and each point corresponds to exactly one real number. A line with a real number associated with each point, and vice versa, as shown in Figure 2, is called a **real number line,** or simply a **real line.** Each number associated with a point is called the **coordinate** of the point.

The point with coordinate 0 is called the **origin.** The arrow on the right end of the line indicates a positive direction. The coordinates of all points to the right of the origin are called **positive real numbers,** and those to the left of the origin are called **negative real numbers.** The real number 0 is neither positive nor negative.

➤ Basic Real Number Properties

We now take a look at some of the basic properties of the real number system that enable us to convert algebraic expressions into *equivalent forms.* These assumed properties become operational rules in the algebra of real numbers.

SUMMARY   Basic Properties of the Set of Real Numbers

Let a, b, and c be arbitrary elements in the set of real numbers R.

Addition Properties

Associative:	$(a + b) + c = a + (b + c)$
Commutative:	$a + b = b + a$
Identity:	0 is the additive identity; that is, $0 + a = a + 0 = a$ for all a in R, and 0 is the only element in R with this property.
Inverse:	For each a in R, $-a$ is its unique additive inverse; that is, $a + (-a) = (-a) + a = 0$, and $-a$ is the only element in R relative to a with this property.

Multiplication Properties

Associative:	$(ab)c = a(bc)$
Commutative:	$ab = ba$

Identity: 1 is the multiplicative identity; that is, $(1)a = a(1) = a$ for all a in R, and 1 is the only element in R with this property.

Inverse: For each a in R, $a \neq 0$, $1/a$ is its unique multiplicative inverse; that is, $a(1/a) = (1/a)a = 1$, and $1/a$ is the only element in R relative to a with this property.

Distributive Properties

$$a(b + c) = ab + ac \qquad (a + b)c = ac + bc$$

Do not be intimidated by the names of these properties. Most of the ideas presented here are quite simple. In fact, you have been using many of these properties in arithmetic for a long time.

You are already familiar with the **commutative properties** for addition and multiplication. They indicate that the order in which the addition or multiplication of two numbers is performed does not matter. For example,

$$7 + 2 = 2 + 7 \qquad \text{and} \qquad 3 \cdot 5 = 5 \cdot 3$$

Is there a commutative property relative to subtraction or division? That is, does $a - b = b - a$ or does $a \div b = b \div a$ for all real numbers a and b (division by 0 excluded)? The answer is no, since, for example,

$$8 - 6 \neq 6 - 8 \qquad \text{and} \qquad 10 \div 5 \neq 5 \div 10$$

When computing

$$3 + 2 + 6 \qquad \text{or} \qquad 3 \cdot 2 \cdot 6$$

why do we not need parentheses to indicate which two numbers are to be added or multiplied first? The answer is to be found in the **associative properties.** These properties allow us to write

$$(3 + 2) + 6 = 3 + (2 + 6) \qquad \text{and} \qquad (3 \cdot 2) \cdot 6 = 3 \cdot (2 \cdot 6)$$

so it does not matter how we group numbers relative to either operation. Is there an associative property for subtraction or division? The answer is no, since, for example,

$$(12 - 6) - 2 \neq 12 - (6 - 2) \quad \text{and} \quad (12 \div 6) \div 2 \neq 12 \div (6 \div 2)$$

Evaluate each side of each equation to see why.

◉ *Insight*   Why are we concerned with the commutative and associative properties? When manipulating algebraic expressions involving addition or multiplication, these properties permit us to change the order of operation at will and insert or remove parentheses as we please. We don't have the same freedom with subtraction or division. ●

What number added to a given number will give that number back again? What number times a given number will give that number back again? The answers are 0 and 1, respectively. Because of this, 0 and 1 are called the **identity elements** for the real numbers. Hence, for any real numbers a and b,

$$0 + 5 = 5 \qquad \text{and} \qquad (a + b) + 0 = a + b$$
$$1 \cdot 4 = 4 \qquad \text{and} \qquad (a + b) \cdot 1 = a + b$$

We now consider **inverses.** For each real number a, there is a unique real number $-a$ such that $a + (-a) = 0$. The number $-a$ is called the **additive**

inverse of a, or the **negative** of a. For example, the additive inverse (or negative) of 7 is -7, since $7 + (-7) = 0$. The additive inverse (or negative) of -7 is $-(-7) = 7$, since $-7 + [-(-7)] = 0$.

◉ **Insight**   Do not confuse negation with the sign of a number. If a is a real number, $-a$ is the negative of a and may be positive or negative. Specifically, if a is negative, then $-a$ is positive and if a is positive, then $-a$ is negative.   ●

For each nonzero real number a, there is a unique real number $1/a$ such that $a(1/a) = 1$. The number $1/a$ is called the **multiplicative inverse** of a, or the **reciprocal** of a. For example, the multiplicative inverse (or reciprocal) of 4 is $\frac{1}{4}$, since $4(\frac{1}{4}) = 1$. (Also note that 4 is the multiplicative inverse of $\frac{1}{4}$.) The number 0 has no multiplicative inverse.

We now turn to the **distributive properties,** which involve both multiplication and addition. Consider the following two computations:

$$5(3 + 4) = 5 \cdot 7 = 35 \qquad 5 \cdot 3 + 5 \cdot 4 = 15 + 20 = 35$$

Thus,

$$5(3 + 4) = 5 \cdot 3 + 5 \cdot 4$$

and we say that multiplication by 5 *distributes* over the sum $(3 + 4)$. In general, **multiplication distributes over addition** in the real number system. Two more illustrations are

$$9(m + n) = 9m + 9n \qquad (7 + 2)u = 7u + 2u$$

EXAMPLE 1   **Real Number Properties** State the real number property that justifies the indicated statement.

STATEMENT	PROPERTY ILLUSTRATED
(A) $x(y + z) = (y + z)x$	Commutative $(\cdot)$
(B) $5(2y) = (5 \cdot 2)y$	Associative $(\cdot)$
(C) $2 + (y + 7) = 2 + (7 + y)$	Commutative $(+)$
(D) $4z + 6z = (4 + 6)z$	Distributive
(E) If $m + n = 0$, then $n = -m$.	Inverse $(+)$

Matched Problem 1   State the real number property that justifies the indicated statement.

(A) $8 + (3 + y) = (8 + 3) + y$
(B) $(x + y) + z = z + (x + y)$
(C) $(a + b)(x + y) = a(x + y) + b(x + y)$
(D) $5xy + 0 = 5xy$
(E) If $xy = 1, x \neq 0$, then $y = 1/x$.

➤ **Further Properties**

Subtraction and *division* can be defined in terms of addition and multiplication, respectively:

DEFINITION Subtraction and Division

For all real numbers a and b,

Subtraction: $a - b = a + (-b)$

$7 - (-5) = 7 + [-(-5)]$
$= 7 + 5 = 12$

Division: $a \div b = a\left(\dfrac{1}{b}\right), b \neq 0$

$9 \div 4 = 9\left(\dfrac{1}{4}\right) = \dfrac{9}{4}$

Thus, to subtract b from a, add the negative (the additive inverse) of b to a. To divide a by b, multiply a by the reciprocal (the multiplicative inverse) of b. Note that division by 0 is not defined, since 0 does not have a reciprocal. Thus, **0 can never be used as a divisor!**

The following properties of negatives can be proved using the preceding assumed properties and definitions.

THEOREM 1 Negative Properties

For all real numbers a and b,

1. $-(-a) = a$

2. $(-a)b = -(ab)$
$= a(-b) = -ab$

3. $(-a)(-b) = ab$

4. $(-1)a = -a$

5. $\dfrac{-a}{b} = -\dfrac{a}{b} = \dfrac{a}{-b}, b \neq 0$

6. $\dfrac{-a}{-b} = -\dfrac{-a}{b} = -\dfrac{a}{-b} = \dfrac{a}{b}, b \neq 0$

We now state two important properties involving 0.

THEOREM 2 Zero Properties

For all real numbers a and b,

1. $a \cdot 0 = 0$ $0 \cdot 0 = 0$ $(-35)(0) = 0$

2. $ab = 0$ if and only if $a = 0$ or $b = 0$
If $(3x + 2)(x - 7) = 0$, then either $3x + 2 = 0$ or $x - 7 = 0$.

EXPLORE & DISCUSS 1

In general, a set of numbers is closed under an operation if performing the operation on numbers in the set always produces another number in the set. For example, the real numbers R are closed under addition, multiplication, subtraction, and division, excluding division by 0. Replace each ? in the following tables with T (true) or F (false), and illustrate each false statement with an example. (See Table 1 for the definitions of the sets N, Z, Q, I, and R.)

	Closed Under Addition	Closed Under Multiplication
N	?	?
Z	?	?
Q	?	?
I	?	?
R	T	T

	Closed Under Subtraction	Closed Under Division*
N	?	?
Z	?	?
Q	?	?
I	?	?
R	T	T

*Excluding division by 0.

➤ Fraction Properties

Recall that the quotient $a \div b (b \neq 0)$ written in the form a/b is called a **fraction.** The quantity a is called the **numerator,** and the quantity b is called the **denominator.**

THEOREM 3   Fraction Properties

For all real numbers $a, b, c, d,$ and k (division by 0 excluded):

1. $\dfrac{a}{b} = \dfrac{c}{d}$ if and only if $ad = bc$ $\dfrac{4}{6} = \dfrac{6}{9}$ since $4 \cdot 9 = 6 \cdot 6$

2. $\dfrac{ka}{kb} = \dfrac{a}{b}$ 3. $\dfrac{a}{b} \cdot \dfrac{c}{d} = \dfrac{ac}{bd}$ 4. $\dfrac{a}{b} \div \dfrac{c}{d} = \dfrac{a}{b} \cdot \dfrac{d}{c}$

   $\dfrac{7 \cdot 3}{7 \cdot 5} = \dfrac{3}{5}$ $\dfrac{3}{5} \cdot \dfrac{7}{8} = \dfrac{3 \cdot 7}{5 \cdot 8}$ $\dfrac{2}{3} \div \dfrac{5}{7} = \dfrac{2}{3} \cdot \dfrac{7}{5}$

5. $\dfrac{a}{b} + \dfrac{c}{b} = \dfrac{a + c}{b}$ 6. $\dfrac{a}{b} - \dfrac{c}{b} = \dfrac{a - c}{b}$ 7. $\dfrac{a}{b} + \dfrac{c}{d} = \dfrac{ad + bc}{bd}$

   $\dfrac{3}{6} + \dfrac{5}{6} = \dfrac{3 + 5}{6}$ $\dfrac{7}{8} - \dfrac{3}{8} = \dfrac{7 - 3}{8}$ $\dfrac{2}{3} + \dfrac{3}{5} = \dfrac{2 \cdot 5 + 3 \cdot 3}{3 \cdot 5}$

Answers to Matched Problems   **1.** (A) Associative (+)   (B) Commutative (+)   (C) Distributive

(D) Identity (+)   (E) Inverse ($\cdot$)

Exercise A-1

All variables represent real numbers.

A *In Problems 1–6, replace each question mark with an appropriate expression that will illustrate the use of the indicated real number property.*

1. Commutative property ($\cdot$): $uv = ?$

2. Commutative property (+): $x + 7 = ?$

3. Associative property (+): $3 + (7 + y) = ?$

4. Associative property ($\cdot$): $x(yz) = ?$

5. Identity property ($\cdot$): $1(u + v) = ?$

6. Identity property (+): $0 + 9m = ?$

In Problems 7–26, indicate true (T) or false (F).

7. $5(8m) = (5 \cdot 8)m$

8. $a + cb = a + bc$

9. $5x + 7x = (5 + 7)x$

10. $uv(w + x) = uvw + uvx$

11. $-2(-a)(2x - y) = 2a(-4x + y)$

12. $8 \div (-5) = 8\left(\frac{1}{-5}\right)$

13. $(x + 3) + 2x = 2x + (x + 3)$

14. $\dfrac{x}{3y} \div \dfrac{5y}{x} = \dfrac{15y^2}{x^2}$

15. $\dfrac{2x}{-(x + 3)} = -\dfrac{2x}{x + 3}$

16. $-\dfrac{2x}{-(x - 3)} = \dfrac{2x}{x - 3}$

17. $(-3)\left(\frac{1}{-3}\right) = 1$

18. $(-0.5) + (0.5) = 0$

19. $-x^2y^2 = (-1)x^2y^2$

20. $[-(x + 2)](-x) = (x + 2)x$

21. $\dfrac{a}{b} + \dfrac{c}{d} = \dfrac{a + c}{b + d}$

22. $\dfrac{k}{k + b} = \dfrac{1}{1 + b}$

23. $(x + 8)(x + 6) = (x + 8)x + (x + 8)6$

24. $u(u - 2v) + v(u - 2v) = (u + v)(u - 2v)$

25. If $(x - 2)(2x + 3) = 0$, then either $x - 2 = 0$ or $2x + 3 = 0$.

26. If either $x - 2 = 0$ or $2x + 3 = 0$, then $(x - 2)(2x + 3) = 0$.

B

27. If $uv = 1$, does either u or v have to be 1? Explain.

28. If $uv = 0$, does either u or v have to be 0? Explain.

29. Indicate whether the following are true (T) or false (F):

(A) All integers are natural numbers.

(B) All rational numbers are real numbers.

(C) All natural numbers are rational numbers.

30. Indicate whether the following are true (T) or false (F):

(A) All natural numbers are integers.

(B) All real numbers are irrational.

(C) All rational numbers are real numbers.

31. Give an example of a real number that is not a rational number.

32. Give an example of a rational number that is not an integer.

33. Given the sets of numbers N (natural numbers), Z (integers), Q (rational numbers), and R (real numbers), indicate to which set(s) each of the following numbers belongs:

(A) 8   (B) $\sqrt{2}$ (C) -1.414 (D) $\frac{-5}{2}$

34. Given the sets of numbers N, Z, Q, and R (see Problem 33), indicate to which set(s) each of the following numbers belongs:

(A) -3 (B) 3.14 (C) π (D) $\frac{2}{3}$

35. Indicate true (T) or false (F), and for each false statement find real number replacements for a, b, and c that will provide a counterexample. For all real numbers a, b, and c,

(A) $a(b - c) = ab - c$

(B) $(a - b) - c = a - (b - c)$

(C) $a(bc) = (ab)c$

(D) $(a \div b) \div c = a \div (b \div c)$

36. Indicate true (T) or false (F), and for each false statement find real number replacements for a and b that will provide a counterexample. For all real numbers a and b,

(A) $a + b = b + a$

(B) $a - b = b - a$

(C) $ab = ba$

(D) $a \div b = b \div a$

C

37. If $c = 0.151\,515\ldots$, then $100c = 15.151\,5\ldots$ and

$$100c - c = 15.151\,5\ldots - 0.151\,515\ldots$$
$$99c = 15$$
$$c = \tfrac{15}{99} = \tfrac{5}{33}$$

Proceeding similarly, convert the repeating decimal $0.090\,909\ldots$ into a fraction. (All repeating decimals are rational numbers, and all rational numbers have repeating decimal representations.)

38. Repeat Problem 37 for $0.181\,818.\ldots$

Use a calculator to express each number in Problems 39 and 40 as a decimal to the capacity of your calculator. Observe the repeating decimal representation of the rational numbers and the nonrepeating decimal representation of the irrational numbers.

39. (A) $\frac{13}{6}$ (B) $\sqrt{21}$ (C) $\frac{7}{16}$ (D) $\frac{29}{111}$

40. (A) $\frac{8}{9}$ (B) $\frac{3}{11}$ (C) $\sqrt{5}$ (D) $\frac{11}{8}$

Section **A-2** | Operations on Polynomials

➤ Natural Number Exponents

➤ Polynomials

➤ Combining Like Terms

➤ Addition and Subtraction

➤ Multiplication

➤ Combined Operations

This section covers basic operations on *polynomials,* a mathematical form that is encountered frequently. Our discussion starts with a brief review of natural number exponents. Integer and rational exponents and their properties will be discussed in detail in subsequent sections. (Natural numbers, integers, and rational numbers are important parts of the real number system; see Table 1 and Figure 1 in Appendix A-1.)

➤ Natural Number Exponents

We define a **natural number exponent** as follows:

> **DEFINITION** Natural Number Exponent
> For n a natural number and b any real number,
> $$b^n = b \cdot b \cdot \cdots \cdot b \qquad n \text{ factors of } b$$
> $$3^5 = 3 \cdot 3 \cdot 3 \cdot 3 \cdot 3 \qquad 5 \text{ factors of } 3$$
> where n is called the **exponent** and b is called the **base.**

Along with this definition, we state the **first property of exponents:**

> **THEOREM 1** First Property of Exponents
> For any natural numbers m and n, and any real number b:
> $$b^m b^n = b^{m+n} \quad (2t^4)(5t^3) = 2 \cdot 5 t^{4+3} = 10t^7$$

➤ Polynomials

Algebraic expressions are formed by using constants and variables and the algebraic operations of addition, subtraction, multiplication, division, raising to powers, and taking roots. Special types of algebraic expressions are called *polynomials.* A **polynomial in one variable** x is constructed by adding or subtracting constants and terms of the form ax^n, where a is a real number and n is a natural number. A **polynomial in two variables** x and y is constructed by adding and subtracting constants and terms of the form $ax^m y^n$, where a is a real number and m and n are natural numbers. Polynomials in three and more variables are defined in a similar manner.

POLYNOMIALS

$$8$$
$$3x^3 - 6x + 7$$
$$2x^2 - 7xy - 8y^2$$
$$2x - 3y + 2$$

$$0$$
$$6x + 3$$
$$9y^3 + 4y^2 - y + 4$$
$$u^5 - 3u^3v^2 + 2uv^4 - v^4$$

NOT POLYNOMIALS

$$\frac{1}{x}$$
$$\sqrt{x^3 - 2x}$$

$$\frac{x - y}{x^2 + y^2}$$
$$2x^{-2} - 3x^{-1}$$

Polynomial forms are encountered frequently in mathematics. For the efficient study of polynomials it is useful to classify them according to their *degree.* If a term in a polynomial has only one variable as a factor, then the **degree of the term** is the power of the variable. If two or more variables are present in a term as factors, then the **degree of the term** is the sum of the powers of the variables. The **degree of a polynomial** is the degree of the nonzero term with the highest degree in the polynomial. Any nonzero constant is defined to be a **polynomial of degree 0.** The number 0 is also a polynomial but is not assigned a degree.

EXAMPLE 1 **Degree**

(A) The degree of the first term in $5x^3 + \sqrt{3}x - \frac{1}{2}$ is 3, the degree of the second term is 1, the degree of the third term is 0, and the degree of the whole polynomial is 3 (the same as the degree of the term with the highest degree).

(B) The degree of the first term in $8u^3v^2 - \sqrt{7}uv^2$ is 5, the degree of the second term is 3, and the degree of the whole polynomial is 5. ∎

Matched Problem 1

(A) Given the polynomial $6x^5 + 7x^3 - 2$, what is the degree of the first term? The second term? The third term? The whole polynomial?

(B) Given the polynomial $2u^4v^2 - 5uv^3$, what is the degree of the first term? The second term? The whole polynomial?

In addition to classifying polynomials by degree, we also call a single-term polynomial a **monomial,** a two-term polynomial a **binomial,** and a three-term polynomial a **trinomial.**

➤ Combining Like Terms

The concept of *coefficient* plays a central role in the process of combining *like terms.* A constant in a term of a polynomial, including the sign that precedes it, is called the **numerical coefficient,** or simply, the **coefficient,** of the term. If a constant does not appear, or only a + sign appears, the coefficient is understood to be 1. If only a − sign appears, the coefficient is understood to be −1. Thus, given the polynomial

$$5x^4 - x^3 - 3x^2 + x - 7 \quad = 5x^4 + (-1)x^3 + (-3)x^2 + 1x + (-7)$$

the coefficient of the first term is 5, the coefficient of the second term is −1, the coefficient of the third term is −3, the coefficient of the fourth term is 1, and the coefficient of the fifth term is −7.

The following distributive properties are fundamental to the process of combining *like terms.*

THEOREM 2   Distributive Properties of Real Numbers

1. $a(b + c) = (b + c)a = ab + ac$
2. $a(b - c) = (b - c)a = ab - ac$
3. $a(b + c + \cdots + f) = ab + ac + \cdots + af$

Two terms in a polynomial are called **like terms** if they have exactly the same variable factors to the same powers. The numerical coefficients may or may not be the same. Since constant terms involve no variables, all constant terms are like terms. If a polynomial contains two or more like terms, these terms can be combined into a single term by making use of distributive properties. The following example illustrates the reasoning behind the process:

$$\begin{aligned}
3x^2y - 5xy^2 + x^2y - 2x^2y &= 3x^2y + x^2y - 2x^2y - 5xy^2 && \text{Note the} \\
&= (3x^2y + 1x^2y - 2x^2y) - 5xy^2 && \text{use of} \\
&= (3 + 1 - 2)x^2y - 5xy^2 && \text{distributive} \\
&= 2x^2y - 5xy^2 && \text{properties.}
\end{aligned}$$

It should be clear that free use is made of the real number properties discussed in Appendix A-1.

👁 *Insight*   The steps shown in the dashed box are usually done mentally. The same result can be obtained by simply adding the numerical coefficients of like terms. ●

How can we simplify expressions such as $4(x - 2y) - 3(2x - 7y)$? We clear the expression of parentheses using distributive properties, and combine like terms:

$$4(x - 2y) - 3(2x - 7y) = 4x - 8y - 6x + 21y$$
$$= -2x + 13y$$

EXAMPLE 2 **Removing Parentheses** Remove parentheses and simplify:

(A) $2(3x^2 - 2x + 5) + (x^2 + 3x - 7)$ $\;= 2(3x^2 - 2x + 5) + 1(x^2 + 3x - 7)$

$$= 6x^2 - 4x + 10 + x^2 + 3x - 7$$
$$= 7x^2 - x + 3$$

(B) $(x^3 - 2x - 6) - (2x^3 - x^2 + 2x - 3)$

$$= 1(x^3 - 2x - 6) + (-1)(2x^3 - x^2 + 2x - 3)$$ *Be careful with the sign here.*

$$= x^3 - 2x - 6 - 2x^3 + x^2 - 2x + 3$$
$$= -x^3 + x^2 - 4x - 3$$

(C) $[3x^2 - (2x + 1)] - (x^2 - 1) = [3x^2 - 2x - 1] - (x^2 - 1)$ *Remove inner*

$$= 3x^2 - 2x - 1 - x^2 + 1$$ *parentheses first.*
$$= 2x^2 - 2x$$ ■

Matched Problem 2 Remove parentheses and simplify:

(A) $3(u^2 - 2v^2) + (u^2 + 5v^2)$
(B) $(m^3 - 3m^2 + m - 1) - (2m^3 - m + 3)$
(C) $(x^3 - 2) - [2x^3 - (3x + 4)]$

➤ Addition and Subtraction

Addition and subtraction of polynomials can be thought of in terms of removing parentheses and combining like terms, as illustrated in Example 2. Horizontal and vertical arrangements are illustrated in the next two examples. You should be able to work either way, letting the situation dictate your choice.

EXAMPLE 3 **Adding Polynomials** Add horizontally and vertically:
$$x^4 - 3x^3 + x^2, \quad -x^3 - 2x^2 + 3x, \quad \text{and} \quad 3x^2 - 4x - 5$$

Solution   Add horizontally:
$$(x^4 - 3x^3 + x^2) + (-x^3 - 2x^2 + 3x) + (3x^2 - 4x - 5)$$
$$= x^4 - 3x^3 + x^2 - x^3 - 2x^2 + 3x + 3x^2 - 4x - 5$$
$$= x^4 - 4x^3 + 2x^2 - x - 5$$

Or vertically, by lining up like terms and adding their coefficients:

$$x^4 - 3x^3 + x^2$$
$$- x^3 - 2x^2 + 3x$$
$$3x^2 - 4x - 5$$
$$\overline{x^4 - 4x^3 + 2x^2 - x - 5}$$

∎

Matched Problem 3   Add horizontally and vertically:

$$3x^4 - 2x^3 - 4x^2, \quad x^3 - 2x^2 - 5x, \quad \text{and} \quad x^2 + 7x - 2$$

EXAMPLE 4   **Subtracting Polynomials**   Subtract $4x^2 - 3x + 5$ from $x^2 - 8$, both horizontally and vertically.

Solution $(x^2 - 8) - (4x^2 - 3x + 5)$ or $x^2 \qquad - 8$
$$= x^2 - 8 - 4x^2 + 3x - 5 \qquad\qquad \underline{-4x^2 + 3x - 5} \quad \leftarrow \text{Change signs}$$
$$= -3x^2 + 3x - 13 \qquad\qquad\qquad -3x^2 + 3x - 13 \qquad \text{and add.}$$
∎

Matched Problem 4   Subtract $2x^2 - 5x + 4$ from $5x^2 - 6$, both horizontally and vertically.

➤ Multiplication

Multiplication of algebraic expressions involves the extensive use of distributive properties for real numbers, as well as other real number properties.

EXAMPLE 5   **Multiplying Polynomials**   Multiply: $(2x - 3)(3x^2 - 2x + 3)$

Solution $(2x - 3)(3x^2 - 2x + 3) \enspace \vdots= 2x(3x^2 - 2x + 3) - 3(3x^2 - 2x + 3) \vdots$
$$= 6x^3 - 4x^2 + 6x - 9x^2 + 6x - 9$$
$$= 6x^3 - 13x^2 + 12x - 9$$

Or, using a vertical arrangement,

$$3x^2 - 2x + 3$$
$$\underline{2x - 3}$$
$$6x^3 - 4x^2 + 6x$$
$$\underline{- 9x^2 + 6x - 9}$$
$$6x^3 - 13x^3 + 12x - 9$$

∎

Matched Problem 5   Multiply: $(2x - 3)(2x^2 + 3x - 2)$

Thus, to multiply two polynomials, multiply each term of one by each term of the other, and combine like terms.

Products of binomial factors occur frequently, so it is useful to develop procedures that will enable us to write down their products by inspection. To find the product $(2x - 1)(3x + 2)$, we proceed as follows:

$$(2x - 1)(3x + 2) \quad \boxed{= 6x^2 + 4x - 3x - 2} \quad \text{The inner and outer products are like terms, so combine into}$$
$$= 6x^2 + x - 2 \qquad\qquad \text{a single term.}$$

To speed the process, we do the step in the dashed box mentally.

Products of certain binomial factors occur so frequently that it is useful to learn formulas for their products. The following formulas are easily verified by multiplying the factors on the left.

THEOREM 3   Special Products

1. $(a - b)(a + b) = a^2 - b^2$
2. $(a + b)^2 = a^2 + 2ab + b^2$
3. $(a - b)^2 = a^2 - 2ab + b^2$

(A) Explain the relationship between special product formula 1 and the areas of the rectangles in the figure.

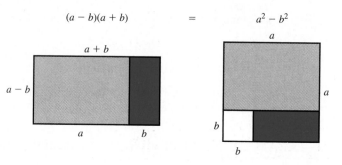

$(a - b)(a + b) \qquad = \qquad a^2 - b^2$

(B) Construct similar figures to provide geometric interpretations for special product formulas 2 and 3.

EXAMPLE 6   **Special Products**   Multiply mentally where possible:

(A) $(2x - 3y)(5x + 2y)$ (B) $(3a - 2b)(3a + 2b)$
(C) $(5x - 3)^2$ (D) $(m + 2n)^3$

Solution   (A) $(2x - 3y)(5x + 2y) \boxed{= 10x^2 + 4xy - 15xy - 6y^2}$

$$= 10x^2 - 11xy - 6y^2$$

(B) $(3a - 2b)(3a + 2b) \boxed{= (3a)^2 - (2b)^2}$

$$= 9a^2 - 4b^2$$

(C) $(5x - 3)^2 \boxed{= (5x)^2 - 2(5x)(3) + 3^2}$

$$= 25x^2 - 30x + 9$$

(D) $(m + 2n)^3 = (m + 2n)^2(m + 2n)$
$= (m^2 + 4mn + 4n^2)(m + 2n)$
$= m^2(m + 2n) + 4mn(m + 2n) + 4n^2(m + 2n)$
$= m^3 + 2m^2n + 4m^2n + 8mn^2 + 4mn^2 + 8n^3$
$= m^3 + 6m^2n + 12mn^2 + 8n^3$ ■

Matched Problem 6   Multiply mentally where possible:

(A) $(4u - 3v)(2u + v)$
(B) $(2xy + 3)(2xy - 3)$
(C) $(m + 4n)(m - 4n)$
(D) $(2u - 3v)^2$
(E) $(2x - y)^3$

➤ Combined Operations

We complete this section by considering several examples that use all the operations just discussed. Note that in simplifying, we usually remove grouping symbols starting from the inside. That is, we remove parentheses ( ) first, then brackets [ ], and finally braces { }, if present. Also,

DEFINITION   Order of Operations

Multiplication and division precede addition and subtraction, and taking powers precedes multiplication and division.

$$2 \cdot 3 + 4 = 6 + 4 = 10, \quad \text{not} \quad 2 \cdot 7 = 14$$

$$\frac{10^2}{2} = \frac{100}{2} = 50, \quad \text{not} \quad 5^2 = 25$$

EXAMPLE 7   **Combined Operations** Perform the indicated operations and simplify:

(A) $3x - \{5 - 3[x - x(3 - x)]\} = 3x - \{5 - 3[x - 3x + x^2]\}$
$= 3x - \{5 - 3x + 9x - 3x^2\}$
$= 3x - 5 + 3x - 9x + 3x^2$
$= 3x^2 - 3x - 5$
(B) $(x - 2y)(2x + 3y) - (2x + y)^2 = 2x^2 - xy - 6y^2 - (4x^2 + 4xy + y^2)$
$= 2x^2 - xy - 6y^2 - 4x^2 - 4xy - y^2$
$= -2x^2 - 5xy - 7y^2$ ■

Matched Problem 7   Perform the indicated operations and simplify:

(A) $2t - \{7 - 2[t - t(4 + t)]\}$
(B) $(u - 3v)^2 - (2u - v)(2u + v)$

Answers to Matched Problems   **1.** (A) $5, 3, 0, 5$ (B) $6, 4, 6$

2. (A) $4u^2 - v^2$ (B) $-m^3 - 3m^2 + 2m - 4$ (C) $-x^3 + 3x + 2$

3. $3x^4 - x^3 - 5x^2 + 2x - 2$ **4.** $3x^2 + 5x - 10$ **5.** $4x^3 - 13x + 6$

6. (A) $8u^2 - 2uv - 3v^2$ (B) $4x^2y^2 - 9$ (C) $m^2 - 16n^2$

(D) $4u^2 - 12uv + 9v^2$ (E) $8x^3 - 12x^2y + 6xy^2 - y^3$

7. (A) $-2t^2 - 4t - 7$ (B) $-3u^2 - 6uv + 10v^2$

Exercise A-2

A *Problems 1–8 refer to the following polynomials:*

(A) $2x - 3$ (B) $2x^2 - x + 2$ (C) $x^3 + 2x^2 - x + 3$

1. What is the degree of (C)?

2. What is the degree of (A)?

3. Add (B) and (C).

4. Add (A) and (B).

5. Subtract (B) from (C).

6. Subtract (A) from (B).

7. Multiply (B) and (C).

8. Multiply (A) and (C).

In Problems 9–30, perform the indicated operations and simplify.

9. $2(u - 1) - (3u + 2) - 2(2u - 3)$

10. $2(x - 1) + 3(2x - 3) - (4x - 5)$

11. $4a - 2a[5 - 3(a + 2)]$

12. $2y - 3y[4 - 2(y - 1)]$

13. $(a + b)(a - b)$

14. $(m - n)(m + n)$

15. $(3x - 5)(2x + 1)$

16. $(4t - 3)(t - 2)$

17. $(2x - 3y)(x + 2y)$

18. $(3x + 2y)(x - 3y)$

19. $(3y + 2)(3y - 2)$

20. $(2m - 7)(2m + 7)$

21. $-(2x - 3)^2$

22. $-(5 - 3x)^2$

23. $(4m + 3n)(4m - 3n)$

24. $(3x - 2y)(3x + 2y)$

25. $(3u + 4v)^2$

26. $(4x - y)^2$

27. $(a - b)(a^2 + ab + b^2)$

28. $(a + b)(a^2 - ab + b^2)$

29. $[(x - y) + 3z][(x - y) - 3z]$

30. $[a - (2b - c)][a + (2b - c)]$

B *In Problems 31–44, perform the indicated operations and simplify.*

31. $m - \{m - [m - (m - 1)]\}$

32. $2x - 3\{x + 2[x - (x + 5)] + 1\}$

33. $(x^2 - 2xy + y^2)(x^2 + 2xy + y^2)$

34. $(3x - 2y)^2(2x + 5y)$

35. $(5a - 2b)^2 - (2b + 5a)^2$

36. $(2x - 1)^2 - (3x + 2)(3x - 2)$

37. $(m - 2)^2 - (m - 2)(m + 2)$

38. $(x - 3)(x + 3) - (x - 3)^2$

39. $(x - 2y)(2x + y) - (x + 2y)(2x - y)$

40. $(3m + n)(m - 3n) - (m + 3n)(3m - n)$

41. $(u + v)^3$

42. $(x - y)^3$

43. $(x - 2y)^3$

44. $(2m - n)^3$

45. Subtract the sum of the last two polynomials from the sum of the first two: $2x^2 - 4xy + y^2, 3xy - y^2, x^2 - 2xy - y^2, -x^2 + 3xy - 2y^2$

46. Subtract the sum of the first two polynomials from the sum of the last two: $3m^2 - 2m + 5, 4m^2 - m, 3m^2 - 3m - 2, m^3 + m^2 + 2$

C *In Problems 47–50, perform the indicated operations and simplify.*

47. $[(2x - 1)^2 - x(3x + 1)]^2$

48. $[5x(3x + 1) - 5(2x - 1)^2]^2$

49. $2\{(x - 3)(x^2 - 2x + 1) - x[3 - x(x - 2)]\}$

50. $-3x\{x[x - x(2 - x)] - (x + 2)(x^2 - 3)\}$

51. If you are given two polynomials, one of degree m and the other of degree n, where m is greater than n, what is the degree of their product?

52. What is the degree of the sum of the two polynomials in Problem 51?

53. How does the answer to Problem 51 change if the two polynomials can have the same degree?

54. How does the answer to Problem 52 change if the two polynomials can have the same degree?

55. Show by example that, in general, $(a + b)^2 \ne a^2 + b^2$. Discuss possible conditions on a and b that would make this a valid equation.

56. Show by example that, in general, $(a - b)^2 \ne a^2 - b^2$. Discuss possible conditions on a and b that would make this a valid equation.

Applications

Business & Economics

57. *Investment.* You have $10,000 to invest, part at 9% and the rest at 12%. If x is the amount invested at 9%, write an algebraic expression that represents the total annual income from both investments. Simplify the expression.

58. *Investment.* A person has $100,000 to invest. If $x are invested in a money market account yielding 7% and twice that amount in certificates of deposit yielding 9%, and if the rest is invested in high-grade bonds yielding 11%, write an algebraic expression that represents the total annual income from all three investments. Simplify the expression.

59. *Gross receipts.* Four thousand tickets are to be sold for a musical show. If x tickets are to be sold for $10 each and three times that number for $30 each, and if the rest are sold for $50 each, write an algebraic expression that represents the gross receipts from ticket sales, assuming all tickets are sold. Simplify the expression.

60. *Gross receipts.* Six thousand tickets are to be sold for a concert, some for $9 each and the rest for $15 each. If x is the number of $9 tickets sold, write an algebraic expression that represents the gross receipts from ticket sales, assuming all tickets are sold. Simplify the expression.

Life Sciences

61. *Nutrition.* Food mix A contains 2% fat, and food mix B contains 6% fat. A 10 kilogram diet mix of foods A and B is formed. If x kilograms of food A are used, write an algebraic expression that represents the total number of kilograms of fat in the final food mix. Simplify the expression.

62. *Nutrition.* Each ounce of food M contains 8 units of calcium, and each ounce of food N contains 5 units of calcium. A 160-ounce diet mix is formed using foods M and N. If x is the number of ounces of food M used, write an algebraic expression that represents the total number of units of calcium in the diet mix. Simplify the expression.

Section **A-3** | Factoring Polynomials

➤ Common Factors
➤ Factoring by Grouping
➤ Factoring Second-Degree Polynomials
➤ Special Factoring Formulas
➤ Combined Factoring Techniques

A polynomial is written in factored form if it is written as the product of two or more polynomials. The following polynomials are written in factored form:

$$4x^2y - 6xy^2 = 2xy(2x - 3y) \qquad 2x^3 - 8x = 2x(x - 2)(x + 2)$$
$$x^2 - x - 6 = (x - 3)(x + 2) \qquad 5m^2 + 20 = 5(m^2 + 4)$$

AGREEMENT   Factoring Polynomials

Unless stated to the contrary, we will limit our discussion of factoring of polynomials to polynomials with integer coefficients.

A polynomial with integer coefficients is said to be **factored completely** if each factor cannot be expressed as the product of two or more polynomials with integer coefficients, other than itself or 1. All the polynomials above, as we will see by the conclusion of this section, are factored completely.

Writing polynomials in completely factored form is often a difficult task. But accomplishing it can lead to the simplification of certain algebraic expressions and to the solution of certain types of equations and inequalities. The distributive properties for real numbers are central to the factoring process.

➤ Common Factors

Generally, a first step in any factoring procedure is to factor out all factors common to all terms.

EXAMPLE 1 **Common Factors** Factor out all factors common to all terms:

(A) $3x^3y - 6x^2y^2 - 3xy^3$

(B) $3y(2y + 5) + 2(2y + 5)$

Solution (A) $3x^3y - 6x^2y^2 - 3xy^3 = (3xy)x^2 - (3xy)2xy - (3xy)y^2$

$$= 3xy(x^2 - 2xy - y^2)$$

(B) $3y(2y + 5) + 2(2y + 5) = 3y(2y + 5) + 2(2y + 5)$

$$= (3y + 2)(2y + 5)$$ ∎

Matched Problem 1 Factor out all factors common to all terms:

(A) $2x^3y - 8x^2y^2 - 6xy^3$ (B) $2x(3x - 2) - 7(3x - 2)$

➤ Factoring by Grouping

Occasionally, polynomials can be factored by grouping terms in such a way that we obtain results that look like Example 1B. We can then complete the factoring following the steps used in that example. This process will prove useful in the next subsection, where an efficient method is developed for factoring a second-degree polynomial as the product of two first-degree polynomials, if such factors exist.

EXAMPLE 2 **Factoring by Grouping** Factor by grouping:

(A) $3x^2 - 3x - x + 1$

(B) $4x^2 - 2xy - 6xy + 3y^2$

(C) $y^2 + xz + xy + yz$

Solution (A) $3x^2 - 3x - x + 1$

$\qquad = (3x^2 - 3x) - (x - 1)$ *Group the first two and the last two terms.*

$\qquad = 3x(x - 1) - (x - 1)$ *Factor out any common factors from each group. The common factor $(x - 1)$ can be taken out, and the factoring is complete.*

$\qquad = (x - 1)(3x - 1)$

(B) $4x^2 - 2xy - 6xy + 3y^2 = (4x^2 - 2xy) - (6xy - 3y^2)$

$\qquad\qquad\qquad\qquad\qquad = 2x(2x - y) - 3y(2x - y)$

$\qquad\qquad\qquad\qquad\qquad = (2x - y)(2x - 3y)$

(C) If, as in parts (A) and (B), we group the first two terms and the last two terms of $y^2 + xz + xy + yz$, no common factor can be taken out of each group to complete the factoring. However, if the two middle terms are reversed, we can proceed as before:

$$\begin{aligned}
y^2 + xz + xy + yz &= y^2 + xy + xz + yz \\
&= (y^2 + xy) + (xz + yz) \\
&= y(y + x) + z(x + y) \\
&= y(x + y) + z(x + y) \\
&= (x + y)(y + z)
\end{aligned}$$

Matched Problem 2   Factor by grouping:

(A) $6x^2 + 2x + 9x + 3$ (B) $2u^2 + 6uv - 3uv - 9v^2$

(C) $ac + bd + bc + ad$

➤ Factoring Second-Degree Polynomials

We now turn our attention to factoring second-degree polynomials of the form

$$2x^2 - 5x - 3 \quad \text{and} \quad 2x^2 + 3xy - 2y^2$$

into the product of two first-degree polynomials with integer coefficients. Since many second-degree polynomials with integer coefficients cannot be factored in this way, it would be useful to know ahead of time that the factors we are seeking actually exist. The factoring approach we use, involving the *ac test,* determines at the beginning whether first-degree factors with integer coefficients do exist. Then, if they exist, the test provides a simple method for finding them.

THEOREM 1   *ac* Test for Factorability

If in polynomials of the form

$$ax^2 + bx + c \quad \text{or} \quad ax^2 + bxy + cy^2 \tag{1}$$

the product ac has two integer factors p and q whose sum is the coefficient b of the middle term; that is, if integers p and q exist so that

$$pq = ac \quad \text{and} \quad p + q = b \tag{2}$$

then the polynomials have first-degree factors with integer coefficients. If no integers p and q exist that satisfy equations (2), then the polynomials in equations (1) will not have first-degree factors with integer coefficients.

If integers p and q exist that satisfy equations (2) in the *ac* test, the factoring always can be completed as follows:

Using $b = p + q$, split the middle terms in equations (1) to obtain

$$ax^2 + bx + c = ax^2 + px + qx + c$$
$$ax^2 + bxy + cy^2 = ax^2 + pxy + qxy + cy^2$$

Complete the factoring by grouping the first two terms and the last two terms as in Example 2. This process always works, and it does not matter if the two middle terms on the right are interchanged.

Several examples should make the process clear. After a little practice, you will perform many of the steps mentally and will find the process fast and efficient.

EXAMPLE 3 **Factoring Second-Degree Polynomials** Factor, if possible, using integer coefficients:

(A) $4x^2 - 4x - 3$

(B) $2x^2 - 3x - 4$

(C) $6x^2 - 25xy + 4y^2$

Solution (A) $4x^2 - 4x - 3$

Step 1. Use the *ac* test to test for factorability. Comparing $4x^2 - 4x - 3$ with $ax^2 + bx + c$, we see that $a = 4$, $b = -4$, and $c = -3$. Multiply *a* and *c* to obtain

$$ac = (4)(-3) = -12$$

pq	
$(1)(-12)$	
$(-1)(12)$	
$(2)(-6)$	All factor pairs
$(-2)(6)$	of $-12 = ac$
$(3)(-4)$	
$(-3)(4)$	

List all pairs of integers whose product is -12, as shown in the margin. These are called **factor pairs** of -12. Then try to find a factor pair that sums to $b = -4$, the coefficient of the middle term in $4x^2 - 4x - 3$. (In practice, this part of step 1 is often done mentally and can be done rather quickly.) Notice that the factor pair 2 and -6 sums to -4. Thus, by the *ac* test, $4x^2 - 4x - 3$ has first-degree factors with integer coefficients.

Step 2. Split the middle term, using $b = p + q$, and complete the factoring by grouping. Using $-4 = 2 + (-6)$, we split the middle term in $4x^2 - 4x - 3$ and complete the factoring by grouping:

$$\begin{aligned}
4x^2 - 4x - 3 &= 4x^2 + 2x - 6x - 3 \\
&= (4x^2 + 2x) - (6x + 3) \\
&= 2x(\mathbf{2x + 1}) - 3(\mathbf{2x + 1}) \\
&= (\mathbf{2x + 1})(2x - 3)
\end{aligned}$$

The result can be checked by multiplying the two factors to obtain the original polynomial.

(B) $2x^2 - 3x - 4$

Step 1. Use the *ac* test to test for factorability:

$$ac = (2)(-4) = -8$$

pq	
$(-1)(8)$	
$(1)(-8)$	All factor pairs
$(-2)(4)$	of $-8 = ac$
$(2)(-4)$	

Does -8 have a factor pair whose sum is -3? None of the factor pairs listed in the margin sums to $-3 = b$, the coefficient of the middle term in $2x^2 - 3x - 4$. According to the *ac* test, we can conclude that $2x^2 - 3x - 4$ does not have first-degree factors with integer coefficients, and we say that the polynomial is **not factorable.**

(C) $6x^2 - 25xy + 4y^2$

Step 1. Use the *ac* test to test for factorability:

$$ac = (6)(4) = 24$$

Mentally checking through the factor pairs of 24, keeping in mind that their sum must be $-25 = b$, we see that if $p = -1$ and $q = -24$, then

$$pq = (-1)(-24) = 24 = ac$$

and

$$p + q = (-1) + (-24) = -25 = b$$

Thus, the polynomial is factorable.

Step 2. Split the middle term, using $b = p + q$, and complete the factoring by grouping. Using $-25 = (-1) + (-24)$, we split the middle term in $6x^2 - 25xy + 4y^2$ and complete the factoring by grouping:

$$\begin{aligned}
6x^2 - 25xy + 4y^2 &= 6x^2 - xy - 24xy + 4y^2 \\
&= (6x^2 - xy) - (24xy - 4y^2) \\
&= x(6x - y) - 4y(6x - y) \\
&= (6x - y)(x - 4y)
\end{aligned}$$

The check is left to the reader. ∎

Matched Problem 3 Factor, if possible, using integer coefficients:

(A) $2x^2 + 11x - 6$ (B) $4x^2 + 11x - 6$ (C) $6x^2 + 5xy - 4y^2$

➤ Special Factoring Formulas

The factoring formulas listed in the following box will enable us to factor certain polynomial forms that occur frequently. These formulas can be established by multiplying the factors on the right.

THEOREM 2 Special Factoring Formulas

Perfect square: 1. $u^2 + 2uv + v^2 = (u + v)^2$

Perfect square: 2. $u^2 - 2uv + v^2 = (u - v)^2$

Difference of squares: 3. $u^2 - v^2 = (u - v)(u + v)$

Difference of cubes: 4. $u^3 - v^3 = (u - v)(u^2 + uv + v^2)$

Sum of cubes: 5. $u^3 + v^3 = (u + v)(u^2 - uv + v^2)$

Caution

Notice that $u^2 + v^2$ is not included in the list of special factoring formulas. In general,

$$u^2 + v^2 \neq (au + bv)(cu + dv)$$

for any choice of real number coefficients a, b, c, and d.

EXAMPLE 4 **Factoring** Factor completely:

(A) $4m^2 - 12mn + 9n^2$ (B) $x^2 - 16y^2$

(C) $z^3 - 1$ (D) $m^3 + n^3$

(E) $a^2 - 4(b + 2)^2$

Solution (A) $4m^2 - 12mn + 9n^2 = (2m - 3n)^2$

(B) $x^2 - 16y^2 = x^2 - (4y)^2 = (x - 4y)(x + 4y)$

(C) $z^3 - 1 = (z - 1)(z^2 + z + 1)$ Use the ac test to verify that $z^2 + z + 1$ cannot be factored.

(D) $m^3 + n^3 = (m + n)(m^2 - mn + n^2)$ *Use the ac test to verify that*
$\qquad\qquad\qquad\qquad\qquad\qquad\qquad$ *$m^2 - mn + n^2$ cannot be factored.*

(E) $a^2 - 4(b + 2)^2 = [a - 2(b + 2)][a + 2(b + 2)]$ ■

Matched Problem 4   Factor completely:

(A) $x^2 + 6xy + 9y^2$ $\qquad$ (B) $9x^2 - 4y^2$ $\qquad\qquad$ (C) $8m^3 - 1$

(D) $x^3 + y^3z^3$ $\qquad\qquad$ (E) $9(m - 3)^2 - 4n^2$ $\qquad$ ────────■

(A) Verify the following factoring formulas for $u^4 - v^4$:

$$u^4 - v^4 = (u - v)(u + v)(u^2 + v^2)$$
$$= (u - v)(u^3 + u^2v + uv^2 + v^3)$$

(B) Discuss the pattern in the following formulas:

$$u^2 - v^2 = (u - v)(u + v)$$
$$u^3 - v^3 = (u - v)(u^2 + uv + v^2)$$
$$u^4 - v^4 = (u - v)(u^3 + u^2v + uv^2 + v^3)$$

(C) Use the pattern you discovered in part (B) to write similar formulas for $u^5 - v^5$ and $u^6 - v^6$. Verify your formulas by multiplication.

➤ Combined Factoring Techniques

We complete this section by considering several factoring problems that involve combinations of the preceding techniques.

PROCEDURE   Factoring Polynomials

Step 1. Take out any factors common to all terms.

Step 2. Use any of the special formulas listed in Theorem 2 that are applicable.

Step 3. Apply the *ac* test to any remaining second degree polynomial factors.

Note: It may be necessary to perform some of these steps more than once. Furthermore, the order of applying these steps can vary.

EXAMPLE 5   **Combined Factoring Techniques**   Factor completely:

(A) $3x^3 - 48x$

(B) $3u^4 - 3u^3v - 9u^2v^2$

(C) $3m^4 - 24mn^3$

(D) $3x^4 - 5x^2 + 2$

Solution   (A) $3x^3 - 48x = 3x(x^2 - 16) = 3x(x - 4)(x + 4)$

(B) $3u^4 - 3u^3v - 9u^2v^2 = 3u^2(u^2 - uv - 3v^2)$

(C) $3m^4 - 24mn^3 = 3m(m^3 - 8n^3) = 3m(m - 2n)(m^2 + 2mn + 4n^2)$

(D) $3x^4 - 5x^2 + 2 = (3x^2 - 2)(x^2 - 1) = (3x^2 - 2)(x - 1)(x + 1)$ ■

Matched Problem 5 Factor completely:

(A) $18x^3 - 8x$ (B) $4m^3n - 2m^2n^2 + 2mn^3$ (C) $2t^4 - 16t$

(D) $2y^4 - 5y^2 - 12$

Answers to Matched Problems

1. (A) $2xy(x^2 - 4xy - 3y^2)$ (B) $(2x - 7)(3x - 2)$
2. (A) $(3x + 1)(2x + 3)$ (B) $(u + 3v)(2u - 3v)$ (C) $(a + b)(c + d)$
3. (A) $(2x - 1)(x + 6)$ (B) Not factorable   (C) $(3x + 4y)(2x - y)$
4. (A) $(x + 3y)^2$ (B) $(3x - 2y)(3x + 2y)$
   (C) $(2m - 1)(4m^2 + 2m + 1)$ (D) $(x + yz)(x^2 - xyz + y^2z^2)$
   (E) $[3(m - 3) - 2n][3(m - 3) + 2n]$
5. (A) $2x(3x - 2)(3x + 2)$ (B) $2mn(2m^2 - mn + n^2)$
   (C) $2t(t - 2)(t^2 + 2t + 4)$ (D) $(2y^2 + 3)(y - 2)(y + 2)$

Exercise A-3

A *In Problems 1–8, factor out all factors common to all terms.*

1. $6m^4 - 9m^3 - 3m^2$
2. $6x^4 - 8x^3 - 2x^2$
3. $8u^3v - 6u^2v^2 + 4uv^3$
4. $10x^3y + 20x^2y^2 - 15xy^3$
5. $7m(2m - 3) + 5(2m - 3)$
6. $5x(x + 1) - 3(x + 1)$
7. $4ab(2c + d) - (2c + d)$
8. $12a(b - 2c) - 15b(b - 2c)$

In Problems 9–18, factor by grouping.

9. $2x^2 - x + 4x - 2$
10. $x^2 - 3x + 2x - 6$
11. $3y^2 - 3y + 2y - 2$
12. $2x^2 - x + 6x - 3$
13. $2x^2 + 8x - x - 4$
14. $6x^2 + 9x - 2x - 3$
15. $wy - wz + xy - xz$
16. $ac + ad + bc + bd$
17. $am - 3bm + 2na - 6bn$
18. $ab + 6 + 2a + 3b$

B *In Problems 19–56, factor completely. If a polynomial cannot be factored, say so.*

19. $3y^2 - y - 2$
20. $2x^2 + 5x - 3$
21. $u^2 - 2uv - 15v^2$
22. $x^2 - 4xy - 12y^2$
23. $m^2 - 6m - 3$
24. $x^2 + x - 4$
25. $w^2x^2 - y^2$
26. $25m^2 - 16n^2$
27. $9m^2 - 6mn + n^2$
28. $x^2 + 10xy + 25y^2$
29. $y^2 + 16$
30. $u^2 + 81$
31. $4z^2 - 28z + 48$
32. $6x^2 + 48x + 72$
33. $2x^4 - 24x^3 + 40x^2$
34. $2y^3 - 22y^2 + 48y$

35. $4xy^2 - 12xy + 9x$
36. $16x^2y - 8xy + y$
37. $6m^2 - mn - 12n^2$
38. $6s^2 + 7st - 3t^2$
39. $4u^3v - uv^3$
40. $x^3y - 9xy^3$
41. $2x^3 - 2x^2 + 8x$
42. $3m^3 - 6m^2 + 15m$
43. $8x^3 - 27y^3$
44. $5x^3 + 40y^3$
45. $x^4y + 8xy$
46. $8a^3 - 1$

C

47. $(x + 2)^2 - 9y^2$
48. $(a - b)^2 - 4(c - d)^2$
49. $5u^2 + 4uv - 2v^2$
50. $3x^2 - 2xy - 4y^2$
51. $6(x - y)^2 + 23(x - y) - 4$
52. $4(A + B)^2 - 5(A + B) - 6$
53. $y^4 - 3y^2 - 4$
54. $m^4 - n^4$
55. $15y(x - y)^3 + 12x(x - y)^2$
56. $15x^2(3x - 1)^4 + 60x^3(3x - 1)^3$

In Problems 57–60, discuss the validity of each statement. If the statement is true, explain why. If not, give a counterexample.

57. If n is a positive integer greater than 1, then $u^n - v^n$ can be factored.

58. If m and n are positive integers and $m \neq n$, then $u^m - v^n$ is not factorable.

59. If n is a positive integer greater than 1, then $u^n + v^n$ can be factored.

60. If k is a positive integer, then $u^{2k+1} + v^{2k+1}$ can be factored.

Section **A-4** | Operations on Rational Expressions

➤ Reducing to Lowest Terms
➤ Multiplication and Division
➤ Addition and Subtraction
➤ Compound Fractions

We now turn our attention to fractional forms. A quotient of two algebraic expressions (division by 0 excluded) is called a **fractional expression.** If both the numerator and the denominator are polynomials, the fractional expression is called a **rational expression.** Some examples of rational expressions are

$$\frac{1}{x^3 + 2x} \qquad \frac{5}{x} \qquad \frac{x + 7}{3x^2 - 5x + 1} \qquad \frac{x^2 - 2x + 4}{1}$$

In this section we discuss basic operations on rational expressions, including multiplication, division, addition, and subtraction.

Since variables represent real numbers in the rational expressions we will consider, the properties of real number fractions summarized in Appendix A-1 will play a central role in much of the work that we will do.

AGREEMENT | **Variable Restriction**

Even though not always explicitly stated, we always assume that variables are restricted so that division by 0 is excluded.

For example, given the rational expression

$$\frac{2x + 5}{x(x + 2)(x - 3)}$$

the variable x is understood to be restricted from being $0, -2$, or 3, since these values would cause the denominator to be 0.

➤ Reducing to Lowest Terms

Central to the process of reducing rational expressions to *lowest terms* is the *fundamental property of fractions,* which we restate here for convenient reference:

THEOREM 1 | **Fundamental Property of Fractions**

If a, b, and k are real numbers with $b, k \neq 0$, then

$$\frac{ka}{kb} = \frac{a}{b} \qquad \frac{5 \cdot 2}{5 \cdot 7} = \frac{2}{7} \qquad \frac{x(x + 4)}{2(x + 4)} = \frac{x}{2}, \quad x \neq -4$$

Using this property from left to right to eliminate all common factors from the numerator and the denominator of a given fraction is referred to as **reducing a fraction to lowest terms.** We are actually dividing the numerator and denominator by the same nonzero common factor.

Using the property from right to left—that is, multiplying the numerator and denominator by the same nonzero factor—is referred to as **raising a fraction to higher terms.** We will use the property in both directions in the material that follows.

EXAMPLE 1 **Reducing to Lowest Terms** Reduce each rational expression to lowest terms.

(A) $\dfrac{6x^2 + x - 1}{2x^2 - x - 1} = \dfrac{(2x + 1)(3x - 1)}{(2x + 1)(x - 1)}$ *Factor numerator and denominator completely.*

$= \dfrac{3x - 1}{x - 1}$ *Divide numerator and denominator by the common factor $(2x + 1)$.*

(B) $\dfrac{x^4 - 8x}{3x^3 - 2x^2 - 8x} = \dfrac{x(x - 2)(x^2 + 2x + 4)}{x(x - 2)(3x + 4)}$

$= \dfrac{x^2 + 2x + 4}{3x + 4}$

Matched Problem 1 Reduce each rational expression to lowest terms.

(A) $\dfrac{x^2 - 6x + 9}{x^2 - 9}$ (B) $\dfrac{x^3 - 1}{x^2 - 1}$

👁 **Insight** Using Theorem 1 to divide the numerator and denominator of a fraction by a common factor is often referred to as **canceling.** This operation can be denoted by drawing a slanted line through each common factor and writing any remaining factors above or below the common factor. Canceling is often incorrectly applied to individual terms in the numerator or denominator, instead of to common factors. For example,

$$\frac{14 - 5}{2} = \frac{9}{2}$$ *Theorem 1 does not apply. There are no common factors in the numerator.*

$$\frac{14 - 5}{2} \neq \frac{\overset{7}{\cancel{14}} - 5}{\underset{1}{\cancel{2}}} = 2$$ *Incorrect use of Theorem 1. To cancel 2 in the denominator, 2 must be a factor of each term in the numerator.*

➤ **Multiplication and Division**

Since we are restricting variable replacements to real numbers, multiplication and division of rational expressions follow the rules for multiplying and dividing real number fractions summarized in Appendix A-1.

THEOREM 2 **Multiplication and Division**

If $a, b, c,$ and d are real numbers, then

1. $\dfrac{a}{b} \cdot \dfrac{c}{d} = \dfrac{ac}{bd}, \quad b, d \neq 0$ $\dfrac{3}{5} \cdot \dfrac{x}{x + 5} = \dfrac{3x}{5(x + 5)}$

2. $\dfrac{a}{b} \div \dfrac{c}{d} = \dfrac{a}{b} \cdot \dfrac{d}{c}, \quad b, c, d \neq 0$ $\dfrac{3}{5} \div \dfrac{x}{x + 5} = \dfrac{3}{5} \cdot \dfrac{x + 5}{x}$

EXPLORE & DISCUSS 1 Write a verbal description of the process of multiplying two rational expressions. Do the same for the quotient of two rational expressions.

EXAMPLE 2 **Multiplication and Division** Perform the indicated operations and reduce to lowest terms.

(A) $\dfrac{10x^3y}{3xy + 9y} \cdot \dfrac{x^2 - 9}{4x^2 - 12x}$ *Factor numerators and denominators. Then divide any numerator and any denominator with a like common factor.*

$$= \dfrac{\overset{5x^2}{\cancel{10x^3\cancel{y}}}}{\underset{3 \cdot 1}{\cancel{3\cancel{y}}(x + 3)}} \cdot \dfrac{\overset{1 \cdot 1}{\cancel{(x - 3)}\cancel{(x + 3)}}}{\underset{2 \cdot 1}{\cancel{4x}\cancel{(x - 3)}}}$$

$$= \dfrac{5x^2}{6}$$

(B) $\dfrac{4 - 2x}{4} \div (x - 2) = \dfrac{\overset{1}{\cancel{2}}(2 - x)}{\underset{2}{\cancel{4}}} \cdot \dfrac{1}{x - 2}$ $x - 2 = \dfrac{x - 2}{1}$

$$= \dfrac{2 - x}{2(x - 2)} = \dfrac{\overset{-1}{\cancel{-(x - 2)}}}{\underset{1}{2\cancel{(x - 2)}}}$$ *b − a = −(a − b), a useful change in some problems*

$$= -\dfrac{1}{2}$$

Matched Problem 2 Perform the indicated operations and reduce to lowest terms.

(A) $\dfrac{12x^2y^3}{2xy^2 + 6xy} \cdot \dfrac{y^2 + 6y + 9}{3y^3 + 9y^2}$ (B) $(4 - x) \div \dfrac{x^2 - 16}{5}$

➤ **Addition and Subtraction**

Again, because we are restricting variable replacements to real numbers, addition and subtraction of rational expressions follow the rules for adding and subtracting real number fractions.

THEOREM 3 Addition and Subtraction

For *a*, *b*, and *c* real numbers,

1. $\dfrac{a}{b} + \dfrac{c}{b} = \dfrac{a + c}{b}$, $b \neq 0$ $\dfrac{x}{x + 5} + \dfrac{8}{x + 5} = \dfrac{x + 8}{x + 5}$

2. $\dfrac{a}{b} - \dfrac{c}{b} = \dfrac{a - c}{b}$, $b \neq 0$ $\dfrac{x}{3x^2y^2} - \dfrac{x + 7}{3x^2y^2} = \dfrac{x - (x + 7)}{3x^2y^2}$

Thus, we add rational expressions with the same denominators by adding or subtracting their numerators and placing the result over the common denominator. If the denominators are not the same, we raise the fractions to higher terms, using the fundamental property of fractions to obtain common denominators, and then proceed as described.

Even though any common denominator will do, our work will be simplified if the *least common denominator (LCD)* is used. Often, the LCD is obvious, but if it is not, the steps in the next box describe how to find it.

PROCEDURE   Least Common Denominator

The least common denominator (LCD) of two or more rational expressions is found as follows:

1. Factor each denominator completely, including integer factors.

2. Identify each different factor from all the denominators.

3. Form a product using each different factor to the highest power that occurs in any one denominator. This product is the LCD.

EXAMPLE 3   **Addition and Subtraction** Combine into a single fraction and reduce to lowest terms.

(A) $\dfrac{3}{10} + \dfrac{5}{6} - \dfrac{11}{45}$ (B) $\dfrac{4}{9x} - \dfrac{5x}{6y^2} + 1$ (C) $\dfrac{1}{x-1} - \dfrac{1}{x} - \dfrac{2}{x^2-1}$

Solution   (A) To find the LCD, factor each denominator completely:

$$\left.\begin{array}{l} 10 = 2 \cdot 5 \\ 6 = 2 \cdot 3 \\ 45 = 3^2 \cdot 5 \end{array}\right\} \quad \text{LCD} = 2 \cdot 3^2 \cdot 5 = 90$$

Now use the fundamental property of fractions to make each denominator 90:

$$\frac{3}{10} + \frac{5}{6} - \frac{11}{45} = \frac{9 \cdot 3}{9 \cdot 10} + \frac{15 \cdot 5}{15 \cdot 6} - \frac{2 \cdot 11}{2 \cdot 45}$$

$$= \frac{27}{90} + \frac{75}{90} - \frac{22}{90}$$

$$= \frac{27 + 75 - 22}{90} = \frac{80}{90} = \frac{8}{9}$$

(B) $\left.\begin{array}{l} 9x = 3^2 x \\ 6y^2 = 2 \cdot 3y^2 \end{array}\right\} \quad \text{LCD} = 2 \cdot 3^2 xy^2 = 18xy^2$

$$\frac{4}{9x} - \frac{5x}{6y^2} + 1 = \frac{2y^2 \cdot 4}{2y^2 \cdot 9x} - \frac{3x \cdot 5x}{3x \cdot 6y^2} + \frac{18xy^2}{18xy^2}$$

$$= \frac{8y^2 - 15x^2 + 18xy^2}{18xy^2}$$

(C) $\dfrac{1}{x-1} - \dfrac{1}{x} - \dfrac{2}{x^2-1}$

$$= \frac{1}{x-1} - \frac{1}{x} - \frac{2}{(x-1)(x+1)} \quad \text{LCD} = x(x-1)(x+1)$$

$$= \frac{x(x+1) - (x-1)(x+1) - 2x}{x(x-1)(x+1)}$$

$$= \frac{x^2 + x - x^2 + 1 - 2x}{x(x-1)(x+1)}$$

$$= \frac{1 - x}{x(x-1)(x+1)}$$

$$= \frac{\overset{-1}{\cancel{-(x-1)}}}{x\underset{1}{\cancel{(x-1)}}(x+1)} = \frac{-1}{x(x+1)}$$

Matched Problem 3 Combine into a single fraction and reduce to lowest terms.

(A) $\dfrac{5}{28} - \dfrac{1}{10} + \dfrac{6}{35}$

(B) $\dfrac{1}{4x^2} - \dfrac{2x+1}{3x^3} + \dfrac{3}{12x}$

(C) $\dfrac{2}{x^2 - 4x + 4} + \dfrac{1}{x} - \dfrac{1}{x-2}$

 EXPLORE & DISCUSS 2

What is the value of $\dfrac{\frac{16}{4}}{2}$?

What is the result of entering $16 \div 4 \div 2$ on a calculator?

What is the difference between $16 \div (4 \div 2)$ and $(16 \div 4) \div 2$?

How could you use fraction bars to distinguish between these two cases when writing $\dfrac{\frac{16}{4}}{2}$?

➤ Compound Fractions

A fractional expression with fractions in its numerator, denominator, or both is called a **compound fraction.** It is often necessary to represent a compound fraction as a **simple fraction**—that is (in all cases we will consider), as the quotient of two polynomials. The process does not involve any new concepts. It is a matter of applying old concepts and processes in the correct sequence.

EXAMPLE 4 **Simplifying Compound Fractions** Express as a simple fraction reduced to lowest terms:

(A) $\dfrac{\dfrac{1}{5+h} - \dfrac{1}{5}}{h}$ (B) $\dfrac{\dfrac{y}{x^2} - \dfrac{x}{y^2}}{\dfrac{y}{x} - \dfrac{x}{y}}$

Solution We will simplify the expressions in parts (A) and (B) using two different methods—each is suited to the particular type of problem.

(A) We simplify this expression by combining the numerator into a single fraction and using division of rational forms.

$$\dfrac{\dfrac{1}{5+h} - \dfrac{1}{5}}{h} = \left[\dfrac{1}{5+h} - \dfrac{1}{5} \right] \div \dfrac{h}{1}$$

$$= \dfrac{5 - 5 - h}{5(5+h)} \cdot \dfrac{1}{h}$$

$$= \dfrac{-h}{5(5+h)h} = \dfrac{-1}{5(5+h)}$$

(B) The method used here makes effective use of the fundamental property of fractions in the form

$$\dfrac{a}{b} = \dfrac{ka}{kb} \qquad b, k \neq 0$$

Multiply the numerator and denominator by the LCD of all fractions in the numerator and denominator—in this case, x^2y^2:

$$\frac{x^2y^2\left(\dfrac{y}{x^2} - \dfrac{x}{y^2}\right)}{x^2y^2\left(\dfrac{y}{x} - \dfrac{x}{y}\right)} = \frac{x^2y^2\dfrac{y}{x^2} - x^2y^2\dfrac{x}{y^2}}{x^2y^2\dfrac{y}{x} - x^2y^2\dfrac{x}{y}} = \frac{y^3 - x^3}{xy^3 - x^3y}$$

$$= \frac{\overset{1}{\cancel{(y - x)}}(y^2 + xy + x^2)}{xy\cancel{(y - x)}(y + x)}$$

$$= \frac{y^2 + xy + x^2}{xy(y + x)} \quad \text{or} \quad \frac{x^2 + xy + y^2}{xy(x + y)} \qquad ∎$$

Matched Problem 4   Express as a simple fraction reduced to lowest terms:

(A) $\dfrac{\dfrac{1}{2 + h} - \dfrac{1}{2}}{h}$

(B) $\dfrac{\dfrac{a}{b} - \dfrac{b}{a}}{\dfrac{a}{b} + 2 + \dfrac{b}{a}}$

Answers to Matched Problems

1. (A) $\dfrac{x - 3}{x + 3}$ (B) $\dfrac{x^2 + x + 1}{x + 1}$ **2.** (A) $2x$ (B) $\dfrac{-5}{x + 4}$

3. (A) $\dfrac{1}{4}$ (B) $\dfrac{3x^2 - 5x - 4}{12x^3}$ (C) $\dfrac{4}{x(x - 2)^2}$

4. (A) $\dfrac{-1}{2(2 + h)}$ (B) $\dfrac{a - b}{a + b}$

Exercise A-4

A *In Problems 1–18, perform the indicated operations and reduce answers to lowest terms.*

1. $\dfrac{d^5}{3a} \div \left(\dfrac{d^2}{6a^2} \cdot \dfrac{a}{4d^3}\right)$

2. $\left(\dfrac{d^5}{3a} \div \dfrac{d^2}{6a^2}\right) \cdot \dfrac{a}{4d^3}$

3. $\dfrac{x^2}{12} + \dfrac{x}{18} - \dfrac{1}{30}$

4. $\dfrac{2y}{18} - \dfrac{-1}{28} - \dfrac{y}{42}$

5. $\dfrac{4m - 3}{18m^3} + \dfrac{3}{4m} - \dfrac{2m - 1}{6m^2}$

6. $\dfrac{3x + 8}{4x^2} - \dfrac{2x - 1}{x^3} - \dfrac{5}{8x}$

7. $\dfrac{x^2 - 9}{x^2 - 3x} \div (x^2 - x - 12)$

8. $\dfrac{2x^2 + 7x + 3}{4x^2 - 1} \div (x + 3)$

9. $\dfrac{2}{x} - \dfrac{1}{x - 3}$

10. $\dfrac{5}{m - 2} - \dfrac{3}{2m + 1}$

11. $\dfrac{2}{(x + 1)^2} - \dfrac{5}{x^2 - x - 2}$

12. $\dfrac{3}{x^2 - 5x + 6} - \dfrac{5}{(x - 2)^2}$

13. $\dfrac{x + 1}{x - 1} - 1$

14. $m - 3 - \dfrac{m - 1}{m - 2}$

15. $\dfrac{3}{a - 1} - \dfrac{2}{1 - a}$

16. $\dfrac{5}{x - 3} - \dfrac{2}{3 - x}$

17. $\dfrac{2x}{x^2 - 16} - \dfrac{x - 4}{x^2 + 4x}$

18. $\dfrac{m+2}{m^2-2m} - \dfrac{m}{m^2-4}$

B In Problems 19–30, perform the indicated operations and reduce answers to lowest terms. Represent any compound fractions as simple fractions reduced to lowest terms.

19. $\dfrac{x^2}{x^2+2x+1} + \dfrac{x-1}{3x+3} - \dfrac{1}{6}$

20. $\dfrac{y}{y^2-y-2} - \dfrac{1}{y^2+5y-14} - \dfrac{2}{y^2+8y+7}$

21. $\dfrac{1-\dfrac{x}{y}}{2-\dfrac{y}{x}}$

22. $\dfrac{2}{5-\dfrac{3}{4x+1}}$

23. $\dfrac{c+2}{5c-5} - \dfrac{c-2}{3c-3} + \dfrac{c}{1-c}$

24. $\dfrac{x+7}{ax-bx} + \dfrac{y+9}{by-ay}$

25. $\dfrac{1+\dfrac{3}{x}}{x-\dfrac{9}{x}}$

26. $\dfrac{1-\dfrac{y^2}{x^2}}{1-\dfrac{y}{x}}$

27. $\dfrac{\dfrac{1}{2(x+h)} - \dfrac{1}{2x}}{h}$

28. $\dfrac{\dfrac{1}{x+h} - \dfrac{1}{x}}{h}$

29. $\dfrac{\dfrac{x}{y}-2+\dfrac{y}{x}}{\dfrac{x}{y}-\dfrac{y}{x}}$

30. $\dfrac{1+\dfrac{2}{x}-\dfrac{15}{x^2}}{1+\dfrac{4}{x}-\dfrac{5}{x^2}}$

In Problems 31–38, imagine that the indicated "solutions" were given to you by a student whom you were tutoring in this class.

(A) Is the solution correct? If the solution is incorrect, explain what is wrong and how it can be corrected.

(B) Show a correct solution for each incorrect solution.

31. $\dfrac{x^2+4x+3}{x+3} = \dfrac{x^2+4x}{x} = x+4$

32. $\dfrac{x^2-3x-4}{x-4} = \dfrac{x^2-3x}{x} = x-3$

33. $\dfrac{(x+h)^2-x^2}{h} = (x+1)^2-x^2 = 2x+1$

34. $\dfrac{(x+h)^3-x^3}{h} = (x+1)^3-x^3 = 3x^2+3x+1$

35. $\dfrac{x^2-3x}{x^2-2x-3} + x-3 = \dfrac{x^2-3x+x-3}{x^2-2x-3} = 1$

36. $\dfrac{2}{x-1} - \dfrac{x+3}{x^2-1} = \dfrac{2x+2-x-3}{x^2-1} = \dfrac{1}{x+1}$

37. $\dfrac{2x^2}{x^2-4} - \dfrac{x}{x-2} = \dfrac{2x^2-x^2-2x}{x^2-4} = \dfrac{x}{x+2}$

38. $x + \dfrac{x-2}{x^2-3x+2} = \dfrac{x+x-2}{x^2-3x+2} = \dfrac{2}{x-2}$

C Represent the compound fractions in Problems 39–42 as simple fractions reduced to lowest terms.

39. $\dfrac{\dfrac{1}{3(x+h)^2} - \dfrac{1}{3x^2}}{h}$

40. $\dfrac{\dfrac{1}{(x+h)^2} - \dfrac{1}{x^2}}{h}$

41. $x - \dfrac{2}{1-\dfrac{1}{x}}$

42. $2 - \dfrac{1}{1-\dfrac{2}{a+2}}$

Section A-5 | Integer Exponents and Scientific Notation

➤ Integer Exponents
➤ Scientific Notation

We now review basic operations on integer exponents and scientific notation and its use.

➤ Integer Exponents

DEFINITION   Integer Exponents

For n an integer and a a real number:

1. For n a positive integer,

$$a^n = a \cdot a \cdot \cdots \cdot a \qquad n \text{ factors of } a \qquad 5^4 = 5\cdot5\cdot5\cdot5$$

2. For $n = 0$,

$$a^0 = 1 \qquad a \neq 0 \qquad 12^0 = 1$$

0^0 is not defined.

3. For n a negative integer,

$$a^n = \frac{1}{a^{-n}} \qquad a \neq 0 \qquad a^{-3} = \frac{1}{a^{-(-3)}} = \frac{1}{a^3}$$

[If n is negative, then $(-n)$ is positive.]
Note: It can be shown that for *all* integers n,

$$a^{-n} = \frac{1}{a^n} \quad \text{and} \quad a^n = \frac{1}{a^{-n}} \qquad a \neq 0 \qquad a^5 = \frac{1}{a^{-5}}, \quad a^{-5} = \frac{1}{a^5}$$

The following integer exponent properties are very useful in manipulating integer exponent forms.

THEOREM 1   Exponent Properties

For n and m integers and a and b real numbers,

1. $a^m a^n = a^{m+n}$ $\qquad\qquad a^8 a^{-3} = a^{8+(-3)} = a^5$

2. $(a^n)^m = a^{mn}$ $\qquad\qquad (a^{-2})^3 = a^{3(-2)} = a^{-6}$

3. $(ab)^m = a^m b^m$ $\qquad\qquad (ab)^{-2} = a^{-2} b^{-2}$

4. $\left(\dfrac{a}{b}\right)^m = \dfrac{a^m}{b^m} \qquad b \neq 0 \qquad \left(\dfrac{a}{b}\right)^5 = \dfrac{a^5}{b^5}$

5. $\dfrac{a^m}{a^n} = a^{m-n} = \dfrac{1}{a^{n-m}} \qquad a \neq 0 \qquad \dfrac{a^{-3}}{a^7} = \dfrac{1}{a^{7-(-3)}} = \dfrac{1}{a^{10}}$

Property 1 in Theorem 1 can be expressed verbally as follows:

To find the product of two exponential forms with the same base, add the exponents and use the same base.

Express the other properties in Theorem 1 verbally. Decide which you find easier to remember—a formula or a verbal description.

Exponent forms are frequently encountered in algebraic applications. You should sharpen your skills in using these forms by reviewing the preceding basic definitions and properties and the examples that follow.

EXAMPLE 1   **Simplifying Exponent Forms** Simplify, and express the answers using positive exponents only.

(A) $(2x^3)(3x^5) = 2 \cdot 3x^{3+5} = 6x^8$

(B) $x^5 x^{-9} = x^{-4} = \dfrac{1}{x^4}$

(C) $\dfrac{x^5}{x^7} = x^{5-7} = x^{-2} = \dfrac{1}{x^2} \qquad \text{or} \qquad \dfrac{x^5}{x^7} = \dfrac{1}{x^{7-5}} = \dfrac{1}{x^2}$

(D) $\dfrac{x^{-3}}{y^{-4}} = \dfrac{y^4}{x^3}$

(E) $(u^{-3}v^2)^{-2} \boxed{= (u^{-3})^{-2}(v^2)^{-2}} = u^6v^{-4} = \dfrac{u^6}{v^4}$

(F) $\left(\dfrac{y^{-5}}{y^{-2}}\right)^{-2} \boxed{= \dfrac{(y^{-5})^{-2}}{(y^{-2})^{-2}} = \dfrac{y^{10}}{y^4}} = y^6$

(G) $\dfrac{4m^{-3}n^{-5}}{6m^{-4}n^3} \boxed{= \dfrac{2m^{-3-(-4)}}{3n^{3-(-5)}}} = \dfrac{2m}{3n^8}$ ∎

Matched Problem 1 Simplify, and express the answers using positive exponents only.

(A) $(3y^4)(2y^3)$ (B) m^2m^{-6} (C) $(u^3v^{-2})^{-2}$

(D) $\left(\dfrac{y^{-6}}{y^{-2}}\right)^{-1}$ (E) $\dfrac{8x^{-2}y^{-4}}{6x^{-5}y^2}$

◉ **Insight** Remember from Section A-2 that taking powers always precedes multiplication and division unless parentheses are used to indicate otherwise. Thus,

$$-5x^3 = -5 \cdot x \cdot x \cdot x$$

while

$$(-5x)^3 = (-5)^3x^3 = -125 \cdot x \cdot x \cdot x$$ ●

EXAMPLE 2 **Converting to a Simple Fraction** Write as a simple fraction with positive exponents:

$$\dfrac{1-x}{x^{-1}-1}$$

Solution First note that

$$\dfrac{1-x}{x^{-1}-1} \neq \dfrac{x(1-x)}{-1}   \textit{A common error}$$

The original expression is a complex fraction, and we proceed to simplify it as follows:

$$\dfrac{1-x}{x^{-1}-1} = \dfrac{1-x}{\dfrac{1}{x}-1}   \textit{Multiply numerator and denominator by x to clear internal fractions.}$$

$$= \dfrac{x(1-x)}{x\left(\dfrac{1}{x}-1\right)}$$

$$= \dfrac{x(1-x)}{1-x} = x$$ ∎

Matched Problem 2 Write as a simple fraction with positive exponents: $\dfrac{1+x^{-1}}{1-x^{-2}}$ ∎

➤ Scientific Notation

In the real world, one often encounters very large numbers. For example,

The public debt in the United States in 1998, to the nearest billion dollars, was

$$\$5,526,000,000,000$$

The world population in the year 2025, to the nearest million, is projected to be

$$7,896,000,000$$

Very small numbers are also encountered:

The sound intensity of a normal conversation is

$$0.000\ 000\ 000\ 316 \text{ watt per square centimeter*}$$

It is generally troublesome to write and work with numbers of this type in standard decimal form. The first and last example cannot even be entered into many calculators as they are written. But with exponents defined for all integers, we can now express any finite decimal form as the product of a number between 1 and 10 and an integer power of 10, that is, in the form

$$a \times 10^n \qquad 1 \leq a < 10, \quad a \text{ in decimal form}, \quad n \text{ an integer}$$

A number expressed in this form is said to be in **scientific notation.** The following are some examples of numbers in standard decimal notation and in scientific notation:

DECIMAL AND SCIENTIFIC NOTATION

$$7 = 7 \times 10^0 \qquad\qquad 0.5 = 5 \times 10^{-1}$$
$$67 = 6.7 \times 10 \qquad\qquad 0.45 = 4.5 \times 10^{-1}$$
$$580 = 5.8 \times 10^2 \qquad\qquad 0.0032 = 3.2 \times 10^{-3}$$
$$43,000 = 4.3 \times 10^4 \qquad\qquad 0.000\ 045 = 4.5 \times 10^{-5}$$
$$73,400,000 = 7.34 \times 10^7 \qquad 0.000\ 000\ 391 = 3.91 \times 10^{-7}$$

Note that the power of 10 used corresponds to the number of places we move the decimal to form a number between 1 and 10. The power is positive if the decimal is moved to the left and negative if it is moved to the right. Positive exponents are associated with numbers greater than or equal to 10; negative exponents are associated with positive numbers less than 1; and a zero exponent is associated with a number that is 1 or greater, but less than 10.

EXAMPLE 3   **Scientific Notation**

(A) Write each number in scientific notation:

$$7,320,000 \qquad \text{and} \qquad 0.000\ 000\ 54$$

(B) Write each number in standard decimal form:

$$4.32 \times 10^6 \qquad \text{and} \qquad 4.32 \times 10^{-5}$$

---

* We write 0.000 000 000 316 in place of 0.000000000316, because it is then easier to keep track of the number of decimal places. We follow this convention when there are more than five decimal places to the right of the decimal.

Solution　(A)　$7{,}320{,}000 = 7.\underset{\text{6 places left}}{320\ 000.} \times 10^6 = 7.32 \times 10^6$

Positive exponent

$0.000\ 000\ 54 = 0.\underset{\text{7 places right}}{000\ 000\ 5.4} \times 10^{-7} = 5.4 \times 10^{-7}$

Negative exponent

(B)　$4.32 \times 10^6 = 4{,}320{,}000$

6 places right

Positive exponent 6

$4.32 \times 10^{-5} = \dfrac{4.32}{10^5} = 0.000\ 043\ 2$

5 places left

Negative exponent −5

Matched Problem 3　(A)　Write each number in scientific notation:　47,100; 2,443,000,000; 1.45

(B)　Write each number in standard decimal form:　3.07×10^8; 5.98×10^{-6}

Scientific and graphing calculators can calculate in either standard decimal mode or scientific notation mode. If the result of a computation in decimal mode is either too large or too small to be displayed, most calculators will automatically display the answer in scientific notation. Read the manual for your calculator and experiment with some operations on very large and very small numbers in both decimal mode and scientific notation mode. For example, show that

$$\frac{216{,}700{,}000{,}000}{0.000\ 000\ 000\ 000\ 078\ 8} = 2.75 \times 10^{24}$$

Answers to Matched Problems　**1.** (A) $6y^7$　(B) $\dfrac{1}{m^4}$　(C) $\dfrac{v^4}{u^6}$　(D) y^4　(E) $\dfrac{4x^3}{3y^6}$　**2.** $\dfrac{x}{x-1}$

3. (A) 4.7×10^4; 2.443×10^9; 1.45×10^0　(B) $307{,}000{,}000$; $0.000\ 005\ 98$

Exercise A-5

A *In Problems 1–14, simplify and express answers using positive exponents only. Variables are restricted to avoid division by 0.*

1. $2x^{-9}$　**2.** $3y^{-5}$　**3.** $\dfrac{3}{2w^{-7}}$

4. $\dfrac{5}{4x^{-9}}$　**5.** $2x^{-8}x^5$　**6.** $3c^{-9}c^4$

7. $\dfrac{w^{-8}}{w^{-3}}$　**8.** $\dfrac{m^{-11}}{m^{-5}}$　**9.** $(2a^{-3})^2$

10. $7d^{-4}d^4$　**11.** $(a^{-3})^2$　**12.** $(5b^{-2})^2$

13. $(2x^4)^{-3}$　**14.** $(a^{-3}b^4)^{-3}$

Write each number in Problems 15–20 in scientific notation.

15. 82,300,000,000　**16.** 5,380,000

17. 0.783　**18.** 0.019

19. 0.000 034　**20.** 0.000 000 007 832

Write each number in Problems 21–28 in standard decimal notation.

21. 4×10^4　**22.** 9×10^6

23. 7×10^{-3}　**24.** 2×10^{-5}

25. 6.171×10^7　**26.** 3.044×10^3

27. 8.08×10^{-4}　**28.** 1.13×10^{-2}

B *In Problems 29–38, simplify and express answers using positive exponents only.*

29. $(22 + 31)^0$　**30.** $(2x^3y^4)^0$

31. $\dfrac{10^{-3} \cdot 10^4}{10^{-11} \cdot 10^{-2}}$

32. $\dfrac{10^{-17} \cdot 10^{-5}}{10^{-3} \cdot 10^{-14}}$

33. $(5x^2y^{-3})^{-2}$

34. $(2m^{-3}n^2)^{-3}$

35. $\left(\dfrac{-5}{2x^3}\right)^{-2}$

36. $\left(\dfrac{2a}{3b^2}\right)^{-3}$

37. $\dfrac{8x^{-3}y^{-1}}{6x^2y^{-4}}$

38. $\dfrac{9m^{-4}n^3}{12m^{-1}n^{-1}}$

In Problems 39–42, write each expression in the form
$ax^p + bx^q$ *or* $ax^p + bx^q + cx^r$, *where a, b, and c are real numbers and p, q, and r are integers. For example,*

$$\dfrac{2x^4 - 3x^2 + 1}{2x^3} = \boxed{\dfrac{2x^4}{2x^3} - \dfrac{3x^2}{2x^3} + \dfrac{1}{2x^3}} = x - \dfrac{3}{2}x^{-1} + \dfrac{1}{2}x^{-3}$$

39. $\dfrac{7x^5 - x^2}{4x^5}$

40. $\dfrac{5x^3 - 2}{3x^2}$

41. $\dfrac{5x^4 - 3x^2 + 8}{2x^2}$

42. $\dfrac{2x^3 - 3x^2 + x}{2x^2}$

Write each expression in Problems 43–46 with positive exponents only, and as a single fraction reduced to lowest terms.

43. $\dfrac{3x^2(x - 1)^2 - 2x^3(x - 1)}{(x - 1)^4}$

44. $\dfrac{5x^4(x + 3)^2 - 2x^5(x + 3)}{(x + 3)^4}$

45. $2x^{-2}(x - 1) - 2x^{-3}(x - 1)^2$

46. $2x(x + 3)^{-1} - x^2(x + 3)^{-2}$

In Problems 47–50, convert each number to scientific notation and simplify. Express the answer in both scientific notation and in standard decimal form.

47. $\dfrac{9,600,000,000}{(1,600,000)(0.000\,000\,25)}$

48. $\dfrac{(60,000)(0.000\,003)}{(0.0004)(1,500,000)}$

49. $\dfrac{(1,250,000)(0.000\,38)}{0.0152}$

50. $\dfrac{(0.000\,000\,82)(230,000)}{(625,000)(0.0082)}$

51. What is the result of entering 2^{3^2} on a calculator?

52. Refer to Problem 51. What is the difference between $2^{(3^2)}$ and $(2^3)^2$? Which agrees with the value of 2^{3^2} obtained with a calculator?

53. If $n = 0$, then property 1 in Theorem 1 implies that $a^m a^0 = a^{m+0} = a^m$. Explain how this helps motivate the definition of a^0.

54. If $m = -n$, then property 1 in Theorem 1 implies that $a^{-n}a^n = a^0 = 1$. Explain how this helps motivate the definition of a^{-n}.

C *Write the fractions in Problems 55–58 as simple fractions reduced to lowest terms.*

55. $\dfrac{u + v}{u^{-1} + v^{-1}}$

56. $\dfrac{x^{-2} - y^{-2}}{x^{-1} + y^{-1}}$

57. $\dfrac{b^{-2} - c^{-2}}{b^{-3} - c^{-3}}$

58. $\dfrac{xy^{-2} - yx^{-2}}{y^{-1} - x^{-1}}$

Applications

Business & Economics

Problems 59 and 60 refer to Table 1.

TABLE 1 Assets of the Five Largest U.S. Commercial Banks, 1998	
Bank	**Assets ($)**
Citigroup, New York	667,400,000,000
BankAmerica, San Francisco	617,679,000,000
Chase Manhattan, New York	365,875,000,000
Bank One, Chicago	261,496,000,000
J.P. Morgan, New York	261,067,000,000

59. *Financial assets*

(A) Write Citigroup's assets in scientific notation.

(B) After converting to scientific notation, determine the ratio of the assets of Citigroup to the assets of Chase Manhattan. Write the answer in standard decimal form to four decimal places.

(C) Repeat part (B) with the banks reversed.

60. *Financial assets*

(A) Write BankAmerica's assets in scientific notation.

(B) After converting to scientific notation, determine the ratio of the assets of BankAmerica to the assets of J. P. Morgan. Write the answer in standard decimal form to four decimal places.

(C) Repeat part (B) with the banks reversed.

Problems 61 and 62 refer to Table 2.

TABLE 2 U.S. Public Debt, Interest on Debt, and Population			
Year	Public Debt ($)	Interest on Debt ($)	Population
1990	3,233,300,000,000	264,800,000,000	248,765,170
1998	5,526,200,000,000	363,800,000,000	270,299,000

61. Public debt. Carry out the following computations using scientific notation, and write final answers in standard decimal form.

(A) What was the per capita debt in 1998 (to the nearest dollar)?

(B) What was the per capita interest paid on the debt in 1998 (to the nearest dollar)?

(C) What was the percentage interest paid on the debt in 1998 (to two decimal places)?

62. Public debt. Carry out the following computations using scientific notation, and write final answers in standard decimal form.

(A) What was the per capita debt in 1990 (to the nearest dollar)?

(B) What was the per capita interest paid on the debt in 1990 (to the nearest dollar)?

(C) What was the percentage interest paid on the debt in 1990 (to two decimal places)?

Life Sciences

Air pollution. *Air quality standards establish maximum amounts of pollutants considered acceptable in the air. The amounts are frequently given in parts per million (ppm). A standard of 30 ppm also can be expressed as follows:*

$$30 \text{ ppm} = \frac{30}{1,000,000} = \frac{3 \times 10}{10^6}$$

$$= 3 \times 10^{-5} = 0.000\,03 = 0.003\%$$

In Problems 63 and 64, express the given standard:

(A) *In scientific notation*

(B) *In standard decimal notation*

(C) *As a percent*

63. 9 ppm, the standard for carbon monoxide, when averaged over a period of 8 hours

64. 0.03 ppm, the standard for sulfur oxides, when averaged over a year

Social Sciences

65. Crime. In 1998, the United States had a violent crime rate of 566.4 per 100,000 people and a population of 270.3 million people. How many violent crimes occurred that year? Compute the answer using scientific notation and convert the answer to standard decimal form (to the nearest thousand).

66. Population density. The United States had a 1998 population of 270.3 million people and a land area of 3,539,000 square miles. What was the population density? Compute the answer using scientific notation and convert the answer to standard decimal form (to one decimal place).

Section A-6 | Rational Exponents and Radicals

➤ nth Roots of Real Numbers

➤ Rational Exponents and Radicals

➤ Properties of Radicals

Square roots may now be generalized to *nth roots*, and the meaning of exponent may be generalized to include all rational numbers.

➤ nth Roots of Real Numbers

Consider a square of side r with area 36 square inches. We can write

$$r^2 = 36$$

and conclude that side r is a number whose square is 36. We say that r is a **square root** of b if $r^2 = b$. Similarly, we say that r is a **cube root** of b if $r^3 = b$. And, in general,

---

DEFINITION   nth Root

For any natural number n,

r is an **nth root** of b if $r^n = b$

Thus, 4 is a square root of 16, since $4^2 = 16$, and -2 is a cube root of -8, since $(-2)^3 = -8$. Since $(-4)^2 = 16$, we see that -4 is also a square root of 16. It can be shown that any positive number has two real square roots, two real 4th roots, and, in general, two real nth roots if n is even. Negative numbers have no real square roots, no real 4th roots, and, in general, no real nth roots if n is even. The reason is that no real number raised to an even power can be negative. For odd roots the situation is simpler. Every real number has exactly one real cube root, one real 5th root, and, in general, one real nth root if n is odd.

Additional roots can be considered in the *complex number system.* But in this book we restrict our interest to *real roots of real numbers,* and "root" will always be interpreted to mean "real root."

➤ Rational Exponents and Radicals

We now turn to the question of what symbols to use to represent nth roots. For n a natural number greater than 1, we use

$$b^{1/n} \qquad \text{or} \qquad \sqrt[n]{b}$$

to represent a **real nth root of b.** The exponent form is motivated by the fact that $(b^{1/n})^n = b$ if exponent laws are to continue to hold for rational exponents. The other form is called an **nth root radical.** In the expression below, the symbol $\sqrt{}$ is called a **radical,** n is the **index** of the radical, and b is the **radicand:**

$$\text{Index} \longrightarrow \overset{\text{Radical}}{\sqrt[n]{b}}$$
$$\underset{\text{Radicand}}{\quad\quad}$$

When the index is 2, it is usually omitted. That is, when dealing with square roots, we simply use $\sqrt{b}$ rather than $\sqrt[2]{b}$ If there are two real nth roots, both $b^{1/n}$ and $\sqrt[n]{b}$ denote the positive root, called the **principal nth root.**

EXAMPLE 1   **Finding nth Roots**   Evaluate each of the following:

(A) $4^{1/2}$ and $\sqrt{4}$ (B) $-4^{1/2}$ and $-\sqrt{4}$ (C) $(-4)^{1/2}$ and $\sqrt{-4}$
(D) $8^{1/3}$ and $\sqrt[3]{28}$ (E) $(-8)^{1/3}$ and $\sqrt[3]{-8}$ (F) $-8^{1/3}$ and $-\sqrt[3]{8}$

Solution   (A) $4^{1/2} = \sqrt{4} = 2$ $(\sqrt{4} \neq \pm 2)$ (B) $-4^{1/2} = -\sqrt{4} = -2$
(C) $(-4)^{1/2}$ and $\sqrt{-4}$ are not real numbers
(D) $8^{1/3} = \sqrt[3]{8} = 2$ (E) $(-8)^{1/3} = \sqrt[3]{-8} = -2$
(F) $-8^{1/3} = -\sqrt[3]{8} = -2$

Matched Problem 1   Evaluate each of the following:

(A) $16^{1/2}$ (B) $-\sqrt{16}$ (C) $\sqrt[3]{-27}$ (D) $(-9)^{1/2}$ (E) $(\sqrt[4]{81})^3$

Common Error

The symbol $\sqrt{4}$ represents the single number 2, not ± 2. Do not confuse $\sqrt{4}$ with the solutions of the equation $x^2 = 4$, which are usually written in the form $x = \pm\sqrt{4} = \pm 2$.

We now define b^r for any rational number $r = m/n$.

DEFINITION   Rational Exponents

If m and n are natural numbers without common prime factors, b is a real number, and b is nonnegative when n is even, then

$$b^{m/n} = \begin{cases} (b^{1/n})^m = (\sqrt[n]{b})^m & 8^{2/3} = (8^{1/3})^2 = (\sqrt[3]{8})^2 = 2^2 = 4 \\ (b^m)^{1/n} = \sqrt[n]{b^m} & 8^{2/3} = (8^2)^{1/3} = \sqrt[3]{8^2} = \sqrt[3]{64} = 4 \end{cases}$$

and

$$b^{-m/n} = \frac{1}{b^{m/n}} \quad b \neq 0 \quad 8^{-2/3} = \frac{1}{8^{2/3}} = \frac{1}{4}$$

Note that the two definitions of $b^{m/n}$ are equivalent under the indicated restrictions on m, n, and b.

👁 **Insight**   All the properties for integer exponents listed in Theorem 1 in Section A-5 also hold for rational exponents, provided that b is nonnegative when n is even. This restriction on b is necessary to avoid nonreal results. For example,

$$(-4)^{3/2} = \sqrt{(-4)^3} = \sqrt{-64} \quad \text{Not a real number}$$

To avoid nonreal results, all variables in the remainder of this discussion represent positive real numbers.   ●

EXAMPLE 2   **From Rational Exponent Form to Radical Form and Vice Versa**
Change rational exponent form to radical form.

(A) $x^{1/7} = \sqrt[7]{x}$

(B) $(3u^2v^3)^{3/5} = \sqrt[5]{(3u^2v^3)^3}$ or $(\sqrt[5]{3u^2v^3})^3$ The first is usually preferred.

(C) $y^{-2/3} = \dfrac{1}{y^{2/3}} = \dfrac{1}{\sqrt[3]{y^2}}$ or $\sqrt[3]{y^{-2}}$ or $\sqrt[3]{\dfrac{1}{y^2}}$

Change radical form to rational exponent form.

(D) $\sqrt[5]{6} = 6^{1/5}$ (E) $-\sqrt[3]{x^2} = -x^{2/3}$

(F) $\sqrt{x^2 + y^2} = (x^2 + y^2)^{1/2}$ Note that $(x^2 + y^2)^{1/2} \neq x + y$. Why?   ■

Matched Problem 2   Convert to radical form.

(A) $u^{1/5}$ (B) $(6x^2y^5)^{2/9}$ (C) $(3xy)^{-3/5}$

Convert to rational exponent form.

(D) $\sqrt[4]{9u}$ (E) $-\sqrt[7]{(2x)^4}$ (F) $\sqrt[3]{x^3 + y^3}$

EXAMPLE 3   **Working with Rational Exponents**   Simplify each and express answers using positive exponents only. If rational exponents appear in final answers, convert to radical form.

(A) $(3x^{1/3})(2x^{1/2}) = 6x^{1/3+1/2} = 6x^{5/6} = 6\sqrt[6]{x^5}$.

(B) $(-8)^{5/3} = [(-8)^{1/3}]^5 = (-2)^5 = -32$

(C) $(2x^{1/3}y^{-2/3})^3 = 8xy^{-2} = \dfrac{8x}{y^2}$

(D) $\left(\dfrac{4x^{1/3}}{x^{1/2}}\right)^{1/2} = \dfrac{4^{1/2}x^{1/6}}{x^{1/4}} = \dfrac{2}{x^{1/4-1/6}} = \dfrac{2}{x^{1/12}} = \dfrac{2}{\sqrt[12]{x}}$

Matched Problem 3 Simplify each and express answers using positive exponents only. If rational exponents appear in final answers, convert to radical form.

(A) $9^{3/2}$ (B) $(-27)^{4/3}$ (C) $(5y^{1/4})(2y^{1/3})$ (D) $(2x^{-3/4}y^{1/4})^4$

(E) $\left(\dfrac{8x^{1/2}}{x^{2/3}}\right)^{1/3}$

EXPLORE & DISCUSS 1

In each of the following, evaluate both radical forms:

$$16^{3/2} = \sqrt{16^3} = (\sqrt{16})^3$$
$$27^{2/3} = \sqrt[3]{27^2} = (\sqrt[3]{27})^2$$

Which radical conversion form is easier to use if you are performing the calculations by hand?

EXAMPLE 4 **Working with Rational Exponents** Multiply, and express answers using positive exponents only.

(A) $3y^{2/3}(2y^{1/3} - y^2)$ (B) $(2u^{1/2} + v^{1/2})(u^{1/2} - 3v^{1/2})$

Solution (A) $3y^{2/3}(2y^{1/3} - y^2) = 6y^{2/3+1/3} - 3y^{2/3+2}$

$= 6y - 3y^{8/3}$

(B) $(2u^{1/2} + v^{1/2})(u^{1/2} - 3v^{1/2}) = 2u - 5u^{1/2}v^{1/2} - 3v$

Matched Problem 4 Multiply, and express answers using positive exponents only.

(A) $2c^{1/4}(5c^3 - c^{3/4})$ (B) $(7x^{1/2} - y^{1/2})(2x^{1/2} + 3y^{1/2})$

EXAMPLE 5 **Working with Rational Exponents** Write the following expression in the form $ax^p + bx^q$, where a and b are real numbers and p and q are rational numbers:

$$\dfrac{2\sqrt{x} - 3\sqrt[3]{x^2}}{2\sqrt[3]{x}}$$

Solution $\dfrac{2\sqrt{x} - 3\sqrt[3]{x^2}}{2\sqrt[3]{x}} = \dfrac{2x^{1/2} - 3x^{2/3}}{2x^{1/3}}$ *Change to rational exponent form.*

$= \dfrac{2x^{1/2}}{2x^{1/3}} - \dfrac{3x^{2/3}}{2x^{1/3}}$ *Separate into two fractions.*

$= x^{1/6} - 1.5x^{1/3}$

Matched Problem 5   Write the following expression in the form $ax^p + bx^q$, where a and b are real numbers and p and q are rational numbers:

$$\frac{5\sqrt[3]{x} - 4\sqrt{x}}{2\sqrt{x^3}}$$

➤ Properties of Radicals

Changing or simplifying radical expressions is aided by several properties of radicals that follow directly from the properties of exponents considered earlier.

THEOREM 1   Properties of Radicals

If c, n, and m are natural numbers greater than or equal to 2, and if x and y are positive real numbers, then

1. $\sqrt[n]{x^n} = x$ $\sqrt[3]{x^3} = x$
2. $\sqrt[n]{xy} = \sqrt[n]{x}\sqrt[n]{y}$ $\sqrt[5]{xy} = \sqrt[5]{x}\sqrt[5]{y}$.
3. $\sqrt[n]{\dfrac{x}{y}} = \dfrac{\sqrt[n]{x}}{\sqrt[n]{y}}$ $\sqrt[4]{\dfrac{x}{y}} = \dfrac{\sqrt[4]{x}}{\sqrt[4]{y}}$

EXAMPLE 6   **Applying Properties of Radicals**   Simplify using properties of radicals:

(A) $\sqrt[4]{(3x^4y^3)^4}$ (B) $\sqrt[4]{8}\sqrt[4]{2}$ (C) $\sqrt[3]{\dfrac{xy}{27}}$

Solution   (A) $\sqrt[4]{(3x^4y^3)^4} = 3x^4y^3$ Property 1

(B) $\sqrt[4]{8}\sqrt[4]{2} = \sqrt[4]{16} = \sqrt[4]{2^4} = 2$ Properties 2 and 1

(C) $\sqrt[3]{\dfrac{xy}{27}} = \dfrac{\sqrt[3]{xy}}{\sqrt[3]{27}} = \dfrac{\sqrt[3]{xy}}{3}$ or $\dfrac{1}{3}\sqrt[3]{xy}$ Properties 3 and 1

Matched Problem 6   Simplify using properties of radicals:

(A) $\sqrt[7]{(x^3 + y^3)^7}$ (B) $\sqrt[3]{8y^3}$ (C) $\dfrac{\sqrt[3]{16x^4y}}{\sqrt[3]{2xy}}$

 EXPLORE & DISCUSS 2   Multiply:

$$(\sqrt{a} - \sqrt{b})(\sqrt{a} + \sqrt{b})$$

How can this product be used to simplify radical forms?

   A question arises regarding the best form in which a radical expression should be left. There are many answers, depending on what use we wish to make of the expression. In deriving certain formulas, it is sometimes useful to clear either a denominator or a numerator of radicals. The process is referred to as **rationalizing** the denominator or numerator. Examples 7 and 8 illustrate the rationalizing process.

EXAMPLE 7   **Rationalizing Denominators**   Rationalize each denominator:

(A) $\dfrac{6x}{\sqrt{2x}}$ (B) $\dfrac{6}{\sqrt{7} - \sqrt{5}}$ (C) $\dfrac{x - 4}{\sqrt{x} + 2}$

Solution   (A) $\dfrac{6x}{\sqrt{2x}} = \dfrac{6x}{\sqrt{2x}} \cdot \dfrac{\sqrt{2x}}{\sqrt{2x}} = \dfrac{6x\sqrt{2x}}{2x} = 3\sqrt{2x}$

(B) $\dfrac{6}{\sqrt{7} - \sqrt{5}} = \dfrac{6}{\sqrt{7} - \sqrt{5}} \cdot \dfrac{\sqrt{7} + \sqrt{5}}{\sqrt{7} + \sqrt{5}}$

$= \dfrac{6(\sqrt{7} + \sqrt{5})}{2} = 3(\sqrt{7} + \sqrt{5})$

(C) $\dfrac{x - 4}{\sqrt{x} + 2} = \dfrac{x - 4}{\sqrt{x} + 2} \cdot \dfrac{\sqrt{x} - 2}{\sqrt{x} - 2}$

$= \dfrac{(x - 4)(\sqrt{x} - 2)}{x - 4} = \sqrt{x} - 2$ ■

Matched Problem 7   Rationalize each denominator:

(A) $\dfrac{12ab^2}{\sqrt{3ab}}$ (B) $\dfrac{9}{\sqrt{6} + \sqrt{3}}$ (C) $\dfrac{x^2 - y^2}{\sqrt{x} - \sqrt{y}}$ _____

EXAMPLE 8   **Rationalizing Numerators**   Rationalize each numerator:

(A) $\dfrac{\sqrt{2}}{2\sqrt{3}}$ (B) $\dfrac{3 + \sqrt{m}}{9 - m}$ (C) $\dfrac{\sqrt{2 + h} - \sqrt{2}}{h}$

Solution   (A) $\dfrac{\sqrt{2}}{2\sqrt{3}} = \dfrac{\sqrt{2}}{2\sqrt{3}} \cdot \dfrac{\sqrt{2}}{\sqrt{2}} = \dfrac{2}{2\sqrt{6}} = \dfrac{1}{\sqrt{6}}$

(B) $\dfrac{3 + \sqrt{m}}{9 - m} = \dfrac{3 + \sqrt{m}}{9 - m} \cdot \dfrac{3 - \sqrt{m}}{3 - \sqrt{m}} = \dfrac{9 - m}{(9 - m)(3 - \sqrt{m})} = \dfrac{1}{3 - \sqrt{m}}$

(C) $\dfrac{\sqrt{2 + h} - \sqrt{2}}{h} = \dfrac{\sqrt{2 + h} - \sqrt{2}}{h} \cdot \dfrac{\sqrt{2 + h} + \sqrt{2}}{\sqrt{2 + h} + \sqrt{2}}$

$= \dfrac{h}{h(\sqrt{2 + h} + \sqrt{2})} = \dfrac{1}{\sqrt{2 + h} + \sqrt{2}}$ ■

Matched Problem 8   Rationalize each numerator:

(A) $\dfrac{\sqrt{3}}{3\sqrt{2}}$ (B) $\dfrac{2 - \sqrt{n}}{4 - n}$ (C) $\dfrac{\sqrt{3 + h} - \sqrt{3}}{h}$ _____

Answers to Matched Problems   **1.** (A) 4   (B) −4   (C) −3
(D) Not a real number   (E) 27
2. (A) $\sqrt[5]{u}$ (B) $\sqrt[9]{(6x^2y^5)^2}$ or $(\sqrt[9]{6x^2y^5})^2$ (C) $1/\sqrt[5]{(3xy)^3}$
(D) $(9u)^{1/4}$ (E) $-(2x)^{4/7}$ (F) $(x^3 + y^3)^{1/3}$ (not $x + y$)
3. (A) 27   (B) 81   (C) $10y^{7/12} = 10\sqrt[12]{y^7}$ (D) $16y/x^3$
(E) $2/x^{1/18} = 2/\sqrt[18]{x}$

4. (A) $10c^{13/4} - 2c$ (B) $14x + 19x^{1/2}y^{1/2} - 3y$ 5. $2.5x^{-7/6} - 2x^{-1}$

6. (A) $x^3 + y^3$ (B) $2y$ (C) $2x$

7. (A) $4b\sqrt{3ab}$ (B) $3(\sqrt{6} - \sqrt{3})$ (C) $(x + y)(\sqrt{x} + \sqrt{y})$

8. (A) $\dfrac{1}{\sqrt{6}}$ (B) $\dfrac{1}{2 + \sqrt{n}}$ (C) $\dfrac{1}{\sqrt{3 + h} + \sqrt{3}}$

Exercise A-6

A *Change each expression in Problems 1–6 to radical form. Do not simplify.*

1. $6x^{3/5}$ 2. $7y^{2/5}$ 3. $(32x^2y^3)^{3/5}$

4. $(7x^2y)^{5/7}$ 5. $(x^2 + y^2)^{1/2}$ 6. $x^{1/2} + y^{1/2}$

Change each expression in Problems 7–12 to rational exponent form. Do not simplify.

7. $5\sqrt[4]{x^3}$ 8. $7m\sqrt[5]{n^2}$ 9. $\sqrt[5]{(2x^2y)^3}$

10. $\sqrt[7]{(8x^4y)^3}$ 11. $\sqrt[3]{x} + \sqrt[3]{y}$ 12. $\sqrt[3]{x^2 + y^3}$

In Problems 13–24, find rational number representations for each, if they exist.

13. $25^{1/2}$ 14. $64^{1/3}$ 15. $16^{3/2}$

16. $16^{3/4}$ 17. $-49^{1/2}$ 18. $(-49)^{1/2}$

19. $-64^{2/3}$ 20. $(-64)^{2/3}$ 21. $\left(\frac{4}{25}\right)^{3/2}$

22. $\left(\frac{8}{27}\right)^{2/3}$ 23. $9^{-3/2}$ 24. $8^{-2/3}$

In Problems 25–34, simplify each expression and write answers using positive exponents only. All variables represent positive real numbers.

25. $x^{4/5}x^{-2/5}$ 26. $y^{-3/7}y^{4/7}$ 27. $\dfrac{m^{2/3}}{m^{-1/3}}$

28. $\dfrac{x^{1/4}}{x^{3/4}}$ 29. $(8x^3y^{-6})^{1/3}$ 30. $(4u^{-2}v^4)^{1/2}$

31. $\left(\dfrac{4x^{-2}}{y^4}\right)^{-1/2}$ 32. $\left(\dfrac{w^4}{9x^{-2}}\right)^{-1/2}$ 33. $\dfrac{(8x)^{-1/3}}{12x^{1/4}}$

34. $\dfrac{6a^{3/4}}{15a^{-1/3}}$

Simplify each expression in Problems 35–40 using properties of radicals. All variables represent positive real numbers.

35. $\sqrt[5]{(2x + 3)^5}$ 36. $\sqrt[3]{(7 + 2y)^3}$

37. $\sqrt{6x}\sqrt{15x^3}\sqrt{30x^7}$ 38. $\sqrt[5]{16a^4}\sqrt[5]{4a^2}\sqrt[5]{8a^3}$

39. $\dfrac{\sqrt{6x}\sqrt{10}}{\sqrt{15x}}$ 40. $\dfrac{\sqrt{8}\sqrt{12y}}{\sqrt{6y}}$

B *In Problems 41–48, multiply, and express answers using positive exponents only.*

41. $3x^{3/4}(4x^{1/4} - 2x^8)$

42. $2m^{1/3}(3m^{2/3} - m^6)$

43. $(3u^{1/2} - v^{1/2})(u^{1/2} - 4v^{1/2})$

44. $(a^{1/2} + 2b^{1/2})(a^{1/2} - 3b^{1/2})$

45. $(6m^{1/2} + n^{-1/2})(6m - n^{-1/2})$

46. $(2x - 3y^{1/3})(2x^{1/3} + 1)$

47. $(3x^{1/2} - y^{1/2})^2$

48. $(x^{1/2} + 2y^{1/2})^2$

Write each expression in Problems 49–54 in the form $ax^p + bx^q$, where a and b are real numbers and p and q are rational numbers.

49. $\dfrac{\sqrt[3]{x^2} + 2}{2\sqrt[3]{x}}$ 50. $\dfrac{12\sqrt{x} - 3}{4\sqrt{x}}$

51. $\dfrac{2\sqrt[4]{x^3} + \sqrt[3]{x}}{3x}$ 52. $\dfrac{3\sqrt[3]{x^2} + \sqrt{x}}{5x}$

53. $\dfrac{2\sqrt[3]{x} - \sqrt{x}}{4\sqrt{x}}$ 54. $\dfrac{x^2 - 4\sqrt{x}}{2\sqrt[3]{x}}$

Rationalize the denominators in Problems 55–60.

55. $\dfrac{12mn^2}{\sqrt{3mn}}$ 56. $\dfrac{14x^2}{\sqrt{7x}}$ 57. $\dfrac{2(x + 3)}{\sqrt{x} - 2}$

58. $\dfrac{3(x + 1)}{\sqrt{x} + 4}$ 59. $\dfrac{7(x - y)^2}{\sqrt{x} - \sqrt{y}}$ 60. $\dfrac{3a - 3b}{\sqrt{a} + \sqrt{b}}$

Rationalize the numerators in Problems 61–66.

61. $\dfrac{\sqrt{5xy}}{5x^2y^2}$ 62. $\dfrac{\sqrt{3mn}}{3mn}$

63. $\dfrac{\sqrt{x + h} - \sqrt{x}}{h}$ 64. $\dfrac{\sqrt{2(a + h)} - \sqrt{2a}}{h}$

65. $\dfrac{\sqrt{t} - \sqrt{x}}{t^2 - x^2}$ 66. $\dfrac{\sqrt{x} - \sqrt{y}}{\sqrt{x} + \sqrt{y}}$

Problems 67–70 illustrate common errors involving rational exponents. In each case, find numerical examples that show that the left side is not always equal to the right side.

67. $(x + y)^{1/2} \neq x^{1/2} + y^{1/2}$

68. $(x^3 + y^3)^{1/3} \neq x + y$

69. $(x + y)^{1/3} \neq \dfrac{1}{(x + y)^3}$

70. $(x + y)^{-1/2} \neq \dfrac{1}{(x + y)^2}$

C *In Problems 71–82, discuss the validity of each statement. If the statement is true, explain why. If not, give a counterexample.*

71. $\sqrt{x^2} = x$ for all real numbers x

72. $\sqrt{x^2} = |x|$ for all real numbers x

73. $\sqrt[3]{x^3} = |x|$ for all real numbers x

74. $\sqrt[3]{x^3} = x$ for all real numbers x

75. If $r < 0$, then r has no cube roots.

76. If $r < 0$, then r has no square roots.

77. If $r > 0$, then r has two square roots.

78. If $r > 0$, then r has three cube roots.

79. The fourth roots of 100 are $\sqrt{10}$ and $-\sqrt{10}$.

80. The square roots of $2\sqrt{6} - 5$ are $\sqrt{3} - \sqrt{2}$ and $\sqrt{2} - \sqrt{3}$.

81. $\sqrt{355 - 60\sqrt{35}} = 5\sqrt{7} - 6\sqrt{5}$

82. $\sqrt[3]{7 - 5\sqrt{2}} = 1 - \sqrt{2}$

In Problems 83–88, simplify by writing each expression as a simple or single fraction reduced to lowest terms and without negative exponents.

83. $-\frac{1}{2}(x - 2)(x + 3)^{-3/2} + (x + 3)^{-1/2}$

84. $2(x - 2)^{-1/2} - \frac{1}{2}(2x + 3)(x - 2)^{-3/2}$

85. $\dfrac{(x - 1)^{1/2} - x(\frac{1}{2})(x - 1)^{-1/2}}{x - 1}$

86. $\dfrac{(2x - 1)^{1/2} - (x + 2)(\frac{1}{2})(2x - 1)^{-1/2}(2)}{2x - 1}$

87. $\dfrac{(x + 2)^{2/3} - x(\frac{2}{3})(x + 2)^{-1/3}}{(x + 2)^{4/3}}$

88. $\dfrac{2(3x - 1)^{1/3} - (2x + 1)(\frac{1}{3})(3x - 1)^{-2/3}(3)}{(3x - 1)^{2/3}}$

In Problems 89–94, evaluate using a calculator. (Refer to the instruction book for your calculator to see how exponential forms are evaluated.)

89. $22^{3/2}$ **90.** $15^{5/4}$ **91.** $827^{-3/8}$

92. $103^{-3/4}$ **93.** $37.09^{7/3}$ **94.** $2.876^{8/5}$

In Problems 95 and 96, evaluate each expression on a calculator and determine which pairs have the same value. Verify these results algebraically.

95. (A) $\sqrt{3} + \sqrt{5}$
   (B) $\sqrt{2 + \sqrt{3}} + \sqrt{2 - \sqrt{3}}$
   (C) $1 + \sqrt{3}$
   (D) $\sqrt[3]{10 + 6\sqrt{3}}$
   (E) $\sqrt{8 + \sqrt{60}}$
   (F) $\sqrt{6}$

96. (A) $2\sqrt[3]{2} + \sqrt{5}$
   (B) $\sqrt{8}$
   (C) $\sqrt{3} + \sqrt{7}$
   (D) $\sqrt{3 + \sqrt{8}} + \sqrt{3 - \sqrt{8}}$
   (E) $\sqrt{10 + \sqrt{84}}$
   (F) $1 + \sqrt{5}$

Section A-7 | Linear Equations and Inequalities in One Variable

- ➤ Linear Equations
- ➤ Linear Inequalities
- ➤ Applications

The equation

$$3 - 2(x + 3) = \frac{x}{3} - 5$$

and the inequality

$$\frac{x}{2} + 2(3x - 1) \geq 5$$

are both first degree in one variable. In general, a **first-degree, or linear, equation** in one variable is any equation that can be written in the form

Standard form: $ax + b = 0$ $a \neq 0$ (1)

If the equality symbol, $=$, in (1) is replaced by $<$, $>$, $\leq$, or $\geq$, the resulting expression is called a **first-degree, or linear, inequality**.

A **solution** of an equation (or inequality) involving a single variable is a number that when substituted for the variable makes the equation (or inequality) true. The set of all solutions is called the **solution set.** When we say that we **solve an equation** (or inequality), we mean that we find its solution set.

Knowing what is meant by the solution set is one thing; finding it is another. We start by recalling the idea of equivalent equations and equivalent inequalities. If we perform an operation on an equation (or inequality) that produces another equation (or inequality) with the same solution set, then the two equations (or inequalities) are said to be **equivalent.** The basic idea in solving equations and inequalities is to perform operations on these forms that produce simpler equivalent forms, and to continue the process until we obtain an equation or inequality with an obvious solution.

➤ Linear Equations

Linear equations are generally solved using the following equality properties:

THEOREM 1   Equality Properties

An equivalent equation will result if

1. The same quantity is added to or subtracted from each side of a given equation.
2. Each side of a given equation is multiplied by or divided by the same nonzero quantity.

Several examples should remind you of the process of solving equations.

EXAMPLE 1   **Solving a Linear Equation** Solve and check:

$$8x - 3(x - 4) = 3(x - 4) + 6$$

Solution

$$8x - 3(x - 4) = 3(x - 4) + 6$$
$$8x - 3x + 12 = 3x - 12 + 6$$
$$5x + 12 = 3x - 6$$
$$2x = -18$$
$$x = -9$$

Check

$$8x - 3(x - 4) = 3(x - 4) + 6$$
$$8(-9) - 3[(-9) - 4] \stackrel{?}{=} 3[(-9) - 4] + 6$$
$$-72 - 3(-13) \stackrel{?}{=} 3(-13) + 6$$
$$-33 \stackrel{?}{=} -33$$

■

Matched Problem 1   Solve and check: $3x - 2(2x - 5) = 2(x + 3) - 8$

EXPLORE & DISCUSS 1

According to equality property 2, multiplying both sides of an equation by a nonzero number always produces an equivalent equation. What is the smallest positive number that you could use to multiply both sides of the following equation to produce an equivalent equation without fractions?

$$\frac{x + 1}{3} - \frac{x}{4} = \frac{1}{2}$$

EXAMPLE 2   **Solving a Linear Equation**   Solve and check: $\dfrac{x + 2}{2} - \dfrac{x}{3} = 5$

Solution   What operations can we perform on

$$\frac{x + 2}{2} - \frac{x}{3} = 5$$

to eliminate the denominators? If we can find a number that is exactly divisible by each denominator, we can use the multiplication property of equality to clear the denominators. The LCD (least common denominator) of the fractions, 6, is exactly what we are looking for! Actually, any common denominator will do, but the LCD results in a simpler equivalent equation. Thus, we multiply both sides of the equation by 6:

$$6\left(\frac{x + 2}{2} - \frac{x}{3}\right) = 6 \cdot 5$$

$$\overset{3}{6} \cdot \frac{(x + 2)}{\underset{1}{2}} - \overset{2}{6} \cdot \frac{x}{\underset{1}{3}} = 30$$

$$3(x + 2) - 2x = 30$$
$$3x + 6 - 2x = 30$$
$$x = 24$$

Check

$$\frac{x + 2}{2} - \frac{x}{3} = 5$$

$$\frac{24 + 2}{2} - \frac{24}{3} \overset{?}{=} 5$$

$$13 - 8 \overset{?}{=} 5$$

$$5 \overset{\checkmark}{=} 5$$

Matched Problem 2   Solve and check: $\dfrac{x + 1}{3} - \dfrac{x}{4} = \dfrac{1}{2}$

In many applications of algebra, formulas or equations must be changed to alternative equivalent forms. The following examples are typical.

EXAMPLE 3   **Solving a Formula for a Particular Variable**   Solve the amount formula for simple interest, $A = P + Prt$, for

(A) r in terms of the other variables
(B) P in terms of the other variables

Solution   (A) $A = P + Prt$ *Reverse equation.*

$\qquad\quad P + Prt = A$ *Now isolate r on the left side.*

$\qquad\qquad\quad Prt = A - P$ *Divide both members by Pt.*

$$\qquad\qquad\quad r = \frac{A - P}{Pt}$$

(B) $A = P + Prt$ Reverse equation.

$P + Prt = A$ Factor out P (note the use of the distributive property).

$P(1 + rt) = A$ Divide by $(1 + rt)$.

$$P = \frac{A}{1 + rt}$$

Matched Problem 3   Solve $M = Nt + Nr$ for:

(A) t (B) N

➤ Linear Inequalities

Before we start solving linear inequalities, let us recall what we mean by $<$ (less than) and $>$ (greater than). If a and b are real numbers, we write

$$a < b \quad \text{a is less than b}$$

if there exists a positive number p such that $a + p = b$. Certainly, we would expect that if a positive number was added to any real number, the sum would be larger than the original. That is essentially what the definition states. If $a < b$, we may also write

$$b > a \quad \text{b is greater than a.}$$

EXAMPLE 4   Inequalities

(A) $3 < 5$ Since $3 + 2 = 5$

(B) $-6 < -2$ Since $-6 + 4 = -2$

(C) $0 > -10$ Since $-10 < 0$

Matched Problem 4   Replace each question mark with either $<$ or $>$.

(A) $2\,?\,8$ (B) $-20\,?\,0$ (C) $-3\,?\,-30$

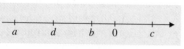

FIGURE 1 $a < b, c > d$

The inequality symbols have a very clear geometric interpretation on the real number line. If $a < b$, then a is to the left of b on the number line; if $c > d$, then c is to the right of d (Fig. 1). Check this geometric property with the inequalities in Example 4.

EXPLORE & DISCUSS 2

Replace ? with $<$ or $>$ in each of the following:

(A) $-1\,?\,3$ and $2(-1)\,?\,2(3)$

(B) $-1\,?\,3$ and $-2(-1)\,?\,-2(3)$

(C) $12\,?\,-8$ and $\dfrac{12}{4}\,?\,\dfrac{-8}{4}$

(D) $12\,?\,-8$ and $\dfrac{12}{-4}\,?\,\dfrac{-8}{-4}$

Based on these examples, describe verbally the effect of multiplying both sides of an inequality by a number.

Now let us turn to the problem of solving linear inequalities in one variable. Recall that a **solution** of an inequality involving one variable is a number that, when substituted for the variable, makes the inequality true. The set of all solutions is called the **solution set.** When we say that we **solve an inequality,** we mean that we find its solution set. The procedures used to solve linear inequalities in one variable are almost the same as those used to solve linear equations in one variable but with one important exception, as noted in property 3 below.

THEOREM 2   Inequality Properties

An equivalent inequality will result and the **sense or direction will remain the same** if each side of the original inequality

   1. Has the same real number added to or subtracted from it.
   2. Is multiplied or divided by the same positive number.

An equivalent inequality will result and the **sense or direction will reverse** if each side of the original inequality:

   3. Is multiplied or divided by the same negative number.

Note: Multiplication by 0 and division by 0 are not permitted.

Thus, we can perform essentially the same operations on inequalities that we perform on equations, with the exception that **the sense of the inequality reverses if we multiply or divide both sides by a negative number.** Otherwise, the sense of the inequality does not change. For example, if we start with the true statement

$$-3 > -7$$

and multiply both sides by 2, we obtain

$$-6 > -14$$

and the sense of the inequality stays the same. But if we multiply both sides of $-3 > -7$ by -2, the left side becomes 6 and the right side becomes 14, so we must write

$$6 < 14$$

to have a true statement. Thus, the sense of the inequality reverses.

If $a < b$, the double inequality $a < x < b$ means that $x > a$ **and** $x < b$; that is, x is between a and b. Other variations, as well as a useful **interval notation,** are given in Table 1 on page 686. Note that an endpoint on a line graph has a square bracket through it if it is included in the inequality and a parenthesis through it if it is not.

The following terminology is useful in connection with the interval notation of Table 1: If $a < b$, an interval of the form $[a, b]$, containing both endpoints, is a *closed interval;* an interval of the form (a, b), containing neither endpoint, is an *open interval;* and intervals of the form $(a, b]$ or $[a, b)$ are *half-open* and *half-closed.*

👁 *Insight*   The notation $(2, 7)$ has two common mathematical interpretations: the ordered pair with first coordinate 2 and second coordinate 7, and the open interval consisting of all real numbers between 2 and 7. The choice of interpretations is usually determined by the context in which the notation is used. The notation $(2, -7)$ also can be interpreted as an ordered pair, but not as an interval. In interval notation, it is always assumed that the left endpoint is less than the right endpoint. Thus, $(-7, 2)$ is correct interval notation, but $(2, -7)$ is not.   ●

TABLE 1

Interval Notation	Inequality Notation	Line Graph
$[a, b]$	$a \leq x \leq b$	
$[a, b)$	$a \leq x < b$	
$(a, b]$	$a < x \leq b$	
(a, b)	$a < x < b$	
$(-\infty, a]$	$x \leq a$	
$(-\infty, a)$	$x < a$	
$[b, \infty)$*	$x \geq b$	
(b, ∞)	$x > b$	

* The symbol ∞ (read "infinity") is not a number. When we write $[b, \infty)$, we are simply referring to the interval starting at b and continuing indefinitely to the right. We would never write $[b, \infty]$.

EXAMPLE 5   Interval and Inequality Notation, and Line Graphs

(A) Write $[-2, 3)$ as a double inequality and graph.

(B) Write $x \geq -5$ in interval notation and graph.

Solution   (A) $[-2, 3)$ is equivalent to $-2 \leq x < 3$.

(B) $x \geq -5$ is equivalent to $[-5, \infty)$.

Matched Problem 5

(A) Write $(-7, 4]$ as a double inequality and graph.

(B) Write $x < 3$ in interval notation and graph.

The solution to Example 5B shows the graph of the inequality $x \geq -5$. What is the graph of $x < -5$? What is the corresponding interval? Describe the relationship between these sets.

EXAMPLE 6   Solving a Linear Inequality   Solve and graph:

$$2(2x + 3) < 6(x - 2) + 10$$

Solution

$$2(2x + 3) < 6(x - 2) + 10$$
$$4x + 6 < 6x - 12 + 10$$
$$4x + 6 < 6x - 2$$
$$-2x + 6 < -2$$
$$-2x < -8$$
$$x > 4 \quad \text{or} \quad (4, \infty)$$ Notice that the sense of the inequality reverses when we divide both sides by -2.

Notice that in the graph of $x > 4$, we use a parenthesis through 4, since the point 4 is not included in the graph. ∎

Matched Problem 6   Solve and graph: $3(x - 1) \leq 5(x + 2) - 5$ ——————————

EXAMPLE 7   **Solving a Double Inequality**   Solve and graph: $-3 < 2x + 3 \leq 9$

Solution   We are looking for all numbers x such that $2x + 3$ is between -3 and 9, including 9 but not -3. We proceed as before except that we try to isolate x in the middle:

$$-3 < 2x + 3 \leq 9$$
$$-3 - 3 < 2x + 3 - 3 \leq 9 - 3$$
$$-6 < 2x \leq 6$$
$$\frac{-6}{2} < \frac{2x}{2} \leq \frac{6}{2}$$
$$-3 < x \leq 3 \quad \text{or} \quad (-3, 3]$$

∎

Matched Problem 7   Solve and graph: $-8 \leq 3x - 5 < 7$ ——————————

Note that a linear equation usually has exactly one solution, while a linear inequality usually has infinitely many solutions.

> **Applications**

To realize the full potential of algebra, we must be able to translate real-world problems into mathematical forms. In short, we must be able to do word problems.

The first example on the next page involves the important concept of **break-even analysis,** which is encountered in several places in this text. Any manufacturing company has **costs, C,** and **revenues, R.** The company will have a **loss** if $R < C$, will **break even** if $R = C$, and will have a **profit** if $R > C$. Costs involve **fixed costs,** such as plant overhead, product design, setup, and promotion; and **variable costs,** which are dependent on the number of items produced at a certain cost per item.

EXAMPLE 8   **Break-Even Analysis** A recording company produces compact disks (CDs). One-time fixed costs for a particular CD are $24,000, which includes costs such as recording, album design, and promotion. Variable costs amount to $6.20 per CD and include the manufacturing, distribution, and royalty costs for each disk actually manufactured and sold to a retailer. The CD is sold to retail outlets at $8.70 each. How many CDs must be manufactured and sold for the company to break even?

Solution   Let x = number of CDs manufactured and sold

C = cost of producing x CDs

R = revenue (return) on sales of x CDs

The company breaks even if $R = C$, with

$$C = \text{fixed costs} + \text{variable costs}$$
$$= \$24{,}000 + \$6.20x$$
$$R = \$8.70x$$

Find x such that $R = C$; that is, such that

$$8.7x = 24{,}000 + 6.2x$$
$$2.5x = 24{,}000$$
$$x = 9{,}600 \text{ CDs}$$

Check   For $x = 9{,}600$,

$$C = 24{,}000 + 6.2x \qquad\qquad R = 8.7x$$
$$= 24{,}000 + 6.2(9{,}600) \qquad\quad = 8.7(9{,}600)$$
$$= \$83{,}520 \qquad\qquad\qquad\quad = \$83{,}520$$

Matched Problem 8   What is the break-even point in Example 8 if fixed costs are $18,000, variable costs are $5.20 per CD, and the CDs are sold to retailers for $7.60 each?

Algebra has many different types of applications—so many, in fact, that no single approach applies to all. However, the following suggestions may help you get started:

PROCEDURE   Solving Word Problems

1. Read the problem very carefully.

2. Write down important facts and relationships.

3. Identify unknown quantities in terms of a single letter, if possible.

4. Write an equation (or inequality) relating the unknown quantities and the facts in the problem.

5. Solve the equation (or inequality).

6. Write all solutions requested in the original problem.

7. Check the solution(s) in the original problem.

EXAMPLE 9

Consumer Price Index The Consumer Price Index (CPI) is a measure of the average change in prices over time from a designated reference period, which equals 100. The index is based on prices of basic consumer goods and services, and is published at regular intervals by the Bureau of Labor Statistics. Table 2 lists the CPI for several years from 1960 to 2000. What net annual salary in 2000 would have the same purchasing power as a net annual salary of $13,000 in 1960? Compute the answer to the nearest dollar.

TABLE 2 CPI
(1982–1984 = 100)

Year	Index
1960	29.6
1970	38.8
1980	82.4
1990	130.7
2000	172.2

Solution To have the same purchasing power, the ratio of a salary in 2000 to a salary in 1960 would have to be the same as the ratio of the CPI in 2000 to the CPI in 1960. Thus, if x is the net annual salary in 2000, we solve the equation

$$\frac{x}{13,000} = \frac{172.2}{29.6}$$

$$x = 13,000 \cdot \frac{172.2}{29.6}$$

$$= \$75,628 \text{ per year}$$

Matched Problem 9

What net annual salary in 1970 would have had the same purchasing power as a net annual salary of $100,000 in 2000? Compute the answer to the nearest dollar.

Answers to Matched Problems

1. $x = 4$ **2.** $x = 2$ **3.** (A) $t = \dfrac{M - Nr}{N}$ (B) $N = \dfrac{M}{t + r}$

4. (A) $<$ (B) $<$ (C) $>$

5. (A) $-7 < x \leq 4$;   (B) $(-\infty, 3)$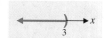

6. $x \geq -4$ or $[-4, \infty)$

7. $-1 \leq x < 4$ or $[-1, 4)$

8. 7,500 CD's   **9.** $22,532

Exercise A-7

A *Solve Problems 1–6.*

1. $2m + 9 = 5m - 6$ **2.** $3y - 4 = 6y - 19$

3. $2x + 3 < -4$ **4.** $5x + 2 > 1$

5. $-3x \geq -12$ **6.** $-4x \leq 8$

Solve Problems 7–10 and graph.

7. $-4x - 7 > 5$ **8.** $-2x + 8 < 4$

9. $2 \leq x + 3 \leq 5$ **10.** $-4 < 2y - 3 < 9$

Solve Problems 11–26.

11. $\dfrac{x}{3} - \dfrac{1}{2} = \dfrac{1}{3}$ **12.** $\dfrac{m}{5} - 2 = \dfrac{3}{5}$

13. $\dfrac{x}{3} > \dfrac{-5}{4}$ **14.** $\dfrac{y}{-2} \leq -1$

15. $\dfrac{y}{3} = 4 - \dfrac{y}{6}$ **16.** $\dfrac{x}{4} = 9 - \dfrac{x}{2}$

B

17. $10x + 25(x - 3) = 275$

18. $-3(4 - x) = 5 - (x + 1)$

19. $3 - y \leq 4(y - 3)$ **20.** $x - 2 \geq 2(x - 5)$

21. $\dfrac{x}{5} - \dfrac{x}{6} = \dfrac{6}{5}$ **22.** $\dfrac{y}{4} - \dfrac{y}{3} = \dfrac{1}{2}$

23. $\dfrac{m}{5} - 3 < \dfrac{3}{5} - \dfrac{m}{2}$ **24.** $\dfrac{u}{2} - \dfrac{2}{3} < \dfrac{u}{3} + 2$

25. $0.1(x - 7) + 0.05x = 0.8$

26. $0.03(2x + 1) - 0.05x = 12$

Solve Problems 27–30 and graph.

27. $2 \leq 3x - 7 < 14$

28. $-4 \leq 5x + 6 < 21$

29. $-4 \leq \frac{9}{5}C + 32 \leq 68$

30. $-1 \leq \frac{2}{3}t + 5 \leq 11$

C *Solve Problems 31–38 for the indicated variable.*

31. $3x - 4y = 12$;   for y

32. $y = -\frac{2}{3}x + 8$;   for x

33. $Ax + By = C$;   for $y (B \neq 0)$

34. $y = mx + b$;   for m

35. $F = \frac{9}{5}C + 32$;   for C

36. $C = \frac{5}{9}(F - 32)$;   for F

37. $A = \frac{2}{3}(Bm - Bn)$;   for B

38. $X = \frac{1}{5}(3CD - C)$;   for C

Solve Problems 39 and 40 and graph.

39. $-3 \leq 4 - 7x < 18$

40. $-10 \leq 8 - 3u \leq -6$

41. What can be said about the signs of the numbers a and b in each case?

(A) $ab > 0$ (B) $ab < 0$

(C) $\dfrac{a}{b} > 0$ (D) $\dfrac{a}{b} < 0$

42. What can be said about the signs of the numbers $a, b,$ and c in each case?

(A) $abc > 0$ (B) $\dfrac{ab}{c} < 0$

(C) $\dfrac{a}{bc} > 0$ (D) $\dfrac{a^2}{bc} < 0$

43. Replace each question mark with $<$ or $>$, as appropriate:

(A) If $a - b = 2$, then a ? b.

(B) If $c - d = -1$, then c ? d.

44. For what c and d is $c + d < c - d$?

45. If both a and b are positive numbers and b/a is greater than 1, then is $a - b$ positive or negative?

46. If both a and b are negative numbers and b/a is greater than 1, then is $a - b$ positive or negative?

In Problems 47–52, discuss the validity of each statement. If the statement is true, explain why. If not, give a counterexample.

47. If the intersection of two open intervals is nonempty, then their intersection is an open interval.

48. If the intersection of two closed intervals is non-empty, then their intersection is a closed interval.

49. The union of any two open intervals is an open interval.

50. The union of any two closed intervals is a closed interval.

51. If the intersection of two open intervals is nonempty, then their union is an open interval.

52. If the intersection of two closed intervals is nonempty, then their union is a closed interval.

Applications

Business & Economics

53. *Puzzle.* A jazz concert brought in $165,000 on the sale of 8,000 tickets. If the tickets sold for $15 and $25 each, how many of each type of ticket were sold?

54. *Puzzle.* An all-day parking meter takes only dimes and quarters. If it contains 100 coins with a total value of $14.50, how many of each type of coin are in the meter?

55. *Investing.* You have $12,000 to invest. If part is invested at 10% and the rest at 15%, how much should be invested at each rate to yield 12% on the total amount?

56. *Investing.* An investor has $20,000 to invest. If part is invested at 8% and the rest at 12%, how much should be invested at each rate to yield 11% on the total amount?

57. *Inflation.* If the price change of cars parallels the change in the CPI (see Table 2 in Example 9), what would a car sell for (to the nearest dollar) in 2000 if a comparable model sold for $5,000 in 1970?

58. *Inflation.* If the price change in houses parallels the CPI (see Table 2 in Example 9), what would a house valued at $200,000 in 2000 be valued at (to the nearest dollar) in 1960?

59. *Break-even analysis.* A publisher for a promising new novel figures fixed costs (overhead, advances, promotion, copy editing, typesetting, and so on) at $55,000, and variable costs (printing, paper, binding, shipping) at $1.60 for each book produced. If the book is sold to distributors for $11 each, what is the break-even point for the publisher?

60. *Break-even analysis.* The publisher of a new book called *Muscle-Powered Sports* figures fixed costs at

$92,000 and variable costs at $2.10 for each book produced. If the book is sold to distributors for $15 each, how many must be sold for the publisher to break even?

61. *Break-even analysis.* The publisher in Problem 59 finds that rising prices for paper increase the variable costs to $2.10 per book.

(A) Discuss possible strategies the company might use to deal with this increase in costs.

(B) If the company continues to sell the books for $11, how many books must they sell now to make a profit?

(C) If the company wants to start making a profit at the same production level as before the cost increase, how much should they sell the book for now?

62. *Break-even analysis.* The publisher in Problem 60 finds that rising prices for paper increase the variable costs to $2.70 per book.

(A) Discuss possible strategies the company might use to deal with this increase in costs.

(B) If the company continues to sell the books for $15, how many books must they sell now to make a profit?

(C) If the company wants to start making a profit at the same production level as before the cost increase, how much should they sell the book for now?

Life Sciences

63. *Wildlife management.* A naturalist for a fish and game department estimated the total number of rainbow trout in a certain lake using the popular capture–mark–recapture technique. He netted, marked, and released 200 rainbow trout. A week later, allowing for thorough mixing, he again netted 200 trout and found 8 marked ones among them. Assuming that the proportion of marked fish in the second sample was the same as the proportion of all marked fish in the total population, estimate the number of rainbow trout in the lake.

64. *Ecology.* If the temperature for a 24 hour period at an Antarctic station ranged between $-49°F$ and $14°F$ (that is, $-49 \leq F \leq 14$), what was the range in degrees Celsius? [*Note:* $F = \frac{9}{5}C + 32$.]

Social Sciences

65. *Psychology.* The IQ (intelligence quotient) is found by dividing the mental age (MA), as indicated on standard tests, by the chronological age (CA) and multiplying by 100. For example, if a child has a mental age of 12 and a chronological age of 8, the calculated IQ is 150. If a 9-year-old girl has an IQ of 140, compute her mental age.

66. *Anthropology.* In their study of genetic groupings, anthropologists use a ratio called the *cephalic index.* This is the ratio of the width of the head to its length (looking down from above) expressed as a percentage. Symbolically,

$$C = \frac{100W}{L}$$

where C is the cephalic index, W is the width, and L is the length. If an Indian tribe in Baja California (Mexico) had an average cephalic index of 66 and the average width of their heads was 6.6 inches, what was the average length of their heads?

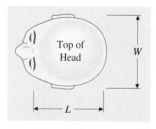

Figure for 66

Section **A-8** | Quadratic Equations

➤ Solution by Square Root
➤ Solution by Factoring
➤ Quadratic Formula
➤ Quadratic Formula and Factoring
➤ Application: Supply and Demand

In this section we consider equations involving second degree polynomials.

DEFINITION   Quadratic Equation

A **quadratic equation** in one variable is any equation that can be written in the form

$$ax^2 + bx + c = 0 \qquad a \neq 0 \quad \text{Standard form}$$

where x is a variable and a, b, and c are constants.

The equations

$$5x^2 - 3x + 7 = 0 \qquad \text{and} \qquad 18 = 32t^2 - 12t$$

are both quadratic equations, since they are either in the standard form or can be transformed into this form.

We restrict our review to finding real solutions to quadratic equations.

➤ Solution by Square Root

The easiest type of quadratic equation to solve is the special form where the first-degree term is missing:

$$ax^2 + c = 0 \qquad a \neq 0$$

The method of solution of this special form makes direct use of the square root property:

THEOREM 1   Square Root Property

If $a^2 = b$, then $a = \pm\sqrt{b}$.

Determine whether each of the following pairs of equations are equivalent. Explain.

(A) $x^2 = 4$ and $x = 2$

(B) $x^2 = 4$ and $x = -2$

(C) $x = \sqrt{4}$ and $x = 2$

(D) $x = \sqrt{4}$ and $x = -2$

(E) $x = -\sqrt{4}$ and $x = -2$

EXAMPLE 1   **Square Root Method**   Use the square root property to solve each equation.

(A) $x^2 - 7 = 0$ (B) $2x^2 - 10 = 0$ (C) $3x^2 + 27 = 0$

(D) $(x - 8)^2 = 9$

Solution   (A) $x^2 - 7 = 0$

$$x^2 = 7 \qquad \text{What real number squared is 7?}$$
$$x = \pm\sqrt{7} \quad \text{Short for } \sqrt{7} \text{ and } -\sqrt{7}$$

(B) $2x^2 - 10 = 0$

$$2x^2 = 10$$
$$x^2 = 5 \qquad \text{What real number squared is 5?}$$
$$x = \pm\sqrt{5}$$

(C) $3x^2 + 27 = 0$

$\qquad 3x^2 = -27$

$\qquad x^2 = -9$ *What real number squared is −9?*

No real solution, since no real number squared is negative.

(D) $(x - 8)^2 = 9$

$\qquad x - 8 = \pm\sqrt{9}$

$\qquad x - 8 = \pm 3$

$\qquad x = 8 \pm 3 = 5 \quad \text{or} \quad 11$ ■

Matched Problem 1   Use the square root property to solve each equation.

(A) $x^2 - 6 = 0$ (B) $3x^2 - 12 = 0$ (C) $x^2 + 4 = 0$

(D) $(x + 5)^2 = 1$

➤ Solution by Factoring

If the left side of a quadratic equation when written in standard form can be factored, the equation can be solved very quickly. The method of solution by factoring rests on a basic property of real numbers, first mentioned in Section A-1.

◉ Insight   Theorem 2 in Section A-1 states that if a and b are real numbers, then $ab = 0$ if and only if $a = 0$ or $b = 0$. To see that this property is useful for solving quadratic equations, consider the following:

$$x^2 - 4x + 3 = 0 \qquad (1)$$
$$(x - 1)(x - 3) = 0$$
$$x - 1 = 0 \quad \text{or} \quad x - 3 = 0$$
$$x = 1 \quad \text{or} \quad x = 3$$

You should check these solutions in equation (1).

If one side of the equation is not 0, then this method cannot be used. For example, consider

$$x^2 - 4x + 3 = 8 \qquad (2)$$
$$(x - 1)(x - 3) = 8$$
$$x - 1 \neq 8 \quad \text{or} \quad x - 3 \neq 8 \quad ab = 8 \text{ does not imply}$$
$$\qquad\qquad\qquad\qquad\qquad\qquad that\ a = 8\ or\ b = 8.$$
$$x = 9 \quad \text{or} \quad x = 11$$

Verify that neither $x = 9$ nor $x = 11$ is a solution for equation (2).   ●

EXAMPLE 2   **Factoring Method**   Solve by factoring using integer coefficients, if possible.

(A) $3x^2 - 6x - 24 = 0$ (B) $3y^2 = 2y$ (C) $x^2 - 2x - 1 = 0$

Solution   (A) $3x^2 - 6x - 24 = 0$ *Divide both sides by 3, since 3 is a factor of each coefficient.*

$\qquad x^2 - 2x - 8 = 0$ *Factor the left side, if possible.*

$\qquad (x - 4)(x + 2) = 0$

$\qquad x - 4 = 0 \quad \text{or} \quad x + 2 = 0$

$\qquad x = 4 \quad \text{or} \qquad x = -2$

(B) $\qquad 3y^2 = 2y$

$3y^2 - 2y = 0$ *We lose the solution y = 0 if both sides are divided*

$y(3y - 2) = 0$ *by y ($3y^2 = 2y$ and $3y = 2$ are not equivalent).*

$y = 0$ or $3y - 2 = 0$

$\qquad\qquad\qquad 3y = 2$

$\qquad\qquad\qquad y = \frac{2}{3}$

(C) $x^2 - 2x - 1 = 0$

This equation cannot be factored using integer coefficients. We will solve this type of equation by another method, considered below. ∎

Matched Problem 2 Solve by factoring using integer coefficients, if possible.

(A) $2x^2 + 4x - 30 = 0$

(B) $2x^2 = 3x$

(C) $2x^2 - 8x + 3 = 0$

Note that an equation such as $x^2 = 25$ can be solved by either the square root or the factoring method, and the results are the same (as they should be). Solve this equation both ways and compare.

Also, note that the factoring method can be extended to higher-degree polynomial equations. Consider the following:

$$x^3 - x = 0$$
$$x(x^2 - 1) = 0$$
$$x(x - 1)(x + 1) = 0$$
$$x = 0 \quad \text{or} \quad x - 1 = 0 \quad \text{or} \quad x + 1 = 0$$
$$\text{Solution:} \quad x = 0, 1, -1$$

Check these solutions in the original equation.

The factoring and square root methods are fast and easy to use when they apply. However, there are quadratic equations that look simple but cannot be solved by either method. For example, as was noted in Example 2C, the polynomial in

$$x^2 - 2x - 1 = 0$$

cannot be factored using integer coefficients. This brings us to the well-known and widely used *quadratic formula.*

➤ Quadratic Formula

There is a method called *completing the square* that will work for all quadratic equations. After briefly reviewing this method, we will then use it to develop the famous quadratic formula—a formula that will enable us to solve any quadratic equation quite mechanically.

EXPLORE & DISCUSS 2

Replace ? in each of the following with a number that makes the equation valid.

(A) $(x + 1)^2 = x^2 + 2x + ?$ (B) $(x + 2)^2 = x^2 + 4x + ?$

(C) $(x + 3)^2 = x^2 + 6x + ?$ (D) $(x + 4)^2 = x^2 + 8x + ?$

Replace ? in each of the following with a number that makes the trinomial a perfect square.

(E) $x^2 + 10x + $?   (F) $x^2 + 12x + $?   (G) $x^2 + bx + $?

The method of **completing the square** is based on the process of transforming a quadratic equation in standard form,

$$ax^2 + bx + c = 0$$

into the form

$$(x + A)^2 = B$$

where A and B are constants. Then, this last equation can be solved easily (if it has a real solution) by the square root method discussed above.

Consider the equation from Example 2C:

$$x^2 - 2x - 1 = 0 \tag{3}$$

Since the left side does not factor using integer coefficients, we add 1 to each side to remove the constant term from the left side:

$$x^2 - 2x = 1 \tag{4}$$

Now we try to find a number that we can add to each side to make the left side a square of a first-degree polynomial. Note the following square of a binomial:

$$(x + m)^2 = x^2 + 2mx + m^2$$

We see that the third term on the right is the square of one-half the coefficient of x in the second term on the right. To complete the square in equation (4), we add the square of one-half the coefficient of x, $(-\frac{2}{2})^2 = 1$, to each side. (This rule works only when the coefficient of x^2 is 1, that is, $a = 1$.) Thus,

$$x^2 - 2x + \mathbf{1} = 1 + \mathbf{1}$$

The left side is the square of $x - 1$, and we write

$$(x - 1)^2 = 2$$

What number squared is 2?

$$x - 1 = \pm\sqrt{2}$$
$$x = 1 \pm \sqrt{2}$$

And equation (3) is solved!

Let us try the method on the general quadratic equation

$$ax^2 + bx + c = 0 \qquad a \neq 0 \tag{5}$$

and solve it once and for all for x in terms of the coefficients a, b, and c. We start by multiplying both sides of equation (5) by $1/a$ to obtain

$$x^2 + \frac{b}{a}x + \frac{c}{a} = 0$$

Add $-c/a$ to both sides:

$$x^2 + \frac{b}{a}x = -\frac{c}{a}$$

Now we complete the square on the left side by adding the square of one-half the coefficient of x, that is, $(b/2a)^2 = b^2/4a^2$, to each side:

$$x^2 + \frac{b}{a}x + \frac{b^2}{4a^2} = \frac{b^2}{4a^2} - \frac{c}{a}$$

Writing the left side as a square and combining the right side into a single fraction, we obtain

$$\left(x + \frac{b}{2a}\right)^2 = \frac{b^2 - 4ac}{4a^2}$$

Now we solve by the square root method:

$$x + \frac{b}{2a} = \pm\sqrt{\frac{b^2 - 4ac}{4a^2}}$$

$$x = -\frac{b}{2a} \pm \frac{\sqrt{b^2 - 4ac}}{2a}$$ Since $\pm\sqrt{4a^2} = \pm 2a$ for any real number a

When this is written as a single fraction, it becomes the **quadratic formula:**

FORMULA Quadratic Formula

If $ax^2 + bx + c = 0, a \neq 0$, then

$$x = \frac{-b \pm \sqrt{b^2 - 4ac}}{2a}$$

TABLE 1	
$b^2 - 4ac$	$ax^2 + bx + c = 0$
Positive	Two real solutions
Zero	One real solution
Negative	No real solutions

This formula is generally used to solve quadratic equations when the square root or factoring methods do not work. The quantity $b^2 - 4ac$ under the radical is called the **discriminant,** and it gives us the useful information about solutions listed in Table 1.

EXAMPLE 3 **Quadratic Formula Method** Solve $x^2 - 2x - 1 = 0$ using the quadratic formula.

Solution

$$x^2 - 2x - 1 = 0$$

$$x = \frac{-b \pm \sqrt{b^2 - 4ac}}{2a}$$ $a = 1, b = -2, c = -1$

$$= \frac{-(-2) \pm \sqrt{(-2)^2 - 4(1)(-1)}}{2(1)}$$

$$= \frac{2 \pm \sqrt{8}}{2} = \frac{2 \pm 2\sqrt{2}}{2} = 1 \pm \sqrt{2} \approx -0.414 \quad \text{or} \quad 2.414$$

Check $x^2 - 2x - 1 = 0$

When $x = 1 + \sqrt{2}$,

$$(1 + \sqrt{2})^2 - 2(1 + \sqrt{2}) - 1 = 1 + 2\sqrt{2} + 2 - 2 - 2\sqrt{2} - 1 = 0$$

When $x = 1 - \sqrt{2}$,

$$(1 - \sqrt{2})^2 - 2(1 - \sqrt{2}) - 1 = 1 - 2\sqrt{2} + 2 - 2 + 2\sqrt{2} - 1 = 0$$ ■

Matched Problem 3 Solve $2x^2 - 4x - 3 = 0$ using the quadratic formula.

If we try to solve $x^2 - 6x + 11 = 0$ using the quadratic formula, we obtain

$$x = \frac{6 \pm \sqrt{-8}}{2}$$

which is not a real number. (Why?)

➤ Quadratic Formula and Factoring

As in Section A-3, we restrict our interest in factoring to polynomials with integer coefficients. If a polynomial cannot be factored as a product of lower-degree polynomials with integer coefficients, we say that the polynomial is **not factorable in the integers.**

☺ Insight   Suppose you were asked to apply the *ac* test discussed in Section A-3 to the following polynomial:

$$x^2 - 13x - 2,310 \tag{6}$$

Your first step would be to construct a table listing the 26 factor pairs for 2,310—a tedious process at best. Fortunately, there is a better way. The quadratic formula provides a simple and efficient method of factoring a second-degree polynomial with integer coefficients as the product of two first-degree polynomials with integer coefficients, if such factors exist.   ●

We illustrate the method using polynomial (6), and generalize the process from this experience. We start by solving the corresponding quadratic equation using the quadratic formula:

$$x^2 - 13x - 2,310 = 0$$

$$x = \frac{-(-13) \pm \sqrt{(-13)^2 - 4(1)(-2,310)}}{2}$$

$$x = \frac{-(-13) \pm \sqrt{9,409}}{2}$$

$$= \frac{13 \pm 97}{2} = 55 \quad \text{or} \quad -42$$

Now we write

$$x^2 - 13x - 2,310 = [x - 55][x - (-42)] = (x - 55)(x + 42)$$

Multiplying the two factors on the right produces the second-degree polynomial on the left.

What is behind this procedure? The following two theorems justify and generalize the process:

THEOREM 2   Factorability Theorem

A second-degree polynomial, $ax^2 + bx + c$, with integer coefficients can be expressed as the product of two first-degree polynomials with integer coefficients if and only if $\sqrt{b^2 - 4ac}$ is an integer.

THEOREM 3   Factor Theorem

If r_1 and r_2 are solutions to the second-degree equation $ax^2 + bx + c = 0$, then

$$ax^2 + bx + c = a(x - r_1)(x - r_2)$$

EXAMPLE 4   **Factoring with the Aid of the Discriminant**   Factor, if possible, using integer coefficients:

(A) $4x^2 - 65x + 264$ (B) $2x^2 - 33x - 306$

Solution   (A) $4x^2 - 65x + 264$

Step 1. Test for factorability:

$$\sqrt{b^2 - 4ac} = \sqrt{(-65)^2 - 4(4)(264)} = 1$$

Since the result is an integer, the polynomial has first-degree factors with integer coefficients.

Step 2. Factor, using the factor theorem. Find the solutions to the corresponding quadratic equation using the quadratic formula:

$$4x^2 - 65x + 264 = 0 \underset{\text{From step 1}}{}$$

$$x = \frac{-(-65) \pm 1}{2 \cdot 4} = \frac{33}{4} \quad \text{or} \quad 8$$

Thus,

$$4x^2 - 65x + 264 = 4\left(x - \frac{33}{4}\right)(x - 8)$$
$$= (4x - 33)(x - 8)$$

(B) $2x^2 - 33x - 306$

Step 1. Test for factorability:

$$\sqrt{b^2 - 4ac} = \sqrt{(-33)^2 - 4(2)(-306)} = \sqrt{3,537}$$

Since $\sqrt{3,537}$ is not an integer, the polynomial is not factorable in the integers.   ∎

Matched
Problem 4   Factor, if possible, using integer coefficients:

(A) $3x^2 - 28x - 464$ (B) $9x^2 + 320x - 144$

➤ **Application: Supply and Demand**

Supply and demand analysis is a very important part of business and economics. In general, producers are willing to supply more of an item as the price of an item increases, and less of an item as the price decreases. Similarly, buyers are willing to buy less of an item as the price increases, and more of an item as the price decreases. Thus, we have a dynamic situation where the price, supply, and demand fluctuate until a price is reached at which the supply is equal to the demand. In economic theory, this point is called the **equilibrium point**—if the price increases from this point, the supply will increase and the demand will decrease; if the price decreases from this point, the supply will decrease and the demand will increase.

EXAMPLE 5

Supply and Demand At a large beach resort in the summer, the weekly supply and demand equations for folding beach chairs are

$$p = \frac{x}{140} + \frac{3}{4} \quad \textit{Supply equation}$$

$$p = \frac{5,670}{x} \quad \textit{Demand equation}$$

The supply equation indicates that the supplier is willing to sell x units at a price of p dollars per unit. The demand equation indicates that consumers are willing to buy x units at a price of p dollars per unit. How many units are required for supply to equal demand? At what price will supply equal demand?

Solution Set the right side of the supply equation equal to the right side of the demand equation and solve for x:

$$\frac{x}{140} + \frac{3}{4} = \frac{5,670}{x} \quad \textit{Multiply by 140x, the LCD.}$$

$$x^2 + 105x = 793,800 \quad \textit{Write in standard form.}$$

$$x^2 + 105x - 793,800 = 0 \quad \textit{Use the quadratic formula.}$$

$$x = \frac{-105 \pm \sqrt{105^2 - 4(1)(-793,800)}}{2}$$

$$x = 840 \text{ units}$$

The negative root is discarded, since a negative number of units cannot be produced or sold. Substitute $x = 840$ back into either the supply equation or the demand equation to find the equilibrium price (we use the demand equation):

$$p = \frac{5,670}{x} = \frac{5,670}{840} = \$6.75$$

Thus, at a price of $6.75 the supplier is willing to supply 840 chairs and consumers are willing to buy 840 chairs during a week. ■

Matched Problem 5

Repeat Example 5 if near the end of summer the supply and demand equations are

$$p = \frac{x}{80} - \frac{1}{20} \quad \textit{Supply equation}$$

$$p = \frac{1,264}{x} \quad \textit{Demand equation}$$

Answers to Matched Problems

1. (A) $\pm\sqrt{6}$ (B) ±2 (C) No real solution   (D) $-6, -4$
2. (A) $-5, 3$ (B) $0, \frac{3}{2}$ (C) Cannot be factored using integer coefficients
3. $(2 \pm \sqrt{10})/2$
4. (A) Cannot be factored using integer coefficients   (B) $(9x - 4)(x + 36)$
5. 320 chairs at $3.95 each

Exercise A-8

Find only real solutions in the problems below. If there are no real solutions, say so.

A *Solve Problems 1–4 by the square root method.*

1. $2x^2 - 22 = 0$ **2.** $3m^2 - 21 = 0$

3. $(3x - 1)^2 = 25$ **4.** $(2x + 1)^2 = 16$

Solve Problems 5–8 by factoring.

5. $2u^2 - 8u - 24 = 0$ **6.** $3x^2 - 18x + 15 = 0$

7. $x^2 = 2x$ **8.** $n^2 = 3n$

Solve Problems 9–12 by using the quadratic formula.

9. $x^2 - 6x - 3 = 0$ **10.** $m^2 + 8m + 3 = 0$

11. $3u^2 + 12u + 6 = 0$ **12.** $2x^2 - 20x - 6 = 0$

B *Solve Problems 13–30 by using any method.*

13. $\dfrac{2x^2}{3} = 5x$ **14.** $x^2 = -\dfrac{3}{4}x$

15. $4u^2 - 9 = 0$ **16.** $9y^2 - 25 = 0$

17. $8x^2 + 20x = 12$ **18.** $9x^2 - 6 = 15x$

19. $x^2 = 1 - x$ **20.** $m^2 = 1 - 3m$

21. $2x^2 = 6x - 3$ **22.** $2x^2 = 4x - 1$

23. $y^2 - 4y = -8$ **24.** $x^2 - 2x = -3$

25. $(2x + 3)^2 = 11$ **26.** $(5x - 2)^2 = 7$

27. $\dfrac{3}{p} = p$ **28.** $x - \dfrac{7}{x} = 0$

29. $2 - \dfrac{2}{m^2} = \dfrac{3}{m}$ **30.** $2 + \dfrac{5}{u} = \dfrac{3}{u^2}$

In Problems 31–38, factor, if possible, as the product of two first-degree polynomials with integer coefficients. Use the quadratic formula and the factor theorem.

31. $x^2 + 40x - 84$

32. $x^2 - 28x - 128$

33. $x^2 - 32x + 144$

34. $x^2 + 52x + 208$

35. $2x^2 + 15x - 108$

36. $3x^2 - 32x - 140$

37. $4x^2 + 241x - 434$

38. $6x^2 - 427x - 360$

C

39. Solve $A = P(1 + r)^2$ for r in terms of A and P; that is, isolate r on the left side of the equation (with coefficient 1) and end up with an algebraic expression on the right side involving A and P but not r. Write the answer using positive square roots only.

40. Solve $x^2 + 3mx - 3n = 0$ for x in terms of m and n.

41. Consider the quadratic equation

$$x^2 + 4x + c = 0$$

where c is a real number. Discuss the relationship between the values of c and the three types of roots listed in Table 1.

42. Consider the quadratic equation

$$x^2 - 2x + c = 0$$

where c is a real number. Discuss the relationship between the values of c and the three types of roots listed in Table 1.

Applications

Business & Economics

43. *Supply and demand.* A company wholesales a certain brand of shampoo in a particular city. Their marketing research department established the following weekly supply and demand equations:

$$p = \frac{x}{450} + \frac{1}{2} \quad \text{Supply equation}$$

$$p = \frac{6{,}300}{x} \quad \text{Demand equation}$$

How many units are required for supply to equal demand? At what price per bottle will supply equal demand?

44. *Supply and demand.* An importer sells a certain brand of automatic camera to outlets in a large metropolitan area. During the summer, the weekly supply and demand equations are

$$p = \frac{x}{6} + 9 \quad \text{Supply equation}$$

$$p = \frac{24{,}840}{x} \quad \text{Demand equation}$$

How many units are required for supply to equal demand? At what price will supply equal demand?

45. *Interest rate.* If P dollars are invested at $100r$ percent compounded annually, at the end of 2 years it will grow to $A = P(1 + r)^2$. At what interest rate will \$484 grow to \$625 in 2 years? [*Note:* If $A = 625$ and $P = 484$ find r.]

46. *Interest rate.* Using the formula in Problem 45, determine the interest rate that will make \$1,000 grow to \$1,210 in 2 years.

Life Sciences

47. *Ecology.* An important element in the erosive force of moving water is its velocity. To measure the velocity v (in feet per second) of a stream, we position a hollow L-shaped tube with one end under the water pointing upstream and the other end pointing straight up a couple of feet out of the water. The water will then be pushed up the tube a certain distance h (in feet) above the surface of the stream. Physicists have shown that $v^2 = 64h$. Approximately how fast is a stream flowing if $h = 1$ foot? If $h = 0.5$ foot?

Social Sciences

48. *Safety research.* It is of considerable importance to know the least number of feet d in which a car can be stopped, including reaction time of the driver, at various speeds v (in miles per hour). Safety research has produced the formula $d = 0.044v^2 + 1.1v$. If it took a car 550 feet to stop, estimate the car's speed at the moment the stopping process was started.

APPENDIX B

SPECIAL TOPICS

Section **B-1** | Sequences, Series, and Summation Notation

➤ Sequences
➤ Series and Summation Notation

If someone asked you to list all natural numbers that are perfect squares, you might begin by writing

$$1, 4, 9, 16, 25, 36$$

But you would soon realize that it is impossible to actually list all the perfect squares, since there are an infinite number of them. However, you could represent this collection of numbers in several different ways. One common method is to write

$$1, 4, 9, \ldots, n^2, \ldots \qquad n \in N$$

where N is the set of natural numbers. A list of numbers such as this is generally called a *sequence*. Sequences and related topics form the subject matter of this section.

➤ Sequences

Consider the function f given by

$$f(n) = 2n + 1 \tag{1}$$

where the domain of f is the set of natural numbers N. Note that

$$f(1) = 3, \quad f(2) = 5, \quad f(3) = 7, \quad \ldots$$

The function f is an example of a sequence. In general, a **sequence** is a function with domain a set of successive integers. Instead of the standard function notation used in equation (1), sequences are usually defined in terms of a special notation.

The range value $f(n)$ is usually symbolized more compactly with a symbol such as a_n. Thus, in place of equation (1), we write

$$a_n = 2n + 1$$

and the domain is understood to be the set of natural numbers unless something is said to the contrary or the context indicates otherwise. The elements in the range are called **terms of the sequence;** a_1 is the first term, a_2 is the second term, and a_n is the **nth term,** or **general term.**

$$a_1 = 2(1) + 1 = 3 \quad \text{First term}$$
$$a_2 = 2(2) + 1 = 5 \quad \text{Second term}$$
$$a_3 = 2(3) + 1 = 7 \quad \text{Third term}$$
$$\vdots$$
$$a_n = 2n + 1 \qquad \text{General term}$$

The ordered list of elements

$$3, 5, 7, \ldots, 2n + 1, \ldots$$

obtained by writing the terms of the sequence in their natural order with respect to the domain values is often informally referred to as a sequence. A sequence also may be represented in the abbreviated form $\{a_n\}$, where a symbol for the nth term is written within braces. For example, we could refer to the sequence $3, 5, 7, \ldots, 2n + 1, \ldots$ as the sequence $\{2n + 1\}$.

If the domain of a sequence is a finite set of successive integers, then the sequence is called a **finite sequence.** If the domain is an infinite set of successive integers, then the sequence is called an **infinite sequence.** The sequence $\{2n + 1\}$ discussed above is an infinite sequence.

EXAMPLE 1   **Writing the Terms of a Sequence** Write the first four terms of each sequence:

(A) $a_n = 3n - 2$ (B) $\left\{ \dfrac{(-1)^n}{n} \right\}$

Solution   (A) $1, 4, 7, 10$ (B) $-1, \dfrac{1}{2}, \dfrac{-1}{3}, \dfrac{1}{4}$

Matched Problem 1   Write the first four terms of each sequence:

(A) $a_n = -n + 3$ (B) $\left\{ \dfrac{(-1)^n}{2^n} \right\}$

EXPLORE & DISCUSS 1

(A) A multiple-choice test question asked for the next term in the sequence

$$2, 4, 8, \ldots$$

and gave the following choices:

(1) 16   (2) 14   (3) $\frac{25}{2}$

Which is the correct answer?

(B) Compare the first four terms of the following sequences:

(1) $a_n = 2^2$ (2) $b_n = n^2 - n + 2$ (3) $c_n = 5n + \dfrac{6}{n} - 9$

Now, which of the choices in part (A) appears to be correct?

Now that we have seen how to use the general term to find the first few terms in a sequence, we consider the reverse problem. That is, can a sequence be defined just by listing the first three or four terms of the sequence? And can we then use these initial terms to find a formula for the nth term? In general, without other information, the answer to the first question is no. As Explore–Discuss 1 illustrates, many different sequences may start off with the same terms. Simply listing the first three terms (or any other finite number of terms) does not specify a particular sequence. In fact, it can be shown that given any list of m numbers, there are an infinite number of sequences whose first m terms agree with these given numbers.

What about the second question? That is, given a few terms, can we find the general formula for at least one sequence whose first few terms agree with the given terms? The answer to this question is a qualified yes. If we can observe a simple pattern in the given terms, we usually can construct a general term that will produce that pattern. The next example illustrates this approach.

EXAMPLE 2   **Finding the General Term of a Sequence** Find the general term of a sequence whose first four terms are

(A) $3, 4, 5, 6, \ldots$ (B) $5, -25, 125, -625, \ldots$

Solution   (A) Since these terms are consecutive integers, one solution is $a_n = n, n \geq 3$. If we want the domain of the sequence to be all natural numbers, another solution is $b_n = n + 2$.

(B) Each of these terms can be written as the product of a power of 5 and a power of -1:

$$5 = (-1)^0 5^1 = a_1$$
$$-25 = (-1)^1 5^2 = a_2$$
$$125 = (-1)^2 5^3 = a_3$$
$$-625 = (-1)^3 5^4 = a_4$$

If we choose the domain to be all natural numbers, a solution is

$$a_n = (-1)^{n-1} 5^n$$

Matched Problem 2   Find the general term of a sequence whose first four terms are

(A) $3, 6, 9, 12, \ldots$ (B) $1, -2, 4, -8, \ldots$

In general, there is usually more than one way of representing the nth term of a given sequence (see the solution of Example 2A). However, unless something is stated to the contrary, we assume that the domain of the sequence is the set of natural numbers N.

➤ **Series and Summation Notation**

If $a_1, a_2, a_3, \ldots, a_n, \ldots$ is a sequence, the expression

$$a_1 + a_2 + a_3 + \cdots + a_n + \cdots$$

is called a **series**. If the sequence is finite, the corresponding series is a **finite series**. If the sequence is infinite, the corresponding series is an **infinite series**.

We consider only finite series in this section. For example,

$$1, 3, 5, 7, 9 \qquad \text{Finite sequence}$$
$$1 + 3 + 5 + 7 + 9 \quad \text{Finite series}$$

Notice that we can easily evaluate this series by adding the five terms:

$$1 + 3 + 5 + 7 + 9 = 25$$

Series are often represented in a compact form called **summation notation.** Consider the following examples:

$$\sum_{k=3}^{6} k^2 = 3^2 + 4^2 + 5^2 + 6^2$$
$$= 9 + 16 + 25 + 36 = 86$$

$$\sum_{k=0}^{2} (4k + 1) = (4 \cdot 0 + 1) + (4 \cdot 1 + 1) + (4 \cdot 2 + 1)$$
$$= 1 + 5 + 9 = 15$$

In each case, the terms of the series on the right are obtained from the expression on the left by successively replacing the **summing index k** with integers, starting with the number indicated below the **summation sign Σ** and ending with the number that appears above Σ. The summing index may be represented by letters other than k and may start at any integer and end at any integer greater than or equal to the starting integer. Thus, if we are given the finite sequence

$$\frac{1}{2}, \frac{1}{4}, \frac{1}{8}, \dots, \frac{1}{2^n}$$

the corresponding series is

$$\frac{1}{2} + \frac{1}{4} + \frac{1}{8} + \dots + \frac{1}{2^n} = \sum_{j=1}^{n} \frac{1}{2^j}$$

where we have used j for the summing index.

EXAMPLE 3   **Summation Notation** Write

$$\sum_{k=1}^{5} \frac{k}{k^2 + 1}$$

without summation notation. Do not evaluate the sum.

Solution
$$\sum_{k=1}^{5} \frac{k}{k^2 + 1} = \frac{1}{1^2 + 1} + \frac{2}{2^2 + 1} + \frac{3}{3^2 + 1} + \frac{4}{4^2 + 1} + \frac{5}{5^2 + 1}$$
$$= \frac{1}{2} + \frac{2}{5} + \frac{3}{10} + \frac{4}{17} + \frac{5}{26}$$

Matched Problem 3   Write

$$\sum_{k=1}^{5} \frac{k + 1}{k}$$

without summation notation. Do not evaluate the sum.

EXPLORE &DISCUSS 2

(A) Find the smallest value of n for which the value of the series

$$\sum_{k=1}^{n} \frac{k}{k^2 + 1}$$

is greater than 3.

(B) Find the smallest value of n for which the value of the series

$$\sum_{j=1}^{n} \frac{1}{2^j}$$

is greater than 0.99. Greater than 0.999.

If the terms of a series are alternately positive and negative, we call the series an **alternating series.** The next example deals with the representation of such a series.

EXAMPLE 4   **Summation Notation** Write the alternating series

$$\frac{1}{2} - \frac{1}{4} + \frac{1}{6} - \frac{1}{8} + \frac{1}{10} - \frac{1}{12}$$

using summation notation with

(A) The summing index k starting at 1
(B) The summing index j starting at 0

Solution   (A) $(-1)^{k+1}$ provides the alternation of sign, and $1/(2k)$ provides the other part of each term. Thus, we can write

$$\frac{1}{2} - \frac{1}{4} + \frac{1}{6} - \frac{1}{8} + \frac{1}{10} - \frac{1}{12} = \sum_{k=1}^{6} \frac{(-1)^{k+1}}{2k}$$

(B) $(-1)^j$ provides the alternation of sign, and $1/[2(j + 1)]$ provides the other part of each term. Thus, we can write

$$\frac{1}{2} - \frac{1}{4} + \frac{1}{6} - \frac{1}{8} + \frac{1}{10} - \frac{1}{12} = \sum_{j=0}^{5} \frac{(-1)^j}{2(j + 1)}$$

Matched Problem 4   Write the alternating series

$$1 - \frac{1}{3} + \frac{1}{9} - \frac{1}{27} + \frac{1}{81}$$

using summation notation with

(A) The summing index k starting at 1
(B) The summing index j starting at 0

Summation notation provides a compact notation for the sum of any list of numbers, even if the numbers are not generated by a formula. For example, suppose that the results of an examination taken by a class of 10 students are given in the following list:

$$87, 77, 95, 83, 86, 73, 95, 68, 75, 86$$

If we let $a_1, a_2, a_3, \ldots, a_{10}$ represent these 10 scores, the average test score is given by

$$\frac{1}{10} \sum_{k=1}^{10} a_k = \frac{1}{10}(87 + 77 + 95 + 83 + 86 + 73 + 95 + 68 + 75 + 86)$$

$$= \frac{1}{10}(825) = 82.5$$

More generally, in statistics, the **arithmetic mean** $\bar{a}$ of a list of n numbers $a_1, a_2, \ldots, a_n$ is defined as

$$\bar{a} = \frac{1}{n} \sum_{k=1}^{n} a_k$$

EXAMPLE 5   **Arithmetic Mean**   Find the arithmetic mean of 3, 5, 4, 7, 4, 2, 3, and 6.

Solution $\bar{a} = \frac{1}{8} \sum_{k=1}^{8} a_k = \frac{1}{8}(3 + 5 + 4 + 7 + 4 + 2 + 3 + 6) = \frac{1}{8}(34) = 4.25$

Matched Problem 5   Find the arithmetic mean of 9, 3, 8, 4, 3, and 6.

Answers to Matched Problems   **1.** (A) $2, 1, 0, -1$ (B) $\frac{-1}{2}, \frac{1}{4}, \frac{-1}{8}, \frac{1}{16}$

2. (A) $a_n = 3n$ (B) $a_n = (-2)^{n-1}$ **3.** $2 + \frac{3}{2} + \frac{4}{3} + \frac{5}{4} + \frac{6}{5}$

4. (A) $\sum_{k=1}^{5} \frac{(-1)^{k-1}}{3^{k-1}}$ (B) $\sum_{j=0}^{4} \frac{(-1)^j}{3^j}$ **5.** 5.5

Exercise B-1

A *Write the first four terms for each sequence in Problems 1–6.*

1. $a_n = 2n + 3$

2. $a_n = 4n - 3$

3. $a_n = \dfrac{n + 2}{n + 1}$

4. $a_n = \dfrac{2n + 1}{2n}$

5. $a_n = (-3)^{n+1}$

6. $a_n = (-\frac{1}{4})^{n-1}$

7. Write the 10th term of the sequence in Problem 1.

8. Write the 15th term of the sequence in Problem 2.

9. Write the 99th term of the sequence in Problem 3.

10. Write the 200th term of the sequence in Problem 4.

In Problems 11–16, write each series in expanded form without summation notation, and evaluate.

11. $\sum_{k=1}^{6} k$

12. $\sum_{k=1}^{5} k^2$

13. $\sum_{k=4}^{7} (2k - 3)$

14. $\sum_{k=0}^{4} (-2)^k$

15. $\sum_{k=0}^{3} \dfrac{1}{10^k}$

16. $\sum_{k=1}^{4} \dfrac{1}{2^k}$

Find the arithmetic mean of each list of numbers in Problems 17–20.

17. 5, 4, 2, 1, and 6

18. 7, 9, 9, 2, and 4

19. 96, 65, 82, 74, 91, 88, 87, 91, 77, and 74

20. 100, 62, 95, 91, 82, 87, 70, 75, 87, and 82

B *Write the first five terms of each sequence in Problems 21–26.*

21. $a_n = \dfrac{(-1)^{n+1}}{2^n}$

22. $a_n = (-1)^n (n - 1)^2$

23. $a_n = n[1 + (-1)^n]$

24. $a_n = \dfrac{1 - (-1)^n}{n}$

25. $a_n = \left(-\dfrac{3}{2}\right)^{n-1}$

26. $a_n = \left(-\dfrac{1}{2}\right)^{n+1}$

In Problems 27–42, find the general term of a sequence whose first four terms agree with the given terms.

27. $-2, -1, 0, 1, \ldots$

28. $4, 5, 6, 7, \ldots$

29. $4, 8, 12, 16, \ldots$

30. $-3, -6, -9, -12, \ldots$

31. $\frac{1}{2}, \frac{3}{4}, \frac{5}{6}, \frac{7}{8}, \ldots$

32. $\frac{1}{2}, \frac{2}{3}, \frac{3}{4}, \frac{4}{5}, \ldots$

33. $1, -2, 3, -4, \ldots$

34. $-2, 4, -8, 16, \ldots$

35. $1, -3, 5, -7, \ldots$

36. $3, -6, 9, -12, \ldots$

37. $1, \frac{2}{5}, \frac{4}{25}, \frac{8}{125}, \ldots$

38. $\frac{4}{3}, \frac{16}{9}, \frac{64}{27}, \frac{256}{81}, \ldots$

39. $x, x^2, x^3, x^4, \ldots$

40. $1, 2x, 3x^2, 4x^3, \ldots$

41. $x, -x^3, x^5, -x^7, \ldots$

42. $x, \dfrac{x^2}{2}, \dfrac{x^3}{3}, \dfrac{x^4}{4}, \ldots$

Write each series in Problems 43–50 in expanded form without summation notation. Do not evaluate.

43. $\displaystyle\sum_{k=1}^{5} (-1)^{k+1}(2k - 1)^2$ **44.** $\displaystyle\sum_{k=1}^{4} \dfrac{(-2)^{k+1}}{2k + 1}$

45. $\displaystyle\sum_{k=2}^{5} \dfrac{2^k}{2k + 3}$ **46.** $\displaystyle\sum_{k=3}^{7} \dfrac{(-1)^k}{k^2 - k}$

47. $\displaystyle\sum_{k=1}^{5} x^{k-1}$ **48.** $\displaystyle\sum_{k=1}^{3} \dfrac{1}{k} x^{k+1}$

49. $\displaystyle\sum_{k=0}^{4} \dfrac{(-1)^k x^{2k+1}}{2k + 1}$ **50.** $\displaystyle\sum_{k=0}^{4} \dfrac{(-1)^k x^{2k}}{2k + 2}$

Write each series in Problems 51–54 using summation notation with

(A) The summing index k starting at k = 1

(B) The summing index j starting at j = 0

51. $2 + 3 + 4 + 5 + 6$ **52.** $1^2 + 2^2 + 3^2 + 4^2$

53. $1 - \frac{1}{2} + \frac{1}{3} - \frac{1}{4}$ **54.** $1 - \frac{1}{3} + \frac{1}{5} - \frac{1}{7} + \frac{1}{9}$

Write each series in Problems 55–58 using summation notation with the summing index k starting at k = 1.

55. $2 + \dfrac{3}{2} + \dfrac{4}{3} + \cdots + \dfrac{n + 1}{n}$

56. $1 + \dfrac{1}{2^2} + \dfrac{1}{3^2} + \cdots + \dfrac{1}{n^2}$

57. $\dfrac{1}{2} - \dfrac{1}{4} + \dfrac{1}{8} - \cdots + \dfrac{(-1)^{n+1}}{2^n}$

58. $1 - 4 + 9 - \cdots + (-1)^{n+1} n^2$

C *In Problems 59–62, discuss the validity of each statement. If the statement is true, explain why. If not, give a counterexample.*

59. For each positive integer n, the sum of the series
$$1 + \frac{1}{2} + \frac{1}{3} + \cdots + \frac{1}{n} \text{ is less than 4.}$$

60. For each positive integer n, the sum of the series
$$\frac{1}{2} + \frac{1}{4} + \frac{1}{8} + \cdots + \frac{1}{2^n} \text{ is less than 1.}$$

61. For each positive integer n, the sum of the series
$$\frac{1}{2} - \frac{1}{4} + \frac{1}{8} - \cdots + \frac{(-1)^{n+1}}{2^n} \text{ is greater than or equal}$$
to $\dfrac{1}{4}$.

62. For each positive integer n, the sum of the series
$$1 - \frac{1}{2} + \frac{1}{3} - \frac{1}{4} + \cdots + \frac{(-1)^{n+1}}{n} \text{ is greater than or}$$
equal to $\dfrac{1}{2}$.

*Some sequences are defined by a **recursion formula**—that is, a formula that defines each term of the sequence in terms of one or more of the preceding terms. For example, if $\{a_n\}$ is defined by*

$$a_1 = 1 \quad and \quad a_n = 2a_{n-1} + 1 \quad for\ n \geq 2$$

then

$$a_2 = 2a_1 + 1 = 2 \cdot 1 + 1 = 3$$
$$a_3 = 2a_2 + 1 = 2 \cdot 3 + 1 = 7$$
$$a_4 = 2a_3 + 1 = 2 \cdot 7 + 1 = 15$$

and so on. In Problems 63–66, write the first five terms of each sequence.

63. $a_1 = 2$ and $a_n = 3a_{n-1} + 2$ for $n \geq 2$

64. $a_1 = 3$ and $a_n = 2a_{n-1} - 2$ for $n \geq 2$

65. $a_1 = 1$ and $a_n = 2a_{n-1}$ for $n \geq 2$

66. $a_1 = 1$ and $a_n = -\frac{1}{3} a_{n-1}$ for $n \geq 2$

If A is a positive real number, the terms of the sequence defined by

$$a_1 = \frac{A}{2} \quad and \quad a_n = \frac{1}{2}\left(a_{n-1} + \frac{A}{a_{n-1}}\right) \quad for\ n \geq 2$$

can be used to approximate $\sqrt{A}$ to any decimal place accuracy desired. In Problems 67 and 68, compute the first four terms of this sequence for the indicated value of A, and compare the fourth term with the value of $\sqrt{A}$ obtained from a calculator.

67. $A = 2$

68. $A = 6$

69. The sequence defined recursively by $a_1 = 1$, $a_2 = 1$, $a_n = a_{n-1} + a_{n-2}$ for $n \geq 3$ is called the *Fibonacci sequence*. Find the first ten terms of the Fibonacci sequence.

70. The sequence defined by $b_n = \dfrac{\sqrt{5}}{5}\left(\dfrac{1 + \sqrt{5}}{2}\right)^n$ is related to the Fibonacci sequence. Find the first ten terms (to three decimal places) of the sequence $\{b_n\}$ and describe the relationship.

Section **B-2** | Arithmetic and Geometric Sequences

- ➤ Arithmetic and Geometric Sequences
- ➤ nth-Term Formulas
- ➤ Sum Formulas for Finite Arithmetic Series
- ➤ Sum Formulas for Finite Geometric Series
- ➤ Sum Formula for Infinite Geometric Series
- ➤ Applications

For most sequences it is difficult to sum an arbitrary number of terms of the sequence without adding term by term. But particular types of sequences—*arithmetic sequences* and *geometric sequences*—have certain properties that lead to convenient and useful formulas for the sums of the corresponding *arithmetic series* and *geometric series*.

➤ Arithmetic and Geometric Sequences

The sequence $5, 7, 9, 11, 13, \ldots, 5 + 2(n - 1), \ldots$, where each term after the first is obtained by adding 2 to the preceding term, is an example of an arithmetic sequence. The sequence $5, 10, 20, 40, 80, \ldots, 5(2)^{n-1}, \ldots$, where each term after the first is obtained by multiplying the preceding term by 2, is an example of a geometric sequence.

DEFINITION   Arithmetic Sequence

A sequence of numbers

$$a_1, a_2, a_3, \ldots, a_n, \ldots$$

is called an **arithmetic sequence** if there is a constant d, called the **common difference**, such that

$$a_n - a_{n-1} = d$$

That is,

$$a_n = a_{n-1} + d \qquad \text{for every } n > 1$$

DEFINITION   Geometric Sequence

A sequence of numbers

$$a_1, a_2, a_3, \ldots, a_n, \ldots$$

is called a **geometric sequence** if there exists a nonzero constant r, called a **common ratio**, such that

$$\frac{a_n}{a_{n-1}} = r$$

That is,

$$a_n = ra_{n-1} \qquad \text{for every } n > 1$$

EXPLORE
&DISCUSS
1

(A) Describe verbally all arithmetic sequences with common difference 2.

(B) Describe verbally all geometric sequences with common ratio 2.

EXAMPLE 1   **Recognizing Arithmetic and Geometric Sequences** Which of the following can be the first four terms of an arithmetic sequence? Of a geometric sequence?

(A) $1, 2, 3, 5, \ldots$ (B) $-1, 3, -9, 27, \ldots$
(C) $3, 3, 3, 3, \ldots$ (D) $10, 8.5, 7, 5.5, \ldots$

Solution   (A) Since $2 - 1 \neq 5 - 3$, there is no common difference, so the sequence is not an arithmetic sequence. Since $2/1 \neq 3/2$, there is no common ratio, so the sequence is not geometric either.

(B) The sequence is geometric with common ratio -3. It is not arithmetic.

(C) The sequence is arithmetic with common difference 0, and is also geometric with common ratio 1.

(D) The sequence is arithmetic with common difference -1.5. It is not geometric.   ∎

Matched Problem 1   Which of the following can be the first four terms of an arithmetic sequence? Of a geometric sequence?

(A) $8, 2, 0.5, 0.125, \ldots$ (B) $-7, -2, 3, 8, \ldots$
(C) $1, 5, 25, 100, \ldots$

➤ nth-Term Formulas

If $\{a_n\}$ is an arithmetic sequence with common difference d, then

$$a_2 = a_1 + d$$
$$a_3 = a_2 + d = a_1 + 2d$$
$$a_4 = a_3 + d = a_1 + 3d$$

This suggests that

THEOREM 1   nth Term of an Arithmetic Sequence

$$a_n = a_1 + (n - 1)d \qquad \text{for all } n > 1 \qquad (1)$$

Similarly, if $\{a_n\}$ is a geometric sequence with common ratio r, then

$$a_2 = a_1 r$$
$$a_3 = a_2 r = a_1 r^2$$
$$a_4 = a_3 r = a_1 r^3$$

This suggests that

THEOREM 2   nth Term of a Geometric Sequence

$$a_n = a_1 r^{n-1} \qquad \text{for all } n > 1 \qquad (2)$$

EXAMPLE 2   **Finding Terms in Arithmetic and Geometric Sequences**

(A) If the 1st and 10th terms of an arithmetic sequence are 3 and 30, respectively, find the 40th term of the sequence.

(B) If the 1st and 10th terms of a geometric sequence are 3 and 30, find the 40th term to three decimal places.

Solution   (A) First use formula (1) with $a_1 = 3$ and $a_{10} = 30$ to find d:

$$a_n = a_1 + (n - 1)d$$
$$a_{10} = a_1 + (10 - 1)d$$
$$30 = 3 + 9d$$
$$d = 3$$

Now find a_{40}:

$$a_{40} = 3 + 39 \cdot 3 = 120$$

(B) First use formula (2) with $a_1 = 3$ and $a_{10} = 30$ to find r:

$$a_n = a_1 r^{n-1}$$
$$a_{10} = a_1 r^{10-1}$$
$$30 = 3r^9$$
$$r^9 = 10$$
$$r = 10^{1/9}$$

Now find a_{40}:

$$a_{40} = 3(10^{1/9})^{39} = 3(10^{39/9}) = 64{,}633.041 \qquad \blacksquare$$

Matched Problem 2   (A) If the 1st and 15th terms of an arithmetic sequence are -5 and 23, respectively, find the 73rd term of the sequence.

(B) Find the 8th term of the geometric sequence

$$\frac{1}{64}, \frac{-1}{32}, \frac{1}{16}, \dots$$

➤ Sum Formulas for Finite Arithmetic Series

If $a_1, a_2, a_3, \dots, a_n$ is a finite arithmetic sequence, then the corresponding series $a_1 + a_2 + a_3 + \cdots + a_n$ is called a *finite arithmetic series*. We will derive two simple and very useful formulas for the sum of a finite arithmetic series. Let d be the common difference of the arithmetic sequence $a_1, a_2, a_3, \dots, a_n$ and let S_n denote the sum of the series $a_1 + a_2 + a_3 + \cdots + a_n$. Then

$$S_n = a_1 + (a_1 + d) + \cdots + [a_1 + (n - 2)d] + [a_1 + (n - 1)d]$$

Reversing the order of the sum, we obtain

$$S_n = [a_1 + (n - 1)d] + [a_1 + (n - 2)d] + \cdots + (a_1 + d) + a_1$$

Something interesting happens if we combine these last two equations by addition (adding corresponding terms on the right sides):

$$2S_n = [2a_1 + (n - 1)d] + [2a_1 + (n - 1)d] + \cdots + [2a_1 + (n - 1)d] + [2a_1 + (n - 1)d]$$

All the terms on the right side are the same, and there are n of them. Thus,

$$2S_n = n[2a_1 + (n - 1)d]$$

and we have the following general formula:

THEOREM 3   Sum of a Finite Arithmetic Series: First Form

$$S_n = \frac{n}{2}[2a_1 + (n - 1)d] \qquad (3)$$

Replacing

$$[a_1 + (n - 1)d] \quad \text{in} \quad \frac{n}{2}[a_1 + a_1 + (n - 1)d]$$

by a_n from equation (1), we obtain a second useful formula for the sum:

THEOREM 4   Sum of a Finite Arithmetic Series: Second Form

$$S_n = \frac{n}{2}(a_1 + a_n) \tag{4}$$

EXAMPLE 3   **Finding a Sum** Find the sum of the first 30 terms in the arithmetic sequence:

$$3, 8, 13, 18, \ldots$$

Solution   Use formula (3) with $n = 30$, $a_1 = 3$, and $d = 5$:

$$S_{30} = \frac{30}{2}[2 \cdot 3 + (30 - 1)5] = 2{,}265$$

Matched Problem 3   Find the sum of the first 40 terms in the arithmetic sequence:

$$15, 13, 11, 9, \ldots$$

EXAMPLE 4   **Finding a Sum** Find the sum of all the even numbers between 31 and 87.

Solution   First, find n using equation (1):

$$a_n = a_1 + (n - 1)d$$
$$86 = 32 + (n - 1)2$$
$$n = 28$$

Now find S_{28} using formula (4):

$$S_n = \frac{n}{2}(a_1 + a_n)$$

$$S_{28} = \frac{28}{2}(32 + 86) = 1{,}652$$

Matched Problem 4   Find the sum of all the odd numbers between 24 and 208.

➤ Sum Formulas for Finite Geometric Series

If $a_1, a_2, a_3, \ldots, a_n$ is a finite geometric sequence, then the corresponding series $a_1 + a_2 + a_3 + \cdots + a_n$ is called a *finite geometric series*. As with arithmetic series, we can derive two simple and very useful formulas for the sum of a finite geometric series. Let r be the common ratio of the geometric sequence

$a_1, a_2, a_3, \ldots, a_n$ and let S_n denote the sum of the series $a_1 + a_2 + a_3 + \cdots + a_n$. Then

$$S_n = a_1 + a_1 r + a_1 r^2 + \cdots + a_1 r^{n-2} + a_1 r^{n-1}$$

If we multiply both sides by r, we obtain

$$r S_n = a_1 r + a_1 r^2 + a_1 r^3 + \cdots + a_1 r^{n-1} + a_1 r^n$$

Now combine these last two equations by subtraction to obtain

$$r S_n - S_n = (a_1 r + a_1 r^2 + a_1 r^3 + \cdots + a_1 r^{n-1} + a_1 r^n) - (a_1 + a_1 r + a_1 r^2 + \cdots + a_1 r^{n-2} + a_1 r^{n-1})$$
$$(r - 1)S_n = a_1 r^n - a_1$$

Notice how many terms drop out on the right side. Solving for S_n, we have

THEOREM 5 Sum of a Finite Geometric Series: First Form

$$S_n = \frac{a_1(r^n - 1)}{r - 1} \qquad r \neq 1 \tag{5}$$

Since $a_n = a_1 r^{n-1}$, or $r a_n = a_1 r^n$, formula (5) also can be written in the form

THEOREM 6 Sum of a Finite Geometric Series: Second Form

$$S_n = \frac{r a_n - a_1}{r - 1} \qquad r \neq 1 \tag{6}$$

EXAMPLE 5 **Finding a Sum** Find the sum of the first ten terms of the geometric sequence:

$$1, 1.05, 1.05^2, \ldots$$

Solution Use formula (5) with $a_1 = 1$, $r = 1.05$, and $n = 10$:

$$S_n = \frac{a_1(r^n - 1)}{r - 1}$$

$$S_{10} = \frac{1(1.05^{10} - 1)}{1.05 - 1}$$

$$\approx \frac{0.6289}{0.05} \approx 12.58$$

Matched Problem 5 Find the sum of the first eight terms of the geometric sequence:

$$100, 100(1.08), 100(1.08)^2, \ldots$$

➤ Sum Formula for Infinite Geometric Series

EXPLORE & DISCUSS 2

(A) For any n, the sum of a finite geometric series with $a_1 = 5$ and $r = \frac{1}{2}$ is given by [see formula (5)]

$$S_n = \frac{5[(\frac{1}{2})^n - 1]}{\frac{1}{2} - 1} = 10 - 10\left(\frac{1}{2}\right)^n$$

Discuss the behavior of S_n as n increases.

(B) Repeat part (A) if $a_1 = 5$ and $r = 2$.

Given a geometric series, what happens to the sum S_n of the first n terms as n increases without stopping? To answer this question, let us write formula (5) in the form

$$S_n = \frac{a_1 r^n}{r - 1} - \frac{a_1}{r - 1}$$

It is possible to show that if $-1 < r < 1$, then r^n will approach 0 as n increases. Thus, the first term above will approach 0 and S_n can be made as close as we please to the second term, $-a_1/(r - 1)$ [which can be written as $a_1/(1 - r)$], by taking n sufficiently large. Thus, if the common ratio r is between -1 and 1, we conclude that the sum of an infinite geometric series is

THEOREM 7   Sum of an Infinite Geometric Series

$$S_\infty = \frac{a_1}{1 - r} \qquad -1 < r < 1 \qquad (7)$$

If $r \le -1$ or $r \ge 1$, then an infinite geometric series has no sum.

> ➤ **Applications**

EXAMPLE 6   **Loan Repayment**   A person borrows $3,600 and agrees to repay the loan in monthly installments over a period of 3 years. The agreement is to pay 1% of the unpaid balance each month for using the money and $100 each month to reduce the loan. What is the total cost of the loan over the 3 years?

Solution   Let us look at the problem relative to a time line:

$3,600	$3,500	$3,400	$\cdots$	$200	$100		Unpaid balance
0	1	2	3	$\cdots$	34	35	36	Months
	0.01(3,600) = 36	0.01(3,500) = 35	0.01(3,400) = 34	$\cdots$	0.01(300) = 3	0.01(200) = 2	0.01(100) = 1	1% of unpaid balance

The total cost of the loan is

$$1 + 2 + \cdots + 34 + 35 + 36$$

The terms form a finite arithmetic series with $n = 36$, $a_1 = 1$, and $a_{36} = 36$, so we can use formula (4):

$$S_n = \frac{n}{2}(a_1 + a_n)$$

$$S_{36} = \frac{36}{2}(1 + 36) = \$666$$

We conclude that the total cost of the loan over the period of 3 years is $666.

Matched Problem 6   Repeat Example 6 with a loan of $6,000 over a period of 5 years.

EXAMPLE 7   **Economy Stimulation** The government has decided on a tax rebate program to stimulate the economy. Suppose that you receive $600 and you spend 80% of this, and each of the people who receive what you spend also spend 80% of what they receive, and this process continues without end. According to the **multiplier principle** in economics, the effect of your $600 tax rebate on the economy is multiplied many times. What is the total amount spent if the process continues as indicated?

Solution   We need to find the sum of an infinite geometric series with the first amount spent being $a_1 = (0.8)(\$600) = \$480$ and $r = 0.8$. Using formula (7), we obtain

$$S_\infty = \frac{a_1}{1 - r}$$

$$= \frac{\$480}{1 - 0.8} = \$2,400$$

Thus, assuming the process continues as indicated, we would expect the $600 tax rebate to result in about $2,400 of spending. ∎

Matched Problem 7   Repeat Example 7 with a tax rebate of $1,000.

Answers to Matched Problems   **1.** (A) The sequence is geometric with $r = \frac{1}{4}$. It is not arithmetic.
(B) The sequence is arithmetic with $d = 5$. It is not geometric.
(C) The sequence is neither arithmetic nor geometric.

2. (A) 139   (B) −2   **3.** −960   **4.** 10,672

5. 1,063.66   **6.** $1,830   **7.** $4,000

Exercise B-2

A *In Problems 1 and 2, determine whether the indicated sequence can be the first three terms of an arithmetic or geometric sequence, and, if so, find the common difference or common ratio and the next two terms of the sequence.*

1. (A) $-11, -16, -21, \dots$ (B) $2, -4, 8, \dots$
(C) $1, 4, 9, \dots$ (D) $\frac{1}{2}, \frac{1}{6}, \frac{1}{18}, \dots$

2. (A) $5, 20, 100, \dots$ (B) $-5, -5, -5, \dots$
(C) $7, 6.5, 6, \dots$ (D) $512, 256, 128, \dots$

B *In Problem 3–8, determine whether the finite series is arithmetic, geometric, both, or neither. If the series is arithmetic or geometric, find its sum.*

3. $\displaystyle\sum_{k=1}^{101} (-1)^{k+1}$

4. $\displaystyle\sum_{k=1}^{200} 3$

5. $1 + \dfrac{1}{2} + \dfrac{1}{3} + \cdots + \dfrac{1}{50}$

6. $3 - 9 + 27 - \cdots - 3^{20}$

7. $5 + 4.9 + 4.8 + \cdots + 0.1$

8. $1 - \dfrac{1}{4} + \dfrac{1}{9} - \cdots - \dfrac{1}{100^2}$

Let $a_1, a_2, a_3, \dots, a_n, \dots$ be an arithmetic sequence. In Problems 9–14, find the indicated quantities.

9. $a_1 = 7; d = 4; a_2 = ?; a_3 = ?$

10. $a_1 = -2; d = -3; a_2 = ?; a_3 = ?$

11. $a_1 = 2; d = 4; a_{21} = ?; S_{31} = ?$

12. $a_1 = 8; d = -10; a_{15} = ?; S_{23} = ?$

13. $a_1 = 18; a_{20} = 75; S_{20} = ?$

14. $a_1 = 203; a_{30} = 261; S_{30} = ?$

Let $a_1, a_2, a_3, \dots, a_n, \dots$ be a geometric sequence. In Problems 15–24, find the indicated quantities.

15. $a_1 = 3; r = -2; a_2 = ?; a_3 = ?; a_4 = ?$

16. $a_1 = 32; r = -\frac{1}{2}; a_2 = ?; a_3 = ?; a_4 = ?$

17. $a_1 = 1; a_7 = 729; r = -3; S_7 = ?$

18. $a_1 = 3; a_7 = 2,187; r = 3; S_7 = ?$

19. $a_1 = 100; r = 1.08; a_{10} = ?$

20. $a_1 = 240; r = 1.06; a_{12} = ?$

21. $a_1 = 100; a_9 = 200; r = ?$

22. $a_1 = 100; a_{10} = 300; r = ?$

23. $a_1 = 500; r = 0.6; S_{10} = ?; S_\infty = ?$

24. $a_1 = 8,000; r = 0.4; S_{10} = ?; S_\infty = ?$

25. $S_{41} = \sum_{k=1}^{41} (3k + 3) = ?$

26. $S_{50} = \sum_{k=1}^{50} (2k - 3) = ?$

27. $S_8 = \sum_{k=1}^{8} (-2)^{k-1} = ?$

28. $S_8 = \sum_{k=1}^{8} 2^k = ?$

29. Find the sum of all the odd integers between 12 and 68.

30. Find the sum of all the even integers between 23 and 97.

31. Find the sum of each infinite geometric sequence (if it exists).

(A) $2, 4, 8, \ldots$ (B) $2, -\frac{1}{2}, \frac{1}{8}, \ldots$

32. Repeat Problem 31 for:

(A) $16, 4, 1, \ldots$ (B) $1, -3, 9, \ldots$

C

33. Find $f(1) + f(2) + f(3) + \cdots + f(50)$ if $f(x) = 2x - 3$.

34. Find $g(1) + g(2) + g(3) + \cdots + g(100)$ if $g(t) = 18 - 3t$.

35. Find $f(1) + f(2) + \cdots + f(10)$ if $f(x) = (\frac{1}{2})^x$.

36. Find $g(1) + g(2) + \cdots + g(10)$ if $g(x) = 2^x$.

37. Show that the sum of the first n odd positive integers is n^2, using appropriate formulas from this section.

38. Show that the sum of the first n even positive integers is $n + n^2$, using formulas in this section.

39. If $r = 1$, neither the first form nor the second form for the sum of a finite geometric series is valid. Find a formula for the sum of a finite geometric series if $r = 1$.

40. If all of the terms of an infinite geometric series are less than 1, could the sum be greater than 1000? Explain.

41. Does there exist a finite arithmetic series with $a_1 = 1$ and $a_n = 1.1$ that has sum equal to 100? Explain.

42. Does there exist a finite arithmetic series with $a_1 = 1$ and $a_n = 1.1$ that has sum equal to 105? Explain.

43. Does there exist an infinite geometric series with $a_1 = 10$ that has sum equal to 6? Explain.

44. Does there exist an infinite geometric series with $a_1 = 10$ that has sum equal to 5? Explain.

Applications

Business & Economics

45. *Loan repayment.* If you borrow \$4,800 and repay the loan by paying \$200 per month to reduce the loan and 1% of the unpaid balance each month for the use of the money, what is the total cost of the loan over 24 months?

46. *Loan repayment.* If you borrow \$5,400 and repay the loan by paying \$300 per month to reduce the loan and 1.5% of the unpaid balance each month for the use of the money, what is the total cost of the loan over 18 months?

47. *Economy stimulation.* The government, through a subsidy program, distributes \$5,000,000. If we assume that each person or agency spends 70% of what is received, and 70% of this is spent, and so on, how much total increase in spending results from this government action? (Let $a_1 = \$3,500,000$.)

48. *Economy stimulation.* Due to reduced taxes, a person has an extra \$1,200 in spendable income.

If we assume that the person spends 65% of this on consumer goods, and the producers of these goods in turn spend 65% on consumer goods, and that this process continues indefinitely, what is the total amount spent (to the nearest dollar) on consumer goods?

49. *Compound interest.* If \$1,000 is invested at 5% compounded annually, the amount A present after n years forms a geometric sequence with common ratio $1 + 0.05 = 1.05$. Use a geometric sequence formula to find the amount A in the account (to the nearest cent) after 10 years. After 20 years. [*Hint:* Use a time line.]

50. *Compound interest.* If \$P is invested at 100r% compounded annually, the amount A present after n years forms a geometric sequence with common ratio $1 + r$. Write a formula for the amount present after n years. [*Hint:* Use a time line.]

Section **B-3** | Binomial Theorem

➤ Factorial
➤ Development of the Binomial Theorem

The binomial form

$$(a + b)^n$$

where n is a natural number, appears more frequently than you might expect. The coefficients in the expansion play an important role in probability studies. The *binomial formula,* which we will derive informally, enables us to expand $(a + b)^n$ directly for n any natural number. Since the formula involves *factorials,* we digress for a moment here to introduce this important concept.

➤ Factorial

For n a natural number, **n factorial,** denoted by **$n!$,** is the product of the first n natural numbers. **Zero factorial** is defined to be 1. That is,

DEFINITION n Factorial

$$n! = n \cdot (n - 1) \cdot \cdots \cdot 2 \cdot 1$$
$$1! = 1$$
$$0! = 1$$

It is also useful to note that $n!$ can be defined recursively.

DEFINITION n Factorial—Recursive Definition

$$n! = n \cdot (n - 1)! \qquad n \geq 1$$

EXAMPLE 1   **Factorial Forms**   Evaluate each:

(A) $5! = 5 \cdot 4 \cdot 3 \cdot 2 \cdot 1 = 120$ (B) $\dfrac{8!}{7!} = \dfrac{8 \cdot 7!}{7!} = 8$

(C) $\dfrac{10!}{7!} = \dfrac{10 \cdot 9 \cdot 8 \cdot 7!}{7!} = 720$

Matched Problem 1   Evaluate each:

(A) $4!$ (B) $\dfrac{7!}{6!}$ (C) $\dfrac{8!}{5!}$

The following important formula involving factorials has applications in many areas of mathematics and statistics. We will use this formula to provide a more concise form for the expressions encountered later in this discussion.

THEOREM 1   For n and r integers satisfying $0 \leq r \leq n$,

$$C_{n,r} = \frac{n!}{r!(n - r)!}$$

EXAMPLE 2   Evaluating $C_{n,r}$

(A) $C_{9,2} = \dfrac{9!}{2!(9-2)!} = \dfrac{9!}{2!7!} = \dfrac{9 \cdot 8 \cdot \cancel{7!}}{2 \cdot \cancel{7!}} = 36$

(B) $C_{5,5} = \dfrac{5!}{5!(5-5)!} = \dfrac{5!}{5!0!} = \dfrac{5!}{5!} = 1$

Matched Problem 2   Find

(A) $C_{5,2}$

(B) $C_{6,0}$

➤ Development of the Binomial Theorem

Let us expand $(a + b)^n$ for several values of n to see if we can observe a pattern that leads to a general formula for the expansion for any natural number n:

$$(a + b)^1 = a + b$$
$$(a + b)^2 = a^2 + 2ab + b^2$$
$$(a + b)^3 = a^3 + 3a^2b + 3ab^2 + b^3$$
$$(a + b)^4 = a^4 + 4a^3b + 6a^2b^2 + 4ab^3 + b^4$$
$$(a + b)^5 = a^5 + 5a^4b + 10a^3b^2 + 10a^2b^3 + 5ab^4 + b^5$$

◉ *Insight*

1. The expansion of $(a + b)^n$ has $(n + 1)$ terms.
2. The power of a decreases by 1 for each term as we move from left to right.
3. The power of b increases by 1 for each term as we move from left to right.
4. In each term, the sum of the powers of a and b always equals n.
5. Starting with a given term, we can get the coefficient of the next term by multiplying the coefficient of the given term by the exponent of a and dividing by the number that represents the position of the term in the series of terms. For example, in the expansion of $(a + b)^4$ above, the coefficient of the third term is found from the second term by multiplying 4 and 3, and then dividing by 2 [that is, the coefficient of the third term $= (4 \cdot 3)/2 = 6$]. ●

We now postulate these same properties for the general case:

$$(a + b)^n = a^n + \frac{n}{1}a^{n-1}b + \frac{n(n-1)}{1 \cdot 2}a^{n-2}b^2 + \frac{n(n-1)(n-2)}{1 \cdot 2 \cdot 3}a^{n-3}b^3 + \cdots + b^n$$

$$= \frac{n!}{0!(n-0)!}a^n + \frac{n!}{1!(n-1)!}a^{n-1}b + \frac{n!}{2!(n-2)!}a^{n-2}b^2 + \frac{n!}{3!(n-3)!}a^{n-3}b^3 + \cdots + \frac{n!}{n!(n-n)!}b^n$$

$$= C_{n,0}a^n + C_{n,1}a^{n-1}b + C_{n,2}a^{n-2}b^2 + C_{n,3}a^{n-3}b^3 + \cdots + C_{n,n}b^n$$

And we are led to the formula in the binomial theorem (a formal proof requires mathematical induction, which is beyond the scope of this book):

THEOREM 2   Binomial Theorem

For all natural numbers n,

$$(a + b)^n = C_{n,0}a^n + C_{n,1}a^{n-1}b + C_{n,2}a^{n-2}b^2 + C_{n,3}a^{n-3}b^3 + \cdots + C_{n,n}b^n$$

EXAMPLE 3 **Using the Binomial Theorem**   Use the binomial formula to expand $(u + v)^6$.

Solution

$$(u + v)^6 = C_{6,0}u^6 + C_{6,1}u^5v + C_{6,2}u^4v^2 + C_{6,3}u^3v^3 + C_{6,4}u^2v^4 + C_{6,5}uv^5 + C_{6,6}v^6$$
$$= u^6 + 6u^5v + 15u^4v^2 + 20u^3v^3 + 15u^2v^4 + 6uv^5 + v^6$$

Matched Problem 3   Use the binomial formula to expand $(x + 2)^5$.

EXAMPLE 4 **Using the Binomial Theorem**   Use the binomial formula to find the sixth term in the expansion of $(x - 1)^{18}$.

Solution $$\text{Sixth term} = C_{18,5}x^{13}(-1)^5 = \frac{18!}{5!(18 - 5)!}x^{13}(-1)$$
$$= -8{,}568x^{13}$$

Matched Problem 4   Use the binomial formula to find the fourth term in the expansion of $(x - 2)^{20}$.

EXPLORE & DISCUSS 1

(A) Use the formula for $C_{n,r}$ to find

$$C_{6,0} + C_{6,1} + C_{6,2} + C_{6,3} + C_{6,4} + C_{6,5} + C_{6,6}$$

(B) Write the binomial theorem for $n = 6$, $a = 1$, and $b = 1$, and compare with the results of part (A).

(C) For any natural number n, find

$$C_{n,0} + C_{n,1} + C_{n,2} + \cdots + C_{n,n}$$

Answers to Matched Problems   **1.** (A) 24   (B) 7   (C) 336   **2.** (A) 10   (B) 1
3. $x^5 + 10x^4 + 40x^3 + 80x^2 + 80x + 32$
4. $-9{,}120x^{17}$

Exercise B-3

A *In Problems 1–20, evaluate each expression.*

1. $6!$

2. $7!$

3. $\dfrac{10!}{9!}$

4. $\dfrac{20!}{19!}$

5. $\dfrac{12!}{9!}$

6. $\dfrac{10!}{6!}$

7. $\dfrac{5!}{2!3!}$

8. $\dfrac{7!}{3!4!}$

9. $\dfrac{6!}{5!(6 - 5)!}$

10. $\dfrac{7!}{4!(7 - 4)!}$

11. $\dfrac{20!}{3!17!}$

12. $\dfrac{52!}{50!2!}$

B

13. $C_{5,3}$ **14.** $C_{7,3}$ **15.** $C_{6,5}$ **16.** $C_{7,4}$
17. $C_{5,0}$ **18.** $C_{5,5}$ **19.** $C_{18,15}$ **20.** $C_{18,3}$

Expand each expression in Problems 21–26 using the binomial formula.

21. $(a + b)^4$ **22.** $(m + n)^5$

23. $(x - 1)^6$ **24.** $(u - 2)^5$

25. $(2a - b)^5$ **26.** $(x - 2y)^5$

Find the indicated term in each expansion in Problems 27–32.

27. $(x - 1)^{18}$; 5th term

28. $(x - 3)^{20}$; 3rd term

29. $(p + q)^{15}$; 7th term

30. $(p + q)^{15}$; 13th term

31. $(2x + y)^{12}$; 11th term

32. $(2x + y)^{12}$; 3rd term

C

33. Show that $C_{n,0} = C_{n,n}$ for $n \geq 0$.

34. Show that $C_{n,r} = C_{n,n-r}$ for $n \geq r \geq 0$.

35. The triangle next is called **Pascal's triangle.** Can you guess what the next two rows at the bottom are?

Compare these numbers with the coefficients of binomial expansions.

$$
\begin{array}{ccccccccc}
 & & & & 1 & & & & \\
 & & & 1 & & 1 & & & \\
 & & 1 & & 2 & & 1 & & \\
 & 1 & & 3 & & 3 & & 1 & \\
1 & & 4 & & 6 & & 4 & & 1
\end{array}
$$

36. Explain why the sum of the entries in each row of Pascal's triangle is a power of 2. [*Hint:* Let $a = b = 1$ in the binomial theorem.]

37. Explain why the alternating sum of the entries (e.g., $1 - 4 + 6 - 4 + 1$) in each row of Pascal's triangle is equal to 0.

38. Show that $C_{n,r} = \frac{n - r + 1}{r} C_{n,r-1}$ for $n \geq r \geq 1$.

39. Show that $C_{n,r-1} + C_{n,r} = C_{n+1,r}$ for $n \geq r \geq 1$.

APPENDIX C

TABLES

TABLE I Basic Geometric Formulas

1. Similar Triangles

(A) Two triangles are similar if two angles of one triangle have the same measure as two angles of the other.

(B) If two triangles are similar, their corresponding sides are proportional:

$$\frac{a}{a'} = \frac{b}{b'} = \frac{c}{c'}$$

2. Pythagorean Theorem

$c^2 = a^2 + b^2$

3. Rectangle

$A = ab$ Area
$P = 2a + 2b$ Perimeter

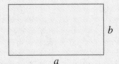

4. Parallelogram

$h = $ height
$A = ah = ab \sin \theta$ Area
$P = 2a + 2b$ Perimeter

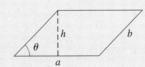

5. Triangle

$h = $ height
$A = \frac{1}{2}hc$ Area
$P = a + b + c$ Perimeter
$s = \frac{1}{2}(a + b + c)$ Semiperimeter
$A = \sqrt{s(s - a)(s - b)(s - c)}$ Area: Heron's formula

6. Trapezoid

Base a is parallel to base b.

$h = $ height
$A = \frac{1}{2}(a + b)h$ Area

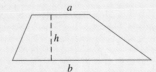

(continued)

TABLE I   *(continued)*

7. Circle

R = radius
D = diameter
$D = 2R$
$A = \pi R^2 = \frac{1}{4}\pi D^2$ Area
$C = 2\pi R = \pi D$ Circumference
$\dfrac{C}{D} = \pi$ For all circles
$\pi \approx 3.141\ 59$

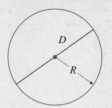

8. Rectangular Solid

$V = abc$ Volume
$T = 2ab + 2ac + 2bc$ Total surface area

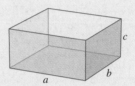

9. Right Circular Cylinder

R = radius of base
h = height
$V = \pi R^2 h$ Volume
$S = 2\pi R h$ Lateral surface area
$T = 2\pi R(R + h)$ Total surface area

10. Right Circular Cone

R = radius of base
h = height
s = slant height
$V = \frac{1}{3}\pi R^2 h$ Volume
$S = \pi R s = \pi R\sqrt{R^2 + h^2}$ Lateral surface area
$T = \pi R(R + s) = \pi R\left(R + \sqrt{R^2 + h^2}\right)$ Total surface area

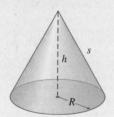

11. Sphere

R = radius
D = diameter
$D = 2R$
$V = \frac{4}{3}\pi R^3 = \frac{1}{6}\pi D^3$ Volume
$S = 4\pi R^2 = \pi D^2$ Surface area

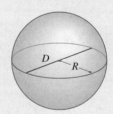

TABLE II   Integration Formulas

[*Note:* The constant of integration is omitted for each integral, but must be included in any particular application of a formula. The variable u is the variable of integration; all other symbols represent constants.]

Integrals Involving u^n

1. $\displaystyle\int u^n\, du = \frac{u^{n+1}}{n+1},\quad n \neq -1$

2. $\displaystyle\int u^{-1}\, du = \int \frac{1}{u}\, du = \ln|u|$

Integrals Involving $a + bu$, $a \neq 0$ and $b \neq 0$

3. $\displaystyle\int \frac{1}{a + bu}\, du = \frac{1}{b}\ln|a + bu|$

4. $\displaystyle\int \frac{u}{a + bu}\, du = \frac{u}{b} - \frac{a}{b^2}\ln|a + bu|$

5. $\displaystyle\int \frac{u^2}{a + bu}\, du = \frac{(a + bu)^2}{2b^3} - \frac{2a(a + bu)}{b^3} + \frac{a^2}{b^3}\ln|a + bu|$

6. $\displaystyle\int \frac{u}{(a + bu)^2}\, du = \frac{1}{b^2}\left(\ln|a + bu| + \frac{a}{a + bu}\right)$

7. $\displaystyle\int \frac{u^2}{(a + bu)^2}\, du = \frac{(a + bu)}{b^3} - \frac{a^2}{b^3(a + bu)} - \frac{2a}{b^3}\ln|a + bu|$

8. $\displaystyle\int u(a + bu)^n\, du = \frac{(a + bu)^{n+2}}{(n + 2)b^2} - \frac{a(a + bu)^{n+1}}{(n + 1)b^2},\quad n \neq -1, -2$

9. $\displaystyle\int \frac{1}{u(a + bu)}\, du = \frac{1}{a}\ln\left|\frac{u}{a + bu}\right|$

10. $\displaystyle\int \frac{1}{u^2(a + bu)}\, du = -\frac{1}{au} + \frac{b}{a^2}\ln\left|\frac{a + bu}{u}\right|$

11. $\displaystyle\int \frac{1}{u(a + bu)^2}\, du = \frac{1}{a(a + bu)} + \frac{1}{a^2}\ln\left|\frac{u}{a + bu}\right|$

12. $\displaystyle\int \frac{1}{u^2(a + bu)^2}\, du = -\frac{a + 2bu}{a^2 u(a + bu)} + \frac{2b}{a^3}\ln\left|\frac{a + bu}{u}\right|$

Integrals Involving $a^2 - u^2$, $a > 0$

13. $\displaystyle\int \frac{1}{u^2 - a^2}\, du = \frac{1}{2a}\ln\left|\frac{u - a}{u + a}\right|$

14. $\displaystyle\int \frac{1}{a^2 - u^2}\, du = \frac{1}{2a}\ln\left|\frac{u + a}{u - a}\right|$

Integrals Involving $(a + bu)$ and $(c + du)$, $b \neq 0$, $d \neq 0$, and $ad - bc \neq 0$

15. $\displaystyle\int \frac{1}{(a + bu)(c + du)}\, du = \frac{1}{ad - bc}\ln\left|\frac{c + du}{a + bu}\right|$

16. $\displaystyle\int \frac{u}{(a + bu)(c + du)}\, du = \frac{1}{ad - bc}\left(\frac{a}{b}\ln|a + bu| - \frac{c}{d}\ln|c + du|\right)$

17. $\displaystyle\int \frac{u^2}{(a + bu)(c + du)}\, du = \frac{1}{bd}u - \frac{1}{ad - bc}\left(\frac{a^2}{b^2}\ln|a + bu| - \frac{c^2}{d^2}\ln|c + du|\right)$

18. $\displaystyle\int \frac{1}{(a + bu)^2(c + du)}\, du = \frac{1}{ad - bc}\frac{1}{a + bu} + \frac{d}{(ad - bc)^2}\ln\left|\frac{c + du}{a + bu}\right|$

19. $\displaystyle\int \frac{u}{(a + bu)^2(c + du)}\, du = -\frac{a}{b(ad - bc)}\frac{1}{a + bu} - \frac{c}{(ad - bc)^2}\ln\left|\frac{c + du}{a + bu}\right|$

20. $\displaystyle\int \frac{a + bu}{c + du}\, du = \frac{bu}{d} + \frac{ad - bc}{d^2}\ln|c + du|$

(continued)

TABLE II *(continued)*

Integrals Involving $\sqrt{a + bu}$, $a \neq 0$ and $b \neq 0$

21. $\displaystyle\int \sqrt{a + bu}\, du = \frac{2\sqrt{(a + bu)^3}}{3b}$

22. $\displaystyle\int u\sqrt{a + bu}\, du = \frac{2(3bu - 2a)}{15b^2}\sqrt{(a + bu)^3}$

23. $\displaystyle\int u^2\sqrt{a + bu}\, du = \frac{2(15b^2u^2 - 12abu + 8a^2)}{105b^3}\sqrt{(a + bu)^3}$

24. $\displaystyle\int \frac{1}{\sqrt{a + bu}}\, du = \frac{2\sqrt{a + bu}}{b}$

25. $\displaystyle\int \frac{u}{\sqrt{a + bu}}\, du = \frac{2(bu - 2a)}{3b^2}\sqrt{a + bu}$

26. $\displaystyle\int \frac{u^2}{\sqrt{a + bu}}\, du = \frac{2(3b^2u^2 - 4abu + 8a^2)}{15b^3}\sqrt{a + bu}$

27. $\displaystyle\int \frac{1}{u\sqrt{a + bu}}\, du = \frac{1}{\sqrt{a}}\ln\left|\frac{\sqrt{a + bu} - \sqrt{a}}{\sqrt{a + bu} + \sqrt{a}}\right|, \quad a > 0$

28. $\displaystyle\int \frac{1}{u^2\sqrt{a + bu}}\, du = -\frac{\sqrt{a + bu}}{au} - \frac{b}{2a\sqrt{a}}\ln\left|\frac{\sqrt{a + bu} - \sqrt{a}}{\sqrt{a + bu} + \sqrt{a}}\right|, \quad a > 0$

Integrals Involving $\sqrt{a^2 - u^2}$, $a > 0$

29. $\displaystyle\int \frac{1}{u\sqrt{a^2 - u^2}}\, du = -\frac{1}{a}\ln\left|\frac{a + \sqrt{a^2 - u^2}}{u}\right|$

30. $\displaystyle\int \frac{1}{u^2\sqrt{a^2 - u^2}}\, du = -\frac{\sqrt{a^2 - u^2}}{a^2u}$

31. $\displaystyle\int \frac{\sqrt{a^2 - u^2}}{u}\, du = \sqrt{a^2 - u^2} - a\ln\left|\frac{a + \sqrt{a^2 - u^2}}{u}\right|$

Integrals Involving $\sqrt{u^2 + a^2}$, $a > 0$

32. $\displaystyle\int \sqrt{u^2 + a^2}\, du = \frac{1}{2}\left(u\sqrt{u^2 + a^2} + a^2\ln|u + \sqrt{u^2 + a^2}|\right)$

33. $\displaystyle\int u^2\sqrt{u^2 + a^2}\, du = \frac{1}{8}\left[u(2u^2 + a^2)\sqrt{u^2 + a^2} - a^4\ln|u + \sqrt{u^2 + a^2}|\right]$

34. $\displaystyle\int \frac{\sqrt{u^2 + a^2}}{u}\, du = \sqrt{u^2 + a^2} - a\ln\left|\frac{a + \sqrt{u^2 + a^2}}{u}\right|$

35. $\displaystyle\int \frac{\sqrt{u^2 + a^2}}{u^2}\, du = -\frac{\sqrt{u^2 + a^2}}{u} + \ln|u + \sqrt{u^2 + a^2}|$

36. $\displaystyle\int \frac{1}{\sqrt{u^2 + a^2}}\, du = \ln|u + \sqrt{u^2 + a^2}|$

37. $\displaystyle\int \frac{1}{u\sqrt{u^2 + a^2}}\, du = \frac{1}{a}\ln\left|\frac{u}{a + \sqrt{u^2 + a^2}}\right|$

38. $\displaystyle\int \frac{u^2}{\sqrt{u^2 + a^2}}\, du = \frac{1}{2}\left(u\sqrt{u^2 + a^2} - a^2\ln|u + \sqrt{u^2 + a^2}|\right)$

39. $\displaystyle\int \frac{1}{u^2\sqrt{u^2 + a^2}}\, du = -\frac{\sqrt{u^2 + a^2}}{a^2u}$

Integrals Involving $\sqrt{u^2 - a^2}$, $a > 0$

40. $\displaystyle\int \sqrt{u^2 - a^2}\, du = \frac{1}{2}\left(u\sqrt{u^2 - a^2} - a^2\ln|u + \sqrt{u^2 - a^2}|\right)$

TABLE II   *(concluded)*

41. $\int u^2 \sqrt{u^2 - a^2}\, du = \frac{1}{8}[u(2u^2 - a^2)\sqrt{u^2 - a^2} - a^4 \ln|u + \sqrt{u^2 - a^2}|]$

42. $\int \frac{\sqrt{u^2 - a^2}}{u^2}\, du = -\frac{\sqrt{u^2 - a^2}}{u} + \ln|u + \sqrt{u^2 - a^2}|$

43. $\int \frac{1}{\sqrt{u^2 - a^2}}\, du = \ln|u + \sqrt{u^2 - a^2}|$

44. $\int \frac{u^2}{\sqrt{u^2 - a^2}}\, du = \frac{1}{2}(u\sqrt{u^2 - a^2} + a^2 \ln|u + \sqrt{u^2 - a^2}|)$

45. $\int \frac{1}{u^2\sqrt{u^2 - a^2}}\, du = \frac{\sqrt{u^2 - a^2}}{a^2 u}$

Integrals Involving e^{au}, $a \neq 0$

46. $\int e^{au}\, du = \frac{e^{au}}{a}$

47. $\int u^n e^{au}\, du = \frac{u^n e^{au}}{a} - \frac{n}{a}\int u^{n-1} e^{au}\, du$

48. $\int \frac{1}{c + de^{au}}\, du = \frac{u}{c} - \frac{1}{ac}\ln|c + de^{au}|, \quad c \neq 0$

Integrals Involving $\ln u$

49. $\int \ln u\, du = u \ln u - u$

50. $\int \frac{\ln u}{u}\, du = \frac{1}{2}(\ln u)^2$

51. $\int u^n \ln u\, du = \frac{u^{n+1}}{n + 1}\ln u - \frac{u^{n+1}}{(n + 1)^2}, \quad n \neq -1$

52. $\int (\ln u)^n\, du = u(\ln u)^n - n\int (\ln u)^{n-1}\, du$

Integrals Involving Trigonometric Functions of au, $a \neq 0$

53. $\int \sin au\, du = -\frac{1}{a}\cos au$

54. $\int \cos au\, du = \frac{1}{a}\sin au$

55. $\int \tan au\, du = -\frac{1}{a}\ln|\cos au|$

56. $\int \cot au\, du = \frac{1}{a}\ln|\sin au|$

57. $\int \sec au\, du = \frac{1}{a}\ln|\sec au + \tan au|$

58. $\int \csc au\, du = \frac{1}{a}\ln|\csc au - \cot au|$

59. $\int (\sin au)^2\, du = \frac{u}{2} - \frac{1}{4a}\sin 2au$

60. $\int (\cos au)^2\, du = \frac{u}{2} + \frac{1}{4a}\sin 2au$

61. $\int (\sin au)^n\, du = -\frac{1}{an}(\sin au)^{n-1}\cos au + \frac{n - 1}{n}\int (\sin au)^{n-2}\, du, \quad n \neq 0$

62. $\int (\cos au)^n\, du = \frac{1}{an}\sin au(\cos au)^{n-1} + \frac{n - 1}{n}\int (\cos au)^{n-2}\, du, \quad n \neq 0$

ANSWERS

Chapter 1

Exercise 1-1

1. Function   **3.** Not a function   **5.** Function   **7.** Function   **9.** Not a function   **11.** Function

15. 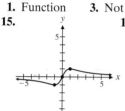   **17.** (A)

x	0	5	10	15	20
$f(x)$	0	375	500	375	0
$g(x)$	150	250	350	450	550
$f(x) - g(x)$	-150	125	150	-75	-550

(B)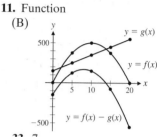

19. $y = 0$ **21.** $y = 4$ **23.** $x = -5, 0, 4$ **25.** $x = -6$ **27.** 1   **29.** -5 **31.** 3   **33.** 7
35. -45 **37.** 0   **39.** All real numbers   **41.** All real numbers except -4 **43.** $x \leq 7$
45. $f(2) = 0$, and 0 is a number; therefore, $f(2)$ exists. On the other hand, $f(3)$ is not defined, since the denominator would be 0; therefore, we say that $f(3)$ does not exist.
47. $g(x) = 2x^3 - 5$ **49.** $G(x) = 2\sqrt{x} - x^2$
51. Function f multiplies the domain element by 2 and subtracts 3 from the result.
53. Function F multiplies the cube of the domain element by 3 and subtracts twice the square root of the domain element from the result.
55. A function with domain R **57.** A function with domain R
59. Not a function; for example, when $x = 1$, $y = \pm 3$ **61.** A function with domain all real numbers except $x = 4$
63. Not a function; for example, when $x = 4$, $y = \pm 3$ **65.** 4   **67.** $h - 1$ **69.** (A) $4x + 4h - 3$ (B) $4h$ (C) 4
71. (A) $4x^2 + 8xh + 4h^2 - 7x - 7h + 6$ (B) $8xh + 4h^2 - 7h$ (C) $8x + 4h - 7$
73. (A) $20x + 20h - x^2 - 2xh - h^2$ (B) $20h - 2xh - h^2$ (C) $20 - 2x - h$
75. $P(w) = 2w + \dfrac{50}{w}, w > 0$ **77.** $A(l) = l(50 - l), 0 \leq l \leq 50$
79. $\$54, \$42$ **81.** (A) $R(x) = (75 - 3x)x, \quad 1 \leq x \leq 20$ (B)

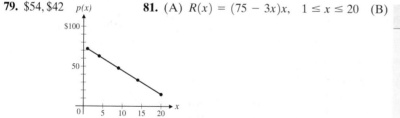

x	$R(x)$
1	72
4	252
8	408
12	468
16	432
20	300

(C)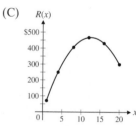

83. (A) $P(x) = 59x - 3x^2 - 125, \quad 1 \leq x \leq 20$ (B)

x	$P(x)$
1	-69
4	63
8	155
12	151
16	51
20	-145

(C)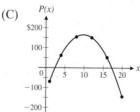

85. (A) $V(x) = x(8 - 2x)(12 - 2x)$ (B) $0 \leq x \leq 4$ (C)

x	$V(x)$
1	60
2	64
3	36

(D)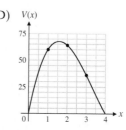

87. (A) The graph indicates that there is a value of x near 2 that will produce a volume of 65. The table shows $x = 1.9$ to one decimal place:

x	1.8	1.9	2
$V(x)$	66.5	65.4	64

(B) $x = 1.93$ to two decimal places

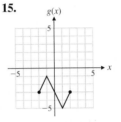

89. $v = \dfrac{75 - w}{15 + w}$; 1.9032 cm/sec

Exercise 1-2

1. Domain: all real numbers; range: all real numbers   **3.** Domain: $[0, \infty)$; range: $(-\infty, 0]$
5. Domain: all real numbers; range: $[0, \infty)$ **7.** Domain: all real numbers; range: all real numbers

9.
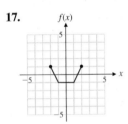

11.
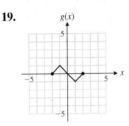

13.
$g(x)$ graph

15.
$g(x)$ graph

17.
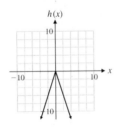

19.
$g(x)$ graph

21. The graph of $g(x) = -|x + 3|$ is the graph of $y = |x|$ reflected in the x axis and shifted 3 units to the left.

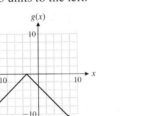

23. The graph of $f(x) = (x - 4)^2 - 3$ is the graph of $y = x^2$ shifted 4 units to the right and 3 units down.

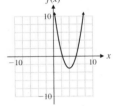

25. The graph of $f(x) = 7 - \sqrt{x}$ is the graph of $y = \sqrt{x}$ reflected in the x axis and shifted 7 units up.

27. The graph of $h(x) = -3|x|$ is the graph of $y = |x|$ reflected in the x axis and vertically expanded by a factor of 3.

29. The graph of the basic function $y = x^2$ is shifted 2 units to the left and 3 units down. Equation: $y = (x + 2)^2 - 3$.
31. The graph of the basic function $y = x^2$ is reflected in the x axis and shifted 3 units to the right and 2 units up. Equation: $y = 2 - (x - 3)^2$.
33. The graph of the basic function $y = \sqrt{x}$ is reflected in the x axis and shifted 4 units up. Equation: $y = 4 - \sqrt{x}$.
35. The graph of the basic function $y = x^3$ is shifted 2 units to the left and 1 unit down. Equation: $y = (x + 2)^3 - 1$.

$f(x)$ graph

$h(x)$ graph

37. $g(x) = \sqrt{x - 2} - 3$ **39.** $g(x) = -|x + 3|$ **41.** $g(x) = -(x - 2)^3 - 1$ **43.**

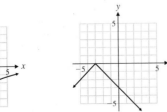

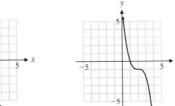

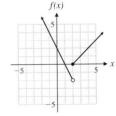

45.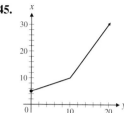

47.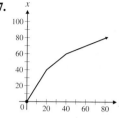

49. The graph of the basic function $y = |x|$ is reflected in the x axis and vertically contracted by a factor of 0.5. Equation: $y = -0.5|x|$.

51. The graph of the basic function $y = x^2$ is reflected in the x axis and vertically expanded by a factor of 2. Equation: $y = -2x^2$.

53. The graph of the basic function $y = \sqrt[3]{x}$ is reflected in the x axis and vertically expanded by a factor of 3. Equation: $y = -3\sqrt[3]{x}$.

55. Reversing the order does not change the result.

57. Reversing the order can change the result.   **59.** Reversing the order can change the result.

61. (A) The graph of the basic function $y = \sqrt{x}$ is reflected in the x axis, vertically expanded by a factor of 4, and shifted up 115 units.

(B)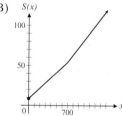

63. (A) The graph of the basic function $y = x^3$ is vertically contracted by a factor of 0.000 48 and shifted right 500 units and up 60,000 units.

(B)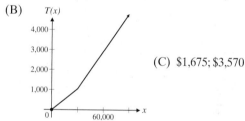

65. (A) $S(x) = \begin{cases} 8.5 + 0.065x & \text{if } 0 \le x \le 700 \\ -9 + 0.09x & \text{if } x > 700 \end{cases}$

(B)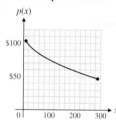

67. (A) $T(x) = \begin{cases} 0.035x & \text{if } 0 \le x \le 30{,}000 \\ 0.0625x - 825 & \text{if } 30{,}000 < x \le 60{,}000 \\ 0.0645x - 945 & \text{if } x > 60{,}000 \end{cases}$

(B)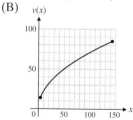

(C) \$1,675; \$3,570

69. (A) The graph of the basic function $y = x$ is vertically expanded by a factor of 5.5 and shifted down 220 units.

(B)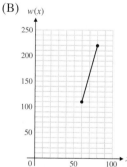

71. (A) The graph of the basic function $y = \sqrt{x}$ is vertically expanded by a factor of 7.08.

(B)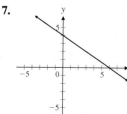

Exercise 1-3

1. (D)   **3. (C)**; slope is 0   **5.** 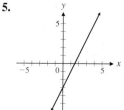   **7.**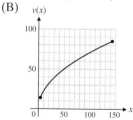

9. Slope $= 3$; y intercept $= 1$

11. Slope $= -\frac{3}{7}$; y intercept $= -6$

13. $y = -2x + 3$

15. $y = \frac{4}{3}x - 4$

17.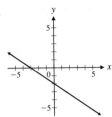

19.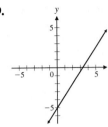

21.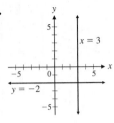

23. -4 **25.** $-\frac{3}{5}$

27.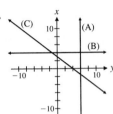

29.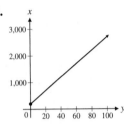

31. (A)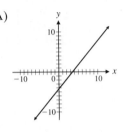

(B) x intercept: 3.5; y intercept: -4.2

(C)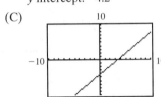

(D) x intercept: 3.5; y intercept: -4.2

(E) $x > 3.5$ or $(3.5, \infty)$

33. $x = 4, y = -3$ **35.** $x = -1.5, y = -3.5$ **37.** $y = -4x + 5$ **39.** $y = \frac{3}{2}x + 1$ **41.** $y = 4.6$

43. (A) $m = \dfrac{2}{3}$ (B) $-2x + 3y = 11$ (C) Linear function   **45.** (A) $m = -\dfrac{5}{4}$ (B) $5x + 4y = -14$ (C) Linear function

47. (A) Not defined (B) $x = 5$ (C) Neither   **49.** (A) $m = 0$ (B) $y = 5$ (C) Constant function

51. The graphs have the same y intercept, $(0, 2)$.

53. (A)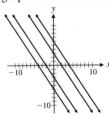

(B) Varying C produces a family of parallel lines. This is verified by observing that varying C does not change the slope of the lines but changes the intercepts.

55. The graph of g is the same as the graph of f for x satisfying $mx + b \geq 0$ and the reflection of the graph of f in the x axis for x satisfying $mx + b < 0$. The function g is never linear.

57. (A) \$130; \$220

(B)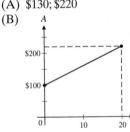

(C) The slope is 6. The amount in the account is growing at the rate of \$6 per year.

59. (A) $C(x) = 180x + 200$

(B) \$2,360

(C)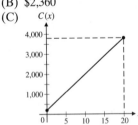

61. (A)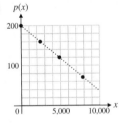

(B) $p(x) = -\frac{1}{60}x + 200$

(C) $p(3,000) = \$150$

(D) The slope is $-\frac{1}{60} \approx -0.02$. The price decreases \$0.02 for each unit increase in demand.

63. (A) Supply: $p = 0.4x - 0.9$; demand: $p = -0.4x + 6.42$ (B) 9.15 million bushels at \$2.76 per bushel

65. (A)

x	0	1	2	3	4
Sales	16.7	19.8	23.6	26.9	32.7
$f(x)$	16.1	20.0	23.9	27.9	31.8

(B)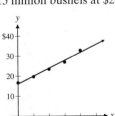

(C) \$55.22 billion, \$74.77 billion

67. (A) $f(x) = -1.25x + 97$

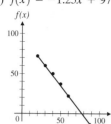

(B) $63.25\%, 30.75\%$ (C) Mid-1997

69. $0.2x + 0.1y = 20$

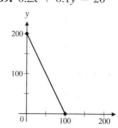

71. (A) 64 g; 35 g   (B)

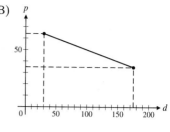

(C) $-\frac{1}{5}$

Exercise 1-4

1. $(x - 2)^2 - 1$ **3.** $-(x - 3)^2 + 5$ **5.** The graph of $f(x)$ is the graph of $y = x^2$ shifted right 2 units and down 1 unit.
7. The graph of $m(x)$ is the graph of $y = x^2$ reflected in the x axis, then shifted right 3 units and up 5 units.
9. (A) m (B) g (C) f (D) n
11. (A) x intercepts: $1, 3$; y intercept: -3 (B) Vertex: $(2, 1)$ (C) Maximum: 1 (D) Range: $y \leq 1$ or $(-\infty, 1]$
  (E) Increasing interval: $x \leq 2$ or $(-\infty, 2]$ (F) Decreasing interval: $x \geq 2$ or $[2, \infty)$
13. (A) x intercepts: $-3, -1$; y intercept: 3 (B) Vertex: $(-2, -1)$ (C) Minimum: -1 (D) Range: $y \geq -1$ or $[-1, \infty)$
  (E) Increasing interval: $x \geq -2$ or $[-2, \infty)$ (F) Decreasing interval: $x \leq -2$ or $(-\infty, -2]$
15. (A) x intercepts: $3 \pm \sqrt{2}$, y intercept: -7 (B) Vertex: $(3, 2)$ (C) Maximum: 2 (D) Range: $y \leq 2$ or $(-\infty, 2]$
17. (A) x intercepts: $-1 \pm \sqrt{2}$, y intercept: -1 (B) Vertex: $(-1, -2)$ (C) Minimum: -2 (D) Range: $y \geq -2$ or $[-2, \infty)$
19. $y = -[x - (-2)]^2 + 5$ or $y = -(x + 2)^2 + 5$ **21.** $y = (x - 1)^2 - 3$
23. Standard form: $(x - 4)^2 - 4$ (A) x intercepts: 2 and 6, y intercept: 12 (B) Vertex: $(4, -4)$ (C) Minimum: -4
  (D) Range: $y \geq -4$ or $[-4, \infty)$
25. Standard form: $-4(x - 2)^2 + 1$ (A) x intercepts: 1.5 and 2.5, y intercept: -15 (B) Vertex: $(2, 1)$ (C) Maximum: 1
  (D) Range: $y \leq 1$ or $(-\infty, 1]$
27. Standard form: $0.5(x - 2)^2 + 3$ (A) x intercepts: none, y intercept: 5 (B) Vertex: $(2, 3)$ (C) Minimum: 3
  (D) Range: $y \geq 3$ or $[3, \infty)$
29. (A) $-4.87, 8.21$ (B) $-3.44, 6.78$ (C) No solution
31. 651.0417 **33.** The vertex of the parabola is on the x axis.
35. $g(x) = 0.25(x - 3)^2 - 9.25$ (A) x intercepts: $-3.08, 9.08$; y intercept: -7 (B) Vertex: $(3, -9.25)$
  (C) Minimum: -9.25 (D) Range: $y \geq -9.25$ or $[-9.25, \infty)$
37. $f(x) = -0.12(x - 4)^2 + 3.12$ (A) x intercepts: $-1.1, 9.1$; y intercept: 1.2 (B) Vertex: $(4, 3.12)$
  (C) Maximum: 3.12 (D) Range: $y \leq 3.12$ or $(-\infty, 3.12]$
39. $x = -5.37, 0.37$ **41.** $-1.37 < x < 2.16$
43. $x \leq -0.74$ or $x \geq 4.19$ **45.** Axis: $x = 2$; vertex: $(2, 4)$; range: $y \geq 4$ or $[4, \infty)$; no x intercepts or $7.61 < x \leq 10$
47. (A)

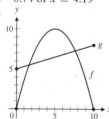

(B) $1.64, 7.61$
(C) $1.64 < x < 7.61$
(D) $0 \leq x < 1.64$

49. (A)

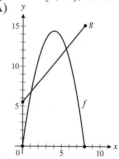

(B) $1.10, 5.57$
(C) $1.10 < x < 5.57$
(D) $0 \leq x < 1.10$
  or $5.57 < x \leq 8$

51. $f(x) = x^2 + 1$ and $g(x) = -(x - 4)^2 - 1$ are two examples. The graphs do not cross the x axis.
53. (A)

x	28	30	32	34	36
Mileage	45	52	55	51	47
$f(x)$	45.3	51.8	54.2	52.4	46.5

(B)

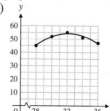

(C) $f(31) = 53.50$ thousand miles; $f(35) = 49.95$ thousand miles

55. (A)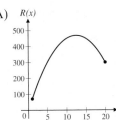

(B) 12,500,000 chips; $468,750,000

(C) $37.50

57. (A)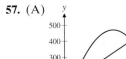

(B) 2,415,000 chips and 17,251,000 chips

(C) Loss: $1 \le x < 2.415$ or $17.251 < x \le 20$; profit: $2.415 < x < 17.251$

59. (A) $P(x) = 59x - 3x^2 - 125$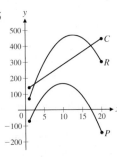

(C) Intercepts and break-even points: 2,415,000 chips and 17,251,000 chips

(E) Maximum profit is $165,083,000 at a production level of 9,833,000 chips. This is much smaller than the maximum revenue of $468,750,000.

61. $x = 0.14$ cm

Chapter 1 Review Exercise

1. 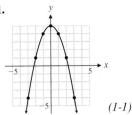 *(1-1)*

2. (A) Not a function (B) A function (C) A function (D) Not a function *(1-1)*

3. (A) -2 (B) -8 (C) 0 (D) Not defined *(1-1)*

4. (A) $y = 4$ (B) $x = 0$ (C) $y = 1$ (D) $x = -1$ or 1 (E) $y = -2$

(F) $x = -5$ or 5 *(1-1)*

5. (A) 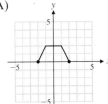 (B) 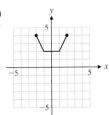 (C) 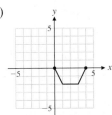 (D) 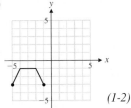 *(1-2)*

6. (A) n (B) g (C) m; slope is zero (D) f; slope is not defined *(1-3)*

7. $y = -\frac{2}{3}x + 6$ *(1-3)*

8. Vertical line: $x = -6$; horizontal line: $y = 5$ *(1-3)*

9. x intercept $= 9$; y intercept $= -6$; slope $= \frac{2}{3}$ *(1-3)*

10. $f(x) = -(x - 2)^2 + 4$. The graph of $f(x)$ is the graph of $y = x^2$ reflected in the x axis, then shifted right 2 units and up 4 units.

11. (A) g (B) m (C) n (D) f *(1-2, 1-4)*

12. (A) x intercepts: $-4, 0$; y intercept: 0 (B) Vertex: $(-2, -4)$

(C) Minimum: -4 (D) Range: $y \ge -4$ or $[-4, \infty)$

(E) Increasing on $[-2, \infty)$ (F) Decreasing on $(-\infty, -2]$ *(1-4)*

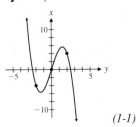

14. 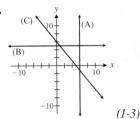 *(1-1)*

15. *(1-3)*

16. Linear functions: (A), (C), (E), (F); constant function: (D) *(1-3)*

17. (A) All real numbers except $x = -2$ and 3

(B) $x < 5$ *(1-1)*

18. Function g multiplies a domain element by 2 and then subtracts 3 times the square root of the domain element from the result. *(1-1)*

19. Standard form: $4(x + \frac{1}{2})^2 - 4$ (A) x intercepts: $-\frac{3}{2}$ and $\frac{1}{2}$; y intercept: -3 (B) Vertex: $(-\frac{1}{2}, -4)$ (C) Minimum: -4
(D) Range: $y \geq -4$ or $[-4, \infty)$

20. The graph of $x = -3$ is a vertical line with x intercept -3, and the graph of $y = 2$ is a horizontal line with y intercept 2. *(1-3)*

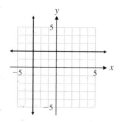

21. (A)

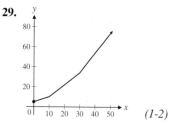

(B) The equation $f(x) = 3$ has one solution; the equation $f(x) = 2$ has two solutions; and the equation $f(x) = 1$ has three solutions.
(C) $f(x) = 3$: $x = -4.28$; $f(x) = 2$: $x = -4.19, 1.19$; $f(x) = 1$: $x = -4.10, 0.35, 1.75$ *(1-1)*

22. (A) -1 (B) $-1 - 2h$ (C) $-2h$ (D) -2 *(1-1)*

23. (A) $a^2 - 3a + 1$ (B) $a^2 + 2ah + h^2 - 3a - 3h + 1$ (C) $2ah + h^2 - 3h$ (D) $2a + h - 3$ *(1-1)*

24. The graph of function m is the graph of $y = |x|$ reflected in the x axis and shifted to the right 4 units. *(1-2)*

25. The graph of function g is the graph of $y = x^3$ vertically contracted by a factor of 0.3 and shifted up 3 units. *(1-2)*

26. The graph of $y = x^2$ is vertically expanded by a factor of 2, reflected in the x axis, and shifted to the left 3 units.
Equation: $y = -2(x + 3)^2$ *(1-2)*

27. $f(x) = 2\sqrt{x + 3} - 1$ *(1-2)*

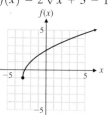

28.

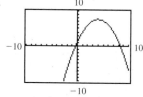

(1-2)

29.

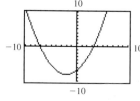

(1-2)

30. (A) $y = -\frac{2}{3}x$ (B) $y = 3$ *(1-3)*

31. (A) $3x + 2y = 1$ (B) $y = 5$ (C) $x = -2$ *(1-3)*

32. $y = -(x - 4)^2 + 3$ *(1-2, 1-4)*

33. $f(x) = -0.4(x - 4)^2 + 7.6$ (A) x intercepts: $-0.4, 8.4$; y intercept: 1.2 (B) Vertex: $(4.0, 7.6)$ (C) Maximum: 7.6
(D) Range: $x \leq 7.6$ or $(-\infty, 7.6]$ *(1-4)*

34.

(A) x intercepts: $-0.4, 8.4$; y intercept: 1.2
(B) Vertex: $(4.0, 7.6)$
(C) Maximum: 7.6
(D) Range: $x \leq 7.6$ or $(-\infty, 7.6]$ *(1-4)*

35. The graph of $y = \sqrt[3]{x}$ is vertically expanded by a factor of 2, reflected in the x axis, and shifted 1 unit left and 1 unit down.
Equation: $y = -2\sqrt[3]{x + 1} - 1$. *(1-2)*

36. The graphs appear to be perpendicular to each other. (It can be shown that if the slopes of two slant lines are the negative reciprocals of each other, then the two lines are perpendicular.) *(1-3)*

37. $G(x) = 0.3(x + 2)^2 - 8.1$ (A) x intercepts: $-7.2, 3.2$; y intercept: -6.9 (B) Vertex: $(-2, -8.1)$ (C) Minimum: -8.1
(D) Range: $x \geq -8.1$ or $[-8.1, \infty)$ (E) Decreasing: $(-\infty, -2]$; increasing: $[-2, \infty)$ *(1-4)*

38.

(A) x intercepts: $-7.2, 3.2$;
y intercept: -6.9
(B) Vertex: $(-2, -8.1)$
(C) Minimum: -8.1
(D) Range: $x \geq -8.1$ or $[-8.1, \infty)$
(E) Decreasing: $(-\infty, -2]$;
increasing: $[-2, \infty)$ *(1-4)*

39. (A) $V(t) = -1,250t + 12,000, 0 \leq t \leq 8$

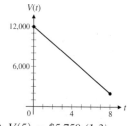

(B) $V(5) = \$5,750$ *(1-3)*

40. (A)

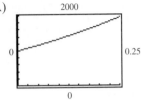

(B) $r = 0.1447$ or 14.47% compounded annually
(1-1, 1-2)

41. (A) $R = 1.6C$
(B) \$192
(C) \$110
(D) 1.6; the slope indicates the change in retail price per unit change in cost. *(1-3)*

42. (A)

x	0	5	10	15	20
Consumption	271	255	233	236	256
f(x)	274	248.5	237	239.5	256

(B)

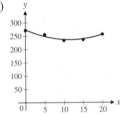

(C) 286.5, 331 *(1-4)*

43. (A) $S(x) = \begin{cases} 3 & \text{if } 0 \le x \le 20 \\ 0.057x + 1.86 & \text{if } 20 < x \le 200 \\ 0.0346x + 6.34 & \text{if } 200 < x \le 1{,}000 \\ 0.0217x + 19.24 & \text{if } x > 1{,}000 \end{cases}$

(B)

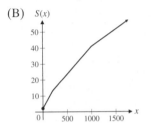

(1-2)

44. (A) Supply: $p = 0.04x - 14.5$; demand: $p = -0.02x + 11$
(B) 425 million bushels at \$2.50 per bushel *(1-3)*

45. (A) $C = 84{,}000 + 15x$; $R = 50x$

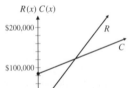

(B) $R = C$ at $x = 2{,}400$ units; $R < C$ for $0 \le x < 2{,}400$; $R > C$ for $x > 2{,}400$
(C) Same as (B) *(1-3)*

46. (A)

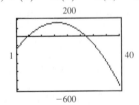

(B) $R = C$ for $x = 4.686$ thousand units (4,686 units) and for $x = 27.314$ thousand units (27,314 units); $R < C$ for $1 \le x < 4.686$ or $27.314 < x \le 40$; $R > C$ for $4.686 < x < 27.314$.
(C) Maximum revenue is 500 thousand dollars (\$500,000). This occurs at an output of 20 thousand units (20,000 units). At this output, the wholesale price is $p(20) = \$25$. *(1-3, 1-4)*

47. (A) $P(x) = R(x) - C(x) = x(50 - 1.25x) - (160 + 10x)$

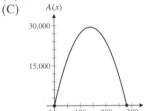

(B) $P = 0$ for $x = 4.686$ thousand units (4,686 units) and for $x = 27.314$ thousand units (27,314 units); $P < 0$ for $1 \le x < 4.686$ or $27.314 < x \le 40$; $P > 0$ for $4.686 < x < 27.314$.
(C) Maximum profit is 160 thousand dollars (\$160,000). This occurs at an output of 16 thousand units (16,000 units). At this output, the wholesale price is $p(16) = \$30$. *(1-4)*

48. (A) $A(x) = -\frac{3}{2}x^2 + 420x$
(B) Domain: $0 \le x \le 280$
(C)

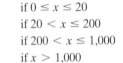

(D) There are two solutions to the equation $A(x) = 25{,}000$, one near 90 and another near 190.
(E) 86 ft; 194 ft
(F) Maximum combined area is 29,400 ft². This occurs for $x = 140$ ft and $y = 105$ ft. *(1-4)*

49. (A) $P(x) = 15x + 20$ (B) 95
(C) 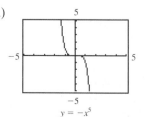   (D) 15 *(1-4)*

50. (A) 1 lb; 3 lb
(B) 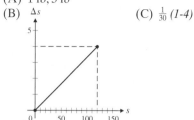   (C) $\frac{1}{30}$ *(1-4)*

Chapter 2

Exercise 2-1

1. (A) 1 (B) $-3/5$ (C) 3   **3.** (A) 2 (B) $3, -3$ (C) -9 **5.** (A) 3 (B) $-3, 2, 5$ (C) 30
7. (A) 2 (B) $-4/3, 9/2$ (C) -36 **9.** (A) 6 (B) None (C) 1   **11.** (A) 3 (B) 4 (C) Negative
13. (A) 4 (B) 5 (C) Negative   **15.** (A) 0 (B) 1 (C) Negative   **17.** (A) 5 (B) 6 (C) Positive   **19.** 7
21. 10   **23.** 1
25. (A) x intercept: -2; y intercept: -1
(B) Domain: all real numbers except 2
(C) Vertical asymptote: $x = 2$; horizontal
asymptote: $y = 1$

27. (A) x intercept: 0; y intercept: 0
(B) Domain: all real numbers except -2
(C) Vertical asymptote: $x = -2$; horizontal
asymptote: $y = 3$

(D) 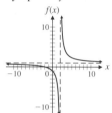   (E)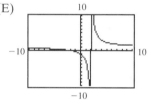

(D) 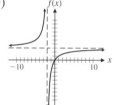   (E)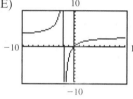

29. (A) x intercept: 2; y intercept: -1
(B) Domain: all real numbers except 4
(C) Vertical asymptote: $x = 4$; horizontal asymptote: $y = -2$
(D) 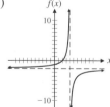   (E)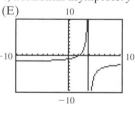

31. The graph will look more and more like the graph
of $y = 2x^4$.

33. The graph will look more and more like the graph
of $y = -x^5$.

35. (A)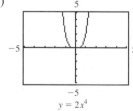
$y = 2x^4$ $y = 2x^4 - 5x^2 + x + 2$
(B)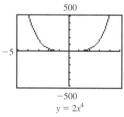
$y = 2x^4$ $y = 2x^4 - 5x^2 + x + 2$

37. (A)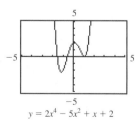
$y = -x^5$ $y = -x^5 + 4x^3 - 4x + 1$
(B)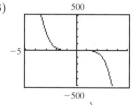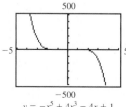
$y = -x^5$ $y = -x^5 + 4x^3 - 4x + 1$

39. $[-9/2, 9/2], -1.84, 0.42, 1.92$ **41.** $[-5, 5], -2.50, -1.22, 0.22, 1.50$ **43.** $[-16, 16], -0.92, 1.30, 11.38$

47. (A) x intercept: 0; y intercept: 0   (B) Vertical asymptotes: $x = -2, x = 3$; horizontal asymptote: $y = 2$

(C) 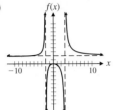   (D)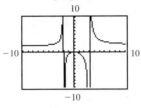

49. (A) x intercept: $\pm\sqrt{3}$; y intercept: $-\frac{2}{3}$ (B) Vertical asymptotes: $x = -3, x = 3$; horizontal asymptote: $y = -2$

(C) 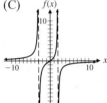   (D)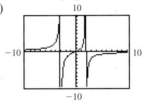

51. (A) x intercept: 0; y intercept: 0   (B) Vertical asymptotes: $x = -3, x = 2$; horizontal asymptote: $y = 0$

(C) 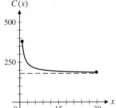   (D)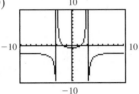

53. $f(x) = x^2 - x - 2$ **55.** $f(x) = 4x - x^3$

57. (A) $C(x) = 180x + 200$ (B) $\overline{C}(x) = \dfrac{180x + 200}{x}$ **59.** (A) $\overline{C}(n) = \dfrac{2{,}500 + 175n + 25n^2}{n}$ (C) 10 yr; $675.00 per year

(C) 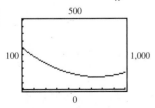   (B) 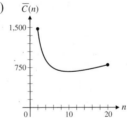   (D) 10 yr; $675.00 per year

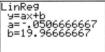

(D) $180 per board

61. (A) $\overline{C}(x) = \dfrac{0.00048(x - 500)^3 + 60{,}000}{x}$ **63.** (A)

(B)

```
LinReg
 y=ax+b
 a=-.0506666667
 b=19.96666667
```

```
QuadReg
 y=ax²+bx+c
 a=2.4444444E-4
 b=-.0065555556
 c=2.086111111
```

(B) $\overline{x} = 195; \overline{p} = \$10.09$

(C) 750 cases per month; $90 per case

65. (A) 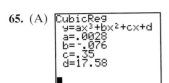 (B) 35.3

67. (A) 0.06 cm/sec   (B)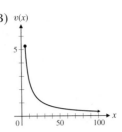

69. (A)  (B) 7.2

Exercise 2-2

1. (A) *k* (B) *g* (C) *h* (D) *f*

3.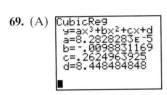

5.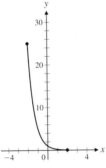

7.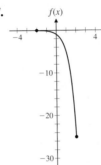

9.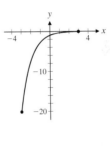

11.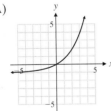

13.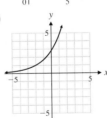

15. 4^{6xy} **17.** *e*   **19.** $8e^{3.6t}$

21. The graph of *g* is a reflection of the graph *f* in the *x* axis.

23. The graph of *g* is the graph of *f* shifted 1 unit to the left.

25. The graph of *g* is the graph of *f* shifted 1 unit up.

27. The graph of *g* is the graph of *f* vertically expanded by a factor of 2 and shifted to the left 2 units.

29. (A)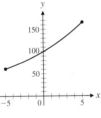

(B)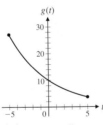

(C)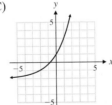

(D)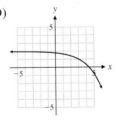

31.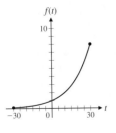

33.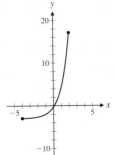

35.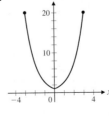

37.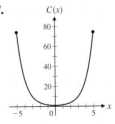

39.

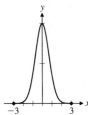

41. $a = 1, -1$ **43.** $x = 1$ **45.** $x = -1, 6$ **47.** $x = 3$
49. $x = 3$ **51.** $x = -3, 0$

53.

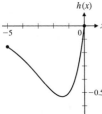

55.

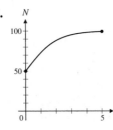

57. $x = 1.40$ **59.** $x = -0.73$
61. (A) $2,633.56   **63.** (A) $11,871.65
         (B) $7,079.54   (B) $20,427.93

65. $10,706   **67.** (A) $10,217.13   (B) $10,200.99   (C) $10,196.91   **69.** $32,201.82
71. N approaches 2 as t increases without bound.   **73.** (A) $5,465,000

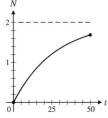

(B) The model gives an average salary of $1,875,000 in 2000.
    Inclusion of the data for 2000 gives an average salary of
    $5,652,000 in 2010.

75. (A) 10%   (B) 1%
77. (A) $N = 60e^{0.08t}$
         (B) 1999: 47,000,000; 2010: 114,000,000
         (C)

79. (A) $P = 6.2e^{0.0125t}$
         (B) 2010: 6.9 billion; 2030: 8.8 billion
         (C)

81. (A) 6,354,000,000

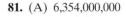

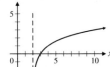

Years since 2002

Years since 2002

Exercise 2-3

1. $27 = 3^3$ **3.** $10^0 = 1$ **5.** $8 = 4^{3/2}$ **7.** $\log_7 49 = 2$ **9.** $\log_4 8 = \frac{3}{2}$ **11.** $\log_b A = u$ **13.** 0   **15.** 1
17. 1   **19.** 3   **21.** -3 **23.** 3   **25.** $\log_b P - \log_b Q$ **27.** $5 \log_b L$ **29.** q^p **31.** $x = 9$ **33.** $y = 2$
35. $b = 10$ **37.** $x = 2$ **39.** $y = -2$ **41.** $b = 100$ **43.** False   **45.** True   **47.** True   **49.** False
51. False   **53.** $x = 2$ **55.** $x = 8$ **57.** $x = 7$ **59.** No solution
61.

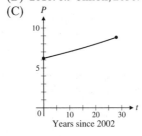

63. The graph of $y = \log_2(x - 2)$ is the graph of $y = \log_2 x$ shifted to the right 2 units.
65. Domain: $(-1, \infty)$; range: all real numbers
67. (A) 3.547 43   (B) $-2.160 32$ (C) 5.626 29   (D) $-3.197 04$
69. (A) 13.4431   (B) 0.0089   (C) 16.0595   (D) 0.1514
71. 1.0792   **73.** 1.4595   **75.** 30.6589   **77.** 18.3559

79. Increasing: $(0, \infty)$

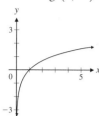

81. Decreasing: $(0,1]$
Increasing: $[1, \infty)$

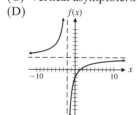

83. Increasing: $(-2, \infty)$

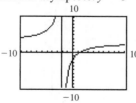

85. Increasing: $(0, \infty)$

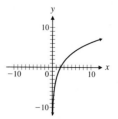

87. Because $b^0 = 1$ for any permissible base b $(b > 0, b \neq 1)$.   **89.** $y = c \cdot 10^{0.8x}$

91. $x > \sqrt{x} > \ln x$ for $1 < x \leq 16$ **93.** 4 yr   **95.** 9.87 yr; 9.80 yr   **97.** 6.758%

99. (A) 5,373   (B) 7,220   **103.** 147.5 bushels/acre   **105.** 817 years

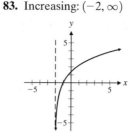

Chapter 2 Review Exercise

1. $v = \ln u$ *(2-3)*   **2.** $y = \log x$ *(2-3)*   **3.** $M = e^N$ *(2-3)*   **4.** $u = 10^v$ *(2-3)*   **5.** 5^{2x} *(2-2)*   **6.** e^{2u^2} *(2-2)*

7. $x = 9$ *(2-3)*   **8.** $x = 6$ *(2-3)*   **9.** $x = 4$ *(2-3)*   **10.** $x = 2.157$ *(2-3)*   **11.** $x = 13.128$ *(2-3)*

12. $x = 1,273.503$ *(2-3)*   **13.** $x = 0.318$ *(2-3)*   **14.** (A) 2   (B) 3   (C) Positive *(2-1)*

15. (A) 3   (B) 4   (C) Negative *(2-1)*

16. (A) x intercept: -4; y intercept: -2 (B) All real numbers, except $x = 2$ (C) Vertical asymptote: $x = 2$;
horizontal asymptote: $y = 1$

(D)

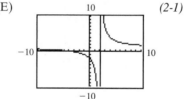

(E)   *(2-1)*

17. (A) x intercept: $\frac{4}{3}$; y intercept: -2 (B) All real numbers, except $x = -2$
(C) Vertical asymptote: $x = -2$; horizontal asymptote: $y = 3$

(D)

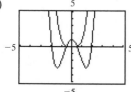

(E)   *(2-1)*

18. $x = 8$ *(2-3)*   **19.** $x = 3$ *(2-3)*   **20.** $x = 3$ *(2-2)*   **21.** $x = -1, 3$ *(2-2)*   **22.** $x = 0, \frac{3}{2}$ *(2-2)*   **23.** $x = -2$ *(2-3)*

24. $x = \frac{1}{2}$ *(2-3)*   **25.** $x = 27$ *(2-3)*   **26.** $x = 13.3113$ *(2-3)*   **27.** $x = 158.7552$ *(2-3)*   **28.** $x = 0.0097$ *(2-3)*

29. $x = 1.4359$ *(2-3)*   **30.** $x = 1.4650$ *(2-3)*   **31.** $x = 92.1034$ *(2-3)*   **32.** $x = 9.0065$ *(2-3)*   **33.** $x = 2.1081$ *(2-3)*

34. $x = 2.8074$ *(2-3)*   **35.** $x = -1.0387$ *(2-3)*   **36.** They look very much alike. *(2-1)*

37. (A)   (B)   *(2-1)*

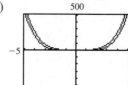

38. $x = -1.14, 6.78$ *(2-1)*   **39.** $(-1.54, -0.79); (0.69, 0.99)$ *(2-2, 2-3)*   **40.** True *(2-1)*   **41.** False *(2-1)*
42. False *(2-1)*   **43.** True *(2-2)*   **44.** True *(2-3)*   **45.** False *(2-3)*   **46.** True *(2-1)*   **47.** False *(2-2)*
48. Increasing: $[-2, 4]$ *(2-2)*   **49.** Decreasing: $[0, \infty)$ *(2-2)*   **50.** Increasing: $(-1, 10]$ *(2-3)*

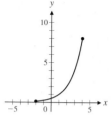

51. $\log 10^\pi = \pi$ and $10^{\log \sqrt{2}} = \sqrt{2}$; $\ln e^\pi = \pi$ and $e^{\ln \sqrt{2}} = \sqrt{2}$ *(2-3)*   **52.** $x = 2$ *(2-3)*   **53.** $x = 2$ *(2-3)*
54. $x = 1$ *(2-3)*   **55.** $x = 300$ *(2-3)*   **56.** $y = ce^{-5t}$ *(2-3)*
57. If $\log_1 x = y$, then $1^y = x$; that is, $1 = x$ for all positive real numbers x, which is not possible. *(2-3)*
58. \$5,971.14 *(2-2)*   **59.** \$5,992.02 *(2-2)*   **60.** 16.7 yr *(2-3)*   **61.** 10.6 yr *(2-3)*

62. (A) $C(x) = 40x + 300; \overline{C}(x) = \dfrac{40x + 300}{x}$ **63.** (A) $\overline{C}(x) = \dfrac{20x^3 - 360x^2 + 2,300x - 1,000}{x}$

(B) $\overline{C}(x)$

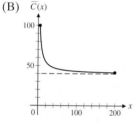

(B)

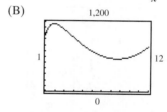

(C) 8.667 thousand cases (8,667)   (D) \$567 per case *(2-1)*

(C) $y = 40$ (D) \$40 per pair *(2-1)*

64. (A) 2,833 sets   (B) 4,836   **65.** (A) 1,879,000,000

```
QuadReg
y=ax²+bx+c
a=5.9477212ε-6
b=-.1024018814
c=422.3467853
```

```
LinReg
y=ax+b
a=.0387421907
b=-7.364689544
```

```
ExpReg
y=a*b^x
a=4.917029881
b=1.346213923
```

(D) Equilibrium price: \$131.59; equilibrium quantity: (B) The model gives 572,000,000 for the number
     3,587 cookware sets *(2-1)*   of wireless subscribers in 2006. *(2-2)*

66. (A) $N = 2^{2t}$ or $N = 4^t$ (B) 15 days *(2-2, 2-3)*   **67.** $k = 0.009\,42$; 489 ft *(2-2, 2-3)*
68. (A) 6,747,000   **69.** 23.4 yr *(2-2, 2-3)*   **70.** 23.1 yr *(2-2, 2-3)*
                                                                    71. (A) \$557 billion   (B) 2009

```
LnReg
y=a+blnx
a=44220.62451
b=-8820.389721
```

```
ExpReg
y=a*b^x
a=43.05517745
b=1.08907428
```

(2-3)   *(2-2)*

Chapter 3

Exercise 3-1

1. (A) 2   (B) 2   (C) 2   (D) 2   **3.** (A) 1   (B) 2   (C) Does not exist   (D) 2   (E) No
5. (A) 1   (B) 2   (C) Does not exist   (D) Does not exist   (E) No
7. (A) 1   (B) 1   (C) 1   (D) 3   (E) Yes, define $g(3) = 1$.
9. (A) -2 (B) -2 (C) -2 (D) 1   (E) Yes   **11.** (A) 2   (B) 2   (C) 2   (D) Does not exist   (E) Yes

13. 12   **15.** 1   **17.** -4 **19.** -1.5 **21.** 3   **23.** 15   **25.** -6 **27.** $\dfrac{7}{5}$ **29.** 10   **31.** 3   **33.** 16

35.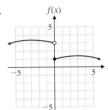

37.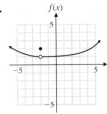

39. (A) 1 (B) 1 (C) 1 (D) 1
41. (A) 2 (B) 1 (C) Does not exist (D) Does not exist
43. (A) −6 (B) Does not exist (C) 6
45. (A) 1 (B) −1 (C) Does not exist (D) Does not exist
47. (A) Does not exist (B) $\frac{1}{2}$ (C) $\frac{1}{4}$
49. (A) −5 (B) −3 (C) 0

51. (A) 0 (B) −1 (C) Does not exist **53.** (A) 1 (B) $\frac{1}{3}$ (C) $\frac{3}{4}$ **55.** 3 **57.** 4

59. $1/(2\sqrt{2})$ **61.** Does not exist **63.** −2

65. (A) $\lim_{x\to 1^-} f(x) = 2$ (B) $\lim_{x\to 1^-} f(x) = 3$ (C) $m = 1.5$ (D) The graph in (A) is broken when
$\lim_{x\to 1^+} f(x) = 3$ $\lim_{x\to 1^+} f(x) = 2$ it jumps from $(1, 2)$ up to $(1, 3)$.
The graph in (B) is also broken
when it jumps down from $(1, 3)$
to $(1, 2)$. The graph in (C) is one
continuous piece, with no breaks
or jumps.

67. $2a$ **69.** $1/(2\sqrt{a})$

71. (A) $F(x) = \begin{cases} 0.99 & \text{if } 0 < x \le 20 \\ 0.07x - 0.41 & \text{if } x \ge 20 \end{cases}$

(B)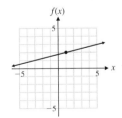

(C) All 3 limits are 0.99.

75. (A) $D(x) = \begin{cases} x & \text{if } 0 \le x < 300 \\ 0.97x & \text{if } 300 \le x < 1,000 \\ 0.95x & \text{if } 1,000 \le x < 3,000 \\ 0.93x & \text{if } 3,000 \le x < 5,000 \\ 0.9x & \text{if } x \ge 5,000 \end{cases}$

(B) $\lim_{x\to 1,000} D(x)$ does not exist because
$\lim_{x\to 1,000^-} D(x) = 970$ and $\lim_{x\to 1,000^+} D(x) = 950$;
$\lim_{x\to 3,000} D(x)$ does not exist because
$\lim_{x\to 3,000^-} D(x) = 2,850$ and $\lim_{x\to 3,000^+} D(x) = 2,790$

77. (A) $F(x) = \begin{cases} 20x & \text{if } 0 < x \le 4,000 \\ 80,000 & \text{if } x \ge 4,000 \end{cases}$

(B) $\lim_{x\to 4,000} F(x) = 80,000$; $\lim_{x\to 8,000} F(x) = 80,000$

79. $\lim_{x\to 5} f(x)$ does not exist; $\lim_{x\to 10} f(x) = 0$;
$\lim_{x\to 5} g(x) = 0$; $\lim_{x\to 10} g(x) = 1$

Exercise 3-2

1. f is continuous at $x = 1$,
since $\lim_{x\to 1} f(x) = f(1)$.

3. f is discontinuous at $x = 1$,
since $\lim_{x\to 1} f(x) \ne f(1)$.

5. f is discontinuous at $x = 1$,
since $\lim_{x\to 1} f(x)$ does not exist.

7. (A) 2 (B) 1 (C) Does not exist (D) 1 (E) No **9.** (A) 1 (B) 1 (C) 1 (D) 3 (E) No
11. (A) 1 (B) 1 (C) 1 (D) 3 (E) No **13.** (A) 2 (B) −1 (C) Does not exist (D) 2 (E) No
15. All x **17.** All x, except $x = -2$ **19.** All x, except $x = -4$ and $x = 1$ **21.** All x

23. All x, except $x = \pm\frac{3}{2}$

25. (A) 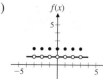   (B) 1   (C) 2   (D) No   (E) All integers

27. $-3 < x < 4; (-3, 4)$

29. $x < 3$ or $x > 7; (-\infty, 3) \cup (7, \infty)$

31. $x < -2$ or $0 < x < 2; (-\infty, -2) \cup (0, 2)$

33. $-5 < x < 0$ or $x > 3; (-5, 0) \cup (3, \infty)$

35. (A) $(-4, -2) \cup (0, 2) \cup (4, \infty)$ **37.** (A) $(-\infty, -2.5308) \cup (-0.7198, \infty)$
(B) $(-\infty, -4) \cup (-2, 0) \cup (2, 4)$ (B) $(-2.5308, -0.7198)$

39. (A) $(-\infty, -2.1451) \cup (-1, -0.5240) \cup (1, 2.6691)$
(B) $(-2.1451, -1) \cup (-0.5240, 1) \cup (2.6691, \infty)$

41. $[6, \infty)$ **43.** $(-\infty, \infty)$ **45.** $(-\infty, -3] \cup [3, \infty)$ **47.** $(-\infty, \infty)$

49. Since $\lim_{x \to 1^-} f(x) = 2$ and $\lim_{x \to 1^+} f(x) = 4$, $\lim_{x \to 1} f(x)$ does not exist and f is not continuous at $x = 1$.

51. This function is continuous for all x.

53. Since $\lim_{x \to 0} f(x) = 0$ and $f(0) = 1$, $\lim_{x \to 0} f(x) \neq f(0)$ and f is not continuous at $x = 0$.

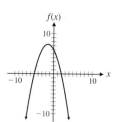

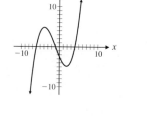

55. Since $\lim_{x \to 2^-} f(x) = 0$ and $\lim_{x \to 2^+} f(x) = 4$, $\lim_{x \to 2} f(x)$ does not exist. Furthermore, $f(2)$ is not defined. Thus, f is not continuous at $x = 2$.

57. Since $f(-1)$ and $f(1)$ are not defined, f is not continuous at $x = -1$ and $x = 1$, even though $\lim_{x \to -1} f(x) = 2$ and $\lim_{x \to 1} f(x) = 2$.

59. (A) Yes   (B) Yes   (C) Yes   (D) Yes

61. (A) Yes   (B) No   (C) Yes   (D) No   (E) Yes

63. x intercepts: $x = -5, 2$ **65.** x intercepts: $x = -6, -1, 4$

67. No, but this does not contradict Theorem 2, since f is discontinuous at $x = 1$.

69. The following sketches illustrate that either condition is possible. Theorem 2 implies that one of these two conditions must occur.

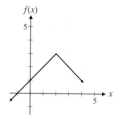

71. (A) $P(x) = \begin{cases} 0.37 & \text{if } 0 < x \le 1 \\ 0.60 & \text{if } 1 < x \le 2 \\ 0.83 & \text{if } 2 < x \le 3 \\ 1.06 & \text{if } 3 < x \le 4 \\ 1.29 & \text{if } 4 < x \le 5 \\ \vdots \\ \vdots \end{cases}$ (B) 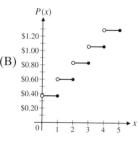   (C) Yes; no

75. (A) $S(x) = \begin{cases} 5 + 0.63x & \text{if } 0 \le x \le 50 \\ 14 + 0.45x & \text{if } 50 < x \end{cases}$ (B) 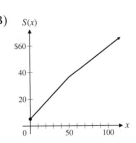   (C) Yes

77. (A) 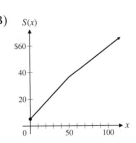   (B) $\lim_{s \to 10,000} E(s) = \$1,000$;
$E(10,000) = \$1,000$
(C) $\lim_{s \to 20,000} E(s)$ does not exist;
$E(20,000) = \$2,000$
(D) Yes; no

79. (A) t_2, t_3, t_4, t_6, t_7
(B) $\lim_{t \to t_5} N(t) = 7; N(t_5) = 7$
(C) $\lim_{t \to t_3} N(t)$ does not exist; $N(t_3) = 4$

Exercise 3-3

1. (A) -3; slope of the secant line through $(1, f(1))$ and $(2, f(2))$
(B) $-2 - h$; slope of the secant line through $(1, f(1))$ and $(1 + h, f(1 + h))$
(C) -2; slope of the tangent line at $(1, f(1))$

3. (A) 15   (B) 15   (C) $6 + 3h$ (D) 6   (E) 6   (F) 6   (G) $y = 6x - 3$

5. $f'(x) = 0; f'(1) = 0, f'(2) = 0, f'(3) = 0$ **7.** $f'(x) = 3; f'(1) = 3, f'(2) = 3, f'(3) = 3$

9. $f'(x) = -6x; f'(1) = -6, f'(2) = -12, f'(3) = -18$ **11.** $f'(x) = 2x + 6; f'(1) = 8, f'(2) = 10, f'(3) = 12$

13. $f'(x) = 4x - 7; f'(1) = -3, f'(2) = 1, f'(3) = 5$ **15.** $f'(x) = -2x + 4; f'(1) = 2, f'(2) = 0, f'(3) = -2$

17. $f'(x) = 6x^2; f'(1) = 6, f'(2) = 24, f'(3) = 54$ **19.** $f'(x) = -\dfrac{4}{x^2}; f'(1) = -4, f'(2) = -1, f'(3) = -\dfrac{4}{9}$

21. $f'(x) = \dfrac{3}{2\sqrt{x}}; f'(1) = \dfrac{3}{2}, f'(2) = \dfrac{3}{2\sqrt{2}}$ or $\dfrac{3\sqrt{2}}{4}, f'(3) = \dfrac{3}{2\sqrt{3}}$ or $\dfrac{\sqrt{3}}{2}$

23. $f'(x) = \dfrac{5}{\sqrt{x + 5}}; f'(1) = \dfrac{5}{\sqrt{6}}$ or $\dfrac{5\sqrt{6}}{6}, f'(2) = \dfrac{5}{\sqrt{7}}$ or $\dfrac{5\sqrt{7}}{7}, f'(3) = \dfrac{5}{2\sqrt{2}}$ or $\dfrac{5\sqrt{2}}{4}$

25. $f'(x) = \dfrac{6}{(x + 2)^2}; f'(1) = \dfrac{2}{3}, f'(2) = \dfrac{3}{8}, f'(3) = \dfrac{6}{25}$

27. (A) 5   (B) $3 + h$ (C) 3   (D) $y = 3x - 1$ **29.** (A) 5 m/s   (B) $3 + h$ m/s   (C) 3 m/s

31. Yes   **33.** No   **35.** Yes   **37.** Yes

39. (A) $f'(x) = 2x - 4$ (B) $-4, 0, 4$
(C)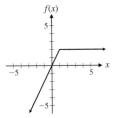

41. $v = f'(x) = 8x - 2; 6$ ft/s, 22 ft/s, 38 ft/s

43. (A) The graphs of g and h are vertical translations of the graph of f. All three functions should have the same derivative.
(B) $2x$

45. (A) The slope of the graph of f is 0 at any point on the graph.

47. f is nondifferentiable at $x = 1$

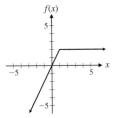

49. f is differentiable for all real numbers

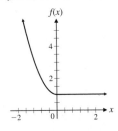

51. No   **53.** No

55. $f'(0) = 0$ **57.** 6 s; 192 ft/s

59. (A) \$8.75   (B) $R'(x) = 60 - 0.05x$
  (C) $R(1,000) = 35,000; R'(1,000) = 10$; At a production level of 1,000 car seats, the revenue is \$35,000 and is increasing at the rate of \$10 per seat.

61. (A) $S'(t) = 1/\sqrt{t} + 10$
  (B) $S(15) = 10; S'(15) = 0.2$. After 15 months, the total sales are \$10 million and are increasing at the rate of \$0.2 million, or \$200,000, per month.
  (C) The estimated total sales are \$10.2 million after 16 months and \$10.4 million after 17 months.

63. (A) $p'(t) = 28t - 6.6$
  (B) $p(15) = 3,653.4; p'(15) = 413.4$; In 2010, 3,653.4 thousand tons of zinc are produced and this quantity is increasing at the rate of 413.4 thousand tons per year.

65. (A)

```
QuadReg
 y=ax²+bx+c
 a=-.0583731517
 b=-1.509819783
 c=50.23597577
```

  (B) In 2010, retail sales will be 1,546.8 billion kilowatthours and will be increasing at the rate of 41.9 billion kilowatthours per year.

67. (A) $P'(t) = 12 - 2t$
  (B) $P(3) = 107; P'(3) = 6$. After 3 hours, the ozone level is 107 ppb and is increasing at the rate of 6 ppb per hour.

69. (A) $f'(t) = 0.022t - 1$
  (B) $f(40) = 7.4; f'(40) = -0.12$; In 2000, the number of male infant deaths per 100,000 births was 7.4 and was decreasing at the rate of -0.12 death per 100,000 births per year.

Exercise 3-4

1. 0   **3.** $9x^8$ **5.** $3x^2$ **7.** $-4x^{-5}$ **9.** $\frac{8}{3}x^{5/3}$ **11.** $-\frac{10}{x^{11}}$ **13.** $10x$ **15.** $2.8x^6$

17. $\frac{x^2}{6}$ **19.** 12   **21.** 2   **23.** 9   **25.** 2   **27.** $4t - 3$ **29.** $-10x^{-3} - 9x^{-2}$

31. $1.5u^{-0.7} - 8.8u^{1.2}$ **33.** $0.5 - 3.3t^2$ **35.** $-\frac{8}{5}x^{-5}$ **37.** $3x + \frac{14}{5}x^{-3}$

39. $-\frac{20}{9}w^{-5} + \frac{5}{3}w^{-2/3}$ **41.** $2u^{-1/3} - \frac{5}{3}u^{-2/3}$ **43.** $-\frac{9}{5}t^{-8/5} + 3t^{-3/2}$ **45.** $-\frac{1}{3}x^{-4/3}$ **47.** $-0.6x^{-3/2} + 6.4x^{-3} + 1$

49. (A) $f'(x) = 6 - 2x$ (B) $f'(2) = 2; f'(4) = -2$ (C) $y = 2x + 4; y = -2x + 16$ (D) $x = 3$

51. (A) $f'(x) = 12x^3 - 12x$ (B) $f'(2) = 72; f'(4) = 720$ (C) $y = 72x - 127; y = 720x - 2,215$ (D) $x = -1, 0, 1$

53. (A) $v = f'(x) = 176 - 32x$ (B) $f'(0) = 176$ ft/s; $f'(3) = 80$ ft/s   (C) 5.5 s

55. (A) $v = f'(x) = 3x^2 - 18x + 15$ (B) $f'(0) = 15$ ft/s; $f'(3) = -12$ ft/s   (C) $x = 1$ s, $x = 5$ s

57. $f'(x) = 2x - 3 - 2x^{-1/2} = 2x - 3 - \frac{2}{x^{1/2}}; x = 2.1777$ **59.** $f'(x) = 4\sqrt[3]{x} - 3x - 3; x = -2.9018$

61. $f'(x) = 0.2x^3 + 0.3x^2 - 3x - 1.6; x = -4.4607, -0.5159, 3.4765$

63. $f'(x) = 0.8x^3 - 9.36x^2 + 32.5x - 28.25; x = 1.3050$

69. $8x - 4$ **71.** $-20x^{-2}$ **73.** $-\frac{1}{4}x^{-2} + \frac{2}{3}x^{-3}$ **75.** $2x - 3 - 10x^{-3}$

81. (A) $S'(t) = 0.09t^2 + t + 2$
  (B) $S(5) = 29.25, S'(5) = 9.25$. After 5 months, sales are \$29.25 million and are increasing at the rate of \$9.25 million per month.
  (C) $S(10) = 103, S'(10) = 21$. After 10 months, sales are \$103 million and are increasing at the rate of \$21 million per month.

83. (A) $N'(x) = 3,780/x^2$
  (B) $N'(10) = 37.8$. At the \$10,000 level of advertising, sales are increasing at the rate of 37.8 boats per \$1,000 spent on advertising.
  $N'(20) = 9.45$. At the \$20,000 level of advertising, sales are increasing at the rate of 9.45 boats per \$1,000 spent on advertising.

85. (A)
```
CubicReg
y=ax³+bx²+cx+d
a=7.445341406
b=-218.3357137
c=1657.552951
d=2545.706745
```
(B) In 1992, 3,900 limousines were produced and limousine production was decreasing at the rate of 400 limousines per year.
(C) In 1998, 3,900 limousines were produced and limousine production was increasing at the rate of 600 limousines per year.

87. (A) -1.37 beats/min   **(B)** -0.58 beat/min   **89. (A)** 25 items/h   **(B)** 8.33 items/h

Exercise 3-5

1. $2x^3(2x) + (x^2 - 2)(6x^2) = 10x^4 - 12x^2$ **3.** $(x - 3)(2) + (2x - 1)(1) = 4x - 7$

5. $\dfrac{(x - 3)(1) - x(1)}{(x - 3)^2} = \dfrac{-3}{(x - 3)^2}$ **7.** $\dfrac{(x - 2)(2) - (2x + 3)(1)}{(x - 2)^2} = \dfrac{-7}{(x - 2)^2}$

9. $(x^2 + 1)(2) + (2x - 3)(2x) = 6x^2 - 6x + 2$ **11.** $(0.4x + 2)(0.5) + (0.5x - 5)(0.4) = 0.4x - 1$

13. $\dfrac{(2x - 3)(2x) - (x^2 + 1)(2)}{(2x - 3)^2} = \dfrac{2x^2 - 6x - 2}{(2x - 3)^2}$ **15.** $(x^2 + 2)2x + (x^2 - 3)2x = 4x^3 - 2x$

17. $\dfrac{(x^2 - 3)2x - (x^2 + 2)2x}{(x^2 - 3)^2} = \dfrac{-10x}{(x^2 - 3)^2}$ **19.** $xf'(x) + f(x)$ **21.** $x^3 f'(x) + 3x^2 f(x)$ **23.** $\dfrac{x^2 f'(x) - 2xf(x)}{x^4}$

25. $\dfrac{f(x) - xf'(x)}{[f(x)]^2}$ **27.** $(2x + 1)(2x - 3) + (x^2 - 3x)(2) = 6x^2 - 10x - 3$

29. $(2.5t - t^2)(4) + (4t + 1.4)(2.5 - 2t) = -12t^2 + 17.2t + 3.5$

31. $\dfrac{(x^2 + 2x)(5) - (5x - 3)(2x + 2)}{(x^2 + 2x)^2} = \dfrac{-5x^2 + 6x + 6}{(x^2 + 2x)^2}$

33. $\dfrac{(w^2 - 1)(2w - 3) - (w^2 - 3w + 1)(2w)}{(w^2 - 1)^2} = \dfrac{3w^2 - 4w + 3}{(w^2 - 1)^2}$

35. $f'(x) = (1 + 3x)(-2) + (5 - 2x)(3); y = -11x + 29$ **37.** $f'(x) = \dfrac{(3x - 4)(1) - (x - 8)(3)}{(3x - 4)^2}; y = 5x - 13$

39. $f'(x) = (2x - 15)(2x) + (x^2 + 18)(2) = 6(x - 2)(x - 3); x = 2, x = 3$

41. $f'(x) = \dfrac{(x^2 + 1)(1) - x(2x)}{(x^2 + 1)^2} = \dfrac{1 - x^2}{(x^2 + 1)^2}; x = -1, x = 1$ **43.** $7x^6 - 3x^2$ **45.** $-27x^{-4} = -\dfrac{27}{x^4}$

47. $f'(w) = (3w^2 - 1)(6w) + (3w^2 - 1)(6w) = 36w^3 - 12w$

49. $\dfrac{(4x^2 + 5x - 1)(6x - 2) - (3x^2 - 2x + 3)(8x + 5)}{(4x^2 + 5x - 1)^2} = \dfrac{23x^2 - 30x - 13}{(4x^2 + 5x - 1)^2}$

51. $9x^{1/3}(3x^2) + (x^3 + 5)(3x^{-2/3}) = \dfrac{30x^3 + 15}{x^{2/3}}$ **53.** $\dfrac{(x^2 - 3)(2x^{-2/3}) - 6x^{1/3}(2x)}{(x^2 - 3)^2} = \dfrac{-10x^2 - 6}{(x^2 - 3)^2 x^{2/3}}$

55. $g'(t) = \dfrac{(3t^2 - 1)(0.2) - (0.2t)(6t)}{(3t^2 - 1)^2} = \dfrac{-0.6t^2 - 0.2}{(3t^2 - 1)^2}$ **57.** $x^{-2/3}(3x^2 - 4x) + (x^3 - 2x^2)(-\tfrac{2}{3}x^{-5/3}) = -\tfrac{8}{3}x^{1/3} + \tfrac{7}{3}x^{4/3}$

59. $\dfrac{(x^2 + 1)[(2x^2 - 1)(2x) + (x^2 + 3)(4x)] - (2x^2 - 1)(x^2 + 3)(2x)}{(x^2 + 1)^2} = \dfrac{4x^5 + 8x^3 + 16x}{(x^2 + 1)^2}$

61. $x = 1.2117$ **63.** $x = -3.7212, x = -1, x = 1.3586, x = 3.3626$

65. (A) $S'(t) = \dfrac{(t^2 + 50)(180t) - 90t^2(2t)}{(t^2 + 50)^2} = \dfrac{9,000t}{(t^2 + 50)^2}$

(B) $S(10) = 60; S'(10) = 4$. After 10 months, the total sales are 60,000 CDs, and sales are increasing at the rate of 4,000 CDs per month.
(C) Approximately 64,000 CDs

67. (A) $\dfrac{dx}{dp} = \dfrac{(0.1p + 1)(0) - 4,000(0.1)}{(0.1p + 1)^2} = \dfrac{-400}{(0.1p + 1)^2}$

(B) $x = 800; dx/dp = -16$. At a price level of \$40, the demand is 800 CD players per week, and demand is decreasing at the rate of 16 players per dollar.
(C) Approximately 784 CD players

69. (A) $C'(t) = \dfrac{(t^2 + 1)(0.14) - 0.14t(2t)}{(t^2 + 1)^2} = \dfrac{0.14 - 0.14t^2}{(t^2 + 1)^2}$

(B) $C'(0.5) = 0.0672$. After 0.5 h, concentration is increasing at the rate of 0.0672 mg/cm^3 per hour.
$C'(3) = -0.0112$. After 3 h, concentration is decreasing at the rate of 0.0112 mg/cm^3 per hour.

71. (A) $N'(x) = \dfrac{(x + 32)(100) - (100x + 200)}{(x + 32)^2} = \dfrac{3{,}000}{(x + 32)^2}$

(B) $N'(4) = 2.31$; $N'(68) = 0.30$

Exercise 3-6

1. 3   **3.** $(-4x)$ **5.** $(2 + 6x)$ **7.** $6(2x + 5)^2$ **9.** $-8(5 - 2x)^3$ **11.** $5(4 + 0.2x)^4(0.2) = (4 + 0.2x)^4$

13. $30x(3x^2 + 5)^4$ **15.** $8(x^3 - 2x^2 + 2)^7(3x^2 - 4x)$ **17.** $(2x - 5)^{-1/2} = \dfrac{1}{(2x - 5)^{1/2}}$

19. $-8x^3(x^4 + 1)^{-3} = \dfrac{-8x^3}{(x^4 + 1)^3}$ **21.** $f'(x) = 6(2x - 1)^2$; $y = 6x - 5$; $x = \frac{1}{2}$

23. $f'(x) = 2(4x - 3)^{-1/2} = \dfrac{2}{(4x - 3)^{1/2}}$; $y = \dfrac{2}{3}x + 1$; none   **25.** $12(x^2 - 2)^3(2x) = 24x(x^2 - 2)^3$

27. $-6(t^2 + 3t)^{-4}(2t + 3) = \dfrac{-6(2t + 3)}{(t^2 + 3t)^4}$ **29.** $\dfrac{1}{2}(w^2 + 8)^{-1/2}(2w) = \dfrac{w}{\sqrt{w^2 + 8}}$

31. $\dfrac{1}{3}(3x + 4)^{-2/3}(3) = \dfrac{1}{\sqrt[3]{(3x + 4)^2}}$ **33.** $\dfrac{1}{4}(0.8x + 3.6)^{-3/4}(0.8) = \dfrac{0.2}{\sqrt[4]{(0.8x + 3.6)^3}}$

35. $\dfrac{1}{2}(t^2 - 4t + 2)^{-1/2}(2t - 4) = \dfrac{t - 2}{\sqrt{t^2 - 4t + 2}}$ **37.** $-(2x + 4)^{-2}(2) = \dfrac{-2}{(2x + 4)^2}$

39. $-5(w^3 + 4)^{-6}(3w^2) = \dfrac{-15w^2}{(w^3 + 4)^6}$ **41.** $5(3x^{1/2} - 1)^4 \dfrac{3}{2}x^{-1/2} = \dfrac{15(3\sqrt{x} - 1)^4}{2\sqrt{x}}$

43. $4\left(-\dfrac{1}{2}\right)(t^2 - 3t)^{-3/2}(2t) = \dfrac{-4t + 6}{\sqrt{(t^2 - 3t)^3}}$ **45.** $f'(x) = (4 - x)^3 - 3x(4 - x)^2 = 4(4 - x)^2(1 - x)$; $y = -16x + 48$

47. $f'(x) = \dfrac{(2x - 5)^3 - 6x(2x - 5)^2}{(2x - 5)^6} = \dfrac{-4x - 5}{(2x - 5)^4}$; $y = -17x + 54$

49. $f'(x) = (2x + 2)^{1/2} + x(2x + 2)^{-1/2} = \dfrac{3x + 2}{(2x + 2)^{1/2}}$; $y = \frac{5}{2}x - \frac{1}{2}$

51. $f'(x) = 2x(x - 5)^3 + 3x^2(x - 5)^2 = 5x(x - 5)^2(x - 2)$; $x = 0, 2, 5$

53. $f'(x) = \dfrac{(2x + 5)^2 - 4x(2x + 5)}{(2x + 5)^4} = \dfrac{5 - 2x}{(2x + 5)^3}$; $x = \frac{5}{2}$

55. $f'(x) = (x^2 - 8x + 20)^{-1/2}(x - 4) = \dfrac{x - 4}{(x^2 - 8x + 20)^{1/2}}$; $x = 4$ **57.** $-1.4903, 0.4752, 1.7651$

59. $0.0000, 1.5465$ **61.** $-1.7723, 0.0835, 1.6888$ **63.** $18x^2(x^2 + 1)^2 + 3(x^2 + 1)^3 = 3(x^2 + 1)^2(7x^2 + 1)$

65. $\dfrac{24x^5(x^3 - 7)^3 - (x^3 - 7)^4 6x^2}{4x^6} = \dfrac{3(x^3 - 7)^3(3x^3 + 7)}{2x^4}$

67. $(2x - 3)^2[12x(2x^2 + 1)^2] + (2x^2 + 1)^3[4(2x - 3)] = 4(2x^2 + 1)^2(2x - 3)(8x^2 - 9x + 1)$

69. $4x^3(x^2 - 1)^{-1/2} + 8x(x^2 - 1)^{1/2} = \dfrac{12x^3 - 8x}{(x^2 - 1)^{1/2}}$ **71.** $\dfrac{(x - 3)^{1/2}(2) - x(x - 3)^{-1/2}}{x - 3} = \dfrac{x - 6}{(x - 3)^{3/2}}$

73. $\frac{1}{2}[(2x - 1)^3(x^2 + 3)^4]^{-1/2}[8x(2x - 1)^3(x^2 + 3)^3 + 6(x^2 + 3)^4(2x - 1)^2] = (2x - 1)^{1/2}(x^2 + 3)(11x^2 - 4x + 9)$

75. (A) $C'(x) = (2x + 16)^{-1/2} = \dfrac{1}{(2x + 16)^{1/2}}$

(B) $C'(24) = \frac{1}{8}$, or \$12.50. At a production level of 24 calculators, total cost is increasing at the rate of \$12.50 per calculator; also, the cost of producing the 25th calculator is approximately \$12.50.
$C'(42) = \frac{1}{10}$, or \$10.00. At a production level of 42 calculators, total cost is increasing at the rate of \$10.00 per calculator; also, the cost of producing the 43rd calculator is approximately \$10.00.

77. (A) $\dfrac{dx}{dp} = 40(p + 25)^{-1/2} = \dfrac{40}{(p + 25)^{1/2}}$

(B) $x = 400$ and $dx/dp = 4$. At a price of $75, the supply is 400 speakers per week, and supply is increasing at the rate of 4 speakers per dollar.

79. $4,000(1 + \frac{1}{12}r)^{47}$ **81.** $\dfrac{(4 \times 10^6)x}{(x^2 - 1)^{5/3}}$

83. (A) $f'(n) = n(n - 2)^{-1/2} + 2(n - 2)^{1/2}$

(B) $f'(11) = \frac{29}{3} = 9.67$. When the list contains 11 items, the learning time is increasing at the rate of 9.67 min per item.
$f'(27) = \frac{77}{5} = 15.4$. When the list contains 27 items, the learning time is increasing at the rate of 15.4 min per item.

Exercise 3-7

1. (A) $29.50   (B) $30

3. (A) $420

(B) $\overline{C}'(500) = -0.24$. At a production level of 500 frames, average cost is decreasing at the rate of 24¢ per frame.

(C) Approximately $419.76

5. (A) $14.70   (B) $15

7. (A) $P'(450) = 0.5$. At a production level of 450 cassettes, profit is increasing at the rate of 50¢ per cassette.

(B) $P'(750) = -2.5$. At a production level of 750 cassettes, profit is decreasing at the rate of $2.50 per cassette.

9. (A) $13.50

(B) $\overline{P}'(50) = \$0.27$. At a production level of 50 mowers, the average profit per mower is increasing at the rate of $0.27 per mower.

(C) Approximately $13.77

11. (A) $p = 100 - 0.025x$, domain: $0 \le x \le 4,000$

(B) $R(x) = 100x - 0.025x^2$, domain: $0 \le x \le 4,000$

(C) $R'(1,600) = 20$. At a production level of 1,600 radios, revenue is increasing at the rate of $20 per radio.

(D) $R'(2,500) = -25$. At a production level of 2,500 radios, revenue is decreasing at the rate of $25 per radio.

13. (A) $p = 200 - \frac{1}{30}x$, domain: $0 \le x \le 6,000$

(B) $C'(x) = 60$

(C) $R(x) = 200x - (x^2/30)$, domain: $0 \le x \le 6,000$

(D) $R'(x) = 200 - (x/15)$

(E) $R'(1,500) = 100$. At a production level of 1,500 saws, revenue is increasing at the rate of $100 per saw.
$R'(4,500) = -100$. At a production level of 4,500 saws, revenue is decreasing at the rate of $100 per saw.

(F) Break-even points; $(600, 108,000)$ and $(3,600, 288,000)$ (G) $P(x) = -(x^2/30) + 140x - 72,000$

(H) $P'(x) = -(x/15) + 140$

(I) $P'(1,500) = 40$. At a production level of 1,500 saws, profit is increasing at the rate of $40 per saw. $P'(3,000) = -60$. At a production level of 3,000 saws, profit is decreasing at the rate of $60 per saw.

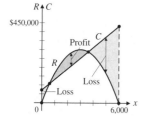

15. (A) $p = 20 - 0.02x$, domain: $0 \le x \le 1,000$ (B) $R(x) = 20x - 0.02x^2$, domain: $0 \le x \le 1,000$

(C) $C(x) = 4x + 1,400$ (D) Break-even points: $(100, 1,800)$ and $(700, 4,200)$ (E) $P(x) = 16x - 0.02x^2 - 1,400$

(F) $P'(250) = 6$. At a production level of 250 toasters, profit is increasing at the rate of $6 per toaster. $P'(475) = -3$. At a production level of 475 toasters, profit is decreasing at the rate of $3 per toaster.

17. (A) $x = 500$ (B) $P(x) = 176x - 0.2x^2 - 21,900$
(C) $x = 440$
(D) Break-even points: (150, 25,500) and
(730, 39,420); x intercepts for $P(x)$: $x = 150$
and $x = 730$

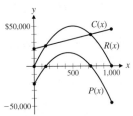

19. (A) $R(x) = 20x - x^{3/2}$
(B) Break-even points: (44, 588), (258, 1,016)

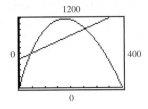

21. (A)
```
QuadReg
y=ax²+bx+c
a=1.4101002e-5
b=-.2732556676
c=1320.924694
```
(B) Fixed costs ≈ $721,680
Variable costs ≈ $121
```
LinReg
y=ax+b
a=120.7047281
b=721680.1282
r=.9934384133
```
(C) (713, 807,703), (5,423, 1,376,227)
(D) $254 \le p \le \$1,133$

Chapter 3 Review Exercise

1. (A) 16   (B) 8   (C) 8   (D) 4   (E) 4   (F) 4 *(3-3)*   **2.** $f'(x) = -3$ *(3-3)*
3. (A) 22   (B) 8   (C) 2   (D) -5 *(3-1)*   **4.** (A) 1   (B) 1   (C) 1   (D) 1 *(3-1)*
5. (A) 2   (B) 3   (C) Does not exist   (D) 3 *(3-1)*   **6.** (A) 4   (B) 4   (C) 4   (D) Does not exist *(3-1)*
7. (A) Does not exist   (B) 3   (C) No *(3-2)*   **8.** (A) 2   (B) Not defined   (C) No *(3-2)*
9. (A) 1   (B) 1   (C) Yes *(3-2)*   **10.** $f'(x) = 10x$ *(3-3)*

11. (A) -11 (B) -14 (C) $\frac{5}{2}$ (D) -8 *(3-4, 3-5, 3-6)*   (E) 15   (F) $-\dfrac{23}{49}$

12. $(6x + 4)$ *(3-6)*   **13.** $x^2 - 10x$ *(3-4)*   **14.** $x^{-1/2} - 3 = \dfrac{1}{x^{1/2}} - 3$ *(3-4)*   **15.** 0 *(3-4)*

16. $-\dfrac{3}{2}x^{-2} + \dfrac{15}{4}x^2 = \dfrac{-3}{2x^2} + \dfrac{15x^2}{4}$ *(3-4)*   **17.** $-2x^{-5} + x^3 = \dfrac{-2}{x^5} + x^3$ *(3-4)*

18. $(2x - 1)(3) + (3x + 2)(2) = 12x + 1$ *(3-5)*   **19.** $(x^2 - 1)(3x^2) + (x^3 - 3)(2x) = 5x^4 - 3x^2 - 6x$ *(3-5)*

20. $(0.2x - 1.5)(0.5) + (0.5x + 0.4)(0.2) = 0.2x - 0.67$ *(3-5)*   **21.** $\dfrac{(x^2 + 2)2 - 2x(2x)}{(x^2 + 2)^2} = \dfrac{4 - 2x^2}{(x^2 + 2)^2}$ *(3-5)*

22. $(-1)(3x + 2)^{-2}(3) = \dfrac{-3}{(3x + 2)^2}$ *(3-6)*   **23.** $3(2x - 3)^2(2) = 6(2x - 3)^2$ *(3-6)*

24. $-2(x^2 + 2)^{-3}(2x) = \dfrac{-4x}{(x^2 + 2)^3}$ *(3-6)*   **25.** (A) 4   (B) 6   (C) Does not exist   (D) 6   (E) No *(3-2)*

26. (A) 3   (B) 3   (C) 3   (D) 3   (E) Yes *(3-2)*   **27.** (A) $(8, \infty)$ (B) $[0, 8]$ *(3-2)*   **28.** $(-3, 4)$ *(3-2)*
29. $(-3, 0) \cup (5, \infty)$ *(3-2)*   **30.** $(-2.3429, -0.4707) \cup (1.8136, \infty)$ *(3-2)*   **31.** (A) 3   (B) $2 + 0.5h$ (C) 2 *(3-3)*
32. $-x^{-4} + 10x^{-3}$ *(3-4)*   **33.** $(2x^2 - 3x + 2)(2x + 2) + (x^2 + 2x - 1)(4x - 3) = 8x^3 + 3x^2 - 12x + 7$ *(3-5)*
34. $\dfrac{(x - 1)^2(2) - (2x - 3)(2)(x - 1)}{(x - 1)^4} = \dfrac{4 - 2x}{(x - 1)^3}$ *(3-5)*   **35.** $\dfrac{3}{4}x^{-1/2} - \dfrac{5}{6}x^{-3/2} = \dfrac{3}{4\sqrt{x}} - \dfrac{5}{6\sqrt{x^3}}$ *(3-4)*

36. $0.6x^{-2/3} - 0.3x^{-4/3} = \dfrac{0.6}{x^{2/3}} - \dfrac{0.3}{x^{4/3}}$ *(3-4)*

37. $(x^2 - 1)[2(2x + 1)(2)] + (2x + 1)^2(2x) = 2(2x + 1)(4x^2 + x - 2)$ *(3-5, 3-6)*
38. $\dfrac{1}{3}(x^3 - 5)^{-2/3}(3x^2) = \dfrac{x^2}{(x^3 - 5)^{2/3}}$ *(3-6)*   **39.** $-\dfrac{3}{5}(-3)x^{-4} = \dfrac{9}{5x^4}$ *(3-4)*
40. $\dfrac{(2x - 3)(4)(x^2 + 2)^3(2x) - (x^2 + 2)^4(2)}{(2x - 3)^2} = \dfrac{2(x^2 + 2)^3(7x^2 - 12x - 2)}{(2x - 3)^2}$ *(3-5, 3-6)*

41. (A) $m = f'(1) = 2$ (B) $y = 2x + 3$ *(3-3, 3-4)*   **42.** (A) $m = f'(1) = 16$ (B) $y = 16x - 12$ *(3-3, 3-5)*
43. $x = 5$ *(3-4)*   **44.** $x = -5, x = 3$ *(3-5)*   **45.** $x = -2, x = 2$ *(3-5)*   **46.** $x = 0, x = 3, x = \frac{15}{2}$ *(3-5)*
47. $x = -1.3401, 0.5771, 2.2630$ *(3-4)*   **48.** $x = -0.4074, 1.7968$ *(3-5)*   **49.** $x = -0.8944, 0, 0.8944$ *(3-5, 3-6)*
50. (A) $v = f'(x) = 16x - 4$ (B) 44 ft/sec *(3-4)*   **51.** (A) $v = f'(x) = -10x + 16$ (B) $x = 1.6$ sec *(3-4)*
52. (A) The graph of g is the graph of f shifted 4 units to the   (B) The graph of g' is the graph of f' shifted 4 units to
right, and the graph of h is the graph of f shifted   the right, and the graph of h' is the graph of f' shifted
3 units to the left: 3 units to the left:

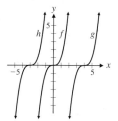

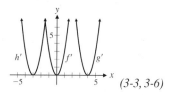
(3-3, 3-6)

53. (A) The graph of g is a horizontal translation of the graph of f, and the graph of g' is a horizontal translation of the
graph of f'.
  (B) The graph of g is a vertical translation of the graph of f, and the graph of g' is the same as the graph of f'. *(3-3)*
54. $(-\infty, \infty)$ *(3-2)*   **55.** $(-\infty, 2) \cup (2, \infty)$ *(3-2)*   **56.** $(-\infty, -4) \cup (-4, 1) \cup (1, \infty)$ *(3-2)*   **57.** $(-\infty, \infty)$ *(3-2)*
58. $[-2, 2]$ *(3-2)*   **59.** (A) -1 (B) Does not exist   (C) $-\frac{2}{3}$ *(3-1)*
60. (A) $\frac{1}{2}$ (B) 0   (C) Does not exist *(3-1)*   **61.** (A) -1 (B) 1   (C) Does not exist *(3-1)*
62. (A) $-\frac{1}{6}$ (B) Does not exist   (C) $-\frac{1}{3}$ *(3-1)*   **63.** (A) 0   (B) -1 (C) Does not exist *(3-1)*
64. 4 *(3-1)*   **65.** $\frac{-1}{(x + 2)^2}$ *(3-1)*
66. (A) $\lim_{x \to -2^-} f(x) = -6$; $\lim_{x \to -2^+} f(x) = 6$; $\lim_{x \to -2} f(x)$ does not exist   (B) $\lim_{x \to 0} f(x) = 4$
  (C) $\lim_{x \to 2^-} f(x) = 2$; $\lim_{x \to 2^+} f(x) = -2$; $\lim_{x \to 2} f(x)$ does not exist *(3-1)*
67. $2x - 1$ *(3-3)*   **68.** $1/(2\sqrt{x})$ *(3-3)*   **69.** No *(3-3)*   **70.** No *(3-3)*   **71.** No *(3-3)*   **72.** Yes *(3-3)*
73. $(x - 4)^4(3)(x + 3)^2 + (x + 3)^3(4)(x - 4)^3 = 7x(x - 4)^3(x + 3)^2$ *(3-5, 3-6)*
74. $5x^3(2)(x^2 - 1)(2x) + 15x^2(x^2 - 1)^2 = 5x^2(x^2 - 1)(7x^2 - 3)$ *(3-5, 3-6)*
75. $\dfrac{(2x + 1)^4(5x^4) - x^5(4)(2x + 1)^3(2)}{(2x + 1)^8} = \dfrac{x^4(2x + 5)}{(2x + 1)^5}$ *(3-5, 3-6)*
76. $\dfrac{x(\frac{1}{2})(x^2 - 1)^{-1/2}(2x) - (x^2 - 1)^{1/2}}{x^2} = \dfrac{1}{x^2(x^2 - 1)^{1/2}}$ *(3-5, 3-6)*
77. $\dfrac{(x^2 + 4)^{1/2} - x(\frac{1}{2})(x^2 + 4)^{-1/2}(2x)}{x^2 + 4} = \dfrac{4}{(x^2 + 4)^{3/2}}$ *(3-5, 3-6)*
78. The domain of $f'(x)$ is all real numbers except $x = 0$. At $x = 0$, the graph of $y = f(x)$ is smooth, but it has a vertical
tangent. *(3-3)*
79. (A) $\lim_{x \to 1^-} f(x) = 1$; $\lim_{x \to 1^+} f(x) = -1$ (B) $\lim_{x \to 1^-} f(x) = -1$; $\lim_{x \to 1^+} f(x) = 1$ (C) $m = 1$

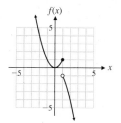
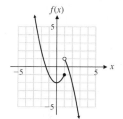
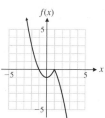

  (D) The graphs in (A) and (B) have discontinuities at $x = 1$; the graph in (C) does not. *(3-2)*
80. (A) 1   (B) -1 (C) Does not exist   (D) No *(3-3)*

81. (A) $S(x) = \begin{cases} 7.47 + 0.4x & \text{if } 0 \le x \le 90 \\ 24.786 + 0.2076x & \text{if } 90 < x \end{cases}$ (B)

(C) Yes *(3-2)*

82. (A) \$179.90   (B) \$180 *(3-7)*

83. (A) $C(100) = 9,500$; $C'(100) = 50$. At a production level of 100 bicycles, the total cost is \$9,500, and cost is increasing at the rate of \$50 per bicycle.

(B) $\overline{C}(100) = 95$; $\overline{C}'(100) = -0.45$. At a production level of 100 bicycles, the average cost is \$95, and average cost is decreasing at a rate of \$0.45 per bicycle. *(3-7)*

84. The approximate cost of producing the 201st printer is greater than that of the 601st printer. Since these marginal costs are decreasing, the manufacturing process is becoming more efficient. *(3-7)*

85. (A) $C'(x) = 2$; $\overline{C}(x) = 2 + \dfrac{9,000}{x}$; $\overline{C}'(x) = \dfrac{-9,000}{x^2}$

(B) $R(x) = xp = 25x - 0.01x^2$; $R'(x) = 25 - 0.02x$; $\overline{R}(x) = 25 - 0.01x$; $\overline{R}'(x) = -0.01$

(C) $P(x) = R(x) - C(x) = 23x - 0.01x^2 - 9,000$; $P'(x) = 23 - 0.02x$;

$\overline{P}(x) = 23 - 0.01x - \dfrac{9,000}{x}$; $\overline{P}'(x) = -0.01 + \dfrac{9,000}{x^2}$

(D) $(500, 10,000)$ and $(1,800, 12,600)$

(E) $P'(1,000) = 3$. Profit is increasing at the rate of \$3 per umbrella.

$P'(1,150) = 0$. Profit is flat.

$P'(1,400) = -5$. Profit is decreasing at the rate of \$5 per umbrella.

(F)

(3-7)

86. (A) 2 components/day   (B) 3.2 components/day *(3-5)*

87. $N(5) = 15$; $N'(5) = 3.833$. After 5 months, the total sales are 15,000 pools, and sales are increasing at the rate of 3,833 pools per month. *(3-6)*

88. (A)
```
CubicReg
y=ax³+bx²+cx+d
a=.001225
b=-.0819285714
c=1.564642857
d=12.08428571
```
(B) $N(50) = 38.6$; $N'(50) = 2.6$. In 2010, natural gas consumption is 38.6 trillion cubic feet and is increasing at the rate of 2.6 trillion cubic feet per year *(3-3)*

89. (A)
```
LinReg
y=ax+b
a=-.0384180791
b=13.59887006
r=-.9897782666
```
(B) Fixed costs: \$484.21; variable costs per kringle: \$2.11

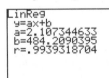
```
LinReg
y=ax+b
a=2.107344633
b=484.2090395
r=.9939318704
```

(C) $(51, 591.15)$, $(248, 1,007.62)$

(D) \$4.07 $< p <$ \$11.64 *(3-7)*

90. $C'(9) = -1$ ppm/m; $C'(99) = -0.001$ ppm/m *(3-6)*

91. $F(3) = 100$; $F'(3) = -0.25$. After 3 h, the body temperature is 100°F, and the temperature is decreasing at the rate of 0.25°F/h. *(3-6)*

92. (A) 10 items/h   (B) 5 items/h *(3-4)*

Chapter 4

Exercise 4-1

1. $(a, b); (d, f); (g, h)$ **3.** $(b, c); (c, d); (f, g)$ **5.** c, d, f **7.** b, f

9. Local maximum at $x = a$; local minimum at $x = c$; no local extrema at $x = b$ and $x = d$ **11.** e **13.** d **15.** f

17. c **19.** Decreasing on $(-\infty, 1)$; increasing on $(1, \infty)$; $f(1) = -2$ is a local minimum

21. Increasing on $(-\infty, -4)$; decreasing on $(-4, \infty)$; local maximum at $x = -4$ **23.** Increasing for all x; no local extrema

25. Increasing on $(-\infty, 0)$ and $(4, \infty)$; decreasing on $(0, 4)$; $f(0) = 1$ is a local maximum; $f(4) = -31$ is a local minimum

27. Increasing on $(-\infty, -2)$ and $(3, \infty)$; decreasing on $(-2, 3)$; local maximum at $x = -2$, local minimum at $x = 3$

29. Decreasing on $(-\infty, 1)$; increasing on $(1, \infty)$; $f(1) = 4$ is a local minimum

31. Increasing on $(-\infty, 2)$; decreasing on $(2, \infty)$; local maximum at $x = 2$

33. Decreasing on $(-\infty, -0.39)$; increasing on $(-0.39, \infty)$; local minimum at $x = -0.39$

35. Decreasing on $(-\infty, -0.77)$ and $(1.08, 2.69)$; increasing on $(-0.77, 1.08)$ and $(2.69, \infty)$; local minima at $x = -0.77$ and $x = 2.69$; local maximum at $x = 1.08$

37. Decreasing on $(-\infty, -1.22)$ and $(0.35, 2.38)$; increasing on $(-1.22, 0.35)$ and $(2.38, \infty)$; local minima at $x = -1.22$ and $x = 2.38$; local maximum at $x = 0.35$

39. Increasing on $(-\infty, 4)$
Decreasing on $(4, \infty)$
Horizontal tangent at $x = 4$

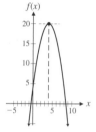

41. Increasing on $(-\infty, -1), (1, \infty)$
Decreasing on $(-1, 1)$
Horizontal tangents at $x = -1, 1$

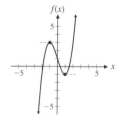

43. Decreasing for all x
Horizontal tangent at $x = 2$

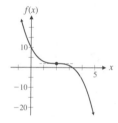

45. Decreasing on $(-\infty, -3)$ and $(0, 3)$; increasing on $(-3, 0)$ and $(3, \infty)$

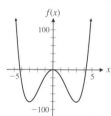

47.

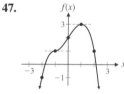

49.

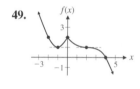

51.

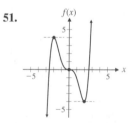

53.

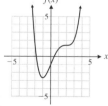

55. g_4 **57.** g_6 **59.** g_2 **61.** Increasing on $(-1, 2)$; decreasing on $(-\infty, -1)$ and $(2, \infty)$; local minimum at $x = -1$; local maximum at $x = 2$

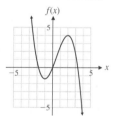

63. Increasing on $(-1, 2)$ and $(2, \infty)$; decreasing on $(-\infty, -1)$; local minimum at $x = -1$

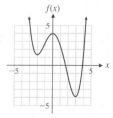

65. Increasing on $(-2, 0)$ and $(3, \infty)$; decreasing on $(-\infty, -2)$ and $(0, 3)$; local minima at $x = -2$ and $x = 3$; local maximum at $x = 0$

67. $f'(x) > 0$ on $(-\infty, -1)$ and $(3, \infty)$; $f'(x) < 0$ on $(-1, 3)$; $f'(x) = 0$ at $x = -1$ and $x = 3$

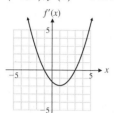

69. $f'(x) > 0$ on $(-2, 1)$ and $(3, \infty)$; $f'(x) < 0$ on $(-\infty, -2)$ and $(1, 3)$; $f'(x) = 0$ at $x = -2, x = 1$, and $x = 3$

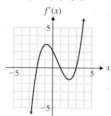

71. Critical values: $x = -2, x = 2$; increasing on $(-\infty, -2)$ and $(2, \infty)$; decreasing on $(-2, 0)$ and $(0, 2)$; local maximum at $x = -2$; local minimum at $x = 2$

73. Critical value: $x = -2$; increasing on $(-2, 0)$; decreasing on $(-\infty, -2)$ and $(0, \infty)$; local minimum at $x = -2$

75. Critical values: $x = 0, x = 4$; increasing on $(-\infty, 0)$ and $(4, \infty)$; decreasing on $(0, 2)$ and $(2, 4)$; local maximum at $x = 0$; local minimum at $x = 4$

77. Critical values: $x = 0, x = 4, x = 6$; increasing on $(0, 4)$ and $(6, \infty)$; decreasing on $(-\infty, 0)$ and $(4, 6)$; local maximum at $x = 4$; local minima at $x = 0$ and $x = 6$

79. Critical value: $x = 2$; increasing on $(2, \infty)$; decreasing on $(-\infty, 2)$; local minimum at $x = 2$

81. Critical value: $x = 0$; decreasing on $(-\infty, 0)$; increasing on $(0, \infty)$; $f(0) = 0$ is a local minimum

83. (A) There are no critical values and no local extrema. The function is increasing for all x.

　(B) There are two critical values, $x = \pm\sqrt{-k/3}$. The function increases on $(-\infty, -\sqrt{-k/3})$ to a local maximum at $x = -\sqrt{-k/3}$, decreases on $(-\sqrt{-k/3}, \sqrt{-k/3})$ to a local minimum at $x = \sqrt{-k/3}$, and increases on $(\sqrt{-k/3}, \infty)$.

　(C) The only critical value is $x = 0$. There are no local extrema. The function is increasing for all x.

85. (A) The marginal profit is positive on $(0, 600)$, 0 at $x = 600$, and negative on $(600, 1,000)$.

　(B) $P'(x)$

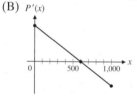

87. (A) The price decreases for the first 15 months to a local minimum, increases for the next 40 months to a local maximum, and then decreases for the remaining 15 months.

　(B) $B(t)$

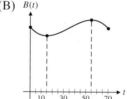

89. (A) $\overline{C}(x) = 0.05x + 20 + \dfrac{320}{x}$

　(B) Critical value: $x = 80$; decreasing for $0 < x < 80$; increasing for $80 < x < 150$; local minimum at $x = 80$

91. $P(x)$ is increasing over (a, b) if $P'(x) = R'(x) - C'(x) > 0$ over (a, b); that is, if $R'(x) > C'(x)$ over (a, b).

93. Critical value: $t = 2$; increasing on $(0, 2)$; decreasing on $(2, 24)$; $C(2) = 0.07$ is a local maximum.

95. Critical value: $t = 7$; increasing for $0 < t < 7$; decreasing for $7 < t < 24$; local maximum at $t = 7$.

Exercise 4-2

1. (A) $(a, c), (c, d), (e, g)$　(B) $(d, e), (g, h)$　(C) $(d, e), (g, h)$　(D) $(a, c), (c, d), (e, g)$　(E) $(a, c), (c, d), (e, g)$
　(F) $(d, e), (g, h)$　(G) d, e, g　(H) d, e, g

3. (C)　**5.** (D)　**7.** $12x - 8$　**9.** $4x^{-3} - 18x^{-4}$　**11.** $2 + \dfrac{9}{2}x^{-3/2}$

13. $8(x^2 + 9)^3 + 48x^2(x^2 + 9)^2 = 8(x^2 + 9)^2(7x^2 + 9)$　**15.** Concave upward for all x; no inflection points

17. Concave downward on $(-\infty, \frac{4}{3})$; concave upward on $(\frac{4}{3}, \infty)$; inflection point at $x = \frac{4}{3}$

19. Concave downward on $(-\infty, 0)$ and $(6, \infty)$; concave upward on $(0, 6)$; inflection points at $x = 0$ and $x = 6$

21.

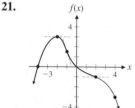

23.

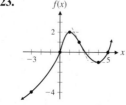

25.

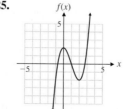

27.

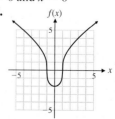

29. Local maximum at $x = 0$
Local minimum at $x = 4$
Inflection point at $x = 2$

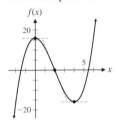

31. Inflection point at $x = 0$

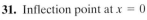
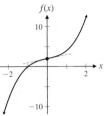

33. Domain: All real numbers
y intercept: 0; x intercepts: 0, 4
Increasing on $(-\infty, 3)$
Decreasing on $(3, \infty)$
Local maximum at $x = 3$
Concave upward on $(0, 2)$
Concave downward on $(-\infty, 0)$ and $(2, \infty)$
Inflection points at $x = 0$ and $x = 2$

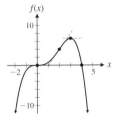

35. Domain: All real numbers
y intercept: 0; x intercepts: 0, 1
Increasing on $(0.25, \infty)$
Decreasing on $(-\infty, 0.25)$
Local minimum at $x = 0.25$
Concave upward on $(-\infty, 0.5)$ and $(1, \infty)$
Concave downward on $(0.5, 1)$
Inflection points at $x = 0.5$ and $x = 1$

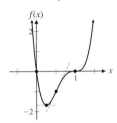

37. Domain: All real numbers
y intercept: 27; x intercepts: $-3, 3$
Increasing on $(-\infty, -\sqrt{3})$ and $(0, \sqrt{3})$
Decreasing on $(-\sqrt{3}, 0)$ and $(\sqrt{3}, \infty)$
Local maxima at $x = -\sqrt{3}$ and $x = \sqrt{3}$
Local minimum at $x = 0$
Concave upward on $(-1, 1)$
Concave downward on $(-\infty, -1)$ and $(1, \infty)$
Inflection points at $x = -1$ and $x = 1$

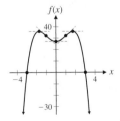

39. Domain: All real numbers
y intercept: 16; x intercepts: $-2, 2$
Decreasing on $(-\infty, -2)$ and $(0, 2)$
Increasing on $(-2, 0)$ and $(2, \infty)$
Local minima at $x = -2$ and $x = 2$
Local maximum at $x = 0$
Concave upward on $(-\infty, -2\sqrt{3}/3)$ and $(2\sqrt{3}/3, \infty)$
Concave downward on $(-2\sqrt{3}/3, 2\sqrt{3}/3)$
Inflection points at $x = -2\sqrt{3}/3$ and $x = 2\sqrt{3}/3$

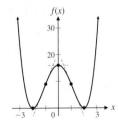

41. Domain: All real numbers
y intercept: 0; x intercepts: 0, 1.5
Decreasing on $(-\infty, 0)$ and $(0, 1.25)$
Increasing on $(1.25, \infty)$
Local minimum at $x = 1.25$
Concave upward on $(-\infty, 0)$ and $(1, \infty)$
Concave downward on $(0, 1)$
Inflection points at $x = 0$ and $x = 1$

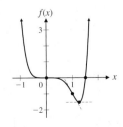

43.

x	$f'(x)$	$f(x)$
$-\infty < x < -1$	Positive and decreasing	Increasing and concave downward
$x = -1$	x intercept	Local maximum
$-1 < x < 0$	Negative and decreasing	Decreasing and concave downward
$x = 0$	Local minimum	Inflection point
$0 < x < 2$	Negative and increasing	Decreasing and concave upward
$x = 2$	Local maximum	Inflection point
$2 < x < \infty$	Negative and decreasing	Decreasing and concave downward

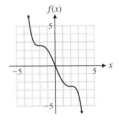

45.

x	$f'(x)$	$f(x)$
$-\infty < x < -2$	Negative and increasing	Decreasing and concave upward
$x = -2$	Local maximum	Inflection point
$-2 < x < 0$	Negative and decreasing	Decreasing and concave downward
$x = 0$	Local minimum	Inflection point
$0 < x < 2$	Negative and increasing	Decreasing and concave upward
$x = 2$	Local maximum	Inflection point
$2 < x < \infty$	Negative and decreasing	Decreasing and concave downward

47. Domain: All real numbers
  x intercepts: $-1.18, 0.61, 1.87, 3.71$
  y intercept: -5
  Decreasing on $(-\infty, -0.53)$ and $(1.24, 3.04)$
  Increasing on $(-0.53, 1.24)$ and $(3.04, \infty)$
  Local minima at $x = -0.53$ and $x = 3.04$
  Local maximum at $x = 1.24$
  Concave upward on $(-\infty, 0.22)$ and $(2.28, \infty)$
  Concave downward on $(0.22, 2.28)$
  Inflection points at $x = 0.22$ and $x = 2.28$

49. Domain: All real numbers
  y intercept: 100; x intercepts: $8.01, 13.36$
  Increasing on $(-0.10, 4.57)$ and $(11.28, \infty)$
  Decreasing on $(-\infty, -0.10)$ and $(4.57, 11.28)$
  Local maximum at $x = 4.57$
  Local minima at $x = -0.10$ and $x = 11.28$
  Concave upward on $(-\infty, 1.95)$ and $(8.55, \infty)$
  Concave downward on $(1.95, 8.55)$
  Inflection points at $x = 1.95$ and $x = 8.55$

51. Domain: All real numbers
  x intercepts: $-2.40, 1.16$; y intercept: 3
  Increasing on $(-\infty, -1.58)$
  Decreasing on $(-1.58, \infty)$
  Local maximum at $x = -1.58$
  Concave downward on $(-\infty, -0.88)$ and $(0.38, \infty)$
  Concave upward on $(-0.88, 0.38)$
  Inflection points at $x = -0.88$ and $x = 0.38$

53. Domain: All real numbers
  x intercepts: $-6.68, -3.64, -0.72$; y intercept: 30
  Decreasing on $(-5.59, -2.27)$ and $(1.65, 3.82)$
  Increasing on $(-\infty, -5.59)$, $(-2.27, 1.65)$, and $(3.82, \infty)$
  Local minima at $x = -2.27$ and $x = 3.82$
  Local maxima at $x = -5.59$ and $x = 1.65$
  Concave upward on $(-4.31, -0.40)$ and $(2.91, \infty)$
  Concave downward on $(-\infty, -4.31)$ and $(-0.40, 2.91)$
  Inflection points at $x = -4.31, x = -0.40$, and $x = 2.91$

55. If $f'(x)$ has a local extremum at $x = c$, then $f'(x)$ must change from increasing to decreasing or from decreasing to increasing at $x = c$. Thus, the graph of $y = f(x)$ must change concavity at $x = c$, and there must be an inflection point at $x = c$.

57. If there is an inflection point on the graph of $y = f(x)$ at $x = c$, then $f(x)$ must change concavity at $x = c$. Consequently, $f'(x)$ must change from increasing to decreasing or from decreasing to increasing at $x = c$, and $x = c$ is a local extremum for $f'(x)$.

59. The graph of the CPI is concave upward.

61. The graph of $y = C'(x)$ is positive and decreasing. Since marginal costs are decreasing, the production process is becoming more efficient as production increases.

63. (A) Local maximum at $x = 60$ (B) Concave downward on the whole interval $(0, 80)$

65. Increasing on $(0, 10)$; decreasing on $(10, 15)$; point of diminishing returns is $x = 10$, max $T'(x) = T'(10) = 500$

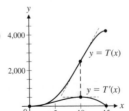

67. Increasing on $(24, 36)$; decreasing on $(36, 45)$; point of diminishing returns is $x = 36$, max $N'(x) = N'(36) = 3888$

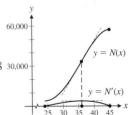

69. (A)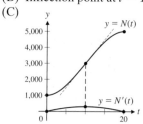

(B) 32 ads to sell 574 cars per month

71. (A) Increasing on $(0, 10)$; decreasing on $(10, 20)$
(B) Inflection point at $t = 10$
(C)

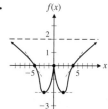

(D) $N'(10) = 300$

73. (A) Increasing on $(5, \infty)$; decreasing on $(0, 5)$
(B) Inflection point at $n = 5$

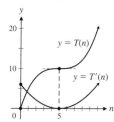

(C) $T'(5) = 0$

Exercise 4-3

1. (A) $(-\infty, b), (0, e), (e, g)$ (B) $(b, d), (d, 0), (g, \infty)$ (C) $(b, d), (d, 0), (g, \infty)$ (D) $(-\infty, b), (0, e), (e, g)$ (E) $x = 0$
(F) $x = b, x = g$ (G) $(-\infty, a), (d, e), (h, \infty)$ (H) $(a, d), (e, h)$ (I) $(a, d), (e, h)$ (J) $(-\infty, a), (d, e), (h, \infty)$
(K) $x = a, x = h$ (L) $y = L$ (M) $x = d, x = e$
3. Horizontal asymptote: $y = 3$; vertical asymptote: $x = 0$ **5.** Horizontal asymptote: $y = 1$; no vertical asymptotes
7. Horizontal asymptote: $y = 0$; vertical asymptotes: $x = -1, x = 1$
9. No horizontal asymptote; vertical asymptotes: $x = -4, x = 4$
11. Horizontal asymptote $y = 2$; vertical asymptote: $x = 1$
13. Horizontal asymptote: $y = \frac{3}{2}$; vertical asymptotes: $x = -4, x = \frac{5}{2}$
15.   **17.**   **19.**   **21.**

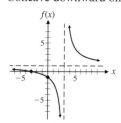   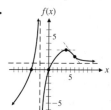   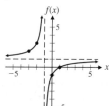   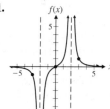

23. Domain: All real numbers, except 3
y intercept: -1; x intercept: -3
Horizontal asymptote: $y = 1$
Vertical asymptote: $x = 3$
Decreasing on $(-\infty, 3)$ and $(3, \infty)$
Concave upward on $(3, \infty)$
Concave downward on $(-\infty, 3)$

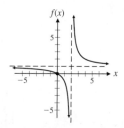

25. Domain: All real numbers, except 2
y intercept: 0; x intercept: 0
Horizontal asymptote: $y = 1$
Vertical asymptote: $x = 2$
Decreasing on $(-\infty, 2)$ and $(2, \infty)$
Concave downward on $(-\infty, 2)$
Concave upward on $(2, \infty)$

27. Domain: All real numbers, except ± 2
y intercept: 0; x intercept: 0
Horizontal asymptote: $y = 0$
Vertical asymptotes: $x = -2, x = 2$
Decreasing on $(-\infty, -2), (-2, 2)$, and $(2, \infty)$
Concave upward on $(-2, 0)$ and $(2, \infty)$
Concave downward on $(-\infty, -2)$ and $(0, 2)$
Inflection point at $x = 0$

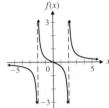

29. Domain: All real numbers
y intercept: 1
Horizontal asymptote: $y = 0$
Increasing on $(-\infty, 0)$
Decreasing on $(0, \infty)$
Local maximum at $x = 0$
Concave upward on $(-\infty, -\sqrt{3}/3)$ and $(\sqrt{3}/3, \infty)$
Concave downward on $(-\sqrt{3}/3, \sqrt{3}/3)$
Inflection points at $x = -\sqrt{3}/3$ and $x = \sqrt{3}/3$

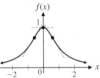

31. Domain: All real numbers except -1 and 1
y intercept: 0; x intercept: 0
Horizontal asymptote: $y = 0$
Vertical asymptote: $x = -1$ and $x = 1$
Increasing on $(-\infty, -1), (-1, 1)$, and $(1, \infty)$
Concave upward on $(-\infty, -1)$ and $(0, 1)$
Concave downward on $(-1, 0)$ and $(1, \infty)$
Inflection point at $x = 0$

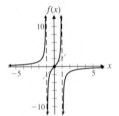

33. Domain: All real numbers except 1
y intercept: 0; x intercept: 0
Horizontal asymptote: $y = 0$
Vertical asymptote: $x = 1$
Increasing on $(-\infty, -1)$ and $(1, \infty)$
Decreasing on $(-1, 1)$
Local maximum at $x = -1$
Concave upward on $(-\infty, -2)$
Concave downward on $(-2, 1)$ and $(1, \infty)$
Inflection point at $x = -2$

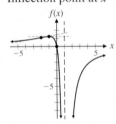

35. Domain: All real numbers except 0
Vertical asymptote: $x = 0$
Increasing on $(-\infty, -\sqrt{2})$ and $(\sqrt{2}, \infty)$
Decreasing on $(-\sqrt{2}, 0)$ and $(0, \sqrt{2})$
Local minimum at $x = \sqrt{2}$
Local maximum at $x = -\sqrt{2}$
Concave upward on $(0, \infty)$
Concave downward on $(-\infty, 0)$

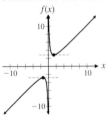

37. Domain: All real numbers except 0
Horizontal asymptote: $y = 1$
Vertical asymptote: $x = 0$
Increasing on $(0, 4)$
Decreasing on $(-\infty, 0)$ and $(4, \infty)$
Local maximum at $x = 4$
Concave upward on $(6, \infty)$
Concave downward on $(-\infty, 0)$ and $(0, 6)$
Inflection point at $x = 6$

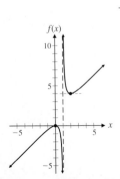

39. Domain: All real numbers except 1
y intercept: 0; x intercept: 0
Vertical asymptote: $x = 1$
Increasing on $(-\infty, 0)$ and $(2, \infty)$
Decreasing on $(0, 1)$ and $(1, 2)$
Local maximum at $x = 0$
Local minimum at $x = 2$
Concave upward on $(1, \infty)$
Concave downward on $(-\infty, 1)$

41. Domain: All real numbers except $-3, 3$
  y intercept: 0; x intercept: 0
  Horizontal asymptote: $y = 3$
  Vertical asymptotes: $x = -3, x = 3$
  Increasing on $(-\infty, -3)$ and $(-3, 0)$
  Decreasing on $(0, 3)$ and $(3, \infty)$
  Local maximum at $x = 0$
  Concave upward on $(-\infty, -3)$ and $(3, \infty)$
  Concave downward on $(-3, 3)$

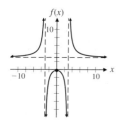

43. Domain: All real numbers except 2
  y intercept: 0; x intercept: 0
  Vertical asymptote: $x = 2$
  Increasing on $(3, \infty)$
  Decreasing on $(-\infty, 2)$ and $(2, 3)$
  Local minimum at $x = 3$
  Concave upward on $(-\infty, 0)$ and $(2, \infty)$
  Concave downward on $(0, 2)$
  Inflection point at $x = 0$

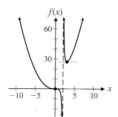

45. Domain: All real numbers except $-4, 2$
  y intercept: $-1/8$
  Horizontal asymptote: $y = 0$
  Vertical asymptote: $x = -4, x = 2$
  Increasing on $(-\infty, -4)$ and $(-4, -1)$
  Decreasing on $(-1, 2)$ and $(2, \infty)$
  Local maximum at $x = -1$
  Concave upward on $(-\infty, -4)$ and $(2, \infty)$
  Concave downward on $(-4, 2)$

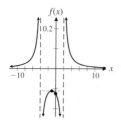

47. Domain: All real numbers except $-2, 2$
  y intercept: 0; x intercept: 0
  Horizontal asymptote: $y = 0$
  Vertical asymptote: $x = -2, x = 2$
  Decreasing on $(-\infty, -2)$, $(-2, 2)$ and $(2, \infty)$
  Concave upward on $(-2, 0)$ and $(2, \infty)$
  Concave downward on $(-\infty, -2)$ and $(0, 2)$
  Inflection point at $x = 0$

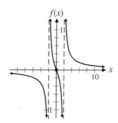

49. Domain: All real numbers except 4
  y intercept: 0; x intercept: 0
  Vertical asymptote: $x = 4$
  Increasing on $(-\infty, 4)$ and $(12, \infty)$
  Decreasing on $(4, 12)$
  Local minimum at $x = 12$
  Concave upward on $(0, 4)$ and $(4, \infty)$
  Concave downward on $(-\infty, 0)$
  Inflection point at $x = 0$

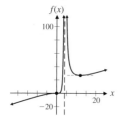

51. Domain: All real numbers except $-\sqrt{3}, \sqrt{3}$
  y intercept: 0; x intercept: 0
  Vertical asymptote: $x = -\sqrt{3}, x = \sqrt{3}$
  Increasing on $(-3, -\sqrt{3})$, $(-\sqrt{3}, \sqrt{3})$ and $(\sqrt{3}, 3)$
  Decreasing on $(-\infty, -3)$ and $(3, \infty)$
  Local maximum at $x = 3$
  Local minimum at $x = -3$
  Concave upward on $(-\infty, -\sqrt{3})$ and $(0, \sqrt{3})$
  Concave downward on $(-\sqrt{3}, 0)$ and $(\sqrt{3}, \infty)$
  Inflection point at $x = 0$

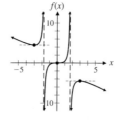

53. Domain: All real numbers except 0
Vertical asymptote: $x = 0$
Oblique asymptote: $y = x$
Increasing on $(-\infty, -2)$ and $(2, \infty)$
Decreasing on $(-2, 0)$ and $(0, 2)$
Local maximum at $x = -2$
Local minimum at $x = 2$
Concave upward on $(0, \infty)$
Concave downward on $(-\infty, 0)$

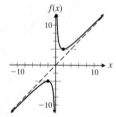

55. Domain: All real numbers except 0
x intercept: $\sqrt[3]{4}$
Vertical asymptote: $x = 0$
Oblique asymptote: $y = x$
Increasing on $(-\infty, -2)$ and $(0, \infty)$
Local maximum at $x = -2$
Decreasing on $(-2, 0)$
Concave downward on $(-\infty, 0)$ and $(0, \infty)$

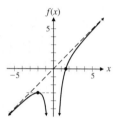

57. Domain: All real numbers except 0
x intercepts: $-\sqrt{3}, \sqrt{3}$
Vertical asymptote: $x = 0$
Oblique asymptote: $y = x$
Increasing on $(-\infty, 0)$ and $(0, \infty)$
Concave upward on $(-\infty, 0)$
Concave downward on $(0, \infty)$

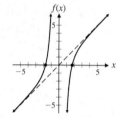

59. Domain: All real numbers except 0
Vertical asymptote: $x = 0$
Oblique asymptote: $y = x$
Increasing on $(-\infty, -2)$ and $(2, \infty)$
Decreasing on $(-2, 0)$ and $(0, 2)$
Local maximum at $x = -2$
Local minimum at $x = 2$
Concave upward on $(0, \infty)$
Concave downward on $(-\infty, 0)$

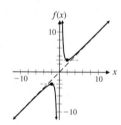

61. Domain: All real numbers except $2, 4$
y intercept: $-3/4$; x intercept: -3
Vertical asymptote: $x = 4$
Horizontal asymptote: $y = 1$
Decreasing on $(-\infty, 2)$, $(2, 4)$, and $(4, \infty)$
Concave upward on $(4, \infty)$
Concave downward on $(-\infty, 2)$ and $(2, 4)$

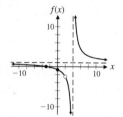

63. Domain: All real numbers except $-3, 3$
y intercept: $5/3$; x intercept: 2.5
Vertical asymptote: $x = 3$
Horizontal asymptote: $y = 2$
Decreasing on $(-\infty, -3)$, $(-3, 3)$, and $(3, \infty)$
Concave upward on $(3, \infty)$
Concave downward on $(-\infty, -3)$ and $(-3, 3)$

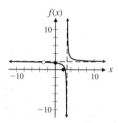

65. Domain: All real numbers except $-1, 2$
y intercept: 0; x intercepts: 0, 3
Vertical asymptote: $x = -1$
Increasing on $(-\infty, -3)$, $(1, 2)$, and $(2, \infty)$
Decreasing on $(-3, -1)$ and $(-1, 1)$
Local maximum at $x = -3$
Local minimum at $x = 1$
Concave upward on $(-1, 2)$ and $(2, \infty)$
Concave downward on $(-\infty, -1)$

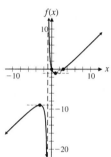

67. Domain: All real numbers except 1
y intercept: -2; x intercept: -2
Vertical asymptote: $x = 1$
Horizontal asymptote: $y = 1$
Decreasing on $(-\infty, 1)$ and $(1, \infty)$
Concave upward on $(1, \infty)$
Concave downward on $(-\infty, 1)$

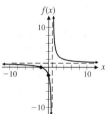

69.

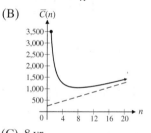

71. (A) Increasing on $(0, 1)$
(B) Concave upward on $(0, 1)$
(C) $x = 1$ is a vertical asymptote
(D) The origin is both an x and a y intercept
(E)

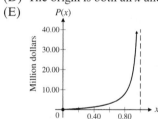

73. (A) $\overline{C}(n) = \dfrac{3{,}200}{n} + 250 + 50n$

(B) $\overline{C}(n)$

(C) 8 yr

75. (A) y

(B) 25 at $x = 100$

77. (A)
```
QuadReg
y=ax²+bx+c
a=.0100714286
b=.7835714286
c=316
```

(B) Minimum average cost is $4.35
when 177 pizzas are produced daily.

79. $C(t)$

81. $N(t)$

Exercise 4-4

1. Min $f(x) = f(0) = 0$; Max $f(x) = f(10) = 14$ **3.** Min $f(x) = f(0) = 0$; Max $f(x) = f(3) = 9$
5. Min $f(x) = f(1) = f(7) = 5$; Max $f(x) = f(10) = 14$ **7.** Min $f(x) = f(1) = f(7) = 5$; Max $f(x) = f(3) = f(9) = 9$
9. Min $f(x) = f(5) = 7$; Max $f(x) = f(3) = 9$ **11.** Min $f(x) = f(1) = 2$; no maximum
13. Max $f(x) = f(-3) = 18$; no minimum   **15.** No absolute extrema   **17.** Max $f(x) = f(3) = 54$; no minimum
19. No absolute extrema   **21.** Min $f(x) = f(0) = 0$; no maximum   **23.** Max $f(x) = f(1) = 1$; min $f(x) = f(-1) = -1$
25. Min $f(x) = f(0) = -1$, no maximum   **27.** Min $f(x) = f(2) = -2$ **29.** Max $f(x) = f(2) = 4$
31. Min $f(x) = f(2) = 0$ **33.** No maximum   **35.** Max $f(x) = f(2) = 8$ **37.** Min $f(x) = f(4) = 22$
39. Min $f(x) = f(\sqrt{10}) = 14/\sqrt{10}$
41. (A) Max $f(x) = f(5) = 14$; Min $f(x) = f(-1) = -22$ (B) Max $f(x) = f(1) = -2$; Min $f(x) = f(-1) = -22$
(C) Max $f(x) = f(5) = 14$; Min $f(x) = f(3) = -6$
43. (A) Max $f(x) = f(0) = 126$; Min $f(x) = f(2) = -26$ (B) Max $f(x) = f(7) = 49$; Min $f(x) = f(2) = -26$
(C) Max $f(x) = f(6) = 6$; Min $f(x) = f(3) = -15$

45. (A) Max $f(x) = f(-1) = 10$; min $f(x) = f(2) = -11$ (B) Max $f(x) = f(0) = f(4) = 5$; min $f(x) = f(3) = -22$
(C) Max $f(x) = f(-1) = 10$; min $f(x) = f(1) = 2$
47. Local minimum   **49.** Unable to determine   **51.** Neither   **53.** Local maximum

Exercise 4-5

1. Exactly in half   **3.** 15 and -15 **5.** A square of side 25 cm; maximum area $= 625$ cm^2
7. If x and y are the dimensions of the rectangle and A is the fixed area, the model is: Minimize $C = 2Bx + 2AB/x, x > 0$. This mathematical problem always has a solution. This agrees with our economic intuition that there should be a cheapest way to build the fence.
9. If x and y are the dimensions of the rectangle and C is the fixed amount to be spent, the model is:
Maximize $A = x(C - 2Bx)/(2B), 0 \le x \le C/(2B)$. This mathematical problem always has a solution. This agrees with our economic intuition that there should be a largest area that can be enclosed with a fixed amount of fencing.
11. (A) Maximum revenue is $125,000 when 500 phones are produced and sold for $250 each.
(B) Maximum profit is $46,612.50 when 365 phones are produced and sold for $317.50 each.
13. (A) Max $R(x) = R(3,000) = \$300,000$
(B) Maximum profit is $75,000 when 2,100 sets are manufactured and sold for $130 each.
(C) Maximum profit is $64,687.50 when 2,025 sets are manufactured and sold for $132.50 each.
15. (A)

```
QuadReg
y=ax²+bx+c
a=-2.352941E-5
b=-.0325964781
c=288.9535407
```

(B)

```
LinReg
y=ax+b
a=53.50318471
b=82245.22293
```

(C) The maximum profit is $118,996 when the price per saw is $195.

17. (A) $4.80 (B) $8   **19.** $35; $6,125   **21.** 40 trees; 1,600 lb   **23.** $(10 - 2\sqrt{7})/3 = 1.57$ in. squares
25. 20 ft by 40 ft (with the expensive side being one of the short sides)   **27.** 8 production runs per year
29. 10,000 books in 5 printings   **31.** (A) $x = 5.1$ mi (B) $x = 10$ mi   **33.** 4 days; 20 bacteria/cm^3
35. 50 mice per order   **37.** 1 month; 2 ft   **39.** 4 yr from now

Chapter 4 Review Exercise

1. $(a, c_1), (c_3, c_6)$ *(4-1, 4-2)*   **2.** $(c_1, c_3), (c_6, b)$ *(4-1, 4-2)*   **3.** $(a, c_2), (c_4, c_5), (c_7, b)$ *(4-1, 4-2)*   **4.** c_3 *(4-1)*
5. c_1, c_6 *(4-1)*   **6.** c_1, c_3, c_5 *(4-1)*   **7.** c_4, c_6 *(4-1)*   **8.** c_2, c_4, c_5, c_7 *(4-2)*
9. *(4-2)*

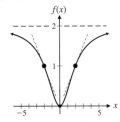

10. *(4-2)*

11. $f''(x) = 12x^2 + 30x$ *(4-2)*   **12.** $y'' = 8/x^3$ *(4-2)*
13. Domain: All real numbers
y intercept: 0; x intercepts: 0, 9
Increasing on $(-\infty, 3)$ and $(9, \infty)$
Decreasing on $(3, 9)$
Local maximum at $x = 3$
Local minimum at $x = 9$
Concave upward on $(6, \infty)$
Concave downward on $(-\infty, 6)$
Inflection point at $x = 6$ *(4-2)*

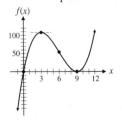

14. Domain: All real numbers
y intercept: 16; x intercepts: $-4, 2$
Increasing on $(-\infty, -2)$ and $(2, \infty)$
Decreasing on $(-2, 2)$
Local maximum at $x = -2$
Local minimum at $x = 2$
Concave upward on $(0, \infty)$
Concave downward on $(-\infty, 0)$
Inflection point at $x = 0$ *(4-2)*

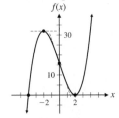

15. Domain: All real numbers
y intercept: 0; x intercepts: 0, 4
Increasing on $(-\infty, 3)$
Decreasing on $(3, \infty)$
Local maximum at $x = 3$
Concave upward on $(0, 2)$
Concave downward on
$(-\infty, 0)$ and $(2, \infty)$
Inflection points at $x = 0$ and $x = 2$ *(4-2)*

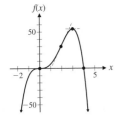

16. Domain: all real numbers
y intercept: -3; x intercepts: $-3, 1$
No vertical or horizontal asymptotes
Increasing on $(-2, \infty)$
Decreasing on $(-\infty, -2)$
Local minimum at $x = -2$
Concave upward on $(-\infty, -1)$ and $(1, \infty)$
Concave downward on $(-1, 1)$
Inflection points at $x = -1$ and $x = 1$ *(4-2)*

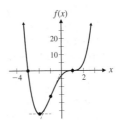

17. Domain: All real numbers, except -2
y intercept: 0; x intercept: 0
Horizontal asymptote: $y = 3$
Vertical asymptote: $x = -2$
Increasing on $(-\infty, -2)$ and $(-2, \infty)$
Concave upward on $(-\infty, -2)$
Concave downward on $(-2, \infty)$ *(4-3)*

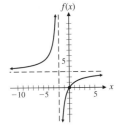

18. Domain: All real numbers
y intercept: 0; x intercept: 0
Horizontal asymptote: $y = 1$
Increasing on $(0, \infty)$
Decreasing on $(-\infty, 0)$
Local minimum at $x = 0$
Concave upward on $(-3, 3)$
Concave downward on $(-\infty, -3)$ and $(3, \infty)$
Inflection points at $x = -3, 3$ *(4-3)*

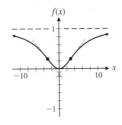

19. Domain: All real numbers except $x = -2$
y intercept: 0; x intercept: 0
Horizontal asymptote: $y = 0$
Vertical asymptote: $x = -2$
Increasing on $(-2, 2)$
Decreasing on $(-\infty, -2)$ and $(2, \infty)$
Local maximum at $x = 2$
Concave upward on $(4, \infty)$
Concave downward on $(-\infty, -2)$ and $(-2, 4)$
Inflection point at $x = 4$ *(4-3)*

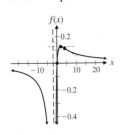

20. Domain: All real numbers
y intercept: 0; x intercept: 0
Increasing on $(-\infty, \infty)$
Concave upward on $(-\infty, -3)$ and $(0, 3)$
Concave downward on $(-3, 0)$ and $(3, \infty)$
Inflection points at $x = -3, 0, 3$ *(4-3)*

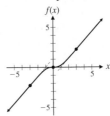

21.

x	f'(x)	f(x)	
$-\infty < x < -2$	Negative and increasing	Decreasing and concave upward	
$x = -2$	x intercept	Local minimum	
$-2 < x < -1$	Positive and increasing	Increasing and concave upward	
$x = -1$	Local maximum	Inflection point	
$-1 < x < 1$	Positive and decreasing	Increasing and concave downward	
$x = 1$	Local minimum	Inflection point	
$1 < x < \infty$	Positive and increasing	Increasing and concave upward	

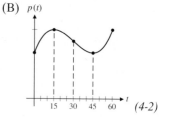

(4-2)

22. (C) *(4-2)*   **23.** Local maximum at $x = -1$; local minimum at $x = 5$ *(4-4)*

24. Min $f(x) = f(2) = -4$; Max $f(x) = f(5) = 77$ *(4-4)*   **25.** Min $f(x) = f(2) = 8$ *(4-4)*

26. Yes. Since f is continuous on $[a, b]$, f has an absolute maximum on $[a, b]$. But each endpoint is a local minimum; hence, the absolute maximum must occur between a and b. *(4-4)*

27. No, increasing/decreasing properties apply to intervals in the domain of f. It is correct to say that $f(x)$ is decreasing on $(-\infty, 0)$ and $(0, \infty)$. *(4-1)*

28. A critical value for $f(x)$ is a partition number for $f'(x)$ that is also in the domain of f. For example, if $f(x) = x^{-1}$, then 0 is a partition number for $f'(x) = -x^{-2}$, but 0 is not a critical value for $f(x)$ since 0 is not in the domain of f. *(4-1)*

29. Max $f'(x) = f'(2) = 12$ *(4-2, 4-4)*   **30.** Each number is 20; minimum sum is 40 *(4-5)*

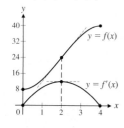

31. Domain: All real numbers
x intercepts: 0.79, 1.64; y intercept: 4
Increasing on $(-1.68, -0.35)$ and $(1.28, \infty)$
Decreasing on $(-\infty, -1.68)$ and $(-0.35, 1.28)$
Local minima at $x = -1.68$ and $x = 1.28$
Local maximum at $x = -0.35$
Concave downward on $(-1.10, 0.60)$
Concave upward on $(-\infty, -1.10)$ and $(0.60, \infty)$
Inflection points at $x = -1.10$ and $x = 0.60$ *(4-2)*

32. Domain: All real numbers
x intercepts; 0, 11.10; y intercept: 0
Increasing on $(1.87, 4.19)$ and $(8.94, \infty)$
Decreasing on $(-\infty, 1.87)$ and $(4.19, 8.94)$
Local maximum at $x = 4.19$
Local minima at $x = 1.87$ and $x = 8.94$
Concave upward on $(-\infty, 2.92)$ and $(7.08, \infty)$
Concave downward on $(2.92, 7.08)$
Inflection points at $x = 2.92$ and $x = 7.08$ *(4-2)*

33. (A) For the first 15 months, the graph of the price is increasing and concave downward, with a local maximum at $t = 15$. For the next 15 months, the graph of the price is decreasing and concave downward, with an inflection point at $t = 30$. For the next 15 months, the graph of the price is decreasing and concave upward, with a local minimum at $t = 45$. For the remaining 15 months, the graph of the price is increasing and concave upward.

(B)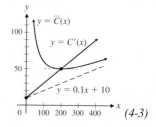

(4-2)

34. (A) Max $R(x) = R(10,000) = \$2,500,000$
(B) Maximum profit is $175,000 when 3,000 stoves are manufactured and sold for $425 each.
(C) Maximum profit is $119,000 when 2,600 stoves are manufactured and sold for $435 each. *(4-5)*

35. (A) The expensive side is 50 ft; the other side is 100 ft.   (B) The expensive side is 75 ft; the other side is 150 ft. *(4-5)*

36. $49; $6,724 *(4-5)*   **37.** 12 orders/yr *(4-5)*   **38.** Min $\overline{C}(x) = \overline{C}(200) = 50$

(4-3)

39. Increasing on $(0, 18)$; decreasing on $(18, 24)$; point of diminishing returns is $x = 18$, max $N'(x) = N'(18) = 972$ *(4-2)*

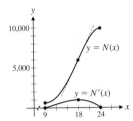

40. 20.39 feet *(4-5)*

41. (A)
```
QuadReg
 y=ax²+bx+c
 a=.0061285714
 b=.1224285714
 c=102.2
```

(B) Min $\overline{C}(x) = \overline{C}(129) = \$1.71$ *(4-3)*

42. (A)
```
CubicReg
 y=ax³+bx²+cx+d
 a=-.01
 b=.83
 c=-2.3
 d=221
```

(B) 28 ads to sell 588 refrigerators per month *(4-2)*

43. 3 days *(4-1)*

44. 2 yr from now *(4-1)*

Chapter 5

Exercise 5-1

1. \$1,221.40; \$1,648.72; \$2,225.54   **3.**

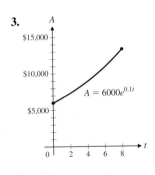

5. 11.55   **7.** 10.99   **9.** 0.14

11.

n	$[1 + (1/n)]^n$
10	2.593 74
100	2.704 81
1,000	2.716 92
10,000	2.718 15
100,000	2.718 27
1,000,000	2.718 28
10,000,000	2.718 28
↓	↓
∞	$e = 2.718\ 281\ 828\ 459\ldots$

13. $\lim_{n \to \infty}(1 + n)^{1/n} = 1$ **15.**

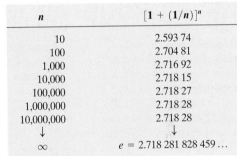

17. (A) \$17,349.87   (B) 7.36 yr   **19.** \$11,890.41

21. 8.11%   **23.** (A)

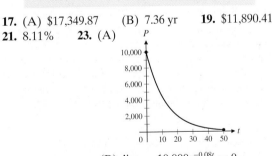

(B) $\lim_{t \to \infty} 10{,}000e^{-0.08t} = 0$

25. 9.90 yr   **27.** 8.66%   **29.** 7.3 yr

Exercise 5-2

1. $(3x^2 + 2)^3$ **3.** e^{-x^2} **5.** $y = u^4; u = 3x^2 - x + 5$ **7.** $y = e^u; u = 1 + x + x^2$ **9.** $f'(x) = 12x^2 + 5e^x$

11. $\dfrac{dy}{dx} = 4e^x - 3ex^{e-1}$ **13.** $y' = 3e^{-x} + 2e^x$ **15.** $x^3e^x + 3x^2e^x = x^2e^x(x + 3)$ **17.** $6e^{2x}$ **19.** $-15e^{-3x}$

21. $-100e^{-0.5x}$ **23.** $x\dfrac{d}{dx}(e^{-2x}) + e^{-2x}\dfrac{d}{dx}(x) = e^{-2x}(1 - 2x)$ **25.** $\dfrac{(x^2 + 9)e^x - 2xe^x}{(x^2 + 9)^2} = \dfrac{e^x(x^2 - 2x + 9)}{(x^2 + 9)^2}$

27. $(6x - 2)e^{3x^2 - 2x}$ **29.** $4(e^{2x} - 1)^3(2e^{2x}) = 8e^{2x}(e^{2x} - 1)^3$ **31.** $\dfrac{2xe^x - (x^2 + 1)e^x}{(e^x)^2} = \dfrac{2x - x^2 - 1}{e^x}$

33. $(x^2 + 1)(-e^{-x}) + e^{-x}(2x) = e^{-x}(2x - x^2 - 1)$ **35.** $xe^x + e^x - e^x = xe^x$

37. Yes, she is correct. In fact, for any real number c, the tangent line to $y = e^x$ at the point (c, e^c) has equation $y - e^c = e^c(x - c)$, and thus the tangent line passes through the point $(c - 1, 0)$.

39. Min $f(x) = f(2) = \dfrac{e^2}{4} \approx 1.847$ **41.** Max $f(x) = f(3) = \dfrac{27}{e^3} \approx 1.344$

43. Domain: $(-\infty, \infty)$
y intercept: 0; x intercept: 0
Horizontal asymptote: $y = 1$
Increasing on $(-\infty, \infty)$
Concave downward on $(-\infty, \infty)$

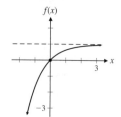

45. Domain: $(-\infty, \infty)$
y intercept: 10
Horizontal asymptote: $y = 5$
Decreasing on $(-\infty, \infty)$
Concave upward on $(-\infty, \infty)$

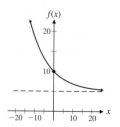

47. Domain: $(-\infty, \infty)$
y intercept: 0; x intercept: 0
Horizontal asymptote: $y = 0$
Increasing on $(-\infty, 5)$
Decreasing on $(5, \infty)$
Local maximum at $x = 5$
Concave upward on $(10, \infty)$
Concave downward on $(-\infty, 10)$
Inflection point at $x = 10$

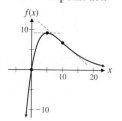

49. Domain: All real numbers
y intercept: 3; x intercept: 3
Horizontal asymptote: $y = 0$
Increasing on $(-\infty, 2)$
Decreasing on $(2, \infty)$
Local maximum at $x = 2$
Concave upward on $(-\infty, 1)$
Concave downward on $(1, \infty)$
Inflection point at $x = 1$

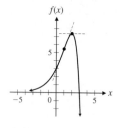

51. Domain: $(-\infty, \infty)$
y intercept: 1
Horizontal asymptote: $y = 0$
Increasing on $(-\infty, 0)$
Decreasing on $(0, \infty)$
Local maximum at $x = 0$
Concave upward on $(-\infty, -1)$ and $(1, \infty)$
Concave downward on $(-1, 1)$
Inflection points at $x = -1$ and $x = 1$

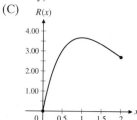

53. Critical values: $x = 0.36$, $x = 2.15$
Increasing on $(-\infty, 0.36)$ and $(2.15, \infty)$
Decreasing on $(0.36, 2.15)$
Local maximum at $x = 0.36$
Local minimum at $x = 2.15$

55. $(-0.82, 0.44)$, $(1.43, 4.18)$, $(8.61, 5503.66)$

57. (A) When the demand is 800, the price is decreasing at the rate of $4.49 per week

(B) At $3.68 each, the maximum revenue will be $3,680/wk (in the test city).

(C)

$R(x)$

59. A maximum revenue of $735.80 is realized at a production level of 20 units at $36.79 each.

61. A maximum profit of $224.61 is realized at a production level of 17 units at $42.74 each.

63. $-\$27,145/\text{yr}$; $-\$18,196/\text{yr}$; $-\$11,036/\text{yr}$

65. (A) 23 days; $26,685; about 50%
(B)

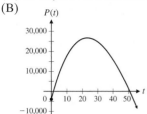

67. (A) After 1 hr, the concentration is decreasing at the rate of 1.60 mg/mL per hour; after 4 hr, the concentration is decreasing at the rate of 0.08 mg/mL per hour.

(B)

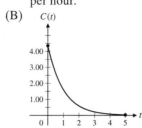

69.

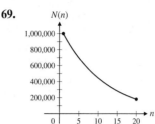

Exercise 5-3

1. $\dfrac{1}{x-3}$ **3.** $\dfrac{-2}{3-2t}$ **5.** $y' = \dfrac{3}{x}$ **7.** $\dfrac{6(\ln x)^5}{x}$ **9.** $x^3 + 4x^3 \ln x = x^3(1 + 4 \ln x)$ **11.** $\dfrac{4}{x+1}$

13. $\dfrac{x^3 - 4x^3 \ln x}{x^8} = \dfrac{1 - 4 \ln x}{x^5}$ **15.** $3(x+2)^2 \ln x + \dfrac{(x+2)^3}{x} = (x+2)^2\left(3 \ln x + \dfrac{x+2}{x}\right)$

17. $\dfrac{1}{x^2+1}\dfrac{d}{dx}(x^2+1) = \dfrac{2x}{x^2+1}$ **19.** $\dfrac{x}{x^2+1}$ **21.** $\dfrac{1}{2}[\ln(x^2+1)]^{-1/2}\dfrac{d}{dx}\ln(x^2+1) = \dfrac{x}{(x^2+1)[\ln(x^2+1)]^{1/2}}$

23. $(\ln x)^3 + 3(\ln x)^2 = (\ln x)^2(\ln x + 3)$ **25.** $\dfrac{1}{2}(1 + \ln x)^{-1/2}\left(\dfrac{1}{x}\right) = \dfrac{1}{2x(1 + \ln x)^{1/2}}$

27. $2x^2\left(\dfrac{1}{x}\right) + 4x \ln x - 2x = 4x \ln x$ **29.** $\dfrac{e^{-x}}{x} - e^{-x} \ln x = \dfrac{e^{-x}(1 - x \ln x)}{x}$ **31.** $\dfrac{-2x}{(1+x^2)[\ln(1+x^2)]^2}$

33. $\dfrac{-2x}{3(1-x^2)[\ln(1-x^2)]^{2/3}}$ **35.** $y = \dfrac{1}{e}x$ **37.** $y = -2x + 2$

41. Domain: $(-\infty, 1)$
y intercept: 0; x intercept: 0
Vertical asymptote: $x = 1$
Decreasing on $(-\infty, 1)$
Concave downward on $(-\infty, 1)$

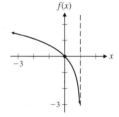

43. Domain: $(0, \infty)$
Vertical asymptote: $x = 0$
Increasing on $(1, \infty)$
Decreasing on $(0, 1)$
Local minimum at $x = 1$
Concave upward on $(0, \infty)$

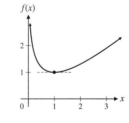

45. Domain: $(0, \infty)$
x intercept: 1
Increasing on $(e^{-1/2}, \infty)$
Decreasing on $(0, e^{-1/2})$
Local minimum at $x = e^{-1/2}$
Concave upward on $(e^{-3/2}, \infty)$
Concave downward on $(0, e^{-3/2})$
Inflection point at $x = e^{-3/2}$

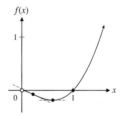

47. Domain: $(0, \infty)$
x intercept: 1
Vertical asymptote: $x = 0$
Increasing on $(1, \infty)$
Decreasing on $(0, 1)$
Local minimum at $x = 1$
Concave upward on $(0, e)$
Concave downward on (e, ∞)
Inflection point at $x = e$

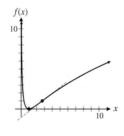

49. Max $f(x) = f(e^{1.5}) = 2e^{1.5} \approx 8.963$ **51.** Max $f(x) = f(e^{2.5}) = \dfrac{e^5}{2} \approx 74.207$ **53.** Max $f(x) = f(1) = -1$

55. $\dfrac{1}{\ln 2}\left(\dfrac{6x}{3x^2 - 1}\right)$ **57.** $(2x + 1)(10^{x^2+x})(\ln 10)$ **59.** $\dfrac{12x^2 + 5}{(4x^3 + 5x + 7) \ln 3}$ **61.** $2^{x^3-x^2+4x+1}(3x^2 - 2x + 4) \ln 2$

63. $(0.49, 0.49)$ **65.** $(3.65, 1.30), (332,105.11, 12.71)$ **67.** $f'(x) = g'(x) = \dfrac{8x}{x^2 + 3}$ **69.** $p = \$2$

71. $\text{Min } \overline{C}(x) = \overline{C}(e^7) \approx \$99.91$ **73.** $p = \$27.57$ **75.** $\$159.68$

77. At the 40-lb weight level, blood pressure would increase at the rate of 0.44 mm of mercury per pound of weight gain. At the 90-lb weight level, blood pressure would increase at the rate of 0.19 mm of mercury per pound of weight gain.

79. 2.27 mm of mercury/yr; 0.81 mm of mercury/yr; 0.41 mm of mercury/yr

81. $A'(t) = 2(\ln 2)5{,}000e^{2t\ln 2} = 10{,}000(\ln 2)2^{2t}; A'(1) = 27{,}726$ bacteria/hr (rate of change at the end of the first hour); $A'(5) = 7{,}097{,}827$ bacteria/hr (rate of change at the end of the fifth hour)

83. $dR/dS = k/S$

Exercise 5-4

1. $\dfrac{dy}{du} = 2u, \dfrac{du}{dx} = e^x, \dfrac{dy}{dx} = 2(2 + e^x)e^x$ **3.** $\dfrac{dy}{du} = e^u, \dfrac{du}{dx} = -4x^3, \dfrac{dy}{dx} = e^{2-x^4}(-4x^3)$

5. $\dfrac{dy}{du} = \dfrac{1}{u}, \dfrac{du}{dx} = 20x^4, \dfrac{dy}{dx} = \dfrac{1}{4x^5 - 7}20x^4$ **7.** $\dfrac{dy}{dw} = 2w, \dfrac{dw}{du} = \dfrac{1}{u}, \dfrac{du}{dx} = e^x, \dfrac{dy}{dx} = \dfrac{2e^x\ln(2 + e^x)}{2 + e^x}$

9. $\dfrac{dy}{dw} = \dfrac{1}{w}, \dfrac{dw}{du} = 2u, \dfrac{du}{dx} = e^x, \dfrac{dy}{dx} = \dfrac{2e^{2x}}{1 + e^{2x}}$ **11.** $\dfrac{dy}{dw} = 2(w + 4), \dfrac{dw}{du} = \dfrac{1}{u}, \dfrac{du}{dx} = e^x, \dfrac{dy}{dx} = 2(x + 4)$ **13.** $\dfrac{1}{x + 50}$

15. $\dfrac{100 - x}{100x - 0.5x^2}$ **17.** $-\dfrac{2}{1 + 2e^{2x}}$ **19.** $\dfrac{28 + 3\ln x}{25x + 3x\ln x}$ **21.** (A) Inelastic   (B) Unit elasticity   (C) Elastic

23. (A) Inelastic   (B) Unit elasticity   (C) Elastic

25. (A) $x = 6{,}000 - 200p$ $0 \le p \le 30$ (B) $E(p) = \dfrac{p}{30 - p}$ (C) $E(10) = 0.5; 5\%$ decrease
(D) $E(25) = 5; 50\%$ decrease   (E) $E(15) = 1; 10\%$ decrease

27. (A) $x = 3{,}000 - 50p$ $0 \le p \le 60$ (B) $R(p) = 3{,}000p - 50p^2$ (C) $E(p) = \dfrac{p}{60 - p}$
(D) Elastic on $(30, 60)$; inelastic on $(0, 30)$ (E) Increasing on $(0, 30)$; decreasing on $(30, 60)$
(F) Decrease   (G) Increase

29. Elastic on $(10, 30)$; inelastic on $(0, 10)$ **31.** Elastic on $(48, 72)$; inelastic on $(0, 48)$

33. Elastic on $(25, 25\sqrt{2})$; inelastic on $(0, 25)$ **35.** $R(p) = 20p(10 - p)$ **37.** $R(p) = 40p(p - 15)^2$

39. $R(p) = 30p - 10p\sqrt{p}$

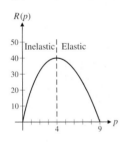

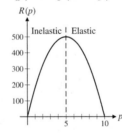

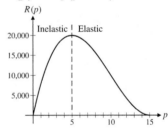

41. $\dfrac{3}{2}$ **43.** $\dfrac{1}{2}$ **45.** k **47.** \$25 per day   **49.** Increase   **51.** Decrease   **53.** \$2.50

55.

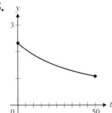

57. -0.13 robberies annually per 1,000 population age 12 and over.

Exercise 5-5

1. $y' = -\dfrac{3}{5}$ **3.** $y' = \dfrac{3x}{2}$ **5.** $y' = 10x$; 10   **7.** $y' = \dfrac{2x}{3y^2}$; $\dfrac{4}{3}$ **9.** $y' = -\dfrac{3}{2y+2}$; $-\dfrac{3}{4}$ **11.** $y' = -\dfrac{y}{x}$; $-\dfrac{3}{2}$

13. $y' = -\dfrac{2y}{2x+1}$; 4   **15.** $y' = \dfrac{6-2y}{x}$; -1 **17.** $y' = \dfrac{2x}{e^y-2y}$; 2   **19.** $y' = \dfrac{3x^2y}{y+1}$; $\dfrac{3}{2}$ **21.** $y' = \dfrac{6x^2y - y\ln y}{x+2y}$; 2

23. $x' = \dfrac{2tx - 3t^2}{2x - t^2}$; 8   **25.** $y'|_{(1.6,\,1.8)} = -\dfrac{3}{4}$; $y'|_{(1.6,\,0.2)} = \dfrac{3}{4}$ **27.** $y = -x + 5$ **29.** $y = \frac{2}{5}x - \frac{12}{5}$; $y = \frac{3}{5}x + \frac{12}{5}$

31. $y' = -\dfrac{1}{x}$ **33.** $y' = \dfrac{1}{3(1+y)^2 + 1}$; $\dfrac{1}{13}$ **35.** $y' = \dfrac{3(x-2y)^2}{6(x-2y)^2 + 4y}$; $\dfrac{3}{10}$ **37.** $y' = \dfrac{3x^2(7+y^2)^{1/2}}{y}$; 16

39. $y' = \dfrac{y}{2xy^2 - x}$; 1   **41.** $y = 0.63x + 1.04$ **43.** $p' = \dfrac{1}{2p-2}$ **45.** $p' = -\dfrac{\sqrt{10,000 - p^2}}{p}$ **47.** $\dfrac{dL}{dV} = \dfrac{-(L+m)}{V+n}$

Exercise 5-6

1. 30   **3.** $-\frac{16}{3}$ **5.** $-\frac{16}{7}$ **7.** Decreasing at 9 units/sec   **9.** Approx. -3.03 ft/sec   **11.** $dA/dt \approx 126$ ft^2/sec
13. 3,768 cm^3/min   **15.** 6 lb/in.^{2}/hr   **17.** $-\frac{9}{4}$ ft/sec   **19.** $\frac{20}{3}$ ft/sec
21. 0.0214 ft/sec; 0.0135 ft/sec; yes, at $t = 0.000\,19$ sec   **23.** 3.835 units/sec
25. (A) $dC/dt = \$15,000/$wk   (B) $dR/dt = -\$50,000/$wk   (C) $dP/dt = -\$65,000/$wk   **27.** $ds/dt = \$2,207/$wk
29. (A) $dx/dt = -12.73$ units/month   (B) $dp/dt = \$1.53/$month   **31.** Approximately 100 ft^3/min

Chapter 5 Review Exercise

1. \$3,136.62; \$4,919.21; \$12,099.29 *(5-1)*   **2.** $\dfrac{2}{x} + 3e^x$ *(5-2)*   **3.** $2e^{2x-3}$ *(5-2)*   **4.** $\dfrac{2}{2x+7}$ *(5-3)*

5. (A) $y = \ln(3 + e^x)$ (B) $\dfrac{dy}{dx} = \dfrac{e^x}{3+e^x}$ *(5-4)*   **6.** $y' = \dfrac{9x^2}{4y}$; $\dfrac{9}{8}$ *(5-5)*   **7.** $dy/dt = 216$ *(5-6)*

8. (A) $x = 1,000 - 25p$ (B) $\dfrac{p}{40-p}$ (C) 0.6; demand is inelastic and insensitive to small changes in price.
  (D) $1,000p - 25p^2$ (E) Revenue increases *(5-4)*

9. Domain: All real numbers   **10.** $\lim\limits_{n\to\infty}\left(1 + \dfrac{2}{n}\right)^n = e^2 \approx 7.389\,06$ *(5-1)*   **11.** $\dfrac{7[(\ln z)^6 + 1]}{z}$ *(5-3)*
y intercept: 100
Horizontal asymptote: $y = 0$ **12.** $x^5(1 + 6\ln x)$ *(5-3)*   **13.** $\dfrac{e^x(x-6)}{x^7}$ *(5-2)*
Decreasing on $(-\infty, \infty)$
Concave upward on $(-\infty, \infty)$ *(5-2)*   **14.** $\dfrac{6x^2 - 3}{2x^3 - 3x}$ *(5-3)*   **15.** $(3x^2 - 2x)e^{x^3 - x^2}$ *(5-3)*

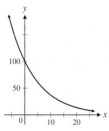

16. $\dfrac{1 - 2x\ln 5x}{xe^{2x}}$ *(5-3)*   **17.** $y = -x + 2$; $y = -ex + 1$ *(5-2)*

18. $y' = \dfrac{3y - 2x}{8y - 3x}$; $\dfrac{8}{19}$ *(5-5)*   **19.** $x' = \dfrac{4tx}{3x^2 - 2t^2}$; -4 *(5-5)*

20. $y' = \dfrac{1}{e^y + 2y}$; 1 *(5-5)*   **21.** $y' = \dfrac{2xy}{1 + 2y^2}$; $\dfrac{2}{3}$ *(5-5)*

22. $dy/dt = -2$ units/sec *(5-6)*   **23.** 0.27 ft/sec *(5-6)*   **24.** $dR/dt = 1/\pi \approx 0.318$ in./min *(5-6)*
25. Elastic for $5 < p < 15$; inelastic for $0 < p < 5$ *(5-4)*
26.

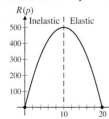

(5-4)

27. Max $f(x) = f(e^{4.5}) = 2e^{4.5} \approx 180.03$ *(5-3)*
28. Max $f(x) = f(0.5) = 5e^{-1} \approx 1.84$ *(5-2)*
29. Max $f(x) = f(1.373) = 2.487$ *(5-2)*
30. Max $f(x) = f(1.763) = 0.097$ *(5-3)*

31. Domain: All real numbers
y intercept: 0; x intercept: 0
Horizontal asymptote: $y = 5$
Increasing on $(-\infty, \infty)$
Concave downward on $(-\infty, \infty)$

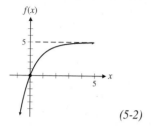

(5-2)

32. Domain: $(0, \infty)$
x intercept: 1
Increasing on $(e^{-1/3}, \infty)$
Decreasing on $(0, e^{-1/3})$
Local minimum at $x = e^{-1/3}$
Concave upward on $(e^{-5/6}, \infty)$
Concave downward on $(0, e^{-5/6})$
Inflection point at $x = e^{-5/6}$

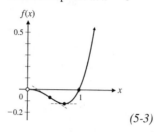

(5-3)

33. (A) $y = [\ln(4 - e^x)]^3$

(B) $\dfrac{dy}{dx} = \dfrac{-3e^x[\ln(4 - e^x)]^2}{4 - e^x}$ (5-4)

34. $2x(5^{x^2-1})(\ln 5)$ (5-3)

35. $\left(\dfrac{1}{\ln 5}\right)\dfrac{2x - 1}{x^2 - x}$ (5-3)

36. $\dfrac{2x + 1}{2(x^2 + x)\sqrt{\ln(x^2 + x)}}$ (5-3)

37. $y' = \dfrac{2x - e^{xy}y}{xe^{xy} - 1}$; 0 (5-5)

38. The rate of increase of area is proportional to the radius R, so it is smallest when $R = 0$, and has no largest value. (5-6)
39. Yes, for $-\sqrt{3}/3 < x < \sqrt{3}/3$ (5-6)   **40.** (A) 15 yr   (B) 13.9 yr (5-1)
41. $A'(t) = 10e^{0.1t}$; $A'(1) = \$11.05/\text{yr}$; $A'(10) = \$27.18/\text{yr}$ (5-1)   **42.** $R'(x) = (1,000 - 20x)e^{-0.02x}$ (5-3)
43. A maximum revenue of \$18,394 is realized at a production level of 50 units at \$367.88 each. (5-3)
44.

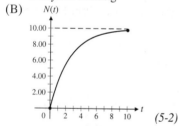

(5-3)

45. \$549.15; \$9,864 (5-3)   **46.** \$1.52 (5-3)   **47.** Min $\overline{C}(x) = \overline{C}(e^5) \approx \$49.66$ (5-3)

48. $p' = \dfrac{-(5,000 - 2p^3)^{1/2}}{3p^2}$ (5-5)   **49.** $dR/dt = \$110/\text{day}$ (5-6)

50. Increase price (5-4)   **51.** 0.02378 (5-4)
52. -1.111 mg/mL per hour; -0.335 mg/mL per hour (5-2)
53. $dR/dt = -3/(2\pi)$; approx. 0.477 mm/day (5-6)

54. (A) Increasing at the rate of 2.68 units/day at the end of 1 day of training; increasing at the rate of 0.54 unit/day after 5 days of training
(B)

N(t) graph (5-2)

55. $dT/dt = -1/27 \approx -0.037$ min/operation hour (5-6)

Chapter 6

Exercise 6-1

1. $(x^3/3) + C$ **3.** $(x^8/8) + C$ **5.** $2x + C$ **7.** $-(5t^{-2}/2) + C$ **9.** $\pi^2 x + C$ **11.** $3t^2 + 3t + C$
13. $3e^t + C$ **15.** $6 \ln|x| + C$ **17.** $10x^{3/2} + C$ **19.** $-21t^{-1/3} + C$ **21.** $\frac{1}{2}x^2 - \frac{2}{3}x^{3/2} + C$ **23.** $y = 40x^5 + C$
25. $P = 24x - 3x^2 + C$ **27.** $y = \frac{1}{3}u^6 - u^3 - u + C$ **29.** $y = e^x + 3x + C$ **31.** $x = 5 \ln|t| + t + C$
33. (A) False   (B) True   **35.** No, since one graph cannot be obtained from another by a vertical translation.
37. Yes, since one graph can be obtained from another by a vertical translation.   **39.** $(5x^2/2) - (5x^3/3) + C$
41. $6x + (5x^3/3) + (x^5/5) + C$ **43.** $2\sqrt{u} + C$ **45.** $-(x^{-2}/8) + C$ **47.** $4 \ln|u| + u + C$ **49.** $5e^z + 4z + C$
51. $x^3 + 2x^{-1} + C$ **53.** $2x^5 + 2x^{-4} - 2x + C$ **55.** $2x^{3/2} + 4x^{1/2} + C$ **57.** $\frac{3}{5}x^{5/3} + 2x^{-2} + C$
59. $(e^x/4) - (3x^2/8) + C$ **61.** $-4z^{-3} - \frac{5}{2}z^{-2} - 3 \ln|z| + C$ **63.** $\frac{2}{5}x^3 - \frac{2}{3}\ln|x| + C$ **65.** $y = x^2 - 3x + 5$
67. $C(x) = 2x^3 - 2x^2 + 3,000$ **69.** $x = 40\sqrt{t}$ **71.** $y = -2x^{-1} + 3 \ln|x| - x + 3$ **73.** $x = 4e^t - 2t - 3$

75. $y = 2x^2 - 3x + 1$ **77.** $x^2 + x^{-1} + C$ **79.** $\frac{1}{2}x^2 + x^{-2} + C$ **81.** $e^x - 2\ln|x| + C$ **83.** $M = t + t^{-1} + \frac{3}{4}$
85. $y = 3x^{5/3} + 3x^{2/3} - 6$ **87.** $p(x) = 10x^{-1} + 10$ **89.** x^3 **91.** $x^4 + 3x^2 + C$
99. $\overline{C}(x) = 15 + \dfrac{1,000}{x}$; $C(x) = 15x + 1,000$; $C(0) = \$1,000$

101. (A) The cost function increases from 0 to 8, is concave downward from 0 to 4, and is concave upward from 4 to 8. There is an inflection point at $x = 4$.

(B) $C(x) = x^3 - 12x^2 + 53x + 30$; $C(4) = \$114,000$; $C(8) = \$198,000$ (C)

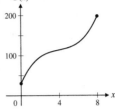

(D) Manufacturing plants are often inefficient at low and high levels of production.

103. $S(t) = 2,000 - 15t^{5/3}$; $80^{3/5} \approx 14$ mo
105. $S(t) = 2,000 - 15t^{5/3} - 70t$; $t \approx 8.92$ mo
107. $L(x) = 4,800x^{1/2}$; $L(25) = 24,000$ labor-hours
109. $W(h) = 0.0005h^3$; $W(70) = 171.5$ lb
111. 19,400

Exercise 6-2

1. $\frac{1}{3}(3x + 5)^3 + C$ **3.** $\frac{1}{6}(x^2 - 1)^6 + C$ **5.** $-\frac{1}{2}(5x^3 + 1)^{-2} + C$ **7.** $e^{5x} + C$ **9.** $\ln|1 + x^2| + C$
11. $\frac{2}{3}(1 + x^4)^{3/2} + C$ **13.** $\frac{1}{11}(x + 3)^{11} + C$ **15.** $-\frac{1}{6}(6t - 7)^{-1} + C$ **17.** $\frac{1}{12}(t^2 + 1)^6 + C$ **19.** $\frac{1}{2}e^{x^2} + C$
21. $\frac{1}{5}\ln|5x + 4| + C$ **23.** $-e^{1-t} + C$ **25.** $-\frac{1}{18}(3t^2 + 1)^{-3} + C$ **27.** $\frac{1}{3}(4 - x^3)^{-1} + C$
29. $\frac{2}{5}(x + 4)^{5/2} - \frac{8}{3}(x + 4)^{3/2} + C$ **31.** $\frac{2}{3}(x - 3)^{3/2} + 6(x - 3)^{1/2} + C$ **33.** $\frac{1}{11}(x - 4)^{11} + \frac{2}{5}(x - 4)^{10} + C$
35. $\frac{1}{8}(1 + e^{2x})^4 + C$ **37.** $\frac{1}{2}\ln|4 + 2x + x^2| + C$ **39.** $-\frac{1}{12}(x^4 + 2x^2 + 1)^{-3} + C$

41. (A) Differentiate the right side to get the integrand on the left side.

(B) Wrong, since $\dfrac{d}{dx}[\ln|2x - 3| + C] = \dfrac{2}{2x - 3} \neq \dfrac{1}{2x - 3}$. If $u = 2x - 3$, then $du = 2\,dx$. The integrand was not adjusted for the missing constant factor 2.

(C) $\displaystyle\int \frac{1}{2x - 3}\,dx = \frac{1}{2}\int \frac{2}{2x - 3}\,dx = \frac{1}{2}\ln|2x - 3| + C$ Check: $\dfrac{d}{dx}\left[\dfrac{1}{2}\ln|2x - 3| + C\right] = \dfrac{1}{2x - 3}$

43. (A) Differentiate the right side to get the integrand on the left side.

(B) Wrong, since $\dfrac{d}{dx}[e^{x^4} + C] = 4x^3e^{x^4} \neq x^3e^{x^4}$. If $u = x^4$, then $du = 4x^3\,dx$. The integrand was not adjusted for the missing constant factor 4.

(C) $\displaystyle\int x^3e^{x^4}\,dx = \frac{1}{4}\int 4x^3e^{x^4}\,dx = \frac{1}{4}e^{x^4} + C$ Check: $\dfrac{d}{dx}\left[\dfrac{1}{4}e^{x^4} + C\right] = x^3e^{x^4}$

45. (A) Differentiate the right side to get the integrand on the left side.

(B) Wrong, since $\dfrac{d}{dx}\left[\dfrac{(x^2 - 2)^2}{3x} + C\right] = \dfrac{3x^4 - 4x^2 - 4}{3x^2} \neq 2(x^2 - 2)^2$. If $u = x^2 - 2$, then $du = 2x\,du$. It appears that the student moved a variable factor across the integral sign as follows (which is *not* valid):
$$\int 2(x^2 - 2)^2\,dx = \frac{1}{x}\int 2x(x^2 - 2)^2\,dx.$$

(C) $\displaystyle\int 2(x^2 - 2)^2\,dx = \int (2x^4 - 8x^2 + 8)\,dx = \frac{2}{5}x^5 - \frac{8}{3}x^3 + 8x + C$

Check: $\dfrac{d}{dx}\left[\dfrac{2}{5}x^5 - \dfrac{8}{3}x^3 + 8x + C\right] = 2x^4 - 8x^2 + 8 = 2(x^2 - 2)^2$

47. $\frac{1}{9}(3x^2 + 7)^{3/2} + C$ **49.** $\frac{1}{8}x^8 + \frac{4}{5}x^5 + 2x^2 + C$ **51.** $\frac{1}{9}(x^3 + 2)^3 + C$ **53.** $\frac{1}{4}(2x^4 + 3)^{1/2} + C$ **55.** $\frac{1}{4}(\ln x)^4 + C$
57. $e^{-1/x} + C$ **59.** $x = \frac{1}{3}(t^3 + 5)^7 + C$ **61.** $y = 3(t^2 - 4)^{1/2} + C$ **63.** $p = -(e^x - e^{-x})^{-1} + C$
67. $p(x) = 2,000/(3x + 50)$; 250 bottles   **69.** $C(x) = 12x + 500\ln(x + 1) + 2,000$; $\overline{C}(1,000) = \$17.45$
71. (A) $S(t) = 10t + 100e^{-0.1t} - 100$, $0 \le t \le 24$ (B) $S(12) \approx \$50$ million   (C) 18.41 mo
73. $Q(t) = 100\ln(t + 1) + 5t$, $0 \le t \le 20$; $Q(9) \approx 275$ thousand barrels
75. $W(t) = 2e^{0.1t}$; $W(8) \approx 4.45$ g
77. (A) $-1,000$ bacteria/mL per day   (B) $N(t) = 5,000 - 1,000\ln(1 + t^2)$; 385 bacteria/mL   (C) 7.32 days
79. $N(t) = 100 - 60e^{-0.1t}$, $0 \le t \le 15$; $N(15) \approx 87$ words/min
81. $E(t) = 12,000 - 10,000(t + 1)^{-1/2}$; $E(15) = 9,500$ students

Exercise 6-3

1. $y = 3x^2 + C$ **3.** $y = 7 \ln|x| + C$ **5.** $y = 50e^{0.02x} + C$ **7.** $y = \dfrac{x^3}{3} - \dfrac{x^2}{2}$ **9.** $y = e^{-x^2} + 2$

11. $y = 2 \ln|1 + x| + 5$

13. Figure B. When $x = 1$, the slope $dy/dx = 1 - 1 = 0$ for any y. When $x = 0$, the slope $dy/dx = 0 - 1 = -1$ for any y. Both are consistent with the slope field shown in Figure B.

15. $y = \dfrac{x^2}{2} - x + C$; $y = \dfrac{x^2}{2} - x - 2$

17.

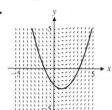

19. $y = Ce^{2t}$ **21.** $y = 100e^{-0.5x}$ **23.** $x = Ce^{-5t}$ **25.** $x = -(5t^2/2) + C$

27. Figure A. When $y = 1$, the slope $dy/dx = 1 - 1 = 0$ for any x. When $y = 2$, the slope $dy/dx = 1 - 2 = -1$ for any x. Both are consistent with the slope field shown in Figure A.

29. $y = 1 - e^{-x}$

31.

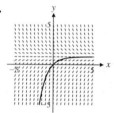

33.

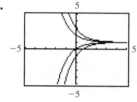

35.

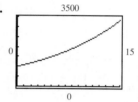

37.

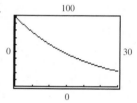

39.

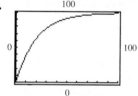

41.

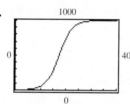

43. Apply the second-derivative test to $f(y) = ky(M - y)$.

45. 1999   **47.** $A = 1,000e^{0.08t}$

49. $A = 8,000e^{0.06t}$

51. (A) $p(x) = 100e^{-0.05x}$
(B) $60.65 per unit
(C)

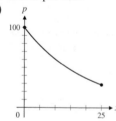

53. (A) $N = L(1 - e^{-0.051t})$
(B) 22.5%   (C) 32 days
(D)

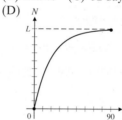

55. $I = I_0 e^{-0.00942x}$; $x \approx 74$ ft

57. (A) $Q = 3e^{-0.04t}$ (B) $Q(10) = 2.01$ mL
(C) 27.47 hr   (D)

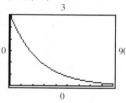
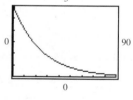

59. 0.023 117   **61.** Approx. 24,200 yr   **63.** 104 times; 67 times

65. (A) 7 people; 353 people   (B) 400
(C)

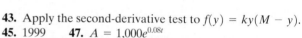

Exercise 6-4

1.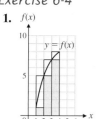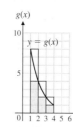

3. Figure A: $L_3 = 13, R_3 = 20$; Figure B: $L_3 = 14, R_3 = 7$

5. $L_3 \le \int_1^4 f(x)\,dx \le R_3$; $R_3 \le \int_1^4 g(x)\,dx \le L_3$; since $f(x)$ is increasing, L_3 underestimates the area and R_3 overestimates the area; since $g(x)$ is decreasing, the reverse is true.

7. In both figures the error bound for L_3 and R_3 is 7.

9. $S_5 = -260$ **11.** $S_4 = -1,194$ **13.** $S_3 = -33.01$ **15.** $S_6 = -38$
17. -2.475 **19.** 4.266 **21.** 2.474 **23.** -5.333 **25.** 1.067 **27.** -1.066
29. 15   **31.** 58.5   **33.** -54 **35.** 248   **37.** 0   **39.** -183

41. (A) False (B) True   **43.** $L_{10} = 286,100 \text{ ft}^2$; error bound is $50,000 \text{ ft}^2$; $n \ge 200$
45. $L_6 = -3.53, R_6 = -0.91$; error bound for L_6 and R_6 is 2.63. Geometrically, the definite integral over the interval $[2, 5]$ is the sum of the areas between the curve and the x axis from $x = 2$ to $x = 5$, with the areas below the x axis counted negatively and those above the x axis counted positively.
47. Increasing on $(-\infty, 0]$; decreasing on $[0, \infty)$ **49.** Increasing on $[-1, 0]$ and $[1, \infty)$; decreasing on $(-\infty, -1]$ and $[0, 1]$
51. $n \ge 22$ **53.** $n \ge 104$ **55.** $L_3 = 2,580, R_3 = 3,900$; error bound for L_3 and R_3 is 1,320
57. (A) $L_5 = 3.72; R_5 = 3.37$ (B) $R_5 = 3.37 \le \int_0^5 A'(t)\,dt \le 3.72 = L_5$
59. $L_3 = 114, R_3 = 102$; error bound for L_3 and R_3 is 12

Exercise 6-5

1. (A) $F(15) - F(10) = 375$ **3.** (A) $F(15) - F(10) = 85$ **5.** 5   **7.** 5   **9.** 2   **11.** $-\frac{7}{3} \approx -2.333$
(B) 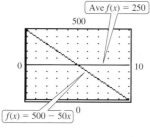   (B)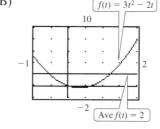

13. 2   **15.** $\frac{1}{2}(e^2 - 1) \approx 3.195$

17. $2 \ln 3.5 \approx 2.506$ **19.** $\frac{3}{4}$ **21.** 12   **23.** -2

25. 14   **27.** $5^6 = 15,625$ **29.** $\ln 4 \approx 1.386$
31. $20(e^{0.25} - e^{-0.5}) \approx 13.550$ **33.** $\frac{1}{2}$

35. $\frac{8}{3} \approx 2.667$ **37.** $\frac{1}{2}(1 - e^{-1}) \approx 0.316$

39. $-\frac{3}{2} - \ln 2 \approx -2.193$

41. (A) Average $f(x) = 250$ **43.** (A) Average $f(t) = 2$ **45.** (A) Average $f(x) = \frac{45}{28} \approx 1.61$
(B)   (B)   (B)

47. (A) Average $f(x) = 2(1 - e^{-2}) \approx 1.73$ **49.** $\frac{1}{6}(15^{3/2} - 5^{3/2}) \approx 7.819$ **51.** $\frac{1}{2}(\ln 2 - \ln 3) \approx -0.203$ **53.** 0
(B)

55. 4.566   **57.** 2.214   **61.** $\int_{300}^{900} \left(500 - \frac{x}{3}\right) dx = \$180,000$

63. $\int_0^5 500(t - 12)\,dt = -\$23,750$; $\int_5^{10} 500(t - 12)\,dt = -\$11,250$

65. (A) 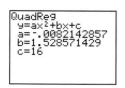   (B) 6,505   **67.** Useful life $= \sqrt{\ln 55} \approx 2$ yr; total
profit $= \frac{51}{22} - \frac{5}{2}e^{-4} \approx 2.272$ or \$2,272
69. (A) \$420 (B) \$135,000

71. (A)

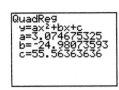

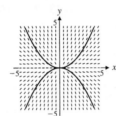

(B) $100,505

73. $50e^{0.6} - 50e^{0.4} - 10 \approx \$6.51$

75. 4,800 labor-hours

77. (A) $I = -200t + 600$
(B) $\frac{1}{3}\int_0^3 (-200t + 600)\, dt = 300$

79. $100 \ln 11 + 50 \approx 290$ thousand barrels;
$100 \ln 21 - 100 \ln 11 + 50 \approx 115$
thousand barrels

81. $2e^{0.8} - 2 \approx 2.45$ g; $2e^{1.6} - 2e^{0.8} \approx 5.45$ g

83. 10°C   **85.** $0.6 \ln 2 + 0.1 \approx 0.516$; $(4.2 \ln 625 + 2.4 - 4.2 \ln 49)/24 \approx 0.546$

Chapter 6 Review Exercise

1. $3x^2 + 3x + C$ (6-1)   **2.** 50 (6-5)   **3.** -207 (6-5)   **4.** $-\frac{1}{8}(1 - t^2)^4 + C$ (6-2)   **5.** $\ln|u| + \frac{1}{4}u^4 + C$ (6-1)

6. 0.216 (6-5)   **7.** e^{-x} (6-1)   **8.** $\sqrt{4 + 5x} + C$ (6-1)   **9.** $y = f(x) = x^3 - 2x + 4$ (6-3)

10. (A) $2x^4 - 2x^2 - x + C$ (B) $e^t - 4\ln|t| + C$ (6-1)   **11.** $R_2 = 72$; error bound for R_2 is 48 (6-4)

12. $\int_1^5 (x^2 + 1)\, dx = \dfrac{136}{3} \approx 45.33$; actual error is $\dfrac{80}{3} \approx 26.67$ (6-5)   **13.** $L_4 = 30.8$ (6-4)   **14.** 7 (6-5)

15. Width $= 2 - (-1) = 3$; height $=$ average $f(x) = 7$ (6-5)   **16.** $S_4 = 368$ (6-4)   **17.** $S_5 = 906$ (6-4)   **18.** -10 (6-4)

19. 0.4 (6-4)   **20.** 1.4 (6-4)   **21.** 0 (6-4)   **22.** 0.4 (6-4)   **23.** 2 (6-4)   **24.** -2 (6-4)   **25.** -0.4 (6-4)

26. (A) 1;1   (B) 4;4 (6-3)

27. $dy/dx = (2y)/x$; the slopes computed in Problem 26A are compatible with the slope field shown. (6-3)

29. $y = \frac{1}{4}x^2$; $y = -\frac{1}{4}x^2$ (6-3)   **30.** (6-3)

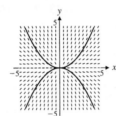

31. (6-3)

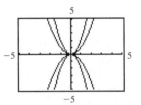

32. $\frac{2}{3}(2)^{3/2} \approx 1.886$ (6-5)   **33.** $\frac{1}{6} \approx 0.167$ (6-5)   **34.** $-5e^{-t} + C$ (6-1)   **35.** $\frac{1}{2}(1 + e^2)$ (6-1)   **36.** $\frac{1}{6}e^{3x^2} + C$ (6-2)

37. $2(\sqrt{5} - 1) \approx 2.472$ (6-5)   **38.** $\frac{1}{2}\ln 10 \approx 1.151$ (6-5)   **39.** 0.45 (6-5)   **40.** $\frac{1}{48}(2x^4 + 5)^6 + C$ (6-2)

41. $-\ln(e^{-x} + 3) + C$ (6-2)   **42.** $-(e^x + 2)^{-1} + C$ (6-2)   **43.** $y = f(x) = 3\ln|x| + x^{-1} + 4$ (6-2, 6-3)

44. $y = 3x^2 + x - 4$ (6-3)

45. (A) Average $f(x) = 6.5$ (B)

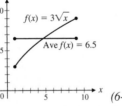

$f(x) = 3\sqrt{x}$

Ave $f(x) = 6.5$

(6-5)

46. $\frac{1}{3}(\ln x)^3 + C$ (6-2)

47. $\frac{1}{8}x^8 - \frac{2}{5}x^5 + \frac{1}{2}x^2 + C$ (6-2)

48. $\frac{2}{3}(6 - x)^{3/2} - 12(6 - x)^{1/2} + C$ (6-2)

49. $\frac{1,234}{15} \approx 82.267$ (6-5)

50. $\frac{64}{15} \approx 4.267$ (6-5)

51. $y = 3e^{x^3} - 1$ (6-3)

52. $N = 800e^{0.06t}$ (6-3)

53. Limited growth

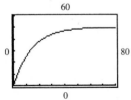

(6-3)

54. Exponential decay

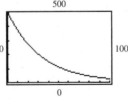

(6-3)

55. Unlimited growth

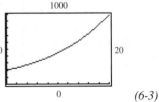

(6-3)

56. Logistic growth

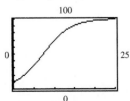

(6-3)

57. 1.167 (6-5)   **58.** 99.074 (6-5)   **59.** -0.153 (6-5)

60. $L_2 = \$180,000$; $R_2 = \$140,000$; $\$140,000 \le \int_{200}^{600} C'(x)\, dx \le \$180,000$ (6-4)

61. $\displaystyle\int_{200}^{600}\left(600 - \frac{x}{2}\right) dx = \$160,000$ (6-5)   **62.** $\displaystyle\int_{10}^{40}\left(150 - \frac{x}{10}\right) dx = \$4,425$ (6-5)

63. $P(x) = 100x - 0.01x^2$; $P(10) = \$999$ (6-3)

64. $\int_0^{15}(60 - 4t)\, dt = 450$ thousand barrels (6-5)

65. 109 items *(6-5)*   **66.** $16e^{2.5} - 16e^2 - 8 \approx \$68.70$ *(6-5)*

67. Useful life = $10 \ln \frac{20}{3} \approx 19$ yr; total profit = $143 - 200e^{-1.9} \approx 113.086$ or \$113,086 *(6-5)*

68. $S(t) = 50 - 50e^{-0.08t}$; $50 - 50e^{-0.96} \approx \$31$ million; $-(\ln 0.2)/0.08 \approx 20$ mo *(6-3)*   **69.** 1 cm^2 *(6-3)*   **70.** 800 gal *(6-5)*

71. (A) 145 million   (B) About 46 years *(6-3)*

72. $\dfrac{-\ln 0.04}{0.000\ 123\ 8} \approx 26{,}000$ yr *(6-3)*   **73.** $N(t) = 95 - 70e^{-0.1t}$; $N(15) \approx 79$ words/min *(6-3)*

Chapter 7

Exercise 7-1

1. $\int_a^b g(x)\,dx$ **3.** $\int_a^b [-h(x)]\,dx$

5. Since the shaded region in Figure C is below the x axis, $h(x) \leq 0$; thus, $\int_a^b h(x)\,dx$ represents the negative of the area of the region.

7. 20   **9.** $\frac{7}{3} \approx 2.333$ **11.** 6   **13.** 7.021   **15.** 0.693   **17.** $\int_a^b [-f(x)]\,dx$ **19.** $\int_b^c f(x)\,dx + \int_c^d [-f(x)]\,dx$

21. $\int_c^d [f(x) - g(x)]\,dx$ **23.** $\int_a^b [f(x) - g(x)]\,dx + \int_b^c [g(x) - f(x)]\,dx$

25. Find the intersection points by solving $f(x) = g(x)$ on the interval $[a, d]$ to determine b and c. Then observe that $f(x) \geq g(x)$ over $[a, b]$, $g(x) \geq f(x)$ over $[b, c]$, and $f(x) \geq g(x)$ over $[c, d]$. Thus,

area = $\int_a^b [f(x) - g(x)]\,dx + \int_b^c [g(x) - f(x)]\,dx + \int_c^d [f(x) - g(x)]\,dx$.

27. 2.5   **29.** 7.667   **31.** 12   **33.** 15   **35.** 32   **37.** 36   **39.** 9   **41.** 2.832   **43.** 18   **45.** 1.858

47. 52.616   **49.** 8   **51.** 101.75   **53.** 8   **55.** 17.979   **57.** 5.113   **59.** 8.290   **61.** 3.166   **63.** 1.385

65. Total production from the end of the fifth year to the end of the 10th year is $50 + 100 \ln 20 - 100 \ln 15 \approx 79$ thousand barrels.

67. Total profit over the 5-yr useful life of the game is $20 - 30e^{-1.5} \approx 13.306$ or \$13,306.

69. 1935: 0.412; 1947: 0.231; income was more equally distributed in 1947.

71. 1963: 0.818; 1983: 0.846; total assets were less equally distributed in 1983.

73. (A) $f(x) = 0.3125x^2 + 0.7175x - 0.015$ (B) 0.104   **75.** Total weight gain during the first 10 hr is $3e - 3 \approx 5.15$ g.

77. Average number of words learned during the second 2 hr is $15 \ln 4 - 15 \ln 2 \approx 10$.

Exercise 7-2

1. 4.12   **3.** 509.14   **5.** (A) 10.72   (B) 3.28   (C) 10.72

7. (A) .75   (B) .11   **9.** 8 yr   **11.** (A) .11   (B) .10   **13.** $P(t \geq 12) = 1 - P(0 \leq t \leq 12) = .89$

(C)   **15.** \$12,500

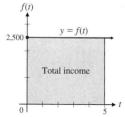

17. If $f(t)$ is the rate of flow of a continuous income stream, then the total income produced from 0 to 5 yr is the area under the graph of $y = f(t)$ from $t = 0$ to $t = 5$.

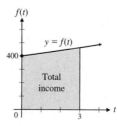

19. $8{,}000(e^{0.15} - 1) \approx \$1{,}295$

21. If $f(t)$ is the rate of flow of a continuous income stream, the total income produced from 0 to 3 yr is the area under the graph of $y = f(t)$ from $t = 0$ to $t = 3$.

23. $255,562; $175,562   **25.** $20,000(e^{0.25} - e^{-0.08}) \approx \$7,218$ **27.** $875

29. Clothing store: $FV = 120,000(e^{0.5} - 1) \approx \$77,847$; computer store: $FV = 200,000(e^{0.5} - e^{0.25}) \approx \$72,939$; the clothing store is the better investment.

31. Bond: $FV = 10,000e^{0.4} \approx \$14,918$; business: $FV = 25,000(e^{0.4} - 1) \approx \$12,296$; the bond is the better investment.

33. $55,230   **35.** $\dfrac{k}{r}(e^{rT} - 1)$ **37.** $625,000

39. The shaded area is the consumers' surplus and represents the total savings to consumers who are willing to pay more than $150 for a product but are still able to buy the product for $150.

41. $9,900

43. The area of the region PS is the producers' surplus and represents the total gain to producers who are willing to supply units at a lower price than $67 but are still able to supply the product at $67.

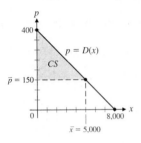

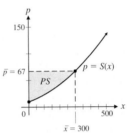

45. $CS = \$3,380$; $PS = \$1,690$ **47.** $CS = \$6,980$; $PS = \$5,041$ **49.** $CS = \$7,810$; $PS = \$8,336$

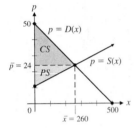

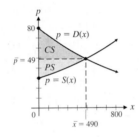

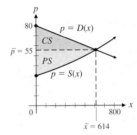

51. $CS = \$8,544$; $PS = \$11,507$ **53.** (A) $\bar{x} = 21.457$; $\bar{p} = \$6.51$ (B) $CS = 1.774$ or $1,774$; $PS = 1.087$ or $1,087$

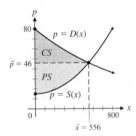

Exercise 7-3

1. $\frac{1}{3}xe^{3x} - \frac{1}{9}e^{3x} + C$ **3.** $\dfrac{x^3}{3}\ln x - \dfrac{x^3}{9} + C$ **5.** $u = x + 2; \dfrac{(x+2)(x+1)^6}{6} - \dfrac{(x+1)^7}{42} + C$ **7.** $-xe^{-x} - e^{-x} + C$

9. $\frac{1}{2}e^{x^2} + C$ **11.** $(xe^x - 4e^x)|_0^1 = -3e + 4 \approx -4.1548$ **13.** $(x\ln 2x - x)|_1^3 = (3\ln 6 - 3) - (\ln 2 - 1) \approx 2.6821$

15. $\ln(x^2 + 1) + C$ **17.** $(\ln x)^2/2 + C$ **19.** $\frac{2}{3}x^{3/2}\ln x - \frac{4}{9}x^{3/2} + C$

21. The integral represents the negative of the area between the graph of $y = (x - 3)e^x$ and the x axis from $x = 0$ to $x = 1$.

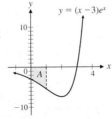

23. The integral represents
the area between the
graph of $y = \ln 2x$ and
the x axis from $x = 1$
to $x = 3$.

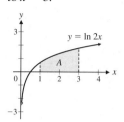

25. $(x^2 - 2x + 2)e^x + C$ **27.** $\dfrac{xe^{ax}}{a} - \dfrac{e^{ax}}{a^2} + C$

29. $\left(-\dfrac{\ln x}{x} - \dfrac{1}{x}\right)\Big|_1^e = -\dfrac{2}{e} + 1 \approx 0.2642$

31. $6 \ln 6 - 4 \ln 4 - 2 \approx 3.205$ **33.** $xe^{x-2} - e^{x-2} + C$

35. $\frac{1}{2}(1 + x^2)\ln(1 + x^2) - \frac{1}{2}(1 + x^2) + C$ **37.** $(1 + e^x)\ln(1 + e^x) - (1 + e^x) + C$

39. $x(\ln x)^2 - 2x \ln x + 2x + C$ **41.** $x(\ln x)^3 - 3x(\ln x)^2 + 6x \ln x - 6x + C$

43. 1.56   **45.** 34.98   **47.** $\int_0^5 (2t - te^{-t})\,dt = \$24$ million

49. The total profit for the first 5 yr (in
millions of dollars) is the same as
the area under the marginal profit
function, $P'(t) = 2t - te^{-t}$, from
$t = 0$ to $t = 5$.

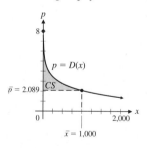

51. \$3,278   **53.** 0.264

55. The area bounded by $y = x$ and the Lorenz curve $y = xe^{x-1}$, divided by the area under the graph of $y = x$ from $x = 0$ to $x = 1$ is
the Gini index of income concentration. The closer this index is
to 0, the more equally distributed income is; the closer this index
is to 1, the more concentrated income is in a few hands.

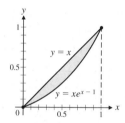

57. $S(t) = 1,600 + 400e^{0.1t} - 40te^{0.1t}$; 15 mo

59. \$977

61. The area bounded by the price–demand
equation, $p = 9 - \ln(x + 4)$, and the price
equation, $y = \bar{p} = 2.089$, from $x = 0$ to
$x = \bar{x} = 1,000$, represents the consumers'
surplus. This is the amount consumers who
are willing to pay more than \$2,089 save.

63. 2.1388 ppm

65. $N(t) = -4te^{-0.25t} - 40e^{-0.25t} + 80$; 8 wk; 78 words/min

67. 20,980

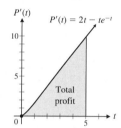

Exercise 7-4

1. $\ln\left|\dfrac{x}{1 + x}\right| + C$ **3.** $\dfrac{1}{3 + x} + 2\ln\left|\dfrac{5 + 2x}{3 + x}\right| + C$ **5.** $\dfrac{2(x - 32)}{3}\sqrt{16 + x} + C$ **7.** $-\ln\left|\dfrac{1 + \sqrt{1 - x^2}}{x}\right| + C$

9. $\dfrac{1}{2}\ln\left|\dfrac{x}{2 + \sqrt{x^2 + 4}}\right| + C$ **11.** $\frac{1}{3}x^3 \ln x - \frac{1}{9}x^3 + C$ **13.** $x - \ln|1 + e^x| + C$ **15.** $9 \ln\frac{3}{2} - 2 \approx 1.6492$

17. $\frac{1}{2}\ln\frac{12}{5} \approx 0.4377$ **19.** $\ln 3 \approx 1.0986$ **21.** $-\dfrac{\sqrt{4x^2 + 1}}{x} + 2\ln|2x + \sqrt{4x^2 + 1}| + C$ **23.** $\frac{1}{2}\ln|x^2 + \sqrt{x^4 - 16}| + C$

25. $\frac{1}{6}(x^3\sqrt{x^6 + 4} + 4\ln|x^3 + \sqrt{x^6 + 4}|) + C$ **27.** $-\dfrac{\sqrt{4 - x^4}}{8x^2} + C$ **29.** $\dfrac{1}{5}\ln\left|\dfrac{3 + 4e^x}{2 + e^x}\right| + C$

31. $\frac{2}{3}(\ln x - 8)\sqrt{4 + \ln x} + C$ **33.** $\frac{1}{5}x^2e^{5x} - \frac{2}{25}xe^{5x} + \frac{2}{125}e^{5x} + C$ **35.** $-x^3e^{-x} - 3x^2e^{-x} - 6xe^{-x} - 6e^{-x} + C$

37. $x(\ln x)^3 - 3x(\ln x)^2 + 6x \ln x - 6x + C$ **39.** $\frac{64}{3}$ **41.** $\frac{1}{2}\ln\frac{9}{5} \approx 0.2939$ **43.** $\dfrac{-1 - \ln x}{x} + C$

45. $\sqrt{x^2 - 1} + C$ **47.** 31.38   **49.** 5.48   **51.** $3{,}000 + 1{,}500 \ln\frac{1}{3} \approx \$1{,}352$

53.

55. $C(x) = 200x + 1{,}000 \ln(1 + 0.05x) + 25{,}000$; 608; \$198,773

57. $100{,}000e - 250{,}000 \approx \$21{,}828$

59. 0.1407

61. As the area bounded by the two curves gets smaller, the Lorenz curve approaches $y = x$ and the distribution of income approaches perfect equality—all persons share equally in the income available.

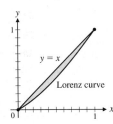

63. $S(t) = 1 + t - \dfrac{1}{1 + t} - 2 \ln|1 + t|$; $24.96 - 2 \ln 25 \approx \$18.5$ million

65. The total sales (in millions of dollars) over the first 2 yr (24 mo) is the area under the graph of $y = S'(t)$ from $t = 0$ to $t = 24$.

67. $P(x) = \dfrac{2(9x - 4)}{135}(2 + 3x)^{3/2} - 2{,}000.83$; 54; \$37,932

69. $100 \ln 3 \approx 110$ ft   **71.** $60 \ln 5 \approx 97$ items

73. The area under the graph of $y = N'(t)$ from $t = 0$ to $t = 12$ represents the total number of items learned in that time interval.

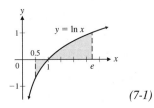

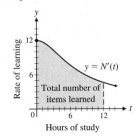

Chapter 7 Review Exercise

1. $\int_a^b f(x)\, dx$ (7-1)   **2.** $\int_b^c[-f(x)]\, dx$ (7-1)   **3.** $\int_a^b f(x)\, dx + \int_b^c[-f(x)]\, dx$ (7-1)

4. Area = 1.153

5. $\frac{1}{4}xe^{4x} - \frac{1}{16}e^{4x} + C$ (7-3, 7-4)   **6.** $\frac{1}{2}x^2 \ln x - \frac{1}{4}x^2 + C$ (7-3, 7-4)

7. $\dfrac{(\ln x)^2}{2} + C$ (6-2)   **8.** $\dfrac{\ln(1 + x^2)}{2} + C$ (7-2)   **9.** $\dfrac{1}{1 + x} + \ln\left|\dfrac{x}{1 + x}\right| + C$ (7-4)

10. $-\dfrac{\sqrt{1 + x}}{x} - \dfrac{1}{2}\ln\left|\dfrac{\sqrt{1 + x} - 1}{\sqrt{1 + x} + 1}\right| + C$ (7-4)   **11.** $\int_a^b[f(x) - g(x)]\, dx$ (7-1)

12. $\int_b^c[g(x) - f(x)]\, dx$ (7-1)   **13.** $\int_b^c[g(x) - f(x)]\, dx + \int_c^d[f(x) - g(x)]\, dx$ (7-1)

14. $\int_a^b[f(x) - g(x)]\, dx + \int_b^c[g(x) - f(x)]\, dx + \int_c^d[f(x) - g(x)]\, dx$ (7-1)

15. Area = 20.833

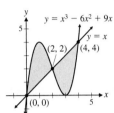

$y = x^2 - 6x + 9$

$(0, 9)$

$(5, 4)$

$y = 9 - x$

(7-1)

16. 1 *(7-3, 7-4)*   **17.** $\frac{15}{2} - 8 \ln 8 + 8 \ln 4 \approx 1.955$ *(7-4)*

18. $\frac{1}{6}(3x\sqrt{9x^2 - 49} - 49 \ln|3x + \sqrt{9x^2 - 49}|) + C$ *(7-4)*

19. $-2te^{-0.5t} - 4e^{-0.5t} + C$ *(7-3, 7-4)*   **20.** $\frac{1}{3}x^3 \ln x - \frac{1}{9}x^3 + C$ *(7-3, 7-4)*

21. $x - \ln|1 + 2e^x| + C$ *(7-4)*

22. (A) Area = 8   (B) Area = 8.38

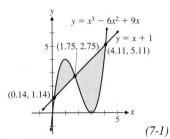

$y = x^3 - 6x^2 + 9x$

$y = x$

$(2, 2)$ $(4, 4)$

$(0, 0)$

$y = x^3 - 6x^2 + 9x$

$y = x + 1$

$(1.75, 2.75)$ $(4.11, 5.11)$

$(0.14, 1.14)$

(7-1)

23. $\frac{1}{3}(\ln x)^3 + C$ *(6-2)*

24. $\frac{1}{2}x^2(\ln x)^2 - \frac{1}{2}x^2 \ln x + \frac{1}{4}x^2 + C$ *(7-3, 7-4)*

25. $\sqrt{x^2 - 36} + C$ *(6-2)*

26. $\frac{1}{2}\ln|x^2 + \sqrt{x^4 - 36}| + C$ *(7-4)*

27. $50 \ln 10 - 42 \ln 6 - 24 \approx 15.875$ *(7-3, 7-4)*

28. $x(\ln x)^2 - 2x \ln x + 2x + C$ *(7-3, 7-4)*

29. $-\frac{1}{4}e^{-2x^2} + C$ *(6-2)*

30. $-\frac{1}{2}x^2e^{-2x} - \frac{1}{2}xe^{-2x} - \frac{1}{4}e^{-2x} + C$ *(7-3, 7-4)*

31. 1.703 *(7-1)*   **32.** (A) .189   (B) .154 *(7-2)*

33. The probability that the product will fail during the second year of warranty is the area under the probability density function $y = f(t)$ from $t = 1$ to $t = 2$. *(7-2)*

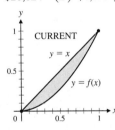

$y = f(t)$

34. $R(x) = 65x - 6[(x + 1) \ln(x + 1) - x]$; 618/wk; $29,506 *(7-3)*

35. (A)

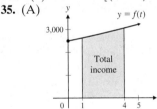

$y = f(t)$

3,000

Total income

(B) $8,507 *(7-2)*

36. (A) $20,824   (B) $6,623 *(7-2)*

37. (A)

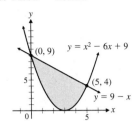

CURRENT

$y = x$

$y = f(x)$

PROJECTED

$y = x$

$y = g(x)$

(B) More equitably distributed, since the area bounded by the two curves will have decreased.

(C) Current = 0.3; projected = 0.2; income will be more equitably distributed 10 years from now. *(7-1)*

38. (A) CS = $2,250; PS = $2,700   (B) CS = $2,890; PS = $2,278

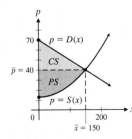

70   $p = D(x)$

CS

$\bar{p} = 40$

PS

$p = S(x)$

200

$\bar{x} = 150$

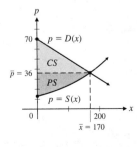

70   $p = D(x)$

CS

$\bar{p} = 36$

PS

$p = S(x)$

200

$\bar{x} = 170$

(7-2)

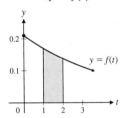

39. (A) 25.403 or 25,403 lb   (B) $PS = 121.6$ or $1,216 (7-2)$
40. 4.522 mL; 1.899 mL *(6-5, 7-4)*
41.

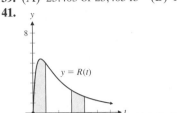

42. .667; .333 *(7-2)*
43. The probability that the doctor will spend more than an hour with a randomly selected patient is the area under the probability density function $y = f(t)$ from $t = 1$ to $t = 3$. *(7-2)*

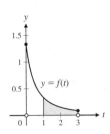

(6-5, 7-1)

44. 45 thousand *(6-5, 7-1)*   **45.** .368 *(7-2)*

Chapter 8

Exercise 8-1

1. -4 **3.** 11   **5.** 4   **7.** Not defined   **9.** 59   **11.** -1 **13.** -64 **15.** 16π **17.** 791   **19.** 0.192
21. 118   **23.** 36,095.07   **25.** $-1.926, 0.599$ **27.** $2x + h$ **29.** $2y^2$ **31.** $E(0, 0, 3); F(2, 0, 3)$
33. (A) In the plane $y = c$, c any constant, $z = x^2$.
   (B) The y axis; the horizontal line parallel to the y axis and passing through the point $(1, 0, 1)$; the horizontal line parallel to the y axis and passing through the point $(2, 0, 4)$ (C) A parabolic "trough" lying on top of the y axis
35. (A) Upper semicircles whose centers lie on the y axis   (B) Upper semicircles whose centers lie on the x axis
   (C) The upper hemisphere of radius 6 with center at the origin
37. (A) $a^2 + b^2$ and $c^2 + d^2$ both equal the square of the radius of the circle.
   (B) Bell-shaped curves with maximum values of 1 at the origin
   (C) A bell, with maximum value 1 at the origin, extending infinitely far in all directions.
39. \$4,400; \$6,000; \$7,100   **41.** $R(p, q) = -5p^2 + 6pq - 4q^2 + 200p + 300q; R(2, 3) = \$1,280; R(3, 2) = \$1,175$
43. 30,065 units   **45.** (A) \$272,615.08 (B) 12.2%
47. $T(70, 47) \approx 29$ min; $T(60, 27) = 33$ min   **49.** $C(6, 8) = 75; C(8.1, 9) = 90$ **51.** $Q(12, 10) = 120; Q(10, 12) \approx 83$

Exercise 8-2

1. 4   **3.** -20 **5.** $18y^2 - 6xy$ **7.** $36y - 6x$ **9.** -19 **11.** $-14x + 10y - 9$ **13.** -17 **15.** 10   **17.** -14
19. $2y^3e^x + 20x^3 \ln y$ **21.** $6e^2 + 80$ **23.** $6y^2e^x + 20x^3y^{-1}$ **25.** $8xe^{4x^2+5y}$ **27.** $40xe^{4x^2+5y}$ **29.** $40e^4$ **31.** $8e^5$
33. $f_x(x, y) = 6x(x^2 - y^3)^2; f_y(x, y) = -9y^2(x^2 - y^3)^2$ **35.** $f_x(x, y) = 24xy(3x^2y - 1)^3; f_y(x, y) = 12x^2(3x^2y - 1)^3$
37. $f_x(x, y) = 2x/(x^2 + y^2); f_y(x, y) = 2y/(x^2 + y^2)$ **39.** $f_x(x, y) = y^4e^{xy^2}; f_y(x, y) = 2xy^3e^{xy^2} + 2ye^{xy^2}$
41. $f_x(x, y) = 4xy^2/(x^2 + y^2)^2; f_y(x, y) = -4x^2y/(x^2 + y^2)^2$
45. $f_{xx}(x, y) = 2y^2 + 6x; f_{xy}(x, y) = 4xy = f_{yx}(x, y); f_{yy}(x, y) = 2x^2$
47. $f_{xx}(x, y) = -2y/x^3; f_{xy}(x, y) = (-1/y^2) + (1/x^2) = f_{yx}(x, y); f_{yy}(x, y) = 2x/y^3$
49. $f_{xx}(x, y) = (2y + xy^2)e^{xy}; f_{xy}(x, y) = (2x + x^2y)e^{xy} = f_{yx}(x, y); f_{yy}(x, y) = x^3e^{xy}$
51. $x = 2$ and $y = 4$ **53.** $x = 1.200$ and $y = -0.695$
55. (A) $-\frac{13}{3}$ (B) The function $f(0, y)$, for example, has values less than $-\frac{13}{3}$.
57. (A) $c = 1.145$ (B) $f_x(c, 2) = 0; f_y(c, 2) = 92.021$
59. $f_{xx}(x, y) + f_{yy}(x, y) = (2y^2 - 2x^2)/(x^2 + y^2)^2 + (2x^2 - 2y^2)/(x^2 + y^2)^2 = 0$ **61.** (A) $2x$ (B) $4y$
63. $P_x(1,200, 1,800) = 24$; profit will increase approx. \$24 per unit increase in production of type A calculators at the $(1,200, 1,800)$ output level; $P_y(1,200, 1,800) = -48$; profit will decrease approx. \$48 per unit increase in production of type B calculators at the $(1,200, 1,800)$ output level
65. $\partial x/\partial p = -5$: a \$1 increase in the price of brand A will decrease the demand for brand A by 5 lb at any price level (p, q); $\partial y/\partial p = 2$: a \$1 increase in the price of brand A will increase the demand for brand B by 2 lb at any price level (p, q)
67. (A) $f_x(x, y) = 7.5x^{-0.25}y^{0.25}; f_y(x, y) = 2.5x^{0.75}y^{-0.75}$
   (B) Marginal productivity of labor $= f_x(600, 100) \approx 4.79$; Marginal productivity of capital $= f_y(600, 100) \approx 9.58$
   (C) Capital
69. Competitive   **71.** Complementary
73. (A) $f_w(w, h) = 6.65w^{-0.575}h^{0.725}; f_h(w, h) = 11.34w^{0.425}h^{-0.275}$
   (B) $f_w(65, 57) = 11.31$: for a 65 lb child 57 in. tall, the rate of change in surface area is 11.31 in.^{2} for each pound gained in weight (height is held fixed); $f_h(65, 57) = 21.99$: for a child 57 in. tall, the rate of change in surface area is 21.99 in.^{2} for each inch gained in height (weight is held fixed)

75. $C_W(6, 8) = 12.5$: index increases approx. 12.5 units for 1 in. increase in width of head (length held fixed) when $W = 6$ and $L = 8$; $C_L(6, 8) = -9.38$: index decreases approx. 9.38 units for 1 in. increase in length (width held fixed) when $W = 6$ and $L = 8$

Exercise 8-3

1. $f_x(x, y) = 4$; $f_y(x, y) = 5$; the functions $f_x(x, y)$ and $f_y(x, y)$ never have the value 0.
3. $f_x(x, y) = -1.2 + 4x^3$; $f_y(x, y) = 6.8 + 0.6y^2$; the function $f_y(x, y)$ never has the value 0.
5. $f(-2, 0) = 10$ is a local maximum   **7.** $f(-1, 3) = 4$ is a local minimum   **9.** f has a saddle point at $(3, -2)$
11. $f(3, 2) = 33$ is a local maximum   **13.** $f(2, 2) = 8$ is a local minimum   **15.** f has a saddle point at $(0, 0)$
17. f has a saddle point at $(0, 0)$; $f(1, 1) = -1$ is a local minimum
19. f has a saddle point at $(0, 0)$; $f(3, 18) = -162$ and $f(-3, -18) = -162$ are local minima
21. The test fails at $(0, 0)$; f has saddle points at $(2, 2)$ and $(2, -2)$ **23.** f has a saddle point at $(0.614, -1.105)$
25. $f(x, y)$ is nonnegative and equals 0 when $x = 0$, so f has a local minimum at each point of the y axis.
27. (B) Local minimum   **29.** 2,000 type A and 4,000 type B; Max $P = P(2, 4) = \$15$ million
31. (A) When $p = \$10$ and $q = \$12$, $x = 56$ and $y = 16$; when $p = \$11$ and $q = \$11$, $x = 6$ and $y = 56$.
    (B) A maximum weekly profit of \$288 is realized for $p = \$10$ and $q = \$12$.
33. $P(x, y) = P(4, 2)$ **35.** 8 in. by 4 in. by 2 in.   **37.** 20 in. by 20 in. by 40 in.

Exercise 8-4

1. Max $f(x, y) = f(3, 3) = 18$ **3.** Min $f(x, y) = f(3, 4) = 25$
5. $F_x = -3 + 2\lambda = 0$ and $F_y = 4 + 5\lambda = 0$ have no simultaneous solution.
7. Max $f(x, y) = f(3, 3) = f(-3, -3) = 18$; Min $f(x, y) = f(3, -3) = f(-3, 3) = -18$
9. Maximum product is 25 when each number is 5   **11.** Min $f(x, y, z) = f(-4, 2, -6) = 56$
13. Max $f(x, y, z) = f(2, 2, 2) = 6$; Min $f(x, y, z) = f(-2, -2, -2) = -6$ **15.** Max $f(x, y) = f(0.217, 0.885) = 1.055$
17. $F_x = e^x + \lambda = 0$ and $F_y = 3e^y - 2\lambda = 0$ have no simultaneous solution.
19. Maximize $f(x, 5)$, a function of just one independent variable.
21. (A) Max $f(x, y) = f(0.707, 0.5) = f(-0.707, 0.5) = 0.47$
23. 60 of model A and 30 of model B will yield a minimum cost of \$32,400 per week
25. (A) 8,000 units of labor and 1,000 units of capital; Max $N(x, y) = N(8,000, 1,000) \approx 263,902$ units
    (B) Marginal productivity of money ≈ 0.6598; increase in production $\approx 32,990$ units
27. 8 in. by 8 in. by $\frac{8}{3}$ in.   **29.** $x = 50$ ft and $y = 200$ ft; maximum area is 10,000 ft^2

Exercise 8-5

1.
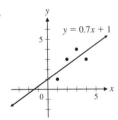

3.
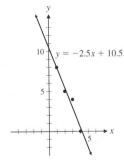

5.
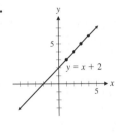

7. $y = -1.5x + 4.5$; $y = 0.75$ when $x = 2.5$ **9.** $y = 2.12x + 10.8$; $y = 63.8$ when $x = 25$
11. $y = -1.2x + 12.6$; $y = 10.2$ when $x = 2$ **13.** $y = -1.53x + 26.67$; $y = 14.4$ when $x = 8$
15.
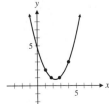

$y = 0.75x^2 - 3.45x + 4.75$

21. (A) $y = 1.52x - 0.16$; $y = 0.73x^2 - 1.39x + 1.30$ (B) The quadratic function.
23. The normal equations form a system of 4 linear equations in the 4 variables a, b, c, and d, which can be solved using Gauss–Jordan elimination.
25. (A) $y = 110.5x + 1,834$ (B) 4,044,000
27. (A) $y = -0.48x + 4.38$ (B) \$6.56 per bottle
29. (A) $P = -0.66T + 48.8$ (B) 11.18 beats/min

31. (A) $y = 0.0086x + 56.48$ (B) $58.19°F$
33. (A) $D = -3.1A + 54.6$ (B) 45% **35.** (A) $y = 0.0871x + 10.80$ (B) 21.25 ft

Exercise 8-6

1. (A) $3x^2y^4 + C(x)$ (B) $3x^2$ **3.** (A) $2x^2 + 6xy + 5x + E(y)$ (B) $35 + 30y$

5. (A) $\sqrt{y + x^2} + E(y)$ (B) $\sqrt{y + 4} - \sqrt{y}$ **7.** (A) $\dfrac{\ln x \ln y}{x} + C(x)$ (B) $\dfrac{2 \ln x}{x}$

9. 9   **11.** 330   **13.** $(56 - 20\sqrt{5})/3$ **15.** 1   **17.** 16   **19.** 49   **21.** $\frac{1}{8}\int_1^5\int_{-1}^1 (x + y)^2 \, dy \, dx = \frac{32}{3}$

23. $\frac{1}{15}\int_1^4\int_2^7 (x/y) \, dy \, dx = \frac{1}{2}\ln\frac{7}{2} \approx 0.6264$ **25.** $\frac{4}{3}$ cubic units   **27.** $\frac{32}{3}$ cubic units   **29.** $\int_0^1\int_1^2 xe^{xy} \, dy \, dx = \frac{1}{2} + \frac{1}{2}e^2 - e$

31. $\int_0^1\int_{-1}^1 \dfrac{2y + 3xy^2}{1 + x^2} \, dy \, dx = \ln 2$

35. (A) $\frac{1}{3} + \frac{1}{4}e^{-2} - \frac{1}{4}e^2$ (B)

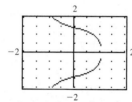

(C) Points to the right of the graph in part (B) are greater than 0; points to the left of the graph are less than 0.

37. $\dfrac{1}{0.4}\int_{0.6}^{0.8}\int_5^7 \dfrac{y}{1 - x} \, dy \, dx = 30 \ln 2 \approx \$20.8$ billion

39. $\frac{1}{10}\int_{10}^{20}\int_1^2 x^{0.75}y^{0.25} \, dy \, dx = \frac{8}{175}(2^{1.25} - 1)(20^{1.75} - 10^{1.75}) \approx 8.375$ or $8,375$ units

41. $\frac{1}{192}\int_{-8}^8\int_{-6}^6 [10 - \frac{1}{10}(x^2 + y^2)] \, dy \, dx = \frac{20}{3}$ insects/ft^2 **43.** $\frac{1}{8}\int_{-2}^2\int_{-1}^1 [100 - 15(x^2 + y^2)] \, dy \, dx = 75$ ppm

45. $\frac{1}{10,000}\int_{2,000}^{3,000}\int_{50}^{60} 0.000\,013\,3xy^2 \, dy \, dx \approx 100.86$ ft   **47.** $\frac{1}{16}\int_8^{16}\int_{10}^{12} 100\frac{x}{y} \, dy \, dx = 600 \ln 1.2 \approx 109.4$

Chapter 8 Review Exercise

1. $f(5, 10) = 2,900; f_x(x, y) = 40; f_y(x, y) = 70$ (8-1, 8-2)   **2.** $\partial^2 z/\partial x^2 = 6xy^2; \partial^2 z/\partial x \, \partial y = 6x^2 y$ (8-2)
3. $2xy^3 + 2y^2 + C(x)$ (8-6)   **4.** $3x^2y^2 + 4xy + E(y)$ (8-6)   **5.** 1 (8-6)
6. $f_x(x, y) = 5 + 6x + 3x^2; f_y(x, y) = -2$; the function $f_y(x, y)$ never has the value 0. (8-3)
7. $f(2, 3) = 7; f_y(x, y) = -2x + 2y + 3; f_y(2, 3) = 5$ (8-1, 8-2)   **8.** $(-8)(-6) - (4)^2 = 32$ (8-2)
9. $(1, 3, -\frac{1}{2}), (-1, -3, \frac{1}{2})$ (8-4)   **10.** $y = -1.5x + 15.5; y = 0.5$ when $x = 10$ (8-5)   **11.** 18 (8-6)
12. $f_x(x, y) = 2xe^{x^2+2y}; f_y(x, y) = 2e^{x^2+2y}; f_{xy}(x, y) = 4xe^{x^2+2y}$ (8-2)
13. $f_x(x, y) = 10x(x^2 + y^2)^4; f_{xy}(x, y) = 80xy(x^2 + y^2)^3$ (8-2)
14. $f(2, 3) = -25$ is a local minimum; f has a saddle point at $(-2, 3)$ (8-3)   **15.** Max $f(x, y) = f(6, 4) = 24$ (8-4)
16. Min $f(x, y, z) = f(2, 1, 2) = 9$ (8-4)   **17.** $y = \frac{116}{165}x + \frac{100}{3}$ (8-5)   **18.** $\frac{27}{5}$ (8-6)   **19.** 4 cubic units (8-6)
20. 0 (8-6)   **21.** (A) 12.56   (B) No (8-6)
22. $F_x = 12x^2 + 3\lambda = 0, F_y = -15y^2 + 2\lambda = 0$, and $F_\lambda = 3x + 2y - 7 = 0$ have no simultaneous solution. (8-4)
23. (A) $P_x(1, 3) = 8$; profit will increase \$8,000 for a 100 unit increase in product A if production of product B is held fixed at an output level of $(1, 3)$.
(B) For 200 units of A and 300 units of B, $P(2, 3) = \$100$ thousand is a local maximum. (8-2, 8-3)
24. 8 in. by 6 in. by 2 in. (8-3)   **25.** $y = 0.63x + 1.33$; profit in sixth year is \$5.11 million (8-4)
26. (A) Marginal productivity of labor ≈ 8.37; marginal productivity of capital ≈ 1.67; management should encourage increased use of labor.
(B) 80 units of labor and 40 units of capital; Max $N(x, y) = N(80, 40) \approx 696$ units; marginal productivity of money ≈ 0.0696; increase in production ≈ 139 units

(C) $\dfrac{1}{1,000}\int_{50}^{100}\int_{20}^{40} 10x^{0.8}y^{0.2} \, dy \, dx = \dfrac{(40^{1.2} - 20^{1.2})(100^{1.8} - 50^{1.8})}{216} = 621$ items (8-4)

27. $T_x(70, 17) = -0.924$ min/ft increase in depth when $V = 70$ ft^3 and $x = 17$ ft (8-2)
28. $\frac{1}{16}\int_{-2}^2\int_{-2}^2 [100 - 24(x^2 + y^2)] \, dy \, dx = 36$ ppm (8-6)   **29.** 50,000 (8-1)
30. $y = \frac{1}{2}x + 48; y = 68$ when $x = 40$ (8-5)
31. (A) $y = 0.4933x + 25.20$ (B) 84.40 people/mi^2 (C) 89.30 people/mi^2; 97.70 people/mi^2 (8-5)
32. (A) $y = 1.069x + 0.522$ (B) 64.68 yr   (C) 64.78 yr; 64.80 yr (8-5)

Chapter 9

Exercise 9-1

1. $\pi/10$ rad   **3.** $\pi/2$ rad   **5.** 3π rad   **7.** I   **9.** II   **11.** III   **13.** -1 **15.** 0   **17.** 0   **19.** $120°$
21. $360°$ **23.** $135°$ **25.** $1/2$ **27.** $-1/2$ **29.** $-\sqrt{2}/2$ **31.** 0.1411 **33.** -0.6840 **35.** 0.7970
37. $3\pi/20$ rad   **39.** $15°$ **41.** 1   **43.** 2   **45.** $1/\sqrt{3}$ or $\sqrt{3}/3$
49. 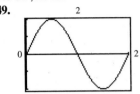   **51.**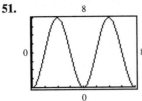

53. (A) $P(13) = 5$, $P(26) = 10$, $P(39) = 5$, $P(52) = 0$
   (B) $P(30) \approx 9.43$, $P(100) \approx 0.57$; thus, 30 weeks after January 1 the profit on a week's sales of bathing suits is \$943, and 100 weeks after January 1 the profit on a week's sales of bathing suits is \$57.
   (C)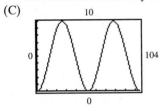

55. (A) $V(0) = 0.10$, $V(1) = 0.45$, $V(2) = 0.80$, $V(3) = 0.45$, $V(7) = 0.45$
   (B) $V(3.5) \approx 0.20$, $V(5.7) \approx 0.76$; thus, the volume of air in the lungs of a normal seated adult 3.5 sec after exhaling is approximately 0.20 L, and 5.7 sec after exhaling is approx. 0.76 L.
   (C)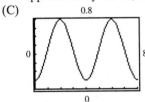

57. (A) $-5.6°$ (B) $-4.7°$

Exercise 9-2

1. $-\sin t$ **3.** $3x^2 \cos x^3$ **5.** $t \cos t + \sin t$ **7.** $(\cos x)^2 - (\sin x)^2$ **9.** $5(\sin x)^4 \cos x$ **11.** $\dfrac{\cos x}{2\sqrt{\sin x}}$

13. $-\dfrac{x^{-1/2}}{2} \sin\sqrt{x} = \dfrac{-\sin\sqrt{x}}{2\sqrt{x}}$ **15.** $f'\left(\dfrac{\pi}{6}\right) = \cos\dfrac{\pi}{6} = \dfrac{\sqrt{3}}{2}$

17. Increasing on $[-\pi, 0]$; decreasing on $[0, \pi]$; concave upward on $[-\pi, -\pi/2]$ and $[\pi/2, \pi]$; concave downward on $[-\pi/2, \pi/2]$; local maximum at $x = 0$; $f'(x) = -\sin x$; $f(x) = \cos x$.

19. $\dfrac{(\cos x)^2 + (\sin x)^2}{(\cos x)^2} = \dfrac{1}{(\cos x)^2} = (\sec x)^2$ **21.** $\dfrac{x \cos \sqrt{x^2 - 1}}{\sqrt{x^2 - 1}}$

23. $2e^x \cos x$ **25.**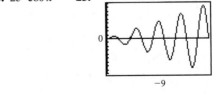

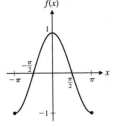

27.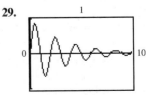

31. (A) $P'(t) = \dfrac{5\pi}{26}\sin\dfrac{\pi t}{26}, 0 < t < 104$

(B) $P'(8)$ = \$0.50 hundred or \$50 per week; $P'(26)$ = \$0 per week; $P'(50)$ = −\$0.14 hundred or −\$14 per week

(C)

t	$P(t)$	
26	\$1,000	Local maximum
52	\$0	Local minimum
78	\$1,000	Local maximum

(D)

t	$P(t)$	
0	\$0	Absolute minimum
26	\$1,000	Absolute maximum
52	\$0	Absolute minimum
78	\$1,000	Absolute maximum
104	\$0	Absolute minimum

(E) Same answer as for part (C)

33. (A) $V'(t) = \dfrac{0.35\pi}{2}\sin\dfrac{\pi t}{2}, 0 \le t \le 8$ (B) $V'(3) = -0.55$ L/sec; $V'(4) = 0.00$ L/sec; $V'(5) = 0.55$ L/sec

(C)

t	$V(t)$	
2	0.80	Local maximum
4	0.10	Local minimum
6	0.80	Local maximum

(D)

t	$V(t)$	
0	0.10	Absolute minimum
2	0.80	Absolute maximum
4	0.10	Absolute minimum
6	0.80	Absolute maximum
8	0.10	Absolute minimum

(E) Same answer as for part (C)

Exercise 9-3

1. $-\cos t + C$ **3.** $\frac{1}{3}\sin 3x + C$ **5.** $\frac{1}{13}(\sin x)^{13} + C$ **7.** $-\frac{3}{4}(\cos x)^{4/3} + C$ **9.** $\frac{1}{3}\sin x^3 + C$ **11.** 1   **13.** 1
15. $\sqrt{3}/2 - \frac{1}{2} \approx 0.366$ **17.** 1.4161   **19.** 0.0678   **21.** $e^{\sin x} + C$ **23.** $\ln|\sin x| + C$ **25.** $-\ln|\cos x| + C$
27. (A) 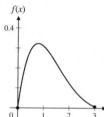   (B) $L_6 \approx 0.498$

29. (A) \$520 hundred or \$52,000
(B) \$106.38 hundred or \$10,638
(C)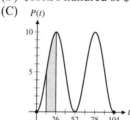

31. (A) 104 tons
(B) 31 tons
(C)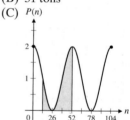

Chapter 9 Review Exercise

1. (A) $\pi/6$ (B) $\pi/4$ (C) $\pi/3$ (D) $\pi/2$ *(12-1)*   **2.** (A) -1 (B) 0 (C) 1 *(12-1)*   **3.** $-\sin m$ *(12-2)*
4. $\cos u$ *(12-2)*   **5.** $(2x - 2)\cos(x^2 - 2x + 1)$ *(12-2)*   **6.** $-\frac{1}{3}\cos 3t + C$ *(12-3)*
7. (A) 30° (B) 45° (C) 60° (D) 90° *(12-1)*   **8.** (A) $\frac{1}{2}$ (B) $\sqrt{2}/2$ (C) $\sqrt{3}/2$ *(12-1)*
9. (A) -0.6543 (B) 0.8308 *(12-1)*   **10.** $(x^2 - 1)\cos x + 2x\sin x$ *(12-2)*   **11.** $6(\sin x)^5\cos x$ *(12-2)*
12. $(\cos x)/[3(\sin x)^{2/3}]$ *(12-2)*   **13.** $\frac{1}{2}\sin(t^2 - 1) + C$ *(12-3)*   **14.** 2 *(12-3)*   **15.** $\sqrt{3}/2$ *(12-3)*   **16.** -0.243 *(12-3)*
17. $-\sqrt{2}/2$ *(12-2)*   **18.** $\sqrt{2}$ *(12-3)*
19. (A)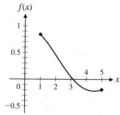

(B) $R_4 \approx 0.121$ *(6-4, 9-3)*

20. $\pi/12$ *(12-1)*   **21.** (A) -1 (B) $-\sqrt{3}/2$ (C) $-\frac{1}{2}$ *(12-1)*
22. $1/(\cos u)^2 = (\sec u)^2$ *(12-2)*   **23.** $-2x(\sin x^2)e^{\cos x^2}$ *(12-2)*
24. $e^{\sin x} + C$ *(12-3)*   **25.** $-\ln|\cos x| + C$ *(12-3)*   **26.** 15.2128 *(12-3)*
27. *(12-2, 12-3)*   **28.** *(12-2, 12-3)*

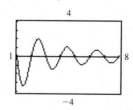

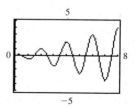

29. *(12-2, 12-3)*

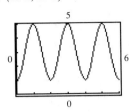

30. (A) $R(0) = \$5$ thousand; $R(2) = \$4$ thousand; $R(3) = \$3$ thousand; $R(6) = \$1$ thousand

(B) $R(1) = \$4.732$ thousand, $R(22) = \$4$ thousand; thus, the revenue is \$4,732 for a month of sweater sales 1 month after January 1, and \$4,000 for a month of sweater sales 22 months after January 1. *(12-1)*

31. (A) $R'(t) = -\dfrac{\pi}{3}\sin\dfrac{\pi t}{6}, 0 \le t \le 24$

(B) $R'(3) = -\$1.047$ thousand or $-\$1,047/\text{mo}$; $R'(10) = \$0.907$ thousand or $\$907/\text{mo}$; $R'(18) = \$0.000$ thousand

(C)

t	$P(t)$	
6	\$1,000	Local minimum
12	\$5,000	Local maximum
18	\$1,000	Local minimum

(D)

t	$P(t)$	
0	\$5,000	Absolute maximum
6	\$1,000	Absolute minimum
12	\$5,000	Absolute maximum
18	\$1,000	Absolute minimum
24	\$5,000	Absolute maximum

(E) Same answer as for part (C) *(12-2)*

32. (A) \$72 thousand or \$72,000   (B) \$6.270 thousand or \$6,270   (C)

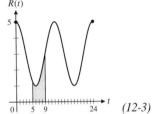

(12-3)

Appendix A

Self-Test on Basic Algebra

1. (A) $(y + z)x$ (B) $(2 + x) + y$ (C) $2x + 3x$ *(A-1)*   **2.** $x^3 - 3x^2 + 4x + 8$ *(A-2)*   **3.** $x^3 + 3x^2 - 2x + 12$ *(A-2)*
4. $-3x^5 + 2x^3 - 24x^2 + 16$ *(A-2)*   **5.** (A) 1 (B) 1 (C) 2 (D) 3 *(A-2)*   **6.** (A) 3 (B) 1 (C) -3 (D) 1 *(A-2)*
7. $14x^2 - 30x$ *(A-2)*   **8.** $6x^2 - 5xy - 4y^2$ *(A-2)*   **9.** $4a^2 - 12ab + 9b^2$ *(A-2)*   **10.** $4xy - 2y^2$ *(A-2)*
11. $9x^6 - 12x^3y + 4y^2$ *(A-2)*   **12.** $x^3 - 6x^2y + 12xy^2 - 8y^3$ *(A-2)*   **13.** (A) 4.065×10^{12} (B) 7.3×10^{-3} *(A-5)*
14. (A) 255,000,000 (B) 0.000 406 *(A-5)*   **15.** (A) T (B) F *(A-1)*
16. 0 and -3 are two examples of infinitely many. *(A-1)*   **17.** $6x^5y^{15}$ *(A-5)*   **18.** $3u^4/v^2$ *(A-5)*   **19.** 6×10^2 *(A-5)*
20. x^6/y^4 *(A-5)*   **21.** $u^{7/3}$ *(A-6)*   **22.** $3a^2/b$ *(A-6)*   **23.** $\frac{5}{9}$ *(A-5)*   **24.** $x + 2x^{1/2}y^{1/2} + y$ *(A-6)*
25. $6x + 7x^{1/2}y^{1/2} - 3y$ *(A-6)*   **26.** $(3x - 1)(4x + 3)$ *(A-3)*   **27.** $(4x - 3y)(2x - 3y)$ *(A-3)*
28. Not factorable relative to the integers *(A-3)*   **29.** $3n(2n - 5)(n + 1)$ *(A-3)*
30. $(x - y)(7x - y)$ *(A-3)*   **31.** $3x(2x + 1)(2 - x)$ *(A-3)*
32. $\dfrac{12a^3b - 40b^2 - 5a}{30a^3b^2}$ *(A-4)*   **33.** $\dfrac{7x - 4}{6x(x - 4)}$ *(A-4)*   **34.** $\dfrac{-8(x + 2)}{x(x - 4)(x + 4)}$ *(A-4)*
35. $2x + y$ *(A-4)*   **36.** $\dfrac{-1}{7(7 + h)}$ *(A-4)*   **37.** $\dfrac{xy}{y - x}$ *(A-6)*
38. (A) Subtraction (B) Commutative $(+)$ (C) Distributive (D) Associative $(\cdot)$ (E) Negatives
(F) Identity $(+)$ *(A-1)*   **39.** $6x^{2/5} - 7(x - 1)^{3/4}$ *(A-6)*
40. $2\sqrt{x} - 3\sqrt[3]{x^2}$ *(A-6)*   **41.** $2 - \frac{3}{2}x^{-1/2}$ *(A-6)*   **42.** $\sqrt{3x}$ *(A-6)*   **43.** $\sqrt{x} + \sqrt{5}$ *(A-6)*   **44.** $\dfrac{1}{\sqrt{x} - 5}$ *(A-6)*
45. $\dfrac{1}{\sqrt{u + h} + \sqrt{u}}$ *(A-6)*   **46.** $x = 2$ *(A-7)*   **47.** $x = 0, 5$ *(A-8)*   **48.** $x = \pm\sqrt{7}$ *(A-8)*   **49.** $x = -4, 5$ *(A-8)*
50. $x = 1, \frac{1}{6}$ *(A-8)*   **51.** $x < 4$ or $(-\infty, 4)$ *(A-7)*   **52.** $x \ge \frac{9}{2}$ or $[\frac{9}{2}, \infty)$ *(A-7)*

53. $1 \le x < 3$ or $[1, 3)$ x *(A-7)*   **54.** $y = \frac{2}{3}x - 2$ *(A-7)*   **55.** $y = 2x/(3x - 1)$ *(A-7)*

56. $3.1487 \times 10^4 = \$31{,}487$ per person *(A-5)*   **57.** \$20,000 at 8%; \$40,000 at 14% *(A-7)*   **58.** 4,000 tapes *(A-7)*

Exercise A-1

1. vu **3.** $(3 + 7) + y$ **5.** $u + v$ **7.** T   **9.** T   **11.** F   **13.** T   **15.** T   **17.** T   **19.** T   **21.** F
23. T   **25.** T   **27.** No   **29.** (A) F   (B) T   (C) T   **31.** $\sqrt{2}$ and π are two examples of infinitely many.
33. (A) N, Z, Q, R (B) R (C) Q, R (D) Q, R
35. (A) F, since, for example, $2(3 - 1) \ne 2 \cdot 3 - 1$ (B) F, since, for example, $(8 - 4) - 2 \ne 8 - (4 - 2)$ (C) T
(D) F, since, for example, $(8 \div 4) \div 2 \ne 8 \div (4 \div 2)$.
37. $\frac{1}{11}$ **39.** (A) $2.166\,666\,666\ldots$ (B) $4.582\,575\,69\ldots$ (C) $0.437\,500\,000\ldots$ (D) $0.261\,261\,261\ldots$

Exercise A-2

1. 3   **3.** $x^3 + 4x^2 - 2x + 5$ **5.** $x^3 + 1$ **7.** $2x^5 + 3x^4 - 2x^3 + 11x^2 - 5x + 6$ **9.** $-5u + 2$ **11.** $6a^2 + 6a$
13. $a^2 - b^2$ **15.** $6x^2 - 7x - 5$ **17.** $2x^2 + xy - 6y^2$ **19.** $9y^2 - 4$ **21.** $-4x^2 + 12x - 9$ **23.** $16m^2 - 9n^2$
25. $9u^2 + 24uv + 16v^2$ **27.** $a^3 - b^3$ **29.** $x^2 - 2xy + y^2 - 9z^2$ **31.** 1   **33.** $x^4 - 2x^2y^2 + y^4$ **35.** $-40ab$
37. $-4m + 8$ **39.** $-6xy$ **41.** $u^3 + 3u^2v + 3uv^2 + v^3$ **43.** $x^3 - 6x^2y + 12xy^2 - 8y^3$ **45.** $2x^2 - 2xy + 3y^2$
47. $x^4 - 10x^3 + 27x^2 - 10x + 1$ **49.** $4x^3 - 14x^2 + 8x - 6$ **51.** $m + n$ **53.** No change
55. $(1 + 1)^2 \ne 1^2 + 1^2$; either a or b must be 0   **57.** $0.09x + 0.12(10{,}000 - x) = 1{,}200 - 0.03x$
59. $10x + 30(3x) + 50(4{,}000 - x - 3x) = 200{,}000 - 100x$ **61.** $0.02x + 0.06(10 - x) = 0.6 - 0.04x$

Exercise A-3

1. $3m^2(2m^2 - 3m - 1)$ **3.** $2uv(4u^2 - 3uv + 2v^2)$ **5.** $(7m + 5)(2m - 3)$ **7.** $(4ab - 1)(2c + d)$
9. $(2x - 1)(x + 2)$ **11.** $(y - 1)(3y + 2)$ **13.** $(x + 4)(2x - 1)$ **15.** $(w + x)(y - z)$
17. $(a - 3b)(m + 2n)$ **19.** $(3y + 2)(y - 1)$ **21.** $(u - 5v)(u + 3v)$ **23.** Not factorable   **25.** $(wx - y)(wx + y)$
27. $(3m - n)^2$ **29.** Not factorable   **31.** $4(z - 3)(z - 4)$ **33.** $2x^2(x - 2)(x - 10)$ **35.** $x(2y - 3)^2$
37. $(2m - 3n)(3m + 4n)$ **39.** $uv(2u - v)(2u + v)$ **41.** $2x(x^2 - x + 4)$ **43.** $(2x - 3y)(4x^2 + 6xy + 9y^2)$
45. $xy(x + 2)(x^2 - 2x + 4)$ **47.** $[(x + 2) - 3y][(x + 2) + 3y]$ **49.** Not factorable   **51.** $(6x - 6y - 1)(x - y + 4)$
53. $(y - 2)(y + 2)(y^2 + 1)$ **55.** $3(x - y)^2(5xy - 5y^2 + 4x)$ **57.** True   **59.** False

Exercise A-4

1. $8d^6$ **3.** $\dfrac{15x^2 + 10x - 6}{180}$ **5.** $\dfrac{15m^2 + 14m - 6}{36m^3}$ **7.** $\dfrac{1}{x(x - 4)}$ **9.** $\dfrac{x - 6}{x(x - 3)}$ **11.** $\dfrac{-3x - 9}{(x - 2)(x + 1)^2}$ **13.** $\dfrac{2}{x - 1}$

15. $\dfrac{5}{a - 1}$ **17.** $\dfrac{x^2 + 8x - 16}{x(x - 4)(x + 4)}$ **19.** $\dfrac{7x^2 - 2x - 3}{6(x + 1)^2}$ **21.** $\dfrac{x(y - x)}{y(2x - y)}$ **23.** $\dfrac{-17c + 16}{15(c - 1)}$ **25.** $\dfrac{1}{x - 3}$

27. $\dfrac{-1}{2x(x + h)}$ **29.** $\dfrac{x - y}{x + y}$ **31.** (A) Incorrect   (B) $x + 1$ **33.** (A) Incorrect   (B) $2x + h$

35. (A) Incorrect   (B) $\dfrac{x^2 - x - 3}{x + 1}$ **37.** (A) Correct   **39.** $\dfrac{-2x - h}{3(x + h)^2 x^2}$ **41.** $\dfrac{x(x - 3)}{x - 1}$

Exercise A-5

1. $2/x^9$ **3.** $3w^7/2$ **5.** $2/x^3$ **7.** $1/w^5$ **9.** $4/a^6$ **11.** $1/a^6$ **13.** $1/8x^{12}$ **15.** 8.23×10^{10} **17.** 7.83×10^{-1}
19. 3.4×10^{-5} **21.** $40{,}000$ **23.** 0.007 **25.** $61{,}710{,}000$ **27.** $0.000\,808$ **29.** 1   **31.** 10^{14} **33.** $y^6/25x^4$

35. $4x^6/25$ **37.** $4y^3/3x^5$ **39.** $\frac{7}{4} - \frac{1}{4}x^{-3}$ **41.** $\frac{5}{2}x^2 - \frac{3}{2} + 4x^{-2}$ **43.** $\dfrac{x^2(x - 3)}{(x - 1)^3}$ **45.** $\dfrac{2(x - 1)}{x^3}$

47. 2.4×10^{10}; $24{,}000{,}000{,}000$ **49.** 3.125×10^4; $31{,}250$ **51.** 64   **55.** uv **57.** $\dfrac{bc(c + b)}{c^2 + bc + b^2}$
59. (A) 6.674×10^{11} (B) 1.8241 (C) 0.5482 **61.** (A) \$20,445   (B) \$1,346   (C) 6.58%
63. (A) 9×10^{-6} (B) $0.000\,009$ (C) 0.0009% **65.** $1{,}531{,}000$

Exercise A-6

1. $6\sqrt[5]{x^3}$ **3.** $8xy\sqrt[5]{xy^4}$ **5.** $\sqrt{x^2 + y^2}$ (not $x + y$)   **7.** $5x^{3/4}$ **9.** $(2x^2y)^{3/5}$ **11.** $x^{1/3} + y^{1/3}$ **13.** 5   **15.** 64

17. -7 **19.** -16 **21.** $\frac{8}{125}$ **23.** $\frac{1}{27}$ **25.** $x^{2/5}$ **27.** m **29.** $2x/y^2$ **31.** $xy^2/2$ **33.** $1/24x^{7/12}$ **35.** $2x + 3$

37. $30x^5\sqrt{3x}$ **39.** 2   **41.** $12x - 6x^{35/4}$ **43.** $3u - 13u^{1/2}v^{1/2} + 4v$ **45.** $36m^{3/2} - \dfrac{6m^{1/2}}{n^{1/2}} + \dfrac{6m}{n^{1/2}} - \dfrac{1}{n}$

47. $9x - 6x^{1/2}y^{1/2} + y$ **49.** $\frac{1}{2}x^{1/3} + x^{-1/3}$ **51.** $\frac{2}{3}x^{-1/4} + \frac{1}{3}x^{-2/3}$ **53.** $\frac{1}{2}x^{-1/6} - \frac{1}{4}$ **55.** $4n\sqrt{3mn}$

57. $\dfrac{2(x + 3)\sqrt{x - 2}}{x - 2}$ **59.** $7(x - y)(\sqrt{x} + \sqrt{y})$ **61.** $\dfrac{1}{xy\sqrt{5xy}}$ **63.** $\dfrac{1}{\sqrt{x + h} + \sqrt{x}}$ **65.** $\dfrac{1}{(t + x)(\sqrt{t} + \sqrt{x})}$

67. $x = y = 1$ is one of many choices.   **69.** $x = y = 1$ is one of many choices.   **71.** False   **73.** False   **75.** False

77. True   **79.** True   **81.** False   **83.** $\dfrac{x + 8}{2(x + 3)^{3/2}}$ **85.** $\dfrac{x - 2}{2(x - 1)^{3/2}}$ **87.** $\dfrac{x + 6}{3(x + 2)^{5/3}}$ **89.** 103.2   **91.** 0.0805

93. 4,588   **95.** (A) and (E);   (B) and (F);   (C) and (D)

Exercise A-7

1. $m = 5$ **3.** $x < -\frac{7}{2}$ **5.** $x \leq 4$ **7.** $x < -3$ or $(-\infty, -3)$

9. $-1 \leq x \leq 2$ or $[-1, 2]$ **11.** $x = \frac{5}{2}$ **13.** $x > -\frac{15}{4}$ **15.** $y = 8$ **17.** $x = 10$ **19.** $y \geq 3$

21. $x = 36$ **23.** $m < \frac{36}{7}$ **25.** $x = 10$ **27.** $3 \leq x < 7$ or $[3, 7)$

29. $-20 \leq C \leq 20$ or $[-20, 20]$ **31.** $y = \frac{3}{4}x - 3$ **33.** $y = -(A/B)x + (C/B) = (-Ax + C)/B$

35. $C = \frac{5}{9}(F - 32)$ **37.** $B = 3A/2(m - n)$ **39.** $-2 < x \leq 1$ or $(-2, 1]$

41. (A) and (C): $a > 0$ and $b > 0$, or $a < 0$ and $b < 0$ (B) and (D): $a > 0$ and $b < 0$, or $a < 0$ and $b > 0$
43. (A) $>$ (B) $<$ **45.** Negative   **47.** True   **49.** False   **51.** True   **53.** 3,500 $15 tickets; 4,500 $25 tickets
55. $7,200 at 10%; $4,800 at 15%   **57.** $22,191   **59.** 5,851 books   **61.** (B) 6,180 books   (C) At least $11.50
63. 5,000   **65.** 12.6 yr

Exercise A-8

1. $\pm\sqrt{11}$ **3.** $-\frac{4}{3}, 2$ **5.** $-2, 6$ **7.** $0, 2$ **9.** $3 \pm 2\sqrt{3}$ **11.** $-2 \pm \sqrt{2}$ **13.** $0, \frac{15}{2}$ **15.** $\pm\frac{3}{2}$ **17.** $\frac{1}{2}, -3$
19. $(-1 \pm \sqrt{5})/2$ **21.** $(3 \pm \sqrt{3})/2$ **23.** No real solution   **25.** $(-3 \pm \sqrt{11})/2$ **27.** $\pm\sqrt{3}$ **29.** $-\frac{1}{2}, 2$
31. $(x - 2)(x + 42)$ **33.** Not factorable in the integers   **35.** $(2x - 9)(x + 12)$ **37.** $(4x - 7)(x + 62)$
39. $r = \sqrt{A/P} - 1$
41. If $c < 4$, there are two distinct real roots; if $c = 4$, there is one real double root; and if $c > 4$, there are no real roots.
43. 1,575 bottles at $4 each   **45.** 13.64%   **47.** 8 ft/sec; $4\sqrt{2}$ or 5.66 ft/sec

Appendix B

Exercise B-1

1. $5, 7, 9, 11$ **3.** $\frac{3}{2}, \frac{4}{3}, \frac{5}{4}, \frac{6}{5}$ **5.** $9, -27, 81, -243$ **7.** 23   **9.** $\frac{101}{100}$ **11.** $1 + 2 + 3 + 4 + 5 + 6 = 21$
13. $5 + 7 + 9 + 11 = 32$ **15.** $1 + \frac{1}{10} + \frac{1}{100} + \frac{1}{1,000} = \frac{1,111}{1,000}$ **17.** 3.6   **19.** 82.5   **21.** $\frac{1}{2}, -\frac{1}{4}, \frac{1}{8}, -\frac{1}{16}, \frac{1}{32}$ **23.** $0, 4, 0, 8, 0$
25. $1, -\frac{3}{2}, \frac{9}{4}, -\frac{27}{8}, \frac{81}{16}$ **27.** $a_n = n - 3$ **29.** $a_n = 4n$ **31.** $a_n = (2n - 1)/2n$ **33.** $a_n = (-1)^{n+1}n$
35. $a_n = (-1)^{n+1}(2n - 1)$ **37.** $a_n = \left(\frac{2}{5}\right)^{n-1}$ **39.** $a_n = x^n$ **41.** $a_n = (-1)^{n+1}x^{2n-1}$ **43.** $1 - 9 + 25 - 49 + 81$

45. $\frac{4}{7} + \frac{8}{9} + \frac{16}{11} + \frac{32}{13}$ **47.** $1 + x + x^2 + x^3 + x^4$ **49.** $x - \frac{x^3}{3} + \frac{x^5}{5} - \frac{x^7}{7} + \frac{x^9}{9}$ **51.** (A) $\sum_{k=1}^{5} (k + 1)$ (B) $\sum_{j=0}^{4} (j + 2)$

53. (A) $\sum_{k=1}^{4} \frac{(-1)^{k+1}}{k}$ (B) $\sum_{j=0}^{3} \frac{(-1)^j}{j + 1}$ **55.** $\sum_{k=1}^{n} \frac{k + 1}{k}$ **57.** $\sum_{k=1}^{n} \frac{(-1)^{k+1}}{2^k}$ **59.** False   **61.** True   **63.** $2, 8, 26, 80, 242$

65. $1, 2, 4, 8, 16$ **67.** $1, \frac{3}{2}, \frac{17}{12}, \frac{577}{408}; a_4 = \frac{577}{408} \approx 1.414\,216, \sqrt{2} \approx 1.414\,214$ **69.** $1, 1, 2, 3, 5, 8, 13, 21, 34, 55$

Exercise B-2

1. (A) Arithmetic, with $d = -5; -26, -31$ (B) Geometric, with $r = 2; -16, 32$
(C) Neither   (D) Geometric, with $r = \frac{1}{3}; \frac{1}{54}, \frac{1}{162}$
3. Geometric; 1   **5.** Neither   **7.** Arithmetic; 127.5   **9.** $a_2 = 11, a_3 = 15$ **11.** $a_{21} = 82, S_{31} = 1{,}922$
13. $S_{20} = 930$ **15.** $a_2 = -6, a_3 = 12, a_4 = -24$ **17.** $S_7 = 547$ **19.** $a_{10} = 199.90$ **21.** $r = 1.09$
23. $S_{10} = 1{,}242, S_{\infty} = 1{,}250$ **25.** $2{,}706$ **27.** -85 **29.** $1{,}120$ **31.** (A) Does not exist   (B) $S_{\infty} = \frac{8}{5} = 1.6$
33. $2{,}400$ **35.** 0.999 **37.** Use $a_1 = 1$ and $d = 2$ in $S_n = (n/2)[2a_1 + (n - 1)d]$.   **39.** $S_n = na_1$ **41.** No
43. Yes   **45.** $\$48 + \$46 + \cdots + \$4 + \$2 = \$600$ **47.** About \$11,670,000   **49.** \$1,628.89; \$2,653.30

Exercise B-3

1. 720   **3.** 10   **5.** 1,320   **7.** 10   **9.** 6   **11.** 1,140   **13.** 10   **15.** 6   **17.** 1   **19.** 816
21. $C_{4,0}a^4 + C_{4,1}a^3b + C_{4,2}a^2b^2 + C_{4,3}ab^3 + C_{4,4}b^4 = a^4 + 4a^3b + 6a^2b^2 + 4ab^3 + b^4$
23. $x^6 - 6x^5 + 15x^4 - 20x^3 + 15x^2 - 6x + 1$ **25.** $32a^5 - 80a^4b + 80a^3b^2 - 40a^2b^3 + 10ab^4 - b^5$ **27.** $3{,}060x^{14}$
29. $5{,}005p^9q^6$ **31.** $264x^2y^{10}$ **33.** $C_{n,0} = \frac{n!}{0!n!} = 1; C_{n,n} = \frac{n!}{n!0!} = 1$ **35.** 1 5 10 10 5 1; 1 6 15 20 15 6 1

INDEX

APPLICATIONS INDEX